D0274583

Collins

Collins
German
Dictionary

HarperCollins Publishers
Westerhill Road
Bishopbriggs
Glasgow
G64 2QT
Great Britain

Eighth Edition 2006

©William Collins Sons & Co. Ltd. 1978, 1988
© HarperCollins Publishers 1993, 1997, 1999, 2000, 2003, 2006

ISBN-13 978-0-00-722398-5
ISBN-10 0-00-722398-6

Collins Gem® and Bank of English® are registered trademarks of HarperCollins Publishers Limited

www.collins.co.uk

A catalogue record for this book is available from the British Library

Typeset by Hagedorn medien[design]

Printed in Italy by Legoprint S.P.A.

Acknowledgements
We would like to thank those authors and publishers who kindly gave permission for copyright material to be used in the Collins Word Web. We would also like to thank Times Newspapers Ltd for providing valuable data.

INHALT

CONTENTS

WARENZEICHEN

NOTE ON TRADEMARKS

This book is set in Collins Fedra, a typeface specially created for Collins
Dictionaries by Peter Bil'ak.

William Collins' dream of knowledge for all began with the publication of his first book in 1819. A self-educated mill worker, he not only enriched millions of lives, but also founded a flourishing publishing house. Today, staying true to this spirit, Collins books are packed with inspiration, innovation, and practical expertise. They place you at the centre of a world of possibility and give you exactly what you need to explore it.

Language is the key to this exploration, and at the heart of Collins Dictionaries is language as it is really used. New words, phrases, and meanings spring up every day, and all of them are captured and analysed by the Collins Word Web. Constantly updated, and with over 2.5 billion entries, this living language resource is unique to our dictionaries.

Words are tools for life. And a Collins Dictionary makes them work for you.

Collins. Do more.

EINFÜHRUNG

Wir freuen uns sehr, dass Sie sich zum Kauf eines Collins Wörterbuchs Deutsch entschlossen haben. Wir wünschen Ihnen viel Spaß beim Gebrauch in der Schule, zu Hause, im Urlaub und im Beruf.

Diese Einführung wird Ihnen einige nützliche Hinweise dazu geben, wie Sie am besten von Ihrem neuen Wörterbuch profitieren. Schließlich bietet Ihnen das Wörterbuch nicht nur Stichwörter und Übersetzungen, sondern auch zahlreiche Zusatzinformationen in jedem einzelnen Eintrag. Mit Hilfe all dieser Informationen können Sie zum einen modernes Deutsch lesen und verstehen, zum anderen auch aktiv auf Deutsch kommunizieren.

Das Collins Wörterbuch Deutsch gibt Ihnen vor dem eigentlichen Wörterbuchtextteil selbst eine Liste aller verwendeten Abkürzungen sowie eine Übersicht zu Aussprache und Gebrauch phonetischer Umschrift. Darüber hinaus finden Sie noch eine Auflistung zu den regelmäßigen deutschen Substantivendungen sowie zu unregelmäßigen englischen und deutschen Verben. Auf den letzten Seiten Ihres Wörterbuchs finden Sie in einem „kleinen Reise-ABC" zahlreiche nützliche Phrasen für verschiedenste Situationen am Urlaubsort.

WIE FINDE ICH WAS?

Die verschiedenen Schriftarten, Schriftgrößen, Symbole, Abkürzungen und Klammern helfen Ihnen dabei, sich innerhalb der Informationen, die das Wörterbuch bietet, zurechtzufinden. Die Konventionen, die diesem Wörterbuch zugrunde liegen, sowie auch der Gebrauch verschiedener Symbole werden im Folgenden näher erläutert.

STICHWÖRTER

Die Wörter, die Sie in Ihrem Wörterbuch nachschlagen, die Stichwörter, sind in alphabetischer Reihenfolge angeordnet. Sie sind **fett** gedruckt und in blauer Farbe, sodass Sie sie schnell finden. Die Stichwörter, die rechts und links oben auf jeder Seite erscheinen, sind das jeweils erste Stichwort einer Seite, wenn es sich dabei um eine linke Seite handelt, bzw. das letzte Stichwort einer Seite, wenn es sich um eine rechte Seite handelt. Informationen zu Form und Gebrauch des jeweiligen Stichworts werden im Anschluss an die Lautschrift in Klammern angegeben. Normalerweise sind diese Angaben in abgekürzter Form und *kursiver* Schrift (z.B. *(fam)* für umgangssprachlich oder *(Comm)* als Sachgebietsangabe für Wirtschaft).

Wo es sich anbietet, werden zusammengehörige Wörter und Wortgruppen in einem Eintrag zusammengefasst (z.B. **gather**, **gathering**; **höflich**, **Höflichkeit**). Hierbei sind die Stichwörter innerhalb des Nests von der Schriftgröße etwas kleiner als das erste Stichwort. Geläufige Ausdrücke, in denen das Stichwort vorkommt, erscheinen ebenfalls **fett**, aber in einer anderen Schriftgröße. Die Tilde (~) steht hierbei für das Hauptstichwort am Anfang eines Eintrags. So steht beispielsweise im Eintrag ,**Mitte**' der Ausdruck ,**~ Juni**' für ,**Mitte Juni**'.

PHONETISCHE UMSCHRIFT

Die Aussprache jedes Stichworts findet sich in phonetischer Umschrift in eckigen Klammern jeweils direkt hinter dem Stichwort selbst (z.B. **mountain**['mauntin]). Eine Liste der Lautschriftzeichen mit Erklärungen finden Sie auf S. xiii.

BEDEUTUNGEN

Die Übersetzung der Stichwörter ist in Normalschrift angegeben. Gibt es mehrere Bedeutungen oder Gebrauchsmöglichkeiten, so sind diese durch einen Strichpunkt voneinander zu unterscheiden. Sie finden oft weitere Angaben in Klammern vor den jeweiligen Übersetzungen. Diese zeigen Ihnen typische Kontexte auf, in denen das Stichwort verwendet werden kann (z.B. **breakup** *(of meeting, organisation)*), oder sie liefern Synonyme (z.B. **fit** *(suitable)*).

GRAMMATISCHE HINWEISE

Die Wortartangabe finden Sie als Abkürzung und in *kursiver Schrift* direkt hinter der Ausspracheinformation zum jeweiligen Stichwort (z.B. *vt, adj, n*).

Die Genusangaben zu deutschen Substantiven werden wie folgt angegeben: *m* für Maskulinum, *f* für Femininum und *nt* für Neutrum. Darüber hinaus finden Sie neben dem Stichwort in Klammern Genitiv- und Pluralform (**Abenteuer***(-s, -)*).

Die Genusangabe zur deutschen Übersetzung findet sich ebenfalls in *kursiver Schrift* direkt hinter dem Hauptbestandteil der Übersetzung.

INTRODUCTION

We are delighted you have decided to buy the Collins German Dictionary and hope you will enjoy and benefit from using it at school, at home, on holiday or at work.

This introduction gives you a few tips on how to get the most out of your dictionary - not simply from its comprehensive wordlist but also from the information provided in each entry. This will help you to read and understand modern German, as well as to communicate and express yourself in the language.

The Collins German Dictionary begins by listing the abbreviations used in the text and illustrating the sounds shown by the phonetic symbols. Next you will find regular German noun endings and English irregular verbs followed by a section on German irregular verbs. Finally, the new Phrasefinder supplement gives you hundreds of useful phrases which are intended to give you practical help in everyday situations when travelling.

USING YOUR COLLINS DICTIONARY

A wealth of information is presented in the dictionary, using various typefaces, sizes of type, symbols, abbreviations and brackets. The conventions and symbols used are explained in the following sections.

HEADWORDS

The words you look up in the dictionary – 'headwords' – are listed alphabetically. They are printed in **colour** for rapid identification. The headwords appearing at the top of each page indicate the first (if it appears on a left-hand page) and last word (if it appears on a right-hand page) dealt with on the page in question.

Information about the usage or form of certain headwords is given in brackets after the phonetic spelling. This usually appears in abbreviated form and in italics (e.g. (*fam*), (*Comm*)).

Where appropriate, words related to headwords are grouped in the same entry (**gather, gathering; höflich, Höflichkeit**) in a slightly smaller bold type than the headword. Common expressions in which the headword appears are shown in a different size of bold roman type. The swung dash, ~, represents the main headword at the start of each entry. For example, in the entry for 'Mitte', the phrase '~ Juni' should be read 'Mitte Juni'.

PHONETIC SPELLINGS

The phonetic spelling of each headword (indicating its pronunciation) is given in square brackets immediately after the headword (e.g. **mountain** ['maʊntɪn]). A list of these spellings is given on page xiii.

MEANINGS

Headword translations are given in ordinary type and, where more than one meaning or usage exists, they are separated by a semicolon. You will often find other words in italics in brackets before the translations. These offer suggested contexts in which the headword might appear (e.g. **breakup** (of meeting, organisation)) or provide synonyms (e.g. **fit** (suitable)).

GRAMMATICAL INFORMATION

Parts of speech are given in abbreviated form in italics after the phonetic spellings of headwords (e.g. *vt*, *adj*, *n*).

Genders of German nouns are indicated as follows: *m* for a masculine, *f* for a feminine, and *nt* for a neuter noun. Genitive and plural forms of nouns are also shown next to the headword (**Abenteuer** (-s, -)).

The gender of the German translation appears in italics immediately following the key element of the translation.

ABKÜRZUNGEN

ABBREVIATIONS

auch	*a.*	also
Abkürzung	*abk, abbr*	abbreviation
Akronym	*acr*	acronym
Adjektiv	*adj*	adjective
Adverb	*adv*	adverb
Landwirtschaft	*Agr*	agriculture
Akkusativ	*akk*	accusative
Akronym	*akr*	acronym
Anatomie	*Anat*	anatomy
Artikel	*art*	article
Bildende Künste	*Art*	fine arts
Astronomie, Astrologie	*Astr*	astronomy, astrology
Auto, Verkehr	*Auto*	automobiles, traffic
Luftfahrt	*Aviat*	aviation
Biologie	*Bio*	biology
Botanik	*Bot*	botany
britisch	*BRIT*	British
schweizerisch	*CH*	Swiss
Chemie	*Chem*	chemistry
Film	*Cine*	cinema
Wirtschaft	*Comm*	commerce
Konjunktion	*conj*	conjunction
Dativ	*dat*	dative
Eisenbahn	*Eisenb*	railways
Elektrizität	*Elek, Elec*	electricity
besonders	*esp*	especially
und so weiter	*etc*	et cetera
etwas	*etw*	
Femininum	*f*	feminine
umgangssprachlich	*fam*	familiar, informal
übertragen	*fig*	figurative
Finanzen, Börse	*Fin*	finance
Fotografie	*Foto*	photography
Gastronomie	*Gastr*	cooking, gastronomy
Genitiv	*gen*	genitive
Geographie, Geologie	*Geo*	geography, geology
Geschichte	*Hist*	history
Imperativ	*imper*	imperative
Imperfekt	*imperf*	past tense
Informatik und Computer	*Inform*	computing
Interjektion, Ausruf	*interj*	interjection
unveränderlich	*inv*	invariable
unregelmäßig	*irr*	irregular
jemand	*jd*	
jemandem	*jdm*	
jemanden	*jdn*	

jemandes	jds	
Rechtsprechung	Jur	law
Konjunktion	konj	conjunction
Bildende Künste	Kunst	fine arts
Sprachwissenschaft, Grammatik	Ling	linguistics, grammar
Maskulinum	m	masculine
Mathematik	Math	mathematics
Medizin	Med	medicine
Meteorologie	Meteo	meteorology
Maskulinum und Femininum	mf	masculine and feminine
Militär	Mil	military
Musik	Mus	music
Substantiv	n	noun
Seefahrt	Naut	nautical, naval
Neutrum	nt	neuter
Zahlwort	num	numeral
oder	o	or
pejorativ, abwertend	pej	pejorative
Physik	Phys	physics
Plural	pl	plural
Politik	Pol	politics
Partizip Perfekt	pp	past participle
Präfix	pref	prefix
Präposition	prep	preposition
Pronomen	pron	pronoun
1. Vergangenheit	pt	past tense
Warenzeichen	®	registered trademark
Radio	Radio	radio
Eisenbahn	Rail	railways
Religion	Rel	religion
siehe	s.	see
	sb	someone, somebody
schottisch	SCOT	Scottish
Singular	sing	singular
Skisport	Ski	skiing
Sport	Sport	sports
	sth	something
Technik	Tech	technology
Nachrichtentechnik	Tel	telecommunications
Theater	Theat	theatre
Fernsehen	TV	television
Typographie, Buchdruck	Typo	printing
unpersönlich	unpers	impersonal
(nord)amerikanisch	US	(North) American
Verb	vb	verb
Hilfsverb	vb aux	auxiliary verb
intransitives Verb	vi	intransitive verb
reflexives Verb	vr	reflexive verb

transitives Verb	*vt*	transitive verb
vulgär	*vulg*	vulgar
Zoologie	*Zool*	zoology
zwischen zwei Sprechern	-	change of speaker
ungefähre Entsprechung	≈	cultural equivalent
abtrennbares Präfix	|	separable prefix

LAUTSCHRIFT   PHONETIC SYMBOLS

[ː] Längezeichen, length mark
['] Betonung, stress mark
[*] Bindungs-R, 'r' pronounced before a vowel

alle Vokallaute sind nur ungefähre Entsprechungen
all vowel sounds are approximate only

VOKALE UND DIPHTHONGE

plant, arm, father	[ɑː]	Bahn
fiancé	[ãː]	Ensemble
life	[aɪ]	weit
house	[aʊ]	Haut
man, sad	[æ]	
but, son	[ʌ]	Butler
get, bed	[ɛ]	Metall
name, lame	[eɪ]	
ago, better	[ə]	bitte
bird, her	[ɜː]	
there, care	[ɛə]	mehr
it, wish	[ɪ]	Bischof
bee, me, beat, belief	[iː]	viel
here	[ɪə]	Bier
no, low	[əʊ]	
not, long	[ɒ]	Post
law, all	[ɔː]	Mond
boy, oil	[ɔɪ]	Heu
push, look	[ʊ]	Pult
you, do	[uː]	Hut
poor, sure	[ʊə]	

KONSONANTEN

been, blind	[b]	Ball
do, had	[d]	dann
jam, object	[dʒ]	
father, wolf	[f]	Fass
go, beg	[g]	Gast
house	[h]	Herr
youth, Indian	[j]	ja
keep, milk	[k]	kalt
lamp, oil, ill	[l]	Laut
man, am	[m]	Mast
no, manner	[n]	Nuss
long, sing	[ŋ]	lang

El Niño	[ɲ]	El Niño
paper, happy	[p]	Pakt
red, dry	[r]	rot
stand, sand, yes	[s]	Rasse
ship, station	[ʃ]	Schal
tell, fat	[t]	Tal
thank, death	[θ]	
this, father	[ð]	
church, catch	[tʃ]	Rutsch
voice, live	[v]	was
water, we, which	[w]	
loch	[x]	Bach
zeal, these, gaze	[z]	Hase
pleasure	[ʒ]	Genie

REGULAR GERMAN NOUN ENDINGS

nominative		genitive	plural	nominative		genitive	plural
-ade	f	-ade	-aden	-ist	m	-isten	-isten
-ant	m	-anten	-anten	-ium	nt	-iums	-ien
-anz	f	-anz	-anzen	-ius	m	-ius	-iusse
-ar	m	-ars	-are	-ive	f	-ive	-iven
-är	m	-ärs	-äre	-keit	f	-keit	-keiten
-at	nt	-at(e)s	-ate	-lein	nt	-leins	-lein
-atte	f	-atte	-atten	-ling	m	-lings	-linge
-chen	nt	-chens	-chen	-ment	nt	-ments	-mente
-ei	f	-ei	-eien	-mus	m	-mus	-men
-elle	f	-elle	-ellen	-nis	f	-nis	-nisse
-ent	m	-enten	-enten	-nis	nt	-nisses	-nisse
-enz	f	-enz	-enzen	-nom	m	-nomen	-nomen
-ette	f	-ette	-etten	-rich	m	-richs	-riche
-eur	m	-eurs	-eure	-schaft	f	-schaft	-schaften
-euse	f	-euse	-eusen	-sel	nt	-sels	-sel
-heit	f	-heit	-heiten	-tät	f	-tät	-täten
-ie	f	-ie	-ien	-tiv	nt, m	-tivs	-tive
-ik	f	-ik	-iken	-tor	m	-tors	-toren
-in	f	-in	-innen	-tum	m, nt	-tums	-tümer
-ine	f	-ine	-inen	-ung	f	-ung	-ungen
-ion	f	-ion	-ionen	-ur	f	-ur	-uren

Substantive, die mit einem geklammerten 'r' oder 's' enden (z.B. **Angestellte(r)** *mf*, **Beamte(r)** *m*, **Gute(s)** *nt*) werden wie Adjektive dekliniert:

Nouns listed with an 'r' or an 's' in brackets (eg **Angestellte(r)** *mf*, **Beamte(r)** *m*, **Gute(s)** *nt*) take the same endings as adjectives:

der Angestellte *m*   die Angestellte *f*   die Angestellten *pl*
ein Angestellter *m*   eine Angestellte *f*   Angestellte *pl*
der Beamte *m*
ein Beamter *m*   die Beamten *pl*
das Gute *nt*   Beamte *pl*
ein Gutes *nt*

UNREGELMÄßIGE ENGLISCHE VERBEN

present	past tense	past participle	present	past tense	past participle
arise (arising)	arose	arisen	drink	drank	drunk
awake (awaking)	awoke	awaked	drive (driving)	drove	driven
be (am, is, are; being)	was, were	been	eat	ate	eaten
			fall	fell	fallen
			feed	fed	fed
bear	bore	born(e)	feel	felt	felt
beat	beat	beaten	fight	fought	fought
become (becoming)	became	become	find	found	found
			flee	fled	fled
begin (beginning)	began	begun	fling	flung	flung
			fly (flies)	flew	flown
bend	bent	bent	forbid (forbidding)	forbade	forbidden
bet (betting)	bet	bet			
bid (bidding)	bid	bid	foresee	foresaw	foreseen
bind	bound	bound	forget (forgetting)	forgot	forgotten
bite (biting)	bit	bitten			
bleed	bled	bled	forgive (forgiving)	forgave	forgiven
blow	blew	blown	freeze (freezing)	froze	frozen
break	broke	broken			
breed	bred	bred	get (getting)	got	got, (US) gotten
bring	brought	brought			
build	built	built	give (giving)	gave	given
burn	burnt (o burned)	burnt (o burned)	go (goes)	went	gone
burst	burst	burst	grind	ground	ground
buy	bought	bought	grow	grew	grown
can	could	(been able)	hang	hung (o hanged)	hung (o hanged)
cast	cast	cast			
catch	caught	caught	have (has; having)	had	had
choose (choosing)	chose	chosen	hear	heard	heard
cling	clung	clung	hide (hiding)	hid	hidden
come (coming)	came	come	hit (hitting)	hit	hit
cost	cost	cost	hold	held	held
creep	crept	crept	hurt	hurt	hurt
cut (cutting)	cut	cut	keep	kept	kept
deal	dealt	dealt	kneel	knelt (o kneeled)	knelt (o kneeled)
dig (digging)	dug	dug			
do (does)	did	done	know	knew	known
draw	drew	drawn	lay	laid	laid
dream	dreamed (o dreamt)	dreamed (o dreamt)	lead	led	led

present	past tense	past participle	present	past tense	past participle
lean	leant (o learned)	leant (o leaned)	shoot	shot	shot
leap	leapt (o leaped)	leapt (o leaped)	show	showed	shown
			shrink	shrank	shrunk
learn	learnt (o learned)	learnt (o learned)	shut (shutting)	shut	shut
			sing	sang	sung
leave (leaving)	left	left	sink	sank	sunk
			sit (sitting)	sat	sat
lend	lent	lent	sleep	slept	slept
let (letting)	let	let	slide (sliding)	slid	slid
lie (lying)	lay	lain	sling	slung	slung
light	lit (o lighted)	lit (o lighted)	slit (slitting)	slit	slit
lose (losing)	lost	lost	smell	smelt (o smelled)	smelt (o smelled)
make (making)	made	made			
may	might	–	sow	sowed	sown (o sowed)
mean	meant	meant			
meet	met	met	speak	spoke	spoken
mow	mowed	mown (o mowed)	speed	sped (o speeded)	sped (o speeded)
must	(had to)	(had to)	spell	spelt (o spelled)	spelt (o spelled)
pay	paid	paid	spend	spent	spent
put (putting)	put	put	spin (spinning)	spun	spun
quit (quitting)	quit (o quitted)	quit (o quitted)	spit (spitting)	spat	spat
read	read	read	split (splitting)	split	split
rid (ridding)	rid	rid			
ride (riding)	rode	ridden	spoil	spoiled (o spoilt)	spoiled (o spoilt)
ring	rang	rung			
rise (rising)	rose	risen	spread	spread	spread
run (running)	ran	run	spring	sprang	sprung
			stand	stood	stood
saw	sawed	sawn	steal	stole	stolen
say	said	said	stick	stuck	stuck
see	saw	seen	sting	stung	stung
seek	sought	sought	stink	stank	stunk
sell	sold	sold	strike (striking)	struck	struck
send	sent	sent			
set (setting)	set	set	strive (striving)	strove	striven
shake (shaking)	shook	shaken	swear	swore	sworn
shall	should	–	sweep	swept	swept
shine (shining)	shone	shone	swell	swelled	swollen (o swelled)

present	past tense	past participle	present	past tense	past participle
swim (swimming)	swam	swum	wake (waking)	woke (o waked)	woken (o waked)
swing	swung	swung	wear	wore	worn
take (taking)	took	taken	weave (weaving)	wove (o weaved)	woven (o weaved)
teach	taught	taught	weep	wept	wept
tear	tore	torn	win (winning)	won	won
tell	told	told			
think	thought	thought	wind	wound	wound
throw	threw	thrown	write (writing)	wrote	written
thrust	thrust	thrust			
tread	trod	trodden			

GERMAN IRREGULAR VERBS

Infinitiv	Präsens 2., 3. Singular	Imperfekt	Partizip Perfekt
backen	bäckst, backt	backte o buk	gebacken
befehlen	befiehlst, befiehlt	befahl	befohlen
beginnen	beginnst, beginnt	begann	begonnen
beißen	beißt, beißt	biss	gebissen
bergen	birgst, birgt	barg	geborgen
betrügen	betrügst, betrügt	betrog	betrogen
biegen	biegst, biegt	bog	gebogen
bieten	bietest, bietet	bot	geboten
binden	bindest, bindet	band	gebunden
bitten	bittest, bittet	bat	gebeten
blasen	bläst, bläst	blies	geblasen
bleiben	bleibst, bleibt	blieb	geblieben
braten	brätst, brät	briet	gebraten
brechen	brichst, bricht	brach	gebrochen
brennen	brennst, brennt	brannte	gebrannt
bringen	bringst, bringt	brachte	gebracht
denken	denkst, denkt	dachte	gedacht
dringen	dringst, dringt	drang	gedrungen
dürfen	darfst, darf	durfte	gedurft
empfangen	empfängst, empfängt	empfing	empfangen
empfehlen	empfiehlst, empfiehlt	empfahl	empfohlen
empfinden	empfindest, empfindet	empfand	empfunden
erschrecken	erschrickst, erschrickt	erschrak	erschrocken
essen	isst, isst	aß	gegessen
fahren	fährst, fährt	fuhr	gefahren
fallen	fällst, fällt	fiel	gefallen
fangen	fängst, fängt	fing	gefangen
finden	findest, findet	fand	gefunden
flechten	flichtst, flicht	flocht	geflochten
fliegen	fliegst, fliegt	flog	geflogen
fließen	fließt, fließt	floss	geflossen
fressen	frisst, frisst	fraß	gefressen
frieren	frierst, friert	fror	gefroren
geben	gibst, gibt	gab	gegeben
gehen	gehst, geht	ging	gegangen
gelingen	-, gelingt	gelang	gelungen
gelten	giltst, gilt	galt	gegolten
genießen	genießt, genießt	genoss	genossen
geraten	gerätst, gerät	geriet	geraten
geschehen	-, geschieht	geschah	geschehen
gewinnen	gewinnst, gewinnt	gewann	gewonnen
gießen	gießt, gießt	goss	gegossen
gleichen	gleichst, gleicht	glich	geglichen
gleiten	gleitest, gleitet	glitt	geglitten

Infinitiv	Präsens 2., 3. Singular	Imperfekt	Partizip Perfekt
graben	gräbst, gräbt	grub	gegraben
greifen	greifst, greift	griff	gegriffen
haben	hast, hat	hatte	gehabt
halten	hältst, hält	hielt	gehalten
hängen	hängst, hängt	hing	gehangen
hauen	haust, haut	haute	gehauen
heben	hebst, hebt	hob	gehoben
heißen	heißt, heißt	hieß	geheißen
helfen	hilfst, hilft	half	geholfen
kennen	kennst, kennt	kannte	gekannt
klingen	klingst, klingt	klang	geklungen
kneifen	kneifst, kneift	kniff	gekniffen
kommen	kommst, kommt	kam	gekommen
können	kannst, kann	konnte	gekonnt
kriechen	kriechst, kriecht	kroch	gekrochen
laden	lädst, lädt	lud	geladen
lassen	lässt, lässt	ließ	gelassen
laufen	läufst, läuft	lief	gelaufen
leiden	leidest, leidet	litt	gelitten
leihen	leihst, leiht	lieh	geliehen
lesen	liest, liest	las	gelesen
liegen	liegst, liegt	lag	gelegen
lügen	lügst, lügt	log	gelogen
mahlen	mahlst, mahlt	mahlte	gemahlen
meiden	meidest, meidet	mied	gemieden
messen	misst, misst	maß	gemessen
misslingen	-, misslingt	misslang	misslungen
mögen	magst, mag	mochte	gemocht
müssen	musst, muss	musste	gemusst
nehmen	nimmst, nimmt	nahm	genommen
nennen	nennst, nennt	nannte	genannt
pfeifen	pfeifst, pfeift	pfiff	gepfiffen
quellen	quillst, quillt	quoll	gequollen
raten	rätst, rät	riet	geraten
reiben	reibst, reibt	rieb	gerieben
reißen	reißt, reißt	riss	gerissen
reiten	reitest, reitet	ritt	geritten
rennen	rennst, rennt	rannte	gerannt
riechen	riechst, riecht	roch	gerochen
ringen	ringst, ringt	rang	gerungen
rufen	rufst, ruft	rief	gerufen
salzen	salzt, salzt	salzte	gesalzen
saufen	säufst, säuft	soff	gesoffen
saugen	saugst, saugt	sog o saugte	gesogen o gesaugt
schaffen	schaffst, schafft	schuf	geschaffen
scheiden	scheidest, scheidet	schied	geschieden

Infinitiv	Präsens 2., 3. Singular	Imperfekt	Partizip Perfekt
scheinen	scheinst, scheint	schien	geschienen
scheißen	scheißt, scheißt	schiss	geschissen
schieben	schiebst, schiebt	schob	geschoben
schließen	schießt, schießt	schoss	geschossen
schlafen	schläfst, schläft	schlief	geschlafen
schlagen	schlägst, schlägt	schlug	geschlagen
schleichen	schleichst, schleicht	schlich	geschlichen
schleifen	schleifst, schleift	schliff	geschliffen
schließen	schließt, schließt	schloss	geschlossen
schmelßen	schmeißt, schmeißt	schmiss	geschmissen
schmelzen	schmilzt, schmilzt	schmolz	geschmolzen
schneiden	schneidest, schneidet	schnitt	geschnitten
schreiben	schreibst, schreibt	schrieb	geschrieben
schreien	schreist, schreit	schrie	geschrie(e)n
schweigen	schweigst, schweigt	schwieg	geschwiegen
schwellen	schwillst, schwillt	schwoll	geschwollen
schwimmen	schwimmst, schwimmt	schwamm	geschwommen
schwören	schwörst, schwört	schwor	geschworen
sehen	siehst, sieht	sah	gesehen
sein	bist, ist	war	gewesen
senden	sendest, sendet	sandte	gesandt
singen	singst, singt	sang	gesungen
sinken	sinkst, sinkt	sank	gesunken
sitzen	sitzt, sitzt	saß	gesessen
sollen	sollst, soll	sollte	gesollt
spinnen	spinnst, spinnt	spann	gesponnen
sprechen	sprichst, spricht	sprach	gesprochen
springen	springst, springt	sprang	gesprungen
stechen	stichst, sticht	stach	gestochen
stehen	stehst, steht	stand	gestanden
stehlen	stiehlst, stiehlt	stahl	gestohlen
steigen	steigst, steigt	stieg	gestiegen
sterben	stirbst, stirbt	starb	gestorben
stinken	stinkst, stinkt	stank	gestunken
stoßen	stößt, stößt	stieß	gestoßen
streichen	streichst, streicht	strich	gestrichen
streiten	streitest, streitet	stritt	gestritten
tragen	trägst, trägt	trug	getragen
treffen	triffst, trifft	traf	getroffen
treiben	treibst, treibt	trieb	getrieben
treten	trittst, tritt	trat	getreten
trinken	trinkst, trinkt	trank	getrunken
tun	tust, tut	tat	getan
verderben	verdirbst, verdirbt	verdarb	verdorben
vergessen	vergisst, vergisst	vergaß	vergessen
verlieren	verlierst, verliert	verlor	verloren

Infinitiv	Präsens 2., 3. Singular	Imperfekt	Partizip Perfekt
verschwinden	verschwindest, verschwindet	verschwand	verschwunden
verzeihen	verzeihst, verzeiht	verzieh	verziehen
wachsen	wächst, wächst	wuchs	gewachsen
waschen	wäschst, wäscht	wusch	gewaschen
weisen	weist, weist	wies	gewiesen
wenden	wendest, wendet	wandte	gewandt
werben	wirbst, wirbt	warb	geworben
werden	wirst, wird	wurde	geworden
werfen	wirfst, wirft	warf	geworfen
wiegen	wiegst, wiegt	wog	gewogen
wissen	weißt, weiß	wusste	gewusst
wollen	willst, will	wollte	gewollt
ziehen	ziehst, zieht	zog	gezogen
zwingen	zwingst, zwingt	zwang	gezwungen

DEUTSCH – ENGLISCH
GERMAN – ENGLISH

à prep ` at ... each; **4 Tickets ~ 8 Euro** 4 tickets at 8 euros each

A abk = **Autobahn** ≈ M (BRIT), ≈ I (US)

Aal (-(e)s, -e) m eel

ab prep +dat from; **von jetzt ~** from now on; **Berlin ~ 16:30 Uhr** departs Berlin 16.30; **~ Seite 17** from page 17; **~ 18** (Alter) from the age of 18 ▷ adv off; **links ~** to the left; **~ und zu** (o **an**) now and then (o again); **der Knopf ist ~** the button has come off

ab|bauen irr vt (Zelt) to take down; (verringern) to reduce

ab|beißen irr vt to bite off

ab|bestellen vt to cancel

ab|biegen irr vt to turn off; (Straße) to bend; **nach links/rechts ~** to turn left/right; **Abbiegespur** f filter lane

Abbildung f illustration

ab|blasen irr vt (fig) to call off

ab|blenden vt, vi (Auto) (die

Scheinwerfer) ~ to dip (BRIT) (o to dim (US)) one's headlights; **Abblendlicht** nt dipped (BRIT) (o dimmed (US)) headlights pl

ab|brechen irr vt to break off; (Gebäude) to pull down; (aufhören) to stop; (Computerprogramm) to abort

ab|bremsen vt to brake, to slow down

ab|bringen irr vt; **jdn von einer Idee ~** to talk sb out of an idea; **jdn vom Thema ~** to get sb away from the subject; **davon lasse ich mich nicht ~** nothing will make me change my mind about it

ab|buchen vt to debit (von to)

ab|danken vi to resign

ab|drehen vt (Gas, Wasser) to turn off; (Licht) to switch off ▷ vi (Schiff, Flugzeug) to change course

Abend (-s, -e) m evening; **am ~** in the evening; **zu ~ essen** to have dinner; **heute/morgen/gestern ~** this/tomorrow/yesterday evening; **guten ~!** good evening; **Abendbrot** nt supper; **Abendessen** nt dinner; **Abendgarderobe** f evening dress (o gown); **Abendkasse** f box office; **Abendkleid** nt evening dress (o gown); **Abendkurs** m evening class; **Abendmahl** nt **das ~** (Holy) Communion; **abends** adv in the evening; **montags ~** on Monday evenings

Abenteuer (-s, -) nt adventure; **Abenteuerurlaub** m adventure holiday

aber conj but; (jedoch) however; **oder ~** alternatively; **~ ja!** (but) of course; **das ist ~ nett von Ihnen** that's really nice of you

abergläubisch adj superstitious

ab|fahren *irr vi* to leave (*o* to depart) (*nach* for); (*Ski*) to ski down; **Abfahrt** *f* departure; (*von Autobahn*) exit; (*Ski*) descent; (*Piste*) run; **Abfahrtslauf** *m* (*Ski*) downhill; **Abfahrtszeit** *f* departure time

Abfall *m* waste; (*Müll*) rubbish (*BRIT*), garbage (*US*); **Abfalleimer** *m* rubbish bin (*BRIT*), garbage can (*US*)

abfällig *adj* disparaging; **~ von jdm sprechen** to make disparaging remarks about sb

ab|färben *vi* (*Wäsche*) to run; (*fig*) to rub off

ab|fertigen *vt* (*Pakete*) to prepare for dispatch; (*an der Grenze*) to clear; **Abfertigungsschalter** *m* (*am Flughafen*) check-in desk

ab|finden *irr vt* to pay off ▷ *vr* **sich mit etw ~** to come to terms with sth; **Abfindung** *f* (*Entschädigung*) compensation; (*von Angestellten*) redundancy payment

ab|fliegen *irr vi* (*Flugzeug*) to take off; (*Passagier a.*) to fly off; **Abflug** *m* departure; (*Start*) takeoff; **Abflughalle** *f* departure lounge; **Abflugzeit** *f* departure time

Abfluss *m* drain; (*am Waschbecken*) plughole (*BRIT*); **Abflussrohr** *nt* waste pipe; (*außen*) drainpipe

ab|fragen *vt* to test; (*Inform*) to call up

ab|führen *vi* (*Med*) to have a laxative effect ▷ *vt* (*Steuern, Abgaben*) to pay; **jdn ~ lassen** to take sb into custody; **Abführmittel** *nt* laxative

Abgabe *f* handing in; (*von Ball*) pass; (*Steuer*) tax; (*einer Erklärung*) making; **abgabenfrei** *adj* tax-free; **abgabenpflichtig** *adj* liable to tax

Abgase *pl* (*Auto*) exhaust fumes *pl*; **Abgas(sonder)untersuchung** *f* exhaust emission test

ab|geben *irr vt* (*Gepäck, Schlüssel*)

to leave (*bei* with); (*Schularbeit etc*) to hand in; (*Wärme*) to give off; (*Erklärung, Urteil*) to make ▷ *vr* **sich mit jdm ~** to associate with sb; **sich mit etw ~** to bother with sth

abgebildet *adj* **wie oben ~** as shown above

ab|gehen *irr vi* (*Post*) to go; (*Knopf etc*) to come off; (*abgezogen werden*) to be taken off; (*Straße*) to branch off; **von der Schule ~** to leave school; **sie geht mir ab** I really miss her; **was geht denn hier ab?** (*fam*) what's going on here?

abgehetzt *adj* exhausted, shattered

abgelaufen *adj* (*Pass*) expired; (*Zeit, Frist*) up; **die Milch ist ~** the milk is past its sell-by date

abgelegen *adj* remote

abgemacht *interj* OK, it's a deal, that's settled, then

abgeneigt *adj* **einer Sache** (*dat*) **~ sein** to be averse to sth; **ich wäre nicht ~, das zu tun** I wouldn't mind doing that

Abgeordnete(r) *mf* Member of Parliament

abgepackt *adj* prepacked

abgerissen *adj* **der Knopf ist ~** the button has come off

abgesehen *adj* **es auf jdn/etw ~ haben** to be after sb/sth; **~ von** apart from

abgespannt *adj* (*Person*) exhausted, worn out

abgestanden *adj* stale; (*Bier*) flat

abgestorben *adj* (*Pflanze*) dead; (*Finger*) numb

abgestumpft *adj* (*Person*) insensitive

abgetragen *adj* (*Kleidung*) worn

ab|gewöhnen *vt* **jdm etw ~** to cure sb of sth; **sich etw ~** to give sth up

ab|haken *vt* to tick off; **das**

(Thema) **ist schon abgehakt** that's been dealt with

ab|halten vt (Versammlung) to hold; **jdn von etw ~** (fernhalten) to keep sb away from sth; (hindern) to keep sb from sth

abhanden adj **~ kommen** to get lost

Abhang m slope

ab|hängen vt (Bild) to take down, (Anhänger) to uncouple; (Verfolger) to shake off ▷ vi **von etw ~** to depend on sb/sth; **das hängt davon ab, ob ...** it depends on whether ...; **abhängig** adj dependent (von on)

ab|hauen irr vt (abschlagen) to cut off ▷ vi (fam: verschwinden) to clear off; **hau ab!** get lost!, beat it!

ab|heben irr vt (Geld) to withdraw; (Telefonhörer, Spielkarte) to pick up ▷ vi (Flugzeug) to take off; (Rakete) to lift off; (Karten) to cut

ab|holen vt to collect; (am Bahnhof etc) to meet; (mit dem Auto) to pick up; **Abholmarkt** m cash and carry

ab|horchen vt (Med) to listen to

ab|hören vt (Vokabeln) to test; (Telefongespräch) to tap; (Tonband etc) to listen to

Abitur (-s, -e) nt German school-leaving examination; ≈ A levels (BRIT), ≈ High School Diploma (US)

ABITUR

- The **Abitur** is the German school-leaving examination which is taken at the age of 18 or 19 by pupils at a **Gymnasium**. It is taken in four subjects and is necessary for entry to university.

ab|kaufen vt **jdm etw ~** to buy sth from sb; **das kauf ich dir nicht ab!** (fam: glauben) I don't believe you

ab|klingen irr vi (Schmerz) to ease,

(Wirkung) to wear off

ab|kommen irr vi to get away; **von der Straße ~** to leave the road; **von einem Plan ~** to give up a plan; **vom Thema ~** to stray from the point

Abkommen (-s, -) nt agreement

ab|koppeln vt (Anhänger) to un-hitch

ab|kratzen vt to scrape off ▷ vi (fam: sterben) to kick the bucket, to croak

ab|kühlen vi, vt to cool down ▷ vr **sich ~** to cool down

ab|kürzen vt (Wort) to abbreviate; **den Weg ~** to take a short cut; **Abkürzung** f (Wort) abbreviation; (Weg) short cut

ab|laden irr vt to unload

Ablage f (für Akten) tray; (Aktenordnung) filing system

Ablauf m (Abfluss) drain; (von Ereignissen) course; (einer Frist, Zeit) expiry; **ab|laufen** irr vi (abfließen) to drain away; (Freignisse) to happen; (Frist, Zeit, Pass) to expire

ab|legen vt to put down; (Kleider) to take off; (Gewohnheit) to get rid of; (Prüfung) to take, to sit; (Akten) to file away ▷ vi (Schiff) to cast off

ab|lehnen vt to reject; (Einladung) to decline; (missbilligen) to disapprove of; (Bewerber) to turn down ▷ vi to decline

ab|lenken vt to distract; **jdn von der Arbeit ~** to distract sb from their work; **vom Thema ~** to change the subject; **Ablenkung** f distraction

ab|lesen vt (Text, Rede) to read; **das Gas/den Strom ~** to read the gas/electricity meter

ab|liefern vt to deliver

ab|machen vt (entfernen) to take off; (vereinbaren) to agree; **Abmachung** f agreement

ab|melden vt (Zeitung) to cancel; (Auto) to take off the road ▷ vr **sich ~** to give notice of one's departure; (im Hotel) to check out; (vom Verein) to cancel one's membership

ab|messen irr vt to measure

ab|nehmen irr vt to take off, to remove; (Hörer) to pick up; (Führerschein) to take away; (Geld) to get (jdm out of sb); (kaufen, umg: glauben) to buy (jdm from sb) ▷ vi to decrease; (schlanker werden) to lose weight; (Tel) to pick up the phone; **fünf Kilo ~** to lose five kilos

Abneigung f dislike (gegen); (stärker) aversion (gegen)

ab|nutzen vt to wear out ▷ vr **sich ~** to wear out

Abonnement (-s, -s) nt subscription; **Abonnent(in)** m(f) subscriber; **abonnieren** vt to subscribe to

ab|raten irr vi jdm von etw ~ to advise sb against sth

ab|räumen vt **den Tisch ~** to clear the table; **das Geschirr ~** to clear away the dishes; (Preis etc) to walk off with

Abrechnung f settlement; (Rechnung) bill

ab|regen vr **sich ~** (fam) to calm (o to cool) down; **reg dich ab!** take it easy

Abreise f departure; **ab|reisen** vi to leave (nach for)

ab|reißen irr vt (Haus) to pull down; (Blatt) to tear off; **den Kontakt nicht ~ lassen** to stay in touch ▷ vi (Knopf etc) to come off

ab|runden vt **eine Zahl nach oben / unten ~** to round a number up / down

abrupt adj abrupt

ABS nt abk = **Antiblockiersystem** (Auto) ABS

Abs. abk = **Absender** from

ab|sagen vt to cancel, to call off;

(Einladung) to turn down ▷ vi (ablehnen) to decline; **ich muss leider ~** I'm afraid I can't come

Absatz m (Comm) sales pl; (neuer Abschnitt) paragraph; (Schuh) heel

ab|schaffen vt to abolish, to do away with

ab|schalten vt, vi (a. fig) to switch off

ab|schätzen vt to estimate; (Lage) to assess; **jdn ~** to size sb up

abscheulich adj disgusting

ab|schicken vt to send off

ab|schieben irr vt (ausweisen) to deport

Abschied (-(e)s, -e) m parting; **~ nehmen** to say good-bye (von jdm to sb); **Abschiedsfeier** f farewell party

Abschlagszahlung f interim payment

Abschleppdienst m (Auto) breakdown service; **ab|schleppen** vt to tow; **Abschleppseil** nt towrope; **Abschleppwagen** m breakdown truck (BRIT), tow truck (US)

ab|schließen irr vt (Tür) to lock; (beenden) to conclude, to finish; (Vertrag, Handel) to conclude; **Abschluss** m (Beendigung) close, conclusion; (von Vertrag, Handel) conclusion

ab|schmecken vt (kosten) to taste; (würzen) to season

ab|schminken vr **sich ~** to take one's make-up off ▷ vt (fam) **sich** (dat) **etw ~** to get sth out of one's mind

ab|schnallen vr **sich ~** to undo one's seatbelt

ab|schneiden irr vt to cut off ▷ vi **gut / schlecht ~** to do well / badly

Abschnitt m (von Buch, Text) section; (Kontrollabschnitt) stub

ab|schrauben vt to unscrew

ab|schrecken vt to deter, to put off

ab|schreiben irr vt to copy (bei, von from, off); (verloren geben) to write off; (Comm: absetzen) to deduct

abschüssig adj steep

ab|schwächen vt to lessen; (Behauptung, Kritik) to tone down

ab|schwellen irr vi (Entzündung) to go down; (Lärm) to die down

absehbar adj foreseeable; **in ~er Zeit** in the foreseeable future; **ab|sehen** irr vt (Ende, Folgen) to foresee ▷ vi **von etw ~** to refrain from sth

abseits adv out of the way; (Sport) offside ▷ prep +gen away from; **Abseits** nt (Sport) offside; **Abseitsfalle** f (Sport) offside trap

ab|senden irr vt to send off; (Post) to post; **Absender(in)** (-s, -) m(f) sender

ab|setzen vt (Glas, Brille etc) to put down; (aussteigen lassen) to drop (off); (Comm) to sell; (Fin) to deduct; (streichen) to drop ▷ vr **sich ~** (sich entfernen) to clear off; (sich ablagern) to be deposited

Absicht f intention; **mit ~** on purpose; **absichtlich** adj intentional, deliberate

absolut adj absolute

ab|speckan vi (fam) to lose weight

ab|speichern vt (Inform) to save

ab|sperren vt to block (o to close) off; (Tür) to lock; **Absperrung** f (Vorgang) blocking (o closing) off; (Sperre) barricade

ab|spielen vt (CD etc) to play ▷ vr **sich ~** to happen

ab|springen irr vi to jump down / off; (von etw Geplantem) to drop out (von of)

ab|spülen vt to rinse; (Geschirr) to wash (up)

Abstand m distance; (zeitlich) in-

terval; **~ halten** to keep one's distance

ab|stauben vt, vi to dust; (fam: stehlen) to pinch

Abstecher (-s, -) m detour

ab|steigen irr vi (vom Rad etc) to get off, to dismount; (in Gasthof) to stay (in etat at)

ab|stellen vt (niederstellen) to put down; (Auto) to park; (ausschalten) to switch off; (Missstand, Unsitte) to stop; **Abstellraum** m store room

Abstieg (-(e)s, -e) m (vom Berg) descent; (Sport) relegation

ab|stimmen vi to vote ⊳ vt (Termine, Ziele) to fit in (auf +akk with); **Dinge aufeinander ~** to coordinate things ▷ vr **sich ~** to come to an agreement (o arrangement)

abstoßend adj repulsive

abstrakt adj abstract

ab|streiten irr vt to deny

Abstrich m (Med) smear; **~e machen** to cut back (an etwt on), (weniger erwarten) to lower one's sights

Absturz m fall; (Aviat, Inform) crash; **ab|stürzen** irr vi to fall; (Aviat, Inform) to crash

absurd adj absurd

Abszess (-es, -e) m abscess

ab|tauen vt, vi to thaw; (Kühlschrank) to defrost

Abtei (-, -en) f abbey

Abteil (-(e)s, -e) nt compartment

Abteilung f (in Firma, Kaufhaus) department; (in Krankenhaus) section

ab|treiben irr vt (Kind) to abort ▷ vi to be driven off course; (Med: Abtreibung vornehmen) to carry out an abortion; (Abtreibung vornehmen lassen) to have an abortion; **Abtreibung** f abortion

ab|trocknen vt to dry

ab|warten vt to wait for; **das bleibt abzuwarten** that remains to be seen ▷ vi to wait

abwärts adv down

Abwasch (-(e)s) m washing-up; **ab|waschen** irr vt (Schmutz) to wash off; (Geschirr) to wash (up)

Abwasser (-s, Abwässer) nt sewage

ab|wechseln vr sich ~ to alternate; **sich mit jdm ~** to take turns with sb; **abwechselnd** adv alternately; **Abwechslung** f change; **zur ~** for a change

ab|weisen irr vt to turn away; (Antrag) to turn down; **abweisend** adj unfriendly

abwesend adj absent; **Abwesenheit** f absence

ab|wiegen irr vt to weigh (out)

ab|wischen vt (Gesicht, Tisch etc) to wipe; (Schmutz) to wipe off

ab|zählen vt to count; (Geld) to count out

Abzeichen nt badge

ab|zeichnen vt to draw, to copy; (Dokument) to initial ▷ vr sich ~ to stand out; (fig: bevorstehen) to loom

ab|ziehen irr vt to take off; (Bett) to strip; (Schlüssel) to take out; (subtrahieren) to take away, to subtract ▷ vi to go away

Abzug m (Foto) print; (Öffnung) vent; (Truppen) withdrawal; (Betrag) deduction; **nach ~ der Kosten** charges deducted; **abzüglich** prep +gen minus; **~ 20% Rabatt** less 20% discount

ab|zweigen vi to branch off ▷ vt to set aside; **Abzweigung** f junction

Accessoires pl accessories pl

ach interj oh; **~ so!** oh, I see; **~ was!** (Überraschung) really?; (Ärger) don't talk nonsense

Achse (-, -n) f axis; (Auto) axle

Achsel (-, -n) f shoulder; (Achselhöhle) armpit

acht num eight; **heute in ~ Tagen** in a week('s time), a week from today

Acht (-) f **sich in ~ nehmen** to be careful (vor +dat of), to watch out (vor +dat for); **~ geben** to take care (auf +akk of); **etw außer ~ lassen** to disregard sth

achte(r, s) adj eighth; siehe auch **dritte**; **Achtel** (-s, -) nt (Bruchteil) eighth; (Wein etc) eighth of a litre; (Glas Wein) ≈ small glass

achten vt to respect ▷ vi to pay attention (auf +akk to)

Achterbahn f big dipper, roller coaster

achthundert num eight hundred; **achtmal** adv eight times

Achtung f attention; (Ehrfurcht) respect ▷ interj look out

achtzehn num eighteen; **achtzehnte(r, s)** adj eighteenth; siehe auch **dritte**; **achtzig** num eighty; **in den ~er Jahren** in the eighties; **achtzigste(r, s)** adj eightieth

Acker (-s, Äcker) m field

Action (-, -s) f (fam) action; **Actionfilm** m action film

Adapter (-s, -) m adapter

addieren vt to add (up)

Adel (-s) m nobility; **adelig** adj noble

Ader (-, -n) f vein

Adjektiv nt adjective

Adler (-s, -) m eagle

adoptieren vt to adopt; **Adoption** f adoption; **Adoptiveltern** pl adoptive parents pl; **Adoptivkind** nt adopted child

Adrenalin (-s) nt adrenalin

Adressbuch nt directory; (persönliches) address book; **Adresse** (-, -n) f address; **adressieren** vt to address (an +akk to)

Advent (-s, -) m Advent; **Adventskranz** m Advent wreath

Adverb nt adverb

Aerobic (-s) nt aerobics sing

Affäre (-, -n) f affair

Affe (-n, -n) m monkey

Afghanistan (-s) nt Afghanistan

Afrika (-s) nt Africa; **Afrikaner(in)** (-s, -) m(f) African; **afrikanisch** adj African

After (-s, -) m anus

Aftershave (-(s), -s) nt aftershave

AG (-, -s) f abk = **Aktiengesellschaft** plc (BRIT), corp (US)

Agent(in) m(f) agent; **Agentur** f agency

aggressiv adj aggressive

Ägypten (-s) nt Egypt

ah interj ah, ooh

äh interj (Sprechpause) er, um; (angeekelt) ugh

aha interj I see, aha

ähneln vi +dat to be like, to resemble ▷ vr **sich ~** to be alike (o similar)

ahnen vt to suspect; **du ahnst es nicht!** would you believe it?

ähnlich adj similar (dat to); **jdm ~ sehen** to look like sb; **Ähnlichkeit** f similarity

Ahnung f idea; (Vermutung) suspicion; **keine ~!** no idea; **ahnungslos** adj unsuspecting

Ahorn (-s, -e) m maple

Aids (-) nt Aids; **aidskrank** adj suffering from Aids; **aidspositiv** adj tested positive for Aids; **Aidstest** m Aids test

Airbag (-s, -s) m (Auto) airbag; **Airbus** m airbus

Akademie (-, -n) f academy; **Akademiker(in)** (-s, -) m(f) (university) graduate

akklimatisieren vr **sich ~** to acclimatize oneself

Akkordeon (-s, -s) nt accordion

Akku (-s, -s) m (storage) battery

Akkusativ m accusative (case)

Akne (,) f acne

Akrobat(in) (-s, -en) m(f) acrobat

Akt (-(e)s, -e) m act; (Kunst) nude

Akte (-, -n) f file; **etw zu den ~n legen** (a. fig) to file sth away; **Aktenkoffer** m briefcase

Aktie (-, -n) f share; **Aktiengesellschaft** f public limited company (BRIT), corporation (US)

Aktion f (Kampagne) campaign; (Einsatz) operation

Aktionär(in) (-s, -e) m(f) shareholder

aktiv adj active

aktualisieren vt to update; **aktuell** adj (Thema) topical; (modern) up-to-date; (Problem) current; **nicht mehr ~** no longer relevant

Akupunktur f acupuncture

akustisch adj acoustic; **Akustik** f acoustics sing

akut adj acute

AKW (-s, -s) nt abk = **Atomkraftwerk** nuclear power station

Akzent (-(e)s, -e) m accent; (Betonung) stress; **mit starkem schottischen ~** with a strong Scottish accent

akzeptieren vt to accept

Alarm (-(e)s, -e) m alarm; **Alarmanlage** f alarm system; **alarmieren** vt to alarm; **die Polizei ~** to call the police

Albanien (-s) nt Albania

Albatros (-ses, -se) m albatross

albern adj silly

Albtraum m nightmare

Album (-s, Alben) nt album

Algen pl algae pl; (Meeresalgen) seaweed sing

Algerien (-s) nt Algeria

Alibi (-s, -s) nt alibi

Alimente pl maintenance sing

Alkohol (-s, -e) m alcohol; **alkoholfrei** adj non-alcoholic; **-es Getränk** soft drink; **Alkoholiker(in)** (-s, -) m(f) alcoholic; **alkoholisch**

adj alcoholic

All (-s) *nt* universe

alle(r, s) *pron* all; **~ Passagiere** all passengers; **wir ~** all of us; **~ beide** both of us / you / them; **~ vier Jahre** every four years; **~ 100 Meter** every 100 metres; *siehe auch* **alles** ▷ *adj* (*fam: zu Ende*) finished

Allee (-, -n) *f* avenue

allein *adj, adv* alone; (*ohne Hilfe*) on one's own, by oneself; **nicht ~** (*nicht nur*) not only; **~ erziehende Mutter** single mother; **~ stehend** single, unmarried; **Alleinerziehende(r)** *mf* single mother / father / parent

allerbeste(r, s) *adj* very best

allerdings *adv* (*zwar*) admittedly; (*gewiss*) certainly, sure (US)

allererste(r, s) *adj* very first; **zu allererst** first of all

Allergie *f* allergy; **Allergiker(in)** (-s, -) *m(f)* allergy sufferer; **allergisch** *adj* allergic (*gegen* to)

allerhand *adj inv* (*fam*) all sorts of; **das ist doch ~!** (*Vorwurf*) that's the limit; **~!** (*lobend*) that's pretty good

Allerheiligen (-) *nt* All Saints' Day

allerhöchste(r, s) *adj* very highest; **allerhöchstens** *adv* at the very most; **allerlei** *adj inv* all sorts of; **allerletzte(r, s)** *adj* very last; **allerwenigste(r, s)** *adj* very least

alles *pron* everything; **~ in allem** all in all; *siehe auch* **alle**

Alleskleber (-s, -) *m* all-purpose glue

allgemein *adj* general; **im Allgemeinen** in general

Alligator (-s, -en) *m* alligator

alljährlich *adj* annual

allmählich *adj* gradual ▷ *adv* gradually

Allradantrieb *m* all-wheel drive

Alltag *m* everyday life; **alltäglich** *adj* everyday; (*gewöhnlich*) ordinary; (*tagtäglich*) daily

allzu *adv* all too

Allzweckreiniger (-s, -) *m* multi--purpose cleaner

Alpen *pl* **die ~** the Alps *pl*

Alphabet (-(e)s, -e) *nt* alphabet; **alphabetisch** *adj* alphabetical

Alptraum *m siehe* **Albtraum**

als *conj* (*vergleichend*) than; (*zeitlich*) when; **das Zimmer ist größer ~ das andere** this room is bigger than the other; **das Essen war billiger ~ ich erwartet hatte** the meal was cheaper than I expected (it to be); **~ Kind** as a child; **nichts ~** (*Ärger*) nothing but (trouble); **anders ~** different from; **erst ~** only when; **~ ob** as if

also *conj* (*folglich*) so, therefore ▷ *adv, interj* so; **~ gut** (*o* **schön**)**!** okay then

alt *adj* old; **wie ~ sind Sie?** how old are you?; **28 Jahre ~** 28 years old; **vier Jahre älter** four years older

Altar (-(e)s, Altäre) *m* altar

Alter (-s, -) *nt* age; (*hohes*) old age; **im ~ von** at the age of; **er ist in meinem ~** he's my age

alternativ *adj* alternative; (*umweltbewusst*) ecologically minded; (*Landwirtschaft*) organic; **Alternative** *f* alternative

Altersheim *nt* old people's home

Altglas *nt* used glass; **Altglascontainer** *m* bottle bank; **altmodisch** *adj* old-fashioned; **Altöl** *nt* used (*o* waste) oil; **Altpapier** *nt* waste paper; **Altstadt** *f* old town

Alt-Taste *f* Alt key

Alufolie *f* tin (*o* kitchen) foil

Aluminium (-s) *nt* aluminium (BRIT), aluminum (US)

Alzheimerkrankheit *f* Alzheimer's (disease)

am *kontr von* **an dem**; **~ 2. Januar** on January 2(nd); **~ Morgen** in the morning; **~ Strand** on the beach; **~**

Bahnhof at the station; **was gefällt ihnen ~ besten?** what do you like best?; **~ besten bleiben wir hier** it would be best if we stayed here

Amateur(in) m(f) amateur

ambulant adj outpatient; **kann ich ~ behandelt werden?** can I have it done as an outpatient?; **Ambulanz** f (Krankenwagen) ambulance; (in der Klinik) outpatients' department

Ameise (-, -n) f ant

amen interj amen

Amerika (-s) nt America; **Amerikaner(in)** (-s, -) m(f) American; **amerikanisch** adj American

Ampel (-, -n) f traffic lights pl

Amphitheater nt amphitheatre

Amsel (-, -n) f blackbird

Amt (-(e)s, Ämter) nt (Dienststelle) office, department; (Posten) post; **amtlich** adj official; **Amtszeichen** nt (Tel) dialling tone (BRIT), dial tone (US)

amüsant adj amusing; **amüsieren** vt to amuse ▷ vr **sich ~** to enjoy oneself, to have a good time

an prep +dat ~ **der Wand** on the wall; ~ **der Themse** on the Thames; **alles ist ~ seinem Platz** everything is in its place; ~ **einem kalten Tag** on a cold day; ~ **Ostern** at Easter ▷ prep +akk ~ **die Tür klopfen** to knock at the door; **ans Meer fahren** to go to the seaside; ~ **die 40 Grad** (fast) nearly 40 degrees ▷ adv **von ... ~** from ... on; **das Licht / Radio ist ~** the light / radio is on

anal adj anal

analog adj analogous; (Inform) analog

Analyse (-, -n) f analysis; **analysieren** vt to analyse

Ananas (-, - o -se) f pineapple

an|baggern vt (fam) to chat up (BRIT), to come on to (US)

Anbau m (Agr) cultivation; (Gebäude) extension; **an|bauen** vt (Agr) to cultivate; (Gebäudeteil) to build on

an|behalten irr vt to keep on

anbei adv enclosed; ~ **sende ich ...** please find enclosed ...

an|beten vt to worship

an|bieten irr vt to offer ▷ vr **sich ~** to volunteer

an|binden irr vt to tie up

Anblick m sight

an|braten irr vt to brown

an|brechen irr vt to start; (Vorräte, Ersparnisse) to break into; (Flasche, Packung) to open ▷ vi to start; (Tag) to break; (Nacht) to fall

an|brennen irr vt, vi to burn; **das Fleisch schmeckt angebrannt** the meat tastes burnt

an|bringen irr vt (herbeibringen) to bring; (befestigen) to fix, to attach

Andacht (-, -en) f devotion; (Gottesdienst) prayers pl

an|dauern vi to continue, to go on; **andauernd** adj continual

Andenken (-s, -) nt memory; (Gegenstand) souvenir

andere(r, s) adj (weitere) other; (verschieden) different; (folgend) next; **am ~n Tag** the next day; **von etw / jmd ~m sprechen** to talk about sth / sb else; **unter ~m** among other things; **andererseits** adv on the other hand

ändern vt to alter, to change ▷ vr **sich ~** to change

andernfalls adv otherwise

anders adv differently (als from); **jemand / irgendwo ~** someone / somewhere else; **sie ist ~ als ihre Schwester** she's not like her sister; **es geht nicht ~** there's no other way; **anders(he)rum** the other way round; **anderswo** adv somewhere else

anderthalb num one and a half

Änderung f change, alteration

an|deuten vt to indicate; (Wink geben) to hint at

Andorra (-s) nt Andorra

Andrang m es herrschte großer ~ there was a huge crowd

an|drohen vt jdm etw ~ to threaten sb with sth

aneinander adv at/on/to one another (ø each other); ~ denken think of each other; ~ geraten to clash; sich ~ gewöhnen to get used to each other; ~ legen to put together

Anemone (-, -n) f anemone

an|erkennen irr vt (Staat, Zeugnis etc) to recognize; (würdigen) to appreciate; **Anerkennung** f recognition; (Würdigung) appreciation

an|fahren irr vt (fahren gegen) to run into; (Ort, Hafen) to stop (ø call) at; (liefern) to deliver; jdn ~ (fig: schimpfen) to jump on sb ▷ vi to start; (losfahren) to drive off

Anfall m (Med) attack; **anfällig** adj delicate; (Maschine) temperamental; ~ für prone to

Anfang m (-(e)s, Anfänge) m beginning, start; zu/am ~ to start with; ~ Mai at the beginning of May; sie ist ~ 20 she's in her early twenties; **an|fangen** irr vt, vi to begin, to start; damit kann ich nichts ~ that's no use to me; **Anfänger(in)** (-s, -) m(f) beginner; **anfangs** adv at first; **Anfangsbuchstabe** m first (ø initial) letter

an|fassen vt (berühren) to touch ▷ vi kannst du mal mit ~? can you give me a hand? ▷ vr sich weich ~ to feel soft

Anflug m (Aviat) approach; (Hauch) trace

an|fordern vt to demand; **Anforderung** f request (von for); (Anspruch) demand

Anfrage f inquiry

an|freunden vr sich mit jdm ~ to make (ø to become) friends with sb

an|fühlen vr sich ~ to feel; es fühlt sich gut an it feels good

Anführungszeichen pl quotation marks pl

Angabe f (Tech) specification; (fam: Prahlerei) showing off; (Tennis) serve; ~n pl (Auskunft) particulars pl; die ~n waren falsch (Info) the information was wrong; **an|geben** irr vt (Name, Grund) to give; (zeigen) to indicate; (bestimmen) to set ▷ vi (fam: prahlen) to boast; (Sport) to serve; **Angeber(in)** (-s, -) m(f) (fam) show-off; **angeblich** adj alleged

angeboren adj inborn

Angebot nt offer; (Comm) supply (an +dat of); ~ und Nachfrage supply and demand

angebracht adj appropriate

angebunden adj kurz ~ curt

angeheitert adj tipsy

an|gehen irr vt to concern; das geht dich nichts an that's none of your business; ein Problem ~ to tackle a problem; was ihn angeht as far as he's concerned, as for him ▷ vi (Feuer) to catch; (fam: beginnen) to begin; **angehend** adj prospective

Angehörige(r) mf relative

Angeklagte(r) mf accused, defendant

Angel (-, -n) f fishing rod; (an der Tür) hinge

Angelegenheit f affair, matter

Angelhaken m fish hook; **an|geln** vt to catch ▷ vi to fish; **Angeln** (-s) nt angling, fishing; **Angelrute** (-, -) f fishing rod

angemessen adj appropriate, suitable

angenehm adj pleasant; ~! (bei Vorstellung) pleased to meet you;

das ist mir gar nicht ~ I don't like the idea of that

angenommen adj assumed ▷ conj **~, es regnet, was machen wir dann?** suppose it rains, what do we do then?

angesehen adj respected

angesichts prep in view of, considering

Angestellte(r) mf employee

angetan adj **von jdm/etw ~ sein** to be impressed by (o taken with) sb/sth

angewiesen adj **auf jdn/etw ~ sein** to be dependent on sb/sth

an|gewöhnen vt **sich etw ~** to get used to doing sth; **Angewohnheit** f habit

Angina (-, Anginen) f tonsillitis; **Angina Pectoris** (-) f angina

Angler(in) (-s, -) m(f) angler

Angora (-s) nt angora

an|greifen irr vt to attack; (anfassen) to touch; (beschädigen) to damage; **Angriff** m attack; **etw in ~ nehmen** to get started on sth

Angst (-, Ängste) f fear; **~ haben** to be afraid (o scared) (vor +dat of); **jdm ~ machen** to scare sb; **ängstigen** vt to frighten ▷ vr **sich ~** to worry (um, wegen +dat about); **ängstlich** adj nervous; (besorgt) worried

an|haben irr vt (Kleidung) to have on, to wear; (Licht) to have on

an|halten irr vi to stop; (andauern) to continue; **anhaltend** adj continuous; **Anhalter(in)** (-s, -) m(f) hitch-hiker; **per ~ fahren** to hitch-hike

anhand prep +gen with; **~ von** by means of

an|hängen vt to hang up; (Eisenb: Wagen) to couple; (Zusatz) to add (on); **jdm etw ~** (fam: unterschieben) to pin sth on sb; **Anhänger** (-s, -) m (Auto) trailer; (am Koffer) tag;

(Schmuck) pendant; **Anhänger(in)** (-s, -) m(f) supporter; **Anhängerkupplung** f towbar; **anhänglich** adj affectionate; (pej) clinging

Anhieb m **auf ~** straight away; **das kann ich nicht auf ~ sagen** I can't say offhand

an|himmeln vt to worship, to idolize

an|hören vt to listen to ▷ vr **sich ~** to sound; **das hört sich gut an** that sounds good

Animateur(in) m(f) host/hostess

Anis (-es, -e) m aniseed

Anker (-s, -) m anchor; **ankern** vt, vi to anchor; **Ankerplatz** m anchorage

Ankleidekabine f changing cubicle

an|klicken vt (Inform) to click on

an|klopfen vi to knock (an +akk on)

an|kommen irr vi to arrive; **bei jdm gut ~** to go down well with sb; **es kommt darauf an** it depends (ob on whether); **darauf kommt es nicht an** that doesn't matter

an|kotzen vt (vulg) **es kotzt mich an** it makes me sick

an|kreuzen vt to mark with a cross

an|kündigen vt to announce

Ankunft (-, Ankünfte) f arrival; **Ankunftszeit** f arrival time

Anlage f (Veranlagung) disposition; (Begabung) talent; (Park) gardens pl, grounds pl; (zu Brief etc) enclosure; (Stereoanlage) stereo (system); (Tech) plant; (Fin) investment

Anlass (-es, Anlässe) m cause (zu for); (Ereignis) occasion; **aus diesem ~** for this reason; **an|lassen** irr vt (Motor) to start; (Licht, Kleidung) to leave on; **Anlasser** (-s, -) m (Auto) starter; **anlässlich** prep +gen on the occasion of

Anlauf m run-up; **an|laufen** irr vi to begin; (Film) to open; (Fenster) to mist up; (Metall) to tarnish

an|legen vt to put (an +akk against / on); (Schmuck) to put on; (Garten) to lay out; (Geld) to invest; (Gewehr) to aim (auf +akk at); **es auf etw** (akk) **~ to be out for sth** ▷ vi (Schiff) to berth, to dock ▷ vr **sich mit jdm ~** (fam) to pick a quarrel with sb; **Anlegestelle** f moorings pl

an|lehnen vt to lean (an +akk against); (Tür) to leave ajar ▷ vr **sich ~** to lean (an +akk against)

an|leiern vt **etw ~** (fam) to get sth going

Anleitung f instructions pl

Anliegen (-s, -) nt matter; (Wunsch) request

Anlieger(in) (-s, -) m(f) resident; **~ frei** residents only

an|lügen irr vt to lie to

an|machen vt (befestigen) to attach; (einschalten) to switch on; (Salat) to dress; (fam: aufreizen) to turn on; (fam: ansprechen) to chat up (BRIT), to come on to (US); (fam: beschimpfen) to have a go at

Anmeldeformular nt application form; (bei Amt) registration form; **an|melden** vt (Besuch etc) to announce ▷ vr **sich ~** (beim Arzt etc) to make an appointment; (bei Amt, für Kurs etc) to register; **Anmeldeschluss** m deadline for applications, registration deadline; **Anmeldung** f registration; (Antrag) application

an|nähen vt **einen Knopf (an den Mantel) ~** to sew a button on (one's coat)

annähernd adv roughly; **nicht ~** nowhere near

Annahme (-, -n) f acceptance;

(Vermutung) assumption; **annehmbar** adj acceptable; **an|nehmen** irr vt to accept; (Namen) to take; (Kind) to adopt; (vermuten) to suppose, to assume

Annonce (-, -n) f advertisement

an|öden vt (fam) to bore stiff (o silly)

annullieren vt to cancel

anonym adj anonymous

Anorak (-s, -s) m anorak

an|packen vt (Problem, Aufgabe) to tackle; **mit ~** to lend a hand

an|passen vt (fig) to adapt (dat to) ▷ vr **sich ~** to adapt (an +akk to)

an|pfeifen vt (Fußballspiel) **das Spiel ~** to start the game; **Anpfiff** m (Sport) (starting) whistle; (Beginn) kick-off; (fam: Tadel) roasting

an|probieren vt to try on

Anrede f form of address; **an|reden** vt to address

an|regen vt to stimulate; **Anregung** f stimulation; (Vorschlag) suggestion

Anreise f journey; **der Tag der ~** the day of arrival; **an|reisen** vi to arrive

Anreiz m incentive

an|richten vt (Speisen) to prepare; (Schaden) to cause

Anruf m call; **Anrufbeantworter** (-s, -) m answering machine, answerphone; **an|rufen** irr vt (Tel) to call, to phone, to ring (BRIT)

ans kontr von **an das**

Ansage f announcement; (auf Anrufbeantworter) recorded message; **an|sagen** vt to announce; **angesagt sein** to be recommended; (modisch sein) to be in the thing; **Spannung ist angesagt** we are in for some excitement ▷ vr **er sagte sich an** he said he would come

an|schaffen vt to buy

an|schauen vt to look at

Anschein m appearance; **dem** (o **allem**) ~ **nach ...** it looks as if ...; **den ~ erwecken, hart zu arbeiten** to give the impression of working hard; **anscheinend** adj apparent ▷ adv apparently

an|schieben irr vt **könnten Sie mich mal ~?** (Auto) could you give me a push?

Anschlag m notice; (Attentat) attack, an|schlagen irr vt (Plakat) to put up; (beschädigen) to chip ▷ vi (wirken) to take effect; **mit etw an etw** (akk) ~ to bang sth against sth

an|schließen irr vt (Elek, Tech) to connect (an +akk to); (mit Stecker) to plug in ▷ vi, vr (sich) **an etw** (akk) ~ (Gebäude etc) to adjoin sth; (zeitlich) to follow sth ▷ vr **sich ~** to join (jdm / einer Gruppe sb / a group); **anschließend** adj adjacent; (zeitlich) subsequent ▷ adv afterwards; **~ an** (+akk) following; **Anschluss** m (Elek, Eisenb) connection; (von Wasser, Gas etc) supply; **im ~ an** (+akk) following; **kein ~ unter dieser Nummer** (Tel) the number you have dialled has not been recognized; **Anschlussflug** m connecting flight

an|schnallen vt (Skier) to put on ▷ vr **sich ~** to fasten one's seat belt

Anschrift f address

an|schwellen irr vi to swell (up)

an|sehen irr vt to look at, (bei etw zuschauen) to watch; **jdn / etw als etw ~** to look on sb / sth as sth; **das sieht man ihm an** he looks it

an sein irr vi siehe **an**

an|setzen vt (Termin) to fix; (zubereiten) to prepare ▷ vi (anfangen) to start, to begin; **zu etw ~** to prepare to do sth

Ansicht f (Meinung) view, opinion; (Anblick) sight; **meiner ~ nach** in my opinion; **zur ~** on approval; **Ansichtskarte** f postcard

ansonsten adv otherwise

Anspiel nt (Sport) start of play; **anspielen** vi **auf etw** (akk) ~ to allude to sth; **Anspielung** f allusion (auf +akk to)

an|sprechen irr vt to speak to; (gefallen) to appeal to ▷ vi **auf etw** (akk) ~ (Patient) to respond to sth; **ansprechend** adj attractive, **Ansprechpartner(in)** m(f) contact

an|springen irr vi (Auto) to start

Anspruch m claim; (Recht) right (auf +akk to); **etw in ~ nehmen** to take advantage of sth; **~ auf etw haben** to be entitled to sth; **anspruchslos** adj undemanding; (bescheiden) modest; **anspruchsvoll** adj demanding

Anstalt (-, -en) f institution

Anstand m decency; **anständig** adj decent; (fig, fam) proper; (groß) considerable

an|starren vt to stare at

anstatt prep +gen instead of

an|stecken vt to pin on; (Med) to infect; **jdn mit einer Erkältung ~** to pass one's cold on to sb ▷ vr **ich habe mich bei ihm angesteckt** I caught it from him ▷ vi (fig) to be infectious; **ansteckend** adj infectious; **Ansteckungsgefahr** f danger of infection

an|stehen irr vi (in Warteschlange) to queue (BRIT), to stand in line (US); (erledigt werden müssen) to be on the agenda

anstelle prep +gen instead of

an|stellen vt (einschalten) to turn on; (Arbeit geben) to employ; (machen) to do; **was hast du wieder angestellt?** what have you been up to now? ▷ vr **sich ~** to queue (BRIT), to stand in line (US); (fam) **stell dich nicht so an!** stop making such a fuss

Anstoß m impetus; (Sport) kick-off;

an|stoßen irr vt to push; (mit Fuß) to kick ▷ vi to knock, to bump; (mit Gläsern) to drink (a toast) (auf +akk to); **anstößig** adj offensive; (Kleidung etc) indecent

an|strengen vt to strain ▷ vr **sich ~** to make an effort; **anstrengend** adj tiring

Antarktis f Antarctic

Anteil m share (an +dat at); **~ nehmen an** (+dat) (mitleidig) to sympathize with; (sich interessieren) to take an interest in

Antenne (-, -n) f aerial

Antibabypille f **die ~** the pill; **Antibiotikum** (-s, Antibiotika) nt (Med) antibiotic

antik adj antique

Antilope (-, -n) f antelope

Antiquariat nt (für Bücher) second-hand bookshop

Antiquitäten pl antiques pl; **Antiquitätenhändler(in)** m(f) antique dealer

an|törnen vt (fam) to turn on

Antrag (-(e)s, Anträge) m proposal; (Pol) motion; (Formular) application form; **einen ~ stellen auf** (+akk) to make an application for

an|treffen irr vt to find

an|treiben irr vt to drive; (anschwemmen) to wash up; **jdn zur Arbeit ~** to make sb work

an|treten irr vt **eine Reise ~** to set off on a journey

Antrieb m (Tech) drive; (Motivation) impetus

an|tun irr vt **jdm etwas ~** to do sth to sb; **sich** (dat) **etwas ~** (Selbstmord begehen) to kill oneself

Antwort (-, -en) f answer, reply; **um ~ wird gebeten** RSVP (répondez s'il vous plaît); **antworten** vi to answer, to reply; **jdm ~** to answer sb; **auf etw** (akk) **~** to answer sth

an|vertrauen vt **jdm etw ~** to

entrust sb with sth

Anwalt (-s, Anwälte) m, **Anwältin** f lawyer

an|weisen irr vt (anleiten) to instruct; (zuteilen) to allocate (jdm etw sth to sb); **Anweisung** f instruction; (von Geld) money order

an|wenden irr vt to use; (Gesetz, Regel) to apply; **Anwender(in)** (-s, -) m(f) user; **Anwendung** f use; (Inform) application

anwesend adj present; **Anwesenheit** f presence

an|widern vt to disgust

Anwohner(in) (-s, -) m(f) resident

Anzahl f number (an +dat of); **an|zahlen** vt to pay a deposit on; **100 Euro ~** to pay 100 euros as a deposit; **Anzahlung** f deposit

Anzeichen nt sign; (Med) symptom

Anzeige (-, -n) f (Werbung) advertisement; (elektronisch) display; (bei Polizei) report; **an|zeigen** vt (Temperatur, Zeit) to indicate, to show; (elektronisch) to display; (bekannt geben) to announce; **jdn/einen Autodiebstahl bei der Polizei ~** to report sb/a stolen car to the police

an|ziehen irr vt to attract; (Kleidung) to put on; (Schraube, Seil) to tighten ▷ vr **sich ~** to get dressed; **anziehend** adj attractive

Anzug m suit

anzüglich adj suggestive

an|zünden vt to light; (Haus etc) to set fire to

an|zweifeln vt to doubt

Aperitif (-s, -s (o -e)) m aperitif

Apfel (-s, Äpfel) m apple; **Apfelbaum** m apple tree; **Apfelkuchen** m apple cake; **Apfelmus** nt apple purée; **Apfelsaft** m apple juice; **Apfelsine** f orange; **Apfelwein** m cider

Apostroph (-s, -e) m apostrophe

Apotheke (-, -n) f chemist's (shop) (BRIT), pharmacy (US); **apothekenpflichtig** adj only available at the chemist's (o pharmacy); **Apotheker(in)** (-s, -) m(f) chemist (BRIT), pharmacist (US)

Apparat (-(e)s, -e) m (piece of) apparatus, (Tel) telephone, (Radio, TV) set; **am -!** (Tel) speaking; **am bleiben** (Tel) to hold the line

Appartement (-s, -s) nt studio flat (BRIT) (o apartment (US))

Appetit (-(e)s, -e) m appetite; **guten -!** bon appétit; **appetitlich** adj appetizing

Applaus (-es, -e) m applause

Aprikose (-, -n) f apricot

April (-(s), -e) m April; siehe auch Juni **-, -!** April fool!; **Aprilscherz** (-es, -e) m April fool's joke

apropos adv by the way; **- Urlaub** ... while we're on the subject of holidays

Aquaplaning (-(s)) nt aquaplaning

Aquarell (-s, -e) nt watercolour

Aquarium nt aquarium

Äquator m equator

Araber(in) (-s, -) m(f) Arab; **arabisch** adj Arab; (Ziffer, Sprache) Arabic; (Meer, Wüste) Arabian

Arbeit (-, -en) f work; (Stelle) job; (Erzeugnis) piece of work; **arbeiten** vi to work; **Arbeiter(in)** (-s, -) m(f) worker; (ungelernt) labourer; **Arbeitgeber(in)** (-s, -) m(f) employer; **Arbeitnehmer(in)** (-s, -) m(f) employee; **Arbeitsamt** nt job centre (BRIT), employment office (US); **arbeitslos** adj unemployed; **Arbeitslose(r)** f(m) unemployed person, die im o) (the unemployed pl; **Arbeitslosengeld** nt (income related) unemployment benefit; jobseeker's allowance (BRIT); **Arbeits**

losenhilfe f (non-income related) unemployment benefit; **Arbeitslosigkeit** f unemployment; **Arbeitsplatz** m job; (Ort) workplace; **Arbeitsspeicher** m (Inform) main memory; **Arbeitszeit** f working hours pl; **gleitende -** flexible working hours pl, flexitime; **Arbeitszimmer** nt study

Archäologe (-n, -n) m, **Archäologin** f archaeologist

Architekt(in) (-en, -en) m(f) architect; **Architektur** f architecture

Archiv (-s, -e) nt archives pl

arg adj bad; (schrecklich) awful ▷ adv (sehr) terribly

Argentinien (-s) nt Argentina

Ärger (-s) m annoyance; (stärker) anger; (Unannehmlichkeiten) trouble; **ärgerlich** adj (zornig) angry; (lästig) annoying; **ärgern** vt to annoy ▷ vr **sich -** to get annoyed

Argument (-s, e) nt argument

Arktis (-) f Arctic

arm adj poor

Arm (-(e)s, -e) m arm; (Fluss) branch

Armaturenbrett nt instrument panel; (Auto) dashboard

Armband nt bracelet; **Armbanduhr** f (wrist)watch

Armee (-, -n) f army

Ärmel (-s, -) m sleeve; **Ärmelkanal** m (English) Channel

Armut (-) f poverty

Aroma (-s, Aromen) nt aroma; **Aromatherapie** f aromatherapy

arrogant adj arrogant

Arsch (-es, Ärsche) m (vulg) arse (BRIT), ass (US); **Arschloch** nt (vulg: Person) arsehole (BRIT), asshole (US)

Art (-, -en) f (Weise) way; (Sorte) kind, sort; (bei Tieren) species; **nach ~ des Hauses** à la maison; **auf diese Art und Weise** in this way; **das ist nicht seine ~** that's not like him

Arterie (-, -n) f artery

artig *adj* good, well-behaved
Artikel (-s, -) *m* (*Ware*) article, item; (*Zeitung*) article
Artischocke (-, -n) *f* artichoke
Artist(in) (-en, -en) *m(f)* (circus) performer
Arznei *f* medicine; **Arzt** (-es, *Ärzte*) *m* doctor; **Arzthelfer(in)** *m(f)* doctor's assistant; **Ärztin** *f* (female) doctor; **ärztlich** *adj* medical; **sich ~ behandeln lassen** to undergo medical treatment
Asche (-, -n) *f* ashes *pl*; (*von Zigarette*) ash; **Aschenbecher** *m* ashtray; **Aschermittwoch** *m* Ash Wednesday
Asiat(in) (-en, -en) *m(f)* Asian; **asiatisch** *adj* Asian; **Asien** (-s) *nt* Asia
Aspekt (-(e)s, -e) *m* aspect
Asphalt (-(e)s, -e) *m* asphalt
Aspirin® (-s, -e) *nt* aspirin
aß *imperf von* **essen**
Ass (-es, -e) *nt* (*Karten, Tennis*) ace
Assistent(in) *m(f)* assistant
Ast (-(e)s, *Äste*) *m* branch
Asthma (-s) *nt* asthma
Astrologie *f* astrology; **Astronaut(in)** (-en, -en) *m(f)* astronaut; **Astronomie** *f* astronomy
ASU (-, -s) *f abk* = **Abgassonderuntersuchung** exhaust emission test
Asyl (-s, -e) *nt* asylum; (*Heim*) home; (*für Obdachlose*) shelter; **Asylant(in)** *m(f)*, **Asylbewerber(in)** *m(f)* asylum seeker
Atelier (-s, -s) *nt* studio
Atem (-s) *m* breath; **atemberaubend** *adj* breathtaking; **Atembeschwerden** *pl* breathing difficulties *pl*; **atemlos** *adj* breathless; **Atempause** *f* breather
Athen *nt* Athens
Äthiopien (-s) *nt* Ethiopia
Athlet(in) (-en, -en) *m(f)* athlete

Atlantik (-s) *m* Atlantic (Ocean)
Atlas (- *o Atlasses, Atlanten*) *m* atlas
atmen *vt, vi* to breathe; **Atmung** *f* breathing
Atom (-s, -e) *nt* atom; **Atombombe** *f* atom bomb; **Atomkraftwerk** *nt* nuclear power station; **Atommüll** *m* nuclear waste; **Atomwaffen** *pl* nuclear weapons *pl*
Attentat (-(e)s, -e) *nt* assassination (*auf +akk of*); (*Versuch*) assassination attempt
Attest (-(e)s, -e) *nt* certificate
attraktiv *adj* attractive
Attrappe (-, -n) *f* dummy
ätzend *adj* (*fam*) revolting; (*schlecht*) lousy
au *interj* ouch; **~ ja!** yeah
Aubergine (-, -n) *f* aubergine, eggplant (*US*)
auch *conj* also, too; (*selbst, sogar*) even; (*wirklich*) really; **oder ~** or; **ich ~ so** so I; **ich ~ nicht** me neither; **wer/was ~ immer** whoever/whatever; **ich gehe jetzt - ich ~** I'm going now - so am I; **das weiß ich ~ nicht** I don't know either
audiovisuell *adj* audiovisual
auf *prep +akk o dat* (*räumlich*) on; **~ der Reise/dem Tisch** on the way/the table; **~ der Post®/der Party** at the post office/the party; **etw ~ den Tisch stellen** to put sth on the table; **~ Deutsch** in German ▷ *prep +akk* (*hinauf*) up; (*in Richtung*) to; (*nach*) after; **~ eine Party gehen** to go to a party; **bis ~ ihn** except for him; **~ einmal** suddenly; (*gleichzeitig*) at once ▷ *adv* (*offen*) open; **~ sein** (*fam*) to be open; (*Mensch*) to be up; **~ und ab** up and down; **~!** (*los!*) come on!; **~ dass** so that
aufatmen *vi* to breathe a sigh of relief
aufbauen *vt* (*errichten*) to put up; (*schaffen*) to build up; (*gestalten*) to

construct; (gründen) to found, to base (auf +akk on); **sich eine Existenz ~** to make a life for oneself

auf|bewahren vt to keep, to store

auf|bleiben irr vi (Tür, Laden etc) to stay open; (Mensch) to stay up

auf|blenden vi, vt (**die Scheinwerfer**) ~ to put one's headlights on full beam

auf|brechen irr vt to break open ▷ vi to burst open; (gehen) to leave; (abreisen) to set off; **Aufbruch** m departure

auf|drängen vt **jdm etw ~** to force sth on sb ▷ vr **sich ~** to intrude (jdm on sb); **aufdringlich** adj pushy

aufeinander adv (übereinander) on top of each other; **~ achten** to look after each other; **~ schießen** to shoot at each other; **~ vertrauen** to trust each other; **~ folgen** to follow one another; **~ prallen** to crash into one another

Aufenthalt m stay; (Zug) stop; **Aufenthaltsgenehmigung** f residence permit; **Aufenthaltsraum** m lounge

auf|essen irr vt to eat up

auf|fahren irr vi (Auto) to run (o to crash) (auf +akk into); (herankommen) to drive up; **Auffahrt** f (am Haus) drive; (Autobahn) slip road (BRIT), ramp (US); **Auffahrunfall** m rear-end collision; (mehrere Fahrzeuge) pile-up

auf|fallen irr vi to stand out; **jdm ~** to strike sb; **das fällt gar nicht auf** nobody will notice; **auffallend** adj striking; **auffällig** adj conspicuous; (Kleidung, Farbe) striking

auf|fangen irr vt (Ball) to catch; (Stoß) to cushion

auf|fassen vt to understand; **Auffassung** f (view); (Meinung) opinion; (Auslegung) concept; (Auffassungsgabe) grasp

auf|fordern vt (befehlen) to call upon; (bitten) to ask

auf|frischen vt (Kenntnisse) to brush up

auf|führen vt (Theat) to perform; (in einem Verzeichnis) to list; (Beispiel) to give ▷ vr **sich ~** (sich benehmen) to behave; **Aufführung** f (Theat) performance

Aufgabe f job, task; (Schule) exercise; (Hausaufgabe) homework

Aufgang m (Treppe) staircase

auf|geben vt (verzichten auf) to give up; (Paket) to post; (Gepäck) to check in; (Bestellung) to place; (Inserat) to insert; (Rätsel, Problem) to set ▷ vi to give up

auf|gehen irr vi (Sonne, Teig) to rise; (sich öffnen) to open; (klar werden) to dawn (jdm on sb)

aufgelegt adj **gut/schlecht ~** in a good/bad mood

aufgeregt adj excited

aufgeschlossen adj open(minded)

aufgeschmissen adj (fam) in a fix

aufgrund, auf Grund prep +gen on the basis of; (wegen) because of

auf|haben irr vt (Hut etc) to have on; **viel ~** (Schule) to have a lot of homework to do ▷ vi (Geschäft) to be open

auf|halten irr vt (jdn) to detain; (Entwicklung) to stop; (Tür, Hund) to hold open; (Augen) to keep open ▷ vr **sich ~** (wohnen) to live; (vorübergehend) to stay

auf|hängen irr vt to hang up

auf|heben irr vt (vom Boden etc) to pick up; (aufbewahren) to keep

auf|holen vt (Zeit) to make up ▷ vi to catch up

auf|hören vi to stop; **~, etw zu tun** to stop doing sth

auf|klären vt (Geheimnis etc) to

clear up; **jdn ~** to enlighten sb; (*sexuell*) to tell sb the facts of life

Aufkleber (*-s, -*) *m* sticker

auf|kommen *irr vi* (*Wind*) to come up; (*Zweifel, Gefühl*) to arise; (*Mode etc*) to appear on the scene; **für den Schaden ~** to pay for the damage

auf|laden *irr vt* to load; (*Handy etc*) to charge; **Aufladegerät** *nt* charger

Auflage *f* edition; (*von Zeitung*) circulation; (*Bedingung*) condition

auf|lassen *vt* (*Hut, Brille*) to keep on; (*Tür*) to leave open

Auflauf *m* (*Menschen*) crowd; (*Speise*) bake

auf|legen *vt* (*CD, Schminke etc*) to put on; (*Hörer*) to put down ▷ *vi* (*Tel*) to hang up

auf|leuchten *vi* to light up

auf|lösen *vt* (*in Flüssigkeit*) to dissolve ▷ *vr* **sich ~** (*in Flüssigkeit*) to dissolve; **der Stau hat sich aufgelöst** traffic is back to normal; **Auflösung** *f* (*von Rätsel*) solution; (*von Bildschirm*) resolution

auf|machen *vt* to open; (*Kleidung*) to undo ▷ *vr* **sich ~** to set out (*nach for*)

aufmerksam *adj* attentive; **jdn auf etw** (*akk*) **~ machen** to draw sb's attention to sth; **Aufmerksamkeit** *f* attention; (*Konzentration*) attentiveness; (*Geschenk*) small token

auf|muntern *vt* (*ermutigen*) to encourage; (*aufheitern*) to cheer up

Aufnahme (*-, -n*) *f* (*Foto*) photo(graph); (*einzelne*) shot; (*in Verein, Krankenhaus etc*) admission; (*Beginn*) beginning; (*auf Tonband etc*) recording; **Aufnahmeprüfung** *f* entrance exam; **auf|nehmen** *irr vt* (*in Krankenhaus, Verein etc*) to admit; (*Musik*) to record; (*beginnen*) to take up; (*in Liste*) to include; (*begreifen*) to

take in; **mit jdm Kontakt ~** to get in touch with sb

auf|passen *vi* (*aufmerksam sein*) to pay attention; (*vorsichtig sein*) to take care; **auf jdn/etw ~** to keep an eye on sb/sth

Aufprall (*-s, -e*) *m* impact; **auf|prallen** *vi* **auf etw** (*akk*) **~** to hit sth, to crash into sth

Aufpreis *m* extra charge

auf|pumpen *vt* to pump up

Aufputschmittel *nt* stimulant

auf|räumen *vt, vi* (*Dinge*) to clear away; (*Zimmer*) to tidy up

aufrecht *adj* upright

auf|regen *vt* to excite; (*ärgern*) to annoy ▷ *vr* **sich ~** to get worked up; **aufregend** *adj* exciting; **Aufregung** *f* excitement

auf|reißen *irr vt* (*Tüte*) to tear open; (*Tür*) to fling open; (*fam: Person*) to pick up

Aufruf *m* (*Aviat, Inform*) call; (*öffentlicher*) appeal; **auf|rufen** *irr vt* (*auffordern*) to call upon (*zu for*); (*Namen*) to call out; (*Aviat*) to call; (*Inform*) to call up

auf|runden *vt* (*Summe*) to round up

aufs *kontr von* **auf das**

Aufsatz *m* essay

auf|schieben *irr vt* (*verschieben*) to postpone; (*verzögern*) to put off; (*Tür*) to slide open

Aufschlag *m* (*auf Preis*) extra charge; (*Tennis*) service; **auf|schlagen** *irr vt* (*öffnen*) to open; (*verletzen*) to cut open; (*Zelt*) to pitch, to put up; (*Lager*) to set up ▷ *vi* (*Tennis*) to serve; **auf etw** (*+akk*) **~** (*aufprallen*) to hit sth

auf|schließen *irr vt* to unlock, to open up ▷ *vi* (*aufrücken*) to close up

auf|schneiden *irr vt* to cut open; (*in Scheiben*) to slice ▷ *vi* (*angeben*) to boast, to show off

Aufschnitt m (slices pl of) cold meat; (bei Käse) (assorted) sliced cheeses pl

auf|schreiben irr vt to write down

Aufschrift f inscription; (Etikett) label

Aufschub m (Verzögerung) delay; (Vertagung) postponement

Aufsehen (-s) nt stir; **großes ~ erregen** to cause a sensation; **Aufseher(in)** (-s, -) m(f) guard; (im Betrieb) supervisor; (im Museum) attendant; (im Park) keeper

auf sein irr vi siehe **auf**

auf|setzen vt to put on; (Dokument) to draw up ▷ vi (Flugzeug) to touch down

Aufsicht f supervision; (bei Prüfung) invigilation; **die ~ haben** to be in charge

auf|spannen vt (Schirm) to put up

auf|sperren vt (Mund) to open wide; (aufschließen) to unlock

auf|springen irr vi to jump (auf +akk onto); (hochspringen) to jump up; (sich öffnen) to spring open

auf|stehen irr vi to get up; (Tür) to be open

auf|stellen vt (aufrecht stellen) to put up; (aufreihen) to line up; (nominieren) to put up; (Liste, Programm) to draw up; (Rekord) to set up

Aufstieg (-(e)s, -e) m (auf Berg) ascent; (Fortschritt) rise; (beruflich, im Sport) promotion

Aufstrich m spread

auf|tanken vt, vi (Auto) to tank up; (Flugzeug) to refuel

auf|tauchen vi to turn up; (aus Wasser etc) to surface; (Frage, Problem) to come up

auf|tauen vt (Speisen) to defrost ▷ vi to thaw; (fig: Person) to unbend

Auftrag (-(e)s, Aufträge) m (Comm) order; (Arbeit) job; (Anweisung) instructions pl; (Aufgabe) task; **im ~**

von on behalf of; **auf|tragen** irr vt (Salbe etc) to apply; (Essen) to serve

auf|treten irr vi to appear; (Problem) to come up; (sich verhalten) to behave; **Auftritt** m (des Schauspielers) entrance; (fig: Szene) scene

auf|wachen vi to wake up

auf|wachsen irr vi to grow up

Aufwand (-(e)s) m expenditure; (Kosten a.) expense; (Anstrengung) effort; **aufwändig** adj costly; **das ist zu ~** that's too much trouble

auf|wärmen vt to warm up ▷ vr **sich ~** to warm up

aufwärts adv upwards; **mit etw geht es ~** things are looking up for sth

auf|wecken vt to wake up

aufwendig adj siehe **aufwändig**

auf|wischen vt to wipe up; (Fußboden) to wipe

auf|zählen vt to list; **Aufzählungszeichen** nt bullet

auf|zeichnen vt to sketch; (schriftlich) to jot down; (auf Band etc) to record; **Aufzeichnung** f (schriftlich) note; (Tonband etc) recording; (Film) record

auf|ziehen irr vt (öffnen) to pull open, (Uhr) to wind (up), (fam: necken) to tease; (Kinder) to bring up; (Tiere) to rear ▷ vi (Gewitter) to come up

Aufzug m (Fahrstuhl) lift (BRIT), elevator (US); (Kleidung) get-up; (Theat) act

Auge (-s, -n) nt eye; **jdm etw aus ~ drücken** (fam) to force sth on sb, **ins ~ gehen** (fam) to go wrong; **unter vier ~n** in private; **etw im ~ behalten** to keep sth in mind; **Augenarzt** m, **Augenärztin** f eye specialist, eye doctor (US); **Augenblick** m moment, **im ~** at the moment; **Augenbraue** (-, -n) f eyebrow; **Augenbrauenstift** m eyebrow pencil; **Augenfarbe** f eye colour; **seine ~** the colour of his eyes; **Augenlid** *nt* eyelid; **Augenoptiker(in)** (*-s*, *-*) *m(f)* optician; **Augentropfen** *pl* eyedrops *pl*; **Augenzeuge** *m*, **Augenzeugin** *f* eyewitness

August (*-(e)s* o *-*, *-e*) *m* August; *siehe auch* **Juni**

Auktion *f* auction

aus *prep* +*dat* (*aus dem Innern von*) out of; (*von ... her*) from; (*Material*) (made) of; **~ Berlin kommen** to come from Berlin; **~ Versehen** by mistake; **~ Angst** out of fear ▷ *adv* out; (*beendet*) finished, over; **ein /~** (*Tech*) on / off; **~ sein** (*fam*: *Sport*) to be out; (*zu Ende*) to be over; **auf etw** (*akk*) **~ sein** to be after sth; **von mir ~** (*was mich angeht*) as far as I'm concerned; **von mir ~!** (*mir ist es egal*) I don't care; **zwischen uns ist es ~** we're finished; **Aus** (*-*) *nt* (*Sport*) touch; (*fig*) end

aus|atmen *vt* to breathe out

aus|bauen *vt* (*Haus*, *Straße*) to extend; (*Motor etc*) to remove

aus|bessern *vt* to repair; (*Kleidung*) to mend

aus|bilden *vt* to educate; (*Lehrling etc*) to train; (*Fähigkeiten*) to develop; **Ausbildung** *f* education; (*von Lehrling etc*) training; (*von Fähigkeiten*) development

Ausblick *m* view; (*fig*) outlook

aus|brechen *irr vi* to break out; **in Tränen ~** to burst into tears; **in Gelächter ~** to burst out laughing

aus|breiten *vt* to spread (out); (*Arme*) to stretch out ▷ *vr* **sich ~** to spread

Ausbruch *m* (*Krieg*, *Seuche etc*) outbreak; (*Vulkan*) eruption; (*Gefühle*) outburst; (*von Gefangenen*) escape

aus|buhen *vt* to boo

Ausdauer *f* perseverance; (*Sport*) stamina

aus|dehnen *vt* to stretch; (*fig*:

Macht) to extend

aus|denken *irr vt* **sich** (*dat*) **etw ~** to come up with sth

Ausdruck *m* (*Ausdrücke*) expression ▷ *m* (*Computerausdruck*) print-out; **aus|drucken** *vt* (*Inform*) to print (out)

aus|drücken *vt* (*formulieren*) to express; (*Zigarette*) to put out; (*Zitrone etc*) to squeeze ▷ *vr* **sich ~** to express oneself; **ausdrücklich** *adj* express ▷ *adv* expressly

auseinander *adv* (*getrennt*) apart; **~ gehen** (*Menschen*) to separate; (*Meinungen*) to differ; (*Gegenstand*) to fall apart; **~ halten** to tell apart; **~ schreiben** to write as separate words; **~ setzen** (*erklären*) to explain; **sich ~ setzen** (*sich beschäftigen*) to look (mit *at*); (*sich streiten*) to argue (mit *with*); **Auseinandersetzung** *f* (*Streit*) argument; (*Diskussion*) debate

Ausfahrt *f* (*des Zuges etc*) departure; (*Autobahn*, *Garage etc*) exit

aus|fallen *vi* (*Haare*) to fall out; (*nicht stattfinden*) to be cancelled; (*nicht funktionieren*) to break down; (*Strom*) to be cut off; (*Resultat haben*) to turn out; **groß/klein ~** (*Kleidung*, *Schuhe*) to be too big / too small

ausfindig machen *vt* to discover

aus|flippen *vi* (*fam*) to freak out

Ausflug *m* excursion, outing; **Ausflugsziel** *nt* destination

Ausfluss *m* (*Med*) discharge

aus|fragen *vt* to question

Ausfuhr (*-*, *-en*) *f* export

aus|führen *vt* (*verwirklichen*) to carry out; (*Person*) to take out; (*Comm*) to export; (*darlegen*) to explain

ausführlich *adj* detailed ▷ *adv* in detail

aus|füllen *vt* to fill up; (*Fragebogen etc*) to fill in (*o* out)

Ausgabe *f* (*Geld*) expenditure; (*Inform*) output; (*Buch*) edition; (*Num-*

mer) issue

Ausgang m way out, exit; (*Flugsteig*) gate; (*Ende*) end; (*Ergebnis*) result; „**kein ~**" 'no exit'

aus|geben *irr vt* (*Geld*) to spend; (*austeilen*) to distribute; **jdm etw ~** (*spendieren*) to buy sb sth ▷ *vr* **sich für etw/jdn ~** to pass oneself off as sth/sb

ausgebucht *adj* fully booked

ausgefallen *adj* (*ungewöhnlich*) unusual

aus|gehen *irr vi* (*abends etc*) to go out; (*Benzin, Kaffee etc*) to run out; (*Haare*) to fall out; (*Feuer, Licht etc*) to go out; (*Resultat haben*) to turn out; **davon ~, dass** to assume that; **ihm ging das Geld aus** he ran out of money

ausgelassen *adj* exuberant

ausgeleiert *adj* worn out

ausgenommen *conj, prep +gen o dat* except

ausgerechnet *adv* **~ du** you of all people; **~ heute** today of all days

ausgeschildert *adj* signposted

ausgeschlafen *adj* **bist du ~?** have you had enough sleep?

ausgeschlossen *adj* (*unmöglich*) impossible, out of the question

ausgesprochen *adj* (*absolut*) out-and-out; (*unverkennbar*) marked ▷ *adv* extremely; **~ gut** really good

ausgezeichnet *adj* excellent

ausgiebig *adj* (*Gebrauch*) thorough; (*Essen*) substantial

aus|gießen *irr vt* (*Getränk*) to pour out; (*Gefäß*) to empty

aus|gleichen *irr vt* to even out ▷ *vi* (*Sport*) to equalize

Ausguss m (*Spüle*) sink; (*Abfluss*) outlet

aus|halten *irr vt* to bear, to stand; **nicht auszuhalten sein** to be unbearable ▷ *vi* to hold out

aus|händigen *vt* **jdm etw ~** to

hand sth over to sb

Aushang m notice

Aushilfe f temporary help; (*im Büro*) temp

aus|kennen *irr vr* **sich ~** to know a lot (*bei, mit* about); (*an einem Ort*) to know one's way around

aus|kommen *irr vi* **gut/schlecht mit jdm ~** to get on well / badly with sb; **mit etw ~** to get by with sth

Auskunft (-, *Auskünfte*) f information; (*nähere*) details pl; (*Schalter*) information desk; (*Tel*) (directory) enquiries *sing* (*kein Artikel*, BRIT), information (*US*)

aus|lachen *vt* to laugh at

aus|laden *irr vt* (*Gepäck etc*) to unload; **jdn ~** (*Gast*) to tell sb not to come

Auslage f window display; **~n** pl (*Kosten*) expenses

Ausland nt foreign countries pl; **im/ins ~** abroad; **Ausländer(in)** (*-s, -*) m(f) foreigner; **ausländerfeindlich** *adj* hostile to foreigners, xenophobic; **ausländisch** *adj* foreign; **Auslandsgespräch** nt international call; **Auslandskrankenschein** m health insurance certificate for foreign countries, ≈ E111 (BRIT); **Auslandsschutzbrief** m international (motor) insurance cover (*documents pl*)

aus|lassen *irr vt* to leave out (*Wort etc a.*) to omit; (*überspringen*) to skip; (*Wut, Ärger*) to vent (*an +dat* on) ▷ *vr* **sich über etw** (*akk*) **~** to speak one's mind about sth

aus|laufen *irr vi* (*Flüssigkeit*) to run out; (*Tank etc*) to leak; (*Schiff*) to leave port; (*Vertrag*) to expire

aus|legen *vt* (*Waren*) to display; (*Geld*) to lend; (*Text etc*) to interpret; (*technisch ausstatten*) to design (*für, auf +akk* for)

aus|leihen *irr vt* (*verleihen*) to lend;

sich (dat) **etw ~** to borrow sth
aus|loggen vi (Inform) to log out (o
off)
aus|lösen vt (Explosion, Alarm) to
set off; (hervorrufen) to cause; **Auslöser** (-s, -) m (Foto) shutter release
aus|machen vt (Licht, Radio) to
turn off; (Feuer) to put out; (Termin,
Preis) to fix; (vereinbaren) to agree;
(Anteil darstellen, betragen) to represent; (bedeuten) to matter; **macht es
ihnen etwas aus, wenn ...?** would
you mind if ...?; **das macht mir
nichts aus** I don't mind
Ausmaß nt extent
Ausnahme (-, -n) f exception;
ausnahmsweise adv as an exception, just this once
aus|nutzen vt (Zeit, Gelegenheit,
Einfluss) to use; (jdn, Gutmütigkeit) to
take advantage of
aus|packen vt to unpack
aus|probieren vt to try (out)
Auspuff (-(e)s, -e) m (Tech) exhaust;
Auspuffrohr nt exhaust (pipe);
Auspufftopf m (Auto) silencer
(BRIT), muffler (US)
aus|rauben vt to rob
aus|räumen vt (Dinge) to clear
away; (Schrank, Zimmer) to empty;
(Bedenken) to put aside
aus|rechnen vt to calculate, to
work out
Ausrede f excuse
aus|reden vi to finish speaking ▷
vt **jdm etw ~** to talk sb out of sth
ausreichend adj sufficient, satisfactory; (Schulnote) ≈ D
Ausreise f departure; **bei der ~** on
leaving the country; **Ausreiseer-
laubnis** f exit visa; **aus|reisen** vi
to leave the country
aus|reißen irr vt to tear out ▷ vi
to come off; (fam: davonlaufen) to run
away
aus|renken vt **sich** (dat) **den Arm**

~ to dislocate one's arm
aus|richten vt (Botschaft) to de-
liver; (Gruß) to pass on; (erreichen)
ich konnte bei ihr nichts ~
I couldn't get anywhere with her;
jdm etw ~ to tell sb sth
aus|rufen vt (über Lautsprecher)
to announce; **jdn ~ lassen** to page
sb; **Ausrufezeichen** nt exclamation mark
aus|ruhen vi to rest ▷ vr **sich ~** to
rest
Ausrüstung f equipment
aus|rutschen vi to slip
aus|schalten vt to switch off; (fig)
to eliminate
Ausschau f **~ halten** to look out
(nach for)
aus|scheiden irr vt (Med) to give
off, to secrete ▷ vi to leave (aus etw
sth); (Sport) to be eliminated
aus|schlafen irr vi to have a lie-in
▷ vr **sich ~** to have a lie-in ▷ vt to
sleep off
Ausschlag m (Med) rash; **den ~
geben** (fig) to tip the balance;
aus|schlagen irr vt (Zahn) to knock
out; (Einladung) to turn down ▷ vi
(Pferd) to kick out; **ausschlagge-
bend** adj decisive
aus|schließen irr vt to lock out;
(fig) to exclude; **ausschließlich** adv
exclusively ▷ prep +gen excluding
Ausschnitt m (Teil) section; (von
Kleid) neckline; (aus Zeitung) cutting
Ausschreitungen pl riots pl
aus|schütten vt (Flüssigkeit) to
pour out; (Gefäß) to empty
aus|sehen irr vi to look; **krank ~**
to look ill; **gut ~** (Person) to be good-
looking; (Sache) to be looking good;
es sieht nach Regen aus it looks
like rain; **es sieht schlecht aus**
things look bad
aus sein irr vi siehe **aus**
außen adv outside; **nach ~** out-

wards; **von ~** from (the) outside;
Außenbordmotor m outboard
motor; **Außenminister(in)** m(f)
foreign minister, Foreign Secretary
(BRIT); **Außenseite** f outside; **Au-
ßenseiter(in)** m(f) outsider; **Au-
ßenspiegel** m wing mirror (BRIT),
side mirror (US)

außer prep +dat (abgesehen von)
except (for); **nichts ~** nothing but; **~
Betrieb** out of order; **~ sich sein** to
be beside oneself (vor with); **~ Atem**
out of breath ▷ conj (ausgenommen)
except; **~ wenn** unless; **~ dass** except; **außerdem** conj besides

äußere(r, s) adj outer, external
außergewöhnlich adj unusual ▷
adv exceptionally; **~ kalt** exceptionally cold; **außerhalb** prep +gen
outside

äußerlich adj external
äußern vt to express; (zeigen) to
show ▷ vr **sich ~** to give one's
opinion; (sich zeigen) to show itself
außerordentlich adj extraordinary; **außerplanmäßig** adj un-
scheduled

äußerst adv extremely; **äußers-
te(r, s)** adj utmost, (räumlich) farthest; (Termin) last possible

Äußerung f remark

aus|setzen vt (Kind, Tier) to
abandon; (Belohnung) to offer; **ich
habe nichts daran auszusetzen**
I have no objection to it ▷ vi (aufhören) to stop; (Pause machen) to
drop out; (beim Spiel) to miss a turn

Aussicht f (Blick) view; (Chance)
prospect; **aussichtslos** adj hopeless; **Aussichtsplattform** f observation platform; **Aussichtsturm**
m observation tower

Aussiedler(in) (-s, -) m(f) émigré
(person of German descent from Eastern
Europe)

aus|spannen vi (erholen) to relax

▷ vt **er hat ihm die Freundin
ausgespannt** (fam) he's nicked his
girlfriend

aus|sperren vt to lock out ▷ vr
sich ~ to lock oneself out

Aussprache f (von Wörtern) pronunciation; (Gespräch) (frank) dis-
cussion; **aus|sprechen** irr vt to
pronounce; (äußern) to express ▷ vr
sich ~ to talk (über +akk about) ▷ vi
(zu Ende sprechen) to finish speaking

aus|spülen vt to rinse (out)

Ausstattung f (Ausrüstung)
equipment; (Einrichtung) furnishings
pl; (von Auto) fittings pl

aus|stehen irr vt to endure; **ich
kann ihn nicht ~** I can't stand him ▷
vi (noch nicht da sein) to be outstanding

aus|steigen irr vi to get out (aus
of); **aus dem Bus/Zug ~** to get off
the bus/train; **Aussteiger(in)** m(f)
dropout

aus|stellen vt to display; (auf
Messe, in Museum etc) to exhibit; (fam:
ausschalten) to switch off; (Scheck etc)
to make out; (Pass etc) to issue;
Ausstellung f exhibition

aus|sterben irr vi to die out

aus|strahlen vt to radiate; (Pro-
gramm) to broadcast; **Ausstrah-
lung** f (Radio, TV) broadcast; (fig: von
Person) charisma

aus|strecken vr **sich ~** to stretch
out ▷ vt (Hand) to reach out (nach for)

aus|suchen vt to choose

Austausch m exchange; **aus|
tauschen** vt to exchange (gegen
for)

aus|teilen vt to distribute; (aus-
händigen) to hand out

Auster (-, -n) f oyster; **Austernpilz**
m oyster mushroom

aus|tragen irr vt (Post) to deliver;
(Wettkampf) to hold

Australien (-s) nt Australia; **Aus-**

tralier(in) (-s, -) m(f) Australian; **australisch** adj Australian

aus|trinken irr vt (Glas) to drain; (Getränk) to drink up ▷ vi to finish one's drink

aus|trocknen vi to dry out; (Fluss) to dry up

aus|üben vt (Beruf, Sport) to practise; (Einfluss) to exert

Ausverkauf m sale; **ausverkauft** adj (Karten, Artikel) sold out

Auswahl f selection, choice (an +dat of); **aus|wählen** vt to select, to choose

aus|wandern vi to emigrate

auswärtig adj (nicht am/vom Ort) not local; (ausländisch) foreign; **auswärts** adv (außerhalb der Stadt) out of town; (Sport) **~ spielen** to play away; **Auswärtsspiel** nt away match

aus|wechseln vt to replace; (Sport) to substitute

Ausweg m way out

aus|weichen irr vi to get out of the way; **jdm/einer Sache ~** to move aside for sb/sth; (fig) to avoid sb/sth

Ausweis (-es, -e) m (Personalausweis) identity card, ID; (für Bibliothek etc) card; **aus|weisen** irr vt to expel ▷ vr **sich ~** to prove one's identity; **Ausweiskontrolle** f ID check; **Ausweispapiere** pl identification documents pl

auswendig adv by heart

aus|wuchten vt (Auto: Räder) to balance

aus|zahlen vt (Summe) to pay (out); (Person) to pay off ▷ vr **sich ~** to be worth it

aus|zeichnen vt (ehren) to honour; (Comm) to price ▷ vr **sich ~** to distinguish oneself

aus|ziehen vt (Kleidung) to take off ▷ vr **sich ~** to undress ▷ vi (aus Wohnung) to move out

Auszubildende(r) mf trainee

Auto (-s, -s) nt car; **~ fahren** to drive; **Autoatlas** m road atlas; **Autobahn** f motorway (BRIT), freeway (US); **Autobahnauffahrt** f motorway access road (BRIT), on-ramp (US); **Autobahnausfahrt** f motorway exit (BRIT), off-ramp (US); **Autobahngebühr** f toll; **Autobahnkreuz** nt motorway interchange; **Autobahnring** m motorway ring (BRIT), beltway (US); **Autobombe** f car bomb; **Autofähre** f car ferry; **Autofahrer(in)** m(f) driver, motorist; **Autofahrt** f drive

Autogramm (-s, -e) nt autograph

Automarke f make of car

Automat (-en, -en) m vending machine

Automatik (-, -en) f (Auto) automatic transmission; **Automatikschaltung** f automatic gear change (BRIT) (o shift (US)); **Automatikwagen** m automatic

automatisch adj automatic ▷ adv automatically

Automechaniker(in) m(f) car mechanic; **Autonummer** f registration (BRIT) (o license (US)) number; **Autoradio** nt car radio; **Autoreifen** m car tyre; **Autoreisezug** m Motorail train® (BRIT), auto train (US); **Autorennen** nt motor racing; (einzelnes Rennen) motor race; **Autoschlüssel** m car key; **Autotelefon** nt car phone; **Autounfall** m car accident; **Autoverleih** m, **Autovermietung** f car hire (BRIT) (o rental (US)); (Firma) car hire (BRIT) (o rental (US)) company; **Autowaschanlage** f car wash; **Autowerkstatt** f car repair shop, garage; **Autozubehör** nt car accessories pl

Avocado (-, -s) f avocado

Axt (-, Äxte) f axe

Azubi (-s, -s) m (-, -s) f akr = **Auszubildende** trainee

b

B *abk* = **Bundesstraße**

Baby (-s, -s) *nt* baby; **Babybett** *nt* cot (BRIT), crib (US); **Babyfläschchen** *nt* baby's bottle; **Babynahrung** *f* baby food; **Babysitter(in)** *m(f)* babysitter; **Babysitz** *m* child seat; **Babywickelraum** *m* baby-changing room

Bach (-(e)s, Bäche) *m* stream

Backblech *nt* baking tray (BRIT), cookie sheet (US)

Backbord *nt* port (side)

Backe (, *n*) *f* cheek

backen (backte, gebacken) *vt, vi* to bake

Backenzahn *m* molar

Bäcker(in) (-s, -) *m(f)* baker; **Bäckerei** *f* bakery, (Laden) baker's (shop)

Backofen *m* oven; **Backpulver** *nt* baking powder

Backspace-Taste *f* (Inform) backspace key

Backstein *m* brick

Backwaren *pl* bread, cakes and pastries *pl*

Bad (-(e)s, Bäder) *nt* bath; (Schwimmen) swim; (Ort) spa; **ein ~ nehmen** to have (o take) a bath; **Badeanzug** *m* swimsuit, swimming costume (BRIT); **Badehose** *f* swimming trunks *pl*; **Badekappe** *f* swimming cap; **Bademantel** *m* bathrobe, **Bademeister(in)** *m(f)* pool attendant; **Bademütze** *f* swimming cap

baden *vi* to have a bath; (schwimmen) to swim, to bathe (BRIT) ▷ *vt* to bath (BRIT), to bathe (US)

Baden-Württemberg (-s) *nt* Baden-Württemberg

Badeort *m* spa; **Badesachen** *pl* swimming things *pl*; **Badetuch** *nt* bath towel; **Badewanne** *f* bath (tub); **Badezimmer** *nt* bathroom

Badminton *nt* badminton

baff *adj* **~ sein** (fam) to be flabbergasted (o gobsmacked)

Bagger (-s, -) *m* excavator; **Baggersee** *m* artificial lake in quarry etc, used for bathing

Bahamas *pl* **die ~** the Bahamas *pl*

Bahn (-, -en) *f* (Eisenbahn) railway (BRIT), railroad (US); (Rennbahn) track; (für Läufer) lane; (Astr) orbit; **bahnbrechend** *adj* groundbreaking; **BahnCard®** (-, -s) *f* rail card (allowing 50% or 25% reduction on tickets); **Bahnfahrt** *f* railway (BRIT) (o railroad US) journey; **Bahnhof** *m* station; **am (o auf dem) ~** at the station; **Bahnlinie** *f* railway (BRIT) (o railroad US) line; **Bahnpolizei** *f* railway (BRIT) (o railroad US) police; **Bahnsteig** (-(e)s, -e) *m* platform; **Bahnstrecke** *f* railway (BRIT) (o railroad US) line; **Bahnübergang** *m* level crossing (BRIT), grade crossing (US)

Bakterien *pl* bacteria *pl*, germs *pl*

bald *adv* (zeitlich) soon; (beinahe)

almost; **bis ~!** see you soon (*o later*); **baldig** *adj* quick, speedy

Balkan (-s) *m* **der ~** the Balkans *pl*

Balken (-s, -) *m* beam

Balkon (-s, -s *o* -e) *m* balcony

Ball (-(e)s, **Bälle**) *m* ball; (*Tanz*) dance, ball

Ballett (-s,) *nt* ballet

Ballon (-s, -s) *m* balloon

Ballspiel *nt* ball game

Ballungsgebiet *nt* conurbation

Baltikum (-s) *nt* **das ~** the Baltic States *pl*

Bambus (-ses, -se) *m* bamboo; **Bambussprossen** *pl* bamboo shoots *pl*

banal *adj* banal; (*Frage, Bemerkung*) trite

Banane (-, -n) *f* banana

band *imperf von* **binden**

Band (-(e)s, **Bände**) *m* (*Buch*) volume ▷ (-(e)s, **Bänder**) *nt* (*aus Stoff*) ribbon, tape; (*Fließband*) production line; (*Tonband*) tape; (*Anat*) ligament; **etw auf ~ aufnehmen** to tape sth ▷ (-, -s) *f* (*Musikgruppe*) band

Bandage (-, -n) *f* bandage; **bandagieren** *vt* to bandage

Bande (-, -n) *f* (*Gruppe*) gang

Bänderriss *m* (*Med*) torn ligament

Bandscheibe *f* (*Anat*) disc; **Bandwurm** *m* tapeworm

Bank (-, **Bänke**) *f* (*Sitzbank*) bench ▷ (-, -en) *f* (*Fin*) bank

Bankautomat *m* cash dispenser; **Bankkarte** *f* bank card; **Bankkonto** *nt* bank account; **Bankleitzahl** *f* bank sort code; **Banknote** *f* banknote; **Bankverbindung** *f* (*Kontonummer etc*) banking (*o account*) details *pl*

bar *adj* **-es Geld** cash; **etw (in) ~ bezahlen** to pay sth (in) cash

Bar (-, -s) *f* bar

Bär (-en, -en) *m* bear

barfuß *adj* barefoot

barg *imperf von* **bergen**

Bargeld *nt* cash; **bargeldlos** *adj* non-cash

Barkeeper (-s, -) *m* , **Barmann** *m* barman, bartender (*US*)

barock *adj* baroque

Barometer (-s, -) *m* barometer

barsch *adj* brusque

Barsch (-(e)s, -e) *m* perch

Barscheck *m* open (*o* uncrossed) cheque

Bart (-(e)s, **Bärte**) *m* beard; **bärtig** *adj* bearded

Barzahlung *f* cash payment

Basar (-s, -e) *m* bazaar

Baseballmütze *f* baseball cap

Basel (-s) *nt* Basle

Basilikum (-s) *nt* basil

Basis (-, **Basen**) *f* basis

Baskenland *nt* Basque region

Basketball *m* basketball

Bass (-es, **Bässe**) *m* bass

basta *interj* **und damit ~!** and that's that

basteln *vt* to make ▷ *vi* to make things, to do handicrafts

bat *imperf von* **bitten**

Batterie *f* battery; **batteriebetrieben** *adj* battery-powered

Bau (-(e)s) *m* (*Bauen*) building, construction; (*Aufbau*) structure; (*Baustelle*) building site ▷ *m* (*Baue*) (*Tier*) burrow ▷ *m* (*Bauten*) (*Gebäude*) building; **Bauarbeiten** *pl* construction work *sing*; (*Straßenbau*) roadworks *pl* (*BRIT*), roadwork (*US*); **Bauarbeiter(in)** *m(f)* construction worker

Bauch (-(e)s, **Bäuche**) *m* stomach; **Bauchnabel** *m* navel; **Bauchredner(in)** *m(f)* ventriloquist; **Bauchschmerzen** *pl* stomach-ache *sing*; **Bauchspeicheldrüse** *f* pancreas; **Bauchtanz** *m* belly dance; (*das Tanzen*) belly dancing; **Bauchweh** (-s) *nt* stomach-ache

Baudenkmal nt monument
bauen vt, vi to build; (Tech) to construct
Bauer (-n o -s, -n) m farmer; (Schach) pawn; **Bäuerin** f farmer; (Frau des Bauern) farmer's wife; **Bauernhof** m farm
baufällig adj dilapidated; **Baujahr** adj year of construction; **der Wagen ist ~ 2002** the car is a 2002 model, the car was made in 2002
Baum (-(e)s, Bäume) m tree
Baumarkt m DIY centre
Baumwolle f cotton
Bauplatz m building site; **Baustein** m (für Haus) stone; (Spielzeug) brick; (fig) element; **elektronischer ~** chip; **Baustelle** f building site; (bei Straßenbau) roadworks pl (BRIT), roadwork (US); **Bauteil** nt prefabricated part; **Bauunternehmer(in)** m(f) building contractor; **Bauwerk** nt building
Bayern (-s) nt Bavaria
beabsichtigen vt to intend
beachten vt (Aufmerksamkeit schenken) to pay attention to; (Vorschrift etc) to observe; **nicht ~** to ignore, disregard; **beachtlich** adj considerable
Beachvolleyball nt beach volleyball
Beamte(r) (-n, -n) m, **Beamtin** f official; (Staatsbeamter) civil servant
beanspruchen vt to claim; (Zeit, Platz) to take up; **jdn ~** to keep sb busy
beanstanden vt to complain about
beantragen vt to apply for
beantworten vt to answer
bearbeiten vt to work on; (Material, Daten) to process; (Chem) to treat; (Fall etc) to deal with; (Buch etc) to revise; (fam: beeinflussen wollen) to work on; **Bearbeitungsgebühr** f

handling (o service) charge
beatmen vt **jdn ~** to give sb artificial respiration
beaufsichtigen vt to supervise; (bei Prüfung) to invigilate
beauftragen vt to instruct; **jdn mit etw ~** to give sb the job of doing sth
Becher (-s, -) m mug; (ohne Henkel) tumbler; (für Joghurt) pot; (aus Pappe) tub
Becken (-s, -) nt basin; (Spüle) sink; (zum Schwimmen) pool; (Mus) cymbal; (Anat) pelvis
bedanken vr **sich ~** to say thank you; **sich bei jdm für etw ~** to thank sb for sth
Bedarf (-(e)s) m need (an +dat for); (Comm) demand (an +dat for); **je nach ~** according to demand; **bei ~** if necessary; **Bedarfshaltestelle** f request stop, flag stop (US)
bedauerlich adj regrettable; **bedauern** vt to regret; (bemitleiden) to feel sorry for; **bedauernswert** adj (Zustände) regrettable; (Mensch) unfortunate
bedeckt adj covered; (Himmel) overcast
bedenken irr vt to consider; **Bedenken** (-s, -) nt (Überlegen) consideration; (Zweifel) doubt; (Skrupel) scruples pl; **bedenklich** adj dubious; (Zustand) serious
bedeuten vt to mean; **jdm nichts / viel ~** to mean nothing / a lot to sb; **bedeutend** adj important; (beträchtlich) considerable; **Bedeutung** f meaning; (Wichtigkeit) importance
bedienen vt to serve; (Maschine) to operate ▷ vr **sich ~** (beim Essen) to help oneself; **Bedienung** f service; (Kellner / Kellnerin) waiter / waitress; (Verkäufer(in)) shop assistant; (Zu-

schlag) service (charge); **Bedienungsanleitung** f operating instructions pl; **Bedienungshandbuch** nt instruction manual; **Bedingung** f condition; **unter der ~, dass** on condition that; **unter diesen ~en** under these circumstances
bedrohen vt to threaten
Bedürfnis nt need
beeilen vr **sich ~** to hurry
beeindrucken vt to impress
beeinflussen vt to influence
beeinträchtigen vt to affect
beenden vt to end; *(fertigstellen)* to finish
beerdigen vt to bury; **Beerdigung** f burial; *(Feier)* funeral
Beere (-, -n) f berry; *(Traubenbeere)* grape
Beet (-(e)s, -e) nt bed
befahl imperf von **befehlen**
befahrbar adj passable; *(Naut)* navigable; **befahren** irr vt *(Straße)* to use; *(Pass)* to drive over; *(Fluss etc)* to navigate ▷ adj **stark / wenig ~** busy / quiet
Befehl (-(e)s, -e) m order; *(Inform)* command; **befehlen** *(befahl, befohlen)* vt to order; **jdm ~, etw zu tun** to order sb to do sth ▷ vi to give orders
befestigen vt to fix; *(mit Schnur, Seil)* to attach; *(mit Klebestoff)* to stick
befeuchten vt to moisten
befinden irr vr **sich ~** to be
befohlen pp von **befehlen**
befolgen vt *(Rat etc)* to follow
befördern vt *(transportieren)* to transport; *(beruflich)* to promote; **Beförderung** f transport; *(beruflich)* promotion; **Beförderungsbedingungen** pl conditions pl of carriage
Befragung f questioning; *(Umfrage)* opinion poll

befreundet adj friendly; **~ sein** to be friends *(mit jdm* with sb)
befriedigen vt to satisfy; **befriedigend** adj satisfactory; *(Schulnote)* ≈ C; **Befriedigung** f satisfaction
befristet adj limited *(auf +akk* to)
befruchten vt to fertilize; *(fig)* to stimulate
Befund (-(e)s, -e) m findings pl; *(Med)* diagnosis
befürchten vt to fear
befürworten vt to support
begabt adj gifted, talented; **Begabung** f talent, gift
begann imperf von **beginnen**
begegnen vi to meet *(jdm* sb), to meet with *(einer Sache dat* sth)
begehen irr vt *(Straftat)* to commit; *(Jubiläum etc)* to celebrate
begehrt adj sought-after; *(Junggeselle)* eligible
begeistern vt to fill with enthusiasm; *(inspirieren)* to inspire ▷ vr **sich für etw ~** to be / get enthusiastic about sth; **begeistert** adj enthusiastic
Beginn (-(e)s) m beginning; **zu ~** at the beginning; **beginnen** *(begann, begonnen)* vt, vi to start, to begin
beglaubigen vt to certify; **Beglaubigung** f certification
begleiten vt to accompany; **Begleiter(in)** m(f) companion; **Begleitung** f company; *(Mus)* accompaniment
beglückwünschen vt to congratulate *(zu* on)
begonnen pp von **beginnen**
begraben irr vt to bury; **Begräbnis** nt burial; *(Feier)* funeral
begreifen irr vt to understand
Begrenzung f boundary; *(fig)* restriction
Begriff (-(e)s, -e) m concept; *(Vorstellung)* idea; **im ~ sein, etw zu tun** to be on the point of doing sth;

schwer von ~ sein to be slow on the uptake

begründen vt (rechtfertigen) to justify; **Begründung** f explanation; (Rechtfertigung) justification

begrüßen vt to greet; (willkommen heißen) to welcome; **Begrüßung** f greeting; (Empfang) welcome

behaart adj hairy

behalten irr vt to keep; (im Gedächtnis) to remember; **etw für sich ~** to keep sth to oneself

Behälter (-s,) m container

behandeln vt to treat; **Behandlung** f treatment

behaupten vt to claim, to maintain ▷ vr **sich ~** to assert oneself; **Behauptung** f claim

beheizen vt to heat

behelfen irr vr **sich mit/ohne etw ~** to make do with/without sth

beherbergen vt to accommodate

beherrschen vt (Situation, Gefühle) to control; (Instrument) to master ▷ vr **sich ~** to control oneself; **Beherrschung** f control (über +akk of); **die ~ verlieren** to lose one's self-control

behilflich adj helpful; **jdm ~ sein** to help sb (bei with)

behindern vt to hinder; (Verkehr, Sicht) to obstruct; **Behinderte(r)** mf disabled person; **behindertengerecht** adj suitable for disabled people

Behörde (-, n) f authority; **die ~n** pl the authorities pl

bei prep +dat (örtlich: in der Nähe von) near, by; (zum Aufenthalt) at; (zeitlich: an, während) during; (Umstand) in; **~m Friseur** at the hairdresser's; **~ uns zuhause** at our place; (in unserem Land) in our country; **~ Nacht** at night; **~ Tag** by day; **~ Nebel** in fog; **~ Regen findet die Veranstaltung im Saal statt** if

it rains the event will take place in the hall; **etw ~ sich haben** to have sth on one; **~m Fahren** while driving

bei|behalten irr vt to keep

Beiboot nt dinghy

bei|bringen irr vt **jdm etw ~** (mitteilen) to break sth to sb, (lehren) to teach sb sth

beide(s) pron both; **meine ~n Brüder** my two brothers, both my brothers; **wir ~ both** (o the two) of us; **keiner von ~n** neither of them; **alle ~** both (of them); **~s ist sehr schön** both are very nice; **30 ~** (beim Tennis) 30 all

beieinander adv together

Beifahrer(in) m(f) passenger; **Beifahrerairbag** m passenger airbag; **Beifahrersitz** m passenger seat

Beifall (-(e)s) m applause

beige adj inv beige

Beigeschmack m aftertaste

Beil (-(e)s, -e) nt axe

Beilage f (Gastr) side dish; (Gemüse) vegetables pl; (zu Buch etc) supplement

beiläufig adj casual ▷ adv casually

Beileid nt condolences pl; (mein) **herzliches ~** please accept my sincere condolences

beiliegend adj enclosed

beim kontr von **bei dem**

Bein (-(e)s, -e) nt leg

beinah(e) adv almost, nearly

beinhalten vt to contain

Beipackzettel m instruction leaflet

beisammen adv together; **Beisammensein** nt get-together

Beischlaf m sexual intercourse

beiseite adv aside, etw ~ legen (sparen) to put sth by

Beispiel (-(e)s, -e) nt example; **sich** (dat) **an jdm/etw ein ~ nehmen** to take sb/sth as an example; **zum ~** for example

beißen (biss, gebissen) vt to bite ▷ vi to bite; (stechen: Rauch, Säure) to sting ▷ vr **sich ~** (Farben) to clash

Beitrag (-(e)s, Beiträge) m contribution; (für Mitgliedschaft) subscription; (Versicherung) premium; **beitragen** irr vt, vi to contribute (zu to)

bekannt adj well-known; (nicht fremd) familiar; **mit jdm ~ sein** to know sb; **~ geben** to announce; **jdn mit jdm ~ machen** to introduce sb to sb; **Bekannte(r)** mf friend; (entfernter) acquaintance; **bekanntlich** adv as everyone knows; **Bekanntschaft** f acquaintance

bekiffen vr **sich ~** (fam) to get stoned

beklagen vr **sich ~** to complain

Bekleidung f clothing

bekommen irr vt to get; (erhalten) to receive; (Kind) to have; (Zug, Grippe) to catch, to get; **wie viel ~ Sie dafür?** how much is that? ▷ vi **jdm ~** (Essen) to agree with sb; **wir ~ schon** (bedient werden) we're being served

beladen irr vt to load

Belag (-(e)s, Beläge) m coating; (auf Zähnen) plaque; (auf Zunge) fur

belasten vt to load; (Körper) to strain; (Umwelt) to pollute; (fig: mit Sorgen etc) to burden; (Comm: Konto) to debit; (Jur) to incriminate

belästigen vt to bother; (stärker) to pester; (sexuell) to harass; **Belästigung** f annoyance; **sexuelle ~** sexual harassment

belebt adj (Straße etc) busy

Beleg (-(e)s, -e) m (Comm) receipt; (Beweis) proof; **belegen** vt (Brot) to spread; (Platz) to reserve; (Kurs, Vorlesung) to register for; (beweisen) to prove

belegt adj (Tel) engaged (BRIT), busy (US); (Hotel) full; (Zunge) coated; **~es Brötchen** sandwich; **der Platz ist ~** this seat is taken; **Belegtzeichen** nt (Tel) engaged tone (BRIT), busy tone (US)

beleidigen vt to insult; (kränken) to offend; **Beleidigung** f insult; (Jur) slander; (schriftliche) libel

beleuchten vt to light; (bestrahlen) to illuminate; (fig) to examine; **Beleuchtung** f lighting; (Bestrahlung) illumination

Belgien (-s) nt Belgium; **Belgier(in)** (-s, -) m(f) Belgian; **belgisch** adj Belgian

belichten vt to expose; **Belichtung** f exposure; **Belichtungsmesser** (-s, -) m light meter

Belieben nt (ganz) **nach ~** (just) as you wish

beliebig adj **jedes ~e Muster** any pattern; **jeder ~e** anyone ▷ adv **~ lange** as long as you like; **~ viel** as many (o much) as you like

beliebt adj popular; **sich bei jdm ~ machen** to make oneself popular with sb

beliefern vt to supply

bellen vi to bark

Belohnung f reward

Belüftung f ventilation

belügen irr vt to lie to

bemerkbar adj noticeable; **sich ~ machen** (Mensch) to attract attention; (Zustand) to become noticeable; **bemerken** vt (wahrnehmen) to notice; (sagen) to remark; **bemerkenswert** adj remarkable; **Bemerkung** f remark

bemitleiden vt to pity

bemühen vr **sich ~** to try (hard), to make an effort; **Bemühung** f effort

bemuttern vt to mother

benachbart adj neighbouring

benachrichtigen vt to inform; **Benachrichtigung** f notification
benachteiligen vt to (put at a) disadvantage; (wegen Rasse etc) to discriminate against
benehmen irr vr **sich ~** to behave; **Benehmen** (-s) nt behaviour
beneiden vt to envy; **jdn um etw ~** to envy sb sth
Beneluxländer pl Benelux countries pl
benommen adj dazed
benötigen vt to need
benutzen vt to use, **Benutzer(in)** (-s, -) m(f) user; **benutzerfreundlich** adj user-friendly; **Benutzerhandbuch** nt user's guide; **Benutzerkennung** f user ID; **Benutzeroberfläche** f (Inform) user/system interface
Benzin (-s, -e) nt (Auto) petrol (BRIT), gas (US); **Benzingutschein** m petrol (BRIT) (o gas (US)) coupon; **Benzinkanister** m petrol (BRIT) (o gas (US)) can; **Benzinpumpe** f petrol (BRIT) (o gas (US)) pump; **Benzintank** m petrol (BRIT) (o gas (US)) tank; **Benzinuhr** f fuel gauge
beobachten vt to observe; **Beobachtung** f observation
bequem adj comfortable; (Ausrede) convenient; (faul) lazy; **machen Sie es sich ~** make yourself at home; **Bequemlichkeit** f comfort; (Faulheit) laziness
beraten irr vt to advise; (besprechen) to discuss ▷ vr **sich ~** to consult; **Beratung** f advice; (bei Arzt etc) consultation
berauben vt to rob
berechnen vt to calculate; (Comm) to charge; **berechnend** adj (Mensch) calculating
berechtigen vt to entitle (zu to); (fig) to justify; **berechtigt** adj justified; **zu etw ~ sein** to be entitled

to sth
bereden vt (besprechen) to discuss
Bereich (-(e)s, -e) m area; (Ressort, Gebiet) field
bereisen vt to travel through
bereit adj ready; **zu etw ~ sein** to be ready for sth; **sich ~ erklären, etw zu tun** to agree to do sth
bereiten vt to prepare; (Kummer) to cause; (Freude) to give
bereitlegen vt to lay out
bereitmachen vr **sich ~** to get ready
bereits adv already
Bereitschaft f readiness; **~ haben** (Arzt) to be on call
bereitstehen vi to be ready
bereuen vt to regret
Berg (-(e)s, -e) m mountain; (kleiner) hill; **in die -e fahren** to go to the mountains; **bergab** adv downhill; **bergauf** adv uphill; **Bergbahn** f mountain railway (BRIT) (o railroad (US))
bergen (barg, geborgen) vt (retten) to rescue; (enthalten) to contain
Bergführer(in) m(f) mountain guide; **Berghütte** f mountain hut, **hergig** adj mountainous; **Bergkette** f mountain range; **Bergschuh** m climbing boot; **Bergsteigen** (-s) nt mountaineering; **Bergsteiger(in)** (-s, -) m(f) mountaineer; **Bergtour** f mountain hike
Bergung f (Rettung) rescue; (von Toten, Fahrzeugen) recovery
Bergwacht (-, -en) f mountain rescue service; **Bergwerk** nt mine
Bericht (-(e)s, -e) m report; **berichten** vt, vi to report
berichtigen vt to correct
Bermudadreieck nt Bermuda triangle: **Bermudainseln** pl Bermuda sing; **Bermudashorts** pl Bermuda shorts pl
Bernstein m amber

berüchtigt adj notorious, infamous

berücksichtigen vt to take into account; (Antrag, Bewerber) to consider

Beruf (-(e)s, -e) m occupation; (akademische) profession; (Gewerbe) trade; **was sind Sie von ~?** what do you do (for a living)?; **beruflich** adj professional

Berufsausbildung f vocational training; **Berufsschule** f vocational college; **berufstätig** adj employed; **Berufsverkehr** m commuter traffic

beruhigen vt to calm ▷ vr **sich ~** (Mensch, Situation) to calm down; **beruhigend** adj reassuring; **Beruhigungsmittel** nt sedative

berühmt adj famous

berühren vt to touch; (gefühlsmäßig bewegen) to move; (betreffen) to affect; (flüchtig erwähnen) to mention, to touch on ▷ vr **sich ~** to touch

besaufen irr vr **sich ~** (fam) to get plastered

beschädigen vt to damage

beschäftigen vt to occupy; (beruflich) to employ ▷ vr **sich mit etw ~** to occupy oneself with sth; (sich befassen) to deal with sth; **beschäftigt** adj busy, occupied; **Beschäftigung** f (Beruf) employment; (Tätigkeit) occupation; (geistige) preoccupation (mit with)

Bescheid (-(e)s, -e) m information; **~ wissen** to be informed (o know) (über +akk about); **ich weiß ~** I know; **jdm ~ geben** (o **sagen**) to let sb know

bescheiden adj modest

bescheinigen vt to certify; (bestätigen) to acknowledge; **Bescheinigung** f certificate; (Quittung) receipt

bescheißen irr vt (vulg) to cheat (um out of)

beschimpfen vt (mit Kraftausdrücken) to swear at

Beschiss (-es) m **das ist ~** (vulg) that's a rip-off; **beschissen** adj (vulg) shitty

beschlagnahmen vt to confiscate

Beschleunigung f acceleration; **Beschleunigungsspur** f acceleration lane

beschließen irr vt to decide on; (beenden) to end; **Beschluss** m decision

beschränken vt to limit, to restrict (auf +akk to) ▷ vr **sich ~** to restrict oneself (auf +akk to); **Beschränkung** f limitation, restriction

beschreiben irr vt to describe; (Papier) to write on; **Beschreibung** f description

beschuldigen vt to accuse (gen of); **Beschuldigung** f accusation

beschummeln vt, vi (fam) to cheat (um out of)

beschützen vt to protect (vor +dat from)

Beschwerde (-, -n) f complaint; **~n** pl (Leiden) trouble sing; **beschweren** vt to weight down; (fig) to burden ▷ vr **sich ~** to complain

beschwipst adj tipsy

beseitigen vt to remove; (Problem) to get rid of; (Müll) to dispose of; **Beseitigung** f removal; (von Müll) disposal

Besen (-s, -) m broom

besetzen vt (Haus, Land) to occupy; (Platz) to take; (Posten) to fill; (Rolle) to cast; **besetzt** adj full; (Tel) engaged (BRIT), busy (US); (Platz) taken; (WC) engaged; **Besetztzeichen** nt engaged tone (BRIT), busy tone (US)

besichtigen vt (Museum) to visit; (Sehenswürdigkeit) to have a look at, (Stadt) to tour

besiegen vt to defeat

Besitz (-es) m possession; (Eigentum) property; **besitzen** irr vt to own; (Eigenschaft) to have; **Besitzer(in)** (-s, -) m(f) owner

besoffen adj (fam) plastered

besondere(r, s) adj special, (bestimmt) particular, (eigentümlich) peculiar; **nichts ~s** nothing special; **Besonderheit** f special feature; (besondere Eigenschaft) peculiarity; **besonders** adv especially, particularly; (getrennt) separately

besorgen vt (beschaffen) to get (jdm for sb); (kaufen a.) to purchase; (erledigen: Geschäfte) to deal with

besprechen irr vt to discuss; **Besprechung** f discussion; (Konferenz) meeting

besser adj better; **es geht ihm ~** he feels better; **~ gesagt** or rather; **~ werden** to improve; **bessern** vt to improve ▷ vr **sich ~** to improve; (Mensch) to mend one's ways; **Besserung** f improvement; **gute ~!** get well soon

beständig adj constant; (Wetter) settled

Bestandteil m component

bestätigen vt to confirm; (Empfang, Brief) to acknowledge; **Bestätigung** f confirmation; (von Brief) acknowledgement

beste(r, s) adj best; **das ~ wäre, wir ...** it would be best if we ... ▷ adv **sie singt am ~n** she sings best; **so ist es am ~n** it's best that way; **am ~n gehst du gleich** you'd better go at once

bestechen irr vt to bribe; **Bestechung** f bribery

Besteck (-(e)s, -e) nt cutlery

bestehen irr vi to be, to exist;

(andauern) to last; **~ auf** (+dat) to insist on, **~ aus** to consist of ▷ vt (Probe, Prüfung) to pass; (Kampf) to win

bestehlen irr vt to rob

bestellen vt to order; (reservieren) to book; (Grüße, Auftrag) to pass on (jdm to sb); (kommen lassen) to send for; **Bestellnummer** f order number; **Bestellung** f (Comm) order; (das Bestellen) ordering

bestens adv very well

bestimmen vt to determine; (Regeln) to lay down; (Tag, Ort) to fix; (ernennen) to appoint; (vorsehen) to mean (für for); **bestimmt** adj definite; (gewiss) certain; (entschlossen) firm ▷ adv definitely; (wissen) for sure; **Bestimmung** f (Verordnung) regulation; (Zweck) purpose

Best.-Nr. abk = **Bestellnummer** order number

bestrafen vt to punish

bestrahlen vt to illuminate; (Med) to treat with radiotherapy

bestreiten irr vt (leugnen) to deny

Bestseller (-s, -) m bestseller

bestürzt adj dismayed

Besuch (-(e)s, -e) m visit; (Mensch) visitor; **~ haben** to have visitors/a visitor; **besuchen** vt to visit; (Schule, Kino etc) to go to; **Besucher(in)** (-s, -) m(f) visitor; **Besuchszeit** f visiting hours pl

betäuben vt (Med) to anaesthetize; **Betäubungsmittel** nt anaesthetic

Bete (-, -n) f **Rote ~** beetroot

beteiligen vr **sich an etw** (dat) **~** to take part in sth, to participate in sth ▷ vt **jdn an etw** (dat) **~** to involve sb in sth; **Beteiligung** f participation; (Anteil) share; (Besucherzahl) attendance

beten vi to pray

Beton (-s, -s) m concrete

betonen vt to stress; (hervorheben) to emphasize; **Betonung** f stress; (fig) emphasis

Betr. abk = **Betreff** re

Betracht m **in ~ ziehen** to take into consideration; **in ~ kommen** to be a possibility; **nicht in ~ kommen** to be out of the question; **betrachten** vt to look at; **~ als** to regard as; **beträchtlich** adj considerable

Betrag (-(e)s, Beträge) m amount, sum; **betragen** irr vt to amount (o come) to ▷ vr **sich ~** to behave

betreffen irr vt to concern; (Regelung etc) to affect; **was mich betrifft** as for me; **betreffend** adj relevant, in question

betreten irr vt to enter; (Bühne etc) to step onto; **„Betreten verboten"** 'keep off/out'

betreuen vt to look after; (Reisegruppe, Abteilung) to be in charge of; **Betreuer(in)** (-s, -) m(f) (Pfleger) carer; (von Kind) child minder; (von Reisegruppe) groupleader

Betrieb (-(e)s, -e) m (Firma) firm; (Anlage) plant; (Tätigkeit) operation; (Treiben) bustle; **außer ~ sein** to be out of order; **in ~ sein** to be in operation; **betriebsbereit** adj operational; **Betriebsrat** m (Gremium) works council; **Betriebssystem** nt (Inform) operating system

betrinken irr vr **sich ~** to get drunk

betroffen adj (bestürzt) shaken; **von etw ~ werden/sein** to be affected by sth

betrog imperf von **betrügen**; **betrogen** pp von **betrügen**

Betrug (-(e)s) m deception; (Jur) fraud; **betrügen** (betrog, betrogen) vt to deceive; (Jur) to defraud; (Partner) to cheat on; **Betrüger(in)** (-s, -) m(f) cheat

betrunken adj drunk

Bett (-(e)s, -en) nt bed; **ins** (o zu) **~ gehen** to go to bed; **das ~ machen** to make the bed; **Bettbezug** m duvet cover; **Bettdecke** f blanket

betteln vi to beg

Bettlaken nt sheet

Bettler(in) (-s, -) m(f) beggar

Bettsofa nt sofa bed; **Betttuch** nt sheet; **Bettwäsche** f bed linen; **Bettzeug** m bedding

beugen vt to bend ▷ vr **sich ~** to bend; (sich fügen) to submit (dat to)

Beule (-, -n) f (Schwellung) bump; (Delle) dent

beunruhigen vt to worry ▷ vr **sich ~** to worry

beurteilen vt to judge

Beute (-) f (von Dieb) booty, loot; (von Tier) prey

Beutel (-, -) m bag

Bevölkerung f population

bevollmächtigt adj authorized (zu etw to do sth)

bevor conj before; **bevor|stehen** irr vi (Schwierigkeiten) to lie ahead; (Gefahr) to be imminent; **jdm ~** (Überraschung etc) to be in store for sb; **bevorstehend** adj forthcoming; **bevorzugen** vt to prefer

bewachen vt to guard; **bewacht** adj **~er Parkplatz** supervised car park (BRIT), guarded parking lot (US)

bewegen vt to move; **jdn dazu ~, etw zu tun** to get sb to do sth ▷ vr **sich ~** to move; **es bewegt sich etwas** (fig) things are beginning to happen; **Bewegung** f movement; (Phys) motion; (innere) emotion; (körperlich) exercise; **Bewegungsmelder** (-s, -) m sensor (which reacts to movement)

Beweis (-es, -e) m proof; (Zeugnis) evidence; **beweisen** irr vt to prove; (zeigen) to show

bewerben irr vr **sich ~** to apply

(um for); **Bewerbung** f application;
Bewerbungsunterlagen pl application documents pl
bewilligen vt to allow; (Geld) to grant
bewirken vt to cause, to bring about
bewohnen vt to live in; **Bewohner(in)** (-s, -) m(f) inhabitant, (von Haus) resident
bewölkt adj cloudy, overcast; **Bewölkung** f clouds pl
bewundern vt to admire; **bewundernswert** adj admirable
bewusst adj conscious; (absichtlich) deliberate; **sich** (dat) **einer Sache** (gen) **- sein** to be aware of sth ▷ adv consciously; (absichtlich) deliberately; **bewusstlos** adj unconscious; **Bewusstlosigkeit** f unconsciousness; **Bewusstsein** (-s) nt consciousness; **bei - sein** conscious
bezahlen vt to pay; (Ware, Leistung) to pay for; **kann ich bar / mit Kreditkarte -?** can I pay cash / by credit card?; **sich bezahlt machen** to be worth it; **Bezahlung** f payment
bezeichnen vt (kennzeichnen) to mark; (nennen) to call; (beschreiben) to describe; **Bezeichnung** f (Name) name; (Begriff) term
beziehen irr vt (Bett) to change; (Haus, Position) to move into; (erhalten) to receive; (Zeitung) to take; **einen Standpunkt -** (fig) to take up a position ▷ vr **sich -** to refer (auf +akk to); **Beziehung** f (Verbindung) connection; (Verhältnis) relationship; **-en haben** (vorteilhaft) to have connections (p contacts); **in dieser -** in this respect; **beziehungsweise** adv or; (genauer gesagt) or rather
Bezirk (-(e)s, -e) m district
Bezug (-(e)s, Bezüge) m (Überzug) cover; (von Kopfkissen) pillowcase; **in - auf** (+akk) with regard to; **be-**

züglich prep +gen concerning
bezweifeln vt to doubt
BH (-s, -s) m bra
Bhf. abk = **Bahnhof** station
Biathlon (-s, -s) m biathlon
Bibel (-, -n) f Bible
Biber (-s, -) m beaver
Bibliothek (-, -en) f library
biegen (bog, gebogen) vt to bend ▷ vr **sich -** to bend ▷ vi to turn (in +akk into); **Biegung** f bend
Biene (-, -n) f bee
Bier (-(e)s, -e) nt beer; **helles - ≈** lager (BRIT), beer (US); **dunkles - ≈** brown ale (BRIT), dark beer (US); **zwei -, bitte!** two beers, please; **Biergarten** m beer garden; **Bierzelt** nt beer tent
bieten (bot, geboten) vt to offer; (bei Versteigerung) bid; **sich** (dat) **etw - lassen** to put up with sth ▷ vr **sich - (Gelegenheit)** to present itself (dat to)
Bikini (-s, -s) m bikini
Bild (-(e)s, -er) nt picture; (gedanklliches) image; (Foto) photo
bilden vt to form; (geistig) to educate; (ausmachen) to constitute ▷ vr **sich - (entstehen)** to form; (lernen) to educate oneself
Bilderbuch nt picture book
Bildhauer(in) (-s, -) m(f) sculptor
Bildschirm m screen; **Bildschirmschoner** (-s, -) m screen saver; **Bildschirmtext** m viewdata, videotext
Bildung f formation; (Wissen, Benehmen) education; **Bildungsurlaub** m educational holiday; (von Firma) study leave
Billard nt billiards sing
billig adj cheap; (gerecht) fair
Binde (-, -n) f bandage; (Armbinde) band; (Damenbinde) sanitary towel (BRIT), sanitary napkin (US)
Bindehautentzündung f con-

junctivitis

binden (band, gebunden) vt to tie; (Buch) to bind; (Soße) to thicken

Bindestrich m hyphen

Bindfaden m string

Bindung f bond, tie; (Skibindung) binding

Bio- in zW bio-; **Biokost** f health food

● **BIOLADEN**

A **Bioladen** is a shop which specializes in selling environmentally friendly products such as phosphate-free washing powders, recycled paper and organically grown vegetables.

Biologie f biology; **biologisch** adj biological; (Anbau) organic

Birke (-, -n) f birch

Birne (-, -n) f (Obst) pear; (Elek) (light) bulb

bis prep +akk (räumlich, bis zu / an) to, as far as; (zeitlich) till, until; (bis spätestens) by; **Sie haben ~ Dienstag Zeit** you have until (0 till) Tuesday; **~ Dienstag muss es fertig sein** it must be ready by Tuesday; **~ hierher** this far; **~ in die Nacht** into the night; **~ auf weiteres** until further notice; **~ bald / gleich!** see you later / soon; **~ auf etw** (akk) (einschließlich) including sth; (ausgeschlossen) except; **zu** up to; **von ... ~ ...** from ... to ... ▷ conj (zeitlich) till; (zeitlich) until, till

Bischof (-s, Bischöfe) m bishop

bisher adv up to now, so far

Biskuit (-(e)s, -s o -e) nt sponge

biss imperf von **beißen**

Biss (-es, -e) m bite

bisschen adj **ein ~** a bit of; **ein ~ Salz / Liebe** a bit of salt / love; **ich habe kein ~ Hunger** I'm not a bit hungry ▷ adv **ein ~** a bit; **kein ~** not at all

bissig adj (Hund) vicious; (Bemerkung) cutting

Bit (-s, -s) nt (Inform) bit

bitte interj please; (wie) ~? (I beg your) pardon?; ~ (schön) you're welcome, that's alright; **hier, ~** here you are; **Bitte** (-, -n) f request; **bitten** (bat, gebeten) vt, vi to ask (um for)

bitter adj bitter

Blähungen pl (Med) wind sing

blamieren vr **sich ~** to make a fool of oneself ▷ vt **jdn ~** to make sb look a fool

Blankoscheck m blank cheque

Blase (-, -n) f bubble; (Med) blister; (Anat) bladder

blasen (blies, geblasen) vi to blow; **jdm einen ~** (vulg) to give sb a blow job

Blasenentzündung f cystitis

blass adj pale

Blatt (-(e)s, Blätter) nt leaf; (von Papier) sheet; **blättern** vi (Inform) to scroll; **in etw** (dat) ~ to leaf through sth; **Blätterteig** m puff pastry; **Blattsalat** m green salad; **Blattspinat** m spinach

blau adj blue; (fam: betrunken) plastered; (Gastr) boiled; **~es Auge** black eye; **~er Fleck** bruise; **Blaubeere** f bilberry, blueberry; **Blaulicht** nt flashing blue light; **blaumachen** vi to skip work; (in Schule) to skip school; **Blauschimmelkäse** m blue cheese

Blazer (-s, -) m blazer

Blech (-(e)s, -e) nt sheet metal; (Backblech) baking tray (BRIT), cookie sheet (US); **Blechschaden** m (Auto) damage to the bodywork

Blei (-(e)s, -e) nt lead

bleiben (blieb, geblieben) vi to stay; **lass das ~!** stop it; **das bleibt unter uns** that's (just) between ourselves; **mir bleibt keine andere Wahl** I have no other choice

bleich adj pale; **bleichen** vt to bleach

bleifrei adj (Benzin) unleaded; **bleihaltig** adj (Benzin) leaded

Bleistift m pencil

Blende (-, -n) f (Foto) aperture

Blick (-(e)s, -e) m look; (kurz) glance; (Aussicht) view, **auf den ersten ~** at first sight; **einen ~ auf etw** (akk) **werfen** to have a look at sth; **blicken** vi to look; **sich ~ lassen** to show up

blieb imperf von **bleiben**

blies imperf von **blasen**

blind adj blind; (Glas etc) dull; **Blinddarm** m appendix; **Blinddarmentzündung** f appendicitis; **Blinde(r)** mf blind person/man/woman; **die ~n** pl the blind; **Blindenhund** m guide dog; **Blindenschrift** f braille

blinken vi (Stern, Lichter) to twinkle; (aufleuchten) to flash; (Auto) to indicate; **Blinker** (-s, -) m (Auto) indicator (BRIT), turn signal (US)

blinzeln vi (mit beiden Augen) to blink; (mit einem Auge) to wink

Blitz (-es, -e) m (flash of) lightning; (Foto) flash; **blitzen** vi (Foto) to use a/the flash; **es blitzte und donnerte** there was thunder and lightning; **Blitzlicht** nt flash

Block (-(e)s, Blöcke) m (a. fig) block; (von Papier) pad; **Blockflöte** f recorder; **Blockhaus** nt log cabin; **blockieren** vt to block ▷ vi to jam; (Räder) to lock; **Blockschrift** f block letters pl

blöd adj stupid; **blödeln** vi (fam) to fool around

blond adj blond; (Frau) blonde; **bloß** adj (unbedeckt) bare; (alleinig) mere ▷ adv only; **geh mir ~ aus dem Weg** just get out of my way

blühen vi to bloom; (fig) to flourish

Blume (-, -n) f flower; (von Wein) bouquet; **Blumenkohl** m cauliflower; **Blumenladen** m flower shop; **Blumenstrauß** m bunch of flowers; **Blumentopf** m flowerpot; **Blumenvase** f vase

Bluse (-, -n) f blouse

Blut (-(e)s) nt blood; **Blutbild** nt blood count; **Blutdruck** m blood pressure

Blüte (-, -n) f (Pflanzenteil) flower, bloom; (Baumblüte) blossom; (fig) prime

bluten vi to bleed

Blütenstaub m pollen

Bluter (-s, -) m (Med) haemophiliac; **Bluterguss** m haematoma; (blauer Fleck) bruise; **Blutgruppe** f blood group; **blutig** adj bloody; **Blutkonserve** f unit of stored blood; **Blutprobe** f blood sample; **Blutspende** f blood donation; **Bluttransfusion** f blood transfusion; **Blutung** f bleeding; **Blutvergiftung** f blood poisoning; **Blutwurst** f black pudding (BRIT), blood sausage (US)

BLZ abk = **Bankleitzahl**

Bob (-s, -s) m bob(sleigh)

Bock (-(e)s, Böcke) m (Reh) buck; (Schaf) ram; (Gestell) trestle; (Sport) vaulting horse; **ich hab keinen ~ (drauf)** (fam) I don't feel like it

Boden (-s, Böden) m ground; (Fußboden) floor; (von Meer, Fass) bottom; (Speicher) attic; **Bodennebel** m ground mist; **Bodenpersonal** nt ground staff; **Bodenschätze** pl mineral resources pl

Bodensee m **der ~** Lake Constance

Body (-s, -s) m body; **Bodybuilding** (-s) nt bodybuilding

bog imperf von **biegen**

Bogen (-s, -) m (Biegung) curve; (in der Architektur) arch; (Waffe, Instrument) bow; (Papier) sheet

Bohne (-, -n) f bean; **grüne ~n** pl green (o French (BRIT)) beans pl; **weiße ~n** pl haricot beans pl; **Bohnenkaffee** m real coffee; **Bohnensprosse** f bean sprout

bohren vt to drill; **Bohrer** (-s, -) m drill

Boiler (-s, -) m water heater

Boje (-, -n) f buoy

Bolivien (-s) nt Bolivia

Bombe (-, -n) f bomb

Bon (-s, -s) m (Kassenzettel) receipt; (Gutschein) voucher, coupon

Bonbon (-s, -s) nt sweet (BRIT), candy (US)

Bonus (o -ses, -se o Boni) m bonus; (Punktvorteil) bonus points pl; (Schadenfreiheitsrabatt) no-claims bonus

Boot (-(e)s, -e) nt boat; **Bootsverleih** m boat hire (BRIT) (o rental (US))

Bord (-(e)s, -e) nt an ~ (eines Schiffes) on board (a ship); **an ~ gehen** (Schiff) to go on board; (Flugzeug) to board; **von ~ gehen** to disembark; **Bordcomputer** m dashboard computer

Bordell (-s, -e) nt brothel

Bordkarte f boarding card

Bordstein m kerb (BRIT), curb (US)

borgen vt to borrow; **jdm etw ~** to lend sb sth; **sich** (dat) **etw ~** to borrow sth

Börse (-, -n) f stock exchange; (Geldbörse) purse

bös adj siehe **böse**; **bösartig** adj malicious; (Med) malignant

Böschung f slope; (Uferböschung) embankment

böse adj bad; (stärker) evil; (Wunde) nasty; (zornig) angry; **bist du mir ~?** are you angry with me?

boshaft adj malicious

Bosnien (-s) nt Bosnia; **Bosnien-Herzegowina** (-s) nt Bosnia-Herzegowina

böswillig adj malicious

bot imperf von **bieten**

botanisch adj **~er Garten** botanical gardens pl

Botschaft f message; (Pol) embassy; **Botschafter(in)** m(f) ambassador

Botsuana (-s) nt Botswana

Bouillon (-, -s) f stock

Boutique (-, -n) f boutique

Bowle (-, -n) f punch

Box (-, -en) f (Behälter, Pferdebox) box; (Lautsprecher) speaker; (bei Autorennen) pit

boxen vi to box; **Boxer** (-s, -) m (Hund, Sportler) boxer; **Boxershorts** pl boxer shorts pl; **Boxkampf** m boxing match

Boykott (-s, -e) m boycott

brach imperf von **brechen**

brachte imperf von **bringen**

Brainstorming (-s) nt brainstorming

Branchenverzeichnis nt yellow pages® pl

Brand (-(e)s, Brände) m fire; **einen ~ haben** (fam) to be parched

Brandenburg (-s) nt Brandenburg

Brandsalbe f ointment for burns

Brandung f surf

Brandwunde f burn

brannte imperf von **brennen**

Brasilien (-s) nt Brazil

braten (briet, gebraten) vt to roast; (auf dem Rost) to grill; (in der Pfanne) to fry; **Braten** (-s, -) m roast; (roher) joint; **Bratensoße** f gravy; **Brathähnchen** nt roast chicken; **Bratkartoffeln** pl fried potatoes pl; **Bratpfanne** f frying pan; **Bratspieß** m spit; **Bratwurst** f fried sausage; (gegrillte) grilled sausage

Brauch (-s, Bräuche) m custom

brauchen vt (nötig haben) to need (für, zu for); (erfordern) to require; (Zeit) to take; (gebrauchen) to use; **wie lange wird er ~?** how long will it take him?; **du brauchst es nur zu sagen** you only need to say; **das braucht (seine) Zeit** it takes time; **ihr braucht es nicht zu tun** you don't have (ø need) to do it; **sie hätte nicht zu kommen** ~ she needn't have come

brauen vt to brew; **Brauerei** f brewery

braun adj brown; (von Sonne) tanned; **Bräune** (-, -n) f brownness; (von Sonne) tan; **Bräunungsstudio** nt tanning studio

Brause (-, -n) f (Dusche) shower; (Getränk) fizzy drink (BRIT), soda (US)

Braut (-, Bräute) f bride; **Bräutigam** (-s, -e) m bridegroom

brav adj (artig) good, well-behaved

bravo interj well done

BRD (-) f abk = **Bundesrepublik Deutschland** FRG

● **BRD**

● The BRD is the official name for
● the Federal Republic of Germany.
● It comprises 16 Länder (see Land).
● It was the name given to the for-
● mer West Germany as opposed to
● East Germany (the DDR). The two
● Germanies were reunited on 3rd
● October 1990.

brechen (brach, gebrochen) vt to break; (erbrechen) to bring up; **sich** (dat) **den Arm** ~ to break one's arm ▷ vi to break; (erbrechen) to vomit, to be sick; **Brechreiz** m nausea

Brei (-(e)s, -e) m (Breimasse) mush, pulp; (Haferbrei) porridge; (für Kinder) pap

breit adj wide; (Schultern) broad; **zwei Meter** ~ two metres wide; **Breite** (-, -n) f breadth; (bei Maßangaben) width; (Geo) latitude; **der** ~ **nach** widthways; **Breitengrad** m (degree of) latitude

Bremen (-s) nt Bremen

Bremsbelag m brake lining; **Bremse** (-, -n) f brake; (Zool) horsefly; **bremsen** vi to brake ▷ vt (Auto) to brake; (fig) to slow down; **Bremsflüssigkeit** f brake fluid; **Bremslicht** nt brake light; **Bremspedal** nt brake pedal; **Bremsspur** f tyre marks pl; **Bremsweg** m braking distance

brennen (brannte, gebrannt) vi to burn, (in Flammen stehen) to be on fire; es brennt! fire!; mir ~ die Augen my eyes are smarting; das Licht ~ lassen to leave the light on; **Brennholz** nt firewood; **Brennnessel** f stinging nettle; **Brennspiritus** m methylated spirits pl; **Brennstab** m fuel rod; **Brennstoff** m fuel

Brett (-(e)s, -er) nt board; (länger) plank; (Regal) shelf; (Spielbrett) board; **schwarzes** ~ notice board, bulletin board (US); ~er pl (ski) skis pl; **Brettspiel** nt board game

Brezel (-, -n) f pretzel

Brief (-(e)s, -e) m letter, **Briefbombe** f letter bomb; **Brieffreund(in)** m(f) penfriend, pen pal; **Briefkasten** m letterbox (BRIT), mailbox (US); **elektronischer** ~ electronic mailbox; **Briefmarke** f stamp; **Briefpapier** nt writing paper; **Brieftasche** f wallet; **Briefträger(in)** m(f) postman/-woman; **Briefumschlag** m envelope; **Briefwaage** f letter scales pl

briet imperf von **braten**

Brille (-, -n) f glasses pl; (Schutzbrille) goggles pl; **Brillenetui** nt glasses case

bringen (brachte, gebracht) vt (herbringen) to bring; (mitnehmen, vom Sprecher weg) to take; (holen, herbringen) to get, to fetch; (Theat, Cine) to show; (Radio, TV) to broadcast ~ **Sie mir bitte noch ein Bier** could

you bring me another beer, please?;
jdn nach Hause ~ to take sb home;
jdn dazu ~, etw zu tun to make sb
do sth; **jdn auf eine Idee ~** to give
sb an idea

Brise (-, -n) f breeze

Brite (-n, -n) m, **Britin** f British
person, Briton; **er ist ~** he is British;
die ~n the British; **britisch** adj
British

Brocken (-s, -) m bit; (größer) lump,
chunk

Brokkoli m broccoli

Brombeere f blackberry

Bronchitis (-) f bronchitis

Bronze (-, -n) f bronze

Brosche (-, -n) f brooch

Brot (-(e)s, -e) nt bread; (Laib) loaf;
Brotaufstrich m spread; **Brötchen** nt roll; **Brotzeit** f (Pause)
break; (Essen) snack; **~ machen** to
have a snack

Browser (-s, -) m (Inform) browser

Bruch (-(e)s, Brüche) m (Brechen)
breaking; (Bruchstelle; mit Partei,
Tradition etc) break; (Med: Eingeweidebruch) rupture, hernia; (Knochenbruch) fracture; (Math) fraction;
brüchig adj brittle

Brücke (-, -n) f bridge

Bruder (-s, Brüder) m brother

Brühe (-, -n) f (Suppe) (clear) soup;
(Grundlage) stock; (pej: Getränk)
muck; **Brühwürfel** m stock cube

brüllen vi to roar; (Stier) to bellow;
(vor Schmerzen) to scream (with pain)

brummen vi (Bär, Mensch) to
growl; (brummeln) to mutter; (Insekt)
to buzz; (Motor, Radio) to drone ▷ vt
to growl

brünett adj brunette

Brunnen (-s, -) m fountain; (tief)
well; (natürlich) spring

Brust (-, Brüste) f breast; (beim Mann)
chest; **Brustschwimmen** (-s) nt
breaststroke; **Brustwarze** f nipple

brutal adj brutal

brutto adv gross

BSE (-) nt abk = **bovine spongiforme Enzephalopathie** BSE

Bube (-n, -n) m boy, lad; (Karten) jack

Buch (-(e)s, Bücher) nt book

Buche (-, -n) f beech (tree)

buchen vt to book; (Betrag) to enter

Bücherei f library

Buchfink m chaffinch

Buchhalter(in) m(f) accountant

Buchhandlung f bookshop

Büchse (-, -n) f tin (BRIT), can;
Büchsenfleisch nt tinned meat
(BRIT), canned meat; **Büchsenmilch** f tinned milk (BRIT), canned
milk; **Büchsenöffner** m tin opener
(BRIT), can opener

Buchstabe (-ns, -n) m letter;
buchstabieren vt to spell

Bucht (-, -en) f bay

Buchung f booking; (Comm) entry

Buckel (-s, -) m hump

bücken vr **sich ~** to bend down

Buddhismus (-) m Buddhism

Bude (-, -en) f (auf Markt) stall; (fam:
Wohnung) pad, place

Büfett (-s, -s) nt sideboard; **kaltes
~** cold buffet

Büffel (-s, -) m buffalo

Bügel (-s, -) m (Kleidung) hanger;
(Steigbügel) stirrup; (Brille) sidepiece;
(von Skilift) T-bar; **Bügelbrett** nt
ironing board; **Bügeleisen** nt iron;
Bügelfalte f crease; **bügelfrei** adj
non-iron; **bügeln** vt, vi to iron

buh interj boo

Bühne (-, -n) f stage; **Bühnenbild**
nt set

Bulgare (-n, -n) m, **Bulgarin** f
Bulgarian; **Bulgarien** (-s) nt Bulgaria; **bulgarisch** adj Bulgarian;
Bulgarisch nt Bulgarian

Bulimie f bulimia

Bulle (-n, -n) m bull; (fam: Polizist) cop

Bummel (-s, -) m stroll; **bummeln**

vi to stroll; (trödeln) to dawdle; (faulenzen) to loaf around; **Bummelzug** m slow train

bums interj bang

bumsen vi (vulg) to screw

Bund (-(e)s, Bünde) m (von Hose, Rock) waistband; (Freundschaftsbund) bond; (Organisation) association; (Pol) confederation; **der ~** (fam: Bundeswehr) the army ▷ (-(e)s, -e) nt bunch; (von Stroh etc) bundle

Bundes- in zW Federal; (auf Deutschland bezogen a.) German; **Bundesbahn** f German railway company; **Bundeskanzler(in)** m(f) Chancellor; **Bundesland** nt state, Land; **Bundesliga** f **erste/zweite ~** First/Second Division; **Bundespräsident(in)** m(f) President; **Bundesrat** m (in Deutschland) Upper House of the German Parliament; (in der Schweiz) Council of Ministers; **Bundesregierung** f Federal Government; **Bundesrepublik** f Federal Republic; **~ Deutschland** Federal Republic of Germany; **Bundesstraße** f ≈ A road (BRIT), ≈ state highway (US); **Bundestag** m Lower House (of the German Parliament); **Bundeswehr** f (German) armed forces pl

● **BUNDESWEHR**
● The **Bundeswehr** is the name for
● the German armed forces. It was
● established in 1955, first of all for
● volunteers, but since 1956 there
● has been compulsory military ser-
● vice for all able-bodied young men
● of 18. In peacetime the Defence
● Minister is the head of the 'Bun-
● deswehr', but in wartime the
● **Bundeskanzler** takes over. The
● 'Bundeswehr' comes under the ju-
● risdiction of NATO.

Bündnis nt alliance

Bungalow (-s, -s) m bungalow

Bungeejumping (-s) nt bungee jumping

bunt adj colourful; (von Programm etc) varied; **~e Farben** bright colours ▷ adv (anstreichen) in bright colours; **Buntstift** m crayon, coloured pencil

Burg (-, -en) f castle

Bürger(in) (-s, -) m(f) citizen; **bürgerlich** adj (Rechte, Ehe etc) civil; (vom Mittelstand) middle-class; (pej) bourgeois; **Bürgermeister(in)** m(f) mayor; **Bürgersteig** (-(e)s, -e) m pavement (BRIT), sidewalk (US)

Büro (-s, -s) nt office; **Büroklammer** f paper clip

Bürokratie f bureaucracy

Bursche (-n, -n) m lad; (Typ) guy

Bürste (-, -n) f brush; **bürsten** vt to brush

Bus (-ses, -se) m bus; (Reisebus) coach (BRIT), bus; **Busbahnhof** m bus station

Busch (-(e)s, Büsche) m bush; (Strauch) shrub

Busen (-s, -) m breasts pl, bosom

Busfahrer(in) m(f) bus driver; **Bushaltestelle** f bus stop

Businessclass (-) f business class

Busreise f coach tour (BRIT), bus tour

Bußgeld nt fine

Büstenhalter (-s, -) m bra

Busverbindung f bus connection

Butter (-) f butter; **Butterbrot** nt slice of bread and butter; **Butterkäse** m type of mild, full-fat cheese; **Buttermilch** f buttermilk; **Butterschmalz** nt clarified butter

Button (-s, -s) m badge (BRIT), button (US)

b. w. abk = **bitte wenden** pto

Byte (-s, -s) nt byte

bzw. adv abk = **beziehungsweise**

C

ca. adv abk = **circa** approx
Cabrio (-s, -s) nt convertible
Café (-s, -s) nt café
Cafeteria (-, -s) f cafeteria
Call-Center (-s, -) nt call centre
campen vi to camp; **Camping** (-s) nt camping; **Campingbus** m camper; **Campingplatz** m campsite, camping ground (US)
Cappuccino (-s, -) m cappuccino
Carving (-s) nt (Ski) carving; **Carvingski** m carving ski
CD (-, -s) f abk = **Compact Disc** CD; **CD-Brenner** (-s, -) m CD burner, CD writer; **CD-Player** (-s, -) m CD player; **CD-ROM** (-, -s) f abk = **Compact Disc Read Only Memory** CD-ROM; **CD-ROM-Laufwerk** nt CD-ROM drive, **CD-Spieler** m CD player
Cello (-s, -s o Celli) nt cello
Celsius (-) nt; **20 Grad ~** 20 degrees Celsius, 68 degrees Fahrenheit
Cent (-, -s) m (von Dollar und Euro)

cent
Chamäleon (-s, -s) nt chameleon
Champagner (-s, -) m champagne
Champignon (-s, -s) m mushroom
Champions League (-, -s) f Champions League
Chance (-, -n) f chance; **die ~n stehen gut** the prospects are good
Chaos (-) nt chaos; **Chaot(in)** (-en, -en) m(f) (fam) disorganized person, scatterbrain; **chaotisch** adj chaotic
Charakter (-s, -e) m character; **charakteristisch** adj characteristic (für of)
Charisma (-s, Charismen o Charismata) nt charisma
charmant adj charming
Charterflug m charter flight; **chartern** vt to charter
checken vt (überprüfen) to check; (fam: verstehen) to get
Check-in (-s, -s) m check-in; **Check-in-Schalter** m check-in desk
Chef(in) (-s, -s) m(f) boss; **Chefarzt** m, **Chefärztin** f senior consultant (BRIT), medical director (US)
Chemie (-) f chemistry; **chemisch** adj chemical; **~e Reinigung** dry cleaning
Chemotherapie f chemotherapy
Chicoree (-s) m chicory
Chiffre (-, -n) f (Geheimzeichen) cipher; (in Zeitung) box number
Chile (-s) nt Chile
Chili (-s, -s) m chilli
China (-s) nt China; **Chinakohl** m Chinese leaves pl (BRIT), bok choy (US); **Chinarestaurant** nt Chinese restaurant; **Chinese** (-n, -n) m Chinese; **Chinesin** (-, -nen) f Chinese (woman); **sie ist ~** she's Chinese; **chinesisch** adj Chinese; **Chinesisch** nt Chinese
Chip (-s, -s) m (Inform) chip; **Chip-**

karte f smart card

Chips pl (Kartoffelchips) crisps pl (BRIT), chips pl (US)

Chirurg(in) (-en, -en) m(f) surgeon

Chlor (-s) nt chlorine

Choke (s, s) m choke

Cholera ( ) f cholera

Cholesterin (-s) nt cholesterol

Chor (-(e), Chöre) m choir; (Theat) chorus

Choreografie f choreography

Christ(in) (-en, -en) m(f) Christian; **Christbaum** m Christmas tree; **Christi Himmelfahrt** f the Ascension (of Christ); **Christkind** nt baby Jesus; (das Geschenke bringt) ≈ Father Christmas, Santa Claus; **christlich** adj Christian

Chrom (-s) nt chrome; (Chem) chromium

chronisch adj chronic

chronologisch adj chronological ▷ adv in chronological order

Chrysantheme (-, -n) f chrysanthemum

circa adv about, approximately

City (-) f city centre, downtown (US)

Clementine (, -n) f clementine

clever adj clever, smart

Clique (-, -n) f group; (pej) clique; **David und seine ~** David and his lot o crowd

Clown (-s, -s) m clown

Club (s, s) m club; **Cluburlaub** m club holiday (BRIT), club vacation (US)

Cocktail (-s, -s) m cocktail; **Cocktailtomate** f cherry tomato

Cognac (-s) m cognac

Cola (-, -s) f Coke®, cola

Comic (-s, -s) m comic strip; (Heft) comic

Compact Disc (-, -s) f compact disc

Computer (-s, -) m computer; **Computerfreak** m computer nerd;

computergesteuert adj computer-controlled; **Computergrafik** f computer graphics pl, computer lesbar adj machine-readable; **Computerspiel** nt computer game; **Computertomografie** f computer tomography, scan, **Computervirus** m computer virus

Container (-s, -) m (zum Transport) container; (für Bauschutt etc) skip

Control-Taste f control key

Cookie (-s, -s) nt (Inform) cookie

cool adj (fam) cool

Cornflakes pl cornflakes pl

Couch (-, -en) f couch; **Couchtisch** m coffee table

Coupé (-s, -s) nt coupé

Coupon (-s, -s) m coupon

Cousin (-s, -s) m cousin; **Cousine** f cousin

Crack (-s) nt (Droge) crack

Creme (-, -s) f cream; (Gastr) mousse

Creutzfeld-Jakob-Krankheit f Creutzfeld-Jakob disease, CJD

Croissant (-s, -s) nt croissant

Curry (-s) m curry powder ▷ (-s) nt (indisches Gericht) curry; **Currywurst** f fried sausage with ketchup and curry powder

Cursor (-s, -) m (Inform) cursor

Cybercafé nt cybercafé; **Cyberspace** (-) m cyberspace

d

da adv (dort) there; (hier) here; (dann) then; ~ **oben / drüben** up / over there; ~, **wo** where; ~ **sein** to be there; **ist jemand ~?** is there anybody there?; **ich bin gleich wieder** ~ I'll be right back; **ist noch Brot ~?** is there any bread left?; **es ist keine Milch mehr** ~ we've run out of milk; ~, **bitte!** there you are; ~ **kann man nichts machen** there's nothing you can do ▷ conj as

dabei adv (räumlich) close to it; (zeitlich) at the same time; (obwohl, doch) though; **sie hörte Radio und rauchte** ~ she was listening to the radio and smoking (at the same time); ~ **fällt mir ein ...** that reminds me ...; ~ **kam es zu einem Unfall** this led to an accident; ... **und** ~ **hat er gar keine Ahnung** ~ even though he has no idea; **ich finde nichts** ~ I don't see anything wrong with it; **es bleibt** ~ that's settled; ~ **sein** (anwesend) to be present; (beteiligt) to be involved;

ich bin ~! count me in; **er war gerade** ~ **zu gehen** he was just (o on the point of) leaving

dabei|bleiben irr vi to stick with it; **ich bleibe dabei** I'm not changing my mind

dabei|haben irr vt **er hat seine Schwester dabei** he's brought his sister; **ich habe kein Geld dabei** I haven't got any money on me

Dach (-(e)s, Dächer) nt roof; **Dachboden** m attic, loft; **Dachgepäckträger** m roofrack; **Dachrinne** f gutter

Dachs (-es, -e) m badger

dachte imperf von **denken**

Dackel (-s, -) m dachshund

dadurch adv (räumlich) through it; (durch diesen Umstand) in that way; (deshalb) because of that, for that reason ▷ conj ~, **dass** because; ~, **dass er hart arbeitete** (indem) by working hard

dafür adv for it; (anstatt) instead; ~ **habe ich 50 Euro bezahlt** I paid 50 euros for it; **ich bin** ~ **zu bleiben** I'm for (o in favour of) staying; ~ **ist er ja da** that's what he's there for; **er kann nichts** ~ he can't help it

dagegen adv against it; (im Vergleich damit) in comparison; (bei Tausch) for it; **ich habe nichts** ~ I don't mind

daheim adv at home

daher adv (räumlich) from there; (Ursache) that's why ▷ conj (deshalb) that's why

dahin adv (räumlich) there; (zeitlich) then; (vergangen) gone; **bis** ~ (zeitlich) till then; (örtlich) up to there; **bis** ~ **muss die Arbeit fertig sein** the work must be finished by then

dahinter adv behind it; ~ **kommen** to find out

dahinterkommen vi to find out

Dahlie f dahlia

Dalmatiner (-s, -) m dalmatian

damals adv at that time, then

Dame (-, -n) f lady; (Karten) queen; (Spiel) draughts sing (BRIT), checkers sing (US); **Damenbinde** f sanitary towel (BRIT), sanitary napkin (US); **Damenfriseur** m ladies' hairdresser; **Damenkleidung** f ladies' wear; **Damentoilette** f ladies' toilet (o restroom (US))

damit adv with it; (begründend) by that; **was meint er -?** what does he mean by that?; **genug -!** that's enough ▷ conj so that

Damm (-(e)s, Dämme) m dyke (Staudamm) dam; (am Hafen) mole; (Bahn-, Straßendamm) embankment

Dämmerung f twilight; (am Morgen) dawn; (am Abend) dusk

Dampf (-(e)s, Dämpfe) m steam; (Dunst) vapour; **Dampfbad** nt Turkish bath; **Dampfbügeleisen** nt steam iron; **dampfen** vi to steam

dämpfen vt (Gastr) to steam; (Geräusch) to deaden; (Begeisterung) to dampen

Dampfer (-s, -) m steamer

Dampfkochtopf m pressure cooker

danach adv after that; (zeitlich a.) afterwards; (demgemäß) accordingly; **mir ist nicht -** I don't feel like it; **- sieht es aus** that's what it looks like

Däne (-n, -n) m Dane

daneben adv beside it; (im Vergleich) in comparison

Dänemark (-s) nt Denmark; **Dänin** f Dane, Danish woman / girl; **dänisch** adj Danish; **Dänisch** nt Danish

dank präp (dat o gen) thanks to;

Dank (-(e)s) m thanks pl; **vielen -!** thank you very much; **jdm - sagen** to thank sb; **dankbar** adj grateful;

(Aufgabe) rewarding; **danke** interj thank you, thanks; **nein -!** no, thank you; **-, gerne!** yes, please; **-, gleichfalls!** thanks, and the same to you; **danken** vi **jdm für etw -** to thank sb for sth; **nichts zu -!** you're welcome

dann adv then; **bis -I** see you (later); **- eben nicht** okay, forget it, suit yourself

daran adv (räumlich) on it; (befestigen) to it; (stoßen) against it; **es liegt -, dass ...** it's because ...

darauf adv (räumlich) on it; (zielgerichtet) towards it; (danach) afterwards; **es kommt ganz - an, ob ...** it all depends whether ...; **ich freue mich -** I'm looking forward to it; **am Tag -** the next day; **- folgend** (Tag, Jahr) next, following

darauffolgend adj (Tag, Jahr) next, following

daraus adv from it; **was ist - geworden?** what became of it?

darin adv in it; **das Problem liegt -, dass ...** the basic problem is that ...

Darm (-(e)s, Därme) m intestine; (Wurstdarm) skin; **Darmgrippe** f gastroenteritis

darstellen vt to represent; (Theat) to play; (beschreiben) to describe; **Darsteller(in)** m(f) actor / actress; **Darstellung** f representation; (Beschreibung) description

darüber adv (räumlich) above it, over it; (fahren) over it; (mehr) more; (währenddessen) meanwhile; (sprechen, streiten, sich freuen) about it

darum adv (deshalb) that's why; **es geht -, dass ...** the point (o thing) is that ...

darunter adv (räumlich) under it;

(*dazwischen*) among them; (*weniger*) less; **was verstehen Sie ~?** what do you understand by that?; **~ fallen** to be included

darunterfallen *vi* to be included

das *art* the; **~ Auto da** that car; **er hat sich ~ Bein gebrochen** he's broken his leg; **vier Euro ~ Kilo** four euros a kilo ▷ *pron* that (one), this (one); (*relativ, Sache*) that, which; (*relativ, Person*) who, that; (*demonstrativ*) this/that one; **~ Auto da** that car; **ich nehme ~ da** I'll take that one; **~ Auto, ~ er kaufte** the car (that (o which)) he bought; **~ Mädchen, ~ nebenan wohnt** the girl who (o that) lives next door; **~ heißt** that is; **~ sind Amerikaner** they're American

da sein *irr vi siehe* **da**

dass *conj* that; **so ~** so that; **es sei denn, ~** unless; **ohne ~ er grüßte** without saying hello

dasselbe *pron* the same

Datei (*Inform*) file; **Dateimanager** *m* file manager

Daten *pl* data *pl*; **Datenbank** *f* database; **Datenmissbrauch** *m* misuse of data; **Datenschutz** *m* data protection; **Datenträger** *m* data carrier; **Datenverarbeitung** *f* data processing

datieren *vt* to date

Dativ *m* dative (case)

Dattel (-, *-n*) *f* date

Datum (*-s, Daten*) *nt* date

Dauer (-, *-n*) *f* duration; (*Länge*) length; **auf die ~** in the long run; **für die ~ von zwei Jahren** for (a period of) two years; **Dauerauftrag** *m* (*Fin*) standing order; **dauerhaft** *adj* lasting; (*Material*) durable; **Dauerkarte** *f* season ticket; **dauern** *vi* to last; (*Zeit benötigen*) to take; **es**

hat sehr lange gedauert, bis er ... it took him a long time to ...; **wie lange dauert es denn noch?** how much longer will it be?; **das dauert mir zu lange** I can't wait that long; **dauernd** *adj* lasting; (*ständig*) constant ▷ *adv* always, constantly; **er lachte ~** he kept laughing; **unterbrich mich nicht ~** stop interrupting me; **Dauerwelle** *f* perm (*BRIT*), permanent (*US*)

Daumen (-s, *-*) *m* thumb

Daunendecke *f* eiderdown

davon *adv* (*räumlich*) away; (*weg von*) from it; (*Grund*) because of it; **ich hätte gerne ein Kilo ~** I'd like one kilo of that; **~ habe ich gehört** I've heard of it; (*Geschehen*) I've heard about it; **das kommt ~, wenn ...** that's what happens when ...; **was habe ich ~?** what's the point?; **auf und ~** up and away; **davon|laufen** *irr vi* to run away

davor *adv* (*räumlich*) in front of it; (*zeitlich*) before; **ich habe Angst ~** I'm afraid of it

dazu *adv* (*zusätzlich*) on top of that, as well; (*zu diesem Zweck*) for it, for that purpose; **ich möchte Reis ~** I'd like rice with it; **und ~ noch** and in addition; **~ fähig sein, etw zu tun** to be capable of doing sth; **wie kam es ~?** how did it happen?; **dazu|gehören** *vi* to belong to it; **dazu|kommen** *irr vi* (*zu jdm ~*) to join sb; **kommt noch etwas dazu?** anything else?

dazwischen *adv* in between; (*Unterschied etc*) between them; (*in einer Gruppe*) among them

dazwischen|kommen *irr vi* **wenn nichts dazwischenkommt** if all goes well; **mir ist etwas dazwischengekommen** something has cropped up

DDR (-) *f abk* = **Deutsche Demo-**

kratische Republik (Hist) GDR

dealen vi (fam. mit Drogen) to deal in drugs; **Dealer(in)** (-s, -) m(f) (fam) dealer, pusher

Deck (-(e)s, -s o -e) nt deck; **an ~** on deck

Decke (-, -n) f cover; (für Bett) blanket; (für Tisch) tablecloth; (von Zimmer) ceiling

Deckel (-s, -) m lid

decken vt to cover; (Tisch) to lay, to set ▷ vr **sich ~** (Interessen) to coincide; (Aussagen) to correspond ▷ vi (den Tisch decken) to lay (o set) the table

Decoder (-s, -) m decoder

defekt adj faulty; **Defekt** (-(e)s, -e) m fault, defect

definieren vt to define; **Definition** (-, -en) f definition

deftig adj (Preise) steep; **ein ~es Essen** a good solid meal

dehnbar adj flexible, elastic; **dehnen** vt to stretch ▷ vr **sich ~** to stretch

Deich (-(e)s, -e) m dyke

dein pron (adjektivisch) your; **deine(r, s)** pron (substantivisch) yours, of you; **deiner** pron gen von **du**, of you; **deinetwegen** adv (wegen dir) because of you; (dir zuliebe) for your sake; (um dich) about you

deinstallieren vt (Programm) to uninstall

Dekolleté (-s, -s) nt low neckline

Dekoration f decoration; (in Laden) window dressing; **dekorativ** adj decorative; **dekorieren** vt to decorate; (Schaufenster) to dress

Delfin (-s, -e) m dolphin

delikat adj (lecker) delicious; (heikel) delicate

Delikatesse (-, -n) f delicacy

Delle (-, -en) f (fam) dent

Delphin (-s, e) m dolphin

dem dat sing von **der / das; wie ~**

auch sein mag be that as it may

demnächst adv shortly, soon

Demo (-, -s) f (fam) demo

Demokratie (-, -n) f democracy; **demokratisch** adj democratic

demolieren vt to demolish

Demonstration f demonstration; **demonstrieren** vt, vi to demonstrate

den art akk sing, dat pl von **der; sie nat sich ~ Arm gebrochen** she's broken her arm ▷ pron him; (Sache) that one; (relativ: Person) who, that, whom; (relativ: Sache) which, that; **~ hab ich schon ewig nicht mehr gesehen** I haven't seen him in ages ▷ pron (Person) who, that, whom; (Sache) which, that; **der Typ, auf ~ sie steht** the guy (who) she fancies; **der Berg, auf ~ wir geklettert sind** the mountain (that) we climbed

denkbar adj **das ist ~** that's possible ▷ adv **~ einfach** extremely simple; **denken** (dachte, gedacht) vt vi to think (über +akk about); an **jdn / etw ~** to think of sb / sth; (sich erinnern, berücksichtigen) to remember sb / sth; **woran denkst Du?** what are you thinking about?; **denk an den Kaffee!** don't forget the coffee ▷ vr **sich ~** (sich vorstellen) to imagine; **das kann ich mir ~** I can (well) imagine

Denkmal (-s, Denkmäler) nt monument; **Denkmalschutz** m monument preservation; **unter ~ stehen** to be listed

denn conj for, because ▷ adv then; (nach Komparativ) than; **was ist ~?** what's wrong?; **ist das ~ so schwierig?** is it really that difficult?

dennoch conj still, nevertheless

Deo (-s, -s) nt **Deodorant** (-s, -s) nt deodorant; **Deoroller** m roll-on deodorant. **Deospray** m o nt deodorant spray

Deponie (-, -n) f waste disposal site, tip

Depressionen pl **an ~ leiden** to suffer from depression sing; **deprimieren** vt to depress

der art the; (Dativ) to the; (Genitiv) of the; **~ Vater ~ Besitzerin** the owner's father ▷ pron (Person) he; (Sache) that (one), this (one); (relativ, auf Person) who, that; (relativ, auf Sache) which, that; **~ mit ~ Brille** the one (o him) with the glasses; **~ schreibt nicht mehr** (Stift etc) that one doesn't write any more; **jeder, ~ ...** anyone who ...; **er war ~ erste, ~ es erfuhr** he was the first to know ▷ pron (Person) who, that; (Sache) which, that; **jeder, ~ ...** anyone who ...; **er war ~ erste, ~ es erfuhr** he was the first to know

derart adv so; (solcher Art) such; **derartig** adj **ein ~er Fehler** such a mistake, a mistake like that

deren gen von **die** ▷ pron (Person) her; (Sache) its; (Plural) their ▷ pron (Person) whose; (Sache) of which; **meine Freundin und ~ Mutter** my friend and her mother; **das sind ~ Sachen** that's their stuff; **die Frau, ~ Tochter ...** the woman whose daughter ...; **ich bin mir ~ bewusst** I'm aware of that

dergleichen pron **und ~ mehr** and the like, and so on; **nichts ~** no such thing

derjenige pron the one; **der ~** (relativ) the one who (o that)

dermaßen adv so much; (mit Adj) so

derselbe pron the same (person / thing)

deshalb adv therefore; **~ frage ich ja** that's why I'm asking

Design (-s, -s) nt design; **Desig-**

ner(in) (-s, -) m(f) designer

Desinfektionsmittel nt disinfectant; **desinfizieren** vt to disinfect

dessen gen von **der, das** ▷ pron (Person) his; (Sache) its; **ich bin mir ~ bewusst** I'm aware of that ▷ pron (Person) whose; (Sache) of which; **mein Freund und ~ Mutter** my friend and his mother; **der Mann, ~ Tochter ...** the man whose daughter ...; **ich bin mir ~ bewusst** I'm aware of that

Dessert (-s, -s) nt dessert; **zum** (o **als**) **~** for dessert

destilliert adj distilled

desto adv **je eher, ~ besser** the sooner, the better

deswegen conj therefore

Detail (-s, -s) nt detail; **ins ~ gehen** to go into detail

Detektiv(in) (-s, -e) m(f) detective

deutlich adj clear; (Unterschied) distinct

deutsch adj German; **Deutsch** nt German; **auf ~** in German; **ins ~e übersetzen** to translate into German; **Deutsche(r)** mf German; **Deutschland** nt Germany

Devise (-, -n) f motto; **~n** pl (Fin) foreign currency sing; **Devisenkurs** m exchange rate

Dezember (-(s), -) m December; siehe auch **Juni**

dezent adj discreet

d.h. abk von **das heißt** i.e. (gesprochen: i.e. oder that is)

Dia (-s, -s) nt slide

Diabetes (-, -) m (Med) diabetes; **Diabetiker(in)** (-s, -) m(f) diabetic

Diagnose (-, -n) f diagnosis

diagonal adj diagonal

Dialekt (-(e)s, -e) m dialect

Dialog (-(e)s, -e) m dialogue; (Inform) dialog

Dialyse (-, -n) f (Med) dialysis

Diamant m diamond

Diaprojektor m slide projector

Diät (-, -en) f diet; **eine ~ machen** to be on a diet; (anfangen) to go on a diet

dich pron akk von **du** you; **~ (selbst)** (reflexiv) yourself; **pass auf ~ auf** look after yourself; **reg ~ nicht auf** don't get upset

dicht adj dense (Nebel) thick; (Gewebe) close; (wasserdicht) watertight; (Verkehr) heavy ▷ adv **~ an/bei** close to, **~ bevölkert** densely populated

Dichter(in) (-s, -) m(f) poet; (Autor) writer

Dichtung f (Auto) gasket; (Dichtungsring) washer; (Gedichte) poetry

Dichtungsring m (Tech) washer

dick adj thick; (Person) fat; **jdn ~ haben** to be sick of sb; **Dickdarm** m colon; **Dickkopf** m stubborn (o pig-headed) person; **Dickmilch** f sour milk

die art the; **~ arme Sarah** poor Sarah ▷ pron (sing, Person, als Subjekt) she; (Person, als Subjekt, Plural) they; (Person, als Objekt) her; (Person, als Objekt, Plural) them; (Sache) that (one), this (one); (Plural) those (ones), this (ones); (relativ, auf Person) who, that; (relativ, auf Sache) which, that; **mit den langen Haaren** the one (o her) with the long hair; **sie war ~ erste, ~ es erfuhr** she was the first to know; **ich nehme ~ da** I'll take that one / those ▷ pl von **der, die, das**

Dieb(in) (-(e)s, -e) m(f) thief; **Diebstahl** (-(e)s, Diebstähle) m theft; **Diebstahlsicherung** f burglar alarm

diejenige pron the one; **~, die** (relativ) the one who (o that); **~n** pl those pl, the ones

Diele (-, -n) f hall

Dienst (-(e)s, -e) m service, **außer ~** retired; **~ haben** to be on duty; **der ~ habende Arzt** the doctor on duty

Dienstag m Tuesday; siehe auch **Mittwoch**; **dienstags** adv on Tuesdays; siehe auch **mittwochs**

Dienstbereitschaft f haben (Arzt) to be on call; **Dienstleistung** f service; **dienstlich** adj official; **er ist ~ unterwegs** he's away on business; **Dienstreise** f business trip; **Dienststelle** f department; **Dienstwagen** m company car; **Dienstzeit** f office hours pl; (Mil) period of service

diesbezüglich adj (formell) on this matter

diese(r, s) pron this (one); pl these; **~ Frau** this woman; **~r Mann** this man; **~s Mädchen** this girl; **~ Leute** these people; **ich nehme ~/~n/~s (hier)** I'll take this one; (dort) I'll take that one; **ich nehme ~ pl (hier)** I'll take these (ones); (dort) I'll take those (ones)

Diesel (-s, -) m (Auto) diesel

dieselbe pron the same; **es sind immer ~** it's always the same people

Dieselmotor m diesel engine; **Dieselöl** nt diesel (oil)

diesig adj hazy, misty

diesmal adv this time

Dietrich (-s, -e) m skeleton key

Differenz (-, -en) f difference

digital adj digital; **Digital-** in zW (Kamera, Anzeige etc) digital

Diktat (-(e)s, -e) nt dictation

Diktatur f dictatorship

Dill (-s) m dill

DIN abk = **Deutsche Industrienorm** DIN; **~ A4** A4

Ding (-(e)s, -e) nt thing; **vor allen ~en** above all; **der Stand der ~e** the state of affairs; **das ist nicht mein ~**

(fam) it's not my sort of thing *(ρ* cup of tea); **Dingsbums** (-) *nt (fam)* thingy, thingummybob

Dinosaurier *m* dinosaur

Diphtherie *f* diphtheria

Diplom (-*(e)s*, -*e*) *nt* diploma

Diplomat(in) (-*en*, -*en*) *m(f)* diplomat

dir *pron dat von* **du** (to) you; **hat er ~ geholfen?** did he help you?; **ich werde es ~ erklären** I'll explain it to you; *(reflexiv)* **wasch ~ die Hände** go and wash your hands; **ein Freund von ~** a friend of yours

direkt *adj* direct; *(Frage)* straight; **~e Verbindung** through service ▷ *adv* directly; *(sofort)* immediately; **~ am Bahnhof** right next to the station; **Direktflug** *m* direct flight

Direktor(in) *m(f)* director; *(Schule)* headmaster / -mistress *(BRIT)*, principal *(US)*

Direktübertragung *f* live broadcast

Dirigent(in) *m(f)* conductor; **dirigieren** *vt* to direct; *(Mus)* to conduct

Discman® (-*s*, -*s*) *m* Discman®

Diskette *f* disk, diskette; **Diskettenlaufwerk** *nt* disk drive

Diskjockey (-*s*, -*s*) *m* disc jockey; **Disko** (-, -*s*) *f (fam)* disco, club; **Diskothek** (-, -*en*) *f* discotheque, club

diskret *adj* discreet

diskriminieren *vt* to discriminate against

Diskussion *f* discussion; **diskutieren** *vt*, *vi* to discuss

Display (-*s*, -*s*) *nt* display

disqualifizieren *vt* to disqualify

Distanz *f* distance

Distel (-, -*n*) *f* thistle

Disziplin (-, -*en*) *f* discipline

divers *adj* various

dividieren *vt* to divide *(durch* by);

8 dividiert durch 2 ist 4 8 divided by 2 is 4

DJ (-*s*, -*s*) *m abk* = **Diskjockey** DJ

doch *adv* **das ist nicht wahr!** — **~!** that's not true — yes it is; **nicht ~!** oh no; **er kommt ~!** he will come, won't he?; **er hat es ~ gemacht** he did it after all; **setzen Sie sich ~** do sit down, please ▷ *conj (aber)* but

Doktor(in) *m(f)* doctor

Dokument *nt* document; **Dokumentarfilm** *m* documentary (film); **dokumentieren** *vt* to document; **Dokumentvorlage** *f (Inform)* document template

Dolch (-*(e)s*, -*e*) *m* dagger

Dollar (-*(s)*, -*s*) *m* dollar

dolmetschen *vt*, *vi* to interpret; **Dolmetscher(in)** (-*s*, -) *m(f)* interpreter

Dolomiten *pl* Dolomites *pl*

Dom (-*(e)s*, -*e*) *m* cathedral

Domäne (-, -*n*) *f* domain, province; *(Inform: Domäin)* domain

Dominikanische Republik *f* Dominican Republic

Domino (-*s*, -*s*) *nt* dominoes *sing*

Donau (-) *f* Danube

Döner (-*s*, -) *m*, **Döner Kebab** (-*(s)*, -*s*) *m* doner kebab

Donner (-*s*, -) *m* thunder; **donnern** *vi* **es donnert** it's thundering

Donnerstag *m* Thursday; *siehe auch* **Mittwoch**; **donnerstags** *adv* on Thursdays; *siehe auch* **mittwochs**

doof *adj (fam)* stupid

dopen *vt* to dope; **Doping** (-*s*) *nt* doping; **Dopingkontrolle** *f* drugs test

Doppel (-*s*, -) *nt* duplicate; *(Sport)* doubles *sing*; **Doppelbett** *nt* double bed; **Doppeldecker** *m* double-decker; **Doppelhaushälfte** *f* semi-detached house *(BRIT)*, duplex *(US)*; **doppelklicken** *vi* to double-click; **Doppelname** *m* double-barrelled

name; **Doppelpunkt** m colon;
Doppelstecker m two-way adaptor; **doppelt** adj double; **in -er
Ausführung** in duplicate; **Doppelzimmer** nt double room
Dorf (-(e)s, Dörfer) nt village
Dorn (-(e)s, -en) m (Bot) thorn
Dörrobst nt dried fruit
Dorsch (-(e)s, -e) m cod
dort adv there; ~ **drüben** over
there; **dorther** adv from there
Dose (-, -n) f box; (Blechdose) tin
(BRIT), can; (Bierdose) can
dösen vi to doze
Dosenbier nt canned beer; **Dosenmilch** f canned milk, tinned
milk (BRIT); **Dosenöffner** m tin
opener (BRIT), can opener
Dotter (-s, -) m (egg) yolk
downloaden vt to download
Downsyndrom (-(e)s, -e) nt (Med)
Down's syndrome
Dozent(in) m(f) lecturer
Dr. abk = **Doktor**
Drache (-n, -n) m dragon; **Drachen**
(-s, -) m (Spielzeug) kite; (Sport) hang-glider; **Drachenfliegen** (-s) nt
hang-gliding; **Drachenflieger(in)**
(-s, -) m(f) hang-glider
Draht (-(e)s, Drähte) m wire;
Drahtseilbahn f cable railway
Drama (-s, Dramen) nt drama;
dramatisch adj dramatic
dran adv (fam) kontr von **daran**, **gut
~ sein** (reich) to be well-off; (glücklich) to be fortunate; (gesundheitlich)
to be well; **schlecht ~ sein** to be in a
bad way; **wer ist ~?** whose turn is it?; **ich bin ~!** it's my turn; **bleib ~!**
(Tel) hang on
drang imperf von **dringen**
Drang (-(e)s, Dränge) m (Trieb) urge
(nach für); (Druck) pressure
drängeln vt, vi to push
drängen vt (schieben) to push;
(antreiben) to urge ▷ vi (eilig sein) to

be urgent; (Zeit) to press; **auf etw**
(akk) ~ to press for sth
dran|kommen irr vi **wer kommt
dran?** who's turn is it?, who's next?
drauf (fam) kontr von **darauf**; **gut /
schlecht ~ sein** to be in a good / bad
mood
Draufgänger(in) (-s, -) m(f)
daredevil
drauf|kommen irr vi to remember; **ich komme nicht drauf** I can't
think of it
drauf|machen vi (fam) **einen ~** to
go on a binge
draußen adv outside
Dreck ((e)s) m dirt, filth; **dreckig**
adj dirty, filthy
drehen vt, vi to turn; (Zigaretten) to
roll; (Film) to shoot ▷ vr **sich ~** to
turn; (um Achse) to rotate; **sich ~ um**
(handeln von) to be about
Drehstrom m three-phase current; **Drehtür** f revolving door;
Drehzahlmesser m rev counter
drei num three; ~ **viertel voll**
three-quarters full; **es ist ~ viertel
neun** it's a quarter to nine; **Drei** (-,
-en) f three; (Schulnote) ≈ C; **Dreieck** nt triangle; **dreieckig** adj
triangular; **dreifach** adj triple ▷
adv three times; **dreihundert** num
three hundred; **Dreikönigstag** m
Epiphany; **dreimal** adv three
times; **Dreirad** nt tricycle; **dreispurig** adj three-lane
dreißig num thirty; **dreißigste(r,
s)** adj thirtieth; siehe auch **dritte**
Dreiviertelstunde f **eine ~** three
quarters of an hour
dreizehn num thirteen; **dreizehnte(r, s)** adj thirteenth; siehe
auch **dritte**
dressieren vt to train
Dressing (-s, -s) nt (salad) dressing
Dressman (s, Dressmen) m (male)
model

Dressur (-, -en) f training

drin (fam) kontr von **darin** in it; **mehr war nicht ~** that was the best I could do

dringen (drang, gedrungen) vi (Wasser, Licht, Kälte) to penetrate (durch through, in +akk into); **auf etw** (akk) **~** to insist on sth; **dringend, dringlich** adj urgent

drinnen adv inside

dritt adv **wir sind zu ~** there are three of us; **dritte(r, s)** adj third; **die Dritte Welt** the Third World; **7. Juni** 7(th) June (gesprochen: the seventh of June); **am 7. Juni** on 7(th) June, on June 7(th) (gesprochen: on the seventh of June); **München, den 7. Juni** Munich, June 7(th); **Drittel** (-s, -) nt (Bruchteil) third; **drittens** adv thirdly

Droge (-, -n) f drug; **drogenab-hängig, drogensüchtig** adj addicted to drugs

Drogerie f chemist's (BRIT), drugstore (US); **Drogeriemarkt** m discount chemist's (BRIT) (o drugstore (US))

● **DROGERIE**

● The **Drogerie** as opposed to the
● **Apotheke** sells medicines not re-
● quiring a prescription. It tends to
● be cheaper and also sells cosmet-
● ics, perfume and toiletries.

drohen vi to threaten (jdm sb); **mit etw ~** to threaten to do sth

dröhnen vi (Motor) to roar; (Stimme, Musik) to boom; (Raum) to resound

Drohung f threat
Drossel (-, -n) f thrush
drüben adv over there; (auf der anderen Seite) on the other side
drüber (fam) kontr von **darüber**
Druck (-(e)s, Drücke) m (Phys) pres-

sure; (fig: Belastung) stress; **jdn un-ter ~ setzen** to put sb under pressure ▷ (-(e)s, -e) m (Typo: Vorgang) printing; (Produkt, Schriftart) print; **Druckbuchstabe** m block letter; **in ~n schreiben** to print; **drucken** vt, vi to print

drücken vt, vi (Knopf, Hand) to press; (zu eng sein) to pinch; (fig: Preise) to keep down; **jdm etw in die Hand ~** to press sth into sb's hand ▷ **vr sich vor etw** (dat) **~** to get out of sth; **drückend** adj oppressive

Drucker (-s, -) m (Inform) printer; **Druckertreiber** m printer driver
Druckknopf m press stud (BRIT), snap fastener (US); **Drucksache** f printed matter; **Druckschrift** f block letters pl

drunten adv down there
drunter (fam) kontr von **darunter**
Drüse (-, -n) f gland
Dschungel (-s, -) m jungle
du pron you; **bist ~ es?** is it you?; **wir sind per ~** we're on first-name terms
Dübel (-s, -) m Rawlplug®
ducken vt to duck ▷ **vr sich ~** to duck

Dudelsack m bagpipes pl
Duett (-s, -e) nt duet
Duft (-(e)s, Düfte) m scent; **duften** vi to smell nice; **es duftet nach ...** it smells of ...
dulden vt to tolerate
dumm adj stupid; **Dummheit** f stupidity; (Tat) stupid thing; **Dummkopf** m idiot
dumpf adj (Ton) muffled; (Erinnerung) vague; (Schmerz) dull
Düne (-, -n) f dune
Dünger (-s, -) m fertilizer
dunkel adj dark; (Stimme) deep; (Ahnung) vague; (rätselhaft) obscure; (verdächtig) dubious; **im Dunkeln tappen** (fig) to be in the dark;

dunkelblau *adj* dark blue; **dunkelblond** *adj* light brown; **dunkelhaarig** *adj* dark-haired; **Dunkelheit** *f* darkness

dünn *adj* thin; *(Kaffee)* weak

Dunst *(-es, Dünste)* *m* haze; *(leichter Nebel)* mist; *(Chem)* vapour

dünsten *vt (Gastr)* to steam

Duo *(-s, -s)* *nt* duo

Dur *(-) nt (Mus)* major (key); **in G- **in G major

durch *prep* +akk through; *(mittels)* by; *(Zeit)* during; **~ Amerika reisen** to travel across the USA; **er verdient seinen Lebensunterhalt ~ den Verkauf von Autos** he makes his living by selling cars ▷ *adv (Fleisch)* cooked through, well done; **das ganze Jahr ~** all through the year, the whole year long; **darf ich bitte ~?** can I get through, please?

durchaus *adv* absolutely; **~ nicht** not at all

Durchblick *m* view; **den ~ haben** *(fig)* to know what's going on; **durchblicken** *vi* to look through; *(fam: verstehen)* to understand *(bei etw sth)*; **etw ~ lassen** *(fig)* to hint at sth

Durchblutung *f* circulation

durchbrennen *irr vi (Sicherung)* to blow; *(Draht)* to burn through; *(fam: davonlaufen)* to run away

durchdacht *adv* **gut ~** well thought-out

durchdrehen *vt (Fleisch)* to mince ▷ *vi (Räder)* to spin; *(fam: nervlich)* to crack up

durcheinander *adv* in a mess; *(fam: verwirrt)* confused; **~ bringen** to mess up; *(verwirren)* to confuse; **~ reden** to talk all at the same time; **~ trinken** to mix one's drinks; **Durcheinander** *(-s) nt (Verwirrung)* confusion; *(Unordnung)* mess

Durchfahrt *f* way through; **„~**

verboten!" 'no thoroughfare'

Durchfall *m (Med)* diarrhoea

durchfallen *irr vi* to fall through; *(in Prüfung)* to fail

durchfragen *vr* **sich ~** to ask one's way

durchführen *vt* to carry out

Durchgang *m* passage; *(Sport)* round; *(bei Wahl)* ballot; **Durchgangsverkehr** *m* through traffic

durchgebraten *adj* well done

durchgefroren *adj* frozen to the bone

durchgehen *irr vi* to go through *(durch etw sth)*; *(ausreißen: Pferd)* to break loose; *(Mensch)* to run away; **durchgehend** *adj (Zug)* through; **~ geöffnet** open all day

durchhalten *irr vi* to hold out ▷ *vt (Tempo)* to keep up; **etw ~** *(bis zum Schluss)* to see sth through

durchkommen *irr vi* to get through; *(Patient)* to pull through

durchlassen *irr vt (jdn)* to let through; *(Wasser)* to let in

Durchlauf(wasser)erhitzer *(-s, -) m* instantaneous water heater

durchlesen *irr vt* to read through

durchleuchten *vt* to X-ray

durchmachen *vt* to go through; *(Entwicklung)* to undergo; **die Nacht ~** to make a night of it, to have an all-nighter

Durchmesser *(-s, -) m* diameter

Durchreise *f* journey through; **auf der ~** passing through; *(Güter)* in transit; **Durchreisevisum** *nt* transit visa

durchreißen *irr vt, vi* to tear (in two)

durchs *kontr von* **durch das**

Durchsage *(-, -n) f* announcement

durchschauen *vt (jdn, Lüge)* to see through

durchschlagen *irr vr* **sich ~** to struggle through

durchschneiden | 54

durch|schneiden *irr vt* to cut (in two)

Durchschnitt *m* (Mittelwert) average; **im ~** on average; **durchschnittlich** *adj* average ▷ *adv* (im Durchschnitt) on average; **Durchschnittsgeschwindigkeit** *f* average speed

durch|setzen *vt* to get through ▷ *vr* **sich ~** (Erfolg haben) to succeed; (sich behaupten) to get one's way

durchsichtig *adj* transparent, see-through

durch|stellen *vt* (Tel) to put through

durch|streichen *irr vt* to cross out

durchsuchen *vt* to search (nach for); **Durchsuchung** *f* search

durchwachsen *adj* (Speck) streaky; (fig: mittelmäßig) so-so

Durchwahl *f* direct dialling; (Nummer) extension

durch|ziehen *irr vt* (Plan) to carry through

Durchzug *m* draught

dürfen (durfte, gedurft) *vi* **etw tun ~** (Erlaubnis) to be allowed to do sth; **darf ich?** may I?; **das darfst du nicht (tun)!** you mustn't do that; **was darf es sein?** what can I do for you?; **er dürfte schon dort sein** he should be there by now

dürftig *adj* (ärmlich) poor; (unzulänglich) inadequate

dürr *adj* dried-up; (Land) arid; (mager) skinny

Durst (-(e)s) *m* thirst; **~ haben** to be thirsty; **durstig** *adj* thirsty

Dusche (-, -n) *f* shower; **duschen** *vi* to have a shower ▷ *vr* **sich ~** to have a shower; **Duschgel** *nt* shower gel; **Duschvorhang** *m* shower curtain

Düse (-, -n) *f* nozzle; (Tech) jet; **Düsenflugzeug** *nt* jet (aircraft)

Dussel (-s, -) *m* (fam) dope; **dus-s(e)lig** *adj* (fam) stupid

düster *adj* dark; (Gedanken, Zukunft) gloomy

Dutyfreeshop (-s, -s) *m* duty-free shop

Dutzend (-s, -e) *nt* dozen

duzen *vt* to address sb 'du' ▷ *vr* **sich ~ (mit jdm)** to address each other as 'du', to be on first-name terms

DVD (-, -s) *f abk* = Digital Versatile Disk DVD

dynamisch *adj* dynamic

Dynamo (-s, -s) *m* dynamo

D-Zug *m* fast train

Ebbe (-, -n) f low tide

eben adj level; (glatt) smooth ▷ adv just; (bestätigend) exactly

Ebene (-, -n) f plain; (fig) level

ebenfalls adv also, as well, (Antwort: gleichfalls!) you too; **ebenso** adv just as; **~ gut** just as well; **~ viel** just as much

Eber (-s, -) m boar

EC (-, -s) m abk = **Eurocityzug**

Echo (-s, -s) nt echo

echt adj (Leder, Gold) real, genuine; **ein ~er Verlust** a real loss

EC-Karte f = debit card

Ecke (-, -n) f corner; (Math) angle; **an der ~** at the corner; **gleich um die ~** just round the corner; **eckig** adj rectangular; **Eckzahn** m canine

Economyclass (-) f coach (class), economy class

Ecstasy (-) f (Droge) ecstasy

edel adj noble; **Edelstein** m precious stone

EDV (-) f abk = **elektronische Datenverarbeitung** EDP

Efeu (-s) m ivy

Effekt (-s, -e) m effect

egal adj **das ist ~** it doesn't matter; **das ist mir ~** I don't care, it's all the same to me; **~ wie teuer** no matter how expensive

egoistisch adj selfish

ehe conj before

Ehe (-, -n) f marriage; **Ehefrau** f wife; (verheiratete Frau) married woman; **Eheleute** pl married couple sing

ehemalig adj former; **ehemals** adv formerly

Ehemann m husband; (verheirateter Mann) married man; **Ehepaar** nt married couple

eher adv (früher) sooner; (lieber) rather, sooner; (mehr) more; **je ~, desto besser** the sooner the better

Ehering m wedding ring

eheste(r, s) adj (früheste) first ▷ adv **am ~n** (am wahrscheinlichsten) most likely

Ehre (-, -n) f honour; **ehren** vt to honour; **ehrenamtlich** adj voluntary; **Ehrengast** m guest of honour; **Ehrenwort** nt word of honour; **~! I promise, ich gebe dir mein ~** I give you my word

ehrgeizig adj ambitious

ehrlich adj honest

Ei (-(e)s, -er) nt egg; **hart gekochtes/weiches ~** hard-boiled/soft-boiled egg

Eiche (-, -n) f oak (tree); **Eichel** (-, -n) f acorn

Eichhörnchen nt squirrel

Eid (-(e)s, -e) m oath

Eidechse (-, -n) f lizard

Eierbecher m eggcup; **Eierstock** m ovary; **Eieruhr** f egg timer

Eifersucht f jealousy; **eifersüchtig** adj jealous (auf +akk of)

Eigelb (-(e)s, -) nt egg yolk

eigen adj own; (typisch) characteristic (*jdm of sb*); (*eigenartig*) peculiar; **eigenartig** *adj* peculiar; **Eigenschaft** *f* quality; (*Chem, Phys*) property; (*Merkmal*) characteristic

eigentlich *adj* actual, real ▷ *adv* actually, really; **was denken Sie sich ~ dabei?** what on earth do you think you're doing?

Eigentum *nt* property; **Eigentümer(in)** *m(f)* owner; **Eigentumswohnung** *f* owner-occupied flat (*BRIT*), condominium (*US*)

eignen *vr* **sich ~ für** to be suited for; **er würde sich als Lehrer ~** he'd make a good teacher

Eilbrief *m* express letter, special-delivery letter; **Eile** (-) *f* hurry; **eilen** *vi* (*dringend sein*) to be urgent; **es eilt nicht** there's no hurry; **eilig** *adj* hurried; (*dringlich*) urgent; **es ~ haben** to be in a hurry

Eimer (*-s, -*) *m* bucket

ein *adv* **nicht ~ noch aus wissen** not to know what to do; **~ - aus** (*Schalter*) on - off

ein(e) *art* a; (*vor gesprochenem Vokal*) an; **~ Mann** a man; **~ Apfel** an apple; **~e Stunde** an hour; **~ Haus** a house; **~ (gewisser) Herr Miller** a (certain) Mr Miller; **~es Tages** one day

einander *pron* one another, each other

ein|arbeiten *vt* to train ▷ *vr* **sich ~** to get used to the work

ein|atmen *vt, vi* to breathe in

Einbahnstraße *f* one-way street

ein|bauen *vt* to build in; (*Motor etc*) to install, to fit; **Einbauküche** *f* fitted kitchen

ein|biegen *irr vi* to turn (*in +akk* into)

ein|bilden *vt* **sich** (*dat*) **etw ~** to imagine sth

ein|brechen *irr vi* (*in Haus*) to break in; (*Dach etc*) to fall in, to collapse; **Einbrecher(in)** (*-s, -*) *m(f)*

burglar

ein|bringen *irr vt* (*Ernte*) to bring in; (*Gewinn*) to yield; **jdm etw ~** to bring (*o earn*) sb sth ▷ *vr* **sich in** (*akk*) **etw ~** to make a contribution to sth

Einbruch *m* (*Haus*) break-in, burglary; **bei ~ der Nacht** at nightfall

Einbürgerung *f* naturalization

ein|checken *vt* to check in

ein|cremen *vt* to put some cream on ▷ *vr* **sich ~** to put some cream on

eindeutig *adj* clear, obvious ▷ *adv* clearly; **~ falsch** clearly wrong

ein|dringen *irr vi* (*gewaltsam*) to force one's way in (*in +akk* -to); (*in Haus*) to break in (*in +akk* -to); (*Gas, Wasser*) to get in (*in +akk* -to)

Eindruck *m* impression; **großen ~ auf jdn machen** to make a big impression on sb

eine(r, s) *pron* one; (*jemand*) someone; **~r meiner Freunde** one of my friends; **~r nach dem andern** one after the other

eineiig *adj* (*Zwillinge*) identical

eineinhalb *num* one and a half

einerseits *adv* on the one hand

einfach *adj* (*nicht kompliziert*) simple; (*Mensch*) ordinary; (*Essen*) plain; (*nicht mehrfach*) single; **~e Fahrkarte** single ticket (*BRIT*), one-way ticket (*US*) ▷ *adv* simply; (*nicht mehrfach*) once

Einfahrt *f* (*Vorgang*) driving in; (*eines Zuges*) arrival; (*Ort*) entrance

Einfall *m* (*Idee*) idea; **ein|fallen** *irr vi* (*Licht etc*) to fall in; (*einstürzen*) to collapse; **ihm fiel ein, dass ...** it occurred to him that ...; **ich werde mir etwas ~ lassen** I'll think of something; **was fällt Ihnen ein!** what do you think you're doing?

Einfamilienhaus *nt* detached house

einfarbig *adj* all one colour; (*Stoff etc*) self-coloured

Einfluss m influence

ein|frieren irr vt, vi to freeze

ein|fügen vt to fit in; (zusätzlich) to add; (Inform) to insert; **Einfügetaste** f (Inform) insert key

Einfuhr (-, -en) f import; **Einfuhrbestimmungen** pl import regulations pl

ein|führen vt to introduce; (Ware) to import; **Einführung** f introduction

Eingabe f (Dateneingabe) input; **Eingabetaste** f (Inform) return (o enter) key

Eingang m entrance; **Eingangshalle** f entrance hall, lobby (US)

ein|geben irr vt (Daten etc) to enter, to key in

eingebildet adj imaginary; (eitel) arrogant

Eingeborene(r) mf native

ein|gehen irr vi (Sendung, Geld) to come in, to arrive; (Tier, Pflanze) to die; (Stoff) to shrink; **auf etw (akk) ~** to agree to sth; **auf jdn ~** to respond to sb ▷ vt (Vertrag) to enter into; (Wette) to make; (Risiko) to take

eingelegt adj (in Essig) pickled

eingeschaltet adj (switched) on

eingeschlossen adj locked in; (inklusive) included

ein|gewöhnen vr **sich ~** to settle in

ein|gießen irr vt to pour

ein|greifen irr vi to intervene; **Eingriff** m intervention; (Operation) operation

ein|halten vt (Versprechen etc) to keep

ein|hängen vt (Telefon) **(den Hörer) ~** to hang up

einheimisch adj (Produkt, Mannschaft) local; **Einheimische(r)** mf local

Einheit f (Geschlossenheit) unity; (Maß) unit; **einheitlich** adj uniform

ein|holen vt (Vorsprung aufholen) to catch up with; (Verspätung) to make up for; (Rat, Erlaubnis) to ask for

Einhorn nt unicorn

einhundert num one (o a) hundred

einig adj (vereint) united; **sich** (dat) **~ sein** to agree

einige pron pl some; (mehrere) several ▷ adj some; **nach ~er Zeit** after some time; **~e hundert Euro** some hundred euros

einigen vr **sich ~** to agree (auf +akk on)

einigermaßen adv fairly, quite; (leidlich) reasonably

einiges pron something; (ziemlich viel) quite a bit; (mehreres) a few things; **es gibt noch ~ zu tun** there's still a fair bit to do

Einkauf m purchase; **Einkäufe (machen)** (to do one's) shopping; **ein|kaufen** vt to buy ▷ vi to go shopping; **Einkaufsbummel** m shopping trip; **Einkaufstasche** f. **Einkaufstüte** f shopping bag; **Einkaufswagen** m shopping trolley (BRIT) (o cart (US)); **Einkaufszentrum** nt shopping centre (BRIT) (o mall (US))

ein|klemmen vt to jam; **er hat sich** (dat) **den Finger eingeklemmt** he got his finger caught

Einkommen (-s, -) nt income

ein|laden irr vt (o jdn) to invite; (Gegenstände) to load; **jdn zum Essen ~** to take sb out for a meal; **ich lade dich ein** (bezahle) it's my treat; **Einladung** f invitation

Einlass (-es, Einlässe) m admittance; **~ ab 18 Uhr** doors open at 6 pm; **ein|lassen** irr vr **sich mit jdm/auf etw** (akk) **~** to get involved with sb / sth

ein|leben vr **sich ~** to settle down

ein|legen vt (Film etc) to put in; (marinieren) to marinate; **eine Pause**

~ to take a break

ein|leiten vt to start; (Maßnahmen) to introduce; (Geburt) to induce; **Einleitung** f introduction; (von Geburt) induction

ein|leuchten vi jdm ~ to be (o become) clear to sb; **einleuchtend** adj clear

ein|loggen vi (Inform) to log on (o in)

ein|lösen vt (Scheck) to cash; (Gutschein) to redeem; (Versprechen) to keep

einmal adv once; (früher) before; (in Zukunft) some day; (erstens) first; ~ **im Jahr** once a year; **noch** ~ once more, again; **ich war schon ~ hier** I've been here before; **warst du schon ~ in London?** have you ever been to London?; **nicht** ~ not even; **auf** ~ suddenly; (gleichzeitig) at once; **einmalig** adj unique; (einmal geschehend) single; (prima) fantastic

ein|mischen vr sich ~ to interfere (in +akk with)

Einnahme (-, -n) f (Geld) takings pl; (von Medizin) taking; **ein|nehmen** irr vt (Medizin) to take; (Geld) to take in; (Standpunkt, Raum) to take up; **jdn für sich ~** to win sb over

ein|ordnen vt to put in order, (klassifizieren) to classify; (Akten) to file ▷ vr sich ~ (Auto) to get in lane; **sich rechts/links ~** to get into the right/left lane

ein|packen vt to pack (up)

ein|parken vt, vi to park

ein|planen vt to allow for

ein|prägen vt sich (dat) etw ~ to remember (o memorize) sth

ein|räumen vt (Bücher, Geschirr) to put away; (Schrank) to put things in

ein|reden vt jdm/sich etw ~ to talk sb/oneself into (believing) sth

ein|reiben irr vt sich mit etw ~ to rub sth into one's skin

ein|reichen vt to hand in; (Antrag) to submit

Einreise f entry; **Einreisebestimmungen** pl entry regulations pl; **Einreiseerlaubnis** f, **Einreisegenehmigung** f entry permit; **ein|reisen** vi to enter (in ein Land a country); **Einreisevisum** nt entry visa

ein|renken vt (Arm, Bein) to set

ein|richten vt (Wohnung) to furnish; (gründen) to establish, to set up; (arrangieren) to arrange ▷ vr sich ~ (in Haus) to furnish one's home; (sich vorbereiten) to prepare oneself (auf +akk for); (sich anpassen) to adapt (auf +akk to); **Einrichtung** f (Wohnung) furnishings pl; (öffentliche Anstalt) institution; (Schwimmbad etc) facility

eins num one; **Eins** (-, -en) f one; (Schulnote) ≈ A

einsam adj lonely

ein|sammeln vt to collect

Einsatz m (Teil) insert; (Verwendung) use; (Spieleinsatz) stake; (Risiko) risk; (Mus) entry

ein|schalten vt (Elek) to switch on

ein|schätzen vt to estimate, to assess

ein|schenken vt to pour

ein|schiffen vr sich ~ to embark (nach for)

ein|schlafen irr vi to fall asleep, to drop off; **mir ist der Arm eingeschlafen** my arm's gone to sleep

ein|schlagen irr vt (Fenster) to smash; (Zähne, Schädel) to smash in; (Weg, Richtung) to take ▷ vi to hit (in etw akk sth, auf jdn sb); (Blitz) to strike; (Anklang finden) to be a success

ein|schließen irr vt (jdn) to lock in; (Gegenstand) to lock away; (umgeben) to surround; (fig: beinhalten) to include; **einschließlich** adv inclusive ▷ *prep* +*gen* including; **von Montag bis Freitag** from Monday up to and including Friday, Monday through Friday (US)

ein|schränken *vt* to limit, to restrict; (*verringern*) to cut down on ▷ *vr* **sich ~** to cut down (on expenditure)

ein|schreiben *irr vt* **sich ~** to register; (*Schule*) to enrol; **Einschreiben** (-s, -) *nt* registered letter; **etw per ~ schicken** to send sth by special delivery

ein|schüchtern *vt* to intimidate

ein|sehen *irr vt* (*verstehen*) to see; (*Fehler*) to recognize; (*Akten*) to have a look at

einseitig *adj* one-sided

ein|senden *irr vt* to send in

ein|setzen *vt* to put in; (*in Amt*) to appoint; (*Geld*) to stake; (*verwenden*) to use ▷ *vi* (*beginnen*) to set in; (*Mus*) to enter, to come in ▷ *vr* **sich ~** to work hard; **sich für jdn/etw ~** to support sb/sth

Einsicht *f* insight; **zu der ~ kommen, dass ...** to come to realize that ...

ein|sperren *vt* to lock up

ein|spielen *vt* (*Geld*) to bring in

ein|springen *irr vi* (*aushelfen*) to step in (für for)

Einspruch *m* objection (gegen to)

einspurig *adj* single-lane

Einstand *m* (*Tennis*) deuce

ein|stecken *vt* to pocket; (*Elek: Stecker*) to plug in; (*Brief*) to post, to mail (US); (*mitnehmen*) to take; (*hinnehmen*) to swallow

ein|steigen *irr vi* (*in Auto*) to get in; (*in Bus, Zug, Flugzeug*) to get on; (*sich beteiligen*) to get involved

ein|stellen *vt* (*beenden*) to stop; (*Geräte*) to adjust; (*Kamera*) to focus; (*Sender, Radio*) to tune in; (*unterstellen*) to put, (*in Firma*) to employ, to take on

▷ *vr* **sich auf jdn/etw ~** to adapt to sb / prepare oneself for sth; **Einstellung** *f* (*von Gerät*) adjustment; (*von Kamera*) focusing; (*von Arbeiter*) taking on; (*Meinung*) attitude

ein|stürzen *vi* to collapse

einträgig *adj* one-day

ein|tauschen *vt* to exchange (*gegen* for)

eintausend *num* one (o a) thousand

ein|teilen *vt* (*in Teile*) to divide (up) (*in +akk* into); (*Zeit*) to organize

eintönig *adj* monotonous

Eintopf *m* stew

ein|tragen *irr vt* (*in eine Liste*) to put down, to enter ▷ *vr* **sich ~** to put one's name down, to register

ein|treffen *irr vi* to happen; (*ankommen*) to arrive

ein|treten *irr vi* (*hineingehen*) to enter (*in etw akk* sth); (*in Klub, Partei*) to join (*in etw akk* sth); (*sich ereignen*) to occur; **~ für** to support; **Eintritt** *m* admission; **„~ frei"** 'admission free'; **Eintrittskarte** *f* (*entrance*) ticket; **Eintrittspreis** *m* admission charge

einverstanden *interj* okay, all right ▷ *adj* **mit etwas ~ sein** to agree to sth, to accept sth

Einwanderer *m*, **Einwanderin** *f* immigrant, **einwandern** *vi* to immigrate

einwandfrei *adj* perfect, flawless

Einwegflasche *f* non-returnable bottle; **Einwegwaschlappen** *m* disposable flannel (BRIT) (o washcloth (US))

ein|weichen *vt* to soak

ein|weihen *vt* (*Gebäude*) to inaugurate, to open; **jdn in etw** (*akk*) **~** to let sb in on sth; **Einweihungsparty** *f* housewarming party

ein|werfen *irr vt* (*Ball, Bemerkung etc*) to throw in; (*Brief*) to post, to mail (US); (Geld) to put in, to insert; (Fenster) to smash

ein|wickeln vt to wrap up; (fig) **jdn ~** to take sb in

Einwohner(in) (-s, -) m(f) inhabitant; **Einwohnermeldeamt** nt registration office for residents

Einwurf m (Öffnung) slot; (Sport) throw-in

Einzahl f singular

ein|zahlen vt to pay in (auf ein Konto -to an account)

Einzel (-s, -) nt (Tennis) singles sing; **Einzelbett** nt single bed; **Einzelfahrschein** m single ticket (BRIT), one-way ticket (US); **Einzelgänger(in)** m(f) loner; **Einzelhandel** m retail trade; **Einzelkind** nt only child

einzeln adj individual; (getrennt) separate; (einzig) single; **~e ...** several ..., some ...; **der/die Einzelne** the individual; **im Einzelnen** in detail ▷ adv separately; (verpacken, aufführen) individually; **~ angeben** to specify; **~ eintreten** to enter one by one

Einzelzimmer nt single room; **Einzelzimmerzuschlag** m single-room supplement

ein|ziehen irr vt **den Kopf ~** to duck ▷ vi (in ein Haus) to move in

einzig adj only; (einzeln) single; (einzigartig) unique; **kein ~er Fehler** not a single mistake; **das Einzige** the only thing; **der/die Einzige** the only person ▷ adv only; **die ~ richtige Lösung** the only correct solution; **einzigartig** adj unique

Eis (-es, -) nt ice; (Speiseeis) ice-cream; **~ laufen** to skate; **Eisbahn** f ice(-skating) rink; **Eisbär** m polar bear; **Eisbecher** m (ice-cream) sundae; **Eisberg** m iceberg; **Eiscafé** nt, **Eisdiele** f ice-cream parlour

Eisen (-s, -) nt iron; **Eisenbahn** f

railway (BRIT), railroad (US); **eisern** adj iron

eisgekühlt adj chilled; **Eishockey** nt ice hockey; **Eiskaffee** m iced coffee; **eiskalt** adj ice-cold; (Temperatur) freezing; **Eiskunstlauf** m figure skating; **Eissalat** m iceberg lettuce; **Eisschokolade** f iced chocolate; **Eisschrank** m fridge, ice-box (US); **Eistee** m iced tea; **Eiswürfel** m ice cube; **Eiszapfen** m icicle

eitel adj vain

Eiter (-s) m pus

Eiweiß (-es, -e) nt egg white; (Chem, Bio) protein

ekelhaft, **ek(e)lig** adj disgusting, revolting; **ekeln** vt **sich ~** to be disgusted (vor +dat at)

EKG (-s, -s) nt abk = **Elektrokardiogramm** ECG

Ekzem (-s, -e) nt (Med) eczema

Elastikbinde f elastic bandage; **elastisch** adj elastic

Elch (-(e)s, -e) m elk; (nordamerikanischer) moose

Elefant m elephant

elegant adj elegant

Elektriker(in) (-s, -) m(f) electrician; **elektrisch** adj electric; **Elektrizität** f electricity; **Elektroauto** nt electric car; **Elektrogerät** nt electrical appliance; **Elektrogeschäft** nt electrical shop; **Elektroherd** m electric cooker; **Elektromotor** m electric motor; **Elektronik** f electronics sing; **elektronisch** adj electronic; **Elektrorasierer** (-s, -) m electric razor

Element (-s, -e) nt element

elend adj miserable; **Elend** (-(e)s) nt misery

elf num eleven; **Elf** (-, -en) f (Sport) eleven

Elfenbein nt ivory

Elfmeter m (Sport) penalty (kick)

elfte(r, s) adj eleventh; siehe auch dritte

Ell(en)bogen m elbow

Elster (-, -n) f magpie

Eltern pl parents pl

EM f abk - **Europameisterschaft** European Championship(s)

Email (s, s) nt enamel

E-Mail (-, -s) f (Inform) e-mail; **jdm eine ~ schicken** to e-mail sb, to send sb an e-mail; **jdm etwas per ~ schicken** to e-mail sth to sb; **E-Mail-Adresse** f e-mail address; **e-mailen** vt to e-mail

Emoticon (-s, -s) nt emoticon

emotional adj emotional

empfahl imperf von **empfehlen**

empfand imperf von **empfinden**

Empfang (-(e)s, Empfänge) m (Rezeption; Veranstaltung) reception; (Erhalten) receipt; **in ~ nehmen** to receive; **empfangen** (empfing, empfangen) vt to receive; **Empfänger(in)** (-s, -) m(f) recipient; (Adressat) addressee⊳ m (Tech) receiver; **Empfängnisverhütung** f contraception; **Empfangshalle** f reception area

empfehlen (empfahl, empfohlen) vt to recommend; **Empfehlung** f recommendation

empfinden (empfand, empfunden) vt to feel; **empfindlich** adj (Mensch) sensitive; (Stelle) sore; (reizbar) touchy; (Material) delicate

empfing imperf von **empfangen**

empfohlen pp von **empfehlen**

empfunden pp von **empfinden**

empört adj indignant (über +akk at)

Ende (-s, -n) nt end; (Film, Roman) ending; **am ~** at the end; (schließlich) in the end; **~ Mai** at the end of May; **~ der Achtzigerjahre** in the late eighties; **sie ist ~ zwanzig** she's in her late twenties; **zu ~** over, finished; **enden** vi to end; **der Zug**

endet hier this service (o train) terminates here; **endgültig** adj final; (Beweis) conclusive

Endivie f endive

endlich adv at last, finally; (am Ende) eventually; **Endspiel** nt final; (Endrunde) finals pl; **Endstation** f terminus; **Endung** f ending

Energie f energy; **~ sparend** energy-saving; **Energiebedarf** m energy requirement; **Energieverbrauch** m energy consumption

energisch adj (entschlossen) forceful

eng adj narrow; (Kleidung) tight; (fig: Freundschaft, Verhältnis) close; **das wird ~** (fam: zeitlich) we're running out of time, it's getting tight ⊳ adv **~ befreundet sein** to be close friends

engagieren vt to engage ⊳ vr **sich ~** to commit oneself, to be committed (für to)

Engel (-s, -) m angel

England nt England; **Engländer(in)** (-s, -) m(f) Englishman/-woman; **die ~** pl the English pl; **englisch** adj English; (Gastr) rare; **Englisch** nt English; **ins ~ übersetzen** to translate into English

Enkel (-s, -) m grandson; **Enkelin** f granddaughter

enorm adj enormous; (fig) tremendous

Entbindung f (Med) delivery

entdecken vt to discover; **Entdeckung** f discovery

Ente (-, -n) f duck

Enter-Taste f (Inform) enter (o return) key

entfernen vt to remove; (Inform) to delete ⊳ vr **sich ~** to go away; **entfernt** adj distant; **15 km von X ~** 15 km away from X; **20 km voneinander ~** 20 km apart; **Entfernung** f distance; **aus der ~** from a distance

entführen vt to kidnap; **Entführer(in)** m(f) kidnapper; **Entführung** f kidnapping

entgegen prep +dat contrary to ▷ adv towards; **dem Wind ~** against the wind; **entgegengesetzt** adj (Richtung) opposite; (Meinung) opposing; **entgegen|kommen** irr vi **jdm ~** to come to meet sb; (fig) to accommodate sb; **entgegenkommend** adj (Verkehr) oncoming; (fig) obliging

entgegnen vt to reply (auf +akk to)

entgehen irr vi **jdm ~** to escape sb's notice; **sich** (dat) **etw ~ lassen** to miss sth

entgleisen vi (Eisenb) to be derailed; (fig: Mensch) to misbehave

Enthaarungscreme f hair remover

enthalten irr vt (Behälter) to contain; (Preis) to include ▷ vr **sich ~** to abstain (gen from)

entkoffeiniert adj decaffeinated

entkommen irr vi to escape

entkorken vt to uncork

entlang prep +akk o dat **~ dem Fluss, den Fluss ~** along the river; **entlang|gehen** irr vi to walk along

entlassen vt (Patient) to discharge; (Arbeiter) to dismiss

entlasten vt **~ (Arbeit abnehmen)** to relieve sb of some of his / her work

entmutigen vt to discourage

entnehmen vt to take (dat from)

entrahmt adj (Milch) skimmed

entschädigen vt to compensate; **Entschädigung** f compensation

entscheiden irr vt, vi to decide ▷ vr **sich ~** to decide; **sich für / gegen etw ~** to decide on / against sth; **wir haben uns entschieden, nicht zu gehen** we decided not to go; **das**

entscheidet sich morgen that'll be decided tomorrow; **entscheidend** adj decisive; (Stimme) casting; (Frage, Problem) crucial; **Entscheidung** f decision

entschließen irr vr **sich ~** to decide (zu, für on), to make up one's mind; **Entschluss** m decision

entschuldigen vt to excuse ▷ vr **sich ~** to apologize; **sich bei jdm für etw ~** to apologize to sb for sth ▷ vi **entschuldige!, ~ Sie!** (vor einer Frage) excuse me; (Verzeihung!) (I'm) sorry, excuse me (US); **Entschuldigung** f apology; (Grund) excuse; **jdn um ~ bitten** to apologize to sb; **~!** (bei Zusammenstoß) (I'm) sorry, excuse me (US); (vor einer Frage) excuse me; (wenn man etw nicht verstanden hat) (I beg your) pardon?

entsetzlich adj dreadful, appalling

entsorgen vt to dispose of

entspannen vt (Körper) to relax; (Pol: Lage) to ease ▷ vr **sich ~** to relax; (fam) to chill out; **Entspannung** f relaxation

entsprechen irr vi +dat to correspond to; (Anforderungen, Wünschen etc) to comply with; **entsprechend** adj appropriate ▷ adv accordingly ▷ prep +dat according to, in accordance with

entstehen irr vi (Schwierigkeiten) to arise; (gebaut werden) to be built; (hergestellt werden) to be created

enttäuschen vt to disappoint; **Enttäuschung** f disappointment

entweder conj **~ ... oder ...** either ... or ...; **~ oder!** take it or leave it

entwerfen vt (Möbel, Kleider) to design; (Plan, Vertrag) to draft

entwerten vt to devalue; (Fahrschein) to cancel; **Entwerter** (-s, -) m ticket-cancelling machine

entwickeln vt (a. Foto) to develop;

(Mut, Energie) to show, to display ▷ vr **sich ~** to develop; **Entwicklung** f development; *(Foto)* developing; **Entwicklungshelfer(in)** *(-s, -)* m(f) development worker; **Entwicklungsland** nt developing country

Entwurf m outline; *(Design)* design; *(Vertragsentwurf, Konzept)* draft

entzückend adj delightful, charming

Entzug m withdrawal; *(Behandlung)* detox; **Entzugserscheinung** f withdrawal symptom

entzünden vt to catch fire; *(Med)* to become inflamed; **Entzündung** f *(Med)* inflammation

Epidemie f epidemic

Epilepsie f epilepsy

er pron *(Person)* he; *(Sache)* it; **er ists** it's him; **wo ist mein Mantel? - ~ ist ...** where's my coat? - it's ...

Erbe *(-n, -n)* m heir ▷ *(-s)* nt inheritance; *(fig)* heritage; **erben** vt to inherit; **Erbin** f heiress; **erblich** adj hereditary

erbrechen irr vt to vomit ▷ vr **sich ~** to vomit; **Erbrechen** nt vomiting

Erbschaft f inheritance

Erbse *(-, -n)* f pea

Erdapfel m potato; **Erdbeben** nt earthquake; **Erdbeere** f strawberry; **Erde** *(-, -n)* f *(Planet)* earth; *(Boden)* ground; **Erdgas** nt natural gas, **Erdgeschoss** nt ground floor *(BRIT)*, first floor *(US)*; **Erdkunde** f geography; **Erdnuss** f peanut; **Erdöl** nt *(mineral)* oil; **Erdrutsch** m landslide; **Erdteil** m continent

ereignen vr sich ~ to happen, to take place; **Ereignis** nt event

erfahren irr vt to learn, to find out; *(erleben)* to experience ▷ adj experienced; **Erfahrung** f experience

erfinden irr vt to invent; **erfinderisch** adj inventive, creative; **Er-**

findung f invention

Erfolg *(-(e)s, -e)* m success; *(Folge)* result; **~ versprechend** promising; **viel ~!** good luck; **erfolglos** adj unsuccessful; **erfolgreich** adj successful

erforderlich adj necessary

erforschen vt to explore; *(untersuchen)* investigate

erfreulich adj pleasing, pleasant; *(Nachricht)* good; **erfreulicherweise** adv fortunately

erfrieren irr vi to freeze to death; *(Pflanzen)* to be killed by frost

Erfrischung f refreshment

erfüllen vt *(Raum)* to fill; *(Bitte, Wunsch etc)* to fulfil ▷ vr **sich ~** to come true

ergänzen vt *(hinzufügen)* to add; *(vervollständigen)* to complete ▷ vr **sich ~** to complement one another; **Ergänzung** f completion; *(Zusatz)* supplement

ergeben irr vt *(Betrag)* to come to; *(zum Ergebnis haben)* to result in ▷ irr vr **sich ~** to surrender; *(folgen)* to result *(aus from)* ▷ adj devoted; *(demütig)* humble

Ergebnis nt result

ergreifen irr vt to seize; *(Beruf)* to take up; *(Maßnahme, Gelegenheit)* to take; *(rühren)* to move

erhalten irr vt *(bekommen)* to receive; *(bewahren)* to preserve; **gut ~** sein to be in good condition; **erhältlich** adj available

erheblich adj considerable

erhitzen vt to heat up)

erhöhen vt to raise; *(verstärken)* to increase ▷ vr **sich ~** to increase

erholen vr **sich ~** to recover; *(sich ausruhen)* to have a rest; **erholsam** adj restful; **Erholung** f recovery; *(Entspannung)* relaxation, rest

erinnern vt to remind *(an +akk of)* ▷ vr **sich ~** to remember *(an etw akk* sth); **Erinnerung** f memory; (*Andenken*) souvenir; (*Mahnung*) reminder

erkälten vr **sich ~** to catch a cold; **erkältet** adj (**stark**) **~ sein** to have a (bad) cold; **Erkältung** f cold

erkennen irr vt to recognize; (*sehen, verstehen*) to see; **~, dass ...** to realize that ...; **erkenntlich** adj **sich ~ zeigen** to show one's appreciation

Erker (-s, -) m bay

erklären vt to explain; (*kundtun*) to declare; **Erklärung** f explanation; (*Aussage*) declaration

erkundigen vr **sich ~** to enquire (*nach* about)

erlauben vt to allow, to permit; **jdm ~, etw zu tun** to allow (*o permit*) sb to do sth; **sich** (*dat*) **etw ~** to permit oneself sth; **~ Sie(, dass ich rauche)?** do you mind (if I smoke)?; **was ~ Sie sich?** what do you think you're doing?; **Erlaubnis** f permission

Erläuterung f explanation; (*zu Text*) comment

erleben vt to experience; (*schöne Tage etc*) to have; (*Schlimmes*) to go through; (*miterleben*) to witness; (*noch miterleben*) to live to see; **Erlebnis** nt experience

erledigen vt (*Angelegenheit, Aufgabe*) to deal with; (*fam: ruinieren*) to finish; **erledigt** adj (*beendet*) finished; (*gelöst*) dealt with; (*fam: erschöpft*) whacked, knackered (*BRIT*)

erleichtert adj relieved

Erlös (-es, -e) m proceeds pl

ermahnen vt (*warnend*) to warn

ermäßigt adj reduced; **Ermäßigung** f reduction

ermitteln vt to find out; (*Täter*) to trace ▷ vi (*Jur*) to investigate

ermöglichen vt to make possible (*dat* for)

ermorden vt to murder

ermüdend adj tiring

ermutigen vt to encourage

ernähren vt to feed; (*Familie*) to support ▷ vr **sich ~ von** to live on; **Ernährung** f (*Essen*) food; **Ernährungsberater(in)** m(f) nutritional (*o dietary*) adviser

erneuern vt to renew; (*restaurieren*) to restore; (*renovieren*) to renovate; (*auswechseln*) to replace

ernst adj serious ▷ adv **jdn/etw ~ nehmen** take sb / sth seriously; **Ernst** (-es) m seriousness; **das ist mein ~** I'm quite serious; **im ~?** seriously?; **ernsthaft** adj serious ▷ adv seriously

Ernte (-, -n) f harvest; **Erntedankfest** nt harvest festival (*BRIT*), Thanksgiving (Day) (*US: 4. Donnerstag im November*); **ernten** vt to harvest; (*Lob etc*) to earn

erobern vt to conquer

eröffnen vt to open; **Eröffnung** f opening

erogen adj erogenous

erotisch adj erotic

erpressen vt (*jdn*) to blackmail; (*Geld etc*) to extort; **Erpressung** f blackmail; (*von Geld*) extortion

erraten irr vt to guess

erregen vt to excite; (*sexuell*) to arouse; (*ärgern*) to annoy; (*hervorrufen*) to arouse ▷ vr **sich ~** to get worked up; **Erreger** (-s, -) m (*Med*) germ; (*Virus*) virus

erreichbar adj **~ sein** to be within reach; (*Person*) to be available; **das Stadtzentrum ist zu Fuß / mit dem Wagen leicht ~** the city centre is within easy walking / driving distance; **erreichen** vt to reach; (*Zug etc*) to catch

Ersatz (-es) m replacement; (*aufZeit*) substitute; (*Ausgleich*) compensation: **Ersatzreifen** m (Auto) spare tyre; **Ersatzteil** nt spare (part)

erscheinen irr vi to appear; (wirken) to seem

erschöpft adj exhausted; **Erschöpfung** f exhaustion

erschrecken vt to frighten ▷ (erschrak, erschrocken) vi to get a fright; **erschreckend** adj alarming; **erschrocken** adj frightened

erschwinglich adj affordable

ersetzen vt to replace; (Auslagen) to reimburse

erst adv first; (anfangs) at first; (nicht früher, nur) only; (nicht bis) not until, ~ **jetzt/gestern** only now/yesterday; ~ **morgen** not until tomorrow; **es ist ~ 10 Uhr** it's only ten o'clock; ~ **recht** all the more; ~ **recht nicht** even less

erstatten vt (Kosten) to refund; **Bericht ~** to report (über +akk on); **Anzeige gegen jdn ~** to report sb to the police

erstaunlich adj astonishing; **erstaunt** adj surprised

erstbeste(r, s) adj das ~ **Hotel** any old hotel; **der Erstbeste** just anyone

erste(r, s) adj first; siehe auch **dritte zum ~n Mal** for the first time; **er wurde Erster** he came first; **auf den ~n Blick** at first sight

erstens adv first(ly), in the first place

ersticken vi (Mensch) to suffocate; **in Arbeit ~** to be snowed under with work

erstklassig adj first-class; **erstmals** adv for the first time

erstrecken vr **sich ~** to extend, to stretch (auf +akk to; über +akk over)

ertappen vt to catch

erteilen vt (Rat, Erlaubnis) to give

Ertrag (-(e)s, Erträge) m yield; (Comm) proceeds pl; **ertragen** irr vt

(Schmerzen) to bear, to stand; (dulden) to put up with; **erträglich** adj bearable; (nicht zu schlecht) tolerable

ertrinken irr vi to drown

erwachsen adj grown-up; ~ **werden** to grow up; **Erwachsene(r)** mf adult, grown-up

erwähnen vt to mention

erwarten vt to expect; (warten auf) to wait for; **ich kann den Sommer kaum ~** I can hardly wait for the summer

erwerbstätig adj employed

erwidern vt to reply; (Gruß, Besuch) to return

erwischen vt (fam) to catch (bei etw doing sth)

erwünscht adj desired; (willkommen) welcome

Erz (-es, -e) nt ore

erzählen vt to tell (jdm etw sb sth); **Erzählung** f story, tale

erzeugen vt to produce; (Strom) to generate; **Erzeugnis** nt product

erziehen irr vt to bring up; (geistig) to educate; (Tier) to train; **Erzieher(in)** (-s, -) m(f) educator; (Kindergarten) (nursery school) teacher; **Erziehung** f upbringing; (Bildung) education

es pron (Sache, im Nom und Akk) it; (Baby, Tier) he; (she); **ich bin ~** it's me; ~ **ist kalt** it's cold; ~ **gibt** ... there is .../there are ...; **ich hoffe ~** I hope so; **ich kann ~** I can do it

Escape-Taste f (Inform) escape key

Esel (-s, -) m donkey

Espresso (-s, -) m espresso

essbar adj edible; **essen** (aß, gegessen) vt, vi to eat; **zu Mittag/Abend ~** to have lunch/dinner; **was gibt's zu ~?** what's for lunch/dinner?; **gehen** to eat out; **gegessen sein** (fig, fam) to be history; **Essen** (-s, -) nt (Mahlzeit) meal; (Nahrung) food

Essig (-s, -e) m vinegar; **Essiggurke** f gherkin

Esslöffel m dessert spoon; **Esszimmer** nt dining room

Estland nt Estonia

Etage (-, -n) f floor, storey; **in** (o **auf**) **der ersten ~** on the first (BRIT) (o second (US)) floor; **Etagenbett** nt bunk bed

Etappe (-, -n) f stage

ethnisch adj ethnic

Etikett (-(e)s, -e) nt label

etliche pron pl several, quite a few; **etliches** pron quite a lot

etwa adv (ungefähr) about; (vielleicht) perhaps; (beispielsweise) for instance

etwas pron something; (verneinend, fragend) anything; (ein wenig) a little; **~ Neues** something / anything new; **~ zu essen** something to eat; **~ Salz** some salt; **wenn ich noch ~ tun kann ...** if I can do anything else ... ▷ adv a bit, a little; **~ mehr** a little more

EU (-) f abk = **Europäische Union** EU

euch pron akk, dat von **ihr**; you, (to) you; **~ (selbst)** (reflexiv) yourselves; **wo kann ich ~ treffen?** where can I meet you; **sie schickt es ~** she'll send it to you; **ein Freund von ~** a friend of yours; **setzt ~ bitte** please sit down; **habt ihr ~ amüsiert?** did you enjoy yourselves?

euer pron (adjektivisch) your; **~ David** (am Briefende) Yours, David ▷ pron gen von **ihr**; of you; **euere(r, s)** pron siehe **eure**

Eule (-, -n) f owl

eure(r, s) pron (substantivisch) yours; **das ist ~** that's yours; **euretwegen** adv (wegen euch) because of you; (euch zuliebe) for your sake; (um euch) about you

Euro (-, -) m (Währung) euro; **Eurocent** m eurocent; **Eurocity** (-(s), -s) f

m , **Eurocityzug** m European Intercity train; **Europa** (-s) nt Europe; **Europäer(in)** (-s, -) m(f) European; **europäisch** adj European; **Europäische Union** European Union; **Europameister(in)** m(f) European champion; (Mannschaft) European champions pl; **Europaparlament** nt European Parliament

Euter (-s, -) nt udder

evangelisch adj Protestant

eventuell adj possible ▷ adv possibly, perhaps

ewig adj eternal; **er hat ~ gebraucht** it took him ages; **Ewigkeit** f eternity

Ex- in zW ex-, former; **~frau** ex-wife; **~minister** former minister

exakt adj precise

Examen (-s, -) nt exam

Exemplar (-s, -e) nt specimen; (Buch) copy

Exil (-s, -e) nt exile

Existenz f existence; (Unterhalt) livelihood, living; **existieren** vi to exist

exklusiv adj exclusive; **exklusive** adv, prep +gen excluding

exotisch adj exotic

Experte (-n, -n) m, **Expertin** f expert

explodieren vi to explode; **Explosion** f explosion

Export (-(e)s, -e) m export; **exportieren** vt to export

Express (-es) m, **Expresszug** m express (train)

extra adj inv (fam: gesondert) separate; (zusätzlich) extra ▷ adv (gesondert) separately; (speziell) specially; (absichtlich) on purpose; **Extra** (-s, -s) nt extra

extrem adj extreme ▷ adv extremely; **~ kalt** extremely cold

exzellent adj excellent

Eyeliner (-s, -) m eyeliner

f

fabelhaft *adj* fabulous, marvellous

Fabrik *f* factory

Fach (-(e)s, Fächer) *nt* compartment; (*Schulfach, Sachgebiet*) subject; **Facharzt** *m*, **Fachärztin** *f* specialist; **Fachausdruck** (-s, Fachausdrücke) *m* technical term

Fächer (-s, -) *m* fan

Fachfrau *f* specialist, expert; **Fachmann** (-leute) *m* specialist, expert; **Fachwerkhaus** *nt* half-timbered house

Fackel (-, -n) *f* torch

fad(e) *adj* (*Essen*) bland; (*langweilig*) dull

Faden (-s, Fäden) *m* thread

fähig *adj* capable (*zu, gen ot*); **Fähigkeit** *f* ability

Fahndung *f* search

Fahne (-, -n) *f* flag

Fahrausweis *m* ticket; **Fahrausweisautomat** *m* ticket machine; **Fahrausweiskontrolle** *f* ticket inspection

Fahrbahn *f* road; (*Spur*) lane

Fähre (-, -n) *f* ferry

fahren (fuhr, gefahren) *vt* to drive; (*Rad*) to ride; (*befördern*) to drive, to take; **50 km/h** ~ to drive at (o drive) 50 kph ▷ *vi* (*sich bewegen*) to go; (*Autofahrer*) to drive; (*Schiff*) to sail; (*abfahren*) to leave; **mit dem Auto/Zug** ~ to go by car/train; **rechts** ~ keep to the right; **Fahrer(in)** (-s, -) *m(f)* driver; **Fahrerairbag** *m* driver airbag; **Fahrerflucht** *f* ~ **begehen** to fail to stop after an accident; **Fahrersitz** *m* driver's seat

Fahrgast *m* passenger; **Fahrgeld** *nt* fare; **Fahrgemeinschaft** *f* car pool; **Fahrkarte** *f* ticket; **Fahrkartenautomat** *m* ticket machine; **Fahrkartenschalter** *m* ticket office

fahrlässig *adj* negligent

Fahrlehrer(in) *m(f)* driving instructor; **Fahrplan** *m* timetable; **Fahrplanauszug** *m* individual timetable; **fahrplanmäßig** *adj* (*Eisenb*) scheduled; **Fahrpreis** *m* fare; **Fahrpreisermäßigung** *f* fare reduction; **Fahrrad** *nt* bicycle; **Fahrradschlauch** *m* bicycle tube; **Fahrradschloss** *nt* bicycle lock; **Fahrradverleih** *m* cycle hire (*BRIT*) (o rental (*US*)); **Fahrradweg** *m* cycle path; **Fahrschein** *m* ticket; **Fahrscheinautomat** *m* ticket machine; **Fahrscheinentwerter** *m* ticket-cancelling machine; **Fahrschule** *f* driving school; **Fahrschüler(in)** *m(f)* learner (driver) (*BRIT*), student driver (*US*); **Fahrspur** *f* lane; **Fahrstreifen** *m* lane; **Fahrstuhl** *m* lift (*BRIT*), elevator (*US*)

Fahrt (-, -en) *f* journey; (*kurz*) trip; (*Auto*) drive; **auf der** ~ **nach London** on the way to London; **nach drei Stunden** ~ after travelling for three hours; **gute** ~! have a good trip;

Fahrtkosten pl travelling expenses pl; **Fahrtrichtung** f direction of travel

fahrtüchtig f (Person) fit to drive; (Fahrzeug) roadworthy

Fahrtunterbrechung f break in the journey, stop

Fahrverbot nt ~ **erhalten/haben** to be banned from driving; **Fahrzeug** nt vehicle; **Fahrzeugbrief** m (vehicle) registration document; **Fahrzeughalter(in)** m(f) registered owner; **Fahrzeugpapiere** pl vehicle documents pl

fair adj fair

Fakultät f faculty

Falke (-n, -n) m falcon

Fall (-(e)s, Fälle) m (Sturz) fall; (Sachverhalt, juristisch) case; **auf jeden ~, auf alle Fälle** in any case; (bestimmt) definitely; **auf keinen ~** on no account; **für den ~, dass …** in case …

Falle (-, -n) f trap

fallen (fiel, gefallen) vi to fall; **etw ~ lassen** to drop sth

fällig adj due

falls adv if; (für den Fall, dass) in case

Fallschirm m parachute; **Fallschirmspringen** nt parachuting, parachute jumping; **Fallschirmspringer(in)** m(f) parachutist

falsch adj (unrichtig) wrong; (unehrlich, unecht) false; (Schmuck) fake; **~ verbunden** sorry, wrong number; **fälschen** vt to forge; **Falschfahrer(in)** m(f) person driving the wrong way on the motorway; **Falschgeld** nt counterfeit money; **Fälschung** f forgery, fake

Faltblatt nt leaflet

Falte (-, -n) f (Knick) fold; (Haut) wrinkle; (Rock) pleat; (Bügel) crease; **falten** vt to fold; **faltig** adj (zerknittert) creased; (Haut, Gesicht) wrinkled

Familie f family; **Familienange-** **hörige(r)** mf family member; **Familienname** m surname; **Familienstand** m marital status

Fan (-s, -s) m fan

fand imperf von **finden**

fangen (fing, gefangen) vt to catch ▷ vr **sich ~** (nicht fallen) to steady oneself; (fig) to compose oneself

Fantasie f imagination

fantastisch adj fantastic

Farbbild nt colour photograph; **Farbdrucker** m colour printer; **Farbe** (-, -n) f colour; (zum Malen etc) paint; (für Stoff) dye; **farbecht** adj colourfast; **färben** vt to colour; (Stoff, Haar) to dye; **Farbfernsehen** nt colour television; **Farbfilm** m colour film; **Farbfoto** nt colour photo; **farbig** adj coloured; **Farbkopierer** m colour copier; **farblos** adj colourless; **Farbstoff** m dye; (für Lebensmittel) colouring

Farn (-(e)s, -e) m fern

Fasan (-(e)s, -e(n)) m pheasant

Fasching (-s, -e) m carnival, Mardi Gras (US); **Faschingsdienstag** (-s, -e) m Shrove Tuesday, Mardi Gras (US)

Faschismus m fascism

Faser (-, -n) f fibre

Fass (-es, Fässer) nt barrel; (Öl) drum

fassen vt (ergreifen) to grasp; (enthalten) to hold; (Entschluss) to take; (verstehen) to understand; **nicht zu ~!** unbelievable ▷ vr **sich ~** to compose oneself; **Fassung** f (Umrahmung) mount; (Brille) frame; (Lampe) socket; (Wortlaut) version; (Beherrschung) composure; **jdn aus der ~ bringen** to throw sb off; **die ~ verlieren** to lose one's cool

fast adv almost, nearly

fasten vi to fast; **Fastenzeit** f die **~** (christlich) Lent; (muslimisch) Ramadan

Fast Food (-s) nt fast food

Fastnacht f (*Fasching*) carnival

fatal adj (*verhängnisvoll*) disastrous; (*peinlich*) embarrassing

faul adj (*Obst, Gemüse*) rotten; (*Mensch*) lazy; (*Ausreden*) lame; **faulen** vi to rot

faulenzen vi to do nothing, to hang around; **Faulheit** f laziness

faulig adj (*Geruch, Geschmack*) foul

Faust (-, *Fäuste*) f fist; **Fausthandschuh** m mitten

Fax (-, *-(e)*) nt fax; **faxen** vi, vt to fax; **Faxgerät** nt fax machine; **Faxnummer** f fax number

FCKW (, s) nt abk = **Fluorchlorkohlenwasserstoff** CFC

Februar (-(s), -e) m February; *siehe auch* **Juni**

Fechten nt fencing

Feder (-, -n) f feather; (*Schreibfeder*) (pen-)nib; (*Tech*) spring; **Federball** m (*Ball*) shuttlecock; (*Spiel*) badminton; **Federung** f suspension

Fee (-, -n) f fairy

fegen vi, vt to sweep

fehl adj ~ **am Platz** o **Ort** out of place

fehlen vi (*abwesend sein*) to be absent; **etw fehlt jdm** sb lacks sth; **was fehlt ihm?** what's wrong with him?; **du fehlst mir** I miss you; **es fehlt an ...** there's no...

Fehler (-s, -) m mistake, error; (*Mangel, Schwäche*) fault; **Fehlermeldung** f (*Inform*) error message

Fehlzündung f (*Auto*) misfire

Feier (-, -n) f celebration; (*Party*) party; **Feierabend** m end of the working day ~ **haben** to finish work; **nach** ~ after work; **feierlich** adj solemn; **feiern** vt, vi to celebrate, to have a party; **Feiertag** m holiday; **gesetzlicher** ~ public (o bank (*BRIT*) o legal (*US*)) holiday

feig(e) adj cowardly

Feige (-, -n) f fig

Feigling m coward

Feile (-, -n) f file

fein adj fine; (*vornehm*) refined; ~! great!; **das schmeckt** ~ that tastes delicious

Feind(in) (-(e)s, -e) m(f) enemy; **feindlich** adj hostile

Feinkost (-) f delicacies pl, **Feinkostladen** m delicatessen; **Feinschmecker(in)** (-s, -) m(f) gourmet

Feinwaschmittel nt washing powder for delicate fabrics

Feld (-(e)s, -er) nt field; (*Schach*) square; (*Sport*) pitch; **Feldsalat** m lamb's lettuce; **Feldweg** m path across the fields

Felge (-, -n) f (*wheel*) rim

Fell (-(e)s, -e) nt fur; (*von Schaf*) fleece

Fels (-en, -en) m, **Felsen** (-s, -) m rock; (*Klippe*) cliff; **felsig** adj rocky

feminin adj feminine; **Femininum** (s, *Feminina*) nt (*Ling*) feminine noun

feministisch adj feminist

Fenchel (-s, -) m fennel

Fenster (-s, -) nt window; **Fensterbrett** nt windowsill; **Fensterladen** m shutter; **Fensterplatz** m window seat; **Fensterscheibe** f windowpane

Ferien (-) (*holidays pl (BRIT*), vacation *sing (US*)) ~ **haben/machen** to be/go on holiday (*BRIT*) (o vacation (*US*)); **Ferienhaus** nt holiday (*BRIT*) (o vacation (*US*)) home; **Ferienkurs** m holiday (*BRIT*) (o vacation (*US*)) course; **Ferienlager** nt holiday camp (*BRIT*), vacation camp (*US*); (*für Kinder im Sommer*) summer camp; **Ferienort** m holiday (*BRIT*) (o vacation (*US*)) resort; **Ferienwohnung** f holiday flat (*BRIT*), vacation apartment (*US*)

Ferkel (-s, -) nt piglet

fern adj distant, far-off; **von** ~ from a distance; **Fernabfrage** f remote-

control access; **Fernbedienung** f remote control; **Ferne** f distance; **aus der ~** from a distance
ferner adj, adv further; (außerdem) besides
Fernflug m long-distance flight; **Ferngespräch** nt long-distance call; **ferngesteuert** adj remote--controlled; **Fernglas** nt binoculars pl; **Fernlicht** nt full beam (BRIT), high beam (US)
Fernsehapparat m TV (set); **fern|sehen** irr vi to watch television; **Fernsehen** nt television; **im ~** on television; **Fernseher** m TV (set); **Fernsehkanal** m TV channel; **Fernsehprogramm** nt (Sendung) TV programme; (Zeitschrift) TV guide; **Fernsehserie** f TV series sing; **Fernsehturm** m TV tower; **Fernsehzeitschrift** f TV guide
Fernstraße f major road; **Fern-tourismus** m long-haul tourism; **Fernverkehr** m long-distance traffic
Ferse (-, -n) f heel
fertig adj (bereit) ready; (beendet) finished; (gebrauchsfertig) ready--made; **~ machen** (beenden) to finish; **jdn ~ machen** (kritisieren) to give sb hell; (zur Verzweiflung bringen) to drive sb mad; (deprimieren) to get sb down; **sich ~ machen** to get ready; **mit etw ~ werden** to be able to cope with sth; **auf die Plätze, ~, los!** on your marks, get set, go!; **Fertiggericht** nt ready meal
fest adj firm; (Nahrung) solid; (Gehalt) regular; (Schuhe) sturdy; (Schlaf) sound
Fest (-(e)s, -e) nt party; (Rel) festival
Festbetrag m fixed amount
fest|binden irr vt to tie (an +dat to); **fest|halten** irr vt to hold onto ▷ vr **sich ~** to hold on (an +dat to)
Festiger (-s, -) m setting lotion

Festival (-s, -s) nt festival
Festland nt mainland; **das europäische ~** the (European) continent
fest|legen vt to fix ▷ vr **sich ~** to commit oneself
festlich adj festive
fest|machen vt to fasten; (Termin etc) to fix; **fest|nehmen** irr vt to arrest; **Festnetz** nt (Tel) fixed-line network; **Festplatte** f (Inform) hard disk
fest|setzen vt to fix
Festspiele pl festival sing
fest|stehen irr vi to be fixed
fest|stellen vt to establish; (sagen) to comment
Feststelltaste f shift lock
Festung f fortress
Festzelt nt marquee
Fete (-, -n) f party
fett adj (dick) fat; (Essen etc) greasy; (Schrift) bold; **Fett** (-(e)s, -e) nt fat; (Tech) grease; **fettarm** adj low-fat; **fettig** adj fatty; (schmierig) greasy
fetzig adj (fam: Musik) funky
feucht adj damp; (Luft) humid; **Feuchtigkeit** f dampness; (Luftfeuchtigkeit) humidity; **Feuchtigkeitscreme** f moisturizing cream
Feuer (-s, -) nt fire; **haben Sie ~?** have you got a light?; **Feueralarm** m fire alarm; **feuerfest** adj fireproof; **feuergefährlich** adj inflammable; **Feuerlöscher** (-s, -) m fire extinguisher; **Feuermelder** (-s, -) m fire alarm; **Feuertreppe** f fire escape; **Feuerwehr** (-, -en) f fire brigade; **Feuerwehrfrau** f firewoman, fire fighter; **Feuerwehrmann** m fireman, fire fighter; **Feuerwerk** nt fireworks pl; **Feuerzeug** nt (cigarette) lighter
Fichte (-, -n) f spruce
ficken vt, vi (vulg) to fuck
Fieber (-s, -) nt temperature, fever; **~ haben** to have a high tempera-

ture; Fieberthermometer nt
thermometer

fiel imperf von **fallen**

fies adj (fam) nasty

Figur (-, -en) f figure; (im Schach)
piece

Filet (-s, -s) nt fillet; **filetieren** vt
to fillet; **Filetsteak** nt fillet steak

Filiale (-, -n) f (Comm) branch

Film (-(e)s, -e) m film movie; **filmen** vt, vi to film

Filter (-s, -) m filter; **Filterkaffee**
m filter coffee; **filtern** vt to filter;
Filterpapier nt filter paper

Filz (-es, -e) m felt; **Filzschreiber**
m, **Filzstift** m felt(-tip) pen, felt
-tip

Finale (-s, -) nt (Sport) final

Finanzamt nt tax office; **finanziell** adj financial; **finanzieren** vt
to finance

finden (fand, gefunden) vt to find;
(meinen) to think; **Ich finde nichts
dabei, wenn ...** I don't see what's
wrong if ...; **Ich finde es gut/
schlecht** I like/don't like it ▷ vr **es
fanden sich nur wenige Helfer**
there were only a few helpers

fing imperf von **fangen**

Finger (-s, -) m finger; **Fingerabdruck** m fingerprint; **Fingerhandschuh** m glove; **Fingernagel** m
fingernail

Fink (-en, -en) m finch

Finne (-n, -n) m, **Finnin** f Finn,
Finnish man/woman; **finnisch** adj
Finnish; **Finnisch** nt Finnish;
Finnland nt Finland

finster adj dark; (verdächtig) dubious; (verdrossen) grim; (Gedanke)
dark; **Finsternis** f darkness

Firewall (-, -s) f (Inform) firewall

Firma (-, Firmen) f firm

Fisch (-(e)s, -e) m fish; **-e** pl (Astr)
Pisces sing; **fischen** vt, vi to fish;
Fischer(in) (-s, -) m(f) fisher-

man/-woman; **Fischerboot** nt
fishing boat; **Fischgericht** nt fish
dish; **Fischhändler(in)** m(f) fishmonger; **Fischstäbchen** nt fish
finger (BRIT) (o stick (US))

Fisole (-, -n) f French bean

fit adj fit; **Fitness** (-) f fitness,
Fitnesscenter (-s, -) nt fitness
centre

fix adj (schnell) quick; **- und fertig**
exhausted

fixen vi (fam) to shoot up; **Fixer(in)** (-s, -) m(f) (fam) junkie

FKK f abk = **Freikörperkultur**
nudism; **FKK-Strand** m nudist
beach

flach adj flat; (Gewässer; Teller)
shallow; **-er Absatz** low heel;
Flachbildschirm m flat screen

Fläche (-, -n) f area; (Oberfläche)
surface

Flagge (-, -n) f flag

flambiert adj flambé(ed)

Flamme (-, -n) f flame

Flanell (-s) m flannel

Flasche (-, -n) f bottle; **eine - sein**
(fam) to be useless; **Flaschenbier**
nt bottled beer; **Flaschenöffner**
m bottle opener; **Flaschenpfand**
nt deposit; **Flaschentomate** f
plum tomato

flatterhaft adj fickle; **flattern** vi
to flutter

flauschig adj fluffy

Flausen pl (fam) daft ideas pl

Flaute (-, -n) f calm; (Comm) recession

Flechte (-, -n) f plait; (Med) scab;
(Bot) lichen; **flechten** (flocht, geflochten) vt to plait; (Kranz) to bind

Fleck (-(e)s, -e) m, **Flecken** (-s, -) m
spot; (Schmutz) stain; (Stoff-) patch;
(Makel) blemish; **Fleckentferner** (-s,
-) m stain remover; **fleckig** adj
spotted; (mit Schmutzflecken) stained

Fledermaus f bat

Fleisch (-(e)s) nt flesh; (Essen) meat; Fleischbrühe f meat stock; Fleischer(in) (-s, -) m(f) butcher; Fleischerei f butcher's (shop); Fleischtomate f beef tomato

fleißig adj diligent, hard-working

flexibel adj flexible

flicken vt to mend; Flickzeug nt repair kit

Flieder (-s, -) m lilac

Fliege (-, -n) f fly; (Krawatte) bow tie

fliegen (flog, geflogen) vt, vi to fly

Fliese (-, -n) f tile

Fließband nt conveyor belt; (als Einrichtung) production (o assembly) line; fließen (floss, geflossen) vi to flow; fließend adj (Rede, Deutsch) fluent; (Übergänge) smooth; ~(es) Wasser running water

Flipper (-s, -) m pinball machine; flippern vi to play pinball

flippig adj (fam) eccentric

flirten vi to flirt

Flitterwochen pl honeymoon sing

flocht imperf von flechten

Flocke (-, -n) f flake

flog imperf von fliegen

Floh (-(e)s, Flöhe) m flea; Flohmarkt m flea market

Flop (-s, -) m flop

Floskel (-, -n) f empty phrase

floss imperf von fließen

Floß (-es, Flöße) nt raft

Flosse (-, -n) f fin; (Schwimmflosse) flipper

Flöte (-, -n) f flute; (Blockflöte) recorder

flott adj lively; (elegant) smart; (Naut) afloat

Fluch (-(e)s, Flüche) m curse; fluchen vi to swear, to curse

Flucht (-, -en) f (a. fig) flight; flüchten vi to flee (vor +dat from); flüchtig adj ich kenne ihn nur ~ I don't know him very well at all; Flüchtling m refugee

Flug (-(e)s, Flüge) m flight; Flugbegleiter(in) (-s, -) m(f) flight attendant; Flugblatt nt leaflet

Flügel (-s, -) m wing; (Mus) grand piano

Fluggast m passenger (on a plane); Fluggesellschaft f airline; Flughafen m airport; Fluglotse m air-traffic controller; Flugnummer f flight number; Flugplan m flight schedule; Flugplatz m airport; (klein) airfield; Flugschein m plane ticket; Flugschreiber m flight recorder, black box; Flugsteig (-s, -e) m gate; Flugstrecke f air route; Flugticket nt plane ticket; Flugverbindung f flight connection; Flugverkehr m air traffic; Flugzeit f flying time; Flugzeug nt plane; Flugzeugentführung f hijacking

Flunder (-, -n) f flounder

Fluor (-s) nt fluorine

Flur (-(e)s, -e) m hall

Fluss (-es, Flüsse) m river; (Fließen) flow

flüssig adj liquid; Flüssigkeit f liquid

flüstern vt, vi to whisper

Flut (-, -en) f (a. fig) flood; (Gezeiten) high tide; Flutlicht nt floodlight

Fohlen (-s, -) nt foal

Föhn (-(e)s, -e) m hairdryer; (Wind) foehn; föhnen vt to dry; (beim Friseur) to blow-dry

Folge (-, -n) f (Reihe, Serie) series sing; (Aufeinanderfolge) sequence; (Fortsetzung eines Romans) instalment; (Fortsetzung einer Fernsehserie) episode; (Auswirkung) result; etw zur ~ haben to result in sth; ~n haben to have consequences; folgen vi to follow (jdm sb); (gehorchen) to obey (jdm sb); jdm ~ können (fig) to be able to follow sb;

folgend adj following; **folgendermaßen** adv as follows; **folglich** adv consequently

Folie f foil; (für Projektor) transparency

Fön® m siehe **Föhn**

Fondue (-s, -s) nt fondue

fönen vt siehe **fönnen**

fordern vt to demand

fördern vt to promote; (unterstützen) to help

Forderung f demand

Forelle f trout

Form (-, -en) f form; (Gestalt) shape; (Gussform) mould; (Backform) baking tin (BRIT) (u pan (US)); **in ~ sein** to be in good form; **Formalität** f formality; **Format** nt format; **von internationalem ~** of international standing; **formatieren** vt (Diskette) to format; (Text) to edit

Formblatt nt form; **formen** vt to form, to shape; **förmlich** adj formal; (buchstäblich) real; **formlos** adj informal; **Formular** (-s, -e) nt form; **formulieren** vt to formulate

forschen vi to search (nach for); (wissenschaftlich) to (do) research; **Forscher(in)** m(f) researcher; **Forschung** f research

Förster(in) (-s, -) m(f) forester; (für Wild) gamekeeper

fort adv away; (verschwunden) gone; **fortbewegen** vt to move away ▷ vr **sich ~** to move; **Fortbildung** f further education; (im Beruf) further training; **fortfahren** irr vi to go away; (weitermachen) to continue; **fortgehen** irr vi to go away; **fortgeschritten** adj advanced; **Fortpflanzung** f reproduction

Fortschritt m progress; **~e machen** to make progress; **fortschrittlich** adj progressive

fortsetzen vt to continue; **Fortsetzung** f continuation; (folgender

Teil) instalment; **~ folgt** to be continued

Foto (-s, -s) nt photo ▷ (-s, -s) m (Fotoapparat) camera; **Fotograf(in)** (-en, -en) m(f) photographer; **Fotografie** f photography; (Bild) photograph; **fotografieren** vt to photograph ▷ vi to take photographs; **Fotokopie** f photocopy; **fotokopieren** vt to photocopy

Foul (-s, -s) nt foul

Foyer (-s, -s) nt foyer

Fr. f abk = **Frau** Mrs; (unverheiratet, neutral) Ms

Fracht (-, -en) f freight; (Naut) cargo; (Preis) carriage; **Frachter** (-s,) m freighter

Frack (-(e)s, Fräcke) m tails pl

Frage (-, -n) f question; **das ist eine ~ der Zeit** that's a matter (o question) of time; **das kommt nicht in ~** that's out of the question; **Fragebogen** m questionnaire; **fragen** vt, vi to ask; **Fragezeichen** nt question mark; **fragwürdig** adj dubious

Franken (-s, -) m (Schweizer Währung) Swiss franc ▷ (-s) nt (Land) Franconia

frankieren vt to stamp; (maschinell) to frank

Frankreich (-s) nt France; **Franzose** (-n, -n) m Frenchman/-woman; **die ~n** pl the French pl; **französisch** adj French; **Französisch** nt French

fraß imperf von **fressen**

Frau (-, -en) f woman; (Ehefrau) wife; (Anrede) Mrs; (unverheiratet, neutral) Ms; **Frauenarzt** m, **Frauenärztin** f gynaecologist; **Frauenbewegung** f women's movement; **frauenfeindlich** adj misogynous; **Frauenhaus** nt refuge (for battered women)

Fräulein nt (junge Dame) young

lady; (veraltet als Anrede) Miss
Freak (-s, -s) m (fam) freak
frech adj cheeky; **Frechheit** f
cheek; **so eine ~!** what a cheek
Freeclimbing (-s) nt free climbing
frei adj free; (Straße) clear; (Mitarbeiter) freelance; **ein ~er Tag** a day
off; **~e Arbeitsstelle** vacancy;
Zimmer ~ room(s) to let (BRIT),
room(s) for rent (US); **im Freien** in
the open air; **Freibad** nt open-air
(swimming) pool; **freiberuflich** adj
freelance; **freig(i)ebig** adj generous; **Freiheit** f freedom; **Freikarte** f free ticket; **frei|lassen** irr vt
to (set) free
freilich adv of course
Freilichtbühne f open-air theatre; **frei|machen** vr **sich ~** to undress; **frei|nehmen** irr vt **sich** (dat)
einen Tag ~ to take a day off;
Freisprechanlage f hands-free
phone; **Freistoß** m free kick
Freitag m Friday; **siehe auch
Mittwoch**; **freitags** adv on Fridays; **siehe auch mittwochs**
freiwillig adj voluntary
Freizeichen nt (Tel) ringing tone
Freizeit f spare (o free) time;
Freizeithemd nt sports shirt;
Freizeitkleidung f leisure wear;
Freizeitpark m leisure park
fremd adj (nicht vertraut) strange;
(ausländisch) foreign; (nicht eigen)
someone else's; **Fremde(r)** mf
(Unbekannter) stranger; (Ausländer)
foreigner; **fremdenfeindlich** adj
anti-foreigner, xenophobic; **Fremdenführer(in)** m(f) (tourist) guide;
Fremdenverkehr m tourism;
Fremdenverkehrsamt nt tourist
information office; **Fremdenzimmer** nt (guest) room; **Fremdsprache** f foreign language;
Fremdsprachenkenntnisse pl
knowledge sing of foreign lan-

guages; **Fremdwort** nt foreign
word
Frequenz f (Radio) frequency
fressen (fraß, gefressen) vt, vi (Tier)
to eat; (Mensch) to guzzle
Freude (-, -n) f joy, delight; **freuen**
vt to please; **es freut mich, dass ...**
I'm pleased that ... ▷ vr **sich ~** to be
pleased (über +akk about); **sich auf
etw** (akk) **~** to look forward to sth
Freund (-(e)s, -e) m friend; (in Beziehung) boyfriend; **Freundin** f
friend; (in Beziehung) girlfriend;
freundlich adj friendly; (liebenswürdig) kind; **freundlicherweise**
adv kindly; **Freundlichkeit** f
friendliness; (Liebenswürdigkeit)
kindness; **Freundschaft** f friendship
Frieden (-s, -) m peace; **Friedhof**
m cemetery; **friedlich** adj peaceful
frieren (fror, gefroren) vt, vi to freeze;
ich friere, es friert mich I'm
freezing
Frikadelle f rissole
Frisbeescheibe® f frisbee®
frisch adj fresh; (lebhaft) lively; **„~
gestrichen"** 'wet paint'; **sich ~
machen** to freshen up; **Frischhaltefolie** f clingfilm® (BRIT), plastic
wrap (US); **Frischkäse** m cream
cheese
Friseur m, **Friseuse** f hairdresser; **frisieren** vt **jdn ~** to do sb's hair
▷ vr **sich ~** to do one's hair; **Frisör**
(-s, -e) m, **Frisöse** (-, -n) f hairdresser
Frist (-, -en) f period; (Zeitpunkt)
deadline; **innerhalb einer ~ von
zehn Tagen** within a ten-day period; **eine ~ einhalten** to meet a
deadline; **die ~ ist abgelaufen** the
deadline has expired; **fristgerecht**
adj, adv within the specified time;
fristlos adj **~e Entlassung** dismissal without notice

Frisur f hairdo, hairstyle

frittieren vt to deep-fry

Frl. f abk = **Fräulein** Miss

froh adj happy; **~e Weihnachten!** Merry Christmas

fröhlich adj happy, cheerful

Fronleichnam (-(e)s) m Corpus Christi

frontal adj frontal; **Frontalzusammenstoß** m head-on collision

fror imperf von **frieren**

Frosch (-(e)s, Frösche) m frog

Frost (-(e)s, Fröste) m frost; **bei ~** in frosty weather; **Frostschutzmittel** nt anti-freeze

Frottee nt terry(cloth); **frottieren** vt to rub down; **Frottier(hand)-tuch** nt towel

Frucht (-, Früchte) f (a. fig) fruit; (Getreide) corn; **Fruchteis** nt fruit-flavoured ice-cream; **Früchtetee** m fruit tea; **fruchtig** adj fruity; **Fruchtpresse** f juicer; **Fruchtsaft** m fruit juice; **Fruchtsalat** m fruit salad

früh adj, adv early; **heute ~** this morning; **um fünf Uhr ~** at five (o'clock) in the morning; **~ genug** soon enough; **früher** adj earlier; (ehemalig) former ▷ adv formerly, in the past; **frühestens** adv at the earliest

Frühjahr nt, **Frühling** m spring; **Frühlingsrolle** f spring roll; **Frühlingszwiebel** f spring onion (BRIT), scallion (US)

frühmorgens adv early in the morning

Frühschicht f **~ haben** to be on the early shift

Frühstück nt breakfast; **frühstücken** vi to have breakfast; **Frühstücksbüfett** nt breakfast buffet; **Frühstücksfernsehen** nt breakfast television; **Frühstücksspeck** m bacon

frühzeitig adj early

Frust (-s) m (fam) frustration; **frustrieren** vt to frustrate

Fuchs (-es, Füchse) m fox

fühlen vt, vi to feel ▷ vr **sich ~** to feel

fuhr imperf von **fahren**

führen vt to lead; (Geschäft) to run; (Name) to bear; (Buch) to keep ▷ vi to lead, to be in the lead ▷ vr to behave; **Führerschein** m driving licence (BRIT), driver's license (US); **Führung** f leadership; (eines Unternehmens) management; (Mil) command; (in Museum, Stadt) guided tour; **in ~ liegen** to be in the lead

füllen vt to fill; (Gastr) to stuff ▷ vr **sich ~** to fill

Füller (-s, -) m, **Füllfederhalter** (-s, -) m fountain pen

Füllung f filling

Fund (-(e)s, -e) m find; **Fundbüro** nt lost property office (BRIT), lost and found (US); **Fundsachen** pl lost property sing

fünf num five; **Fünf** (-, -en) f five; (Schulnote) ≈ E; **fünfhundert** num five hundred; **fünfmal** adv five times; **fünfte(r, s)** adj fifth; siehe auch **dritte**; **Fünftel** (-s, -) nt (Bruchteil) fifth; **fünfzehn** num fifteen; **fünfzehnte(r, s)** adj fifteenth; siehe auch **dritte**; **fünfzig** num fifty; **fünfzigste(r, s)** adj fiftieth

Funk (-s) m radio; **über ~** by radio

Funke (-ns, -n) m spark; **funkeln** vi to sparkle

Funkgerät nt radio set; **Funktaxi** nt radio taxi, radio cab

Funktion f function; **funktionieren** vi to work, to function; **Funktionstaste** f (Inform) function key

für prep +akk for; **was ~ (ein) ...?** what kind (o sort) of ...?; **Tag ~ Tag** day after day

Furcht (-) f fear; **furchtbar** adj terrible; **fürchten** vt to be afraid of, to fear ▷ vr **sich ~** to be afraid (vor +dat of); **fürchterlich** adj awful

füreinander adv for each other

fürs kontr von **für das**

Fürst(in) (-en, -en) m(f) prince/ princess; **Fürstentum** nt principality; **fürstlich** adj (fig) splendid

Furunkel (-s, -) nt boil

Furz (-es, -e) m (vulg) fart; **furzen** vi (vulg) to fart

Fuß (-es, Füße) m foot; (von Glas, Säule etc) base; (von Möbel) leg; **zu ~** on foot; **zu ~ gehen** to walk; **Fußball** m football (BRIT), soccer; **Fußballmannschaft** f football (BRIT) (◊ soccer) team; **Fußballplatz** m football pitch (BRIT), soccer field (US); **Fußballspiel** nt football (BRIT) (◊ soccer) match; **Fußballspieler(in)** m(f) footballer (BRIT), soccer player; **Fußboden** m floor; **Fußgänger(in)** (-s, -) m(f) pedestrian; **Fußgängerüberweg** m pedestrian crossing (BRIT), crosswalk (US); **Fußgängerzone** f pedestrian precinct (BRIT) (◊ zone (US)); **Fußgelenk** nt ankle; **Fußpilz** m athlete's foot; **Fußtritt** m kick; **jdm einen ~ geben** to give sb a kick, to kick sb; **Fußweg** m footpath

Futon (-s, -s) m futon

futsch adj (fam: kaputt) broken; (zerschlagen) smashed; (weg, verloren) gone

Futter (-s, -) nt feed; (Heu etc) fodder; (Stoff) lining; **füttern** vt to feed; (Kleidung) to line

Futur (-s, -e) nt (Ling) future (tense)

Fuzzi (-s, -s) m (fam) guy

gab imperf von **geben**

Gabe (-, -n) f gift

Gabel (-, -n) f fork; **Gabelung** f fork

gaffen vi to gape

Gage (-, -n) f fee

gähnen vi to yawn

Galerie f gallery

Galle (-, -n) f gall; (Organ) gall bladder; **Gallenstein** m gallstone

Galopp (-s) m gallop; **galoppieren** vi to gallop

galt imperf von **gelten**

Gameboy® (-s, -s) m Gameboy®

gammeln vi to loaf (◊ hang) around; **Gammler(in)** (-s, -) m(f) layabout

gang adj **~ und gäbe sein** to be quite normal

Gang (-(e)s, Gänge) m walk; (im Flugzeug) aisle; (Essen, Ablauf) course; (Flur etc) corridor; (Durchgang) passage; (Auto) gear; **den zweiten ~ einlegen** to change into second (gear); **etw in ~ bringen** to get sth going; **Gangschaltung** f gears pl; **Gangway** (-, -s) f (Aviat) steps pl; (Naut) gangway

Gans (-, Gänse) f goose; **Gänseblümchen** nt daisy; **Gänsehaut** f goose pimples pl (BRIT), goose bumps pl (US)

ganz adj whole; (vollständig) complete; ~ **Europa** all of Europe; **sein ~es Geld** all his money; **den ~en Tag** all day; **die ~e Zeit** all the time ▷ adv quite; (völlig) completely; **es hat mir ~ gut gefallen** I quite liked it; ~ **schön viel** quite a lot; ~ **und gar nicht** not at all; **das ist etwas ~ anderes** that's a completely different matter; **ganztägig** adj all-day; (Arbeit, Stelle) full-time

gar adj done, cooked ▷ adv at all; ~ **nicht / nichts / keiner** not / nothing / nobody at all; ~ **nicht schlecht** not bad at all

Garage (-, -n) f garage

Garantie (-) f guarantee; **garantieren** vt to guarantee

Garderobe (-, -n) f (Kleidung) wardrobe; (Abgabe) cloakroom

Gardine f curtain

Garn (-(e)s, -e) nt thread

Garnele (-, -n) f shrimp

garnieren vt to decorate; (Speisen) to garnish

Garten (-s, Gärten) m garden; **Gärtner(in)** (-s, -) m(f) gardener; **Gärtnerei** f nursery; (Gemüsegärtnerei) market garden (BRIT), truck farm (US)

Garzeit f cooking time

Gas (-es, -e) nt gas; ~ **geben** (Auto) to accelerate; (fig) to get a move on; **Gasanzünder** m gas lighter; **Gasbrenner** m gas burner; **Gasflasche** f gas bottle; **Gasheizung** f gas heating; **Gasherd** m gas stove, gas cooker (BRIT); **Gaskocher** m camping stove; **Gaspedal** nt accelerator, gas pedal (US)

Gasse (-, -n) f alley

Gast (-es, Gäste) m guest; **Gäste haben** to have guests; **Gastarbeiter(in)** m(f) foreign worker; **Gästebett** nt spare bed; **Gästebuch** nt visitors' book; **Gästehaus** nt guest house; **Gästezimmer** nt guest room; **gastfreundlich** adj hospitable; **Gastgeber(in)** (-s, -) m(f) host / hostess; **Gasthaus** nt, **Gasthof** m inn; **Gastland** nt host country

Gastritis (-) f gastritis

Gastronomie f (Gewerbe) catering trade

Gastspiel nt (Sport) away game, **Gaststätte** f restaurant; (Trinklokal) pub (BRIT), bar; **Gastwirt(in)** m(f) landlord / -lady

GAU (-s, -s) m akr = **größter anzunehmender Unfall** MCA

Gaumen (-s, -) m palate

Gaze (-, -n) f gauze

geb. adj abk = **geboren** b. b.; ▷ adj abk = **geborene** née; siehe **geboren**

Gebäck (-(e)s, -e) nt pastries pl; (Kekse) biscuits pl (BRIT), cookies pl (US)

gebacken pp von **backen**

Gebärdensprache f sign language

Gebärmutter f womb

Gebäude (-s, -) nt building

geben (gab, gegeben) vt, vi to give (jdm etw sb sth, sth to sb); (Karten) to deal; **lass dir eine Quittung ~** ask for a receipt ▷ vt impers **es gibt** there is / are; (in Zukunft) there will be; **das gibt's nicht** I don't believe it ▷ vr **sich ~** (sich verhalten) to behave, to act; **das gibt sich wieder** it'll sort itself out

Gebet (-(e)s, -e) nt prayer

gebeten pp von **bitten**

Gebiet (-(e)s, -e) nt area, (Hoheitsgebiet) territory; (fig) field

gebildet adj educated; (belesen) well-read

Gebirge (-s, -) nt mountains pl; **gebirgig** adj mountainous

Gebiss (-es, -e) nt teeth pl; (künstlich) dentures pl; **gebissen** pp von **beißen**; **Gebissreiniger** m denture tablets pl

Gebläse (-s, -) nt fan, blower

geblasen pp von **blasen**

geblieben pp von **bleiben**

gebogen pp von **biegen**

geboren pp von **gebären** ▷ adj born; **Andrea Jordan, ~e Christian** Andrea Jordan, née Christian

geborgen pp von **bergen** ▷ adj secure, safe

geboten pp von **bieten**

gebracht pp von **bringen**

gebrannt pp von **brennen**

gebraten pp von **braten**

gebrauchen vt to use; **Gebrauchsanweisung** f directions pl for use; **gebrauchsfertig** adj ready to use; **gebraucht** adj used; **etw ~ kaufen** to buy sth secondhand; **Gebrauchtwagen** m secondhand (o used) car

gebräunt adj tanned

gebrochen pp von **brechen**

Gebühr (-, -en) f charge; (Maut) toll; (Honorar) fee; **Gebühreneinheit** f (Tel) unit; **gebührenfrei** adj free of charge; (Telefonnummer) freefone® (BRIT), toll-free (US); **gebührenpflichtig** adj subject to charges; **~e Straße** toll road

gebunden pp von **binden**

Geburt (-, -en) f birth; **gebürtig** adj **er ist ~er Schweizer** he is Swiss by birth; **Geburtsdatum** nt date of birth; **Geburtsjahr** nt year of birth; **Geburtsname** m birth name; (einer Frau) maiden name; **Geburtsort** m birthplace; **Geburtstag** m birthday; **herzlichen Glückwunsch zum**

~! Happy Birthday; **Geburtsurkunde** f birth certificate

Gebüsch (-(e)s, -e) nt bushes pl

gedacht pp von **denken**

Gedächtnis nt memory; **im ~ behalten** to remember

Gedanke (-ns, -n) m thought; **sich** (dat) **über etw** (akk) **~n machen** to think about sth; (besorgt) to be worried about sth; **Gedankenstrich** m dash

Gedeck (-(e)s, -e) nt place setting; (Speisenfolge) set meal

Gedenkstätte f memorial; **Gedenktafel** f commemorative plaque

Gedicht (-(e)s, -e) nt poem

Gedränge (-s) nt crush, crowd

gedrungen pp von **dringen**

Geduld (-) f patience; **geduldig** adj patient

gedurft pp von **dürfen**

geehrt adj **Sehr ~er Herr Young** Dear Mr Young

geeignet adj suitable

Gefahr (-, -en) f danger; **auf eigene ~** at one's own risk; **außer ~** out of danger; **gefährden** vt to endanger

gefahren pp von **fahren**

gefährlich adj dangerous

Gefälle (-s, -) nt gradient, slope

gefallen pp von **fallen** ▷ irr vi **jdm ~** to please sb; **er/es gefällt mir** I like him/it; **sich** (dat) **etw ~ lassen** to put up with sth

Gefallen (-s, -) m favour; **jdm einen ~ tun** to do sb a favour

gefälligst adv ..., will you!; **sei ~ still!** be quiet, will you!

gefangen pp von **fangen**

Gefängnis nt prison

Gefäß (-es, -e) nt (Behälter) container, receptacle; (Anat, Bot) vessel

gefasst adj composed, calm; **auf etw** (akk) **~ sein** to be prepared (o ready) for sth

geflochten pp von **flechten**

geflogen pp von **fliegen**

geflossen pp von **fließen**

Geflügel (-s) nt poultry

gefragt adj in demand

gefressen pp von **fressen**

Gefrierbeutel m freezer bag; **gefrieren** irr vi to freeze; **Gefrierfach** nt freezer compartment; **Gefrierschrank** m (upright) freezer; **Gefriertruhe** f (chest) freezer

gefroren pp von **frieren**

Gefühl (-(e)s, -e) nt feeling

gefunden pp von **finden**

gegangen pp von **gehen**

gegeben pp von **geben**, **gegebenenfalls** adv if need be

gegen prep +akk against; (im Austausch für) (in return) for; **~ 8 Uhr** about 8 o'clock; **Deutschland ~ England** Germany versus England; **etwas ~ Husten** (Mittel) something for coughs

Gegend (-, -en) f area, **hier in der ~** around here

gegeneinander adv against one another

Gegenfahrbahn f opposite lane; **Gegenmittel** nt remedy (gegen for); **Gegenrichtung** f opposite direction; **Gegensatz** m contrast; **im ~ zu** in contrast to; **gegensätzlich** adj conflicting; **gegenseitig** adj mutual; **sich ~ helfen** to help each other

Gegenstand m object; (Thema) subject

Gegenteil nt opposite; **im ~** on the contrary; **gegenteilig** adj opposite, contrary

gegenüber prep +dat opposite; (zu jdm) to(wards); (angesichts) in the face of ▷ adv opposite, **gegenüberstehen** vt to face; (Problemen) to be faced with; **gegenüberstellen** vt to confront (dat with); (fig)

compare (dat with)

Gegenverkehr m oncoming traffic; **Gegenwart** (-) f present (tense)

Gegenwind m headwind

gegessen pp von **essen**

geglichen pp von **gleichen**

geglitten pp von **gleiten**

Gegner(in) (-s, -) m(f) opponent

gegolten pp von **gelten**

gegossen irr von **gießen**

gegraben pp von **graben**

gegriffen pp von **greifen**

gehabt pp von **haben**

Gehackte(s) nt mince(d meat) (BRIT), ground meat (US)

Gehalt (-(e)s, -e) m content ▷ (-(e)s, Gehälter) nt salary

gehalten pp von **halten**

gehangen pp von **hängen**

gehässig adj spiteful, nasty

gehauen pp von **hauen**

gehbehindert adj **sie ist ~** she can't walk properly

geheim adj secret; **etw ~ halten** to keep sth secret; **Geheimnis** nt secret; (rätselhaft) mystery; **geheimnisvoll** adj mysterious; **Geheimnummer** f, **Geheimzahl** f (von Kreditkarte) PIN number

geheißen pp von **heißen**

gehen (ging, gegangen) vt, vi to go; (zu Fuß) to walk; (funktionieren) to work; **über die Straße ~** to cross the street; **~ nach** (Fenster) to face ▷ vi impers **wie geht es** (dir)? how are you (o things)?; **mir/ihm geht es gut** I'm / he's (doing) fine; **geht das?** is that possible?; **geht's noch?** can you still manage?; **es geht** not too bad, OK; **das geht nicht** that's not on; **es geht um ...** it's about ...

Gehirn (-(e)s, -e) nt brain; **Gehirnerschütterung** f concussion

gehoben pp von **heben**

geholfen pp von **helfen**

Gehör (-(e)s) nt hearing

gehorchen vi to obey (jdm sb)

gehören vi to belong (jdm to sb); **wem gehört das Buch?** whose book is this?; **gehört es dir?** is it yours? ▷ vr impers **das gehört sich nicht** it's not done

gehörlos adj deaf

gehorsam adj obedient

Gehsteig m

Gehweg (-s, -e) m pavement (BRIT), sidewalk (US)

Geier (-s, -) m vulture

Geige (-, -n) f violin

geil adj randy (BRIT), horny (US); (fam: toll) fantastic

Geisel (-, -n) f hostage

Geist (-(e)s, -er) m spirit; (Gespenst) ghost; (Verstand) mind; **Geisterbahn** f ghost train, tunnel of horror (US); **Geisterfahrer(in)** m(f) person driving the wrong way on the motorway

geizig adj stingy

gekannt pp von **kennen**

geklungen pp von **klingen**

geknickt adj (fig) dejected

gekniffen pp von **kneifen**

gekommen pp von **kommen**

gekonnt pp von **können** ▷ adj skilful

gekrochen pp von **kriechen**

Gel (-s, -s) nt gel

Gelächter (-s, -) nt laughter

geladen pp von **laden** ▷ adj loaded; (Elek) live; (fig) furious

gelähmt adj paralysed

Gelände (-s, -) nt land, terrain; (Fabrik, Sportgelände) grounds pl; (Baugelände) site

Geländer (-s, -) nt railing; (Treppengeländer) banister

Geländewagen m off-road vehicle

gelang imperf von **gelingen**

gelassen pp von **lassen** ▷ adj calm, composed

Gelatine f gelatine

gelaufen pp von **laufen**

gelaunt adj: **gut/schlecht ~** in a good/bad mood

gelb adj yellow; (Ampel) amber, yellow (US); **gelblich** adj yellowish; **Gelbsucht** f jaundice

Geld (-(e)s, -er) nt money; **Geldautomat** m cash machine (o dispenser (BRIT)), ATM (US); **Geldbeutel** m, **Geldbörse** f purse; **Geldbuße** f fine; **Geldschein** m (bank)note (BRIT), bill (US); **Geldstrafe** f fine; **Geldstück** nt coin; **Geldwechsel** m exchange of money; (Ort) bureau de change; **Geldwechselautomat** m, **Geldwechsler** (-s, -) m change machine

Gelee (-s, -s) nt jelly

gelegen pp von **liegen** ▷ adj situated; (passend) convenient; **etw kommt jdm ~** sth is convenient for sb

Gelegenheit f opportunity; (Anlass) occasion

gelegentlich adj occasional ▷ adv occasionally; (bei Gelegenheit) some time (or other)

Gelenk (-(e)s, -e) nt joint

gelernt adj skilled

gelesen pp von **lesen**

geliehen pp von **leihen**

gelingen (gelang, gelungen) vi to succeed; **es ist mir gelungen, ihn zu erreichen** I managed to get hold of him

gelitten pp von **leiden**

gelockt adj curly

gelogen pp von **lügen**

gelten (galt, gegolten) vt (wert sein) to be worth; **jdm viel/wenig ~** to mean a lot/not to mean much to sb ▷ vi (gültig sein) to be valid; (erlaubt sein) to be allowed; **jdm ~** (gemünzt sein auf) to be meant for (o aimed at) sb; **etw ~ lassen** to accept sth; **als**

etw ~ to be considered to be sth;
Geltungsdauer f **eine ~ von fünf
Tagen haben** to be valid for five
days

gelungen pp von **gelingen**

gemahlen pp von **mahlen**

Gemälde (-s, -) nt painting, picture

gemäß prep +dat in accordance
with ▷ adj appropriate (dat to)

gemein adj (niederträchtig) mean,
nasty; (gewöhnlich) common

Gemeinde (-, -n) f district, community; (Pfarrgemeinde) parish; (Kir-
chengemeinde) congregation

gemeinsam adj joint, common ▷
adv together, jointly; **das Haus
gehört uns beiden ~** the house
belongs to both of us

Gemeinschaft f community; **~
Unabhängiger Staaten** Commonwealth of Independent States

gemeint pp von **meinen**; **das war
nicht so** - I didn't mean it like that

gemessen pp von **messen**

gemieden pp von **meiden**

gemischt adj mixed

gemocht pp von **mögen**

Gemüse (-s, -) nt vegetables pl;
Gemüsehändler(in) m(f) greengrocer

gemusst pp von **müssen**

gemustert adj patterned

gemütlich adj comfortable, cosy;
(Mensch) good-natured, easy-going;
mach es dir - make yourself at home

genannt pp von **nennen**

genau adj exact, precise ▷ adv
exactly, precisely; **~ in der Mitte**
right in the middle; **es mit etw ~
nehmen** to be particular about sth;
~ genommen strictly speaking; **ich
weiß es** - I know for certain (o for
sure); **genauso** adv exactly the
same (way); **~ gut/viel/viele
Leute** just as well/much/many
people (wie as)

genehmigen vt to approve; **sich**
(dat) **etw ~** to indulge in sth; **Genehmigung** f approval

Generalkonsulat nt consulate
general

Generation f generation

Genf (-s) nt Geneva; **~er See** Lake
Geneva

genial adj brilliant

Genick (-(e)s, -e) nt (back of the) neck

Genie (-s, -s) nt genius

genieren vr **sich ~** to feel awkward; **ich geniere mich vor ihm** he
makes me feel embarrassed

genießen (genoss, genossen) vt to
enjoy

Genitiv m genitive (case)

genommen pp von **nehmen**

genoss imperf von **genießen**

genossen pp von **genießen**

genug adv enough

genügen vi to be enough (jdm for
sb); **danke, das genügt** thanks,
that's enough (o that will do)

Genuss (-es, Genüsse) m pleasure;
(Zusichnehmen) consumption

geöffnet adj (Geschäft etc) open

Geografie f geography

Geologie f geology

Georgien (-s) nt Georgia

Gepäck (-(e)s) nt luggage (BRIT),
baggage; **Gepäckabfertigung** f
luggage (BRIT) (o baggage) check-in;
Gepäckablage f luggage (BRIT) (o
baggage) rack; **Gepäckannahme** f
(zur Beförderung) luggage (BRIT) (o
baggage) office; (zur Aufbewahrung)
left-luggage office (BRIT), baggage
checkroom (US); **Gepäckaufbewahrung** f left-luggage office
(BRIT), baggage checkroom (US);
Gepäckausgabe f luggage (BRIT) (o
baggage) office; (am Flughafen) baggage reclaim; **Gepäckband** nt
luggage (BRIT) (o baggage) conveyor;
Gepäckkontrolle f luggage (BRIT)

(o baggage) check; **Gepäckstück**
nt item of luggage (BRIT) (o baggage
(US)); **Gepäckträger** m porter; (an
Fahrrad) carrier; **Gepäckversiche-
rung** f luggage (BRIT) (o baggage)
insurance; **Gepäckwagen** m luggage van (BRIT), baggage car (US)

gepfiffen pp von **pfeifen**
gepflegt adj well-groomed; (Park)
well looked after
gequollen pp von **quellen**
gerade adj straight; (Zahl) even ▷
adv (genau) exactly; (eben) just;
warum ~ ich? why me (of all people)?; ~ **weil** precisely because; ~
noch only just; ~ **neben** right next
to; **geradeaus** adv straight ahead
gerannt pp von **rennen**
geraspelt adj grated
Gerät (-(e)s, -e) nt device, gadget;
(Werkzeug) tool; (Radio, Fernseher)
set; (Zubehör) equipment
geraten pp von **raten** ▷ irrvi to turn
out; **gut / schlecht ~** to turn out
well / badly; **an jdn ~** to come across
sb; **in etw** (akk) ~ to get into sth
geräuchert adj smoked
geräumig adj roomy
Geräusch (-(e)s, -e) nt sound; (unangenehm) noise
gerecht adj fair; (Strafe, Belohnung)
just; **jdm / einer Sache ~ werden**
to do justice to sb / sth
gereizt adj irritable
Gericht (-(e)s, -e) nt (Jur) court;
(Essen) dish
gerieben pp von **reiben**
gering adj small; (unbedeutend)
slight; (niedrig) low; (Zeit) short;
geringfügig adj slight, minor ▷
adv slightly
gerissen pp von **reißen**
geritten pp von **reiten**
gern(e) adv willingly, gladly; ~
haben, ~ **mögen** to like; **etw ~ tun**
to like doing sth; ~ **geschehen**

you're welcome

gerochen pp von **riechen**
Gerste (-, -n) f barley; **Gerstenkorn** nt (im Auge) stye
Geruch (-(e)s, **Gerüche**) m smell
Gerücht (-(e)s, -e) nt rumour
gerufen pp von **rufen**
Gerümpel (-s) nt junk
gerungen pp von **ringen**
Gerüst (-(e)s, -e) nt (auf Bau) scaffolding; (Gestell) trestle; (fig) framework (zu of)
gesalzen pp von **salzen**
gesamt adj whole, entire; (Kosten)
total; (Werke) complete; **Gesamt-
schule** f ≈ comprehensive school
gesandt pp von **senden**
Gesäß (-es, -e) nt bottom
geschaffen pp von **schaffen**
Geschäft (-(e)s, -e) nt business;
(Laden) shop; (Geschäftsabschluss)
deal; **geschäftlich** adj commercial
▷ adv on business; **Geschäftsfrau**
f businesswoman; **Geschäftsfüh-
rer(in)** m(f) managing director;
(von Laden) manager; **Geschäftsmann** m businessman; **Ge-
schäftsreise** f business trip; **Ge-
schäftsstraße** f shopping street;
Geschäftszeiten pl business (o
opening) hours pl
geschehen (geschah, geschehen) vi
to happen
Geschenk (-(e)s, -e) nt present, gift;
Geschenkgutschein m gift
voucher; **Geschenkpapier** nt gift-
-wrapping paper, giftwrap
Geschichte (-, -n) f story; (Sache)
affair; (Hist) history
geschickt adj skilful
geschieden pp von **scheiden** ▷
adj divorced
geschienen pp von **scheinen**
Geschirr (-(e)s, -e) nt crockery; (zum
Kochen) pots and pans pl; (von Pferd)
harness; ~ **spülen** to do (o wash) the

dishes, to do the washing-up (BRIT),
Geschirrspülmaschine f dishwasher; **Geschirrspülmittel** nt
washing-up liquid (BRIT), dishwashing liquid (US); **Geschirrtuch** nt tea
towel (BRIT), dish towel (US)
geschissen pp von **scheißen**
geschlafen pp von **schlafen**
geschlagen pp von **schlagen**
Geschlecht ((e)s, er) nt sex; (Ling)
gender; **Geschlechtskrankheit** f
sexually transmitted disease, STD;
Geschlechtsorgan nt sexual organ; **Geschlechtsverkehr** m sexual intercourse
geschlichen pp von **schleichen**
geschliffen pp von **schleifen**
geschlossen adj closed
Geschmack (-(e)s, Geschmäcke) m
taste; **geschmacklos** adj tasteless;
Geschmack(s)sache f das ist ~
that's a matter of taste; **geschmackvoll** adj tasteful
geschmissen pp von **schmeißen**
geschmolzen pp von **schmelzen**
geschnitten pp von **schneiden**
geschoben pp von **schieben**
Geschoss (-es, -e) nt (Stockwerk)
floor
geschossen pp von **schießen**
Geschrei (s) nt cries pl; (fig) fuss
geschrieben pp von **schreiben**
geschrie(e)n pp von **schreien**
geschützt adj protected
Geschwätz (-es) nt chatter;
(Klatsch) gossip; **geschwätzig** adj
talkative, gossipy
geschweige adv ~ (denn) let alone
geschwiegen pp von **schweigen**
Geschwindigkeit f speed; (Phys)
velocity; **Geschwindigkeitsbegrenzung** f speed limit
Geschwister pl brothers and sisters pl
geschwollen adj (angeschwollen)
swollen; (Rede) pompous

geschwommen pp von **schwimmen**
geschworen pp von **schwören**
Geschwulst (-, Geschwülste) f
growth
Geschwür (-(e)s, -e) nt ulcer
gesehen pp von **sehen**
gesellig adj sociable; **Gesellschaft** f society; (Begleitung) company; (Abend) party); ~ **mit ba**
schränkter Haftung limited company (BRIT), limited corporation (US)
gesessen pp von **sitzen**
Gesetz (-es, -e) nt law; **gesetzlich**
adj legal; **~er Feiertag** public (o
bank (BRIT) o legal (US)) holiday;
gesetzwidrig adj illegal
Gesicht (-(e)s, -er) nt face; (Miene)
expression; **mach doch nicht so ein
~!** stop pulling such a face; **Gesichtscreme** f face cream; **Gesichtswasser** nt toner
gesoffen pp von **saufen**
gesogen pp von **saugen**
gespannt adj tense; (begierig) eager; **ich bin ~, ob ...** I wonder if ...;
auf etw/jdn ~ sein to look forward
to sth/to seeing sb
Gespenst (-(e)s, -er) nt ghost
gesperrt adj closed
gesponnen pp von **spinnen**
Gespräch ((e)s, -e) nt talk, conversation; (Diskussion) discussion;
(Anruf) call
gesprochen pp von **sprechen**
gesprungen pp von **springen**
Gestalt (-, -en) f form, shape;
(Mensch) figure
gestanden pp von **stehen**, **gestehen**
Gestank (-(e)s) m stench
gestatten vt to permit, to allow;
~ **Sie?** may I?
Geste (-, -n) f gesture
gestehen irr vt to confess
gestern adv yesterday; ~ **Abend /**

Morgen yesterday evening / morning

gestiegen pp von **steigen**

gestochen pp von **stechen**

gestohlen pp von **stehlen**

gestorben pp von **sterben**

gestört adj disturbed; (Empfang) poor

gestoßen pp von **stoßen**

gestreift adj striped

gestrichen pp von **streichen**

gestritten pp von **streiten**

gestunken pp von **stinken**

gesund adj healthy; **wieder ~ werden** to get better; **Gesundheit** f health; **~!** I bless you!; **gesundheitsschädlich** adj unhealthy

gesungen pp von **singen**

gesunken pp von **sinken**

getan pp von **tun**

getragen pp von **tragen**

Getränk (-(e)s, -e) nt drink; **Getränkeautomat** m drinks machine; **Getränkekarte** f list of drinks

Getreide (-s, -) nt cereals pl, grain

getrennt adj separate; **~ leben** to live apart; **~ zahlen** to pay separately

getreten pp von **treten**

Getriebe (-s, -) nt (Auto) gearbox

getrieben pp von **treiben**

Getriebeschaden m gearbox damage

getroffen pp von **treffen**

getrunken pp von **trinken**

Getue nt fuss

geübt adj experienced

gewachsen pp von **wachsen** ▷ adj **jdm / einer Sache ~ sein** to be a match for sb / up to sth

Gewähr (-) f guarantee; **keine ~ übernehmen für** to accept no responsibility for

Gewalt (-, -en) f (Macht) power; (Kontrolle) control; (große Kraft) force; (~taten) violence; **mit aller ~** with all one's might; **gewaltig** adj

tremendous; (Irrtum) huge

gewandt pp von **wenden** ▷ adj (flink) nimble; (geschickt) skilful

gewann imperf von **gewinnen**

gewaschen pp von **waschen**

Gewebe (-s, -) nt (Stoff) fabric; (Bio) tissue

Gewehr (-(e)s, -e) nt rifle, gun

Geweih (-(e)s, -e) nt antlers pl

gewellt adj (Haare) wavy

gewendet pp von **wenden**

Gewerbe (-s, -) nt trade; **Gewerbegebiet** nt industrial estate (BRIT) (o park (US)); **gewerblich** adj commercial

Gewerkschaft f trade union

gewesen pp von **sein**

Gewicht (-(e)s, -e) nt weight; (fig) importance

gewiesen pp von **weisen**

Gewinn (-(e)s, -e) m profit; (bei Spiel) winnings pl; **gewinnen** (gewann, gewonnen) vt to win; (erwerben) to gain; (Kohle, Öl) to extract ▷ vi to win; (profitieren) to gain; **Gewinner(in)** (-s, -) m(f) winner

gewiss adj certain ▷ adv certainly

Gewissen (-s, -) nt conscience; **ein gutes / schlechtes ~ haben** to have a clear / bad conscience

Gewitter (-s, -) nt thunderstorm; **gewittern** vi impers **es gewittert** it's thundering

gewogen pp von **wiegen**

gewöhnen vt **jdn an etw** (akk) **~** to accustom sb to sth ▷ vr **sich an jdn / etw ~** to get used (o accustomed) to sb / sth; **Gewohnheit** f habit; (Brauch) custom; **gewöhnlich** adj usual; (durchschnittlich) ordinary; (pej) common; **wie ~** as usual; **gewohnt** adj usual; **etw ~ sein** to be used to sth

Gewölbe (-s, -) nt (Deckengewölbe) vault

gewonnen pp von **gewinnen**

geworben pp von **werben**

geworden pp von **werden**

geworfen pp von **werfen**

Gewürz (-es, -e) nt spice; **Gewürznelke** f clove; **gewürzt** adj seasoned

gewusst pp von **wissen**

Gezeiten pl tides pl

gezogen pp von **ziehen**

gezwungen nn von **zwingen**

Gibraltar (-s) nt Gibraltar

Gicht (-) f gout

Giebel (-s, -) m gable

gierig adj greedy

gießen (goss, gegossen) vt to pour; (Blumen) to water; (Metall) to cast; **Gießkanne** f watering can

Gift (-(e)s, -e) nt poison; **giftig** adj poisonous

Gigabyte nt gigabyte

Gin (-s, -s) m gin

ging imperf von **gehen**; **Gin Tonic** (-(s), -s) m gin and tonic

Gipfel (-s, -) m summit, peak, (Pol) summit; (fig: Höhepunkt) height

Gips (-es, -e) m (a. Med) plaster; **Gipsbein** nt **sie hat ein ~** she's got her leg in plaster; **Gipsverband** m plaster cast

Giraffe (-, -n) f giraffe

Girokonto nt current account (BRIT), checking account (US)

Gitarre (-, -n) f guitar

Gitter (-s, -) nt bars pl

glänzen vi (a. fig) to shine; **glänzend** adj shining; (fig) brilliant

Glas (-es, Gläser) nt glass; (Marmelade) jar; **zwei ~ Wein** two glasses of wine; **Glascontainer** m bottle bank; **Glaser(in)** m(f) glazier; **Glasscheibe** f pane (of glass); **Glassplitter** m splinter of glass

Glasur f glaze; (Gastr) icing

glatt adj smooth; (rutschig) slippery; (Lüge) downright; **Glatteis** nt (black) ice

Glatze (-, -n) f bald head; (fam: Skinhead) skinhead

glauben vt, vi to believe (an +akk in); (meinen) to think; **jdm ~** to believe sb

gleich adj equal; (identisch) same, identical; **alle Menschen sind ~** all people are the same; **es ist mir ~** it's all the same to me ▷ adv equally; (sofort) straight away; (bald) in a minute; **~ groß/alt** the same size/age; **~ nach/an** right after/at; **Gleichberechtigung** f equal rights pl; **gleichen** (glich, geglichen) vi **jdm/einer Sache ~** to be like sb/sth ▷ vr **sich ~** to be alike; **gleichfalls** adv likewise; **danke ~!** thanks, and the same to you; **gleichgültig** indifferent; **gleichmäßig** adj regular; (Verteilung) even, equal; **gleichzeitig** adj simultaneous ▷ adv at the same time

Gleis (-es, -e) nt track, rails pl; (Bahnsteig) platform

gleiten (glitt, geglitten) vi to glide; (rutschen) to slide; **Gleitschirmfliegen** (-s) nt paragliding

Gletscher (-s, -) m glacier; **Gletscherskifahren** nt glacier skiing; **Gletscherspalte** f crevasse

glich imperf von **gleichen**

Glied ((e)s, er) nt (Arm, Dein) limb; (von Kette) link; (Penis) penis; **Gliedmaßen** pl limbs pl

glitschig adj slippery

glitt imperf von **gleiten**

glitzern vi to glitter; (Sterne) to twinkle

Glocke (-, -n) f bell; **Glockenspiel** nt chimes pl

Glotze (-, -n) f (fam: TV) box; **glotzen** vi (fam) to stare

Glück (-(e)s) nt luck; (Freude) happiness; **~ haben** to be lucky; **viel ~!** good luck; **zum ~** fortunately; **glücklich** adj lucky; (froh) happy;

glücklicherweise adj fortunately; **Glückwunsch** m congratulations pl; **herzlichen ~ zur bestandenen Prüfung** congratulations on passing your exam; **herzlichen ~ zum Geburtstag!** Happy Birthday

Glühbirne f light bulb; **glühen** vi to glow; **Glühwein** m mulled wine

GmbH (-, -s) f abk = **Gesellschaft mit beschränkter Haftung** ≈ Ltd (BRIT), ≈ Inc (US)

Gokart (-(s), -s) m go-kart

Gold (-(e)s) nt gold; **golden** adj gold; (fig) golden; **Goldfisch** m goldfish; **Goldmedaille** f gold medal; **Goldschmied(in)** m(f) goldsmith

Golf (-(e)s, -e) m gulf; **der ~ von Biskaya** the Bay of Biscay ▷ (-s) nt golf; **Golfplatz** m golf course; **Golfschläger** m golf club

Gondel (-, -n) f gondola; (Seilbahn) cable-car

gönnen vt **ich gönne es ihm** I'm really pleased for him; **sich** (dat) **etw ~** to allow oneself sth

goss imperf von **gießen**

gotisch adj Gothic

Gott (-es, Götter) m God; (Gottheit) god; **Gottesdienst** m service; **Göttin** f goddess

Grab (-(e)s, Gräber) nt grave

graben (grub, gegraben) vt to dig; **Graben** (-s, Gräben) m ditch

Grabstein m gravestone

Grad (-(e)s, -e) m degree; **wir haben 30 ~ Celsius** it's 30 degrees Celsius, it's 86 degrees Fahrenheit; **bis zu einem gewissen ~** up to a certain extent

Graf (-en, -en) m count; (in Großbritannien) earl

Graffiti pl graffiti sing

Grafik (-, -en) f graph; (Kunstwerk) graphic; (Illustration) diagram; **Grafikkarte** f (Inform) graphics card; **Grafikprogramm** nt (Inform)

graphics software

Gräfin (-, -nen) f countess

Gramm (-s) nt gram(me)

Grammatik f grammar

Grapefruit (-, -s) f grapefruit

Graphik f siehe **Grafik**

Gras (-es, Gräser) nt grass

grässlich adj horrible

Gräte (-, -n) f (fish)bone

gratis adj, adv free (of charge)

gratulieren vi **jdm (zu etw) ~** to congratulate sb (on sth); **(ich) gratuliere!** congratulations!

grau adj grey, gray (US); **grauhaarig** adj grey-haired

grausam adj cruel

gravierend adj (Fehler) serious

greifen (griff, gegriffen) vt to seize; **zu etw ~** (fig) to resort to sth ▷ vi (Regel etc) to have an effect (bei on)

grell adj harsh

Grenze (-, -n) f boundary; (Staat) border; (Schranke) limit; **grenzen** vi to border (an +akk on sth); **Grenzkontrolle** f border control; **Grenzübergang** m border crossing point; **Grenzverkehr** m border traffic

Grieche (-n, -n) m Greek; **Griechenland** nt Greece; **Griechin** f Greek; **griechisch** adj Greek; **Griechisch** nt Greek

griesgrämig adj grumpy

Grieß (-es, -e) m (Gastr) semolina

griff imperf von **greifen**

Griff (-(e)s, -e) m grip; (Tür etc) handle; **griffbereit** adj handy

Grill (-s, -s) m grill; (im Freien) barbecue

Grille (-, -n) f cricket

grillen vt to grill ▷ vi to have a barbecue; **Grillfest** nt, **Grillfete** f barbecue; **Grillkohle** f charcoal

grinsen vi to grin; (höhnisch) to sneer

Grippe (-, -n) f flu; **Grippeschutzimpfung** f flu vaccination

grob adj coarse; (Fehler, Verstoß) gross; (Einschätzung) rough

Grönland (-s) nt Greenland

groß adj big, large; (hoch) tall; (fig) great; (Buchstabe) capital; (erwachsen) grown-up; **im Großen und Ganzen** on the whole ▷ adv greatly; **großartig** adj wonderful

Großbritannien (-s) nt (Great) Britain

Großbuchstabe m capital letter

Größe (-, -n) f size; (Länge) height; (fig) greatness; **welche - haben Sie?** what size do you take?

Großeltern pl grandparents pl; **Großhandel** m wholesale trade; **Großmarkt** m hypermarket; **Großmutter** f grandmother; **Großraum** m **der ~ Manchester** Greater Manchester; **groß|schreiben** irr vt to write with a capital letter; **Großstadt** f city; **Großvater** m grandfather; **großzügig** adj generous; (Planung) on a large scale

Grotte (-, -n) f grotto

grub imperf von **graben**

Grübchen nt dimple

Grube (-, -n) f pit

grüezi interj (schweizerisch) hello

Gruft -, -en f vault

grün adj green; **~er Salat** lettuce; **~e Bohnen** French beans; **die Bananen sind noch zu ~** the bananas aren't ripe yet; **der ~ Punkt** symbol for recyclable packaging im **~en Bereich** hunky-dory

Grünanlage f park

Grund (-(e)s, Gründe) m (Ursache) reason; (Erdboden) ground; (See, Gefäß) bottom; (Grundbesitz) land, property; **aus gesundheitlichen Gründen** for health reasons; **im ~e** basically; **aus diesem ~** for this reason

gründen vt to found; **Gründer(in)** m(f) founder

Grundgebühr f basic charge; **Grundgesetz** nt (German) Constitution

gründlich adj thorough

Gründonnerstag m Maundy Thursday

grundsätzlich adj fundamental, basic, **sie kommt ~ zu spät** she's always late; **Grundschule** f primary school; **Grundstück** nt plot; (Anwesen) estate; (Baugrundstück) site; **Grundwasser** nt ground water

Grüne(r) mf (Pol) Green; **die ~n** the Green Party

Gruppe (-, -n) f group; **Gruppenermäßigung** f group discount; **Gruppenreise** f group tour

Gruß (-es, Grüße) m greeting; **viele Grüße** best wishes; **Grüße an** (+akk) regards to; **mit freundlichen Grüßen** Yours sincerely (BRIT), Sincerely yours (US); **sag ihm einen schönen ~ von mir** give him my regards; **grüßen** vt to greet; **grüß deine Mutter von mir** give your mother my regards; **Julia lässt (euch) ~** Julia sends (you) her regards

gucken vi to look

Gulasch (-(e)s, -e) nt goulash

gültig adj valid

Gummi (-s, -s) m o nt rubber; **Gum-**

miband nt rubber (◊ elastic (BRIT))
band; **Gummibärchen** pl gums pl
(in the shape of a bear) (BRIT), gum-
drops pl (in the shape of a bear) (US);
Gummihandschuhe pl rubber
gloves pl; **Gummistiefel** m wel-
lington (boot) (BRIT), rubber boot (US)

günstig adj favourable; (Preis) good

gurgeln vi to gurgle; (im Mund) to
gargle

Gurke (-, -n) f cucumber; **saure ~**
gherkin

Gurt (-(e)s, -e) m belt

Gürtel (-s, -) m belt; (Geo) zone;
Gürtelrose f shingles sing

GUS (-) f akr = **Gemeinschaft Unabhängiger Staaten** CIS

gut adj good; (Schulnote) ≈ B; **sehr ~**
very good, excellent; (Schulnote) ≈ A;
alles Gute! all the best ▷ adv well;
~ gehen (gut ausgehen) to go well; **es
geht ihm ~** he's doing fine; **jdm ~
tun** to do sb good; **~ aussehend**
good-looking; **~ gelaunt** in a good
mood; **~ gemeint** well meant;
schon ~! it's all right; **das kann ~
sein** that's quite possible; **machs ~!**
take care, bye

Gutachten (-s, -) nt report; **Gut-
achter(in)** (-s, -) m(f) expert

gutartig adj (Med) benign

Güter pl goods pl; **Güterbahnhof**
m goods station; **Güterzug** m
goods train

gutgläubig adj trusting; **Guthaben** (-s) nt (credit) balance

gutmütig adj good-natured

Gutschein m voucher; **Gut-
schrift** f credit

Gymnasium nt ≈ grammar
school (BRIT), ≈ high school (US)

Gymnastik f exercises pl, keep-fit

Gynäkologe m, **Gynäkologin** f
gynaecologist

Gyros (-, -) nt doner kebab

Haar (-(e)s, -e) nt hair; **um ein ~**
nearly; **sich** (dat) **die ~e schneiden
lassen** to have one's hair cut;
Haarbürste f hairbrush; **Haarfes-
tiger** m setting lotion; **Haargel**
nt hair gel; **haarig** adj hairy; (fig)
nasty; **Haarschnitt** m haircut;
Haarspange f hair slide (BRIT),
barrette (US); **Haarspliss** m split
ends pl; **Haarspray** nt hair spray;
Haartrockner (-s, -) m hairdryer;
Haarwaschmittel nt shampoo;
Haarwasser nt hair tonic

haben (hatte, gehabt) vt, vaux to
have; **Hunger/Angst ~** to be hun-
gry/afraid; **Ferien ~** to be on holiday (BRIT) (◊ vacation (US)); **welches
Datum ~ wir heute?** what's the
date today?; **ich hätte gerne ...** I'd
like ...; **hätten Sie etwas dagegen,
wenn ...?** would you mind if ...?;
was hast du denn? what's the
matter (with you)?

Haben nt (Comm) credit

Habicht (-(e)s, -e) m hawk

Hacke (-, -n) f (im Garten) hoe; (Ferse) heel; **hacken** vt to chop; (Loch) to hack; (Erde) to hoe; **Hacker(in)** (-s, -) m(f) (Inform) hacker; **Hackfleisch** nt mince(d meat) (BRIT), ground meat (US)

Hafen (-s, Häfen) m harbour, (große) port; **Hafenstadt** f port

Hafer (-s, -) m oats pl; **Haferflocken** pl rolled oats pl

Haft (-) f custody; **haftbar** adj liable, responsible; **haften** vi to stick; ~ **für** to be liable (o responsible) for; **Haftnotiz** f Post-it®; **Haftpflichtversicherung** f third party insurance; **Haftung** f liability

Hagebutte (-, -n) f rose hip

Hagel (-s) m hail; **hageln** vi impers to hail

Hahn (-(e)s, Hähne) m cock; (Wasserhahn) tap (BRIT), faucet (US); **Hähnchen** nt cockerel; (Gastr) chicken

Hai(fisch) (-(e)s, -e) m shark

häkeln vi, vt to crochet; **Häkelnadel** f crochet hook

Haken (-s, -) m hook; (Zeichen) tick

halb adj half; ~ **eins** half past twelve; (fam) half twelve, **eine ~e Stunde** half an hour; ~ **offen** half-open; **Halbfinale** nt semifinal; **halbieren** vt to halve; **Halbinsel** f peninsula; **Halbjahr** nt half-year; **halbjährlich** adj half-yearly; **Halbmond** m (Astr) half moon; (Symbol) crescent; **Halbpension** f half board; **halbseitig** adj ~ **gelähmt** paralyzed on one side; **halbtags** adv (arbeiten) part-time; **halbwegs** adv (leidlich) reasonably; **Halbzeit** f half; (Pause) half-time

half imperf von **helfen**; **Hälfte** (-, -n) f half

Halle (-, -n) f hall; **Hallenbad** nt indoor (swimming) pool

hallo interj hello, hi

Halogenlampe f halogen lamp; **Halogenscheinwerfer** m halogen headlight

Hals (-es, Hälse) m neck; (Kehle) throat; **Halsband** nt (für Tiere) collar; **Halsentzündung** f sore throat; **Halskette** f necklace; **Hals-Nasen-Ohren-Arzt** m, **Hals-Nasen-Ohren-Ärztin** f ear, nose and throat specialist; **Halsschmerzen** pl sore throat sing; **Halstuch** nt scarf

halt interj stop ▷ adv **das ist ~ so** that's just the way it is; **Halt** (-(e)s, -e) m stop; (fester) hold; (innerer) stability

haltbar adj durable; (Lebensmittel) non-perishable; **Haltbarkeitsdatum** nt best-before date

halten (hielt, gehalten) vt to keep; (festhalten) to hold; ~ **für** to regard as; ~ **von** to think of; **den Elfmeter** ~ to save the penalty; **eine Rede** ~ to give (o make) a speech ▷ vi to hold; (frisch bleiben) to keep; (stoppen) to stop; **zu jdm** ~ to stand by sb ▷ vr **sich** ~ (frisch bleiben) to keep; (sich behaupten) to hold out

Haltestelle f stop; **Halteverbot** nt **hier ist** ~ you can't stop here

Haltung f (Körper) posture; (fig) attitude; (Selbstbeherrschung) composure; ~ **bewahren** to keep one's composure

Hamburg (-s) nt Hamburg; **Hamburger** (-s, -) m (Gastr) hamburger

Hammelfleisch nt mutton

Hammer (-s, Hämmer) m hammer; (fig, fam: Fehler) howler; **das ist der** ~ (unerhört) that's a bit much

Hämorr(ho)iden pl haemorrhoids pl, piles pl

Hamster (-s, -) m hamster

Hand (-, Hände) f hand; **jdm die ~ geben** to shake hands with sb; **jdn bei der ~ nehmen** to take sb by the hand; **eine ~ voll Reis/Leute** a handful of rice/people; **zu Händen von** attention; **Handarbeit** f (*Schulfach*) handicraft; **~ sein** to be handmade; **Handball** m handball; **Handbremse** f handbrake; **Handbuch** nt handbook, manual; **Handcreme** f hand cream; **Händedruck** m handshake

Handel (-s) m trade; (*Geschäft*) transaction; **handeln** vi to act; (*Comm*) to trade; **~ von** to be about ▷ vr impers **sich ~ um** to be about; **es handelt sich um …** it's about …; **Handelskammer** f chamber of commerce; **Handelsschule** f business school

Handfeger (-s, -) m brush; **Handfläche** f palm; **Handgelenk** nt wrist; **handgemacht** adj handmade; **Handgepäck** nt hand luggage (*BRIT*) (*o baggage*)

Händler(in) (-s, -) m(f) dealer

handlich adj handy

Handlung f act, action; (*von Roman, Film*) plot

Handschellen pl handcuffs pl; **Handschrift** f handwriting; **Handschuh** m glove; **Handschuhfach** nt glove compartment; **Handtasche** f handbag, purse (*US*); **Handtuch** nt towel; **Handwerk** nt trade; (*Kunst~*) craft; **Handwerker** (-s, -) m workman

Handy (-s, -s) nt mobile (phone), cell phone (*US*)

Hanf (-(e)s) m hemp

Hang (-(e)s, *Hänge*) m (*Abhang*) slope; (*fig*) tendency

Hängebrücke f suspension bridge; **Hängematte** f hammock

hängen (*hing, gehangen*) vi to hang; **an der Wand/an der Decke ~** to hang on the wall/from the ceiling; **an jdm ~** (*fig*) to be attached to sb; **~ bleiben** to get caught (*an +dat on*);

(*fig*) to get stuck ▷ vt to hang (*an +akk on*)

Hantel (-, -n) f dumbbell

Hardware (-, -s) f (*Inform*) hardware

Harfe (-, -n) f harp

harmlos adj harmless

harmonisch adj harmonious

Harn (-(e)s, -e) m urine; **Harnblase** f bladder

Harpune (-, -n) f harpoon

hart adj hard; (*fig*) harsh; **zu jdm ~ sein** to be hard on sb; **~ gekocht** (*Ei*) hard-boiled; **hartnäckig** adj stubborn

Haschee (-s, -s) nt hash

Haschisch (-) nt hashish

Hase (-n, -n) m hare

Haselnuss f hazelnut

Hasenscharte f (*Med*) harelip

Hass (-es) m hatred (*auf, gegen +akk of*), hate; **einen ~ kriegen** (*fam*) to see red; **hassen** vt to hate

hässlich adj ugly; (*gemein*) nasty

Hast (-) f haste, hurry; **hastig** adj hasty

hatte imperf von **haben**

Haube (-, -n) f hood; (*Mütze*) cap; (*Auto*) bonnet (*BRIT*), hood (*US*)

Hauch (-(e)s, -e) m breath; (*Luft~*) breeze; (*fig*) trace; **hauchdünn** adj (*Schicht, Scheibe*) wafer-thin

hauen (*haute, gehauen*) vt to hit

Haufen (-s, -) m pile; **ein ~ Geld** (*viel Geld*) a lot of money

häufig adj frequent ▷ adv frequently, often

Haupt- in zW main; **Hauptbahnhof** m central (*o main*) station; **Hauptdarsteller(in)** m(f) leading actor/lady; **Haupteingang** m main entrance; **Hauptgericht** nt main course; **Hauptgeschäftszeiten** pl peak shopping hours pl; **Hauptgewinn** m first prize

Häuptling m chief

Hauptquartier nt headquarters

_pl_; **Hauptreisezeit** _f_ peak tourist season; **Hauptrolle** _f_ leading role; **Hauptsache** _f_ main thing; **hauptsächlich** _adv_ mainly, chiefly; **Hauptsaison** _f_ high (o peak) sea son; **Hauptsatz** _m_ main clause; **Hauptschule** _f_ ≈ secondary school (_BRIT_), ≈ junior high school (_US_); **Hauptspeicher** _m_ (_Inform_) main storage (o memory); **Hauptstadt** _f_ capital; **Hauptstraße** _f_ main road, (_im Stadtzentrum_) main street; **Hauptverkehrszeit** _f_ rush hour

Haus (-_es_, _Häuser_) _nt_ house; **nach ~e** home; **zu ~e** at home; **jdn nach ~e bringen** to take sb home; **bei uns zu ~e** (_Heimat_) where we come from; (_Familie_) in my family; (_Haus_) at our place; **Hausarbeit** _f_ housework; **Hausaufgabe** _f_ (_Schule_) homework; **~n** _pl_ homework sing; **Hausbesitzer(in)** (-_s_, -) _m(f)_ house owner; (_Vermieter_) landlord/-lady; **Hausbesuch** _m_ home visit; **Hausbewohner(in)** (-_s_, -) _m(f)_ occupant; **Hausflur** _m_ hall, **Hausfrau** _f_ housewife; **hausgemacht** _adj_ homemade; **Haushalt** _m_ household, (_Pol_) budget; **Haushalten** (_irr_) _m(f)_ host/hostess; (_Vermieter_) landlord/-lady

häuslich _adj_ domestic **Hausmann** _m_ house-husband; **Hausmannskost** _f_ good plain cooking; **Hausmeister(in)** _m(f)_ caretaker (_BRIT_), janitor (_US_); **Hausnummer** _f_ house number; **Hausordnung** _f_ (_house_) rules _pl_; **Hausschlüssel** _m_ front-door key; **Hausschuh** _m_ slipper; **Haustier** _nt_ pet; **Haustür** _f_ front door **Haut** (-, _Häute_) _f_ skin; (_Tier_) hide; **Hautarzt** _m_, **Hautärztin** _f_ dermatologist; **Hautausschlag** _m_ skin rash; **Hautcreme** _f_ skin cream; **Hautfarbe** _f_ skin colour;

Hautkrankheit _f_ skin disease **Hawaii** (-_s_) _nt_ Hawaii **Hbf.** _abk_ = **Hauptbahnhof** central station **Hebamme** (, _n_) _f_ midwife **Hebel** (-_s_, -) _m_ lever **heben** (_hob_, _gehoben_) _vt_ to raise, to lift **Hebräisch** ( ) _nt_ Hebrew **Hecht** (-_(e)s_, -_e_) _m_ pike **Heck** (-_(e)s_, -_e_) _nt_ (_von Boot_) stern, (_von Auto_) rear; **Heckantrieb** _m_ rear-wheel drive **Hecke** (-, -_n_) _f_ hedge **Heckklappe** _f_ tailgate; **Hecklicht** _nt_ tail-light; **Heckscheibe** _f_ rear window; **Heckscheibenheizung** _f_ rear-window defroster **Hefe** (-, -_n_) _f_ yeast **Heft** (-_(e)s_, -_e_) _nt_ notebook, exercise book; (_Ausgabe_) issue **heftig** _adj_ violent; (_Kritik, Streit_) fierce **Heftklammer** _f_ paper clip; **Heftpflaster** _nt_ plaster (_BRIT_), Band--Aid® (_US_) **Heide** (-, -_n_) _f_ heath, moor; **Heidekraut** _nt_ heather **Heidelbeere** _f_ bilberry, blueberry **heidnisch** _adj_ (_Brauch_) pagan **heikel** _adj_ (_Angelegenheit_) awkward, (_wählerisch_) fussy **hell** _adj_ (_Suche_) in one piece, intact; (_Person_) unhurt, **helbar** _adj_ curable **Hellhurt** ((_f_)_s_, -_e_) _m_ halibut **heilen** _vt_ to cure ▷ _vi_ to heal **heilig** _adj_ holy; **Heiligabend** _m_ Christmas Eve; **Heilige(r)** _mf_ saint **Heilmittel** _n_ remedy, cure (_gegen_ for); **Heilpraktiker(in)** (-_s_, -) _m(f)_ non-medical practitioner **heim** _adv_ home; **Heim** (-_(e)_, -_e_) _nt_ home **Heimat** (-, -_en_) _f_ home (town/ country); **Heimatland** _nt_ home country

heim|fahren irr vi to drive home;
Heimfahrt f journey home; **hei-
misch** adj (Bevölkerung, Brauchtum)
local; (Tiere, Pflanzen) native; **heim|
kommen** irr vi to come (o return)
home

heimlich adj secret

Heimreise f journey home;
Heimspiel nt (Sport) home game;
Heimvorteil m (Sport) home advantage; **Heimweg** m way home;
Heimweh (-s) nt homesickness; ~
haben to be homesick; **Heimwer-
ker(in)** m(f) DIY enthusiast

Heirat (-, -en) f marriage; **heiraten**
vi to get married ▷ vt to marry;
Heiratsantrag m proposal; **er hat
ihr einen ~ gemacht** he proposed
to her

heiser adj hoarse

heiß adj hot; (Diskussion) heated;
mir ist ~ I'm hot

heißen (hieß, geheißen) vi to be
called; (bedeuten) to mean; **ich
heiße Tom** my name is Tom; **wie ~
Sie?** what's your name?; **wie heißt
sie mit Nachnamen?** what's her
surname?; **wie heißt das auf Englisch?** what's that in English? ▷ vi
impers **es heißt** (man sagt) it is said;
es heißt in dem Brief ... it says in
the letter ...; **das heißt** that is

Heißluftherd m fan-assisted ov-
en

heiter adj cheerful; (Wetter) bright

heizen vt to heat; **Heizkissen** nt
(Med) heated pad; **Heizkörper** m
radiator; **Heizöl** nt fuel oil; **Heizung** f heating

Hektar (-s, -) nt hectare

Hektik (-, -en) f **nur keine ~!** take it
easy; **hektisch** adj hectic

Held (-en, -en) m hero; **Heldin** f
heroine

helfen (half, geholfen) vi to help (jdm
bei etw sb with sth); (nützen) to be of

use; **sie weiß sich** (dat) **zu ~** she can
manage ▷ vi impers **es hilft nichts,
du musst ...** it's no use, you have to
...; **Helfer(in)** m(f) helper; (Mitarbeiter) assistant

Helikopter-Skiing (-s) nt heliski-
ing, helicopter skiing

hell adj bright; (Farbe) light; (Hautfarbe) fair; **hellblau** adj light blue;
hellblond adj ash-blond; **hellgelb**
adj pale yellow; **hellgrün** adj light
green; **Hellseher(in)** m(f) clair-
voyant

Helm (-(e)s, -e) m helmet; **Helm-
pflicht** f compulsory wearing of
helmets

Hemd (-(e)s, -en) nt shirt; (Unter~)
vest

hemmen vt to check; (behindern)
to hamper; **gehemmt sein** to be
inhibited; **Hemmung** f (psychisch)
inhibition; **sie hatte keine ~, ihn zu
betrügen** she had no scruples
about deceiving him; (moralisch)
scruple

Henkel (-s, -) m handle

Henna (-s) nt henna

Henne (-, -n) f hen

Hepatitis (-, Hepatitiden) f hepatitis

her adv here; **wo ist sie ~?** where is
she from?; **das ist zehn Jahre ~** that
was ten years ago

herab adv down; **herablassend**
adj (Bemerkung) condescending;
herab|sehen irr vt **auf jdn ~** to
look down on sb; **herab|setzen** vt
to reduce; (fig) to disparage

heran adv **näher ~!** come closer;
heran|kommen irr vi to approach;
~ an (+akk) to be able to get at; (fig)
to be able to get hold of; **heran|
wachsen** irr vi to grow up

herauf adv up; **herauf|beschwö-
ren** irr vt to evoke; (verursachen) to
cause; **herauf|ziehen** irr vt to pull
up ▷ vi to approach; (Sturm) to

gather
heraus adv out; **heraus|bekommen** irr vt (Geheimnis) to find out; (Rätsel) to solve; **ich bekomme noch zwei Euro heraus** I've got two euros change to come; **heraus|bringen** irr vt to bring out; **heraus|finden** irr vt to find out; **her aus|fordern** vt to challenge; **her ausforderung** f challenge; **her aus|geben** irr vt (Buch) to edit; (veröffentlichen) to publish; **jdm zwei Euro ~** to give sb two euros change; **geben Sie mir bitte auf 20 Euro heraus** could you give me change for 20 euros, please?; **heraus|holen** vt to get out (aus of); **heraus| kommen** irr vi to come out; **dabei kommt nichts heraus** nothing will come of it; **heraus|stellen** vi **sich ~** to turn out (als to be); **heraus| ziehen** irr vt to pull out

Herbst (-(e)s, -e) m autumn, fall (US)
Herd (-(e)s, -e) m cooker, stove
Herde (-, -n) f herd; (Schafe) flock
herein adv in; **~!** come in; **her ein|fallen** irr vi **wir sind auf einen Betrüger hereingefallen** we were taken in by a swindler; **herein|le gen** vt **jdn ~** (fig) to take sb for a ride

Herfahrt f journey here; **auf der ~** on the way here
Hergang m course (of events); **schildern Sie mir den ~** tell me what happened
Hering (-s, -e) m herring
her|kommen irr vi to come; **wo kommt sie her?** where does she come from?
Heroin (-s) nt heroin
Herpes (-) m (Med) herpes
Herr ((e)n, -en) m (vor Namen) Mr; (Mann) gentleman; (Adliger, Gott) Lord; **mein ~!** sir; **meine ~en!** gen tlemen; **Sehr geehrte Damen und**

~en Dear Sir or Madam; **herrenlos** adj (Gepäckstück) abandoned; (Tier) stray; **Herrentoilette** f men's toilet, gents
her|richten vt to prepare
herrlich adj marvellous, splendid
Herrschaft f rule; (Macht) power; **meine ~en!** ladies and gentlemen!
herrschen vi to rule; (bestehen) to be
her|stellen vt to make; (industriell) to manufacture; **Hersteller(in)** m(f) manufacturer; **Herstellung** f production
herüber adv over
herum adv around; (im Kreis) round; **um etw ~** around sth; **du hast den Pulli falsch ~ an** you're wearing your sweater inside out; **anders ~** the other way round; **he rum|fahren** irr vi to drive around; **herum|führen** vt **jdn in der Stadt ~** to show sb around the town; (s) **die Straße führt um das Zentrum herum** the road goes around the city centre; **herum|kommen** irr vi **sie ist viel in der Welt herumge kommen** she's been around the world; **um etw ~** (vermeiden) to get out of sth; **herum|kriegen** vt to talk round; **herum|treiben** irr vr **sich ~** to hang around
herunter adv down; **herunter gekommen** adj (Gebäude, Gegend) run down; (Person) down at heel; **herunter|handeln** vt to get down; **herunter|holen** vt to bring down; **herunter|kommen** irr vi to come down; **herunter|laden** irr vt (In form) to download
hervor adv out; **hervor|bringen** irr vt to produce; (Wort) to utter; **hervor|heben** irr vt to emphasize, to stress; **hervorragend** adj ex cellent; **hervor|rufen** irr vt to cause, to give rise to

Herz (-ens, -en) nt heart; (Karten) hearts pl; **von ganzem ~en** wholeheartedly; **sich** (dat) **etw zu ~en nehmen** to take sth to heart; **Herzanfall** m heart attack; **Herzbeschwerden** pl heart trouble sing; **Herzfehler** m heart defect; **herzhaft** adj (Essen) substantial; **~ lachen** to have a good laugh; **Herzinfarkt** m heart attack; **Herzklopfen** (-s) nt (Med) palpitations pl; **ich hatte ~** (vor Aufregung) my heart was pounding (with excitement); **herzkrank** adj **sie ist ~** she's got a heart condition; **herzlich** adj (Empfang, Mensch) warm; **~en Glückwunsch** congratulations

Herzog(in) (-s, Herzöge) m(f) duke/duchess

Herzschlag m heartbeat; (Herzversagen) heart failure; **Herzschrittmacher** m pacemaker; **Herzstillstand** m cardiac arrest

Hessen (-s) nt Hessen

heterosexuell adj heterosexual; **Heterosexuelle(r)** mf heterosexual

Hetze (-, -n) f (Eile) rush; **hetzen** vt to rush ▷ vr **sich ~** to rush

Heu (-(e)s) nt hay

heuer adv this year

heulen vi to howl; (weinen) to cry

Heuschnupfen m hay fever; **Heuschrecke** (-, -n) f grasshopper; (größer) locust

heute adv today; **~ Abend/früh** this evening/morning; **~ Nacht** tonight; (letzte Nacht) last night; **~ in acht Tagen** a week (from) today; **sie hat bis ~ nicht bezahlt** she hasn't paid to this day; **heutig** adj **die ~e Zeitung/Generation** today's paper/generation; **heutzutage** adv nowadays

Hexe (-, -n) f witch; **Hexenschuss**

m lumbago

hielt imperf von **halten**

hier adv here; **~ entlang** this way; **~ bleiben** to stay here; **~ lassen** to leave here; **ich bin auch nicht ~** I'm a stranger here myself; **hier-her** adv here; **das gehört nicht ~** that doesn't belong here; **hiermit** adv with this; **hierzulande, hier zu Lande** adv in this country

hiesig adj local

hieß imperf von **heißen**

Hi-Fi-Anlage f hi-fi (system)

high adj (fam) high; **Highlife** (-s) nt high life; **~ machen** to live it up; **Hightech** (-s) nt high tech

Hilfe (-, -n) f help; (für Notleidende, finanziell) aid; **~!** help!; **erste ~ leisten** to give first aid; **um ~ bitten** to ask for help; **hilflos** adj helpless; **hilfsbereit** adj helpful; **Hilfsmittel** nt aid

Himbeere f raspberry

Himmel (-s, -) m sky; (Rel) heaven; **Himmelfahrt** f Ascension; **Himmelsrichtung** f direction; **himmlisch** adj heavenly

hin adv there; **~ und her** to and fro; **~ und zurück** there and back; **bis zur Mauer ~** up to the wall; **das ist noch lange ~** (zeitlich) that's a long way off

hinab adv down; **hinab|gehen** irr vi to go down

hinauf adv up; **hinauf|gehen** irr vi, vt to go up; **hinauf|steigen** irr vi to climb (up)

hinaus adv out; **hinaus|gehen** irr vi to go out; **das Zimmer geht auf den See hinaus** the room looks out onto the lake; **~ über** (+akk) to exceed; **hinaus|laufen** irr vi to run out; **~ auf** (+akk) to come to, to amount to; **hinaus|schieben** irr vi to put off, to postpone; **hinaus|werfen** irr vt to throw out; (aus

Firma) to fire, to sack (BRIT); **hinaus|zögern** vr sich ~ to take longer than expected

Hinblick m in (*o im*) ~ **auf** (+*akk*) with regard to; (*wegen*) in view of

hin|bringen *irr vt* **ich bringe Sie hin** I'll take you there

hindern *vt* to prevent; **jdn daran ~, etw zu tun** to stop (*o* prevent) sb from doing sth; **Hindernis** *nt* obstacle

Hinduismus m Hinduism

hindurch *adv* through; **das ganze Jahr ~** throughout the year, all year round; **die ganze Nacht ~** all night (long)

hinein *adv* in; **hinein|gehen** *irr vi* to go in; **~ in** (+*akk*) to go into, to enter; **hinein|passen** *vi* to fit in: **~ in** (+*akk*) to fit into

hin|fahren *irr vi* to go there ▷ *vt* to take there; **Hinfahrt** *f* outward journey

hin|fallen *irr vi* to fall (down)

Hinflug m outward flight

hing *imperf von* **hängen**

hin|gehen *irr vi* to go there; (*Zeit*) to pass; **hin|halten** *irr vt* to hold out; (*warten lassen*) to put off

hinken *vi* to limp; **der Vergleich hinkt** the comparison doesn't work

hin|knien vr sich ~ to kneel down; **hin|legen** vt to put down ▷ vr sich ~ to lie down; **hin|nehmen** *irr vt* (*fig*) to put up with, to take; **Hinreise** *f* outward journey; **hin|setzen** vr sich ~ to sit down; **hinsichtlich** *prep* +*gen* with regard to; **hin|stellen** vt to put (down) ▷ vr sich ~ to stand

hinten *adv* at the back; (*im Auto*) in the back; (*dahinter*) behind

hinter *prep* +*akk o* +*dat* behind; (*nach*) after; ~ **jdm her sein** to be after sb; **etw ~ sich** (*akk*) **bringen** to get sth over (and done) with; **Hin-**

terachse *f* rear axle; **Hinterausgang** m rear exit; **Hinterbein** *nt* hind leg; **Hinterbliebene(r)** *mf* dependant; **hintere(r, s)** *adj* rear, back; **hintereinander** *adv* (*in einer Reihe*) one behind the other; (*hintereinander her*) one after the other; **drei Tage ~** three days running (*o* in a row); **Hintereingang** m rear entrance; **Hintergedanke** m ulterior motive; **hintergehen** *irr vt* to deceive; **Hintergrund** m background; **hinterher** *adv* (*zeitlich*) afterwards; **los, ~!** come on, after him / her / them; **Hinterkopf** m back of the head; **hinterlassen** vt to leave a message for sb; **hinterlegen** vt to leave (*bei* with)

Hintern (-, -) m (*fam*) backside, bum

Hinterradantrieb m (*Auto*) rear-wheel drive; **Hinterteil** *nt* back (part); (*Hintern*) behind; **Hintertür** *f* back door

hinüber *adv* over; ~ **sein** (*fam*: *kaputt*) to be ruined; (*verdorben*) to have gone bad; **hinüber|gehen** *irr vi* to go over

hinunter *adv* down; **hinunter|gehen** *irr vi, vt* to go down; **hinunter|schlucken** vt (*a. fig*) to swallow

Hinweg m outward journey

hinweg|setzen vr sich über etw (*akk*) ~ to ignore sth

Hinweis (-es, -e) m (*Andeutung*) hint; (*Anweisung*) instruction; (*Verweis*) reference; **hin|weisen** *irr vi* **jdn auf etw** (*acc*) ~ to point sth out to sb; **jdn nochmal auf etw ~** to remind sb of sth

hinzu *adv* in addition; **hinzu|fügen** vt to add; **hinzu|kommen** *irr vi* **zu jdm ~** to join sb; **es war kalt, hinzu kam, dass es auch noch regnete** it was cold, and on top of that it was raining

Hirn (-(e)s, -e) nt brain; (Verstand) brains pl; **Hirnhautentzündung** f meningitis; **hirnverbrannt** adj crazy

Hirsch (-(e)s, -e) m deer; (als Speise) venison

Hirse (-, -n) f millet

Hirte (-n, -n) m shepherd

historisch adj historical

Hit (-s, -s) m (fig, Mus, Inform) hit; **Hitliste** f, **Hitparade** f charts pl

Hitze (-) f heat; **hitzebeständig** adj heat-resistant; **Hitzewelle** f heatwave; **hitzig** adj hot-tempered; (Debatte) heated; **Hitzschlag** m heatstroke

HIV (-(s), (-s)) nt abk = **Human Immunodeficiency Virus** HIV; **HIV-negativ** adj HIV-negative; **HIV-positiv** adj HIV-positive

H-Milch f long-life milk

hob imperf von **heben**

Hobby (-s, -s) nt hobby

Hobel (-s, -) m plane

hoch adj high; (Baum, Haus) tall; (Schnee) deep; **der Zaun ist drei Meter ~** the fence is three metres high; **~ auflösend** high-resolution; **~ begabt** extremely gifted; **das ist mir zu ~** that's above my head; **~ soll sie leben!, sie lebe ~!** three cheers for her; **4 ~ 2 ist 16** 4 squared is 16; **4 ~ 5** 4 to the power of 5

Hoch (-s, -s) nt (Ruf) cheer; (Meteo) high; **hochachtungsvoll** adv (in Briefen) Yours faithfully; **Hochbetrieb** m **es herrscht ~** they/we are extremely busy; **Hochdeutsch** nt High German; **Hochgebirge** nt high mountains pl; **Hochgeschwindigkeitszug** m high-speed train; **Hochhaus** nt high rise; **hoch|heben** irr vt to lift (up); **hochprozentig** adj (Alkohol) high-proof; **Hochsaison** f high season;

Hochschule f college; (Universität) university; **hochschwanger** adj heavily pregnant; **Hochsommer** m midsummer; **Hochspannung** f great tension; (Elek) high voltage; **Hochsprung** m high jump

höchst adv highly, extremely; **höchste(r, s)** adj highest; (äußerste) extreme; **höchstens** adv at the most; **Höchstgeschwindigkeit** f maximum speed; **Höchstparkdauer** f maximum stay

Hochstuhl m high chair

höchstwahrscheinlich adv very probably

Hochwasser nt high water; (Überschwemmung) floods pl; **hochwertig** adj high-quality

Hochzeit (-, -en) f wedding; **Hochzeitsnacht** f wedding night; **Hochzeitsreise** f honeymoon; **Hochzeitstag** m wedding day; (Jahrestag) wedding anniversary

hocken vi to squat, to crouch

Hocker (-s, -) m stool

Hockey (-s) nt hockey

Hoden (-s, -) m testicle

Hof (-(e)s, Höfe) m (Hinterhof) yard; (Innenhof) courtyard; (Bauernhof) farm; (Königshof) court

hoffen vi to hope (auf +akk for); **ich hoffe es** I hope so; **hoffentlich** adv hopefully; **~ nicht** I hope not; **Hoffnung** f hope; **hoffnungslos** adj hopeless

höflich adj polite; **Höflichkeit** f politeness

hohe(r, s) adj siehe **hoch**

Höhe (-, -n) f height; (Anhöhe) hill; (einer Summe) amount; **in einer ~ von 5000 Metern** at an altitude of 5,000 metres; (Flughöhe) altitude; **Höhenangst** f vertigo; **Höhensonne** f sun lamp

Höhepunkt m (einer Reise) high point; (einer Veranstaltung) highlight;

(eines Films; sexuell) climax

höher *adj, adv* higher

hohl *adj* hollow

Höhle (-, -n) *f* cave

holen *vt* to get, to fetch; *(abholen)* to pick up; *(Atem)* to catch; **die Polizei ~** to call the police; **jdn/etw ~ lassen** to send for sb/sth

Holland *nt* Holland; **Holländer(in)** (-s, -) *m(f)* Dutchman/-woman; **holländisch** *adj* Dutch

Hölle (-, -n) *f* hell

Hologramm *nt* hologram

holperig *adj* bumpy

Holunder (-s, -) *m* elder

Holz (-es, Hölzer) *nt* wood; **Holzboden** *m* wooden floor; **hölzern** *adj* wooden; **holzig** *adj (Stängel)* woody; **Holzkohle** *f* charcoal

Homebanking (-s) *nt* home banking, online banking; **Homepage** (-, -s) *f* home page; **Hometrainer** *m* exercise machine

homöopathisch *adj* homeopathic

homosexuell *adj* homosexual; **Homosexuelle(r)** *mf* homosexual

Honig (-s, -e) *m* honey; **Honigmelone** *f* honeydew melon

Honorar (-s, -e) *nt* fee

Hopfen (-s, -) *m (Bot)* hop; *(beim Brauen)* hops pl

hoppla *interj* whoops, oops

horchen *vi* to listen *(auf +akk* to); *(an der Tür)* to eavesdrop

hören *vt, vi (passiv, mitbekommen)* to hear; *(zufällig)* to overhear; *(aufmerksam zuhören; Radio, Musik)* to listen to; **ich habe schon viel von Ihnen gehört** I've heard a lot about you; **Hörer** *m (Tel)* receiver; **Hörer(in)** *m(f)* listener; **Hörgerät** *nt* hearing aid

Horizont (-(e)s, -e) *m* horizon; **das geht über meinen ~** that's beyond me

Hormon (-s, -e) *nt* hormone

Hornhaut *f* hard skin; *(des Auges)* cornea

Hornisse (-, -n) *f* hornet

Horoskop (-s, -e) *nt* horoscope

Hörsaal *m* lecture hall; **Hörsturz** *m* acute hearing loss; **Hörweite** *f* **in/außer ~** within/out of earshot

Höschenwindel (-, -n) *f* nappy *(BRIT)*, diaper *(US)*

Hose (-, -n) *f* trousers *pl (BRIT)*, pants *pl (US)*; *(Unterhose)* (under)pants *pl*; **eine ~** a pair of trousers/pants; **kurze ~** (pair of) shorts *pl*; **Hosenanzug** *m* trouser suit *(BRIT)*, pantsuit *(US)*; **Hosenschlitz** *m* fly, flies *(BRIT)*; **Hosentasche** *f* trouser pocket *(BRIT)*, pant pocket *(US)*; **Hosenträger** *m* braces *pl (BRIT)*, suspenders *pl (US)*

Hospital (-s, Hospitäler) *nt* hospital

Hotdog (-s, -s) *nt o m* hot dog

Hotel (-s, -s) *nt* hotel, **in welchem ~ seid ihr?** which hotel are you staying at?; **Hoteldirektor(in)** *m(f)* hotel manager; **Hotelkette** *f* hotel chain; **Hotelzimmer** *nt* hotel room

Hotline (-, -s) *f* hot line

Hubraum *m* cubic capacity

hübsch *adj (Mädchen, Kind, Kleid)* pretty; *(gutaussehend: Mann, Frau)* good-looking, cute

Hubschrauber (-s, -) *m* helicopter

Huf (-(e)s, -e) *m* hoof; **Hufeisen** *nt* horseshoe

Hüfte (-, -n) *f* hip

Hügel (-s, -) *m* hill; **hügelig** *adj* hilly

Huhn (-(e)s, Hühner) *nt* hen; *(Gastr)* chicken; **Hühnchen** *nt* chicken; **Hühnerauge** *nt* corn; **Hühnerbrühe** *f* chicken broth

Hülle (-, -n) *f* cover; *(für Ausweis)* case; *(Zellophan)* wrapping

Hummel (-, -n) *f* bumblebee

Hummer (-s, -) *m* lobster, **Hum-**

merkrabbe f king prawn

Humor (-s) m humour; **~ haben** to have a sense of humour; **humorvoll** adj humorous

humpeln vi hobble

Hund (-(e)s, -e) m dog; **Hundeleine** f dog lead (BRIT), dog leash (US)

hundert num hundred; **Hundertjahrfeier** f centenary; **hundertprozentig** adj, adv one hundred per cent; **hundertste(r, s)** adj hundredth

Hündin f bitch

Hunger (-s) m hunger; **~ haben/bekommen** to be/get hungry; **hungern** vi to go hungry; (ernsthaft, dauernd) to starve

Hupe (-, -n) f horn; **hupen** vi to sound one's horn

Hüpfburg f bouncy castle®; **hüpfen** vi to hop; (springen) to jump

Hürde (-, -n) f hurdle

Hure (-, -n) f whore

hurra interj hooray

husten vi to cough; **Husten** (-s) m cough; **Hustenbonbon** nt cough sweet; **Hustensaft** m cough mixture

Hut (-(e)s, Hüte) m hat

hüten vt to look after ▷ vr **sich ~** to watch out; **sich ~, etw zu tun** to take care not to do sth; **sich ~ vor** (+dat) to beware of

Hütte (-, -n) f hut, cottage; **Hüttenkäse** m cottage cheese

Hyäne (-, -n) f hyena

Hydrant m hydrant

hygienisch adj hygienic

Hyperlink (-s, -s) m hyperlink

Hypnose (-, -n) f hypnosis; **Hypnotiseur(in)** m(f) hypnotist; **hypnotisieren** vt to hypnotize

Hypothek (-, -en) f mortgage

hysterisch adj hysterical

i. A. abk = **im Auftrag** pp

IC (-, -s) m abk = **Intercityzug** Intercity (train)

ICE (-, -s) m abk = **Intercityexpresszug** German high-speed train

ich pron I; **~ bin's** it's me; **~ nicht** not me; **du und ~** you and me; **hier bin ~!** here I am; **~ Idiot!** stupid me

Icon (-s, -s) nt (Inform) icon

IC-Zuschlag m Intercity supplement

ideal adj ideal; **Ideal** (-s, -e) nt ideal

Idee (-, -n) f idea

identifizieren vt to identify ▷ vr **sich mit jdm/etw ~** to identify with sb/sth

identisch adj identical

Idiot(in) (-en, -en) m(f) idiot; **idiotisch** adj idiotic

Idol (-s, -e) nt idol

Idylle (-, -n) f idyll; **idyllisch** adj idyllic

Igel (-s, -) m hedgehog

ignorieren vt to ignore

ihm pron dat sing von **er/es**; (to)

him, (to) it; **wie geht es ~?** how is he?; **ein Freund von ~** a friend of his ▷ *pron dat von* **es**; (to) it

ihn *pron akk sing von* **er**; *(Person)* him; *(Sache)* it

ihnen *pron dat pl von* **sie**; (to) them; **wie geht es ~?** how are they?; **ein Freund von ~** a friend of theirs

Ihnen *pron dat sing u pl von* **Sie**; (to) you; **wie geht es ~?** how are you?; **ein Freund von ~** a friend of yours

ihr *pron (2. Person pl)* you; **~ seid's** it's you ▷ *pron (Dat sing) von* **sie**; *(Person)* (to) her; *(Sache)* (to) it; **er schickte es ~** he sent it to her; **er hat ~ die Haare geschnitten** he cut her hair; **wie geht es ~?** how is she?; **ein Freund von ~** a friend of hers ▷ *pron (adjektivisch, sing, Person)* her; *(sing, Sache)* its; *(pl)* their; **~ Vater** her father; **~ Auto** *(mehrere Besitzer)* their car

Ihr *pron von* **Sie**; *(adjektivisch)* your; **~(e) XY** *(am Briefende)* Yours, XY

ihre(r, s) *pron (substantivisch, sing)* hers; *(pl)* theirs; **das ist ~/r/ihr(e)s** that's hers; *(pl)* that's theirs

Ihre(r, s) *pron (substantivisch)* yours; **das ist ~/r/'lhr(e)s** that's yours

ihretwegen *adv (wegen ihr)* because of her; *(Ihr zuliebe)* for her sake; *(um Sie)* about her; *(von ihr aus)* as far as she is concerned ▷ *adv (wegen ihnen)* because of them; *(ihnen zuliebe)* for their sake; *(um sie)* about them; *(von ihnen aus)* as far as they are concerned; **Ihretwegen** *adv (wegen ihnen)* because of you; *(Ihnen zuliebe)* for your sake; *(um Sie)* about you; *(von Ihnen aus)* as far as you are concerned

Ikone (-, -n) *f* icon

illegal *adj* illegal

Illusion *f* illusion; **sich** *(dat)* **-en machen** to delude oneself; **illuso-**

risch *adj* illusory

Illustration *f* illustration

Illustrierte (-n, -n) *f* (glossy) magazine

im *kontr von* **in dem**; **~ Bett** in bed; **~ Fernsehen** on TV; **~ Radio** on the radio; **~ Bus / Zug** on the bus / train; **~ Januar** in January; **~ Stehen** (while) standing up

Imbiss *(-es, -e) m* snack; **Imbiss-Bude** *f*, **Imbissstube** *f* snack bar

Imbussschlüssel *m* hex key

immer *adv* always; **~ mehr** more and more; **~ wieder** again and again; **~ noch** still; **~ noch nicht** still not; **für ~** forever; **~ wenn ich ...** every time I ...; **~ schöner / trauriger** more and more beautiful / sad-der and sadder; **was / wer / wo / wann (auch) ~** whatever / whoev-er / wherever / whenever; **immer-hin** *adv* after all; **immerzu** *adv* all the time

Immigrant(in) *m(f)* immigrant

Immobilien *pl* property sing, real estate sing; **Immobilienmakler(in)** *m(f)* estate agent (BRIT), realtor (US)

immun *adj* immune (**gegen** to); **Immunschwäche** *f* immunodefi-ciency; **Immunschwächekrank-heit** *f* immune deficiency syn-drome; **Immunsystem** *nt* immune system

impfen *vt* to vaccinate; **ich muss mich gegen Pocken ~ lassen** I've got to get myself vaccinated against smallpox; **Impfpass** *m* vaccination card; **Impfstoff** *m* vaccine; **Imp-fung** *f* vaccination

imponieren *vi* to impress (*jdm* sb)

Import *(-(e)s, -e) m* import; **impor-tieren** *vt* to import

impotent *adj* impotent

imstande *adj* **~ sein** to be in a position; *(fähig)* to be able

in *prep* **+akk** in(to); (to); **~ die Stadt**

into town; ~ **die Schule gehen** to go to school ▷ *prep* +*dat* in; (*zeitlich*) in; (*während*) during; (*innerhalb*) within; ~ **der Stadt** in town; ~ **der Schule** at school; **noch ~ dieser Woche** by the end of this week; **heute ~ acht Tagen** a week (from) today; **Dienstag ~ einer Woche** a week on Tuesday ▷ *adv* ~ **sein** (*modisch*) to be in

inbegriffen *adj* included

indem *conj* **sie gewann, ~ sie mogelte** she won by cheating

Inder(in) (-s, -) *m(f)* Indian

Indianer(in) (-s, -) *m(f)* American Indian, Native American; **indianisch** *adj* American Indian, Native American

Indien (-s) *nt* India

indirekt *adj* indirect

indisch *adj* Indian

indiskret *adj* indiscreet

individuell *adj* individual

Indonesien (-s) *nt* Indonesia

Industrie *f* industry; **Industrie-** in *zW* industrial; **Industriegebiet** *nt* industrial area; **industriell** *adj* industrial

ineinander *adv* in(to) one another (*o* each other)

Infarkt (-(e)s, -e) *m* (*Herzinfarkt*) heart attack

Infektion *f* infection; **Infektionskrankheit** *f* infectious disease; **infizieren** *vt* to infect ▷ *vr* **sich ~** to be infected

Info (-, -s) *f* (*fam*) info

infolge *prep* +*gen* as a result of, owing to; **infolgedessen** *adv* consequently

Informatik *f* computer science; **Informatiker(in)** (-s, -) *m(f)* computer scientist

Information *f* information; **Informationsschalter** *m* information desk; **informieren** *vt* to in-

form; **falsch ~** to misinform ▷ *vr* **sich ~** to find out (*über* +*akk* about)

infrage *adv* **das kommt nicht ~** that's out of the question; **etw ~ stellen** to question sth

Infrastruktur *f* infrastructure

Infusion *f* infusion

Ingenieur(in) *m(f)* engineer

Ingwer (-s) *m* ginger

Inhaber(in) (-s, -) *m(f)* owner; (*Haus~*) occupier; (*von Lizenz*) holder; (*Fin*) bearer

Inhalt (-(e)s, -e) *m* contents *pl*; (*eines Buchs etc*) content; (*Math*) volume; (*Flächeninhalt*) area; **Inhaltsangabe** *f* summary; **Inhaltsverzeichnis** *nt* table of contents

Initiative *f* initiative; **die ~ ergreifen** to take the initiative

Injektion *f* injection

inklusive *adv, prep* inclusive (*gen* of)

inkonsequent *adj* inconsistent

Inland *nt* (*Pol, Comm*) home; **im ~** at home; (*Geo*) inland; **inländisch** *adj* domestic; **Inlandsflug** *m* domestic flight; **Inlandsgespräch** *nt* national call

Inlineskates *pl* Rollerblades® *pl*, inline skates *pl*

innen *adv* inside; **Innenarchitekt(in)** *m(f)* interior designer; **Innenhof** *m* (inner) courtyard; **Innenminister(in)** *m(f)* minister of the interior, Home Secretary (*BRIT*); **Innenseite** *f* inside; **Innenspiegel** *m* rearview mirror; **Innenstadt** *f* town centre; (*von Großstadt*) city centre

innere(r, s) *adj* inner; (*im Körper, inländisch*) internal; **Innere(s)** *nt* inside; (*Mitte*) centre; (*fig*) heart

Innereien *pl* innards *pl*

innerhalb *adv, prep* +*gen* within; (*räumlich*) inside

innerlich *adj* internal; (*geistig*) inner

innerste(r, s) *adj* innermost

Innovation *f* innovation; **innovativ** *adj* innovative

inoffiziell *adj* unofficial; *(zwanglos)* informal

ins *kontr von* **in das**

Insasse (*n, m*)*m*, **Insassin** *f* *(Auto)* passenger; *(Anstalt)* inmate

insbesondere *adv* particularly, in particular

Inschrift *f* inscription

Insekt *(-(e)s, -en)* *nt* insect, bug *(US)*; **Insektenschutzmittel** *nt* insect repellent; **Insektenstich** *m* insect bite

Insel (*·, -n*) *f* island

Inserat *nt* advertisement

insgesamt *adv* altogether, all in all

Insider(in) *(-s, -)* *m(f)* insider

insofern *adv* in that respect; *(deshalb)* (and) so ▷ *conj* if; **~ als** in so far as

Installateur(in) *m(f)* *(Klempner)* plumber; *(Elektroinstallateur)* electrician; **installieren** *vt* *(Inform)* to install

Instinkt *(-(e)s, -e)* *m* instinct

Institut *(-(e)s, -e)* *nt* institute

Institution *f* institution

Instrument *nt* instrument

Insulin *(-s)* *nt* insulin

Inszenierung *f* production

intakt *adj* intact

Intellektuell *adj* intellectual

intelligent *adj* intelligent; **Intelligenz** *f* intelligence

intensiv *adj* *(gründlich)* intensive; *(Gefühl, Schmerz)* intense; **Intensivkurs** *m* crash course; **Intensivstation** *f* intensive care unit

interaktiv *adj* interactive

Intercityexpress(zug) *m* German high-speed train; **Intercityzug** *m* Intercity (train); **Intercityzu-**

schlag *m* Intercity supplement

interessant *adj* interesting; **Interesse** *(-s, -n)* *nt* interest; **~ haben an** *(+dat)* to be interested in; **interessieren** *vt* to interest ▷ *vr* **sich ~** to be interested *(für in)*

Interface *(-, -)* *nt* *(Inform)* interface

Internat *nt* boarding school

international *adj* international

Internet *(-s)* *nt* Internet, Net; **im ~** on the Internet; **im ~ surfen** to surf the Net; **Internetcafé** *nt* Internetcafé, cybercafé; **Internetfirma** *f* dotcom company; **Internethandel** *m* e-commerce; **Internetseite** *f* web page

interpretieren *vt* to interpret *(als as)*

Interpunktion *f* punctuation

Interregio *(-s, -s)* *m* regional train

Interview *(-s, -s)* *nt* interview; **interviewen** *vt* to interview

intim *adj* intimate

intolerant *adj* intolerant

investieren *vt* to invest

inwiefern *adv* in what way; *(in welchem Ausmaß)* to what extent; **inwieweit** *adv* to what extent

inzwischen *adv* meanwhile

Irak *(-s)* *m* **(der) ~** Iraq

Iran *(-s)* *m* **(der) ~** Iran

Ire *(-n, n)* *m* Irishman

irgend *adv* **~ so ein Idiot** some idiot; **wenn ~ möglich** if at all possible; **irgendein** *pron*, **irgendeine(r, s)** *adj* some; *(fragend, im Bedingungssatz; beliebig)* any; **irgendetwas** *pron* something; *(fragend, im Bedingungssatz)* anything; **irgendjemand** *pron* somebody; *(fragend, im Bedingungssatz)* anybody; **irgendwann** *adv* sometime; *(zu beliebiger Zeit)* any time; **irgendwie** *adv* somehow; **irgendwo** *adv* somewhere; *(fragend, im Bedingungssatz)* anywhere

Irin f Irishwoman; **irisch** adj Irish; **Irland** nt Ireland

ironisch adj ironic

irre adj crazy, mad; (toll) terrific; **Irre(r)** mf lunatic; **irreführen** irr vt to mislead; **irremachen** vt to confuse; **irren** vi to be mistaken; (umherirren) to wander ▷ vr **sich ~** to be mistaken; **wenn ich mich nicht irre** if I'm not mistaken; **sich in der Nummer ~** (Telefon) to get the wrong number; **irrsinnig** adj mad, crazy; **Irrtum** (-s, -tümer) m mistake, error; **irrtümlich** adj mistaken ▷ adv by mistake

ISBN (-) nt abk = **industrial standard business network** ISBN ▷ (-) f abk = **Internationale Standard Buchnummer** ISBN

Ischias (-) m sciatica

ISDN (-) nt abk = **integrated services digital network** ISDN

Islam (-s) m Islam; **islamisch** adj Islamic

Island nt Iceland; **Isländer(in)** (-s, -) m(f) Icelander; **isländisch** adj Icelandic; **Isländisch** nt Icelandic

Isolierband nt insulating tape; **isolieren** vt to isolate; (Elek) to insulate

Isomatte f thermomat, karrymat®

Israel (-s) nt Israel; **Israeli** (-(s), -(s)) m (-, -(s)) f Israeli; **israelisch** adj Israeli

IT (-) f abk = **Informationstechnologie** IT

Italien (-s) nt Italy; **Italiener(in)** (-s, -) m(f) Italian; **italienisch** adj Italian; **Italienisch** nt Italian

ja adv yes; **aber ~!** yes, of course; **~, wissen Sie ...** well, you know ...; **ich glaube ~** I think so; **~?** (am Telefon) hello?; **sag's ihr ~ nicht!** don't you dare tell her; **das sag ich ~** that's what I'm trying to say; **ich komme ~ schon** I'm coming

Jacht (-, -en) f yacht; **Jachthafen** m marina

Jacke (-, -n) f jacket; (Wolljacke) cardigan

Jackett (-s, -s o -e) nt jacket

Jagd (-, -en) f hunt; (Jagen) hunting; **jagen** vi to hunt ▷ vt to hunt; (verfolgen) to chase; **Jäger(in)** m(f) hunter

Jaguar (-s, -e) m jaguar

Jahr (-(e)s, -e) nt year; **ein halbes ~** six months pl; **Anfang der neunziger ~e** in the early nineties; **mit sechzehn ~en** at (the age of) sixteen; **Jahrestag** m anniversary; **Jahreszahl** f date, year; **Jahreszeit** f season; **Jahrgang** m (Wein) year, vintage; **der ~ 1989** (Personen) those born in 1989; **Jahrhundert** (-s, -e) nt century; **jährlich** adj yearly, annual; **Jahrmarkt** m fair; **Jahrtausend** nt millennium; **Jahrzehnt** nt decade

jähzornig adj hot-tempered

Jakobsmuschel f scallop

Jalousie f (venetian) blind

Jamaika (-s) nt Jamaica

jämmerlich adj pathetic

jammern vi to moan

Januar (-(s), -e) m January; siehe auch **Juni**

Japan (-s) nt Japan; **Japaner(in)** (-s, -) m(f) Japanese; **japanisch** adj Japanese; **Japanisch** nt Japanese

jaulen vi to howl

jawohl adv yes (of course)

Jazz (-) m jazz

je adv ever; (jeweils) each; ~ **nach** depending on; ~ **nachdem** it depends; ~ **schneller desto besser** the faster the better

Jeans (-, -) f jeans pl

jede(r, s) unbest Zahlwort (insgesamt gesehen) every; (einzeln gesehen) each; (jede(r, s) beliebige) any; ~s **Mal** every time, each time; ~n **zweiten Tag** every other day; **sie hat an ~m Finger einen Ring** she's got a ring on each finger; ~r **Computer reicht aus** any computer will do; **bei ~m Wetter** in any weather ▷ pron everybody; (jeder Einzelne) each; ~r **von euch/uns** each of you/us; **jedenfalls** adv in any case; **jederzeit** adv at any time; **jedesmal** adv every time

jedoch adv however

jemals adv ever

jemand pron somebody; (in Frage und Verneinung) anybody

Jemen (-(s)) m Yemen

jene(r, s) adj that, those pl ▷ pron that (one), those pl

jenseits adv on the other side ▷

prep +gen on the other side of; (fig) beyond

Jetlag (-s) m jet lag

jetzt adj present

jetzt adv now; **erst** ~ only now; ~ **gleich** right now; **bis** ~ so far, up to now; **von** ~ **an** from now on

jeweils adv ~ **zwei zusammen** two at a time; **zu** ~ **5 Euro** at 5 euros each

Job (-s, -s) m job; **jobben** vi (fam) to work, to have a job

Jod (-(e)s) nt iodine

Joga (-s) nt yoga

joggen vi to jog; **Jogging** (-s) nt jogging; **Jogginganzug** m jogging suit, tracksuit; **Jogginghose** f jogging pants pl

Jog(h)urt (-s, -s) m o nt yoghurt

Johannisbeere f **Schwarze** ~ blackcurrant; **Rote** ~ redcurrant

Joint (-s, -s) m (fam) joint

jonglieren vi to juggle

Jordanien (-s) nt Jordan

Joule (-(s), -) nt joule

Journalist(in) m(f) journalist

Joystick (-s, -s) m (Inform) joystick

jubeln vi to cheer

Jubiläum (-s, Jubiläen) nt jubilee; (Jahrestag) anniversary

jucken vi to itch ▷ vt **es juckt mich am Arm** my arm is itching; **das juckt mich nicht** (fam) I couldn't care less; **juckreiz** m itch

Jude (-n, -n) m, **Jüdin** f Jew; **sie ist Jüdin** she's Jewish; **jüdisch** adj Jewish

Judo (-(s)) nt judo

Jugend (-) f youth; **jugendfrei** adj **ein ~er Film** a U-rated film (BRIT), a G-rated film (US); **nicht ~er Film** an X-rated film; **Jugendherberge** (-, -n) f youth hostel; **jugendlich** adj youthful; **Jugendliche(r)** mf young person; **Jugendstil** m art nouveau; **Jugendzentrum** nt youth centre

Jugoslawien (-s) nt (Hist) Yugoslavia; **das ehemalige ~** the former Yugoslavia
Juli (-(s), -s) m July; siehe auch **Juni**
jung adj young
Junge (-n, -n) m boy
Junge(s) (-n, -n) nt young animal; **die ~n** pl the young pl
Jungfrau f virgin; (Astr) Virgo
Junggeselle (-n, -n) m bachelor; **Junggesellin** f single woman
Juni (-(s), -s) m June; **im ~** in June; **am 4. ~** on 4(th) June, on June 4(th) (gesprochen: on the fourth of June); **Anfang/Mitte/Ende ~** at the beginning/in the middle/at the end of June; **letzten/nächsten ~** last/next June
Jupiter (-s) m Jupiter
Jura ohne Artikel (Studienfach) law; **~ studieren** to study law; **Jurist(in)** m(f) lawyer; **juristisch** adj legal
Justiz (-) f justice; **Justizminister(in)** m(f) minister of justice
Juwel (-s, -en) nt jewel; **Juwelier(in)** (-s, -e) m(f) jeweller
Jux (-es, -e) m joke, lark

k

Kabel (-s, -) nt (Elek) wire; (stark) cable; **Kabelfernsehen** nt cable television
Kabeljau (-s, -e o -s) m cod
Kabine f cabin; (im Schwimmbad) cubicle
Kabrio (-s, -s) nt convertible
Kachel (-, -n) f tile; **Kachelofen** m tiled stove
Käfer (-s, -) m beetle, bug (US)
Kaff (-s, -s) nt dump, hole
Kaffee (-s, -s) m coffee; **~ kochen** to make some coffee; **Kaffeefilter** m coffee filter; **Kaffeekanne** f coffeepot; **Kaffeeklatsch** (-(e)s, -e) m chat over coffee and cakes, coffee klatch (US); **Kaffeelöffel** m coffee spoon; **Kaffeemaschine** f coffee maker (o machine); **Kaffeetasse** f coffee cup
Käfig (-s, -e) m cage
kahl adj (Mensch, Kopf) bald; (Baum, Wand) bare
Kahn (-(e)s, Kähne) m boat; (Lastkahn) barge

Kal (-s, -e o -s) m quay

Kaiser (-s, -) m emperor; **Kaiserin** f empress; **Kaiserschnitt** m (Med) caesarean (section)

Kajak (-s, -s) nt kayak

Kajal (-s) m kohl

Kajüte (-, -n) f cabin

Kakao (-s, -s) m cocoa; (Getränk) (hot) chocolate

Kakerlake (-, -n) f cockroach

Kaki (-, -s) f kaki

Kaktee (-, -n) f, **Kaktus** (-, -se) m cactus

Kalb (-(e)s, Kälber) nt calf; **Kalbfleisch** nt veal; **Kalbsbraten** m roast veal, **Kalbsschnitzel** nt veal cutlet; (paniert) escalope of veal

Kalender (-s, -) m calendar; (Taschenkalender) diary

Kalk (-(e)s, -e) m lime; (in Knochen) calcium

Kalorie f calorie; **kalorienarm** adj low-calorie

kalt adj cold; **mir ist (es)** - I'm cold; **kaltblütig** adj cold-blooded; **Kälte** (-) f cold; (fig) coldness

kam imperf von **kommen**

Kambodscha (-s) nt Cambodia

Kamel (-(e)s, -e) nt camel

Kamera (-, -s) f camera

Kamerad(in) (-en, -en) m(f) friend; (als Begleiter) companion

Kamerafrau f, **Kameramann** m camerawoman/-man

Kamille (-, -n) f camomile; **Kamillentee** m camomile tea

Kamin (-s, -e) m (außen) chimney; (innen) fireplace

Kamm (-(e)s, Kämme) m comb; (Berg) ridge; (Hahn) crest; **kämmen** vr **sich ~, sich** (dat) **die Haare ~** to comb one's hair; **Kammermusik** f chamber music

Kampf (-(e)s, Kämpfe) m fight; (Schlacht) battle; (Wettbewerb) contest; (fig Anstrengung) struggle;

kämpfen vi to fight (für, um for); **Kampfsport** m martial art

Kanada (-s) nt Canada; **Kanadier(in)** (-s, -) m(f) Canadian; **kanadisch** adj Canadian

Kanal (-s, Kanäle) m (Fluss) canal; (Rinne, TV) channel; (für Abfluss) drain; **der ~** (Ärmelkanal) the (English) Channel; **Kanalinseln** pl Channel Islands pl; **Kanalisation** f sewerage system; **Kanaltunnel** m Channel Tunnel

Kanarienvogel m canary

Kandidat(in) (-en, -en) m(f) candidate

Kandis(zucker) (-) m rock candy

Känguru (-s, -s) nt kangaroo

Kaninchen nt rabbit

Kanister (-s, -) m can

Kännchen nt pot; **ein ~ Kaffee / Tee** a pot of coffee / tea; **Kanne** (-, -n) f (Krug) jug; (Kaffeekanne) pot; (Milchkanne) churn; (Gießkanne) can

kannte imperf von **kennen**

Kante (-, -n) f edge

Kantine f canteen

Kanton (-s, -e) m canton

Kanu (-s, -s) nt canoe

Kanzler(in) (-s, -) m(f) chancellor

Kap (-s, -s) nt cape

Kapazität f capacity; (Fachmann) authority

Kapelle f (Gebäude) chapel; (Mus) band

Kaper (-, -n) f caper

kapieren vt, vi (fam) to understand; **kapiert?** got it?

Kapital (-s, -e o -ien) nt capital

Kapitän (-s, -e) m captain

Kapitel (-s, -) nt chapter

Kappe (-, -n) f cap

Kapsel (-, -n) f capsule

kaputt adj (fam) broken; (Mensch) exhausted, **kaputtgehen** irr vi to break; (Schuhe) to fall apart; (Firma) to go bust; (Stoff) to wear out; **ka-**

putt|machen vt to break; (jdn) to wear out

Kapuze (-, -n) f hood

Kap Verde (-s) nt Cape Verde

Karaffe (-, -n) f carafe; (mit Stöpsel) decanter

Karambole (-, -n) f star fruit, carambola

Karamell (-s) m caramel, toffee

Karaoke (-(s)) nt karaoke

Karat (-s, -e) nt carat

Karate (-s) nt karate

Kardinal (-s, Kardinäle) m cardinal

Karfreitag m Good Friday

kariert adj checked; (Papier) squared

Karies (-) f (tooth) decay

Karikatur f caricature

Karneval (-s, -e o -s) m carnival

● **KARNEVAL**

● **Karneval** is the name given to the
● days immediately before Lent
● when people gather to sing,
● dance, eat, drink and generally
● make merry before the fasting
● begins. **Rosenmontag**, the day
● before Shrove Tuesday, is the most
● important day of 'Karneval' on the
● Rhine. Most firms take a day's
● holiday on that day to enjoy the
● parades and revelry. In South
● Germany 'Karneval' is called
● **Fasching**.

Kärnten (-s) nt Carinthia

Karo (-s, -s) nt square; (Karten) diamonds pl

Karosserie f (Auto) body(work)

Karotte (-, -n) f carrot

Karpfen (-s, -) m carp

Karriere (-, -n) f career

Karte (-, -n) f card; (Landkarte) map; (Speisekarte) menu; (Eintrittskarte, Fahrkarte) ticket; **mit ~ bezahlen** to pay by credit card; **~n spielen** to

play cards; **die ~n mischen/geben** to shuffle/deal the cards

Kartei f card index; **Karteikarte** f index card

Kartenspiel nt card game; **Kartentelefon** nt cardphone; **Kartenvorverkauf** m advance booking

Kartoffel (-, -n) f potato; **Kartoffelbrei** m mashed potatoes pl; **Kartoffelchips** pl crisps pl (BRIT), chips pl (US); **Kartoffelpuffer** m potato cake (made from grated potatoes); **Kartoffelpüree** m mashed potatoes pl; **Kartoffelsalat** m potato salad

Karton (-s, -s) m cardboard; (Schachtel) (cardboard) box

Kartusche (-, -n) f cartridge

Karussell (-s, -s) nt roundabout (BRIT), merry-go-round

Kaschmir (-s, e) m (Stoff) cashmere

Käse (-s, -) m cheese; **Käsekuchen** m cheesecake; **Käseplatte** f cheeseboard

Kasino (-s, -s) nt (Spielkasino) casino

Kaskoversicherung f comprehensive insurance

Kasper(l) (-s, -) m Punch; (fig) clown; **Kasperl(e)theater** nt (Vorstellung) Punch and Judy show; (Gebäude) Punch and Judy theatre

Kasse (-, -n) f (in Geschäft) till, cash register; (im Supermarkt) checkout; (Geldkasten) cashbox; (Theater) box office; (Kino) ticket office; (Krankenkasse) health insurance; (Spar~) savings bank; **Kassenbon** (-s, -s) m, **Kassenzettel** m receipt; **Kassenzettel** m receipt

Kassette f (small) box; (Tonband) cassette; **Kassettenrekorder** m cassette recorder

kassieren vt to take ▷ vi **darf ich ~?** would you like to pay now?; **Kassierer(in)** m(f) cashier

Kastanie f chestnut

Kasten (-s, Kästen) m (Behälter) box; (Getränkekasten) crate

Kat m abk = **Katalysator**

Katalog (-(e)s, -e) m catalogue

Katalysator m (Auto) catalytic converter; (fig) catalyst

Katar (-s) nt Qatar

Katarr(h) (-s, -e) m catarrh

Katastrophe (-, n) f catastrophe, disaster

Kategorie (-, n) f category

Kater (-s, -) m tomcat; (fam: nach zu viel Alkohol) hangover

Kathedrale (-, -n) f cathedral

Katholik(in) m(f) Catholic; **katholisch** adj Catholic

Katze (-, -n) f cat

Kauderwelsch (-(s)) nt (unverständlich) gibberish; (Fachjargon) jargon

kauen vt, vi to chew

Kauf (-(e)s, Käufe) m purchase; (Kaufen) buying; **ein guter ~** a bargain; **etw in ~ nehmen** to put up with sth; **kaufen** vt to buy; **Käufer(in)** m(f) buyer; **Kauffrau** f businesswoman; **Kaufhaus** nt department store; **Kaufmann** m businessman; (im Einzelhandel) shopkeeper (BRIT), storekeeper (US); **Kaufpreis** m purchase price; **Kaufvertrag** m purchase agreement

Kaugummi m chewing gum

Kaulquappe (-, -n) f tadpole

kaum adv hardly, scarcely

Kaution f deposit; (Jur) bail

Kaviar m caviar

KB (-, -) nt, **Kbyte** (-, -) nt abk = **Kilobyte** KB

Kebab (-(s), -s) m kebab

Kegel (-s, -) m skittle; (beim Bowling) pin; (Math) cone; **Kegelbahn** f bowling alley; **kegeln** vi to play skittles; (bowlen) to bowl

Kehle (-, -n) f throat; **Kehlkopf** m larynx

Kehre (-, -n) f sharp bend

kehren vt (fegen) to sweep

Keilriemen m (Auto) fan belt

kein pron no, not ... any; **ich habe ~ Geld** I have no money, I don't have any; **~ Mensch** no one; **du bist ~ Kind mehr** you're not a child any more; **keine(r, s)** pron (Person) no one, nobody; (Sache) not any, none; **~r von ihnen** none of them; (bei zwei Personen/Sachen) neither of them; **ich will keins von beiden** I don't want either (of them); **keinesfalls** adv on no account, under no circumstances

Keks (-es, -e) m biscuit (BRIT), cookie (US); **jdm auf den ~ gehen** (fam) to get on sb's nerves

Keller (-s, -) m cellar; (Geschoss) basement

Kellner (-s, -) m waiter; **Kellnerin** f waitress

Kenia (-s) nt Kenya

kennen (kannte, gekannt) vt to know; **wir ~ uns seit 1990** we've known each other since 1990; **wir ~ uns schon** we've already met; **kennst du mich noch?** do you remember me?; **~ lernen** to get to know; **sich ~ lernen** to get to know each other; (zum ersten Mal) to meet; **Kenntnis** f knowledge; **seine ~se** his knowledge

Kennwort nt (a. Inform) password; **Kennzeichen** nt mark, sign; (Auto) number plate (BRIT), license plate (US); **besondere ~** distinguishing marks

Kerl (-s, -e) m guy, bloke (BRIT)

Kern (-(e)s, -e) m (Obst) pip; (Pfirsich, Kirsche etc) stone; (Nuss) kernel; (Atomkern) nucleus; (fig) heart, core; **Kernenergie** f nuclear energy; **Kernkraft** f nuclear power; **Kernkraftwerk** nt nuclear power station

Kerze (-, -n) f candle; (*Zündkerze*) plug

Ket(s)chup (-(s), -s) m ont ketchup

Kette (-, -n) f chain; (*Halskette*) necklace

keuchen vi to pant; **Keuchhusten** m whooping cough

Keule (-, -n) f club; (*Gastr*) leg; (*von Hähnchen a.*) drumstick

Keyboard (-s, -s) nt (*Mus*) keyboard

Kfz nt abk = **Kraftfahrzeug**

Kfz-Brief m ≈ logbook

Kfz-Steuer f ≈ road tax (*BRIT*), vehicle tax (*US*)

KG (-, -s) f abk = **Kommanditgesellschaft** limited partnership

Kichererbse f chick pea

kichern vi to giggle

Kickboard® (-s, -s) nt micro scooter

Kicker (-s, -) m (*Spiel*) table football (*BRIT*), foosball (*US*)

kidnappen vt to kidnap

Kidney-Bohne f kidney bean

Kiefer (-s, -) m jaw ▷ (-, -n) f pine

Kieme (-, -n) f gill

Kies (-es, -e) m gravel; **Kiesel** (-s, -) m, **Kieselstein** m pebble

kiffen vi (*fam*) to smoke pot

Kilo (-s, -(s)) nt kilo; **Kilobyte** nt kilobyte; **Kilogramm** nt kilogram; **Kilojoule** nt kilojoule; **Kilometer** m kilometre; **Kilometerstand** m ≈ mileage; **Kilometerzähler** m ≈ mileometer; **Kilowatt** nt kilowatt

Kind (-(e)s, -er) nt child; **sie bekommt ein ~** she's having a baby; **Kinderarzt** m, **Kinderärztin** f paediatrician; **Kinderbetreuung** f childcare; **Kinderbett** nt cot (*BRIT*), crib (*US*); **Kinderfahrkarte** f child's ticket; **Kindergarten** m nursery school, kindergarten; **Kindergärtnerin** f nursery-school teacher; **Kindergeld** nt child benefit; **Kin-**

derkrankheit f children's illness; **Kinderkrippe** f crèche (*BRIT*), day-care center (*US*); **Kinderlähmung** f polio; **Kindermädchen** nt nanny (*BRIT*), nurse(maid); **kindersicher** adj childproof; **Kindersicherung** f childproof safety catch; (*an Flasche*) childproof cap; **Kindersitz** m child seat; **Kindertagesstätte** f day nursery; **Kinderteller** m (*im Restaurant*) children's portion; **Kinderwagen** m pram (*BRIT*), baby carriage (*US*); **Kinderzimmer** nt children's (bed)room; **Kindheit** f childhood; **kindisch** adj childish; **kindlich** adj childlike

Kinn (-(e)s, -e) nt chin

Kino (-s, -s) nt cinema (*BRIT*), movie theater (*US*); **ins ~ gehen** to go to the cinema (*BRIT*) (o to the movies (*US*))

Kiosk (-(e)s, -e) m kiosk

Kippe f (*fam: Zigarettenstummel*) cigarette end, fag end (*BRIT*)

kippen vi to tip over ▷ vt to tilt; (*Regierung, Minister*) to topple

Kirche (-, -n) f church; **Kirchturm** m church tower; (*mit Spitze*) steeple

Kirmes (-, -sen) f fair

Kirsche (-, -n) f cherry; **Kirschtomate** f cherry tomato

Kissen (-s, -) nt cushion; (*Kopfkissen*) pillow; **Kissenbezug** m cushion cover; (*für Kopfkissen*) pillowcase

Kiste (-, -n) f box; (*Truhe*) chest

kitschig adj kitschy, cheesy

kitzelig adj (a. fig) ticklish; **kitzeln** vt, vi to tickle

Kiwi (-, -s) f (*Frucht*) kiwi (fruit)

Klage (-, -n) f complaint; (*Jur*) lawsuit; **klagen** vi to complain (*über +akk* about, *bei* to); **kläglich** adj wretched

Klammer (-, -n) f (*in Text*) bracket; (*Büroklammer*) clip; (*Wäscheklammer*) peg (*BRIT*), clothespin (*US*); (*Zahn-*

klammer) brace; **Klammeraffe** m (fam) at-sign, @; **klammern** vr **sich ~ to** cling (an +akk to)

klang imperf von **klingen**

Klang (-(e)s, Klänge) m sound

Klappbett nt folding bed

klappen vi impers (gelingen) to work; **es hat gut geklappt** it went well

klappern vi to rattle (Geschirr) to clatter; **Klapperschlange** f rattlesnake

Klappfahrrad nt folding bicycle; **Klappstuhl** m folding chair

klar adj clear; **sich** (dat) **im Klaren sein** to be clear (über +akk about), **alles ~?** everything okay?

klären vt (Flüssigkeit) to purify; (Probleme, Frage) to clarify ▷ vr **sich ~** to clear itself up

Klarinette (-, -n) f clarinet

klar|kommen irr vi **mit etw ~** to cope with something; **kommst du klar?** are you managing all right?; **mit jdm ~** to get along with sb; **klar|machen** vt **jdm etw ~** to make sth clear to sb; **Klarsichtfolie** f clingfilm (BRIT), plastic wrap (US); **klar|stellen** vt to clarify

Klärung f (von Frage, Problem) clarification

klasse adj inv (fam) great, brilliant

Klasse (-, -n) f class; (Schuljahr) form (BRIT), grade (US); **erster ~ reisen** to travel first class; **in welche ~ gehst du?** which form (BRIT) (o grade (US)) are you in?; **Klassenarbeit** f test; **Klassenlehrer(in)** m(f) class teacher; **Klassenzimmer** nt classroom

Klassik f (Zeit) classical period; (Musik) classical music

Klatsch (-(e)s, -e) m (Gerede) gossip; **klatschen** vi (schlagen) to smack; (Beifall) to applaud, to clap, (reden) to gossip; **Klatschmohn** m (corn)

poppy; **klatschnass** adj soaking (wet)

Klaue (-, -n) f claw; (fam: Schrift) scrawl; **klauen** vt (fam) to pinch

Klavier (-s, -e) nt piano

Klebeband nt adhesive tape; **kleben** vt to stick (an +akk to) ▷ vi (klebrig sein) to be sticky; **klebrig** adj sticky; **Klebstoff** m glue; **Klebstreifen** m adhesive tape

Klecks (-es, -e) m blob; (Tinte) blot

Klee (-s) m clover

Kleid ((e)s, -er) nt (Frauen~) dress; **~er** pl (Kleidung) clothes pl; **Kleiderbügel** m coat hanger; **Kleiderschrank** m wardrobe (BRIT), closet (US); **Kleidung** f clothing

klein adj small, little; (Finger) little; **mein ~er Bruder** my little (o younger) brother; **als ich noch ~ war** when I was a little boy/girl; **etw ~ schneiden** to chop sth up; **etw ~ schreiben** to write sth with a small letter; **Kleinanzeige** f classified ad; **Kleinbuchstabe** m small letter; **Kleinbus** m minibus; **Kleingeld** nt change; **Kleinigkeit** f trifle; (Zwischenmahlzeit) snack; **Kleinkind** nt toddler; **klein|schreiben** vt to write with a small letter; **Kleinstadt** f small town

Kleister (-s, -) m paste

Klempner(in) m(f) plumber

klettern vi to climb

Klettverschluss m Velcro® fastening

klicken vi (a. Inform) to click

Klient(in) (-en, -en) m(f) client

Klima (-s, -s) nt climate; **Klimaanlage** f air conditioning; **klimatisiert** adj air-conditioned

Klinge (-, -n) f blade

Klingel (-, -n) f bell; **klingeln** vi to ring

klingen (klang, geklungen) vi to sound

Klinik f clinic; (*Krankenhaus*) hospital

Klinke (-, -n) f handle

Klippe (-, -n) f cliff; (*im Meer*) reef; (*fig*) hurdle

Klischee (-s, -s) nt (*fig*) cliché

Klo (-s, -s) nt (*fam*) loo (BRIT), john (US); **Klobrille** f toilet seat; **Klopapier** nt toilet paper

klopfen vt, vi to knock; (*Herz*) to thump

Kloß (-es, Klöße) m (*im Hals*) lump; (*Gastr*) dumpling

Kloster (-s, Klöster) nt (*für Männer*) monastery; (*für Frauen*) convent

Klub (-s, -s) m club

klug adj clever

knabbern vt, vi to nibble

Knäckebrot nt crispbread

knacken vt, vi to crack

Knall (-(e)s, -e) m bang; **Knallbonbon** m cracker; **knallen** vi to bang

knapp adj (*kaum ausreichend*) scarce; (*Sieg*) narrow; ~ **bei Kasse sein** to be short of money; ~ **zwei Stunden** just under two hours

Knauf (-s, Knäufe) m knob

Knautschzone f (*Auto*) crumple zone

kneifen (kniff, gekniffen) vt, vi to pinch; (*sich drücken*) to back out (vor +dat of); **Kneifzange** f pincers pl

Kneipe (-, -n) f (*fam*) pub (BRIT), bar

Knete (-) f (*fam: Geld*) dough; **kneten** vt to knead; (*formen*) to mould

knicken vt, vi (*brechen*) to break; (*Papier*) to fold; **geknickt sein** (*fig*) to be downcast

Knie (-s, -) nt knee; **in die ~ gehen** to bend one's knees; **Kniebeuge** f knee bend; **Kniegelenk** nt knee joint; **Kniekehle** f back of the knee; **knien** vi to kneel; **Kniescheibe** f kneecap; **Knieschoner** (-s, -) m , **Knieschützer** (-s, -) m knee pad; **Kniestrumpf** m knee-

-length sock

kniff imperf von **kneifen**

knipsen vt to punch; (*Foto*) to snap ▷ vi (*Foto*) to take snaps

knirschen vi to crunch; **mit den Zähnen** ~ to grind one's teeth

knitterfrei adj non-crease; **knittern** vi to crease

Knoblauch m garlic; **Knoblauchbrot** nt garlic bread; **Knoblauchzehe** f clove of garlic

Knöchel (-s, -) m (*Finger*) knuckle; (*Fuß*) ankle

Knochen (-s, -) m bone; **Knochenbruch** m fracture; **Knochenmark** nt marrow

Knödel (-s, -) m dumpling

Knollensellerie m celeriac

Knopf (-(e)s, Knöpfe) m button; **Knopfdruck** m **auf** ~ at the touch of a button; **Knopfloch** nt buttonhole

Knospe (-, -n) f bud

knoten vt to knot; **Knoten** (-s, -) m knot; (*Med*) lump

Know-how (-(s)) nt know-how, expertise

knurren vi (*Hund*) to growl; (*Magen*) to rumble; (*Mensch*) to grumble

knusprig adj crisp; (*Keks*) crunchy

knutschen vi (*fam*) to smooch

k. o. adj inv (*Sport*) knocked out; (*fig*) knackered

Koalition f coalition

Koch (-(e)s, Köche) m cook; **Kochbuch** nt cookery book, cookbook; **kochen** vt, vi to cook; (*Wasser*) to boil; (*Kaffee, Tee*) to make; **Köchin** f cook; **Kochlöffel** m wooden spoon; **Kochnische** f kitchenette; **Kochplatte** f hotplate; **Kochrezept** nt recipe; **Kochtopf** m saucepan

Kode (-s, -s) m code

Köder (-s, -) m bait

Koffein (-s) nt caffeine; **koffeinfrei** adj decaffeinated

Koffer (s,) m (suit)case; **Kofferraum** m (Auto) boot (BRIT), trunk (US)

Kognak (-s, -s) m brandy

Kohl (-(e)s, -e) m cabbage

Kohle (-, -n) f coal; (Holzkohle) charcoal; (Chem) carbon; (fam: Geld) cash, dough; **Kohlehydrat** nt carbohydrate; **Kohlendioxid** nt carbon dioxide; **Kohlensäure** f (in Getränken) fizz; **ohne ~** still, non-carbonated (US); **mit ~** sparkling, carbonated (US); **Kohletablette** f charcoal tablet

Kohlrabi (-(s), -(s)) m kohlrabi

Kohlrübe f swede (BRIT), rutabaga (US)

Koje (-, -n) f cabin; (Bett) bunk

Kokain (-s) nt cocaine

Kokosnuss f coconut

Kolben (s,) m (Tech) piston; (Mais~) cob

Kolik (-, -en) f colic

Kollaps (-es, -e) m collapse

Kollege (-n, -n) m, **Kollegin** f colleague

Köln (-s) nt Cologne

Kolonne (-, -n) f convoy; **in ~ fahren** to drive in convoy

Kölsch (-, -) nt (Bier) (strong) lager (from the Cologne region)

Kolumbien (s) nt Columbia

Koma (-s, -s) nt coma

Kombi (-(s), -s) m estate (car) (BRIT), station wagon (US); **Kombination** f combination; (Folgerung) deduction; (Hemdhose) combinations pl; (Aviat) flying suit; **kombinieren** vt to combine b vi to reason; (vermuten) to guess; **Kombizange** f (pair of) pliers pl

Komfort (-s) m conveniences pl; (Bequemlichkeit) comfort

Komiker(in) m(f) comedian, comic; **komisch** adj funny

Komma (-s, -s) nt comma

Kommanditgesellschaft f limited partnership

kommen (kam, gekommen) vi to come; (näher kommen) to approach; (passieren) to happen; (gelangen, geraten) to get; (erscheinen) to appear; (in die Schule, das Gefängnis etc) to go: **~ lassen** to send for: **zu sich ~** to come round (o to); **zu etw ~** (bo kommen) to acquire sth; (Zeit dazu finden) to get round to sth; **wer kommt zuerst?** who's first?; kommend adj coming; **~e Woche** next week; **in den ~en Jahren** in the years to come

Kommentar m commentary; **kein ~** no comment

Kommilitone (-n, -n) m, **Kommilitonin** f fellow student

Kommissar(in) m(f) inspector

Kommode (-, -n) f chest of drawers

Kommunikation f communication

Kommunion f (Rel) communion

Kommunismus m communism

Komödie f comedy

kompakt adj compact

Kompass (-es, -e) m compass

kompatibel adj compatible

kompetent adj competent

komplett adj complete

Kompliment nt compliment, **jdm ein ~ machen** to pay sb a compliment; **~!** congratulations

Komplize (-n, -n) m accomplice

kompliziert adj complicated

Komponist(in) m(f) composer

Kompost (-(e)s, -e) m compost; **Komposthaufen** m compost heap; **kompostierbar** adj biodegradable

Kompott (-(e)s, -e) nt stewed fruit

Kompresse (-, -n) f compress

Kompromiss (-es, -e) m compromise

Kondensmilch f condensed milk, evaporated milk

Kondition f (*Leistungsfähigkeit*) condition; **sie hat eine gute ~** she's in good shape

Konditorei f cake shop; (*mit Café*) café

Kondom (*-s, -e*) nt condom

Konfektionsgröße f size

Konferenz f conference

Konfession f religion; (*christlich*) denomination

Konfetti (*-(s)*) nt confetti

Konfirmation f (*Rel*) confirmation

Konfitüre (*-, -n*) f jam

Konflikt (*-(e)s, -e*) m conflict

konfrontieren vt to confront

Kongo (*-s*) m Congo

Kongress (*-es, -e*) m conference; **der ~** (*Parlament der USA*) Congress

König (*-(e)s, -e*) m king; **Königin** f queen; **Königinpastete** f vol-au-vent; **königlich** adj royal; **Königreich** nt kingdom

Konkurrenz f competition

können (*konnte, gekonnt*) vt, vi to be able to, can; (*wissen*) to know; **~ Sie Deutsch?** can (o do) you speak German?; **ich kann nicht kommen** I can't come; **das kann sein** that's possible; **ich kann nicht mehr** (*essen / weitergehen*) I can't eat any more / carry on; **ich kann nichts dafür** it's not my fault

konsequent adj consistent; **Konsequenz** f consequence

konservativ adj conservative

Konserven pl tinned food sing (*BRIT*), canned food sing; **Konservendose** f tin (*BRIT*), can

konservieren vt to preserve; **Konservierungsmittel** nt preservative

Konsonant m consonant

Konsul(in) (*-s, -n*) m(f) consul; **Konsulat** nt consulate

Kontakt (*-(e)s, -e*) m contact; **kontaktarm** adj **er ist ~** he lacks

contact with other people; **kontaktfreudig** adj sociable; **Kontaktlinsen** pl contact lenses pl

Kontinent m continent

Konto (*-s, Konten*) nt account; **Kontoauszug** m (bank) statement; **Kontoauszugsdrucker** m bank-statement machine; **Kontoinhaber(in)** m(f) account holder; **Kontonummer** f account number; **Kontostand** m balance

Kontrabass m double bass

Kontrast (*-(e)s, -e*) m contrast

Kontrolle (*-, -n*) f control; (*Aufsicht*) supervision; (*Passkontrolle*) passport control; **kontrollieren** vt to control; (*nachprüfen*) to check

Konzentration f concentration; **Konzentrationslager** nt (*Hist*) concentration camp; **konzentrieren** vt to concentrate ▷ vr **sich ~** to concentrate

Konzept (*-(e)s, -e*) nt rough draft; **jdn aus dem ~ bringen** to put sb off

Konzert (*-(e)s, -e*) nt concert; (*Stück*) concerto; **Konzertsaal** m concert hall

koordinieren vt to coordinate

Kopf (*-(e)s, Köpfe*) m head; **pro ~** per person; **sich den ~ zerbrechen** to rack one's brains; **Kopfhörer** m headphones pl; **Kopfkissen** nt pillow; **Kopfsalat** m lettuce; **Kopfschmerzen** pl headache sing; **Kopfstütze** f headrest; **Kopftuch** nt headscarf; **kopfüber** adv headfirst

Kopie f copy; **kopieren** vt (a. Inform) to copy; **Kopierer** (*-s, -*) m, **Kopiergerät** nt copier

Kopilot(in) m(f) co-pilot

Koralle (*-, -n*) f coral

Koran (*-s*) m (*Rel*) Koran

Korb (*-(e)s, Körbe*) m basket; **jdm einen ~ geben** (*fig*) to turn sb down

Kord (*-(e)s, -e*) m corduroy

Kordel (-, -n) f cord

Korinthe (e, n) f currant

Kork (-(e)s, -e) m cork; **Korken** (-s, -) m cork; **Korkenzieher** (-s, -) m corkscrew

Korn (-(e)s, Körner) nt grain; **Kornblume** f cornflower

Körper (-s, -) m body, **Körperbau** m build; **Körperbehindert** adj disabled; **Körpergeruch** m body odour; **Körpergröße** f height; **körperlich** adj physical; **Körperteil** m part of the body; **Körperverletzung** f physical injury

korrekt adj correct

Korrespondent(in) m(f) correspondent; **Korrespondenz** f correspondence

korrigieren vt to correct

Kosmetik f cosmetics pl; **Kosmetikkoffer** m vanity case; **Kosmetiksalon** m beauty parlour; **Kosmetiktuch** nt paper tissue

Kost (-) f (Nahrung) food; (Verpflegung) board

kostbar adj precious; (teuer) costly, expensive

kosten vt to cost ▷ vt, vi (versuchen) to taste; **Kosten** pl costs pl, cost; (Ausgaben) expenses pl; **auf ~ von** at the expense of; **kostenlos** adj free (of charge); **Kostenvoranschlag** m estimate

köstlich adj (Essen) delicious; (Einfall) delightful; **sich ~ amüsieren** to have a marvellous time

Kostprobe f taster; (fig) sample; **kostspielig** adj expensive

Kostüm (-s, -e) nt costume; (Damenkostüm) suit

Kot (-(e)s) m excrement

Kotelett (-(e)s, -e o -s) nt chop, cutlet

Koteletten pl sideboards pl (BRIT), sideburns pl (US)

Kotflügel m (Auto) wing

kotzen vi (vulg) to puke, to throw up

Krabbe (-, -n) f shrimp; (größer) prawn; (Krebs) crab

krabbeln vi to crawl

Krach (-(e)s, s o -e) m crash; (andauernd) noise; (fam: Streit) row

Kraft (-, Kräfte) f strength; (Pol, Phys) force; (Fähigkeit) power; (Arbeits-) worker; **in ~ treten** to come into effect; **Kraftausdruck** m swearword; **Kraftfahrzeug** nt motor vehicle; **Kraftfahrzeugbrief** m ~ logbook; **Kraftfahrzeugschein** m vehicle registration document; **Kraftfahrzeugsteuer** f ~ road tax (BRIT), vehicle tax (US); **Kraftfahrzeugversicherung** f car insurance; **kräftig** adj strong; (gesund) healthy; (Farben) intense, strong; **Kraftstoff** m fuel; **Kraftwerk** nt power station

Kragen (-s, -) m collar

Krähe (, n) f crow

Kralle (-, -n) f claw; (Parkkralle) wheel clamp

Kram (-(e)s) m stuff

Krampf (-(e)s, Krämpfe) m cramp; (zuckend) spasm; **Krampfader** f varicose vein

Kran (-(e)s, Kräne) m crane

Kranich (-s, -e) m (Zool) crane

krank adj ill, sick

kränken vt to hurt

Krankengymnastik f physiotherapy; **Krankenhaus** nt hospital; **Krankenkasse** f health insurance; **Krankenpfleger** (-s, -) m (male) nurse; **Krankenschein** m health insurance certificate; **Krankenschwester** f nurse; **Krankenversicherung** f health insurance; **Krankenwagen** m ambulance; **Krankheit** f illness; (durch Infektion hervorgerufen) disease

Kränkung f insult

Kranz (-es, Kränze) m wreath

krass adj crass; (fam: toll) wicked

kratzen vt, vi to scratch; **Kratzer** (-s, -) m scratch

kraulen vi (schwimmen) to do the crawl ▷ vt (streicheln) to pet

Kraut (-(e)s, Kräuter) nt plant; (Gewürz) herb; (Gemüse) cabbage; **Kräuter** pl herbs pl; **Kräuterbutter** f herb butter; **Kräutertee** m herbal tea; **Krautsalat** m coleslaw

Krawatte f tie

kreativ adj creative

Krebs (-es, -e) m (Zool) crab; (Med) cancer; (Astr) Cancer

Kredit (-(e)s, -e) m credit; **auf ~** on credit; **einen ~ aufnehmen** to take out a loan; **Kreditkarte** f credit card

Kreide (-, -n) f chalk

Kreis (-es, -e) m circle; (Bezirk) district

kreischen vi to shriek; (Bremsen, Säge) to screech

Kreisel (-s, -) m (Spielzeug) top; (Verkehrskreisel) roundabout (BRIT), traffic circle (US)

Kreislauf m (Med) circulation; (fig: der Natur etc) cycle; **Kreislaufstörungen** pl (Med) **ich habe ~** I've got problems with my circulation; **Kreisverkehr** m roundabout (BRIT), traffic circle (US)

Kren (-s) m horseradish

Kresse (-, -n) f cress

Kreuz (-es, -e) nt cross; (Anat) small of the back; (Karten) clubs pl; **mir tut das ~ weh** I've got backache; **Kreuzband** m cruciate ligament; **kreuzen** vt to cross ▷ vr **sich ~** to cross ▷ vi (Naut) to cruise; **Kreuzfahrt** f cruise; **Kreuzgang** m cloisters pl; **Kreuzotter** (-, -n) f adder; **Kreuzschlitzschraubenzieher** m Phillips® screwdriver; **Kreuzschlüssel** m (Auto) wheel brace; **Kreuzschmerzen** pl backache sing; **Kreuzung** f (Verkehrskreuzung) crossroads sing, intersection; (Züchtung) cross; **Kreuzworträtsel** nt crossword (puzzle)

kriechen (kroch, gekrochen) vi to crawl; (unauffällig) to creep; (fig, pej) **(vor jdm) ~** to crawl (to sb); **Kriechspur** f crawler lane

Krieg (-(e)s, -e) m war

kriegen vt (fam) to get; (erwischen) to catch; **sie kriegt ein Kind** she's having a baby; **ich kriege noch Geld von dir** you still owe me some money

Krimi (-s, -s) m (fam) thriller; **Kriminalität** f criminality; **Kriminalpolizei** f detective force, ≈ CID (BRIT), ≈ FBI (US); **Kriminalroman** m detective novel; **kriminell** adj criminal

Krippe (-, -n) f (Futterkrippe) manger; (Weihnachtskrippe) crib (BRIT), crèche (US); (Kinderkrippe) crèche (BRIT), daycare center (US)

Krise (-, -n) f crisis

Kristall (-s, -e) m crystal ▷ (-s) nt (Glas) crystal

Kritik f criticism; (Rezension) review; **Kritiker(in)** m(f) critic; **kritisch** adj critical

kritzeln vt, vi to scribble, to scrawl

Kroate (-n, -n) m Croat; **Kroatien** (-s) nt Croatia; **Kroatin** f Croat; **kroatisch** adj Croatian; **Kroatisch** nt Croatian

kroch imperf von **kriechen**

Krokodil (-s, -e) nt crocodile

Krokus (-, - o -se) m crocus

Krone (-, -n) f crown; **Kronleuchter** m chandelier

Kropf (-(e)s, Kröpfe) m (Med) goitre; (von Vogel) crop

Kröte (-, -n) f toad

Krücke (-, -n) f crutch

Krug (-(e)s, Krüge) m jug; (Bierkrug) mug

Krümel (-s, -) m crumb

krumm adj crooked

Krüppel (-s, -) m cripple

Kruste (-, -n) f crust

Kruzifix (-es, -e) nt crucifix

Kuba (-s) nt Cuba

Kübel (-s, -) m tub; (Eimer) bucket

Kubikmeter m cubic metre

Küche (-, -n) f kitchen; (Kochen) cooking

Kuchen (-s, -) m cake; (mit Teigdeckel) pie; **Kuchengabel** f cake fork

Küchenmaschine f food processor; **Küchenpapier** nt kitchen roll; **Küchenschrank** m (kitchen) cupboard

Kuckuck (-s, -e) m cuckoo

Kugel (-, -n) f ball; (Math) sphere; (Mil) bullet; (Weihnachtskugel) bauble; **Kugellager** nt ball bearing; **Kugelschreiber** m (ball-point) pen, biro® (BRIT); **Kugelstoßen** (-s) nt shot put

Kuh (-, Kühe) f cow

kühl adj cool; **Kühlakku** (-s, -s) m ice pack; **Kühlbox** f cool box; **kühlen** vt to cool, **Kühler** (-s, -) m (Auto) radiator; **Kühlerhaube** f (Auto) bonnet (BRIT), hood (US); **Kühlschrank** m fridge, refrigerator; **Kühltasche** f cool bag; **Kühltruhe** f freezer; **Kühlwasser** nt (Auto) radiator water

Kuhstall m cowshed

Kuken (-s, -) nt chick

Kuli (-s, -s) m (fam: Kugelschreiber) pen, biro® (BRIT)

Kulisse (-, -n) f scenery

Kult (-s, -e) m cult; **Kultfigur** f cult figure

Kultur f culture; (Lebensform) civilization; **Kulturbeutel** m toilet bag (BRIT), washbag; **kulturell** adj cultural

Kümmel (-s, -) m caraway seeds pl

Kummer (-s) m grief, sorrow

kümmern vr **sich um jdn ~** to look

after sb; **sich um etw ~** to see to sth; **▷ vt** to concern; **das kümmert mich nicht** that doesn't worry me

Kumpel (-s, -) m (fam) mate, pal

Kunde (-n, -n) m customer; **Kundendienst** m after-sales (o customer) service; **Kunden(lreditkarte** f storecard, chargecard; **Kundennummer** f customer number

kündigen vi to hand in one's notice; (Mieter) to give notice that one is moving out; **jdm ~** to give sb his / her notice, (Vermieter) to give sb notice to quit ▷ vt to cancel; (Vertrag) to terminate; **jdm die Stellung ~** to give sb his / her notice; **jdm die Wohnung ~** to give sb notice to quit; **Kündigung** f (Arbeitsverhältnis) dismissal; (Vertrag) termination; (Abonnement) cancellation; (Frist) notice; **Kündigungsfrist** f period of notice

Kundin f customer; **Kundschaft** f customers pl

künftig adj future

Kunst (-, Künste) f art; (Können) skill; **Kunstausstellung** f art exhibition; **Kunstgewerbe** nt arts and crafts pl; **Künstler(in)** (-s, -) m(f) artist; **künstlerisch** adj artistic

künstlich adj artificial

Kunststoff m synthetic material; **Kunststück** nt trick; **Kunstwerk** nt work of art

Kupfer (-s, -) nt copper

Kuppel (-, -n) f dome

kuppeln vi (Auto) to operate the clutch; **Kupplung** f coupling; (Auto) clutch

Kur (-, -en) f course of treatment; (am Kurort) cure

Kür (-, -en) f (Sport) free programme

Kurbel (-, -n) f crank; (von Rollo, Fenster) winder

Kürbis (-ses, -se) m pumpkin

Kurierdienst m courier service

kurieren vt to cure
Kurort m health resort
Kurs (-es, -e) m course; (Fin) rate; (Wechselkurs) exchange rate
kursiv adj italic ▷ adv in italics
Kursleiter(in) m(f) course tutor; **Kursteilnehmer(in)** m(f) (course) participant; **Kurswagen** m (Eisenb) through carriage
Kurve (-, -n) f curve; (Straßenkurve) bend; **kurvenreich** adj (Straße) winding
kurz adj short; (zeitlich a.) brief; **~ vorher / darauf** shortly before / after; **kannst du ~ kommen?** could you come here for a minute?; **~ gesagt** in short; **kurzärmelig** adj short-sleeved; **kürzen** vt to cut short; (in der Länge) to shorten; (Gehalt) to reduce; **kurzerhand** adv on the spot; **kurzfristig** adj short-term; **das Konzert wurde ~ abgesagt** the concert was called off at short notice; **Kurzgeschichte** f short story; **kurzhaarig** adj short-haired; **kürzlich** adv recently; **Kurznachrichten** pl news summary sing; **Kurzparkzone** f short-stay (BRIT) (o short-term (US)) parking zone; **Kurzschluss** m (Elek) short circuit; **kurzsichtig** adj short-sighted; **Kurzurlaub** m short holiday (BRIT), short vacation (US); **Kurzwelle** f short wave
Kusine f cousin
Kuss (-(e)s, Küsse) m kiss; **küssen** vt to kiss ▷ vr **sich ~** to kiss
Küste (-, -n) f coast; (Ufer) shore; **Küstenwache** f coastguard
Kutsche (-, -n) f carriage; (geschlossene) coach
Kuvert (-s, -s) nt envelope
Kuvertüre (-, -n) f coating
Kuwait (-s) nt Kuwait
KZ (-s, -s) nt abk = **Konzentrationslager** (Hist) concentration camp

Labor (-s, -e o -s) nt lab
Labyrinth (-s, -e) nt maze
Lache (-, -n) f (Pfütze) puddle; (Blut~, Öl~) pool
lächeln vi to smile; **Lächeln** (-s) nt smile; **lachen** vi to laugh; **lächerlich** adj ridiculous
Lachs (-es, -e) m salmon
Lack (-(e)s, -e) m varnish; (Farblack) lacquer; (an Auto) paint; **lackieren** vt to varnish; (Auto) to spray; **Lackschaden** m scratch (on the paintwork)
Ladegerät nt (battery) charger; **laden** (lud, geladen) vt (a. Inform) to load; (einladen) to invite; (Handy etc) to charge
Laden (-s, Läden) m shop; (Fensterladen) shutter; **Ladendieb(in)** m(f) shoplifter; **Ladendiebstahl** m shoplifting; **Ladenschluss** m closing time
Ladung f load; (Naut, Aviat) cargo; (Jur) summons sing
lag imperf von **liegen**

Lage (-, -n) f position, situation; (Schicht) layer; **in der ~ sein zu** to be in a position to

Lager (-s, -) nt camp; (Comm) warehouse; (Tech) bearing; **Lagerfeuer** nt campfire; **lagern** vi (Dinge) to be stored; (Menschen) to camp ▷ vt to store

Lagune f lagoon

lahm adj lame; (langweilig) dull; **lähmen** vt to paralyse; **Lähmung** f paralysis

Laib (-s, -e) m loaf

Laie (-n, -n) m layman

Laken (-s, -) nt sheet

Lakritze (-, -n) f liquorice

Lamm (-(e)s, Lämmer) nt (a. Lammfleisch) lamb

Lampe (-, -n) f lamp; (Glühbirne) bulb; **Lampenfieber** nt stage fright; **Lampenschirm** m lampshade

Lampion (-s, -s) m Chinese lantern

Land (-(e)s, Länder) nt (Gelände) land; (Nation) country; (Bundesland) state, Land; **auf dem ~(e)** in the country

● **LAND**

● A **Land** (plural **Länder**) is a
● member state of the **BRD**. There
● are 16 **Länder**, namely Baden-
● Württemberg, Bayern, Berlin,
● Brandenburg, Bremen, Hamburg,
● Hessen, Mecklenburg-Vorpom-
● mern, Niedersachsen, Nordrhein-
● Westfalen, Rheinland-Pfalz, Saar-
● land, Sachsen, Sachsen-Anhalt,
● Schleswig-Holstein and Thüringen.
● Each 'Land' has its own parliament
● and constitution.

Landebahn f runway; **landen** vt, vi to land; (Schiff) to dock

Länderspiel nt international (match)

Landesgrenze f national border,

frontier; **Landesinnere** nt interior; **landesüblich** adj customary; **Landeswährung** f national currency; **landesweit** adj nationwide

Landhaus nt country house; **Landkarte** f map; **Landkreis** m administrative region, ≈ district

ländlich adj rural

Landschaft f countryside; (schöne) scenery; (Kunst) landscape; **Landstraße** f country road, B road (BRIT)

Landung f landing; **Landungsbrücke** f, **Landungssteg** m gangway

Landwirt(in) m(f) farmer; **Landwirtschaft** f agriculture, farming; **landwirtschaftlich** adj agricultural

lang adj long; (Mensch) tall; **ein zwei Meter ~er Tisch** a table two metres long; **den ganzen Tag ~** all day long; **die Straße ~** along the street; **langärmelig** adj long-sleeved; **lange** adv (for) a long time, **ich musste ~ warten** I had to wait (for) a long time; **ich bleibe nicht ~** I won't stay long; **es ist ~ her, dass wir uns gesehen haben** it's a long time since we saw each other; **Länge** (-, -n) f length; (Geo) longitude

langen vi (fam: ausreichen) to be enough; (fam: fassen) to reach (nach for); **mir langt's** I've had enough

Langeweile f boredom

langfristig adj long-term ▷ adv in the long term

Langlauf m cross-country skiing

längs prep +gen **die Bäume ~ der Straße** the trees along(side) the road ▷ adv **die Streifen laufen ~ über das Hemd** the stripes run lengthways down the shirt

langsam adj slow ▷ adv slowly

Langschläfer(in) (-s, -) m(f) late

riser

längst adv **das ist ~ fertig** that was finished a long time ago; **sie sollte ~ da sein** she should have been here long ago; **als sie kam, waren wir ~ weg** when she arrived we had long since left

Langstreckenflug m long-haul flight

Languste (-, -n) f crayfish, crawfish (US)

langweilen vt to bore; **ich langweile mich** I'm bored; **langweilig** adj boring; **Langwelle** f long wave

Laos (-) nt Laos

Lappen (-s, -) m cloth, rag; (Staublappen) duster

läppisch adj silly; (Summe) ridiculous

Laptop (-s, -s) m laptop

Lärche (-, -n) f larch

Lärm (-(e)s) m noise

las imperf von **lesen**

Lasche (-, -n) f flap

Laser (-s, -) m laser; **Laserdrucker** m laser printer

lassen (ließ, gelassen) vi, vt (erlauben) to let; (an einem Ort, in einem Zustand) to leave; (aufhören mit) to stop; **etw machen ~** to have sth done; **sich** (dat) **die Haare schneiden ~** to have one's hair cut; **jdn etw machen ~** to make sb do sth; **lass das!** stop it!; **es lässt sich machen** it's doable

lässig adj casual

Last (-, -en) f load; (Bürde) burden; (Naut, Aviat) cargo

Laster (-s, -) nt vice; (fam) truck, lorry (BRIT)

lästern vi **über jdn/etw ~** to make nasty remarks about sb / sth

lästig adj annoying; (Person) tiresome

Last-Minute-Flug m last-minute flight; **Last-Minute-Ticket** nt last-minute ticket

Lastwagen m truck, lorry (BRIT)

Latein (-s) nt Latin

Laterne (-, -n) f lantern; (Straßenlaterne) streetlight

Latte (-, -n) f slat; (Sport) bar

Latz (-es, Lätze) m bib; **Lätzchen** nt bib; **Latzhose** f dungarees pl

lau adj (Wind, Luft) mild

Laub (-(e)s) nt foliage; **Laubfrosch** m tree frog; **Laubsäge** f fretsaw

Lauch (-(e)s, -e) m leeks pl; **eine Stange ~** a leek; **Lauchzwiebel** f spring onions pl (BRIT), scallions pl (US)

Lauf (-(e)s, Läufe) m run; (Wettlauf) race; (Entwicklung) course; (Schach) barrel; **Laufbahn** f career; **laufen** (lief, gelaufen) vi, vt to run; (gehen) to walk; (funktionieren) to work; **mir läuft die Nase** my nose is running; **was läuft im Kino?** what's on at the cinema?; **wie läuft's so?** how are things?; **laufend** adj running; (Monat, Ausgaben) current; **auf dem Laufenden sein/halten** to be/to keep up-to-date; **Läufer** (-s, -) m (Teppich) rug; (Schach) bishop; **Läufer(in)** m(f) (Sport) runner; **Laufmasche** f ladder (BRIT), run (US); **Laufwerk** nt (Inform) drive

Laune (-, -n) f mood; **gute/schlechte ~ haben** to be in a good / bad mood; **launisch** adj moody

Laus (-, Läuse) f louse

lauschen vi to listen; (heimlich) to eavesdrop

laut adj loud ▷ adv loudly; (lesen) aloud ▷ prep +gen o dat according to

läuten vt, vi to ring

lauter adv (fam: nichts als) nothing but

Lautsprecher m loudspeaker; **Lautstärke** f loudness; (Radio, Tv) volume

lauwarm adj lukewarm

Lava (-, Laven) f lava

Lavendel (-s, -) m lavender

Lawine f avalanche

LCD-Anzeige f LCD-display

leasen vt to lease; **Leasing** (-s) nt leasing

leben vt, vi to live; **(am Leben** *sein*) to be alive; **wie lange ~ Sie schon hier?** how long have you been living here?; **von ... ~** *(Nahrungsmittel etc)* to live on ...; *(Beruf, Beschäftigung)* to make one's living from ...; **Leben** (-s, -) nt life; **lebend** adj living; **lebendig** adj alive; *(lebhaft)* lively; **lebensgefährlich** adj very dangerous; *(Verletzung)* critical; **Lebensgefährte** m, **Lebensgefährtin** f partner; **Lebenshaltungskosten** pl cost sing of living; **lebenslänglich** adj for life; **~ bekommen** to get life; **Lebenslauf** m curriculum vitae (BRIT), CV (BRIT), resumé (US); **Lebensmittel** pl food sing; **Lebensmittelgeschäft** nt grocer's (shop); **Lebensmittelvergiftung** f food poisoning; **lebensnotwendig** adj vital; **Lebensretter(in)** m(f) rescuer; **Lebensstandard** m standard of living; **Lebensunterhalt** m livelihood; **Lebensversicherung** f life insurance (assurance (BRIT)); **Lebenszeichen** nt sign of life

Leber (-, -n) f liver; **Leberfleck** m mole; **Leberpastete** f liver pâté

Lebewesen nt living being

lebhaft adj lively; *(Erinnerung, Eindruck)* vivid; **Lebkuchen** m gingerbread; **ein ~** a piece of gingerbread; **leblos** adj lifeless

Leck nt leak

lecken vi *(Loch haben)* to leak ▷ vt, vi *(schlecken)* to lick

lecker adj delicious, tasty

Leder (-s, -) nt leather

ledig adj single

leer adj empty; *(Seite)* blank; *(Bat-*

terie) dead; **leeren** vt to empty ▷ vr **sich ~** to empty; **Leerlauf** m *(Gang)* neutral; **Leertaste** f space bar; **Leerung** f emptying; *(Postkasten)* collection; **Leerzeichen** nt blank, space

legal adj legal, lawful

legen vt to put, to place; *(Eier)* to lay ▷ vr **sich ~** to lie down; *(Sturm, Begeisterung)* to die down; *(Schmerz, Gefühl)* to wear off

Legende (-, -n) f legend

leger adj casual

Lehm (-(e)s, -e) m loam; *(Ton)* clay

Lehne (-, -n) f arm(rest); *(Rückenlehne)* back(rest); **lehnen** vt to lean ▷ vr **sich ~** to lean *(an/gegen +akk* against); **Lehnstuhl** m armchair

Lehrbuch nt textbook; **Lehre** (-, -n) f teaching; *(berufliche)* apprenticeship; *(moralisch)* lesson; **lehren** vt to teach; **Lehrer(in)** (-s, -) m(f) teacher; **Lehrgang** m course; **Lehrling** m apprentice; **lehrreich** adj instructive

Leib (-(e)s, -er) m body; **Leibgericht** nt, **Leibspeise** f favourite dish; **Leibwächter(in)** m(f) bodyguard

Leiche (-, -n) f corpse; **Leichenhalle** f mortuary; **Leichenwagen** m hearse

leicht adj light; *(einfach)* easy, simple; *(Erkrankung)* slight; **jdm ~ fallen** to be easy for sb; **es sich (dat) ~ machen** to take the easy way out ▷ adv *(mühelos, schnell)* easily; *(geringfügig)* slightly; **Leichtathletik** f athletics sing; **leichtsinnig** adj careless; *(stärker)* reckless

leid adj **jdn/etw ~ sein** to be tired of sb/sth; **Leid** (-(e)s) nt grief, sorrow; **es tut mir/ihm ~** I'm/he's sorry; **er tut mir ~** I'm sorry for him; **~ tun**: *siehe auch* **leidtun**; **leiden** *(litt, gelitten)* vi, vt to suffer *(an, unter +dat* from); **ich kann ihn/es nicht**

~ I can't stand him / it; **Leiden** (-s, -)
nt suffering; (Krankheit) illness
Leidenschaft f passion; **leiden-**
schaftlich adj passionate
leider adv unfortunately; **wir**
müssen jetzt ~ gehen I'm afraid we
have to go now; **~ ja / nein** I'm
afraid so / not
leidtun vi **es tut mir / ihm ~**
I'm / he's sorry; **er tut mir ~** I'm sorry
for him
Leihbücherei f lending library
leihen (lieh, geliehen) vt **jdm etw ~**
to lend sb sth; **sich** (dat) **etw von**
jdm ~ to borrow sth from sb;
Leihfrist f lending period; **Leih-**
gebühr f hire charge; (für Buch)
lending charge; **Leihwagen** m hire
car (BRIT), rental car (US)
Leim (-(e)s, -e) m glue
Leine (-, -n) f cord; (für Wäsche) line;
(Hundeleine) lead (BRIT), leash (US)
Leinen (-s, -) nt linen; **Leintuch** nt
(für Bett) sheet; **Leinwand** f (Kunst)
canvas; (Cine) screen
leise adj quiet; (sanft) soft ▷ adv
quietly
Leiste (-, -n) f ledge; (Zierleiste) strip;
(Anat) groin
leisten vt (Arbeit) to do; (vollbrin-
gen) to achieve; **jdm Gesellschaft ~**
to keep sb company; **sich** (dat) **etw**
~ (gönnen) to treat oneself to sth; **ich**
kann es mir nicht ~ I can't afford it
Leistenbruch m hernia
Leistung f performance; (gute)
achievement
Leitartikel m leading article
(BRIT), editorial (US)
leiten vt to lead; (Firma) to run; (in
eine Richtung) to direct; (Elek) to
conduct
Leiter (-, -n) f ladder
Leiter(in) (-s, -) m(f) (von Geschäft)
manager
Leitplanke (-, -n) f crash barrier

Leitung f (Führung) direction; (Tel)
line; (von Firma) management;
(Wasserleitung) pipe; (Kabel) cable;
eine lange ~ haben to be slow on
the uptake; **Leitungswasser** nt
tap water
Lektion f lesson
Lektüre (-, -n) f (Lesen) reading;
(Lesestoff) reading matter
Lende (-, -n) f (Speise) loin; (vom
Rind) sirloin; **die ~n** pl (Med) the
lumbar region sing
lenken vt to steer; (Blick) to direct
(auf +akk towards); **jds Aufmerk-**
samkeit auf etw ~ to draw
sb's attention to sth; **Lenker** m
(von Fahrrad, Motorrad) handlebars pl;
Lenkrad nt steering wheel; **Lenk-**
radschloss nt steering lock;
Lenkstange f handlebars pl
Leopard (-en, -en) m leopard
Lepra (-) f leprosy
Lerche (-, -n) f lark
lernen vt, vi to learn; (für eine
Prüfung) to study, to revise
lesbisch adj lesbian
Lesebuch nt reader; **lesen** (las,
gelesen) vt, vi to read; (ernten) to
pick; **Leser(in)** m(f) reader; **Le-**
serbrief m letter to the editor;
leserlich adj legible; **Lesezeichen**
nt bookmark
Lettland nt Latvia
letzte(r, s) adj last; (neueste) latest; (endgültig) final; **zum ~n Mal** for
the last time; **am ~n Montag** last
Monday; **in ~r Zeit** lately, recently;
letztens adv (vor kurzem) recently;
letztere(r, s) adj the latter
Leuchtanzeige f illuminated
display; **Leuchte** (-, -n) f lamp,
light; **leuchten** vi to shine; (Feuer,
Zifferblatt) to glow; **Leuchter** (-s, -)
m candlestick; **Leuchtfarbe** f fluorescent colour; (Anstrichfarbe) luminous paint; **Leuchtreklame** f

neon sign; **Leuchtstift** *m* highlighter; **Leuchtstoffröhre** *f* strip light; **Leuchtturm** *m* lighthouse

leugnen *vt* to deny ▷ *vi* to deny everything

Leukämie *f* leukaemia (*BRIT*), leukemia (*US*)

Leukoplast® *(-(e)s, -e)* *nt* Elastoplast® (*BRIT*), Band-Aid® (*US*)

Leute *pl* people *pl*

Lexikon *(-s, Lexika)* *nt* encyclopaedia (*BRIT*), encyclopedia (*US*); (*Wörterbuch*) dictionary

Libanon *(-s)* *m* **der ~** Lebanon

Libelle *f* dragonfly

liberal *adj* liberal

Libyen *(-s)* *nt* Libya

Licht *(-(e)s, -er)* *nt* light; **Lichtblick** *m* ray of hope; **lichtempfindlich** *adj* sensitive to light; **Lichtempfindlichkeit** *f* (*Foto*) speed; **Lichthupe** *f* **die ~ betätigen** to flash one's lights; **Lichtjahr** *nt* light year; **Lichtmaschine** *f* dynamo; **Lichtschalter** *m* light switch; **Lichtschranke** *f* light barrier; **Lichtschutzfaktor** *m* sun protection factor, SPF

Lichtung *f* clearing

Lid *(-(e)s, -er)* *nt* eyelid; **Lidschatten** *m* eyeshadow

lieb *adj* (*nett*) nice; (*teuer, geliebt*) dear; (*liebenswert*) sweet; **das ist ~ von dir** that's nice of you; **Lieber Herr X** Dear Mr X; **Liebe** *(-, -n)* *f* love; **lieben** *vt* to love; (*sexuell*) to make love to; **liebenswürdig** *adj* kind; **lieber** *adv* rather; **ich möchte ~ nicht** I'd rather not; **welches ist dir ~?** which one do you prefer?; *siehe auch* **gern, lieb**; **Liebesbrief** *m* love letter; **Liebeskummer** *m* **haben** to be lovesick; **Liebespaar** *nt* lovers *pl*; **liebevoll** *adj* loving; **Liebhaber(in)** *(-s, -)* *m(f)* lover; **lieblich** *adj* lovely;

(*Wein*) sweet; **Liebling** *m* darling; (*Günstling*) favourite; **Lieblings-** *in zW* favourite; **liebste(r, s)** *adj* favourite; **liebsten** *adv* **am ~ esse ich ...** my favourite food is ...; **am ~ würde ich bleiben** I'd really like to stay

Liechtenstein *(-s)* *nt* Liechtenstein

Lied *(-(e)s, -er)* *nt* song; (*Rel*) hymn

lief *imperf von* **laufen**

Lieferant(in) *m(f)* supplier

lieferbar *adj* available

liefern *vt* to deliver; (*beschaffen*) to supply

Lieferschein *m* delivery note; **Lieferung** *f* delivery; **Lieferwagen** *m* delivery van

Liege *(-, -n)* *f* (*beim Arzt*) couch; (*Notbett*) campbed; (*Gartenliege*) lounger; **liegen** (*lag, gelegen*) *vi* to lie; (*sich befinden*) to be; **mir liegt nichts / viel daran** it doesn't matter to me / it matters a lot to me; **woran liegt es nur, dass ...?** why is it that ...?; **~ bleiben** (*Mensch*) to stay lying down; (*im Bett*) to stay in bed; (*Ding*) to be left (behind); **~ lassen** (*vergessen*) to leave behind; **Liegestuhl** *m* deck chair; **Liegestütz** *m* press-up (*BRIT*), push-up (*US*); **Liegewagen** *m* (*Eisenb*) couchette car

lieh *imperf von* **leihen**

ließ *imperf von* **lassen**

Lift *(-(e)s, -e o -s)* *m* lift, elevator (*US*)

Liga *(-, Ligen)* *f* league, division

light *adj* (*Cola*) diet; (*fettarm*) low-fat; (*kalorienarm*) low-calorie; (*Zigaretten*) mild

Likör *(-s, -e)* *m* liqueur

lila *adj inv* purple

Lilie *f* lily

Limette *(-, -n)* *f* lime

Limo *(-, -s)* *f* (*fam*) fizzy drink (*BRIT*), soda (*US*); **Limonade** *f* fizzy drink (*BRIT*), soda (*US*); (*mit Zitronenge-*

schmack) lemonade
Limone (-, -n) f lime
Limousine (-, -n) f saloon (car) (BRIT), sedan (US); (fam) limo
Linde (-, -n) f lime tree
lindern vt to relieve, to soothe
Lineal (-s, -e) nt ruler
Linie f line; **Linienflug** m scheduled flight; **Linienrichter** m linesman; **liniert** adj ruled, lined
Linke (-n, -n) f left-hand side; (Hand) left hand; (Pol) left (wing); **linke(r, s)** adj left; **auf der ~n Seite** on the left, on the left-hand side; **links** adv on the left; **~ abbiegen** to turn left; **~ von** to the left of; **~ oben** at the top left; **Linksaußen** m left winger; **Linkshänder(in)** (-s, -) m(f) left-hander; **linksherum** adv to the left of, anticlockwise; **Linksverkehr** m driving on the left
Linse (-, -n) f lentil; (optisch) lens; **Linsensuppe** f lentil soup
Lippe (-, -n) f lip; **Lipgloss** nt lip gloss; **Lippenstift** m lipstick
lispeln vi to lisp
List (-, -en) f cunning; (Trick) trick
Liste (-, -n) f list
Litauen (-s) nt Lithuania
Liter (-s, -) m o nt litre
literarisch adj literary; **Literatur** f literature
Litschi (-, -s) f lychee, litchi
litt imperf von **leiden**
live adv (Radio, TV) live
Lizenz f licence
Lkw (-(s), -(s)) m abk = **Lastkraftwagen** truck, lorry (BRIT)
Lob (-(e)s) nt praise; **loben** vt to praise
Loch (-(e)s, Löcher) nt hole; **lochen** vt to punch; **Locher** (-s, -) m (hole) punch
Locke (-, -n) f curl; **locken** vt (anlocken) to lure; (Haare) to curl; **Lockenstab** m curling tongs pl

(BRIT), curling irons pl (US); **Lockenwickler** (-s, -) m curler
locker adj (Schraube, Zahn) loose; (Haltung) relaxed; (Person) easy-going; **das schaffe ich ~** (fam) I'll manage it, no problem; **lockern** vt to loosen ▷ vr **sich ~** to loosen up
lockig adj curly
Löffel (-s, -) m spoon; **einen ~ Mehl zugeben** add a spoonful of flour; **Löffelbiskuit** (-s, -s) m sponge finger
log imperf von **lügen**
Loge (-, -n) f (Theat) box
logisch adj logical
Logo (-s, -s) nt logo
Lohn (-(e)s, Löhne) m reward; (Arbeitslohn) pay, wages pl
lohnen vr **sich ~** to be worth it; **es lohnt sich nicht zu warten** it's no use waiting
Lohnerhöhung f pay rise (BRIT), pay raise (US); **Lohnsteuer** f income tax
Lokal (-(e)s, -e) nt (Gaststätte) restaurant; (Kneipe) pub (BRIT), bar
Lokomotive f locomotive
London (-s) nt London
Lorbeer (-s, -en) m laurel; **Lorbeerblatt** nt (Gastr) bay leaf
los adj loose; **~!** go on!; **jdn/etw ~ sein** to be rid of sb/sth; **was ist ~?** what's the matter?, what's up?; **dort ist nichts/viel ~** there's nothing/a lot going on there
Los (-es, -e) nt (Schicksal) lot, fate; (Lotterie etc) ticket
los|binden irr vt to untie
löschen vt (Feuer, Licht) to put out, to extinguish; (Durst) to quench; (Tonband) to erase; (Daten, Datei) to delete; **Löschtaste** f delete key
lose adj loose
Lösegeld nt ransom
losen vi to draw lots
lösen vt (lockern) to loosen; (Rätsel)

to solve; (Chem) to dissolve; (Fahrkarte) to buy ▷ vr sich ~ (abgehen) to come off; (Zucker etc) to dissolve; (Problem, Schwierigkeit) to (re)solve itself

los|fahren irr vi to leave; **los|gehen** irr vi to set out; (anfangen) to start; **los|lassen** irr vt to let go

löslich adj soluble

Lösung f (eines Rätsels, Problems, Flüssigkeit) solution

los|werden irr vt to get rid of

Lotterie f lottery; **Lotto** (-s) nt National Lottery; ~ **spielen** to play the lottery

Löwe (-n, -n) m (Zool) lion; (Astr) Leo; **Löwenzahn** m dandelion

Luchs (-es, -e) m lynx

Lücke (-, -n) f gap; **Lückenbüßer(in)** (-s, -) m(f) stopgap

lud imperf von **laden**

Luft (-, Lüfte) f air; (Atem) breath; **Luftballon** m balloon; **Luftblase** f (air) bubble; **luftdicht** adj airtight; **Luftdruck** m (Meteo) atmospheric pressure; (in Reifen) air pressure

lüften vt to air; (Geheimnis) to reveal

Luftfahrt f aviation; **Luftfeuchtigkeit** f humidity; **Luftfilter** m air filter; **Luftfracht** f air freight; **Luftkissenfahrzeug** nt hovercraft; **Luftlinie** f 10 km = 10 km as the crow flies; **Luftmatratze** f airbed; **Luftpirat(in)** m(f) hijacker; **Luftpost** f airmail; **Luftpumpe** f (bicycle) pump; **Luftröhre** f windpipe

Lüftung f ventilation

Luftveränderung f change of air; **Luftverschmutzung** f air pollution; **Luftwaffe** f air force; **Luftzug** m draught (BRIT), draft (US)

Lüge (-, -n) f lie; **lügen** (log, gelogen) vi to lie; **Lügner(in)** (-s, -) m(f) liar

Luke (-, -n) f hatch

Lumpen (-s, -) m rag

Lunchpaket nt packed lunch

Lunge (-, -n) f lungs pl; **Lungenentzündung** f pneumonia

Lupe (-, -n) f magnifying glass; **etw unter die ~ nehmen** (fig) to have a close look at sth

Lust (-, Lüste) f joy, delight; (Neigung) desire; ~ **auf etw** (akk) **haben** to feel like sth; ~ **haben, etw zu tun** to feel like doing sth

lustig adj (komisch) amusing, funny; (fröhlich) cheerful

lutschen vt to suck ▷ vi ~ **an** (+dat) to suck; **Lutscher** (-s, -) m lollipop

Luxemburg (-s) nt Luxembourg

luxuriös adj luxurious

Luxus (-) m luxury

Lymphdrüse f lymph gland; **Lymphknoten** m lymph node

Lyrik (-) f poetry

m

machbar *adj* feasible
machen *vt* (herstellen, verursachen) to make; (tun, erledigen) to do; (kosten) to be; **das Essen / einen Fehler ~** to make dinner / a mistake; **ein Foto ~** to take a photo; **was machst du?** what are you doing?; (beruflich) what do you do (for a living)?; **das kann man doch nicht ~!** you can't do that; **das Bett ~** to make the bed; **das Zimmer ~** (o to tidy (up)) the room; **was macht das?** (kostet) how much is that?; **das macht zwanzig Euro** that's twenty euros; **einen Spaziergang ~** to go for a walk; **Urlaub ~** to go on holiday; **eine Pause ~** to take a break; **einen Kurs ~** to take a course; **das macht nichts** it doesn't matter; **da kann man nichts ~** it's just one of those things ▷ *vr* **sie macht sich gut** she's coming along well; **sich auf den Weg ~** to set out; **sich an die Arbeit ~** to get down to work
Macho (-s, -s) *m* (fam) macho (type)

Macht (-s, *Mächte*) *f* power; **mächtig** *adj* powerful; (fam: ungeheuer) enormous; **machtlos** *adj* powerless; **da ist man ~** there's nothing you can do (about it)
Mädchen *nt* girl; **Mädchenname** *m* maiden name
Made (-, -n) *f* maggot
Magazin (-s, -e) *nt* magazine
Magen (-s, - o *Mägen*) *m* stomach; **Magenbeschwerden** *pl* stomach trouble sing; **Magen-Darm-Infektion** *f* gastroenteritis; **Magengeschwür** *nt* stomach ulcer; **Magenschmerzen** *pl* stomachache sing
mager *adj* (Fleisch, Wurst) lean; (Person) thin; (Käse, Joghurt) low-fat; **Magermilch** *f* skimmed milk; **Magersucht** *f* anorexia; **magersüchtig** *adj* anorexic
magisch *adj* magical
Magnet (-s o -en, -en) *m* magnet
mähen *vt*, *vi* to mow
mahlen (mahlte, gemahlen) *vt* to grind
Mahlzeit *f* meal; (für Baby) feed ▷ *interj* (guten Appetit) enjoy your meal
Mähne (-, -n) *f* mane
mahnen *vt* to urge; **jdn schriftlich ~** to send sb a reminder; **Mahngebühr** *f* fine; **Mahnung** *f* warning; (schriftlich) reminder
Mai (-(s), -e) *m* May; siehe auch **Juni**; **Maifeiertag** *m* May Day; **Maiglöckchen** *nt* lily of the valley; **Maikäfer** *m* cockchafer
Mail (-, -s) *f* e-mail; **Mailbox** *f* (Inform) mailbox; **mailen** *vi*, *vt* to e-mail
Mais (-es, -e) *m* maize, corn (US); **Maiskolben** *m* corn cob; (Gastr) corn on the cob
Majestät (-, -en) *f* Majesty
Majonäse (-, -n) *f* mayonnaise

Majoran (-s, -e) m marjoram

makaber adj macabre

Make-up (-s, -s) nt make-up

Makler(in) (-s, -s) m(f) broker; (Immobilienmakler) estate agent (BRIT), realtor (US)

Makrele (, -n) f mackerel

Makro (-s, -s) nt (Inform) macro

Makrone (, -n) f macaroon

mal adv (beim Rechnen) times, multiplied by; (beim Messen) by; (fam: einmal = früher) once. (einmal = zukünftig) some day; **4 ~ 3 ist 12** 4 times 3 is (o equals) twelve; **da habe ich ~ gewohnt** I used to live there; **irgendwann ~ werde ich dort hinfahren** I'll go there one day; **das ist nun ~ so** well, that's just the way it is (o goes); **Mal** (-(e)s, -e) nt (Zeitpunkt) time; (Markierung) mark; **jedes ~** every time; **ein paar ~** a few times; **ein einziges ~** just once

Malaria (-) f malaria

Malaysia (-s) nt Malaysia

Malbuch nt colouring book

Malediven pl Maldives pl

malen vt, vi to paint; **Maler(in)** (-s, -) m(f) painter; **Malerei** f painting; **malerisch** adj picturesque

Mallorca (-s) nt Majorca, Mallorca

mal|nehmen irr vt to multiply (mit by)

Malta (-s) nt Malta

Malventee m mallow tea

Malz (-es) nt malt; **Malzbier** nt malt beer

Mama (-, -s) f mum(my) (BRIT), mom(my) (US)

man pron you; (förmlich) one; (jemand) someone, somebody; (je Leute) they, people pl; **wie schreibt ~ das?** how do you spell that?; **~ hat mir das Fahrrad gestohlen** someone stole her bike; **~ sagt, dass ...** they (o people) say that ...

managen vt (fam) to manage; **Manager(in)** (-s, -) m(f) manager

manche(r, s) adj many a; (mit pl) a number of, some ▷ pron (einige) some; (viele) many; **~ Politiker** many politicians pl, many a politician; **manchmal** adv sometimes

Mandant(in) m(f) client

Mandarine f mandarin, tangerine

Mandel (-, -n) f almond; **~n** (Anat) tonsils pl; **Mandelentzündung** f tonsillitis

Manege (-, -n) f ring

Mangel (-s, Mängel) m (Fehlen) lack; (Knappheit) shortage (an +dat of); (Fehler) defect, fault; **mangelhaft** adj (Ware) faulty; (Schulnote) ≈ E

Mango (-, -s) f mango

Mangold (-s) m mangel(wurzel)

Manieren pl manners pl

Maniküre (-, -n) f manicure

manipulieren vt to manipulate

Manko (-s, -s) nt deficiency

Mann (-(e)s, Männer) m man; (Ehemann) husband; **Männchen** nt es **ist ein ~** (Tier) it's a he; **männlich** adj masculine; (Bio) male

Mannschaft f (Sport, fig) team; (Naut, Aviat) crew

Mansarde (-, -n) f attic

Manschettenknopf m cufflink

Mantel (-s, Mäntel) m coat; (Tech) casing, jacket

Mappe (, -n) f briefcase; (Aktenmappe) folder

Maracuja (-, -s) f passion fruit

Marathon (-s, -s) m marathon

Märchen nt fairy tale

Marder (-s, -) m marten

Margarine f margarine

Marienkäfer m ladybird (BRIT), ladybug (US)

Marihuana (-s) nt marijuana

Marille (-, -n) f apricot

Marinade f marinade

Marine f navy

marinieren vt to marinate
Marionette f puppet
Mark (-(e)s) nt (Knochenmark) marrow; (Fruchtmark) pulp
Marke (-, -n) f (Warensorte) brand; (Fabrikat) make; (Briefmarke) stamp; (Essenmarke) voucher, ticket; (aus Metall etc) disc; (Messpunkt) mark; **Markenartikel** m branded item, brand name product; **Markenzeichen** nt trademark
markieren vt to mark; **Markierung** f marking; (Zeichen) mark
Markise (-, -n) f awning
Markt (-(e)s, Märkte) m market; **auf den ~ bringen** to launch; **Markthalle** f covered market; **Marktlücke** f gap in the market; **Marktplatz** m market place; **Marktwirtschaft** f market economy
Marmelade f jam; (Orangenmarmelade) marmalade
Marmor (-s, -e) m marble; **Marmorkuchen** m marble cake
Marokko (-s) nt Morocco
Marone (-, -n) f chestnut
Mars (-) m Mars
Marsch (-(e)s, Märsche) m march
Märtyrer(in) (-s, -) m(f) martyr
März (-(es), -e) m March; siehe auch **Juni**
Marzipan (-s, -e) nt marzipan
Maschine (-, -n) f machine; (Motor) engine; **maschinell** adj mechanical, machine-; **Maschinenbau** m mechanical engineering
Masern pl (Med) measles sing
Maske (-, -n) f mask; **Maskenball** m fancy-dress ball; **maskieren** vr **sich ~** (Maske aufsetzen) to put on a mask; (verkleiden) to dress up
Maskottchen nt mascot
maß imperf von **messen**
Maß (-es, -e) nt measure; (Mäßigung) moderation; (Grad) degree, extent; **-e** (Person) measurements;

(Raum) dimensions; **in gewissem / hohem ~e** to a certain / high degree; **in zunehmendem ~e** increasingly
Mass (-, -(en)) f (Bier) litre of beer
Massage (-, -n) f massage
Masse (-, -n) f mass; (von Menschen) crowd; (Großteil) majority; **massenhaft** adv masses (o loads) of; **am See sind ~ Mücken** there are masses of mosquitoes at the lake; **Massenkarambolage** f pile-up; **Massenmedien** pl mass media pl; **Massenproduktion** f mass production; **Massentourismus** m mass tourism
Masseur(in) m(f) masseur / masseuse
maßgeschneidert adj (Kleidung) made-to-measure
massieren vt to massage
mäßig adj moderate
massiv adj solid; (fig) massive
maßlos adj extreme
Maßnahme (-, -n) f measure, step
Maßstab m rule, measure; (fig) standard; **im ~ von 1:5** on a scale of 1:5
Mast (-(e)s, -e(n)) m mast; (Elek) pylon
Material (-s, -ien) nt material; (Arbeitsmaterial) materials pl; **materialistisch** adj materialistic
Materie f matter; **materiell** adj material
Mathematik f mathematics sing; **Mathematiker(in)** m(f) mathematician
Matinee (-, -n) f ≈ matinee
Matratze (-, -n) f mattress
Matrose (-n, -n) m sailor
Matsch (-(e)s) m mud; (Schnee) slush; **matschig** adj (Boden) muddy; (Schnee) slushy; (Obst) mushy
matt adj weak; (glanzlos) dull; (Foto) matt; (Schach) mate

Matte (-, -n) f mat

Matura (-) f Austrian school-leaving examination; ≈ A-levels (BRIT); ≈ High School Diploma (US)

Mauer (-, -n) f wall

Maul (-(e)s, Mäuler) nt mouth; (fam) gob; **halt's ~!** shut your face (o gob); **Maulbeere** f mulberry; **Maulesel** m mule; **Maulkorb** m muzzle; **Maul und Klauenseuche** f foot-and-mouth disease; **Maulwurf** m mole

Maurer(in) (-s, -) m(f) bricklayer

Mauritius (-) nt Mauritius

Maus (-, Mäuse) f mouse; **Mausefalle** f mousetrap; **Mausklick** (-s, -s) m mouse click; **Mauspad** (-s, -s) nt mouse mat (o pad); **Maustaste** f mouse key (o button)

Maut (-, -en) f toll; **Mautgebühr** f toll; **mautpflichtig** adj **~e Straße** toll road, turnpike (US); **Mautstelle** f tollbooth, tollgate; **Mautstraße** f toll road, turnpike (US)

maximal adv **ihr habt ~ zwei Stunden Zeit** you've got two hours at (the) most; **~ vier Leute** a maximum of four people

Mayonnaise f siehe **Majonäse**

Mazedonien (-s) nt Macedonia

MB (-, -) nt, **Mbyte** (-, -) nt abk = **Megabyte** MB

Mechanik f mechanics sing; (Getriebe) mechanics pl; **Mechaniker(in)** (-s, -) m(f) mechanic; **mechanisch** adj mechanical; **Mechanismus** m mechanism

meckern vi (Ziege) to bleat; (fam: schimpfen) to moan

Mecklenburg-Vorpommern (-s) nt Mecklenburg-Western Pomerania

Medaille (-, -n) f medal

Medien (-s) nt media pl

Medikament nt medicine

Meditation f meditation; **medi-**

tieren vi to meditate

medium adj (Steak) medium

Medizin (-, -en) f medicine (gegen for); **medizinisch** adj medical

Meer (-(e)s, -e) nt sea; **am ~** by the sea; **Meerenge** f straits pl; **Meeresfrüchte** pl seafood sing; **Meeresspiegel** m sea level; **Meerrettich** m horseradish; **Meerschweinchen** nt guinea pig; **Meerwasser** nt seawater

Megabyte nt megabyte; **Megahertz** nt megahertz

Mehl (-(e)s, -e) nt flour; **Mehlspeise** f sweet dish made from flour, eggs and milk

mehr pron, adv more; **~ will ich nicht ausgeben** I don't want to spend any more, that's as much as I want to spend; **was willst du ~?** what more do you want? ▷ adv **immer ~** (Leute) more and more (people); **~ als fünf Minuten** more than five minutes; **je ~ ..., desto besser** the more ..., the better; **ich kann nicht ~ stehen** I can't stand any more (o longer); **es ist kein Brot ~ da** there's no bread left; **nie ~** never again; **mehrdeutig** adj ambiguous; **mehrere** pron several; **mehreres** pron several things; **mehrfach** adj multiple; (wiederholt) repeated; **Mehrfachstecker** m multiple plug; **Mehrheit** f majority; **mehrmals** adv repeatedly; **mehrsprachig** adj multilingual; **Mehrwegflasche** f returnable bottle, deposit bottle; **Mehrwertsteuer** f value added tax, VAT; **Mehrzahl** f majority; (Plural) plural

meiden (mied, gemieden) vt to avoid

Meile (-, -n) f mile

mein pron (adjektivisch) my; **meine(r, s)** pron (substantivisch) mine

meinen vt, vi (glauben, der Ansicht sein) to think; (sagen) to say; (sagen wollen, beabsichtigen) to mean; **das war nicht so gemeint** I didn't mean it like that

meinetwegen adv (wegen mir) because of me; (mir zuliebe) for my sake; (von mir aus) as far as I'm concerned

Meinung f opinion; **meiner ~ nach** in my opinion; **Meinungsumfrage** f opinion poll; **Meinungsverschiedenheit** f disagreement (über +akk about)

Meise (-, -n) f tit; **eine ~ haben** (fam) to be crazy

Meißel (-s, -) m chisel

meist adv mostly; **meiste(r, s)** pron (adjektivisch) most; **die ~n** (Leute) most people; **die ~ Zeit** most of the time; **das ~** (davon) most of it; **die ~n von ihnen** most of them; (substantivisch) most of them; **am ~n** (the) most; **meistens** adv mostly; (zum größten Teil) for the most part

Meister(in) (-s, -) m(f) master; (Sport) champion; **Meisterschaft** f championship; **Meisterwerk** nt masterpiece

melden vt to report ▷ vr **sich ~** to report (bei to); (Schule) to put one's hand up; (freiwillig) to volunteer; (auf etw, am Telefon) to answer; **Meldung** f announcement; (Bericht) report; (Inform) message

Melodie f tune, melody

Melone (-, -n) f melon

Memoiren pl memoirs pl

Menge (-, -n) f quantity; (Menschen) crowd; **eine ~** (große Anzahl) a lot (gen of); **Mengenrabatt** m bulk discount

Meniskus (-, Menisken) m meniscus

Mensa (-, Mensen) f canteen, cafeteria (US)

Mensch (-en, -en) m human being, man; (Person) person; **kein ~** no-

body; **~!** (bewundernd) wow!; (verärgert) bloody hell!; **Menschenmenge** f crowd; **Menschenrechte** pl human rights pl; **Menschenverstand** m **gesunder ~** common sense; **Menschheit** f humanity, mankind; **menschlich** adj human; (human) humane

Menstruation f menstruation

Mentalität f mentality, mindset

Menthol (-s) nt menthol

Menü (-s, -s) nt set meal; (Inform) menu; **Menüleiste** f (Inform) menu bar

Merkblatt nt leaflet; **merken** vt (bemerken) to notice; **sich** (dat) **etw ~** to remember sth; **Merkmal** nt feature

Merkur (-s) m Mercury

merkwürdig adj odd

Messbecher m measuring jug

Messe (-, -n) f fair; (Rel) mass; **Messebesucher(in)** m(f) visitor to a / the fair; **Messegelände** nt exhibition site

messen (maß, gemessen) vt to measure; (Temperatur, Puls) to take ▷ vr **sich ~** to compete; **sie kann sich mit ihm nicht ~** she's no match for him

Messer (-s, -) nt knife

Messgerät nt measuring device, gauge

Messing (-s) nt brass

Metall (-s, -e) nt metal

Meteorologe m, **Meteorologin** f meteorologist

Meter (-s, -) m o nt metre; **Metermaß** nt tape measure

Methode f method

Metzger(in) (-s, -) m(f) butcher; **Metzgerei** f butcher's (shop)

Mexiko (-s) nt Mexico

MEZ f abk = **mitteleuropäische Zeit** CET

miau interj miaow

mich pron akk von **ich** me; ~ (**selbst**) (reflexiv) myself; **stell dich hinter ~** stand behind me; **ich fühle ~ wohl** I feel fine

mied imperf von **meiden**

Miene (~, -n) f look, expression

mies adj (fam) lousy

Miesmuschel f mussel

Mietauto nt siehe **Mietwagen**; **Miete** (~, -n) f rent; **mieten** vt to rent; (Auto) to hire (BRIT), to rent (US); **Mieter(in)** (-s, -) m(f) tenant; **Mietshaus** nt block of flats (BRIT), apartment house (US); **Mietvertrag** m rental agreement; **Mietwagen** m hire car (BRIT), rental car (US); **sich** (dat) **einen ~ nehmen** to hire (BRIT) o rent (US) a car

Migräne (~, -n) f migraine

Mikrofon (-s, -e) nt microphone

Mikrowelle (~, -n) f, **Mikrowellenherd** m microwave (oven)

Milch (~) f milk; **Milcheis** nt ice-cream (made with milk); **Milchglas** nt (dickes, trübes Glas) frosted glass; **Milchkaffee** m milky coffee; **Milchprodukte** pl dairy products pl; **Milchpulver** nt powdered milk; **Milchreis** m rice pudding; **Milchshake** m milk shake; **Milchstraße** f Milky Way

mild adj mild; (Richter) lenient; (freundlich) kind

Militär (-s) nt military, army

Milliarde (~, -n) f billion; **Milligramm** nt milligram; **Milliliter** m milllitre; **Millimeter** m millimetre; **Million** f million; **Millionär(in)** m(f) millionaire

Milz (~, -en) f spleen

Mimik f facial expression(s)

Minderheit f minority

minderjährig adj underage

minderwertig adj inferior; **Minderwertigkeitskomplex** m inferiority complex

Mindest- in zW minimum; **mindeste(r, s)** adj least; **mindestens** adv at least; **Mindesthaltbarkeitsdatum** nt best-before date, sell-by date (BRIT)

Mine (~, -n) f mine; (Bleistift) lead; (Kugelschreiber) refill

Mineralwasser nt mineral water

Minibar f minibar; **Minigolf** nt miniature golf, crazy golf (BRIT)

minimal adj minimal

Minimum (-s, Minima) nt minimum

Minirock m miniskirt

Minister(in) (-s, -) m(f) minister; **Ministerium** nt ministry; **Ministerpräsident(in)** m(f) (von Bundesland) Minister President (Prime Minister of a Bundesland)

minus adv minus; **Minus** (-, -) nt deficit; **im ~ sein** to be in the red; (Konto) to be overdrawn

Minute (~, -n) f minute

Minze (~, -n) f mint

Mio. nt abk von **Million(en)** m

mir pron dat von **ich** (to) me; **kannst du ~ helfen?** can you help me?; **kannst du es ~ erklären?** can you explain it to me?; **ich habe ~ einen neuen Rechner gekauft** I bought (myself) a new computer; **ein Freund von ~** a friend of mine

Mirabelle (~, -n) f mirabelle (small yellow plum)

mischen vt to mix; (Karten) to shuffle; **Mischmasch** m (fam) hotchpotch; **Mischung** f mixture (aus of)

missachten vt to ignore; **Missbrauch** m abuse; (falscher Gebrauch) misuse; **missbrauchen** vt to misuse (zu for); (sexuell) to abuse; **Misserfolg** m failure; **Missgeschick** nt (Panne) mishap; **misshandeln** vt to ill-treat

Mission f mission

misslingen (misslang, misslungen)

vi to fail; **der Versuch ist mir misslungen** my attempt failed; **misstrauen** vt +dat to distrust; **Misstrauen** (-s) nt mistrust, suspicion (gegenüber) of; **misstrauisch** adj distrustful; (argwöhnisch) suspicious; **Missverständnis** nt misunderstanding; **missverstehen** irr vt to misunderstand

Mist (-(e)s) m (fam) rubbish; (von Kühen) dung; (als Dünger) manure

Mistel (-, -n) f mistletoe

mit prep +dat with; (mittels) by; ~ **der Bahn** by train; ~ **der Kreditkarte bezahlen** to pay by credit card; ~ **10 Jahren** at the age of 10; **wie wärs ~ ...?** how about ...? ▷ adv along, too; **wollen Sie ~?** do you want to come along?

Mitarbeiter(in) m(f) (Angestellter) employee; (an Projekt) collaborator; (freier) freelancer

mit|bekommen irr vt (fam: aufschnappen) to catch; (hören) to hear; (verstehen) to get

mit|benutzen vt to share

Mitbewohner(in) m(f) (in Wohnung) flatmate (BRIT), roommate (US)

mit|bringen vt to bring along; **Mitbringsel** (-s, -) nt small present

miteinander adv with one another; (gemeinsam) together

mit|erleben vt to see (with one's own eyes)

Mitesser (-s, -) m blackhead

Mitfahrgelegenheit f ≈ lift, ride (US); **Mitfahrzentrale** f agency for arranging lifts

mit|geben irr vt **jdm etw ~** to give sb sth (to take along)

Mitgefühl nt sympathy

mit|gehen irr vi to go/come along

mitgenommen adj worn out, exhausted

Mitglied nt member

mithilfe prep +gen ~ **von** with the help of

mit|kommen irr vi to come along; (verstehen) to follow

Mitleid nt pity; ~ **haben mit** to feel sorry for

mit|machen vt to take part in ▷ vi to take part

mit|nehmen irr vt to take along; (anstrengen) to wear out, to exhaust

mit|schreiben irr vi to take notes ▷ vt to take down

Mitschüler(in) m(f) schoolmate

mit|spielen vi (in Mannschaft) to play; (bei Spiel) to join in; **in einem Film / Stück ~** to act in a film / play

Mittag m midday; **gestern ~** at midday yesterday, yesterday lunchtime; **über ~ geschlossen** closed at lunchtime; **zu ~ essen** to have lunch; **Mittagessen** nt lunch; **mittags** adv at lunchtime, at midday; **Mittagspause** f lunch break

Mitte (-, -n) f middle; ~ **Juni** in the middle of June; **sie ist ~ zwanzig** she's in her mid-twenties

mit|teilen vt **jdm etw ~** to inform sb of sth; **Mitteilung** f notification

Mittel (-s -) nt means sing; (Maßnahme, Methode) method; (Med) remedy (gegen for); **das ist ein gutes ~, um junge Leute zu erreichen** that's a good way of engaging with young people

Mittelalter nt Middle Ages pl; **mittelalterlich** adj medieval; **Mittelamerika** nt Central America; **Mitteleuropa** nt Central Europe; **Mittelfeld** nt midfield; **Mittelfinger** m middle finger; **mittelmäßig** adj mediocre; **Mittelmeer** nt Mediterranean (Sea); **Mittelohrentzündung** f inflammation of the middle ear; **Mittel-**

punkt *m* centre; **im ~ stehen** to be the centre of attention

mittels *prep* +*gen* by means of

Mittelstreifen *m* central reservation (BRIT), median (US); **Mittelstürmer(in)** *m(f)* striker, centreforward; **Mittelwelle** f medium wave

mitten *adv* in the middle; **~ auf der Straße/in der Nacht** in the middle of the street/night

Mitternacht f midnight

mittlere(r, s) *adj* middle; (*durchschnittlich*) average

mittlerweile *adv* meanwhile

Mittwoch (-*s*, -*e*) *m* Wednesday; (**am**) ~ on Wednesday; (**am**) ~ **Morgen/Nachmittag/Abend** (on) Wednesday morning/afternoon/evening; **diesen/letzten/nächsten** ~ this/last/next Wednesday; **jeden** ~ every Wednesday; **~ in einer Woche** a week on Wednesday, Wednesday week; **mittwochs** *adv* on Wednesdays; **~ abends** (*jeden Mittwochabend*) on Wednesday evenings

mixen *vt* to mix, **Mixer** (*s,*) *m* (*Küchengerät*) blender

MKS f *abk* = **Maul- und Klauenseuche** FMD

mobben *vt* to harass (*o* to bully) (at work)

Mobbing (*-s*) *nt* workplace bullying (*o* harassment)

Möbel (*-s*, -) *nt* piece of furniture; **die ~** *pl* the furniture *sing*; **Möbelwagen** *m* removal van

mobil *adj* mobile

Mobilfunknetz *nt* cellular network; **Mobiltelefon** *nt* mobile phone

möblieren *vt* to furnish

mochte *imperf von* **mögen**

Mode (-, -*n*) f fashion

Modell (-*s*, -*e*) *nt* model

Modell (-*s*, -*e*) *nt* model

Modem (-*s*, -*s*) *nt* (*Inform*) modem

Mode(n)schau f fashion show

Moderator(in) *m(f)* presenter

modern *adj* modern; (*modisch*) fashionable

Modeschmuck *m* costume jewellery; **modisch** *adj* fashionable

Modus (-, *Modi*) *m* (*Inform*) mode; (*fig*) way

Mofa (-*s*, -*s*) *nt* moped

mogeln *vi* to cheat

mögen (*mochte, gemocht*) *vt, vi* to like; **ich möchte ...** I would like ...; **ich möchte lieber bleiben** I'd rather stay; **möchtest du lieber Tee oder Kaffee?** would you prefer tea or coffee?

möglich *adj* possible; **so bald wie ~** as soon as possible; **möglicherweise** *adv* possibly; **Möglichkeit** f possibility; **möglichst** *adv* as ... as possible

Mohn (-(*e*)*s*, -*e*) *m* (*Blume*) poppy; (*Samen*) poppy seed

Möhre (-, -*n*) f, **Mohrrübe** f carrot

Mokka (-*s*, -*s*) *m* mocha

Moldawien (-*s*) *nt* Moldova

Molkerei (-, -*en*) f dairy

Moll (-) *nt* minor (key); **a ~** A minor

mollig *adj* cosy; (*dicklich*) plump

Moment (-*e*)*s*, -*e*) *m*; **im ~** at the moment; **einen ~ bitte!** just a minute; **momentan** *adj* momentary ▷ *adv* at the moment

Monaco (-*s*) *nt* Monaco

Monarchie f monarchy

Monat (-(*e*)*s*, -*e*) *m* month; **sie ist im dritten ~** (*schwanger*) she's three months pregnant; **monatlich** *adj, adv* monthly; **~ 100 Euro zahlen** to pay 100 euros a month (*o* every month); **Monatskarte** f monthly season ticket

Mönch (-*s*, -*e*) *m* monk

Mond (-(*e*)*s*, -*e*) *m* moon; **Mond-**

finsternis f lunar eclipse
Mongolei (-) f **die ~** Mongolia
Monitor m (Inform) monitor
monoton adj monotonous
Monsun (-s, -e) m monsoon
Montag m Monday; siehe auch **Mittwoch**; **montags** adv on Mondays; siehe auch **mittwochs**
Montenegro (-s) nt Montenegro
Monteur(in) (-s, -e) m(f) fitter; **montieren** vt to assemble, to set up
Monument nt monument
Moor (-(e)s, -e) nt moor
Moos (-es, -e) nt moss
Moped (-s, -s) nt moped
Moral (-) f (Werte) morals pl; (einer Geschichte) moral; **moralisch** adj moral
Mord (-(e)s, -e) m murder; **Mörder(in)** (-s, -) m(f) murderer / murderess
morgen adv tomorrow; **~ früh** tomorrow morning
Morgen (-s, -) m morning; **am ~** in the morning; **Morgenmantel** m, **Morgenrock** m dressing gown; **Morgenmuffel** m **er ist ein ~** he's not a morning person; **morgens** adv in the morning; **um 3 Uhr ~** at 3 (o'clock) in the morning, at 3 am
Morphium (-s) nt morphine
morsch adj rotten
Mosaik (-s, -e(n)) nt mosaic
Mosambik (-s) nt Mozambique
Moschee (-, -n) f mosque
Moskau (-s) nt Moscow
Moskito (-s) m mosquito; **Moskitonetz** nt mosquito net
Moslem (-s, -s) m, **Moslime** (-, -n) f Muslim
Most (-(e)s, -e) m (unfermented) fruit juice; (Apfelwein) cider
Motel (-s, -s) nt motel
motivieren vt to motivate
Motor m engine; (Elek) motor;

Motorboot nt motorboat; **Motorenöl** nt engine oil; **Motorhaube** f bonnet (BRIT), hood (US); **Motorrad** nt motorbike, motorcycle; **Motorradfahrer(in)** m(f) motorcyclist; **Motorroller** m (motor) scooter; **Motorschaden** m engine trouble
Motte (-, -n) f moth
Motto (-s, -s) nt motto
Mountainbike (-s, -s) nt mountain bike
Möwe (-, -n) f (sea)gull
Mrd. f abk = **Milliarde(n)**
MS (-) f abk = **multiple Sklerose** MS
Mücke (-, -n) f midge; (tropische) mosquito; **Mückenstich** m mosquito bite
müde adj tired
muffig adj (Geruch) musty; (Gesicht, Mensch) grumpy
Mühe (-, -n) f trouble, pains pl; **sich** (dat) **große ~ geben** to go to a lot of trouble
muhen vi to moo
Mühle (-, -n) f mill; (Kaffeemühle) grinder
Mull (-(e)s, -e) m muslin; (Med) gauze
Müll (-(e)s) m rubbish (BRIT), garbage (US); **Müllabfuhr** f rubbish (BRIT) (o garbage (US)) disposal
Mullbinde f gauze bandage
Müllcontainer m waste container; **Mülldeponie** f rubbish (BRIT) (o garbage (US)) dump; **Mülleimer** m rubbish bin (BRIT), garbage can (US); **Mülltonne** f dustbin (BRIT), garbage can (US); **Mülltrennung** f sorting and collecting household waste according to type of material; **Müllverbrennungsanlage** f incineration plant; **Müllwagen** m dustcart (BRIT), garbage truck (US)
multikulturell adj multicultural
Multimedia- in zW multimedia

Multiple-Choice-Verfahren nt multiple choice
multiple Sklerose (-n, -n) f multiple sclerosis
Multiplexkino nt multiplex (cinema)
multiplizieren vt to multiply (mit by)
Mumie f mummy
Mumps (-) m mumps sing
München (-s) nt Munich
Mund (-(e)s, Münder) m mouth; **halt den ~!** shut up; **Mundart** f dialect; **Munddusche** f dental water jet
münden vi to flow (in +akk into)
Mundgeruch m bad breath; **Mundharmonika** (-, -s) f mouth organ
mündlich adj oral
Mundschutz m mask; **Mundwasser** nt mouthwash
Munition f ammunition
Münster (s,) nt minster, cathedral
munter adj lively
Münzautomat m vending machine; **Münze** (-, -n) f coin, **Münzeinwurf** m slot; **Münzrückgabe** f coin return; **Münztelefon** nt pay phone; **Münzwechsler** m change machine
murmeln vt, vi to murmur, to mutter
Murmeltier m marmot
mürrisch adj sullen, grumpy
Mus (es, e) nt puree
Muschel (-, -n) f mussel; (~schale) shell
Museum (-s, Museen) nt museum
Musical (-s, -s) nt musical
Musik f music; **musikalisch** adj musical; **Musiker(in)** (-s, -) m(f) musician; **Musikinstrument** nt musical instrument; **musizieren** vi to play music
Muskat (-(e)s) m nutmeg

Muskel (-s, -n) m muscle; **Muskelkater** m ~ **haben** to be stiff; **Muskelriss** m torn muscle; **Muskelzerrung** f pulled muscle; **muskulös** adj muscular
Müsli (-s, -) nt muesli
Muslim(in) (-s, -s) m(f) Muslim
Muss ( ) nt must
müssen (musste, gemusst) vi must, to have to; **er hat gehen** he (has) had to go; **sie müsste schon längst hier sein** she should have arrived a long time ago; **du musst es nicht tun** you don't have to do it, you needn't do it; **ich muss mal** I need to go to the loo (BRIT), I have to go to the bathroom (US)
Muster (-s, -) nt (Dessin) pattern, design; (Probe) sample; (Vorbild) model; **mustern** vt to have a close look at; **jdn ~** to look sb up and down
Mut (-(e)s) m courage; **jdm ~ machen** to encourage sb; **mutig** adj brave, courageous
Mutter (-, Mütter) f mother ▷ (-, -n) f (Schraubenmutter) nut; **Muttersprache** f mother tongue; **Muttertag** m Mother's Day; **Mutti** f mum(my) (BRIT), mom(my) (US)
mutwillig adj deliberate
Mütze (-, -n) f cap
MwSt. abk = **Mehrwertsteuer** VAT
Myanmar (-r) nt Myanmar

n

N *abk* = **Nord** N

na *interj* **~ also!, ~ bitte!** see?, what did I tell you?; **~ ja** well; **~ und?** so what?

Nabel (-s, -) *m* navel

nach *prep +dat* (*zeitlich*) after; (*in Richtung*) to; (*gemäß*) according to; **~ zwei Stunden** after two hours, two hours later; **es ist fünf ~ sechs** it's five past (*BRIT*) (*o* after (*US*)) six; **der Zug ~ London** the train for (*o* to) London; **~ rechts / links** to the right / left; **~ Hause** home; **~ oben / hinten / unten** up / back / down; **~ und ~** gradually; **nach|ahmen** *vt* to imitate

Nachbar(in) (-n, -n) *m(f)* neighbour; **Nachbarschaft** *f* neighbourhood

nach|bestellen *vt* to order some more

nachdem *conj* after; (*weil*) since; **je ~ (ob/wie)** depending on (whether/how)

nach|denken *irr vi* to think (*über +akk* about); **nachdenklich** *adj* thoughtful

nacheinander *adv* one after another (*o* the other)

Nachfolger(in) (-s, -) *m(f)* successor

nach|forschen *vt* to investigate

Nachfrage *f* inquiry; (*Comm*) demand; **nach|fragen** *vi* to inquire

Nachfüllpack *m* refill pack

nach|geben *irr vi* to give in (*jdm* to sb)

Nachgebühr *f* surcharge; (*für Briefe etc*) excess postage

nach|gehen *irr vi* to follow (*jdm* sb); (*erforschen*) to inquire (*einer Sache dat* into sth); **die Uhr geht (zehn Minuten) nach** this watch is (ten minutes) slow

nachher *adv* afterwards; **bis ~!** see you later

Nachhilfe *f* extra tuition

nach|holen *vt* to catch up with; (*Versäumtes*) to make up for

nach|kommen *irr vi* to follow; **einer Verpflichtung** (*dat*) **~** to fulfil an obligation

nach|lassen *irr vt* (*Summe*) to take off ▸ *vi* to decrease, to ease off; (*schlechter werden*) to deteriorate; **nachlässig** *adj* negligent, careless

nach|laufen *irr vi* to run after, to chase (*jdm* sb)

nach|lösen *vt* **eine Fahrkarte ~** to buy a ticket on the bus / train

nach|machen *vt* to imitate, to copy (*jdm etw* sth from sb); (*fälschen*) to counterfeit

Nachmittag *m* afternoon; **heute ~** this afternoon; **am ~** in the afternoon; **nachmittags** *adv* in the afternoon; **um 3 Uhr ~** at 3 (o'clock) in the afternoon, at 3 pm

Nachnahme (-, -n) *f* cash on delivery; **per ~** COD

Nachname *m* surname

Nachporto nt excess postage

nach|prüfen vt to check

nach|rechnen vt to check

Nachricht (-, -en) f (piece of) news sing; (Mitteilung) message; **Nachrichten** pl news sing

Nachsaison f off-season

nach|schauen vi u to gaze after sb ▷ vt (prüfen) to check

nach|schicken vi u forward

nach|schlagen irr vt to look up

nach|sehen irr vt (prüfen) to check

nach|senden irr vt to forward

Nachspeise f dessert

nächstbeste(r, s) adj der ~ Zug/Job the first train/job that comes along; **nächste(r, s)** adj next; (nächstgelegen) nearest

Nacht (-, -ächte) f night; **in der ~** during the night; (bei Nacht) at night; **Nachtclub** m nightclub; **Nachtdienst** m night duty; ~ **haben** (Apotheke) to be open all night

Nachteil m disadvantage

Nachtflug m night flight; **Nachtfrost** m overnight frost; **Nachthemd** nt (für Damen) nightdress; (für Herren) nightshirt

Nachtigall (-, -en) f nightingale

Nachtisch m dessert, sweet (BRIT), pudding (BRIT); **Nachtleben** nt nightlife

nach|tragen irr vt jdm etw ~ (übel nehmen) to hold sth against sb

nachträglich adv ~ **alles Gute zum Geburtstag!** Happy belated birthday

nachts adv at night; **um 11 Uhr ~** at 11 (o'clock) at night, at 11 pm; **um 2 Uhr ~** at 2 (o'clock) in the morning, at 2 am; **Nachtschicht** f night shift; **Nachttarif** m off-peak rate; **Nachttisch** m bedside table; **Nachtzug** m night train

Nachweis (-es, -e) m proof

Nachwirkung f after-effect

nach|zahlen vi to pay extra ▷ vt **20 Euro ~** to pay 20 euros extra

nach|zählen vt to check

Nacken (-s, -) m (nape of the) neck

nackt adj naked; (Tatsachen) plain, bare; **Nacktbadestrand** m nudist beach

Nadel (-, -n) f needle; (Stecknadel) pin; **Nadelstreifen** pl pinstripes pl

Nagel (-s, Nägel) m nail; **Nagelfeile** f nail-file; **Nagellack** m nail varnish (o polish); **Nagellackentferner** (-s, -) m nail-varnish (o nail-polish) remover; **Nagelschere** f nail scissors pl

nah(e) adj, adv (räumlich) near(by), (zeitlich) near; (Verwandte, Freunde) close; **jdm ~e gehen** to upset sb; **jdm etw ~e legen** to suggest sth to sb; **~e liegen** to be obvious ▷ prep +dat near (to), close to; **Nähe** (-) f (Umgebung) vicinity; **in der ~** nearby; **in der ~ von** near to

nähen vt, vi to sew

nähere(r, s) adj (Erklärung, Erkundigung) more detailed; **die ~ Umgebung** the immediate area; **Nähere(s)** nt details pl; **nähern** vr **sich ~** to approach

nahezu adv virtually, almost

nahm imperf von **nehmen**

Nähmaschine f sewing machine; **Nähnadel** f (sewing) needle

nahrhaft adj nourishing, nutritious; **Nahrung** f food; **Nahrungsmittel** nt food

Naht (-, Nähte) f seam, (Med) stitches pl, suture; (Tech) join

Nahverkehr m local traffic; **Nahverkehrszug** m local train

Nähzeug nt sewing kit

naiv adj naive

Name (-ns, -n) m name

nämlich adv that is to say, namely; (denn) since

nannte imperf von **nennen**

Napf (-(e)s, Näpfe) m bowl, dish

Narbe (-, -n) f scar

Narkose (-, -n) f anaesthetic

Narzisse (-, -n) f narcissus

naschen vt, vi to nibble; **Naschkatze** f (fam) nibbler; **eine ~ sein** to have a sweet tooth

Nase (-, -n) f nose; **Nasenbluten** (-s) nt nosebleed; **~ haben** to have a nosebleed; **Nasenloch** nt nostril; **Nasentropfen** pl nose drops pl

Nashorn nt rhinoceros

nass adj wet; **Nässe** (-) f wetness; **nässen** vi (Wunde) to weep

Nation (-, -en) f nation; **national** adj national; **Nationalfeiertag** m national holiday; **Nationalhymne** (-, -n) f national anthem; **Nationalität** f nationality; **Nationalmannschaft** f national team; **Nationalspieler(in)** m(f) international (player)

NATO (-) f abk = **North Atlantic Treaty Organization** NATO, Nato

Natur f nature; **Naturkost** f health food; **natürlich** adj natural ▷ adv naturally; (selbstverständlich) of course; **Naturpark** m nature reserve; **naturrein** adj natural, pure; **Naturschutz** m conservation; **Naturschutzgebiet** nt nature reserve; **Naturwissenschaft** f (natural) science; **Naturwissenschaftler(in)** m(f) scientist

Navigationssystem nt (Auto) navigation system

n. Chr. abk = **nach Christus** AD

Nebel (-s, -) m fog, mist; **nebelig** adj foggy, misty; **Nebelscheinwerfer** m foglamp; **Nebelschlussleuchte** f (Auto) rear fog light

neben prep +akk o dat next to; (außer) apart from, besides; **nebenan** adv next door; **Nebenausgang** m side exit; **nebenbei** adv

at the same time; (außerdem) additionally; (beiläufig) incidentally; **nebeneinander** adv side by side; **Nebeneingang** m side entrance; **Nebenfach** nt subsidiary subject

nebenher adv (zusätzlich) besides; (gleichzeitig) at the same time; (daneben) alongside

Nebenkosten pl extra charges pl, extras pl; **Nebensache** f minor matter; **nebensächlich** adj minor; **Nebensaison** f low season; **Nebenstelle** f (Geschäft) branch; (Telefon) extension; **Nebenstraße** f side street; **Nebenwirkung** f side effect

neblig adj foggy, misty

necken vt to tease

Neffe (-n, -n) m nephew

negativ adj negative; **Negativ** nt (Foto) negative

nehmen (nahm, genommen) vt to take; **jdm etw ~** to take sth (away) from sb; **wie man's nimmt** it depends on how you look at it; **den Bus/Zug ~** to take the bus/train; **jdn/etw ernst ~** to take sb/sth seriously; **etw zu sich ~** to eat sth; **jdn zu sich ~** to have sb come and live with one; **jdn an die Hand ~** to take sb by the hand

neidisch adj envious

neigen vi **zu etw ~** to tend towards sth; **Neigung** f (des Geländes) slope; (Tendenz) inclination; (Vorliebe) liking

nein adv no

Nektarine f nectarine

Nelke (-, -n) f carnation; (Gewürz) clove

nennen (nannte, genannt) vt to name; (mit Namen) to call

Neonazi (-s, -s) m neo-Nazi

Neonlicht nt neon light; **Neonröhre** f neon tube

Nepal (-s) nt Nepal

Neptun (-s) m Neptune

Nerv (-s, -en) m nerve; **jdm auf die ~en gehen** to get on sb's nerves; **nerven** vt **jdn ~** (fam) to get on sb's nerves; **Nervenzusammenbruch** m nervous breakdown; **nervös** adj nervous

Nest (-(e)s, -er) nt nest; (pej: Ort) dump

nett adj nice, (freundlich) kind; **sei so ~ und ...** do me a favour and ...; **netto** adv net

Netz (-es, -e) nt net; (für Einkauf) string bag; (System) network; (Stromnetz) mains, power (US); **Netzanschluss** m mains connection; **Netzbetreiber(in)** m(f) network operator; (Inform) Internet (o Net) operator; **Netzgerät** nt power pack; **Netzkarte** f season ticket; **Netzwerk** nt (Inform) network; **Netzwerkkarte** f network card

neu adj new; (Sprache, Geschichte) modern; **die ~esten Nachrichten** the latest news; **Neubau** m new building; **neuerdings** adv recently; **Neueröffnung** f (Geschäft) new business; **Neuerung** f innovation; (Reform) reform

Neugier f curiosity; **neugierig** adj curious; (auf +akk about); **ich bin ~, ob ...** I wonder whether (o if) ...; **ich bin ~, was du dazu sagst** I'll be interested to hear what you have to say about it

Neuheit f novelty; **Neuigkeit** f news sing; **eine ~** a piece of news; **Neujahr** nt New Year; **prosit ~!** Happy New Year; **neulich** adv recently, the other day; **Neumond** m new moon

neun num nine; **neunhundert** num nine hundred; **neunmal** adv nine times; **neunte(r, s)** adj ninth; siehe auch **dritte**; **Neuntel** (-s, -) nt

ninth; **neunzehn** num nineteen; **neunzehnte(r, s)** adj nineteenth; siehe auch **dritte**; **neunzig** num ninety; **in den ~er Jahren** in the nineties; **Neunzigerjahre** pl nineties pl; **neunzigste(r, s)** adj ninetieth

neureich adj nouveau riche

Neurologe m, **Neurologin** f neurologist; **Neurose** (-, n) f neurosis; **neurotisch** adj neurotic

Neuseeland nt New Zealand

Neustart m (Inform) restart, reboot

neutral adj neutral

neuwertig adj nearly new

Nicaragua (-s) nt Nicaragua

nicht adv not; **er kommt ~** (überhaupt nicht) he doesn't come; (diesmal) he isn't coming; **er kommt, ~ wahr?** he's coming, isn't he?; **er kommt ~, wahr?** he isn't coming, is he?; **sie wohnt ~ mehr hier** she doesn't live here any more; **gar ~** not at all; **ich kenne ihn auch ~** I don't know him either; **auch ~** either; **noch ~** not yet; **~ berühren!** do not touch ▷ präf non-

Nichte (-, n) f niece

Nichtraucher(in) m(f) nonsmoker; **Nichtraucherabteil** nt non-smoking compartment; **Nichtraucherzone** f non-smoking area

nichts pron nothing; **für und wieder ~** for nothing at all; **ich habe ~ gesagt** I didn't say anything; **~ sagend** meaningless; **macht ~** never mind

Nichtschwimmer(in) m(f) nonswimmer

nicken vi to nod

Nickerchen nt nap

nie adv never; **~ wieder** (o mehr) never again; **fast ~** hardly ever

nieder adj (niedrig) low; (gering) inferior ▷ adv down; **niedergeschlagen** adj depressed; **Nieder-**

lage f defeat
Niederlande pl Netherlands pl;
Niederländer(in) m(f) Dutchman / Dutchwoman; **niederländisch** adj Dutch; **Niederländisch**
nt Dutch
Niederlassung f branch
Niederösterreich nt Lower
Austria; **Niedersachsen** nt Lower
Saxony
Niederschlag m (Meteo) precipitation; (Regen) rainfall
niedlich adj sweet, cute
niedrig adj low; (Qualität) inferior
niemals adv never
niemand pron nobody, no one;
ich habe ~en gesehen I haven't
seen anyone; **~ von ihnen** none of
them
Niere (-, -n) f kidney; **Nierenentzündung** f kidney infection; **Nierensteine** pl kidney stones pl
nieseln vi impers to drizzle; **Nieselregen** m drizzle
niesen vi to sneeze
Niete (-, -n) f (Los) blank; (Reinfall)
flop; (pej: Mensch) failure; (Tech) rivet
Nigeria (-s) nt Nigeria
Nikotin (-s) nt nicotine; **nikotinarm** adj low in nicotine
Nilpferd nt hippopotamus
nippen vi to sip; **an etw** (dat) **~** to
sip sth
nirgends adv nowhere
Nische (-, -n) f niche
Nitrat nt nitrate
Niveau (-s, -s) nt level; **sie hat ~**
she's got class
nobel adj (großzügig) generous;
(fam: luxuriös) classy, posh; **Nobelpreis** m Nobel Prize
noch adv still; (außerdem) else; **wer
kommt ~?** who else is coming?; **~
nie** never; **~ nicht** not yet; **immer ~**
still; **~ einmal** (once) again; **~ am
selben Tag** that (very) same day; **~**

besser / mehr / jetzt even better /
more / now; **wie heißt sie ~?** what's
her name again?; **~ ein Bier, bitte**
another beer, please ▷ conj nor;
nochmal(s) adv again, once more
Nominativ m nominative (case)
Nonne (-, -n) f nun
Non-Stop-Flug m nonstop flight
Nord north; **Nordamerika** nt
North America; **Norddeutschland**
nt Northern Germany; **Norden** (-s)
m north; **im ~ Deutschlands** in the
north of Germany; **Nordeuropa** nt
Northern Europe; **Nordirland** nt
Northern Ireland; **nordisch** adj
(Völker, Sprache) Nordic; **Nordkorea**
(-s) nt North Korea; **nördlich** adj
northern; (Kurs, Richtung) northerly;
Nordost(en) m northeast; **Nordpol** m North Pole; **Nordrhein-Westfalen** (-s) nt North Rhine-Westphalia; **Nordsee** f North Sea;
nordwärts adv north, northwards;
Nordwest(en) m northwest;
Nordwind m north wind
nörgeln vi to grumble
Norm (-, -en) f norm; (Größenvorschrift) standard
normal adj normal; **Normalbenzin** nt regular (petrol (BRIT)) o gas
(US)); **normalerweise** adv normally
normen vt to standardize
Norwegen (-s) nt Norway; **Norweger(in)** m(f) Norwegian; **norwegisch** adj Norwegian; **Norwegisch** nt Norwegian
Not (-, Nöte) f need; (Armut) poverty; (Elend) hardship; (Bedrängnis)
trouble; (Mangel) want; (Mühe)
trouble; (Zwang) necessity; **zur ~** if
necessary; (gerade noch) just about
Notar(in) m(f) public notary; **notariell ~ beglaubigt** attested
by a notary
Notarzt m, **Notärztin** f emer-

gency doctor; **Notarztwagen** m emergency ambulance; **Notaus gang** m emergency exit; **Notbremse** f emergency brake; **Notdienst** m emergency service, afterhours service; **notdürftig** adj scanty; (behelfsmäßig) makeshift

Note (-, -n) f note; (in Schule) mark grade (US); (Mus) note

Notebook ((s), s) nt (Inform) notebook

Notfall m emergency; **notfalls** adv if necessary

notieren vt to note down

nötig adj necessary; **etw ~ haben** to need sth

Notiz (-, -en) f note; (Zeitungs~) item; **Notizblock** m notepad; **Notizbuch** nt notebook

Notlage f crisis; (Elend) plight; **notlanden** vi to make a forced (o emergency) landing; **Notruf** m emergency call; **Notrufnummer** f emergency number; **Notrufsäule** f emergency telephone

notwendig adj necessary

Nougat (-s, -s) m od nt nougat

November ((s),) m November; siehe auch **Juni**

Nr. abk = **Nummer** No., no.

Nu m **im ~** in no time

nüchtern adj sober; (Magen) empty

Nudel (-, -n) f noodle; **~n** pl (italienische) pasta sing; **Nudelsuppe** f noodle soup

null num zero; (Tel) O (BRIT), zero (US); **~ Fehler** no mistakes; **~ Uhr** midnight; **Null** (-, -en) f nought, zero; (pej: Mensch) dead loss; **Nulltarif** m **zum ~** free of charge

Numerus clausus (-) m restriction on the number of students allowed to study a particular subject

Nummer (-, -n) f number; **nummerieren** vt to number; **Num-**

mernschild nt (Aut) number plate (BRIT), license plate (US)

nun adv now; **von ~ an** from now on ▷ interj well; **~ gut!** all right, then; **es ist ~ mal so** that's the way it is

nur adv only; **nicht ~ ..., sondern auch ...** not only ... but also ...; **~ Anna nicht** except Anna

Nürnberg (s) nt Nuremberg

Nuss (-, Nüsse) f nut; **Nussknacker** (-s, -) m nutcracker; **Nuss-Nougat-Creme** f chocolate nut cream

Nutte (-, -n) f (fam) tart

nutz, **nütze** adj **zu nichts ~ sein** to be useless; **nutzen**, **nützen** vt to use (zu etw for sth); **was nützt es?** what use is it? ▷ vi to be of use; **das nützt nicht viel** that doesn't help much; **es nützt nichts(, es zu tun)** it's no use (doing it); **Nutzen** (-s, -) m usefulness; (Gewinn) profit; **nützlich** adj useful

Nylon (-s) nt nylon

o *interj* oh

O *abk* = **Ost** E

Oase (-, -n) f oasis

ob *conj* if, whether; **so als** ~ as if; **er tut so, als** ~ **er krank wäre** he's pretending to be sick; **und** ~**!** you bet

obdachlos *adj* homeless

oben *adv* (am oberen Ende) at the top; (obenauf) on (the) top; (im Haus) upstairs; (in einem Text) above; ~ **erwähnt** (o **genannt**) above-mentioned; **mit dem Gesicht nach** ~ face up; **da** ~ up there; **von** ~ **bis unten** from top to bottom; **siehe** ~ see above

Ober (-s, -) m waiter

obere(r, s) *adj* upper, top

Oberfläche f surface; **oberfläch-lich** *adj* superficial; **Oberge-schoss** *nt* upper floor

oberhalb *adv, prep +gen* above

Oberhemd *nt* shirt; **Oberkörper** m upper body; **Oberlippe** f upper lip; **Oberösterreich** *nt* Upper Austria; **Oberschenkel** m thigh

oberste(r, s) *adj* very top, top-most

Oberteil *nt* top; **Oberweite** f bust / chest measurement

obig *adj* above(-mentioned)

Objekt (-(e)s, -e) *nt* object

objektiv *adj* objective; **Objektiv** *nt* lens

obligatorisch *adj* compulsory, obligatory

Oboe (-, -n) f oboe

Observatorium *nt* observatory

Obst (-(e)s) *nt* fruit; **Obstkuchen** m fruit tart; **Obstsalat** m fruit salad

obszön *adj* obscene

obwohl *conj* although

Ochse (-n, -n) m ox; **Ochsen-schwanzsuppe** f oxtail soup

ocker *adj* ochre

öd(e) *adj* waste; (unbebaut) barren; (fig) dull

oder *conj* or; ~ **aber** or else; **er kommt doch,** ~**?** he's coming, isn't he?

Ofen (-s, Öfen) m oven; (Heizofen) heater; (Kohleofen) stove; (Herd) cooker, stove; **Ofenkartoffel** f baked (o jacket) potato

offen *adj* open; (aufrichtig) frank; (Stelle) vacant ▷ *adv* frankly; ~ **ge-sagt** to be honest

offenbar *adj* obvious; **offen-sichtlich** *adj* evident, obvious

öffentlich *adj* public; **Öffentlich-keit** f (Leute) public; (einer Ver-sammlung etc) public nature

offiziell *adj* official

offline *adv* (Inform) offline

öffnen *vt* to open ▷ *vr* **sich** ~ to open; **Öffner** (-s, -) m opener; **Öffnung** f opening; **Öffnungs-zeiten** *pl* opening times *pl*

oft *adv* often; **schon** ~ many times; **öfter** *adv* more often (o frequent-ly); **öfters** *adv* often, frequently

ohne *conj, prep +akk* without; ~

weiteres without a second thought; (*sofort*) immediately; **~ ein Wort zu sagen** without saying a word; **~ mich** count me out

Ohnmacht (*-machten*) *f* unconsciousness; (*Hilflosigkeit*) helplessness; **in ~ fallen** to faint; **ohnmächtig** *adj* unconscious; **sie ist ~** she has fainted

Ohr ((e)s, en) *nt* ear; (*Gehör*) hearing

Öhr ((e)s, e) *nt* eye

Ohrenarzt *m*, **Ohrenärztin** *f* ear specialist; **Ohrenschmerzen** *pl* earache; **Ohrentropfen** *pl* ear drops *pl*; **Ohrfeige** *f* slap (in the face); **Ohrläppchen** *nt* earlobe; **Ohrringe** *pl* earrings *pl*

oje *interj* oh dear

okay *interj* OK, okay

Ökoladen *m* health food store; **ökologisch** *adj* ecological; **~e Landwirtschaft** organic farming

ökonomisch *adj* economic, (*sparsam*) economical

Ökosystem *nt* ecosystem

Oktanzahl *f* (*bei Benzin*) octane rating

Oktober (*-(s)*, *-*) *m* October; **siehe auch Juni**

● OKTOBERFEST

● The annual October beer festival, the **Oktoberfest**, takes place in Munich on a huge field where beer
● tents, roller coasters and many
● other amusements are set up.
● People sit at long wooden tables,
● drink beer from enormous litre
● beer mugs, eat pretzels and listen
● to brass bands. It is a great attraction for tourists and locals
● alike.

Öl (*-(e)s*, *-e*) *nt* oil; **Ölbaum** *m* olive tree; **ölen** *vt* to oil; (*Tech*) to lubricate; **Ölfarbe** *f* oil paint; **Ölfilter** *m* oil filter; **Ölgemälde** *nt* oil painting; **Ölheizung** *f* oil-fired central heating; **ölig** *adj* oily

oliv *adj inv* olive-green; **Olive** (*-*, *-n*) *f* olive; **Olivenöl** *nt* olive oil

Ölmessstab *m* dipstick; **Ölofen** *m* oil stove; **Ölpest** *f* oil pollution; **Ölsardine** *f* sardine in oil; **Ölstandanzeiger** *m* (*Auto*) oil gauge; **Ölteppich** *m* oil slick; **Ölwechsel** *m* oil change

Olympiade *f* Olympic Games *pl*; **olympisch** *adj* Olympic

Oma *f*, **Omi** (*-s*, *-s*) *f* grandma, gran(ny)

Omelett (*-(e)s*, *-s*) *nt*, **Omelette** *f* omelette

Omnibus *m* bus

onanieren *vi* to masturbate

Onkel (*-s*, *-*) *m* uncle

online *adv* (*Inform*) online; **Online-dienst** *m* (*Inform*) online service

OP (*-s*, *-s*) *m abk* = **Operationssaal** operating theatre (*BRIT*) (*o room* (*US*))

Opa *m*, **Opi** (*-s*, *-s*) *m* grandpa, grandad

Openairkonzert *nt* open-air concert

Oper (*-*, *-n*) *f* opera; (*Gebäude*) opera house

Operation *f* operation

Operette *f* operetta

operieren *vi* to operate ▷ *vt* to operate on

Opernsänger(in) *m(f)* opera singer

Opfer (*-s*, *-*) *nt* sacrifice; (*Mensch*) victim; **ein ~ bringen** to make a sacrifice

Opium (*-s*) *nt* opium

Opposition *f* opposition

Optiker(in) (*-s*, *-*) *m(f)* optician

optimal *adj* optimal, optimum

optimistisch *adj* optimistic

oral *adj* oral; **Oralverkehr** *m* oral

sex

orange adj inv orange; **Orange** (-, -n) f orange; **Orangenmarmelade** f marmalade; **Orangensaft** m orange juice

Orchester (-s, -) nt orchestra

Orchidee (-, -n) f orchid

Orden (-s, -) m (Rel) order; (Mil) decoration

ordentlich adj (anständig) respectable; (geordnet) tidy, neat; (fam: annehmbar) not bad; (fam: tüchtig) proper ▷ adv properly

ordinär adj common, vulgar; (Witz) dirty

ordnen vt to sort out; **Ordner** (-s, -) m (bei Veranstaltung) steward; (Aktenordner) file; **Ordnung** f order; (Geordnetsein) tidiness; **(geht) in ~!** (that's) all right; **mit dem Drucker ist etwas nicht in ~** there's something wrong with the printer

Oregano (-s) m oregano

Organ (-s, -e) nt organ; (Stimme) voice

Organisation f organization; **organisieren** vt to organize; (fam: beschaffen) to get hold of ▷ vr **sich ~** to organize

Organismus m organism

Orgasmus m orgasm

Orgel (-, -n) f organ

Orgie (-, -n) f orgy

orientalisch adj oriental

orientieren vr **sich ~** to get one's bearings; **Orientierung** f orientation; **Orientierungssinn** m sense of direction

original adj original; (echt) genuine; **Original** (-s, -e) nt original; **Originalfassung** f original version

originell adj original; (komisch) witty

Orkan (-(e)s, -e) m hurricane

Ort (-(e)s, -e) m place; (Dorf) village; **an ~ und Stelle, vor ~** on the spot

Orthopäde (-n, -n) m, **Orthopädin** f orthopaedist

örtlich adj local; **Ortschaft** f village, small town; **Ortsgespräch** nt local call; **Ortstarif** m local rate; **Ortszeit** f local time

● OSSI

● **Ossi** is a colloquial and rather
● derogatory word used to describe
● a German from the former **DDR**.

Ost east; **Ostdeutschland** nt (als Landesteil) Eastern Germany; (Hist) East Germany; **Osten** (-s) m east

Osterei nt Easter egg; **Osterglocke** f daffodil; **Osterhase** m Easter bunny; **Ostermontag** m Easter Monday; **Ostern** (-, -) nt Easter; **an** (o zu) **~** at Easter; **frohe ~** Happy Easter

Österreich (-s) nt Austria; **Österreicher(in)** (-s, -) m(f) Austrian; **österreichisch** adj Austrian

Ostersonntag m Easter Sunday

Osteuropa nt Eastern Europe; **Ostküste** f east coast; **östlich** adj eastern; (Kurs, Richtung) easterly; **Ostsee** f **die ~** the Baltic (Sea); **Ostwind** m east(erly) wind

OSZE (-) f abk = **Organisation für Sicherheit und Zusammenarbeit in Europa** OSCE

Otter (-s, -) m otter

out adj (fam) out; **outen** vt to out

oval adj oval

Overheadprojektor m overhead projector

Ozean (-s, -e) m ocean; **der Stille ~** the Pacific (Ocean)

Ozon (-s) nt ozone; **Ozonbelastung** f ozone level; **Ozonloch** nt hole in the ozone layer; **Ozonschicht** f ozone layer; **Ozonwerte** pl ozone levels pl

P

paar adj inv **ein ~** a few; **ein ~ Mal** a few times; **ein ~ Äpfel** some apples

Paar (-(e)s, -e) nt pair; (Ehepaar) couple; **ein ~ Socken** a pair of socks

pachten vt to lease

Päckchen nt package; (Zigaretten) packet; (zum Verschicken) small parcel; **packen** vt to pack; (fassen) to grasp, to seize; (fam: schaffen) to manage; (fig: fesseln) to grip; **Packpapier** nt brown paper; **Packung** f packet, pack (US), **Packungsbeilage** f package insert, patient information leaflet

Pädagoge (-n, -n) m, **Pädagogin** f teacher; **pädagogisch** adj educational; **~e Hochschule** college of education

Paddel (-s, -) nt paddle; **Paddelboot** nt canoe; **paddeln** vi to paddle

Paket (-(e)s, -e) nt packet; (Postpaket) parcel; (Inform) package; **Paketbombe** f parcel bomb; **Paketkar-**

te f dispatch form (to be filled in with details of the sender and the addressee when handing in a parcel at the post office)

Pakistan (s) nt Pakistan

Palast (-es, Paläste) m palace

Palästina (-s) nt Palestine; **Palästinenser(in)** (s,) m(f) Palestinian

Palatschinken pl filled pancakes pl

Palette f (von Maler) palette, (auf depalette) pallet; (Vielfalt) range

Palme (-, -n) f palm (tree); **Palmsonntag** m Palm Sunday

Pampelmuse (-, -n) f grapefruit

pampig adj (fam: frech) cheeky; (breiig) gooey

Panda(bär) (-s, -s) m panda

panieren vt (Gastr) to coat with breadcrumbs; **paniert** adj breaded

Panik f panic

Panne (-, -n) f (Auto) breakdown; (Missgeschick) slip; **Pannendienst** m, **Pannenhilfe** f breakdown (o rescue) service

Pant(h)er (-s, -) m panther

Pantoffel (-s, -n) m slipper

Pantomime (-, -n) f mime

Panzer (-s, -) m (Panzerung) armour (plating); (Mil) tank

Papa (-s, -s) m dad(dy), pa (US)

Papagei (-s, -en) m parrot

Papaya (-, -s) f papaya

Papier (-s, -e) nt paper; **~e** pl (Ausweispapiere) papers pl; (Dokumente, Urkunden) papers pl, documents pl; **Papiercontainer** m paper bank; **Papierformat** nt paper size; **Papiergeld** nt paper money; **Papierkorb** m wastepaper basket; (Inform) recycle bin; **Papiertaschentuch** nt (paper) tissue; **Papiertonne** f paper bank

Pappbecher m paper cup; **Pappe** (-, -n) f cardboard; **Pappkarton** m cardboard box; **Pappteller** m paper plate

Paprika (-s, -s) m (Gewürz) paprika; (Schote) pepper

Papst (-(e)s, Päpste) m pope

Paradeiser (-s, -) m tomato

Paradies (-es, -e) nt paradise

Paragliding (-s) nt paragliding

Paragraph (-en, -en) m paragraph; (Jur) section

parallel adj parallel

Paranuss f Brazil nut

Parasit (-en, -en) m parasite

parat adj ready; **etw ~ haben** to have sth ready

Pärchen nt couple

Parfüm (-s, -s o -e) nt perfume; **Parfümerie** f perfumery; **parfümieren** vt to scent, to perfume

Pariser (-s, -) m (fam: Kondom) rubber

Park (-s, -s) m park

Park-and-ride-System nt park-and-ride system; **Parkanlage** f park; (um Gebäude) grounds pl; **Parkbank** f park bench; **Parkdeck** nt parking level; **parken** vt, vi to park

Parkett (-s, -e) nt parquet flooring; (Theat) stalls pl (BRIT), orchestra (US)

Parkhaus nt multi-storey car park (BRIT), parking garage (US)

parkinsonsche Krankheit f Parkinson's disease

Parkkralle f (Auto) wheel clamp; **Parklicht** nt parking light; **Parklücke** f parking space; **Parkplatz** m (für ein Auto) parking space; (für mehrere Autos) car park (BRIT), parking lot (US); **Parkscheibe** f parking disc; **Parkscheinautomat** m pay point; (Parkscheinausgabegerät) ticket machine; **Parkuhr** f parking meter; **Parkverbot** nt (Stelle) no-parking zone; **hier ist ~** you can't park here

Parlament nt parliament

Parmesan (-s) m Parmesan (cheese)

Partei f party

Parterre (-s, -s) nt ground floor (BRIT), first floor (US)

Partie f part; (Spiel) game; (Mann, Frau) catch; **mit von der ~ sein** to be in on it

Partitur f (Mus) score

Partizip (-s, -ien) nt participle

Partner(in) (-s, -) m(f) partner; **Partnerschaft** f partnership; **eingetragene ~** civil partnership; **Partnerstadt** f twin town

Party (-, -s) f party; **Partymuffel** (-s, -) m party pooper; **Partyservice** m catering service

Pass (-es, Pässe) m pass; (Ausweis) passport

passabel adj reasonable

Passagier (-s, -e) m passenger

Passamt nt passport office

Passant(in) m(f) passer-by; **Passbild** nt passport photo

passen vi (Größe) to fit; (Farbe, Stil) to go (zu with); (auf Frage) to pass; **passt (es) dir morgen?** does tomorrow suit you?; **das passt mir gut** that suits me fine; **passend** adj suitable; (zusammenpassend) matching; (angebracht) fitting; (Zeit) convenient; **haben Sie es nicht ~?** (Kleingeld) have you got the right change?

passieren vi to happen

passiv adj passive

Passkontrolle f passport control

Passwort nt password

Paste (-, -n) f paste

Pastellfarbe f pastel colour

Pastete (-, -n) f (warmes Gericht) pie; (Pastetchen) vol-au-vent; (ohne Teig) pâté

Pastor, in (-s, -en) m(f) minister, vicar

Pate (-n, -n) m godfather; **Patenkind** nt godchild

Patient(in) m(f) patient

Patin f godmother

Patrone (-, -n) f cartridge

patsch interj splat; **Patsche** (-, -n) f (Fliegen~) swat; (Bedrängnis) mess; **patschnass** adj soaking wet

pauschal adj (Kosten) inclusive; (Urteil) sweeping; **Pauschale** (-, -n) f, **Pauschalgebühr** f flat rate (charge); **Pauschalpreis** m flat rate; (für Hotel, Reise) all-inclusive price; **Pauschalreise** f package tour

Pause (-, -n) f break; (Theat) interval; (Kino etc) intermission; (Innehalten) pause

Pavian (-s, -e) m baboon

Pavillon (-s, -s) m pavilion

Pay-TV (-s) nt pay per view television, pay TV

Pazifik (-s) m Pacific (Ocean)

PC (-s, -s) m abk = **Personalcomputer** PC

Pech (-s, -e) nt (fig) bad luck, ~ **haben** to be unlucky; ~ **gehabt!** tough (luck)

Pedal (-s, -e) nt pedal

Pediküre (-, -en) f pedicure

Peeling (-s, -s) nt (facial / body) scrub

peinlich adj (unangenehm) embarrassing, awkward; (genau) painstaking; **es war mir sehr ~** I was totally embarrassed

Peitsche (-, -n) f whip

Pelikan (-s, -e) m pelican

Pellkartoffeln pl potatoes pl boiled in their skins

Pelz (-es, -e) m fur; **pelzig** adj (Zunge) furred

pendeln vi (Zug, Bus) to shuttle; (Mensch) to commute; **Pendelverkehr** m shuttle traffic; (für Pendler) commuter traffic; **Pendler(in)** (-s, -) m(f) commuter

penetrant adj sharp; (Mensch)

pushy

Penis (-, -se) m penis

Pension f (Geld) pension; (Ruhestand) retirement; (für Gäste) guesthouse, B&B; **pensioniert** adj retired; **Pensionsgast** m guest (in a guesthouse)

Peperoni (-, -) f chilli

per prep +akk by, per; (pro) per; (bis) by

perfekt adj perfect

Pergamentpapier nt greaseproof paper

Periode (-, -n) f period

Perle (-, -n) f (a. fig) pearl

perplex adj dumbfounded

Person (-, -en) f person; **ein Tisch für drei ~en** a table for three; **Personal** (-s) nt staff, personnel; (Bedienung) servants pl; **Personalausweis** m identity card; **Personalien** pl particulars pl; **Personenschaden** m injury to persons; **Personenwaage** f (bathroom) scales pl; **Personenzug** m passenger train; **persönlich** adj personal; (auf Briefen) private ▷ adv personally; (selbst) in person; **Persönlichkeit** f personality

Peru (-s) nt Peru

Perücke (-, -n) f wig

pervers adj perverted

pessimistisch adj pessimistic

Pest (-) f plague

Petersilie f parsley

Petroleum (-s) nt paraffin (BRIT), kerosene (US)

Pfad (-(e)s, -e) m path; **Pfadfinder** (-s, -) m boy scout; **Pfadfinderin** f girl guide

Pfahl (-(e)s, Pfähle) m post, stake

Pfand (-(e)s, Pfänder) nt security; (Flaschenpfand) deposit; (im Spiel) forfeit; **Pfandflasche** f returnable bottle

Pfanne (-, -n) f (frying) pan

Pfannkuchen m pancake

Pfarrei f parish; **Pfarrer(in)** (-s, -) m(f) priest

Pfau (-(e)s, -en) m peacock

Pfeffer (-s, -) m pepper; **Pfefferkuchen** m gingerbread; **Pfefferminze** (-e) f peppermint; **Pfefferminztee** m peppermint tea; **Pfeffermühle** f pepper mill; **pfeffern** vt to put pepper on / in; **Pfefferstreuer** (-s, -) m pepper pot

Pfeife (-, -n) f whistle; (für Tabak, von Orgel) pipe; **pfeifen** (pfiff, gepfiffen) vt, vi to whistle

Pfeil (-(e)s, -e) m arrow

Pfeiltaste f (Inform) arrow key

Pferd (-(e)s, -e) nt horse; **Pferdeschwanz** m (Frisur) ponytail; **Pferdestall** m stable; **Pferdestärke** f horsepower

pfiff imperf von **pfeifen**

Pfifferling m chanterelle

Pfingsten (-, -) nt Whitsun, Pentecost (US); **Pfingstmontag** m Whit Monday; **Pfingstsonntag** m Whit Sunday, Pentecost (US); **Pfingstrose** f peony

Pfirsich (-s, -e) m peach

Pflanze (-, -n) f plant; **pflanzen** vt to plant; **Pflanzenfett** nt vegetable fat

Pflaster (-s, -) nt (für Wunde) plaster, Band Aid® (US); (Straßenpflaster) road surface, pavement (US)

Pflaume (-, -n) f plum

Pflege (-, -n) f care; (Krankenpflege) nursing; (von Autos, Maschinen) maintenance; **pflegebedürftig** adj in need of care; **pflegeleicht** adj easy-care; (fig) easy to handle; **pflegen** vt to look after; (Kranke) to nurse; (Beziehungen) to foster; (Fingernägel, Gesicht) to take care of; (Daten) to maintain; **Pflegepersonal** nt nursing staff; **Pflegeversicherung** f long-term care insur-

ance

Pflicht (-, -en) f duty; (Sport) compulsory section; **pflichtbewusst** adj conscientious; **Pflichtfach** nt (Schule) compulsory subject; **Pflichtversicherung** f compulsory insurance

pflücken vt to pick

Pforte (-, -n) f gate; **Pförtner(in)** (-s, -) m(f) porter

Pfosten (-s, -) m post

Pfote (-, -n) f paw

pfui interj ugh

Pfund (-(e)s, -e) nt pound

pfuschen vi (fam) to be sloppy

Pfütze (-, -n) f puddle

Phantasie f siehe **Fantasie**; **phantastisch** adj siehe **fantastisch**

Phase (-, -n) f phase

Philippinen pl Philippines pl

Philosophie f philosophy

Photo nt siehe **Foto**

pH-neutral adj pH-balanced; **pH-Wert** m pH-value

Physalis (-, Physalen) f physalis

Physik f physics sing

physisch adj physical

Pianist(in) (-en, -en) m(f) pianist

Pickel (-s, -) m pimple; (Werkzeug) pickaxe; (Berg~) ice-axe

Picknick (-s, -e o -s) nt picnic; **ein ~ machen** to have a picnic

piepsen vi to chirp

piercen vt **sich die Nase ~ lassen** to have one's nose pierced; **Piercing** (-s) nt (body) piercing

pieseln vi (fam) to pee

Pik (-, -) nt (Karten) spades pl

pikant adj spicy

Pilger(in) m(f) pilgrim; **Pilgerfahrt** f pilgrimage

Pille (-, -n) f pill; **sie nimmt die ~** she's on the pill

Pilot(in) (-en, -en) m(f) pilot

Pilz (-es, -e) m (essbar) mushroom;

(giftig) toadstool; *(Med)* fungus

PIN (-, -s) f PIN (number)

pingelig *adj* (fam) fussy

Pinguin (-s, -e) m penguin

Pinie f pine; **Pinienkern** m pine nut

pink *adj* shocking pink

pinkeln *vi* (fam) to pee

Pinsel (-s, -) m (paint)brush

Pinzette f tweezers pl

Pistazie f pistachio

Piste (-, -n) f (Ski) piste; (Aviat) runway

Pistole (-, -n) f pistol

Pixel (-s) nt (Inform) pixel

Pizza (-, -s) f pizza; **Pizzaservice** m pizza delivery service; **Pizzeria** (-, Pizzerien) f pizzeria

Pkw (-(s), -(s)) m abk = **Personenkraftwagen** car

Plakat nt poster

Plakette f (Schildchen) badge; (Aufkleber) sticker

Plan (-(e)s, Pläne) m plan; (Karte) map; **planen** vt to plan

Planet (-en, -en) m planet; **Planetarium** nt planetarium

planmäßig *adj* scheduled

Plan(t)schbecken nt paddling pool; **plan(t)schen** vi to splash around

Planung f planning

Plastik f sculpture ▷ (-s) nt (Kunststoff) plastic; **Plastikfolie** f plastic film; **Plastiktüte** f plastic bag

Platin (-s) nt platinum

platsch *interj* splash

platt *adj* flat; (fam: überrascht) flabbergasted; (fig: geistlos) flat, boring

Platte (-, -n) f (Foto, Tech, Gastr) plate; (Steinplatte) flag; (Schallplatte) record; **Plattenspieler** m record player

Plattform f platform; **Plattfuß** m flat foot; (Reifen) flat (tyre)

Platz (-es, Plätze) m place; (Sitzplatz) seat; (freier Raum) space, room; (in Stadt) square; (Sportplatz) playing field; **nehmen Sie ~** please sit down, take a seat; **ist dieser ~ frei?** is this seat taken?; **Platzanweiser(in)** m(f) usher/usherette

Plätzchen nt spot; (Gebäck) biscuit

platzen vi to burst; (Bombe) to explode

Platzkarte f seat reservation; **Platzreservierung** f seat reservation; **Platzverweis** m er erhielt einen ~ he was sent off; **Platzwunde** f laceration, cut

plaudern vi to chat, to talk

pleite *adj* (fam) broke; **Pleite** (-, -n) f (Bankrott) bankruptcy; (fam: Reinfall) flop

Plombe (-, -n) f lead seal; (Zahnplombe) filling; **plombieren** vt (Zahn) to fill

plötzlich *adj* sudden ▷ *adv* suddenly, all at once

plump *adj* clumsy; (Hände) ungainly; (Körper) shapeless

plumps *interj* thud; (in Flüssigkeit) plop

Plural (-s, -e) m plural

plus *adv* plus; **fünf ~ sieben ist zwölf** five plus seven is (o are) twelve; **zehn Grad ~** ten degrees above zero; **Plus** (,) nt plus; (Fin) profit; (Vorteil) advantage

Plüsch (-(e)s, -e) m plush

Pluto (-) m Pluto

PLZ *abk* = **Postleitzahl** postcode (BRIT), zip code (US)

Po (-s, -s) m (fam) bottom, bum

Pocken pl smallpox sing

poetisch *adj* poetic

Pointe (-, -n) f punch line

Pokal (-s, -e) m goblet; (Sport) cup

pökeln vt to pickle

Pol (-s, -e) m pole

Pole (-n, -n) m Pole; **Polen** (-s) nt

Poland
Police (-, -n) f (insurance) policy
polieren vt to polish
Polin f Pole, Polish woman
Politik f politics sing; (eine bestimmte) policy; **Politiker(in)** m(f) politician; **politisch** adj political
Politur f polish
Polizei f police pl; **Polizeibeamte(r)** m, **Polizeibeamtin** f police officer; **polizeilich** adj police; **sie wird ~ gesucht** the police are looking for her; **Polizeirevier** nt, **Polizeiwache** f police station; **Polizeistunde** f closing time; **Polizeiwache** f police station; **Polizist(in)** m(f) policeman /-woman
Pollen (-s, -) m pollen; **Pollenflug** (-s) m pollen count
polnisch adj Polish; **Polnisch** nt Polish
Polo (-s) nt polo; **Polohemd** nt polo shirt
Polster (-s, -) nt cushion; (Polsterung) upholstery; (in Kleidung) padding; (fig: Geld) reserves pl; **Polstergarnitur** f living-room suite; **Polstermöbel** pl upholstered furniture sing; **polstern** vt to upholster; (Kleidung) to pad
Polterabend m party prior to a wedding, at which old crockery is smashed to bring good luck
poltern vi (Krach machen) to crash; (schimpfen) to rant
Polyester (-s) m polyester
Polypen pl (Med) adenoids pl
Pommes frites pl chips pl (BRIT), French fries pl (US)
Pony (-s, -s) m (Frisur) fringe (BRIT), bangs pl (US) ▷ (-s, -s) nt (Pferd) pony
Popcorn (-s) nt popcorn
Popmusik f pop (music)
populär adj popular
Pore (-, -n) f pore

Pornografie f pornography
Porree (-s, -s) m leeks pl; **eine Stange ~** a leek
Portemonnaie, Portmonee (-s, -s) nt purse
Portier (-s, -s) m porter; siehe auch **Pförtner**
Portion f portion, helping
Porto (-s, -s) nt postage
Porträt, Porträt (-s, -s) nt portrait
Portugal (-s) nt Portugal; **Portugiese** (-n, -n) m Portuguese; **Portugiesin** (-, -nen) f Portuguese; **portugiesisch** adj Portuguese; **Portugiesisch** nt Portuguese
Portwein (-s, -e) m port
Porzellan (-s, -e) nt china
Posaune (-, -n) f trombone
Position f position
positiv adj positive
Post® (-, -en) f post office; (Briefe) post (BRIT), mail; **Postamt** nt post office; **Postanweisung** f postal order (BRIT), money order (US); **Postbank** f German post office bank; **Postbote** m, **-botin** f postman /-woman
Posten (-s, -) m post, position; (Comm) item; (auf Liste) entry
Poster (-s, -) nt poster
Postfach nt post-office box, PO box; **Postkarte** f postcard; **postlagernd** adv poste restante; **Postleitzahl** f postcode (BRIT), zip code (US)
postmodern adj postmodern
Postsparkasse f post office savings bank; **Poststempel** m postmark; **Postweg** m **auf dem ~** by mail
Potenz f (Math) power; (eines Mannes) potency
PR (-, -s) f abk = Public Relations PR
prächtig adj splendid
prahlen vi to boast, to brag

Praktikant(in) m(f) trainee; **Praktikum** (-s, Praktika) nt practical training; **praktisch** adj practical; **~er Arzt** general practitioner

Praline f chocolate

Prämie f (bei Versicherung) premium; (Belohnung) reward; (von Arbeitgeber) bonus

Präparat nt (Med) medicine; (Bio) preparation

Präservativ nt condom

Präsident(in) m(f) president

Praxis (-, Praxen) f practice; (Behandlungsraum) surgery; (von Anwalt) office

präzise adj precise, exact

predigen vt, vi to preach; **Predigt** (-, -en) f sermon

Preis (-es, -e) m (zu zahlen) price; (bei Sieg) prize; **den ersten ~ gewinnen** to win first prize; **Preisausschreiben** nt competition

Preiselbeere f cranberry

preisgünstig adj inexpensive; **Preislage** f price range; **Preisliste** f price list; **Preisschild** nt price tag; **Preisträger(in)** m(f) prizewinner; **preiswert** adj inexpensive

Prellung f bruise

Premiere (-, -n) f premiere, first night

Premierminister(in) m(f) prime minister, premier

Presse (-, -n) f press; **pressen** vt to press

prickeln vi to tingle

Priester(in) (-s, -) m(f) priest / (-) woman) priest

Primel (-, -n) f primrose

primitiv adj primitive

Prinz (-en, -en) m prince; **Prinzessin** f princess

Prinzip (-s, -ien) nt principle; **im ~** basically; **aus ~** on principle

Priorität f priority

privat adj private; **Privatfernse-** hen nt commercial television; **Privatgrundstück** nt private property; **privatisieren** vt to privatize; **Privatquartier** nt private accommodation

pro prep +akk per; **5 Euro ~ Stück / Person** 5 euros each / per person; **Pro** (-) nt pro

Probe (-, -n) f test; (Teststück) sample; (Theat) rehearsal; **Probefahrt** f test drive: **eine ~ machen** to go for a test drive; **Probezeit** f trial period; **probieren** vt, vi to try; (Wein, Speise) to taste, to sample

Problem (-s, -e) nt problem

Produkt (-(e)s, -e) nt product; **Produktion** f production; (produzierte Menge) output; **produzieren** vt to produce

Professor(in) (-s, -en) m(f) professor

Profi (-s, -s) m pro

Profil (-s, -e) nt profile; (von Reifen, Schuhsohle) tread

Profit (-(e)s, -e) m profit; **profitieren** vi to profit (von from)

Prognose (-, -n) f prediction; (Wetter) forecast

Programm (-s, -e) nt programme; (Inform) program; (TV) channel; **Programmheft** nt programme; **programmieren** vt to program; **Programmierer(in)** (-s, -) m(f) programmer; **Programmkino** nt arts (o repertory US)) cinema

Projekt (-(e)s, -e) nt project

Projektor m projector

Promenade (-, -n) f promenade

Promille (-(s), -) nt (blood) alcohol level; **0,8 ~** 0.08 per cent; **Promillegrenze** f legal alcohol limit

prominent adj prominent; **Prominenz** f VIPs pl, prominent figures pl; (fam: Stars) the glitterati pl

Propeller (-s, -) m propeller

prosit interj cheers

Prospekt (-(e)s, -e) m leaflet, brochure

prost interj cheers

Prostituierte(r) mf prostitute

Protest (-(e)s, -e) m protest

Protestant(in) m(f) Protestant; **protestantisch** adj Protestant; **protestieren** vi to protest (gegen against)

Prothese (-, -n) f artificial arm/leg; (Gebiss) dentures pl

Protokoll (-s, -e) nt (bei Sitzung) minutes pl; (diplomatisch) (Inform) protocol; (bei Polizei) statement

protzen vi to show off; **protzig** adj flashy

Proviant (-s, -e) m provisions pl

Provider (-s, -) m (Inform) (service) provider

Provinz (-, -en) f province

Provision f (Comm) commission

provisorisch adj provisional

provozieren vt to provoke

Prozent (-(e)s, -e) nt per cent

Prozess (-es, -e) m (Vorgang) process; (Jur) trial; (Rechtsfall) (court) case; **prozessieren** vi to go to law (mit against)

Prozession f procession

Prozessor (-s, -en) m (Inform) processor

prüde adj prudish

prüfen vt to test; (nachprüfen) to check; **Prüfung** f (Schule) exam; (Überprüfung) check; **eine ~ machen** (Schule) to take an exam

Prügelei f fight; **prügeln** vt to beat ▷ vr **sich ~** to fight

PS abk = **Pferdestärke** hp ▷ abk = **Postskript(um)** PS

pseudo- präf pseudo; **Pseudokrupp** (-s) m (Med) pseudocroup; **Pseudonym** (-s, -e) nt pseudonym

pst interj ssh

Psychiater(in) (-s, -) m(f) psychiatrist; **psychisch** adj psycho-

logical; (Krankheit) mental; **Psychoanalyse** f psychoanalysis; **Psychologe** (-n, -n) m, **Psychologin** f psychologist; **Psychologie** f psychology

Psychopharmaka pl mind-affecting drugs pl, psychotropic drugs pl; **psychosomatisch** adj psychosomatic; **Psychoterror** m psychological intimidation; **Psychotherapie** f psychotherapy

Pubertät f puberty

Publikum (-s) nt audience; (Sport) crowd

Pudding (-s, -e o -s) m blancmange

Pudel (-s, -) m poodle

Puder (-s, -) m powder; **Puderzucker** m icing sugar

Puerto Rico (-s) nt Puerto Rico

Pulli (-s) m, **Pullover** (-s, -) m sweater, pullover, jumper (BRIT)

Puls (-es, -e) m pulse

Pulver (-s, -) nt powder; **Pulverkaffee** m instant coffee; **Pulverschnee** m powder snow

pummelig adj chubby

Pumpe (-, -n) f pump; **pumpen** vt to pump; (fam: verleihen) to lend; (fam: sich ausleihen) to borrow

Pumps pl court shoes pl (BRIT), pumps pl (US)

Punk (-s, -s) m (Musik, Mensch) punk

Punkt (-(e)s, -e) m point; (bei Muster) dot; (Satzzeichen) full stop (BRIT), period (US); **~ zwei Uhr** at two o'clock sharp

pünktlich adj punctual, on time; **Pünktlichkeit** f punctuality

Punsch (-(e)s, -e) m punch

Pupille (-, -n) f pupil

Puppe (-, -n) f doll

pur adj pure; (völlig) sheer; (Whisky) neat

Püree (-s, -s) nt puree; (Kartoffelpüree) mashed potatoes pl

Puste (-) f (fam) puff; **außer ~ sein**

to be puffed

Pustel (-, -n) f pustule; (Pickel) pimple; **pusten** vi to blow; (keuchen) to puff

Pute (-, -n) f turkey; **Putenschnitzel** nt turkey escalope

Putsch (-es, -e) m putsch

Putz (-es) m (Mörtel) plaster

putzen vt to clean; **sich** (dat) **die Nase ~** to blow one's nose; **sich** (dat) **die Zähne ~** to brush one's teeth; **Putzfrau** f cleaner; **Putzlappen** m cloth, **Putzmann** m cleaner; **Putzmittel** nt cleaning agent, cleaner

Puzzle (-s, -s) nt jigsaw (puzzle)

Pyjama (-s, -s) m pyjamas pl

Pyramide (-, -n) f pyramid

Python (-s, -s) m python

Quadrat nt square; **quadratisch** adj square; **Quadratmeter** m square metre

quaken vi (Frosch) to croak; (Ente) to quack

Qual (-, -en) f pain, agony; (seelisch) anguish, **quälen** vt to torment ▷ vr **sich ~** to struggle; (geistig) to torment oneself; **Quälerei** f torture, torment

qualifizieren vt to qualify; (einstufen) to label ▷ vr **sich ~** to qualify

Qualität f quality

Qualle (-, -n) f jellyfish

Qualm ((e)s) m thick smoke; **qualmen** vt, vi to smoke

Quantität f quantity

Quarantäne (-, -n) f quarantine

Quark (-s) m quark; (fam: Unsinn) rubbish

Quartett (-s, -e) nt quartet; (Kartenspiel) happy families sing

Quartier (-s, -e) nt accommodation

quasi adv more or less

Quatsch (-es) m (fam) rubbish; **quatschen** vi (fam) to chat

Quecksilber nt mercury

Quelle (-, -n) f spring; (eines Flusses) source

quellen vi to pour

quer adv crossways, diagonally; (rechtwinklig) at right angles; ~ **über die Straße** straight across the street; **querfeldein** adv across country; **Querflöte** f flute; **Querschnitt** m cross section; **querschnittsgelähmt** adj paraplegic; **Querstraße** f side street

quetschen vt to squash, to crush; (Med) to bruise; **Quetschung** f bruise

Queue (-s, -s) m (billiard) cue

quietschen vi to squeal; (Tür, Bett) to squeak; (Bremsen) to screech

Quirl (-s, -e) m whisk

quitt adj quits, even

Quitte (-, -n) f quince

Quittung f receipt

Quiz (-, -) nt quiz

Quote (-, -n) f rate; (Comm) quota

r

Rabatt (-(e)s, -e) m discount

Rabbi (-(s), -s) m rabbi; **Rabbiner** (-s, -) m rabbi

Rabe (-n, -n) m raven

Rache (-) f revenge, vengeance

Rachen (-s, -) m throat

rächen vt to avenge ▷ vr **sich** ~ to take (one's) revenge (an +dat on)

Rad (-(e)s, Räder) nt wheel; (Fahrrad) bike; ~ **fahren** to cycle; **mit dem** ~ **fahren** to go by bike

Radar (-s) m o nt radar; **Radarfalle** f speed trap; **Radarkontrolle** f radar speed check

radeln vi (fam) to cycle; **Radfahrer(in)** m(f) cyclist; **Radfahrweg** m cycle track (⊘ path)

Radicchio (-s) m (Salatsorte) radicchio

radieren vt to rub out, to erase; **Radiergummi** m rubber (BRIT), eraser; **Radierung** f (Kunst) etching

Radieschen nt radish

radikal adj radical

Radio (-s, -s) nt radio; **im** ~ on the

radio

radioaktiv adj radioactive

Radiologe (-n, -n) m, **Radiologin** f radiologist

Radiorekorder m radio cassette recorder; **Radiosender** m radio station; **Radiowecker** m radio alarm (clock)

Radkappe f (Auto) hub cap

Radler(in) (-s, -) m(f) cyclist

Radler (-s, -) nt ≈ shandy

Radlerhose f cycling shorts pl; **Radrennen** nt cycle racing; (einzelnes Rennen) cycle race; **Radtour** f cycling tour; **Radweg** m cycle track (ø path)

raffiniert adj crafty, cunning; (Zucker) refined

Rafting (-s) nt white water rafting

Ragout (-s, -s) nt ragout

Rahm (-s) m cream

rahmen vt to frame; **Rahmen** (-s, -) m frame

Rakete (-, -n) f rocket

rammen vt to ram

Rampe (-, -n) f ramp

ramponieren vt (fam) to damage, to batter

Ramsch (-(e)s, -e) m junk

ran (fam) kontr von **heran**

Rand (-(e)s, Ränder) m edge; (von Brille, Tasse etc) rim; (auf Papier) margin; (Schmutzrand, unter Augen) ring; (fig) verge, brink

randalieren vi to (go on the) rampage; **Randalierer(in)** (-s, -) m(f) hooligan

Randstein m kerb (BRIT), curb (US); **Randstreifen** m shoulder

rang imperf von **ringen**

Rang (-(e)s, Ränge) m rank; (in Wettbewerb) place; (Theat) circle

rannte imperf von **rennen**

ranzig adj rancid

Rap ((s), s) m (Mus) rap; **rappen** vi (Mus) to rap; **Rapper(in)** (-s, -) m(f)

(Mus) rapper

rar adj rare, scarce

rasant adj quick, rapid

rasch adj quick

rascheln vi to rustle

rasen vi (sich schnell bewegen) to race; (toben) to rave; **gegen einen Baum ~** to crash into a tree

Rasen (-s, -) m lawn

rasend adj (vor Wut) furious

Rasenmäher (-s, -) m lawnmower

Rasierapparat m razor; (elektrischer) shaver; **Rasiercreme** f shaving cream; **rasieren** vt to shave ▷ vr **sich ~** to shave; **Rasierer** m shaver; **Rasiergel** nt shaving gel; **Rasierklinge** f razor blade; **Rasiermesser** m (cut-throat) razor; **Rasierpinsel** m shaving brush; **Rasierschaum** m shaving foam

Rasse (-, -n) f race; (Tiere) breed

Rassismus m racism; **Rassist(in)** m(f) racist; **rassistisch** adj racist

Rast (-, -en) f rest, break; **~ machen** to have a rest (ø break); **rasten** vi to rest; **Rastplatz** m (Auto) rest area; **Raststätte** f (Auto) service area; (Gaststätte) motorway (BRIT) (ø highway (US)) restaurant

Rasur f shave

Rat ((e)s, Ratschläge) m (piece of) advice; **sie hat mir einen ~ gegeben** she gave me some advice; **um ~ fragen** to ask for advice

Rate (-, -n) f instalment; **etw auf ~n kaufen** to buy sth in instalments (BRIT), to buy sth on the instalment plan (US)

raten (riet, geraten) vt, vi to guess; (empfehlen) to advise (jdm sb)

Rathaus nt town hall

Ration f ration

ratlos adj at a loss, helpless; **ratsam** adj advisable

Rätsel (-s, -) nt puzzle; (Worträtsel)

riddle; **das ist mir ein ~** it's a mystery to me; **rätselhaft** adj mysterious

Ratte (-, -n) f rat

rau adj rough, coarse; (Wetter) harsh

Raub (-(e)s) m robbery; (Beute) loot, booty; **rauben** vt to steal; **jdm etw ~** to rob sb of sth; **Räuber(in)** (-s, -) m(f) robber; **Raubfisch** m predatory fish; **Raubkopie** f pirate copy; **Raubmord** m robbery with murder; **Raubtier** nt predator; **Raubüberfall** m mugging; **Raubvogel** m bird of prey

Rauch (-(e)s) m smoke; (Abgase) fumes pl; **rauchen** vt, vi to smoke; **Raucher(in)** (-s, -) m(f) smoker; **Raucherabteil** nt smoking compartment

Räucherlachs m smoked salmon; **räuchern** vt to smoke

rauchig adj smoky; **Rauchmelder** m smoke detector; **Rauchverbot** nt smoking ban; **hier ist ~** there's no smoking here

rauf (fam) kontr von **herauf**

rauh adj alte **rau**; **Rauhreif** m siehe **Raureif**

Raum (-(e)s, Räume) m space; (Zimmer, Platz) room; (Gebiet) area

räumen vt to clear; (Wohnung, Platz) to vacate; (wegbringen) to shift, to move; (in Schrank etc) to put away

Raumfähre f space shuttle; **Raumfahrt** f space travel; **Raumschiff** nt spacecraft, spaceship; **Raumsonde** f space probe; **Raumstation** f space station

Raumtemperatur f room temperature

Räumungsverkauf m clearance sale, closing-down sale

Raupe (-, -n) f caterpillar

Raureif m hoarfrost

raus (fam) kontr von **heraus, hinaus**; **~!** (get) out!

Rausch (-(e)s, Räusche) m intoxication; **einen ~ haben/kriegen** to be/get drunk

rauschen vi (Wasser) to rush; (Baum) to rustle; (Radio etc) to hiss; **Rauschgift** nt drug; **Rauschgiftsüchtige(r)** mf drug addict

raus|fliegen irr vi (fam) to be kicked out

raus|halten irr vr (fam) **halt du dich da raus!** you (just) keep out of it

räuspern vr **sich ~** to clear one's throat

raus|schmeißen irr vt (fam) to throw out

Razzia (-, Razzien) f raid

reagieren vi to react (auf +akk to); **Reaktion** f reaction

real adj real; **realisieren** vt (merken) to realize; (verwirklichen) to implement; **realistisch** adj realistic; **Realität** (-, -en) f reality; **Reality-TV** (-s) nt reality TV

Realschule f ≈ secondary school, junior high (school) (US)

Rebe (-, -n) f vine

rebellieren vi to rebel

Rebhuhn nt partridge

rechnen vt, vi to calculate; **~ mit** to expect; (bauen auf) to count on ▷ vr **sich ~** to pay off, to turn out to be profitable; **Rechner** (-s, -) m calculator; (Computer) computer; **Rechnung** f calculation(s); (Comm) bill (BRIT), check (US); **die ~, bitte!** can I have the bill, please?; **das geht auf meine ~** this is on me

recht adj (richtig, passend) right; **mir soll's ~ sein** it's alright by me; **mir ist es ~** I don't mind ▷ adv really, quite; (richtig) right(ly); **ich weiß nicht ~** I don't really know; **es geschieht ihm ~** it serves him right

Recht *(-(e)s, -e)* nt right: *(Jur)* law: ~ **haben** to be right; **jdm ~ geben** to agree with sb

Rechte *(-n, -n)* f right-hand side; *(Hand)* right hand; *(Pol)* right (wing); **rechte(r, s)** adj right; **auf der ~n Seite** on the right, on the right-hand side; **Rechte(s)** nt right thing; **etwas/nichts ~s** something/nothing proper

Rechteck *(-s, -e)* nt rectangle; **rechteckig** adj rectangular

rechtfertigen vt to justify ▷ vr **sich ~** to justify oneself

rechtlich adj legal; **rechtmäßig** adj legal, lawful

rechts adv on the right; **~ abbiegen** to turn right; **~ von** to the right of; **~ oben** at the top right

Rechtsanwalt m, **-anwältin** f lawyer

Rechtschreibung f spelling

Rechtshänder(in) *(-s, -)* m(f) right-hander; **rechtsherum** adv to the right, clockwise; **rechtsradikal** adj *(Pol)* extreme right-wing

Rechtsschutzversicherung f legal costs insurance

Rechtsverkehr m driving on the right

rechtswidrig adj illegal

rechtwinklig adj right-angled; **rechtzeitig** adj timely ▷ adv in time

recycelbar adj recyclable; **recyceln** vt to recycle; **Recycling** *(-s)* nt recycling; **Recyclingpapier** nt recycled paper

Redakteur(in) m(f) editor; **Redaktion** f editing, *(Leute)* editorial staff; *(Büro)* editorial office(s)

Rede *(, n)* f speech; *(Gespräch)* talk; **eine ~ halten** to make a speech; **reden** vi to talk, to speak ▷ vt to say; *(Unsinn etc)* to talk; **Redewendung** f idiom; **Redner(in)** m(f)

speaker

reduzieren vt to reduce

Referat *(-s, -e)* nt paper; **ein ~ halten** to give a paper *(über +akk* on)

reflektieren vt to reflect

Reform *(-, -en)* f reform; **Reformhaus** nt health food shop; **reformieren** vt to reform

Regal *(-s, -e)* nt shelf; *(Möbelstück)* shelves pl

Regel *(-, -n)* f rule; *(Med)* period; **regelmäßig** adj regular; **regeln** vt to regulate, to control; *(Angelegenheit)* to settle ▷ vr **sich von selbst ~** to sort itself out; **Regelung** f regulation

Regen *(-s, -)* m rain; **Regenbogen** m rainbow; **Regenmantel** m raincoat; **Regenrinne** f gutter; **Regenschauer** m shower; **Regenschirm** m umbrella; **Regenwald** m rainforest; **Regenwurm** m earthworm

Regie f direction

regieren vt, vi to govern, to rule; **Regierung** f government; *(von Monarch)* reign

Region f region; **regional** adj regional

Regisseur(in) m(f) director

registrieren vt to register; *(bemerken)* to notice

regnen vi impers to rain; **regnerisch** adj rainy

regulär adj regular; **regulieren** vt to regulate, to adjust

Reh *(-(e)s, -e)* nt deer; *(Fleisch)* venison

Rehabilitationszentrum nt *(Med)* rehabilitation centre

Reibe *(-, -n)* f, **Reibeisen** nt grater; **reiben** *(rieb, gerieben)* vt to rub; *(Gastr)* to grate; **reibungslos** adj smooth

reich adj rich

Reich *(-(e)s, -e)* nt empire; *(eines*

Königs) kingdom

reichen vi to reach; (genügen) to be enough, to be sufficient (jdm for sb) ▷ vt to hold out; (geben) to pass, to hand; (anbieten) to offer

reichhaltig adj ample, rich; **reichlich** adj (Trinkgeld) generous; (Essen) ample; **~ Zeit** plenty of time; **Reichtum** (-s, -tümer) m wealth

reif adj ripe; (Mensch, Urteil) mature

Reif (-(e)s) m (Raureif) hoarfrost ▷ (-(e)s, -e) m (Ring) ring, hoop

reifen vi to mature; (Obst) to ripen

Reifen (-s, -) m ring, hoop; (von Auto) tyre; **Reifendruck** m tyre pressure; **Reifenpanne** f puncture; **Reifenwechsel** m tyre change

Reihe (-, -n) f row; (von Tagen etc, fam: Anzahl) series sing; **der ~ nach** one after the other; **er ist an der ~** it's his turn; **Reihenfolge** f order, sequence; **Reihenhaus** nt terraced house (BRIT), row house (US)

Reiher (-s, -) m heron

rein (fam) kontr von **herein, hinein** ▷ adj pure; (sauber) clean

Reinfall m (fam) letdown; **rein|-fallen** irr vi (fam) **auf etw** (akk) **~** to fall for sth

reinigen vt to clean; **Reinigung** f cleaning; (Geschäft) (dry) cleaner's; **Reinigungsmittel** nt cleaning agent, cleaner

rein|legen vt jdn **~** to take sb for a ride

Reis (-es, -e) m rice

Reise (-, -n) f journey; (auf Schiff) voyage; **Reiseapotheke** f first-aid kit; **Reisebüro** nt travel agent's; **Reisebus** m coach; **Reiseführer(in)** m(f) (Mensch) courier; (Buch) guide(book); **Reisegepäck** nt luggage (BRIT), baggage; **Reisegesellschaft** f (Veranstalter) tour operator; **Reiseleiter(in)** m(f) courier;

reisen vi to travel; **~ nach** to go to; **Reisende(r)** mf traveller; **Reisepass** m passport; **Reiseroute** f route, itinerary; **Reiserücktrittversicherung** f holiday cancellation insurance; **Reisescheck** m traveller's cheque; **Reisetasche** f holdall (BRIT), carryall (US); **Reiseveranstalter** m tour operator; **Reiseverkehr** m holiday traffic; **Reiseversicherung** f travel insurance; **Reiseziel** nt destination

reißen (riss, gerissen) vt, vi to tear; (ziehen) to pull, to drag; (Witz) to crack

Reißnagel m drawing pin (BRIT), thumbtack (US); **Reißverschluss** m zip (BRIT), zipper (US); **Reißzwecke** f drawing pin (BRIT), thumbtack (US)

reiten (ritt, geritten) vt, vi to ride; **Reiter(in)** m(f) rider; **~ Reithose** f riding breeches pl; **Reitsport** m riding; **Reitstiefel** m riding boot

Reiz (-es, -e) m stimulus; (angenehm) charm; (Verlockung) attraction; **reizen** vt to stimulate; (unangenehm) to annoy; (verlocken) to appeal to, to attract; **reizend** adj charming; **Reizgas** nt irritant gas; **Reizung** f irritation

Reklamation f complaint

Reklame (-, -n) f advertising; (Einzelwerbung) advertisement; (im Fernsehen) commercial

reklamieren vi to complain (wegen about)

Rekord (-(e)s, -e) m record

relativ adj relative ▷ adv relatively

relaxen vi to relax, to chill out

Religion f religion; **religiös** adj religious

Remoulade (-, -n) f tartar sauce

Renaissance f renaissance, revival; (Hist) Renaissance

Rennbahn f racecourse; (Auto)

racetrack; **rennen** (rannte, gerannt)
vt, vi to run; **Rennen** (-s, -) nt
running; (Wettbewerb) race; **Rennfahrer(in)** m(f) racing driver;
Rennrad nt racing bike; **Rennwagen** m racing car

renommiert adj famous, noted
(wegen, für for)

renovieren vt to renovate; **Renovierung** f renovation

rentabel adj profitable

Rente (-, -n) f pension; **Rentenversicherung** f pension scheme

Rentier nt reindeer

rentieren vr **sich ~** to pay, to be
profitable

Rentner(in) (-s, -) m(f) pensioner,
senior citizen

Reparatur (-, -en) f repair; **Reparaturwerkstatt** f repair shop; (Auto)
garage; **reparieren** vt to repair

Reportage f report; **Reporter(in)** (-s, -) m(f) reporter

Reptil (-s, -ien) nt reptile

Republik f republic

Reservat (-(e)s, -e) nt nature reserve;
(für Ureinwohner) reservation; **Reserve** (-, -n) f reserve; **Reservekanister** m spare can; **Reserverad**
nt (Auto) spare wheel; **Reservespieler(in)** m(f) reserve; **reservieren** vt to reserve; **Reservierung** f
reservation

resignieren vi to give up; **resigniert** adj resigned

Respekt (-(e)s) m respect; **respektieren** vt to respect

Rest (-(e)s, -e) m rest, remainder;
(Überreste) remains pl; **der ~ ist für
Sie** (zur Bedienung) keep the change

Restaurant (-s, -s) nt restaurant

restaurieren vt to restore

Restbetrag m balance; **restlich**
adj remaining; **restlos** adj complete

Resultat nt result

retten vt to save, to rescue

Rettich (-s, -e) m radish (large white
or red variety)

Rettung f rescue; (Hilfe) help;
(Rettungsdienst) ambulance service;
Rettungsboot nt lifeboat; **Rettungshubschrauber** m rescue
helicopter; **Rettungsring** m lifebelt, life preserver (US); **Rettungswagen** m ambulance

Reue (-) f remorse; (Bedauern) regret; **reuen** vt **es reut ihn** he regrets it

revanchieren vr **sich ~** (sich rächen) to get one's own back, to get
one's revenge; (für Hilfe etc) to return
the favour

Revolution f revolution

Rezept (-(e)s, -e) nt (Gastr) recipe;
(Med) prescription; **rezeptfrei** adj
over-the-counter, non-prescription

Rezeption f (im Hotel) reception

rezeptpflichtig adj available only
on prescription

R-Gespräch nt reverse-charge
(BRIT) (o collect (US)) call

Rhabarber (-s) m rhubarb

Rhein (-s) m Rhine; **Rheinland-Pfalz** (-) nt Rhineland-Palatinate

Rheuma (-s) nt rheumatism

Rhythmus m rhythm

richten vt (lenken) to direct (auf
+akk to); (Waffe, Kamera) to point (auf
+akk at); (Brief, Anfrage) to address
(an +akk to); (einstellen) to adjust;
(instand setzen) to repair; (zurechtmachen) to prepare ▷ vr **sich ~ nach**
(Regel etc) to keep to; (Mode, Beispiel)
to follow; (abhängen von) to depend
on

Richter(in) (-s, -) m(f) judge

Richtgeschwindigkeit f recommended speed

richtig adj right, correct; (echt)
proper; **etw ~ stellen** to correct sth
▷ adv (fam: sehr) really

Richtlinie f guideline
Richtung f direction; (Tendenz) tendency
rieb imperf von **reiben**
riechen (roch, gerochen) vt, vi to smell; **nach etw ~** to smell of sth; **an etw** (dat) **~** to smell sth
rief imperf von **rufen**
Riegel (-s, -) m bolt; (Gastr) bar
Riemen (-s, -) m strap; (Gürtel) belt
Riese (-n, -n) m giant; **Riesengarnele** f king prawn; **riesengroß** adj gigantic, huge; **Riesenrad** nt big wheel; **riesig** adj enormous, huge
riet imperf von **raten**
Riff (-(e)s, -e) nt reef
Rind (-(e)s, -er) nt cow; (Bulle) bull; (Gastr) beef; **-er** pl cattle pl
Rinde (-, -n) f (Baum) bark; (Käse) rind; (Brot) crust
Rinderbraten m roast beef; **Rinderwahn(sinn)** m mad cow disease; **Rindfleisch** nt beef
Ring (-(e)s, -e) m ring; (Straße) ring road; **Ringbuch** nt ring binder
ringen (rang, gerungen) vi to wrestle; **Ringer(in)** m(f) wrestler; **Ringfinger** m ring finger; **Ringkampf** m wrestling match; **ringsherum** adv round about
Rippe (-, -n) f rib; **Rippenfellentzündung** f pleurisy
Risiko (-s, -s o Risiken) nt risk; **auf eigenes ~** at one's own risk; **riskant** adj risky; **riskieren** vt to risk
riss imperf von **reißen**
Riss (-es, -e) m tear; (in Mauer, Tasse etc) crack; (Haut) chapped
ritt imperf von **reiten**
Ritter (-s, -) m knight
Rivale (-n, -n) m, **Rivalin** f rival
Rizinusöl nt castor oil
Robbe (-, -n) f seal
Roboter (-s, -) m robot

robust adj robust
roch imperf von **riechen**
Rock (-(e)s, Röcke) m skirt
Rockband f (Musikgruppe) rock band; **Rockmusik** f rock (music)
Rodelbahn f toboggan run; **rodeln** vi to toboggan
Roggen (-s, -) m rye; **Roggenbrot** nt rye bread
roh adj raw; (Mensch) coarse, crude; **Rohkost** f raw vegetables and fruit pl
Rohr (-(e)s, -e) nt pipe; (Bot) cane; (Schilf) reed; **Röhre** (-, -n) f tube; (Leitung) pipe; (Elek) valve; (Backröhre) oven; **Rohrzucker** m cane sugar
Rohstoff m raw material
Rokoko (-s) nt rococo
Rolle (-, -n) f (etw Zusammengerolltes) roll; (Theat) role
rollen vt, vi to roll
Roller (-s, -) m scooter
Rollerblades® pl; **Rollerskates** pl roller skates pl
Rollkragenpullover m polo-neck (BRIT) (o turtleneck (US)) sweater; **Rollladen**, **Rollo** (-s, -s) m (roller) shutters pl; **Rollschuh** m roller skate; **Rollstuhl** m wheelchair; **rollstuhlgerecht** adj suitable for wheelchairs; **Rolltreppe** f escalator
Roman (-s, -e) m novel
Romantik f romance; **romantisch** adj romantic
römisch-katholisch adj Roman Catholic
röntgen vt to X-ray; **Röntgenaufnahme** f, **Röntgenbild** nt X-ray; **Röntgenstrahlen** pl X-rays pl
rosa adj inv pink
Rose (-, -n) f rose
Rosenkohl m (Brussels) sprouts pl
Rosé(wein) m rosé (wine)
rosig adj rosy

Rosine f raisin
Rosmarin (-s) m rosemary
Rosskastanie f horse chestnut
Rost (-(e)s, -e) m rust; (zum Braten) grill, gridiron; **Rostbratwurst** f grilled sausage; **rosten** vi to rust; **rösten** vt to roast, to grill; (Brot) to toast, **rostfrei** adj rustproof; (Stahl) stainless; **rostig** adj rusty; **Rostschutz** m rustproofing
rot adj red; ~ **werden** to blush; ~**e Karte** red card; ~**e Be(e)te** beetroot; **bei Rot über die Ampel fahren** to jump the lights; **das Rote Kreuz** the Red Cross
Röteln pl German measles sing
röten vt to redden ▷ vr **sich** ~ to redden
rothaarig adj red-haired
rotieren vi to rotate; **am Rotieren sein** (fam) to be rushing around like a mad thing
Rotkehlchen nt robin; **Rotkohl** m, **Rotkraut** nt red cabbage; **Rotlichtviertel** nt red-light district; **Rotwein** m red wine
Rouge (-s, -s) nt rouge
Route (-, -n) f route
Routine f experience; (Trott) routine
Rubbellos nt scratchcard; **rubbeln** vt to rub
Rübe (-, -n) f turnip; **Gelbe ~** carrot; **Rote ~** beetroot
rüber (fam) kontr von **herüber, hinüber**
Rubin (-s, -e) m ruby
rücken vt, vi to move; **könntest du ein bisschen ~?** could you move over a bit?
Rücken (-s, -) m back; **Rückenlehne** f back(rest); **Rückenmark** nt spinal cord; **Rückenschmerzen** pl backache sing; **Rückenschwimmen** (-s) nt backstroke; **Rückenwind** m tailwind

Rückerstattung f refund;
Rückfahrkarte f return ticket (BRIT), round-trip ticket (US); **Rückfahrt** f return journey; **Rückfall** m relapse; **Rückflug** m return flight; **Rückgabe** f return; **rückgängig** adj; **etw ~ machen** to cancel sth; **Rückgrat** (-(e)s, -e) nt spine, backbone; **Rückkehr** (-, -en) f return; **Rücklicht** nt rear light; **Rückreise** f return journey; **auf der ~** on the way back
Rucksack m rucksack, backpack; **Rucksacktourist(in)** m(f) backpacker
Rückschritt m step back; **Rückseite** f back; (hinterer Teil) rear; **siehe ~** see overleaf; **Rücksicht** f consideration; ~ **nehmen auf** (+akk) to show consideration for; **rücksichtslos** adj inconsiderate; (Fahren) reckless; (unbarmherzig) ruthless; **rücksichtsvoll** adj considerate; **Rücksitz** m back seat; **Rückspiegel** m (Auto) rear-view mirror; **Rückstand** m sie sind zwei Tore **im ~** they're two goals down; **im ~ sein mit** (Arbeit, Miete) to be behind with; **Rücktaste** f backspace key; **Rückvergütung** f refund; **rückwärts** adv backwards; back; **Rückwärtsgang** m (Auto) reverse (gear); **Rückweg** m return journey; way back; **Rückzahlung** f repayment; **Rückzieher** m **einen ~ machen** to back out
Ruder (-s, -) nt oar; (Steuer) rudder; **Ruderboot** nt rowing boat (BRIT), rowboat (US); **rudern** vt, vi to row
Ruf (-(e)s, -e) m call, cry; (Ansehen) reputation; **rufen** (rief, gerufen) vt, vi to call; (schreien) to cry; **Rufnummer** f telephone number
Ruhe (-) f rest; (Ungestörtheit) peace, quiet; (Gelassenheit, Stille) calm; (Schweigen) silence; **lass mich**

in **~**! leave me alone; **ruhen** vi to rest; **Ruhestand** m retirement; **im ~ sein** to be retired; **Ruhestörung** f disturbance of the peace; **Ruhetag** m closing day; **montags ~ haben** to be closed on Mondays

ruhig adj quiet; (bewegungslos) still; (Hand) steady; (gelassen) calm

Ruhm (-(e)s) m fame, glory

Rührei nt scrambled egg(s); **rühren** vt to move; (umrühren) to stir ▷ vr **sich ~** to move; (sich bemerkbar machen) to say something; **rührend** adj touching, moving; **Rührung** f emotion

Ruine (-, -n) f ruin; **ruinieren** vt to ruin

rülpsen vi to burp, to belch

rum (fam) kontr von **herum**

Rum (-s, -s) m rum

Rumänien (-s) nt Romania

Rummel (-s) m (Trubel) hustle and bustle; (Jahrmarkt) fair; (Medienrummel) hype; **Rummelplatz** m fairground

rumoren vi **es rumort in meinem Bauch / Kopf** my stomach is rumbling / my head is spinning

Rumpf (-(e)s, Rümpfe) m (Anat) trunk; (Aviat) fuselage; (Naut) hull

rümpfen vt **die Nase ~** to turn one's nose up (über at)

Rumpsteak nt rump steak

rund adj round ▷ adv (etwa) around; **~ um etw** (a)round sth; **Runde** (-, -n) f round; (in Rennen) lap; **Rundfahrt** f tour (durch of); **Rundfunk** m broadcasting; (Rundfunkanstalt) broadcasting service; **im ~** on the radio; **Rundgang** m tour (durch of); (von Wächter) round

rundlich adj plump; **Rundreise** f tour (durch of)

runter (fam) kontr von **herunter, hinunter**; **runterscrollen** vt (In-form) to scroll down

runzeln vt **die Stirn ~** to frown; **runzelig** adj wrinkled

ruppig adj gruff

Rüsche (-, -n) f frill

Ruß (-es) m soot

Russe (-n, -n) m Russian

Rüssel (-s, -) m (Elefant) trunk; (Schwein) snout

Russin f Russian; **russisch** adj Russian; **Russisch** nt Russian; **Russland** nt Russia

Rüstung f (mit Waffen) arming; (Ritterrüstung) armour; (Waffen) armaments pl

Rutsch (-(e)s, -e) m **guten ~ (ins neue Jahr)!** Happy New Year; **Rutschbahn** f, **Rutsche** f slide; **rutschen** vi to slide; (ausrutschen) to slip; **rutschig** adj slippery

rütteln vt, vi to shake

S *abk* = **Süd** S

s. *abk* = **siehe** see; **S.** *abk* = **Seite** p.

Saal(-(e)s, *Säle*) m hall; (für Sitzungen) room

Saarland nt Saarland

sabotieren vt to sabotage

Sache (-, -n) f thing; (Angelegenheit) affair, business; (Frage) matter; **bei der ~ bleiben** to keep to the point; **sachkundig** adj competent; **Sachlage** f situation; **sachlich** adj (objektiv) objective; (nüchtern) matter of fact; **sächlich** adj (Ling) neuter; **Sachschaden** m material damage

Sachsen (-s) nt Saxony; **Sachsen-Anhalt**(-s) nt Saxony-Anhalt

sacht(e) adv softly, gently

Sachverständige(r) mf expert

Sack (-(e)s, *Säcke*) m sack; (pej: Mensch) bastard, bugger; **Sackgasse** f dead end, cul-de-sac

Safe (-s, -s) m safe

Safer Sex m safe sex

Safran (-s, -e) m saffron

Saft (-(e)s, *Säfte*) m juice; **saftig** adj juicy

Sage (-, -n) f legend

Säge (-, -n) f saw; **Sägemehl** nt sawdust

sagen vt, vi to say (jdm to sb), to tell (jdm sb); **wie sagt man ... auf Englisch?** what's ... in English?; **ich will dir mal was ~** let me tell you something

sägen vt, vi to saw

sagenhaft adj legendary; (fam: großartig) fantastic

sah imperf von **sehen**

Sahne (-) f cream; **Sahnetorte** f gateau

Saison (-, -s) f season; **außerhalb der ~** out of season

Saite (-, -n) f string

Sakko (-s, -s) nt jacket

Salami (-, -s) f salami

Salat (-(e)s, -e) m salad; (Kopfsalat) lettuce; **Salatbar** f salad bar; **Salatschüssel** f salad bowl, **Salatsoße** f salad dressing

Salbe (-, -n) f ointment

Salbei (-s) m sage

Salmonellenvergiftung f salmonella (poisoning)

salopp adj (Kleidung) casual; (Sprache) slangy

Salsamusik f salsa (music)

Salto (-s, -s) m somersault

Salz (-es, -e) nt salt; **salzarm** adj low-salt; **salzen** (salzte, gesalzen) vt to salt; **Salzgurke** f pickled gherkin; **Salzhering** m pickled herring; **salzig** adj salty; **Salzkartoffeln** pl boiled potatoes pl; **Salzstange** f pretzel stick; **Salzstreuer** m salt cellar (BRIT) (o shaker (US)); **Salzwasser** nt salt water

Samba (-, -s) f samba

Samen (-s, -) m seed; (Sperma) sperm

sammeln vt to collect; **sammle-**

r(in) *m(f)* collector; **Sammlung** *f* collection; (*Ansammlung, Konzentration*) concentration

Samstag *m* Saturday; *siehe auch* **Mittwoch**; **samstags** *adv* on Saturdays; *siehe auch* **mittwochs**

samt *prep +dat* (along) with, together with

Samt (-(e)s, -e) *m* velvet

sämtliche(r, s) *adj* all (the)

Sanatorium (-s, Sanatorien) *nt* sanatorium (BRIT), sanitarium (US)

Sand (-(e)s, -e) *m* sand

Sandale (-, -n) *f* sandal

sandig *adj* sandy; **Sandkasten** *m* sandpit (BRIT), sandbox (US); **Sandpapier** *nt* sandpaper; **Sandstrand** *m* sandy beach

sandte *imperf von* **senden**

sanft *adj* soft, gentle

sang *imperf von* **singen**; **Sänger(in)** (-s, -) *m(f)* singer

Sangria (-, -) *f* sangria

sanieren *vt* to redevelop; (*Gebäude*) to renovate; (*Betrieb*) to restore to profitability

sanitär *adj* sanitary; **~e Anlagen** *pl* sanitation

Sanitäter(in) (-s, -) *m(f)* ambulance man/woman, paramedic

sank *imperf von* **sinken**

Sankt Gallen (-s) *nt* St Gallen

Saphir (-s, -e) *m* sapphire

Sardelle *f* anchovy

Sardine *f* sardine

Sarg (-(e)s, Särge) *m* coffin

saß *imperf von* **sitzen**

Satellit (-en, -en) *m* satellite; **Satellitenfernsehen** *nt* satellite TV; **Satellitenschüssel** *f* (*fam*) satellite dish

Satire (-, -n) *f* satire (*auf +akk* on)

satt *adj* full; (*Farbe*) rich, deep; **~ sein** (*gesättigt*) to be full; **~ machen** to be filling; **jdn/etw ~ sein** (*o haben*) to be fed up with sb/sth

Sattel (-s, Sättel) *m* saddle

Saturn (-s) *m* Saturn

Satz (-es, Sätze) *m* (*Ling*) sentence; (*Mus*) movement; (*Tennis*) set; (*Kaffee*) grounds *pl*; (*Comm*) rate; (*Sprung*) jump; (*Comm*) rate

Satzzeichen *nt* punctuation mark

Sau (-, Säue) *f* sow; (*pej: Mensch*) dirty bugger

sauber *adj* clean; (*ironisch*) fine; **~ machen** to clean; **Sauberkeit** *f* cleanness; (*von Person*) cleanliness; **säubern** *vt* to clean

saublöd *adj* (*fam*) really stupid, dumb

Sauce (-, -n) *f* sauce; (*zu Braten*) gravy

Saudi-Arabien (-s) *nt* Saudi Arabia

sauer *adj* sour; (*Chem*) acid; (*fam: verärgert*) cross; **saurer Regen** acid rain; **Sauerkirsche** *f* sour cherry; **Sauerkraut** *nt* sauerkraut; **säuerlich** *adj* slightlhy sour; **Sauermilch** *f* sour milk; **Sauerrahm** *m* sour cream; **Sauerstoff** *m* oxygen

saufen (*soff, gesoffen*) *vt* to drink; (*fam: Mensch*) to knock back ▷ *vi* to drink; (*fam: Mensch*) to booze

saugen (*sog o saugte, gesogen o gesaugt*) *vt, vi* to suck; (*mit Staubsauger*) to vacuum, to hoover (BRIT)

Sauger (-s, -) *m* (*auf Flasche*) teat; **Säugetier** *nt* mammal; **Säugling** *m* infant, baby

Säule (-, -n) *f* column, pillar

Saum (-s, Säume) *m* hem; (*Naht*) seam

Sauna (-, -s) *f* sauna

Säure (-, -n) *f* acid

sausen *vi* (*Ohren*) to buzz; (*Wind*) to howl; (*Mensch*) to rush

Saustall *m* pigsty; **Sauwetter** *nt* **was für ein ~** (*fam*) what lousy weather

Saxophon (-s, -e) nt saxophone

S-Bahn f suburban railway; **S-Bahn-Haltestelle** f, **S-Bahnhof** m suburban (train) station

scannen vt to scan; **Scanner** (-s, -) m scanner

schäblig adj shabby

Schach (-s, -s) nt chess, (Stellung) check; **Schachbrett** nt chessboard; **Schachfigur** f chess piece; **schachmatt** adj checkmate

Schacht (-(e)s, Schächte) m shaft

Schachtel (-, -n) f box

schade interj what a pity

Schädel (-s, -) m skull; **Schädelbruch** m fractured skull

schaden vi to damage, to harm (jdm sb); **das schadet nichts** it won't do any harm; **Schaden** (-s, Schäden) m damage; (Verletzung) injury; (Nachteil) disadvantage; **einen ~ verursachen** to cause damage; **Schadenersatz** m compensation, damages pl; **schadhaft** adj faulty; (beschädigt) damaged; **schädigen** vt to damage; (jdn) to do harm to, to harm; **schädlich** adj harmful (für to); **Schadstoff** m harmful substance; **schadstoffarm** adj low-emission

Schaf (-(e)s, -e) nt sheep; **Schafbock** m ram; **Schäfer** (-s, -) m shepherd; **Schäferhund** m Alsatian (BRIT), German shepherd; **Schäferin** f shepherdess

schaffen (schuf, geschaffen) vt to create; (Platz) to make ▷ vt (erreichen) to manage, to do; (erledigen) to finish; (Prüfung) to pass; (transportieren) to take; **jdm zu ~ machen** to cause sb trouble

Schaffner(in) (-s, -) m(f) (in Bus) conductor/conductress; (Eisenb) guard

Schafskäse m sheep's (milk) cheese

schal adj (Getränk) flat

Schal (-s, -e o -s) m scarf

Schälchen nt (small) bowl

Schale (-, -n) f skin; (abgeschält) peel; (Nuss, Muschel, Ei) shell; (Geschirr) bowl, dish

schälen vt to peel; (Tomate, Mandel) to skin; (Erbsen, Eier, Nüsse) to shell; (Getreide) to husk ▷ vr **sich ~** to peel

Schall (-(e)s, -e) m sound; **Schalldämpfer** (-s, -) m (Auto) silencer (BRIT), muffler (US); **Schallplatte** f record

Schalotte (-, -n) f shallot

schalten vt to switch ▷ vi (Auto) to change gear; (fam: begreifen) to catch on; **Schalter** (-s, -) m (auf Post, Bank) counter; (an Gerät) switch; **Schalterhalle** f main hall; **Schalteröffnungszeiten** pl business hours pl

Schaltfläche f (Inform) button; **Schalthebel** m gear lever (BRIT) (o shift (US)); **Schaltjahr** nt leap year; **Schaltknüppel** m gear lever (BRIT) (o shift (US)); **Schaltung** f gear change (BRIT), gearshift (US)

Scham (-) f shame; (Schamgefühl) modesty; **schämen** vr **sich ~** to be ashamed

Schande (-) f disgrace

Schanze (-, -n) f ski jump

Schar (-, -en) f (von Vögeln) flock; (Menge) crowd, **in ~en** in droves

scharf adj (Messer, Kritik) sharp; (Essen) hot; **auf etw** (akk) **~ sein** (fam) to be keen on sth

Schärfe (-, -n) f sharpness; (Strenge) rigour; (Foto) focus

Scharlach (-s) m (Med) scarlet fever

Scharnier (-s, -e) nt hinge

Schaschlik (-s, -s) m o nt (shish) kebab

Schatten (-s, -) m shadow; **30 Grad im ~** 30 degrees in the shade;

schattig adj shady
Schatz (-es, Schätze) m treasure; (Mensch) love
schätzen vt (abschätzen) to estimate; (Gegenstand) to value; (würdigen) to value, to esteem; (vermuten) to reckon; **Schätzung** f estimate; (das Schätzen) estimation; (von Wertgegenstand) valuation; **schätzungsweise** adv roughly, approximately
Schau (-, -en) f show; (Ausstellung) exhibition
schauen vi to look; **ich schau mal, ob ...** I'll go and have a look whether ...; **schau, dass ...** see (to it) that ...
Schauer (-s, -) m (Regen) shower; (Schreck) shudder
Schaufel (-, -n) f shovel; **~ und Besen** dustpan and brush; **schaufeln** vt to shovel; **Schnee ~** to clear the snow away
Schaufenster nt shop window; **Schaufensterbummel** m window-shopping expedition
Schaukel (-, -n) f swing; **schaukeln** vi to rock; (mit Schaukel) to swing; **Schaukelstuhl** m rocking chair
Schaulustige(r) mf gawper (BRIT), rubbernecker (US)
Schaum (-(e)s, Schäume) m foam; (Seifenschaum) lather; (Bierschaum) froth; **Schaumbad** nt bubble bath; **schäumen** vi to foam; **Schaumfestiger** (-s, -) m styling mousse; **Schaumgummi** m foam (rubber); **Schaumwein** m sparkling wine
Schauplatz m scene; **Schauspiel** nt spectacle; (Theat) play; **Schauspieler(in)** m(f) actor/actress
Scheck (-s, -s) m cheque; **Scheckheft** nt chequebook; **Scheckkarte** f cheque card
Scheibe (-, -n) f disc; (von Brot, Käse etc) slice; (Glasscheibe) pane; Schei-

benbremse f (Auto) disc brake; **Scheibenwaschanlage** f (Auto) windscreen (BRIT) o windshield (US) washer unit; **Scheibenwischer** (-s, -) m (Auto) windscreen (BRIT) o windshield (US) wiper
Scheich (-s, -s/-e) m sheik(h)
Scheide (-, -n) f (Anat) vagina
scheiden (schied, geschieden) vt (trennen) to separate; (Ehe) to dissolve; **sich ~ lassen** to get a divorce; **sie hat sich von ihm ~ lassen** she divorced him; **Scheidung** f divorce
Schein (-(e)s, -e) m light; (Anschein) appearance; (Geld) (bank)note; **scheinbar** adj apparent; **scheinen** (schien, geschienen) vi (Sonne) to shine; (den Anschein haben) to seem; **Scheinwerfer** (-s, -) m floodlight; (Theat) spotlight; (Auto) headlight
Scheiß- in zW (vulg) damned, bloody (BRIT); **Scheiße** (-) f (vulg) shit, crap; **scheißegal** adj (vulg) **das ist mir ~** I don't give a damn (o toss); **scheißen** (schiss, geschissen) vi (vulg) to shit
Scheitel (-s, -) m parting (BRIT), part (US)
scheitern vi to fail (an +dat because of)
Schellfisch m haddock
Schema (-s, -s o Schemata) nt scheme, plan; (Darstellung) diagram
Schenkel (-s, -) m thigh
schenken vt to give; **er hat es mir geschenkt** he gave it to me (as a present); **sich** (dat) **etw ~** (fam: weglassen) to skip sth
Scherbe (-, -n) f broken piece, fragment
Schere (-, -n) f scissors pl; (groß) shears pl; **eine ~** a pair of scissors/shears
Scherz (-es, -e) m joke
scheu adj shy
scheuen vr **sich ~ vor** (+dat) to be

afraid of, to shrink from ▷ vt to shun ▷ vi (Pferd) to shy

scheuern vt to scrub; **jdm eine ~** (fam) to slap sb in the face

Scheune (-, -n) f barn

scheußlich adj dreadful

Schi (-s, -er) m siehe **Ski**

Schicht (-, -en) f layer; (in Gesellschaft) class; (in Fabrik etc) shift

schick adj stylish, chic

schicken vt to send ▷ vr **sich ~** (sich beeilen) to hurry up

Schickimicki (-(s), -s) m (fam) trendy

Schicksal (-s, -e) nt fate

Schiebedach nt (Auto) sunroof;
schieben (schob, geschoben) vt to push; **die Schuld auf jdn ~** to put the blame on sb; **Schiebetür** f sliding door

schied imperf von **scheiden**

Schiedsrichter(in) m(f) referee;
(Tennis) umpire; (Schlichter) arbitrator

schief adj crooked; (Blick) funny ▷ adv crooked(ly); **~ gehen** (fam) to go wrong

schielen vi to squint

schien imperf von **scheinen**

Schienbein nt shin

Schiene (-, -n) f rail; (Med) splint

schier adj pure; (fig) sheer ▷ adv nearly, almost

schießen (schoss, geschossen) vt to shoot; (Ball) to kick; (Tor) to score;
(Foto) to take ▷ vi to shoot (auf +akk at)

Schiff (-(e)s, -e) nt ship; (in Kirche) nave; **Schifffahrt** f shipping;
Schiffsreise f voyage

schikanieren vt to harass; (Schule) to bully

Schild (-(e)s, -e) m (Schutz) shield ▷ (-(e)s, -er) nt sign; **was steht auf dem ~?** what does the sign say?

Schilddrüse f thyroid gland

schildern vt to describe

Schildkröte f tortoise; (Wasserschildkröte) turtle

Schimmel (-s, -) m mould; (Pferd) white horse; **schimmelig** adj mouldy

schimpfen vt to tell off ▷ vi (sich beklagen) to complain; **mit jdm ~** to tell sb off; **Schimpfwort** nt swearword

Schinken (-s, -) m ham

Schirm (-(e)s, -e) m (Regenschirm) umbrella; (Sonnenschirm) parasol, sunshade

schiss imperf von **scheißen**

Schlacht (-, -en) f battle; **schlachten** vt to slaughter; **Schlachter(in)** (-s, -) m(f) butcher;
Schlachtfeld nt battlefield

Schlaf (-(e)s) m sleep; **Schlafanzug** m pyjamas pl; **Schlafcouch** f bed settee

Schläfe (-, -n) f temple

schlafen (schlief, geschlafen) vi to sleep; **schläfst gut! sleep well! hast du gut geschlafen?** did you sleep all right?; **er schläft noch** he's still asleep; **~ gehen** to go to bed

schlaff adj slack; (kraftlos) limp;
(erschöpft) exhausted

Schlafgelegenheit f place to sleep; **Schlaflosigkeit** f sleeplessness; **Schlafmittel** nt sleeping pill;
schläfrig adj sleepy

Schlafsaal m dormitory; **Schlafsack** m sleeping bag; **Schlaftablette** f sleeping pill; **er ist eine richtige ~** (fam: langweilig) he's such a bore; **Schlafwagen** m sleeping car, sleeper; **Schlafzimmer** nt bedroom

Schlag (-(e)s, Schläge) m blow; (Puls) beat, (Elek) shock; (fam: Portion) helping; (Art) kind, type; **Schlagader** f artery; **Schlaganfall** m (Med) stroke; **schlagartig** adj sudden; **Schlagbohrmaschine** f hammer drill

schlagen (schlug, geschlagen) vt to hit; (besiegen) to beat; (Sahne) to whip; **jdn zu Boden ~** to knock sb down ▷ vi (Herz) to beat; (Uhr) to strike; **mit dem Kopf gegen etw ~** to bang one's head against sth ▷ vr **sich ~** to fight

Schläger (-s, -) m (Sport) bat; (Tennis) racket; (Golf) (golf) club; (Hockey) hockey stick; (Mensch) brawler; **Schlägerei** f fight, brawl

schlagfertig adj quick-witted; **Schlagloch** nt pothole; **Schlagsahne** f whipping cream; (geschlagen) whipped cream; **Schlagzeile** f headline; **Schlagzeug** nt drums pl; (in Orchester) percussion

Schlamm (-(e)s, -e) m mud

schlampig adj (fam) sloppy

schlang imperf von **schlingen**

Schlange (-, -n) f snake; (von Menschen) queue (BRIT), line (US); **~ stehen** to queue (BRIT), to stand in line (US); **Schlangenlinie** f wavy line; **in ~n fahren** to swerve about

schlank adj slim

schlapp adj limp; (locker) slack

Schlappe (-, -n) f (fam) setback

schlau adj clever, smart; (raffiniert) crafty, cunning

Schlauch (-(e)s, Schläuche) m hose; (in Reifen) inner tube; **Schlauchboot** nt rubber dinghy

schlecht adj bad; **mir ist ~** I feel sick; **jdn ~ machen** to run sb down; **die Milch ist ~** the milk has gone off ▷ adv badly; **es geht ihm ~** he's having a hard time; (gesundheitlich) he's not feeling well; (finanziell) he's pretty hard up

schleichen (schlich, geschlichen) vi to creep

Schleier (-s, -) m veil

Schleife (-, -n) f (Inform, Aviat, Elek) loop; (Band) bow

schleifen vt (ziehen, schleppen) to drag ▷ (schliff, geschliffen) vt (schärfen) to grind; (Edelstein) to cut

Schleim (-(e)s, -e) m slime; (Med) mucus; **Schleimer** (-s, -) m (fam) creep; **Schleimhaut** f mucous membrane

schlendern vi to stroll

schleppen vt to drag; (Auto, Schiff) to tow; (tragen) to lug; **Schlepplift** m ski tow

Schleswig-Holstein (-s) nt Schleswig-Holstein

Schleuder (-, -n) f catapult; (für Wäsche) spin-dryer; **schleudern** vt to hurl; (Wäsche) to spin-dry ▷ vi (Auto) to skid; **Schleudersitz** m ejector seat

schleunigst adv straight away

schlich imperf von **schleichen**

schlicht adj simple, plain

schlichten vt (Streit) to settle

schlief imperf von **schlafen**

schließen (schloss, geschlossen) vt, vi to close, to shut; (beenden) to close; (Freundschaft, Ehe) to enter into; (folgern) to infer (aus from) ▷ vr **sich ~** to close, to shut; **Schließfach** nt locker

schließlich adv finally; (schließlich doch) after all

schliff imperf von **schleifen**

schlimm adj bad; **schlimmer** adj worse; **schlimmste(r, s)** adj worst; **schlimmstenfalls** adv at (the) worst

Schlinge (-, -n) f loop; (Med) sling

Schlips (-es, -e) m tie

Schlitten (-s, -) m sledge, toboggan; (mit Pferden) sleigh; **Schlittenfahren** (-s) nt tobogganing

Schlittschuh m ice skate; **~ laufen** to ice-skate

Schlitz (-es, -e) m slit; (für Münze) slot; (an Hose) flies pl

schloss imperf von **schließen**

Schloss (-es, Schlösser) nt lock; (Burg) castle

Schlosser(in) m(f) mechanic

Schlucht (-, -en) f gorge, ravine

schluchzen vi to sob

Schluck (-(e)s, -e) m swallow; Schluckauf (-s) m hiccups pl; schlucken vt, vi to swallow

schludern vi (fam) to do sloppy work

schlug imperf von schlagen

Schlüpfer (-s, -) m panties pl

schlüpfrig adj slippery; (fig) lewd; (Witz) risqué

schlürfen vt, vi to slurp

Schluss (-es, Schlüsse) m end; (Schlussfolgerung) conclusion; am ~ at the end; mit jdm ~ machen to finish (o split up) with sb

Schlüssel (-s, -) m (a. fig) key; Schlüsselbein nt collarbone; Schlüsselblume f cowslip; Schlüsselbund m bunch of keys; Schlüsseldienst m key-cutting service; Schlüsselloch nt keyhole

Schlussfolgerung f conclusion; Schlusslicht nt tail-light; (fig) tail-ender; Schlusspfiff m final whistle; Schlussverkauf m clearance sale

schmächtig adj frail

schmal adj narrow; (Mensch, Buch etc) slim; (karg) meagre

Schmalz (-es, -e) nt dripping, lard; (fig Sentimentalitäten) schmaltz

schmatzen vi to eat noisily

schmecken vt, vi to taste (nach of); es schmeckt ihm he likes it; lass es dir ~! bon appétit

Schmeichelei f flattery; schmeichelhaft adj flattering, schmeicheln vi jdm ~ to flatter sb

schmeißen (schmiss, geschmissen) vt (fam) to chuck, to throw

schmelzen (schmolz, geschmolzen) vt, vi to melt; (Metall, Erz) to smelt; Schmelzkäse m cheese spread

Schmerz (-es, -en) m pain; (Trauer) grief; ~en haben to be in pain; ~en im Rücken haben to have a pain in one's back; schmerzen vt, vi to hurt; Schmerzensgeld nt compensation; schmerzhaft, schmerzlich adj painful; schmerzlos adj painless; Schmerzmittel nt painkiller; schmerzstillend adj painkilling; Schmerztablette f painkiller

Schmetterling m butterfly

Schmied(in) (-(e)s, -e) m(f) blacksmith; schmieden vt to forge; (Pläne) to make

schmieren vt, vi to smear; (ölen) to lubricate, to grease; (bestechen) to bribe ▷ vt, vi (unsauber schreiben) to scrawl; Schmiergeld nt (fam) bribe; schmierig adj greasy; Schmiermittel nt lubricant; Schmierpapier nt scrap paper; Schmierseife f soft soap

Schminke (-, -n) f make-up; schminken vr sich ~ to put one's make-up on

schmiss imperf von schmeißen

schmollen vi to sulk; schmollend adj sulky

schmolz imperf von schmelzen

Schmuck (-(e)s, -e) m jewellery (BRIT), jewelry (US); (Verzierung) decoration; schmücken vt to decorate

schmuggeln vt, vi to smuggle

schmunzeln vi to smile

schmusen vi to (kiss and) cuddle

Schmutz (-es) m dirt, filth; schmutzig adj dirty

Schnabel (-s, Schnäbel) m beak, bill; (Ausguss) spout

Schnake (-, -n) f mosquito

Schnalle (-, -n) f buckle

Schnäppchen nt (fam) bargain; schnappen vt (fangen) to catch ▷ vi nach Luft ~ to gasp for breath;

Schnappschuss m (Foto) snap(shot)

Schnaps (-es, Schnäpse) m schnapps

schnarchen vi to snore

schnaufen vi to puff, to pant

Schnauzbart m moustache;
Schnauze (-, -n) f snout, muzzle; (Ausguss) spout; (fam: Mund) trap; **die ~ voll haben** to have had enough

schnäuzen vr **sich ~** to blow one's nose

Schnecke (-, -n) f snail; **Schneckenhaus** nt snail's shell

Schnee (-s) m snow; **Schneeball** m snowball; **Schneebob** m snowmobile; **Schneebrille** f snow goggles pl; **Schneeflocke** f snowflake; **Schneegestöber** (-s, -) nt snow flurry; **Schneeglöckchen** nt snowdrop; **Schneegrenze** f snowline; **Schneekanone** f snow thrower; **Schneekette** f (Auto) snow chain; **Schneemann** m snowman; **Schneematsch** m slush; **Schneepflug** m snowplough; **Schneeregen** m sleet; **Schneeschmelze** f thaw; **Schneesturm** m snowstorm, blizzard; **Schneetreiben** nt light blizzard pl; **Schneewehe** f snowdrift

Schneide (-, -n) f edge; (Klinge) blade; **schneiden** (schnitt, geschnitten) vt to cut; **sich** (dat) **die Haare ~ lassen** to have one's hair cut ▷ vr **sich ~** to cut oneself; **Schneider(in)** (-s, -) m(f) tailor; (für Damenmode) dressmaker; **Schneiderin** f dressmaker; **Schneidezahn** m incisor

schneien vi impers to snow

schnell adj quick, fast ▷ adv quickly, fast; **mach ~!** hurry up; **Schnelldienst** m express service; **Schnellhefter** m loose-leaf binder;

Schnellimbiss m snack bar; **Schnellkochtopf** m pressure cooker; **Schnellreinigung** f express dry cleaning; (Geschäft) express (dry) cleaner's; **Schnellstraße** f expressway; **Schnellzug** m fast train

schneuzen vr siehe **schnäuzen**

schnitt imperf von **schneiden**

Schnitt (-(e)s, -e) m cut; (Schnittpunkt) intersection; (Querschnitt) (cross) section; (Durchschnitt) average; (eines Kleides) style; **Schnittblume** f cut flower; **Schnitte** (-, -n) f slice; (belegt) sandwich; **Schnittkäse** m cheese slices pl; **Schnittlauch** m chives pl; **Schnittmuster** nt pattern; **Schnittstelle** f (Inform, fig) interface; **Schnittwunde** f cut, gash

Schnitzel (-s, -) nt (Papier) scrap; (Gastr) escalope

schnitzen vt to carve

Schnorchel (-s, -) m snorkel; **schnorcheln** vi to go snorkelling, to snorkel; **Schnorcheln** (-s) nt snorkelling

schnüffeln vi to sniff

Schnuller (-s, -) m dummy (BRIT), pacifier (US)

Schnulze (-, -n) f (Film, Roman) weepie

Schnupfen (-s, -) m cold

schnuppern vi to sniff

Schnur (-, Schnüre) f string, cord; (Elek) lead; **schnurlos** adj (Telefon) cordless

Schnurrbart m moustache

schnurren vi to purr

Schnürschuh m lace-up (shoe); **Schnürsenkel** (-s, -) m shoelace

schob imperf von **schieben**

Schock (-(e)s, -e) m shock; **unter ~ stehen** to be in a state of shock; **schockieren** vt to shock

Schokolade f chocolate; **Scho-**

koriegel m chocolate bar

Scholle (-, -n) f (Fisch) plaice; (Eis) ice floe

schon adv already: **ist er ~ da?** is he here yet?; **warst du ~ einmal da?** have you ever been there?; **ich war ~ einmal da** I've been there before; **~ damals** even then; **~ 1999** as early (o as long ago) as 1999

schön adj beautiful; (nett) nice; (Frau) beautiful, pretty; (Mann) beautiful, handsome; (Wetter) fine; **~e Grüße** best wishes; **~es Wochenende** have a nice weekend

schonen vt (pfleglich behandeln) to look after ▷ vr **sich ~** to take it easy

Schönheit f beauty

Schonkost f light diet

schöpfen vt to scoop; (mit Kelle) to ladle; **Schöpfkelle** f, **Schöpflöffel** m ladle

Schöpfung f creation

Schuppen (-s, -) m glass (of wine)

Schorf (-(e)s, -e) m scab

Schorle (-, -n) f spritzer

Schornstein m chimney; **Schornsteinfeger(in)** (-s, -) m(f) chimney sweep

schoss imperf von **schießen**

Schoß (-es, Schöße) m lap

Schotte (-n, -n) m Scot, Scotsman; **Schottin** f Scot, Scotswoman; **schottisch** adj Scottish, Scots; **Schottland** nt Scotland

schräg adj slanting; (Dach) sloping; (Linie) diagonal; (fam: unkonventionell) wacky

Schrank (-(e)s, Schränke) m cupboard; (Kleiderschrank) wardrobe (BRIT), closet (US)

Schranke (-, -n) f barrier

Schrankwand f wall unit

Schraube (-, -n) f screw; **schrauben** vt to screw; **Schraubendreher** (-s, -) m screwdriver, **Schraubenschlüssel** m spanner; **Schrau-**

benzieher (s,) m screwdriver; **Schraubverschluss** m screw top, screw cap

Schreck (-(e)s, -e) m, **Schrecken** (-s, -) m terror; (Angst) fright; **jdm einen ~ einjagen** to give sb a fright; **schreckhaft** adj jumpy; **schrecklich** adj terrible; dreadful

Schrei (-(e)s, -e) m scream; (Ruf) shout

Schreibblock m writing pad; **schreiben** (schrieb, geschrieben) vt, vi to write; (buchstabieren) to spell; **wie schreibt man ...?** how do you spell ...?; **Schreiben** (-s, -) nt writing; (Brief) letter; **Schreibfehler** m spelling mistake; **schreibgeschützt** adj (Diskette) write-protected; **Schreibtisch** m desk; **Schreibwaren** pl stationery sing; **Schreibwarenladen** m stationer's

schreien (schrie, geschrie(e)n) vt, vi to scream; (rufen) to shout

Schreiner(in) m(f) joiner; **Schreinerei** f joiner's workshop

schrie imperf von **schreien**

schrieb imperf von **schreiben**

Schrift (-, -en) f writing; (Handschrift) handwriting; (Schriftart) typeface; (Schrifttyp) font; **schriftlich** adj written ▷ adv in writing; **würden Sie uns das bitte ~ geben?** could we have that in writing, please?; **Schriftsteller(in)** (-s, -) m(f) writer

Schritt (-(e)s, -e) m step; **~ für ~** step by step; **~e gegen etw unternehmen** to take steps against sth; **Schrittgeschwindigkeit** f walking speed; **Schrittmacher** m (Med) pacemaker

Schrott (-(e)s, -e) m scrap metal; (fig) rubbish

schrubben vi, vt to scrub; **Schrubber** (-s, -) m scrubbing brush

schrumpfen vi to shrink

Schubkarren (-s, -) m wheelbarrow; **Schublade** f drawer

schubsen vt to shove, to push

schüchtern adj shy

schuf imperf von **schaffen**

Schuh (-(e)s, -e) m shoe; **Schuhcreme** f shoe polish; **Schuhgeschäft** nt shoe shop; **Schuhgröße** f shoe size; **Schuhlöffel** m shoehorn; **Schuhsohle** f sole

Schulabschluss m school-leaving qualification

schuld adj **wer ist ~ daran?** whose fault is it?; **er ist ~** it's his fault, he's to blame; **Schuld** (-) f guilt; (Verschulden) fault; **~ haben** to be to blame (an +dat for); **er hat ~** it's his fault; **sie gibt mir die ~ an dem Unfall** she blames me for the accident; **schulden** vt to owe (jdm etw sb sth); **Schulden** pl debts pl; **~ haben** to be in debt; **~ machen** to run up debts; **seine ~ bezahlen** to pay off one's debts; **schuldig** adj guilty (an +dat of); (gebührend) due; **jdm etw ~ sein** to owe sb sth

Schule (-, -n) f school; **in der ~** at school; **in die ~ gehen** to go to school; **Schüler(in)** (-s, -) m(f) (jüngerer) pupil; (älterer) student; **Schüleraustausch** m school exchange; **Schulfach** nt subject; **Schulferien** pl school holidays pl (BRIT) (o vacation (US)); **schulfrei** adj **morgen ist ~** there's no school tomorrow; **Schulfreund(in)** m(f) schoolmate; **Schuljahr** nt school year; **Schulkenntnisse** pl **~ in Französisch** school(-level) French; **Schulklasse** f class; **Schulleiter(in)** m(f) headmaster/headmistress (BRIT), principal (US)

Schulter (-, -n) f shoulder; **Schulterblatt** nt shoulder blade

Schulung f training; (Veranstaltung) training course

Schund (-(e)s) m trash

Schuppe (-, -n) f (von Fisch) scale; **vt zu ~** to peel; **Schuppen** pl (im Haar) dandruff sing

Schürfwunde f graze

Schürze (-, -n) f apron

Schuss (-es, Schüsse) m shot; **mit einem ~ Wodka** with a dash of vodka

Schüssel (-, -n) f bowl

Schuster(in) (-s, -) m(f) shoemaker

Schutt (-(e)s) m rubble

Schüttelfrost m shivering fit; **schütteln** vt to shake ▷ vr **sich ~** to shake

schütten vt to pour; (Zucker, Kies etc) to tip ▷ vi impers to pour (down)

Schutz (-es) m protection (gegen, vor against, from); (Unterschlupf) shelter; **jdn in ~ nehmen** to stand up for sb; **Schutzblech** nt mudguard; **Schutzbrief** m travel insurance document for drivers; **Schutzbrille** f (safety) goggles pl

Schütze (-n, -n) m (beim Fußball) scorer; (Astr) Sagittarius

schützen vt **jdn gegen / vor etw ~** to protect sb against / from sth; **Schutzimpfung** f inoculation, vaccination

schwach adj weak; **~e Augen** poor eyesight sing; **Schwäche** (-, -n) f weakness; **Schwachstelle** f weak point; **Schwachstrom** m low-voltage current

Schwager (-s, Schwäger) m brother-in-law; **Schwägerin** f sister-in-law

Schwalbe (-, -n) f swallow; (beim Fußball) dive

schwamm imperf von **schwimmen**

Schwamm (-(e)s, Schwämme) m sponge; **~ drüber!** (fam) let's forget it!

Schwan (-(e)s, Schwäne) m swan

schwanger adj pregnant; **im vierten Monat ~ sein** to be four months pregnant; **Schwangerschaft** f pregnancy; **Schwangerschaftsabbruch** m abortion; **Schwangerschaftstest** m pregnancy test

schwanken vi to sway; (Preise, Zahlen) to fluctuate; (zögern) to hesitate; (taumeln) to stagger; **ich schwanke zwischen A und B** I can't decide between A and B

Schwanz (-es, Schwänze) m tail; (vulg: Penis) cock

Schwarm (-(e)s, Schwärme) m swarm; (fam: angehimmelte Person) heartthrob; **schwärmen** vi to swarm; **~ für** to be mad about

schwarz adj black; **~ sehen** (fam) to be pessimistic (für about); **mir wurde ~ vor Augen** everything went black; **Schwarzarbeit** f illicit work; **Schwarzbrot** nt black bread; **schwarzfahren** irr vi to travel without a ticket; (ohne Führerschein) to drive without a licence; **Schwarzfahrer(in)** m(f) fare-dodger; **Schwarzmarkt** m black market; **Schwarzwald** m Black Forest; **schwarzweiß** adj black and white; **Schwarzwurzel** f black salsify

schwatzen vi to chatter; **Schwätzer(in)** (-s, -) m(f) chatterbox; (Schwafler) gasbag; (Klatschmaul) gossip

Schwebebahn f suspension railway; **schweben** vi to float; (hoch) to soar

Schwede (-n, -n) m Swede; **Schweden** (-s) nt Sweden; **Schwedin** f Swede; **schwedisch** adj Swedish; **Schwedisch** nt Swedish

Schwefel (-s) m sulphur

schweigen (schwieg, geschwiegen) vi to be silent; (nicht mehr reden) to stop talking; **Schweigen** (-s) nt silence; **Schweigepflicht** f duty of confidentiality; **die ärztliche ~** medical confidentiality

Schwein (-(e)s, -e) nt pig; (fam: Glück) luck; (fam: gemeiner Mensch) swine; **Schweinebraten** m roast pork; **Schweinefleisch** nt pork; **Schweinerei** f mess; (Gemeinheit) dirty trick

Schweiß (-es) m sweat

schweißen vt, vi to weld

Schweißfüße pl sweaty feet pl

Schweiz (-) f **die ~** Switzerland; **Schweizer(in)** (-s, -) m(f) Swiss; **Schweizerdeutsch** nt Swiss German; **schweizerisch** adj Swiss

Schwelle (-, -n) f doorstep; (a. fig) threshold

schwellen vi to swell (up); **Schwellung** f swelling

schwer adj heavy; (schwierig) difficult, hard; (schlimm) serious, bad; **er ist ~ zu verstehen** it's difficult to understand what he's saying ▷ adv (sehr) really; (verletzt etc) seriously, badly; **jdm ~ fallen** to be difficult for sb; **etw ~ nehmen** to take sth hard; **Schwerbehinderte(r)** m(f) severely disabled person; **schwerhörig** adj hard of hearing

Schwert (-(e)s, -er) nt sword; **Schwertlilie** f iris

Schwester (-, -n) f sister; (Med) nurse

schwieg imperf von **schweigen**

Schwiegereltern pl parents-in-law pl; **Schwiegermutter** f mother-in-law; **Schwiegersohn** m son-in-law; **Schwiegertochter** f daughter-in-law; **Schwiegervater** m father-in-law

schwierig adj difficult, hard;

Schwierigkeit f difficulty; **in ~en kommen** to get into trouble; **jdm ~en machen** to make things difficult for sb

Schwimmbad nt swimming pool; **Schwimmbecken** nt swimming pool; **schwimmen** (schwamm, geschwommen) vi to swim; (treiben) to float; (fig: unsicher sein) to be all at sea; **Schwimmer(in)** m(f) swimmer; **Schwimmflosse** f flipper; **Schwimmflügel** m water wing; **Schwimmreifen** m rubber ring; **Schwimmweste** f life jacket

Schwindel (-s) m dizziness; (Anfall) dizzy spell; (Betrug) swindle; **schwindelfrei** adj **nicht ~ sein** to suffer from vertigo; **~ sein** to have a head for heights; **schwindlig** adj dizzy; **mir ist ~** I feel dizzy

Schwips m **einen ~ haben** to be tipsy

schwitzen vi to sweat

schwoll imperf von **schwellen**

schwor imperf von **schwören**

schwören (schwor, geschworen) vt, vi to swear; **einen Eid ~** to take an oath

schwul adj gay

schwül adj close

Schwung (-(e)s, Schwünge) m swing; (Triebkraft) momentum; (fig: Energie) energy; (fam: Menge) batch; **in ~ kommen** to get going

Schwur (-s, Schwüre) m oath

scrollen vi (Inform) to scroll

sechs num six; **Sechs** (-, -en) f six; (Schulnote) ≈ F; **Sechserpack** m sixpack; **sechshundert** num six hundred; **sechsmal** adv six times; **sechste(r, s)** adj sixth; siehe auch **dritte**; **Sechstel** (-s, -) nt sixth; **sechzehn** num sixteen; **sechzehnte(r, s)** adj sixteenth; siehe auch **dritte**; **sechzig** num sixty; **in den ~er Jahren** in the sixties;

sechzigste(r, s) adj sixtieth

Secondhandladen m secondhand shop

See (-, -n) f sea; **an der ~** by the sea ⊳ (-s, -n) m lake; **am ~** by the lake; **Seegang** m waves; **hoher / schwerer / leichter ~** rough / heavy / calm seas pl; **Seehund** m seal; **Seeigel** m sea urchin; **seekrank** adj seasick

Seele (-, -n) f soul

Seeleute pl seamen pl, sailors pl

seelisch adj mental, psychological

Seelöwe m sea lion; **Seemann** m sailor, seaman; **Seemeile** f nautical mile; **Seemöwe** f seagull; **Seenot** f distress (at sea); **Seepferdchen** nt sea horse; **Seerose** f water lily; **Seestern** m starfish; **Seezunge** f sole

Segel (-s, -) nt sail; **Segelboot** nt yacht; **Segelfliegen** (-s) nt gliding; **Segelflugzeug** nt glider; **segeln** vt, vi to sail; **Segelschiff** nt sailing ship

sehbehindert adj partially sighted

sehen (sah, gesehen) vt, vi to see; (in bestimmter Richtung) to look; **gut / schlecht ~** to have good / bad eyesight; **auf die Uhr ~** to look at one's watch; **kann ich das mal ~?** can I have a look at it?; **wir ~ uns morgen!** see you tomorrow; **ich kenne sie nur von Sehen** I only know her by sight; **Sehenswürdigkeiten** pl sights pl

Sehne (-, -n) f tendon; (an Bogen) string

sehnen vr **sich ~** to long (nach for)

Sehnenscheidenentzündung f (Med) tendovaginitis; **Sehnenzerrung** f (Med) pulled tendon

Sehnsucht f longing; **sehnsüchtig** adj longing

sehr adv (vor Adjektiv, Adverb) very;

(mit Verben) a lot, very much; **zu ~** too much

seicht adj shallow

Seide (-, -n) f silk

Seife (-, -n) f soap; **Seifenoper** f soap (opera); **Seifenschale** f soap dish

Seil (-(e)s, -e) nt rope; (Kabel) cable; **Seilbahn** f cable railway

sein (war, gewesen) vi, vaux to be; **lass das ~!** leave that!; (hör auf) stop that!; **das kann ~** that's possible

sein pron possessive von **er**; (adjektivisch) his ▷ pron possessive von **es**; (adjektivisch) its; (adjektivisch, männlich) his; (weiblich) her; (sächlich) its; **das ist ~e Tasche** that's his bag; **jeder hat ~e Sorgen** everyone has their problems; **seine(r, s)** pron possessive von **er**; (substantivisch) his ▷ pron possessive von **es**; (substantivisch) its; (substantivisch, männlich) his; (weiblich) hers; **das ist ~r/-/-s** that's his / hers; **seiner** pron gen von **er**; of him ▷ pron gen von **es**; of it; **seinetwegen** adv (wegen ihm) because of him; (ihm zuliebe) for his sake; (um ihn) about him; (von ihm aus) as far as he is concerned

seit conj (bei Zeitpunkt) since; (bei Zeitraum) for; **er ist ~ Montag hier** he's been here since Monday; **er ist ~ einer Woche hier** he's been here for a week; **~ langem** for a long time; **seitdem** adv, conj since

Seite (-, -n) f side; (in Buch) page; **zur ~ gehen** to step aside; **Seitenairbag** m side-impact airbag; **Seitenaufprallschutz** m (Auto) side-impact protection; **Seitensprung** m affair; **Seitenstechen** (-s) nt - **haben/bekommen** to have / get a stitch; **Seitenstraße** f side street; **Seitenstreifen** m hard shoulder (BRIT), shoulder (US); **seitenverkehrt** adj the wrong way round;

Seitenwind m crosswind

seither adv since (then)

seitlich adj side

Sekretär(in) m(f) secretary

Sekt (-(e)s, -e) m sparkling wine (similar to champagne)

Sekte (-, -n) f sect

Sekunde (-, -n) f second; **Sekundenkleber** (-s, -) m superglue; **Sekundenschnelle f es geschah al les in ~** it was all over in a matter of seconds

selbst pron **ich ~** I ... myself; **du/ Sie ~** you ... yourself; **er ~** he ... himself; **sie ~** she ... herself; (mehrere) they ... themselves; **wir haben es ~ gemacht** we did it ourselves; **mach es ~** do it yourself; **von ~** by itself; **das versteht sich ja von ~** that goes without saying ▷ adv even; **~ mir gefiel's** even I liked it; **selbständig** adj siehe **selbst-ständig**

Selbstauslöser (-s, -) m (Foto) self-timer; **Selbstbedienung** f self-service; **Selbstbefriedigung** f masturbation; **Selbstbeherrschung** f self-control; **Selbstbeteiligung** f (einer Versicherung) excess; **selbstbewusst** adj (self-)confident; **Selbstbräuner** (-s, -) m self-tanning lotion; **selbstgemacht** adj self-made; **Selbstgespräch** nt **~e führen** to talk to oneself; **selbstklebend** adj self-adhesive; **Selbstkostenpreis** m cost price; **Selbstlaut** m vowel; **Selbstmord** m suicide; **selbstsicher** adj self-assured; **selbstständig** adj independent; (arbeitend) self-employed; **Selbstverpflegung** f self-catering; **selbstverständlich** adj obvious; **ich halte das für ~** I take that for granted ▷ adv naturally; **Selbstvertrauen** nt self-confidence

Sellerie (-s, -(s)) m (-, -n) f (Knol-

lensellerie) celeriac; *(Stangensellerie)* celery

selten *adj* rare ▷ *adv* seldom, rarely

seltsam *adj* strange; **~ schmecken/riechen** to taste/smell strange

Semester *(-s, -)* nt semester; **Semesterferien** *pl* vacation *sing*

Semikolon *(-s, Semikola)* nt semicolon

Seminar *(-s, -e)* nt seminar

Semmel *(-, -n)* f roll; **Semmelbrösel** *pl* breadcrumbs

Senat *(-(e)s, -e)* m senate

senden *(sandte, gesandt)* vt to send ▷ *vt, vi (Radio, Tv)* to broadcast; **Sender** *(-s, -)* m *(TV)* channel; *(Radio)* station; *(Anlage)* transmitter; **Sendung** f *(Radio, Tv)* broadcasting; *(Programm)* programme

Senf *(-(e)s, -e)* m mustard

Senior(in) *m(f)* senior citizen; **Seniorenpass** m senior citizen's travel pass

senken *vt* to lower ▷ *vr* **sich ~** to sink

senkrecht *adj* vertical

Sensation *(-, -en)* f sensation

sensibel *adj* sensitive

sentimental *adj* sentimental

separat *adj* separate

September *(-(s), -)* m September; *siehe auch* **Juni**

Serbien *(-s)* nt Serbia

Serie f series *sing*

seriös *adj (ernsthaft)* serious; *(anständig)* respectable

Serpentine f hairpin (bend)

Serum *(-s, Seren)* nt serum

Server *(-s, -)* m *(Inform)* server

Service *(-(s), -)* nt *(Geschirr)* service ▷ *(-, -s)* m service

servieren *vt, vi* to serve

Serviette f napkin, serviette

Servolenkung f *(Auto)* power

steering

Sesam *(-s, -s)* m sesame seeds *pl*

Sessel *(-s, -)* m armchair; **Sessellift** m chairlift

Set *(-s, -s)* m o nt set; *(Tischset)* tablemat

setzen *vt* to put; *(Baum etc)* to plant; *(Segel)* to set ▷ *vr* **sich ~** to settle; *(hinsetzen)* to sit down; **~ Sie sich doch** please sit down

Seuche *(-, -n)* f epidemic

seufzen *vt, vi* to sigh

Sex *(-(es))* m sex; **Sexismus** m sexism; **sexistisch** *adj* sexist; **Sextourismus** m sex tourism; **Sexualität** f sexuality; **sexuell** *adj* sexual

Seychellen *pl* Seychelles *pl*

sfr *abk* = **Schweizer Franken** Swiss franc(s)

Shampoo *(-s, -s)* nt shampoo

Shareware *(-, -s)* f *(Inform)* shareware

Shorts *pl* shorts *pl*

Shuttlebus *m* shuttle bus

sich *pron (sing männlich)* himself; *(sing weiblich)* herself; *(sing sächlich)* itself; *(pl)* themselves; *(nach Sie)* yourself; *(nach Sie im pl)* yourselves; *(unbestimmt, nach man)* oneself; **er hat ~ verletzt** he hurt himself; **Sie sollten ~ glücklich schätzen** you should consider yourself lucky; **sie kennen ~** they know each other; **sie hat ~ sehr gefreut** she was very pleased; **er hat ~ das Bein gebrochen** he's broken his leg; **er hat noch 20 Kilometer vor ~** he still has 20 kilometres ahead of him

sicher *adj* safe *(vor +dat* from); *(gewiss)* certain *(gen* of); *(zuverlässig)* reliable; *(selbstsicher)* confident; **aber ~!** of course, sure; **Sicherheit** f safety; *(Aufgabe von Sicherheitsbeamten) (Fin)* security; *(Gewissheit)* certainty; *(Selbstsicherheit)* confidence; **mit ~** definitely; **Sicherheitsabstand** m safe distance; **Sicherheitsgurt** m seat belt; **cherheitshalber** adv just to be on the safe side; **Sicherheitsnadel** f safety pin; **Sicherheitsvorkehrung** f safety precaution; **sicherlich** adv certainly; (wahrscheinlich) probably **sichern** vt to secure (gegen against); (schützen) to protect; (Daten) to back up, **Sicherung** f (Sichern) securing; (Vorrichtung) safety device; (an Waffen) safety catch; (ELEK) fuse; (Inform) backup; **die ~ ist durchgebrannt** the fuse has blown **Sicht** (-) f sight; (Aussicht) view; **sichtbar** adj visible; **sichtlich** adj evident, obvious; **Sichtverhältnisse** pl visibility sing; **Sichtweite** f **in/außer ~** within/out of sight **sie** pron (3. Person sing) she; (3. Person pl) they; (akk von sing) her; (akk von pl) them; (für eine Sache) it: **da ist ~ ja** there she is; **da sind ~ ja** there they are; **ich kenne ~** (Frau) I know her; (mehrere Personen) I know them; **~ lag gerade noch hier** (meine Jacke, Uhr) it was here just a minute ago; **ich hab ~ gefunden** (meine Jacke, Uhr) I've found it; **hast du meine Brille/Hose gesehen? - ich kann ~ nirgends finden** have you seen my glasses/trousers? - I can't find them anywhere

Sie pron (Höflichkeitsform, Nom und Akk) you

Sieb (-(e)s, -e) nt sieve; (Teesieb) strainer

sieben num seven; **siebenhundert** num seven hundred; **siebenmal** adv seven times; **siebte(r, s)** adj seventh; siehe auch **dritte**; **Siebtel** (-s, -) nt seventh; **siebzehn** num seventeen; **siebzehnte(r, s)** adj seventeenth; siehe auch **dritte**; **siebzig** num seventy; **in den ~er**

Jahren in the seventies; **siebzigste(r, s)** adj seventieth

Siedlung (-, -en) f (Wohngebiet) housing estate (BRIT) (o development (US))

Sieg (-(e)s, -e) m victory, **siegen** vi to win; **Sieger(in)** (-s, -) m(f) winner; **Siegerehrung** f presentation ceremony

siehe imper see

siezen vt to address as 'Sie'

Signal (-s, -e) nt signal

Silbe (-, -n) f syllable

Silber (-s) nt silver; **Silberhochzeit** f silver wedding; **Silbermedaille** f silver medal

Silikon (-s, -e) nt silicone

Silvester (-s, -) nt, **Silvesterabend** m New Year's Eve, Hogmanay (SCOT)

● **SILVESTER**

● **Silvester** is the German name for New Year's Eve. Although not an official holiday, most businesses close early and shops shut at midday. Most Germans celebrate in the evening and at midnight they let off fireworks and rockets, the revelry usually lasts until the early hours of the morning.

Simbabwe (-s) nt Zimbabwe

simpel adj simple

simultan adj simultaneous

simsen vt, vi (fam) to text

Sinfonie (-, -n) f symphony; **Sinfonieorchester** nt symphony orchestra

Singapur (-s) nt Singapore

singen (sang, gesungen) vt, vi to sing; **richtig/falsch ~** to sing in tune/out of tune

Single (-, -s) f (CD) single ▷ (-s, -s) m (Mensch) single

Singular m singular

sinken (sank, gesunken) vi to sink; (Preise etc) to fall, to go down

Sinn (-(e)s, -e) m (Denken) mind; (Wahrnehmung) sense; (Bedeutung) sense, meaning; **~ machen** to make sense; **das hat keinen ~** it's no use; **sinnlich** adj sensuous; (erotisch) sensual; (Wahrnehmung) sensory; **sinnlos** adj (unsinnig) stupid; (Verhalten) senseless; (zwecklos) pointless; (bedeutungslos) meaningless; **sinnvoll** adj meaningful; (vernünftig) sensible

Sirup (-s, -e) m syrup

Sitte (-, -n) f custom

Situation f situation

Sitz (-es, -e) m seat; **sitzen** (saß, gesessen) vi to sit; (Bemerkung, Schlag) to strike home; (Gelerntes) to have sunk in; **der Rock sitzt gut** the skirt is a good fit; **Sitzgelegenheit** f place to sit down; **Sitzplatz** m seat; **Sitzung** f meeting

Sizilien (-s) nt Sicily

Skandal (-s, -e) m scandal

Skandinavien (-s) nt Scandinavia

Skateboard (-s, -s) nt skateboard; **Skateboardfahrer(in)** m(f) skateboarder

Skelett (-s, -e) nt skeleton

skeptisch adj sceptical

Ski (-s, -er) m ski; **~ laufen** (o **fahren**) to ski; **Skianzug** m ski suit; **Skibrille** f ski goggles pl; **Skifahren** (-s) nt skiing; **Skigebiet** (-s, -e) nt skiing area; **Skihose** f skiing trousers pl; **Skikurs** m skiing course; **Skilanglauf** m cross-country skiing; **Skiläufer(in)** m(f) skier; **Skilehrer(in)** m(f) ski instructor; **Skilift** m ski-lift

Skinhead (-s, -s) m skinhead

Skipiste f ski run; **Skischanze** (-, -n) f ski jump; **Skischuh** m ski boot; **Skischule** f ski school; **Skispringen** (-s, -n) nt ski jumping;

Skistiefel (-s, -) m ski boot; **Skistock** m ski pole; **Skiträger** m ski rack; **Skiurlaub** m skiing holiday (BRIT) (o vacation (US))

Skizze (-, -n) f sketch

Skonto (-s, -s) m o nt discount

Skorpion (-s, -e) m (Zool) scorpion; (Astr) Scorpio

Skulptur (-, -en) f sculpture

S-Kurve f double bend

Slalom (-s, -s) m slalom

Slip (-s, -s) m (pair of) briefs pl; **Slipeinlage** f panty liner

Slowakei (-) f Slovakia; **slowakisch** adj Slovakian; **Slowakische Republik** Slovak Republic; **Slowakisch** nt Slovakian

Slowenien (-s) nt Slovenia; **slowenisch** adj Slovenian; **Slowenisch** nt Slovenian

Smiley (-s, -s) m smiley

Smog (-s) m smog; **Smogalarm** m smog alert

Smoking (-s, -s) m dinner jacket (BRIT), tuxedo (US)

SMS nt abk = **Short Message Service** ▷ f (Nachricht) text message; **ich schicke dir eine ~** I'll text you, I'll send you a text (message)

Snowboard (-s, -s) nt snowboard; **Snowboardfahren** (-s) nt snowboarding; **Snowboardfahrer(in)** m(f) snowboarder

so adv so; (auf diese Weise) like this; (ungefähr) about; **fünf Euro oder ~** five euros or so; **~ ein** such a; **~ ... wie ...** as ... as ...; **und ~ weiter** and so on; **~ genannt** so-called; **~ viel** as much (wie as); **~ weit sein** to be ready; **~ weit wie (o als) möglich** as far as possible ▷ conj so; (vor Adjektiv) as

s. o. abk = **siehe oben** see above

sobald conj as soon as

Socke (-, -n) f sock

Sodbrennen (-s) nt heartburn

Sofa (-s, -s) nt sofa

sofern conj if, provided (that)

soff imperf von **saufen**

sofort adv immediately, at once; **Sofortbildkamera** f instant camera

Softeis nt soft ice-cream

Software (-, -s) f software

sog imperf von **saugen**

sogar adv even; **kalt, ~ sehr kalt** cold, in fact very cold

Sohle (-, -n) f sole

Sohn (-(e)s, Söhne) m son

Soja (-, Sojen) f soya; **Sojasprossen** pl bean sprouts pl

solang(e) conj as long as

Solarium nt solarium

Solarzelle f solar cell

solche(r, s) pron such; **eine ~ Frau, solch eine Frau** such a woman, a woman like that; **~ Sachen** things like that, such things; **ich habe ~ Kopfschmerzen** I've got such a headache; **ich habe ~n Hunger** I'm so hungry

Soldat(in) (-en, -en) m(f) soldier

solidarisch adj showing solidarity; **sich ~ erklären mit** to declare one's solidarity with

solid(e) adj solid; (Leben, Mensch) respectable

Soll (-(s), -(s)) nt (Fin) debit; (Arbeitsmenge) quota, target

sollen vi to be supposed to, (Verpflichtung) shall, ought to, **soll ich?** shall I?; **du solltest besser nach Hause gehen** you'd better go home; **sie soll sehr reich sein** she's said to be very rich; **was soll das?** what's all that about?

Solo (-s, -) nt solo

Sommer (-s, -) m summer; **Sommerfahrplan** m summer timetable; **Sommerferien** pl summer holidays pl (BRIT) (n vacation sing (US)); **sommerlich** adj summery;

(Sommer-) summer; **Sommerreifen** m normal tyre; **Sommersprossen** pl freckles pl; **Sommerzeit** f summertime; (Uhrzeit) daylight saving time

Sonderangebot nt special offer; **sonderbar** adj strange, odd; **Sondermarke** f special stamp; **Sondermaschine** f special plane; **Sondermüll** m hazardous waste

sondern conj but; **nicht nur ..., ~ auch** not only ..., but also

Sonderpreis m special price; **Sonderschule** f special school; **Sonderzeichen** nt (Inform) special character; **Sonderzug** m special train

Song (-s, -s) m song

Sonnabend m Saturday; siehe auch **Mittwoch**; **sonnabends** adv on Saturdays; **~ morgens** on Saturday mornings; siehe auch **mittwochs**

Sonne (-, -n) f sun; **sonnen** vr **sich ~** to sunbathe; **Sonnenallergie** f sun allergy; **Sonnenaufgang** m sunrise; **Sonnenblume** f sunflower; **Sonnenblumenkern** m sunflower seed; **Sonnenbrand** m sunburn; **Sonnenbrille** f sunglasses pl, shades pl; **Sonnencreme** f sun cream; **Sonnendach** nt (an Haus) awning; (Auto) sunroof; **Sonnendeck** nt sun deck; **Sonnenmilch** f suntan lotion; **Sonnenöl** nt suntan oil; **Sonnenschein** m sunshine; **Sonnenschirm** m parasol, sunshade; **Sonnenschutzcreme** f sunscreen; **Sonnenstich** m sunstroke; **Sonnenstudio** nt solarium; **Sonnenuhr** f sundial; **Sonnenuntergang** m sunset; **sonnig** adj sunny

Sonntag m Sunday; siehe auch **Mittwoch**; **sonntags** adv on Sundays; siehe auch **mittwochs**

sonst adv , conj (außerdem) else; (andernfalls) otherwise, (or) else; (mit Pron, in Fragen) else; (normalerweise) normally, usually; **~ noch etwas?** anything else?; **~ nichts** nothing else

sooft conj whenever

Sopran (-s, -e) m soprano

Sorge (-, -n) f worry; (Fürsorge) care; **sich** (dat) **um jdn ~n machen** to be worried about sb; **sorgen** vi **für jdn ~** to look after sb; **für etw ~** to take care of sth, to see to sth ▷ vr **sich ~** to worry (um about); **sorgfältig** adj careful

sortieren vt to sort (out)

Sortiment nt assortment

sosehr conj however much

Soße (-, -n) f sauce; (zu Braten) gravy

Soundkarte f (Inform) sound card

Souvenir (-s, -s) nt souvenir

soviel conj as far as

soweit conj as far as

sowie conj (wie auch) as well as; (sobald) as soon as

sowohl conj **~ ... als** (o wie) **auch** both ... and

sozial adj social; **Sozialhilfe** f income support (BRIT), welfare (aid) (US); **Sozialismus** m socialism; **Sozialversicherung** f social security; **Sozialwohnung** f council flat (BRIT), state-subsidized apartment (US)

Soziologie f sociology

sozusagen adv so to speak

Spachtel (-s, -) m spatula

Spag(h)etti pl spaghetti sing

Spalte (-, -n) f crack; (Gletscher) crevasse; (in Text) column

spalten vt to split ▷ vr **sich ~** to split

Spange (-, -n) f clasp; (Haarspange) hair slide (BRIT), barrette (US)

Spanien (-s) nt Spain; **Spanier(in)** (-s, -) m(f) Spaniard; **spanisch** adj

Spanish; **Spanisch** nt Spanish

spann imperf von **spinnen**

spannen vt (straffen) to tighten; (befestigen) to brace ▷ vi to be tight

spannend adj exciting, gripping; **Spannung** f tension; (Elek) voltage; (fig) suspense

Sparbuch nt savings book; (Konto) savings account; **sparen** vt, vi to save

Spargel (-s, -) m asparagus; **Spargelsuppe** f asparagus soup

Sparkasse f savings bank; **Sparkonto** f savings account

spärlich adj meagre; (Bekleidung) scanty

sparsam adj economical; **Sparschwein** nt piggy bank

Spaß (-es, Späße) m joke; (Freude) fun; **es macht mir ~** I enjoy it, it's (great) fun; **viel ~!** have fun

spät adj, adv late; **zu ~ kommen** to be late

Spaten (-s, -) m spade

später adj, adv later; **spätestens** adv at the latest; **Spätlese** f late vintage (wine); **Spätvorstellung** f late-night performance

Spatz (-en, -en) m sparrow

spazieren vi to stroll, to walk; **~ gehen** to go for a walk; **Spaziergang** m walk

Specht (-(e)s, -e) m woodpecker

Speck (-(e)s, -e) m bacon fat; (durchwachsen) bacon

Spedition f (für Umzug) removal firm

Speiche (-, -n) f spoke

Speichel (-s) m saliva

Speicher (-s, -) m storehouse; (Dachboden) attic; (Inform) memory; **speichern** vt (Inform) to store; (sichern) to save

Speise (-, -n) f food; (Gericht) dish; **Speisekarte** f menu; **Speiseröhre** f gullet, oesophagus; **Speise-**

saal m dining hall; **Speisewagen** m dining car

Spende (-, -n) f donation; **spenden** vt to donate, to give

spendieren vt **jdm etw ~** to treat sb to sth

Sperre (-, -n) f barrier; (Verbot) ban; **sperren** vt to block; (Sport) to suspend; (verbieten) to ban

Sperrgepäck nt bulky luggage; **Sperrmüll** m bulky refuse; **Sperrstunde** f closing time; **Sperrung** f closing

Spesen pl expenses pl

spezialisieren vr **sich ~** to specialize (auf +akk in); **Spezialist(in)** m(f) specialist; **Spezialität** f speciality (BRIT), specialty (US); **speziell** adj special ▷ adv especially

Spiegel (-s, -) m mirror; **Spiegelei** nt fried egg (sunny-side up (US)); **spiegelglatt** adj very slippery; **Spiegelreflexkamera** f reflex camera

Spiel (-(e)s, -e) nt game; (Tätigkeit) play(ing); (Karten) pack, deck; (Tech) (free) play; **Spielautomat** m (ohne Geldgewinn) gaming machine; (mit Geldgewinn) slot machine, **spielen** vt, vi to play; (um Geld) to gamble; (Theat) to perform, to act; **Klavier ~** to play the piano; **spielend** adv easily; **Spieler(in)** (-s, -) m(f) player; (um Geld) gambler; **Spielfeld** nt (für Fußball, Hockey) field; (für Basketball) court; **Spielfilm** m feature film; **Spielkasino** nt casino; **Spielplatz** m playground; **Spielraum** m room to manoeuvre; **Spielregel** f rule; **sich an die ~n halten** to stick to the rules; **Spielsachen** pl toys pl; **Spielverderber(in)** (-s, -) m(f) spoilsport; **Spielzeug** nt toys pl; (einzelnes) toy

Spieß (-es, -e) m spear; (Bratspieß) spit, **Spießer(in)** (-s, -) m(f) square,

stuffy type; **spießig** adj square, uncool

Spikes pl (Sport) spikes pl; (Auto) studs pl

Spinat (-(e)s, -e) m spinach

Spinne (-, -n) f spider; **spinnen** (spann, gesponnen) vt, vi to spin; (fam: Unsinn reden) to talk rubbish; (verrückt sein) to be crazy; **du spinnst!** you must be mad; **Spinnwebe** (-, -n) f cobweb

Spion(in) (-s, -e) m(f) spy; **spionieren** vi to spy; (fig) to snoop around

Spirale (-, -n) f spiral; (Med) coil

Spirituosen pl spirits pl, liquor sing (US)

Spiritus (-, -se) m spirit

spitz adj (Nase, Kinn) pointed; (Bleistift, Messer) sharp; (Winkel) acute; **Spitze** (-, -n) f point; (von Finger, Nase) tip; (Bemerkung) taunt, dig; (erster Platz) lead; (Gewebe) lace; **Spitzengeschwindigkeit** f top speed; **Spitzer** (-s, -) m pencil sharpener; **Spitzname** m nickname

Spliss (-) m split ends pl

sponsern vt to sponsor; **Sponsor(in)** (-s, -en) m(f) sponsor

spontan adj spontaneous

Sport (-(e)s, -e) m sport; **~ treiben** to do sport; **Sportanlage** f sports grounds pl, **Sportart** f sport; **Sportbekleidung** f sportswear; **Sportgeschäft** nt sports shop; **Sporthalle** f gymnasium, gym; **Sportlehrer(in)** (-s, -) m(f) sports instructor; (Schule) PE teacher; **Sportler(in)** (-s, -) m(f) sportsman /-woman; **sportlich** adj sporting; (Mensch) sporty; **Sportplatz** m playing field; **Sporttauchen** nt (skin-)diving; (mit Gerät) scuba-diving; **Sportverein** m sports club, **Sportwagen** m sports car

sprach imperf von **sprechen**

Sprache (-, -n) f language; (Sprechen) speech; **Sprachenschule** f language school; **Sprachführer** m phrasebook; **Sprachkenntnisse** pl knowledge sing of languages; **gute englische ~ haben** to have a good knowledge of English; **Sprachkurs** m language course; **Sprachunterricht** m language teaching

sprang imperf von **springen**

Spray (-s, -s) m o nt spray

Sprechanlage f intercom; **sprechen** (sprach, gesprochen) vt, vi to speak (jdn, mit jdm to sb); (sich unterhalten) to talk (mit to, über, von about); **~ Sie Deutsch?** do you speak German?; **kann ich bitte mit David ~?** (am Telefon) can I speak to David, please?; **Sprecher(in)** m(f) speaker; (Ansager) announcer; **Sprechstunde** f consultation; (Arzt) surgery hours pl; (Anwalt etc) office hours pl; **Sprechzimmer** nt consulting room

Sprengstoff m explosive

Sprichwort nt proverb

Springbrunnen m fountain

springen (sprang, gesprungen) vi to jump; (Glas) to crack; (mit Kopfsprung) to dive

Sprit (-(e)s, -e) m (fam: Benzin) petrol (BRIT), gas (US)

Spritze (-, -n) f (Gegenstand) syringe; (Injektion) injection; (an Schlauch) nozzle; **spritzen** vt to spray; (Med) to inject ▷ vi to splash; (Med) to give injections

Spruch (-(e)s, Sprüche) m saying

Sprudel (-s, -) m sparkling mineral water; (süßer) fizzy drink (BRIT), soda (US); **sprudeln** vi to bubble

Sprühdose f aerosol (can); **sprühen** vt, vi to spray; (fig) to sparkle; **Sprühregen** m drizzle

Sprung (-(e)s, Sprünge) m jump; (Riss) crack; **Sprungbrett** nt springboard; **Sprungschanze** f ski jump; **Sprungturm** m diving platforms pl

Spucke (-) f spit; **spucken** vt, vi to spit; (fam: sich erbrechen) to vomit; **Spucktüte** f sick bag

spuken vi (Geist) to walk; **hier spukt es** this place is haunted

Spülbecken nt sink

Spule (-, -n) f spool; (Elek) coil

Spüle (-, -n) f sink; **spülen** vt, vi to rinse; (Geschirr) to wash up; (Toilette) to flush; **Spülmaschine** f dishwasher; **Spülmittel** nt washing-up liquid (BRIT), dishwashing liquid (US); **Spültuch** nt dishcloth; **Spülung** f (von WC) flush

Spur (-, -en) f track; (Fußspur, Radspur) track; (Fährte) trail; (Fahrspur) lane; **die ~ wechseln** to change lanes pl

spüren vt to feel; (merken) to notice; **Spürhund** m sniffer dog

Squash (-) nt squash; **Squashschläger** m squash racket

Sri Lanka (-s) nt Sri Lanka

Staat (-(e)s, -en) m state; **staatlich** adj state(-); (vom Staat betrieben) state-run; **Staatsangehörigkeit** f nationality; **Staatsanwalt** m, **-anwältin** f prosecuting counsel (BRIT), district attorney (US); **Staatsbürger(in)** m(f) citizen; **Staatsbürgerschaft** f nationality; **doppelte ~** dual nationality; **Staatsexamen** nt final exam taken by trainee teachers, medical and law students

Stab (-(e)s, Stäbe) m rod; (Gitter) bar; **Stäbchen** nt (Esstäbchen) chopstick; **Stabhochsprung** m pole vault

stabil adj stable; (Möbel) sturdy

stach imperf von **stechen**

Stachel (-s, -n) m spike; (von Tier) spine; (von Insekten) sting; **Stachelbeere** f gooseberry; **Stacheldraht** m barbed wire; **stachelig** adj prickly

Stadion (-s, Stadien) nt stadium

Stadt (-, Städte) f town; (groß) city; **in der -** in town; **Stadtautobahn** f urban motorway (BRIT) (o expressway (US)); **Stadtbummel** (-s, -) m einen ~ machen to go round town; **Städtepartnerschaft** f twinning; **Stadtführer** m (Heft) city guide; **Stadtführung** f city sightseeing tour; **Stadthalle** f municipal hall; **städtisch** adj municipal; **Stadtmauer** f city wall(s); **Stadtmitte** f town/city centre, downtown (US); **Stadtplan** m (street) map; **Stadtrand** m outskirts pl; **Stadtrundfahrt** f city tour; **Stadtteil** m, **Stadtviertel** m district, part of town; **Stadtzentrum** nt town/city centre, downtown (US)

stahl imperf von **stehlen**

Stahl (-(e)s, Stähle) m steel

Stall (-(e)s, Ställe) m stable; (Kaninchen) hutch; (Schweine) pigsty; (Hühner) henhouse

Stamm (-(e)s, Stämme) m (Baum) trunk; (von Menschen) tribe; **stammen** vi ~ **aus** to come from; **Stammgast** m regular (guest); **Stammkunde** m, **Stammkundin** f regular (customer); **Stammtisch** m table reserved for regulars

stampfen vt, vi to stamp; (mit Werkzeug) to pound; (stapfen) to tramp

stand imperf von **stehen**

Stand (-(e)s, Stände) m (Wasser, Benzin) level; (Stehen) standing position; (Zustand) state; (Spielstand) score; (auf Messe etc) stand; (Klasse) class; **im -e sein** to be in a position; (fähig) to be able

Standby-Betrieb m stand by; **Standby-Ticket** nt stand-by ticket

Ständer (-s, -) m (Gestell) stand; (fam: Erektion) hard-on

Standesamt nt registry office

ständig adj permanent; (ununterbrochen) constant, continual

Standlicht nt sidelights pl (BRIT), parking lights pl (US); **Standort** m position; **Standpunkt** m stand point; **Standspur** f (Auto) hard shoulder (BRIT), shoulder (US)

Stange (-, -n) f stick, (Stab) pole; (Metall) bar; (Zigaretten) carton; **Stangenbohne** f runner (BRIT) (o string (US)) bean; **Stangenbrot** nt French stick; **Stangensellerie** m celery

stank imperf von **stinken**

Stapel (-s, -) m pile

Star (-(e)s, -e) m (Vogel) starling; (Med) cataract ▷ (-s, -s) m (in Film etc) star

starb imperf von **sterben**

stark adj strong; (heftig, groß) heavy; (Mußangabe) thick; **Stärke** (-, -n) f strength; (Dicke) thickness; (Wäschestärke Speisestärke) starch; **stärken** vt to strengthen; (Wäsche) to starch; **Starkstrom** m high-voltage current; **Stärkung** f strengthening; (Essen) refreshment

starr adj stiff; (unnachgiebig) rigid, (Blick) staring

starren vi to stare

Start (-(e)s, -e) m start, (Aviat) takeoff; **Startautomatik** f automatic choke; **Startbahn** f runway; **starten** vt, vi to start; (Aviat) to take off; **Starthilfekabel** nt jump leads pl (BRIT), jumper cables pl (US); **Startmenü** nt (Inform) start menu

Station f (Haltestelle) stop; (Bahnhof) station; (im Krankenhaus) ward; **stationär** adj stationary; **~e Behandlung** in-patient treatment; **jdn**

~ behandeln to treat sb as an in-patient

Statistik f statistics pl

Stativ nt tripod

statt conj, prep +gen or dat instead of; **~ zu arbeiten** instead of working

statt|finden irr vi to take place

Statue (-, -n) f statue

Statusleiste f, **Statuszeile** f (inform) status bar

Stau (-(e)s, -e) m (im Verkehr) (traffic) jam; **im ~ stehen** to be stuck in a traffic jam

Staub (-(e)s) m dust; **~ wischen** to dust; **staubig** adj dusty; **staub-saugen** vt, vi to vacuum, to hoover (BRIT); **Staubsauger** m vacuum cleaner, hoover® (BRIT); **Staubtuch** nt duster

Staudamm m dam

staunen vi to be astonished (über +akk at)

Stausee m reservoir; **Stauung** f (von Wasser) damming-up; (von Blut, Verkehr) congestion; **Stauwarnung** f traffic report

Std. abk = **Stunde** h

Steak (-s, -s) nt steak

stechen (stach, gestochen) vt, vi (mit Nadel etc) to prick; (mit Messer) to stab; (mit Finger) to poke; (Biene) to sting; (Mücke) to bite; (Sonne) to burn; (Kartenspiel) to trump; **Ste-chen** (-s, -) nt sharp pain, stabbing pain; **Stechmücke** f mosquito

Steckdose f socket; **stecken** vt to put; (Nadel) to stick; (beim Nähen) to pin ▷ vi (festsitzen) to be stuck; (Nadeln) to be sticking); **der Schlüssel steckt** the key is in the door; **Stecker** (-s, -) m plug; **Stecknadel** f pin; **Steckrübe** f swede (BRIT), rutabaga (US)

Steg (-s, -e) m bridge

stehen (stand, gestanden) vi to stand (zu by); (sich befinden) to be; (still-stehen) to have stopped; **was steht im Brief?** what does it say in the letter?; **jdm (gut) ~** to suit sb; **~ bleiben** (Uhr) to stop; **~ lassen** to leave ▷ vi impers **wie steht's?** (Sport) what's the score?; **Stehlampe** f standard lamp (BRIT), floor lamp (US)

stehlen (stahl, gestohlen) vt to steal

Stehplatz m (im Konzert etc) standing ticket

Steiermark (-) f Styria

steif adj stiff

steigen (stieg, gestiegen) vi (Preise, Temperatur) to rise; (klettern) to climb; **~ in/auf** (+akk) to get in/on

steigern vt to increase ▷ vr **sich ~** to increase

Steigung f incline, gradient

steil adj steep; **Steilhang** m steep slope; **Steilküste** f steep coast

Stein (-(e)s, -e) m stone; **Steinbock** m (Zool) ibex; (Astr) Capricorn; **Steinbutt** (-s, -e) m turbot; **steinig** adj stony; **Steinschlag** m falling rocks pl

Stelle (-, -n) f place, spot; (Arbeit) post, job; (Amt) office; **ich an deiner ~** if I were you; **auf der ~** straight-away; **stellen** vt to put; (Uhr etc) to set (auf +akk to); (zur Verfügung stel-len) to provide ▷ vr **sich ~** (bei Po-lizei) to give oneself up; **sich schla-fend ~** to pretend to be asleep; **Stellenangebot** nt job offer, va-cancy; **stellenweise** adv in places; **Stellenwert** m (fig) status; **einen hohen ~ haben** to play an impor-tant role; **Stellplatz** m parking space; **Stellung** f position; **zu etw ~ nehmen** to comment on sth; **Stellvertreter(in)** m(f) represent-ative; (amtlich) deputy; (von Arzt) locum (BRIT), locum tenens (US)

Stempel (-s, -) m stamp; **stem-peln** vt to stamp; (Briefmarke) to cancel

sterben (starb, gestorben) vi to die

Stereoanlage f stereo (system)

steril adj sterile; **sterilisieren** vt to sterilize

Stern (-(e)s, -e) m star; **ein Hotel mit vier -en** a four-star hotel; **Sternbild** nt constellation, (Sternzeichen) star sign, sign of the zodiac; **Sternfrucht** f star fruit; **Sternschnuppe** (-, -n) f shooting star; **Sternwarte** (-e, -n) f observatory; **Sternzeichen** nt star sign, sign of the zodiac; **welches ~ bist du?** what's your star sign?

stets adv always

Steuer (-s, -) nt (Auto) steering wheel ▷ (-, -n) f tax; **Steuerberater(in)** m(f) tax adviser; **Steuerbord** nt starboard; **Steuererklärung** f tax declaration; **steuerfrei** adj tax-free; (Waren) duty-free; **Steuerknüppel** m control column; (Aviat, Inform) joystick; **steuern** vt, vi to steer; (Flugzeug) to pilot; (Entwicklung, Tonstärke) (Inform) to control; **steuerpflichtig** adj taxable; **Steuerung** f (Auto) steering; (Vorrichtung) controls pl; (Aviat) piloting; (fig) control; **Steuerungstaste** f (Inform) control key

Stich (-(e)s, -e) m (von Insekt) sting; (von Mücke) bite; (durch Messer) stab; (beim Nähen) stitch; (Färbung) tinge; (Kartenspiel) trick; (Kunst) engraving; **Stichprobe** f spot check

sticken vt, vi to embroider

Sticker (-s, -) m sticker

Stickerei f embroidery

stickig adj stuffy, close

Stiefbruder m stepbrother

Stiefel (-s, -) m boot

Stiefmutter f stepmother

Stiefmütterchen nt pansy

Stiefschwester f stepsister; **Stiefsohn** m stepson; **Stieftochter** f stepdaughter; **Stiefvater** m

stepfather

stieg imperf von **steigen**

Stiege (-, -n) f steps pl

Stiel (-(e)s, -e) m handle; (Bot) stalk; **ein Eis am ~** an ice lolly (BRIT), a Popsicle® (US)

Stier (-(e)s, -e) m (Zool) bull; (Astr) Taurus; **Stierkampf** m bullfight; **Stierkämpfer(in)** m(f) bullfighter

stieß imperf von **stoßen**

Stift (-(e)s, -e) m (aus Holz) peg; (Nagel) tack; (zum Schreiben) pen; (Farbstift) crayon; (Bleistift) pencil

Stil (-s, -e) m style

still adj quiet; (unbewegt) still

stillen vt (Säugling) to breast-feed

stillhalten irr vi to keep still; **Stillleben** nt still life; **stillstehen** irr vi to stand still

Stimme (-, -n) f voice; (bei Wahl) vote

stimmen vi to be right; **stimmt!** that's right; **hier stimmt was nicht** there's something wrong here; **stimmt so!** (beim Bezahlen) keep the change

Stimmung f mood; (Atmosphäre) atmosphere

Stinkefinger m (fam) **jdm den ~ zeigen** to give sb the finger (≈ bird (US))

stinken (stank, gestunken) vi to stink (nach of)

Stipendium nt scholarship; (als Unterstützung) grant

Stirn (-, -en) f forehead; **Stirnhöhle** f sinus

Stock (-(e)s, Stöcke) m stick; (Bot) stock ▷ m (Stockwerke) floor, storey; **Stockbett** nt bunk bed; **Stöckelschuhe** pl high-heels; **Stockwerk** nt floor; **im ersten ~** on the first floor (BRIT), on the second floor (US)

Stoff (-(e)s, -e) m (Gewebe) material; (Materie) matter; (von Buch etc) subject (matter); (fam: Rauschgift) stuff

stöhnen vi to groan (vor with)
stolpern vi to stumble, to trip
stolz adj proud
stopp interj hold it!; (Moment mal!) hang on a minute; **stoppen** vt, vi to stop; (mit Uhr) to time; **Stoppschild** nt stop sign; **Stoppuhr** f stopwatch
Stöpsel (-s, -) m plug; (für Flaschen) stopper
Storch (-(e)s, Störche) m stork
stören vt to disturb; (behindern) to interfere with; **darf ich dich kurz ~?** can I trouble you for a minute?; **stört es dich, wenn ...?** do you mind if ...?
stornieren vt to cancel; **Stornogebühr** f cancellation fee
Störung f disturbance; (in der Leitung) fault
Stoß (-es, Stöße) m (Schub) push; (Schlag) blow; (mit Fuß) kick; (Haufen) pile; (mit Fuß) kick; **Stoßdämpfer** (-s, -) m shock absorber
stoßen (stieß, gestoßen) vt (mit Druck) to shove, to push; (mit Schlag) to knock; (mit Fuß) to kick; (anstoßen) to bump; (zerkleinern) to pulverize ▷ vr **sich ~** to bang oneself; **sich ~ an** (+dat) (fig) to take exception to
Stoßstange f (Auto) bumper
stottern vt, vi to stutter
Str. abk von **Straße** St, Rd
Strafe (-, -n) f punishment; (Sport) penalty; (Gefängnisstrafe) sentence; (Geldstrafe) fine; **strafen** vt to punish; **Strafraum** m penalty area; **Strafstoß** m penalty kick; **Straftat** f (criminal) offence; **Strafzettel** m ticket
Strahl (-s, -en) m ray, beam; (Wasser) jet; **strahlen** vi to radiate; (fig) to beam
Strähne (-, -n) f strand; (weiß, gefärbt) streak

Strand (-(e)s, Strände) m beach; **am ~** on the beach; **Strandcafé** nt beach café; **Strandkorb** m wicker beach chair with a hood; **Strandpromenade** f promenade
strapazieren vt (Material) to be hard on; (Mensch, Kräfte) to be a strain on
Straße (-, -n) f road; (in der Stadt) street; **Straßenarbeiten** pl roadworks pl (BRIT), road repairs pl (US); **Straßenbahn** f tram (BRIT), streetcar (US); **Straßencafé** nt pavement café (BRIT), sidewalk café (US); **Straßenfest** nt street party; **Straßenglätte** f slippery roads pl; **Straßenkarte** f road map; **Straßenrand** m **am ~** at the roadside; **Straßenschild** nt street sign; **Straßensperre** f roadblock; **Straßenverhältnisse** pl road conditions pl
Strategie (-, -n) f strategy
Strauch (-(e)s, Sträucher) m bush, shrub; **Strauchtomate** f vine-ripened tomato
Strauß (-es, Sträuße) m bunch; (als Geschenk) bouquet ▷ m (Strauße) (Vogel) ostrich
Strecke (-, -n) f route; (Entfernung) distance; (Eisenb) line
strecken vt to stretch ▷ vr **sich ~** to stretch
streckenweise adv (teilweise) in parts; (zeitweise) at times
Streich (-(e)s, -e) m trick, prank
streicheln vt to stroke
streichen (strich, gestrichen) vt (anmalen) to paint; (berühren) to stroke; (auftragen) to spread; (durchstreichen) to delete; (nicht genehmigen) to cancel
Streichholz nt match; **Streichholzschachtel** f matchbox; **Streichkäse** m cheese spread
Streifen (-s, -) m (Linie) stripe;

(Stück) strip; (Film) film

Streifenwagen m patrol car

Streik (-(e)s, -s) m strike; **streiken** vi to be on strike

Streit (-(e)s, -e) m argument (um, wegen about, over); **streiten** (stritt, gestritten) vi to argue (um, wegen about, over) ▷ vr **sich ~** to argue (um, wegen about, over)

streng adj (Blick) severe; (Lehrer) strict; (Geruch) sharp

Stress (-es) m stress; **stressen** vt to stress (out); **stressig** adj (fam) stressful

Stretching (-s) nt (Sport) stretching exercises pl

streuen vt to scatter; **die Straßen ~** to grit the roads; (mit Salz) to put salt down on the roads; **Streufahrzeug** nt gritter lorry (BRIT), salt truck (US)

strich imperf von **streichen**

Strich (-(e)s, -e) m (Linie) line; Strichcher m (fam: Strichjunge) rent boy (BRIT), boy prostitute; **Strichkode** (-s, -s) m bar code; **Stricherin** f (fam: Strichmädchen) hooker; **Strichpunkt** m semicolon

Strick (-(e)s, -e) m rope

stricken vt, vi to knit; **Strickjacke** f cardigan; **Stricknadel** f knitting needle

Stripper(in) m(f) stripper; **Striptease** (-) m striptease

stritt imperf von **streiten**

Stroh (-(e)s) nt straw; **Strohdach** nt thatched roof; **Strohhalm** m (drinking) straw; **Strohhut** m straw hat

Strom (-(e)s, Ströme) m river; (fig) stream; (Elek) current; **Stromanschluss** m connection; **Stromausfall** m power failure

strömen vi to stream, to pour; **Strömung** f current

Stromverbrauch m power con-

sumption; **Stromzähler** m electricity meter

Strophe (-, -n) f verse

Strudel (-s, -) m (in Fluss) whirlpool; (Gebäck) strudel

Struktur f structure; (von Material) texture

Strumpf (-(e)s, Strümpfe) m (Damenstrumpf) stocking; (Socke) sock; **Strumpfhose** f (nair of) tights pl (BRIT), pantyhose (US)

Stück (-(e)s, -e) nt piece; (von Zucker) lump; (etwas) bit; (Zucker) lump; (Theat) play; **ein ~ Käse** a piece of cheese

Student(in) m(f) student; **Studentenausweis** m student card; **Studentenwohnheim** nt hall of residence (BRIT), dormitory (US); **Studienabschluss** m qualification (at the end of a course of higher education); **Studienfahrt** f study trip; **Studienplatz** m university/college place; **studieren** vt, vi to study; **Studium** nt studies pl; **während seines ~s** while he is/was studying

Stufe (-, -n) f step; (Entwicklungsstufe) stage

Stuhl (-(e)s, Stühle) m chair

stumm adj silent; (Med) dumb

stumpf adj blunt; (teilnahmslos, glanzlos) dull; **stumpfsinnig** adj dull

Stunde (-, -n) f hour; (Unterricht) lesson; **eine halbe ~** half an hour; **Stundenkilometer** m **80 ~** 80 kilometres an hour; **stundenlang** adv for hours; **Stundenlohn** m hourly wage; **Stundenplan** m timetable; **stündlich** adj hourly

Stuntman (-s, Stuntmen) m stuntman; **Stuntwoman** (-, Stuntwomen) f stuntwoman

stur adj stubborn; (störrisch) pigheaded

Sturm (-(e)s, Stürme) m storm;
stürmen vi (Wind) to blow hard;
(rennen) to storm; **Stürmer(in)**
m(f) striker, forward; **Sturmflut** f
storm tide; **stürmisch** adj stormy;
(fig) tempestuous; (Zeit) turbulent;
(Liebhaber) passionate; (Beifall, Begrüßung) tumultuous; **Sturmwar-
nung** f gale warning

Sturz (-es, Stürze) m fall; (Pol) overthrow; **stürzen** vt (werfen) to hurl;
(Pol) to overthrow; (umkehren) to
overturn ▷ vi to fall; (rennen) to
dash; **Sturzhelm** m crash helmet

Stute (-, -n) f mare

Stütze (-, -n) f support; (Hilfe) help;
(fam: Arbeitslosenunterstützung) dole
(BRIT), welfare (US)

stützen vt to support; (Ellbogen) to
prop

stutzig adj perplexed, puzzled;
(misstrauisch) suspicious

Styropor® (-s) nt polystyrene
(BRIT), styrofoam (US)

subjektiv adj subjective

Substanz (-, -en) f substance

subtrahieren vt to subtract

Subvention f subsidy; **subventi-
onieren** vt to subsidize

Suche f search (nach for); **auf der ~
nach etw sein** to be looking for sth;
suchen vt to look for; (Inform) to
search ▷ vi to look, to search (nach
for); **Suchmaschine** f (Inform)
search engine

Sucht (-, Süchte) f mania; (Med) ad-
diction; **süchtig** adj addicted;
Süchtige(r) mf addict

Süd south; **Südafrika** nt South
Africa; **Südamerika** nt South
America; **Süddeutschland** nt
Southern Germany; **Süden** (-s) m
south; **im ~ Deutschlands** in the
south of Germany; **Südeuropa** nt
Southern Europe; **Südkorea** (-s) nt
South Korea; **südlich** adj southern;

(Kurs, Richtung) southerly; **Verkehr
in ~er Richtung** southbound traffic; **Südost(en)** m southeast;
Südpol m South Pole; **Südstaa-
ten** pl (der USA) the Southern
States pl, the South sing; **südwärts**
adv south, southwards; **Südwes-
t(en)** m southwest; **Südwind** m
south wind

Sultanine f sultana

Sülze (-, -n) f jellied meat

Summe (-, -n) f sum; (Gesamtsumme) total

summen vi, vt to hum; (Insekt) to
buzz

Sumpf (-(e)s, Sümpfe) m marsh;
(subtropischer) swamp; **sumpfig**
adj marshy

Sünde (-, -n) f sin

super adj (fam) super, great; **Super**
(-s) nt (Benzin) four star (petrol)
(BRIT), premium (US); **Supermarkt**
m supermarket

Suppe (-, -n) f soup; **Suppengrün**
nt bunch of herbs and vegetables for
flavouring soup; **Suppenlöffel** m
soup spoon; **Suppenschüssel** f
soup tureen; **Suppentasse** f soup
cup; **Suppenteller** m soup plate;
Suppenwürfel m stock cube

Surfbrett nt surfboard; **surfen** vi
to surf; **im Internet ~** to surf the
Internet; **Surfer(in)** (-s, -) m(f)
surfer

Surrealismus m surrealism

süß adj sweet; **süßen** vt to
sweeten; **Süßigkeit** f (Bonbon etc)
sweet (BRIT), candy (US); **Süßkar-
toffel** f sweet potato, yam (US);
süßsauer adj sweet-and-sour;
Süßspeise f dessert; **Süßstoff** m
sweetener; **Süßwasser** nt fresh
water

Sweatshirt (-s, -s) nt sweatshirt

Swimmingpool (-s, -s) m (swimming) pool

Sylvester nt siehe **Silvester**

Symbol (-s, e) nt symbol; **Symbolleiste** f (Inform) toolbar

Symmetrie (-, -n) f symmetry; **symmetrisch** adj symmetrical

sympathisch adj nice; **jdn ~ finden** to like sb

Symphonie (-, -n) f symphony

Symptom (-s, -e) nt symptom (für of)

Synagoge (-, -n) f synagogue

synchronisiert adj (Film) dubbed; **Synchronstimme** f dubbing voice

Synthesizer (-s, -) m (Mus) synthesizer

Synthetik (-, -en) f synthetic (fibre); **synthetisch** adj synthetic

Syrien (-s) nt Syria

System (-s, -e) nt system; **systematisch** adj systematic; **Systemsteuerung** f (Inform) control panel

Szene (-, -n) f scene

Tabak (-s, -e) m tobacco; **Tabakladen** m tobacconist's

Tabelle f table

Tablett (-s, -s) nt tray

Tablette f tablet, pill

Tabulator m tabulator, tab

Tacho(meter) (-s, -) m (Auto) speedometer

Tafel (-, -n) f (a. Math) table; (Anschlagtafel) board; (Wandtafel) blackboard; (Schiefer~) slate; (Gedenktafel) plaque; **eine ~ Schokolade** a bar of chocolate; **Tafelwasser** nt table water; **Tafelwein** m table wine

Tag (-(e)s, -e) m day; (Tageslicht) daylight; **guten ~!** good morning/afternoon; **am ~** during the day; **sie hat ihre ~e** she's got her period; **eines ~es** one day; **~ der Arbeit** Labour Day; **Tagebuch** nt diary; **tagelang** adj for days (on end); **Tagesanbruch** m daybreak; **Tagesausflug** m day trip; **Tagescreme** f day cream; **Tagesdecke** f bedspread; **Tagesgericht** nt dish of the day; **Tageskarte** f (Fahrkarte) day ticket; **die ~** (Speisekarte) today's menu; **Tageslicht** nt daylight; **Tagesmutter** f child minder; **Tagesordnung** f agenda; **Tagestour** f day trip; **Tageszeitung** f daily newspaper; **täglich** adj, adv daily; **tags(über)** adv during the day; **Tagung** f conference

Tai Chi (-) nt tai chi

Taille (-, -n) f waist; **tailliert** adj fitted

Taiwan (-s) nt Taiwan

Takt (-(e)s, -e) m (Taktgefühl) tact; (Mus) time

Taktik (-, -en) f tactics pl

taktlos adj tactless; **taktvoll** adj tactful

Tal (-(e)s, Täler) nt valley

Talent (-(e)s, -e) nt talent; **talentiert** adj talented

Talkmaster(in) (s,) m(f) talk-show host; **Talkshow** (-, -s) f talk-show

Tampon (-s, -s) m tampon

Tandem (-s, -s) nt tandem

Tang (-s, -e) m seaweed

Tank (-s, -s) m tank; **Tankanzeige** f fuel gauge; **Tankdeckel** m fuel cap; **tanken** vi to get some petrol (BRIT) (o gas (US)); (Aviat) to refuel; **Tanker** (-s, -) m (oil) tanker; **Tankstelle** f petrol station (BRIT), gas station (US); **Tankwart(in)** (-s, -e) m(f) petrol pump attendant (BRIT), gas station attendant (US)

Tanne (-, -n) f fir; **Tannenzapfen** m fir cone

Tansania (-s) nt Tanzania

Tante (-, -n) f aunt; **Tante-Emma-Laden** m corner shop (BRIT), grocery store

Tanz (-es, Tänze) m dance; **tanzen** vt, vi to dance; **Tänzer(in)** m(f) dancer; **Tanzfläche** f dance floor; **Tanzkurs** m dancing course;

Tanzlehrer(in) m(f) dancing instructor; **Tanzstunde** f dancing lesson

Tapete (-, -n) f wallpaper; **tapezieren** vt, vi to wallpaper

Tarantel (-, -n) f tarantula

Tarif (-s, -e) m tariff, (scale of) fares / charges pl

Tasche (-, -n) f bag; (Hosentasche) pocket; (Handtasche) bag (BRIT), purse (US); **Taschen-** in zW pocket; **Taschenbuch** nt paperback; **Taschendieb(in)** m(f) pickpocket; **Taschengeld** nt pocket money; **Taschenlampe** f torch (BRIT), flashlight (US); **Taschenmesser** nt penknife; **Taschenrechner** m pocket calculator; **Taschentuch** nt handkerchief

Tasse (-, -n) f cup; **eine ~ Kaffee** a cup of coffee

Tastatur f keyboard; **Taste** (-, -n) f button; (von Klavier, Computer) key; **Tastenkombination** f (Inform) shortcut; **Tastentelefon** nt push-button telephone

tat imperf von **tun**

Tat (-, -en) f action

Tatar (-s, -s) nt raw minced beef

Täter(in) (-s, -) m(f) culprit

tätig adj active; **in einer Firma ~ sein** to work for a firm; **Tätigkeit** f activity; (Beruf) occupation

tätowieren vt to tattoo; **Tätowierung** f tattoo (an +dat on)

Tatsache f fact; **tatsächlich** adj actual ▷ adv really

Tau (-(e)s, -e) nt (Seil) rope ▷ (-(e)s) m dew

taub adj deaf; (Füße etc) numb (vor Kälte with cold)

Taube (-, -n) f pigeon; (Turtel~, fig: Friedenssymbol) dove

taubstumm adj deaf-and-dumb; **Taubstumme(r)** mf deaf-mute

tauchen vt to dip ▷ vi to dive;

(*Naut*) to submerge; **Tauchen** (-s) *nt* diving; **Taucher(in)** (-s, -) *m(f)* diver; **Taucheranzug** *m* diving (*o* wet) suit; **Taucherbrille** *f* diving goggles *pl*; **Tauchermaske** *f* diving mask; **Tauchkurs** *m* diving course; **Tauchsieder** (-s, -) *m* portable immersion coil for heating water

tauen *vi impers* to thaw

Taufe (-, -n) *f* baptism; **taufen** *vt* to baptize (*nennen*) to christen

taugen *vi* to be suitable (**für** for); **nichts ~** to be no good

Tausch (-(e)s, -e) *m* exchange; **tauschen** *vt* to exchange, to swap

täuschen *vt* to deceive ▷ *vi* to be deceptive ▷ *vr* **sich ~** to be wrong; **täuschend** *adj* deceptive; **Täuschung** *f* deception; (*optisch*) illusion

tausend *num* a thousand; **vierfour thousand; ~ Dank!** thanks a lot; **tausendmal** *adv* a thousand times; **tausendste(r, s)** *adj* thousandth; **Tausendstel** (-s, -) *nt* (*Bruchteil*) thousandth

Tauwetter *nt* thaw

Taxi *nt* taxi; **Taxifahrer(in)** *m(f)* taxi driver; **Taxistand** *m* taxi rank (*BRIT*), taxi stand (*US*)

Team (-s, -s) *nt* team; **Teamarbeit** *f* team work; **teamfähig** *adj* able to work in a team

Technik *f* technology; (*angewandte*) engineering; (*Methode*) technique; **Techniker(in)** (-s, -) *m(f)* engineer; (*Sport, Mus*) technician; **technisch** *adj* technical

Techno (-s) *m* (*Mus*) techno

Teddybär *m* teddy bear

Tee (-s, -s) *m* tea; **Teebeutel** *m* teabag; **Teekanne** *f* teapot; **Teelöffel** *m* teaspoon

Teer (-(e)s, -e) *m* tar

Teesieb *nt* tea strainer; **Teetasse** *f* teacup

Teich (-(e)s, -e) *m* pond

Teig (-(e)s, -e) *m* dough; **Teigwaren** *pl* pasta sing

Teil (-(e)s, -e) *m* part; (*Anteil*) share; **zum ~** in part; (-(e)s, -e) *nt* part; (*Bestandteil*) component; **teilen** *vt* to divide; (*mit jdm*) to share (**mit** with); **20 durch 4 ~** to divide 20 by 4 ▷ *vr* **sich ~** to divide

Teilkaskoversicherung *f* third party, fire and theft insurance

teilmöbliert *adj* partly furnished

Teilnahme (-, -n) *f* participation (**an** +*dat* in); **teilnehmen** *irr vi* to take part (**an** +*dat* in); **Teilnehmer(in)** (-s, -) *m(f)* participant

teils *adv* partly; **teilweise** *adv* partially, in part; **Teilzeit** *f* ~ **arbeiten** to work part-time

Teint (-s, -s) *m* complexion

Tel. *abk von* **Telefon** tel.

Telefon (-s, -e) *nt* telephone; **Telefonanruf** *m*, **Telefonat** *nt* (tele)phone call; **Telefonanschluss** *m* telephone connection; **Telefonauskunft** *f* directory enquiries *pl* (*BRIT*), directory assistance (*US*); **Telefonbuch** *nt* telephone directory; **Telefongebühren** *pl* telephone charges *pl*; **Telefongespräch** *nt* telephone conversation; **telefonieren** *vi* **ich telefoniere gerade (mit ...)** I'm on the phone (to ...); **telefonisch** *adj* telephone; (*Benachrichtigung*) by telephone; **Telefonkarte** *f* phonecard; **Telefonnummer** *f* (tele)phone number; **Telefonrechnung** *f* phone bill; **Telefonverbindung** *f* telephone connection; **Telefonzelle** *f* phone box (*BRIT*), phone booth; **Telefonzentrale** *f* switchboard; **über die ~** through the switchboard

Telegramm *nt* telegram; **Teleobjektiv** *nt* telephoto lens; **Teleshopping** (-s) *nt* teleshopping; **Te-**

leskop (-s, -e) nt telescope
Teller (-s, -) m plate
Tempel (-s, -) m temple
Temperament nt temperament; (Schwung) liveliness; **temperamentvoll** adj lively
Temperatur f temperature; **bei ~en von 30 Grad** at temperatures of 30 degrees; **~ haben** to have a temperature; **~ bei jdm messen** to take sb's temperature
Tempo (-s, -s) nt (Geschwindigkeit) speed; **Tempolimit** (-s, -s) nt speed limit
Tempotaschentuch® nt (Papiertaschentuch) (paper) tissue, ≈ Kleenex®
Tendenz f tendency; (Absicht) intention
Tennis (-) nt tennis; **Tennisball** m tennis ball; **Tennisplatz** m tennis court; **Tennisschläger** m tennis racket; **Tennisspieler(in)** m(f) tennis player; **Tennisturnier** nt tennis tournament
Tenor (-s, Tenöre) m tenor
Teppich (-s, -e) m carpet; **Teppichboden** m (wall-to-wall) carpet
Termin (-s, -e) m (Zeitpunkt) date; (Frist) deadline; (Arzttermin etc) appointment
Terminal (-s, -s) nt (Inform, Aviat) terminal
Terminkalender m diary; **Terminplaner** m (in Buchform) personal organizer, Filofax®; (Taschencomputer) personal digital assistant, PDA
Terpentin (-s, -e) nt turpentine, turps sing
Terrasse (-, -n) f terrace; (hinter einem Haus) patio
Terror (-s) m terror; **Terroranschlag** m terrorist attack; **terrorisieren** vt to terrorize; **Terrorismus** m terrorism; **Terrorist(in)**

m(f) terrorist
Tesafilm® m ≈ sellotape® (BRIT), ≈ Scotch tape® (US)
Test (-s, -s) m test
Testament nt will; **das Alte/Neue ~** the Old/New Testament
testen vt to test; **Testergebnis** nt test results pl
Tetanus (-) m tetanus; **Tetanusimpfung** f (anti-)tetanus injection
teuer adj expensive, dear (BRIT)
Teufel (-s, -) m devil; **was/wo zum ~** what/where the devil; **Teufelskreis** m vicious circle
Text (-(e)s, -e) m text; (Liedertext) words pl, lyrics pl; **Textmarker** (-s, -) m highlighter; **Textverarbeitung** f word processing; **Textverarbeitungsprogramm** nt word processing program
Thailand nt Thailand
Theater (-s, -) nt theatre; (fam) fuss; **ins ~ gehen** to go to the theatre; **Theaterkasse** f box office; **Theaterstück** nt (stage) play; **Theatervorstellung** f (stage) performance
Theke (-, -n) f (Schanktisch) bar; (Ladentisch) counter
Thema (-s, Themen) nt subject, topic; **kein ~!** no problem
Themse (-) f Thames
Theologie f theology
theoretisch adj theoretical; **~ stimmt das** that's right in theory; **Theorie** f theory
Therapeut(in) m(f) therapist; **Therapie** f therapy; **eine ~ machen** to undergo therapy
Thermalbad nt thermal bath; (Ort) thermal spa; **Thermometer** (-s, -) nt thermometer
Thermosflasche® f, **Thermoskanne®** f Thermos® (flask); **Thermostat** (-(e)s, -e) m thermostat

These (-, -en) f theory

Thron ((e)s, -e) m throne

Thunfisch m tuna

Thüringen (-s) nt Thuringia

Thymian (-s, -e) m thyme

Tick (-(e)s, -s) m tic; (Eigenart) quirk; (Fimmel) craze; **ticken** vi to tick; **er tickt nicht ganz richtig** he's off his rocker

Ticket (-s, -s) nt (plane) ticket

Tiebreak (-s, -s) m (Sport: Tennis) tie break(er)

tief adj deep; (Ausschnitt, Ton, Sonne) low; **2 Meter ~** 2 metres deep; **Tief** (-s, -s) nt (Meteo) low; (seelisch) depression; **Tiefdruck** m (Meteo) low pressure; **Tiefe** (-, -n) f depth; **Tiefgarage** f underground car park (BRIT) (o garage (US)); **tiefgekühlt** adj frozen; **Tiefkühlfach** nt freezer compartment; **Tiefkühlkost** f frozen food; **Tiefkühltruhe** f freezer; **Tiefpunkt** m low

Tier (-(e)s, -e) nt animal; **Tierarzt** m, **Tierärztin** f vet; **Tiergarten** m zoo; **Tierhandlung** f pet shop; **Tierheim** nt animal shelter; **tierisch** adj animal ⊳ adv (fam) really; **~ ernst** deadly serious; **ich hatte ~ Angst** I was dead scared; **Tierkreiszeichen** nt sign of the zodiac; **Tierpark** m zoo; **Tierquälerei** f cruelty to animals; **Tierschutzer(in)** (-s, -) m(f) animal rights campaigner; **Tierversuch** m animal experiment

Tiger (-s, -) m tiger

timen vt to time; **Timing** (-s) nt timing

Tinte (-, -n) f ink; **Tintenfisch** m cuttlefish; (klein) squid; (achtarmig) octopus; **Tintenfischringe** pl calamari pl; **Tintenstrahldrucker** m ink-jet printer

Tipp (-s, -s) m tip; **tippen** vt, vi to tap; (fam: schreiben) to type; (fam:

raten) to guess

Tirol (-s) nt Tyrol

Tisch (-(e)s, -e) m table; **Tischdecke** f tablecloth; **Tischlerei** f joiner's workshop; (Arbeit) joinery; **Tischtennis** nt table tennis; **Tischtennisschläger** m table-tennis bat

Titel (-s, -) m title; **Titelbild** nt cover picture; **Titelmusik** f theme music; **Titelverteidiger(in)** m(f) defending champion

Toast ((e)s, -s) m toast; **toasten** vt to toast; **Toaster** (-s, -) m toaster

Tochter (-, Töchter) f daughter

Tod (-(e)s, -e) m death; **Todesopfer** nt casualty; **Todesstrafe** f death penalty; **todkrank** adj terminally ill; (sehr krank) seriously ill; **tödlich** adj deadly, fatal; **er ist ~ verunglückt** he was killed in an accident; **todmüde** adj (fam) dead tired; **todsicher** adj (fam) dead certain

Tofu (-(s)) m tofu, bean curd

Toilette f toilet, restroom (US); **Toilettenpapier** nt toilet paper

toi, toi, toi interj good luck

tolerant adj tolerant (gegen of)

toll adj mad; (Treiben) wild; (fam. großartig) great; **Tollkirsche** f deadly nightshade; **Tollwut** f rabies sing

Tomate (-, -n) f tomato; **Tomatenmark** nt tomato purée (BRIT) (o paste (US)); **Tomatensaft** m tomato juice

Tombola (-, -s) f raffle, tombola (BRIT)

Ton (-(e)s, -e) m (Erde) clay ⊳ m (Töne) (Laut) sound; (Mus) note; (Redeweise) tone; (Farbton, Nuance) shade; **Tonband** nt tape; **Tonbandgerät** nt tape recorder

tönen vi to sound ⊳ vt to shade; (Haare) to tint

Toner (-s, -) m toner; **Tonerkassette** f toner cartridge

Tonne (-, -n) f (Faß) barrel; (Gewicht) tonne, metric ton

Tontechniker(in) m(f) sound engineer

Tönung f hue; (für Haar) rinse

Top (-s, -s) nt top

Topf (-(e)s, Töpfe) m pot

Töpfer(in) (-s, -) m(f) potter; **Töpferei** f pottery; (Gegenstand) piece of pottery

Tor (-(e)s, -e) nt gate; (Sport) goal; **ein ~ schießen** to score a goal; **Torhüter(in)** m(f) goalkeeper

torkeln vi to stagger

Torlinie f goal line

Tornado (-s, -s) m tornado

Torpfosten m goalpost; **Torschütze** m, **Torschützin** f (goal)scorer

Torte (-, -n) f cake; (Obsttorte) flan; (Sahnetorte) gateau

Torwart(in) (-s, -e) m(f) goalkeeper

tot adj dead; **~er Winkel** blind spot

total adj total, complete; **Totalschaden** m complete write-off

Tote(r) mf dead man/woman; (Leiche) corpse; **töten** vt, vi to kill; **Totenkopf** m skull

tot|lachen vr **sich ~** to kill oneself laughing

Toto (-s, -s) m o nt pools pl

tot|schlagen irr vt to beat to death; **die Zeit ~** to kill time

Touchscreen (-s, -s) m touch screen

Toupet (-s, -s) nt toupee

Tour (-, -en) f trip; (Rundfahrt) tour; **eine ~ nach York machen** to go on a trip to York; **Tourenski** m touring ski

Tourismus m tourism; **Tourist(in)** m(f) tourist; **Touristenklasse** f tourist class; **touristisch**

adj tourist; (pej) touristy

traben vi to trot

Tournee (-, -n) f tour

Tracht (-, -en) f (Kleidung) traditional costume

Trackball (-s, -s) m (Inform) trackball

Tradition f tradition; **traditionell** adj traditional

traf imperf von **treffen**

Trafik (-, -en) f tobacconist's

Tragbahre (-, -n) f stretcher

tragbar adj portable

träge adj sluggish, slow

tragen (trug, getragen) vt to carry; (Kleidung, Brille, Haare) to wear; (Namen, Früchte) to bear; **Träger** (-s, -) m (an Kleidung) strap; (Hosen~) braces pl (BRIT), suspenders pl (US); (in der Architektur) beam; (Stahl~, Eisen~) girder

Tragfläche f wing; **Tragflügelboot** nt hydrofoil

tragisch adj tragic; **Tragödie** f tragedy

Trainer(in) (-s, -) m(f) trainer, coach; **trainieren** vt, vi to train; (jdn a.) to coach; (Übung) to practise; **Training** nt training; **Trainingsanzug** m tracksuit

Traktor m tractor

Trambahn f tram (BRIT), streetcar (US)

trampen vi to hitchhike; **Tramper(in)** m(f) hitchhiker

Träne (-, -n) f tear; **tränen** vi to water; **Tränengas** nt teargas

trank imperf von **trinken**

Transfusion f transfusion

Transitverkehr m transit traffic; **Transitvisum** nt transit visa

Transplantation f transplant; (Hauttransplantation) graft

Transport (-(e)s, -e) m transport; **transportieren** vt to transport; **Transportmittel** nt means sing of transport; **Transportunterneh-men** nt haulage firm

Transvestit (-en, -en) m transvestite

trat imperf von **treten**

Traube (-, -n) f (einzelne Beere) grape; (ganze Frucht) bunch of grapes; **Traubensaft** m grape juice; **Traubenzucker** m glucose

trauen vi jdm/einer Sache ~ to trust sb/sth; **ich traute meinen Ohren nicht** I couldn't believe my ears ▷ vr **sich** ~ to dare ▷ vt to marry; **sich ~ lassen** to get married

Trauer (-) f sorrow; (für Verstorbenen) mourning

Traum (-(e)s, Träume) m dream; **träumen** vt, vi to dream (von of, about); **traumhaft** adj dreamlike; (fig) wonderful

traurig adj sad (über +akk about)

Trauschein m marriage certificate; **Trauung** f wedding ceremony; **Trauzeuge** m, **Trauzeugin** f witness (at wedding ceremony), ≈ best man/maid of honour

Travellerscheck m traveller's cheque

treffen (traf, getroffen) vr **sich** ~ to meet ▷ vt, vi to hit; (Bemerkung) to hurt; (begegnen) to meet; (Entscheidung) to make; (Maßnahmen) to take; **Treffen** (-s, -) nt meeting; **Treffer** (-s, -) m (Tor) goal; **Treffpunkt** m meeting place

treiben (trieb, getrieben) vt to drive; (Sport) to do ▷ vi (im Wasser) to drift; (Pflanzen) to sprout; (Tee, Kaffee) to be diuretic; **Treiber** (-s, -) m (Inform) driver

Treibgas nt propellant; **Treibhaus** nt greenhouse; **Treibstoff** m fuel

trennen vt to separate; (teilen) to divide ▷ vr **sich** ~ to separate; **sich von jdm** ~ to leave sb; **sich von etw** ~ to part with sth; **Trennung** f separation

Treppe (-, -n) f stairs pl; (im Freien) steps pl; **Treppengeländer** nt banister; **Treppenhaus** nt staircase

Tresen (-, -) m (in Kneipe) bar; (in Laden) counter

Tresor (-s, -e) m safe

Tretboot nt pedal boat; **treten** (trat, getreten) vi to step; ~ **nach** to kick at; **mit jdm in Verbindung** ~ to get in contact with sb ▷ vt to kick; (nieder~) to tread

treu adj (gegenüber Partner) faithful; (Kunde, Fan) loyal; **Treue** (-) f (eheliche) faithfulness; (von Kunde, Fan) loyalty

Triathlon (-s, -s) m triathlon

Tribüne (-, -n) f stand; (Rednertribüne) platform

Trick (-s, -e o -s) m trick; **Trickfilm** m cartoon

trieb imperf von **treiben**

Trieb (-(e)s, -e) m urge; (Instinkt) drive; (Neigung) inclination; (an Baum etc) shoot; **Triebwerk** nt engine

Trikot (-s, -s) nt shirt, jersey

Trimm-Dich-Pfad m fitness trail

trinkbar adj drinkable; **trinken** (trank, getrunken) vt, vi to drink; **einen ~ gehen** to go out for a drink; **trinkgeld** nt tip; **Trinkhalm** m (drinking) straw; **trinkschokolade** f drinking chocolate; **Trinkwasser** nt drinking water

Trio (-s, -s) nt trio

Tripper (-s, -) m gonorrhoea

Tritt (-(e)s, -e) m (Schritt) step; (Fußtritt) kick; **Trittbrett** nt running board

Triumph (-(e)s, -e) m triumph; **triumphieren** vi to triumph (über +akk over)

trivial adj trivial

trocken adj dry; **Trockenhaube** f

hair-dryer; **Trockenheit** f dryness;
trocken|legen vt (Baby) to
change; **trocknen** vt, vi to dry;
Trockner (-s, -) m dryer
Trödel (-s) m (fam) junk; **Trödel-
markt** m flea market
trödeln vi (fam) to dawdle
Trommel (-, -n) f drum; **Trommelfell** nt eardrum; **trommeln** vt,
vi to drum
Trompete (-, -n) f trumpet
Tropen pl tropics pl
Tropf (-(e)s, -e) m (Med) drip; **am ~
hängen** to be on a drip; **tröpfeln**
vi to drip; **es tröpfelt** it's drizzling;
tropfen vt, vi to drip; **Tropfen** (-s,
-) m drop; **tropfenweise** adv drop
by drop; **tropfnass** adj dripping
wet; **Tropfsteinhöhle** f stalactite
cave
tropisch adj tropical
Trost (-es) m consolation, comfort;
trösten vt to console, to comfort;
trostlos adj bleak; (Verhältnisse)
wretched; **Trostpreis** m consolation prize
Trottoir (-s, -s) nt pavement (BRIT),
sidewalk (US)
trotz prep +gen o dat in spite of;
Trotz (-es) m defiance; **trotzdem**
adv nevertheless ▷ conj although;
trotzig adj defiant
trüb adj dull; (Flüssigkeit, Glas)
cloudy; (fig) gloomy
Trüffel (-, -n) f truffle
trug imperf von **tragen**
trügerisch adj deceptive
Truhe (-, -n) f chest
Trümmer pl wreckage sing; (Bau~)
ruins pl
Trumpf (-(e)s, Trümpfe) m trump
Trunkenheit f intoxication; **~ am
Steuer** drink driving (BRIT), drunk
driving (US)
Truthahn m turkey
Tscheche (-n, -n) m, **Tschechin** f

Czech; **Tschechien** (-s) nt Czech
Republic; **tschechisch** adj Czech;
Tschechische Republik Czech Re-
public; **Tschechisch** nt Czech
Tschetschenien (-s) nt Chechnya
tschüs(s) interj bye
T-Shirt (-s, -s) nt T-shirt
Tube (-, -n) f tube
Tuberkulose (-, -n) f tuberculosis,
TB
Tuch (-(e)s, Tücher) nt cloth; (Halstuch) scarf; (Kopftuch) headscarf
tüchtig adj competent; (fleißig)
efficient; (fam: kräftig) good
Tugend (-, -en) f virtue; **tugendhaft** adj virtuous
Tulpe (-, -n) f tulip
Tumor (-s, -en) m tumour
Tümpel (-s, -) m pond
tun (tat, getan) vt (machen) to do;
(legen) to put; **was tust du da?** what
are you doing?; **das tut man nicht**
you shouldn't do that; **jdm etw ~**
(antun) to do sth to sb; **das tut es
auch** that'll do ▷ vi to act; **so ~, als
ob** to act as if ▷ vr impers **es tut
sich etwas/viel** something/a lot
is happening
Tuner (-s, -) m tuner
Tunesien (-s) nt Tunisia
Tunfisch m siehe **Thunfisch** tuna
Tunnel (-s, -s o -) m tunnel
Tunte (-, -n) f (pej, fam) fairy
tupfen vt, vi to dab; (mit Farbe) to
dot; **Tupfen** (-s, -) m dot
Tür (-, -en) f door; **vor/an der ~** at
the door; **an die ~ gehen** to answer
the door
Türke (-n, -n) m Turk; **Türkei** (-) f
die ~ Turkey; **Türkin** f Turk
Türkis (-es, -e) m turquoise
türkisch adj Turkish; **Türkisch** nt
Turkish
Turm (-(e)s, Türme) m tower; (spitzer
Kirchturm) steeple; (Sprung~) diving
platform; (Schach) rook, castle

turnen vi to do gymnastics; **Turnen** (-s) nt gymnastics sing; (Schule) physical education, PE; **Turner(in)** m(f) gymnast; **Turnhalle** f gym(-nasium); **Turnhose** f gym shorts pl

Turnier (-s, -e) nt tournament

Turnschuh m gym shoe, sneaker (US)

Turschild nt doorplate; **Tür schloss** nt lock

tuscheln vt, vi to whisper

Tussi (-, -s) f (pej, fam) chick

Tüte (-, -n) f bag

TÜV (-s, -s) m abk = **Technischer Überwachungsverein** ≈ MOT (BRIT), vehicle inspection (US)

● **TÜV**
● The **TÜV** is the organization re-
● sponsible for checking the safety of
● machinery, particularly vehicles.
● Cars over three years old have to
● be examined every two years for
● their safety and for their exhaust
● emissions. **TÜV** is also the name
● given to the test itself.

TÜV-Plakette f badge attached to a vehicle's numberplate, indicating that it has passed the 'TÜV'

Tweed (-s, -s) m tweed

Typ (-s, -en) m type; (Auto) model; (Mann) guy, bloke

Typhus (-) m typhoid

typisch adj typical (für of); **ein ~er Fehler** a common mistake; **~ Marcus!** that's just like Marcus; **~ amerikanisch!** that's so American

u. abk = **und**

u. a. abk = **und andere(s)** and others; = **unter anderem, unter anderen** among other things

u. A. w. g. abk = **um Antwort wird gebeten** RSVP

U-Bahn f underground (BRIT), subway (US)

übel adj bad; (moralisch) wicked; **mir ist ~** I feel sick; **diese Bemerkung hat er mir ~ genommen** he took offence at my remark; **Übelkeit** f nausea

üben vt, vi to practise

über prep +dat o akk (werfen, springen) over; (hoch über) above; (quer über) across; (oberhalb von) above; (Route) via; (betreffend) about; (mehr als) over, more than; **~ das Wochenende** over the weekend

überall adv everywhere

überanstrengen vr **sich ~** to overexert oneself

überbacken adj (mit Käse) **~ au gratin; überbelichten** vt (Foto) to overexpose; **überbieten** irr vt to outbid; (übertreffen) to surpass; (Rekord) to break

Überbleibsel (-s, -) nt remnant

Überblick m overview; (fig: in Darstellung) survey; (Fähigkeit zu verstehen) grasp (über +akk of)

überbuchen vt to overbook; **Überbuchung** f overbooking

überdurchschnittlich adj above average

übereinander adv on top of each other; (sprechen etc) about each other

überein|stimmen vi to agree (mit with)

überempfindlich adj hypersensitive

überfahren irr vt (Auto) to run over; **Überfahrt** f crossing

Überfall m (Banküberfall) robbery; (Mil) raid; (auf jdn) assault; **überfallen** irr vt to attack; (Bank) to raid

überfällig adj overdue

überfliegen irr vt to fly over; (Buch) to skim through

Überfluss m overabundance, excess (an +dat of); **überflüssig** adj superfluous

überfordern vt to demand too much of; (Kräfte) to overtax; **da bin ich überfordert** (bei Antwort) you've got me there

Überführung f (Brücke) flyover (BRIT), overpass (US)

überfüllt adj overcrowded

Übergabe f handover

Übergang m crossing; (Wandel, Überleitung) transition; **Übergangslösung** f temporary solution, stopgap

übergeben irr vt to hand over ▷ vr **sich ~** to be sick, to vomit

Übergepäck nt excess baggage

Übergewicht nt excess weight; **(10 Kilo) ~ haben** to be (10 kilos) overweight

überglücklich adj overjoyed; (fam) over the moon

Übergröße f outsize

überhaupt adv at all; (im Allgemeinen) in general; (besonders) especially; **was willst du ~?** what is it you want?

überheblich adj arrogant

überholen vt to overtake; (Tech) to overhaul; **Überholspur** f overtaking (BRIT) (o passing (US)) lane; **überholt** adj outdated

Überholverbot nt **hier herrscht ~** you can't overtake here

überhören vt to miss, not to catch; (absichtlich) to ignore; **überladen** irr vt to overload ▷ adj (fig) cluttered; **überlassen** irr vt **jdm etw ~** to leave sth to sb; **über|laufen** irr vi (Flüssigkeit) to overflow

überleben vt, vi to survive; **Überlebende(r)** mf survivor

überlegen vt to consider; **sich** (dat) **etw ~** to think about sth; **er hat es sich** (dat) **anders überlegt** he's changed his mind ▷ adj superior (dat to); **Überlegung** f consideration

überm kontr von **über dem**

übermäßig adj excessive

übermorgen adv the day after tomorrow

übernächste(r, s) adj **~ Woche** the week after next

übernachten vi to spend the night (bei jdm at sb's place); **übernächtigt** adj bleary-eyed, very tired; **Übernachtung** f overnight stay; **~ mit Frühstück** bed and breakfast

übernehmen irr vt to take on; (Amt, Geschäft) to take over ▷ vr **sich ~** to take on too much

überprüfen vt to check; **Überprüfung** f check; (Überprüfen) checking

überqueren vt to cross
überraschen vt to surprise;
Überraschung f surprise
überreden vt to persuade; **er hat mich überredet** he talked me into it
überreichen vt to hand over
übers kontr von **über das**
überschätzen vt to overestimate; **überschlagen** irr vt (berechnen) to estimate; (auslassen: Seite) to skip ▷ vr **sich ~** to somersault; (Auto) to overturn; (Stimme) to crack;
überschneiden irr vr **sich ~** (Linien etc) to intersect; (Termine) to clash
Überschrift f heading
Überschwemmung f flood
Übersee f **nach/in ~** overseas
übersehen irr vt (Gelände) to look (out) over; (nicht beachten) to overlook
übersetzen vt to translate (aus from, in +akk into); **Übersetzer(in)** (-s, -) m(f) translator; **Übersetzung** f translation
Übersicht f overall view; (Darstellung) survey; **übersichtlich** adj clear
überstehen irr vt (durchstehen) to get over; (Winter etc) to get through
überstürzen irr vt overtime sing
überstürzt adj hasty
überteuert adj overpriced
übertragbar adj transferable; (Med) infectious; **übertragen** irr vt to transfer (auf +akk to); (Radio) to broadcast; (Krankheit) to transmit ▷ vr to spread (auf +akk to) ▷ adj figurative; **Übertragung** f (Radio) broadcast; (von Daten) transmission
übertreffen irr vt to surpass
übertreiben irr vt, vi to exaggerate, to overdo; **Übertreibung** f exaggeration; **übertrieben** adj exaggerated, overdone
überwachen vt to supervise; (Verdächtigen) to keep under surveillance

überwand imperf von **überwinden**
überweisen irr vt to transfer; (Patienten) to refer (an +akk to);
Überweisung f transfer; (von Patienten) referral
überwiegend adv mainly
überwinden (überwand, überwunden) vt to overcome ▷ vr **sich ~** to make an effort, to force oneself;
überwunden pp von **überwinden**
Überzelt nt flysheet
überzeugen vt to convince;
Überzeugung f conviction
überziehen irr vt (bedecken) to cover; (Jacke etc) to put on; (Konto) to overdraw; **die Betten frisch ~** to change the sheets; **Überziehungskredit** m overdraft facility
üblich adj usual
übrig adj remaining; **ist noch Saft ~?** is there any juice left?; **für jdn etwas ~ haben** (fam) to have a soft spot for sb; **die Übrigen** pl the rest pl; **im Übrigen** besides; **~ bleiben** to be left (over); **mir blieb nichts anderes ~(, als zu gehen)** I had no other choice (but to go); **übrigens** adv besides, (nebenbei bemerkt) by the way
Übung f practice; (im Sport, Aufgabe etc) exercise
Ufer (-s, -) nt (Fluss) bank; (Meer, See) shore; **am ~** on the bank/shore
Ufo (-(s), -s) nt abk von **unbekanntes Flugobjekt** UFO
Uhr (-, -en) f clock; (am Arm) watch; **wie viel ~ ist es?** what time is it?; **1 ~** 1 o'clock; **20 ~** 8 o'clock, 8 pm;
Uhrzeigersinn m im ~ clockwise;
gegen den ~ anticlockwise (BRIT), counterclockwise (US); **Uhrzeit** f time (of day)
Ukraine (-) f **die ~** the Ukraine
UKW abk = **Ultrakurzwelle** VHF
Ulme (-, -n) f elm

Ultrakurzwelle f very high frequency; **Ultraschallaufnahme** f
(Med) scan

um prep +akk (räumlich) (a)round;
(zeitlich) at; ~ **etw kämpfen** to fight
for sth; ~ ... **willen** for the sake of ▷
conj (damit) (in order) to; **zu klug,** ~
zu ... too clever to ... ▷ adv (ungefähr) about; **die Ferien sind** ~ the
holidays are over; **die Zeit ist** ~
time's up; **siehe auch umso**

umarmen vt to embrace

Umbau m rebuilding; (zu etwas)
conversion (zu etwas); **um|bauen** vt
to rebuild; (zu etwas) to convert (zu
into)

um|blättern vt, vi to turn over
um|bringen irr vt to kill
um|buchen vi to change one's
reservation / flight

um|drehen vt to turn (round);
(obere Seite nach unten) to turn over ▷
vr **sich** ~ to turn (round); **Umdrehung** f turn; (Phys, Auto) revolution
um|fahren irr vt to knock down
um|fallen irr vi to fall over

Umfang m (Ausmaß) extent; (von
Buch) size; (Reichweite) range; (Math)
circumference; **umfangreich** adj
extensive

Umfeld nt environment
Umfrage f survey

Umgang m company; (mit jdm)
dealings pl; **umgänglich** adj sociable; **Umgangssprache** f colloquial language, slang

Umgebung f surroundings pl;
(Milieu) environment; (Personen)
people around one

umgehen irr vi (Gerücht) to go
round; ~ **(können) mit** (know how
to) handle ▷ irr vt to avoid;
(Schwierigkeit, Verbot) to get round
um|gehen irr vi **mit etw** ~ to
handle sth; **Umgehungsstraße** f
bypass

umgekehrt adj reverse; (gegenteilig) opposite ▷ adv the other way
round; **und** ~ and vice versa
um|hören vr **sich** ~ to ask around;
um|kehren vi to turn back ▷ vt to
reverse; (Kleidungsstück) to turn in-
side out; **um|kippen** vt to tip over
▷ vi to overturn; (fig) to change
one's mind; (fam: ohnmächtig werden)
to pass out

Umkleidekabine f changing cubicle (BRIT), dressing room (US);
Umkleideraum m changing room
Umkreis m neighbourhood; **im** ~
von within a radius of
um|leiten vt to divert; **Umlei-
tung** f diversion
um|rechnen vt to convert (in +akk
into); **Umrechnung** f conversion;
Umrechnungskurs m rate of exchange

Umriss m outline
um|rühren vt, vi to stir
ums kontr von **um das**
Umsatz m turnover
um|schalten vt to turn over
Umschlag m cover; (Buch) jacket;
(Med) compress; (Brief) envelope
Umschulung f retraining
um|sehen irr vr **sich** ~ to look
around; (suchen) to look out (nach für)
umso adv all the; ~ **mehr** all the
more; ~ **besser** so much the better
umsonst adv (vergeblich) in vain;
(gratis) for nothing
Umstand m circumstance; **Umstände** (pl) (fig) fuss; **in anderen
Umständen sein** to be pregnant;
jdm Umstände machen to cause
sb a lot of trouble; **machen Sie
bitte keine Umstände** please,
don't put yourself out; **unter diesen /keinen Umständen** under
these / no circumstances; **unter
Umständen** possibly; **umständlich** adj (Methode) complicated!

(*Ausdrucksweise*) long-winded; (*Mensch*) ponderous; **Umstandsmode** f maternity wear

um|steigen irr vi to change (trains/buses)

um|stellen vt (*an anderen Ort*) to change round; (*Tech*) to convert ▷ vr **sich ~** to adapt (*auf +akk* to); **Umstellung** f change, (*Umgewöhnung*) adjustment; (*Tech*) conversion

Umtausch m exchange; **um|tauschen** vt to exchange; (*Währung*) to change

Umweg m detour

Umwelt f environment; **Umweltbelastung** f ecological damage; **umweltbewusst** adj environmentally aware; **umweltfreundlich** adj environment-friendly; **Umweltpapier** nt recycled paper; **umweltschädlich** adj harmful to the environment; **Umweltschutz** m environmental protection; **Umweltschützer(in)** (-s, -) m(f) environmentalist; **Umweltverschmutzung** f pollution; **umweltverträglich** adj environment-friendly

um|werfen irr vt to knock over; (*fig: ändern*) to upset, (*fig, fam: jdn*) to flabbergast

um|ziehen irr vt to change ▷ vr **sich ~** to change; (*house*) **Umzug** m (*Straßenumzug*) procession; (*Wohnungsumzug*) move

unabhängig adj independent; **Unabhängigkeitstag** m Independence Day, Fourth of July (*US*)

unabsichtlich adv unintentionally

unangenehm adj unpleasant; **Unannehmlichkeit** f inconvenience; **~en** pl trouble sing

unanständig adj indecent; **appetitlich** adj (*Essen*) unappetizing; (*abstoßend*) off-putting; **unbeabsichtigt** adj unintentional; **un-**

bedeutend adj insignificant, unimportant; (*Fehler*) slight

unbedingt adj unconditional ▷ adv absolutely

unbefriedigend adj unsatisfactory; **unbegrenzt** adj unlimited; **unbekannt** adj unknown; **unbeliebt** adj unpopular; **unbemerkt** adj unnoticed; **unbequem** adj (*Stuhl, Mensch*) uncomfortable; (*Regelung*) inconvenient; **unbeständig** adj (*Wetter*) unsettled; (*Lage*) unstable; (*Mensch*) unreliable, **unbestimmt** adj indefinite; **unbeteiligt** adj (*nicht dazugehörig*) uninvolved; (*innerlich nicht beteiligt*) indifferent, unconcerned; **unbewacht** adj unguarded; **unbewusst** adj unconscious; **unbezahlt** adj unpaid; **unbrauchbar** adj useless

und conj and; **~ so weiter** and so on; **na ~?** so what?

undankbar adj (*Person*) ungrateful; (*Aufgabe*) thankless; **undenkbar** adj inconceivable; **undeutlich** adj indistinct; **undicht** adj leaky; **uneben** adj uneven; **unecht** adj (*Schmuck etc*) fake; **unehelich** adj (*Kind*) illegitimate; **unendlich** adj endless; (*Math*) infinite; **unentbehrlich** adj indispensable; **unentgeltlich** adj free (of charge)

unentschieden adj undecided; **~ enden** (*Sport*) to end in a draw

unerfreulich adj unpleasant

unerhört adj unheard-of; (*Bitte*) outrageous; **unerlässlich** adj indispensable; **unerträglich** adj unbearable; **unerwartet** adj unexpected

unerwünscht adj unwelcome; (*Eigenschaften*) undesirable; **unfähig** adj incompetent; **~ sein, etw zu tun** to be incapable of doing sth; **unfair** adj unfair

Unfall m accident; **Unfallbericht**

m accident report; **Unfallflucht** f failure to stop after an accident; **Unfallhergang** m **den ~ schildern** to give details of the accident; **Unfallstation** f casualty ward; **Unfallstelle** f scene of the accident; **Unfallversicherung** f accident insurance

unfreundlich adj unfriendly

Ungarn (-s) nt Hungary

Ungeduld f impatience; **ungeduldig** adj impatient

ungeeignet adj unsuitable

ungefähr adj approximate ▷ adv approximately; **~ 10 Kilometer** about 10 kilometres; **wann ~?** about what time?; **wo ~?** whereabouts?

ungefährlich adj harmless; (sicher) safe

ungeheuer adj huge ▷ adv (fam) enormously; **Ungeheuer** (-s, -) nt monster

ungehorsam adj disobedient (gegenüber to)

ungelegen adj inconvenient; **ungemütlich** adj unpleasant; (Mensch) disagreeable; **ungenießbar** adj inedible; (Getränk) undrinkable; **ungenügend** adj unsatisfactory; (Schulnote) ≈ F; **ungepflegt** adj (Garten) untended; (Aussehen) unkempt; (Hände) neglected; **ungerade** adj odd

ungerecht adj unjust; **ungerechtfertigt** adj unjustified; **Ungerechtigkeit** f injustice, unfairness

ungern adv reluctantly; **ungeschickt** adj clumsy; **ungeschminkt** adj without make-up; **ungesund** adj unhealthy; **ungewiss** adj uncertain; **ungewöhnlich** adj unusual

Ungeziefer (-s) nt vermin pl

ungezogen adj ill-mannered

ungezwungen adj relaxed

ungiftig adj non-toxic

unglaublich adj incredible

Unglück (-(e)s, -e) nt (Unheil) misfortune; (Pech) bad luck; (Unglücksfall) disaster; (Verkehrs~) accident; **das bringt ~** that's unlucky; **unglücklich** adj unhappy; (erfolglos) unlucky; (unerfreulich) unfortunate; **unglücklicherweise** adv unfortunately

ungültig adj invalid

ungünstig adj inconvenient

unheilbar adj incurable; **~ krank sein** to be terminally ill

unheimlich adj eerie ▷ adv (fam) incredibly

unhöflich adj impolite

uni adj plain

Uni (-, -s) f uni

Uniform (-, -en) f uniform

Universität f university

Unkenntnis f ignorance

unklar adj unclear

Unkosten f expenses pl; **Unkostenbeitrag** m contribution (towards expenses)

Unkraut nt weeds pl, ~art, weed

unlogisch adj illogical

unmissverständlich adj unambiguous

unmittelbar adj immediate; **~ darauf** immediately afterwards

unmöbliert adj unfurnished

unmöglich adj impossible

unnahbar adj unapproachable

unnötig adj unnecessary

UNO (-) f akr **= United Nations Organization** UN

unordentlich adj untidy; **Unordnung** f disorder

unpassend adj inappropriate; (Zeit) inconvenient; **unpersönlich** adj impersonal; **unpraktisch** adj impractical

Unrecht nt wrong; **zu ~** wrongly; **~ haben, im ~ sein** to be wrong

unregelmäßig adj irregular; un-

reif adj unripe; **unruhig** adj restless, **~ schlafen** to have a bad night

uns pron akk, dat von **wir**, us, (to) us; **~ (selbst)** (reflexiv) ourselves; **sehen Sie ~?** can you see us?; **er schickte es ~** he sent it to us; **lasst ~ in Ruhe** leave us alone; **ein Freund von ~** a friend of ours; **wir haben ~ hingesetzt** we sat down; **wir haben ~ amüsiert** we enjoyed ourselves; **wir mögen ~** we like each other

unscharf adj (Foto) blurred, out of focus

unscheinbar adj insignificant; (Aussehen) unprepossessing

unschlüssig adj undecided

unschuldig adj innocent

unser pron (adjektivisch) our ▷ pron gen von **wir**, of us; **unsere(r, s)** pron (substantivisch) ours; **unseretwegen** adv (wegen uns) because of us; (uns zuliebe) for our sake; (um uns) about us; (von uns aus) as far as we are concerned

unseriös adj dubious; **unsicher** adj (ungewiss) uncertain; (Person, Job) insecure

Unsinn m nonsense

unsterblich adj immortal, **~ verliebt** madly in love

unsympathisch adj unpleasant; **er ist mir ~** I don't like him

unten adv below; (im Haus) downstairs; (an der Treppe etc) at the bottom; **nach ~** down; **unter** prep +akk o dat under, below; (bei Menschen) among; (während) during

Unterarm m forearm

unterbelichtet adj (Foto) underexposed

Unterbewusstsein nt subconscious

unterbrechen irr vt to interrupt; **Unterbrechung** f interruption; **ohne ~** nonstop

unterdrücken vt to suppress;

(Leute) to oppress

unterdurchschnittlich adj below average

untere(r, s) adj lower

untereinander adv (räumlich) one below the other; (gegenseitig) each other; (miteinander) among themselves / yourselves / ourselves

Unterführung f underpass

untergehen irr vi to go down; (Sonne) to set; (Volk) to perish; (Welt) to come to an end; (im Lärm) to be drowned out

Untergeschoss nt basement; **Untergewicht** nt (3 Kilo) **~ haben** to be (3 kilos) underweight; **Untergrund** m foundation; (Pol) underground; **Untergrundbahn** f underground, subway (US)

unterhalb adv, prep +gen below; **~ von** below

Unterhalt m maintenance; **unterhalten** irr vt to maintain; (belustigen) to entertain ▷ vr **sich ~** to talk; (sich belustigen) to enjoy oneself; **Unterhaltung** f (Belustigung) entertainment; (Gespräch) talk, conversation

Unterhemd nt vest (BRIT), undershirt (US); **Unterhose** f underpants pl; (für Damen) briefs pl

unterirdisch adj underground

Unterkiefer m lower jaw

Unterkunft (-, -künfte) f accommodation

Unterlage f (Beleg) document; (Schreibunterlage) pad

unterlassen irr vt **es~, etw zu tun** (versäumen) to fail to do sth; (bleiben lassen) to refrain from doing sth

unterlegen adj inferior (dat to); (besiegt) defeated

Unterleib m abdomen

Unterlippe f lower lip

Untermiete f **zur ~ wohnen** to be a subtenant; **Untermieter(in)**

m(f) subtenant

unternehmen *irr vt (Reise)* to go on; *(Versuch)* to make; **etwas ~** to do something *(gegen* about); **Unternehmen** *(-s, -) nt* undertaking; *(Comm)* company; **Unternehmensberater(in)** *(-s, -) m(f)* management consultant; **Unternehmer(in)** *(-s, -) m(f)* entrepreneur

Unterricht *(-(e)s, -e) m* lessons *pl*; **unterrichten** *vt* to teach

unterschätzen *vt* to underestimate

unterscheiden *irr vt* to distinguish *(von* from, *zwischen +dat* between)▷ *vr* **sich ~** to differ *(von* from)

Unterschenkel *m* lower leg

Unterschied *(-(e)s, -e) m* difference; **im ~ zu dir** unlike you; **unterschiedlich** *adj* different

unterschreiben *irr vt* to sign; **Unterschrift** *f* signature

Untersetzer *(-s, -) m* tablemat; *(für Gläser)* coaster

unterste(r, s) *adj* lowest, bottom

unter|stellen *vr* **sich ~** to take shelter

unterstellen *vt (rangmäßig)* to subordinate *(dat* to); *(fig)* to impute *(jdm etw* sth to sb)

unterstreichen *irr vt (a. fig)* to underline

Unterstrich *m (Inform)* underscore

unterstützen *vt* to support; **Unterstützung** *f* support

untersuchen *vt (Med)* to examine; *(Polizei)* to investigate; **Untersuchung** *f* examination; *(polizeiliche)* investigation

untertags *adv* during the day

Untertasse *f* saucer

Unterteil *nt* lower part, bottom

Untertitel *m* subtitle

untervermieten *vt* to sublet

Unterwäsche *f* underwear

unterwegs *adv* on the way

unterzeichnen *vt* to sign

untreu *adj* unfaithful

untröstlich *adj* inconsolable; **unüberlegt** *adj* ill-considered ▷ *adv* without thinking; **unüblich** *adj* unusual; **unverantwortlich** *adj* irresponsible; *(unentschuldbar)* inexcusable

unverbindlich *adj* not binding; *(Antwort)* noncommittal ▷ *adv (Comm)* without obligation

unverbleit *adj* unleaded; **unverheiratet** *adj* unmarried, single; **unvermeidlich** *adj* unavoidable; **unvernünftig** *adj* silly; **unverschämt** *adj* impudent; **unverständlich** *adj* incomprehensible; **unverträglich** *adj (Person)* quarrelsome; *(Essen)* indigestible

unverwüstlich *adj* indestructible; *(Mensch)* irrepressible

unverzeihlich *adj* unpardonable; **unverzüglich** *adj* immediate; **unvollständig** *adj* incomplete; **unvorsichtig** *adj* careless

unwahrscheinlich *adj* improbable, unlikely ▷ *adv (fam)* incredibly

Unwetter *nt* thunderstorm

unwichtig *adj* unimportant

unwiderstehlich *adj* irresistible

unwillkürlich *adj* involuntary ▷ *adv* instinctively; **ich musste ~ lachen** I couldn't help laughing

unwohl *adj* unwell, ill

unzählig *adj* innumerable, countless

unzerbrechlich *adj* unbreakable; **unzertrennlich** *adj* inseparable; **unzufrieden** *adj* dissatisfied; **unzugänglich** *adj* inaccessible; **unzumutbar** *adj* unacceptable

unzusammenhängend *adj* disconnected; *(Äußerung)* incoherent; **unzutreffend** *adj* inapplicable; *(unwahr)* incorrect; **unzuverlässig** *adj* unreliable

Update (-s, -s) nt (Inform) update

üppig adj (Essen) lavish; (Vegetation) lush

uralt adj ancient, very old

Uran (-s) nt uranium

Uranus (-) m Uranus

Uraufführung f premiere

Urenkel m great grandson; **Urenkelin** f great-granddaughter; **Urgroßeltern** pl great-grandparents pl; **Urgroßmutter** f great-grandmother; **Urgroßvater** m great-grandfather

Urheber(in) (-s, -) m(f) originator; (Autor) author

Urin (-s, -e) m urine; **Urinprobe** f urine specimen

Urkunde (-, -n) f document

Urlaub (-(e)s, -e) m holiday (BRIT), vacation (US); **im ~** on holiday (BRIT), on vacation (US); **in ~ fahren** to go on holiday (BRIT) (o vacation (US)); **Urlauber(in)** (-s,-) m(f) holiday maker (BRIT), vacationer (US); **Urlaubsort** m holiday resort; **urlaubsreif** adj ready for a holiday (BRIT) (o vacation (US)); **Urlaubszeit** f holiday season (BRIT), vacation period (US)

Urne (-, -n) f urn

Urologe m, **Urologin** f urologist

Ursache f cause (für of); **keine ~!** not at all; (bei Entschuldigung) that's all right

Ursprung m origin; (von Fluss) source; **ursprünglich** adj original ▷ adv originally; **Ursprungsland** nt country of origin

Urteil (-s, -e) nt (Meinung) opinion; (Jur) verdict, (Strafmaß) sentence; **urteilen** vi to judge

Uruguay (-s) nt Uruguay

Urwald m jungle

USA pl USA sing

User(in) (-s, -) m(f) (Inform) user

usw. abk = **und so weiter** etc

Utensilien pl utensils pl

vage adj vague

Vagina (-, Vaginen) f vagina

vakuumverpackt adj vacuum-packed

Valentinstag m St Valentine's Day

Vandalismus m vandalism

Vanille (-) f vanilla

variieren vt, vi to vary

Vase (-, -n) f vase

Vaseline (-) f Vaseline®

Vater (-s, Väter) m father; **väterlich** adj paternal; **Vaterschaft** f fatherhood; (Jur) paternity; **Vatertag** m Father's Day; **Vaterunser** nt **das ~ (beten)** (to say) the Lord's Prayer

V-Ausschnitt m V-neck

v. Chr. abk = **vor Christus** BC

Veganer(in) (-s, -) m(f) vegan; **Vegetarier(in)** (-s, -) m(f) vegetarian; **vegetarisch** adj vegetarian

Veilchen nt violet

Velo (-s, -s) nt (schweizerisch) bicycle

Vene (-, -n) f vein

Venedig (-s) nt Venice

Venezuela (-s) nt Venezuela

Ventil (-s, -e) nt valve

Ventilator m ventilator

Venus (-) f Venus

Venusmuschel f clam

verabreden vt to arrange ▷ vr
sich ~ to arrange to meet (mit jdm
sb); **ich bin schon verabredet** I'm
already meeting someone; **Verabredung** f arrangement; (Termin)
appointment; (zum Ausgehen) date

verabschieden vt (Gäste) to say
goodbye to; (Gesetz) to pass ▷ vr
sich ~ to say goodbye

verachten vt to despise; **verächtlich** adj contemptuous; (verachtenswert) contemptible; **Verachtung** f contempt

verallgemeinern vt to generalize

Veranda (-, Veranden) f veranda,
porch (US)

veränderlich adj changeable;
verändern vt to change ▷ vr sich ~
to change; **Veränderung** f change

veranlassen vt to cause

veranstalten vt to organize;
Veranstalter(in) (-s, -) m(f) organizer; **Veranstaltung** f event;
Veranstaltungsort m venue

verantworten vt to take responsibility for ▷ vr sich für etw ~
to answer for sth; **verantwortlich**
adj responsible (für for); **Verantwortung** f responsibility (für for)

verärgern vt to annoy

verarschen vt (fam) to take the
piss out of (BRIT), to make a sucker
out of (US)

Verb (-s, -en) nt verb

Verband m (Med) bandage; (Bund)
association; **Verband(s)kasten** m
first-aid box; **Verband(s)zeug** nt
dressing material

verbergen irr vt to hide (vor +dat
from) ▷ vr sich ~ to hide (vor +dat

from)

verbessern vt to improve; (berichtigen) to correct ▷ vr sich ~ to
improve; (berichtigen) to correct
oneself; **Verbesserung** f improvement; (Berichtigung) correction

verbiegen irr vi to bend ▷ vr sich
~ to bend

verbieten irr vt to forbid; **jdm ~,
etw zu tun** to forbid sb to do sth

verbilligt adj reduced

verbinden irr vt to connect;
(kombinieren) to combine; (Med) to
bandage; **können Sie mich mit ...
~?** (Tel) can you put me through to
...?; **ich verbinde** (Tel) I'm putting
you through ▷ vr (Chem) sich ~ to
combine

verbindlich adj binding; (freundlich) friendly; **Verbindung** f connection

verbleit adj leaded

verblüffen vt to amaze

verblühen vi to fade

verborgen adj hidden

Verbot (-(e)s, -e) nt ban (für, von on);
verboten adj forbidden; **es ist ~**
it's not allowed; **es ist ~, hier zu
parken** you're not allowed to park
here; **Rauchen ~** no smoking

verbrannt adj burnt

Verbrauch (-(e)s) m consumption;
verbrauchen vt to use up; **Verbraucher(in)** (-s, -) m(f) consumer

Verbrechen (-s, -) nt crime; **Verbrecher(in)** (-s, -) m(f) criminal

verbreiten vt to spread ▷ vr sich
~ to spread

verbrennen irr vt to burn; **Verbrennung** f burning; (in Motor)
combustion

verbringen irr vt to spend

verbunden adj falsch ~ sorry,
wrong number

Verdacht (-(e)s) m suspicion; **verdächtig** adj suspicious; **verdäch-**

tigen *vt* to suspect

verdammt *interj (fam)* damn

verdanken *vt* **jdm etw ~** to owe sth to sb

verdarb *imperf von* **verderben**

verdauen *vt (a. fig)* to digest; **verdaulich** *adj* digestible; **das ist schwer ~** that is hard to digest; **Verdauung** *f* digestion

Verdeck *(-(e)s, -e) nt* top

verderben (verdarb, verdorben) *vt* to spoil; *(schädigen)* to ruin; *(moralisch)* to corrupt; **es sich** *(dat)* **mit jdm ~** to get into sb's bad books; **ich habe mir den Magen verdorben** I've got an upset stomach ▷ *vi (Lebensmittel)* to go off

verdienen *vt* to earn; *(moralisch)* to deserve; **Verdienst** *(-(e)s, -e) m* earnings *pl* ▷ *(-(e)s, -e) nt* merit; *(Leistung)* service (*um* to)

verdoppeln *vt* to double

verdorben *pp von* **verderben** ▷ *adj* spoilt; *(geschädigt)* ruined; *(moralisch)* corrupt

verdrehen *vt* to twist; *(Augen)* to roll; **jdm den Kopf ~** *(fig)* to turn sb's head

verdünnen *vt* to dilute

verdunsten *vi* to evaporate

verdursten *vi* to die of thirst

verehren *vt* to admire; *(Rel)* to worship; **Verehrer(in)** *(-s, -) m(f)* admirer

Verein *(-(e)s, -e) m* association; *(Klub)* club

vereinbar *adj* compatible

vereinbaren *vt* to arrange; **Vereinbarung** *f* agreement, arrangement

vereinigen *vt* to unite ▷ *vr* **sich ~** to unite; **Vereinigtes Königreich** *nt* United Kingdom; **Vereinigte Staaten (von Amerika)** *pl* United States *sing* (of America); **Vereinigung** *f* union; *(Verein)* association;

Vereinte Nationen *pl* United Nations *pl*

vereisen *vi (Straße)* to freeze over; *(Fenster)* to ice up ▷ *vt (Med)* to freeze

vererben *vt* **jdm etw ~** to leave sth to sb; *(Bio)* to pass sth on to sb ▷ *vr* **sich ~** to be hereditary; **vererblich** *adj* hereditary

verfahren *irr vi* to proceed ▷ *vr* **sich ~** to get lost; **Verfahren** *(-s, -) nt* procedure; *(Tech)* method; *(Jur)* proceedings *pl*

verfallen *irr vi* to decline; *(Haus)* to be falling apart; *(Fin)* to lapse; *(Fahrkarte etc)* to expire; **~ in** *(+akk)* to lapse into; **Verfallsdatum** *nt* expiry *(BRIT)* (*o* expiration (US)) date; *(von Lebensmitteln)* best-before date

verfärben *vr* **sich ~** to change colour; *(Wäsche)* to discolour

Verfasser(in) *(-s, -) m(f)* author, writer; **Verfassung** *f (gesundheitlich)* condition; *(Pol)* constitution

verfaulen *vi* to rot

verfehlen *vt* to miss

verfeinern *vt* to refine

Verfilmung *f* film (*o* screen) version

verfluchen *vt* to curse

verfolgen *vt* to pursue; *(Pol)* to persecute

verfügbar *adj* available; **verfügen über etw** *(akk)* **~** to have sth at one's disposal; **Verfügung** *f (Pol* order; **jdm zur ~ stehen** to be at sb's disposal; **jdm etw zur ~ stellen** to put sth at sb's disposal

verführen *vt* to tempt; *(sexuell)* to seduce; **verführerisch** *adj* seductive

vergangen *adj* past; **~e Woche** last week; **Vergangenheit** *f* past

Vergaser *(-s, -) m (Auto)* carburettor

vergaß *imperf von* **vergessen**

vergeben *irr vt* to forgive *(jdm etw* sb for sth); *(weggeben)* to award, to allocate; **vergebens** adv in vain; **vergeblich** adv in vain ▷ adj vain, futile

vergehen irr vi to pass ▷ vr **sich an jdm ~** to indecently assault sb; **Vergehen** (-s, -) nt offence

Vergeltung f retaliation

vergessen (vergaß, vergessen) vt to forget; **vergesslich** adj forgetful

vergeuden vt to squander, to waste

vergewaltigen vt to rape; **Vergewaltigung** f rape

vergewissern vr **sich ~** to make sure

vergiften vt to poison; **Vergiftung** f poisoning

Vergissmeinnicht (-(e)s, -e) nt forget-me-not

Vergleich (-(e)s, -e) m comparison; (Jur) settlement; **im ~ zu** compared to (o with); **vergleichen** irr vt to compare (mit to, with)

Vergnügen (-s, -) nt pleasure; **viel ~!** enjoy yourself; **vergnügt** adj cheerful; **Vergnügungspark** m amusement park

vergoldet adj gold-plated

vergriffen adj (Buch) out of print; (Ware) out of stock

vergrößern vt to enlarge; (Menge) to increase; (mit Lupe) to magnify; **Vergrößerung** f enlargement; (Menge) increase; (mit Lupe) magnification; **Vergrößerungsglas** nt magnifying glass

verh. adj abk = **verheiratet** married

verhaften vt to arrest

verhalten irr vr **sich ~** (sich benehmen) to behave; (Sache) to be; **Verhalten** (-s) nt behaviour

Verhältnis nt relationship (zu with); (Math) ratio; **-se** pl circumstances pl, conditions pl; **im ~ von 1 zu 2** in a ratio of 1 to 2; **verhält-**

nismäßig adj relative ▷ adv relatively

verhandeln vi to negotiate (über etw akk sth); **Verhandlung** f negotiation

verheimlichen vt to keep secret (jdm from sb)

verheiratet adj married

verhindern vt to prevent; **sie ist verhindert** she can't make it

Verhör (-(e)s, -e) nt interrogation; (gerichtlich) examination; **verhören** vt to interrogate; (bei Gericht) to examine ▷ vr **sich ~** to mishear

verhungern vi to starve to death

verhüten vt to prevent; **Verhütung** f prevention; (mit Pille, Kondom etc) contraception; **Verhütungsmittel** nt contraceptive

verirren vr **sich ~** to get lost

Verkauf m sale; **verkaufen** vt to sell; **zu ~** for sale; **Verkäufer(in)** m(f) seller; (beruflich) salesperson; (in Laden) shop assistant (BRIT), salesperson (US); **verkäuflich** adj for sale

Verkehr (-s, -e) m traffic; (Sex) intercourse; (Umlauf) circulation; **verkehren** vi (Bus etc) to run; **~ in** to frequent; **~ mit** to associate (o mix) with; **Verkehrsampel** f traffic lights pl; **Verkehrsamt** nt tourist information office; **verkehrsfrei** adj traffic-free; **Verkehrsfunk** m travel news sing; **Verkehrsinsel** f traffic island; **Verkehrsmeldung** f traffic report; **Verkehrsmittel** nt means sing of transport; **öffentliche ~ pl** public transport sing; **Verkehrsschild** nt traffic sign; **Verkehrstote(r)** mf road casualty; **die Zahl der ~n** the number of deaths on the road; **Verkehrsunfall** m road accident; **Verkehrszeichen** nt traffic sign

verkehrt adj wrong; (verkehrt herum) the wrong way round; (Pullover etc) inside out, **du machst es ~** you're doing it wrong

verklagen vt to take to court

verkleiden vt to dress up (als as) ▷ vr **sich ~** to dress up (als as); (um unerkannt zu bleiben) to disguise oneself; **Verkleidung** f (Karneval) fancy dress; (um nicht erkannt zu werden) disguise

verkleinern vt to reduce; (Zimmer, Gebiet etc) to make smaller

verkneifen irr vt **sich** (dat) **etw ~** (Lachen) to stifle sth; (Schmerz) to hide sth; (sich versagen) to do without sth; **verkommen** irr vi to deteriorate; (Mensch) to go downhill ▷ adj (Haus) dilapidated; (moralisch) depraved; **verkraften** vt to cope with

verkratzt adj scratched

verkühlen vr **sich ~** to get a chill

verkürzen vt to shorten

Verlag (-(e)s, -e) m publishing company

verlangen vt (fordern) to demand; (wollen) to want; (Preis) to ask; (Qualifikation) to require; (erwarten) to ask (von sb); (fragen nach) to ask for; (Pass etc) to ask to see; **► Sie Herrn X** ask for Mr X ▷ vi **~ nach** to ask for

verlängern vt to extend; (Pass, Erlaubnis) renew; **Verlängerung** f extension; (Sport) extra time; (von Pass, Erlaubnis) renewal; **Verlängerungsschnur** f extension cable; **Verlängerungswoche** f extra week

verlassen irr vt to leave ▷ irr vr **sich ~** to rely (auf +akk on) ▷ adj desolate; (Mensch) abandoned; **verlässlich** adj reliable

Verlauf m course; **verlaufen** irr vi (Weg, Grenze) to run (entlang along); (zeitlich) to pass; (Farben) to run ▷ vr

sich ~ to get lost; (Menschenmenge) to disperse

verlegen vt to move; (verlieren) to mislay; (Buch) to publish ▷ adj embarrassed; **Verlegenheit** f embarrassment; (Situation) difficulty

Verleih (-(e)s, -e) m (Firma) hire company (BRIT), rental company (US); **verleihen** irr vt to lend; (vermieten) to hire (out) (BRIT), to rent (out) (US); (Preis, Medaille) to award

verleiten vt **jdn dazu ~, etw zu tun** to induce sb to do sth

verlernen vt to forget

verletzen vt to injure; (fig) to hurt; **Verletzte(r)** mf injured person; **Verletzung** f injury; (Verstoß) violation

verlieben vr **sich ~** to fall in love (in jdn with sb); **verliebt** adj in love

verlieren (verlor, verloren) vt, vi to lose

verloben vr **sich ~** to get engaged (mit to); **Verlobte(r)** mf fiancé/ fiancée; **Verlobung** f engagement

verlor imperf von **verlieren**

verloren pp von **verlieren** ▷ adj lost; (Eier) poached; **~ gehen** to go missing

verlosen vt to raffle; **Verlosung** f raffle

Verlust (-(e)s, -e) m loss

vermehren vt to multiply; (Menge) to increase ▷ vr **sich ~** to multiply; (Menge) to increase

vermeiden irr vt to avoid

vermeintlich adj supposed

vermieten vt to rent (out), to let (out) (BRIT); (Auto) to hire (out) (BRIT), to rent (out) (US); **Vermieter(in)** m(f) landlord/-lady

vermischen vt to mix ▷ vr **sich ~** to mix

vermissen vt to miss; **vermisst** adj missing; **jdn als ~ melden** to report sb missing

Vermittlung f (bei Streit) mediation; (Herbeiführung) arranging; (Stelle) agency

Vermögen (-s, -) nt fortune

vermuten vt to suppose; (argwöhnen) to suspect; **vermutlich** adj probable ▷ adv probably; **Vermutung** f supposition; (Verdacht) suspicion

vernachlässigen vt to neglect

vernichten vt to destroy; **vernichtend** adj (fig) crushing; (Blick) withering; (Kritik) scathing

Vernunft (-) f reason; **ich kann ihn nicht zur ~ bringen** I can't make him see reason; **vernünftig** adj sensible; (Preis) reasonable

veröffentlichen vt to publish

verordnen vt (Med) to prescribe; **Verordnung** f order; (Med) prescription

verpachten vt to lease (out) (an +akk to)

verpacken vt to pack; (einwickeln) to wrap up

Verpackung f packaging; **Verpackungskosten** pl packing charges pl

verpassen vt to miss

verpflegen vt to feed; **Verpflegung** f feeding; (Kost) food; (in Hotel) board

verpflichten vt to oblige; (anstellen) to engage ▷ vr **sich ~** to commit oneself (etw zu tun to doing sth)

verpfuschen vt (fam) to make a mess of; (vulg) to fuck up

verprügeln vt to beat up

verraten irr vt to betray; (Geheimnis) to divulge; **aber nicht ~!** but don't tell anyone ▷ vr **sich ~** to give oneself away

verrechnen vt **~ mit** to set off against ▷ vr **sich ~** to miscalculate; **Verrechnungsscheck** m crossed

cheque (BRIT), check for deposit only (US)

verregnet adj rainy

verreisen vi to go away (nach to); **sie ist (geschäftlich) verreist** she's away (on business); **verrenken** vt to contort; (Med) to dislocate; **sich** (dat) **den Knöchel ~** to sprain (o twist) one's ankle; **verringern** vt to reduce

verrostet adj rusty

verrückt adj mad, crazy; **es macht mich ~** it's driving me mad

versagen vi to fail; **Versagen** (-s) nt failure; **Versager(in)** (-s, -) m(f) failure

versalzen irr vt to put too much salt in / on

versammeln vt to assemble, to gather ▷ vr **sich ~** to assemble, to gather; **Versammlung** f meeting

Versand (-(e)s) m dispatch; (Abteilung) dispatch department; **Versandhaus** nt mail-order company

versäumen vt to miss; (unterlassen) to neglect; **~, etw zu tun** to fail to do sth

verschätzen vr **sich ~** to miscalculate

verschenken vt to give away; (Chance) to waste

verschicken vt to send off

verschieben vt irr (auf später) to postpone, to put off; (an anderen Ort) to move

verschieden adj (unterschiedlich) different; (mehrere) various; **sie sind ~ groß** they are of different sizes; **Verschiedene** pl various people / things pl; **Verschiedenes** various things pl

verschimmelt adj mouldy

verschlafen irr vt to sleep through; (fig) to miss ▷ vi to oversleep

verschlechtern vr **sich ~** to deteriorate, to get worse; **Ver-schlechterung** f deterioration

Verschleiß (-es) m wear and tear

verschließbar adj lockable; **ver-schließen** irr vt to close; (mit Schlüssel) to lock

verschlimmern vt to make worse ▷ vr **sich** ~ to get worse

verschlossen adj locked; (fig) reserved

verschlucken vt to swallow ▷ vr **sich** ~ to choke (an +dat on)

Verschluss m lock; (von Kleid) fastener; (Foto) shutter; (Stöpsel) stopper

verschmutzen vt to get dirty; (Umwelt) to pollute

verschnaufen vi **ich muss mal** ~ I need to get my breath back

verschneit adj snow-covered

verschnupft adj ~ **sein** to have a cold; (fam: beleidigt) to be peeved

verschonen vt to spare (jdn mit etw sb sth)

verschreiben irr vt (Med) to prescribe; **verschreibungspflichtig** adj available only on prescription

verschwand imperf von **ver-schwinden**

verschweigen irr vt to keep secret; **jdm etw** ~ to keep sth from sb

verschwenden vt to waste; **Verschwendung** f waste

verschwiegen adj discreet; (Ort) secluded

verschwinden (verschwand, verschwunden) vi to disappear, to vanish; **verschwinde!** get lost!; **ver-schwunden** pp von **verschwinden**

Versehen (-s, -) nt **aus** ~ by mistake; **versehentlich** adv by mistake

versenden irr vt to send off

versessen adj ~ **auf** (+akk) mad about

versetzen vt to transfer; (verpfänden) to pawn; (fam: bei Verabredung)

to stand up ▷ vr **sich in jdn** (n jds **Lage**) ~ to put oneself in sb's place

verseuchen vt to contaminate

versichern vt to insure; (bestätigen) to assure; **versichert sein** to be insured; **Versichertenkarte** f health-insurance card; **Versiche-rung** f insurance; **Versicherungs-karte** f **grüne** ~ green card (BRIT); insurance document for driving abroad; **Versicherungspolice** f insurance policy

versilbert adj silver plated

versinken irr vi to sink

Version f version

versöhnen vt to reconcile ▷ vr **sich** ~ to become reconciled

versorgen vt to provide, to supply (mit with); (Familie) to look after ▷ vr **sich** ~ to look after oneself; **Versorgung** f provision; (Unter-halt) maintenance; (für Alter etc) benefit

verspäten vr **sich** ~ to be late; **verspätet** adj late; **Verspätung** f delay; (eine Stunde) ~ **haben** to be (an hour) late

versprechen irr vt to promise ▷ vr **ich habe mich versprochen** I didn't mean to say that

Verstand m mind; (Vernunft) (common) sense; **den** ~ **verlieren** to lose one's mind; **verständigen** vt to inform ▷ vr **sich** ~ to communicate; (sich einigen) to come to an understanding; **Verständigung** f communication; **verständlich** adj understandable; **Verständnis** nt understanding (für of); (Mitgefühl) sympathy; **verständnisvoll** adj understanding

Verstärker (-s, -) m amplifier

verstauchen vt to sprain

Versteck (-(e)s, -e) nt hiding place; ~ **spielen** to play hide-and-seek; **ver-stecken** vt to hide (vor +dat from) ▷

vr **sich ~** to hide (*vor +dat* from)

verstehen *irr vt* to understand; **falsch ~** to misunderstand ▷ *vr* **sich ~** to get on (*mit* with)

Versteigerung *f* auction

verstellbar *adj* adjustable; **verstellen** *vt* to move; (*Uhr*) to adjust; (*versperren*) to block; (*Stimme, Handschrift*) to disguise ▷ *vr* **sich ~** to pretend, to put on an act

verstopfen *vt* to block up; (*Med*) to constipate; **Verstopfung** *f* obstruction; (*Med*) constipation

Verstoß *m* infringement, violation (*gegen* of)

Versuch *(-(e)s, -e) m* attempt; (*wissenschaftlich*) experiment; **versuchen** *vt* to try

vertauschen *vt* to exchange; (*versehentlich*) to mix up

verteidigen *vt* to defend; **Verteidiger(in)** *(-s, -) m(f)* (*Sport*) defender; (*Jur*) defence counsel; **Verteidigung** *f* defence

verteilen *vt* to distribute

Vertrag *(-(e)s, Verträge) m* contract; (*Pol*) treaty

vertragen *irr vt* to stand, to bear ▷ *vr* **sich ~** to get along (with each other); (*sich aussöhnen*) to make it up

verträglich *adj* (*Mensch*) good-natured; (*Speisen*) digestible

vertrauen *vi* **jdm/einer Sache ~** to trust sb/sth; **Vertrauen** *(-s) nt* trust (*in +akk* in, *zu* in); **ich habe kein ~ zu ihm** I don't trust him; **ich hab's ihm im ~ gesagt** I told him in confidence; **vertraulich** *adj* (*geheim*) confidential; **vertraut** *adj* **sich mit etw ~ machen** to familiarize oneself with sth

vertreten *irr vt* to represent; (*Ansicht*) to hold; **Vertreter(in)** *(-s, -) m(f)* representative

Vertrieb *(-(e)s, -e) m* (*Abteilung*) sales department

vertrocknen *vi* to dry up

vertun *irr vr* **sich ~** to make a mistake

vertuschen *vt* to cover up

verunglücken *vi* to have an accident; **tödlich ~** to be killed in an accident

verunsichern *vt* to make uneasy

verursachen *vt* to cause

verurteilen *vt* to condemn

vervielfältigen *vt* to make copies of

verwackeln *vt* (*Foto*) to blur

verwählen *vr* **sich ~** to dial the wrong number

verwalten *vt* to manage; (*behördlich*) to administer; **Verwalter(in)** *(-s, -) m(f)* manager; (*Vermögens~*) trustee; **Verwaltung** *f* management; (*amtlich*) administration

verwandt *adj* related (*mit* to); **Verwandte(r)** *mf* relative, relation; **Verwandtschaft** *f* relationship; (*Menschen*) relations *pl*

verwarnen *vt* to warn; (*Sport*) to caution

verwechseln *vt* to confuse (*mit* with); (*halten für*) to mistake (*mit* for)

verweigern *vt* to refuse

verwenden *vt* to use; (*Zeit*) to spend; **Mühe auf etw (akk) ~** to take trouble over sth; **Verwendung** *f* use

verwirklichen *vt* to realize; **sich selbst ~** to fulfil oneself

verwirren *vt* to confuse; **Verwirrung** *f* confusion

verwitwet *adj* widowed

verwöhnen *vt* to spoil

verwunderlich *adj* surprising; **Verwunderung** *f* astonishment

verwüsten *vt* to devastate

verzählen *vr* **sich ~** to miscount

verzehren *vt* to consume

Verzeichnis nt (Liste) list; (Katalog) catalogue; (in Buch) index; (Inform) directory

verzeihen (verzieh, verziehen) vt, vi to forgive (jdm etw sb for sth); **~ Sie bitte, ...** (vor Frage etc) excuse me, ...; **~ Sie die Störung** sorry to disturb you; **Verzeihung** f **~!** sorry, **~, ...** (vor Frage etc) excuse me, ...; (jdn) **um ~ bitten** to apologize (to sb)

verzichten vi **auf etw** (akk) **~** to do without sth; (aufgeben) to give sth up

verzieh imperf von **verzeihen**

verziehen pp von **verzeihen**

verziehen irr vt (Kind) to spoil; **das Gesicht ~** to pull a face ▷ vr **sich ~** to go out of shape; (Gesicht) to contort; (verschwinden) to disappear

verzieren vt to decorate

verzögern vt to delay ▷ vr **sich ~** to be delayed; **Verzögerung** f delay

verzweifeln vi to despair (an idat of); **verzweifelt** adj desperate; **Verzweiflung** f despair

Veterinär(in) (-s, -e) m(f) veterinary surgeon (BRIT), veterinarian (US)

Vetter (-s, -n) m cousin

vgl. abk = **vergleiche** cf

Viagra® (-s) nt Viagra®

Vibrator (-s, -en) m vibrator; **vibrieren** vi to vibrate

Video (-s, -s) nt video; **auf ~ aufnehmen** to video; **Videoclip** (-s, -s) m video clip; **Videofilm** m video; **Videogerät** nt video (recorder); **Videokamera** f video camera; **Videokassette** f video (cassette); **Videorekorder** m video recorder; **Videospiel** nt video game; **Videothek** (-, -en) f video library

Vieh (-(e)s) nt cattle

viel pron a lot (of), lots of; **~ Arbeit** a lot of work, lots of work; **~e Leute** a lot of people, lots of people, many

people; **zu ~** too much; **zu ~e** too many; **sehr ~** a great deal of; **sehr ~e** a great many; **ziemlich ~/-e** quite a lot of; **nicht ~** not much, not a lot of; **nicht ~e** not many, not a lot of ▷ pron a lot; **sie sagt nicht ~** she doesn't say a lot; **nicht ~** not much, not a lot of; **nicht ~e** not many, not a lot of; **gibt es ~?** is there much?, is there a lot?; **gibt es ~e?** are there many?, are there a lot? ▷ adv a lot; **er geht ~ ins Kino** he goes a lot to the cinema; **sehr ~** a great deal; **ziemlich ~** quite a lot; **~ besser** much better; **~ teurer** much more expensive; **~ zu ~** far too much

vielleicht adv perhaps; **~ ist sie krank** perhaps she's ill, she might be ill; **weißt du ~, wo er ist?** do you know where he is (by any chance)?

vielmal(s) adv many times; **danke ~s** many thanks; **vielmehr** adv rather, vielseitig adj very varied; (Mensch, Gerät) versatile

vier num four; **auf allen ~en** on all fours; **unter ~ Augen** in private, privately; **Vier** (-, -en) f four; (Schulnote) = D; **Vierbettzimmer** nt four-bed room; **Viereck** (-(e)s, -e) nt four-sided figure; (Quadrat) square; **viereckig** adj four-sided; (quadratisch) square; **vierfach** adj **die ~e Menge** four times the amount; **vierhundert** num four hundred; **viermal** adv four times; **vierspurig** adj four lane

viert adv **wir sind zu ~** there are four of us; **vierte(r, s)** adj fourth; siehe auch **dritte**

Viertel (-s, -n) nt (Stadtviertel) quarter, district; (Bruchteil) quarter; (Viertelliter) quarter-litre; (Uhrzeit) quarter; **~ vor/nach drei** a quarter to/past three; **viertel drei** a quarter past two; **drei viertel drei** a quarter to three; **Viertelfinale** nt quarter-final; **vierteljährlich** adj quarterly; **Viertelstunde** f quarter of an hour

vierzehn num fourteen; **in ~ Tagen** in two weeks, in a fortnight (BRIT); **vierzehntägig** adj two-week, fortnightly (BRIT); **vierzehnte(r, s)** adj fourteenth; *siehe auch* **dritte**; **vierzig** num forty; **vierzigste(r, s)** adj fortieth

Vietnam (-s) nt Vietnam

Vignette f (Autobahn~) motorway (BRIT) (o freeway US)) permit

Villa (-, *Villen*) f villa

violett adj purple

Violine f violin

Virus (-, *Viren*) m o nt virus

Visitenkarte f card

Visum (-s, *Visa* o *Visen*) nt visa

Vitamin (-s, -e) nt vitamin

Vitrine (-, -n) f (glass) cabinet; (*Schaukasten*) display case

Vogel (-s, *Vögel*) m bird; **vögeln** vi, vt (*vulg*) to screw

Voicemail (-, -s) f voice mail

Vokal (-s, -e) m vowel

Volk (-(e)s, *Völker*) nt people pl; (*Nation*) nation; **Volksfest** nt festival; (*Jahrmarkt*) funfair; **Volkshochschule** f adult education centre; **Volkslied** nt folksong; **Volksmusik** f folk music; **volkstümlich** adj (*einfach und beliebt*) popular; (*herkömmlich*) traditional; (*Kunst*) folk

voll adj full (von of); **~ machen** to fill (up); **~ tanken** to fill up

Vollbart m beard; **Vollbremsung** f **eine ~ machen** to slam on the brakes; **vollends** adv completely

Volleyball m volleyball

Vollgas nt **mit ~** at full throttle; **~ geben** to step on it

völlig adj complete ▷ adv completely

volljährig adj of age; **Vollkasko-**

versicherung f fully comprehensive insurance; **vollklimatisiert** adj fully air-conditioned; **vollkommen** adj perfect; **~er Unsinn** complete rubbish ▷ adv completely

Vollkornbrot nt wholemeal (BRIT) (o whole wheat (US)) bread

Vollmacht (-, -en) f authority; (*Urkunde*) power of attorney

Vollmilch f full-fat milk (BRIT), whole milk (US); **Vollmilchschokolade** f milk chocolate; **Vollmond** m full moon; **Vollnarkose** f general anaesthetic; **Vollpension** f full board

vollständig adj complete

Volltreffer m direct hit; **Vollwaschmittel** nt all-purpose washing powder; **Vollwertkost** f wholefood; **vollzählig** adj complete

Volt (-, -) nt volt

Volumen (-s, -) nt volume

vom kontr von **von dem** (*räumlich, zeitlich, Ursache*) from; **ich kenne sie nur ~ Sehen** I only know her by sight

von prep +dat (*räumlich, zeitlich*) from; (*statt Gen, bestehend aus*) of; (*im Passiv*) by; **ein Freund ~ mir** a friend of mine; **~ mir aus** (*fam*) if you like; **~ wegen!** no way; **voneinander** adv from each other

vor prep +dat o akk (*zeitlich*) before; (*räumlich*) in front of; **fünf ~ drei** five to three; **~ 2 Tagen** 2 days ago; **~ Wut / Liebe** with rage / love; **~ allem** above all

voran|gehen irr vi to go ahead; **einer Sache** (dat) **~** to precede sth; **voran|kommen** irr vi to make progress

Vorarlberg (-s) nt Vorarlberg

voraus adv **jdm ~ sein** to be ahead of sb; **im Voraus** in advance; **voraus|fahren** irr vi to drive on ahead;

vorausgesetzt *conj* provided (that); **Voraussage** *f* prediction; (Wetter) forecast; **voraus|sagen** *vt* to predict; **voraus|sehen** *irr vt* to foresee; **voraus|setzen** *vt* to assume; **Voraussetzung** *f* requirement, prerequisite; **voraussichtlich** *adj* expected ▷ *adv* probably; **voraus|zahlen** *vt* to pay in advance

Vorbehalt (-(e)s, -e) *m* reservation; **vorbehalten** *irr vt* **sich/jdm etw ~** to reserve sth (for oneself)/for sb

vorbei *adv* past, over, finished; **vorbei|bringen** *irr vt* to drop by (o in); **vorbei|fahren** *irr vi* to drive past; **vorbei|gehen** *irr vi* to pass by, to go past; (verstreichen, aufhören) to pass; **vorbei|kommen** *irr vi* to drop by; **vorbei|lassen** *irr vt* **kannst du die Leute ~?** could you let these people pass?; **lässt du mich bitte mal vorbei?** can I get past, please?; **vorbei|reden** *vi* **aneinander ~** to talk at cross-purposes

vor|bereiten *irr vt* to prepare ▷ *vr* **sich ~** to get ready (auf +akk, für for); **Vorbereitung** *f* preparation

vor|bestellen *vt* to book in advance; (Essen) to order in advance; **Vorbestellung** *f* booking, reservation

vor|beugen *vi* to prevent (dat sth); **vorbeugend** *adj* preventive; **Vorbeugung** *f* prevention

Vorbild *nt* (role) model; **vorbildlich** *adj* model, ideal

Vorderachse *f* front axle; **vordere(r, s)** *adj* front; **Vordergrund** *m* foreground; **Vorderradantrieb** *m* (Auto) front-wheel drive; **Vorderseite** *f* front; **Vordersitz** *m* front seat; **Vorderteil** *m o nt* front (part)

vor|drängen *vr* **sich ~** to push forward

Vordruck *m* form

voreilig *adj* hasty, rash, **~e Schlüsse ziehen** to jump to conclusions; **voreingenommen** *adj* biased

vor|enthalten *irr vt* **jdm etw ~** to withhold sth from sb

vorerst *adv* for the moment

vor|fahren *irr vi* (vorausfahren) to drive on ahead; **vor das Haus ~** to drive up to the house, **fahren Sie bis zur Ampel vor** drive as far as the traffic lights

Vorfahrt *f* (Auto) right of way; **~ achten** give way (BRIT), yield (US); **Vorfahrtsschild** *nt* give way (BRIT) (o yield (US)) sign; **Vorfahrtsstraße** *f* major road

Vorfall *m* incident

vor|führen *vt* to demonstrate; (Film) to show; (Theaterstück, Trick) to perform

Vorgänger(in) *m(f)* predecessor

vor|gehen *irr vi* (vorausgehen) to go on ahead; (nach vorn) to go forward; (handeln) to act, to proceed; (Uhr) to be fast; (Vorrang haben) to take precedence; (passieren) to go on; **Vorgehen** (-s) *nt* procedure

Vorgesetzte(r) *mf* superior

vorgestern *adv* the day before yesterday

vor|haben *irr vt* to plan; **hast du schon was vor?** have you got anything on?; **ich habe vor, nach Rom zu fahren** I'm planning to go to Rome

vor|halten *irr vt* **jdm etw ~** to accuse sb of sth

Vorhand *f* forehand

vorhanden *adj* existing; (erhältlich) available

Vorhang *m* curtain

Vorhängeschloss *nt* padlock

Vorhaut *f* foreskin

vorher *adv* before; **zwei Tage ~** two days before; **~ essen wir** we'll eat first; **Vorhersage** *f* forecast;

vorher|sehen irr vt to foresee

vorhin adv just now, a moment ago

vorig adj previous; (Woche etc) last

Vorkenntnisse pl previous knowledge sing

vor|kommen irr vi (nach vorne kommen) to come forward; (geschehen) to happen; (sich finden) to occur; (scheinen) to seem (to be); **sich** (dat) **dumm ~** to feel stupid

Vorlage f model

vor|lassen irr vt **jdn ~** to let sb go first

vorläufig adj temporary

vor|lesen irr vt to read out

Vorlesung f lecture

vorletzte(r, s) adj last but one; **am ~n Samstag** (on) the Saturday before last

Vorliebe f preference

vor|machen vt **kannst du es mir ~?** can you show me how to do it?; **jdm etwas ~** (fig: täuschen) to fool sb

vor|merken vt to note down; (Plätze) to book

Vormittag m morning; **am ~** in the morning; **heute ~** this morning; **vormittags** adv in the morning; **um 9 Uhr ~** at 9 (o'clock) in the morning, at 9 am

vorn(e) adv in front; **von ~ anfangen** to start at the beginning; **nach ~** to the front; **weiter ~** further up; **von ~ bis hinten** from beginning to end

Vorname m first name; **wie heißt du mit ~** what's your first name?

vornehm adj (von Rang) distinguished; (Benehmen) refined; (fein, elegant) elegant

vor|nehmen irr vt **sich** (dat) **etw ~** to start on sth; **sich** (dat) **~, etw zu tun** (beschließen) to decide to do sth

vornherein adv **von ~** from the start

Vorort m suburb

vorrangig adj priority

Vorrat m stock, supply; **vorrätig** adj in stock; **Vorratskammer** f pantry

Vorrecht nt privilege

Vorruhestand m early retirement

Vorsaison f early season

Vorsatz m intention; (Jur) intent; **vorsätzlich** adj intentional; (Jur) premeditated

Vorschau f preview; (Film) trailer

Vorschlag m suggestion, proposal; **vorschlagen** irr vt to suggest, to propose; **ich schlage vor, dass wir gehen** I suggest we go

vor|schreiben irr vt (befehlen) to stipulate; **jdm etw ~** to dictate sth to sb

Vorschrift f regulation, rule; (Anweisung) instruction; **vorschriftsmäßig** adj correct

Vorschule f nursery school, preschool (US)

Vorsicht f care; **~!** look out; (Schild) caution; **~ Stufe!** mind the step; **vorsichtig** adj careful; **vorsichtshalber** adv just in case

Vorsorge f precaution; (Vorbeugung) prevention; **Vorsorgeuntersuchung** f checkup; **vorsorglich** adv as a precaution

Vorspann (-(e)s, -e) m credits pl

Vorspeise f starter

Vorsprung m projection; (Abstand) lead

vor|stellen vt (bekannt machen) to introduce; (Uhr) to put forward; (vor etw) to put in front; **sich** (dat) **etw ~** to imagine sth; **Vorstellung** f (Bekanntmachung) introduction; (Theat) performance; (Gedanke) idea; **Vorstellungsgespräch** nt interview

vor|täuschen vt to feign

Vorteil m advantage (*gegenüber* over); **die Vor- und Nachteile** the pros and cons; **vorteilhaft** adj advantageous

Vortrag (-(e)s, Vorträge) m talk (*über* +akk on); (*akademisch*) lecture; **einen ~ halten** to give a talk

vorüber adv over; **vorüber|gehen** irr vi to pass; **vorübergehend** adj temporary ▷ adv temporarily, for the time being

Vorurteil nt prejudice

Vorverkauf m advance booking

vor|verlegen vt to bring forward

Vorwahl f (Tel) dialling code (BRIT), area code (US)

Vorwand (-(e)s, Vorwände) m pretext, excuse; **unter dem ~, dass** with the excuse that

vorwärts adv forward; **~ gehen** (*fig*) to progress; **Vorwärtsgang** m (Auto) forward gear

vorweg adv in advance; **vorweg|nehmen** irr vt to anticipate

Vorweihnachtszeit f pre-Christmas period, run-up to Christmas (BRIT)

vor|werfen irr vt jdm etw ~ to accuse sb of sth

vorwiegend adv mainly

Vorwort nt preface

Vorwurf m reproach; **sich** (dat) **Vorwürfe machen** to reproach oneself; **jdm Vorwürfe machen** to accuse sb; **vorwurfsvoll** adj reproachful

vor|zeigen vt to show

vorzeitig adj premature, early

vor|ziehen irr vt (lieber haben) to prefer

Vorzug m preference; (gute Eigenschaft) merit; (Vorteil) advantage

vorzüglich adj excellent

vulgär adj vulgar

Vulkan (-s, -e) m volcano; **Vulkanausbruch** m volcanic eruption

W abk = **West** W

Waage (-, -n) f scales pl; (Astr) Libra; **waagerecht** adj horizontal

wach adj awake; **~ werden** to wake up; **Wache** (-, -n) f guard

Wachs (-es, -e) nt wax

wachsen (wuchs, gewachsen) vi to grow

wachsen vt (Skier) to wax

Wachstum nt growth

Wachtel (-, -n) f quail

Wächter(in) (-s, -) m(f) guard; (auf Parkplatz) attendant

wackelig adj wobbly; (fig) shaky; **Wackelkontakt** m loose connection; **wackeln** vi (Stuhl) to be wobbly; (Zahn, Schraube) to be loose; **mit dem Kopf ~** to waggle one's head

Wade (-, -n) f (Anat) calf

Waffe (-, -n) f weapon

Waffel (-, -n) f waffle; (Keks, Eiswaffel) wafer

wagen vt to risk; **es ~, etw zu tun** to dare to do sth

Wagen (-s, -) m (Auto) car; (Eisenb) carriage; **Wagenheber** (-s, -) m jack; **Wagentyp** m model, make

Wahl (-, -en) f choice; (Pol) election

wählen vt to choose; (Tel) to dial; (Pol) to vote for; (durch Wahl ermitteln) to elect ▷ vi to choose; (Tel) to dial; (Pol) to vote; **Wähler(in)** (-s, -) m(f) voter; **wählerisch** adj choosy

Wahlkampf m election campaign; **wahllos** adv at random; **Wahlwiederholung** f redial

Wahnsinn m madness; **~!** amazing!; **wahnsinnig** adj insane, mad ▷ adv (fam) incredibly

wahr adj true; **das darf doch nicht ~ sein!** I don't believe it; **nicht ~?** that's right, isn't it?

während prep +gen during ▷ conj while; **währenddessen** adv meanwhile, in the meantime

Wahrheit f truth

wahrnehmbar adj noticeable, perceptible; **wahr|nehmen** irr vt to perceive

Wahrsager(in) (-s, -) m(f) fortune-teller

wahrscheinlich adj probable, likely ▷ adv probably; **ich komme ~ zu spät** I'll probably be late; **Wahrscheinlichkeit** f probability

Währung f currency

Wahrzeichen nt symbol

Waise (-, -n) f orphan

Wal (-(e)s, -e) m whale

Wald (-(e)s, Wälder) m wood; (groß) forest; **Waldbrand** m forest fire; **Waldlauf** m cross-country run; **Waldsterben** nt forest dieback

Wales (-) nt Wales; **Waliser(in)** m(f) Welshman / Welshwoman; **walisisch** adj Welsh; **Walisisch** nt Welsh

Walkie-Talkie (-(s), -s) nt walkie-talkie

Walkman® (-s, -s) m walkman®,

personal stereo

Wall (-(e)s, Wälle) m embankment

Wallfahrt f pilgrimage; **Wallfahrtsort** m place of pilgrimage

Walnuss f walnut

Walross (-es, -e) nt walrus

wälzen vt to roll; (Bücher) to pore over; (Probleme) to deliberate on ▷ vr **sich ~** to wallow; (vor Schmerzen) to roll about; (im Bett) to toss and turn

Walzer (-s, -) m waltz

Wand (-, Wände) f wall; (Trenn~) partition; (Berg~) (rock) face

Wandel (-s) m change; **wandeln** vt to change ▷ vr **sich ~** to change f

Wanderer (-s, -) m, **Wanderin** f hiker; **Wanderkarte** f hiking map; **wandern** vi to hike; (Blick) to wander; (Gedanken) to stray; **Wanderschuh** m walking shoe; **Wanderstiefel** m hiking boot; **Wanderung** f hike; **eine ~ machen** to go on a hike; **Wanderweg** m walking (ó hiking) trail

Wandleuchte f wall lamp; **Wandmalerei** f mural; **Wandschrank** m built-in cupboard (BRIT), closet (US)

wandte imperf von **wenden**

Wange (-, -n) f cheek

wann adv when; **seit ~ ist sie da?** how long has she been here?; **bis ~ bleibt ihr?** how long are you staying?

Wanne (-, -n) f (bath) tub

Wappen (-s, -) nt coat of arms

war imperf von **sein**

warb imperf von **werben**

Ware (-, -n) f product; **~n** goods pl; **Warenhaus** nt department store; **Warenprobe** f sample; **Warensendung** f consignment; **Warenzeichen** nt trademark

warf imperf von **werfen**

warm adj warm; (Essen) hot; **~**

laufen to warm up; **mir ist es zu ~** I'm too warm; **Wärme** (-, -n) f warmth; **wärmen** vt to warm, (Essen) to warm (o to heat) up ▷ vi (Kleidung, Sonne) to be warm ▷ vr **sich ~** (o) (gegenseitig) to keep each other warm; **Wärmflasche** f hot-water bottle; **Warmstart** m (Inform) warm start

Warnblinkanlage f (Auto) warning flasher; **Warndreieck** nt (Auto) warning triangle; **warnen** vt to warn (vor +dat about, of); **Warnung** f warning

Warteliste f waiting list; **warten** vi to wait (auf +akk for); **warte mal!** wait (o hang on) a minute ▷ vt (Tech) to service

Warter(in) m(f) attendant

Wartesaal m, **Wartezimmer** nt waiting room

Wartung f service; (das Warten) servicing

warum adv why

Warze (-, -n) f wart

was pron what; (fam: etwas) something; **~ kostet das?** what does it cost? how much is it?; **~ für ein Auto ist das?** what kind of car is that?; **~ für eine Farbe/Größe?** what colour/size?; **~?** (fam: wie bitte?) what?; **~ ist/gibt's?** what is it? what's up? **du weißt, ~ ich meine** you know what I mean; **~ (auch) immer** whatever; **soll ich dir ~ mitbringen?** do you want me to bring you anything?; **alles, ~ er hat** everything he's got

Waschanlage f (Auto) car wash; **waschbar** adj washable; **Waschbär** m raccoon; **Waschbecken** nt washbasin

Wäsche (-, -n) f washing; (schmutzig) laundry; (Bettwäsche) linen; (Unterwäsche) underwear; **in der ~** in the wash; **Wäscheklammer** f

clothes peg (BRIT) (o pin (US)); **Wäscheleine** f clothesline

waschen (wusch, gewaschen) vt, vi to wash; **Waschen und Legen** shampoo and set ▷ vr **sich ~** (o) (have a) wash; **sich (dat) die Haare ~** to wash one's hair

Wäscherei f laundry; **Wäscheschleuder** f spin-drier; **Wäscheständer** m clothes horse; **Wäschetrockner** m tumble-drier

Waschgelegenheit f washing facilities pl; **Waschlappen** m flannel (BRIT), washcloth (US); (fam: Mensch) wet blanket; **Waschmaschine** f washing machine; **Waschmittel** nt, **Waschpulver** nt washing powder; **Waschraum** m washroom; **Waschsalon** (-s, -s) m launderette (BRIT), laundromat (US); **Waschstraße** f car wash

Wasser (-s, -) nt water; **fließendes ~** running water; **Wasserball** m (Sport) water polo; **Wasserbob** m jet ski; **wasserdicht** adj watertight; (Uhr etc) waterproof; **Wasserfall** m waterfall; **Wasserfarbe** f watercolour; **wasserfest** adj watertight, waterproof; **Wasserhahn** m tap (BRIT), faucet (US); **wässerig** adj watery; **Wasserkessel** m kettle; **Wasserkocher** m electric kettle; **Wasserleitung** f water pipe; **wasserlöslich** adj water soluble; **Wassermann** m (Astr) Aquarius; **Wassermelone** f water melon; **Wasserrutsche** f water chute; **Wasserschaden** m water damage; **wasserscheu** adj scared of water; **Wasserigel** m water-skiing; **W~** (Wasserstand) surface of... **Wassersport** m water... **Wasserverbrauch** f flush; **wasserundurchlässig** adj... spouterproof; **Wasserver-**

brauch *m* water consumption; **Wasserversorgung** *f* water supply; **Wasserwaage** *f* spirit level; **Wasserwerk** *nt* waterworks *pl*
waten *vi* to wade
Watt (-(*e*)*s*, -*en*) *nt* (*Geo*) mud flats *pl* ▷ (-*s*, -) *nt* (*Elek*) watt
Watte (-, -*n*) *f* cotton wool; **Wattepad** (-*s*, -*s*) *m* cotton pad; **Wattestäbchen** *nt* cotton bud, Q-tip® (*US*)
WC (-*s*, -*s*) *nt* toilet, restroom (*US*); **WC-Reiniger** *m* toilet cleaner
Web (-*s*) *nt* (*Inform*) Web; **Webseite** *f* (*Inform*) web page
Wechsel (-*s*, -) *m* change; (*Spieler~*) (*Sport*) substitution; **Wechselgeld** *nt* change; **wechselhaft** *adj* (*Wetter*) changeable; **Wechseljahre** *pl* menopause *sing*; **Wechselkurs** *m* exchange rate; **wechseln** *vt* to change; (*Blicke*) to exchange; **Geld ~** to change some money; (*in Kleingeld*) to get some change; **Euro in Pfund ~** to change euros into pounds ▷ *vi* to change; **kannst du ~?** can you change this?; **Wechselstrom** *m* alternating current, AC; **Wechselstube** *f* bureau de change
Weckdienst *m* wake-up call service; **wecken** *vt* to wake (up); **Wecker** (-*s*, -) *m* alarm clock; **Weckruf** *m* wake-up call
wedeln *vi* (*Ski*) to wedel; **mit etw ~** to wave sth; **mit dem Schwanz ~** to wag its tail; **der Hund wedelte mit dem Schwanz** the dog wagged its tail
weder *conj* **~ ... noch ...** neither ... nor
weg [illegible] (*los, ab*) (*entfernt, verreist*) away; [illegible] already left; [illegible] **war schon ~** he had [illegible] off; **weit ~** a[illegible]; **Hände ~!** hands off
Weg (-(*e*)*s*, -*e*) *m* [illegible] away (*o* off) (*Route*) route; **jdn** [illegible] (*Pfad*) path; [illegible] **~ fragen** to ask sb the [illegible] **m ~**

sein to be on the way
weg|bleiben *irr vi* to stay away; **weg|bringen** *irr vt* to take away
wegen *prep +gen o dat* because of
weg|fahren *irr vi* to drive away; (*abfahren*) to leave; (*in Urlaub*) to go away; **Wegfahrsperre** *f* (*Auto*) (engine) immobilizer; **weg|gehen** *irr vi* to go away; **weg|kommen** *irr vi* to get away; (*fig*) **gut / schlecht ~** to come off well / badly; **weg|lassen** *irr vt* to leave out; **weg|laufen** *irr vi* to run away; **weg|legen** *vt* to put aside; **weg|machen** *vt* (*fam*) to get rid of; **weg|müssen** *irr vi* **ich muss weg** I've got to go; **weg|nehmen** *irr vt* to take away; **weg|räumen** *vt* to clear away; **weg|rennen** *irr vi* to run away; **weg|schicken** *vt* to send away; **weg|schmeißen** *irr vt* to throw away; **weg|sehen** *irr vi* to look away; **weg|tun** *irr vt* to put away
Wegweiser (-*s*, -) *m* signpost
weg|werfen *irr vt* to throw away; **Wegwerfflasche** *f* non-returnable bottle; **weg|wischen** *vt* to wipe off; **weg|ziehen** *irr vi* to move (away)
weh *adj* sore; *siehe auch* **wehtun**
wehen *vt, vi* to blow; (*Fahne*) to flutter
Wehen *pl* labour pains *pl*
Wehrdienst *m* military service
wehren *vr* **sich ~** to defend oneself
weh|tun *irr vi* to hurt; **jdm / sich ~** to hurt sb / oneself
Weibchen *nt* **es ist ein ~** (*Tier*) it's a she; **weiblich** *adj* feminine; (*Bio*) female
weich *adj* soft; **~ gekocht** (*Ei*) soft-boiled
Weichkäse *m* soft cheese; (*Streichkäse*) cheese spread; **weichlich** *adj* soft; (*körperlich*) weak;

Weichspüler (-s, -) m (für Wäsche) (fabric) softener

Weide (-, -n) f (Baum) willow; (Grasfläche) meadow

weigern vr **sich** ~ to refuse; **Weigerung** f refusal

Weiher (-s, -) m pond

Weihnachten (-, -) nt Christmas, **Weihnachtsabend** m Christmas Eve; **Weihnachtsbaum** m Christmas tree; **Weihnachtsfeier** f Christmas party; **Weihnachtsferien** pl Christmas holidays pl (BRIT), Christmas vacation sing (US); **Weihnachtsgeschenk** nt Christmas present; **Weihnachtslied** nt Christmas carol; **Weihnachtsmann** m Father Christmas, Santa (Claus)

● WEIHNACHTSMARKT

- The **Weihnachtsmarkt** is a mar-
- ket held in most large towns in
- Germany in the weeks prior to
- Christmas. People visit it to buy
- presents, toys and Christmas dec
- orations, and to enjoy the festive
- atmosphere. Food and drink as-
- sociated with the Christmas fes-
- tivities can also be eaten and drunk
- there, for example, gingerbread
- and mulled wine.

Weihnachtsstern m (Bot) poin-
settia; **Weihnachtstag** m **erster** ~
Christmas Day; **zweiter** ~ Boxing
Day; **Weihnachtszeit** f Christmas
season

weil conj because

Weile (-) f while, short time; **es
kann noch eine ~ dauern** it could
take some time

Wein (-(e)s, -e) m wine; (Pflanze) vine;
Weinbeere f grape, **Weinberg** m
vineyard; **Weinbergschnecke** f
snail; **Weinbrand** m brandy

weinen vt, vi to cry

Weinglas nt wine glass; **Weinkarte** f wine list; **Weinkeller** m
wine cellar; **Weinlese** (-, -n) f vintage; **Weinprobe** f wine tasting;
Weintraube f grape

weise adj wise

Weise (-, -n) f manner, way; **auf
diese** (Art und) ~ this way

weisen (wies, gewiesen) vr to show

Weisheit f wisdom; **Weisheitszahn** m wisdom tooth

weiß adj white; **Weißbier** nt ~
wheat beer; **Weißbrot** nt white
bread; **weißhaarig** adj white-
-haired; **Weißkohl** m, **Weißkraut**
nt (white) cabbage; **Weißwein** m
white wine

weit adj wide; (Begriff) broad; (Reise,
Wurf) long; (Kleid) loose; **wie ~ ist es
...?** how far is it ...?; **so ~ sein** to be
ready ▷ adv far; ~ **verbreitet** widespread; ~ **gereist** widely travelled; ~
offen wide open; **das geht zu ~**
that's going too far, that's pushing it

weiter adj wider; (~ weg) farther
(away); (zusätzlich) further; ~**e Informationen** further information
sing ▷ adv further; ~! go on; (weitergehen!) keep moving; ~ **nichts/
niemand** nothing/nobody else;
und so ~ and so on; **weiter|arbei-
ten** vi to carry on working; **Weiterbildung** f further training (o
education); **weiter|empfehlen** irr
vt to recommend; **weiter|erzäh-
len vt nicht ~!** don't tell anyone;
weiter|fahren irr vi to go on (nach
to, bis as far as); **weiter|geben** irr
vt to pass on; **weiter|gehen** irr vi
to go on; **weiter|helfen** irr vi **jdm** ~
to help sb; **weiterhin** adv etw ~
tun to go on doing sth; **weiter|
machen** vt, vi to continue; **wei-
ter|reisen** vi to continue one's
journey

weitgehend adj considerable ▷ adv largely; **weitsichtig** adj long-sighted; (fig)far-sighted; **Weitspringer(in)** m(f) long jumper; **Weitsprung** m long jump; **Weitwinkelobjektiv** nt (Foto) wide-angle lens

Weizen (-s, -) m wheat; **Weizenbier** nt ≈ wheat beer

welche(r, s) pron what; (auswählend) which (one); **~r Vater würde ...?** what father would ...?; **~ Geschmacksrichtung willst du?** which flavour do you want?; **~r ist es?** which (one) is it? ▷ pron (interrogativ) what; (interrogativ, auswählend) which (one); (Person) who; (Sache) which, that; (unbestimmt, fam) some; **~ ein Anblick** what a sight; **zeig mir, ~r es war** show me which one of them it was ▷ pron (fam) some; **hast du Kleingeld? - ja, ich hab' ~s** have you got any change? - yes, I've got some

welk adj withered; **welken** vi to wither

Welle (-, -n) f wave; **Wellengang** m waves pl; **starker ~** heavy seas pl; **Wellenlänge** f (a. fig) wavelength; **Wellenreiten** nt surfing; **Wellensittich** (-s, -e) m budgerigar, budgie; **wellig** adj wavy

Welpe (-n, -n) m puppy

Welt (-, -en) f world; **auf der ~** in the world; **auf die ~ kommen** to be born; **Weltall** nt universe; **weltbekannt** adj world-famous; **Weltkrieg** m world war; **Weltmacht** f world power; **Weltmeister(in)** m(f) world champion; **Weltmeisterschaft** f world championship; (im Fußball) World Cup; **Weltraum** m space; **Weltreise** f trip round the world; **Weltrekord** m world record; **Weltstadt** f metropolis; **weltweit** adj worldwide, global

wem pron dat von **wer** who ... to, (to) whom; **~ hast du's gegeben?** who did you give it to?; **~ gehört es?** who does it belong to?, whose is it?; **~ auch immer es gehört** whoever it belongs to

wen pron akk von **wer** who, whom; **~ hast du besucht?** who did you visit?; **~ möchten Sie sprechen?** who would you like to speak to?; **~ auch immer du gesprochen hast** whoever you talked to

Wende (-, -n) f turning point; (Veränderung) change; **die ~** (Hist) the fall of the Berlin Wall; **Wendekreis** m (Auto) turning circle

Wendeltreppe f spiral staircase

wenden (wendete o wandte, gewendet o gewandt) vt, vi to turn (round); (um 180°) to make a U-turn; **sich an jdn ~** to turn to sb; **bitte ~!** please turn over, PTO ▷ vr **sich ~** to turn; **sich an jdn ~** to turn to sb

wenig pron, adv little; **~(e)** pl few; **(nur) ein (klein)** ~ (just) a little (bit); **ein ~ Zucker** a little bit of sugar, a little sugar; **wir haben ~ Zeit** we haven't got much time; **zu ~** too little; pl too few; **nur ~ wissen** only a few know ▷ adv **er spricht ~** he doesn't talk much; **~ bekannt** little known; **wenige** pron pl few pl; **wenigste(r, s)** adj least; **wenigstens** adv at least

wenn conj (falls) if; (zeitlich) when; **wennschon** adv **na ~** so what?

wer pron who; **~ war das?** who was that?; **~ von euch?** which (one) of you? ▷ pron anybody who, anyone who; **~ das glaubt, ist dumm** anyone who believes that is stupid; **~ auch immer** whoever ▷ pron somebody, someone; (in Fragen) anybody, anyone; **ist da ~?** is (there) anybody there?

Werbefernsehen nt TV commercials *pl*; **Werbegeschenk** *nt* promotional gift; **werben** (*warb, geworben*) *vt* to win; (*Mitglied*) to recruit ▷ *vi* to advertise; **Werbespot** (-s, -s) *m* commercial; **Werbung** *f* advertising

werden (*wurde, geworden*) *vi* to get, to become; **alt/müde/reich** ~ to get old/tired/rich, **was willst du** ~? what do you want to be? ▷ *vaux* (*Futur*) will; (*Entschluss*) to be going to; (*Passiv*) to be; **er wird uns (schon) fahren** he'll drive us; **ich werde kommen** I'll come; **er wird uns abholen** he's going to pick us up; **wir** ~ **dafür bezahlt** we're paid for it; **er wird gerade diskutiert** he's being discussed

werfen (*warf, geworfen*) *vt* to throw

Werft (-, -en) *f* shipyard, dockyard

Werk (-(e)s, -e) *nt* (*Kunstwerk, Buch etc*) work; (*Fabrik*) factory; (*Mechanismus*) works *pl*; **Werkstatt** (-, -stätten) *f* workshop; (*Auto*) garage; **Werktag** *m* working day; **werktags** *adv* on weekdays, during the week; **Werkzeug** *nt* tool; **Werkzeugkasten** *m* toolbox

wert *adj* worth, **es ist etwa 50 Euro** ~ it's worth about 50 euros; **das ist nichts** ~ it's worthless; **Wert** (-(e)s, -e) *m* worth; (*Zahlen*~) (*Fin*) value; ~ **legen auf** (*+akk*) to attach importance to; **es hat doch keinen** ~ (*Sinn*) it's pointless; **Wertangabe** *f* declaration of value; **Wertbrief** *m* insured letter; **Wertgegenstand** *m* valuable object; **wertlos** *adj* worthless; **Wertmarke** *f* token; **Wertpapiere** *pl* securities *pl*; **Wertsachen** *pl* valuables *pl*; **Wertstoff** *m* recyclable waste; **wertvoll** *adj* valuable

Wesen (-s, -) *nt* being, (*Natur, Charakter*) nature

wesentlich *adj* significant; (*beträchtlich*) considerable ▷ *adv* considerably

weshalb *adv* why

Wespe (-, -n) *f* wasp; **Wespenstich** *m* wasp sting

wessen *pron gen von* **wer**; whose

● **WESSI**

● A **Wessi** is a colloquial and often
● derogatory word used to describe
● a German from the former West
● Germany. The expression 'Besser-
● wessi' is used by East Germans to
● describe a West German who is
● considered to be a know-all.

West west; **Westdeutschland** *nt* (*als Landesteil*) Western Germany; (*Hist*) West Germany

Weste (-, -n) *f* waistcoat (*BRIT*), vest (*US*); (*Wollweste*) cardigan

Westen (-s) *m* west; **im** ~ **Englands** in the west of England; **der Wilde** ~ the Wild West; **Westeuropa** *nt* Western Europe; **Westküste** *f* west coast; **westlich** *adj* western; (*Kurs, Richtung*) westerly; **Westwind** *m* west(erly) wind

weswegen *adv* why

Wettbewerb *m* competition; **Wettbüro** *nt* betting office; **Wette** (-, -n) *f* bet; **eine** ~ **abschließen** to make a bet; **die** ~ **gilt!** you're on; **wetten** *vt, vi* to bet (*auf +akk* on); **ich habe mit ihm gewettet, dass** ... I bet him that ...; **ich wette mit dir um 50 Euro** I'll bet you 50 euros; ~, **dass?** wanna bet?

Wetter (-s, -) *nt* weather; **Wetterbericht** *m*, **Wettervorhersage** *f* weather forecast; **Wetterkarte** *f* weather map; **Wetterlage** *f* weather situation; **Wettervorhersage** *f* weather forecast

Wettkampf *m* contest; **Wettlauf** *m* race; **Wettrennen** *nt* race

WG (-, -s) f abk = **Wohngemein-schaft**

Whirlpool® (-s, -s) m jacuzzi®

Whisky (-s, -s) m (schottisch) whis-ky; (irisch, amerikanisch) whiskey

wichtig adj important

wickeln vt (Schnur) to wind (um round); (Schal, Decke) to wrap (um round); **ein Baby ~** to change a baby's nappy (BRIT) (o diaper (US)); **Wickel-raum** m baby-changing room; **Wi-ckeltisch** m baby-changing table

Widder (-s, -) m (Zool) ram; (Astr) Aries sing

wider prep +akk against

widerlich adj disgusting

widerrufen irr vt to withdraw; (Auftrag, Befehl etc) to cancel

widersprechen irr vi to contra-dict (jdm sb); **Widerspruch** m contradiction

Widerstand m resistance; **wider-standsfähig** adj resistant (gegen to)

widerwärtig adj disgusting

widerwillig adj unwilling, reluc-tant

widmen vt to dedicate ▷ vr **sich jdm/etw ~** to devote oneself to sb/sth; **Widmung** f dedication

wie adv how; **~ viel** how much; **~ viele Menschen?** how many peo-ple?; **~ gehts?** how are you?; **~ ist das neue Zimmer?** what's the new room like?; **~ das?** how come?; **~ bitte?** pardon?, sorry? (BRIT) ▷ (so) **schön ~ ...** as beautiful as ...; **~ du weißt** as you know; **~ ich das hörte** when I heard that; **ich sah, ~ er rauskam** I saw him coming out

wieder adv again; **~ ein(e) ...** an-other ...; **~ erkennen** to recognize; **etw ~ gutmachen** to make up for sth; **~ verwerten** to recycle

wieder|bekommen irr vt to get back

wiederholen vt to repeat; **Wie-**derholung f repetition

Wiederhören nt (Tel) **auf ~** goodbye

wieder|kommen irr vi to come back

wieder|sehen irr vt to see again; (wieder treffen) to meet again; **Wie-dersehen** (-s) nt reunion; **auf ~!** goodbye

Wiedervereinigung f reunifica-tion

Wiege (-, -n) f cradle; **wiegen** (wog, gewogen) vt, vi (Gewicht) to weigh

Wien (-s) nt Vienna

wies imperf von **weisen**

Wiese (-, -n) f meadow

Wiesel (-s, -) nt weasel

wieso adv why

wievielmal adv how often; **wie-vielte(r, s)** adj **zum ~n Mal?** how many times?; **den Wievielten haben wir heute?** what's the date today?; **am Wievielten hast du Geburts-tag?** which day is your birthday?

wieweit conj to what extent

wild adj wild

Wild (-(e)s) nt game

wildfremd adj (fam) **ein ~er Mensch** a complete (o total) stran-ger; **Wildleder** nt suede; **Wildpark** m game park; **Wildschwein** nt (wild) boar; **Wildwasserfahren** (-s) nt whitewater canoeing (o rafting)

Wille (-ns, -n) m will

willen prep +gen **um ... ~** for the sake of ...; **um Himmels ~!** (vor-wurfsvoll) for heaven's sake; (betrof-fen) goodness me

willkommen adj welcome

Wimper (-, -n) f eyelash; **Wim-perntusche** f mascara

Wind (-(e)s, -e) m wind

Windel (-, -n) f nappy (BRIT), diaper (US)

windgeschützt adj sheltered from the wind; **windig** adj windy;

(fig) dubious; **Windjacke** f windcheater; **Windmühle** f windmill; **Windpocken** pl chickenpox sing; **Windschutzscheibe** f *(Auto)* windscreen *(BRIT)*, windshield *(US)*; **Windstärke** f wind force; **Windsurfen** *(-s)* nt windsurfing; **Windsurfer(in)** m(f) windsurfer

Winkel *(-s, -)* m *(Math)* angle; *(Gerät)* set square; *(in Raum)* corner; **im rechten ~ zu** at right angles to

winken vt, vi to wave

Winter *(-s, -)* m winter; **Winterausrüstung** f *(Auto)* winter equipment; **Winterfahrplan** m winter timetable; **winterlich** adj wintry; **Wintermantel** m winter coat; **Winterreifen** m winter tyre; **Winterschlussverkauf** m winter sales pl; **Wintersport** m winter sports pl; **Winterzeit** f *(Uhrzeit)* winter time *(BRIT)*, standard time *(US)*

winzig adj tiny

wir pron we; **~ selbst** we ourselves; **~ alle** all of us; **~ drei** the three of us; **~ sind's** it's us; **~ nicht** not us

Wirbel *(-s, -)* m whirl; *(Trubel)* hurly-burly; *(Aufsehen)* fuss; *(Anat)* vertebra; **Wirbelsäule** f spine

wirken vi to be effective; *(erfolgreich sein)* to work; *(scheinen)* to seem

wirklich adj real; **Wirklichkeit** f reality

wirksam adj effective; **Wirkung** f effect

wirr adj confused; **Wirrwarr** *(-s)* m confusion

Wirsing *(-s)* m savoy cabbage

Wirt *(-(e)s, -e)* m landlord; **Wirtin** f landlady

Wirtschaft f *(Comm)* economy; *(Gaststätte)* pub; **wirtschaftlich** adj *(Pol, Comm)* economic; *(sparsam)* economical

Wirtshaus nt pub

wischen vt, vi to wipe; **Wischer** *(-s,*

-) m wiper; **Wischlappen** m cloth

wissen *(wusste, gewusst)* vt to know; **weißt du schon, ...?** did you know ...?; **woher weißt du das?** how do you know?; **das musst du selbst ~** that's up to you; **Wissen** *(-s)* nt knowledge

Wissenschaft f science; **Wissenschaftler(in)** *(-s, -)* m(f) scientist; *(Geisteswissenschaftler)* academic; **wissenschaftlich** adj scientific; *(geisteswissenschaftlich)* academic

Witwe *(-, -n)* f widow; **Witwer** *(-s, -)* m widower

Witz *(-(e)s, -e)* m joke; **mach keine ~e!** you're kidding!; **das soll wohl ein ~ sein** you've got to be joking; **witzig** adj funny

wo adv where; **zu einer Zeit, ~ ...** at a time when ...; **überall, ~ ich hingehe** wherever I go ▷ conj **jetzt, ~ du da bist** now that you're here; **~ ich dich gerade spreche** while I'm talking to you, **woanders** adv somewhere else

wobei adv **~ mir einfällt ...** which reminds me ...

Woche *(-, -n)* f week; **während** *(n unter)* der **~** during the week; **einmal die ~** once a week; **Wochenende** nt weekend; **am ~** at *(BRIT)* *(o an (US))* the weekend; **wir fahren übers ~ weg** we're going away for the weekend; **Wochenendhaus** nt weekend cottage; **Wochenkarte** f weekly (season) ticket; **wochenlang** adv for weeks (on end); **Wochenmarkt** m weekly market; **Wochentag** m weekday; **wöchentlich** adj, adv weekly

Wodka *(-s, -s)* m vodka

wodurch adv **~ unterscheiden sie sich?** what's the difference between them?; **~ hast du es gemerkt?** how did you notice?; **wofür** adv *(relativ)* for which; *(Frage)* what

... for; **~ brauchst du das?** what do you need that for?

wog *imperf von* **wiegen**

woher *adv* where ... from; **wohin** *adv* where ... to

wohl *adv* well; (*behaglich*) at ease, comfortable; (*vermutlich*) probably; (*gewiss*) certainly; **Wohl** (-(e)s) *nt* **zum ~!** cheers; **wohlbehalten** *adv* safe and sound; **wohlgemerkt** *adv* mind you; **Wohlstand** *m* prosperity, affluence

Wohlwollen (-s) *nt* goodwill

Wohnblock *m* block of flats (BRIT), apartment house (US); **wohnen** *vi* to live; **Wohngemeinschaft** *f* shared flat (BRIT) (o apartment (US)); **ich wohne in einer ~** I share a flat (o apartment); **wohnhaft** *adj* resident; **Wohnküche** *f* kitchen-cum-living-room; **Wohnmobil** (-s, -e) *nt* camper, RV (US); **Wohnort** *m* place of residence; **Wohnsitz** *m* place of residence; **Wohnung** *f* flat (BRIT), apartment (US); **Wohnungstür** *f* front door; **Wohnwagen** *m* caravan; **Wohnzimmer** *nt* living room

Wolf (-(e)s, **Wölfe**) *m* wolf

Wolke (-, -n) *f* cloud; **Wolkenkratzer** *m* skyscraper; **wolkenlos** *adj* cloudless; **wolkig** *adj* cloudy

Wolldecke *f* (woollen) blanket; **Wolle** (-, -n) *f* wool

wollen *vaux* to want; **sie wollte ihn nicht sehen** she didn't want to see him; **~ wir gehen?** shall we go?; **~ Sie bitte ...** will (o would) you please ... ▷ *vt* to want; **er will lieber bleiben** I'd prefer to stay; **er will, dass ich aufhöre** he wants me to stop; **ich wollte, ich wäre/hätte ...** I wish I were/had ... ▷ *vi* to want to; **ich will nicht** I don't want to; **was du willst** whatever you like; **ich will nach Hause** I want

to go home; **wo willst du hin?** where do you want to go?; (*wohin gehst du?*) where are you going?

Wolljacke *f* cardigan

womit *adv* what ... with; **~ habe ich das verdient?** what have I done to deserve that?

womöglich *adv* possibly

woran *adv* **~ denkst du?** what are you thinking of?; **~ ist er gestorben?** what did he die of?; **~ sieht man das?** how can you tell?

worauf *adv* **~ wartest du?** what are you waiting for?

woraus *adv* **~ ist das gemacht?** what is it made of?

Workshop (-s, -s) *m* workshop

World Wide Web *nt* World Wide Web

Wort (-(e)s, **Wörter**) *nt* (*Vokabel*) word ▷ (-(e)s, -e) *nt* (*Äußerung*) word; **mit anderen ~en** in other words; **jdn beim ~ nehmen** to take sb at his/her word; **Wörterbuch** *nt* dictionary; **wörtlich** *adj* literal

worüber *adv* **~ redet sie?** what is she talking about?

worum *adv* **~ gehts?** what is it about?

worunter *adv* **~ leidet er?** what is he suffering from?

wovon *adv* (*relativ*) from which; **~ redest du?** what are you talking about?; **wozu** *adv* (*relativ*) to/for which; (*interrogativ*) what ... for/to; (*warum*) why; **~?** what for?; **~ brauchst du das?** what do you need it for?; **~ soll das gut sein?** what's it for?; **~ hast du Lust?** what do you feel like doing?

Wrack (-(e)s, -s) *nt* wreck

Wucher (-s) *m* profiteering; **das ist ~!** that's daylight robbery!

wuchs *imperf von* **wachsen**

wühlen *vi* to rummage; (*Tier*) to root; (*Maulwurf*) to burrow

Wühltisch *m* bargain counter
wund *adj* sore; **Wunde** (-, -n) *f* wound
Wunder (-s, -) *nt* miracle; **es ist kein ~** it's no wonder; **wunderbar** *adj* wonderful, marvellous; **Wunderkerze** *f* sparkler; **Wundermittel** *nt* wonder cure; **wundern** *vr* **sich ~** to be surprised (über +akk at) ▷ *vt* to surprise; **wunderschön** *adj* beautiful; **wundervoll** *adj* wonderful
Wundsalbe *f* antiseptic ointment; **Wundstarrkrampf** *m* tetanus
Wunsch (-(e)s, Wünsche) *m* wish (nach for); **wünschen** *vt* to wish; **sich** (*dat*) **etw ~** to want sth; **ich wünsche dir alles Gute** I wish you all the best; **wünschenswert** *adj* desirable
wurde *imperf von* **werden**
Wurf (-s, Würfe) *m* throw; (Zool) litter
Würfel (-s, -) *m* dice; (Math) cube; **würfeln** *vi* to throw (the dice); (Würfel spielen) to play dice ▷ *vt* (Zahl) to throw; (Gastr) to dice; **Würfelzucker** *m* lump sugar
Wurm (-(e)s, Würmer) *m* worm
Wurst (-, Würste) *f* sausage; **das ist mir** (*fam*) I couldn't care less
Würstchen *nt* frankfurter
Würze (-, -n) *f* seasoning, spice
Wurzel (-, -n) *f* root
würzen *vt* to season, to spice; **würzig** *adj* spicy
wusch *imperf von* **waschen**
wusste *imperf von* **wissen**
wüst *adj* (unordentlich) chaotic; (ausschweifend) wild; (öde) desolate; (fam: heftig) terrible
Wüste (-, -n) *f* desert
Wut (-) *f* rage, fury; **ich habe eine ~ auf ihn** I'm really mad at him; **wütend** *adj* furious
WWW (-) *nt* abk = World Wide Web WWW

X, y

X-Beine *pl* knock-knees *pl*; **x-beinig** *adj* knock kneed
x-beliebig *adj* **ein ~es Buch** any book (you like)
x-mal *adv* umpteen times
Xylophon (-s, -e) *nt* xylophone
Yacht (-, -en) *f* yacht
Yoga (-(s)) *m o nt* yoga
Yuppie (-s, -s) *m* (-, -s) *f* yuppie

Z

Zacke (-, -n) f point; (Säge, Kamm) tooth; (Gabel) prong; **zackig** adj (Linie etc) jagged; (fam: Tempo) brisk

zaghaft adj timid

zäh adj tough; (Flüssigkeit) thick

Zahl (-, -en) f number; **zahlbar** adj payable; **zahlen** vt, vi to pay; **~ bitte!** could I have the bill (BRIT) (o check (US)) please?; **bar ~** to pay cash; **zählen** vt, vi to count (auf +akk on); **~ zu** to be one of; **Zahlenschloss** nt combination lock; **Zähler** (-s, -) m (Gerät) counter; (für Strom, Wasser) meter; **zahlreich** adj numerous; **Zahlung** f payment; **Zahlungsanweisung** f money order; **Zahlungsbedingungen** pl terms pl of payment

zahm adj tame; **zähmen** vt to tame

Zahn (-(e)s, Zähne) m tooth; **Zahnarzt** m, **Zahnärztin** f dentist; **Zahnbürste** f toothbrush; **Zahncreme** f toothpaste; **Zahnersatz**

m dentures pl; **Zahnfleisch** nt gums pl; **Zahnfleischbluten** nt bleeding gums pl; **Zahnfüllung** f filling; **Zahnklammer** f brace; **Zahnpasta**, **Zahnpaste** f toothpaste; **Zahnradbahn** f rack railway (BRIT) (o railroad (US)); **Zahnschmerzen** pl toothache sing; **Zahnseide** f dental floss; **Zahnspange** f brace; **Zahnstocher** (-s, -) m toothpick

Zange (-, -n) f pliers pl; (Zuckerzange) tongs pl; (Beißzange, Zool) pincers pl; (Med) forceps pl

zanken vi to quarrel ▷ vr **sich ~** to quarrel

Zäpfchen nt (Anat) uvula; (Med) suppository

zapfen vt (Bier) to pull; **Zapfsäule** f petrol (BRIT) (o gas (US)) pump

zappeln vi to wriggle; (unruhig sein) to fidget

zappen vi to zap, to channel-hop

zart adj (weich, leise) soft; (Braten etc) tender; (fein, schwächlich) delicate; **zartbitter** adj (Schokolade) plain, dark

zärtlich adj tender, affectionate; **Zärtlichkeit** f tenderness; **~en** pl hugs and kisses pl

Zauber (-s, -) m magic; (Bann) spell; **Zauberei** f magic; **Zauberer** (-s, -) m magician; (Künstler) conjuror; **Zauberformel** f (magic) spell; **zauberhaft** adj enchanting; **Zauberin** f sorceress; **Zauberkünstler(in)** m(f) magician, conjuror; **Zaubermittel** nt magic cure; **zaubern** vi to do magic; (Künstler) to do conjuring tricks; **Zauberspruch** m (magic) spell

Zaun (-(e)s, Zäune) m fence

z. B. abk = **zum Beispiel** e.g., eg

Zebra (-s, -s) nt zebra; **Zebrastreifen** m zebra crossing (BRIT), crosswalk (US)

Zechtour f pub crawl

Zecke (-, -n) f tick

Zehe (-, n) f toe; (Knoblauch) clove; **Zehennagel** m toenail; **Zehenspitze** f tip of the toes

zehn num ten; **Zehnerkarte** f ticket valid for ten trips; **Zehnkampf** m decathlon; **Zehnkämpfer(in)** m(f) decathlete; **zehnmal** adv ten times; **zehntausend** num ten thousand; **zehnte(r, s)** adj tenth; siehe auch **dritte**; **Zehntel** (-s, -) nt (Bruchteil) tenth; **Zehntelsekunde** f tenth of a second

Zeichen (-s, -) nt sign; (Schriftzeichen) character; **Zeichenblock** m sketch pad; **Zeichenerklärung** f key; **Zeichensetzung** f punctuation; **Zeichensprache** f sign language; **Zeichentrickfilm** m cartoon

zeichnen vt, vi to draw; **Zeichnung** f drawing

Zeigefinger m index finger; **zeigen** vt to show; **sie zeigte uns die Stadt** she showed us around the town; **zeig mal!** let me see ▷ vi to point (auf +akk to, at) ▷ vr **sich** ~ to show oneself; **es wird sich** ~ time will tell; **Zeiger** (-s, -) m pointer; (Uhr) hand

Zeile (-, -n) f line

Zeit (-, -en) f time; **ich habe keine Zeit** I haven't got time, **lass dir** ~ take your time; **das hat** ~ there's no rush; **von** ~ **zu** ~ from time to time; **Zeitansage** f (Tel) speaking clock (BRIT), correct time (US); **Zeitarbeit** f temporary work; **zeitgenössisch** adj contemporary, modern; **zeitgleich** adj si-

multaneous ▷ adv at exactly the same time; **zeitig** adj early; **Zeitkarte** f season ticket; **zeitlich** adj (Reihenfolge) chronological; **es passt** ~ **nicht** it isn't a convenient time; **ich schaff es** ~ **nicht** I'm not going to make it; **Zeitlupe** f slow motion; **Zeitplan** m schedule; **Zeitpunkt** m point in time; **Zeitraum** m period (of time); **Zeitschrift** f magazine; (wissenschaftliche) periodical

Zeitung f newspaper; **es steht in der** ~ it's in the paper(s); **Zeitungsanzeige** f newspaper advertisement; **Zeitungsartikel** m newspaper article; **Zeitungskiosk** m, **Zeitungsstand** m newsstand

Zeitunterschied m time difference; **Zeitverschiebung** f time lag; **Zeitvertreib** (-(e)s, -e) m **zum** ~ to pass the time; **zeitweise** adv occasionally; **Zeitzone** f time zone

Zelle (-, -n) f cell

Zellophan® (-s) nt cellophane®

Zelt (-(e)s, -e) nt tent; **zelten** vi to camp, to go camping; **Zeltplatz** m campsite, camping site

Zement (-(e)s, -e) m cement

Zentimeter m or nt centimetre

Zentner (-s, -) m (metric) hundredweight; (in Deutschland) fifty kilos; (in Österreich und der Schweiz) one hundred kilos

zentral adj central; **Zentrale** (-, -n) f central office; (Tel) exchange; **Zentralheizung** f central heating; **Zentralverriegelung** f (Auto) central locking; **Zentrum** (-s, Zentren) nt centre

zerbrechen irr vt, vi to break; **zerbrechlich** adj fragile

Zeremonie (-, -n) f ceremony

zergehen irr vi to dissolve;

(*schmelzen*) to melt
zerkleinern vt to cut up; (*zerhacken*) to chop (up); **zerkratzen** vt to scratch; **zerlegen** vt to take to pieces; (*Fleisch*) to carve; (*Gerät, Maschine*) to dismantle; **zerquetschen** vt to squash; **zerreißen** irr vt to tear to pieces ▷ vi to tear

zerren vt to drag; **sich** (*dat*) **einen Muskel ~** to pull a muscle ▷ vi to tug (*an* +*akk* at); **Zerrung** f (*Med*) pulled muscle
zerschlagen irr vt to smash ▷ vr **sich ~** to come to nothing
zerschneiden irr vt to cut up
Zerstäuber (-s, -) m atomizer
zerstören vt to destroy; **Zerstörung** f destruction
zerstreuen vt to scatter; (*Menge*) to disperse; (*Zweifel etc*) to dispel ▷ vr **sich ~** (*Menge*) to disperse; **zerstreut** adj scattered; (*Mensch*) absent-minded; (*kurzfristig*) distracted
zerteilen vt to split up
Zertifikat (-(*e*)s, -e) nt certificate
Zettel (-s, -) m piece of paper; (*Notizzettel*) note
Zeug (-(*e*)s, -e) nt (*fam*) stuff; (*Ausrüstung*) gear; **dummes ~** nonsense
Zeuge (-n, -n) m, **Zeugin** f witness
Zeugnis nt certificate; (*Schule*) report; (*Referenz*) reference
z. H(d). abk = **zu Händen von** attn
zickig adj (*fam*) touchy, bitchy
Zickzack (-(*e*)s, -e) m **im ~ fahren** to zigzag (across the road)
Ziege (-, -n) f goat
Ziegel (-s, -) m brick; (*Dach*) tile
Ziegenkäse m goat's cheese;
Ziegenpeter m mumps

ziehen (*zog, gezogen*) vt to draw; (*zerren*) to pull; (*Spielfigur*) to move; (*züchten*) to rear ▷ vi (*zerren*) to pull; (*sich bewegen*) to move; (*Rauch, Wolke etc*) to drift; **den Tee ~ lassen** to let the tea stand ▷ vi impers **es zieht** there's a draught ▷ vr **sich ~** (*Treffen, Rede*) to drag on
Ziel (-(*e*)s, -e) nt (*Reise*) destination; (*Sport*) finish; (*Absicht*) goal, aim; **zielen** vi to aim (*auf* +*akk* at); **Zielgruppe** f target group; **ziellos** adj aimless; **Zielscheibe** f target
ziemlich adj considerable; **ein ~es Durcheinander** quite a mess; **mit ~er Sicherheit** with some certainty ▷ adv rather, quite; **~ viel** quite a lot
zierlich adj dainty; (*Frau*) petite
Ziffer (-, -n) f figure; **arabische/römische ~n** pl Arabic / Roman numerals pl; **Zifferblatt** nt dial, face
zig adj (*fam*) umpteen
Zigarette f cigarette; **Zigarettenautomat** m cigarette machine; **Zigarettenpapier** nt cigarette paper; **Zigarettenschachtel** f cigarette packet; **Zigarettenstummel** m cigarette end; **Zigarillo** (-s, -s) m cigarillo; **Zigarre** (-, -n) f cigar
Zigeuner(in) (-s, -) m(f) gipsy
Zimmer (-s, -) nt room; **haben Sie ein ~ für zwei Personen?** do you have a room for two?; **Zimmerlautstärke** f reasonable volume; **Zimmermädchen** nt chambermaid; **Zimmermann** m carpenter; **Zimmerpflanze** f house plant; **Zimmerschlüssel** m room key; **Zimmerservice** m room service; **Zimmervermittlung** f accommodation agency
Zimt (-(*e*)s, -e) m cinnamon; **Zimt-**

stange f cinnamon stick

Zink (-(e)s) nt zinc

Zinn (-(e)s) nt (Element) tin; (legiertes) pewter

Zinsen pl interest sing

Zipfel (-s, -) m corner; (spitz) tip; (Hemd) tail; (Wurst) end; (fam: Penis) willy; **Zipfelmütze** f pointed hat

zirka adv about, approximately

Zirkel (s,) m (Math) (pair of) compasses pl

Zirkus (-, -e) m circus

zischen vi to hiss

Zitat (-(e)s, -e) nt quotation (aus from); **zitieren** vt to quote

Zitronat nt candied lemon peel; **Zitrone** (-, -n) f lemon; **Zitronenlimonade** f lemonade; **Zitronensaft** m lemon juice

zittern vi to tremble (vor +dat with)

zivil adj civilian; (Preis) reasonable; **Zivil** (-s) nt plain clothes pl; (Mil) civilian clothes pl; **Zivildienst** m community service (for conscientious objectors)

zocken vi (fam) to gamble

Zoff (s) m (fam) trouble

zog imperf von **ziehen**

zögerlich adj hesitant; **zögern** vi to hesitate

Zoll (-(e)s, Zölle) m customs pl; (Abgabe) duty; **Zollabfertigung** f customs clearance; **Zollamt** nt customs office; **Zollbeamte(r)** m, -beamtin f customs official; **Zollerklärung** f customs declaration; **zollfrei** adj duty-free; **Zollgebühren** pl customs duties pl, **Zollkontrolle** f customs check; **Zöllner(in)** m(f) customs officer; **zollpflichtig** adj liable to duty

Zombie (-s, -s) m zombie

Zone (-, -n) f zone

Zoo (-s, -s) m zoo

Zoom (-s, -s) nt zoom (shot); (Objektiv) zoom (lens)

Zopf (-(e)s, Zöpfe) m plait (BRIT), braid (US)

Zorn (-(e)s) m anger; **zornig** adj angry (über etw akk about sth, auf jdn with sb)

zu conj (mit Infinitiv) to ▷ prep +dat (bei Richtung, Vorgang) to; (bei Orts-, Zeit-, Preisangabe) at; (Zweck) for; **~r Post®** gehen to go to the post office; **~ Hause** at home; **~ Weihnachten** at Christmas; **fünf Bücher ~ 20 Euro** five books at 20 euros each; **~m Braten brauchst du Fett** you need fat for frying; **~m Fenster herein** through the window; **~ meiner Zeit** in my time ▷ adv (zu sehr) too; **~ viel** too much; **~ wenig** not enough; **auf den Wald ~** towards the forest ▷ adj (fam) shut; **Tür ~!** shut the door

zuallererst adv first of all; **zuallerletzt** adv last of all

Zubehör (-(e)s, -e) nt accessories pl

zu|bereiten vt to prepare; **Zubereitung** f preparation

zu|binden irr vt to do (o tie) up

Zucchini pl courgettes pl (BRIT), zucchini pl (US)

züchten vt (Tiere) to breed, (Pflanzen) to grow

zucken vi to jerk; (krampfhaft) to twitch; (Strahl etc) to flicker, **mit den Schultern ~** to shrug (one's shoulders)

Zucker (-s) m sugar; (Med) diabetes sing; **Zuckerdose** f sugar bowl; **zuckerkrank** adj diabetic; **Zuckerrohr** nt sugar cane; **Zuckerrübe** f sugar beet; **Zuckerwatte** f candy-floss (BRIT), cotton candy (US)

zu|decken vt to cover up

zu|drehen vt to turn off

zueinander adv to one other; (mit Verb) together; **~ halten** to stick together

zuerst adv first; (zu Anfang) at first; **~ einmal** first of all

Zufahrt f access; (Einfahrt) drive(way); **Zufahrtsstraße** f access road; (Autobahn) slip road (BRIT), ramp (US)

Zufall m chance; (Ereignis) coincidence; **durch ~** by accident; **so ein ~!** what a coincidence; **zufällig** adj chance ▷ adv by chance; **weißt du ~, ob ...?** do you happen to know whether ...?

zufrieden adj content(ed); (befriedigt) satisfied; **sich mit etw ~ geben** to settle for sth; **lass sie ~** leave her alone (o in peace); **sie ist schwer ~ zu stellen** she is hard to please; **Zufriedenheit** f contentment; (Befriedigtsein) satisfaction

zu|fügen vt to add (dat to); **jdm Schaden/Schmerzen ~** to cause sb harm/pain

Zug m (-(e)s, Züge) m train; (Luft) draught; (Ziehen) pull; (Gesichtszug) feature; (Schach) move; (Charakterzug) trait; (an Zigarette) puff, drag; (Schluck) gulp

Zugabe f extra; (in Konzert etc) encore

Zugabteil nt train compartment

Zugang m access; **„kein ~!"** 'no entry!'

Zugauskunft f (Stelle) train information office/desk; **Zugbegleiter(in)** m(f) guard (BRIT), conductor (US)

zu|geben irr vt (zugestehen) admit; **zugegeben** adv admittedly

zu|gehen irr vi (schließen) to shut; **auf jdn/etw ~** to walk towards sb/sth; **dem Ende ~** to be coming to a close ▷ vi impers (sich ereignen) to happen; **es ging lustig zu** we/they had a lot of fun; **dort geht es streng zu** it's strict there

Zügel (-s, -) m rein

Zugführer(in) m(f) guard (BRIT), conductor (US)

zugig adj draughty

zügig adj speedy

Zugluft f draught

Zugpersonal nt train staff

zu|greifen irr vi (fig) to seize the opportunity; (beim Essen) to help oneself; **~ auf** (+akk) (Inform) to access

Zugrestauraunt nt dining car, diner (US)

Zugriffsberechtigung f (Inform) access right

zugrunde adv **~ gehen** to perish; **~ gehen an** (+dat) (sterben) to die of

Zugschaffner(in) m(f) ticket inspector; **Zugunglück** nt train crash

zugunsten prep +gen o dat in favour of

Zugverbindung f train connection

zu|haben irr vi to be closed

zu|halten irr vt **sich** (dat) **die Nase ~** to hold one's nose; **sich** (dat) **die Ohren ~** to hold one's hands over one's ears; **die Tür ~** to hold the door shut

Zuhause (-s) nt home

zu|hören vi to listen (dat to); **Zuhörer(in)** m(f) listener

zu|kleben vt to seal

zu|kommen irr vi to come up (auf +akk to); **jdm etw ~ lassen** to give/send sb sth; **etw auf sich** (akk) **~ lassen** to take sth as it comes

zu|kriegen vt **ich krieg den Koffer nicht zu** I can't shut the case

Zukunft (-, Zukünfte) f future; **zukünftig** adj future ▷ adv in future

zu|lassen vt (hereinlassen) to admit; (erlauben) to permit; (Auto) to license; (fam: nicht öffnen) to keep shut; **zulässig** adj permissible, permitted

zuletzt adv finally, at last

zuliebe adv **jdm** ~ for sb's sake

zum kontr von **zu dem**; ~ **dritten Mal** for the third time; ~ **Scherz** as a joke; ~ **Trinken** for drinking

zu|machen vt to shut; (Kleidung) to do up ▷ vi to shut

zumindest adv at least

zu|muten vt **jdm etw** ~ to expect sth of sb ▷ vr **sich** (dat) **zu viel** ~ to overdo things

zunächst adv first of all; ~ **einmal** to start with

Zunahme (-, -n) f increase

Zuname m surname, last name

zünden vt, vi (Auto) to ignite, to fire; **Zündholz** nt match; **Zündkabel** f (Auto) ignition cable; **Zündkerze** f (Auto) spark plug; **Zündschloss** nt ignition lock; **Zündschlüssel** m ignition key; **Zündung** f ignition

zu|nehmen irr vi to increase; (Mensch) to put on weight ▷ vt **5 Kilo** ~ to put on 5 kilos

Zunge (-, -n) f tongue

Zungenkuss m French kiss

zunichte adv ~ **machen** to ruin

zunutze adv **sich** (dat) **etw** ~ **machen** to make use of sth

zu|parken vt to block

zur kontr von **zu der**

zurecht|finden irr vr **sich** ~ to find one's way around; **zurecht|-**

kommen irr vi to cope (mit etw with sth), **zurecht|machen** vt to prepare ▷ vr **sich** ~ to get ready

Zürich (-s) nt Zurich

zurück adv back

zurück|bekommen irr vt to get back; **zurück|blicken** vi to look back (auf +akk at); **zurück|bringen** irr vt (hierhin) to bring back; (woandershin) to take back; **zurück|erstatten** vt to refund; **zurück|fahren** irr vi to go back; **zurück|geben** irr vt to give back; (antworten) to answer; **zurück|gehen** irr vi to go back; (zeitlich) to date back (auf +akk to)

zurück|halten irr vt to hold back; (hindern) to prevent ▷ vr **sich** ~ to hold back; **zurückhaltend** adj reserved

zurück|holen vt to fetch back; **zurück|kommen** irr vi to come back, **auf etw** (akk) ~ to return (or get back) to sth, **zurück|lassen** irr vt to leave behind; **zurück|legen** vt to put back; (Geld) to put by; (reservieren) to keep back; (Strecke) to cover; **zurück|nehmen** irr vt to take back; **zurück|rufen** irr vt to call back; **zurück|schicken** vt to send back; **zurück|stellen** vt to put back; **zurück|treten** irr vi to step back; (von Amt) to retire; **zurück|verlangen** vt **etw** ~ to ask for sth back, **zurück|zahlen** vt to pay back

zurzeit adv at present

Zusage f promise (Annahme) acceptance; **zu|sagen** vt to promise ▷ vi to accept; **jdm** ~ (gefallen) to appeal to sb

zusammen adv together

Zusammenarbeit f collaboration; **zusammen|arbeiten** vi to work together

zusammen|brechen irr vi to

collapse; (*psychisch*) to break down; **Zusammenbruch** m collapse; (*psychischer*) breakdown

zusammen|fassen vt to summarize; (*vereinigen*) to unite; **zusammenfassend** adj summarizing ▷ adv to summarize; **Zusammenfassung** f summary

zusammen|gehören vi to belong together; **zusammen|halten** irr vi to stick together

Zusammenhang m connection; **im/aus dem ~** in/out of context; **zusammen|hängen** irr vi to be connected; **zusammenhängend** adj coherent; **zusammenhang(s)-los** adj incoherent

zusammen|klappen vi, vt to fold up

zusammen|knüllen vt to screw up

zusammen|kommen irr vi to meet; (*sich ereignen*) to happen together; **zusammen|legen** vt to fold up ▷ vi (*Geld sammeln*) to club together; **zusammen|nehmen** irr vt to summon up; **alles zusammengenommen** all in all ▷ vr **sich ~** to pull oneself together; (*fam*) to get a grip, to get one's act together; **zusammen|passen** vi to go together; (*Personen*) to be suited; **zusammen|rechnen** vt to add up

Zusammensein (-s) nt get-together

zusammen|setzen vt to put together ▷ vr **sich ~ aus** to be composed of sth; **Zusammensetzung** f composition

Zusammenstoß m crash, collision; **zusammen|stoßen** irr vi to crash (*mit* into)

zusammen|zählen vt to add up

zusammen|ziehen irr vi (*in*

Wohnung etc) to move in together

Zusatz m addition; **Zusatzgerät** nt attachment; (*Inform*) add-on; **zusätzlich** adj additional ▷ adv in addition

zu|schauen vi to watch; **Zuschauer(in)** (-s, -) m(f) spectator; **die ~** (pl) (*Theat*) the audience sing; **Zuschauertribüne** f stand

zu|schicken vt to send

Zuschlag m extra charge; (*Fahrkarte*) supplement; **zuschlagpflichtig** adj subject to an extra charge; (*Eisenb*) subject to a supplement

zu|schließen irr vt to lock up

zu|sehen irr vi to watch (*jdm* sb); **~, dass** (*dafür sorgen*) to make sure that

zu|sichern vt **jdm etw ~** to assure sb of sth

Zustand m state, condition; **sie bekommt Zustände, wenn sie das sieht** (*fam*) she'll have a fit if she sees that

zustande adv **~ bringen** to bring about; **~ kommen** to come about

zuständig adj (*Behörde*) relevant; **~ für** responsible for

Zustellung f delivery

zu|stimmen vi to agree (*einer Sache dat* to sth, *jdm* with sb); **Zustimmung** f approval

zu|stoßen irr vi (*fig*) to happen (*jdm* to sb)

Zutaten pl ingredients pl

zu|trauen vt **jdm etw ~** to think sb is capable of sth; **das hätte ich ihm nie zugetraut** I'd never have thought he was capable of it; **ich würde es ihr ~** (*etw Negatives*) I wouldn't put it past her; **Zutrauen** (-s) nt confidence (*zu* in); **zutrau-**

lich adj trusting; (Tier) friendly

zu|treffen irr vi to be correct; ~ auf (+akk) to apply to; Zutreffendes bitte streichen please delete as applicable

Zutritt m entry; (Zugang) access; ~ verboten! no entry

zuverlässig adj reliable; Zuverlässigkeit f reliability

Zuversicht f confidence; zuversichtlich adj confident

zuvor adv before; (zunächst) first; zuvor|kommen irr vi jdm ~ to beat sb to it; zuvorkommend adj obliging

Zuwachs (-es, Zuwächse) m increase, growth; (fam: Baby) addition to the family

zuwider adv es ist mir ~ I hate (o detest) it

zuzüglich prep +gen plus

zwang imperf von zwingen

Zwang (-(e)s, Zwänge) m (innerer) compulsion; (Gewalt) force

zwängen vt to squeeze (in +akk into) ▷ vr sich ~ to squeeze (in +akk into)

zwanglos adj informal

zwanzig num twenty, zwanzigste(r, s) adj twentieth; siehe auch dritte

zwar adv und ~ ... (genauer) ..., to be precise, das ist ~ schön, aber ... it is nice, but ...; ich kenne ihn ~, aber ... I know him all right, but ...

Zweck (-(e)s, -e) m purpose; zwecklos adj pointless

zwei num two; Zwei (-, -en) f two; (Schulnote) ≈ B; Zweibettzimmer nt twin room; zweideutig adj ambiguous; (unanständig) suggestive; zweifach adj, adv double

Zweifel (-s,) m doubt; zweifellos adj undoubtedly; zwei-

feln vi to doubt (an etw dat sth); Zweifelsfall m im ~ in case of doubt

Zweig (-(e)s, -e) m branch

Zweigstelle f branch

zweihundert num two hundred; zweimal adv twice; zweisprachig adj bilingual; zweispurig adj (Auto) two-lane; zweit adv wir sind zu ~ there are two of us; zweite(r, s) adj second; siehe auch dritte eine ~ Portion a second helping; zweitens adv secondly; (bei Aufzählungen) second; zweitgrößte(r, s) adj second largest; Zweitschlüssel m spare key

Zwerchfell nt diaphragm

Zwerg(in) (-(e)s, -e) m(f) dwarf

Zwetschge (-, -n) f plum

zwicken vt to pinch

Zwieback (-(e)s, -e) m rusk

Zwiebel (-, -n) f onion; (von Blume) bulb; Zwiebelsuppe f onion soup

Zwilling (-s, -e) m twin; ~e (pl) (Astr) Gemini sing

zwingen (zwang, gezwungen) vt to force

zwinkern vi to blink; (absichtlich) to wink

zwischen prep +akk o dat between

Zwischenablage f (Inform) clipboard

zwischendurch adv in between

Zwischenfall m incident

Zwischenlandung f stopover

zwischenmenschlich adj interpersonal

Zwischenraum m space

Zwischenstopp (-s, -s) m stopover

Zwischensumme f subtotal

Zwischenzeit f in der ~ in the meantime

zwitschern vt, vi to twitter, to

chirp
zwölf *num* twelve; **zwölfte(r, s)** *adj* twelfth; *siehe auch* **dritte**

Zylinder (*-s, -*) *m* cylinder; (*Hut*) top hat; **Zylinderkopfdichtung** *f* cylinder-head gasket

zynisch *adj* cynical

Zypern (*-s*) *nt* Cyprus

Zyste (*-, -n*) *f* cyst

a, an [eɪ, ə; æn, ən] *art* ein/eine/
ein; **~ man** ein Mann; **~ woman** eine
Frau; **~ apple** ein Apfel; **he's ~
student** er ist Student; **~ thousand**
tausend; **three times ~ week** dreimal pro Woche ▷ in der Woche

AA *abbr* = **Automobile Association**
britischer Automobilklub, ≈ ADAC *m*

aback *adv* **taken ~** erstaunt

abandon [əˈbændən] *vt* (*desert*)
verlassen; (*give up*) aufgeben

abbey [ˈæbɪ] *n* Abtei *f*

abbreviate [əˈbriːvɪeɪt] *vt* ab-
kürzen; **abbreviation** [əbriːv-
ɪˈeɪʃən] *n* Abkürzung *f*

ABC [ˈeɪbiːˈsiː] *n* (*a. fig*) Abc *nt*

abdicate [ˈæbdɪkeɪt] *vi* (*king*) ab-
danken; **abdication** [æbdɪˈkeɪʃən]
n Abdankung *f*

abdomen [ˈæbdəmən] *n* Unterleib *m*

ability [əˈbɪlɪtɪ] *n* Fähigkeit *f*;

able [ˈeɪbl] *adj* fähig; **to be ~ to do
sth** etw tun können

abnormal [æbˈnɔːml] *adj* anor-
mal

aboard [əˈbɔːd] *adv, prep* an Bord
+*gen*

abolish [əˈbɒlɪʃ] *vt* abschaffen

aborigine [æbəˈrɪdʒɪniː] *n* Ur-
einwohner(in) *m(f)* (Australiens)

abort [əˈbɔːt] *vt* (*Med: foetus*) ab-
treiben; (*Space: mission*) abbrechen;
abortion [əˈbɔːʃən] *n* Abtreibung *f*

about [əˈbaut] *adv* (*around*) herum, umher; (*approximately*) ungefähr; (*with time*) gegen; **to be ~ to
do** im Begriff sein zu; **there are a lot of
people ~** es sind eine Menge Leute
da ▷ *prep* (*concerning*) über +*akk*;
there is nothing you can do ~ it da
kann man nichts machen

above [əˈbʌv] *adv* oben; **children
aged 8 and ~** Kinder ab 8 Jahren; **on
the floor ~** ein Stockwerk höher ▷
prep über; **~ 40 degrees** über 40
Grad; **~ all** vor allem ▷ *adj* obig

abroad [əˈbrɔːd] *adv* im Ausland;
to go ~ ins Ausland gehen

abrupt [əˈbrʌpt] *adj* (*sudden*)
plötzlich, abrupt

abscess [ˈæbsɪs] *n* Geschwür *nt*

absence [ˈæbsəns] *n* Abwesenheit *f*; **absent** [ˈæbsənt] *adj* abwesend; **to be ~** fehlen, absent-
minded *adj* zerstreut

absolute [ˈæbsəluːt] *adj* absolut;
(*power*) unumschränkt; (*rubbish*)
vollkommen, total; **absolutely** *adv*
absolut; (*true, stupid*) vollkommen;
~! genau!, you're ~ right du hast
Sie haben völlig Recht

absorb [əbˈzɔːb] *vt* absorbieren;
(*fig: information*) in sich aufnehmen;

absorbed adj ~ **in sth** in etw vertieft; **absorbent** adj absorbierend; ~ **cotton** (US) Watte f; **absorbing** adj (fig) faszinierend, fesselnd

abstain [əb'steɪn] vi **to** ~ **(from voting)** sich (der Stimme) enthalten

abstract [æb'strækt] adj abstrakt

absurd [əb'sɜːd] adj absurd

abundance [ə'bʌndəns] n Reichtum m (of an +dat)

abuse [ə'bjuːs] n (rude language) Beschimpfungen pl; (mistreatment) Missbrauch m ▷ [ə'bjuːz] vt (misuse) missbrauchen; **abusive** [ə'bjuːsɪv] adj beleidigend

AC abbr = **alternating current** Wechselstrom m ▷ abbr = **air conditioning** Klimaanlage

a / c abbr = account Kto.

academic [ækə'demɪk] n Wissenschaftler(in) m(f) ▷ adj akademisch, wissenschaftlich

accelerate [æk'seləreɪt] vi (car etc) beschleunigen; (driver) Gas geben; **acceleration** [ækselə'reɪʃən] n Beschleunigung f; **accelerator** [ək'seləreɪtə⁺] n Gas(pedal) nt

accent [æksənt] n Akzent m

accept [ək'sept] vt annehmen; (agree to) akzeptieren; (responsibility) übernehmen; **acceptable** [ək'septəbl] adj annehmbar

access [ækses] n Zugang m; (inform) Zugriff m; **accessible** [æk'sesəbl] adj (easily) zugänglich / erreichbar; (place) (leicht) erreichbar

accessory [æk'sesərɪ] n Zubehörteil nt

access road n Zufahrtsstraße f

accident [æksɪdənt] n Unfall m; **by** ~ zufällig; **accidental** [æksɪ'dentl] adj unbeabsichtigt; (meeting) zufällig; (death) durch Unfall; ~ **damage** Unfallschaden m; **accident-prone** adj vom Pech verfolgt

acclimatize [ə'klaɪmətaɪz] vt **to**

~ **oneself** sich gewöhnen (to an +akk)

accommodate [ə'kɒmədeɪt] vt unterbringen; **accommodation(s)** [əkɒmə'deɪʃən(z)] n Unterkunft f

accompany [ə'kʌmpənɪ] vt begleiten

accomplish [ə'kʌmplɪʃ] vt erreichen

accord [ə'kɔːd] n **of one's own** ~ freiwillig; **according to** prep nach, laut +dat

account [ə'kaʊnt] n (in bank etc) Konto nt; (narrative) Bericht m; **on** ~ of wegen; **on no** ~ auf keinen Fall; **to take into** ~ berücksichtigen, in Betracht ziehen; **accountant** [ə'kaʊntənt] n Buchhalter(in) m(f); **account for** vt (explain) erklären; (expenditure) Rechenschaft ablegen für; **account number** n Kontonummer f

accumulate [ə'kjuːmjʊleɪt] vt ansammeln ▷ vi sich ansammeln

accuracy [ækjʊrəsɪ] n Genauigkeit f; **accurate** [ækjʊrɪt] adj genau

accusation [ækjʊ'zeɪʃən] n Anklage f, Beschuldigung f

accusative [ə'kjuːzətɪv] n Akkusativ m

accuse [ə'kjuːz] vt beschuldigen; (Jur) anklagen (of wegen +gen); ~ **sb of doing sth** jdn beschuldigen, etw getan zu haben; **accused** n (Jur) Angeklagte(r) mf

accustom [ə'kʌstəm] vt gewöhnen (to an +akk); **accustomed** adj gewohnt; **to get** ~ **to sth** sich an etw akk gewöhnen

ace [eɪs] n Ass nt ▷ adj Star-

ache [eɪk] n Schmerz m ▷ vi wehtun

achieve [ə'tʃiːv] vt erreichen; **achievement** n Leistung f

acid [æsɪd] n Säure f ▷ adj sauer;

~ rain saurer Regen

acknowledge [əkˈnɒlɪdʒ] vt (recognize) anerkennen; (admit) zugeben; (receipt of letter etc) bestätigen; **acknowledgement** n Anerkennung f; (of letter) Empfangsbestätigung f

acne [ˈæknɪ] n Akne f

acorn [ˈeɪkɔːn] n Eichel f

acoustic [əˈkuːstɪk] adj akustisch; **acoustics** [əˈkuːstɪks] npl Akustik f

acquaintance [əˈkweɪntəns] n (person) Bekannte(r) f

acquire [əˈkwaɪə*] vt erwerben, sich aneignen; **acquisition** [ækwɪˈzɪʃn] n (of skills etc) Erwerb m; (object) Anschaffung f

acrobat [ˈækrəbæt] n Akrobat(in) m(f)

across [əˈkrɒs] prep über +akk; **he lives ~ the street** er wohnt auf der anderen Seite der Straße ▷ adv hinüber, herüber; **100m ~** 100m breit

act [ækt] n (deed) Tat f; (Jur: law) Gesetz nt; (Theat) Akt m; (fig: pretence) Schau f; **it's all an ~** es ist alles nur Theater; **to be in the ~ of doing sth** gerade dabei sein, etw zu tun ▷ vi (take action) handeln; (behave) sich verhalten; (Theat) spielen; **to ~ as** (person) fungieren als; (thing) dienen als ▷ vt (a part) spielen

action [ˈækʃən] n (of play, novel etc) Handlung f; (in film etc) Action f; (Mil) Kampf m; **to take ~** etwas unternehmen; **out of ~** (machine) außer Betrieb; **to put a plan into ~** einen Plan in die Tat umsetzen; **action replay** n (Sport, TV) Wiederholung f

active [ˈæktɪv] adj aktiv; (child) lebhaft; **activity** [ækˈtɪvɪtɪ] n Aktivität f; (occupation) Beschäftigung f; (organized event) Veranstaltung f

actor [ˈæktə*] n Schauspieler(in) m(f); **actress** [ˈæktrɪs] n Schau-

spielerin f

actual [ˈæktjʊəl] adj wirklich; **actually** adv eigentlich; (said in surprise) tatsächlich

acupuncture [ˈækjʊpʌŋktʃə*] n Akupunktur f

acute [əˈkjuːt] adj (pain) akut; (sense of smell) fein; (Math: angle) spitz

ad [æd] abbr = advertisement

AD abbr = Anno Domini nach Christi, n. Chr.

adapt [əˈdæpt] vi sich anpassen (to +dat) ▷ vt anpassen (to +dat); (rewrite) bearbeiten (for für); **adaptable** adj anpassungsfähig; **adaptation** n (of book etc) Bearbeitung f; **adapter** n (Elec) Zwischenstecker m, Adapter m

add [æd] vt (ingredient) hinzufügen; (numbers) addieren; **add up** vi (make sense) stimmen ▷ vt (numbers) addieren

addict [ˈædɪkt] n Süchtige(r) mf; **addicted** [əˈdɪktɪd] adj **~ to alcohol/drugs** alkohol-/drogensüchtig

addition [əˈdɪʃən] n Zusatz m; (to bill) Aufschlag m; (Math) Addition f; **in ~** außerdem, zusätzlich (to zu); **additional** adj zusätzlich, weiter; **additive** [ˈædɪtɪv] n Zusatz m; **add-on** [ˈædɒn] n Zusatzgerät nt

address [əˈdrɛs] n Adresse f ▷ vt (letter) adressieren; (person) anreden

adequate [ˈædɪkwɪt] adj (appropriate) angemessen; (sufficient) ausreichend; (time) genügend

adhesive [ədˈhiːsɪv] n Klebstoff m; **adhesive tape** n Klebestreifen m

adjacent [əˈdʒeɪsənt] adj benachbart

adjective [ˈædʒəktɪv] n Adjektiv nt

adjoining [əˈdʒɔɪnɪŋ] adj benachbart, Neben-

adjust [əˈdʒʌst] vt einstellen; (put

right also) richtig stellen; (*speed, flow*) regulieren; (*in position*) verstellen ▷ vi sich anpassen (*to +dat*); **adjustable** *adj* verstellbar

admin [ædˈmɪn] *n* (*fam*) Verwaltung *f*; **administration** [ædmɪnɪsˈtreɪʃən] *n* Verwaltung *f*; (*Pol*) Regierung *f*

admirable [ˈædmərəbl] *adj* bewundernswert; **admiration** [ædmɪˈreɪʃən] *n* Bewunderung *f*; **admire** [ədˈmaɪə*] *vt* bewundern

admission [ədˈmɪʃən] *n* (*entrance*) Zutritt *m*; (*to university etc*) Zulassung *f*; (*fee*) Eintritt *m*; (*confession*) Eingeständnis *nt*; **admission charge**, **admission fee** *n* Eintrittspreis *m*; **admit** [ədˈmɪt] *vt* (*let in*) hereinlassen (*to in +akk*); (*to university etc*) zulassen; (*confess*) zugeben, gestehen; **to be ~ted to hospital** ins Krankenhaus eingeliefert werden

adolescent [ædəˈlesnt] *n* Jugendliche(r) *mf*

adopt [əˈdɒpt] *vt* (*child*) adoptieren; (*idea*) übernehmen; **adoption** [əˈdɒptʃn] *n* (*of child*) Adoption *f*; (*of idea*) Übernahme *f*

adorable [əˈdɔːrəbl] *adj* entzückend; **adore** [əˈdɔː*] *vt* anbeten; (*person*) über alles lieben, vergöttern

adult [ˈædʌlt] *adj* (*person*) erwachsen; (*film etc*) für Erwachsene ▷ *n* Erwachsene(r) *mf*

adultery [əˈdʌltəri] *n* Ehebruch *m*

advance [ədˈvɑːns] *n* (*money*) Vorschuss *m*; (*progress*) Fortschritt *m*; **in ~** im Voraus; **to book in ~** vorbestellen ▷ vi (*move forward*) vorrücken ▷ vt (*money*) vorschießen; **advance booking** *n* Reservierung *f*; (*Theat*) Vorverkauf *m*; **advanced** *adj* (*modern*) fortschrittlich; (*course, study*) für Fortgeschrittene; **advance payment** *n* Vorauszahlung *f*

advantage [ədˈvɑːntɪdʒ] *n* Vorteil *m*; **to take ~ of** (*exploit*) ausnutzen; (*profit from*) Nutzen ziehen aus; **it's to your ~** es ist in deinem / Ihrem Interesse

adventure [ədˈventʃə*] *n* Abenteuer *nt*; **adventure holiday** *n* Abenteuerurlaub *m*; **adventure playground** *n* Abenteuerspielplatz *m*; **adventurous** [ədˈventʃərəs] *adj* (*person*) abenteuerlustig

adverb [ˈædvɜːb] *n* Adverb *nt*

adverse [ˈædvɜːs] *adj* (*conditions etc*) ungünstig; (*effect, comment etc*) negativ

advert [ˈædvɜːt] *n* Anzeige *f*; **advertise** [ˈædvətaɪz] *vt* werben für; (*in newspaper*) inserieren; (*job*) ausschreiben ▷ vi Reklame machen; (*in newspaper*) annoncieren (*for* für); **advertisement** [ədˈvɜːtɪsmənt] *n* Werbung *f*; (*announcement*) Anzeige *f*; **advertising** *n* Werbung *f*

advice [ədˈvaɪs] *n* Rat(schlag) *m*; **word o piece of ~** Ratschlag *m*; **take my ~** hör auf mich; **advisable** [ədˈvaɪzəbl] *adj* ratsam; **advise** [ədˈvaɪz] *vt* raten (*sb* jdm); **to ~ sb to do sth / not to do sth** jdm zuraten / abraten, etw zu tun

Aegean [iːˈdʒiːən] *n* **the ~ (Sea)** die Ägäis

aerial [ˈɛəriəl] *n* Antenne *f* ▷ *adj* Luft-

aerobatics [ɛərəʊˈbætɪks] *npl* Kunstfliegen *nt*

aerobics [ɛəˈrəʊbɪks] *nsing* Aerobic *nt*

aeroplane [ˈɛərəpleɪn] *n* Flugzeug *nt*

afaik *abbr* = **as far as I know**; (*SMS*) ≈ soweit ich weiß

affair [əˈfɛə*] *n* (*matter, business*) Sache *f*, Angelegenheit *f*; (*scandal*) Affäre *f*; (*love affair*) Verhältnis *nt*

affect [əˈfekt] *vt* (*influence*) (ein)-

wirken auf +akk; (health, organ) angreifen; (move deeply) berühren; (concern) betreffen; **affection** [ə'fekʃən] n Zuneigung f; **affectionate** [ə'fekʃənɪt] adj liebevoll

affluent ['æfluənt] adj wohlhabend

afford [ə'fɔːd] vt sich leisten; **I can't ~ it** ich kann es mir nicht leisten; **affordable** [ə'fɔːdəbl] adj erschwinglich

Afghanistan [æf'gænɪstæn] n Afghanistan nt

aforementioned [əfɔː'menʃənd] adj oben genannt

afraid [ə'freɪd] adj **to be ~** Angst haben (of vor +dat); **to be ~ that …** fürchten, dass …; **I'm ~ I don't know** das weiß ich leider nicht

Africa ['æfrɪkə] n Afrika nt; **African** adj afrikanisch ▷ n Afrikaner(in) m(f); **African American**, **Afro-American** n Afroamerikaner(in) m(f)

after ['ɑːftə*] prep nach; **ten ~ five** (US) zehn nach fünf; **to be ~ sb/sth** (following, seeking) hinter jdm / etw her sein; **~ all** schließlich; (in spite of everything) (schließlich) doch ▷ conj nachdem ▷ adv **soon ~** bald danach; **aftercare** n Nachbehandlung f; **after-effect** n Nachwirkung f

afternoon n Nachmittag m; **~, good ~** guten Tag!; **in the ~** nach mittags

afters npl Nachtisch m; **after-sales service** n Kundendienst m; **after-shave (lotion)** n Rasierwasser nt; **after-sun lotion** n After-Sun-Lotion f; **afterwards** adv nachher; (after that) danach

again [ə'gen] adv wieder; (one more time) noch einmal; **not ~!** (nicht) schon wieder!; **~ and ~** immer wieder; **the same ~ please** das Gleiche

noch mal bitte

against [ə'genst] prep gegen; **~ my will** wider Willen; **~ the law** unrechtmäßig, illegal

age [eɪdʒ] n Alter nt; (period of history) Zeitalter nt; **at the ~ of four** im Alter von vier (Jahren); **what ~ is she?, what is her ~?** wie alt ist sie?; **to come of ~** volljährig werden; **under ~** minderjährig ▷ vi altern, alt werden; **aged** adj: **~ thirty** dreißig Jahre alt; **a son ~ twenty** ein zwanzigjähriger Sohn ▷ adj ['eɪdʒɪd] (elderly) betagt; **age group** n Altersgruppe f; **ageism** n Diskriminierung f aufgrund des Alters; **age limit** n Altersgrenze f

agency ['eɪdʒənsɪ] n Agentur f

agenda [ə'dʒendə] n Tagesordnung f

agent ['eɪdʒənt] n (Comm) Vertreter(in) m(f); (for writer, actor etc) Agent(in) m(f)

aggression [ə'greʃn] n Aggression f; **aggressive** [ə'gresɪv] adj aggressiv

agitated adj aufgeregt; **to get ~** sich aufregen

AGM abbr = **Annual General Meeting** JHV f

ago [ə'gəu] adv **two days ~** heute vor zwei Tagen; **not long ~** (erst) vor kurzem

agonize ['ægənaɪz] vi sich den Kopf zerbrechen (over über dat); **agonizing** adj qualvoll; **agony** ['ægənɪ] n Qual f

agree [ə'griː] vt (date, price etc) vereinbaren; **to ~ to do sth** sich bereit erklären, etw zu tun; **to ~ that …** sich darauf einigen, dass …; (deride) beschließen, dass …; (admit) zugeben, dass … ▷ vi (have same opinion, correspond) übereinstimmen (with mit); (consent) zustimmen; (come to an agreement) sich einigen (*about, on* auf +akk); (*food*) **not to ~ with sb** jdm nicht bekommen; **agreement** n (*agreeing*) Übereinstimmung f; (*contract*) Abkommen nt, Vereinbarung f

agricultural [ægrɪˈkʌltʃərəl] adj landwirtschaftlich, Landwirtschafts-; **agriculture** ['ægrɪkʌltʃə*] n Landwirtschaft f

ahead [əˈhed] adv to be ~ führen, vorne liegen; **~ of** vor +dat; **to be ~ of sb** (*person*) jdm voraus sein; (*fig*) vor jdm liegen; **to be 3 metres ~** 3 Meter Vorsprung haben

aid [eɪd] n Hilfe f; **in ~ of** zugunsten +gen; **with the ~ of** mithilfe +gen ▷ vt helfen +dat; (*support*) unterstützen

Aids [eɪdz] n acr = **acquired immune deficiency syndrome** Aids nt

aim [eɪm] vt (*gun, camera*) richten (*at* auf +akk) ▷ vi **to ~ at** (*with gun etc*) zielen auf +akk; (*fig*) abzielen auf +akk; **to ~ to do sth** beabsichtigen, etw zu tun ▷ n Ziel nt

air [ɛə*] n Luft f; **in the open ~** im Freien; (*Radio, Tv*) **to be on the ~** (*programme*) auf Sendung sein; (*station*) senden ▷ vt lüften; **airbag** n (*Auto*) Airbag m; **air-conditioned** adj mit Klimaanlage; **air-conditioning** n Klimaanlage f; **aircraft** n Flugzeug nt; **airfield** n Flugplatz m; **air force** n Luftwaffe f; **airgun** n Luftgewehr nt; **airline** n Fluggesellschaft f; **airmail** n Luftpost f; **by ~** mit Luftpost; **airplane** n (*US*) Flugzeug nt; **air pollution** n Luftverschmutzung f; **airport** n Flughafen m; **airsick** adj luftkrank; **airtight** adj luftdicht; **air-traffic controller** n Fluglotse m, Fluglotsin f; **airy** adj luftig; (*manner*) lässig

aisle [aɪl] n Gang m; (*in church*) Seitenschiff nt; **~ seat** Sitz m am Gang

ajar [əˈdʒɑː*] adj (*door*) angelehnt

alarm [əˈlɑːm] n (*warning*) Alarm m; (*bell etc*) Alarmanlage f ▷ vt beunruhigen; **alarm clock** n Wecker m; **alarmed** adj (*protected*) alarmgesichert; **alarming** adj beunruhigend

Albania [ælˈbeɪnɪə] n Albanien nt; **Albanian** adj albanisch ▷ n (*person*) Albaner(in) m(f); (*language*) Albanisch nt

album ['ælbəm] n Album nt

alcohol ['ælkəhɒl] n Alkohol m; **alcohol-free** adj alkoholfrei; **alcoholic** [ælkəˈhɒlɪk] adj (*drink*) alkoholisch ▷ n Alkoholiker(in) m(f); **alcoholism** n Alkoholismus m

ale [eɪl] n Ale nt (*helles englisches Bier*)

alert [əˈlɜːt] adj wachsam ▷ n Alarm m ▷ vt warnen (*to* vor +dat)

algebra ['ældʒɪbrə] n Algebra f

Algeria [ælˈdʒɪərɪə] n Algerien nt

alibi ['ælɪbaɪ] n Alibi nt

alien ['eɪlɪən] n (*foreigner*) Ausländer(in) m(f); (*from space*) Außerirdische(r) mf

align [əˈlaɪn] vt ausrichten (*with* auf +akk)

alike [əˈlaɪk] adj, adv gleich; (*similar*) ähnlich

alive [əˈlaɪv] adj lebendig; **to keep sth ~** etw am Leben erhalten; **he's still ~** er lebt noch

all [ɔːl] adj (*plural, every one of*) alle; (*singular, the whole of*) ganz; **~ the children** alle Kinder; **~ the time** die ganze Zeit; **~ his life** sein ganzes Leben; **why me ~ people?** warum ausgerechnet ich? ▷ pron (*everything*) alles; (*everybody*) alle; **~ of** ganz; **~ of them came** sie kamen alle ▷ adv (*completely*) ganz; **it's ~ over** es ist ganz aus; **~ along** von Anfang an; **~ at once** auf einmal; **~ the nicer** umso netter

allegation [ælɪ'geɪʃən] n Behauptung f; **alleged** adj angeblich

allergic [ə'lɜːdʒɪk] adj allergisch (to gegen); **allergy** ['ælədʒɪ] n Allergie f

alleviate [ə'liːvɪeɪt] vt (pain) lindern

alley ['ælɪ] n (enge) Gasse; (passage) Durchgang m; (bowling) Bahn f

alliance [ə'laɪəns] n Bündnis nt

alligator ['ælɪgeɪtə*] n Alligator m

all-night (café, cinema) die ganze Nacht geöffnet

allocate ['æləkeɪt] vt zuweisen, zuteilen (to dat)

allotment n (plot) Schrebergarten m

allow [ə'lau] vt (permit) erlauben (sb jdm); (grant) bewilligen; (time) einplanen; **allow for** vt berücksichtigen; (cost etc) einkalkulieren; **allowance** n (from state) Beihilfe f; (from parent) Unterhaltsgeld nt

all right ['ɔːl'raɪt] adj okay, in Ordnung; **I'm ~** mir geht's gut ▷ (satisfactorily) ganz gut ▷ interj okay

all-time adj (record, high) aller Zeiten

allusion [ə'luːʒən] n Anspielung f (to auf +akk)

all-wheel drive ['ɔːlwiːl'draɪv] n (Auto) Allradantrieb m

ally ['ælaɪ] n Verbündete(r) mf; (Hist) Alliierte(r) mf

almond ['aːmənd] n Mandel f

almost ['ɔːlməust] adv fast

alone [ə'ləun] adj, adv allein

along [ə'lɒŋ] prep entlang +akk; **~ the river** den Fluss entlang; (position) am Fluss entlang ▷ adv (onward) weiter; **~ with** zusammen mit; **all ~** die ganze Zeit; **alongside** prep neben +dat ▷ adv (walk) nebenher

aloud [ə'laud] adv laut

alphabet ['ælfəbet] n Alphabet nt

alpine ['ælpaɪn] adj alpin; **Alps**

[ælps] npl **the ~** die Alpen

already [ɔːl'redɪ] adv schon, bereits

Alsace ['ælsæs] n Elsass nt; **Alsatian** [æl'seɪʃən] adj elsässisch ▷ n Elsässer(in) m(f); (BRIT: dog) Schäferhund m

also ['ɔːlsəu] adv auch

altar ['ɔːltə*] n Altar m

alter ['ɔːltə*] vt ändern; **alteration** [ɔːltə'reɪʃən] n Änderung f; **~s** (to building) Umbau m

alternate [ɔːl'tɜːnət] adj abwechselnd ▷ ['ɔːltəneɪt] vi abwechseln (with mit); **alternating current** n Wechselstrom m

alternative [ɔːl'tɜːnətɪv] adj Alternativ- ▷ n Alternative f

although [ɔːl'ðəu] conj obwohl

altitude ['æltɪtjuːd] n Höhe f

altogether [ɔːltə'geðə*] adv (in total) insgesamt; (entirely) ganz und gar

aluminium, **aluminum** (US) [æljʊ-'mɪnɪəm, ə'luːmɪnəm] n Aluminium nt

always ['ɔːlweɪz] adv immer

am [æm] present of **be**; bin

a.m. adv abbr = **ante meridiem** vormittags, vorm.

amateur ['æmətə*] n Amateur(in) m(f) ▷ adj Amateur-; (theatre, choir) Laien-

amaze [ə'meɪz] vt erstaunen; **amazed** adj erstaunt (at über +akk); **amazing** adj erstaunlich

Amazon ['æməzən] n **~ (river)** Amazonas m

ambassador [æm'bæsədə*] n Botschafter m

amber ['æmbə*] n Bernstein m

ambiguity [æmbɪ'gjuɪtɪ] n Zweideutigkeit f; **ambiguous** [æm'bɪgjuəs] adj zweideutig

ambition [æm'bɪʃən] n Ambition f; (ambitious nature) Ehrgeiz m; **am-**

(*ambitious nature*) Ehrgeiz m; **ambitious** [æm'bɪʃəs] *adj* ehrgeizig

ambulance [ˈæmbjʊləns] n Krankenwagen m

amend [əˈmend] vt (*law etc*) ändern

America [əˈmerɪkə] n Amerika nt; **American** *adj* amerikanisch ▷ n Amerikaner(in) m(f); **native ~** Indianer(in) m(f)

amiable [ˈeɪmɪəbl] *adj* liebenswürdig

amicable [ˈæmɪkəbl] *adj* freundlich; (*relations*) freundschaftlich; (*Jur: settlement*) gütlich

amnesia [æmˈniːzɪə] n Gedächtnisverlust m

among(st) [əˈmʌŋ(st)] *prep* unter +dat

amount [əˈmaʊnt] n (*quantity*) Menge f; (*of money*) Betrag m; **a large/small ~ of ...** ziemlich viel/wenig ... ▷ vi **to ~ to** (*total*) sich belaufen auf +akk

amp, ampere [æmp, ˈæmpeəʳ] n Ampere nt

amplifier [ˈæmplɪfaɪəʳ] n Verstärker m

amputate [ˈæmpjʊteɪt] vt amputieren

Amtrak® [ˈæmtræk] n amerikanische Eisenbahngesellschaft

amuse [əˈmjuːz] vt amüsieren; (*entertain*) unterhalten; **amused** *adj* **I'm not ~** das finde ich gar nicht lustig; **amusement** n (*enjoyment*) Vergnügen nt; (*recreation*) Unterhaltung f; **amusement arcade** n Spielhalle f; **amusement park** n Vergnügungspark m; **amusing** *adj* amüsant

an [æn, ən] *art* ein(e)

anaemic [əˈniːmɪk] *adj* blutarm

anaesthetic [ænɪsˈθetɪk] n Narkose f; (*substance*) Narkosemittel nt

analyse, analyze [ˈænəlaɪz] vt

analysieren; **analysis** [əˈnælɪsɪs] n Analyse f

anatomy [əˈnætəmɪ] n Anatomie f; (*structure*) Körperbau m

ancestor [ˈænsestəʳ] n Vorfahr m

anchor [ˈæŋkəʳ] n Anker m ▷ vt verankern; **anchorage** n Ankerplatz m

anchovy [ˈæntʃəvɪ] n Sardelle f

ancient [ˈeɪnʃənt] *adj* alt; (*fam: person, clothes etc*) uralt

and [ænd, ənd] *conj* und

Andorra [ænˈdɔːrə] n Andorra nt

anemic *adj* (US) see **anaemic**

anesthetic n (US) see **anaesthetic**

angel [ˈeɪndʒəl] n Engel m

anger [ˈæŋɡəʳ] n Zorn m ▷ vt ärgern

angina, angina pectoris [ænˈdʒaɪnə(ˈpektərɪs)] n Angina Pectoris f

angle [ˈæŋɡl] n Winkel m; (*fig*) Standpunkt m

angler [ˈæŋɡləʳ] n Angler(in) m(f); **angling** [ˈæŋɡlɪŋ] n Angeln nt

angry [ˈæŋɡrɪ] *adj* verärgert; (*stronger*) zornig; **to be ~ with sb** auf jdn böse sein

angular [ˈæŋɡjʊləʳ] *adj* eckig; (*face*) kantig

animal [ˈænɪməl] n Tier nt; **animal rights** npl Tierrechte pl

animated [ˈænɪmeɪtɪd] *adj* lebhaft; **~ film** Zeichentrickfilm m

aniseed [ˈænɪsiːd] n Anis m

ankle [ˈæŋkl] n (Fuß)knöchel m

annex [ˈæneks] n Anbau m

anniversary [ænɪˈvɜːsərɪ] n Jahrestag m

announce [əˈnaʊns] vt bekannt geben; (*officially*) bekannt machen; (*on radio, TV etc*) (*Radio, TV*) ansagen; **announcement** n Bekanntgabe f; (*official*) Bekanntmachung f; (*Radio, TV*) Ansage f; **announcer** n (*Radio, TV*) Ansager(in) m(f)

ance n Ärger m; **annoyed** adj
ärgerlich; **to be ~ with sb (about
sth)** sich über jdn (über etw) ärgern;
annoying adj ärgerlich; (person)
lästig, nervig

annual ['ænjʊəl] adj jährlich ▷ n
Jahrbuch nt

anonymous [ə'nɒnɪməs] adj
anonym

anorak ['ænəræk] n Anorak m;
(BRIT fam: pej) Freak m

anorexia [ænə'reksɪə] n Magersucht f; **anorexic** adj magersüchtig

another [ə'nʌðə*] adj, pron (different) ein(e) andere(r, s); (additional)
noch eine(r, s); **let me put it ~ way**
lass es mich anders sagen

answer ['ɑːnsə*] n Antwort f (to auf
+akk); (solution) Lösung f (+gen ▷ vi
antworten; (on phone) sich melden ▷
vt (person) antworten +dat; (letter,
question) beantworten; (telephone)
gehen an +akk, abnehmen; (door)
öffnen; **answer back** vi widersprechen; **answering machine** n Answerphone n Anrufbeantworter m

ant [ænt] n Ameise f

Antarctic [ænt'ɑːktɪk] n Antarktis f; **Antarctic Circle** n südlicher
Polarkreis

antelope ['æntɪləʊp] n Antilope f

antenna [æn'tenə] (pl **antennae**)
n (Zool) Fühler m; (Radio) Antenne f

anti- ['æntɪ] pref Anti-, anti-; **antibiotic** ['æntɪbaɪ'ɒtɪk] n Antibiotikum nt

anticipate [æn'tɪsɪpeɪt] vt (expect:
trouble, question) erwarten, rechnen
mit; **anticipation** [æntɪsɪ'peɪʃən]
n Erwartung f

anticlimax [æntɪ'klaɪmæks] n
Enttäuschung f; **anticlockwise**
[æntɪ'klɒkwaɪz] adv entgegen
dem Uhrzeigersinn

antidote ['æntɪdəʊt] n Gegenmittel nt; **antifreeze** n Frost-

schutzmittel nt

Antipodes [æn'tɪpədiːz] npl
Australien und Neuseeland

antiquarian [æntɪ'kweərɪən] adj
~ bookshop Antiquariat nt

antique [æn'tiːk] n Antiquität f ▷
adj antik; **antique shop** n Anti-
quitätengeschäft nt

anti-Semitism [æntɪ'semɪtɪzm]
n Antisemitismus m; **antiseptic**
[æntɪ'septɪk] n Antiseptikum nt ▷
adj antiseptisch; **antisocial** adj
(person) ungesellig, (behaviour) un-
sozial, asozial

antlers ['æntləz] npl Geweih nt

anxiety [æŋ'zaɪətɪ] n Sorge f
(about um); **anxious** ['æŋkʃəs] adj
besorgt (about um); (apprehensive)
ängstlich

any ['enɪ] adj (in question: untrans-
lated) **do you have ~ money?** hast
du Geld?; (with negative) **I don't have
~ money** ich habe kein Geld;
(whichever one likes) **take ~ card**
nimm irgendeine Karte ▷ pron (in
question) **do you want ~?** (singular)
willst du etwas (davon)?; (plural)
willst du welche?; (with negative) **I
don't have ~** ich habe keine/kei-
nen/keins; (whichever one likes) **you
can take ~ of them** du kannst je-
de(n, s) beliebige(n) nehmen ▷ adv
(in question) **are there ~ more
strawberries?** gibt es noch Erd-
beeren?; **can't you work ~ faster?**
kannst du nicht schneller arbeiten?;
(with negative) **not ~ longer** nicht
mehr; **this isn't ~ better** das ist
auch nicht besser; **anybody** pron
(whoever one likes) irgendjemand;
(everyone) jeder; (in question) jemand;
anyhow adv **I don't want to talk
about it, not now ~** ich möchte
nicht darüber sprechen, jedenfalls
nicht jetzt; **if I can help you ~** wenn
ich Ihnen irgendwie helfen kann;

they asked me not to go, but I went ~ sie baten mich, nicht hinzugehen, aber ich bin trotzdem hingegangen; **anyone** pron (whoever one likes) irgendjemand; (everyone) jeder; (in question) jemand; **isn't there ~ you can ask?** gibt es denn niemanden, den du fragen kannst?; **anyplace** adv (US) irgendwo; (direction) irgendwohin; (everywhere) überall; **anything** pron (whatever one likes, in question) irgend(etwas; (everything) alles; ~ **else?** sonst noch etwas?; ~ **but that** alles, nur das nicht; **she didn't tell me ~** sie hat mir nichts gesagt; **anytime** adv jederzeit; **anyway** adv **I didn't want to go there** ~ ich wollte da sowieso nicht hingehen; **thanks ~** trotzdem danke; ~, **as I was saying, ...** jedenfalls, wie ich schon sagte, ...; **anywhere** adv irgendwo; (direction) irgendwohin; (everywhere) überall

apart [ə'pɑːt] adv auseinander; ~ **from** außer; **live ~** getrennt leben **apartment** [ə'pɑːtmənt] n (esp US) Wohnung f; **apartment block** n (esp US) Wohnblock m **ape** [eɪp] n (Menschen)affe m **aperitif** [ə'peritif] n Aperitif m **aperture** ['æpətjʊə*] n Öffnung f; (Foto) Blende f **apologize** [ə'pɒlədʒaɪz] vi sich entschuldigen; **apology** n Entschuldigung f **apostrophe** [ə'pɒstrəfi] n Apostroph m **appalled** [ə'pɔːld] adj entsetzt (at über +akk); **appalling** adj entsetzlich **apparatus** [æpə'reɪtəs] n Apparat m; (piece of apparatus) Gerät nt **apparent** [ə'pærənt] adj (obvious) offensichtlich (to für); (seeming) scheinbar; **apparently** adv an-

scheinend

appeal [ə'piːl] vi (dringend) bitten (for um, to +akk); (Jur) Berufung einlegen; **to ~ to sb** (be attractive) jdm zusagen ▷ n Aufruf m (to an +akk); (Jur) Berufung f; (attraction) Reiz m; **appealing** adj ansprechend, attraktiv **appear** [ə'pɪə*] vi erscheinen; (Theat) auftreten; (seem) scheinen; **appearance** n Erscheinen nt; (Theat) Auftritt m; (look) Aussehen nt **appendicitis** [əpendɪ'saɪtɪs] n Blinddarmentzündung f; **appendix** [ə'pendɪks] n Blinddarm m; (to book) Anhang m **appetite** ['æpɪtaɪt] n Appetit m; (fig: desire) Verlangen nt; (sexual) Lust f; **appetizing** ['æpɪtaɪzɪŋ] adj appetitlich, appetitanregend **applause** [ə'plɔːz] n Beifall m, Applaus m **apple** ['æpl] n Apfel m; **apple crumble** n mit Streuseln bestreutes Apfeldessert; **apple juice** n Apfelsaft m; **apple pie** n gedeckter Apfelkuchen m; **apple puree, apple sauce** n Apfelmus nt; **apple tart** n Apfelkuchen m; **apple tree** n Apfelbaum m **appliance** [ə'plaɪəns] n Gerät nt; **applicable** [ə'plɪkəbl] adj anwendbar; (on forms) zutreffend; **applicant** ['æplɪkənt] n Bewerber(in) m(f); **application** [æplɪ'keɪʃən] n (request) Antrag m (for auf +akk); (for job) Bewerbung f (for um); **application form** n Anmeldeformular nt; **apply** [ə'plaɪ] vi (be relevant) zutreffen (to auf +akk); (for job etc) sich bewerben (for um) ▷ vt (cream, paint etc) auftragen; (put into practice) anwenden; (brakes) betätigen **appoint** [ə'pɔɪnt] vt (to post) ernennen; **appointment** n Verabredung f; (at doctor, hairdresser etc, in business) Termin m; **by** ~ nach Vereinbarung

appreciate [ə'priːʃɪeɪt] vt (value) zu schätzen wissen; (understand) einsehen, **to be much ~d** richtig gewürdigt werden ▷ vi (increase in value) im Wert steigen; **appreciation** [əpriːʃɪ'eɪʃən] n (esteem) Anerkennung f, Würdigung f; (of person also) Wertschätzung f

apprehensive [æprɪ'hensɪv] adj ängstlich

apprentice [ə'prentɪs] n Lehrling m

approach [ə'prəʊtʃ] vi sich nähern ▷ vt (place) sich nähern +dat; (person) herantreten an +akk; (problem) angehen

appropriate [ə'prəʊprɪət] adj passend; (to occasion) angemessen; (remark) treffend; **appropriately** adv passend; (expressed) treffend

approval [ə'pruːvəl] n (show of satisfaction) Anerkennung f; (permission) Zustimmung f (of zu); **approve** [ə'pruːv] vt billigen ▷ vi **to ~ of sth/sb** etw billigen/von jdm etwas halten; **I don't ~** ich missbillige das

approx [ə'prɒks] abbr = **approximately** ca.; **approximate** [ə'prɒksɪmɪt] adj ungefähr; **approximately** adv ungefähr, circa

apricot ['eɪprɪkɒt] n Aprikose f

April ['eɪprəl] n April m; see also **September**

apron ['eɪprən] n Schürze f

aptitude ['æptɪtjuːd] n Begabung f

aquaplaning ['ækwəpleɪnɪŋ] n (Auto) Aquaplaning nt

aquarium [ə'kweərɪəm] n Aquarium nt

Aquarius [ə'kweərɪəs] n (Astr) Wassermann m

Arab ['ærəb] n Araber(in) m(f); (horse) Araber m; **Arabian** [ə'reɪbɪən] adj arabisch; **Arabic** ['ærəbɪk] n (language) Arabisch nt ▷ adj arabisch

arbitrary ['ɑːbɪtrərɪ] adj willkürlich

arcade [ɑː'keɪd] n Arkade f; (shopping arcade) Einkaufspassage f

arch [ɑːtʃ] n Bogen m

archaeologist, archeologist (US) [ɑːkɪ'ɒlədʒɪst] n Archäologe m, Archäologin f; **archaeology, archeology** (US) [ɑːkɪ'ɒlədʒɪ] n Archäologie f

archaic [ɑː'keɪɪk] adj veraltet

archbishop [ɑːtʃ'bɪʃəp] n Erzbischof m

archery ['ɑːtʃərɪ] n Bogenschießen nt

architect ['ɑːkɪtekt] n Architekt(in) m(f); **architecture** [ɑːkɪ'tektʃə] n Architektur f

archive(s) ['ɑːkaɪv(z)] n(pl) Archiv nt

archway ['ɑːtʃweɪ] n Torbogen m

Arctic ['ɑːktɪk] n Arktis f; **Arctic Circle** n nördlicher Polarkreis

are [ɑː], unstressed [ə'*] present of **be**

area ['eərɪə] n (region, district) Gebiet nt, Gegend f; (amount of space) Fläche f; (part of building etc) Bereich m, Zone f; (fig: field) Bereich m; **the London** ~ der Londoner Raum; **area code** n (US) Vorwahl f

aren't [ɑːnt] contr of **are not**

Argentina [ɑːdʒən'tiːnə] n Argentinien nt

argue ['ɑːgjuː] vi streiten (about, over über +akk); **to ~ that** ... behaupten, dass ...; **to ~ for/against** ... sprechen für/gegen ...; **argument** n (reasons) Argument nt; (quarrel) Streit m; **to have an** ~ sich streiten

Aries ['eərɪːz] nsing (Astr) Widder m

arise [ə'raɪz] (**arose, arisen**) vi sich ergeben, entstehen; (problem, *question, wind*) aufkommen

aristocracy [ˌærɪsˈtɒkrəsɪ] *n* (*class*) Adel *m*; **aristocrat** [ˈærɪstəkræt] *n* Adlige(r) *mf*; **aristocratic** [ˌærɪstəˈkrætɪk] *adj* aristokratisch, adlig

arm [ɑːm] *n* Arm *m*; (*sleeve*) Ärmel *m*; (*of armchair*) Armlehne *f* ▷ *vt* bewaffnen; **armchair** [ˈɑːmtʃeəʳ] *n* Lehnstuhl *m*

armed [ɑːmd] *adj* bewaffnet

armpit [ˈɑːmpɪt] *n* Achselhöhle *f*

arms [ɑːmz] *npl* Waffen *pl*

army [ˈɑːmɪ] *n* Armee *f*, Heer *nt*

A road [ˈeɪrəʊd] *n* (*BRIT*) ≈ Bundesstraße *f*

aroma [əˈrəʊmə] *n* Duft *m*, Aroma *nt*; **aromatherapy** [ərəʊmə-ˈθerəpɪ] *n* Aromatherapie *f*

arose [əˈrəʊz] *pt of* **arise**

around [əˈraʊnd] *adv* herum, umher; (*present*) hier (irgendwo); (*approximately*) ungefähr; (*with time*) gegen; **he's ~ somewhere** er ist hier irgendwo in der Nähe ▷ *prep* (*surrounding*) um ... (herum); (*about in*) in ... herum

arr. *abbr* = **arrival, arrives** Ank.

arrange [əˈreɪndʒ] *vt* (*put in order*) (an)ordnen; (*alphabetically*) ordnen; (*artistically*) arrangieren; (*agree to: meeting etc*) vereinbaren, festsetzen; (*holidays*) festlegen; (*organize*) planen; **to ~ that ...** es so einrichten, dass ...; **we ~d to meet at eight o'clock** wir haben uns für acht Uhr verabredet; **it's all ~d** es ist alles arrangiert; **arrangement** *n* (*layout*) Anordnung *f*; (*agreement*) Vereinbarung *f*, Plan *m*; **make ~s** Vorbereitungen treffen

arrest [əˈrest] *vt* (*person*) verhaften ▷ *n* Verhaftung *f*; **under ~** verhaftet

arrival [əˈraɪvl] *n* Ankunft *f*; **new ~** (*person*) Neuankömmling *m*; **ar-**

rivals *n* (*airport*) Ankunftshalle *f*;

arrive [əˈraɪv] *vi* ankommen (*at* bei, in *+dat*); **to ~ at a solution** eine Lösung finden

arrogant [ˈærəgənt] *adj* arrogant

arrow [ˈærəʊ] *n* Pfeil *m*

arse [ɑːs] *n* (*vulg*) Arsch *m*

art [ɑːt] *n* Kunst *f*, **~s** (*pl*) Geisteswissenschaften *pl*

artery [ˈɑːtərɪ] *n* Schlagader *f*, Arterie *f*

art gallery *n* Kunstgalerie *f*, Kunstmuseum *nt*

arthritis [ɑːˈθraɪtɪs] *n* Arthritis *f*

artichoke [ˈɑːtɪtʃəʊk] *n* Artischocke *f*

article [ˈɑːtɪkl] *n* Artikel *m*; (*object*) Gegenstand *m*

artificial [ɑːtɪˈfɪʃl] *adj* künstlich, Kunst-; (*smile etc*) gekünstelt

artist [ˈɑːtɪst] *n* Künstler(in) *m(f)*; **artistic** [ɑːˈtɪstɪk] *adj* künstlerisch

as [æz, əz] *adj* (*like*) wie; (*in role of*) als; **such ~** (*for example*) ... wie etwa ...; **~ ... ~ so ...** wie; **~ soon ~ he comes** sobald er kommt; **twice ~ much** zweimal so viel; **not ~ nice** weniger schön; **to use / work ~ ...** verwenden / arbeiten als ...; **~ for / ~ to** betreff: **~ of ...** (*time*) ab ... *+dat* ▷ *conj* (*since*) da, weil; (*while*) als, während; **~ if, ~ though** als ob; **leave it ~ it is** lass es so (wie es ist); **~ it were** sozusagen

asap [ˌeɪeseɪˈpiː, ˈeɪsæp] *acr* = **as soon as possible** möglichst bald

ascertain [æsəˈteɪn] *vt* feststellen

ash [æʃ] *n* (*dust*) Asche *f*; (*tree*) Esche *f*

ashamed [əˈʃeɪmd] *adj* beschämt; **to be ~ (of sb / sth)** sich (für jdn / etw) schämen

ashore [əˈʃɔːʳ] *adv* an Land

ashtray [ˈæʃtreɪ] *n* Aschenbecher *m*

Asia [ˈeɪʃə] *n* Asien *nt*; **Asian** *adj*

asiatisch ▷ n Asiat(in) m(f)

aside [əˈsaɪd] adv beiseite, zur Seite; ~ **from** (esp US) außer

ask [ɑːsk] vt, vi fragen; (question) stellen; (request) bitten um; (invite) einladen; **to ~ sb the way** jdn nach dem Weg fragen; **to ~ sb to do sth** jdn darum bitten, etw zu tun; **ask for** vt bitten um

asleep [əˈsliːp] adj, adv **to be ~** schlafen; **to fall ~** einschlafen

asparagus [əˈspærəgəs] n Spargel m

aspect [ˈæspekt] n Aspekt m

aspirin [ˈæsprɪn] n Aspirin® nt

ass [æs] n (a. fig) Esel m; (US vulg) Arsch m

assassinate [əˈsæsɪneɪt] vt ermorden; **assassination** [əˈsæsɪneɪʃn] n Ermordung f; ~ **attempt** Attentat nt

assault [əˈsɔːlt] n Angriff m; (Jur) Körperverletzung f ▷ vt überfallen, herfallen über +akk

assemble [əˈsembl] vt (parts) zusammensetzen; (people) zusammenrufen ▷ vi sich versammeln; **assembly** [əˈsemblɪ] n (of people) Versammlung f; (putting together) Zusammensetzen nt; **assembly hall** n Aula f

assert [əˈsɜːt] vt behaupten; **assertion** [əˈsɜːʃən] n Behauptung f

assess [əˈses] vt einschätzen; **assessment** n Einschätzung f

asset [ˈæset] n Vermögenswert m, (fig) Vorteil m; ~**s** pl Vermögen nt

assign [əˈsaɪn] vt zuweisen; **assignment** n Aufgabe f; (mission) Auftrag m

assist [əˈsɪst] vt helfen +dat; **assistance** n Hilfe f; **assistant** n Assistent(in) m(f), Mitarbeiter(in) m(f); (in shop) Verkäufer(in) m(f)

associate [əˈsəʊʃieɪt] n (partner) Partner(in) m(f), Teilhaber(in) m(f) ▷

[əˈsəʊʃieɪt] vt verbinden (with mit)

association [əsəʊsɪˈeɪʃən] n (organization) Verband m, Vereinigung f; **in ~ with ...** in Zusammenarbeit mit ...

assorted [əˈsɔːtɪd] adj gemischt; **assortment** n Auswahl f (of an +dat); (of sweets) Mischung f

assume [əˈsjuːm] vt annehmen (that ... dass ...); (role, responsibility) übernehmen; **assumption** [əˈsʌmpʃən] n Annahme f

assurance [əˈʃʊərəns] n Versicherung f; (confidence) Zuversicht f; **assure** [əˈʃʊə*] vt (say confidently) versichern +dat; **to ~ sb of sth** jdm etw zusichern; **to be ~d of sth** einer Sache sicher sein

asterisk [ˈæstərɪsk] n Sternchen nt

asthma [ˈæsmə] n Asthma nt

astonish [əˈstɒnɪʃ] vt erstaunen; **astonished** adj erstaunt (at über); **astonishing** adj erstaunlich; **astonishment** n Erstaunen nt

astound [əˈstaʊnd] vt sehr erstaunen; **astounding** adj erstaunlich

astray [əˈstreɪ] adv **to go ~** (letter etc) verloren gehen; (person) vom Weg abkommen; **to lead ~** irreführen, verführen

astrology [əˈstrɒlədʒɪ] n Astrologie f

astronaut [ˈæstrənɔːt] n Astronaut(in) m(f)

astronomy [əˈstrɒnəmɪ] n Astronomie f

asylum [əˈsaɪləm] n (home) Anstalt f; (political asylum) Asyl nt; **asylum seeker** n Asylbewerber(in) m(f)

at [æt] prep (place) ~ **the door** an der Tür; ~ **home** zu Hause; ~ **John's** bei John; ~ **school** in der Schule; ~ **the theatre / cinema** im Theater / Kino; ~ **lunch / work** beim Essen / bei der Arbeit; (direction) **to point ~**

sb auf jdn zeigen; **he looked ~ me** er sah mich an; (time) **~ 2 o'clock** um 2 Uhr; **~ Easter/Christmas** zu Ostern/Weihnachten; **~ the moment** im Moment; **~ (the age of) 16** im Alter von 16 Jahren, mit 16; (price) **~ £5 each** zu je 5 Pfund; (speed) **~ 20 mph** mit 20 Meilen pro Stunde

ate [et, eɪt] *pt of* **eat**

athlete ['æθliːt] *n* Athlet(in) *m(f)*; (track and field) Leichtathlet(in) *m(f)*; (sportsman) Sportler(in) *m(f)*; **~'s foot** Fußpilz *m*; **athletic** [æθ'letɪk] *adj* sportlich; (build) athletisch; **athletics** *npl* Leichtathletik *f*

Atlantic [ət'læntɪk] *n* **the ~ (Ocean)** der Atlantik

atlas ['ætləs] *n* Atlas *m*

ATM *abbr* = **automated teller machine** Geldautomat *m*

atmosphere ['ætməsfɪə*] *n* Atmosphäre *f*; (fig) Stimmung *f*

atom ['ætəm] *n* Atom *nt*; **atom(ic) bomb** *n* Atombombe *f*; **atomic** [ə'tɒmɪk] *adj* Atom-; **~ energy** Atomenergie *f*; **~ power** Atomkraft *f*

A to Z® ['eɪtə'zed] *n* Stadtplan *m* (in Buchform)

atrocious [ə'trəʊʃəs] *adj* grauenhaft; **atrocity** [ə'trɒsɪti] *n* Grausamkeit *f*; (deed) Gräueltat *f*

attach [ə'tætʃ] *vt* befestigen, anheften (to an +dat); **to ~ importance to sth** Wert auf etw akk legen; **to be ~ed to sb/sth** an jdm/etw hängen; **attachment** [ə'tætʃmənt] *n* (affection) Zuneigung *f*; (Inform) Attachment *m*, Anhang *m*, Anlage *f*

attack [ə'tæk] *vt*, *vi* angreifen ▷ *n* Angriff *m*+*akk* (on auf *m*); (Med) Anfall *m*

attempt [ə'tempt] *n* Versuch *m*; **to make an ~ to do sth** versuchen, etw zu tun ▷ *vt* versuchen

attend [ə'tend] *vt* (go to) teilnehmen an +*dat*; (lectures, school) besuchen ▷ *vi* (be present) anwesend sein; **attend to** *vt* sich kümmern um; (customer) bedienen; **attendance** *n* (presence) Anwesenheit *f*; (people present) Teilnehmerzahl *f*; **attendant** *n* (in car park etc) Wächter(in) *m(f)*; (in museum) Aufseher(in) *m(f)*

attention [ə'tenʃən] *n* Aufmerksamkeit *f*; **(your) ~ please** Achtung!; **to pay ~ to sth** etw beachten; **to pay ~ to sb** jdm aufmerksam zuhören; (listen) jdm/etw aufmerksam zuhören; **for the ~ of ...** zu Händen von ...; **attentive** [ə'tentɪv] *adj* aufmerksam

attic ['ætɪk] *n* Dachboden *m*; (lived in) Mansarde *f*

attitude ['ætɪtjuːd] *n* (mental) Einstellung *f* (to, towards zu); (more general, physical) Haltung *f*

attorney [ə'tɜːnɪ] *n* (US: lawyer) Rechtsanwalt *m*, Rechtsanwältin *f*

attract [ə'trækt] *vt* anziehen; (attention) erregen; **to be ~ed to** **by sb** sich zu jdm hingezogen fühlen; **attraction** [ə'trækʃən] *n* Anziehungskraft *f*; (thing) Attraktion *f*; **attractive** *adj* attraktiv; (thing, idea) reizvoll

aubergine ['əʊbəʒiːn] *n* Aubergine *f*

auction ['ɔːkʃən] *n* Versteigerung *f*, Auktion *f* ▷ *vt* versteigern

audible ['ɔːdɪbl] *adj* hörbar

audience ['ɔːdɪəns] *n* Publikum *nt*; (Radio) Zuhörer *pl*; (TV) Zuschauer *pl*

audio ['ɔːdɪəʊ] *adj* Ton-

audition [ɔː'dɪʃən] *n* Probe *f* ▷ *vi* (Theat) vorspielen, vorsingen

auditorium [ɔːdɪ'tɔːrɪəm] *n* Zuschauerraum *m*

Aug *abbr* = **August**

August ['ɔːgəst] n August m; see also **September**

aunt [ɑːnt] n Tante f

au pair [əʊˈpeə*] n Aupairmädchen nt, Aupairjunge m

Australia [ɒˈstreɪlɪə] n Australien nt; **Australian** adj australisch ▷ n Australier(in) m(f)

Austria ['ɒstrɪə] n Österreich nt; **Austrian** adj österreichisch ▷ n Österreicher(in) m(f)

authentic [ɔːˈθentɪk] adj echt; (signature) authentisch; **authenticity** [ɔːθenˈtɪsɪtɪ] n Echtheit f

author ['ɔːθə*] n Autor(in) m(f); (of report etc) Verfasser(in) m(f)

authority [ɔːˈθɒrɪtɪ] n (power, expert) Autorität f; **an ~ on sth** eine Autorität auf dem Gebiet einer Sache; **the authorities** (pl) die Behörden pl; **authorize** ['ɔːθəraɪz] vt (permit) genehmigen; **to be ~d to do sth** offiziell berechtigt sein, etw zu tun

auto ['ɔːtəʊ] (pl -s) n (US) Auto nt

autobiography [ɔːtəbaɪˈɒgrəfɪ] n Autobiographie f; **autograph** ['ɔːtəgrɑːf] n Autogramm nt

automatic [ɔːtəˈmætɪk] adj automatisch; **~ gear change** (BRIT), **~ gear shift** (US) Automatikschaltung f ▷ n (car) Automatikwagen m

automobile ['ɔːtəməbiːl] n (US) Auto(mobil) nt; **autotrain** ['ɔːtəʊtreɪn] n (US) Autoreisezug m

autumn ['ɔːtəm] n (BRIT) Herbst m

auxiliary [ɔːgˈzɪlɪərɪ] adj Hilfs-; **verb** Hilfsverb nt ▷ n Hilfskraft f

availability [əveɪləˈbɪlɪtɪ] n (of product) Lieferbarkeit f; (of resources) Verfügbarkeit f; **available** adj erhältlich; (existing) vorhanden; (product) lieferbar; (person) erreichbar; **to be/make ~ to sb** jdm zur Verfügung stehen/stellen; **they're only ~ in black** es gibt sie nur in Schwarz

sie sind nur in Schwarz erhältlich

avalanche ['ævəlɑːnʃ] n Lawine f

Ave abbr = **avenue**

avenue ['ævənjuː] n Allee f

average ['ævərɪdʒ] n Durchschnitt m; **on ~** im Durchschnitt ▷ adj durchschnittlich; **~ speed** Durchschnittsgeschwindigkeit f; **of ~ height** von mittlerer Größe

aviation [eɪvɪˈeɪʃən] n Luftfahrt f

avocado [ævəˈkɑːdəʊ] (pl -s) n Avocado f

avoid [əˈvɔɪd] vt vermeiden; **to ~ sb** jdm aus dem Weg gehen; **avoidable** adj vermeidbar

awake [əˈweɪk] (awoke, awoken) vi aufwachen ▷ adj wach

award [əˈwɔːd] n (prize) Preis m; (for bravery etc) Auszeichnung f ▷ vt zuerkennen (to sb jdm); (present) verleihen (to sb jdm)

aware [əˈweə*] adj bewusst; **to be ~ of sth** sich dat einer Sache gen bewusst sein; **I was not ~ that ...** es war mir nicht klar, dass ...

away [əˈweɪ] adv weg; **to look ~** wegsehen; **he's ~** er ist nicht da; (on a trip) er ist verreist; (from school, work) er fehlt; (Sport) **they are (playing) ~** sie spielen auswärts; (with distance) **three miles ~** drei Meilen (von hier) entfernt; **to work ~** drauflos arbeiten

awful ['ɔːfʊl] adj schrecklich, furchtbar; **awfully** adv furchtbar

awkward ['ɔːkwəd] adj (clumsy) ungeschickt; (embarrassing) peinlich; (difficult) schwierig

awning ['ɔːnɪŋ] n Markise f

awoke [əˈwəʊk] pt of **awake**; **awoken** [əˈwəʊkən] pp of **awake**

ax (US), **axe** [æks] n Axt f

axle ['æksl] n (Tech) Achse f

BA _abbr_ = **Bachelor of Arts**
BSc _abbr_ = **Bachelor of Science**
babe [beɪb] _n_ (_fam_) Baby _nt_; (_fam:
affectionate_) Schatz _m_, Kleine(r) _mf_
baby ['beɪbɪ] _n_ Baby _nt_; (_of animal_)
Junge(s) _nt_; (_fam: affectionate_) Schatz
_m_, Kleine(r) _mf_; **to have a ~** ein Kind
bekommen; **it's your ~** (_fam: re-
sponsibility_) das ist dein Bier; **baby
carriage** _n_ (_US_) Kinderwagen _m_;
baby food _n_ Babynahrung _f_; **ba-
byish** _adj_ kindisch; **baby shower**
_n_ (_US_) Party für die werdende Mutter;
baby-sit _irr vi_ babysitten; **baby-
-sitter** _n_ Babysitter(in) _m(f)_
bachelor ['bætʃələ*] _n_ Junggeselle
_m_; **Bachelor of Arts / Science** erster
akademischer Grad, ≈ Magister / Diplom; **bachelorette** _n_ Junggesellin _f_;
bachelorette party _n_ (_US_) Junggesellinnenabschied; **bachelor party** _n_
(_US_) Junggesellenabschied
back [bæk] _n_ (_of person, animal_)
Rücken _m_; (_of house, coin etc_) Rückseite _f_; (_of chair_) Rückenlehne _f_; (_of

car_) Rücksitz _m_; (_of train_) Ende _nt_;
(_Sport: defender_) Verteidiger(in) _m(f)_;
at the ~ of ..., (_US_) **in ~ of** (_inside_)
hinten in ...; (_outside_) hinter ...; **~ to
front** verkehrt herum ▷ _vt_ (_support_)
unterstützen; (_car_) rückwärts fahren
▷ _vi_ (_go backwards_) rückwärts gehen
o fahren ▷ _adj_ Hinter-; **~ wheel**
Hinterrad _nt_ ▷ _adv_ zurück; **they're
~** sie sind wieder da; **back away** _vi_
sich zurückziehen; **back down** _vi_
nachgeben; **back up** _vi_ (_car etc_)
zurücksetzen ▷ _vt_ (_support_) unterstützen; (_Inform_) sichern; (_car_) zu-
rückfahren
backache _n_ Rückenschmerzen _pl_;
backbone _n_ Rückgrat _nt_; **back-
date** _vt_ zurückdatieren; **back-
door** _n_ Hintertür _f_; **backfire** _vi_
(_plan_) fehlschlagen; (_Auto_) fehlzün-
den; **background** _n_ Hintergrund
_m_; (_Sport_) Rückhand _f_; **backhand** _n_ (_Sport_) Rückhand _f_;
backlog _n_ (_of work_) Rückstand _m_;
backpack _n_ (_US_) Rucksack _m_;
backpacker _n_ Rucksacktourist(in)
_m(f)_; **backpacking** _n_ Rucksack-
tourismus _m_; **back seat** _n_ Rücksitz
_m_; **backside** _n_ (_fam_) Po _m_; **back
street** _n_ Seitenstraßchen _nt_;
backstroke _n_ Rückenschwimmen
_nt_; **back-up** _n_ (_support_) Unterstützung _f_; **~ copy**) (_Inform_) Siche-
rungskopie _f_; **backward** _adj_ (_child_)
zurückgeblieben; (_region_) rückstän-
dig; **~ movement** Rückwärtsbe-
wegung _f_; **backwards** _adv_ rückwärts; **backyard** _n_ Hinterhof _m_
bacon ['beɪkən] _n_ Frühstücksspeck _m_
bacteria [bæk'tɪərɪə] _npl_ Bakterien _pl_
bad [bæd] (_worse, worst_) _adj_
schlecht, schlimm; (_smell_) übel; **I
have a ~ back** mir tut der Rücken
weh; **I'm ~ at maths / sport** ich bin
schlecht in Mathe / Sport; **to go ~**

badge [bædʒ] n Abzeichen nt

badger ['bædʒə*] n Dachs m

badly ['bædlɪ] adv schlecht; **~ wounded** schwer verwundet; **to need sth ~** etw dringend brauchen; **bad-tempered** ['bæd'tempəd] adj schlecht gelaunt

bag [bæg] n (small) Tüte f; (larger) Beutel m; (handbag) Tasche f; **my ~s** (luggage) mein Gepäck; **it's not my ~** (fam) das ist nicht mein Ding

baggage ['bægɪdʒ] n Gepäck nt; **baggage allowance** n Freigepäck nt; **baggage (re)claim** n Gepäckrückgabe f

baggy ['bægɪ] adj (zu) weit; (trousers, suit) ausgebeult

bag lady ['bæglerdɪ] n Stadtstreicherin f

bagpipes ['bægpaɪps] npl Dudelsack m

Bahamas [bə'hɑ:məz] npl **die ~**, die Bahamas pl

bail [beɪl] n (money) Kaution f

bait [beɪt] n Köder m

bake [beɪk] vt, vi backen; **baked beans** npl weiße Bohnen in Tomatensoße, **baked potato** (pl **-es**) n in der Schale gebackene Kartoffel, Ofenkartoffel f; **baker** n Bäcker(in) m(f); **bakery** ['beɪkərɪ] n Bäckerei f; **baking powder** n Backpulver nt

balance ['bæləns] n (equilibrium) Gleichgewicht nt ▷ vt (make up for) ausgleichen; **balanced** adj ausgeglichen; **balance sheet** n Bilanz f

balcony ['bælkənɪ] n Balkon m

bald [bɔ:ld] adj kahl; **to be ~** eine Glatze haben

Balkans ['bɔ:lkənz] npl **the ~** der Balkan, die Balkanländer pl

ball [bɔ:l] n Ball m; **to have a ~** (fam) sich prima amüsieren

ballet ['bæleɪ] n Ballett nt; **ballet dancer** n Balletttänzer(in) m(f)

balloon [bə'lu:n] n (Luft)ballon m

ballot ['bælət] n (geheime) Abstimmung; **ballot box** n Wahlurne f; **ballot paper** n Stimmzettel m

ballpoint (pen) ['bɔ:lpɔɪnt] n Kugelschreiber m

ballroom ['bɔ:lru:m] n Tanzsaal m

Baltic ['bɔ:ltɪk] adj = **Sea Ostsee** f; **the ~ States** die baltischen Staaten

bamboo [bæm'bu:] n Bambus m; **bamboo shoots** npl Bambussprossen pl

ban [bæn] n Verbot nt ▷ vt verbieten

banana [bə'nɑ:nə] n Banane f; **he's ~s** er ist völlig durchgeknallt; **banana split** n Bananensplit m

band [bænd] n (group) Gruppe f; (of criminals) Bande f; (Mus) Kapelle f; (pop, rock etc) Band f; (strip) Band nt

bandage ['bændɪdʒ] n Verband m; (elastic) Bandage f ▷ vt verbinden

B & B abbr = **bed and breakfast**

bang [bæŋ] n (noise) Knall m; (blow) Schlag m ▷ vt, vi knallen; (door) zuschlagen, zuknallen; **banger** ['bæŋə*] n (BRIT fam: firework) Knallkörper m; (sausage) Würstchen nt; (fam: old car) Klapperkiste f

bangs [bæŋz] npl (US: of hair) Pony m

banish ['bænɪʃ] vt verbannen

banister(s) ['bænɪstə*] n (Treppen)geländer nt

bank [bæŋk] n (Fin) Bank f; (of river etc) Ufer nt; **bank account** n Bankkonto nt; **bank balance** n Kontostand m; **bank card** n Bankkarte f; **bank code** n Bankleitzahl f; **bank holiday** n gesetzlicher Feiertag

● BANK HOLIDAY

● Als **bank holiday** wird in Großbritannien ein gesetzlicher Feiertag bezeichnet, an dem die Banken geschlossen sind. Die meisten dieser Feiertage, abgesehen von Weihnachten und Ostern, fallen auf Montage im Mai und August. An diesen langen Wochenenden (bank holiday weekends) fahren viele Briten in Urlaub, so dass dann auf den Straßen, Flughäfen und bei der Bahn sehr viel Betrieb ist.

bank manager n Filialleiter(in) m(f); **banknote** n Banknote f

bankrupt vt ruinieren; **to go ~** Pleite gehen

bank statement n Kontoauszug m

baptism ['bæptɪzəm] n Taufe f; **baptize** [bæp'taɪz] vt taufen

bar [baː*] n (for drinks) Bar f; (less smart) Lokal nt; (rod) Stange f; (of chocolate etc) Riegel m, Tafel f; (of soap) Stück nt; (counter) Theke f ▷ prep außer; **~ none** ohne Ausnahme

barbecue ['baːbɪkjuː] n (device) Grill m; (party) Barbecue nt, Grillfete f; **to have a ~** grillen

barbed wire ['baːbd'waɪə*] n Stacheldraht m

barber ['baːbə*] n (Herren)friseur m

bar code ['baːkəʊd] n Strichcode m

bare [bɛə*] adj nackt; **~ patch** kahle Stelle; **barefoot** adj, adv barfuß; **bareheaded** adj, adv ohne Kopfbedeckung; **barely** adv kaum; (with age) knapp

bargain ['baːgɪn] n (cheap offer) günstiges Angebot, Schnäppchen nt; (transaction) Geschäft nt; **what a ~** das ist aber günstig! ▷ vi (ver)handeln

barge [baːdʒ] n (for freight) Lastkahn m; (unpowered) Schleppkahn m

bark [baːk] n (of tree) Rinde f; (of dog) Bellen nt ▷ vi (dog) bellen

barley ['baːlɪ] n Gerste f

barmaid [baː'meɪd] n Bardame f;
barman ['baːmən] (pl **-men**) n Barkeeper m

barn [baːn] n Scheune f

barometer [bə'rɒmɪtə*] n Barometer m

baroque [bə'rɒk] adj barock, Barock-

barracks ['bærəks] npl Kaserne f

barrel ['bærəl] n Fass nt; **barrel organ** n Drehorgel f

barricade [bærɪ'keɪd] n Barrikade f

barrier ['bærɪə*] n (obstruction) Absperrung f, Barriere f; (across road etc) Schranke f

barrow ['bærəʊ] n (cart) Schubkarren m

bartender ['baːtendə*] n (US) Barkeeper m

base [beɪs] n Basis f; (of lamp, pillar etc) Fuß m; (Mil) Stützpunkt m ▷ vt gründen (on auf +akk); **to be ~d on sth** auf etw dat basieren; **baseball** n Baseball nt; **baseball cap** n Baseballmütze f; **basement** n Kellergeschoss nt

bash [bæʃ] (fam) n Schlag m; (fam) Party f ▷ vt hauen

basic ['beɪsɪk] adj einfach; (fundamental) Grund-; (importance, difference) grundlegend; (in principle) grundsätzlich; **the accomodation is very ~** die Unterkunft ist sehr bescheiden; **basically** adv im Grunde; **basics** npl **the ~** das Wesentliche

basil ['bæzl] n Basilikum nt

basin ['beɪsn] n (for washing, valley) (Wasch)becken nt

basis ['beɪsɪs] n Basis f; **on the ~ of** aufgrund +gen; **on a monthly ~** monatlich

basket ['baːskɪt] n Korb m; **bas-**

ketball n Basketball m

Basque [bæsk] n (person) Baske m, Baskin f; (language) Baskisch nt ▷ adj baskisch

bass [beɪs] n (Mus) Bass m; (Zool) Barsch m ▷ adj (Mus) Bass-

bastard ['bɑːstəd] n (lit) uneheliches Kind nt; (vulg: awful person) Arschloch nt

bat [bæt] n (Zool) Fledermaus f; (Sport: cricket, baseball) Schlagholz nt; (table tennis) Schläger m

batch [bætʃ] n Schwung m; (fam: of letters, books etc) Stoß m

bath [bɑːθ] n Bad nt; (tub) Badewanne f; **to have a ~** baden ▷ vt (child etc) baden

bathe [beɪð] vt, vi (wound etc) baden; **bathing cap** n Badekappe f; **bathing costume**, **bathing suit** (US) n Badeanzug m

bathmat ['bɑːθmæt] n Badevorleger m; **bathrobe** n Bademantel m; **bathroom** n Bad(ezimmer) nt; **baths** [bɑːðz] npl (Schwimm)bad nt; **bath towel** n Badetuch nt; **bathtub** n Badewanne f

baton ['bætən] n (Mus) Taktstock m; (police) Schlagstock m

batter ['bætə*] n Teig m ▷ vt heftig schlagen; **battered** adj übel zugerichtet; (hat, car) verbeult; (wife, baby) misshandelt

battery ['bætərɪ] n (Elec) Batterie f; **battery charger** n Ladegerät nt

battle ['bætl] n Schlacht f; (fig) Kampf m (for um +akk); **battlefield** n Schlachtfeld nt; **battlements** npl Zinnen pl

Bavaria [bə'veərɪə] n Bayern nt; **Bavarian** adj bay(e)risch ▷ n Bayer(in) m(f)

bay [beɪ] n (of sea) Bucht f; (on house) Erker m; (tree) Lorbeerbaum m; **bay leaf** n Lorbeerblatt nt; **bay window** n Erkerfenster nt

BBC abbr = **British Broadcasting Corporation** BBC f

BC abbr = **before Christ** vor Christi Geburt, v. Chr.

be [biː] (was, been) vi sein; (become) werden; (be situated) liegen, sein; **she's French** sie ist Französin; **I'm too hot** mir ist zu warm; **she's not well** (health) ihr geht's nicht gut; **he wants to ~ a doctor** er will Arzt werden; (cost) das Buch kostet 5 Euro; **how much is that altogether?** was macht das zusammen?; **how long have you been here?** wie lange sind Sie schon da?; **have you ever been to Rome?** warst du/waren Sie schon einmal in Rom?; **there is / are** es gibt, es ist / sind; **there are two left** es sind noch zwei übrig ▷ vb aux (passive) werden; **he was run over** er ist überfahren worden, er wurde überfahren; (continuous tenses) **I was walking on the beach** ich ging am Strand spazieren; **they're coming tomorrow** sie kommen morgen; (infinitive: intention, obligation) **the car is to ~ sold** das Auto soll verkauft werden; **you are not to mention it** du darfst es nicht erwähnen

beach [biːtʃ] n Strand m; **beachwear** n Strandkleidung f

bead [biːd] n (of glass, wood etc) Perle f; (drop) Tropfen m

beak [biːk] n Schnabel m

beam [biːm] n (of wood) Balken m; (of light) Strahl m ▷ vi (smile etc) strahlen

bean [biːn] n Bohne f; **bean curd** n Tofu m

bear [beə*] (bore, borne) vt (carry) tragen; (tolerate) ertragen ▷ n Bär m; **bearable** adj erträglich

beard [bɪəd] n Bart m

beast [biːst] n Tier nt; (brutal person) Bestie f; (disliked person) Biest nt

beat [biːt] (**beat, beaten**) vt schlagen; (as punishment) prügeln; **to ~ sb at tennis** jdn im Tennis schlagen ▷ n (of heart, drum etc) Schlag m; (Mus) Takt m; (type of music) Beat m; **beat up** vt zusammenschlagen

beaten ['biːtn] pp of **beat**; **of the ~ track** abgelegen

beautiful ['bjuːtɪful] adj schön; (splendid) herrlich; **beauty** ['bjuːtɪ] n Schönheit f; **beauty spot** n (place) lohnendes Ausflugsziel

beaver ['biːvə*] n Biber m

became [bɪ'keɪm] pt of **become**

because [bɪ'kɒz] adv, conj weil ▷ prep **~ of** wegen +gen o dat

become [bɪ'kʌm] (**became, become**) vt werden; **what's ~ of him?** was ist aus ihm geworden?

bed [bed] n Bett nt; (in garden) Beet nt; **bed and breakfast** n Übernachtung f mit Frühstück; **bedclothes** npl Bettwäsche f; **bedding** n Bettzeug nt; **bed linen** n Bettwäsche f; **bedroom** n Schlafzimmer nt; **bed-sit(ter)** n (fam) möblierte Einzimmerwohnung; **bedspread** n Tagesdecke f; **bedtime** n Schlafenszeit f

bee [biː] n Biene f

beech [biːtʃ] n Buche f

beef [biːf] n Rindfleisch nt; **beefburger** n Hamburger m; **beef tomato** (pl **-es**) n Fleischtomate f

beehive ['biːhaɪv] n Bienenstock m

been [biːn] pp of **be**

beer [bɪə*] n Bier nt; **beer garden** n Biergarten m

beetle ['biːtl] n Käfer m

beetroot ['biːtruːt] n Rote Bete

before [bɪ'fɔː] prep vor; **the year ~ last** vorletztes Jahr; **the day ~ yesterday** vorgestern ▷ conj bevor ▷ adv (of time) vorher; **have you**

been there ~? waren Sie/warst du schon einmal dort?; **beforehand** adv vorher

beg [beg] vt **to ~ sb to do sth** jdn inständig bitten, etw zu tun ▷ vi (beggar) betteln (for um +akk)

began [bɪ'gæn] pt of **begin**

beggar ['begə*] n Bettler(in) m(f)

begin [bɪ'gɪn] (**began, begun**) vt, vi anfangen, beginnen; **to ~ to do sth** anfangen, etw zu tun; **beginner** n Anfänger(in) m(f); **beginning** n Anfang m

begun [bɪ'gʌn] pp of **begin**

behalf [bɪ'hɑːf] n **on ~ of, in ~ of** (US) im Namen/Auftrag von; **on my ~** für mich

behave [bɪ'heɪv] vi sich benehmen; **~ yourself!** benimm dich!; **behavior** (US), **behaviour** [bɪ'heɪvjə*] n Benehmen nt

behind [bɪ'haɪnd] prep hinter; **to be ~ time** Verspätung haben ▷ adv hinten; **to be ~ with one's work** mit seiner Arbeit im Rückstand sein ▷ n (fam) Hinterteil nt

beige [beɪʒ] adj beige

being ['biːɪŋ] n (existence) Dasein nt; (person) Wesen nt

Belarus [bjelæ'ruːs] n Weißrussland nt

belch [beltʃ] n Rülpser m ▷ vi rülpsen

belfry ['belfrɪ] n Glockenturm m

Belgian ['beldʒən] adj belgisch ▷ n Belgier(in) m(f); **Belgium** ['beldʒəm] n Belgien nt

belief [bɪ'liːf] n (church) Glaube m (in an +akk); (conviction) Überzeugung f; **it's my ~ that ...** ich bin der Überzeugung, dass ...; **believe** [bɪ'liːv] vt glauben; **believe in** vi glauben an+akk; **believer** n (Rel) Gläubige(r) mf

bell [bel] n (church) Glocke f; (bicycle, door) Klingel f; **bellboy** ['bel-

bои n (esp US) Page m

bellows ['beləυz] npl (for fire) Blasebalg m

belly ['belɪ] n Bauch m; **bellyache** n Bauchweh nt ▷ vi (fam) meckern; **belly button** n (fam) Bauchnabel m; **bellyflop** n (fam) Bauchklatscher m

belong [bɪ'lɒŋ] vi gehören (to sb jdm); (to club) angehören +dat; **belongings** npl Habe f

below [bɪ'ləυ] prep unter ▷ adv unten

belt [belt] n (round waist) Gürtel m; (safety belt) Gurt m; **below the ~** unter der Gürtellinie ▷ vi (fam: go fast) rasen, düsen; **beltway** n (US) Umgehungsstraße f

bench [bentʃ] n Bank f

bend [bend] vt (bent, bent) (shape) biegen; (head, arm) beugen ▷ vi sich biegen; (person) sich beugen; **bend down** vi sich bücken

beneath [bɪ'ni:θ] prep unter ▷ adv darunter

beneficial [benɪ'fɪʃl] adj gut, nützlich (to für) **benefit** ['benɪfɪt] n (advantage) Vorteil m; (profit) Nutzen m; **for your/his ~** deinetwegen/seinetwegen; **unemployment ~** Arbeitslosengeld nt ▷ vt gut tun +dat ▷ vi Nutzen ziehen (from aus)

Benelux ['benɪlʌks] n Beneluxländer pl

benign [bɪ'naɪn] adj (person) gütig; (climate) mild; (Med) gutartig

bent [bent] pt, pp of **bend** ▷ adj krumm; (fam) korrupt

beret ['bereɪ] n Baskenmütze f

Bermuda [bə'mju:də] n **the ~s** pl die Bermudas pl ▷ adj **~ shorts** pl Bermudashorts pl; **the ~ triangle** das Bermudadreieck

berry ['berɪ] n Beere f

berth [bɜ:θ] n (for ship) Ankerplatz m; (in ship) Koje f, (in train) Bett nt ▷ vt am Kai festmachen ▷ vi anlegen

beside [bɪ'saɪd] prep neben; **the sea/lake** am Meer/See; **besides** [bɪ'saɪdz] prep außer ▷ adv außerdem

besiege [bɪ'si:dʒ] vt belagern

best [best] adj beste(r, s); **my ~ friend** mein bester o engster Freund; **the ~ thing (to do) would be to ...** das Beste wäre zu ...; (on food packaging) **~ before ...** mindestens haltbar bis ... ▷ n der/die/das Beste; **all the ~** alles Gute; **to make the ~ of it** das Beste daraus machen ▷ adv am besten; **I like this ~** das mag ich am liebsten; **best-before date** n Mindesthaltbarkeitsdatum nt; **best man** ['best'mæn] (pl men) n Trauzeuge m; **bestseller** ['best'selə*] n Bestseller m

bet [bet] n (bet, bet) vt, vi wetten (on auf +akk); **I ~ him £5 that ...** ich habe mit ihm um 5 Pfund gewettet, dass ...; **you ~** (fam) und ob!; **I ~ he'll be late** er kommt mit Sicherheit zu spät ▷ n Wette f

betray [bɪ'treɪ] vt verraten; **betrayal** n Verrat m

better ['betə*] adj, adv besser; **to get ~** (healthwise) sich erholen, wieder gesund werden; (improve) sich verbessern; **I'm much ~ today** es geht mir heute viel besser; **you'd ~ go** du solltest lieber gehen; **a change for the ~** eine Wendung zum Guten

betting ['betɪŋ] n Wetten nt; **betting shop** n Wettbüro nt

between [bɪ'twi:n] prep zwischen; (among) unter; **~ you and me, ...** unter uns gesagt, ... ▷ adv **(in) ~** dazwischen

beverage ['bevərɪdʒ] n (formal) Getränk nt

beware [bɪ'wɛə*] vt **to ~ of** sth sich vor etw +dat hüten; **'~ of the dog'** „Vorsicht, bissiger Hund!"

bewildered [bɪ'wɪldəd] adj verwirrt

beyond [bɪ'jɒnd] prep (place) jenseits +gen; (time) über ... hinaus; (out of reach) außerhalb +gen; **it's ~ me** da habe ich keine Ahnung, da bin ich überfragt ▷ adv darüber hinaus

bias ['baɪəs] n (prejudice) Vorurteil nt, Voreingenommenheit f

bias(s)ed adj voreingenommen

bib [bɪb] n Latz m

Bible ['baɪbl] n Bibel f

bicycle ['baɪsɪkl] n Fahrrad nt

bid [bɪd] (bid, bid) vt (offer) bieten ▷ n (attempt) Versuch m; (offer) Gebot nt

big [bɪg] adj groß; **it's no ~ deal** (fam) es ist nichts Besonderes; **big dipper** n (BRIT) Achterbahn f; **bigheaded** [bɪg'hedɪd] adj eingebildet

bike [baɪk] n (fam) Rad nt

bikini [bɪ'ki:nɪ] n Bikini m

bilberry ['bɪlbərɪ] n Heidelbeere f

bilingual [baɪ'lɪŋgwəl] adj zweisprachig

bill [bɪl] n (account) Rechnung f; (US: banknote) Banknote f; (Pol) Gesetzentwurf m; (Zool) Schnabel m; **billfold** ['bɪlfəʊld] n (US) Brieftasche f

billiards ['bɪlɪədz] nsing Billard nt; **billiard table** n Billardtisch m

billion ['bɪlɪən] n Milliarde f

bin [bɪn] n Behälter m; (rubbish bin) (Müll)eimer m; (for paper) Papierkorb m

bind [baɪnd] (bound, bound) vt binden; (bind together) zusammenbinden; (wound) verbinden; **binding** n (ski) Bindung f; (book) Einband m

binge [bɪndʒ] n (fam: drinking) Sauferei f; **to go on a ~** auf Sauftour gehen

bingo ['bɪŋgəʊ] n Bingo nt

binoculars [bɪ'nɒkjʊləz] npl Fernglas nt

biodegradable ['baɪəʊdɪ'greɪdəbl] adj biologisch abbaubar

biography [baɪ'ɒgrəfɪ] n Biografie f

biological [baɪə'lɒdʒɪkəl] adj biologisch; **biology** [baɪ'ɒlədʒɪ] n Biologie f

birch [bɜ:tʃ] n Birke f

bird [bɜ:d] n Vogel m; (BRIT fam: girl, girlfriend) Tussi f; **bird watcher** n Vogelbeobachter(in) m(f)

birth [bɜ:θ] n Geburt f; **birth certificate** n Geburtsurkunde f; **birth control** n Geburtenkontrolle f; **birthday** n Geburtstag m; **happy ~** herzlichen Glückwunsch zum Geburtstag; **birthday card** n Geburtstagskarte f; **birthday party** n Geburtstagsfeier f; **birthplace** n Geburtsort m

biscuit ['bɪskɪt] n (BRIT) Keks m

bisexual [baɪ'seksjʊəl] adj bisexuell

bishop ['bɪʃəp] n Bischof m; (in chess) Läufer m

bit [bɪt] pt of **bite** ▷ n (piece) Stück(chen) nt; (inform) Bit nt; **a ~ (of ...)** (small amount) ein bisschen ...; **a ~ tired** etwas müde; **~ by ~** allmählich; (time) **for a ~** ein Weilchen; **quite a ~** (a lot) ganz schön viel

bitch [bɪtʃ] n (dog) Hündin f; (pej: woman) Miststück nt, Schlampe f; **son of a ~** (US: vulg) Hurensohn m, Scheißkerl m; **bitchy** adj gemein, zickig

bite [baɪt] (**bit**, **bitten**) vt, vi beißen ▷ n Biss m; (mouthful) Bissen m; (insect) Stich m; **to have a ~** eine Kleinigkeit essen; **bitten** pp of **bite**

bitter ['bɪtə*] adj bitter; (memory etc) schmerzlich ▷ n (BRIT: beer) halbdunkles Bier; **bitter lemon** n Bitter Lemon nt

bizarre [bɪˈzɑːʳ] adj bizarr

black [blæk] adj schwarz; **blackberry** n Brombeere f; **blackbird** n Amsel f; **blackboard** n (Wand)tafel f; **black box** n (Aviat) Flugschreiber m; **blackcurrant** n Schwarze Johannisbeere; **black eye** n blaues Auge; **Black Forest** n Schwarzwald m; **Black Forest gateau** n Schwarzwälder Kirschtorte f; **blackmail** n Erpressung f ▷ vt erpressen; **black market** n Schwarzmarkt m; **blackout** n (Med) Ohnmacht f; **to have a ~** ohnmächtig werden; **black pudding** n ≈ Blutwurst f; **Black Sea** n **the ~** das Schwarze Meer; **blacksmith** n Schmied(in) m(f); **black tie** n Abendanzug m, Smoking m; **is it ~?** ist / besteht da Smokingzwang?

bladder [ˈblædəʳ] n Blase f

blade [bleɪd] n (of knife) Klinge f; (of propeller) Blatt nt; (of grass) Halm m

blame [bleɪm] n Schuld f ▷ vt **to ~ sth on sb** jdm die Schuld an etw dat geben; **he is to ~** er ist daran schuld

bland [blænd] adj (taste) fade, (comment) nichts sagend

blank [blæŋk] adj (page, space) leer, unbeschrieben; (look) ausdruckslos, **~ cheque** Blankoscheck m

blanket [ˈblæŋkɪt] n (Woll)decke f

blast [blɑːst] n (of wind) Windstoß m; (of explosion) Druckwelle f ▷ vt (blow up) sprengen; **~!** (fam) Mist!, verdammt!

blatant [ˈbleɪtənt] adj (undisguised) offen; (obvious) offensichtlich

blaze [bleɪz] vi lodern; (sun) brennen ▷ n (building) Brand m; (other fire) Feuer nt; **a ~ of colour** eine Farbenpracht

blazer [ˈbleɪzəʳ] n Blazer m

bleach [bliːtʃ] n Bleichmittel nt ▷ vt bleichen

bleak [bliːk] adj öde, düster; (future) trostlos

bleary [ˈblɪərɪ] adj (eyes) trübe, verschlafen

bleed [bliːd] (bled, bled) vi bluten

bleep [bliːp] n Piepton m ▷ vi piepen; **bleeper** n (fam) Piepser m

blend [blend] n Mischung f ▷ vt mischen ▷ vi sich mischen; **blender** n Mixer m

bless [bles] vt segnen; **~ you!** Gesundheit!; **blessing** n Segen m

blew [bluː] pt of **blow**

blind [blaɪnd] adj blind; (corner) unübersichtlich; **to turn a ~ eye to sth** bei etw ein Auge zudrücken ▷ n (for window) Rollo nt ▷ vt blenden; **blind alley** n Sackgasse f; **blind spot** n (Aut) toter Winkel; (fig) schwacher Punkt

blink [blɪŋk] vi blinzeln; (light) blinken

bliss [blɪs] n (Glück)seligkeit f

blister [ˈblɪstəʳ] n Blase f

blizzard [ˈblɪzəd] n Schneesturm m

bloated [ˈbləʊtɪd] adj aufgedunsen

block [blɒk] n (of wood, stone, ice) Block m, Klotz m; (of buildings) Häuserblock m; **~ of flats** (BRIT) Wohnblock m ▷ vt (road etc) blockieren; (pipe, nose) verstopfen; **blockage** [ˈblɒkɪdʒ] n Verstopfung f; **blockbuster** [ˈblɒkbʌstəʳ] n Knüller m; **block letters** npl Blockschrift f

bloke [bləʊk] n (BRIT fam) Kerl m, Typ m

blonde [blɒnd] adj blond ▷ n (person) Blondine f, blonder Typ

blood [blʌd] n Blut nt; **blood count** n Blutbild nt; **blood donor** n Blutspender(in) m(f); **blood**

group n Blutgruppe f; **blood poisoning** n Blutvergiftung f; **blood pressure** n Blutdruck m; **blood sample** n Blutprobe f; **bloodsports** npl Sportarten, bei denen Tiere getötet werden; **bloodthirsty** adj blutrünstig; **bloody** adj (BRIT fam) verdammt, Scheiß-; (literal sense) blutig

bloom [bluːm] n Blüte f ▷ vi blühen

blossom ['blɒsəm] n Blüte f ▷ vi blühen

blot ['blɒt] n (of ink) Klecks m; Fleck m; (fig)

blouse [blauz] n Bluse f; **big girl's ~** (fam) Schwächling m, femininer Typ

blow [bləʊ] n Schlag m ▷ vi, vt (**blew, blown**) (wind) wehen, blasen; (person: trumpet etc) blasen; **to ~ one's nose** sich dat die Nase putzen; **blow out** vt (candle etc) ausblasen; **blow up** vi explodieren ▷ vt sprengen; (balloon, tyre) aufblasen; (Foto: enlarge) vergrößern; **blow-dry** vt föhnen; **blowjob** n (fam) **to give sb a ~** jdm einen blasen; **blown** [bləʊn] pp of **blow**; **blowout** n (Auto) geplatzter Reifen

BLT n abbr = **bacon, lettuce and tomato sandwich** mit Frühstücksspeck, Kopfsalat und Tomaten belegtes Sandwich

blue [bluː] adj blau; (fam: unhappy) trübsinnig, niedergeschlagen; (film) pornografisch; (joke) anzüglich; (language) derb; **bluebell** n Glockenblume f; **blueberry** n Blaubeere f; **blue cheese** n Blauschimmelkäse m; **blues** npl **the ~** (Mus) der Blues; **to have the ~** (fam) niedergeschlagen sein

blunder ['blʌndə*] n Schnitzer m

blunt [blʌnt] adj (knife) stumpf; (fig) unverblümt; **bluntly** adv ge-

radeheraus

blurred [blɜːd] adj verschwommen, unklar

blush [blʌʃ] vi erröten

board [bɔːd] n (of wood) Brett nt; (committee) Ausschuss m; (of firm) Vorstand m; **~ and lodging** Unterkunft und Verpflegung; **on ~** an Bord ▷ vt (train, bus) einsteigen in +akk; (ship) an Bord gehen; **boarder** n Pensionsgast m; (school) Internatsschüler(in) m(f); **board game** n Brettspiel nt; **boarding card**, **boarding pass** n Bordkarte f, Einsteigekarte f; **boarding school** n Internat nt; **board meeting** n Vorstandssitzung f; **boardroom** n Sitzungssaal m (des Vorstands)

boast [bəʊst] vi prahlen (about mit) ▷ n Prahlerei f

boat [bəʊt] n Boot nt; (ship) Schiff nt; **boatman** n (hirer) Bootsverleiher m; **boat race** n Regatta f; **boat train** n Zug m mit Schiffsanschluss

bob(sleigh) ['bɒbsleɪ] n Bob m

bodily ['bɒdɪlɪ] adj körperlich ▷ adv (forcibly) gewaltsam; **body** ['bɒdɪ] n Körper m; (dead) Leiche f; (of car) Karosserie f; **bodybuilding** n Bodybuilding nt; **bodyguard** n Leibwächter m; (group) Leibwache f; **body jewellery** n Intimschmuck m; **body odour** n Körpergeruch m; **body piercing** n Piercing nt; **bodywork** n Karosserie f

boil [bɔɪl] vt, vi kochen ▷ n (Med) Geschwür nt; **boiler** n Boiler m; **boiling** adj (water etc) kochend (heiß); **I was ~** (hot) mir war fürchterlich heiß; (with rage) ich kochte vor Wut; **boiling point** n Siedepunkt m

bold [bəʊld] adj kühn, mutig; (colours) kräftig; (type) fett

Bolivia [bəˈlɪvɪə] n Bolivien nt

bolt [bəʊlt] n (lock) Riegel m;

(screw) Bolzen m ▷ vt verriegeln

bomb [bɒm] n Bombe f ▷ vt bombardieren

bond [bɒnd] n (link) Bindung f; (Fin) Obligation f

bone [bəʊn] n Knochen m; (of fish) Gräte f; **bone** n (US fam) Schnitzer m; (erection) Ständer m

bonfire ['bɒnfaɪə*] n Feuer nt (im Freien)

bonnet ['bɒnɪt] n (BRIT Auto) Haube f; (for baby) Haubchen nt

bonny ['bɒnɪ] adj (esp Scottish) hübsch

bonus ['bəʊnəs] n Bonus m, Prämie f

boo [buː] vt auspfeifen, ausbuhen ▷ vi buhen ▷ n Buhruf m

book [bʊk] n Buch nt; (of tickets, stamps) Heft nt ▷ vt (ticket etc) bestellen; (hotel, flight etc) buchen; (Sport) verwarnen; **fully ~ed (up)** ausgebucht; (performance) ausverkauft; **book in** vt eintragen; **to be ~ed in at a hotel** ein Zimmer in einem Hotel bestellt haben; **bookable** adj im Vorverkauf erhältlich; **bookcase** n Bücherregal nt; **booking** n Buchung f; **booking office** n (Rail) Fahrkartenschalter m; (Theat) Vorverkaufsstelle f; **book-keeping** n Buchhaltung f; **booklet** n Broschüre f; **bookmark** n (a. Inform) Lesezeichen nt; **bookshelf** n Bücherbord nt; **bookshelves** n Bücherregal nt; **bookshop, bookstore** n (esp US) Buchhandlung f

boom [buːm] n (of business) Boom m; (noise) Dröhnen nt ▷ vi (business) boomen; (fam) florieren; (voice etc) dröhnen

boomerang ['buːməræŋ] n Bumerang m

boost [buːst] n Auftrieb m ▷ vt (production, sales) ankurbeln; (power, profits etc) steigern; **booster** (injec-

tion) n Wiederholungsimpfung f

boot [buːt] n Stiefel m; (BRIT Auto) Kofferraum m ▷ vt (Inform) laden, booten

booth [buːð] n (at fair etc) Bude f; (at trade fair etc) Stand m

booze [buːz] n (fam) Alkohol m ▷ vi (fam) saufen

border ['bɔːdə*] n Grenze f; (edge) Rand m; **north/south of the Border** in Schottland/England; **borderline** n Grenze f

bore [bɔː*] pt of **bear** ▷ vt (hole etc) bohren; (person) langweilen ▷ n (person) Langweiler(in) m(f), langweiliger Mensch; (thing) langweilige Sache; **bored** adj **to be ~** sich langweilen; **boredom** n Langeweile f; **boring** adj langweilig

born [bɔːn] adj **he was ~ in London** er ist in London geboren

borne [bɔːn] pp of **bear**

borough ['bʌrə] n Stadtbezirk m

borrow ['bɒrəʊ] vt borgen

Bosnia-Herzegovina ['bɒznɪəhз:tsəgəʊ'viːnə] n Bosnien-Herzegowina nt; **Bosnian** ['bɒznɪən] adj bosnisch ▷ n Bosnier(in) m(f)

boss [bɒs] n Chef(in) m(f), Boss m; **boss around** vt herumkommandieren; **bossy** adj herrisch

botanical [bə'tænɪkəl] adj botanisch; **~ garden(s)** botanischer Garten

both [bəʊθ] adj beide; **~ the books** beide Bücher ▷ pron (people) beide; (things) beides; **~ (of)** the boys beide Jungs; **I like ~ of them** ich mag sie (alle) beide ▷ adv **~ X and Y** sowohl X als auch Y

bother ['bɒðə*] vt ärgern, belästigen; **it doesn't ~ me** das stört mich nicht; **he can't be ~ed with details** mit Details gibt er sich nicht ab; **I'm not ~ed** das ist mir egal ▷ vi sich kümmern (about um); **don't ~** (das ist) nicht nötig, lass es! ▷ n (trouble) Mühe f; (annoyance) Ärger m

bottle ['bɒtl] n Flasche f ▷ vt (in Flaschen) abfüllen; **bottle out** vi (fam) den Mut verlieren, aufgeben; **bottle bank** n Altglascontainer m; **bottled** adj in Flaschen; **~ beer** Flaschenbier nt; **bottleneck** n (fig) Engpass m; **bottle opener** n Flaschenöffner m

bottom ['bɒtəm] n (of container) Boden m; (underside) Unterseite f; (fam: of person) Po m; **at the ~ of the sea/table/page** auf dem Meeresgrund/am Tabellenende/unten auf der Seite ▷ adj unterste(r, s); **to be ~ of the class/league** Klassenletzte(r)/Tabellenletzte(r) sein; **~ gear** (Auto) erster Gang

bought [bɔːt] pt, pp of **buy**

bounce [baʊns] vi (ball) springen, aufprallen; (cheque) platzen; **~ up and down** (person) herumhüpfen; **bouncy** adj (ball) gut springend; (person) munter; **bouncy castle®** n Hüpfburg f

bound [baʊnd] pt, pp of **bind** ▷ adj (tied up) gebunden; (obliged) verpflichtet; **to be ~ to do sth** (sure to) etw bestimmt tun (werden); (have to) etw tun müssen; **it's ~ to happen** es muss so kommen; **to be ~ for ...** auf dem Weg nach ... sein; **boundary** ['baʊndərɪ] n Grenze f

bouquet [bʊ'keɪ] n (flowers) Strauß m; (of wine) Blume f

boutique [buː'tiːk] n Boutique f

bow [bəʊ] n (ribbon) Schleife f; (instrument, weapon) Bogen m ▷ [baʊ] vi sich verbeugen ▷ n (with head) Verbeugung f; (of ship) Bug m

bowels ['baʊəlz] npl Darm m

bowl [bəʊl] n (basin) Schüssel f; (shallow) Schale f; (for animal) Napf m

▷ vt, vi (in cricket) werfen

bowler ['bəʊlə*] n (in cricket) Werfer(in) m(f); (hat) Melone f

bowling ['bəʊlɪŋ] n Kegeln nt; **bowling alley** n Kegelbahn f; **bowling green** n Rasen m zum Bowling-Spiel; **bowls** [bəʊlz] nsing (game) Bowling-Spiel nt

bow tie [bəʊ'taɪ] n Fliege f

box [bɒks] n Schachtel f; (cardboard) Karton m; (bigger) Kasten m; (space on form) Kästchen nt; (Theat) Loge f; **boxer** n Boxer(in) m(f); **boxers, boxer shorts** npl Boxershorts pl; **boxing** n (Sport) Boxen nt; **Boxing Day** n zweiter Weihnachtsfeiertag

● **BOXING DAY**

● **Boxing Day** ist ein Feiertag in
● Großbritannien. Fällt Weihnach
● ten auf ein Wochenende, wird der
● Feiertag an einem Wochentag
● nachgeholt. Der Name geht auf
● einen alten Brauch zurück: früher
● erhielten Händler und Lieferanten
● an diesem Tag ein Geschenk, die so
● genannte Christmas Box.

boxing gloves npl Boxhandschuhe pl; **boxing ring** n Boxring m

box number n Chiffre f

box office n Kasse f

boy [bɔɪ] n Junge m

boycott ['bɔɪkɒt] n Boykott m ▷ vt boykottieren

boyfriend ['bɔɪfrend] n (fester) Freund m; **boy scout** n Pfadfinder m

bra [brɑː] n BH m

brace [breɪs] n (Tech) Strebe f; (on teeth) Spange f

bracelet ['breɪslɪt] n Armband nt

braces ['breɪsɪz] npl (BRIT) Hosenträger pl

bracket ['brækɪt] n (in text)

Klammer f; (Tech) Träger m ▷ vt einklammern

brag [bræg] vi angeben

Braille [breɪl] n Blindenschrift f

brain [breɪn] n (Anat) Gehirn nt; (mind) Verstand m, ~s (pl) (intelligence) Grips m; **brainwave** n Geistesblitz m; **brainy** adj schlau, clever

braise [breɪz] vt schmoren

brake [breɪk] n Bremse f ▷ vi bremsen; **brake fluid** n Bremsflüssigkeit f; **brake light** n Bremslicht nt; **brake pedal** n Bremspedal nt

branch [brɑːntʃ] n (of tree) Ast m; (of family, subject) Zweig m; (of firm) Filiale f, Zweigstelle f; **branch off** vi (road) abzweigen

brand [brænd] n (Comm) Marke f

brand-new ['brænd'njuː] adj (funkel)nagelneu

brandy ['brændɪ] n Weinbrand m

brass [brɑːs] n Messing nt; (BRIT fam: money) Knete f; **brass band** n Blaskapelle f

brat [bræt] n (pej, fam) Gör nt

brave [breɪv] adj tapfer, mutig; **bravery** ['breɪvərɪ] n Mut m

brawl [brɔːl] n Schlägerei f

brawn [brɔːn] n (strength) Muskelkraft f; (Gastr) Sülze f; **brawny** adj muskulös

Brazil [brə'nɪl] n Brasilien nt; **Brazilian** adj brasilianisch ▷ n Brasilianer(in) m(f); **brazil nut** n Paranuss f

bread [bred] n Brot nt; **breadbin** (BRIT), **breadbox** (US) n Brotkasten m; **breadcrumbs** npl Brotkrumen pl; (Gastr) Paniermehl nt; **breaded** adj paniert; **breadknife** n Brotmesser nt

breadth [bredθ] n Breite f

break [breɪk] n (fracture) Bruch m; (rest) Pause f; (short holiday) Kurzurlaub m; **give me a ~** gib mir eine

Chance, hör auf damit! ▷ vt (broke, broken) (fracture) brechen; (in pieces) zerbrechen; (toy, device) kaputtmachen; (promise) nicht halten; (silence) brechen; (law) verletzen; (journey) unterbrechen; (news) mitteilen (to sb jdm); **I broke my leg** ich habe mir das Bein gebrochen; **he broke it to her gently** er hat es ihr schonend beigebracht ▷ vi (come apart) (auseinander) brechen; (in pieces) zerbrechen; (toy, device) kaputtgehen; (person) zusammenbrechen; (day, dawn) anbrechen; (news) bekannt werden; **break down** vi (car) eine Panne haben; (machine) versagen; (person) zusammenbrechen; **break in** vi (burglar) einbrechen; **break into** vt einbrechen in +akk; **break off** vi, vt abbrechen; **break out** vi ausbrechen; **to ~ in a rash** einen Ausschlag bekommen; **break up** vi auftrennen; (meeting, organisation) sich auflösen; (marriage) in die Brüche gehen; (couple) sich trennen; **school breaks up on Friday** am Freitag beginnen die Ferien ▷ vt auftrennen; (marriage) zerstören; (meeting) auflösen; **breakable** adj zerbrechlich; **breakage** n Bruch m; **breakdown** n (of car) Panne f; (of machine) Versagen nt; (of person, relations, system) Zusammenbruch m; **breakdown service** n Pannendienst m; **breakdown truck** n Abschleppwagen m

breakfast ['brekfəst] n Frühstück nt; **to have ~** frühstücken; **breakfast cereal** n Cornflakes, Muesli etc; **breakfast television** n Frühstücksfernsehen nt

break-in ['breɪkɪn] n Einbruch m; **breakup** ['breɪkʌp] n (of meeting, organization) Auflösung f; (of marriage) Zerrüttung f

breast [brest] n Brust f; **breast-**

feed vt stillen; **breaststroke** n Brustschwimmen nt

breath [breθ] n Atem m; **out of ~** außer Atem; **breathalyse**, **breathalyze** ['breθəlaɪz] vt (ins Röhrchen) blasen lassen; **breathalyser**, **breathalyzer** n Promillemesser m; **breathe** [briːð] vt, vi atmen; **breathe in** vt, vi einatmen; **breathe out** vt, vi ausatmen; **breathless** ['breθlɪs] adj atemlos; **breath-taking** ['breθteɪkɪŋ] adj atemberaubend

bred [bred] pt, pp of **breed**

breed [briːd] n (race) Rasse f ▷ vi (**bred, bred**) sich vermehren ▷ vt züchten; **breeder** n Züchter(in) m(f); (fam) Hetero m; **breeding** n (of animals) Züchtung f; (of person) (gute) Erziehung f

breeze [briːz] n Brise f

brevity ['brevɪtɪ] n Kürze f

brew [bruː] vt (beer) brauen; (tea) kochen; **brewery** n Brauerei f

bribe [braɪb] n Bestechungsgeld nt ▷ vt bestechen; **bribery** ['braɪbərɪ] n Bestechung f

brick [brɪk] n Backstein m; **bricklayer** n Maurer(in) m(f)

bride [braɪd] n Braut f; **bridegroom** n Bräutigam m; **bridesmaid** n Brautjungfer f

bridge [brɪdʒ] n Brücke f; (cards) Bridge nt

brief [briːf] adj kurz ▷ vt instruieren (on über +akk); **briefcase** n Aktentasche f; **briefs** npl Slip m

bright [braɪt] adj hell; (colour) leuchtend; (cheerful) heiter; (intelligent) intelligent; (idea) glänzend; **brighten up** vt aufhellen; (person) aufheitern ▷ vi sich aufheitern; (person) fröhlicher werden

brilliant ['brɪljənt] adj (sunshine, colour) strahlend; (person) brillant; (idea) glänzend; (BRIT fam) **it was ~**

es war fantastisch

brim [brɪm] n Rand m

bring [brɪŋ] (**brought, brought**) vt bringen; (with one) mitbringen; **bring about** vt herbeiführen, bewirken; **bring back** vt zurückbringen; (memories) wecken; **bring down** vt (reduce) senken; (government etc) zu Fall bringen; **bring in** vt hereinbringen; (introduce) einführen; **bring out** vt herausbringen; **bring round, bring to** vt wieder zu sich bringen; **bring up** vt (child) aufziehen; (question) zur Sprache bringen

brisk [brɪsk] adj (trade) lebhaft; (wind) frisch

bristle ['brɪsl] n Borste f

Brit [brɪt] n (fam) Brite m, Britin f; **Britain** ['brɪtn] n Großbritannien nt; **British** ['brɪtɪʃ] adj britisch; **the ~ Isles** (pl) die Britischen Inseln pl ▷ n **the ~** (pl) die Briten pl

Brittany ['brɪtənɪ] n die Bretagne

brittle ['brɪtl] adj spröde

broad [brɔːd] adj breit; (accent) stark; **in ~ daylight** am helllichten Tag ▷ (US fam) Frau f

B road ['biːrəʊd] n (BRIT) ≈ Landstraße f

broadcast ['brɔːdkɑːst] n Sendung f ▷ irr vt, vi senden; (event) übertragen

broaden ['brɔːdn] vt **to ~ the mind** den Horizont erweitern; **broad-minded** adj tolerant

broccoli ['brɒkəlɪ] n Brokkoli pl

brochure ['brəʊʃjʊə*] n Prospekt m, Broschüre f

broke [brəʊk] pt of **break** ▷ adj (BRIT fam) pleite; **broken** ['brəʊkən] pp of **break**; **broken-hearted** adj untröstlich

broker ['brəʊkə*] n Makler(in) m(f)

brolly ['brɒlɪ] n (BRIT fam) Schirm

m

bronchitis [brɒŋ'kaɪtɪs] *n* Bronchitis *f*

bronze [brɒnz] *n* Bronze *f*

brooch [brəʊtʃ] *n* Brosche *f*

broom [bruːm] *n* Besen *m*

Bros [brɒs] *abbr* = **brothers** Gebr.

broth [brɒθ] *n* Fleischbrühe *f*

brothel ['brɒθl] *n* Bordell *nt*

brother ['brʌðə*] *n* Bruder *m*; **~s** (*pl*) (*Comm*) Gebrüder *pl*; **brother-in-law** (*pl* **brothers-in-law**) *n* Schwager *m*

brought [brɔːt] *pt, pp of* **bring**

brow [braʊ] *n* (*eyebrow*) (Augen)braue *f*; (*forehead*) Stirn *f*

brown [braʊn] *adj* braun; **brown bread** *n* Mischbrot *nt*; (*wholemeal*) Vollkornbrot *nt*; **brownie** ['braʊnɪ] *n* (*Gastr*) Brownie *m*; (*BRIT*) junge Pfadfinderin; **brown paper** *n* Packpapier *nt*; **brown rice** *n* Naturreis *m*; **brown sugar** *n* brauner Zucker

browse [braʊz] *vi* (*in book*) blättern; (*in shop*) schmökern, herumschauen; **browser** *n* (*Inform*) Browser *m*

bruise [bruːz] *n* blauer Fleck ⊳ *vt* **to ~ one's arm** sich *dat* einen blauen Fleck (am Arm) holen

brunette [bruː'net] *n* Brünette *f*

brush [brʌʃ] *n* Bürste *f*; (*for sweeping*) Handbesen *m*; (*for painting*) Pinsel *m* ⊳ *vt* bürsten; (*sweep*) fegen; **to ~ one's teeth** sich *dat* die Zähne putzen; **brush up** *vt* (*French etc*) auffrischen

Brussels sprouts [brʌsl'spraʊts] *npl* Rosenkohl *m*, Kohlsprossen *pl*

brutal ['bruːtl] *adj* brutal; **brutality** [bruː'tælɪtɪ] *n* Brutalität *f*

BSE *abbr* = **bovine spongiform encephalopathy** BSE *f*

bubble ['bʌbl] *n* Blase *f*; **bubble bath** *n* Schaumbad *nt*; **bubbly** ['bʌblɪ] *adj* sprudelnd; (*person*)

temperamentvoll ⊳ *n* (*fam*) Schampus *m*

buck [bʌk] *n* (*animal*) Bock *m*; (*US fam*) Dollar *m*

bucket ['bʌkɪt] *n* Eimer *m*

● **BUCKINGHAM PALACE**

● Der **Buckingham Palace** ist die
● offizielle Londoner Residenz der
● britischen Monarchen und liegt am
● St James's Park. Der Palast wurde
● 1703 für den Herzog von Bucking-
● ham erbaut, 1762 von George III
● gekauft, zwischen 1821 und 1836
● von John Nash umgebaut, und
● Anfang des 20. Jahrhunderts teil-
● weise neu gestaltet. Teile des Bu-
● ckingham Palace sind heute der
● Öffentlichkeit zugänglich.

buckle ['bʌkl] *n* Schnalle *f* ⊳ *vi* (*Tech*) sich verbiegen ⊳ *vt* zuschnallen

bud [bʌd] *n* Knospe *f*

Buddhism ['bʊdɪzəm] *n* Buddhismus *m*; **Buddhist** *adj* buddhistisch ⊳ *n* Buddhist(in) *m(f)*

buddy ['bʌdɪ] *n* (*fam*) Kumpel *m*

budget ['bʌdʒɪt] *n* Budget *nt*

budgie ['bʌdʒɪ] *n* (*fam*) Wellensittich *m*

buff [bʌf] *adj* (*US*) muskulös, **in the ~** nackt ⊳ *n* (*enthusiast*) Fan *m*

buffalo ['bʌfələʊ] (*pl* **-es**) *n* Büffel *m*

buffer ['bʌfə*] *n* (*a. Inform*) Puffer *m*

buffet ['bʊfeɪ] *n* (*food*) (kaltes) Büfett *nt*

bug [bʌg] *n* (*Inform*) Bug *m*, Programmfehler *m*; (*listening device*) Wanze *f*; (*US: insect*) Insekt *nt*; (*fam: illness*) Infektion *f* ⊳ *vt* (*fam*) nerven

bugger ['bʌgə*] *n* (*vulg*) Scheißkerl *m* ⊳ *interj* (*vulg*) Scheiße *f*; **bugger off** *vi* (*vulg*) abhauen, Leine ziehen

buggy® ['bʌgɪ] *n* (*for baby*) Buggy®

m; (US: pram) Kinderwagen m

build [bɪld] (built, built) vt bauen; **build up** vt aufbauen; **builder** n Bauunternehmer(in) m(f); **building** n Gebäude nt; **building site** n Baustelle f; **building society** n Bausparkasse f

built pt, pp of **build**; **built-in** adj (cupboard) Einbau-, eingebaut

bulb [bʌlb] n (Bot) (Blumen)zwiebel f; (Elec) Glühbirne f

Bulgaria [bʌlˈgeərɪə] n Bulgarien nt; **Bulgarian** adj bulgarisch ▷ n (person) Bulgare m, Bulgarin f; (language) Bulgarisch nt

bulimia [bəˈlɪmɪə] n Bulimie f

bulk [bʌlk] n (size) Größe f; (greater part) Großteil m (of +gen); **in ~** en gros; **bulky** adj (goods) sperrig; (person) stämmig

bull [bʊl] n Stier m; **bulldog** n Bulldogge f; **bulldoze** [ˈbʊldəʊz] vt planieren; **bulldozer** n Planierraupe f

bullet [ˈbʊlɪt] n Kugel f

bulletin [ˈbʊlɪtɪn] n Bulletin nt; (announcement) Bekanntmachung f; (Med) Krankenbericht m; **bulletin board** n (US: Inform) schwarzes Brett

bullfight [ˈbʊlfaɪt] n Stierkampf m; **bullshit** n (fam) Scheiß m

bully [ˈbʊlɪ] n Tyrann m

bum [bʌm] n (BRIT fam: backside) Po m; (US: vagrant) Penner m; (worthless person) Rumtreiber m; **bum around** vi herumgammeln

bumblebee [ˈbʌmblbiː] n Hummel f

bump [bʌmp] n (fam: swelling) Beule f; (road) Unebenheit f; (blow) Stoß m ▷ vt stoßen; **to ~ one's head** vt sich dat den Kopf anschlagen (on an +dat); **bump into** vt stoßen gegen; (fam: meet) (zufällig) begegnen +dat; **bumper** n (Auto) Stoß-

stange f ▷ adj (edition etc) Riesen-; (crop etc) Rekord-; **bumpy** [ˈbʌmpɪ] adj holp(e)rig

bun [bʌn] n süßes Brötchen

bunch [bʌntʃ] n (of flowers) Strauß m; (fam: of people) Haufen m; **~ of keys** Schlüsselbund m; **~ of grapes** Weintraube f

bundle [ˈbʌndl] n Bündel nt

bungalow [ˈbʌŋgələʊ] n Bungalow m

bungee jumping [ˈbʌndʒɪ-dʒʌmpɪŋ] n Bungeejumping nt

bunk [bʌŋk] n Koje f; **bunk bed(s)** n(pl) Etagenbett nt

bunker [ˈbʌŋkə*] n (Mil) Bunker m

bunny [ˈbʌnɪ] n Häschen n

buoy [bɔɪ] n Boje f; **buoyant** [ˈbɔɪənt] adj (floating) schwimmend

BUPA [ˈbuːpə] abbr (BRIT) private Krankenkasse

burden [ˈbɜːdn] n Last f

bureau [ˈbjʊərəʊ] n Büro nt; (government department) Amt nt; **bureaucracy** [bjʊˈrɒkrəsɪ] n Bürokratie f; **bureaucratic** [bjuːrəˈkrætɪk] adj bürokratisch; **bureau de change** [ˈbjuːrəʊ də ˈʃɒnʒ] n Wechselstube f

burger [ˈbɜːgə*] n Hamburger m

burglar [ˈbɜːglə*] n Einbrecher(in) m(f); **burglar alarm** n Alarmanlage f; **burglarize** vt (US) einbrechen in +akk; **burglary** n Einbruch m; **burgle** [ˈbɜːgl] vt einbrechen in +akk

burial [ˈberɪəl] n Beerdigung f

burn [bɜːn] (burnt o burned, burnt o burned) vt verbrennen; (food, slightly) anbrennen; **to ~ one's hand** sich dat die Hand verbrennen ▷ vi brennen ▷ n (injury) Brandwunde f; (on material) verbrannte Stelle; **burn down** vt, vi abbrennen

burp [bɜːp] vi rülpsen ▷ vt (baby)

aufstoßen lassen

bursary ['bɜːsəɹɪ] n Stipendium nt

burst [bɜːst] (burst, burst) vt platzen lassen ▷ vi platzen; **to ~ into tears** in Tränen ausbrechen

bury ['beɹɪ] vt begraben; (in grave) beerdigen; (hide) vergraben

bus [bʌs] n Bus m; **bus driver** n Busfahrer(in) m(f)

bush [bʊʃ] n Busch m

business ['bɪznɪs] n Geschäft nt; (enterprise) Unternehmen nt; (concern, affair) Sache f; **I'm here on** ~ ich bin geschäftlich hier; **it's none of your** ~ das geht dich nichts an; **business card** n Visitenkarte f; **business class** n (Aviat) Businessclass f; **business hours** npl Geschäftsstunden pl; **businessman** (pl -men) n Geschäftsmann m; **business studies** npl Betriebswirtschaftslehre f; **businesswoman** (pl -women) n Geschäftsfrau f

bus service n Busverbindung f; **bus shelter** n Wartehäuschen nt; **bus station** n Busbahnhof m; **bus stop** n Bushaltestelle f

bust [bʌst] n Büste f ▷ adj (broken) kaputt; **to go** ~ Pleite gehen; **bust-up** n (fam) Krach m

busy ['bɪzɪ] adj beschäftigt; (street, place) belebt; (esp US: telephone) besetzt; ~ **signal** (US) Besetztzeichen nt

but [bʌt, bət] conj aber; (only) nur, not this ~ that nicht dies, sondern das ▷ prep (except) außer; **any colour** ~ **blue** jede Farbe, nur nicht blau; **nothing** ~ ... nichts als ...; **the last / next house** ~ **one** das vorletzte / übernächste Haus

butcher ['bʊtʃə*] n Fleischer(in) m(f), Metzger(in) m(f)

butler ['bʌtlə*] n Butler m

butter ['bʌtə*] n Butter f ▷ vt buttern; **buttercup** n Butterblume

butterfly n Schmetterling m

buttocks ['bʌtəks] npl Gesäß nt

button ['bʌtn] n Knopf m; (badge) Button m ▷ vt zuknöpfen; **buttonhole** n Knopfloch nt

buy [baɪ] n Kauf m ▷ vt (bought, bought) kaufen (from von); **he bought me a ring** er hat mir einen Ring gekauft; **buyer** n Käufer(in) m(f)

buzz [bʌz] n Summen nt; **to give sb a** ~ (fam) jdn anrufen ▷ vi summen; **buzzer** ['bʌzə*] n Summer m; **buzz word** n (fam) Modewort nt

by [baɪ] prep (cause, author) von; (means) mit; (beside, near) bei, an; (via) durch; (before) bis; (according to) nach; **to go** ~ **train / bus / car** mit dem Zug / Bus / Auto fahren; **to send** ~ **post** mit der Post schicken; **a house** ~ **the river** ein Haus am o beim Fluss; ~ **her side** neben ihr, an ihrer Seite; **to leave** ~ **the back door** durch die Hintertür rausgehen; ~ **day / night** tags / nachts; **they'll be here** ~ **five** bis fünf Uhr müssten sie hier sein; **to judge** ~ **appearances** nach dem Äußeren urteilen; **to rise** ~ **10%** um 10% steigen; **it missed me** ~ **inches** es hat mich um Zentimeter verfehlt; **divided / multiplied** ~ **7** dividiert durch / multipliziert mit 7; **a room 3 metres** ~ **5** ein Zimmer 3 mal 5 Meter; ~ **oneself** allein ▷ adv (past) vorbei; **to rush** ~ vorbeirasen

bye-bye ['baɪ'baɪ] interj (fam) Wiedersehen, tschüss

by-election n Nachwahl f; **bypass** n Umgehungsstraße f; (Med) Bypass m; **byproduct** n Nebenprodukt nt; **byroad** n Nebenstraße f; **bystander** n Zuschauer(in) m(f)

byte [baɪt] n Byte nt

C [si:] *abbr* = **Celsius** C

c *abbr* = **circa** ca

cab [kæb] *n* Taxi *nt*

cabbage ['kæbɪdʒ] *n* Kohl *m*

cabin ['kæbɪn] *n* (*Naut*) Kajüte *f*; (*Aviat*) Passagierraum *m*; (*wooden house*) Hütte *f*; **cabin crew** *n* Flugbegleitpersonal *nt*; **cabin cruiser** *n* Kajütboot *nt*

cabinet ['kæbɪnɪt] *n* Schrank *m*; (*for display*) Vitrine *f*; (*Pol*) Kabinett *nt*

cable ['keɪbl] *n* (*Elec*) Kabel *nt*; **cable-car** *n* Seilbahn *f*; **cable railway** *n* Drahtseilbahn *f*; **cable television, cablevision** (*US*) *n* Kabelfernsehen *nt*

cactus ['kæktəs] *n* Kaktus *m*

CAD ['kæfeɪ] *n* = **computer-aided design** CAD *nt*

Caesarean [si:'zeərɪən] *adj* ~ (**section**) Kaiserschnitt *m*

café ['kæfeɪ] *n* Café *nt*; **cafeteria** [kæfɪ'tɪərɪə] *n* Cafeteria *f*; **cafetiere** [kæfə'tjɛə*] *n* Kaffeebereiter *m*

caffein(e) ['kæfi:n] *n* Koffein *nt*

cage [keɪdʒ] *n* Käfig *m*

Cairo ['kaɪərəʊ] *n* Kairo *nt*

cake [keɪk] *n* Kuchen *m*; **cake shop** *n* Konditorei *f*

calamity [kə'læmɪtɪ] *n* Katastrophe *f*

calculate ['kælkjʊleɪt] *vt* berechnen; (*estimate*) kalkulieren; **calculating** *adj* berechnend; **calculation** [kælkjʊ'leɪʃən] *n* Berechnung *f*; (*estimate*) Kalkulation *f*; **calculator** ['kælkjʊleɪtə*] *n* Taschenrechner *m*

calendar ['kælɪndə*] *n* Kalender *m*

calf [kɑ:f] (*pl* **calves**) *n* Kalb *nt*; (*Anat*) Wade *f*

California [kælɪ'fɔ:nɪə] *n* Kalifornien *nt*

call [kɔ:l] *vt* rufen; (*name, describe as*) nennen; (*Tel*) anrufen; (*Inform, Aviat*) aufrufen; **what's this ~ed?** wie heißt das?; **that's what I ~ service** das nenne ich guten Service ▷ *vi* (*shout*) rufen (*for help* um Hilfe); (*visit*) vorbeikommen; **to ~ at the doctor's** beim Arzt vorbeigehen; (*of train*) **to ~ at ...** in ... halten ▷ *n* (*shout*) Ruf *m*; (*Tel*) Anruf; (*Inform, Aviat*) Aufruf *m*; **to make a ~** telefonieren; **to give sb a ~** jdn anrufen; **to be on ~** Bereitschaftsdienst haben; **call back** *vi, vt* zurückrufen; **call for** *vt* (*come to pick up*) abholen; (*demand, require*) verlangen; **call off** *vt* absagen

call centre *n* Callcenter *nt*; **caller** *n* Besucher(in) *m(f)*; (*Tel*) Anrufer(in) *m(f)*

calm [kɑ:m] *n* Stille *f*; (*also of person*) Ruhe *f*; (*of sea*) Flaute *f* ▷ *vt* beruhigen ▷ *adj* ruhig; **calm down** *vi* sich beruhigen

calorie ['kælərɪ] *n* Kalorie *f*

calves [kɑ:vz] *pl of* **calf**

Cambodia [kæm'bəʊdɪə] *n* Kambodscha *nt*

camcorder ['kæmkɔːdə*] *n* Camcorder *m*

came [keɪm] *pt of* **come**

camel ['kæməl] *n* Kamel *nt*

camera ['kæmərə] *n* Fotoapparat *m*, Kamera *f*

camomile ['kæməmaɪl] *n* Kamille *f*

camouflage ['kæməflɑːʒ] *n* Tarnung *f*

camp [kæmp] *n* Lager *nt*; (*camping place*) Zeltplatz *m* ▷ *vi* zelten, campen ▷ *adj* (*fam*) theatralisch, tuntig

campaign [kæm'peɪn] *n* Kampagne *f*; (*Pol*) Wahlkampf *m* ▷ *vi* sich einsetzen (*for / against* für / gegen)

campbed ['kæmpbed] *n* Campingliege *f*; **camper** ['kæmpə*] *n* (*person*) Camper(in) *m(f)*; (*van*) Wohnmobil *nt*; **camping** ['kæmpɪŋ] *n* Zelten *nt*, Camping *nt*; **campsite** ['kæmpsaɪt] *n* Zeltplatz *m*, Campingplatz *m*

campus ['kæmpəs] *n* (*of university*) Universitätsgelände *nt*, Campus *m*

can [kæn] (*could, been able*) *vb aux* (*be able*) können; (*permission*) dürfen; **I ~not** *o* **~'t see** ich kann nichts sehen; **~ I go now?** darf ich jetzt gehen? ▷ *n* (*for food, beer*) Dose *f*; (*for water, milk*) Kanne *f*

Canada ['kænədə] *n* Kanada *nt*; **Canadian** [kə'neɪdɪən] *adj* kanadisch ▷ *n* Kanadier(in) *m(f)*

canal [kə'næl] *n* Kanal *m*

canary [kə'nɛərɪ] *n* Kanarienvogel *m*

cancel ['kænsəl] *vt* (*plans*) aufgeben, (*meeting, event*) absagen, (*comm. order etc*) stornieren, (*contract*) kündigen; (*Inform*) löschen; (*Aviat: flight*) streichen; **to be ~led** (*event, train,*

bus) ausfallen; **cancellation** [kænsə'leɪʃən] *n* Absage *f*; (*Comm*) Stornierung *f*; (*Aviat*) gestrichener Flug

cancer ['kænsə*] *n* (*Med*) Krebs *m*; **Cancer** *n* (*Astr*) Krebs *m*

candid ['kændɪd] *adj* (*person, conversation*) offen

candidate ['kændɪdət] *n* (*for post*) Bewerber(in) *m(f)*; (*Pol*) Kandidat(in) *m(f)*

candle ['kændl] *n* Kerze *f*; **candlelight** *n* Kerzenlicht *nt*; **candlestick** *n* Kerzenhalter *m*

candy ['kændɪ] *n* (*US*) Bonbon *nt*; (*quantity*) Süßigkeiten *pl*; **candy-floss** *n* (*BRIT*) Zuckerwatte *f*

cane [keɪn] *n* Rohr *nt*; (*stick*) Stock *m*

cannabis ['kænəbɪs] *n* Cannabis *m*

canned [kænd] *adj* Dosen-

cannot ['kænɒt] *contr of* **can not**

canny ['kænɪ] *adj* (*shrewd*) schlau

canoe [kə'nuː] *n* Kanu *nt*; **canoeing** *n* Kanufahren *nt*

can opener ['kænəʊpnə*] *n* Dosenöffner *m*

canopy ['kænəpɪ] *n* Baldachin *m*; (*awning*) Markise *f*; (*over entrance*) Vordach *nt*

can't [kɑːnt] *contr of* **can not**

canteen [kæn'tiːn] *n* (*in factory*) Kantine *f*; (*in university*) Mensa *f*

canvas ['kænvəs] *n* (*for sails, shoes*) Segeltuch *nt*; (*for tent*) Zeltstoff *m*; (*for painting*) Leinwand *f*

canvass ['kænvəs] *vi* um Stimmen werben (*for* für)

canyon ['kænjən] *n* Felsenschlucht *f*, **canyoning** ['kænjənɪŋ] *n* Canyoning *nt*

cap [kæp] *n* Mütze *f*; (*lid*) Verschluss *m*, Deckel *m*

capability [keɪpə'bɪlɪtɪ] *n* Fähigkeit *f*; **capable** ['keɪpəbl] *adj* fähig; **to be ~ of sth** zu etw fähig (*o* imstande) sein; **to be ~ of doing sth** etw tun können

capacity [kə'pæsɪtɪ] n (of building, container) Fassungsvermögen nt; (ability) Fähigkeit f; (function) **in his ~ as ...** in seiner Eigenschaft als ...

cape [keɪp] n (garment) Cape nt, Umhang m; (Geo) Kap nt

caper ['keɪpə*] n (for cooking) Kaper f

capital ['kæpɪtl] n (Fin) Kapital nt; (letter) Großbuchstabe m; **~ (city)** Hauptstadt f; **capitalism** n Kapitalismus m; **capital punishment** n die Todesstrafe

Capricorn ['kæprɪkɔːn] n (Astr) Steinbock m

capsize [kæp'saɪz] vi kentern

capsule ['kæpsjuːl] n Kapsel f

captain ['kæptɪn] n Kapitän m; (army) Hauptmann m

caption ['kæpʃən] n Bilderunterschrift f

captive ['kæptɪv] n Gefangene(r) mf; **capture** ['kæptʃə*] vt (person) fassen, gefangen nehmen; (town etc) einnehmen; (Inform: data) erfassen ▷ n Gefangennahme f; (Inform) Erfassung f

car [kɑː*] n Auto nt; (US Rail) Wagen m

carafe [kə'ræf] n Karaffe f

carambola [kærəm'bəʊlə] n Sternfrucht f

caramel ['kærəməl] n Karamelle f

caravan ['kærəvæn] n Wohnwagen m; **caravan site** n Campingplatz m für Wohnwagen

caraway (seed) ['kærəweɪ] n Kümmel m

carbohydrate [kɑːbəʊ'haɪdreɪt] n Kohle(n)hydrat nt

car bomb n Autobombe f

carbon ['kɑːbən] n Kohlenstoff m

car boot sale n auf einem Parkplatz stattfindender Flohmarkt

carburettor, carburetor (US) ['kɑːbjʊretə*] n Vergaser m

card [kɑːd] n Karte f; (material) Pappe f; **cardboard** n Pappe f; **~ (box)** Karton m; (smaller) Pappschachtel f; **card game** n Kartenspiel nt

cardiac ['kɑːdɪæk] adj Herz-

cardigan ['kɑːdɪɡən] n Strickjacke f

card index n Kartei f; **cardphone** ['kɑːdfəʊn] n Kartentelefon nt

care [kɛə*] n (worry) Sorge f; (carefulness) Sorgfalt f; (looking after things, people) Pflege f; **with ~** sorgfältig; (cautiously) vorsichtig; **to take ~** (watch out) vorsichtig sein; (in address) **~ of** bei; **to take ~ of** sorgen für, sich kümmern um ▷ vi **I don't ~** es ist mir egal; **to ~ about sth** Wert auf etw akk legen; **he ~s about her** sie liegt ihm am Herzen; **care for** vt (look after) sorgen für, sich kümmern um; (like) mögen

career [kə'rɪə*] n Karriere f, Laufbahn f; **career woman** (pl **career women**) n Karrierefrau f; **careers adviser** n Berufsberater(in) m(f)

carefree ['kɛəfriː] adj sorgenfrei; **careful, carefully** adj, adv sorgfältig; (cautious, cautiously) vorsichtig; **careless, carelessly** adj, adv nachlässig; (driving etc) leichtsinnig; (remark) unvorsichtig; **carer** ['kɛərə*] n Betreuer(in) m(f), Pfleger(in) m(f); **caretaker** ['kɛəteɪkə*] n Hausmeister(in) m(f); **careworker** n Pfleger(in) m(f)

car-ferry ['kɑːfɛrɪ] n Autofähre f

cargo ['kɑːɡəʊ] (pl **-(e)s**) n Ladung f

car hire, car hire company n Autovermietung f

Caribbean [kærɪ'biːən] n Karibik f ▷ adj karibisch

caring ['kɛərɪŋ] adj mitfühlend;

(parent, partner) liebevoll; (looking after sb) fürsorglich

car insurance n Kraftfahrzeugversicherung f

carnation [kɑːˈneɪʃən] n Nelke f

carnival [ˈkɑːnɪvəl] n Volksfest nt; (before Lent) Karneval m

carol [ˈkærəl] n Weihnachtslied nt

carp [kɑːp] n (fish) Karpfen m

car park n (BRIT) Parkplatz m; (multi-storey car park) Parkhaus nt

carpenter [ˈkɑːpəntə*] n Zimmermann m; **carpet** [ˈkɑːpɪt] n Teppich m

car phone n Autotelefon nt; **car pool** n Fahrgemeinschaft f; (vehicles) Fuhrpark m ▷ vi eine Fahrgemeinschaft bilden; **car rental** n Autovermietung f

carriage [ˈkærɪdʒ] n (BRIT Rail: coach) Wagen m; (compartment) Abteil nt; (horse-drawn) Kutsche f; (transport) Beförderung f; **carriageway** n (BRIT: on road) Fahrbahn f

carrier [ˈkærɪə*] n (comm) Spediteur(in) m(f), **carrier bag** n Tragetasche f

carrot [ˈkærət] n Karotte f

carry [ˈkærɪ] vt tragen; (in vehicle) befördern; (have on one) bei sich haben; **carry on** vi (continue) weitermachen; (fam: make a scene) ein Theater machen ▷ vt (continue) fortführen; **carry on working** weiter arbeiten; **carry out** vt (orders, plan) ausführen, durchführen

carrycot n Babytragetasche f

carsick [ˈkɑːsɪk] adj **he gets ~** ihm wird beim Autofahren übel

cart [kɑːt] n Wagen m, Karren m; (US: shopping trolley) Einkaufswagen m

carton [ˈkɑːtən] n (Papp)karton m; (of cigarettes) Stange f

cartoon [kɑːˈtuːn] n Cartoon m o nt; (one drawing) Karikatur f; (film)

(Zeichen)trickfilm m

cartridge [ˈkɑːtrɪdʒ] n (for film) Kassette f; (for gun, pen, printer) Patrone f; (for copier) Kartusche f

carve [kɑːv] vt, vi (wood) schnitzen; (stone) meißeln; (meat) schneiden, tranchieren; **carving** n (in wood) Schnitzerei f; (in stone) Skulptur f; (Ski) Carving nt

car wash n Autowaschanlage f

case [keɪs] n (crate) Kiste f; (box) Schachtel f; (for jewels) Schatulle f; (for spectacles) Etui nt; (Jur, matter) Fall m; **in ~** falls; **in that ~** in dem Fall; **in ~ of** fire bei Brand; **it's a ~ of ...** es handelt sich hier um ...

cash [kæʃ] n Bargeld nt; **in ~** bar; **~ on delivery** per Nachnahme ▷ vt (cheque) einlösen; **cash desk** n Kasse f; **cash dispenser** n Geldautomat m; **cashier** [kæˈʃɪə*] n Kassierer(in) m(f); **cash machine** n (BRIT) Geldautomat m

cashmere [ˈkæʃmɪə*] n Kaschmirwolle f

cash payment n Barzahlung f; **cashpoint** n (BRIT) Geldautomat m

casing [ˈkeɪsɪŋ] n Gehäuse nt

casino [kəˈsiːnəu] (pl **-s**) n Kasino nt

cask [kɑːsk] n Fass nt

casserole [ˈkæsərəul] n Kasserole f; (food) Schmortopf m

cassette [kæˈset] n Kassette f; **cassette recorder** n Kassettenrekorder m

cast [kɑːst] (cast, cast) vt (throw) werfen; (Theat, Cine) besetzen; (roles) verteilen ▷ n (Theat, Cine) Besetzung f; (Med) Gipsverband m; **cast off** vi (Naut) losmachen

caster [ˈkɑːstə*] n **~ sugar** Streuzucker m

castle [ˈkɑːsl] n Burg f

castrate [kæsˈtreɪt] vt kastrieren

casual [ˈkæʒuəl] adj (arrangement,

remark) beiläufig; (*attitude, manner*) (nach)lässig, zwanglos; (*dress*) leger; (*work, earnings*) Gelegenheits-; (*look, glance*) flüchtig; **~ wear** Freizeitkleidung f; **~ sex** Gelegenheitssex m;

casually *adv* (*remark, say*) beiläufig; (*meet*) zwanglos; (*dressed*) leger

casualty ['kæʒjuəltɪ] n Verletzte(r) mf; (*dead*) Tote(r) mf; (*department in hospital*) Notaufnahme f

cat [kæt] n Katze f; (*male*) Kater m

catalog (US), **catalogue** ['kætəlɒg] n Katalog m ▷ vt katalogisieren

cataract ['kætərækt] n Wasserfall m; (*Med*) grauer Star

catarrh [kə'tɑː*] n Katarr(h) m

catastrophe [kə'tæstrəfɪ] n Katastrophe f

catch [kætʃ] n (*fish etc*) Fang m ▷ vt (**caught, caught**) fangen; (*thief*) fassen; (*train, bus etc*) nehmen; (*not miss*) erreichen; **to ~ a cold** sich erkälten; **to ~ fire** Feuer fangen; **I didn't ~ that** das habe ich nicht mitgekriegt; **catch on** vi (*become popular*) Anklang finden; **catch up** vt, vi **to ~ with sb** jdn einholen; **to ~ on sth** etw nachholen; **catching** *adj* ansteckend

category ['kætɪgərɪ] n Kategorie f

cater ['keɪtə*] vi die Speisen und Getränke liefern (*for* für); **cater for** vt (*have facilities for*) eingestellt sein auf +*akk*; **catering** n Versorgung f mit Speisen und Getränken, Gastronomie f; **catering service** n Partyservice m

caterpillar ['kætəpɪlə*] n Raupe f

cathedral [kə'θiːdrəl] n Kathedrale f, Dom m

Catholic ['kæθəlɪk] *adj* katholisch ▷ n Katholik(in) m(f)

cat nap (*BRIT*) kurzer Schlaf; **cat's eyes** ['kætsaɪz] npl (*in road*)

Katzenaugen pl, Reflektoren pl

catsup ['kætsəp] n (US) Ketchup nt o m

cattle ['kætl] npl Vieh nt

caught [kɔːt] pt, pp of **catch**

cauliflower ['kɒlɪflauə*] n Blumenkohl m; **cauliflower cheese** n Blumenkohl m in Käsesoße

cause [kɔːz] n (*origin*) Ursache f (*of* für); (*reason*) Grund m (*for zu*); (*purpose*) Sache f; **for a good ~** für wohltätige Zwecke; **no ~ for alarm / complaint** kein Grund zur Aufregung / Klage ▷ vt verursachen

causeway ['kɔːzweɪ] n Damm m

caution ['kɔːʃən] n Vorsicht f; (*Jur, Sport*) Verwarnung f ▷ vt verwarnen; **cautious** ['kɔːʃəs] *adj* vorsichtig

cave [keɪv] n Höhle f; **cave in** vi einstürzen

cavity ['kævɪtɪ] n Hohlraum m; (*in tooth*) Loch nt

cayenne (pepper) ['keɪen] n Cayennepfeffer m

CCTV *abbr* = **closed circuit television** Videoüberwachungsanlage f

CD *abbr* = **Compact Disc** CD f; **CD player** n CD-Spieler m; **CD-ROM** *abbr* = **Compact Disc Read Only Memory** CD-ROM f; **CD-RW** *abbr* = **Compact Disc Rewritable** CD-RW f

cease [siːs] vi aufhören ▷ vt beenden; **to ~ doing sth** aufhören, etw zu tun; **cease fire** n Waffenstillstand m

ceiling ['siːlɪŋ] n Decke f

celebrate ['selɪbreɪt] vt, vi feiern; **celebrated** *adj* gefeiert; **celebration** [selɪ'breɪʃən] n Feier f; **celebrity** [sɪ'lebrɪtɪ] n Berühmtheit f, Star m

celeriac [sə'lerɪæk] n (Knollen)sellerie m o f; **celery** ['selərɪ] n (Stangen)sellerie m o f

cell [sel] n Zelle f; (US) see **cell-**

phone

cellar ['selə*] n Keller m

cello ['tʃeləu] (pl -s) n Cello nt

cellphone ['selfəun], cellular phone ['seljulə* 'fəun] n Mobiltelefon nt, Handy nt

Celt [kelt] n Kelte m, Keltin f; Celtic ['keltik] adj keltisch ▷ n (language) Keltisch nt

cement [si'ment] n Zement m

cemetery ['semitri] n Friedhof m

censorship ['sensəʃip] n Zensur f

cent [sent] n (of dollar, euro etc) Cent m

center n (US) see centre

centiliter (US), centilitre ['sentili:tə*] n Zentiliter m; centimeter (US), centimetre ['sentimi:tə*] n Zentimeter m

central ['sentrəl] adj zentral; Central America n Mittelamerika nt; Central Europe n Mitteleuropa nt; central heating n Zentralheizung f; centralize vt zentralisieren; central locking n (Auto) Zentralverriegelung f; central reservation n (BRIT) Mittelstreifen m; central station n Hauptbahnhof m

centre ['sentə*] n Mitte f; (building, of city) Zentrum nt ▷ vt zentrieren; centre forward n (Sport) Mittelstürmer m

century ['sentʃuri] n Jahrhundert nt

ceramic [si'ræmik] adj keramisch

cereal ['siəriəl] n (any grain) Getreide nt; (breakfast cereal) Frühstücksflocken pl

ceremony ['seriməni] n Feier f, Zeremonie f

certain ['sɜːtən] adj sicher (of (+gen); (particular) bestimmt; for ~ mit Sicherheit; certainly adv sicher; (without doubt) bestimmt; ~! aber sicher!; ~ not ganz bestimmt

nicht!

certificate [sə'tifikit] n Bescheinigung f; (in school, of qualification) Zeugnis nt; certify ['sɜːtifai] vt, vi bescheinigen

cervical smear ['sɜːvikəl smiə*] n Abstrich m

CFC abbr = chlorofluorocarbon FCKW nt

chain [tʃein] n Kette f ▷ vt to ~ (up) anketten; chain reaction n Kettenreaktion f; chain store n Kettenladen m

chair [tʃeə*] n Stuhl m; (university) Lehrstuhl m; (armchair) Sessel m; (chairperson) Vorsitzende(r) mf; chairlift n Sessellift m; chairman (pl -men) n Vorsitzende(r) m; (of firm) Präsident m; chairperson n Vorsitzende(r) mf; (of firm) Präsident(in) m(f); chairwoman (pl -women) n Vorsitzende f; (of firm) Präsidentin f

chalet ['ʃælei] n (in mountains) Berghütte f; (holiday dwelling) Ferienhäuschen nt

chalk [tʃɔːk] n Kreide f

challenge ['tʃælindʒ] n Herausforderung f ▷ vt (person) herausfordern; (statement) bestreiten

chambermaid ['tʃeimbə*meid] n Zimmermädchen nt

chamois leather ['ʃæmwɑː 'leðə*] n (for windows) Fensterleder nt

champagne [ʃæm'pein] n Champagner m

champion ['tʃæmpiən] n (Sport) Meister(in) m(f); championship n Meisterschaft f; Champions League n Champions League f

chance [tʃɑːns] n (fate) Zufall m; (possibility) Möglichkeit f; (opportunity) Gelegenheit f; (risk) Risiko nt; by ~ zufällig; he doesn't stand a ~ (of winning) er hat keinerlei Chance(, zu gewinnen)

chancellor [ˈtʃɑːnsələˈ] n Kanzler(in) m(f)

chandelier [ʃændɪˈlɪəˈ] n Kronleuchter m

change [tʃeɪndʒ] vt verändern; (alter) ändern; (money, wheel, nappy) wechseln; (exchange) (um)tauschen; **to ~ one's clothes** sich umziehen; **to ~ trains** umsteigen ▷ vt (Auto) schalten ▷ vi sich ändern; (esp outwardly) sich wandeln; (get changed) sich umziehen ▷ n Veränderung f; (alteration) Änderung f; (money) Wechselgeld nt; (coins) Kleingeld nt; **for a ~** zur Abwechslung; **can you give me ~ for £10?** können Sie mir auf 10 Pfund herausgeben?; **change down** vi (BRIT Auto) herunterschalten; **change over** vi sich umstellen (to auf +akk); **change up** vi (BRIT Auto) hochschalten

changeable adj (weather) veränderlich, wechselhaft; **change machine** n Geldwechsler m; **changing room** n Umkleideraum m

channel [ˈtʃænl] n Kanal m; (Radio, TV) Kanal m, Sender m; **the (English) Channel** der Ärmelkanal; **the Channel Islands** die Kanalinseln; **the Channel Tunnel** der Kanaltunnel; **channel-hopping** n Zappen nt

chaos [ˈkeɪɒs] n Chaos nt; **chaotic** [keɪˈɒtɪk] adj chaotisch

chap [tʃæp] n (BRIT fam) Bursche m, Kerl m

chapel [ˈtʃæpəl] n Kapelle f

chapped [tʃæpt] adj (lips) aufgesprungen

chapter [ˈtʃæptəˈ] n Kapitel nt

character [ˈkærəktəˈ] n Charakter m, Wesen nt; (in a play, novel etc) Figur f; (Typo) Zeichen nt; **he's a real ~** er ist ein echtes Original; **characteristic** [kærəktəˈrɪstɪk] n ty-

pisches Merkmal

charcoal [ˈtʃɑːkəʊl] n Holzkohle f

charge [tʃɑːdʒ] n (cost) Gebühr f; (Jur) Anklage f; **free of ~** gratis, kostenlos; **to be in ~ of** verantwortlich sein für ▷ vt (money) verlangen; (Jur) anklagen; (battery) laden; **charge card** n Kundenkreditkarte f

charity [ˈtʃærɪtɪ] n (institution) wohltätige Organisation f; **a collection for ~** eine Sammlung für wohltätige Zwecke; **charity shop** n Geschäft einer 'charity', in dem freiwillige Helfer gebrauchte Kleidung, Bücher etc verkaufen

charm [tʃɑːm] n Charme m ▷ vt bezaubern; **charming** adj reizend, charmant

chart [tʃɑːt] n Diagramm nt; (map) Karte f; **the ~s** pl die Charts, die Hitliste

charter [ˈtʃɑːtəˈ] n Urkunde f ▷ vt (Naut, Aviat) chartern; **charter flight** n Charterflug m

chase [tʃeɪs] vt jagen, verfolgen ▷ n Verfolgungsjagd f; (hunt) Jagd f

chassis [ˈʃæsɪ] n (Auto) Fahrgestell nt

chat [tʃæt] vi plaudern; (Inform) chatten ▷ n Plauderei f; **chat up** vt anmachen, anbaggern; **chatroom** n (Inform) Chatroom m; **chat show** n Talkshow f; **chatty** adj geschwätzig

chauffeur [ˈʃəʊfəˈ] n Chauffeur(in) m(f), Fahrer(in) m(f)

cheap [tʃiːp] adj billig; (of poor quality) minderwertig

cheat [tʃiːt] vt, vi betrügen; (in school, game) mogeln

Chechen [ˈtʃetʃen] adj tschetschenisch ▷ n Tschetschene m, Tschetschenin f; **Chechnya** [ˈtʃetʃnɪə] n Tschetschenien nt

check [tʃek] vt (examine) überprüfen (for auf +akk); (Tech: adjustment etc) kontrollieren; (US: tick) abhaken; (Aviat: luggage) einchecken; (US: coat) abgeben ⊳ n (examination, restraint) Kontrolle f; (US: restaurant bill) Rechnung f; (pattern) Karo(muster) nt; (US) see **cheque**; check in vt, vi (Aviat) einchecken; (into hotel) sich anmelden; check out vi sich abmelden, auschecken; check up vi nachprüfen, **to ~ on sb** Nachforschungen über jdn anstellen

checkers ['tʃɛkəz] nsing (US) Damespiel nt

check-in ['tʃɛkɪn] n (airport) Check-in m; (hotel) Anmeldung f; **check-in desk** n Abfertigungsschalter m; **checking account** n (US) Scheckkonto nt; **check list** n Kontrolliste f; **checkout** n (supermarket) Kasse f; **checkout time** n (hotel) Abreise(zeit) f; **checkpoint** n Kontrollpunkt m; **checkroom** n (US) Gepäckaufbewahrung f; **checkup** n (Med) (ärztliche) Untersuchung

cheddar ['tʃɛdə*] n Cheddarkäse m

cheek [tʃiːk] n Backe f, Wange f; (insolence) Frechheit f; **what a ~** so eine Frechheit!; **cheekbone** n Backenknochen m; **cheeky** adj frech

cheer [tʃɪə*] n Beifallsruf m; **~s** (when drinking) prost!; (BRIT fam: thanks) danke; (BRIT: goodbye) tschüs ⊳ vt zujubeln also vi jubeln; **cheer up** vt aufmuntern ⊳ vi fröhlicher werden; **~!** Kopf hoch!; **cheerful** adj fröhlich

cheese [tʃiːz] n Käse m; **cheeseboard** n Käsebrett nt; (as course) (gemischte) Käseplatte; **cheesecake** n Käsekuchen m

chef [ʃɛf] n Koch m, (in charge of kitchen) Küchenchef(in) m(f)

chemical ['kɛmɪkəl] adj che-

misch ⊳ Chemikalie f; **chemist** ['kɛmɪst] n (pharmacist) Apotheker(in) m(f); (industrial chemist) Chemiker(in) m(f), **~'s (shop)** Apotheke f; **chemistry** n Chemie f

cheque [tʃɛk] n (BRIT) Scheck m; **cheque account** n (BRIT) Girokonto nt; **cheque book** n (BRIT) Scheckheft nt; **cheque card** n (BRIT) Scheckkarte f

chequered ['tʃɛkəd] adj kariert

cherish ['tʃɛrɪʃ] vt (look after) liebevoll sorgen für; (hope) hegen; (memory) bewahren

cherry ['tʃɛrɪ] n Kirsche f; **cherry tomato** (pl **-es**) n Kirschtomate f

chess [tʃɛs] n Schach nt; **chessboard** n Schachbrett nt

chest [tʃɛst] n Brust f; (box) Kiste f; **~ of drawers** Kommode f

chestnut ['tʃɛsnʌt] n Kastanie f

chew [tʃuː] vt, vi kauen; **chewing gum** n Kaugummi m

chick [tʃɪk] n Küken nt; **chicken** n Huhn nt, (food: roast) Hähnchen nt; (coward) Feigling m; **chicken breast** n Hühnerbrust f; **chicken Kiev** n panierte Hähnchen, mit knoblauchbutter gefüllt; **chickenpox** n Windpocken pl; **chickpea** n Kichererbse f

chicory ['tʃɪkərɪ] n Chicorée f

chief [tʃiːf] n (of department etc) Leiter(in) m(f); (boss) Chef(in) m(f); (of tribe) Häuptling m ⊳ adj Haupt-; **chiefly** adv hauptsächlich

child [tʃaɪld] n (pl **children**) n Kind nt; **child abuse** n Kindesmisshandlung f; **child allowance, child benefit** (BRIT) n Kindergeld nt; **childbirth** n Geburt f, Entbindung f; **childhood** n Kindheit f; **childish** adj kindisch, **child lock** n Kindersicherung f; **childproof** adj kindersicher; **children** ['tʃɪldrən] pl of **child**; **child seat** n Kindersitz m

Chile ['tʃɪlɪ] n Chile nt

chill [tʃɪl] n Kühle f, (Med) Erkältung f ▷ vt (wine) kühlen; **chill out** vi (fam) relaxen; **chilled** adj gekühlt

chilli ['tʃɪlɪ] n Pepperoni pl; (spice) Chili m; **chilli con carne** ['tʃɪlɪkɒn-'kɑːnɪ] n Chili con carne nt

chilly ['tʃɪlɪ] adj kühl, frostig

chimney ['tʃɪmnɪ] n Schornstein m; **chimneysweep** n Schornsteinfeger(in) m(f)

chimpanzee [tʃɪmpæn'ziː] n Schimpanse m

chin [tʃɪn] n Kinn nt

china ['tʃaɪnə] n Porzellan nt

China ['tʃaɪnə] n China nt; **Chinese** [tʃaɪ'niːz] adj chinesisch ▷ n (person) Chinese m, Chinesin f; (language) Chinesisch nt; **Chinese leaves** npl Chinakohl m

chip [tʃɪp] n (of wood etc) Splitter m; (damage) angeschlagene Stelle; (in form) Chip m; **-s** (BRIT: potatoes) Pommes frites pl; (US: crisps) Kartoffelchips pl ▷ vt anschlagen, beschädigen; **chippie** (fam), **chip shop** n Frittenbude f

chiropodist [kɪ'rɒpədɪst] n Fußpfleger(in) m(f)

chirp [tʃɜːp] vi zwitschern

chisel ['tʃɪzl] n Meißel m

chitchat ['tʃɪttʃæt] n Gerede f

chives [tʃaɪvz] npl Schnittlauch m

chlorine ['klɔːriːn] n Chlor nt

chocaholic, chocoholic [tʃɒkə'hɒlɪk] n Schokoladenfreak m; **choc-ice** ['tʃɒkaɪs] n Eis nt mit Schokoladenüberzug; **chocolate** ['tʃɒklɪt] n Schokolade f; (chocolate-coated sweet) Praline f; **a bar of ~** eine Tafel Schokolade; **a box of ~s** eine Schachtel Pralinen; **chocolate cake** n Schokoladenkuchen m; **chocolate sauce** n Schokoladensoße f

choice [tʃɔɪs] n Wahl f; (selection) Auswahl f ▷ adj auserlesen; (product) Qualitäts-

choir ['kwaɪə*] n Chor m

choke [tʃəʊk] vi sich verschlucken; (Sport) die Nerven verlieren ▷ vt erdrosseln ▷ n (Aut) Choke m

cholera ['kɒlərə] n Cholera f

cholesterol [kə'lestərəl] n Cholesterin nt

choose [tʃuːz] (**chose, chosen**) vt wählen; (pick out) sich aussuchen; **there are three to ~ from** es stehen drei zur Auswahl

chop [tʃɒp] vt (zer)hacken; (meat etc) klein schneiden ▷ n (meat) Kotelett nt; **to get the ~** gefeuert werden; **chopper** n Hackbeil nt; (fam: helicopter) Hubschrauber m; **chopsticks** npl Essstäbchen pl

chorus ['kɔːrəs] n Chor m; (in song) Refrain m

chose [tʃəʊz], **chosen** ['tʃəʊzn] pt, pp of **choose**

chowder ['tʃaʊdə*] n (US) dicke Suppe mit Meeresfrüchten

christen ['krɪsn] vt taufen; **christening** n Taufe f; **Christian** ['krɪstʃən] adj christlich ▷ n Christ(in) m(f); **Christian name** n (BRIT) Vorname m

Christmas ['krɪsməs] n Weihnachten pl; **Christmas card** n Weihnachtskarte f; **Christmas carol** n Weihnachtslied nt; **Christmas Day** n der erste Weihnachtstag; **Christmas Eve** n Heiligabend m; **Christmas pudding** n Plumpudding m; **Christmas tree** n Weihnachtsbaum m

chronic ['krɒnɪk] adj (Med, fig) chronisch; (fam: very bad) miserabel

chrysanthemum [krɪ'sænθɪməm] n Chrysantheme f

chubby ['tʃʌbɪ] adj (child) pummelig; (adult) rundlich

chuck [tʃʌk] vt (fam) schmeißen; **chuck in** vi (fam: job) hinschmeißen; **chuck out** vt (fam) rausschmeißen; **chuck up** vi (fam) kotzen

chunk [tʃʌŋk] n Klumpen m; (of bread) Brocken m; (of meat) Batzen m; **chunky** adj (person) stämmig

Chunnel [tʃʌnəl] n (fam) Kanaltunnel m

church [tʃɜːtʃ] n Kirche f; **churchyard** n Kirchhof m

chute [ʃuːt] n Rutsche f

chutney [tʃʌtnɪ] n Chutney m

CIA abbr = **Central Intelligence Agency** (US) CIA f

CID abbr = **Criminal Investigation Department** (BRIT) ≈ Kripo f

cider [saɪdə*] n ≈ Apfelmost m

cigar [sɪˈgɑː*] n Zigarre f; **cigarette** [sɪgəˈret] n Zigarette f

cinema [sɪnəmə] n Kino nt

cinnamon [sɪnəmən] n Zimt m

circa [sɜːkə] prep zirka

circle [sɜːkl] n Kreis m ▷ vi kreisen; **circuit** [sɜːkɪt] n Rundfahrt f; (on foot) Rundgang m; (for racing) Rennstrecke f; (Elec) Stromkreis m; **circular** [sɜːkjʊlə*] adj (kreis)-rund, kreisförmig ▷ n Rundschreiben nt; **circulation** [sɜːkjʊˈleɪʃən] n (of blood) Kreislauf m; (of newspaper) Auflage f

circumstances [sɜːkəmstənsɪz] npl (facts) Umstände pl; (financial condition) Verhältnisse pl; **in / under the ~** unter den Umständen; **under no ~** auf keinen Fall

circus [sɜːkəs] n Zirkus m

cissy [sɪsɪ] n (fam) Weichling m

cistern [sɪstən] n Zisterne f; (of WC) Spülkasten m

cite [saɪt] vt zitieren

citizen [sɪtɪzn] n Bürger(in) m(f); (of nation) Staatsangehörige(r) m(f); **citizenship** n Staatsangehörigkeit

f

city [sɪtɪ] n Stadt f; (large) Großstadt f; **the ~** (London's financial centre) die (Londoner) City; **city centre** n Innenstadt f, Zentrum nt

civil [sɪvɪl] adj (of town) Bürger-; (of state) staatsbürgerlich; (not military) zivil; (polite) höflich; **civil ceremony** n standesamtliche Hochzeit; **civil engineering** n Hoch- und Tiefbau m, Bauingenieurwesen nt; **civilian** [sɪˈvɪljən] n Zivilist(in) m(f); **civilization** [sɪvɪlaɪˈzeɪʃən] n Zivilisation f, Kultur f; **civilized** [sɪvɪlaɪzd] adj zivilisiert, kultiviert; **civil partnership** n eingetragene Partnerschaft, **civil rights** npl Bürgerrechte pl; **civil servant** n (Staats)beamte(r) m, (Staats)beamtin f; **civil service** n Staatsdienst m; **civil war** n Bürgerkrieg m

CJD abbr = **Creutzfeld-Jakob disease** Creutzfeld-Jakob-Krankheit f

cl abbr = **centilitre(s)** cl

claim [kleɪm] vt beanspruchen; (apply for) beantragen; (demand) fordern; (assert) behaupten (that dass) ▷ n (demand) Forderung f (for für); (right) Anspruch m (to auf +akk); ~ **for damages** Schadenersatzforderung f; **to make ○ put in a ~** (insurance) Ansprüche geltend machen; **claimant** n Antragsteller(in) m(f)

clam [klæm] n Venusmuschel f; **clam chowder** n (US) dicke Muschelsuppe (mit Sellerie, Zwiebeln etc)

clap [klæp] vi (Beifall) klatschen

claret [klærɪt] n roter Bordeaux(wein)

clarify [klærɪfaɪ] vt klären

clarinet [klærɪˈnet] n Klarinette f

clarity [klærɪtɪ] n Klarheit f

clash [klæʃ] vi (physically) zusammenstoßen (with mit); (argue) sich auseinandersetzen (with mit); (fig: colours) sich beißen ▷ n Zusammenstoß m; (argument) Auseinandersetzung f

clasp [klɑːsp] n (on belt) Schnalle f

class [klɑːs] n Klasse f ▷ vt einordnen, einstufen

classic ['klæsɪk] adj (mistake, example etc) klassisch ▷ n Klassiker m; **classical** ['klæsɪkəl] adj (music, ballet etc) klassisch

classification [klæsɪfɪ'keɪʃn] n Klassifizierung f; **classify** ['klæsɪfaɪ] vt klassifizieren; **classified advertisement** Kleinanzeige f

classroom ['klɑːsrʊm] n Klassenzimmer nt

classy ['klɑːsɪ] adj (fam) nobel, exklusiv

clatter ['klætə*] vi klappern

clause [klɔːz] n (Ling) Satz m; (Jur) Klausel f

claw [klɔː] n Kralle f

clay [kleɪ] n Lehm m; (for pottery) Ton m

clean [kliːn] adj sauber; ~ **driving licence** Führerschein ohne Strafpunkte ▷ adv (completely) glatt ▷ vt sauber machen; (carpet etc) reinigen; (window, shoes, vegetables) putzen; (wound) säubern; **clean up** vt sauber machen ▷ vi aufräumen; **cleaner** n (person) Putzmann m, Putzfrau f; (substance) Putzmittel nt; **~'s** (firm) Reinigung f

cleanse [klenz] vt reinigen; (wound) säubern; **cleanser** n Reinigungsmittel nt

clear ['klɪə*] adj klar; (distinct) deutlich; (conscience) rein; (free, road etc) frei; **to be ~ about sth** über etw im Klaren sein ▷ adv **to stand ~** zurücktreten ▷ vt (road, room etc) räumen; (table) abräumen; (Jur: find innocent) freisprechen (of von) ▷ vi (fog, mist) sich verziehen; (weather) aufklaren; **clear away** vt wegräumen; (dishes) abräumen; **clear off**

vi (fam) abhauen; **clear up** vi (tidy up) aufräumen; (weather) sich aufklären ▷ vt (room) aufräumen; (litter) wegräumen; (matter) klären

clearance sale n Räumungsverkauf m; **clearing** n Lichtung f; **clearly** adv klar; (speak, remember) deutlich; (obviously) eindeutig; **clearout** n Entrümpelungsaktion f; **clearway** n (BRIT) Straße f mit Halteverbot nt

clench [klentʃ] vt (fist) ballen; (teeth) zusammenbeißen

clergyman ['klɜːdʒɪmæn] (pl **-men**) n Geistliche(r) m

clerk [klɑːk], (US) [klɜːk] n (in office) Büroangestellte(r) mf; (US: salesperson) Verkäufer(in) m(f)

clever ['klevə*] adj schlau, klug; (idea) clever

cliché ['kliːʃeɪ] n Klischee nt

click [klɪk] n Klicken nt; (Inform) Mausklick m ▷ vi klicken; **to ~ on sth** (inform) etw anklicken; **it ~ed** (fam) ich hab's / er hat's etc geschnallt; es hat gefunkt, es hat Klick gemacht; **they ~ed** sie haben sich gleich verstanden; **click on** vt (Inform) anklicken

client ['klaɪənt] n Kunde m, Kundin f; (Jur) Mandant(in) m(f)

cliff [klɪf] n Klippe f

climate ['klaɪmɪt] n Klima nt

climax ['klaɪmæks] n Höhepunkt m

climb [klaɪm] vi (person) klettern; (aircraft, sun) steigen; (road) ansteigen ▷ vt (mountain) besteigen; (tree etc) klettern auf +akk ▷ n Aufstieg m; **climber** n (mountaineer) Bergsteiger(in) m(f); **climbing** n Klettern nt, Bergsteigen nt; **climbing frame** n Klettergerüst nt

cling [klɪŋ] (**clung, clung**) vi sich klammern (**to** an +akk); **cling film®** n Frischhaltefolie f

clinic ['klɪnɪk] n Klinik f; **clinical**
adj klinisch

clip [klɪp] n Klammer f ▷ vt (fix)
anklemmen (to an +akk); (fingernails)
schneiden; **clipboard** n Klemm-
brett nt; **clippers** npl Schere f; (for
nails) Zwicker m

cloak [kləʊk] n Umhang m;
cloakroom n (for coats) Garderobe f

clock [klɒk] n Uhr f; (Aut. fam)
Tacho m; **round the** ~ rund um die
Uhr; **clockwise** adv im Uhrzeiger-
sinn; **clockwork** n Uhrwerk nt

clog [klɒg] n Holzschuh m ▷ vt
verstopfen

cloister ['klɔɪstə*] n Kreuzgang m

clone [kləʊn] n Klon m ▷ vt klo-
nen

close [kləʊs] adj nahe (to +dat);
(friend, contact) eng; (resemblance)
groß; ~ **to the beach** in der Nähe
des Strandes; ~ **win** knapper Sieg;
on ~r examination bei näherer o
genauerer Untersuchung ▷ adv
[kləʊs] dicht; **he lives ~ by** er
wohnt ganz in der Nähe ▷ vt
[kləʊz] schließen; (road) sperren;
(discussion, matter) abschließen ▷ vi
[kləʊz] schließen ▷ n [kləʊz] Ende
nt; **close down** vi schließen; (factory) stillgelegt werden ▷ vt (shop)
schließen; (factory) stilllegen;
closed adj (road) gesperrt; (shop etc)
geschlossen; **closed circuit television** n Videoüberwachungsanlage
f. **closely** adv (related) eng, nah;
(packed, follow) dicht; (attentively)
genau

closet ['klɒzɪt] n (esp US) Schrank
m

close-up ['kləʊsʌp] n Nahauf-
nahme f

closing ['kləʊzɪŋ] adj ~ **date**
letzter Termin; (for competition) Ein-
sendeschluss m; ~ **time** (of shop)
Ladenschluss m; (BRIT: of pub) Poli-

zeistunde f

clot [klɒt] (blood) ~ Blutgerinnsel
nt; (fam, idiot) Trottel m ▷ vi (blood)
gerinnen

cloth [klɒθ] n (material) Tuch nt;
(for cleaning) Lappen m

clothe [kləʊð] vt kleiden;
clothes npl Kleider pl, Kleidung f;
clothes line n Wäscheleine f;
clothes peg, clothespin (US) n
Wäscheklammer f; **clothing**
['kləʊðɪŋ] n Kleidung f

clotted ['klɒtɪd] adj ~ **cream** dicke Sahne (aus erhitzter Milch)

cloud [klaʊd] n Wolke f; **cloudy**
adj (sky) bewölkt; (liquid) trüb

clove [kləʊv] n Gewürznelke f; ~
of garlic Knoblauchzehe f

clover ['kləʊvə*] n Klee m; **clo-
verleaf** (pl **-leaves**) n Kleeblatt n

clown [klaʊn] n Clown m

club [klʌb] n (weapon) Knüppel m;
(society) Klub m, Verein m; (nightclub)
Disko f; (golf club) Golfschläger m; **~s**
npl (Cards) Kreuz nt; **clubbing** n **to go ~**
in die Disko gehen; **club class** n
(Aviat) Businessclass f

clue [kluː] n Anhaltspunkt m,
Hinweis m; **he hasn't a ~** er hat
keine Ahnung

clumsy ['klʌmzɪ] adj unbeholfen,
ungeschickt

clung [klʌŋ] pt, pp of **cling**

clutch [klʌtʃ] n (Aut) Kupplung f
▷ vt umklammern; (book etc) an sich
akk klammern

cm abbr = **centimetre(s)** cm

c/o abbr = **care of** bei

Co abbr = **company** Co

coach [kəʊtʃ] n (BRIT: bus) Reise-
bus m; (Rail) (Personen)wagen m;
(Sport: trainer) Trainer(in) m(f) ▷ vt
Nachhilfeunterricht geben idat;
(Sport) trainieren; **coach (class)** n
(Aviat) Economyclass f; **coach driv-
er** n Busfahrer(in) m(f); **coach**

station n Busbahnhof m; **coach trip** n Busfahrt f; (tour) Busreise f

coal [kəʊl] n Kohle f

coalition [kəʊəˈlɪʃən] n (Pol) Koalition f

coalmine [ˈkəʊlmaɪn] n Kohlenbergwerk nt; **coalminer** n Bergarbeiter m

coast [kəʊst] n Küste f; **coastguard** n Küstenwache f; **coastline** n Küste f

coat [kəʊt] n Mantel m; (jacket) Jacke f; (on animals) Fell nt, Pelz m; (of paint) Schicht f; ~ **of arms** Wappen nt; **coathanger** n Kleiderbügel m; **coating** n Überzug m; (layer) Schicht f

cobble(stone)s [ˈkɒbl(stəʊn)z] npl Kopfsteine pl; (surface) Kopfsteinpflaster nt

cobweb [ˈkɒbwɛb] n Spinnennetz nt

cocaine [kəˈkeɪn] n Kokain nt

cock [kɒk] n Hahn m; (vulg: penis) Schwanz m; **cockerel** [ˈkɒkərəl] n junger Hahn

cockle [ˈkɒkl] n Herzmuschel f

cockpit [ˈkɒkpɪt] n (in plane, racing car) Cockpit nt

cockroach [ˈkɒkrəʊtʃ] n Kakerlake f

cocksure adj todsicher; **cocktail** [ˈkɒkteɪl] n Cocktail m; **to make a ~ of sth** heir etw Mist bauen; **cocky** [ˈkɒkɪ] adj großspurig, von sich selbst überzeugt

cocoa [ˈkəʊkəʊ] n Kakao m

coconut [ˈkəʊkənʌt] n Kokosnuss f

cod [kɒd] n Kabeljau m

COD abbr = **cash on delivery** per Nachnahme

code [kəʊd] n Kode m

coeducational [kəʊɛdjʊˈkeɪʃənl] adj (school) gemischt

coffee [ˈkɒfɪ] n Kaffee m; **coffee bar** n Café nt; **coffee break** n

Kaffeepause f; **coffee maker** n Kaffeemaschine f; **coffee pot** n Kaffeekanne f; **coffee shop** n Café nt; **coffee table** n Couchtisch m

coffin [ˈkɒfɪn] n Sarg m

coil [kɔɪl] n Rolle f; (Elec) Spule f; (Med) Spirale f

coin [kɔɪn] n Münze f

coincide [kəʊɪnˈsaɪd] vi (happen together) zusammenfallen (with mit); **coincidence** [kəʊˈɪnsɪdəns] n Zufall m

coke [kəʊk] n Koks m; **Coke®** Cola f

cola [ˈkəʊlə] n Cola f

cold [kəʊld] adj kalt; **I'm ~** mir ist kalt, ich friere ▷ n Kälte f; (illness) Erkältung f, Schnupfen m; **to catch a ~** sich erkälten; **cold box** n Kühlbox f; **coldness** n Kälte f; **cold sore** n Herpes m; **cold turkey** n (fam) Totalentzug m; (symptoms) Entzugserscheinungen pl

coleslaw [ˈkəʊlslɔː] n Krautsalat m

collaborate [kəˈlæbəreɪt] vi zusammenarbeiten (with mit); **collaboration** [kəlæbəˈreɪʃən] n Zusammenarbeit f; (of one party) Mitarbeit f

collapse [kəˈlæps] vi zusammenbrechen; (building etc) einstürzen ▷ n Zusammenbruch m; (of building) Einsturz m; **collapsible** [kəˈlæpsəbl] adj zusammenklappbar, Klapp-

collar [ˈkɒlə*] n Kragen m; (for dog, cat) Halsband nt; **collarbone** n Schlüsselbein m

colleague [ˈkɒliːg] n Kollege m, Kollegin f

collect [kəˈlɛkt] vt sammeln; (fetch) abholen ▷ vi sich sammeln; **collect call** n (US) R-Gespräch nt; **collected** adj (works) gesammelt; (person) gefasst; **collector** n

Sammler(in) m(f); **collection** [kə-ˈlekʃən] n Sammlung f; (Rel) Kollekte f; (from postbox) Leerung f

college [ˈkɒlɪdʒ] n (residential) College nt; (specialist) Fachhochschule f; (vocational) Berufsschule f; (US: university) Universität f; **to go to ~** (US) studieren

collide [kəˈlaɪd] vi zusammenstoßen; **collision** [kəˈlɪʒən] n /zusammenstoß m

colloquial [kəˈləʊkwɪəl] adj umgangssprachlich

Cologne [kəˈləʊn] n Köln nt

colon [ˈkəʊlən] n (punctuation mark) Doppelpunkt m

colonial [kəˈləʊnɪəl] adj Kolonial-; **colonize** [ˈkɒlənaɪz] vt kolonisieren; **colony** [ˈkɒlənɪ] n Kolonie f

color n (US), **colour** [ˈkʌlə*] n Farbe f; (of skin) Hautfarbe f ▷ vt anmalen; (bias) färben; **colour-blind** adj farbenblind; **coloured** adj farbig, (biased) gefärbt; **colour film** n Farbfilm m; **colourful** adj (lit, fig) bunt; (life, fig) bewegt; **colouring** n (in food etc) Farbstoff m; (complexion) Gesichtsfarbe f; **colourless** adj (lit, fig) farblos; **colour photo(graph)** n Farbfoto nt; **colour television** n Farbfernsehen nt

column [ˈkɒləm] n Säule f; (of print) Spalte f

comb [kəʊm] n Kamm m ▷ vt kämmen; **to ~ one's hair** sich kämmen

combination [kɒmbɪˈneɪʃən] n Kombination f; (mixture) Mischung f (of aus); **combine** [kəmˈbaɪn] vt verbinden (with mit); (two things) kombinieren

come [kʌm] (came (came), come) vi kommen; (arrive) ankommen; (on list, in order) stehen; (with adjective, become) werden; **~ and see us** besu-

chen Sie uns mal; **coming** ich komm ja schon!; **to ~ first / second** erster / zweiter werden; **to ~ true** wahr werden; **to ~ loose** sich lockern; **the years to ~** die kommenden Jahre; **there's one more to ~** es kommt noch eins / noch einer; **how ~ ...?** (fam) wie kommt es, dass ...?; **(I) think of it** (fam) wo es mir gerade einfällt; **come across** vi (find) stoßen auf +akk; **come back** vi zurückkommen; **I'll ~ to that** ich komme darauf zurück; **come down** vi herunterkommen; (rain, snow, price) fallen; **come from** vt (result) kommen von; **where do you ~?** wo kommen Sie her?; **I ~ London** ich komme aus London; **come in** vi hereinkommen; (arrive) ankommen; (in race) **to ~ fourth** Vierter werden; **come off** vi (button, handle etc) abgehen; (succeed) gelingen; **to ~ well / badly** gut / schlecht wegkommen; **come on** vi (progress) vorankommen; **~!** kommt; (hurry) beeil dich!; (encouraging) los!; **come out** vi herauskommen; (photo) was werden; (homosexual) sich outen; **come round** vi (visit) vorbeikommen; (regain consciousness) wieder zu sich kommen; **come to** vi (regain consciousness) wieder zu sich kommen ▷ vt (sum) sich belaufen auf +akk; **when it comes to ...** wenn es ... geht; **come up** vi hochkommen; (sun, moon) aufgehen; **to ~ (for discussion)** zur Sprache kommen; **come up to** vt (approach) zukommen auf +akk; (water) reichen bis zu; (expectations) entsprechen +dat; **come up with** vt (idea) haben; (solution, answer) kommen auf +akk; **to ~ a suggestion** einen Vorschlag machen

comedian [kəˈmiːdɪən] n Komiker(in) m(f)

comedown ['kʌmdaʊn] n Abstieg m

comedy ['kɒmədɪ] n Komödie f

come-on ['kʌmɒn] n **to give sb the ~** (fam) jdn anmachen

comfort ['kʌmfət] n Komfort m; (consolation) Trost m ▷ vt trösten; **comfortable** adj bequem; (income) ausreichend; (temperature, life) angenehm; **comfort station** n (US) Toilette f; **comforting** adj tröstlich

comic ['kɒmɪk] n (magazine) Comic(heft) nt; (comedian) Komiker(in) m(f) ▷ adj komisch

coming ['kʌmɪŋ] adj kommend; (event) bevorstehend

comma ['kɒmə] n Komma nt

command [kə'mɑːnd] n Befehl m; (control) Führung f; (Mil) Kommando nt ▷ vt befehlen +dat

commemorate [kə'meməreɪt] vt gedenken +gen; **commemoration** [kəmeməreɪʃən] n **in ~ of** in Gedenken an +akk

comment ['kɒment] n (remark) Bemerkung f; (note) Anmerkung f; (official) Kommentar m (on zu); **no ~** kein Kommentar ▷ vi sich äußern (on zu); **commentary** ['kɒməntrɪ] n Kommentar m (on zu); (Tv, Sport) Livereportage f; **commentator** ['kɒmənteɪtə*] n Kommentator(in) m(f); (Tv, Sport) Reporter(in) m(f)

commerce ['kɒmɜːs] n Handel m; **commercial** [kə'mɜːʃəl] adj kommerziell; (training) kaufmännisch; **~ break** Werbepause f; **~ vehicle** Lieferwagen m ▷ n (Tv) Werbespot m

commission [kə'mɪʃən] n Auftrag m; (fee) Provision f; (reporting body) Kommission f ▷ vt beauftragen

commit [kə'mɪt] vt (crime) begehen ▷ vr **to ~ oneself** (undertake) sich verpflichten (to zu); **commit-**

ment n Verpflichtung f; (Pol) Engagement nt

committee [kə'mɪtɪ] n Ausschuss m, Komitee nt

commodity [kə'mɒdɪtɪ] n Ware f

common ['kɒmən] adj (experience) allgemein, alltäglich; (shared) gemeinsam; (widespread, frequent) häufig; (pej) gewöhnlich, ordinär; **to have sth in ~** etw gemein haben ▷ n (BRIT: land) Gemeindewiese f; **commonly** adv häufig, allgemein; **commonplace** adj alltäglich; (pej) banal; **commonroom** n Gemeinschaftsraum m; **Commons** n (BRIT Pol) **the (House of) ~** das Unterhaus; **common sense** n gesunder Menschenverstand; **Commonwealth** n Commonwealth nt; **~ of Independent States** Gemeinschaft f Unabhängiger Staaten

communal ['kɒmjʊnl] adj gemeinsam; (of a community) Gemeinschafts-, Gemeinde-

communicate [kə'mjuːnɪkeɪt] vi kommunizieren (with mit); **communication** [kəmjuːnɪ'keɪʃən] n Kommunikation f, Verständigung f; **communications satellite** n Nachrichtensatellit m; **communications technology** n Nachrichtentechnik f; **communicative** adj gesprächig

communion [kə'mjuːnɪən] n **(Holy) Communion** Heiliges Abendmahl; (Catholic) Kommunion f

communism ['kɒmjʊnɪzəm] n Kommunismus m; **communist** ['kɒmjʊnɪst] adj kommunistisch ▷ n Kommunist(in) m(f)

community [kə'mjuːnɪtɪ] n Gemeinschaft f; **community centre** n Gemeindezentrum nt; **community service** n (Jur) Sozialdienst m

commutation ticket [kɒmjuˈteɪʃəntɪkɪt] n (US) Zeitkarte f;

commute [kə'mju:t] vi pendeln;
commuter n Pendler(in) m(f)

compact [kəm'pækt] adj kompakt ▷ ['kɒmpækt] n (for make-up)
Puderdose f; (US: car) ≈ Mittelklassewagen m; **compact camera** n
Kompaktkamera f; **compact disc**
n Compact Disc f, CD f

companion [kəm'pænɪən] n
Begleiter(in) m(f)

company ['kʌmpənɪ] n Gesellschaft f; (Comm) Firma f; **to keep sb** ~
jdm Gesellschaft leisten; **company
car** n Firmenauto nt

comparable ['kɒmpərəbl] adj
vergleichbar (with, to mit)

comparative [kəm'pærətɪv] adj
relativ ▷ n (Ling) Komparativ m;
comparatively adv verhältnismäßig

compare [kəm'peə*] vt vergleichen (with, to mit); **~d with** o **to** im
Vergleich zu; **beyond ~** unvergleichlich; **comparison** [kəm-
'pærɪsn] n Vergleich m; **in ~ with** im
Vergleich mit (o zu)

compartment [kəm'pɑ:tmənt]
n (Rail) Abteil nt; (in desk etc) Fach nt

compass ['kʌmpəs] n Kompass
m; **~es** pl Zirkel m

compassion [kəm'pæʃən] n
Mitgefühl nt

compatible [kəm'pætɪbl] adj
vereinbar (with mit); (Inform) kompatibel; **we're not** ~ wir passen
nicht zueinander

compensate ['kɒmpənseɪt] vt
(person) entschädigen (for für) ▷ vi
to ~ for sth Ersatz für etw leisten;
(make up for) etw ausgleichen;
compensation [kɒmpən'seɪʃən]
n Entschädigung f; (money) Schadenersatz m; (Jur) Abfindung f

compete [kəm'pi:t] vi konkurrieren (for um); (Sport) kämpfen (for
um); (take part) teilnehmen (in an

+dat)

competence ['kɒmpɪtəns] n
Fähigkeit f; (Jur) Zuständigkeit f;
competent adj fähig; (Jur) zuständig

competition [kɒmpɪ'tɪʃən] n
(contest) Wettbewerb m; (Comm)
Konkurrenz f (for um); **competitive**
[kəm'petɪtɪv] adj (firm, price, prod
uct) konkurrenzfähig; **competitor**
[kəm'petɪtə*] n (Comm) Konkurrent(in) m(f); (Sport) Teilnehmer(in)
m(f)

complain [kəm'pleɪn] vi klagen;
(formally) sich beschweren (about
über +akk); **complaint** n Klage f;
(formal) Beschwerde f; (Med) Leiden
nt

complement vt ergänzen

complete [kəm'pli:t] adj vollständig; (finished) fertig; (failure, disaster) total; (happiness) vollkommen;
are we ~? sind wir vollzählig? ▷ vt
vervollständigen; (finish) beenden;
(form) ausfüllen; **completely** adv
völlig; **not ~ ...** nicht ganz ...

complex ['kɒmpleks] adj komplex; (task, theory etc) kompliziert ▷
n Komplex m

complexion [kəm'plekʃən] n
Gesichtsfarbe f, Teint m

complicated ['kɒmplɪkeɪtɪd] adj
kompliziert; **complication** [kɒm-
plɪkeɪʃən] n Komplikation f

compliment n ['kɒmplɪmənt] n
Kompliment nt; **complimentary**
[kɒmplɪ'mentərɪ] adj lobend; (free
of charge) Gratis-; **~ ticket** Freikarte f

comply [kəm'plaɪ] vi **to ~ with
the regulations** den Vorschriften
entsprechen

component [kəm'pəʊnənt] n
Bestandteil m

compose [kəm'pəʊz] vt (music)
komponieren; **to ~ oneself** sich zusammennehmen; **composed** adj

gefasst; **to be ~ of** bestehen aus;
composer n Komponist(in) m(f);
composition [kɒmpə'zɪʃən] n (of
a group) Zusammensetzung f; (Mus)
Komposition f
comprehend [kɒmprɪ'hend] vt
verstehen; **comprehension**
[kɒmprɪ'henʃən] n Verständnis n
comprehensive [kɒmprɪ'hen-
sɪv] adj umfassend; **~ school** Ge-
samtschule f
compress [kəm'pres] vt kompri-
mieren
comprise [kəm'praɪz] vt umfas-
sen, bestehen aus
compromise [kɒmprəmaɪz] n
Kompromiss m ⊳ vi einen Kompromiss schließen
compulsory [kəm'pʌlsərɪ] adj
obligatorisch; **~ subject** Pflichtfach
nt
computer [kəm'pju:tə*] n Computer m; **computer aided** adj
computergestützt; **computer-controlled** adj rechnergesteuert;
computer game n Computerspiel
nt; **computer-literate** adj to be ~
mit dem Computer umgehen können; **computer scientist** n Infor-
matiker(in) m(f); **computing** n
(subject) Informatik f
con [kɒn] (fam) n Schwindel m ⊳
vt betrügen (out of um)
conceal [kən'si:l] vt verbergen
(from vor +dat)
conceivable [kən'si:vəbl] adj
denkbar, vorstellbar; **conceive**
[kən'si:v] vt (imagine) sich vorstellen; (child) empfangen
concentrate [kɒnsəntreɪt] vi
sich konzentrieren (on auf +akk);
concentration [kɒnsən'treɪʃən]
n Konzentration f
concept [kɒnsept] n Begriff m
concern [kən'sɜ:n] n (affair) Angelegenheit f; (worry) Sorge f; (Comm:

firm) Unternehmen nt; **it's not my ~**
das geht mich nichts an; **there's no
cause for ~** kein Grund zur Beun-
ruhigung ⊳ vt (affect) angehen;
(have connection with) betreffen; (be
about) handeln von; **those ~ed** die
Betroffenen; **as far as I'm ~ed** was
mich betrifft; **concerned** adj (anxious) besorgt; **concerning** prep
bezüglich, hinsichtlich +gen
concert [kɒnsət] n Konzert nt; **~
hall** Konzertsaal m
concession [kən'seʃən] n Zuge-
ständnis nt; (reduction) Ermäßigung f
concise [kən'saɪs] adj knapp gefasst, prägnant
conclude [kən'klu:d] vt (end)
beenden; (also:schließen; (infer) folgern (from aus); **to ~ that ...** zu dem
Schluss kommen, dass ...; **conclusion** [kən'klu:ʒən] n Schluss m,
Schlussfolgerung f
concrete [kɒnkri:t] n Beton m ⊳
adj konkret
concussion [kən'kʌʃən] n Gehirnerschütterung f
condemn [kən'dem] vt verdam-
men; (esp Jur) verurteilen
condensed milk n Kondensmilch
f, Dosenmilch f
condition [kən'dɪʃən] n (state)
Zustand m; (requirement) Bedingung
f; **on ~ that ...** unter der Bedingung,
dass ...; **~s** pl (circumstances, weather)
Verhältnisse pl; **conditional** adj
bedingt; (Ling) Konditional-; **conditioner** n Weichspüler m; (for hair)
Pflegespülung f
condo [kɒndəʊ] (pl **-s**) n see
condominium
condolences [kən'dəʊlənsɪz]
npl Beileid nt
condom [kɒndəm] n Kondom nt
condominium [kɒndə'mɪnɪəm]
n (US: apartment) Eigentumswohnung f

conduct ['kɒndʌkt] n (behaviour)
Verhalten nt ▷ [kən'dʌkt] vt führen, leiten; (ɒrtʃiestɾə) dirigieren;
conductor [kən'dʌktə*] n (of orchestra) Dirigent(in) m(f); (in bus)
Schaffner(in) m(f); (US: on train)
Zugführer(in) m(f)

cone [kəʊn] n Kegel m; (for ice cream) Waffeltüte f; (fir cone) (Tannen)zapfen m

conference ['kɒnfərəns] n Konferenz f

confess [kən'fes] vt, vi to ~ that
... gestehen, dass ...; **confession**
[kən'feʃən] n Geständnis nt; (Rel)
Beichte f

confetti [kən'feti] n Konfetti nt

confidence ['kɒnfidəns] n Vertrauen nt (in zu); (assurance) Selbstvertrauen nt; **confident** adj (sure)
zuversichtlich (that ... dass ...),
überzeugt (of von); (self-assured)
selbstsicher; **confidential** [kɒnfi-'denʃəl] adj vertraulich

confine [kən'faɪn] vt beschränken (to auf +akk)

confirm [kən'fɜːm] vt bestätigen;
confirmation [kɒnfə'meɪʃən] n
Bestätigung f; (Rel) Konfirmation f;
confirmed adj überzeugt; (bachelor) eingefleischt

confiscate ['kɒnfiskeit] vt beschlagnahmen, konfiszieren

conflict ['kɒnflikt] n Konflikt m

confuse [kən'fjuːz] vt verwirren;
(sth with sth) verwechseln (mit mit);
(several things) durcheinanderbringen; **confused** adj (person) konfus,
verwirrt; (account) verworren; **confusing** adj verwirrend; **confusion**
[kən'fjuːʒən] n Verwirrung f; (of two things) Verwechslung f; (muddle)
Chaos nt

congested [kən'dʒestɪd] adj verstopft, (overcrowded) überfüllt; **congestion** [kən'dʒestʃən] n Stau m

congratulate [kən'grætjʊleit]
vt gratulieren (on zu); **congratulations** [kəngrætjʊ'leiʃənz] npl
Glückwünsche pl; ~! gratuliere!,
herzlichen Glückwunsch!

congregation [kɒŋgrɪ'geɪʃən] n
(Rel) Gemeinde f

congress ['kɒŋgres] n Kongress
m; (US) **Congress** der Kongress;
congressman (pl -men), **congresswoman** (pl -women) n (US)
Mitglied nt des Repräsentantenhauses

conifer ['kɒnɪfə*] n Nadelbaum m

conjunction [kən'dʒʌŋkʃən] n
(Ling) Konjunktion f; **in ~ with** in
Verbindung mit

conk out [kɒŋk 'aʊt] vi (fam: appliance, car) den Geist aufgeben,
streiken; (person: die) ins Gras beißen

connect [kə'nekt] vt verbinden
(with, to mit); (Elec, Tech: appliance etc)
anschließen (to an +akk) ▷ vi (train,
plane) Anschluss haben (with an
+akk); **~ing flight** Anschlussflug m;
~ing train Anschlusszug m; **connection** [kə'nekʃən] n Verbindung
f; (link) Zusammenhang m; (for train,
plane, electrical appliance) Anschluss
m (with, to an +akk); (business etc)
Beziehung f; **in ~ with** in Zusammenhang mit, **bad ~** (Tel) schlechte
Verbindung f; (Elec) Wackelkontakt m;
connector n (inform: computer)
Stecker m

conscience ['kɒnʃəns] n Gewissen nt; **conscientious** [kɒnʃɪ'enʃəs] adj gewissenhaft

conscious ['kɒnʃəs] adj (act) bewusst; (Med) bei Bewusstsein; **to be ~** bei Bewusstsein sein; **consciousness** n Bewusstsein nt

consecutive [kən'sekjʊtɪv] adj
aufeinander folgend

consent [kən'sent] n Zustimmung f ▷ vi zustimmen (to dat)

consequence ['kɒnsɪkwəns] n
Folge f, Konsequenz f; **consequently** ['kɒnsɪkwəntlɪ] adv
folglich

conservation [kɒnsə'veɪʃən] n
Erhaltung f; (of buildings) Denkmalschutz m; (nature conservation) Naturschutz m; **conservation area** n
Naturschutzgebiet nt; (in town) unter
Denkmalschutz stehendes Gebiet

Conservative [kən'sɜ:vətɪv] adj
(Pol) konservativ

conservatory [kən'sɜ:vətrɪ] n
(greenhouse) Gewächshaus nt; (room)
Wintergarten m

consider [kən'sɪdə*] vt (reflect on)
nachdenken über, sich überlegen;
(take into account) in Betracht ziehen;
(regard) halten für; **he is ~ed (to be)
...** er gilt als ...; **considerable**
[kən'sɪdərəbl] adj beträchtlich;
considerate [kən'sɪdərɪt] adj
aufmerksam, rücksichtsvoll; **consideration** [kənsɪdə'reɪʃən] n
(thoughtfulness) Rücksicht f;
(thought) Überlegung f; **to take sth
into ~** etw in Betracht ziehen;
considering [kən'sɪdərɪŋ] prep in
Anbetracht +gen ◊ conj da

consist [kən'sɪst] vi **to ~ of ...**
bestehen aus ...

consistent [kən'sɪstənt] adj (behaviour, process etc) konsequent;
(statements) übereinstimmend; (argument) folgerichtig; (performance,
results) beständig

consolation [kɒnsə'leɪʃən] n
Trost m; **console** [kən'səʊl] vt
trösten

consolidate [kən'sɒlɪdeɪt] vt
festigen

consonant ['kɒnsənənt] n Konsonant m

conspicuous [kən'spɪkjʊəs] adj
auffällig, auffallend

conspiracy [kən'spɪrəsɪ] n

Komplott nt; **conspire** [kən-
'spaɪə*] vi sich verschwören
(against gegen)

constable ['kʌnstəbl] n (BRIT)
Polizist(in) m(f)

Constance ['kɒnstəns] n Konstanz nt; **Lake ~** der Bodensee

constant ['kɒnstənt] adj (continual) ständig, dauernd; (unchanging:
temperature etc) gleich bleibend;
constantly adv dauernd

consternation [kɒnstə'neɪʃən]
n (dismay) Bestürzung f

constituency [kən'stɪtjʊənsɪ] n
Wahlkreis m

constitution [kɒnstɪ'tjuːʃən] n
Verfassung f; (of person) Konstitution
f

construct [kən'strʌkt] vt bauen;
construction [kən'strʌkʃən] n
(process, result) Bau m; (method)
Bauweise f; **under ~** im Bau befindlich; **construction site** n
Baustelle f; **construction worker**
n Bauarbeiter(in) m(f)

consulate ['kɒnsjʊlət] n Konsulat nt

consult [kən'sʌlt] vt um Rat fragen; (doctor) konsultieren; (book)
nachschlagen in +dat; **consultant**
n (Med) Facharzt m, Fachärztin f;
consultation [kɒnsəl'teɪʃən] n
Beratung f; (Med) Konsultation f

consume [kən'sjuːm] vt verbrauchen; (food) konsumieren; **consumer** n Verbraucher(in) m(f);
consumer-friendly adj verbraucherfreundlich

contact ['kɒntækt] n (touch) Berührung f; (communication) Kontakt
m; (person) Kontaktperson f; **to be /
keep in ~ (with sb)** (mit jdm) in
Kontakt sein / bleiben ◊ vt sich in
Verbindung setzen mit; **contact
lenses** npl Kontaktlinsen pl

contagious [kən'teɪdʒəs] adj

ansteckend

contain [kən'teɪn] vt enthalten; **container** n Behälter m; (for transport) Container m

contaminate [kən'tæmɪneɪt] vt verunreinigen; (chemically) verseuchen; **~d by radiation** strahlenverseucht, verstrahlt; **contamination** [kəntæmɪ'neɪʃən] n Verunreinigung f, (by radiation) Verseuchung f

contemporary [kən'tempərəri] adj zeitgenössisch

contempt [kən'tempt] n Verachtung f; **contemptuous** adj verächtlich; **to be ~** voller Verachtung sein (of für)

content [kən'tent] adj zufrieden

content(s) ['kɒntent(s)] n pl Inhalt m

contest ['kɒntest] n (Wett)kampf m (for um); (competition) Wettbewerb m ▷ [kən'test] vt kämpfen um +akk; (dispute) bestreiten; **contestant** [kən'testənt] n Teilnehmer(in) m(f)

context ['kɒntekst] n Zusammenhang m; **out of ~** aus dem Zusammenhang gerissen

continent ['kɒntɪnənt] n Kontinent m, Festland nt; **the Continent** (BRIT) das europäische Festland, der Kontinent; **continental** [kɒntɪ'nentl] adj kontinental; **~ breakfast** kleines Frühstück mit Brötchen und Marmelade, Kaffee oder Tee

continual [kən'tɪnjʊəl] adj (endless) ununterbrochen; (constant) dauernd, ständig; **continually** adv dauernd; (again and again) immer wieder; **continuation** [kəntɪnjʊ'eɪʃən] n Fortsetzung f; **continue** [kən'tɪnjuː] vi weitermachen (with mit); (esp talking) fortfahren (with mit); (travelling) weiterfahren; (state, conditions) fortdauern, anhalten ▷ vt fortsetzen; **to be ~d** Fortsetzung

folgt; **continuous** [kən'tɪnjʊəs] adj (endless) ununterbrochen; (constant) ständig

contraceptive [kɒntrə'septɪv] n Verhütungsmittel nt

contract ['kɒntrækt] n Vertrag m

contradict [kɒntrə'dɪkt] vt widersprechen +dat; **contradiction** [kɒntrə'dɪkʃən] n Widerspruch m

contrary ['kɒntrəri] n Gegenteil nt; **on the ~** im Gegenteil ▷ adj **~ to** entgegen +dat

contrast ['kɒntrɑːst] n Kontrast m, Gegensatz m; **in ~** im Gegensatz zu ▷ [kən'trɑːst] vt entgegensetzen

contribute [kən'trɪbjuːt] vt, vi beitragen (to zu); (money) spenden (to für); **contribution** [kɒntrɪ'bjuːʃən] n Beitrag m

control [kən'trəʊl] vt (master) beherrschen; (temper etc) im Griff haben; (esp Tech) steuern; **to – oneself** sich beherrschen ▷ n Kontrolle f, (mastery) Beherrschung f; (of business) Leitung f; (esp Tech) Steuerung f, **~s** pl (knobs, switches etc) Bedienungselemente pl; (collectively) Steuerung f; **to be out of ~** außer Kontrolle sein; **control knob** n Bedienungsknopf m; **control panel** n Schalttafel f

controversial [kɒntrə'vɜːʃəl] adj umstritten

convalesce [kɒnvə'les] vi gesund werden; **convalescence** n Genesung f

convenience [kən'viːnɪəns] n (quality, thing) Annehmlichkeit f; **at your ~** wann es Ihnen passt; **with all modern ~s** mit allem Komfort; **convenience food** n Fertiggericht nt; **convenient** adj günstig, passend

convent ['kɒnvənt] n Kloster nt

convention [kən'venʃən] n (cus-

tom) Konvention f; *(meeting)* Konferenz f; **the Geneva Convention** die Genfer Konvention; **conventional** *adj* herkömmlich, konventionell

conversation [kɔnvə'seɪʃən] n Gespräch nt, Unterhaltung f

conversion [kən'vɜːʃən] n Umwandlung f *(into* in *+akk)*; *(of building)* Umbau m *(into* zu); *(calculation)* Umrechnung f; **conversion table** n Umrechnungstabelle f; **convert** [kən'vɜːt] vt umwandeln; *(person)* bekehren; *(Inform)* konvertieren; **to ~ into Euros** in Euro umrechnen; **convertible** n *(Auto)* Kabrio nt ▷ adj umwandelbar

convey [kən'veɪ] vt *(carry)* befördern; *(feelings)* vermitteln; **conveyor belt** n Förderband nt, Fließband nt

convict [kən'vɪkt] vt verurteilen *(of* wegen) ▷ n ['kɔnvɪkt] n Strafgefangene(r) mf; **conviction** n *(Jur)* Verurteilung f; *(strong belief)* Überzeugung f

convince [kən'vɪns] vt überzeugen *(of* von); **convincing** *adj* überzeugend

cook [kʊk] vt, vi kochen ▷ n Koch m, Köchin f; **cookbook** n Kochbuch nt; **cooker** n Herd m; **cookery** n Kochkunst f; **~ book** Kochbuch nt; **cookie** n *(US)* Keks m, Kochen nt; *(style of cooking)* Küche f

cool [kuːl] adj kühl, gelassen; *(fam: brilliant)* cool, stark ▷ vt, vi (ab)kühlen; **~ it** reg dich ab! ▷ n **to keep/lose one's ~** *(fam)* ruhig bleiben/durchdrehen; **cool down** vi abkühlen; *(calm down)* sich beruhigen

cooperate [kəʊ'ɔpəreɪt] vi zusammenarbeiten, kooperieren; **cooperation** [kəʊɒpə'reɪʃən] n Zusammenarbeit f, Kooperation f; **cooperative** [kəʊ'ɒpərətɪv] adj hilfsbereit ▷ n Genossenschaft f

coordinate [kəʊ'ɔːdɪneɪt] vt ko-

ordinieren

cop [kɔp] n *(fam: policeman)* Bulle m

cope [kəʊp] vi zurechtkommen, fertig werden *(with* mit)

Copenhagen [kəʊpən'heɪgən] n Kopenhagen nt

copier ['kɔpɪə*] n Kopierer m

copper ['kɔpə*] n Kupfer nt; *(BRIT fam: policeman)* Bulle m; *(fam: coin)* Kupfermünze f; **~s** Kleingeld nt

copy ['kɔpɪ] n Kopie f; *(of book)* Exemplar nt ▷ vt kopieren; *(imitate)* nachahmen; **copyright** n Urheberrecht nt

coral ['kɔrəl] n Koralle f

cord [kɔːd] n Schnur f; *(material)* Kordsamt m

cordial ['kɔːdɪəl] adj freundlich

cordless ['kɔːdlɪs] adj *(phone)* schnurlos

core [kɔː*] n *(a. fig)* Kern m; *(of apple, pear)* Kerngehäuse nt; **core business** n Kerngeschäft nt

cork [kɔːk] n *(material)* Kork m; *(stopper)* Korken m; **corkscrew** ['kɔːkskruː] n Korkenzieher m

corn [kɔːn] n Getreide nt, Korn nt; *(US: maize)* Mais m; *(on foot)* Hühnerauge nt; **~ on the cob** *(gekochter)* Maiskolben; **corned beef** n Cornedbeef nt

corner ['kɔːnə*] n Ecke f; *(on road)* Kurve f; *(Sport)* Eckstoß m ▷ vt in die Enge treiben; **corner shop** n Laden m an der Ecke

cornflakes ['kɔːfleɪks] npl Cornflakes pl; **cornflour** ['kɔːnflaʊə*] *(BRIT)*, **cornstarch** ['kɔːnstɑːtʃ] *(US)* n Maismehl nt

Cornish ['kɔːnɪʃ] adj kornisch; **~ pasty** mit Fleisch und Kartoffeln gefüllte Pastete; **Cornwall** ['kɔːnwəl] n Cornwall nt

coronary ['kɔrənərɪ] n *(Med)* Herzinfarkt m

coronation [kɔrə'neɪʃən] n Krö-

nung f
corporation [kɔːpəˈreɪʃən] n (US Comm) Aktiengesellschaft f
corpse [kɔːps] n Leiche f
correct [kəˈrekt] adj (accurate) richtig; (proper) korrekt ▷ vt korrigieren, verbessern; **correction** n (esp written) Korrektur f
correspond [kɒrɪˈspɒnd] vi entsprechen (to dat.); (two things) über einstimmen; (exchange letters) korrespondieren; **corresponding** adj entsprechend
corridor [ˈkɒrɪdɔː*] n (in building) Flur m; (in train) Gang m
corrupt [kəˈrʌpt] adj korrupt
cosmetic [kɒzˈmetɪk] adj kosmetisch; **cosmetics** npl Kosmetika pl; **cosmetic surgeon** n Schönheitschirurg(in) m(f); **cosmetic surgery** n Schönheitschirurgie f
cosmopolitan [kɒzməˈpɒlɪtən] adj international; (attitude) weltoffen
cost [kɒst] (cost, cost) vt kosten ▷ n Kosten pl; **at all ~s, at any ~** um jeden Preis; **~ of living** Lebenshaltungskosten pl; **costly** adj kostspielig
costume [ˈkɒstjuːm] n (Theat) Kostüm nt
cosy [ˈkəʊzɪ] adj gemütlich
cot [kɒt] n (BRIT) Kinderbett nt; (US) Campingliege f
cottage [ˈkɒtɪdʒ] n kleines Haus; (country cottage) Landhäuschen nt; **cottage cheese** n Hüttenkäse m; **cottage pie** n Hackfleisch mit Kartoffelbrei überbacken
cotton [ˈkɒtn] n Baumwolle f; **cotton candy** n (US) Zuckerwatte f; **cotton wool** n (BRIT) Watte f
couch [kaʊtʃ] n Couch f; (sofa) Sofa nt; **couchette** [kuːˈʃet] n Liegewagen(platz) m
cough [kɒf] vi husten ▷ n Husten

m; **cough mixture** n Hustensaft m; **cough sweet** n Hustenbonbon nt
could [kʊd] pt of **can** konnte; conditional könnte: **~ you come earlier?** könntest du früher kommen?
couldn't contr of **could not**
council [ˈkaʊnsl] n (Pol) Rat m; (local ~) Gemeinderat m, (town ~) Stadtrat m; **council estate** n Siedlung f des sozialen Wohnungsbaus; **council house** n Sozialwohnung f; **councillor** [ˈkaʊnsɪlə*] n Gemeinderat m, Gemeinderätin f; **council tax** n Gemeindesteuer f
count [kaʊnt] vt, vi zählen; (include) mitrechnen ▷ n Zählung f; (noble) Graf m; **count on** vt (rely on) sich verlassen auf +akk; (expect) rechnen mit
counter [ˈkaʊntə*] n (in shop) Ladentisch m; (in café) Theke f; (in bank, post office) Schalter m; **counter attack** n Gegenangriff m ▷ vi zu rückschlagen; **counter-clockwise** adv (US) entgegen dem Uhrzeigersinn
counterfoil [ˈkaʊntəfɔɪl] n (Kontroll)abschnitt m
counterpart [ˈkaʊntəpɑːt] n Gegenstück nt (of zu)
countess [ˈkaʊntɪs] n Gräfin f
countless [ˈkaʊntlɪs] adj zahllos, unzählig
country [ˈkʌntrɪ] n Land nt; **in the ~** auf dem Land(e); **in this ~** hierzulande; **country cousin** n (fam) Landei nt; **country dancing** n Volkstanz m; **country house** n Landhaus nt; **countryman** n (compatriot) Landsmann m; **country music** n Countrymusic f; **country road** n Landstraße f; **countryside** n Landschaft f; (rural area) Land nt
county [ˈkaʊntɪ] n (BRIT) Grafschaft f; (US) Verwaltungsbezirk m; **county town** n (BRIT) ≈ Kreisstadt f

couple ['kʌpl] n Paar nt; **a ~ of** ein paar

coupon ['ku:pɒn] n (voucher) Gutschein m

courage ['kʌrɪdʒ] n Mut m; **courageous** [kə'reɪdʒəs] adj mutig

courgette [kuə'ʒet] n (BRIT) Zucchini f

courier ['kʊrɪə*] n (for tourists) Reiseleiter(in) m(f); (messenger) Kurier m

course [kɔ:s] n (of study) Kurs m; (for race) Strecke f; (Naut, Aviat) Kurs m; (at university) Studiengang m; (in meal) Gang m; **of ~** natürlich; **in the ~ of** während

court [kɔ:t] n (Sport) Platz m; (Jur) Gericht nt

courteous ['kɜ:tɪəs] adj höflich; **courtesy** ['kɜ:təsɪ] n Höflichkeit f; **~ bus / coach** n (gebührenfreier) Zubringerbus

courthouse ['kɔ:thaʊs] n (US) Gerichtsgebäude nt; **court order** n Gerichtsbeschluss m; **courtroom** n Gerichtssaal m

courtyard ['kɔ:tjɑ:d] n Hof m

cousin ['kʌzn] n (male) Cousin m; (female) Cousine f

cover ['kʌvə*] vt bedecken (in, with mit); (distance) zurücklegen; (loan, costs) decken ▷ n (for bed etc) Decke f; (of cushion) Bezug m; (lid) Deckel m; (of book) Umschlag m; (insurance) Versicherungsschutz m; **cover up** vt zudecken; (error etc) vertuschen; **coverage** n Berichterstattung f (of über +akk); **cover charge** n Kosten pl für ein Gedeck; **covering** n Decke f; **covering letter** n Begleitbrief m; **cover story** n (newspaper) Titelgeschichte f

cow [kaʊ] n Kuh f

coward ['kaʊəd] n Feigling m; **cowardly** adj feig(e)

cowboy ['kaʊbɔɪ] n Cowboy m

coy [kɔɪ] adj gespielt schüchtern, kokett

cozy ['kəʊzɪ] adj (US) gemütlich

CPU abbr = **central processing unit** Zentraleinheit f

crab [kræb] n Krabbe f

crabby ['kræbɪ] adj mürrisch, reizbar

crack [kræk] n Riss m; (in pottery, glass) Sprung m; (drug) Crack nt; **to have a ~ at sth** etw ausprobieren ▷ vi (pottery, glass) einen Sprung bekommen; (wood, ice etc) einen Riss bekommen; **to get ~ing** (fam) loslegen ▷ vt (bone) anbrechen; (nut, code) knacken

cracker ['krækə*] n (biscuit) Kräcker m; (Christmas ~) Knallbonbon nt; **crackers** adj (fam) verrückt; **he's ~** er hat nicht alle Tassen im Schrank

crackle ['krækl] vi knistern; (telephone, radio) knacken; **crackling** n (Gastr) Kruste f (des Schweinebratens)

cradle ['kreɪdl] n Wiege f

craft [krɑ:ft] n Handwerk nt; (art) Kunsthandwerk nt; (Naut) Boot nt; **craftsman** (pl **-men**) n Handwerker m; **craftsmanship** n Handwerkskunst f; (ability) handwerkliches Können

crafty ['krɑ:ftɪ] adj schlau

cram [kræm] vt stopfen (into in +akk); **to be ~med with ...** mit ... voll gestopft sein ▷ vi (revise for exam) pauken (for für)

cramp [kræmp] n Krampf m

cranberry ['krænbərɪ] n Preiselbeere f

crane [kreɪn] n (machine) Kran m; (bird) Kranich m

crap [kræp] n (vulg) Scheiße f; (rubbish) Mist m ▷ adj beschissen, Scheiß-

crash [kræʃ] vi einen Unfall haben; (two vehicles) zusammenstoßen, (plane, computer) abstürzen; (economy) zusammenbrechen; **to ~ into sth** gegen etw knallen ▷ vt einen Unfall haben mit ▷ n (car) Unfall m; (train) Unglück nt; (collision) Zusammenstoß m; (Aviat, Inform) Absturz m; (noise) Krachen nt; **crash barrier** n Leitplanke f; **crash course** n Intensivkurs m; **crash helmet** n Sturzhelm m; **crash landing** n Bruchlandung f

crate [kreɪt] n Kiste f, (of beer) Kasten m

crater ['kreɪtə*] n Krater m

craving ['kreɪvɪŋ] n starkes Verlangen, Bedürfnis nt

crawl [krɔːl] vi kriechen; (baby) krabbeln ▷ n (swimming) Kraul nt; **crawler lane** n Kriechspur f

crayfish ['kreɪfɪʃ] n Languste f

crayon ['kreɪən] n Buntstift m

crazy ['kreɪzɪ] adj verrückt (about nach)

cream [kriːm] n (from milk) Sahne f, Rahm m; (polish, cosmetic) Creme f ▷ adj cremefarben; **cream cake** n (small) Sahnetörtchen nt; (big) Sahnetorte f; **cream cheese** n Frischkäse m; **creamer** n Kaffeeweißer m; **cream tea** n (BRIT) Nachmittagstee mit Törtchen, Marmelade und Schlagsahne; **creamy** adj sahnig

crease [kriːs] n Falte f ▷ vt falten; (untidy) zerknittern

create [kriːˈeɪt] vt schaffen; (cause) verursachen; **creative** [kriːˈeɪtɪv] adj schöpferisch; (person) kreativ; **creature** ['kriːtʃə*] n Geschöpf nt

crèche [kreʃ] n Kinderkrippe f

credible ['kredɪbl] adj (person) glaubwürdig; **credibility** n Glaubwürdigkeit f

credit ['kredɪt] n (Fin: amount allowed) Kredit m; (amount possessed) Guthaben nt; (recognition) Anerkennung f; **~s** (of film) Abspann m; **credit card** n Kreditkarte f

creep [kriːp] (**crept, crept**) vi kriechen; **creeps** n **he gives me the ~** er ist mir nicht ganz geheuer; **creepy** ['kriːpɪ] adj (frightening) gruselig, unheimlich

crept [krept] pt, pp of **creep**

cress [kres] n Kresse f

crest [krest] n Kamm m; (coat of arms) Wappen nt

crew [kruː] n Besatzung f, Mannschaft f

crib [krɪb] n (US) Kinderbett nt

cricket ['krɪkɪt] n (game) Kricket nt; (insect) Grille f

crime [kraɪm] n Verbrechen nt; **criminal** ['krɪmɪnl] n Verbrecher(in) m(f) ▷ adj kriminell, strafbar

cripple ['krɪpl] n Krüppel m ▷ vt verkrüppeln, lähmen

crisis ['kraɪsɪs] (pl **crises**) n Krise f

crisp [krɪsp] adj knusprig; **crisps** npl (BRIT) Chips pl; **crispbread** n Knäckebrot nt

criterion [kraɪˈtɪərɪən] n Kriterium m; **critic** ['krɪtɪk] n Kritiker(in) m(f); **critical** adj kritisch; **critically** adv kritisch; **~ ill / injured** schwer krank / verletzt; **criticism** ['krɪtɪsɪzm] n Kritik f; **criticize** ['krɪtɪsaɪz] vt kritisieren

Croat ['krəʊæt] n Kroate m, Kroatin f; **Croatia** [krəʊˈeɪʃə] n Kroatien nt; **Croatian** [krəʊˈeɪʃən] adj kroatisch

crockery ['krɒkərɪ] n Geschirr nt

crocodile ['krɒkədaɪl] n Krokodil nt

crocus ['krəʊkəs] n Krokus m

crop [krɒp] n (harvest) Ernte f; **crops** npl Getreide nt; **crop up** vi auftauchen

croquette [krəˈket] n Krokette f

cross [krɒs] n Kreuz nt; **to mark sth with a ~** etw ankreuzen ▷ vt (road, river etc) überqueren; (legs) übereinander schlagen; **it ~ed my mind** es fiel mir ein; **to ~ one's fingers** die Daumen drücken ▷ *adj* ärgerlich, böse; **cross out** *vt* durchstreichen

crossbar *n (of bicycle)* Stange *f*; *(Sport)* Querlatte *f*; **cross-country** *adj* ~ **running** Geländelauf *m*; ~ **skiing** Langlauf *m*; **cross-examination** *n* Kreuzverhör *nt*; **cross-eyed** *adj* **to be** ~ schielen; **crossing** *n (crossroads)* (Straßen)kreuzung *f*; *(for pedestrians)* Fußgängerüberweg *m*; *(on ship)* Überfahrt *f*; **crossroads** *nsing o pl* Straßenkreuzung *f*; **cross section** *n* Querschnitt *m*; **crosswalk** *n* (US) Fußgängerüberweg *m*; **crossword (puzzle)** *n* Kreuzworträtsel *nt*

crouch [kraʊtʃ] *vi* hocken

crouton ['kru:tɒn] *n* Croûton *m*

crow [krəʊ] *n* Krähe *f*

crowbar ['krəʊbɑ:*] *n* Brecheisen *nt*

crowd [kraʊd] *n* Menge *f* ▷ *vi* sich drängen *(into* in +*akk; round* um); **crowded** *adj* überfüllt

crown [kraʊn] *n* Krone *f* ▷ *vt* krönen; *(fam)* **and to ~ it all ...** und als Krönung ...; **crown jewels** *npl* Kronjuwelen *pl*

crucial ['kru:ʃəl] *adj* entscheidend

crude [kru:d] *adj* primitiv; *(humour, behaviour)* derb, ordinär ▷ *n* **(oil)** Rohöl *nt*

cruel ['krʊəl] *adj* grausam *(to* zu, *gegen)*; *(unfeeling)* gefühllos; **cruelty** *n* Grausamkeit *f*; ~ **to animals** Tierquälerei *f*

cruise [kru:z] *n* Kreuzfahrt *f* ▷ *vi (ship)* kreuzen; *(car)* mit Reisegeschwindigkeit fahren; **cruise liner** *n* Kreuzfahrtschiff *nt*; **cruise missile** *n* Marschflugkörper *m*; **cruising speed** *n* Reisegeschwindigkeit *f*

crumb [krʌm] *n* Krume *f*

crumble ['krʌmbl] *vt, vi* zerbröckeln ▷ *n mit Streuseln überbackenes Kompott*

crumpet ['krʌmpɪt] *n* weiches Hefegebäck zum Toasten; *(fam: attractive woman)* Schnecke *f*

crumple ['krʌmpl] *vt* zerknittern; **crumple zone** *n (Auto)* Knautschzone *f*

crunchy ['krʌntʃɪ] *adj* (BRIT) knusprig

crusade [kru:'seɪd] *n* Kreuzzug *m*

crush [krʌʃ] *vt* zerdrücken; *(finger etc)* quetschen; *(spices, stone)* zerstoßen ▷ *n* **to have a ~ on sb** in jdn verknallt sein; **crushing** *adj (defeat, remark)* vernichtend

crust [krʌst] *n* Kruste *f*; **crusty** *adj* knusprig

crutch [krʌtʃ] *n* Krücke *f*

cry [kraɪ] *vi (call)* rufen; *(scream)* schreien; *(weep)* weinen ▷ *n (call)* Ruf *m*; *(louder)* Schrei *m*

crypt [krɪpt] *n* Krypta *f*

crystal ['krɪstl] *n* Kristall *m*

cu *abbr* = **see you** (SMS, E-Mail) bis bald

cub [kʌb] *n (animal)* Junge(s) *nt*

Cuba ['kju:bə] *n* Kuba *nt*

cube [kju:b] *n* Würfel *m*

cubic ['kju:bɪk] *adj* Kubik-

cubicle ['kju:bɪkl] *n* Kabine *f*

cuckoo ['kʊku:] *n* Kuckuck *m*

cucumber ['kju:kʌmbə*] *n* Salatgurke *f*

cuddle ['kʌdl] *vt* in den Arm nehmen; *(amorously)* schmusen mit ▷ *n* Liebkosung *f*, Umarmung *f*; **to have a ~** schmusen; **cuddly** *adj* verschmust; **cuddly toy** *n* Plüschtier *nt*

cuff [kʌf] *n* Manschette *f*; (US: *trouser ~)* Aufschlag *m*; **off the ~** aus dem Stegreif; **cufflink** *n* Manschettenknopf *m*

cuisine [kwɪ'zi:n] *n* Kochkunst *f*, Küche *f*

cul-de-sac ['kʌldəsæk] n (BRIT) Sackgasse f

culprit ['kʌlprɪt] n Schuldige(r) mf; (fig) Übeltäter(in) m(f)

cult [kʌlt] n Kult m

cultivate ['kʌltɪveɪt] vt (Agr: land) bepflanzen, (crop) anbauen; **cultivated** adj (person) kultiviert, gebildet

cultural ['kʌltʃərəl] adj kulturell, Kultur-; **culture** ['kʌltʃə*] n Kultur f; **cultured** adj gebildet, kultiviert; **culture vulture** (BRIT fam) n Kulturfanatiker(in) m(f)

cumbersome ['kʌmbəsəm] adj (object) unhandlich

cumin ['kʌmɪn] n Kreuzkümmel m

cunning ['kʌnɪŋ] adj schlau; (person a.) gerissen

cup [kʌp] n Tasse f; (prize) Pokal m; **it's not his ~ of tea** das ist nicht sein Fall; **cupboard** ['kʌbəd] n Schrank m; **cup final** n Pokalendspiel nt; **cup tie** n Pokalspiel nt

cupola ['kju:pələ] n Kuppel f

curable ['kjʊərəbl] adj heilbar

curb [kə:b] n (US see kerb)

curd [kə:d] n ~ **cheese**, ~**s** ≈ Quark m

cure [kjʊə*] n Heilmittel nt (for gegen); (process) Heilung f ⊳ vt heilen; (Culin) pökeln; (smoke) räuchern

curious ['kjʊərɪəs] adj neugierig; (strange) seltsam

curl [kə:l] n Locke f ⊳ vi sich kräuseln; **curly** adj lockig

currant ['kʌrənt] n (dried) Korinthe f; (red, black) Johannisbeere f

currency ['kʌrənsɪ] n Währung f; **foreign** ~ Devisen pl

current ['kʌrənt] n (in water) Strömung f; (electric ~) Strom m ⊳ adj (issue, affairs) aktuell, gegenwärtig; (expression) gängig; **current account** n Girokonto nt; **currently** adv zur Zeit

curriculum [kə'rɪkjʊləm] n Lehr-

plan m; **curriculum vitae** [kə'rɪkjʊləm'vi:taɪ] n (BRIT) Lebenslauf m

curry ['kʌrɪ] n Currygericht nt; **curry powder** n Curry(pulver) nt

curse [kə:s] vi (swear) fluchen (at auf +akk) ⊳ n Fluch m

cursor ['kə:sə*] n (Inform) Cursor m

curt [kə:t] adj schroff, kurz angebunden

curtain ['kə:tn] n Vorhang m; **it was ~s for Benny** für Benny war alles vorbei

curve [kə:v] n Kurve f ⊳ vi einen Bogen machen; **curved** adj gebogen

cushion ['kʊʃən] n Kissen nt

custard ['kʌstəd] n dicke Vanillesoße, die warm oder kalt zu vielen englischen Nachspeisen gegessen wird

custom ['kʌstəm] n Brauch m; (habit) Gewohnheit f; **customary** ['kʌstəmrɪ] adj üblich; **custom-built** adj nach Kundenangaben gefertigt; **customer** ['kʌstəmə*] n Kunde m, Kundin f; **customer loyalty card** n Kundenkarte f; **customer service** n Kundendienst m

customs ['kʌstəmz] npl (organization, location) Zoll m; **to pass through ~** durch den Zoll gehen; **customs officer** n Zollbeamte(r) m, Zollbeamtin f

cut [kʌt] (**cut**, **cut**) vt schneiden; (cake) anschneiden; (wages, benefits) kürzen; (prices) heruntersetzen; **I ~ my finger** ich habe mir in den Finger geschnitten ⊳ n Schnitt m; (wound) Schnittwunde f; (reduction) Kürzung f (in gen); **price/tax ~** Preissenkung/Steuersenkung f; **to be a ~ above the rest** eine Klasse besser als die anderen sein; **cut back** vt (work-force etc) reduzieren; **cut down** vt (tree) fällen, **to ~ on sth** etwas einschränken; **cut in** vi (Auto) scharf einscheren; **to ~ on sb** jdn schneiden; **cut off** vt abschneiden; (gas, *electricity*) abdrehen, abstellen; (*Tel*) **I was ~** ich wurde unterbrochen

cutback n Kürzung f

cute [kjuːt] *adj* putzig, niedlich; (*US: shrewd*) clever

cutlery ['kʌtlərɪ] n Besteck *nt*

cutlet ['kʌtlɪt] n (*pork*) Kotelett *nt*; (*veal*) Schnitzel *nt*

cut-price *adj* verbilligt

cutting ['kʌtɪŋ] n (*from paper*) Ausschnitt *m*; (*of plant*) Ableger *m* ▷ *adj* (*comment*) verletzend

CV *abbr* = **curriculum vitae**

cwt *abbr* = **hundredweight** ≈ Zentner, Ztr.

cybercafé [saɪbəˈkæfeɪ] n Internetcafé *nt*; **cyberspace** n Cyberspace *m*

cyclamen ['sɪkləmən] n Alpenveilchen *nt*

cycle ['saɪkl] n Fahrrad *nt* ▷ *vi* Rad fahren; **cycle lane, cycle path** n Radweg *m*; **cycling** n Radfahren *nt*; **cyclist** ['saɪklɪst] n Radfahrer(in) *m(f)*

cylinder ['sɪlɪndə*] n Zylinder *m*

cynical ['sɪnɪkəl] *adj* zynisch

cypress ['saɪprɪs] n Zypresse f

Cypriot ['sɪprɪət] *adj* zypriotisch ▷ n Zypriote *m*, Zypriotin f; **Cyprus** ['saɪprəs] n Zypern *nt*

czar [zɑː*] n Zar *m*; **czarina** [zaˈriːnə] n Zarin f

Czech [tʃek] *adj* tschechisch ▷ n (*person*) Tscheche *m*, Tschechin f; (*language*) Tschechisch *nt*; **Czech Republic** n Tschechische Republik, Tschechien *nt*

dab [dæb] *vt* (*wound, nose etc*) betupfen (*with* mit)

dachshund ['dækshʊnd] n Dackel *m*

dad(dy) ['dæd(ɪ)] n Papa *m*, Vati *m*; **daddy-longlegs** *nsing* (BRIT) Schnake; (*US*) Weberknecht *m*

daffodil ['dæfədɪl] n Osterglocke f

daft [dɑːft] *adj* (*fam*) blöd, doof

dahlia ['deɪlɪə] n Dahlie f

daily ['deɪlɪ] *adj, adv* täglich ▷ n (*paper*) Tageszeitung f

dairy ['deərɪ] n (*on farm*) Molkerei f; **dairy products** *npl* Milchprodukte *pl*

daisy ['deɪzɪ] n Gänseblümchen *nt*

dam [dæm] n Staudamm *m* ▷ *vt* stauen

damage ['dæmɪdʒ] n Schaden *m*; **~s** *pl* (*Jur*) Schadenersatz *m* ▷ *vt* beschädigen; (*reputation, health*) schädigen, schaden +*dat*

damn [dæm] *adj* (*fam*) verdammt ▷ *vt* (*condemn*) verurteilen; **~ (it)!**

verflucht! ▷ *il* **he doesn't give a ~** es ist ihm völlig egal

damp [dæmp] *adj* feucht ▷ *n* Feuchtigkeit *f*; **dampen** ['dæmp- ən] *vt* befeuchten

dance [dɑːns] *n* Tanz *m*; (event) Tanzveranstaltung *f* ▷ *vi* tanzen; **dance floor** *n* Tanzfläche *f*; **dancer** *n* Tänzer(in) *m(f)*; **dancing** *n* Tanzen *nt*

dandelion ['dændɪlaɪən] *n* Löwenzahn *m*

dandruff ['dændrəf] *n* Schuppen *pl*

Dane [deɪn] *n* Däne *m*, Dänin *f*

danger ['deɪndʒə*] *n* Gefahr *f*; (sign) Achtung!; **to be in ~** in Gefahr sein; **dangerous** *adj* gefährlich

Danish ['deɪnɪʃ] *adj* dänisch ▷ *n* (language) Dänisch *nt*; **the ~** *pl* die Dänen; **Danish pastry** *n* Plundergebäck *nt*

Danube ['dænjuːb] *n* Donau *f*

dare [dɛə*] *vt* **to ~ (to) do sth** es wagen, etw zu tun; **I didn't ~ ask** ich traute mich nicht, zu fragen; **how ~ you** was fällt dir ein!; **daring** *adj* (person) mutig (film, clothes etc) gewagt

dark [dɑːk] *adj* dunkel; (gloomy) düster, trübe; (sinister) finster; **~ chocolate** Bitterschokolade *f*; **~ green / blue** dunkelgrün / dunkelblau ▷ *n* Dunkelheit *f*; **in the ~** im Dunkeln; **dark glasses** *npl* Sonnenbrille *f*; **darkness** *n* Dunkelheit *nt*

darling ['dɑːlɪŋ] *n* Schatz *m*; (also favourite) Liebling *m*

dart [dɑːt] *n* Wurfpfeil *m*; **darts** *nsing* (game) Darts *nt*

dash [dæʃ] *vi* stürzen, rennen ▷ *vt* **to ~ hopes** Hoffnungen zerstören ▷ *n* (in text) Gedankenstrich *m*; (of liquid) Schuss *m*; **dashboard** *n* Armaturenbrett *nt*

data ['deɪtə] *npl* Daten *pl*; **data bank data base** *n* Datenbank *f*; **data capture** *n* Datenerfassung *f*; **data processing** *n* Datenverarbeitung *f*; **data protection** *n* Datenschutz *m*

date [deɪt] *n* Datum *nt*; (for meeting, delivery etc) Termin *m*; (with person) Verabredung *f*; (with girlfriend etc) (fruit) Dattel *f*; **what's the ~ (today)?** der Wievielte ist heute?; **out of ~** *adj* veraltet; **up to ~** *adj* (news) aktuell; (fashion) zeitgemäß ▷ *vt* (letter etc) datieren; (person) gehen mit; **dated** *adj* altmodisch; **date of birth** *n* Geburtsdatum *nt*; **dating agency** *n* Partnervermittlung *f*

dative ['deɪtɪv] *n* Dativ *m*

daughter ['dɔːtə*] *n* Tochter *f*; **daughter-in-law** (*pl* **daughters-in-law**) *n* Schwiegertochter *f*

dawn [dɔːn] *n* Morgendämmerung *f* ▷ *vi* dämmern; **it ~ed on me** mir ging ein Licht auf

day [deɪ] *n* Tag *m*; **one ~** eines Tages; **by ~** bei Tage; **~ after ~, ~ by ~** Tag für Tag; **the ~ after / before** am Tag danach / zuvor; **the ~ before yesterday** vorgestern; **the ~ after tomorrow** übermorgen; **these ~s** heutzutage; **in those ~s** damals; **let's call it a ~** Schluss für heute!; **daybreak** *n* Tagesanbruch *m*; **daydream** *n* Tagtraum *m* ▷ *vi* (mit offenen Augen) träumen; **daylight** *n* Tageslicht *nt*, **in ~** bei Tage; **daylight saving time** *n* Sommerzeit *f*; **day nursery** *n* Kindertagesstätte *f*; **day return** *n* (BRIT Rail) Tagesrückfahrkarte *f*; **daytime** *n* in the ~ bei Tage, tagsüber; **daytrip** *n* Tagesausflug *m*

dazed [deɪzd] *adj* benommen

dazzle ['dæzl] *vt* blenden; **dazzling** *adj* blendend, glänzend

dead [ded] *adj* tot; *(limb)* abgestorben ▷ *adv* genau; *(fam)* total, völlig; ~ **tired** *adj* todmüde; ~ **slow** *(sign)* Schritt fahren; **dead end** *n* Sackgasse *f;* **deadline** *n* Termin *m;* *(period)* Frist *f;* ~ **for applications** Anmeldeschluss *m;* **deadly** *adj* tödlich ▷ *adv* ~ **dull** todlangweilig

deaf [def] *adj* taub; **deafen** *vt* taub machen; **deafening** *adj* ohrenbetäubend

deal [di:l] *(dealt, dealt) vt, vi (cards)* geben, austeilen ▷ *n (business ~)* Geschäft *nt;* *(agreement)* Abmachung *f;* **it's a ~** abgemacht!; **a good/great ~ of** ziemlich / sehr viel; **deal in** *vt* handeln mit; **deal with** *vt (matter)* sich beschäftigen mit; *(book, film)* behandeln; *(successfully: person, problem)* fertig werden mit; *(matter)* erledigen; **dealer** *n (Comm)* Händler(in) *m(f);* *(drugs)* Dealer(in) *m(f);* **dealings** *npl (Comm)* Geschäfte *pl*

dealt [delt] *pt, pp of* **deal**

dear [dɪə*] *adj* lieb, teuer; **Dear Sir or Madam** Sehr geehrte Damen und Herren; **Dear David** Lieber David ▷ *n* Schatz *m;* *(as address)* mein Schatz, Liebling; **dearly** *adv (love)* (heiß und) innig; *(pay)* teuer

death [deθ] *n* Tod *m;* *(of project, hopes)* Ende *nt;* ~**s** *pl* Todesfälle; *(in accident)* Todesopfer; **death certificate** *n* Totenschein *m;* **death penalty** *n* Todesstrafe *f;* **death toll** *n* Zahl *f* der Todesopfer; **death trap** *n* Todesfalle *f*

debatable [dɪ'beɪtəbl] *adj* fraglich; *(question)* strittig; **debate** [dɪ'beɪt] *n* Debatte *f* ▷ *vt* debattieren

debauched [dɪ'bɔ:tʃt] *adj* ausschweifend

debit ['debɪt] *n* Soll *nt* ▷ *vt (account)* belasten; **debit card** *n* Geldkarte *f*

debris ['debri:] *n* Trümmer *pl*

debt [det] *n* Schuld *f;* **to be in ~** verschuldet sein

decade ['dekeɪd] *n* Jahrzehnt *nt*

decadent ['dekədənt] *adj* dekadent

decaff ['di:kæf] *n (fam)* koffeinfreier Kaffee; **decaffeinated** [di:-'kæfɪneɪtɪd] *adj* koffeinfrei

decanter [dɪ'kæntə*] *n* Dekanter *m,* Karaffe *f*

decay [dɪ'keɪ] *n* Verfall *m;* *(rotting)* Verwesung *f;* *(of tooth)* Fäule *f* ▷ *vi* verfallen; *(rot)* verwesen; *(wood)* vermodern; *(teeth)* faulen; *(leaves)* verrotten

deceased [dɪ'si:st] *n* **the ~** der / die Verstorbene

deceit [dɪ'si:t] *n* Betrug *m;* **deceive** [dɪ'si:v] *vt* täuschen

December [dɪ'sembə*] *n* Dezember *m; see also* **September**

decent ['di:sənt] *adj* anständig

deception [dɪ'sepʃən] *n* Betrug *m;* **deceptive** [dɪ'septɪv] *adj* täuschend, irreführend

decide [dɪ'saɪd] *vt (question)* entscheiden; *(body of people)* beschließen; **I can't ~ what to do** ich kann mich nicht entscheiden, was ich tun soll ▷ *vi* sich entscheiden; **to ~ on sth** *(in favour of sth)* sich für etw entscheiden, sich zu etw entschließen; **decided** *adj* entschieden; *(clear)* deutlich; **decidedly** *adv* entschieden

decimal ['desɪməl] *adj* Dezimal-; **decimal system** *n* Dezimalsystem *nt*

decipher [dɪ'saɪfə*] *vt* entziffern

decision [dɪ'sɪʒən] *n* Entscheidung *f* *(on* über *+akk);* *(of committee, jury etc)* Beschluss *m;* **to make a ~** eine Entscheidung treffen; **decisive** [dɪ'saɪsɪv] *adj* entscheidend; *(person)* entscheidungsfreudig

deck [dɛk] n (Naut) Deck nt; (of cards) Blatt nt; **deckchair** n Liegestuhl m

declaration [dɛklə'reɪʃən] n Erklärung f; **declare** [dɪ'klɛə*] vt erklären; (state) behaupten (that dass); (at customs) **have you anything to ~** haben Sie etwas zu verzollen?

decline [dɪ'klaɪn] n Rückgang m ▷ vt (invitation, offer) ablehnen ▷ vi (become less) sinken, abnehmen; (health) sich verschlechtern

decode [diː'kəʊd] vt entschlüsseln

decompose [diːkəm'pəʊz] vi sich zersetzen

decontaminate [diːkən'tæmɪneɪt] vt entgiften; (from radioactivity) entseuchen

decorate ['dɛkəreɪt] vt (aus)schmücken; (wallpaper) tapezieren; (paint) anstreichen; **decoration** [dɛkə'reɪʃən] n Schmuck m; (process) Schmücken nt; (wallpapering) Tapezieren nt; (painting) Anstreichen nt; **Christmas ~s** Weihnachtsschmuck m, **decorator** n Maler(in) m(f)

decrease [diː'kriːs] n Abnahme f ▷ [diː'kriːs] vi abnehmen

dedicate ['dɛdɪkeɪt] vt widmen (to sb jdm); **dedicated** adj (person) engagiert; **dedication** [dɛdɪ'keɪʃən] n Widmung f; (commitment) Hingabe f, Engagement nt

deduce [dɪ'djuːs] vt folgern, schließen (from aus, that dass)

deduct [dɪ'dʌkt] vt abziehen (from von); **deduction** [dɪ'dʌkʃən] n (of money) Abzug m; (conclusion) (Schluss)folgerung f

deed [diːd] n Tat f

deep [diːp] adj tief; **deepen** vt vertiefen; **deep-freeze** n Tiefkühltruhe f; (upright) Gefrierschrank m;

deep-fry vt frittieren

deer [dɪə*] n Reh nt; (with stag) Hirsch m

defeat [dɪ'fiːt] n Niederlage f; **to admit ~** sich geschlagen geben ▷ vt besiegen

defect ['diːfɛkt] n Defekt m, Fehler m; **defective** [dɪ'fɛktɪv] adj fehlerhaft

defence [dɪ'fɛns] n Verteidigung f; **defend** [dɪ'fɛnd] vt verteidigen; **defendant** [dɪ'fɛndənt] n (Jur) Angeklagte(r) mf; **defender** n (Sport) Verteidiger(in) m(f); **defensive** [dɪ'fɛnsɪv] adj defensiv

deficiency [dɪ'fɪʃənsɪ] n Mangel m; **deficient** adj mangelhaft; **deficit** ['dɛfɪsɪt] n Defizit nt

define [dɪ'faɪn] vt (word) definieren; (duties, powers) bestimmen; **definite** ['dɛfɪnɪt] adj (clear) klar, eindeutig; (certain) sicher; **it's ~** es steht fest; **definitely** adv bestimmt; **definition** [dɛfɪ'nɪʃən] n Definition f; (Foto) Schärfe f

deflate [diː'fleɪt] vt die Luft ablassen aus

defrost [diː'frɒst] vt (fridge) abtauen; (food) auftauen

degrading [dɪ'greɪdɪŋ] adj erniedrigend

degree [dɪ'griː] n Grad m; (at university) akademischer Grad; **a certain / high ~ of** ein gewisses / hohes Maß an +dat; **to a certain ~** einigermaßen; **I have a ~ in chemistry** ≈ ich habe Chemie studiert

dehydrated [diːhaɪ'dreɪtɪd] adj (food) getrocknet, Trocken-; (person) ausgetrocknet

de-ice [diː'aɪs] vt enteisen

delay [dɪ'leɪ] vt (postpone) verschieben, aufschieben; **to be ~ed** (event) sich verzögern; **the train / flight was ~ed** der Zug / die Maschine hatte Verspätung ▷ vi warten; (hesitate) zögern ▷ n Verzögerung f; (of train etc) Verspätung f; **without ~** unverzüglich; **delayed** adj (train etc) verspätet

delegate n ['deligət] Delegierte(r) mf▷ ['deligeit] vt delegieren; **delegation** [deli'geiʃən] n Abordnung f; (foreign) Delegation f

delete [di'li:t] vt (aus)streichen; (Inform) löschen; **deletion** n Streichung f; (Inform) Löschung f

deli ['deli] n (fam) Feinkostgeschäft nt

deliberate [di'libərət] adj (intentional) absichtlich; **deliberately** adv mit Absicht, extra

delicate ['delikit] adj (fine) fein; (fragile) zart; (a. Med) empfindlich; (situation) heikel

delicatessen [delikə'tesn] nsing Feinkostgeschäft nt

delicious [di'liʃəs] adj köstlich, lecker

delight [di'lait] n Freude f ▷ vt entzücken; **delighted** adj sehr erfreut (with über +akk); **delightful** adj entzückend; (weather, meal etc) herrlich

deliver [di'livə*] vt (goods) liefern (to sb jdm); (letter, parcel) zustellen; (speech) halten; (baby) entbinden; **delivery** n Lieferung f; (of letter, parcel) Zustellung f; (of baby) Entbindung f; **delivery van** n Lieferwagen m

delude [di'lu:d] vt täuschen; **don't ~ yourself** mach dir nichts vor; **delusion** n Irrglaube m

de luxe [di'lʌks] adj Luxus-

demand [di'mɑ:nd] vt verlangen (from von); (time, patience etc) erfordern ▷ n (request) Forderung f, Verlangen nt (for nach); (Comm: for goods) Nachfrage f; **on ~** auf Wunsch; **very much in ~** sehr ge-

fragt; **demanding** adj anspruchsvoll

demented [di'mentid] adj wahnsinnig

demerara [demə'reərə] n **~ (sugar)** brauner Zucker

demister n Defroster m

demo ['deməu] (pl **-s**) n (fam) Demo f

democracy [di'mɒkrəsi] n Demokratie f; **democrat, Democrat** (US Pol) ['deməkræt] Demokrat(in) m(f); **democratic** adj demokratisch; **the Democratic Party** (US Pol) die Demokratische Partei

demolish [di'mɒliʃ] vt abreißen; (fig) zerstören; **demolition** [demə'liʃən] n Abbruch m

demonstrate ['demənstreit] vt, vi demonstrieren, beweisen; **demonstration** n Demonstration f

demoralize [di'mɒrəlaiz] vt demoralisieren

denationalization ['di:næʃnəlai'zeiʃən] n Privatisierung f

denial [di'naiəl] n Leugnung f; (official ~) Dementi nt

denim ['denim] n Jeansstoff m; **denim jacket** n Jeansjacke f; **denims** npl Bluejeans pl

Denmark ['denmɑ:k] n Dänemark nt

denomination [dinɒmi'neiʃən] n (Rel) Konfession f; (Comm) Nennwert m

dense [dens] adj dicht; (fam: stupid) schwer von Begriff; **density** ['densiti] n Dichte f

dent [dent] n Beule f, Delle f ▷ vt einbeulen

dental ['dentl] adj Zahn-; **~ care** Zahnpflege f; **~ floss** Zahnseide f; **dentist** ['dentist] n Zahnarzt m, Zahnärztin; **dentures** ['dentʃəz] npl Zahnprothese f; (full) Gebiss nt

deny [di'nai] vt leugnen, bestreiten, (refuse) ablehnen

deodorant [di:'əʊdərənt] n Deo(dorant) nt; **~ spray** Deospray nt o m

depart [dɪ'pɑ:t] vi abreisen; (bus, train) abfahren (for nach, from von); (plane) abfliegen (for nach, from von) **department** [dɪ'pɑ:tmənt] n Abteilung f; (at university) Institut nt; (Pol: ministry) Ministerium nt; **department store** n Kaufhaus nt

departure [dɪ'pɑ:tʃə*] n (of person) Weggang m; (on journey) Abreise f (for nach); (of train etc) Abfahrt f (for nach); (of plane) Abflug m (for nach); **departure lounge** n (Aviat) Abflughalle f; **departure time** n Abfahrtzeit f; (Aviat) Abflugzeit f

depend [dɪ'pend] vi **it ~s** es kommt darauf an (whether, if ob); **depend on** vt (thing) abhängig von; (person: rely on) sich verlassen auf +akk; (person, area etc) angewiesen sein auf +akk; **it ~s on the weather** es kommt auf das Wetter an; **dependable** adj zuverlässig; **dependence** n Abhängigkeit f (on von); **dependent** adj abhängig (on von)

deplorable [dɪ'plɔ:rəbl] adj bedauerlich; **deplore** vt bedauern

deport [dɪ'pɔ:t] vt ausweisen, abschieben; **deportation** [di:pɔ:-'teɪʃən] n Abschiebung f

deposit [dɪ'pɒzɪt] n (down payment) Anzahlung f; (security) Kaution f; (for bottle) Pfand nt; (to bank account) Einzahlung f; (in river etc) Ablagerung f ▷ vt (put down) abstellen, absetzen; (to bank account) einzahlen; (sth valuable) deponieren; **deposit account** n Sparkonto nt

depot ['depəʊ] n Depot nt; **depreciate** [dɪ'pri:ʃɪeɪt] vi an Wert verlieren

depress [dɪ'pres] vt (in mood) deprimieren; **depressed** adj (person) niedergeschlagen, deprimiert; **~ area** Notstandsgebiet nt; **depressing** adj deprimierend; **depression** [dɪ'preʃən] n (mood) Depression f; (Meteo) Tief nt

deprive [dɪ'praɪv] vt **to ~ sb of sth** jdn einer Sache berauben; **deprived** adj (child) (sozial) benachteiligt

dept abbr = **department** Abt.

depth [depθ] n Tiefe f

deputy ['depjʊtɪ] adj stellvertretend, Vize- ▷ n Stellvertreter(in) m(f); (US Pol) Abgeordnete(r) mf

derail [dɪ'reɪl] vt entgleisen lassen; **to be ~ed** entgleisen

deranged [dɪ'reɪndʒd] adj geistesgestört

derivation [derɪ'veɪʃən] n Ableitung f; **derive** [dɪ'raɪv] vt ableiten (from von) ▷ abstammen (from von)

dermatitis [dɜ:mə'taɪtɪs] n Hautentzündung f

derogatory [dɪ'rɒgətərɪ] adj abfällig

descend [dɪ'send] vt, vi hinabsteigen, hinuntergehen; (person) **to ~ o be ~ed from** abstammen von; **descendant** n Nachkomme m; **descent** [dɪ'sent] n (coming down) Abstieg m; (origin) Abstammung f

describe [dɪs'kraɪb] vt beschreiben; **description** [dɪs'krɪpʃən] n Beschreibung f

desert [dezət] n Wüste f ▷ [dɪ'zɜ:t] vt verlassen; (abandon) im Stich lassen; **deserted** adj verlassen; (empty) menschenleer

deserve [dɪ'zɜ:v] vt verdienen

design [dɪ'zaɪn] n (plan) Entwurf m; (of vehicle, machine) Konstruktion f; (of object) Design nt; (planning) Gestaltung f ▷ vt entwerfen; (machine etc) konstruieren; **~ed for sb / sth** (intended) für jdn / etw konzipiert

designate ['dezıgneıt] vt bestimmen

designer [dı'zaınə*] n Designer(in) m(f); (Tech) Konstrukteur(in) m(f); **designer drug** n Designerdroge f

desirable [dı'zaıərəbl] adj wünschenswert; (person) begehrenswert; **desire** [dı'zaıə*] n Wunsch m (for nach); (esp sexual) Begierde f (for nach) ▷ vt wünschen; (ask for) verlangen; **if ~d** auf Wunsch

desk [desk] n Schreibtisch m; (reception ~) Empfang m; (at airport etc) Schalter m; **desktop publishing** n Desktoppublishing nt

desolate ['desəlıt] adj trostlos

despair [dıs'peə*] n Verzweiflung f (at über +akk) ▷ vi verzweifeln (of an +dat)

despatch [dı'spætʃ] see **dispatch**

desperate ['despərıt] adj verzweifelt; (situation) hoffnungslos; **to be ~ for sth** etw dringend brauchen, unbedingt wollen; **desperation** [despə'reıʃən] n Verzweiflung f

despicable [dı'spıkəbl] adj verachtenswert; **despise** [dı'spaız] vt verachten

despite [dı'spaıt] prep trotz +gen

dessert [dı'zɜːt] n Nachtisch m; **dessertspoon** n Dessertlöffel m

destination [destı'neıʃən] n (of person) (Reise)ziel nt; (of goods) Bestimmungsort m; **destine** vb **we're ~d for Hull** wir sind auf dem Weg nach Hull; **he was ~d to die young** er sollte früh sterben; **destiny** ['destını] n Schicksal nt

destroy [dı'strɔı] vt zerstören; (completely) vernichten; **destruction** [dı'strʌkʃən] n Zerstörung f; (complete) Vernichtung f; **destructive** [dı'strʌktıv] adj zerstörerisch; (esp fig) destruktiv

detach [dı'tætʃ] vt abnehmen;

(from form etc) abtrennen; (free) lösen (from von); **detachable** adj abnehmbar; (from form etc) abtrennbar; **detached** adj (attitude) distanziert, objektiv; **~ house** Einzelhaus nt

detail ['diːteıl,] (US) [dı'teıl] n Einzelheit f, Detail nt; (further) **~s from ...** Näheres erfahren Sie bei ...; **to go into ~** ins Detail gehen; **in ~** ausführlich; **detailed** adj detailliert, ausführlich

detain [dı'teın] vt aufhalten; (police) in Haft nehmen

detect [dı'tekt] vt entdecken; (notice) wahrnehmen; **detective** [dı'tektıv] n Detektiv(in) m(f); **detective story** n Detektivroman, Krimi m

detention [dı'tenʃən] n Haft f; (Sch) Nachsitzen nt

deter [dı'tɜː*] vt abschrecken (from von)

detergent [dı'tɜːdʒənt] n Reinigungsmittel nt; (soap powder) Waschmittel nt

deteriorate [dı'tıərıəreıt] vi sich verschlechtern

determination [dıtɜːmı'neıʃən] n Entschlossenheit f; **determine** [dı'tɜːmın] vt bestimmen; **determined** adj (fest) entschlossen

deterrent [dı'terənt] n Abschreckungsmittel nt

detest [dı'test] vt verabscheuen; **detestable** adj abscheulich

detour ['diːtʊə*] n Umweg m; (of traffic) Umleitung f

deuce [djuːs] n (Tennis) Einstand m

devalue [diː'væljuː] vt abwerten

devastate ['devəsteıt] vt verwüsten; **devastating** ['devəsteıtıŋ] adj verheerend

develop [dı'veləp] vt entwickeln; (illness) bekommen ▷ vi sich entwickeln; **developing country** n Entwicklungsland nt; **develop-**

ment n Entwicklung f; (of land)
Erschließung f

device [dɪ'vaɪs] n Vorrichtung f,
Gerät nt

devil ['devl] n Teufel m; devilish
adj teuflisch

devote [dɪ'vəʊt] vt widmen (to
dat); devoted adj liebend; (servant
etc) treu ergeben; devotion n
Hingabe f

devour [dɪ'vaʊə*] vt verschlingen

dew [djuː] n Tau m

diabetes [daɪə'biːtiːz] n Diabetes
m, Zuckerkrankheit f; diabetic
[daɪə'betɪk] adj zuckerkrank, für
Diabetiker ⊳ n Diabetiker(in) m(f)

diagnosis [daɪəg'nəʊsɪs] (pl diagnoses) n Diagnose f

diagonal [daɪ'ægənl] adj diagonal

diagram ['daɪəgræm] n Diagramm m

dial ['daɪəl] n Skala f; (of clock)
Zifferblatt nt ⊳ vt (tel) wählen; dial
code n (US) Vorwahl f

dialect ['daɪəlekt] n Dialekt m

dialling code n (BRIT) Vorwahl f;
dialling tone n (BRIT) Amtszeichen nt

dialogue, dialog (US) ['daɪəlɒg] n
Dialog m

dial tone n (US) Amtszeichen nt

dialysis [daɪ'ælɪsɪs] n (Med) Dialyse f

diameter [daɪ'æmɪtə*] n Durchmesser m

diamond ['daɪəmənd] n Diamant
m; (Cards) Karo nt

diaper ['daɪpə*] n (US) Windel f

diarrhoea [daɪə'riːə] n Durchfall
m

diary ['daɪərɪ] n (Taschen)kalender m; (account) Tagebuch nt

dice [daɪs] npl Würfel pl; diced
adj in Würfel geschnitten

dictate [dɪk'teɪt] vt diktieren;

dictation [dɪk'teɪʃən] n Diktat nt

dictator [dɪk'teɪtə*] n Diktator(in) m(f); dictatorship [dɪk'teɪtəʃɪp] n Diktatur f

dictionary ['dɪkʃənrɪ] n Wörterbuch nt

did [dɪd] pt of do

didn't ['dɪdnt] contr of did not

die [daɪ] vi sterben (of an +dat);
(plant, animal) eingehen; (engine)
absterben; to be dying to do sth
darauf brennen, etw zu tun; I'm
dying for a drink ich brauche unbedingt was zu trinken; die away
vi schwächer werden; (wind) sich
legen; die down vi nachlassen; die
out vi aussterben

diesel ['diːzəl] n (fuel, car) Diesel
m; ~ engine Dieselmotor m

diet ['daɪət] n Kost f; (special food)
Diät f ⊳ vi eine Diät machen

differ ['dɪfə*] vi (be different) sich
unterscheiden; (disagree) anderer
Meinung sein; difference ['dɪfrəns] n Unterschied m; it makes
no ~ (to me) es ist (mir) egal; it
makes a big ~ es macht viel aus;
different adj andere(r, s); (with pl)
verschieden; to be quite ~ ganz
anders sein (from als), (two people,
things) völlig verschieden sein; a ~
person ein anderer Mensch; differentiate [dɪfə'renʃieɪt] vt, vi unterscheiden; differently ['dɪfrəntlɪ] adv anders (from als); (from one
another) unterschiedlich

difficult ['dɪfɪkəlt] adj schwierig; I
find it ~ es fällt mir schwer; difficulty n Schwierigkeit f; with ~ nur
schwer; to have ~ in doing sth etw
nur mit Mühe machen können

dig [dɪg] (dug, dug) vt, vi (hole)
graben; dig in vi (fam: food)
reinhauen; ~! greif(t) zu!, dig up vt
ausgraben

digest [daɪ'dʒest] vt (a. fig) verdauen; **digestible** [dɪˈdʒestəbl] adj verdaulich; **digestion** [dɪˈdʒestʃən] n Verdauung f; **digestive** [dɪˈdʒestɪv] adj ~ **biscuit** (BRIT) Vollkornkeks m

digit [ˈdɪdʒɪt] n Ziffer f; **digital** [ˈdɪdʒɪtəl] adj digital; ~ **computer** Digitalrechner m; ~ **watch / clock** Digitaluhr f; **digital camera** n Digitalkamera f

dignified [ˈdɪɡnɪfaɪd] adj würdevoll; **dignity** [ˈdɪɡnɪtɪ] n Würde f

dilapidated [dɪˈlæpɪdeɪtɪd] adj baufällig

dilemma [daɪˈlemə] n Dilemma nt

dill [dɪl] n Dill m

dilute [daɪˈluːt] vt verdünnen

dim [dɪm] adj (light) schwach; (outline) undeutlich; (stupid) schwer von Begriff ▷ vt verdunkeln; (US Auto) abblenden; **~med headlights** (US) Abblendlicht nt

dime [daɪm] n (US) Zehncentstück nt

dimension [daɪˈmenʃən] n Dimension f; **~s** pl Maße pl

diminish [dɪˈmɪnɪʃ] vt verringern ▷ vi sich verringern

dimple [ˈdɪmpl] n Grübchen nt

dine [daɪn] vi speisen; **dine out** vi außer Haus essen; **diner** n Gast m; (Rail) Speisewagen m; (US) Speiselokal nt

dinghy [ˈdɪŋɡɪ] n Ding(h)i nt; (inflatable) Schlauchboot nt

dingy [ˈdɪndʒɪ] adj düster; (dirty) schmuddelig

dining car [ˈdaɪnɪŋkɑː*] n Speisewagen m; **dining room** n Esszimmer nt; (in hotel) Speiseraum m; **dining table** n Esstisch m

dinner [ˈdɪnə*] n Abendessen nt; (lunch) Mittagessen nt; (public) Diner nt; **to be at ~** beim Essen sein; **to have ~** zu Abend / Mittag essen;

dinner jacket n Smoking m; **dinner party** n Abendgesellschaft f (mit Essen); **dinnertime** n Essenszeit f

dinosaur [ˈdaɪnəsɔː*] n Dinosaurier m

dip [dɪp] vt tauchen (in in +akk); **to ~ (one's) headlights** (BRIT Auto) abblenden; **~ped headlights** Abblendlicht nt ▷ n (in ground) Bodensenke f; (sauce) Dip m

diploma [dɪˈpləʊmə] n Diplom nt

diplomat [ˈdɪpləmæt] n Diplomat(in) m(f); **diplomatic** [dɪpləˈmætɪk] adj diplomatisch

dipstick [ˈdɪpstɪk] n Ölmessstab m

direct [daɪˈrekt] adj direkt; (cause, consequence) unmittelbar; ~ **debit** (mandate) Einzugsermächtigung f; (transaction) Abbuchung f im Lastschriftverfahren; ~ **train** durchgehender Zug m ▷ vt (aim, send) richten (at, to an +akk); (film) die Regie führen bei; (traffic) regeln; **direct current** n (Elec) Gleichstrom m

direction [daɪˈrekʃən] n (course) Richtung f; (Cine) Regie f; **in the ~ of** ... in Richtung ...; **~s** pl **for use** Gebrauchsanweisung f; **~s** pl (to a place) Wegbeschreibung f

directly [daɪˈrektlɪ] adv direkt; (at once) sofort

director [daɪˈrektə*] n Direktor(in) m(f); Leiter(in) m(f); (of film) Regisseur(in) m(f)

directory [daɪˈrektərɪ] n Adressbuch nt; (Tel) Telefonbuch nt; ~ **enquiries** pl (Tel) **assistance** (Tel) Auskunft f

dirt [dɜːt] n Schmutz m, Dreck m; **dirt cheap** adj spottbillig; **dirt road** n unbefestigte Straße; **dirty** adj schmutzig

disability [dɪsəˈbɪlɪtɪ] n Behinderung f; **disabled** [dɪsˈeɪbld] behindert, Behinderten ▷ *npl* the ~ die Behinderten

disadvantage [dɪsəd'vɑ:ntɪdʒ] *n* Nachteil *m*; **at a ~** benachteiligt; **disadvantageous** [dɪsædvən-'teɪdʒəs] *adj* nachteilig, ungünstig

disagree [dɪsə'griː] *vi* anderer Meinung sein; (*two people*) sich nicht einig sein; (*two reports etc*) nicht übereinstimmen; **to ~ with sb** jdm nicht übereinstimmen; (*food*) jdm nicht bekommen; **disagreeable** *adj* unangenehm; (*person*) unsympathisch; **disagreement** *n* Meinungsverschiedenheit *f*

disappear [dɪsə'pɪə*] *vi* verschwinden; **disappearance** *n* Verschwinden *nt*

disappoint [dɪsə'pɔɪnt] *vt* enttäuschen; **disappointing** *adj* enttäuschend; **disappointment** *n* Enttäuschung *f*

disapproval [dɪsə'pruːvl] *n* Missbilligung *f*; **disapprove** [dɪsə'pruːv] *vi* missbilligen (*of akk*)

disarm [dɪs'ɑːm] *vt* entwaffnen ▷ *vi* (*Pol*) abrüsten; **disarmament** *n* Abrüstung *f*; **disarming** *adj* (*smile, look*) gewinnend

disaster [dɪ'zɑːstə*] *n* Katastrophe *f*; **disastrous** [dɪ'zɑːstrəs] *adj* katastrophal

disbelief [dɪsbə'liːf] *n* Ungläubigkeit *f*

disc [dɪsk] *n* Scheibe *f*, CD *f*; see also **disk** (*Anat*) Bandscheibe *f*; **disc brake** *n* Scheibenbremse *f*

discharge [dɪs'tʃɑːdʒ] *vt* (*Med*) Ausfluss *m* ▷ [dɪs'tʃɑːdʒ] *vt* (*person*) entlassen; (*emit*) ausstoßen; (*Med*) ausscheiden

discipline ['dɪsɪplɪn] *n* Disziplin *f*

disc jockey ['dɪskdʒɒkɪ] *n* Diskjockey *m*

disclose [dɪs'kləʊz] *vt* bekannt geben; (*secret*) enthüllen

disco ['dɪskəʊ] (*pl* **-s**) *n* Disko *f*, Diskomusik *f*

discomfort [dɪs'kʌmfət] *n* (*slight pain*) leichte Schmerzen *pl*; (*unease*) Unbehagen *nt*

disconnect [dɪskə'nekt] *vt* (*electricity, gas, phone*) abstellen; (*unplug*) **to ~ the TV (from the mains)** den Stecker des Fernsehers herausziehen; (*Tel*) **I've been ~ed** das Gespräch ist unterbrochen worden

discontent [dɪskən'tent] *n* Unzufriedenheit *f*; **discontented** *adj* unzufrieden

discontinue [dɪskən'tɪnjuː] *vt* einstellen; (*product*) auslaufen lassen

discotheque ['dɪskəʊtek] *n* Diskothek *f*

discount ['dɪskaʊnt] *n* Rabatt *m*

discover [dɪs'kʌvə*] *vt* entdecken; **discovery** *n* Entdeckung *f*

discredit [dɪs'kredɪt] *vt* in Verruf bringen ▷ *n* Misskredit *m*

discreet [dɪs'kriːt] *adj* diskret

discrepancy [dɪs'krepənsɪ] *n* Unstimmigkeit *f*, Diskrepanz *f*

discriminate [dɪs'krɪmɪneɪt] *vi* unterscheiden; **to ~ against sb** jdn diskriminieren; **discrimination** [dɪskrɪmɪ'neɪʃən] *n* (*different treatment*) Diskriminierung *f*

discus ['dɪskəs] *n* Diskus *m*

discuss [dɪs'kʌs] *vt* diskutieren, besprechen; **discussion** [dɪs'kʌʃən] *n* Diskussion *f*

disease [dɪ'ziːz] *n* Krankheit *f*

disembark [dɪsɪm'bɑːk] *vi* von Bord gehen

disentangle [dɪsɪn'tæŋgl] *vt* entwirren

disgrace [dɪs'greɪs] *n* Schande *f* ▷ *vt* Schande machen +*dat*; (*family etc*) Schande bringen über +*akk*; (*less strong*) blamieren; **disgraceful** *adj* skandalös; **it's ~ es** ist eine Schande

disguise [dɪs'gaɪz] *vt* verkleiden;

(voice) verstellen ▷ n Verkleidung f; **in ~** verkleidet

disgust [dɪs'ɡʌst] n Abscheu m; (physical) Ekel m ▷ vt anekeln, anwidern; **disgusting** adj widerlich; (physically) ekelhaft

dish [dɪʃ] n Schüssel f; (food) Gericht nt; (crockery) Geschirr nt; **to do/wash the ~es** abwaschen; **dishcloth** n (for washing) Spültuch nt; (for drying) Geschirrtuch nt

dishearten [dɪs'hɑ:tən] vt entmutigen; **don't be ~ed** lass den Kopf nicht hängen!

dishonest [dɪs'ɒnɪst] adj unehrlich

dishonour [dɪs'ɒnə*] n Schande f

dish towel n (US) Geschirrtuch nt; **dish washer** n Geschirrspülmaschine f

dishy ['dɪʃɪ] adj (BRIT fam) klasse, attraktiv

disillusioned [dɪsɪ'lu:ʒənd] adj desillusioniert

disinfect [dɪsɪn'fekt] vt desinfizieren; **disinfectant** n Desinfektionsmittel nt

disintegrate [dɪs'ɪntɪɡreɪt] vi zerfallen; (group) sich auflösen

disjointed [dɪs'dʒɔɪntɪd] adj unzusammenhängend

disk [dɪsk] n (Inform: floppy) Diskette f; **disk drive** n Diskettenlaufwerk nt; **diskette** [dɪs'ket] n Diskette f

dislike [dɪs'laɪk] n Abneigung f ▷ vt nicht mögen; **to ~ doing sth** etw ungern tun

dislocate ['dɪsləʊkeɪt] vt (Med) verrenken, ausrenken

dismal ['dɪzməl] adj trostlos

dismantle [dɪs'mæntl] vt auseinander nehmen; (machine) demontieren

dismay [dɪs'meɪ] n Bestürzung f; **dismayed** adj bestürzt

dismiss [dɪs'mɪs] vt (employee) entlassen; **dismissal** n Entlassung f

disobedience [dɪsə'bi:dɪəns] n Ungehorsam m; **disobedient** adj ungehorsam; **disobey** [dɪsə'beɪ] vt nicht gehorchen +dat

disorder [dɪs'ɔ:də*] n (mess) Unordnung f; (riot) Aufruhr m; (Med) Störung f, Leiden nt

disorganized [dɪs'ɔ:ɡənaɪzd] adj chaotisch

disparaging adj geringschätzig

dispatch [dɪs'pætʃ] vt abschicken, abfertigen

dispensable [dɪs'pensəbl] adj entbehrlich; **dispense** vt verteilen; **dispense with** vt verzichten auf +akk; **dispenser** n Automat m

disperse [dɪs'pɜ:s] vi sich zerstreuen

display [dɪs'pleɪ] n (exhibition) Ausstellung f, Show f; (of goods) Auslage f; (Tech) Anzeige f, Display nt ▷ vt zeigen; (goods) ausstellen

disposable [dɪs'pəʊzəbl] adj (container, razor etc) Wegwerf-; **~ nappy** Wegwerfwindel f; **disposal** [dɪs'pəʊzəl] n Loswerden nt; (of waste) Beseitigung f; **to be at sb's ~** jdm zur Verfügung stehen; **dispose of** vt loswerden; (waste etc) beseitigen

dispute [dɪs'pju:t] n Streit m; (industrial) Auseinandersetzung f ▷ vt bestreiten

disqualification [dɪskwɒlɪfɪ'keɪʃən] n Disqualifikation f; **disqualify** [dɪs'kwɒlɪfaɪ] vt disqualifizieren

disregard [dɪsrɪ'ɡɑ:d] vt nicht beachten

disreputable [dɪs'repjʊtəbl] adj verrufen

disrespect [dɪsrɪ'spekt] n Respektlosigkeit f

disrupt [dɪsˈrʌpt] vt stören; (interrupt) unterbrechen; disruption [dɪsˈrʌpʃən] n Störung f; (interruption) Unterbrechung f

dissatisfied [dɪsˈsætɪsfaɪd] adj unzufrieden

dissent [dɪˈsɛnt] n Widerspruch m

dissolve [dɪˈzɒlv] vt auflösen ⊳ vi sich auflösen

dissuade [dɪˈsweɪd] vt (from abbringen) to ~ sb from doing sth jdn davon abbringen, etw zu tun

distance [ˈdɪstəns] n Entfernung f; in the/from a ~ in/aus der Ferne; distant adj (a. in time) fern; (relative etc) entfernt; (person) distanziert

distaste [dɪsˈteɪst] n Abneigung f (for gegen)

distil [dɪsˈtɪl] vt destillieren; distillery n Brennerei f

distinct [dɪsˈtɪŋkt] adj verschieden; (clear) klar, deutlich; distinction [dɪsˈtɪŋkʃən] n (difference) Unterschied m; (in exam etc) Auszeichnung f; distinctive adj unverkennbar; distinctly adv deutlich

distinguish [dɪsˈtɪŋgwɪʃ] vt unterscheiden (sth from sth etw von etw)

distort [dɪsˈtɔːt] vt verzerren; (truth) verdrehen

distract [dɪsˈtrækt] vt ablenken; distraction [dɪsˈtrækʃən] n Ablenkung f; (diversion) Zerstreuung f

distress [dɪsˈtrɛs] n (need, danger) Not f; (suffering) Leiden nt; (mental) Qual f; (worry) Kummer m ⊳ vt mitnehmen, erschüttern; distressed area n Notstandsgebiet nt; distress signal n Notsignal nt

distribute [dɪsˈtrɪbjuːt] vt verteilen; (Comm: goods) vertreiben; distribution [dɪstrɪˈbjuːʃən] n Verteilung f; (Comm: of goods) Vertrieb

m; distributor [dɪsˈtrɪbjʊtə*] n (Auto) Verteiler m; (Comm) Händler(in) m(f)

district [ˈdɪstrɪkt] n Gegend f; (administrative) Bezirk m; district attorney n (US) Staatsanwalt m, Staatsanwältin f

distrust [dɪsˈtrʌst] vt misstrauen +dat ⊳ n Misstrauen nt

disturb [dɪsˈtɜːb] vt stören; (worry) beunruhigen; disturbance n Störung f; disturbing adj beunruhigend

ditch [dɪtʃ] n Graben m ⊳ vt (fam: person) den Laufpass geben +dat; (plan etc) verwerfen

ditto [ˈdɪtəʊ] n dito, ebenfalls

dive [daɪv] n (into water) Kopfsprung m; (Aviat) Sturzflug m; (fam) zwielichtiges Lokal ⊳ vi (under water) tauchen; diver n Taucher(in) m(f)

diverse [daɪˈvɜːs] adj verschieden; diversion [daɪˈvɜːʃən] n (of traffic) Umleitung f; (distraction) Ablenkung f; divert [daɪˈvɜːt] vt ablenken; (traffic) umleiten

divide [dɪˈvaɪd] vt teilen; (in several parts, between people) aufteilen ⊳ vi sich teilen; dividend [ˈdɪvɪdɛnd] n Dividende f

divine [dɪˈvaɪn] adj göttlich

diving [ˈdaɪvɪŋ] n (Sport) tauchen nt; (jumping in) Springen nt; (Sport: from board) Kunstspringen nt; diving board n Sprungbrett nt; diving goggles npl Taucherbrille f; diving mask n Tauchmaske f

division [dɪˈvɪʒən] n Teilung f; (Math) Division f; (department) Abteilung f; (Sport) Liga f

divorce [dɪˈvɔːs] n Scheidung f ⊳ vt sich scheiden lassen von +dat; divorced adj geschieden; to get ~ sich scheiden lassen; divorcee [dɪvɔːˈsiː] n Geschiedene(r) mf

DIY [diːaɪˈwaɪ] *abbr* = **do-it-yourself**; **DIY centre** *n* Baumarkt *m*

dizzy [ˈdɪzɪ] *adj* schwindlig

DJ [ˈdiːˈdʒeɪ] *abbr* = **dinner jacket** Smoking *m* ▷ *abbr* = **disc jockey** Diskjockey *m*, DJ *m*

DNA *abbr* = **desoxyribonucleic acid** DNS *f*

do [duː] (**did, done**) *vb aux* (*in negatives*) **I don't know** ich weiß es nicht; **he didn't come** er ist nicht gekommen; (*in questions*) **does she swim?** schwimmt sie?; (*for emphasis*) **he does like talking** er redet sehr gern; **~ come and see us** kommen Sie uns doch mal besuchen; (*replacing verb*) **they drink more than we do** sie trinken mehr als wir; **please don't!** bitte tun Sie / tu das nicht!; (*in question tags*) **you know him, don't you?** du kennst ihn doch, oder? ▷ *vt* tun, machen; (*clean: room etc*) saubermachen; (*study*) studieren; (*Auto: speed*) fahren; (*distance*) zurücklegen; **what are you doing?** was machen Sie da?; **she has nothing to ~** sie hat nichts zu tun; **to ~ the dishes** abwaschen; **you can't ~ Cambridge in a day** Cambridge kann man nicht an einem Tag besichtigen; **the car does 100mph** der Wagen fährt 160 km/h ▷ *vi* (*get on*) vorankommen; (*be enough*) reichen; **to ~ well/badly** gut/schlecht vorankommen; (*in exam etc*) gut/schlecht abschneiden; **how are you doing?** wie geht's denn so?; **that (much) should ~** das dürfte reichen ▷ *n* (*pl* **-s**) (*party*) Party *f*; **do away with** *vt* abschaffen; **do up** *vt* (*fasten*) zumachen; (*parcel*) verschnüren; (*renovate*) wieder herrichten; **do with** *vt* (*need*) brauchen; **I could ~ a drink** ich könnte einen Drink gebrauchen; **do without** *vt* auskommen ohne; **I can ~ your**

comments auf deine Kommentare kann ich verzichten

dock [dɒk] *n* Dock *nt*; (*Jur*) Anklagebank *f*; **docker** *n* Hafenarbeiter *m*; **dockyard** *n* Werft *f*

doctor [ˈdɒktə*] *n* Arzt *m*, Ärztin; (*in title, also academic*) Doktor *m*

document [ˈdɒkjʊmənt] *n* Dokument *nt*; **documentary** [dɒkjʊˈmentərɪ] *n* Dokumentarfilm *m*; **documentation** [dɒkjʊmenˈteɪʃən] *n* Dokumentation *f*

docusoap [ˈdɒkjʊsəʊp] *n* Reality-Serie *f*, Dokusoap *f*

doddery [ˈdɒdərɪ] *adj* tatterig

dodgem [ˈdɒdʒəm] *n* Autoskooter *m*

dodgy [ˈdɒdʒɪ] *adj* nicht ganz in Ordnung; (*dishonest, unreliable*) zwielichtig; **he has a ~ stomach** er hat sich den Magen verdorben

dog [dɒg] *n* Hund *m*; **dog food** *n* Hundefutter *nt*; **doggie bag** [ˈdɒgɪbæg] *n* Tüte oder Box, in der Essensreste aus dem Restaurant mit nach Hause genommen werden können

do-it-yourself [ˈduːɪtjəˈself] *n* Heimwerken *nt*, Do-it-yourself *nt* ▷ *adj* Heimwerker-; **do-it-yourselfer** *n* Bastler(in) *m(f)*, Heimwerker(in) *m(f)*

doll [dɒl] *n* Puppe *f*

dollar [ˈdɒlə*] *n* Dollar *m*

dolphin [ˈdɒlfɪn] *n* Delphin *m*

domain [dəˈmeɪn] *n* Domäne *f*; (*Inform*) Domain *f*

dome [dəʊm] *n* Kuppel *f*

domestic [dəˈmestɪk] *adj* häuslich; (*within country*) Innen-, Binnen-; **domestic animal** *n* Haustier *nt*; **domesticated** [dəˈmestɪkeɪtɪd] *adj* (*person*) häuslich; (*animal*) zahm; **domestic flight** *n* Inlandsflug *m*

domicile [ˈdɒmɪsaɪl] *n* (*ständiger*) Wohnsitz

dominant [ˈdɒmɪnənt] *adj* dominierend, vorherrschend; **dominate** ['dɒmɪneɪt] vt beherrschen

dominoes ['dɒmɪnəʊz] npl Domino(spiel) nt

donate [dəʊ'neɪt] vt spenden; **donation** n Spende f

done [dʌn] pp of **do** ▷ adj (cooked) gar; **well ~** durchgebraten

doner (**kebab**) ['dɒnəkɪbæb] n Döner (Kebab) m

donkey ['dɒŋkɪ] n Esel m

donor ['dəʊnə] n Spender(in) m(f)

don't [dəʊnt] contr of **do not**

doom [duːm] n Schicksal nt; (downfall) Verderben nt

door [dɔː*] n Tür f, **doorbell** n Türklingel f; **door handle** n Türklinke f; **doorknob** n Türknauf m; **doormat** n Fußabtreter m; **doorstep** n Türstufe f; **right on our ~** direkt vor unserer Haustür

dope [dəʊp] (Sport) n (for athlete) Aufputschmittel nt ▷ vt dopen; **dopey** adj (fam) bekloppt; (from drugs) benebelt; (sleepy) benommen

dormitory ['dɔːmɪtrɪ] n Schlafsaal m; (US) Studentenwohnheim nt

dosage ['dəʊsɪdʒ] n Dosierung f; **dose** [dəʊs] n Dosis f ▷ vt dosieren

dot [dɒt] n Punkt m; **on the ~ auf** die Minute genau, pünktlich

dotcom ['dɒtkɒm] n ~ (**company**) Internetfirma f, Dotcom-Unternehmen nt

dote on [dəʊt ɒn] vt abgöttisch lieben

dotted line n punktierte Linie

double ['dʌbl] adj, adv doppelt; **~ the quantity** die zweifache Menge, doppelt so viel ▷ vt verdoppeln n (person) Doppelgänger(in) m(f); (Cine) Double nt; **double bass** n Kontrabass m; **double bed** n Doppelbett nt; **double-click** vt (Inform) doppelklicken; **double cream** n Sahne

mit hohem Fettgehalt; **doubledecker** n Doppeldecker m; **double glazing** n Doppelverglasung f; **double-park** vi in zweiter Reihe parken; **double room** n Doppelzimmer nt; **doubles** npl (Sport: also match) Doppel nt

doubt [daʊt] n Zweifel m; **no ~** ohne Zweifel, zweifellos, wahrscheinlich; **to have one's ~s** bedenken haben ▷ vt bezweifeln, (statement, word) anzweifeln; **I ~ it** das bezweifle ich; **doubtful** adj zweifelhaft, zweifelnd; **it is ~ whether ...** es ist fraglich, ob ...; **doubtless** adv ohne Zweifel, sicherlich

dough [dəʊ] n Teig m; **doughnut** n Donut m (rundes Hefegebäck)

dove [dʌv] n Taube f

down [daʊn] n Daunen pl; (fluff) Flaum m ▷ adv unten; (motion) nach unten; (towards speaker) herunter; (away from speaker) hinunter; **~ here/there** hier/dort unten; (downstairs) **they came ~ for breakfast** sie kamen zum Frühstück herunter; (southwards) **he came ~ from Scotland** er kam von Schottland herunter ▷ prep (towards speaker) herunter; (away from speaker) hinunter; **to drive ~ the hill/ road** den Berg/die Straße hinunter fahren; (along) **to walk ~ the street** die Straße entlang gehen; **he's ~ the pub** (fam) er ist in der Kneipe ▷ vt (fam: drink) runterkippen ▷ adj niedergeschlagen, deprimiert

down-and-out adj heruntergekommen ▷ n Obdachlose(r) mf, Penner(in) m(f); **downcast** adj niedergeschlagen; **downfall** n Sturz m; **down-hearted** adj entmutigt; **downhill** adv bergab; **he's going ~** (fig) mit ihm geht es bergab

● **DOWNING STREET**

● **Downing Street** ist die Straße in London, die von Whitehall zum St James's Park führt, und in der sich der offizielle Wohnsitz des Premierministers (Nr. 10) und des Finanzministers (Nr. 11) befindet. Im weiteren Sinne bezieht sich der Begriff „Downing Street" auf die britische Regierung.

download ['daυnləυd] vt downloaden, herunterladen; **downmarket** adj für die Massenmarkt; **down payment** n Anzahlung f; **downpour** n Platzregen m; **downs** npl Hügelland nt; **downsize** vt (business) verkleinern ▷ vi sich verkleinern

Down's syndrome ['daυnz-'sındrəυm] n (Med) Downsyndrom nt

downstairs [daυn'stɛəz] adv unten; (motion) nach unten; **downstream** adv flussabwärts; **downtime** n Ausfallzeit f; **downtown** adv (be, work etc) in der Innenstadt; (go) in die Innenstadt ▷ adj (US) in der Innenstadt; **~ Chicago** die Innenstadt von Chicago; **down under** adv (fam: in/to Australia) in/nach Australien; (in/to New Zealand) in/nach Neuseeland; **downwards** adv, adj nach unten; (movement, trend) Abwärts-

doze [daυz] vi dösen ▷ n Nickerchen nt

dozen ['dΛzn] n Dutzend nt; **two ~ eggs** zwei Dutzend Eier; **~s of times** x-mal

DP abbr = **data processing** DV f

drab [dræb] adj trist; (colour) düster

draft [drɑːft] n (outline) Entwurf m; (US Mil) Einberufung f

drag [dræg] vt schleppen ▷ n

(fam) **to be a ~** (boring) stinklangweilig sein; (laborious) ein ziemlicher Schlauch sein; **drag on** vi sich in die Länge ziehen

dragon ['drægən] n Drache m; **dragonfly** n Libelle f

drain [dreɪn] n Abfluss m ▷ vt (water, oil) ablassen; (vegetables etc) abgießen; (land) entwässern, trockenlegen ▷ vi (of water) abfließen; **drainpipe** n Abflussrohr nt

drama ['drɑːmə] n (a. fig) Drama nt; **dramatic** [drə'mætɪk] adj dramatisch

drank [dræŋk] pt of **drink**

drapes [dreɪps] npl (US) Vorhänge pl

drastic ['dræstɪk] adj drastisch

draught [drɑːft] n (Luft)zug m; **there's a ~** es zieht; **on ~** (beer) vom Fass; **draughts** sing Damespiel nt; **draughty** adj zugig

draw [drɔː] (drew, drawn) vt (pull) ziehen; (crowd) anlocken, anziehen; (picture) zeichnen ▷ n (Sport) unentschieden spielen ▷ n (Sport) Unentschieden nt; (attraction) Attraktion f; (for lottery) Ziehung f; **draw out** vt herausziehen; (money) abheben; **draw up** vt (formulate) entwerfen; (list) erstellen ▷ vi (car) anhalten; **drawback** n Nachteil m; **drawbridge** n Zugbrücke f; **drawer** ['drɔː*] n Schublade f; **drawing** ['drɔːɪŋ] n Zeichnung f; **drawing pin** n Reißzwecke f

drawn [drɔːn] pp of **draw**

dread [dred] n Furcht f (of vor +dat) ▷ vt sich fürchten vor +dat; **dreadful** adj entsetzlich; **dreadlocks** npl Rastalocken pl

dream [driːm] (**dreamed** o **dreamt**, **dreamed** o **dreamt**) vt, vi träumen (about von) ▷ n Traum m; **dreamt** [dremt] pt, pp of **dream**

dreary ['drɪərɪ] adj (weather, place)

trostlos; (book etc) langweilig

drench [drɛntʃ] vt durchnässen

dress [drɛs] n Kleidung f; (garment) Kleid nt ▷ vt anziehen; (Med: wound) verbinden; **to get ~ed** sich anziehen; **dress up** vi sich fein machen; (In costume) sich verkleiden (as als); **dress circle** n (Theat) erster Rang; **dresser** n Anrichte f; (US: dressing table) (Frisier)kommode f; **dressing** n (Gastr) Dressing nt, Soße f; (Med) Verband m; **dressing gown** n Morgenmantel m; **dressing room** n (Sport) Umkleideraum m; (Theat) Künstlergarderobe f; **dressing table** n Frisierkommode f; **dress rehearsal** n (Theat) Generalprobe f

drew [druː] pt of **draw**

dried [draɪd] adj getrocknet; (milk, flowers) Trocken-; **~ fruit** Dörrobst nt; **drier** [draɪə*] n see **dryer**

drift [drɪft] vi treiben ▷ n (of snow) Verwehung f; (fig) Tendenz f; **if you get my ~** wenn du mich richtig verstehst

drill [drɪl] n Bohrer m ▷ vt, vi bohren

drink [drɪŋk] (**drank, drunk**) vt, vi trinken ▷ n Getränk nt, (alcoholic) Drink m; **drink-driving** n (BRIT) Trunkenheit f am Steuer; **drinking water** n Trinkwasser nt

drip [drɪp] n Tropfen m ▷ vi tropfen; **drip-dry** adj bügelfrei; **dripping** n Bratenfett nt ▷ adj ~ **(wet)** tropfnass

drive [draɪv] (**drove, driven**) vt (car, person in car) fahren; (force: person, animal) treiben; (Tech) antreiben; **to ~ sb mad** jdn verrückt machen ▷ vi fahren ▷ n Fahrt f; (entrance) Einfahrt f, Auffahrt f, (inform) Tatkraft f; **to go for a ~** spazieren fahren; **drive away, drive off** vi wegfahren ▷ vt vertreiben

drive-in adj Drive-in-; **~ cinema** (US) Autokino nt

driven [drɪvn] pp of **drive**

driver [draɪvə*] n Fahrer(in) m(f); (Inform) Treiber m; **~'s license** (US) Führerschein m; **~'s seat** Fahrersitz m; **driving** [draɪvɪŋ] n (Auto) Fahren nt; **he likes ~** er fährt gern Auto; **driving lesson** n Fahrstunde f; **driving licence** n (BRIT) Führerschein m; **driving school** n Fahrschule f; **driving seat** n (BRIT) Fahrersitz m; **to be in the ~** alles im Griff haben; **driving test** n Fahrprüfung f

drizzle [drɪzl] n Nieselregen m ▷ vi nieseln

drop [drɒp] n (of liquid) Tropfen m; (fall in price etc) Rückgang m ▷ vt (a. fig: give up) fallen lassen ▷ vi (fall) herunterfallen; (figures, temperature) sinken, zurückgehen; **drop by, drop in** vi vorbeikommen; **drop off** vi (to sleep) einnicken; **drop out** vi (withdraw) aussteigen; (university) das Studium abbrechen; **dropout** n Aussteiger(in) m(f)

drought [draut] n Dürre f

drove [drəuv] pt of **drive**

drown [draun] vi ertrinken ▷ vt ertranken

drowsy [drauzɪ] adj schläfrig

drug [drʌg] n (Med) Medikament nt, Arznei f; (addictive) Droge f; (narcotic) Rauschgift nt; **to be on ~s** drogensüchtig sein ▷ vt (mit Medikamenten) betäuben; **drug addict** n Rauschgiftsüchtige(r) mf; **drug dealer** n Drogenhändler(in) m(f); **druggist** n (US) Drogist(in) m(f); **drugstore** n (US) Drogerie f

drum [drʌm] n Trommel f; **~s** pl Schlagzeug nt; **drummer** n Schlagzeuger(in) m(f)

drunk [drʌŋk] pp of **drink** ▷ adj betrunken; **to get ~** sich betrinken ▷

n Betrunkene(r) *mf*; *(alcoholic)* Trinker(in) *m(f)*; **drunk-driving** *n* (US) Trunkenheit *f* am Steuer; **drunken** *adj* betrunken, besoffen

dry [draɪ] *adj* trocken ▷ *vt* trocknen; *(dishes, oneself, one's hands etc)* abtrocknen ▷ *vi* trocknen, trocken werden; **dry out** *vi* trocknen; **dry up** *vi* austrocknen; **dry-clean** *vt* chemisch reinigen; **dry-cleaning** *n* chemische Reinigung; **dryer** *n* Trockner *m*; *(for hair)* Föhn *m*; *(over head)* Trockenhaube *f*

DTP *abbr* = **desktop publishing** DTP *nt*

dual [ˈdjʊəl] *adj* doppelt; **~ carriageway** *(BRIT)* zweispurige Schnellstraße *f*; **~ nationality** doppelte Staatsangehörigkeit; **dual--purpose** *adj* Mehrzweck-

dubbed [dʌbd] *adj* *(film)* synchronisiert

dubious [ˈdjuːbɪəs] *adj* zweifelhaft

duchess [ˈdʌtʃəs] *n* Herzogin *f*

duck [dʌk] *n* Ente *f*

dude [duːd] *n* (US *fam*) Typ *m*; **a cool ~** ein cooler Typ

due [djuː] *adj* *(time)* fällig; *(fitting)* angemessen; **in ~ course** zu gegebener Zeit; **~ to** infolge +*gen*, wegen +*gen* ▷ *adv* **~ south/north etc** direkt nach Norden/Süden etc

dug [dʌg] *pt, pp* of **dig**

duke [djuːk] *n* Herzog *m*

dull [dʌl] *adj (colour, light, weather)* trübe; *(boring)* langweilig

duly [ˈdjuːlɪ] *adv* ordnungsgemäß; *(as expected)* wie erwartet

dumb [dʌm] *adj* stumm; *(fam: stupid)* doof, blöde

dumb-bell [ˈdʌmbel] *n* Hantel *f*

dummy [ˈdʌmɪ] *n (sham)* Attrappe *f*; *(in shop)* Schaufensterpuppe *f*; *(BRIT: teat)* Schnuller *m*; *(fam: person)* Dummkopf *m* ▷ *adj* unecht,

Schein-; **~ run** Testlauf *m*

dump [dʌmp] *n* Abfallhaufen *m*; *(fam: place)* Kaff *nt* ▷ *vt* *(lit, fig)* abladen; *(fam)* **he ~ed her** er hat mir ihr Schluss gemacht

dumpling [ˈdʌmplɪŋ] *n* Kloß *m*, Knödel *m*

dune [djuːn] *n* Düne *f*

dung [dʌŋ] *n* Dung *m*; *(manure)* Mist *m*

dungarees [dʌŋgəˈriːz] *npl* Latzhose *f*

dungeon [ˈdʌndʒən] *n* Kerker *m*

duplex [ˈdjuːpleks] *n* zweistöckige Wohnung; *(US)* Doppelhaushälfte *f*

duplicate [ˈdjuːplɪkɪt] *n* Duplikat *nt* ▷ [ˈdjuːplɪkeɪt] *vt* *(make copies of)* kopieren; *(repeat)* wiederholen

durable [ˈdjʊərəbl] *adj* haltbar;

duration [djʊəˈreɪʃən] *n* Dauer *f*

during [ˈdjʊərɪŋ] *prep* *(time)* während +*gen*

dusk [dʌsk] *n* Abenddämmerung *f*

dust [dʌst] *n* Staub *m* ▷ *vt* abstauben; **dustbin** *n* *(BRIT)* Mülleimer *m*; **dustcart** *n* *(BRIT)* Müllwagen *m*; **duster** *n* Staubtuch *nt*; **dust jacket** *n* Schutzumschlag *m*; **dustman** *n* *(BRIT)* Müllmann *m*; **dustpan** *n* Kehrschaufel *f*; **dusty** *adj* staubig

Dutch [dʌtʃ] *adj* holländisch ▷ *n (language)* Holländisch *nt*; **to speak/talk double ~** *(fam)* Quatsch reden; **the ~** *pl* die Holländer; **Dutchman** *(pl* -**men)** *n* Holländer *m*; **Dutchwoman** *(pl* -**women)** *n* Holländerin *f*

duty [ˈdjuːtɪ] *n* Pflicht *f*; *(task)* Aufgabe *f*; *(tax)* Zoll *m*; **on/off ~** im Dienst/nicht im Dienst; **to be on ~** Dienst haben; **duty-free** *adj* zollfrei; **~ shop** Dutyfreeshop *m*

duvet [ˈduːveɪ] *n* Federbett *nt*

DVD *n abbr* = **digital versatile**

disk DVD f
dwarf [dwɔːf] (pl **dwarves**) n
Zwerg(in) m(f)
dwelling ['dwelɪŋ] n Wohnung f
dwindle ['dwɪndl] vi schwinden
dye [daɪ] n Farbstoff m ▷ vt färben
dynamic [daɪ'næmɪk] adj dynamisch
dynamo ['daɪnəməʊ] n Dynamo
m
dyslexia [dɪs'leksɪə] n Legasthe-
nie f, **dyslexic** adj legasthenisch;
to be ~ Legastheniker(in) sein
dyspepsia [dɪs'pepsɪə] n Verdauungsstörung f

E [iː] abbr = **east** O
E111 form n ≈ Auslandskrankenschein m
each [iːtʃ] adj jeder / jede / jedes ▷
pron jeder / jede / jedes; **I'll have
one of ~** ich nehme von jedem eins;
they ~ have a car jeder von ihnen
hat ein Auto; **~ other** einander, sich;
for / against ~ other füreinander /
gegeneinander ▷ adv je; **they cost
10 euros ~** sie kosten je 10 Euro, sie
kosten 10 Euro das Stück
eager ['iːɡə*] adj eifrig; **to be ~ to
do sth** darauf brennen, etw zu tun
eagle ['iːɡl] n Adler m
ear [ɪə*] n Ohr nt; **earache** n
Ohrenschmerzen pl; **eardrum** n
Trommelfell nt
earl [ɜːl] n Graf m
early ['ɜːlɪ] adj, adv früh; **to be 10
minutes ~** 10 Minuten zu früh
kommen; **at the earliest** frühestens; **in ~ June / 2008** Anfang Juni /
2008; **~ retirement** vorzeitiger Ruhestand; **~ warning system** Früh-

warnsystem nt

earn [ɜːn] vt verdienen

earnest ['ɜːnɪst] adj ernst; **in ~** im Ernst

earnings ['ɜːnɪŋz] npl Verdienst m, Einkommen nt

earphones ['ɪəfəʊnz] npl Kopfhörer m; **earplug** n Ohrenstöpsel m, Ohropax® nt; **earring** n Ohrring m

earth [ɜːθ] n Erde f; **what on ~ ...?** was in aller Welt ...? ▷ vt erden; **earthenware** n Tonwaren pl; **earthquake** n Erdbeben nt

earwig ['ɪəwɪɡ] n Ohrwurm m

ease [iːz] vt (pain) lindern; (burden) erleichtern ▷ n (easiness) Leichtigkeit f; **to feel at ~** sich wohl fühlen; **to feel ill at ~** sich nicht wohl fühlen; **easily** ['iːzɪlɪ] adv leicht; **he is ~ the best** er ist mit Abstand der Beste

east [iːst] n Osten m; **to the ~ of** östlich von ▷ adv (go, face) nach Osten ▷ adj Ost-; **~ wind** Ostwind m; **eastbound** adj (in) Richtung Osten

Easter ['iːstə*] n Ostern nt; **at ~** zu Ostern; **Easter egg** n Osterei nt; **Easter Sunday** n Ostersonntag m

eastern ['iːstən] adj Ost-, östlich; **Eastern Europe** Osteuropa n; **East Germany** n Ostdeutschland nt; **former ~** die ehemalige DDR, die neuen Bundesländer; **eastwards** ['iːstwədz] adv nach Osten

easy ['iːzɪ] adj leicht; (task, solution) einfach; (life) bequem; (manner) ungezwungen; **easy-care** adj pflegeleicht; **easy-going** adj gelassen

eat [iːt] (**ate, eaten**) vt essen; (animal) fressen; **eat out** vi zum Essen ausgehen; **eat up** vt aufessen; (animal) auffressen

eaten ['iːtn] pp of eat

eavesdrop ['iːvzdrɒp] vi (heimlich) lauschen; **to ~ on sb** jdn belauschen

eccentric [ɪk'sentrɪk] adj exzentrisch

echo ['ekəʊ] (pl **-es**) n Echo nt ▷ vi widerhallen

ecological [iːkə'lɒdʒɪkl] adj ökologisch; **~ disaster** Umweltkatastrophe f; **ecology** [ɪ'kɒlədʒɪ] n Ökologie f

economic [iːkə'nɒmɪk] adj wirtschaftlich, Wirtschafts-; **~ aid** Wirtschaftshilfe f; **economical** adj wirtschaftlich; (person) sparsam; **economics** nsing of npl Wirtschaftswissenschaft f; **economist** [ɪ'kɒn-əmɪst] n Wirtschaftswissenschaftler(in) m(f); **economize** [ɪ'kɒnəmaɪz] vi sparen (on an +dat); **economy** [ɪ'kɒnəmɪ] n (of state) Wirtschaft f; (thrift) Sparsamkeit f; **economy class** n (Aviat) Economyclass f

ecstasy ['ekstəsɪ] n Ekstase f; (drug) Ecstasy f

eczema ['eksɪmə] n Ekzem nt

edge [edʒ] n Rand m; (of knife) Schneide f; **on ~** nervös; **edgy** ['edʒɪ] adj nervös

edible ['edɪbl] adj essbar

Edinburgh ['edɪnbərə] n Edinburg nt

edit ['edɪt] vt (series, newspaper etc) herausgeben; (text) redigieren; (film) schneiden; (Inform) editieren; **edition** [ɪ'dɪʃən] n Ausgabe f, Auflage f; **editor** n Redakteur(in) m(f); (of series etc) Herausgeber(in) m(f); **editorial** [edɪ'tɔːrɪəl] adj Redaktions- ▷ n Leitartikel m

educate ['edjʊkeɪt] vt (child) erziehen; (at school, university) ausbilden; (public) aufklären; **educated** adj gebildet; **education** [edjʊ-

'keɪʃən] n Erziehung f; (studies, training) Ausbildung f; (subject of study) Pädagogik f; (system) Schulwesen nt; (knowledge) Bildung f; educational adj pädagogisch; (instructive) lehrreich; ~ television Schulfernsehen nt

eel [iːl] n Aal m

eerie ['ɪərɪ] adj unheimlich

effect [ɪ'fekt] n Wirkung f (on auf +akk); to come into ~ in Kraft treten; effective adj wirksam, effektiv

effeminate [ɪ'femɪnət] adj (of man) tuntig

efficiency [ɪ'fɪʃənsɪ] n Leistungsfähigkeit f; (of method) Wirksamkeit f; efficient adj (Tech) leistungsfähig; (method) wirksam, effizient

effort ['efət] n Anstrengung f; (attempt) Versuch m; to make an ~ sich anstrengen; effortless adj mühelos

eg abbr = exempli gratia (for example) z. B.

egg [eg] n Ei nt; eggcup n Eierbecher m; eggplant n (US) Aubergine f; eggshell n Eierschale f

ego ['iːgəʊ] (pl -s) n Ich nt; (self-esteem) Selbstbewusstsein nt; ego(t)ist ['egəʊ(t)ɪst] n Egozentriker(in) m(f)

Egypt ['iːdʒɪpt] n Ägypten nt; Egyptian [ɪ'dʒɪpʃən] adj ägyptisch ▷ n Ägypter(in) m(f)

eiderdown ['aɪdədaʊn] n Daunendecke f

eight [eɪt] num acht; at the age of ~ im Alter von acht Jahren; it's ~ (o'clock) es ist acht Uhr ▷ n (a. bus etc) Acht f; (boat) Achter m; eighteen [eɪ'tiːn] num achtzehn ▷ n Achtzehn f; see also eight; eighteenth [eɪ'tiːnθ] adj achtzehnte(r, s); see also eighth; eighth [eɪtθ] adj achte(r, s); the ~ of June der achte Juni ▷ n

(fraction) Achtel nt; an ~ of a litre ein Achtelliter; eightieth ['eɪtɪəθ] adj achtzigste(r, s); see also eighth; eighty ['eɪtɪ] num achtzig ▷ n Achtzig f; see also eight

Eire ['eərə] n die Republik Irland

either ['aɪðə*] conj ~ ... or entweder ... oder ▷ pron ~ of the two eine(r, s) von beiden ▷ adj on ~ side auf beiden Seiten ▷ adv I won't go ~ ich gehe auch nicht

eject [ɪ'dʒekt] vt ausstoßen; (person) vertreiben

elaborate [ɪ'læbərət] adj (complex) kompliziert; (plan) ausgeklügelt; (decoration) kunstvoll ▷ vt [ɪ'læbəreɪt] could you ~ on that? könntest du mehr darüber sagen?

elastic [ɪ'læstɪk] adj elastisch; ~ band Gummiband nt

elbow ['elbəʊ] n Ellbogen m

elder ['eldə*] adj (of two) älter ▷ n Ältere(r) mf; (Bot) Holunder m; elderly adj ältere(r, s) ▷ n the ~ die älteren Leute; eldest ['eldɪst] adj älteste(r, s)

elect [ɪ'lekt] vt wählen; he was ~ed chairman er wurde zum Vorsitzenden gewählt; election [ɪ'lekʃən] n Wahl f; election campaign n Wahlkampf m; electioneering [ɪlekʃə'nɪərɪŋ] n Wahlpropaganda f; electorate [ɪ'lektərɪt] n Wähler pl

electric [ɪ'lektrɪk] adj elektrisch; (car, motor, razor etc) Elektro-; ~ blanket Heizdecke f; ~ cooker Elektroherd m; ~ current elektrischer Strom; ~ shock Stromschlag m; electrical adj elektrisch; ~ goods/appliances Elektrogeräte; electrician [ɪlek'trɪʃən] n Elektriker(in) m(f); electricity [ɪlek'trɪsɪtɪ] n Elektrizität f; electrocute [ɪ'lektrəkjuːt] vt durch einen Stromschlag töten; electronic

[ɪlek'trɒnɪk] adj elektronisch
elegance ['elɪgəns] n Eleganz f;
elegant adj elegant
element ['elɪmənt] n Element nt;
an ~ of truth ein Körnchen Wahrheit; **elementary** [elɪ'mentərɪ]
adj einfach; (basic) grundlegend; **~ stage** Anfangsstadium nt; **~ school**
(US) Grundschule f; **~ maths** /
French Grundkenntnisse in Mathematik / Französisch
elephant ['elɪfənt] n Elefant m
elevator ['elɪveɪtə*] n (US) Fahrstuhl m
eleven [ɪ'levn] num elf ⊳ n (team,
bus etc) Elf f see **eight**; **eleventh**
[ɪ'levnθ] adj elfte(r, s) ⊳ n (fraction)
Elftel nt see **eighth**
eligible ['elɪdʒəbl] adj in Frage
kommend; (for grant etc) berechtigt;
~ for a pension / competition
pensions-/teilnahmeberechtigt; **~
bachelor** begehrter Junggeselle
eliminate [ɪ'lɪmɪneɪt] vt ausschließen (from aus), ausschalten;
(problem etc) beseitigen; **elimination** n Ausschluss m (from aus); (of
problem etc) Beseitigung f
elm [elm] n Ulme f
elope [ɪ'ləʊp] vi durchbrennen
(with sb mit jdm)
eloquent ['eləkwənt] adj redegewandt
else [els] adv anybody / anything
~ (in addition) sonst (noch) jemand /
etwas; (other) ein anderer / etwas
anderes; **somebody ~** jemand anders; **everyone ~** alle anderen; **or ~**
sonst; **elsewhere** adv anderswo,
woanders; (direction) woandershin
ELT abbr = **English Language
Teaching**
e-mail, **E-mail** ['iːmeɪl] vi, vt
mailen (sth to sb jdm etw) ⊳ n
E-Mail f; **e-mail address** n E-Mail-
-Adresse f

emancipated [ɪ'mænsɪpeɪtɪd]
adj emanzipiert
embankment [ɪm'bæŋkmənt]
n Böschung f; (for railway) Bahndamm m
embargo [ɪm'bɑːgəʊ] (pl **-es**) n
Embargo nt
embark [ɪm'bɑːk] vi an Bord gehen
embarrass [ɪm'bærəs] vt in Verlegenheit bringen; **embarrassed**
adj verlegen; **embarrassing** adj
peinlich
embassy ['embəsɪ] n Botschaft f
embrace [ɪm'breɪs] vt umarmen
⊳ n Umarmung f
embroider [ɪm'brɔɪdə*] vt besticken; **embroidery** n Stickerei f
embryo ['embrɪəʊ] (pl **-s**) n Embryo m
emerald ['emərəld] n Smaragd m
emerge [ɪ'mɜːdʒ] vi auftauchen;
it ~d that ... es stellte sich heraus,
dass ...
emergency [ɪ'mɜːdʒənsɪ] n
Notfall m ⊳ adj Not-; **~ exit** Notausgang m; **~ room** (US) Unfallstation f; **~ service** Notdienst m; **~ stop**
Vollbremsung f
emigrate ['emɪgreɪt] vi auswandern
emit [ɪ'mɪt] vt ausstoßen; (heat)
abgeben
emotion [ɪ'məʊʃən] n Emotion f,
Gefühl nt; **emotional** adj (person)
emotional; (experience, moment,
scene) ergreifend
emperor ['empərə*] n Kaiser m
emphasis ['emfəsɪs] n Betonung
f; **emphasize** ['emfəsaɪz] vt betonen; **emphatic**, **emphatically**
[ɪm'fætɪk, -lɪ] adj, adv nachdrücklich
empire ['empaɪə*] n Reich nt
employ [ɪm'plɔɪ] vt beschäftigen;
(hire) anstellen; (use) anwenden;

employee [emplɔɪˈiː] n Angestellte(r) mf; **employer** n Arbeitgeber(in) m(f); **employment** n Beschäftigung f; (position) Stellung f; **employment agency** n Stellenvermittlung f

empress ['empris] n Kaiserin f

empty ['empti] adj leer ▷ vt (contents) leeren; (container) ausleeren

enable [ɪˈneɪbl] vt **to ~ sb to do sth** es jdm ermöglichen, etw zu tun

enamel [ɪˈnæməl] n Email nt; (of teeth) Zahnschmelz m

enchanting [ɪnˈtʃɑːntɪŋ] adj bezaubernd

enclose [ɪnˈkləʊz] vt einschließen; (in letter) beilegen (in, with dat); **enclosure** [ɪnˈkləʊʒə*] n (for animals) Gehege nt; (in letter) Anlage f

encore [ˈɒŋkɔː*] n Zugabe f

encounter [ɪnˈkaʊntə*] n Begegnung f ▷ vt (person) begegnen +dat; (difficulties) stoßen auf +akk

encourage [ɪnˈkʌrɪdʒ] vt ermutigen; **encouragement** n Ermutigung f

encyclopaedia [ensaɪkləʊˈpiːdɪə] n Lexikon nt, Enzyklopädie f

end [end] n Ende nt; (of film, play etc) Schluss m; (purpose) Zweck m; **at the ~ of May** Ende Mai; **in the ~** schließlich; **to come to an ~** zu Ende gehen ▷ vt beenden ▷ vi enden; **end up** vi enden

endanger [ɪnˈdeɪndʒə*] vt gefährden; **~ed species** vom Aussterben bedrohte Art

endeavour [ɪnˈdevə*] n Bemühung f ▷ vi **to ~** sich bemühen (to do sth etw zu tun)

ending ['endɪŋ] n (of book) Ausgang m; (last part) Schluss m; (of word) Endung f

endive ['endaɪv] n Endiviensalat m

endless ['endlɪs] adj endlos; (possibilities) unendlich

endurance [ɪnˈdjʊərəns] n Ausdauer f; **endure** [ɪnˈdjʊə*] vt ertragen

enemy ['enɪmɪ] n Feind(in) m(f) ▷ adj feindlich

energetic [enəˈdʒetɪk] adj energiegeladen; (active) aktiv; **energy** ['enədʒɪ] n Energie f

enforce [ɪnˈfɔːs] vt durchsetzen; (obedience) erzwingen

engage [ɪnˈgeɪdʒ] vt (employ) einstellen; (singer, performer) engagieren; **engaged** adj verlobt; (toilet, telephone line) besetzt; **to get ~** sich verloben (to mit); **engaged tone** n (BRIT Tel) Belegtzeichen nt; **engagement** n (to marry) Verlobung f; **~ ring** Verlobungsring m; **engaging** adj gewinnend

engine ['endʒɪn] n (Auto) Motor m; (Rail) Lokomotive f; **~ failure** (Auto) Motorschaden m; **~ trouble** (Auto) Defekt m am Motor; **engineer** [endʒɪˈnɪə*] n Ingenieur(in) m(f); (US Rail) Lokomotivführer(in) m(f); **engineering** [endʒɪˈnɪərɪŋ] n Technik f; (mechanical ~) Maschinenbau m; (subject) Ingenieurwesen nt; **engine immobilizer** n (Auto) Wegfahrsperre f

England ['ɪŋglənd] n England nt; **English** adj englisch; **he's ~** er ist Engländer; **the ~ Channel** der Ärmelkanal ▷ n (language) Englisch nt; **in ~** auf Englisch; **to translate into ~** ins Englische übersetzen; (people) **the ~** pl die Engländer; **Englishman** (pl -men) n Engländer m; **Englishwoman** (pl -women) n Engländerin f

engrave [ɪnˈgreɪv] vt eingravieren; **engraving** n Stich m

engrossed [ɪnˈgrəʊst] adj vertieft (in sth in etw akk)

enigma [ɪ'nɪgmə] n Rätsel nt

enjoy [ɪn'dʒɔɪ] vt genießen; **I ~ reading** ich lese gern; **he ~s teasing her** es macht ihm Spaß, sie aufzuziehen; **did you ~ the film?** hat dir der Film gefallen?; **enjoyable** [-əbl] adj angenehm; (entertaining) unterhaltsam; **enjoyment** n Vergnügen nt; (stronger) Freude f (of an +dat)

enlarge [ɪn'lɑːdʒ] vt vergrößern; (expand) erweitern; **enlargement** n Vergrößerung f

enormous, **enormously** [ɪ'nɔːməs, -lɪ] adj, adv riesig, ungeheuer

enough [ɪ'nʌf] adj genug; **that's ~** das reicht!; (stop it) Schluss damit!; **I've had ~** das reicht mir; (to eat) ich bin satt ▷ adv genug, genügend

enquire [ɪn'kwaɪə*] vi sich erkundigen (about nach); **enquiry** [ɪn'kwaɪərɪ] n (question) Anfrage f; (for information) Erkundigung f (about über +akk); (investigation) Untersuchung f; **'Enquiries'** „Auskunft"

enrol [ɪn'rəʊl] vi sich einschreiben; (for course, school) sich anmelden; **enrolment** n Einschreibung f, Anmeldung f

en suite [ɒn'swiːt] adj, n **room with ~ (bathroom)** Zimmer nt mit eigenem Bad

ensure [ɪn'ʃʊə*] vt sicherstellen

enter ['entə*] vt eintreten in +akk, betreten; (drive into) einfahren in +akk; (country) einreisen in +akk; (in list) eintragen; (Comput) eingeben; (race, contest) teilnehmen an +dat ▷ vi (towards speaker) hereinkommen; (away from speaker) hineingehen

enterprise ['entəpraɪz] n (Comm) Unternehmen nt

entertain [entə'teɪn] vt (guest) bewirten; (amuse) unterhalten; **entertaining** adj unterhaltsam; **en-tertainment** n (amusement) Unterhaltung f

enthusiasm [ɪn'θjuːzɪæzəm] n Begeisterung f; **enthusiastic** [ɪn-θjuːzɪ'æstɪk] adj begeistert (about von)

entice [ɪn'taɪs] vt locken; (lead astray) verleiten

entire, **entirely** [ɪn'taɪə*, -lɪ] adj, adv ganz

entitle [ɪn'taɪtl] vt (qualify) berechtigen (to zu); (name) betiteln

entrance ['entrəns] n Eingang m; (for vehicles) Einfahrt f; (entering) Eintritt m; (Theat) Auftritt m; **entrance exam** n Aufnahmeprüfung f; **entrance fee** n Eintrittsgeld nt

entrust [ɪn'trʌst] vt **to ~ sb with sth** jdm etw anvertrauen

entry ['entrɪ] n (way in) Eingang m; (entering) Eintritt m; (in vehicle) Einfahrt f; (into country) Einreise f; (admission) Zutritt m; (in diary, accounts) Eintrag m; **'no ~'** „Eintritt verboten"; (for vehicles) „Einfahrt verboten"; **entry phone** n Türsprechanlage f

E-number n (food additive) E-Nummer f

envelope ['envələʊp] n (Brief)umschlag m

enviable ['envɪəbl] adj beneidenswert; **envious** ['envɪəs] adj neidisch

environment [ɪn'vaɪərənmənt] n Umgebung f; (ecology) Umwelt f; **environmental** [ɪnvaɪərən'mən-təl] adj Umwelt-; **~ pollution** Umweltverschmutzung f; **environmentalist** n Umweltschützer(in) m(f)

envy ['envɪ] n Neid m (of auf +akk) ▷ vt beneiden (sb jdn um etw)

epic ['epɪk] n Epos nt; (film) Monumentalfilm m

epidemic [epɪ'demɪk] n Epidemie

f

epilepsy [ˈepɪlepsɪ] n Epilepsie f;
epileptic [epɪˈleptɪk] adj epileptisch

episode [ˈepɪsəʊd] n Episode f;
(TV) Fortsetzung f, Folge f

epoch [ˈiːpɒk] n Zeitalter nt,
Epoche f

equal [ˈiːkwl] adj gleich (to +dat) ▷
n Gleichgestellte(r) mf ▷ vt gleichen; (match) gleichkommen +dat;
two times two ~s four zwei mal
zwei ist gleich vier; **equality**
[ɪˈkwɒlɪtɪ] n Gleichheit f; (equal
rights) Gleichberechtigung f; **equalize** vi (Sport) ausgleichen; **equalizer** n (Sport) Ausgleichstreffer m;
equally adv gleich; (on the other
hand) andererseits; **equation**
[ɪˈkweɪʒən] n (Math) Gleichung f

equator [ɪˈkweɪtə*] n Äquator m

equilibrium [iːkwɪˈlɪbrɪəm] n
Gleichgewicht nt

equip [ɪˈkwɪp] vt ausrüsten;
(kitchen) ausstatten; **equipment** n
Ausrüstung f; (for kitchen) Ausstattung f; **electrical ~** Elektrogeräte pl

equivalent [ɪˈkwɪvələnt] adj
gleichwertig (to sth, corresponding)
entsprechend (to +dat) ▷ n Äquivalent nt; (amount) gleiche Menge; (in
money) Gegenwert m

era [ˈɪərə] n Ära f, Zeitalter nt

erase [ɪˈreɪz] vt ausradieren; (tape,
disk) löschen; **eraser** n Radiergummi m

erect [ɪˈrekt] adj aufrecht ▷ vt
(building, monument) errichten; (tent)
aufstellen; **erection** n Errichtung f;
(Anat) Erektion f

erode [ɪˈrəʊd] vt zerfressen; (land)
auswaschen; (rights, power) aushöhlen; **erosion** [ɪˈrəʊʒən] n Erosion f

erotic [ɪˈrɒtɪk] adj erotisch

err [ɜː*] vi sich irren

errand [ˈerənd] n Besorgung f

erratic [ɪˈrætɪk] adj (behaviour)
unberechenbar; (bus link etc) unregelmäßig; (performance) unbeständig

error [ˈerə*] n Fehler m; **in ~** irrtümlicherweise; **error message** n
(Inform) Fehlermeldung f

erupt [ɪˈrʌpt] vi ausbrechen

escalator [ˈeskəleɪtə*] n Rolltreppe f

escalope [ˈeskələp] n Schnitzel nt

escape [ɪˈskeɪp] n Flucht f; (from
prison etc) Ausbruch m; **to have a
narrow ~** gerade noch davonkommen; **there's no ~** (fig) es gibt keinen
Ausweg ▷ vt (pursuers) entkommen
+dat; (punishment etc) entgehen +dat
▷ vi (from pursuers) entkommen
(from dat); (from prison etc) ausbrechen (from dat); (leak: gas) ausströmen; (water) auslaufen

escort [ˈeskɔːt] n (companion) Begleiter(in) m(f), (guard) Eskorte f ▷ vt
[ɪˈskɔːt] (lady) begleiten

especially [ɪˈspeʃəlɪ] adv besonders

espionage [ˈespɪənaːʒ] n Spionage f

Esquire [ɪˈskwaɪə*] n (BRIT: in
address) **J. Brown, Esq** Herrn J.
Brown

essay [ˈeseɪ] n Aufsatz m; (literary)
Essay m

essential [ɪˈsenʃəl] adj (necessary)
unentbehrlich, unverzichtbar; (basic)
wesentlich ▷ n **the ~s** pl das Wesentliche; **essentially** adv im Wesentlichen

establish [ɪˈstæblɪʃ] vt (set up)
gründen; (introduce) einführen; (relations) aufnehmen; (prove) nachweisen; **to ~ that ...** feststellen, dass ...;
establishment n Institution f;
(business) Unternehmen nt

estate [ɪˈsteɪt] n Gut nt, (of deceased) Nachlass m; (housing ~)

Siedlung f; (country house) Landsitz m; **estate agent** n (BRIT) Grundstücksmakler(in) m(f), Immobilienmakler(in) m(f); **estate car** n (BRIT) Kombiwagen m

estimate ['estɪmət] n Schätzung f; (Comm: of price) Kostenvoranschlag m ▷ ['estɪmeɪt] vt schätzen

estuary ['estjʊərɪ] n Mündung f

etching ['etʃɪŋ] n Radierung f

eternal, eternally [ɪ'tɜːnl, -nəlɪ] adj, adv ewig; **eternity** n Ewigkeit f

ethical ['eθɪkəl] adj ethisch; **ethics** ['eθɪks] npl Ethik f

Ethiopia [iːθɪ'əʊpɪə] n Äthiopien nt

ethnic ['eθnɪk] adj ethnisch; (clothes etc) landesüblich; **~ minority** ethnische Minderheit

EU abbr = **European Union** EU f

euphemism ['juːfɪmɪzəm] n Euphemismus m

euro ['jʊərəʊ] (pl **-s**) n (Fin) Euro m; **~ symbol** Eurozeichen nt; **Eurocheque** ['jʊərəʊtʃek] n Euroscheck m; **Europe** ['jʊərəp] n Europa nt; **European** [jʊərə'piːən] adj europäisch; **~ Parliament** n Europäisches Parlament; **~ Union** Europäische Union f ▷ n Europäer(in) m(f); **Eurosceptic** ['jʊərəʊskeptɪk] n Euroskeptiker(in) m(f); **Eurotunnel** n Eurotunnel m

evacuate [ɪ'vækjʊeɪt] vt (place) räumen; (people) evakuieren

evade [ɪ'veɪd] vt ausweichen +dat; (pursuers) sich entziehen +dat

evaluate [ɪ'væljʊeɪt] vt auswerten

evaporate [ɪ'væpəreɪt] vi verdampfen; (fig) verschwinden; **~d milk** Kondensmilch f

even ['iːvən] adj (flat) eben; (regular) gleichmäßig; (equal) gleich; (number) gerade; **the score is ~** es

steht unentschieden ▷ adv sogar; **~ you** selbst (o sogar) du; **~ if** selbst wenn, wenn auch; **~ though** obwohl; **not ~** nicht einmal; **~ better** noch besser; **even out** vi (prices) sich einpendeln

evening ['iːvnɪŋ] n Abend m; **in the ~** abends, am Abend; **this ~** heute Abend; **evening class** n Abendkurs m; **evening dress** n (generally) Abendkleidung f; (woman's) Abendkleid nt

evenly ['iːvənlɪ] adv gleichmäßig

event [ɪ'vent] n Ereignis nt; (organized) Veranstaltung f; (Sport: discipline) Disziplin f; **in the ~ of** im Falle +gen; **eventful** adj ereignisreich

eventual [ɪ'ventʃʊəl] adj (final) letztendlich; **eventually** [ɪ'ventʃʊəlɪ] adv (at last) am Ende; (given time) schließlich

ever ['evə'] adv (at any time) je(-mals); **don't ~ do that again** tu das ja nie wieder; **he's the best ~** er ist der Beste, den es je gegeben hat; **have you ~ been to the States?** bist du schon einmal in den Staaten gewesen?; **for ~** (für) immer; **for ~ and ~** auf immer und ewig; **~ so ...** (fam) äußerst ...; **~ so drunk** ganz schön betrunken

every ['evrɪ] adj jeder / jede / jedes; **~ day** jeden Tag; (or)jeden zweiten Tag; **~ other day** jeden zweiten Tag; **~ five days** alle fünf Tage; **I have ~ reason to believe that ...** ich habe allen Grund anzunehmen, dass ...; **everybody** pron jeder, alle pl; **everyday** adj (commonplace) alltäglich; (clothes, language etc) Alltags-; **everyone** pron jeder, alle pl; **everything** pron alles; **everywhere** adv überall; (with direction) überallhin

evidence ['evɪdəns] n Beweise pl; (single piece) Beweis m; (testimony)

Aussage f; (signs) Spuren pl; **evident**, **evidently** adj, adv offensichtlich

evil ['iːvl] adj böse n Böse(s) nt, **an ~** ein Übel

evolution [iːvə'luːʃən] n Entwicklung f; (of life) Evolution f; **evolve** [ɪ'vɒlv] vi sich entwickeln

ex- [eks] pref Ex-, ehemalig; **~wife** frühere Frau, Exfrau f; **~** in (am) Verflossene(r) mf, Ex mf

exact [ɪg'zækt] adj genau; **exactly** adv genau; **not ~ fast** nicht gerade schnell

exaggerate [ɪg'zædʒəreɪt] vt, vi übertreiben; **exaggerated** adj übertrieben; **exaggeration** n Übertreibung f

exam [ɪg'zæm] n Prüfung f; **examination** [ɪgzæmɪ'neɪʃən] n (Med etc) Untersuchung f, Prüfung f; (at university) Examen nt; (at customs etc) Kontrolle f; **examine** [ɪg'zæmɪn] vt untersuchen (for auf +akk); (check) kontrollieren, prüfen; **examiner** n Prüfer(in) mf)

example [ɪg'zɑːmpl] n Beispiel n; **for ~** zum Beispiel

excavation [ekskə'veɪʃən] n Ausgrabung f

exceed [ɪk'siːd] vt überschreiten, übertreffen; **exceedingly** adv äußerst

excel [ɪk'sel] vt übertreffen; **he ~led himself** er hat sich selbst übertroffen vi sich auszeichnen (in in +dat, at bei); **excellent**, exc **ellently** ['eksələnt, li] adj, adv ausgezeichnet

except [ɪk'sept] prep ~ außer +dat; **~ for** abgesehen von ▷ vt ausnehmen; **exception** [ɪk'sepʃən] n Ausnahme f; **exceptional**, **exceptionally** [ɪk'sepʃənl, -nəli] adj, adv außergewöhnlich

excess [ek'ses] n Übermaß nt (of an +dat); **excess baggage** n

Übergepäck nt; **excesses** npl Exzesse pl; (drink, sex) Ausschweifungen pl, **excess fare** n Nachlösegebühr f; **excessive, excessively** adj, adv übermäßig; **excess weight** n Übergewicht nt

exchange [ɪks'tʃeɪndʒ] n Austausch m (of gegen); (of bought items) Umtausch m (for gegen); (Tel) Wechsel m; (Tel) Vermittlung f, Zentrale f ▷ vt austauschen; (goods) tauschen; (bought items) umtauschen (for gegen); (money, blows) wechseln; **exchange rate** n Wechselkurs m

excite [ɪk'saɪt] vt erregen; **excited** adj aufgeregt; **to get ~** sich aufregen; **exciting** adj aufregend; (book, film) spannend

exclamation [eksklə'meɪʃən] n Ausruf m; **exclamation mark**, **exclamation point** (US) n Ausrufezeichen nt

exclude [ɪks'kluːd] vt ausschließen; **exclusion** [ɪks'kluːʒən] n Ausschluss m, **exclusive** [ɪks'kluːsɪv] adj (select) exklusiv; (sole) ausschließlich; **exclusively** adv ausschließlich

excrement ['ekskrɪmənt] n Kot m, Exkremente pl

excruciating [ɪks'kruːʃɪeɪtɪŋ] adj fürchterlich, entsetzlich

excursion [ɪks'kɜːʃən] n Ausflug m

excusable [ɪks'kjuːzəbl] adj entschuldbar; **excuse** [ɪks'kjuːz] vt entschuldigen; **~ me** Entschuldigung!; **to ~ sb for sth** jdm etw verzeihen; **to ~ sb from sth** jdn von etw befreien ▷ [ɪks'kjuːs] n Entschuldigung f, Ausrede f

ex-directory [eksdaɪ'rektərɪ] adj **to be ~** (BRIT Tel) nicht im Telefonbuch stehen

execute ['eksɪkjuːt] vt (carry out)

ausführen; (kill) hinrichten; **execution** n (killing) Hinrichtung f; (carrying out) Ausführung f; **executive** [ɪɡˈzekjutɪv] n (Comm) leitender Angestellter, leitende Angestellte

exemplary [ɪɡˈzemplərɪ] adj beispielhaft

exempt [ɪɡˈzempt] adj befreit (from von) ▷ vt befreien

exercise [ˈeksəsaɪz] n (in school, sports) Übung f; (movement) Bewegung f; **to get more ~** mehr Sport treiben; **exercise bike** n Heimtrainer m; **exercise book** n Heft nt

exert [ɪɡˈzɜːt] vt (influence) ausüben

exhaust [ɪɡˈzɔːst] n (fumes) Abgase pl; (Auto) Auspuff m; **exhausted** adj erschöpft; **exhausting** adj anstrengend

exhibit [ɪɡˈzɪbɪt] n (in exhibition) Ausstellungsstück nt; **exhibition** [eksɪˈbɪʃən] n Ausstellung f; **exhibitor** n Aussteller(in) m(f)

exhilarating [ɪɡˈzɪləreɪtɪŋ] adj belebend, erregend

exile [ˈeksaɪl] n Exil nt; (person) Verbannte(r) mf ▷ vt verbannen

exist [ɪɡˈzɪst] vi existieren; (live) leben (on von); **existence** n Existenz f; **to come into ~** entstehen; **existing** adj bestehend

exit [ˈeksɪt] n Ausgang m; (for vehicles) Ausfahrt f; **exit poll** n Umfrage direkt nach dem Wahlgang

exorbitant [ɪɡˈzɔːbɪtənt] adj astronomisch

exotic [ɪɡˈzɒtɪk] adj exotisch

expand [ɪksˈpænd] vt ausdehnen, erweitern ▷ vi sich ausdehnen; **expansion** [ɪksˈpænʃən] n Expansion f, Erweiterung f

expect [ɪksˈpekt] vt erwarten; (suppose) annehmen; **he ~s me to do it** er erwartet, dass ich es mache; **I ~ it'll rain** es wird wohl regnen; **I ~**

so ich denke schon ▷ vi **to be ~ing** ein Kind erwarten

expedition [ekspɪˈdɪʃən] n Expedition f

expenditure [ɪkˈspendɪtʃə*] n Ausgaben pl

expense [ɪkˈspens] n Kosten pl; (single cost) Ausgabe f; **(business) ~s** pl Spesen pl; **at sb's ~** auf jds Kosten; **expensive** [ɪkˈspensɪv] adj teuer

experience [ɪkˈspɪərɪəns] n Erfahrung f; (particular incident) Erlebnis nt; **by/from ~** aus Erfahrung ▷ vt erfahren, erleben; (hardship) durchmachen; **experienced** adj erfahren

experiment [ɪkˈsperɪmənt] n Versuch m, Experiment nt ▷ vi experimentieren

expert [ˈekspɜːt] n Experte m, Expertin f; (professional) Fachmann m, Fachfrau f; (Jur) Sachverständige(r) mf ▷ adj fachmännisch; **expertise** [ekspɜːˈtiːz] n Sachkenntnis f

expire [ɪkˈspaɪə*] vi (end) ablaufen; **expiry date** [ɪkˈspaɪərɪdeɪt] n Verfallsdatum nt

explain [ɪkˈspleɪn] vt erklären (sth to sb jdm etw); **explanation** [ekspləˈneɪʃən] n Erklärung f

explicit [ɪkˈsplɪsɪt] adj ausdrücklich, deutlich

explode [ɪkˈspləʊd] vi explodieren

exploit [ɪkˈsplɔɪt] vt ausbeuten

explore [ɪkˈsplɔː*] vt erforschen

explosion [ɪkˈspləʊʒən] n Explosion f; **explosive** [ɪkˈspləʊsɪv] adj explosiv ▷ n Sprengstoff m

export [ekˈspɔːt] vt, vi exportieren ▷ [ˈekspɔːt] n Export m ▷ adj (trade) Export-

expose [ɪkˈspəʊz] vt (to danger etc) aussetzen (to dat); (uncover) freilegen; (imposter) entlarven; **exposed**

adj (position) ungeschützt; **exposure** [ɪkˈspəʊʒəʳ] *n (Med)* Unterkühlung *f*; **24 ~s** 24 Aufnahmen

express [ɪkˈsprɛs] *adj (speedy)* Express-, Schnell-; **~ delivery** Eilzustellung *f*; **~** *n (rail)* Schnellzug *m* ▷ *vt* ausdrücken ▷ *vr* **to ~ oneself** sich ausdrücken; **expression** [ɪkˈsprɛʃən] *n (phrase)* Ausdruck *m*; *(look)* Gesichtsausdruck *m*; **expressive** *adj* ausdrucksvoll; **expressway** *n (US)* Schnellstraße *f*

extend [ɪkˈstɛnd] *vt (arms)* ausstrecken; *(lengthen)* verlängern; *(building)* vergrößern, ausbauen; *(business, limits)* erweitern; **extension** [ɪkˈstɛnʃən] *n (lengthening)* Verlängerung *f*; *(of building)* Anbau *m*; *(Tel)* Anschluss *m*; *(of business, limits)* Erweiterung *f*; **extensive** [ɪkˈstɛnsɪv] *adj (knowledge)* umfangreich; *(use)* häufig; **extent** [ɪkˈstɛnt] *n (length)* Länge *f*; *(size)* Ausdehnung *f*; *(scope)* Umfang *m*, Ausmaß *nt*; **to a certain/large ~** in gewissem/hohem Maße

exterior [ɛkˈstɪərɪəʳ] *n* Äußere(s) *nt*

external [ɛkˈstɔːnl] *adj* äußere(r, s), Außen-; **externally** *adv* äußerlich

extinct [ɪkˈstɪŋkt] *adj (species)* ausgestorben

extinguish [ɪkˈstɪŋgwɪʃ] *vt* löschen; **extinguisher** *n* Löschgerät *nt*

extra [ˈɛkstrə] *adj* zusätzlich; **~ charge** Zuschlag *m*, **~ time** *(Sport)* Verlängerung *f* ▷ *adv* besonders; **~ large** *(clothing)* übergroß ▷ *n* **~s** zusätzliche Kosten *pl*; *(food)* Beilagen *pl*; *(accessories)* Zubehör *nt*; *(for car etc)* Extras *pl*

extract [ɪkˈstrækt] *vt* herausziehen *(from aus)*; *(tooth)* ziehen ▷

[ˈɛkstrækt] *n (from book etc)* Auszug *m*

extraordinary [ɪkˈstrɔːdnrɪ] *adj* außerordentlich; *(unusual)* ungewöhnlich; *(amazing)* erstaunlich

extreme [ɪkˈstriːm] *adj* äußerste(r, s); *(drastic)* extrem ▷ *n* Extrem *nt*, äußerste(s) *nt*; **extremely** *adv* äußerst, höchst; **extreme sports** *npl* Extremsportarten *pl* **extremist** [ɪkˈstriːmɪst] *adj* extremistisch ▷ *n* Extremist *m*

extricate [ˈɛkstrɪkeɪt] *vt* befreien *(from aus)*

extrovert [ˈɛkstrəʊvɜːt] *adj* extrovertiert

exuberance [ɪgˈzuːbərəns] *n* Überschwang *m*; **exuberant** *adj* überschwänglich

exultation [ɛgzʌlˈteɪʃən] *n* Jubel *m*

eye [aɪ] *n* Auge *nt*; **to keep an ~ on sb/sth** auf jdn/etw aufpassen ▷ *vt* mustern; **eyebrow** *n* Augenbraue *f*; **eyelash** *n* Wimper *f*; **eyelid** *n* Augenlid *nt*; **eyeliner** *n* Eyeliner *m*; **eyeopener** *n* **that was an ~** das hat mir die Augen geöffnet; **eyeshadow** *n* Lidschatten *m*; **eyesight** *n* Sehkraft *f*; **eyesore** *n* Schandfleck *m*; **eye witness** *n* Augenzeuge *m*, Augenzeugin *f*

f

fabric ['fæbrɪk] n Stoff m
fabulous ['fæbjʊləs] adj sagenhaft
façade [fə'sɑːd] n (a. fig) Fassade f
face [feɪs] n Gesicht nt; (of clock) Zifferblatt nt; (of mountain) Wand f; **in the ~ of** trotz +gen; **to be ~ to ~** (people) einander gegenüberstehen ▷ vt, vi (person) gegenüberstehen +dat; (at table) gegenübersitzen +dat; **to ~ north** (room) nach Norden gehen; **to ~ (up to) the facts** den Tatsachen ins Auge sehen; **to be ~d with sth** mit etw konfrontiert sein; **face cream** n Gesichtscreme f; **face lift** n Gesichtsstraffung f; (fig) Verschönerung f; **face powder** n Gesichtspuder m
facet ['fæsɪt] n (fig) Aspekt m
face value n Nennwert m
facial ['feɪʃəl] adj Gesichts- ▷ n (fam) (kosmetische) Gesichtsbehandlung
facilitate [fə'sɪlɪteɪt] vt erleich-

tern
facility [fə'sɪlɪtɪ] n (building etc to be used) Einrichtung f, Möglichkeit f; (installation) Anlage f; (skill) Gewandtheit f
fact [fækt] n Tatsache f; **as a matter of ~, in ~** eigentlich, tatsächlich
factor ['fæktə*] n Faktor m
factory ['fæktərɪ] n Fabrik f; **factory outlet** n Fabrikverkauf m
factual ['fæktjʊəl] adj sachlich
faculty ['fækəltɪ] n Fähigkeit f; (at university) Fakultät f; (US: teaching staff) Lehrkörper m
fade [feɪd] vi (a. fig) verblassen; **faded** adj verblasst, verblichen
faff about ['fæfəbaʊt] vi (BRIT fam) herumwursteln
fag [fæg] n (BRIT fam: cigarette) Kippe f; (US fam pej) Schwule(r) m
Fahrenheit ['færənhaɪt] n Fahrenheit
fail [feɪl] vt (exam) nicht bestehen ▷ vi versagen; (plan, marriage) scheitern; (student) durchfallen; (eyesight) nachlassen; **words ~ me** ich bin sprachlos; **failing** n Schwäche f, Fehler m ▷ prep (person) Versager(in) m(f); (act) (Tech) Versagen nt; (of engine etc) Ausfall m; (of plan, marriage) Scheitern nt
faint [feɪnt] adj schwach; (sound) leise; (fam) **I haven't the ~est (idea)** ich habe keine Ahnung ▷ vi ohnmächtig werden (with vor +dat); **faintness** n (Med) Schwächegefühl nt
fair [feə*] adj (hair) blond; (skin) hell; (just) gerecht, fair; (reasonable) ganz ordentlich; (in school) befriedigend; (weather) schön; (wind) günstig; **a ~ number of /amount of** ziemlich viele /viel ▷ adv **to play ~** fair spielen; (fig) fair sein; **~ enough**

in Ordnung! ▷ n (fun~) Jahrmarkt m; (comm) Messe f; **fair-haired** adj blond; **fairly** adv (honestly) fair; (rather) ziemlich

fairy [ˈfeərɪ] n Fee f; **fairy tale** n Märchen nt

faith [feɪθ] n (trust) Vertrauen nt (in sb zu jdm); (Rel) Glaube m; **faithful, faithfully** adj, adv treu; Yours ~ly Hochachtungsvoll

fake [feɪk] n (thing) Fälschung f ▷ adj vorgetäuscht ▷ vt fälschen

falcon [ˈfɔːlkən] n Falke m

fall [fɔːl] (fell, fallen) vi fallen; (from a height, badly) stürzen; **to ~ ill** krank werden; **to ~ asleep** einschlafen; **to ~ in love** sich verlieben ▷ n Fall m; (accident, fig: of regime) Sturz m; (decrease) Sinken nt (in +gen); (US: autumn) Herbst m; **fall apart** vi auseinanderfallen; **fall behind** vi zurückbleiben; (with work, rent) in Rückstand geraten; **fall down** vi (person) hinfallen; **fall off** vi herunterfallen; (decrease) zurückgehen; **fall out** vi herausfallen; (quarrel) sich streiten; **fall over** vi hinfallen; **fall through** vi (plan etc) ins Wasser fallen

fallen [ˈfɔːlən] pp of fall

fallout [ˈfɔːlaʊt] n radioaktiver Niederschlag, Fall-out m

false [fɔːls] adj falsch; (artificial) künstlich; **raise alarm** n blinder Alarm, **false start** n (Sport) Fehlstart m; **false teeth** npl (künstliches) Gebiss

fame [feɪm] n Ruhm m

familiar [fəˈmɪlɪə*] adj vertraut, bekannt; **to be ~ with** vertraut sein mit, gut kennen; **familiarity** [fəmɪlɪˈærɪtɪ] n Vertrautheit f

family [ˈfæmɪlɪ] n Familie f; (including relations) Verwandtschaft f; **family man** n Familienvater m; **family name** n Familienname m,

Nachname m

famine [ˈfæmɪn] n Hungersnot f; **famished** [ˈfæmɪʃt] adj ausgehungert

famous [ˈfeɪməs] adj berühmt

fan [fæn] n (hand-held) Fächer m; (Elec) Ventilator m; (admirer) Fan m

fanatic [fəˈnætɪk] n Fanatiker(in) m(f)

fancy [ˈfænsɪ] adj (elaborate) kunstvoll; (unusual) ausgefallen ▷ vt (like) gern haben; **he fancies her** er steht auf sie; **~ that** stell dir vor!, so was!; **fancy dress** n Kostüm nt, Verkleidung f

fan heater [ˈfænhiːtə*] n Heizlüfter m; **fanlight** n Oberlicht nt

fan mail n Fanpost f

fantasise [ˈfæntəsaɪz] vi träumen (about von); **fantastic** [fænˈtæstɪk] adj (a. fam) fantastisch; **that's ~** (fam) das ist ja toll!; **fantasy** [ˈfæntəzɪ] n Fantasie f

far [fɑː*] (further o farther, furthest o farthest) adj weit; **the ~ end of the room** das andere Ende des Zimmers; **the Far East** der Ferne Osten ▷ adv weit; **~ better** viel besser; **by ~ the best** bei weitem der/die/das Beste; **as ~ as ...** bis zum o zur ... (with place name) bis nach ...; **as ~ as I'm concerned** was mich betrifft, von mir aus; **so ~** soweit, bisher; **faraway** adj weit entfernt; (look) verträumt

fare [feə*] n Fahrpreis m; (money) Fahrgeld nt

farm [fɑːm] n Bauernhof m, Farm f; **farmer** n Bauer m, Bäuerin f, Landwirt(in) m(f); **farmhouse** n Bauernhaus nt; **farming** n Landwirtschaft f; **farmland** n Ackerland nt; **farmyard** n Hof m

far-reaching [fɑːˈriːtʃɪŋ] adj weitreichend; **far-sighted** adj weitsichtig; (fig) weitblickend

fart [fɑːt] n (fam) Furz m; **old ~** (fam: person) alter Sack ▷ vi (fam) furzen

farther ['fɑːðə*] adj, adv comparative of **far**; see **further**

farthest ['fɑːðɪst] adj, adv superlative of **far**; see **furthest**

fascinating ['fæsɪneɪtɪŋ] adj faszinierend; **fascination** n Faszination f

fascism ['fæʃɪzəm] n Faschismus m; **fascist** ['fæʃɪst] adj faschistisch ▷ Faschist(in) m(f)

fashion ['fæʃən] n (clothes) Mode f; (manner) Art (und Weise) f; **to be in ~** (in) Mode sein; **out of ~** unmodisch; **fashionable, fashionably** adj, adv (clothes, person) modisch; (author, pub etc) in Mode

fast [fɑːst] adj schnell; (dye) waschecht; **to be ~** (clock) vorgehen ▷ adv schnell; (firmly) fest; **to be ~ asleep** fest schlafen ▷ n Fasten nt ▷ vi fasten; **fastback** n (Auto) Fließheck nt

fasten ['fɑːsn] vt (attach) befestigen (to an +dat); (do up) zumachen; **~ your seatbelts** bitte anschnallen; **fastener, fastening** n Verschluss m

fast food n Fast Food nt; **fast forward** n (for tape) Schnellvorlauf m; **fast lane** n Überholspur f

fat [fæt] adj dick; (meat) fett ▷ n Fett nt

fatal ['feɪtl] adj tödlich

fate [feɪt] n Schicksal nt

fat-free adj (food) fettfrei

father ['fɑːðə*] n Vater m; (priest) Pfarrer m ▷ vt (child) zeugen; **Father Christmas** n der Weihnachtsmann; **father-in-law** (pl **fathers-in-law**) n Schwiegervater m

fatigue [fə'tiːg] n Ermüdung f

fattening ['fætnɪŋ] adj **to be ~** dick machen; **fatty** ['fætɪ] adj (food) fettig

faucet ['fɔːsɪt] n (US) Wasserhahn m

fault [fɔːlt] n Fehler m; (Tech) Defekt m; (Geo) Störung f; (blame) Schuld f; **it's your ~** du bist daran schuld; **faulty** adj fehlerhaft; (Tech) defekt

favor (US), **favour** ['feɪvə*] n (approval) Gunst f; (kindness) Gefallen m; **in ~ of** für; **I'm in ~ of (of going)** ich bin dafür(, dass wir gehen); **to do sb a ~** jdm einen Gefallen tun ▷ vt (prefer) vorziehen; (be favourable) günstig (to, for für); **favourite** ['feɪvərɪt] n Liebling m, Favorit(in) m(f) ▷ adj Lieblings-

fax [fæks] vt faxen ▷ n Fax nt; **fax number** n Faxnummer f

faze [feɪz] vt (fam) aus der Fassung bringen

FBI abbr = **Federal Bureau of Investigation** FBI nt

fear [fɪə*] n Angst f (of vor +dat) ▷ vt befürchten; **I ~ that most** davor habe ich am meisten Angst; **fearful** adj (timid) ängstlich, furchtsam; (terrible) fürchterlich; **fearless** adj furchtlos

feasible ['fiːzəbl] adj machbar

feast [fiːst] n Festessen nt

feather ['feðə*] n Feder f

feature ['fiːtʃə*] n (facial) (Gesichts)zug m; (characteristic) Merkmal nt; (of car etc) Ausstattungsmerkmal nt; (in the press) (Cine) Feature nt ▷ vt bringen, (als Besonderheit) zeigen; **feature film** n Spielfilm m

February ['februərɪ] n Februar m; see also **September**

fed [fed] pt, pp of **feed**

federal ['fedərəl] adj Bundes-; **the Federal Republic of Germany**

die Bundesrepublik Deutschland

fed-up [fɛd'ʌp] adj **to be ~ with sth** etw satt haben, **I'm ~** ich habe die Nase voll

fee [fiː] n Gebühr f; (of doctor, lawyer) Honorar nt

feeble ['fiːbl] adj schwach

feed [fiːd] (**fed, fed**) vt (baby, animal) füttern; (support) ernähren ▷ n (for baby) Mahlzeit f; (for animals) Futter nt; (Inform: paper ~) Zufuhr f; **feed in** vt (information) eingeben; **feedback** n (information) Feed-back nt

feel [fiːl] (**felt, felt**) vt (sense) fühlen; (pain) empfinden; (touch) anfassen; (think) meinen ▷ vi (person) sich fühlen; **I ~ cold** mir ist kalt; **do you ~ like a walk?** hast du Lust, spazieren zu gehen?; **feeling** n Gefühl nt

feet [fiːt] pl of **foot**

fell [fɛl] pt of **fall** ▷ vt (tree) fällen

fellow ['fɛləʊ] n Kerl m, Typ m; **~ citizen** Mitbürger(in) m(f); **~ countryman** Landsmann m; **~ worker** Mitarbeiter(in) m(f)

felt [fɛlt] pt, pp of **feel** ▷ n Filz m; **felt tip felt tip pen** n Filzstift m

female ['fiːmeɪl] n (of animals) Weibchen nt ▷ adj weiblich; **~ doctor** Ärztin f; **~ dog** Hündin f; **feminine** ['fɛmɪnɪn] adj weiblich; **feminist** ['fɛmɪnɪst] n (Pol) Feminist(in) m(f) ▷ adj feministisch

fence [fɛns] n Zaun m

fencing n (Sport) Fechten nt

fender ['fɛndə*] n (US Auto) Kotflügel m

fennel ['fɛnl] n Fenchel m

fern [fɜːn] n Farn m

ferocious [fə'rəʊʃəs] adj wild

ferry ['fɛrɪ] n Fähre f ▷ vt übersetzen

fertile ['fɜːtaɪl] adj fruchtbar; **fertility** [fə'tɪlɪtɪ] n Fruchtbarkeit f;

fertilize ['fɜːtɪlaɪz] vt (Bio) befruchten; (Agr: land) düngen; **fertilizer** n Dünger m

festival ['fɛstɪvəl] n (Rel) Fest nt; (Art, Mus) Festspiele pl; (pop music) Festival nt; **festive** ['fɛstɪv] adj festlich; **festivities** [fe'stɪvɪtɪz] n pl Feierlichkeiten pl

fetch [fɛtʃ] vt holen; (collect) abholen; (in sale, money) einbringen; **fetching** adj reizend

fetish ['fɛtɪʃ] n Fetisch m

fetus ['fiːtəs] n (US) Fötus m

fever ['fiːvə*] n Fieber nt; **feverish** adj (Med) fiebrig; (fig) fieberhaft

few [fjuː] adj, pron a few pl; **a ~** pl ein paar; **fewer** adj weniger; **fewest** adj wenigste(r, s)

fiancé [fɪ'ɒnseɪ] n Verlobte(r) m; **fiancée** n Verlobte f

fiasco [fɪ'æskəʊ] (pl **-s** o US **-es**) n Fiasko nt

fiber (US), **fibre** ['faɪbə*] n Faser f; (material) Faserstoff m

fickle ['fɪkl] adj unbeständig

fiction ['fɪkʃən] n (novels) Prosaliteratur f; **fictional**, **fictitious** [fɪk'tɪʃəs] adj erfunden

fiddle ['fɪdl] n Geige f; (trick) Betrug m ▷ vt (accounts, results) frisieren; **fiddle with** vt herumfummeln an +dat; **fiddly** adj knifflig

fidelity [fɪ'dɛlɪtɪ] n Treue f

fidget ['fɪdʒɪt] vi zappeln; **fidgety** adj zappelig

field [fiːld] n Feld nt; (grass-covered) Wiese f; (fig: of work) (Arbeits)gebiet nt

fierce [fɪəs] adj heftig; (animal, appearance) wild; (criticism, competition) scharf

fifteen [fɪf'tiːn] num fünfzehn ▷ n Fünfzehn f; see also **eight**; **fifteenth** adj fünfzehnte(r, s), see also **eighth**; **fifth** [fɪfθ] adj fünfte(r, s)

▷ *n* (*fraction*) Fünftel *nt*; *see also* **eighth**; **fifty** ['fɪftɪ] *num* fünfzig ▷ *n* Fünfzig f; *see also* **eight**; **fiftieth** *adj* fünfzigste(r, s); *see also* **eighth**

fig [fɪg] *n* Feige f

fight [faɪt] (**fought, fought**) *vi* kämpfen (*with, against* gegen, *for, over* um) ▷ *vt* (*person*) kämpfen mit; (*fig: disease, fire etc*) bekämpfen ▷ *n* Kampf *m*; (*brawl*) Schlägerei f; (*argument*) Streit *m*; **fight back** *vi* zurückschlagen; **fight off** *vt* abwehren; **fighter** *n* Kämpfer(in) *m(f)*

figurative ['fɪɡərətɪv] *adj* übertragen

figure ['fɪɡə*] *n* (*person*) Gestalt f; (*of person*) Figur f; (*number*) Zahl f, Ziffer f; (*amount*) Betrag *m*; **a four-figure sum** eine vierstellige Summe ▷ *vt* (*US: think*) glauben ▷ *vi* (*appear*) erscheinen; **figure out** *vt* (*work out*) herausbekommen; **I can't figure him out** ich werde aus ihm nicht schlau; **figure skating** *n* Eiskunstlauf *m*

file [faɪl] *n* (*tool*) Feile f; (*dossier*) Akte f; (*inform*) Datei f; (*folder*) Aktenordner *m*; **on ~** in den Akten ▷ *vt* (*metal, nails*) feilen; (*papers*) ablegen (*under* unter) ▷ *vi* **to ~ in/out** hintereinander hereinkommen/hinausgehen; **filing cabinet** *n* Aktenschrank *m*

fill [fɪl] *vt* füllen; (*tooth*) plombieren; (*post*) besetzen; **fill in** *vt* (*hole*) auffüllen; (*form*) ausfüllen; (*tell*) informieren (*on* über); **fill out** *vt* (*form*) ausfüllen; **fill up** *vi* (*Auto*) voll tanken

fillet ['fɪlɪt] *n* Filet *nt*

filling ['fɪlɪŋ] *n* (*Gastr*) Füllung f; (*for tooth*) Plombe f; **filling station** *n* Tankstelle f

film [fɪlm] *n* Film *m* ▷ *vt* (*scene*) filmen; **film star** *n* Filmstar *m*; **film studio** *n* Filmstudio *nt*

filter ['fɪltə*] *n* Filter *m*; (*traffic lane*) Abbiegespur f ▷ *vt* filtern

filth [fɪlθ] *n* Dreck *m*; **filthy** *adj* dreckig

fin [fɪn] *n* Flosse f

final ['faɪnl] *adj* letzte(r, s); (*stage, round*) End-; (*decision, version*) endgültig; **~ score** Schlussstand *m* ▷ *n* (*Sport*) Endspiel *nt*; (*competition*) Finale *nt*; **~s** *pl* Abschlussexamen *nt*; **finalize** *vt* die endgültige Form geben *+dat*; **finally** *adv* (*lastly*) zuletzt; (*eventually*) schließlich, endlich

finance [faɪ'næns] *n* Finanzwesen *nt*; **~s** *pl* Finanzen *pl* ▷ *vt* finanzieren; **financial** [faɪ'nænʃəl] *adj* finanziell; (*adviser, crisis, policy etc*) Finanz-

find [faɪnd] (**found, found**) *vt* finden; **he was found dead** er wurde tot aufgefunden; **I ~ myself in difficulties** ich befinde mich in Schwierigkeiten; **she ~s it difficult/easy** es fällt ihr schwer/leicht; **find out** *vt* herausfinden; **findings** *npl* (*of report, Med*) Befund *m*

fine [faɪn] *adj* (*thin*) dünn, fein; (*good*) gut; (*splendid*) herrlich; (*clothes*) elegant; (*weather*) schön; **I'm ~** es geht mir gut; **that's ~** das ist OK ▷ *adv* (*well*) gut ▷ *n* (*Jur*) Geldstrafe f ▷ *vt* (*Jur*) mit einer Geldstrafe belegen; **fine arts** *npl* **the ~** die schönen Künste *pl*; **finely** *adv* (*cut*) dünn; (*ground*) fein

finger ['fɪŋɡə*] *n* Finger *m* ▷ *vt* herumfingern an *+dat*; **fingernail** *n* Fingernagel *m*; **fingerprint** *n* Fingerabdruck *m*; **fingertip** *n* Fingerspitze f

finicky ['fɪnɪkɪ] *adj* (*person*) pingelig; (*work*) knifflig

finish ['fɪnɪʃ] *n* Ende *nt*; (*Sport*) Finish *nt*; (*line*) Ziel *nt*; (*of product*)

Verarbeitung f ▷ vt beenden; (book etc) zu Ende lesen; (food) aufessen; (drink) austrinken ▷ vi zu Ende gehen; (song, story) enden; (person) fertig sein; (stop) aufhören; **have you ~ed?** bist du fertig?; **to ~ first / second** (Sport) als erster / zweiter durchs Ziel gehen; **finishing line** n Ziellinie f

Finland ['fɪnlənd] n Finnland nt; **Finn** n Finne m, Finnin f; **Finnish** adj finnisch ▷ n (language) Finnisch nt

fir [fɜ:*] n Tanne f

fire [faɪə*] n Feuer nt; (house etc) Brand m; **to set ~ to sth** etw in Brand stecken; **to be on ~** brennen ▷ vt (bullets, rockets) abfeuern; (fam: dismiss) feuern ▷ vi (Auto: engine) zünden; **to ~ at sb** auf jdn schießen; **fire alarm** n Feuermelder m; **fire brigade** n Feuerwehr f; **fire engine** n Feuerwehrauto nt; **fire escape** n Feuerleiter f; **fire extinguisher** n Feuerlöscher m; **fire-fighter** n Feuerwehrmann m, Feuerwehrfrau f; **fireman** n Feuerwehrmann m; **fireplace** n (offener) Kamin; **fireproof** adj feuerfest; **fire station** n Feuerwache f; **firewood** n Brennholz nt; **fireworks** npl Feuerwerk nt

firm [fɜ:m] adj fest; (person) **to be ~** entschlossen auftreten ▷ n Firma f

first [fɜ:st] adj erste(r, s) ▷ adv (at first) zuerst; (firstly) erstens; (arrive, finish) als erste(r); (happen) zum ersten Mal; **~ of all** zuallererst ▷ n (person) Erste(r) mf; (Auto: gear) erster Gang; **at ~** zuerst, anfangs; **first aid** n erste Hilfe; **first-class** adj erstklassig; (compartment, ticket) erster Klasse; **~ mail** (BRIT) bevorzugt beförderte Post ▷ adv (travel) erster Klasse; **first floor** n (BRIT) erster

Stock; (US) Erdgeschoss nt; **first lady** n (US) Frau f des Präsidenten; **firstly** adv erstens; **first name** n Vorname m; **first night** n (Theat) Premiere f; **first-rate** adj erstklassig

fir tree n Tannenbaum m

fish [fɪʃ] n Fisch m; **~ and chips** (BRIT) frittierter Fisch mit Pommes frites ▷ vi fischen; (with rod) angeln; **to go ~ing** fischen / angeln gehen; **fishbone** n Gräte f; **fishcake** n Fischfrikadelle f; **fish farm** n Fischzucht f; **fish finger** n (BRIT) Fischstäbchen nt; **fishing** ['fɪʃɪŋ] n Fischen nt; (with rod) Angeln nt; (as industry) Fischerei f; **fishing boat** n Fischerboot nt; **fishing line** n Angelschnur f; **fishing rod** n Angelrute f; **fishing village** n Fischerdorf nt; **fishmonger** ['fɪʃmʌŋgə*] n Fischhändler(in) m(f); **fish stick** n (US) Fischstäbchen nt; **fish tank** n Aquarium nt

fishy ['fɪʃɪ] adj (fam: suspicious) faul

fist [fɪst] n Faust f

fit [fɪt] adj (Med) gesund; (Sport) in Form, fit; (suitable) geeignet; **to keep ~** sich in Form halten ▷ vt passen +dat; (attach) anbringen (to an +dat); (install) einbauen (in in +akk) ▷ vi passen (in space, gap) hineinpassen ▷ n (of clothes) Sitz m; (Med) Anfall m; **it's a good ~** es passt gut; **fit in** vt (accommodate) unterbringen; (find time for) einschieben ▷ vi (in space) hineinpassen; (plans, ideas) passen; **he doesn't ~ (here)** er passt nicht hierher; **to ~ with sb's plans** sich mit jds Plänen vereinbaren lassen; **fitness** n (Med) Gesundheit f; (Sport) Fitness f; **fitted carpet** n Teppichboden m; **fitted kitchen** n Einbauküche f; **fitting** adj passend ▷ n (of dress) Anprobe f; **~s** pl Ausstattung f

five [faɪv] num fünf ▷ n Fünf f; see also **eight**; **fiver** n (BRIT fam) Fünfpfundschein m

fix [fɪks] vt befestigen (to an +dat); (settle) festsetzen; (place, time) ausmachen; (repair) reparieren; **fixer** n (drug addict) Fixer(in) m(f); **fixture** ['fɪkstʃə*] n (Sport) Veranstaltung f; (match) Spiel nt; (in building) Installationsteil m; **~s (and fittings)** pl Ausstattung f

fizzy ['fɪzɪ] adj sprudelnd; **~ drink** Limo f

flabbergasted ['flæbəgɑ:stɪd] adj (fam) platt

flabby ['flæbɪ] adj (fat) wabbelig

flag [flæg] n Fahne f; **flagstone** n Steinplatte f

flake [fleɪk] n Flocke f ▷ vi **to ~ (off)** abblättern

flamboyant [flæm'bɔɪənt] adj extravagant

flame [fleɪm] n Flamme f; (person) **an old ~** eine alte Liebe

flan [flæn] n (fruit~) Obstkuchen m

flannel ['flænl] n Flanell m; (BRIT: face ~) Waschlappen m; (fam: waffle) Geschwafel nt ▷ vi herumlabern

flap [flæp] n Klappe f; (fam) **to be in a ~** rotieren ▷ vt (wings) schlagen mit ▷ vi flattern

flared [flɛəd] adj (trousers) mit Schlag; **flares** npl Schlaghose f

flash [flæʃ] n Blitz m; (news ~) Kurzmeldung f; (Foto) Blitzlicht nt; **in a ~** im Nu ▷ vt **to ~ one's (head)lights** die Lichthupe betätigen ▷ vi aufblinken; (brightly) aufblitzen; **flashback** n Rückblende f, Flashback m; **flashlight** ['flæʃlaɪt] n (Photo) Blitzlicht nt; (US: torch) Taschenlampe f; **flashy** adj grell, schrill; (pej) protzig

flat [flæt] adj flach; (surface) eben; (drink) abgestanden; (tyre) platt;

(battery) leer; (refusal) glatt ▷ n (BRIT: rooms) Wohnung f; (Auto) Reifenpanne f; **flat screen** n (in form) Flachbildschirm m; **flatten** vt platt machen, einebnen

flatter ['flætə*] vt schmeicheln +dat; **flattering** adj schmeichelhaft

flatware ['flætwɛə] n (US) Besteck nt

flavor (US), **flavour** ['fleɪvə*] n Geschmack m ▷ vt Geschmack geben +dat; (with spices) würzen; **flavouring** n Aroma nt

flaw [flɔ:] n Fehler m; **flawless** adj fehlerlos; (complexion) makellos

flea [fli:] n Floh m

fled [fled] pt, pp of **flee**

flee [fli:] (**fled, fled**) vi fliehen

fleece [fli:s] n (of sheep) Vlies m; (soft material) Fleece m; (jacket) Fleecejacke f

fleet [fli:t] n Flotte f

Flemish ['flemɪʃ] adj flämisch ▷ n (language) Flämisch nt

flesh [fleʃ] n Fleisch nt

flew [flu:] pt of **fly**

flex [fleks] n (BRIT Elec) Schnur f

flexibility [fleksɪ'bɪlɪtɪ] n Biegsamkeit f; (fig) Flexibilität f; **flexible** ['fleksɪbl] adj biegsam; (plans, person) flexibel; **flexitime** n gleitende Arbeitszeit, Gleitzeit f

flicker ['flɪkə*] vi flackern; (TV) flimmern

flies [flaɪz] pl of **fly** ▷ n

flight [flaɪt] n Flug m; (escape) Flucht f; **~ of stairs** Treppe f; **flight attendant** n Flugbegleiter(in) m(f); **flight recorder** n Flugschreiber m

flimsy ['flɪmzɪ] adj leicht gebaut, nicht stabil; (thin) hauchdünn; (excuse) fadenscheinig

fling [flɪŋ] (**flung, flung**) vt

schleudern ▷ n **to have a ~** eine (kurze) Affäre haben

flint [flɪnt] n Feuerstein m

flip [flɪp] vt schnippen; **to ~ a coin** eine Münze werfen; durchblättern vt (book) durchblättern; **flipchart** n Flipchart m

flipper ['flɪpə*] n Flosse f

flirt [flɜːt] vi flirten

float [fləʊt] n (for fishing) Schwimmer m; (in procession) Festwagen m; (money) Wechselgeld nt ▷ vi schwimmen; (in air) schweben

flock [flɒk] n (of sheep) (Rel) Herde f; (of birds) Schwarm m; (of people) Schar f

flog [flɒg] vt auspeitschen; (BRIT fam) verscheuern

flood [flʌd] n Hochwasser nt, Überschwemmung f; (fig) Flut f ▷ vt überschwemmen; **floodlight** n Flutlicht nt, **floodlit** adj (building) angestrahlt

floor [flɔː*] n Fußboden m; (storey) Stock m; **ground ~** (BRIT), **first ~** (US) Erdgeschoss nt; **first ~** (BRIT), **second ~** (US) erster Stock; **floorboard** n Diele f

flop [flɒp] n (fam: failure) Reinfall m, Flop m ▷ vi misslingen, floppen

floppy disk ['flɒpɪdɪsk] n Diskette f

Florence ['flɒrəns] n Florenz nt

florist ['flɒrɪst] n Blumenhändler(in) m(f)

flounder ['flaʊndə*] n (fish) Flunder f

flour ['flaʊə*] n Mehl nt

flourish ['flʌrɪʃ] vi gedeihen; (business) gut laufen; (boom) florieren ▷ vt (wave about) schwenken; **flourishing** adj blühend

flow [fləʊ] n Fluss m; **to go with the ~** mit dem Strom schwimmen ▷ vi fließen

flower ['flaʊə*] n Blume f ▷ vi blühen; **flower bed** n Blumenbeet nt; **flowerpot** n Blumentopf m

flown [fləʊn] pp of **fly**

flu [fluː] n (Med) Grippe f

fluent adj (Italian etc) fließend; **to be ~ in German** fließend Deutsch sprechen

fluid ['fluːɪd] n Flüssigkeit f ▷ adj flüssig

flung [flʌŋ] pt, pp of **fling**

fluorescent [flʊə'resnt] adj fluoreszierend, Leucht-

flush [flʌʃ] n (lavatory) Wasserspülung f; (blush) Röte f ▷ vi (lavatory) spülen

flute [fluːt] n Flöte f

fly [flaɪ] (flew, flown) vt, vi fliegen; **how time flies** wie die Zeit vergeht! ▷ n (insect) Fliege f; **~/flies** (pl) (on trousers) Hosenschlitz m; **fly-drive** n Urlaub m mit Flug und Mietwagen; **flyover** n (BRIT) Straßenüberführung f, Eisenbahnüberführung f; **flysheet** n Überzelt nt

FM abbr = **frequency modulation** ≈ UKW

FO abbr = **Foreign Office** ≈ AA nt

foal [fəʊl] n Fohlen nt

foam [fəʊm] n Schaum m ▷ vi schäumen

fob off [fɒb ɒf] vt **to fob sb off with sth** jdn etw andrehen

focus ['fəʊkəs] n Brennpunkt m; **in/out of ~** (photo) scharf/unscharf; (camera) scharf/unscharf eingestellt ▷ vt (camera) scharf stellen ▷ vi sich konzentrieren (on auf +akk)

foetus ['fiːtəs] n Fötus m

fog [fɒg] n Nebel m; **foggy** adj neblig, **fog light** n (Auto: at rear) Nebelschlussleuchte f

foil [fɔɪl] vt vereiteln ▷ n Folie f

fold [fəʊld] vt falten ▷ vi (fam:

business) eingehen ▷ n Falte f; **fold up** vt (map etc) zusammenfalten; (chair etc) zusammenklappen ▷ vi (fam: business) eingehen; **folder** n (portfolio) Aktenmappe f; (pamphlet) Broschüre f; (Inform) Ordner m; **folding** adj zusammenklappbar; (bicycle, chair) Klapp-

folk [fəʊk] n Leute pl; (Mus) Folk m; **my ~s** pl (fam) meine Leute ▷ adj Volks-

follow ['fɒləʊ] vt folgen +dat; (pursue) verfolgen; (understand) folgen können +dat; (career, news etc) verfolgen; **as ~s** wie folgt ▷ vi folgen; (result) sich ergeben (from aus); **follow up** vt (request, rumour) nachgehen +dat, weiter verfolgen; **follower** n Anhänger(in) m(f); **following** adj folgend; **the ~ day** am (darauf)folgenden Tag ▷ prep nach; **follow up** n (event, book etc) Fortsetzung f

fond [fɒnd] adj **to be ~ of** gern haben; **fondly** adv (with love) liebevoll; **fondness** n Vorliebe f; (for people) Zuneigung f

fondue ['fɒndu:] n Fondue nt

font [fɒnt] n Taufbecken nt; (Typo) Schriftart f

food [fu:d] n Essen nt, Lebensmittel pl; (for animals) Futter nt; (groceries) Lebensmittel pl; **food poisoning** n Lebensmittelvergiftung f; **food processor** n Küchenmaschine f; **foodstuff** n Lebensmittel nt

fool [fu:l] n Idiot m, Narr m; **to make a ~ of oneself** sich blamieren ▷ vt (deceive) hereinlegen ▷ vi **to ~ around** herumalbern; (waste time) herumtrödeln; **foolish** adj dumm; **foolproof** adj idiotensicher

foot [fʊt] (pl **feet**) n [fi:t] Fuß m; (measure) Fuß m (30,48 cm); **on ~** zu

Fuß ▷ vt (bill) bezahlen; **foot--and-mouth disease** n Maul- und Klauenseuche f; **football** n Fußball m; (US: American ~) Football m; **footballer** n Fußballspieler(in) m(f); **footbridge** n Fußgängerbrücke f; **footing** n (hold) Halt m; **footlights** npl Rampenlicht nt; **footnote** n Fußnote f; **footpath** n Fußweg m; **footprint** n Fußabdruck m; **footwear** n Schuhwerk nt

for [fɔ:*] prep für; **I'm all ~ it** ich bin ganz dafür; **D – David** D wie Dora; (purpose) **what ~?** wozu?; **~ pleasure** zum Vergnügen; **what's ~ lunch?** was gibt es zum Mittagessen?; (destination) **the train ~ London** der Zug nach London; (because of) **~ this reason** aus diesem Grund; **famous ~** bekannt für, berühmt wegen; (with time) **we talked ~ two hours** wir redeten zwei Stunden lang; (up to now) **we have been talking ~ two hours** wir reden seit zwei Stunden; (with distance) **~ miles** (and miles) meilenweit; **bends ~ 2 miles** kurvenreich auf 2 Meilen; **as ~ ...** was ... betrifft ▷ conj denn

forbade [fə'bæd] pt of **forbid**

forbid [fə'bɪd] (forbade, forbidden) vt verbieten

force [fɔ:s] n Kraft f; (compulsion) Zwang m, Gewalt; **to come into ~** in Kraft treten; **the Forces** pl die Streitkräfte ▷ vt zwingen; **forced** adj (smile) gezwungen; **~ landing** Notlandung f; **forceful** adj kraftvoll

forceps ['fɔ:seps] npl Zange f

forearm ['fɔ:rɑ:m] n Unterarm m

forecast ['fɔ:kɑ:st] vt voraussagen; (weather) vorhersagen ▷ n Vorhersage f

forefinger ['fɔ:fɪŋə*] n Zeigefinger m

foreground ['fɔːɡraʊnd] n Vordergrund m

forehand ['fɔːhænd] n (Sport) Vorhand f

forehead ['fɔːhed, 'fɒrɪd] n Stirn f

foreign ['fɒrən] adj ausländisch; **foreigner** n Ausländer(in) m(f); **foreign exchange** n Devisen pl, **foreign language** n Fremdsprache f; **foreign minister** n Außenminister(in) m(f); **foreign secretary** n Außenminister(in) m(f); **foreign policy** n Außenpolitik f

foremost ['fɔːməʊst] adj erste(r, s); (leading) führend

forerunner ['fɔːrʌnə*] n Vorläufer(in) m(f)

foresee [fɔːˈsiː] irr vt vorhersehen; **foreseeable** adj absehbar

forest ['fɒrɪst] n Wald m; **forestry** ['fɒrɪstrɪ] n Forstwirtschaft f

forever [fəˈrevə*] adv für immer

forgave [fəˈɡeɪv] pt of **forgive**

forge [fɔːdʒ] n Schmiede f ⊳ vt schmieden; (fake) fälschen; **forger** n Fälscher(in) m(f); **forgery** n Fälschung f

forget [fəˈɡet] (forgot, forgotten) vt, vi vergessen; **to ~ about sth** etw vergessen; **forgetful** adj vergesslich; **forgetfulness** n Vergesslichkeit f; **forget-me-not** n Vergissmeinnicht nt

forgive [fəˈɡɪv] (forgave, forgiven) irr vt verzeihen; **to ~ sb for sth** jdm etw verzeihen

forgot [fəˈɡɒt] pt of **forget**

forgotten [fəˈɡɒtn] pp of **forget**

fork [fɔːk] n Gabel f; (in road) Gabelung f ⊳ vi (road) sich gabeln

form [fɔːm] n (shape) Form f, Klasse f; (document) Formular nt; (person) **to be in (good) ~** in Form sein ⊳ vt bilden

formal ['fɔːməl] adj förmlich,

formell; **formality** [fɔːˈmælɪtɪ] n Formalität f

format ['fɔːmæt] n Format nt ⊳ vt (Inform) formatieren

former ['fɔːmə*] adj frühere(r, s); (opposite of latter) erstere(r, s); **formerly** adv früher

formidable ['fɔːmɪdəbl] adj gewaltig; (opponent) stark

formula ['fɔːmjʊlə] n Formel f

formulate ['fɔːmjʊleɪt] vt formulieren

forth [fɔːθ] adv **and so ~** und so weiter; **forthcoming** [fɔːθˈkʌmɪŋ] adj kommend, bevorstehend

fortify ['fɔːtɪfaɪ] vt verstärken; (for protection) befestigen

fortieth ['fɔːtɪəθ] adj vierzigste(r, s); see also **eighth**

fortnight ['fɔːtnaɪt] n vierzehn Tage pl

fortress ['fɔːtrɪs] n Festung f

fortunate ['fɔːtʃənɪt] adj glücklich; **I was ~** ich hatte Glück; **fortunately** adv zum Glück; **fortune** ['fɔːtʃən] n (money) Vermögen nt; **good ~** Glück nt; **fortune-teller** n Wahrsager(in) m(f)

forty ['fɔːtɪ] num vierzig ⊳ n Vierzig f; see also **eight**

forward ['fɔːwəd] adv vorwärts ⊳ n (Sport) Stürmer(in) m(f) ⊳ vt (send on) nachsenden; (Inform) weiterleiten, **forwards** adv vorwärts

foster child n ['fɒstətʃaɪld] n Pflegekind nt; **foster parents** npl Pflegeeltern pl

fought [fɔːt] pt, pp of **fight**

foul [faʊl] adj (weather) schlecht; (smell) übel ⊳ n (Sport) Foul nt

found [faʊnd] pt, pp of **find** ⊳ vt (establish) gründen; **foundations** [faʊnˈdeɪʃənz] npl Fundament nt

fountain ['faʊntɪn] n Springbrunnen m; **fountain pen** n Füller *m*

four [fɔː*] *num* vier ▷ *n* Vier *f*; *see also* **eight**; **fourteen** ['fɔː'tiːn] *num* vierzehn ▷ *n* Vierzehn *f*; *see also* **eight**; **fourteenth** *adj* vierzehnte(r, s); *see also* **eighth**; **fourth** [fɔːθ] *adj* vierte(r, s); *see also* **eighth**

four-wheel drive *n* Allradantrieb *m*; *(car)* Geländewagen *m*

fowl [faul] *n* Geflügel *nt*

fox [fɒks] *n* (a. fig) Fuchs *m*

fraction ['frækʃən] *n* (Math) Bruch *m*; *(part)* Bruchteil *m*; **fracture** ['fræktʃə] *n* (Med) Bruch *m* ▷ *vt* brechen

fragile ['frædʒaɪl] *adj* zerbrechlich

fragment ['frægmənt] *n* Bruchstück *nt*

fragrance ['freɪgrəns] *n* Duft *m*; **fragrant** *adj* duftend

frail [freɪl] *adj* gebrechlich

frame [freɪm] *n* Rahmen *m*; *(of spectacles)* Gestell *nt*; **~ of mind** Verfassung *f* ▷ *vt* einrahmen; **to ~ sb** *(fam: incriminate)* jdm etwas anhängen; **framework** *n* Rahmen *m*, Struktur *f*

France [frɑːns] *n* Frankreich *nt*

frank [fræŋk] *adj* offen

frankfurter ['fræŋkfɜːtə*] *n* (Frankfurter) Würstchen *nt*

frankly ['fræŋklɪ] *adv* offen gesagt; **quite ~** ganz ehrlich; **frankness** *n* Offenheit *f*

frantic ['fræntɪk] *adj* *(activity)* hektisch; *(effort)* verzweifelt; **~ with worry** außer sich vor Sorge

fraud [frɔːd] *n* *(trickery)* Betrug *m*; *(person)* Schwindler(in) *m(f)*

freak [friːk] *n* Anomalie *f*; *(animal, person)* Missgeburt *f*; *(fam: fan)* Fan *m*, Freak *m* ▷ *adj* *(conditions)* außergewöhnlich, seltsam; **freak out** *vi* *(fam)* ausflippen

freckle ['frekl] *n* Sommersprosse

f

free [friː] *adj, adv* frei; *(without payment)* gratis, kostenlos; **for ~** umsonst ▷ *vt* befreien; **freebie** ['friːbɪ] *n* Werbegeschenk *nt*; **it was a ~** es war gratis; **freedom** ['friːdəm] *n* Freiheit *f*; **freefone** ['friːfəʊn] *adj* **a ~ number** eine gebührenfreie Nummer; **free kick** *n* (Sport) Freistoß *m*

freelance ['friːlɑːns] *adj* freiberuflich tätig; *(artist)* freischaffend ▷ *n* Freiberufler(in) *m(f)*

free-range ['friː'reɪndʒ] *adj* (hen) frei laufend; **~ eggs** *pl* Freilandeier *pl*

freeway ['friːweɪ] *n* (US) (gebührenfreie) Autobahn

freeze [friːz] **(froze, frozen)** *vi* *(feel cold)* frieren; *(of lake etc)* zufrieren; *(water etc)* gefrieren ▷ *vt* einfrieren; **freezer** *n* Tiefkühltruhe *f*; *(in fridge)* Gefrierfach *nt*; **freezing** *adj* eiskalt; **I'm ~** mir ist eiskalt; **freezing point** *n* Gefrierpunkt *m*

freight [freɪt] *n* *(goods)* Fracht *f*; *(money charged)* Frachtgebühr *f*; **freight car** *n* (US) Güterwagen *m*; **freight train** *n* (US) Güterzug *m*

French [frentʃ] *adj* französisch ▷ *n* *(language)* Französisch *nt*; **the ~** *pl* die Franzosen; **French bean** *n* grüne Bohne; **French bread** *n* Baguette *f*; **French dressing** *n* Vinaigrette *f*; **French fries** (US) *npl* Pommes frites *pl*; **French kiss** *n* Zungenkuss *m*; **Frenchman** (*pl* **-men**) *n* Franzose *m*; **French toast** *n* (US) in Ei und Milch getunktes gebratenes Brot; **French window(s)** *n(pl)* Balkontür *f*, Terrassentür *f*; **Frenchwoman** (*pl* **-women**) *n* Französin *f*

frequency ['friːkwənsɪ] *n* Häufigkeit f; (Phys) Frequenz f; **frequent** ['fri:kwənt] adj häufig, **frequently** adv häufig

fresco ['freskəʊ] (pl **-es**) n Fresko nt

fresh [freʃ] adj frisch; (new) neu; **freshen** vi **to ~ (up)** (person) sich frisch machen; **freshman** (pl **-men**) n Erstsemester nt; **freshwater fish** n Süßwasserfisch m

Fri abbr = **Friday** f;

friction ['frɪkʃən] n (a. fig) Reibung f

Friday ['fraɪdeɪ] n Freitag m; see also **Tuesday**

fridge [frɪdʒ] n Kühlschrank m

fried [fraɪd] adj gebraten; **~ potatoes** Bratkartoffeln pl; **~ egg** Spiegelei nt; **~ rice** gebratener Reis

friend [frend] n Freund(in) m(f); (less close) Bekannte(r) mf; **to make ~s with sb** sich mit jdm anfreunden; **we're good ~s** wir sind gut befreundet; **friendly** adj freundlich; **to be ~ with sb** mit jdm befreundet sein ▷ n (Sport) Freundschaftsspiel nt; **friendship** ['frendʃɪp] n Freundschaft f

fright [fraɪt] n Schrecken m; **frighten** vt erschrecken; **to be ~ed** Angst haben; **frightening** adj beängstigend

frill [frɪl] n Rüsche f, ~s (fam) Schnickschnack

fringe [frɪndʒ] n (edge) Rand m; (on shawl etc) Fransen pl; (hair) Pony m

frivolous ['frɪvələs] adj leichtsinnig; (remark) frivol

frizzy ['frɪzɪ] adj kraus

frog [frɒg] n Frosch m

from [frɒm] prep von; (place, out of) aus; (with date, time) ab; **to travel ~ A to B** von A nach B fahren; **the train ~ Bath** der Zug aus Bath;

where does she come ~? woher kommt sie?; **it's ten miles ~ here** es ist zehn Meilen von hier (entfernt), von hier aus sind es zehn Meilen; **~ May 5th (onwards)** ab dem 5. Mai, vom 5. Mai an

front [frʌnt] n Vorderseite f; (of house) Fassade f; (in war, of weather) Front f; (at seaside) Promenade f; **in ~**, **at the ~** vorne; **in ~ of** vor; **up ~** (in advance) vorher, im Voraus ▷ adj vordere(r, s), Vorder-; (first) vorderste(r, s); **~ door** Haustür f; **~ page** Titelseite f; **~ seat** Vordersitz m; **~ wheel** Vorderrad m

frontier ['frʌntɪə*] n Grenze f

front-wheel drive n (Auto) Frontantrieb m

frost [frɒst] n Frost m; (white ~) Reif m; **frosting** n (US) Zuckerguss m; **frosty** adj frostig

froth [frɒθ] n Schaum m; **frothy** adj schaumig

frown [fraʊn] vi die Stirn runzeln

froze [frəʊz] pt of **freeze**

frozen ['frəʊzn] pp of **freeze** ▷ adj (food) tiefgekühlt, Tiefkühl-

fruit [fru:t] n (as collective, a. type) Obst nt; (single ~, a. fig) Frucht f; **fruit machine** n Spielautomat m; **fruit salad** n Obstsalat m

frustrated [frʌ'streɪtɪd] adj frustriert; **frustration** n Frustration f, Frust m

fry [fraɪ] vt braten; **frying pan** n Bratpfanne f

fuchsia ['fju:ʃə] n Fuchsie f

fuck [fʌk] vt (vulg) ficken, **~ off** verpiss dich!; **fucking** adj (vulg) Scheiß-

fudge [fʌdʒ] n weiche Karamellsüßigkeit

fuel [fjʊəl] n Kraftstoff m; (for heating) Brennstoff m; **fuel consumption** n Kraftstoffverbrauch m; **fuel gauge** n Benzinuhr f; **fuel**

oil n Gasöl nt; **fuel rod** n Brennstab m; **fuel tank** n Tank m; (for oil) Öltank m

fugitive ['fjuːdʒɪtɪv] n Flüchtling m

fulfil [fʊl'fɪl] vt erfüllen

full [fʊl] adj voll; (person: satisfied) satt; (member, employment) Voll(-zeit)-; (complete) vollständig; **~ of** ... voller ... gen; **full beam** n (Auto) Fernlicht nt; **full moon** n Vollmond m; **full stop** n Punkt m; **full-time** adj ~ **job** Ganztagsarbeit f; **fully** adv völlig; (recover) voll und ganz; (discuss) ausführlich

fumble ['fʌmbl] vi herumfummeln (with, at an +dat)

fumes [fjuːmz] npl Dämpfe pl; (of car) Abgase pl

fun [fʌn] n Spaß m; **for ~** zum Spaß; **it's ~** es macht Spaß; **to make ~ of** sich lustig machen über +akk

function ['fʌŋkʃən] n Funktion f; (event) Feier f; (reception) Empfang m ▷ vi funktionieren; **function key** n (Inform) Funktionstaste f

fund [fʌnd] n Fonds m; **~s** pl Geldmittel pl

fundamental [fʌndə'mentl] adj grundlegend; **fundamentally** adv im Grunde

funding ['fʌndɪŋ] n finanzielle Unterstützung

funeral ['fjuːnərəl] n Beerdigung f

funfair ['fʌnfeə*] n Jahrmarkt m

fungus ['fʌŋgəs] (pl **fungi** o **funguses**) n Pilz m

funicular [fjuː'nɪkjʊlə*] n Seilbahn f

funnel ['fʌnl] n Trichter m; (of steamer) Schornstein m

funny ['fʌnɪ] adj (amusing) komisch, lustig; (strange) seltsam

fur [fɜː*] n Pelz m; (of animal) Fell

nt

furious ['fjʊərɪəs] adj wütend (with sb auf jdn)

furnished ['fɜːnɪʃd] adj möbliert;

furniture ['fɜːnɪtʃə*] n Möbel pl; **piece of ~** Möbelstück nt

further ['fɜːðə*] comparative of **far** ▷ adj weiter(e)(r, s); **~ education** Weiterbildung f; **until ~ notice** bis auf weiteres ▷ adv weiter; **furthest** ['fɜːðɪst] superlative of **far** ▷ adj am weitesten entfernt ▷ adv am weitesten

fury ['fjʊərɪ] n Wut f

fuse [fjuːz] n (Elec) Sicherung f ▷ vi (Elec) durchbrennen; **fuse box** n Sicherungskasten m

fuss [fʌs] n Theater nt; **to make a ~** ein Theater machen; **fussy** adj (difficult) schwierig, kompliziert; (attentive to detail) pingelig

future ['fjuːtʃə*] adj künftig ▷ n Zukunft f

fuze (US) see **fuse**

fuzzy ['fʌzɪ] adj (indistinct) verschwommen; (hair) kraus

g

gable ['geɪbl] n Giebel m

gadget ['gædʒɪt] n Vorrichtung f, Gerät nt

Gaelic ['geɪlɪk] adj gälisch ▷ n (language) Gälisch nt

gain [geɪn] vt (obtain, win) gewinnen; (advantage, respect) sich verschaffen; (wealth) erwerben; (weight) zunehmen ▷ vi (improve) gewinnen (in an +dat); (clock) vorgehen ▷ n Gewinn m (in an +dat)

gala [geɪl] n Sturm m

gall bladder ['gɔːlblædə*] n Gallenblase f

gallery ['gælərɪ] n Galerie f, Museum nt

gallon ['gælən] n Gallone f; ((BRIT) 4.546 l, (US) 3.79 l)

gallop ['gæləp] n Galopp m ▷ vi galoppieren

gallstone ['gɔːlstəʊn] n Gallenstein m

Gambia ['gæmbɪə] n Gambia nt

gamble ['gæmbl] vi um Geld spielen, wetten ▷ vt **it's a ~** es ist

riskant; **gambling** n Glücksspiel nt

game [geɪm] n Spiel nt; (animals) Wild nt; **a ~ of chess** eine Partie Schach; **~s** (in school) Sport m; **game show** n (TV) Gameshow f

gammon ['gæmən] n geräucherter Schinken

gang [gæŋ] n (of criminals, youths) Bande f, Gang f, Clique f ▷ vi **to ~ up on** sich verschwören gegen

gangster ['gæŋstə*] n Gangster m

gangway ['gæŋweɪ] n (for ship) Gangway f; (BRIT: aisle) Gang m, Gangway f

gap [gæp] n (hole) Lücke f; (in time) Pause f; (in age) Unterschied m

gape [geɪp] vi (mit offenem Mund) starren

gap year n Jahr zwischen Schulabschluss und Studium, das oft zu Auslandsaufenthalten genutzt wird

garage ['gærɑːʒ] n Garage f; (for repair) (Auto)werkstatt f; (for fuel) Tankstelle f

garbage ['gɑːbɪdʒ] n (US) Müll m; (fam: nonsense) Quatsch m; **garbage can** n (US) Mülleimer m; (outside) Mülltonne f; **garbage truck** n (US) Müllwagen m

garbled ['gɑːbld] adj (story) verdreht

garden ['gɑːdn] n Garten m; (public) **~s** Park m; **garden centre** n Gartencenter nt; **gardener** n Gärtner(in) m(f); **gardening** n Gartenarbeit f

gargle ['gɑːgl] vi gurgeln

gargoyle ['gɑːgɔɪl] n Wasserspeier m

garlic ['gɑːlɪk] n Knoblauch m; **garlic bread** n Knoblauchbrot nt; **garlic butter** n Knoblauchbutter f

gas [gæs] n Gas nt; (US: petrol) Benzin nt; **to step on the ~** Gas geben; **gas cooker** n Gasherd m; **gas cylinder** n Gasflasche f; **gas**

fire n Gasofen m

gasket ['gæskɪt] n Dichtung f

gas lighter n (for cigarettes) Gasfeuerzeug nt; **gas mask** n Gasmaske f; **gas meter** n Gaszähler m

gasoline ['gæsəli:n] n (US) Benzin nt

gasp [gɑ:sp] vi keuchen; (in surprise) nach Luft schnappen

gas pedal n (US) Gaspedal nt; **gas pump** n (US) Zapfsäule f; **gas station** n (US) Tankstelle f; **gas tank** n (US) Benzintank m

gastric ['gæstrɪk] adj Magen-; **~ flu** Magen-Darm-Grippe f; **~ ulcer** Magengeschwür nt

gasworks ['gæswɜ:ks] n Gaswerk nt

gate [geɪt] n Tor nt, (barrier) Schranke f; (Aviat) Gate nt, Flugsteig m

gateau ['gætəʊ] n Torte f

gateway n Tor nt

gather ['gæðə*] vt (collect) sammeln; **to ~ speed** beschleunigen ▷ vi (assemble) sich versammeln; (understand) schließen (from aus); **gathering** n Versammlung f

gauge [geɪdʒ] n Meßgerät nt

gauze [gɔ:z] n Gaze f; (for bandages) Mull m

gave [geɪv] pt of **give**

gay [geɪ] adj (homosexual) schwul

gaze [geɪz] n Blick m ▷ vi starren

GCSE abbr = **general certificate of secondary education** (school) Abschlussprüfung f der Sekundarstufe, ≈ mittlere Reife

gear [gɪə*] n (Auto) Gang m; (equipment) Ausrüstung f; (clothes) Klamotten pl; **to change ~** schalten; **gearbox** n Getriebe nt; **gear change, gear shift** (US) n Gangschaltung f; **gear lever, gear stick** (US) n Schalthebel m

geese [gi:s] pl of **goose**

gel [dʒel] n Gel nt ▷ vi gelieren; **they really ~led** sie verstanden sich auf Anhieb

gelatine ['dʒeləti:n] n Gelatine f

gem [dʒem] n Edelstein m; (fig) Juwel nt

Gemini ['dʒemɪni:] nsing (Astr) Zwillinge pl

gender ['dʒendə*] n Geschlecht nt

gene [dʒi:n] n Gen nt

general ['dʒenərəl] adj allgemein; **~ knowledge** Allgemeinbildung f; **~ election** Parlamentswahlen pl; **generalize** ['dʒenrəlaɪz] vi verallgemeinern; **generally** ['dʒenrəlɪ] adv im Allgemeinen

generation [dʒenə'reɪʃən] n Generation f; **generation gap** n Generationsunterschied m

generator ['dʒenəreɪtə*] n Generator m

generosity [dʒenə'rɒsɪtɪ] n Großzügigkeit f; **generous** ['dʒenərəs] adj großzügig; (portion) reichlich

genetic [dʒɪ'netɪk] adj genetisch; **genetically modified** adj gentechnisch verändert, genmanipuliert; see also **GM**

Geneva [dʒɪ'ni:və] n Genf nt; **Lake ~** der Genfer See

genitals ['dʒenɪtlz] npl Geschlechtsteile pl

genitive ['dʒenɪtɪv] n Genitiv m

genius ['dʒi:nɪəs] n Genie nt

gentle ['dʒentl] adj sanft; (touch) zart; **gentleman** (pl **-men**) n Herr m; (polite man) Gentleman m

gents [dʒents] n '~' (lavatory) "Herren"; **the ~ pl** die Herrentoilette

genuine ['dʒenjʊɪn] adj echt

geographical [dʒɪə'græfɪkəl] adj geografisch; **geography** [dʒɪ'ɒgrəfɪ] n Geografie f; (at school) Erdkunde f

geological [dʒɪəʊ'lɒdʒɪkəl] adj

geologisch; **geology** [dʒɪˈɒlədʒɪ] n Geologie f

geometry [dʒɪˈɒmɪtrɪ] n Geometrie f

geranium [dʒɪˈreɪnɪəm] n Geranie f

germ [dʒɜːm] n Keim m; (Med) Bazillus m

German [ˈdʒɜːmən] adj deutsch; **she's ~** sie ist Deutsche; **~ Deutscher Schäferhund** m ⊳ n (person) Deutsche(r) mf; (language) Deutsch nt; **in ~** auf Deutsch; **German measles** n sing Röteln pl; **Germany** [ˈdʒɜːmənɪ] n Deutschland nt

gesture [ˈdʒestʃə*] n Geste f

get [ɡet] (got, got, o US gotten) vt (receive) bekommen, kriegen; **to ~ a cold/flu** sich erkälten/eine Grippe bekommen; (buy) kaufen; (obtain) sich besorgen; (to keep) sich anschaffen; **to ~ sb sth** jdm etw besorgen; (fetch) jdm etw holen; **where did you ~ that (from)?** woher hast du das?; **to ~ a taxi** ein Taxi nehmen; (persuade) **to ~ sb to do sth** jdn dazu bringen, etw zu tun; (manage) **to ~ sth to work** etw zum Laufen bringen; **I can't ~ the door open** ich kriege die Tür nicht auf; **to ~ sth done** (oneself) etw machen; (by sb else) etw machen lassen; (bring) **this isn't ~ting us anywhere** so kommen wir nicht weiter; (understand) **don't ~ me wrong** versteh mich nicht falsch! ⊳ vi (become) werden; **to ~ old** alt werden; **it's ~ting dark** es wird dunkel; **to ~ dressed/washed** sich anziehen/waschen; **I'll ~ ready** ich mache mich fertig; **to ~ lost** sich verirren; (start) **to ~ going** losfahren; (arrive) **we got to Dover at 5** wir kamen um 5 in Dover an; **to ~ somewhere/nowhere** (fig: in career) es zu etwas/nichts bringen; (with task,

discussion) weiterkommen/nicht weiterkommen; **get across** vt **to ~ sth** über etw akk kommen; **to get sth across** (communicate) etw klarmachen; (get along) vi (manage) zurechtkommen; (people) gut auskommen (with mit); **get at** vt (reach) herankommen an +akk, **what are you getting at?** worauf wollen Sie hinaus?, was meinst du damit?; **get away** vi (leave) weggehen, (escape) entkommen (from dat); **to he got away with it** er kam ungeschoren davon; **get back** vi zurückkommen; (Tel) **to ~ to s.o.** jdn zurückrufen ⊳ vt **to get sth back** etw zurückbekommen; **get by** vi (manage) auskommen (on mit); **get down** vi heruntersteigen; **to ~ to business** zur Sache kommen ⊳ vt **to get sth down** (write) etw aufschreiben; **it gets me down** (fam) es macht mich fertig; **get in** vi (arrive home) heimkommen; (into car etc) einsteigen; **get into** vt (car, bus etc) einsteigen in +akk; (rage, panic etc) geraten in +akk; **to ~ trouble** in Schwierigkeiten kommen; **get off** vi, vt (train etc) aussteigen (aus); (horse) absteigen (von); (fam: be enthusiastic) **to ~ on sth** auf etw abfahren; **get on** vi (progress) vorankommen; (be friends) auskommen (with mit); **to be getting ~** alt werden; **how are you getting ~ with the book?** wie geht's mit dem Buch? ⊳ vi, vt (train etc) einsteigen (in +akk); (horse) aufsteigen (auf +akk); **get out** vi herauskommen; (of vehicle) aussteigen (of aus); **~!** raus! ⊳ vt (take out) herausholen; (stain, nail) herausbekommen; **get over** vt (recover from) hinwegkommen über +akk; (illness) sich erholen von; (loss) sich abfinden mit; **get through** vi durchkommen;

up vi aufstehen; **getaway** n
Flucht f; **get-together** n Treffen nt

Ghana ['gɑːnə] n Ghana nt

gherkin ['gɜːkɪn] n Gewürzgurke f

ghetto ['getəʊ] (pl **-es**) n Ghetto nt

ghost [gəʊst] n Gespenst nt; (of
sb) Geist m

giant ['dʒaɪənt] n Riese m ▷ adj
riesig

giblets ['dʒɪblɪts] npl Geflügelin-
nereien pl

Gibraltar [dʒɪˈbrɔːltə*] n Gibraltar nt

giddy ['gɪdɪ] adj schwindlig

gift [gɪft] n Geschenk nt; (talent)
Begabung f; **gifted** adj begabt;
giftwrap vt als Geschenk verpacken

gigantic [dʒaɪˈgæntɪk] adj riesig

giggle ['gɪgl] vi kichern ▷ n Ge-
kicher nt

gill [gɪl] n (of fish) Kieme f

gimmick ['gɪmɪk] n (for sales,
publicity) Gag m

gin [dʒɪn] n Gin m

ginger ['dʒɪndʒə*] n Ingwer m ▷
adj (colour) kupferrot; (cat) rötlich-
gelb; **ginger ale** n Gingerale nt;
ginger beer n Ingwerlimonade f;
gingerbread n Lebkuchen m (mit
Ingwergeschmack); **ginger(-haired)**
adj rotblond; **gingerly** adv (move)
vorsichtig

gipsy ['dʒɪpsɪ] n Zigeuner(in) m(f)

giraffe [dʒɪˈrɑːf] n Giraffe f

girl [gɜːl] n Mädchen nt; **girlfriend** n (feste) Freundin f; **girl
guide** n (BRIT), **girl scout** n (US)
Pfadfinderin f

gist [dʒɪst] n **to get the ~ (of it)**
das Wesentliche verstehen

give [gɪv] (gave, given) vt geben;
(as present) schenken (to sb jdm);
(state: name etc) angeben; (speech)
halten; (blood) spenden; **to ~ sb sth**
jdm etw geben / schenken ▷ vi

(yield) nachgeben; **give away** vt
(give free) verschenken; (secret) verraten; **give back** vt zurückgeben;
give in vi aufgeben; **give up** vt, vi
aufgeben; **give way** vi (collapse,
yield) nachgeben; (traffic) die Vorfahrt beachten

given ['gɪvn] pp of **give** ▷ adj (fixed)
festgesetzt; (certain) bestimmt; **~
name** (US) Vorname m ▷ conj **~ that
...** angesichts der Tatsache, dass ...

glacier ['glæsɪə*] n Gletscher m

glad [glæd] adj froh (about über); **I
was ~ (to hear) that ...** es hat mich
gefreut, dass ...; **gladly** ['glædlɪ]
adv gerne

glance [glɑːns] n Blick m ▷ vi
einen Blick werfen (at auf +akk)

gland [glænd] n Drüse f; **glan-
dular fever** n Drüsenfieber nt

glare [glɛə*] n grelles Licht; (stare)
stechender Blick ▷ vi (angrily) **to ~
at sb** jdn böse anstarren; **glaring**
adj (mistake) krass

glass [glɑːs] n Glas nt; **~es** pl Brille f

glen [glen] n (SCOT) (enges)
Bergtal nt

glide [glaɪd] vi gleiten; (hover)
schweben; **glider** n Segelflugzeug
nt; **gliding** n Segelfliegen nt

glimmer ['glɪmə*] n (of hope)
Schimmer m

glimpse [glɪmps] n flüchtiger Blick

glitter ['glɪtə*] vi glitzern; (eyes)
funkeln

glitzy ['glɪtsɪ] adj (fam) glanzvoll,
Schickimicki-

global ['gləʊbəl] adj global, Welt-;
~ warming die Erwärmung der
Erdatmosphäre; **globe** [gləʊb] n
(sphere) Kugel f; (world) Erdball m;
(map) Globus m

gloomily ['gluːmɪlɪ], **gloomy**
adv, adj düster

glorious ['glɔːrɪəs] adj (victory,
past) ruhmreich; (weather, day) herr-

lich; **glory** ['glɔːrɪ] n Herrlichkeit f

gloss [glɒs] n (shine) Glanz m

glossary ['glɒsərɪ] n Glossar nt

glossy ['glɒsɪ] adj (surface) glänzend ▷ n (magazine) Hochglanzmagazin nt

glove [glʌv] n Handschuh m; **glove compartment** n Handschuhfach nt

glow [gləʊ] vi glühen

glucose ['gluːkəʊs] n Traubenzucker m

glue [gluː] n Klebstoff m ▷ vt kleben

glutton ['glʌtn] n Vielfraß m; **a ~ for punishment** (fam) Masochist m

GM abbr = **genetically modified** Gen-; **~ foods** gentechnisch veränderte Lebensmittel

GMT abbr = **Greenwich Mean Time** WEZ f

go [gəʊ] (went, gone) vi gehen; (in vehicle, travel) fahren; (plane) fliegen; (road) führen (to nach); (depart: train, bus) (ab)fahren; (person) (fort)gehen; (disappear) verschwinden; (time) vergehen; (function) gehen, funktionieren, (machine, engine) laufen; (fit, suit) passen (with zu); (fail) nachlassen; **I have to ~ to the doctor/to London** ich muss zum Arzt/nach London; **to ~ shopping** einkaufen gehen; **to ~ for a walk/swim** spazieren/schwimmen gehen; **has he gone yet?** ist er schon weg?; **the wine ~es in the cupboard** der Wein kommt in den Schrank; **to get sth ~ing** etw in Gang setzen; **to keep ~ing** weitermachen; (machine etc) weiterlaufen; **how's the job ~ing?** was macht der Job?; **his memory/eyesight is going** sein Gedächtnis lässt nach/seine Augen werden schwach; **~ deaf/mad/grey** taub/verrückt/grau werden ▷ vb aux **to be ~ing to do sth** etw tun werden; **I was ~ing to do it** ich

wollte es tun ▷ n (pl **-es**) (attempt) Versuch m; **can I have another ~?** darf ich noch mal (probieren)?; **it's my ~** ich bin dran; **in one ~** auf einen Schlag; (drink) in einem Zug; **go after** vt nachlaufen +dat, (in vehicle) nachfahren +dat; **go ahead** vi (in front) vorausgehen; (start) anfangen; **go away** vi weggehen; (on holiday, business) verreisen; **go back** vi (return) zurückgehen; **we ~ a long way** (fam) wir kennen uns schon ewig; **go by** vi vorbeigehen; (vehicle) vorbeifahren; (years, time) vergehen ▷ vt (judge by) gehen nach; **go down** vi (sun, ship) untergehen; (flood, temperature) zurückgehen; (price) sinken; **to ~ well/badly** gut/schlecht ankommen; **go in** vi hineingehen; **go into** vt (enter) hineingehen in +akk; (crash) fahren gegen, hineinfahren in +akk; **to ~ teaching/politics/the army** Lehrer werden/in die Politik gehen/zum Militär gehen; **go off** vi (depart) weggehen; (in vehicle) wegfahren; (lights) ausgehen; (milk etc) sauer werden; (gun, bomb, alarm) losgehen ▷ vt (dislike) nicht mehr mögen; **go on** vi (continue) weitergehen; (lights) angehen; **to ~ with o doing sth** etw weitermachen; **go out** vi (leave house) hinausgehen; (fire, light, person socially) ausgehen; **to ~ for a meal** essen gehen; **go up** vi (temperature, price) steigen; (lift) hochfahren; **go without** vt verzichten auf +akk; (food, sleep) auskommen ohne

go-ahead ['gəʊəhed] adj (progressive) fortschrittlich ▷ n grünes Licht

goal [gəʊl] n (aim) Ziel nt; (Sport) Tor nt; **goalie, goalkeeper** n Torwart m, Torfrau f; **goalpost** n Torpfosten m

goat [gəʊt] n Ziege f

gob [gɒb] n (BRIT fam) Maul nt; **shut your ~** halt's Maul! ▷ vi spucken; **gobsmacked** (*fam:* *surprised*) platt

god [gɒd] *n* Gott *m;* **thank God** Gott sei Dank; **godchild** (*pl* -**children**) *n* Patenkind *nt;* **goddaughter** *n* Patentochter *f;* **goddess** ['gɒdes] *n* Göttin *f;* **godfather** *n* Pate *m;* **godmother** *n* Patin *f;* **godson** *n* Patensohn *m*

goggles *npl* Schutzbrille *f;* (*for skiing*) Skibrille *f;* (*for diving*) Taucherbrille *f*

going ['gəʊɪŋ] *adj* (*rate*) üblich; **goings-on** *npl* Vorgänge *m*

go-kart ['gəʊkɑːt] *n* Gokart *m*

gold [gəʊld] *n* Gold *nt* ▷ *adj* golden; **goldfish** *n* Goldfisch *m;* **gold-plated** *adj* vergoldet

golf [gɒlf] *n* Golf *nt;* **golf ball** *n* Golfball *m;* **golf club** *n* Golfschläger *m;* (*association*) Golfklub *m;* **golf course** *n* Golfplatz *m;* **golfer** *n* Golfspieler(in) *m(f)*

gone [gɒn] *pp of* **go**; **he's** ~ er ist weg ▷ *prep* **just** ~ **three** gerade drei Uhr vorbei

good [gʊd] *adj* (*benefit*) Wohl *nt;* (*morally good things*) Gute(s) *nt;* **for the** ~ **of** zum Wohle +*gen;* **it's for your own** ~ es ist zu deinem Besten *o* Vorteil; **it's no** ~ (*doing sth*) es hat keinen Sinn *o* Zweck; (*thing*) es taugt nichts; **for** ~ für immer ▷ *adj* (*better, best*) gut; (*suitable*) passend; (*thorough*) gründlich; (*well-behaved*) brav; (*kind*) nett, lieb; **to be** ~ **at maths** gut in Sport / Mathe sein; **to be no** ~ **at sport / maths** schlecht in Sport / Mathe sein; **it's** ~ **for you** es tut dir gut; **this is** ~ **for colds** das ist gut gegen Erkältungen; **too** ~ **to be true** zu schön, um wahr zu sein; **this is just not** ~ **enough** so geht das nicht; **a** ~ **three hours** gute drei Stunden; ~ **morning / evening** guten Morgen / Abend; ~ **night** gute

Nacht; **to have a** ~ **time** sich gut amüsieren

goodbye [gʊd'baɪ] *interj* auf Wiedersehen

Good Friday *n* Karfreitag *m*

good-looking *adj* gut aussehend

goods [gʊdz] *npl* Waren *pl,* Güter *pl;* **goods train** *n* (BRIT) Güterzug *m*

goodwill [gʊd'wɪl] *n* Wohlwollen *nt*

goose [guːs] (*pl* **geese**) *n* Gans *f* ▷ *vt* (*fam*) **to** ~ **s.o.** jdn in den Arsch kneifen; **gooseberry** ['gʊzbərɪ] *n* Stachelbeere *f;* **goose bumps** *n,* **goose pimples** *npl* Gänsehaut *f*

gorge [gɔːdʒ] *n* Schlucht *f*

gorgeous ['gɔːdʒəs] *adj* wunderschön; **he's** ~ er sieht toll aus

gorilla [gə'rɪlə] *n* Gorilla *m*

gossip ['gɒsɪp] *n* (*talk*) Klatsch *m;* (*person*) Klatschtante *f* ▷ *vi* klatschen, tratschen

got [gɒt] *pt, pp of* **get**

gotten ['gɒtn] (US) *pp of* **get**

govern ['gʌvən] *vt* regieren; (*province etc*) verwalten; **government** *n* Regierung *f;* **governor** *n* Gouverneur(in) *m(f);* **govt** *abbr* = **government** Regierung *f*

gown [gaʊn] *n* Abendkleid *nt;* (*academic*) Robe *f*

GP *abbr* = **General Practitioner** praktischer Arzt

GPS *n abbr* = **global positioning system** GPS *nt*

grab [græb] *vt* packen; (*person*) schnappen

grace [greɪs] *n* Anmut *f;* (*prayer*) Tischgebet *nt;* **5 days'** ~ 5 Tage Aufschub; **graceful** *adj* anmutig

grade [greɪd] *n* Niveau *nt;* (*of goods*) Güteklasse *f;* (*mark*) Note *f;* (US: *year*) Klasse *f;* **to make the** ~ es schaffen; **grade crossing** *n* (US) Bahnübergang *m;* **grade school** *n* (US) Grundschule *f*

gradient ['greidiənt] n (upward) Steigung f; (downward) Gefälle nt

gradual, gradually ['grædjuəl, -lı] adj, adv allmählich

graduate ['grædjuit] n Uniabsolvent(in) m(f), Akademiker(in) m(f), Hochschulabsolvent(in) m(f) ▷ ['grædjueit] vi einen akademischen Grad erwerben

grain [grein] n (cereals) Getreide nt; (of corn, sand) Korn nt; (in wood) Maserung f

gram [græm] n Gramm m

grammar ['græmə*] n Grammatik f; **grammar school** (BRIT) ≈ Gymnasium nt

gran [græn] n (fam) Oma f

grand [grænd] adj (pej) hochnäsig; (posh) vornehm ▷ n (fam) 1000 Pfund bzw. 1000 Dollar

grand(d)ad n (fam) Opa m; **granddaughter** n Enkelin f; **grandfather** n Großvater m; **grandma** n (fam) Oma f; **grandmother** n Großmutter f; **grandpa** n (fam) Opa m; **grandparents** npl Großeltern pl; **grandson** n Enkel m

grandstand n (Sport) Tribüne f

granny ['grænı] n (fam) Oma f

grant [grɑːnt] vt gewähren (sb sth jdm etw); **to take sb/sth for ~ed** jdn/etw als selbstverständlich hinnehmen ▷ n Subvention f, finanzielle Unterstützung f; (for university) Stipendium nt

grape [greip] n Weintraube f; **grapefruit** n Grapefruit f; **grape juice** n Traubensaft m

graph [grɑːf] n Diagramm nt; **graphic** ['græfik] adj grafisch; (description) anschaulich

grasp [grɑːsp] vt ergreifen; (understand) begreifen

grass [grɑːs] n Gras nt; (lawn) Rasen m; **grasshopper** n Heuschrecke f

grate [greit] n Feuerrost m ▷ vi kratzen ▷ vt (cheese) reiben

grateful, gratefully ['greitful, -fəlı] adj, adv dankbar

grater ['greitə*] n Reibe f

gratifying ['grætifaiıŋ] adj erfreulich

gratitude ['grætitjuːd] n Dankbarkeit f

grave [greiv] n Grab nt ▷ adj ernst; (mistake) schwer

gravel ['grævəl] n Kies m

graveyard ['greivjɑːd] n Friedhof m

gravity ['grævitı] n Schwerkraft f; (seriousness) Ernst m

gravy ['greivı] n Bratensoße f

gray [grei] adj (US) grau

graze [greiz] vi (of animals) grasen ▷ vt (touch) streifen; (Med) abschürfen ▷ n (Med) Abschürfung f

grease [griːs] n (fat) Fett nt; (lubricant) Schmiere f ▷ vt schmieren; (Tech) schmieren; **greasy** ['griːzı] adj fettig; (hands, tools) schmierig; (fam: person) schleimig

great [greit] adj groß; (fam: good) großartig, super; **a - deal of** viel; **Great Britain** [greit'britn] n Großbritannien nt, **great-grandfather** n Urgroßvater m; **great-grandmother** n Urgroßmutter f; **greatly** adv sehr; **~ disappointed** zutiefst enttäuscht

Greece [griːs] n Griechenland nt

greed [griːd] n Gier f (for nach); (for food) Gefräßigkeit f; **greedy** adj gierig; (for food) gefräßig

Greek [griːk] adj griechisch ▷ n (person) Grieche m, Griechin f; (language) Griechisch nt

green [griːn] adj grün ▷ n (colour, for golf) Grün nt; (village~) Dorfwiese f; **~s** (vegetables) grünes Gemüse; **the Greens, the Green Party** (Pol) die Grünen; **green card** n (US: work *permit*) Arbeitserlaubnis *f*; (BRIT: for car) grüne Versicherungskarte;

greengage *n* Reneklode *f*; **greengrocer** *n* Obst- und Gemüsehändler(in) *m(f)*; **greenhouse** *n* Gewächshaus *nt*; ~ **effect** Treibhauseffekt *m*; **Greenland** *n* Grönland *nt*; **green pepper** *n* grüner Paprika; **green salad** *n* grüner Salat

Greenwich Mean Time ['grenɪdʒ'miːntaɪm] *n* westeuropäische Zeit

greet [griːt] *vt* grüßen; **greeting** *n* Gruß *m*

grew [gruː] *pt of* **grow**

grey [greɪ] *adj* grau; **grey-haired** *adj* grauhaarig; **greyhound** *n* Windhund *m*

grid [grɪd] *n* Gitter *nt*; **gridlock** *n* Verkehrsinfarkt *m*; **gridlocked** *adj* (roads) völlig verstopft; (talks) festgefahren

grief [griːf] *n* Kummer *m*; (over loss) Trauer *f*

grievance ['griːvəns] *n* Beschwerde *f*

grieve [griːv] *vi* trauern (for an)

grill [grɪl] *n* (on cooker) Grill *m* ▷ *vt* grillen

grim [grɪm] *adj* (face, humour) grimmig; (situation, prospects) trostlos

grin [grɪn] *n* Grinsen *nt* ▷ *vi* grinsen

grind [graɪnd] *vt* mahlen; (sharpen) schleifen; (US: meat) durchdrehen, hacken

grip [grɪp] *n* Griff *m*; **get a** ~ nimm dich zusammen!; **to get to** ~**s with sth** etw in den Griff bekommen ▷ *vt* packen; **gripping** *adj* (exciting) spannend

gristle ['grɪsl] *n* Knorpel *m*

groan [grəʊn] *n* stöhnen (with vor +dat)

grocer ['grəʊsə*] *n* Lebensmittelhändler(in) *m(f)*; **groceries** *npl* Lebensmittel *pl*

groin [grɔɪn] *n* (Anat) Leiste *f*; **groin strain** *n* (Med) Leistenbruch *m*

groom [gruːm] *n* Bräutigam *m* ▷ *vt* **well** ~**ed** gepflegt

groovy ['gruːvɪ] *adj* (fam) cool

grope [grəʊp] *vi* tasten ▷ *vt* (sexually harrass) befummeln

gross [grəʊs] *adj* (coarse) derb; (extreme: negligence, error) grob; (disgusting) ekelhaft; (Comm) brutto; ~ **national product** Bruttosozialprodukt *nt*; ~ **salary** Bruttogehalt *nt*

grotty ['grɒtɪ] *adj* (fam) mies, vergammelt

ground [graʊnd] *pt, pp of* **grind** ▷ *n* Boden *m*, Erde *f*; (Sport) Platz *m*; ~**s** *pl* (around house) (Garten)anlagen *pl*; (reasons) Gründe *pl*; (of coffee) Satz *m*; **on (the)** ~**s of** aufgrund von; **ground floor** *n* (BRIT) Erdgeschoss *nt*; **ground meat** *n* (US) Hackfleisch *nt*

group [gruːp] *n* Gruppe *f* ▷ *vt* gruppieren

grouse [graʊs] *n* (pl ~) (bird) Schottisches Moorhuhn; (complaint) Nörgelei *f*

grow [grəʊ] (**grew, grown**) *vi* wachsen; (increase) zunehmen (in an); (become) werden; **to** ~ **old** alt werden; **to** ~ **into** ... sich entwickeln zu ... ▷ *vt* (crop, plant) ziehen; (commercially) anbauen; **I'm** ~**ing a beard** ich lasse mir einen Bart wachsen; **grow up** *vi* aufwachsen; (mature) erwachsen werden; **growing** *adj* wachsend; **a** ~ **number of people** immer mehr Leute

growl [graʊl] *vi* knurren

grown [grəʊn] *pp of* **grow**

grown-up [grəʊn'ʌp] *adj* erwachsen ▷ *n* Erwachsene(r) *mf*

growth [grəʊθ] *n* Wachstum *nt*; (increase) Zunahme *f*; (Med) Wucherung *f*

grubby ['grʌbɪ] *adj* schmuddelig

h

habit ['hæbɪt] n Gewohnheit f;
habitual [hə'bɪtjʊəl] adj gewohnt; (drinker, liar) gewohnheits-
mäßig

hack [hæk] vt hacken; **hacker** n
(inform) Hacker(in) m(f)

had [hæd] pt, pp of **have**

haddock ['hædək] n Schellfisch m

hadn't ['hædnt] contr of **had not**

haemophiliac, hemophiliac (US)
[hi:məʊ'fɪlɪæk] n Bluter(in) m(f);
haemorrhage, hemorrhage (US)
['hemərɪdʒ] n Blutung f ▷ vi bluten; **haemorrhoids, hemorrhoids**
(US) ['hemərɔɪdz] npl Hämorrhoiden pl

haggis ['hægɪs] n (SCOT) mit
gehackten Schafsinnereien und Hafer-
schrot gefüllter Schafsmagen

Hague [heɪg] n **the ~** Den Haag

hail [heɪl] n Hagel m ▷ vi hageln
▷ vt **to ~ sb as sth** jdn als etw
feiern; **hailstone** n Hagelkorn nt;
hailstorm n Hagelschauer m

hair [heə*] n Haar nt, Haare pl; **to**
do one's ~ sich frisieren; **to get**
one's ~ cut sich dat die Haare
schneiden lassen; **hairbrush** n
Haarbürste f; **hair conditioner** n
Haarspülung f; **haircut** n Haarschnitt m; **to have a ~** sich dat die
Haare schneiden lassen; **hairdo** (pl
-s) n Frisur f; **hairdresser** n Friseur
m, Friseuse f; **hairdryer** n Haartrockner m; (hand-held) Föhn® m; (over
head) Trockenhaube f; **hair gel** n
Haargel nt; **hairpin** n Haarnadel f;
hair remover n Enthaarungsmit-
tel nt; **hair spray** n Haarspray nt;
hair style n Frisur f; **hairy** adj
haarig, behaart; (fam: dangerous)
brenzlig

hake [heɪk] n Seehecht m

half [hɑ:f] (pl **halves**) n Hälfte f;
(Sport: of game) Halbzeit f; **to cut in**
~ halbieren ▷ adj halb; **three and a**
~ pounds dreieinhalb Pfund; **~ an**
hour, a ~ hour eine halbe Stunde;
one and a ~ eineinhalb, anderthalb
▷ adv halb, zur Hälfte: **~ past**
three, ~ three halb vier; **at ~ past**
um halb; **~ asleep** fast eingeschlafen; **she's ~ German** sie ist zur
Hälfte Deutsche; **~ as big (as)** halb
so groß (wie); **half board** n Halbpension f; **half fare** n halber
Fahrpreis; **half-hearted** adj
lieblos; **half hour** n halbe Stunde;
half moon n Halbmond m; **half**
pint n ≈ Viertelliter m o nt; **half**
price n (**at**) **~** zum halben Preis;
half-term n (at school) Ferien pl in
der Mitte des Trimesters; **half-time**
n Halbzeit f; **halfway** adv auf
halbem Wege; **halfwit** n (fam)
Trottel m

halibut ['hælɪbət] n Heilbutt m

hall [hɔ:l] n (building) Halle f; (for
audience) Saal m; (entrance ~) Flur m;
(large) Diele f; **~ of residence** (BRIT)
Studentenwohnheim nt

grudge [grʌdʒ] n Abneigung f
(against gegen) ▷ vt **to ~ sb sth** jdm
etw nicht gönnen

gruelling ['groəlɪŋ] adj aufrei-
bend; (pace) mörderisch

gruesome ['gruːsəm] adj grausig

grumble ['grʌmbl] vi murren
(about über +akk)

grumpy ['grʌmpɪ] adj (fam) mürrisch, grantig

grunt [grʌnt] vi grunzen

G-string ['dʒiːstrɪŋ] n ≈ Tanga m

guarantee [gærən'tiː] n Garantie
f (of für); **it's still under ~** es ist noch
Garantie darauf ▷ vt garantieren

guard [gɑːd] n (sentry) Wache f; (in
prison) Wärter(in) m(f); (BRIT Rail)
Schaffner(in) m(f) ▷ vt bewachen; **a
closely ~ed secret** ein streng ge-
hütetes Geheimnis

guardian ['gɑːdɪən] n Vormund
m; **~ angel** Schutzengel m

guess [ges] n Vermutung f; (estimate) Schätzung f; **have a ~ rate
mal!** ▷ vt, vi raten; (estimate)
schätzen; **I ~ you're right** du hast
wohl recht; **I ~ so** ich glaube schon;
guesstimate n (fam)
grobe Schätzung

guest [gest] n Gast m; **be my ~**
nur zu!; **guest-house** n Pension f;
guest room n Gästezimmer nt

guidance ['gaɪdəns] n (direction)
Leitung f; (advice) Rat m; (counselling)
Beratung f; **for your ~** zu Ihrer Ori-
entierung; **guide** [gaɪd] n (person)
Führer(in) m(f); (tour) Reiseleiter(in)
m(f); (book) Führer m; (girl ~) Pfad-
finderin f ▷ vt führen; **guidebook**
n Reiseführer m; **guide dog** n
Blindenhund m; **guided tour** n
Führung f (of durch); **guidelines** npl
Richtlinien pl

guilt [gɪlt] n Schuld f; **guilty** adj
schuldig (of gen); (look) schuldbe-
wusst; **to have a ~ conscience** ein

schlechtes Gewissen haben

guinea pig ['gɪnɪ pɪg] n Meerschweinchen nt; (person) Versuchs-
kaninchen nt

guitar [gɪ'tɑː] n Gitarre f

gulf [gʌlf] n Golf m; (gap) Kluft f;
Gulf States npl Golfstaaten pl

gull [gʌl] n Möwe f

gullible ['gʌlɪbl] adj leichtgläubig

gulp [gʌlp] n (kräftiger) Schluck f ▷
vi schlucken

gum [gʌm] n (around teeth, usu pl)
Zahnfleisch nt; (chewing ~) Kaugummi m

gun [gʌn] n Schusswaffe f; (rifle)
Gewehr nt; (pistol) Pistole f; **gunfire**
n Schüsse pl, Geschützfeuer nt;
gunpowder n Schießpulver nt;
gunshot n Schuss m

gush [gʌʃ] vi (heraus)strömen
(from aus)

gut [gʌt] n Darm m; **~s** pl (intestines)
Eingeweide; (courage) Mumm m

gutter ['gʌtə*] n (for roof) Dachrinne f; (in street) Rinnstein m, Gosse
f; **gutter press** n Skandalpresse f

guy [gaɪ] n (man) Typ m, Kerl m; **~s**
pl (US) Leute pl

gym [dʒɪm] n Turnhalle f; (for
working out) Fitnesscenter nt; **gymnasium** [dʒɪm'neɪzɪəm] n Turnhalle f; **gymnastics** [dʒɪm'næs-
tɪks] nsing Turnen nt; **gym-toned**
adj durchtrainiert

gynaecologist [gaɪnɪ'kɒlədʒɪst]
n Frauenarzt m, Frauenärztin f,
Gynäkologe m, Gynäkologin f; **gyn-
aecology** n Gynäkologie f, Frau-
enheilkunde f

gypsy ['dʒɪpsɪ] n Zigeuner(in) m(f)

hallmark ['hɔːlmɑːk] n Stempel m; (fig) Kennzeichen nt

hallo [hʌ'ləʊ] interj hallo

Hallowe'en [hæləʊ'iːn] n Halloween nt (Tag vor Allerheiligen, an dem sich Kinder verkleiden und von Tür zu Tür gehen)

HALLOWE'EN

Hallowe'en ist der 31. Oktober, der Vorabend von Allerheiligen und nach altem Glauben der Abend, an dem man Geister und Hexen sehen kann. In Großbritannien und vor allem in den USA feiern die Kinder Hallowe'en, indem sie sich verkleiden und mit selbst gemachten Laternen aus Kürbissen von Tür zu Tür ziehen.

halo ['heɪləʊ] (pl -es) n (of saint) Heiligenschein m

halt [hɔːlt] n Pause f, Halt m; **to come to a ~** zum Stillstand kommen ▷ vt, vi anhalten

halve [hɑːv] vt halbieren

ham [hæm] n Schinken m; **~ and eggs** Schinken mit Spiegelei

hamburger ['hæmbɜːgə*] n (Culin) Hamburger m

hammer ['hæmə*] n Hammer m ▷ vt, vi hämmern

hammock ['hæmək] n Hängematte f

hamper ['hæmpə*] vt behindern ▷ n (as gift) Geschenkkorb m; (for picnic) Picknickkorb m

hamster ['hæmstə*] n Hamster m

hand [hænd] n Hand f; (of clock, instrument) Zeiger m; (in card game) Blatt nt; **to be made by ~** Handarbeit sein; **~s up!** Hände hoch!; (at school) meldet euch!; **~s off!** Finger weg!; **on the one ~ ..., on the other ~...** einerseits ..., andererseits

...; **to give sb a ~** jdm helfen (with bei); **it's in his ~s** er hat es in der Hand; **to be in good ~s** gut aufgehoben sein; **to get out of ~** außer Kontrolle geraten ▷ vt (pass) reichen (to sb jdm); **hand down** vt (tradition) überliefern; (heirloom) vererben; **hand in** vt einreichen; (at school, university etc) abgeben; **hand out** vt verteilen; **hand over** vt übergeben

handbag n Handtasche f; **handbook** n Handbuch nt; **handbrake** n (BRIT) Handbremse f; **hand cream** n Handcreme f; **handcuffs** npl Handschellen pl; **handful** n Handvoll f; **handheld PC** n Handheld m

handicap ['hændɪkæp] n Behinderung f, Handikap nt ▷ vt benachteiligen; **handicapped** adj behindert; **the ~** die Behinderten

handicraft ['hændɪkrɑːft] n Kunsthandwerk nt

handkerchief ['hæŋkətʃɪf] n Taschentuch nt

handle ['hændl] n Griff m; (of door) Klinke f; (of cup etc) Henkel m; (for winding) Kurbel f ▷ vt (touch) anfassen; (deal with: matter) sich befassen mit; (people, machine etc) umgehen mit; (situation, problem) fertig werden mit; **handlebars** npl Lenkstange f

hand luggage ['hændlʌgɪdʒ] n Handgepäck nt; **handmade** adj handgefertigt; **to be ~** Handarbeit sein; **handout** n (sheet) Handout nt, Thesenpapier nt; **handset** n Hörer m; **please replace the ~** bitte legen Sie auf; **hands-free phone** n Freisprechanlage f; **handshake** n Händedruck m

handsome ['hænsəm] adj (man) gut aussehen

hands-on [hændz'ɒn] adj praxisorientiert; **~ experience** praktische Erfahrung

handwriting ['hændraitiŋ] n Handschrift f

handy ['hændi] adj (useful) praktisch

hang [hæŋ] (**hung, hung**) vt (auf)hängen; (execute: hanged, hanged) hängen; **to ~ sth on** etw an etw akk hängen ▷ vi hängen ▷ n **he's got the ~ of it** er hat den Dreh raus; **hang about** vi sich herumtreiben, rumhängen; **hang on** vi sich festhalten (to an +dat); (fam: wait) warten; **to ~ to sth** etw behalten; **hang up** vi (Tel) auflegen ▷ vt aufhängen

hangar ['hæŋə*] n Flugzeughalle f

hanger ['hæŋə*] n Kleiderbügel m

hang glider ['hæŋglaidə*] n (Flug)drachen m; (person) Drachenflieger(in) m(f); **hang-gliding** n Drachenfliegen nt

hangover ['hæŋəuvə*] n (bad head) Kater m; (relic) Überbleibsel nt

hankie ['hæŋki] n (fam) Taschentuch nt

happen ['hæpən] vi geschehen; (sth strange, unpleasant) passieren; **if anything should ~ to me** wenn mir etwas passieren sollte; **it won't ~ again** es wird nicht wieder vorkommen; **I ~ed to be passing** ich kam zufällig vorbei; **happening** n Ereignis nt, Happening nt

happily ['hæpili] adv fröhlich, glücklich; (luckily) glücklicherweise; **happiness** ['hæpinis] n Glück nt; **happy** ['hæpi] adj glücklich; (satisfied) **~ with sth** mit etw zufrieden; (willing) **to be ~ to do sth** etw gerne tun; **Happy Christmas** fröhliche Weihnachten!; **Happy New Year** ein glückliches Neues Jahr!; **Happy Birthday** herzlichen Glückwunsch

zum Geburtstag!; **happy hour** n Happy Hour f (Zeit, in der man in Bars Getränke zu günstigeren Preisen bekommt)

harass ['hærəs] vt (ständig) belästigen; **harassment** n Belästigung f; (at work) Mobbing nt; **sexual ~** sexuelle Belästigung

harbor (US), **harbour** ['hɑ:bə*] n Hafen m

hard [hɑ:d] adj hart; (difficult) schwer, schwierig; (harsh) hart(herzig); **don't be ~ on him** sei nicht zu streng zu ihm; **it's ~ to believe** es ist kaum zu glauben ▷ adv (work) schwer; (rain, snow) stark; **to try ~/~er** sich dat große/mehr Mühe geben; **hardback** n gebundene Ausgabe; **hard-boiled** adj (egg) hart gekocht; **hard copy** n (Inform) Ausdruck m; **hard disk** n (Inform) Festplatte f; **harden** vt härten ▷ vi hart werden; **hardened** adj (person) abgehärtet (to gegen); **hard-hearted** adj hartherzig; **hardliner** n Hardliner(in) m(f); **hardly** ['hɑ:dli] adv kaum; **~ ever** fast nie; **hardship** ['hɑ:dʃip] n Not f; **hard shoulder** n (BRIT) Standspur f; **hardware** n (Inform) Hardware f, Haushalts- und Eisenwaren pl; **hard-working** adj fleißig, tüchtig

hare [hɛə*] n Hase m

harm [hɑ:m] n Schaden m; (bodily) Verletzung f; **it wouldn't do any ~** es würde nicht schaden ▷ vt schaden +dat; (person) verletzen; **harmful** adj schädlich; **harmless** adj harmlos

harp [hɑ:p] n Harfe f

harsh [hɑ:ʃ] adj (climate, voice) rau; (light, sound) grell; (severe) hart, streng

harvest ['hɑ:vist] n Ernte f; (time) Erntezeit f ▷ vt ernten

has [hæz] *pres of* **have**

hash [hæʃ] *n* (*Gastr*) Haschee *nt*; (*fam: hashish*) Haschisch *nt*; **to make a ~ of sth** etw vermasseln; **hash browns** *npl* (*US*) ≈ Kartoffelpuffer *pl*

hassle ['hæsl] *n* Ärger *m*; (*fuss*) Theater *nt*; **no ~** kein Problem ▷ *vt* bedrängen

hasn't ['hæznt] *contr of* **has not**

haste [heist] *n* Eile *f*; **hastily**, **hasty** *adv, adj* hastig; (*rash*) vorschnell

hat [hæt] *n* Hut *m*

hatch [hætʃ] *n* (*Naut*) Luke *f*; (*in house*) Durchreiche *f*; **hatchback** ['hætʃbæk] *n* (*car*) Wagen *m* mit Hecktür

hate [heit] *vt* hassen; **I ~ doing this** ich mache das sehr ungern ▷ *n* Hass *m* (*of auf +akk*)

haul [hɔ:l] *vt* ziehen, schleppen ▷ *n* (*booty*) Beute *f*; **haulage** ['hɔ:lidʒ] *n* Transport *m*; (*trade*) Spedition *f*; **haunted** *adj* **a ~ house** ein Haus, in dem es spukt

have [hæv] (*had, had*) *vt* haben; (*possess*) **~ you got** *o do* **you ~ a light?** haben Sie Feuer?; (*receive*) **I've just had a letter from ...** ich habe soeben einen Brief von ... erhalten; **to ~ a baby** ein Kind bekommen; (*to eat / drink*) **what are you having?** was möchten Sie (essen / trinken)?; **I had too much wine** ich habe zu viel Wein getrunken; **to ~ lunch / dinner** zu Mittag / Abend essen; (*hold*) **to ~ a party** eine Party geben; (*take*) **to ~ a bath / shower** ein Bad nehmen / duschen; (*causative*) **to ~ sth done** etw machen lassen; **they had a good time** sie haben sich amüsiert; (*phrases with* '*it*') **I won't ~ it** das lasse ich mir nicht bieten; **we've had it** (*fam*) wir sind geliefert ▷ *vb aux* (*forming perfect tenses*) ha-

ben / sein; **he has seen it** er hat es gesehen; (*with vbs of motion etc*) sein; **she has come** sie ist gekommen; (*expressing compulsion*) **to ~ (got) to do sth** etw tun müssen; **you don't ~ to go** du musst nicht gehen; (*in tag questions*) **you've been there, ~n't you?** du bist mal dort gewesen, nicht wahr?; **have on** *vt* (*be wearing*) anhaben; (*have arranged*) vorhaben; (*BRIT*) **you're having me on** das meinst du nicht ernst

Hawaii [hə'waiiː] *n* Hawaii *nt*

hawk [hɔ:k] *n* Habicht *m*

hay [hei] *n* Heu *nt*; **hay fever** *n* Heuschnupfen *m*

hazard ['hæzəd] *n* Gefahr *f*; (*risk*) Risiko *nt*; **hazardous** *adj* gefährlich; **~ waste** Sondermüll *m*; **hazard warning lights** *npl* Warnblinkanlage *f*

haze [heiz] *n* Dunst *m*

hazelnut ['heizlnʌt] *n* Haselnuss *f*

hazy ['heizi] *adj* (*misty*) dunstig; (*vague*) verschwommen

he [hiː] *pron* er

head [hed] *n* Kopf *m*; (*leader*) Leiter(in) *m(f)*; (*at school*) Schulleiter(in) *m(f)*; **~ of state** Staatsoberhaupt *nt*; **at the ~ of** an der Spitze von; (*tossing coin*) **~s or tails** Kopf oder Zahl? ▷ *adj* (*leading*) Ober-; **~ boy** Schulsprecher *m*; **~ girl** Schulsprecherin *f* ▷ *vt* anführen; (*organization*) leiten; **head for** *vt* zusteuern auf *+akk*; **he's heading for trouble** er wird Ärger bekommen

headache ['hedeik] *n* Kopfschmerzen *pl*, Kopfweh *nt*; **header** *n* (*football*) Kopfball *m*; (*dive*) Kopfsprung *m*; **headfirst** *adj* kopfüber; **headhunt** *vt* (*Comm*) abwerben; **heading** *n* Überschrift *f*; **headlamp**, **headlight** *n* Scheinwerfer *m*; **headline** *n* Schlagzeile *f*;

headmaster n Schulleiter m;
headmistress n Schulleiterin f;
head-on collision adj Frontalzusammenstoß m; **headphones** npl
Kopfhörer m; **headquarters** npl (of
firm) Zentrale f; **headrest**, **head
restraint** n Kopfstütze f; **headscarf** (pl **-scarves**) n Kopftuch nt;
head teacher n Schulleiter(in) m(f)

heal [hiːl] vt, vi heilen
health [hɛlθ] n Gesundheit f;
good/bad for one's ~ gesund/
ungesund; **your ~!** zum Wohl!;
health centre n Ärztezentrum nt;
health club n Fitnesscenter nt;
health food n Reformkost f; **~
store** Bioladen m; **health insurance** n Krankenversicherung f;
health service n Gesundheitswe-
sen nt; **healthy** adj gesund

heap [hiːp] n Haufen m; **~s of**
(fam) jede Menge ▷ vt, vi häufen
hear [hɪə*] (**heard**, **heard**) vt, vi
hören; **to ~ about sth** von etw erfahren; **I've ~d of it/him** ich habe
schon davon/von ihm gehört;
hearing n Gehör nt; (Jur) Verhandlung f; **hearing aid** n Hörgerät nt; **hearsay** n **from ~** vom
Hörensagen
heart [hɑːt] n Herz nt; **to loose/
take ~** den Mut verlieren/Mut fassen; **to learn by ~** auswendig lernen; (cards) **~s** Herz nt; **queen of ~s**
Herzdame f; **heart attack** n
Herzanfall m; **heartbeat** n Herzschlag m; **heartbreaking** adj
herzzerreißend; **heartbroken** adj
todunglücklich, untröstlich; **heartburn** n Sodbrennen nt; **heart
failure** n Herzversagen nt; **heart-
felt** adj tief empfunden; **heartless**
adj herzlos; **heart-throb** n (fam)
Schwarm m; **heart-to-heart** n offene Aussprache f; **hearty** [hɑːtɪ]
adj (meal, appetite) herzhaft; (wel-

come) herzlich
heat [hiːt] n Hitze f; (pleasant)
Wärme f; (temperature) Temperatur f;
(Sport) Vorlauf m ▷ vt (house, room)
heizen; **heat up** vi warm werden ▷
vt aufwärmen; **heated** adj be-
heizt; (fig) hitzig; **heater** n Heizofen m; (Auto) Heizung f
heath [hiːθ] n (BRIT) Heide f
heather ['hɛðə*] n Heidekraut nt
heating ['hiːtɪŋ] n Heizung f;
heat resistant adj hitzebeständig;
heatstroke n Hitzschlag m;
heatwave n Hitzewelle f
heaven ['hɛvn] n Himmel m;
heavenly adj himmlisch
heavily ['hɛvɪlɪ] adv (rain, drink
etc) stark; **heavy** ['hɛvɪ] adj
schwer; (rain, traffic, smoker etc)
stark; **heavy goods vehicle** n
Lastkraftwagen m
Hebrew ['hiːbruː] adj hebräisch ▷
n (language) Hebräisch nt
hectic ['hɛktɪk] adj hektisch
he'd [hiːd] contr of **he had**; **he
would**
hedge [hɛdʒ] n Hecke f
hedgehog ['hɛdʒhɒg] n Igel m
heel [hiːl] n (Anat) Ferse f; (of shoe)
Absatz m
hefty ['hɛftɪ] adj schwer; (person)
stämmig; (fine, amount) saftig
height [haɪt] n Höhe f; (of person)
Größe f
heir [ɛə*] n Erbe m; **heiress**
['ɛərɪs] n Erbin f
held [hɛld] pt, pp of **hold**
helicopter ['hɛlɪkɒptə*] n Hubschrauber m; **heliport** ['hɛlɪpɔːt]
n Hubschrauberlandeplatz m
hell [hɛl] n Hölle f; **go to ~** scher
dich zum Teufel ▷ interj verdammt;
that's a ~ of a lot of money das ist
verdammt viel Geld
he'll [hiːl] contr of **he will**; **he shall**
hello [hʌ'ləʊ] interj hallo

helmet ['helmɪt] n Helm m

help [help] n Hilfe f ▷ vt, vi helfen +dat (with bei); **to ~ sb (to) do sth** jdm helfen, etw zu tun; **can I ~?** kann ich (Ihnen) behilflich sein?; **I couldn't ~ laughing** ich musste einfach lachen; **I can't ~ it** ich kann nichts dafür; **~ yourself** bedienen Sie sich; **helpful** adj (person) hilfsbereit; (useful) nützlich; **helping** n Portion f; **helpless** adj hilflos

hem [hem] n Saum m

hemophiliac [hiːməʊ'fɪliæk] n (US) Bluter m; **hemorrhage** ['hemərɪdʒ] n (US) Blutung f; **hemorrhoids** ['hemərɔɪdz] npl (US) Hämorrhoiden pl

hen [hen] n Henne f

hen night n (BRIT) Junggesellinnenabschied m

hence [hens] adv (reason) daher

henpecked ['henpekt] adj **to be ~** unter dem Pantoffel stehen

hepatitis [hepə'taɪtɪs] n Hepatitis f

her [hɜː*] adj ihr; **she's hurt ~ leg** sie hat sich dat das Bein verletzt ▷ pron (direct object) sie; (indirect object) ihr; **do you know ~?** kennst du sie?; **can you help ~?** kannst du ihr helfen?; **it's ~** sie ist's

herb [hɜːb] n Kraut nt

herbal medicine ['hɜːbəl-] n Pflanzenheilkunde f; **herbal tea** n Kräutertee m

herd [hɜːd] n Herde f; **herd instinct** n Herdentrieb m

here [hɪə*] adv hier; (to this place) hierher; **come ~** komm her; **I won't be ~ for lunch** ich bin zum Mittagessen nicht da; **~ and there** hier und da, da und dort

hereditary [hɪ'redɪtərɪ] adj erblich; **hereditary disease** n Erbkrankheit f; **heritage** ['herɪtɪdʒ] n Erbe nt

hernia ['hɜːnɪə] n Leistenbruch m, Eingeweidebruch m

hero ['hɪərəʊ] (pl -es) n Held m

heroin ['herəʊɪn] n Heroin nt

heroine ['herəʊɪn] n Heldin f; **heroism** ['herəʊɪzəm] n Heldentum nt

herring ['herɪŋ] n Hering m

hers [hɜːz] pron ihre(r, s); **this is ~** das gehört ihr, **a friend of ~** ein Freund von ihr

herself [hɜː'self] pron (reflexive) sich; **she's bought ~ a flat** sie hat sich eine Wohnung gekauft; **she needs it for ~** sie braucht es für sich (selbst); (emphatic) **she did it ~** sie hat es selbst gemacht; **(all) by ~** allein

he's [hiːz] contr of **he is**; **he has**

hesitant ['hezɪtənt] adj zögernd; **hesitate** ['hezɪteɪt] vi zögern; **don't ~ to ask** fragen Sie ruhig; **hesitation** n Zögern nt; **without ~** ohne zu zögern

heterosexual [hetərəʊ'seksjʊəl] adj heterosexuell ▷ n Heterosexuelle(r) mf

HGV abbr = **heavy goods vehicle** LKW m

hi [haɪ] interj hi, hallo

hiccup ['hɪkʌp] n Schluckauf m; (minor problem) Problemchen nt; **to have (the) ~s** Schluckauf haben

hid [hɪd] pt of **hide**

hidden ['hɪdn] pp of **hide**

hide [haɪd] (hid, hidden) vt verstecken (from vor +dat); (feelings, truth) verbergen; (cover) verdecken ▷ vi sich verstecken (from vor +dat)

hideous ['hɪdɪəs] adj scheußlich

hiding ['haɪdɪŋ] n (beating) Tracht f Prügel; (concealment) **to be in ~** sich versteckt halten; **hiding place** n Versteck nt

hi-fi ['haɪfaɪ] n Hi-Fi nt; (system) Hi-Fi-Anlage f

high [haɪ] adj hoch; (wind) stark; (living) im großen Stil; (on drugs) high ▷ adv hoch ▷ n (Meteo) Hoch nt; **highchair** n Hochstuhl m; **higher** adj höher; **higher education** n Hochschulbildung f; **high flier** n Hochbegabte(r) (m)f; **high heels** npl Stöckelschuhe pl; **high jump** n Hochsprung m; **Highlands** npl (schottisches) Hochland nt; **highlight** n (in hair) Strähnchen nt; (fig) Höhepunkt m ▷ vt (with pen) hervorheben; **highlighter** n Textmarker m; **highly** adj hoch, sehr; ~ **paid** hoch bezahlt; **I think ~ of him** ich habe eine hohe Meinung von ihm; **high-performance** adj Hochleistungs-; **high pressure** n Hochdruck m; **high school** n (US) Highschool f, ≈ Gymnasium nt; **high-speed** adj Schnell-; ~ **train** Hochgeschwindigkeitszug m; **high street** n Hauptstraße f; **high tech** adj Hightech- ▷ n Hightech nt; **high tide** n Flut f; **highway** n (US) ≈ Autobahn f; (BRIT) Landstraße f

hijack [ˈhaɪdʒæk] vt entführen, hijacken; **hijacker** n Entführer(in) m(f), Hijacker m

hike [haɪk] vi wandern ▷ n Wanderung f; **hiker** n Wanderer m, Wanderin f; **hiking** n Wandern nt

hilarious [hɪˈlɛərɪəs] adj zum Schreien komisch

hill [hɪl] n Hügel m, (higher) Berg m; **hilly** adj hügelig

him [hɪm] pron (direct object) ihn; (indirect object) ihm; **do you know ~?** kennst du ihn?; **can you help ~?** kannst du ihm helfen?; **it's ~** er ist's; **~ too** er auch

himself [hɪmˈsɛlf] pron (reflexive) sich; **he's bought ~ a flat** er hat sich eine Wohnung gekauft; **he needs it for ~** er braucht es für sich (selbst);

(emphatic) **he did it ~** er hat es selbst gemacht; **(all) by ~** allein

hinder [ˈhɪndə*] vt behindern; **hindrance** [ˈhɪndrəns] n Behinderung f

Hindu [ˈhɪnduː] adj hinduistisch ▷ n Hindu m; **Hinduism** [ˈhɪnduːɪzəm] n Hinduismus m

hinge [hɪndʒ] n Scharnier nt; (on door) Angel f

hint [hɪnt] n Wink m, Andeutung f; (trace) Spur f ▷ vi andeuten (at akk)

hip [hɪp] n Hüfte f ▷ adj (trend) hip, trendy

hippopotamus [hɪpəˈpɒtəməs] n Nilpferd nt

hire [ˈhaɪə*] vt (worker) anstellen; (car, bike etc) mieten ▷ n Miete f; **for ~** (taxi) frei; **hire(d) car** n Mietwagen m; **hire purchase** n Ratenkauf m

his [hɪz] adj sein; **he's hurt ~ leg** er hat sich dat das Bein verletzt ▷ pron seine(r, s); **it's ~** es gehört ihm; **a friend of ~** ein Freund von ihm

historic [hɪˈstɒrɪk] adj (significant) historisch; **historical** adj (monument etc) historisch; (studies etc) geschichtlich; **history** [ˈhɪstərɪ] n Geschichte f

hit [hɪt] n (blow) Schlag m; (on target) Treffer m; (success) Erfolg m; (Mus) Hit m ▷ vt (**hit, hit**) schlagen; (bullet, stone etc) treffen; **the car ~ the tree** das Auto fuhr gegen einen Baum; **to ~ one's head on sth** sich dat den Kopf an etw dat stoßen; **hit (up)on** vt stoßen auf +akk; **hit-and-run ~ accident** Unfall m mit Fahrerflucht

hitch [hɪtʃ] vt (pull up) hochziehen ▷ n Schwierigkeit f; **without a ~** reibungslos

hitch-hike [ˈhɪtʃhaɪk] vi trampen; **hitch-hiker** n Tramper(in) ilf'), **hitchhiking** n Trampen nt

HIV abbr = **human immunodeficiency virus** HIV nt; **~ positive/negative** HIV-positiv/negativ

hive [haɪv] n Bienenstock m

HM abbr = **His/Her Majesty**

HMS abbr = **His/Her Majesty's Ship**

hoarse [hɔːs] adj heiser

hoax [həʊks] n Streich m, Jux m; (false alarm) blinder Alarm

hob [hɒb] n (of cooker) Kochfeld nt

hobble ['hɒbl] vi humpeln

hobby ['hɒbɪ] n Hobby nt

hobo ['həʊbəʊ] (pl **-es**) n (US) Penner(in) m(f)

hockey ['hɒkɪ] n Hockey nt

hold [həʊld] (held, held) vt halten; (contain) enthalten; (be able to contain) fassen; (post, office) innehaben; (value) beibehalten; (meeting) abhalten; (person as prisoner) gefangen halten; **to ~ one's breath** den Atem anhalten; **to ~ hands** Händchen halten; **~ the line** (Tel) bleiben Sie am Apparat ▷ vi halten; (weather) sich halten ▷ n (grasp) Halt m; (of ship, aircraft) Laderaum m; **hold back** vt zurückhalten; (keep secret) verheimlichen; **hold on** vi sich festhalten; (wait) warten; (Tel) dranbleiben; **to ~ to sth** etw festhalten; **hold out** vt ausstrecken; (offer) hinhalten; (offer) bieten ▷ vi durchhalten; **hold up** vt hochhalten; (support) stützen; (delay) aufhalten; **holdall** n Reisetasche f; **holder** n (person) Inhaber(in) m(f); **holdup** n (in traffic) Stau m; (robbery) Überfall m

hole [həʊl] n Loch nt; (of fox, rabbit) Bau m; **~ in the wall** (cash dispenser) Geldautomat m

holiday ['hɒlɪdeɪ] n (day off) freier Tag; (public ~) Feiertag m; (vacation) Urlaub m; (at school) Ferien pl; **on ~** im Urlaub; **to go on ~** in Urlaub ma

chen; **holiday camp** n Ferienlager nt; **holiday home** n Ferienhaus nt; (flat) Ferienwohnung f; **holidaymaker** n Urlauber(in) m(f); **holiday resort** n Ferienort m

Holland ['hɒlənd] n Holland nt

hollow ['hɒləʊ] adj hohl; (words) leer ▷ n Vertiefung f

holly ['hɒlɪ] n Stechpalme f

holy ['həʊlɪ] adj heilig; **Holy Week** n Karwoche f

home [həʊm] n Zuhause nt; (area, country) Heimat f; (institution) Heim nt; **at ~** zu Hause; **to make oneself at ~** es sich dat bequem machen; **away from ~** verreist ▷ adv **to go** nach Hause gehen/fahren; **home address** n Heimatadresse f; **home country** n Heimatland nt; **home game** n (Sport) Heimspiel nt; **homeless** adj obdachlos; **homely** adj häuslich; (US: ugly) unscheinbar; **home-made** adj selbst gemacht; **home movie** n Amateurfilm m; **Home Office** n (BRIT) Innenministerium nt

homeopathic adj (US) see **homoeopathic**

home page ['həʊmpeɪdʒ] n (Inform) Homepage f; **Home Secretary** n (BRIT) Innenminister(in) m(f); **homesick** adj **to be ~** Heimweh haben; **home town** n Heimatstadt f; **homework** n Hausaufgaben pl

homicide ['hɒmɪsaɪd] n (US) Totschlag m

homoeopathic [həʊmɪəʊ'pæθɪk] adj homöopathisch

homosexual [hɒməʊ'sɛksjʊəl] adj homosexuell ▷ n Homosexuelle(r) mf

Honduras [hɒn'djʊərəs] n Honduras nt

honest ['ɒnɪst] adj ehrlich; **honesty** n Ehrlichkeit f

honey ['hʌnɪ] n Honig m; **hon-**

eycomb n Honigwabe f; **honeydew melon** n Honigmelone f; **honeymoon** n Flitterwochen pl

Hong Kong [hɒŋ 'kɒŋ] n Hongkong nt

honor (US) see **honour**; **honorary** ['ɒnərərɪ] adj (member, title etc) Ehren-, ehrenamtlich; **honour** ['ɒnə*] vt ehren; (cheque) einlösen; (contract) einhalten ▷ n Ehre f; **in ~ of** zu Ehren von; **honourable** adj ehrenhaft; **honours degree** n akademischer Grad mit Prüfung im Spezialfach

hood [hʊd] n Kapuze f; (Auto) Verdeck nt; (US Auto) Kühlerhaube f

hoof [huːf] (pl **hooves**) n Huf m

hook [hʊk] n Haken m; **hooked** adj (keen) besessen (on von); (drugs) abhängig sein (on von)

hooligan ['huːlɪɡən] n Hooligan m

hoot [huːt] vi (Auto) hupen

Hoover® ['huːvə] n Staubsauger m; **hoover** vi, vt staubsaugen

hop [hɒp] vi hüpfen ▷ n (Bot) Hopfen m

hope [həʊp] vi, vt hoffen (for auf +akk); **I ~ so / ~ not** hoffentlich / hoffentlich nicht; **I ~ (that) we'll meet** ich hoffe, dass wir uns sehen werden ▷ n Hoffnung f; **there's no ~** es ist aussichtslos; **hopeful** adj hoffnungsvoll; **hopefully** adv (full of hope) hoffnungsvoll; (I hope so) hoffentlich; **hopeless** adj hoffnungslos; (incompetent) miserabel

horizon [hə'raɪzn] n Horizont m; **horizontal** [hɒrɪ'zɒntl] adj horizontal

hormone ['hɔːməʊn] n Hormon nt

horn [hɔːn] n Horn nt; (Auto) Hupe f

hornet ['hɔːnɪt] n Hornisse f

horny ['hɔːnɪ] adj (fam) geil

horoscope ['hɒrəskəʊp] n Horoskop nt

horrible, horribly ['hɒrɪbl, -blɪ] adj, adv schrecklich; **horrid, horridly** ['hɒrɪd, -lɪ] adj, adv abscheulich; **horrify** ['hɒrɪfaɪ] vt entsetzen; **horror** ['hɒrə*] n Entsetzen nt; **~s** (things) Schrecken pl

hors d'oeuvre [ɔː'dɜːvr] n Vorspeise f

horse [hɔːs] n Pferd nt; **horse chestnut** n Rosskastanie f; **horsepower** n Pferdestärke f, PS nt; **horse racing** n Pferderennen nt; **horseradish** n Meerrettich m; **horse riding** n Reiten nt; **horseshoe** n Hufeisen nt

horticulture ['hɔːtɪkʌltʃə*] n Gartenbau m

hose, hosepipe [həʊz, 'həʊzpaɪp] n Schlauch m

hospitable [hɒ'spɪtəbl] adj gastfreundlich

hospital ['hɒspɪtl] n Krankenhaus nt

hospitality [hɒspɪ'tælɪtɪ] n Gastfreundschaft f

host [həʊst] n Gastgeber m; (Tv: of show) Moderator(in) m(f), Talkmaster(in) m(f) ▷ vt (party) geben; (Tv: TV show) moderieren

hostage ['hɒstɪdʒ] n Geisel f

hostel ['hɒstəl] n Wohnheim nt; (youth ~) Jugendherberge f

hostess ['həʊstɪs] n (of a party) Gastgeberin f

hostile ['hɒstaɪl] adj feindlich; **hostility** [hɒs'tɪlɪtɪ] n Feindseligkeit f

hot [hɒt] adj heiß; (drink, food, water) warm; (spiced) scharf; **I'm (feeling) ~** mir ist heiß; **hot cross bun** n Rosinenbrötchen mit einem Kreuz darauf, hauptsächlich zu Ostern gegessen; **hot dog** n Hotdog nt

hotel [həʊ'tel] n Hotel nt; **hotel**

room n Hotelzimmer nt

hothouse n Treibhaus nt; **hotline** n Hotline f; **hotplate** n Kochplatte f; **hotpot** n Fleischeintopf mit Kartoffeleinlage; **hot-water bottle** n Wärmflasche f

hour ['auə*] n Stunde f; **to wait for ~s** stundenlang warten; **~s** pl (of shops etc) Geschäftszeiten pl; **hourly** adj stündlich

house [haus] (pl **houses**) n Haus nt; **at my ~** bei mir (zu Hause), **to my ~** zu mir (nach Hause); **on the ~** auf Kosten des Hauses; **the House of Commons/Lords** das britische Unterhaus/Oberhaus; **the Houses of Parliament** das britische Parlamentsgebäude ▷ [hauz] vt unterbringen; **houseboat** n Hausboot nt; **household** n Haushalt m; **~ appliance** Haushaltsgerat nt; **house-husband** n Hausmann m; **housekeeping** n Haushaltung f; (money) Haushaltsgeld nt; **house-trained** adj stubenrein; **house-warming (party)** n Einzugsparty f; **housewife** (pl **-wives**) n Hausfrau f; **house wine** n Hauswein m; **housework** n Hausarbeit f

housing ['hauzɪŋ] n (houses) Wohnungen pl; (house building) Wohnungsbau m; **housing benefit** n Wohngeld nt; **housing development, housing estate** (BRIT) n Wohnsiedlung f

hover ['hɒvə*] vi schweben; **hovercraft** n Luftkissenboot nt

how [hau] adv wie; **~ many** wie viele; **~ much** wie viel; **~ are you?** wie geht es Ihnen?; **~ are things?** wie geht's?; **~'s work?** was macht die Arbeit?; **~ about ...?** wie wäre es mit ...?; **however** [hau'evə*] conj (but) jedoch, aber ▷ adv (no matter how) wie ... auch; **~ much it costs** wie viel es auch kostet; **~ you do it** wie man es auch macht

howl [haul] vi heulen; **howler** ['haulə*] n (fam) grober Schnitzer

HP, hp n (BRIT) abbr = **hire purchase** Ratenkauf m ▷ abbr = **horsepower** PS

HQ abbr = **headquarters**

hubcap ['hʌbkæp] n Radkappe f

hug [hʌg] vt umarmen ▷ n Umarmung f

huge [hju:dʒ] adj riesig

hum [hʌm] vi, vt summen

human ['hju:mən] adj menschlich; **~ rights** Menschenrechte pl ▷ n **~ (being)** Mensch m; **humanitarian** [hju:mænɪ'teərɪən] adj humanitär; **humanity** [hju:'mænɪtɪ] n Menschheit f; (kindliness) Menschlichkeit f; **humanities** Geisteswissenschaften pl

humble ['hʌmbl] adj demütig; (modest) bescheiden

humid ['hju:mɪd] adj feucht; **humidity** [hju:'mɪdɪtɪ] n (Luft)feuchtigkeit f

humiliate [hju:'mɪlɪeɪt] vt demütigen; **humiliation** [hju:mɪlɪ'eɪʃn] n Erniedrigung f, Demütigung f

humor (US) see **humour**; **humorous** ['hju:mərəs] adj humorvoll; (story) lustig, witzig; **humour** ['hju:mə*] n Humor m, sense of ~ Sinn m für Humor

hump [hʌmp] n Buckel m

hunch [hʌntʃ] n Gefühl nt, Ahnung f ▷ vt (back) krümmen; **hunchback** n Bucklige(r) mf

hundred ['hʌndrəd] num **one ~, a ~** (ein)hundert; **a ~ and one** hundert(und)eins; **two ~** zweihundert; **hundredth** adj hundertste(r, s) ▷ n (fraction) Hundertstel nt; **hundredweight** n Zentner m (50,8 kg)

hung [hʌŋ] pt, pp of **hang**

Hungarian [hʌŋˈgɛərɪən] *adj* ungarisch ▷ *n* (*person*) Ungar(in) *m(f)*; (*language*) Ungarisch *nt*; **Hungary** [ˈhʌŋgərɪ] *n* Ungarn *nt*

hunger [ˈhʌŋgə*] *n* Hunger *m*; **hungry** [ˈhʌŋgrɪ] *adj* hungrig; **to be ~** Hunger haben

hunk [hʌŋk] *n* (*fam*) gut aussehender Mann

hunt [hʌnt] *n* Jagd *f*; (*search*) Suche *f* (*for* nach) ▷ *vt, vi* jagen; (*search*) suchen (*for* nach); **hunting** *n* Jagen *nt*, Jagd *f*

hurdle [ˈhɜːdl] *n* (*a. fig*) Hürde *f*; **the 400m ~s** der 400m-Hürdenlauf

hurl [hɜːl] *vt* schleudern

hurray [huˈreɪ] *interj* hurra

hurricane [ˈhʌrɪkən] *n* Orkan *m*

hurried [ˈhʌrɪd] *adj* eilig; **hurry** [ˈhʌrɪ] *n* Eile *f*; **to be in a ~** es eilig haben; **there's no ~** es besteht ▷ *vi* sich beeilen; **~ (up)** mach schnell! ▷ *vt* antreiben

hurt [hɜːt] (**hurt, hurt**) *vt* wehtun +*dat*; (*wound: person, feelings*) verletzen; **I've ~ my arm** ich habe mir am Arm wehgetan ▷ *vi* wehtun; **my arm ~s** mir tut der Arm weh

husband [ˈhʌzbənd] *n* Ehemann *m*

husky [ˈhʌskɪ] *adj* rau ▷ *n* Schlittenhund *m*

hut [hʌt] *n* Hütte *f*

hyacinth [ˈhaɪəsɪnθ] *n* Hyazinthe *f*

hybrid [ˈhaɪbrɪd] *n* Kreuzung *f*

hydroelectric [ˈhaɪdrəʊˈlektrɪk] *adj* **~ power station** Wasserkraftwerk *nt*

hydrofoil [ˈhaɪdrəʊfɔɪl] *n* Tragflächenboot *nt*

hydrogen [ˈhaɪdrədʒən] *n* Wasserstoff *m*

hygiene [ˈhaɪdʒiːn] *n* Hygiene *f*; **hygienic** [haɪˈdʒiːnɪk] *adj* hygienisch

hymn [hɪm] *n* Kirchenlied *nt*

hypermarket [ˈhaɪpəmɑːkɪt] *n* Großmarkt *m*; **hypersensitive** *adj* überempfindlich

hyphen [ˈhaɪfən] *n* Bindestrich *m*

hypnosis [hɪpˈnəʊsɪs] *n* Hypnose *f*; **hypnotize** [ˈhɪpnətaɪz] *vt* hypnotisieren

hypochondriac [haɪpəʊˈkɒndrɪæk] *n* eingebildete(r) Kranke(r), eingebildete Kranke

hypocrisy [hɪˈpɒkrəsɪ] *n* Heuchelei *f*; **hypocrite** [ˈhɪpəkrɪt] *n* Heuchler(in) *m(f)*

hypodermic [haɪpəˈdɜːmɪk] *adj*, *n* **~ (needle)** Spritze *f*

hypothetical [haɪpəʊˈθetɪkəl] *adj* hypothetisch

hysteria [hɪˈstɪərɪə] *n* Hysterie *f*; **hysterical** [hɪˈsterɪkəl] *adj* hysterisch; (*amusing*) zum Totlachen

I [aɪ] *pron* ich

ice [aɪs] *n* Eis *nt* ▷ *vt* (*cake*) glasieren; **iceberg** *n* Eisberg *m*; **iceberg lettuce** *n* Eisbergsalat *m*; **icebox** *n* (US) Kühlschrank *m*; **ice-cold** *adj* eiskalt; **ice cream** *n* Eis *nt*; **ice cube** *n* Eiswürfel *m*, **iced** *adj* eisgekühlt; (*coffee, tea*) Eis-; (*cake*) glasiert; **ice hockey** *n* Eishockey *nt*

Iceland [ˈaɪslənd] *n* Island *nt*; **Icelander** *n* Isländer(in) *m(f)*; **Icelandic** [aɪsˈlændɪk] *adj* isländisch ▷ *n* (*language*) Isländisch *nt*

ice lolly [ˈaɪslɒlɪ] *n* (BRIT) Eis *nt* am Stiel; **ice rink** *n* Kunsteisbahn *f*; **ice skating** *n* Schlittschuhlaufen *nt*

icing [ˈaɪsɪŋ] *n* (*on cake*) Zuckerguss *m*

icon [ˈaɪkɒn] *n* Ikone *f*; (*inform*) Icon *nt*, Programmsymbol *nt*

icy [ˈaɪsɪ] *adj* (*slippery*) vereist; (*cold*) eisig

I'd [aɪd] *contr* of **I would; I had**

ID *abbr* = **identification** Ausweis *m*

idea [aɪˈdɪə] *n* Idee *f*; (**I've) no ~** (ich habe) keine Ahnung, **that's my ~ of ...** so stelle ich mir ... vor

ideal [aɪˈdɪəl] *n* Ideal *nt* ▷ *adj* ideal; **ideally** *adv* ideal; (*before statement*) idealerweise

identical [aɪˈdentɪkəl] *adj* identisch; **~ twins** eineiige Zwillinge

identify [aɪˈdentɪfaɪ] *vt* identifizieren; **identity** [aɪˈdentɪtɪ] *n* Identität *f*, **identity card** *n* Personalausweis *m*

idiom [ˈɪdɪəm] *n* Redewendung *f*; **idiomatic** *adj* idiomatisch

idiot [ˈɪdɪət] *n* Idiot(in) *m(f)*

idle [ˈaɪdl] *adj* (*doing nothing*) untätig, (*worker*) unbeschäftigt; (*machines*) außer Betrieb; (*lazy*) faul; (*promise, threat*) leer

idol [ˈaɪdl] *n* Idol *nt*; **idolize** [ˈaɪdəlaɪz] *vt* vergöttern

idyllic [ɪˈdɪlɪk] *adj* idyllisch

i.e. *abbr* = **id est** d.h.

if [ɪf] *conj* wenn, falls; (*whether*) ob; **~ so** wenn ja, **~ I were you** wenn ich du wäre, ich an deiner Stelle; **I don't know - he's coming** ich weiß nicht, ob er kommt

ignition [ɪɡˈnɪʃən] *n* Zündung *f*; **ignition key** *n* (*Auto*) Zündschlüssel *m*

ignorance [ˈɪɡnərəns] *n* Unwissenheit *f*; **ignorant** *adj* unwissend; **ignore** [ɪɡˈnɔː*] *vt* ignorieren, nicht beachten

I'll [aɪl] *contr* of **I will; I shall**

ill [ɪl] *adj* krank; **~ at ease** unbehaglich

illegal [ɪˈliːɡəl] *adj* illegal

illegitimate [ɪlɪˈdʒɪtɪmət] *adj* unzulässig, (*child*) unehelich

illiterate [ɪˈlɪtərət] *adj* **to be ~** Analphabet(in) sein

illness [ˈɪlnɪs] *n* Krankheit *f*

illuminate [ɪˈluːmɪneɪt] *vt* beleuchten, **illuminating** *adj* (*remark*) aufschlussreich

illusion [ɪˈluːʒən] *n* Illusion *f*; **to be under the ~ that ...** sich einbilden, dass ...

illustrate [ˈɪləstreɪt] *vt* illustrieren; **illustration** *n* Abbildung *f*, Bild *nt*

I'm [aɪm] *contr of* **I am**

image [ˈɪmɪdʒ] *n* Bild *nt*; (*public ~*) Image *nt*; **imaginable** [ɪˈmædʒɪnəbl] *adj* denkbar; **imaginary** [ɪˈmædʒɪnərɪ] *adj* eingebildet; **~ world** Fantasiewelt *f*; **imagination** [ɪmædʒɪˈneɪʃən] *n* Fantasie *f*; (*mistaken*) Einbildung *f*; **imaginative** [ɪˈmædʒɪnətɪv] *adj* fantasievoll; **imagine** [ɪˈmædʒɪn] *vt* sich vorstellen; (*wrongly*) sich einbilden; **~I** stell dir vor!

imbecile [ˈɪmbəsiːl] *n* Trottel *m*

imitate [ˈɪmɪteɪt] *vt* nachahmen, nachmachen; **imitation** *n* Nachahmung *f* ▷ *adj* imitiert; **~ leather** Kunstleder *nt*

immaculate [ɪˈmækjʊlɪt] *adj* tadellos; (*spotless*) makellos

immature [ɪməˈtjʊə*] *adj* unreif

immediate [ɪˈmiːdɪət] *adj* unmittelbar; (*instant*) sofortig; (*reply*) umgehend; **immediately** *adv* sofort

immense, immensely [ɪˈmens, -lɪ] *adj, adv* riesig, enorm

immersion heater [ɪˈmɜːʃn hiːtə] *n* Boiler *m*

immigrant [ˈɪmɪgrənt] *n* Einwanderer *m*, Einwanderin *f*; **immigration** [ɪmɪˈgreɪʃən] *n* Einwanderung *f*; (*facility*) Einwanderungskontrolle *f*

immobilize [ɪˈməʊbɪlaɪz] *vt* lähmen; **immobilizer** *n* (*Auto*) Wegfahrsperre *f*

immoral [ɪˈmɒrəl] *adj* unmoralisch

immortal [ɪˈmɔːtl] *adj* unsterblich

immune [ɪˈmjuːn] *adj* (*Med*) immun (*from, to* gegen); **immune system** *n* Immunsystem *nt*

impact [ˈɪmpækt] *n* Aufprall *m*; (*effect*) Auswirkung *f* (*on auf +akk*)

impatience [ɪmˈpeɪʃəns] *n* Ungeduld *f*; **impatient, impatiently** *adj, adv* ungeduldig

impeccable [ɪmˈpekəbl] *adj* tadellos

impede [ɪmˈpiːd] *vt* behindern

imperative [ɪmˈperətɪv] *adj* unbedingt erforderlich ▷ *n* (*Ling*) Imperativ *m*

imperfect [ɪmˈpɜːfɪkt] *adj* unvollkommen; (*goods*) fehlerhaft ▷ *n* (*Ling*) Imperfekt *nt*; **imperfection** [ɪmpəˈfekʃən] *n* Unvollkommenheit *f*; (*fault*) Fehler *m*

imperial [ɪmˈpɪərɪəl] *adj* kaiserlich, Reichs-; **imperialism** *n* Imperialismus *m*

impertinence [ɪmˈpɜːtɪnəns] *n* Unverschämtheit *f*, Zumutung *f*; **impertinent** *adj* unverschämt

implant [ˈɪmplɑːnt] *n* (*Med*) Implantat *nt*

implausible [ɪmˈplɔːzəbl] *adj* unglaubwürdig

implement [ˈɪmplɪmənt] *n* Werkzeug *nt*, Gerät *nt* ▷ [ɪmplɪˈment] *vt* durchführen

implication [ɪmplɪˈkeɪʃən] *n* Folge *f*, Auswirkung *f*; (*logical*) Schlussfolgerung *f*; **implicit** [ɪmˈplɪsɪt] *adj* implizit, unausgesprochen; **imply** [ɪmˈplaɪ] *vt* (*indicate*) andeuten; (*mean*) bedeuten; **are you ~ing that ...** wollen Sie damit sagen, dass ...

impolite [ɪmpəˈlaɪt] *adj* unhöflich

import [ɪmˈpɔːt] *vt* einführen, importieren ▷ *n* [ˈɪmpɔːt] Einfuhr *f*, Import *m*

importance [ɪmˈpɔːtəns] *n* Bedeutung *f*; **of no ~** unwichtig; im-

portant adj wichtig (to sb für jdn); (significant) bedeutend; (influential) einflussreich

import duty ['impɔːtdjuːtɪ] n Einfuhrzoll m; **import licence** n Einfuhrgenehmigung f

impose [im'pəuz] vt (conditions) auferlegen (on dat); (penalty, sanctions) verhängen (on gegen); **imposing** [im'pəuzɪŋ] adj eindrucksvoll, imposant

impossible [im'pɔsəbl] adj unmöglich

impotence ['impətəns] n Machtlosigkeit f; (sexual) Impotenz f; **impotent** adj machtlos; (sexually) impotent

impractical [im'præktɪkl] adj unpraktisch; (plan) undurchführbar

impress [im'pres] vt beeindrucken; **impression** [im'preʃən] n Eindruck m; **impressive** adj eindrucksvoll

imprison [im'prɪzn] vt inhaftieren, **imprisonment** n Inhaftierung f

improbability [improbə'bɪlɪtɪ] n Unwahrscheinlichkeit f; **improbable** [im'prɔbəbl] adj unwahrscheinlich

improper [im'prɔpə*] adj (indecent) unanständig; (use) unsachgemäß

improve [im'pruːv] vt verbessern ▷ vi sich verbessern, besser werden; (patient) Fortschritte machen; **improvement** n Verbesserung f (in +gen, in gegenüber); (in appearance) Verschönerung f

improvise ['imprəvaɪz] vt, vi improvisieren

impulse ['impʌls] n Impuls m; **impulsive** [im'pʌlsɪv] adj impulsiv

in [in] prep in +dat; (expressing motion) in +akk, (in the case of) bei; **put**

it ~ the drawer tu es in die Schublade; **~ the army** beim Militär; **~ itself** an sich; **~ that ...** insofern als ...; (time) **~ the morning / afternoon / evening** am Morgen / Nachmittag / Abend; **at three ~ the afternoon** um drei Uhr nachmittags; **~ 2007** (im Jahre) 2007; **~ July** im Juli; **~ a week** in einer Woche; **~ writing** schriftlich; **~ German** auf Deutsch; **one ~ ten** einer von zehn, jeder zehnte; **~ all** insgesamt ▷ adv (go) hinein; (come) herein; **to be ~** zu Hause sein; (in fashion) in sein, modisch sein; (arrived) angekommen sein; **sb is ~ for sth** jdm steht etw bevor; (sth unpleasant) jmd kann sich auf etw akk gefasst machen; **to be ~ on sth** an etw dat beteiligt sein

inability [inə'bɪlɪtɪ] n Unfähigkeit f

inaccessible [inæk'sesəbl] adj (a. fig) unzugänglich

inaccurate [in'ækjurɪt] adj ungenau

inadequate [in'ædɪkwət] adj unzulänglich

inapplicable [inə'plɪkəbl] adj unzutreffend

inappropriate [inə'prəupriət] adj unpassend; (clothing) ungeeignet; (remark) unangebracht

inborn [in'bɔːn] adj angeboren

incapable [in'keɪpəbl] adj unfähig (of zu); **to be ~ of doing sth** nicht imstande sein, etw zu tun

incense ['insens] n Weihrauch m

incentive [in'sentiv] n Anreiz m

incessant, incessantly [in'sesnt, -lɪ] adj, adv unaufhörlich

incest ['insest] n Inzest m

inch [intʃ] n Zoll m (2,54 cm)

incident ['insɪdənt] n Vorfall m; (disturbance) Zwischenfall m; **incidentally** [insɪ'dentlɪ] adv nebenbei bemerkt, übrigens

inclination [ɪnklɪ'neɪʃən] n Neigung f; **inclined** ['ɪnklaɪnd] adj **to be ~ to do sth** dazu neigen, etw zu tun

include [ɪn'kluːd] vt einschließen; (on list, in group) aufnehmen; **including** prep einschließlich (+gen); **not ~ service** Bedienung nicht inbegriffen; **inclusive** [ɪn'kluːsɪv] adj einschließlich (of +gen); (price) Pauschal-

incoherent [ɪnkəʊ'hɪərənt] adj zusammenhanglos

income ['ɪnkʌm] n Einkommen nt; (from business) Einkünfte pl; **income tax** n Einkommensteuer f; (on wages, salary) Lohnsteuer f; **incoming** ['ɪnkʌmɪŋ] adj ankommend; (mail) eingehend

incompatible [ɪnkəm'pætəbl] adj unvereinbar; (people) unverträglich; (Inform) nicht kompatibel

incompetent [ɪn'kɒmpɪtənt] adj unfähig

incomplete [ɪnkəm'pliːt] adj unvollständig

incomprehensible [ɪnkɒmprɪ'hensəbl] adj unverständlich

inconceivable [ɪnkən'siːvəbl] adj unvorstellbar

inconsiderate [ɪnkən'sɪdərət] adj rücksichtslos

inconsistency [ɪnkən'sɪstənsɪ] n Inkonsequenz f; (contradictory) Widersprüchlichkeit f; **inconsistent** adj inkonsequent; (contradictory) widersprüchlich; (work) unbeständig

inconvenience [ɪnkən'viːnɪəns] n Unannehmlichkeit f; (trouble) Umstände pl; **inconvenient** adj ungünstig, unbequem; (time) **it's ~ for me** es kommt mir ungelegen; **if it's not too ~ for you** wenn es dir passt

incorporate [ɪn'kɔːpəreɪt] vt

aufnehmen (into in +akk); (include) enthalten

incorrect ['ɪnkərekt] adj falsch; (improper) inkorrekt

increase ['ɪnkriːs] n Zunahme f (in an +dat); (in amount, speed) Erhöhung f (in +dat); (in size Vergrößerung f ▷ [ɪn'kriːs] vt (price, taxes, salary, speed etc) erhöhen; (wealth) vermehren; (number) vergrößern; (business) erweitern ▷ vi zunehmen (in an +dat); (prices) steigen; (in size) größer werden; (in number) sich vermehren; **increasingly** [ɪn'kriːsɪŋlɪ] adv zunehmend

incredible, incredibly [ɪn'kredəbl, -blɪ] adj, adv unglaublich; (very good) fantastisch

incredulous [ɪn'kredjʊləs] adj ungläubig, skeptisch

incriminate [ɪn'krɪmɪneɪt] vt belasten

incubator ['ɪnkjʊbeɪtə*] n Brutkasten m

incurable [ɪn'kjʊərəbl] adj unheilbar

indecent [ɪn'diːsnt] adj unanständig

indecisive [ɪndɪ'saɪsɪv] adj (person) unentschlossen; (result) nicht entscheidend

indeed [ɪn'diːd] adv tatsächlich; (as answer) allerdings; **very hot ~** wirklich sehr heiß

indefinite [ɪn'defɪnɪt] adj unbestimmt; **indefinitely** adv endlos; (postpone) auf unbestimmte Zeit

independence [ɪndɪ'pendəns] n Unabhängigkeit f

● **INDEPENDENCE DAY**

● Der **Independence Day**, der 4.
● Juli, ist in den USA ein gesetzlicher
● Feiertag zum Gedenken an die
● Unabhängigkeitserklärung am 4.

Juli 1776, mit der die 13 amerikanischen Kolonien ihre Freiheit und Unabhängigkeit von Großbritannien erklärten.

independent [ɪndɪˈpendənt] adj unabhängig (of von); (person) selbstständig

indescribable [ɪndɪˈskraɪbəbl] adj unbeschreiblich

index ['ɪndeks] n Index m, Verzeichnis nt; **index finger** n Zeigefinger m

India ['ɪndɪə] n Indien nt; **Indian** ['ɪndɪən] adj indisch; (Native American) indianisch ▷ n Inder(in) m(f); (Native American) Indianer(in) m(f); **Indian Ocean** n Indischer Ozean; **Indian summer** n Spätsommer m, Altweibersommer m

indicate ['ɪndɪkeɪt] vt (show) zeigen; (instrument) anzeigen; (suggest) hinweisen auf +akk ▷ vi (Auto) blinken; **Indication** [ɪndɪˈkeɪʃn] n (sign) Anzeichen nt (of für); **indicator** ['ɪndɪkeɪtə*] n (Auto) Blinker m

indifferent [ɪnˈdɪfrənt] adj (not caring) gleichgültig (to, towards gegenüber); (mediocre) mittelmäßig

indigestible [ɪndɪˈdʒestəbl] adj unverdaulich; **indigestion** [ɪndɪˈdʒestʃən] n Verdauungsstörung f

indignity [ɪnˈdɪgnɪtɪ] n Demütigung f

indirect, indirectly [ɪndɪˈrekt, -lɪ] adj, adv indirekt

indiscreet [ɪndɪˈskriːt] adj indiskret

indispensable [ɪndɪˈspensəbl] adj unentbehrlich

indisposed [ɪndɪˈspəʊzd] adj unwohl

indisputable [ɪndɪˈspjuːtəbl] adj unbestreitbar; (evidence) unanfechtbar

individual [ɪndɪˈvɪdjʊəl] n Ein-

zelne(r) m(f) ▷ adj einzeln; (distinctive) eigen, individuell; **~ case** Einzelfall m; **individually** adv (separately) einzeln

Indonesia [ɪndəʊˈniːzjə] n Indonesien nt

indoor ['ɪndɔː*] adj (shoes) Haus-; (plant, games) Zimmer-; (Sport: football, championship, record etc) Hallen-; **indoors** adv drinnen, im Haus

indulge [ɪnˈdʌldʒ] vi **to ~ in sth** sich dat etw gönnen; **indulgence** n Nachsicht f; (enjoyment) (übermäßiger) Genuss; (luxury) Luxus m; **indulgent** adj nachsichtig (with gegenüber)

industrial [ɪnˈdʌstrɪəl] adj Industrie-, industriell; **~ estate** Industriegebiet nt; **industry** ['ɪndəstrɪ] n Industrie f

inedible [ɪnˈedɪbl] adj nicht essbar, ungenießbar

ineffective [ɪnɪˈfektɪv] adj unwirksam, wirkungslos; **inefficient** adj unwirksam; (use, machine) unwirtschaftlich; (method etc) unrationell

ineligible [ɪnˈelɪdʒəbl] adj nicht berechtigt (for zu)

inequality [ɪnɪˈkwɒlɪtɪ] n Ungleichheit f

inevitable [ɪnˈevɪtəbl] adj unvermeidlich; **inevitably** adv zwangsläufig

inexcusable [ɪnɪksˈkjuːzəbl] adj unverzeihlich; **that's ~** das kann man nicht verzeihen

inexpensive [ɪnɪksˈpensɪv] adj preisgünstig

inexperience [ɪnɪksˈpɪərɪəns] n Unerfahrenheit f; **inexperienced** adj unerfahren

inexplicable [ɪnɪksˈplɪkəbl] adj unerklärlich

infallible [ɪnˈfælɪbl] adj unfehlbar

infamous ['ɪnfəməs] *adj* (*person*) berüchtigt (*for wegen*); (*deed*) niederträchtig

infancy ['ɪnfənsɪ] *n* frühe Kindheit; **infant** ['ɪnfənt] *n* Säugling *m*; (*small child*) Kleinkind *nt*; **infant school** *n* Vorschule *f*

infatuated [ɪn'fætjʊeɪtɪd] *adj* vernarrt (*with* in +*akk*), verknallt (*with* in +*akk*)

infect [ɪn'fekt] *vt* (*person*) anstecken; (*wound*) infizieren; **infection** [ɪn'fekʃən] *n* Infektion *f*; **infectious** [ɪn'fekʃəs] *adj* ansteckend

inferior [ɪn'fɪərɪə*] *adj* (*in quality*) minderwertig; (*in rank*) untergeordnet; **inferiority** [ɪnfɪərɪ'ɒrɪtɪ] *n* Minderwertigkeit *f*; **~ complex** Minderwertigkeitskomplex *m*

infertile [ɪn'fɜːtaɪl] *adj* unfruchtbar

infidelity [ɪnfɪ'delɪtɪ] *n* Untreue *f*

infinite ['ɪnfɪnɪt] *adj* unendlich; **infinitive** [ɪn'fɪnɪtɪv] *n* (*Ling*) Infinitiv *m*

infinity [ɪn'fɪnɪtɪ] *n* Unendlichkeit *f*

infirmary [ɪn'fɜːmərɪ] *n* Krankenhaus *nt*

inflame [ɪn'fleɪm] *vt* (*Med*) entzünden; **inflammation** [ɪnflə'meɪʃən] *n* (*Med*) Entzündung *f*

inflatable [ɪn'fleɪtəbl] *adj* aufblasbar; **~ dinghy** Schlauchboot *nt*; **inflate** [ɪn'fleɪt] *vt* aufpumpen; (*by blowing*) aufblasen; (*prices*) hochtreiben

inflation [ɪn'fleɪʃən] *n* Inflation *f*

inflexible [ɪn'fleksəbl] *adj* unflexibel

inflict [ɪn'flɪkt] *vt* **to ~ sth on sb** jdm etw zufügen; (*punishment*) jdm etw auferlegen; (*wound*) jdm etw beibringen

in-flight [ɪn'flaɪt] *adj* (*catering, magazine*) Bord-; **~ entertainment**

Bordprogramm *nt*

influence ['ɪnflʊəns] *n* Einfluss *m* (*on auf* +*akk*) ▷ *vt* beeinflussen; **influential** [ɪnflʊ'enʃəl] *adj* einflussreich

influenza [ɪnflʊ'enzə] *n* Grippe *f*

inform [ɪn'fɔːm] *vt* informieren (*of, about* über +*akk*); **to keep sb ~ed** jdn auf dem Laufenden halten

informal [ɪn'fɔːməl] *adj* zwanglos, ungezwungen

information [ɪnfə'meɪʃən] *n* Auskunft *f*, Informationen *pl*; **for your ~** zu Ihrer Information; **further ~** weitere Informationen, weiteres; **information desk** *n* Auskunftsschalter *m*; **information technology** *n* Informationstechnik *f*; **informative** [ɪn'fɔːmətɪv] *adj* aufschlussreich

infra-red ['ɪnfrə'red] *adj* infrarot

infrastructure *n* Infrastruktur *f*

infuriate [ɪn'fjʊərɪeɪt] *vt* wütend machen; **infuriating** *adj* äußerst ärgerlich

infusion [ɪn'fjuːʒən] *n* (*herbal tea*) Aufguss *m*; (*Med*) Infusion *f*

ingenious [ɪn'dʒiːnɪəs] *adj* (*person*) erfinderisch; (*device*) raffiniert; (*idea*) genial

ingredient [ɪn'griːdɪənt] *n* (*Gastr*) Zutat *f*

inhabit [ɪn'hæbɪt] *vt* bewohnen; **inhabitant** *n* Einwohner(in) *m(f)*

inhale [ɪn'heɪl] *vt* einatmen; (*cigarettes, Med*) inhalieren; **inhaler** *n* Inhalationsgerät *nt*

inherit [ɪn'herɪt] *vt* erben; **inheritance** *n* Erbe *nt*

inhibited [ɪn'hɪbɪtɪd] *adj* gehemmt; **inhibition** [ɪnhɪ'bɪʃən] *n* Hemmung *f*

in-house [ɪn'haʊs] *adj* intern

inhuman [ɪn'hjuːmən] *adj* unmenschlich

initial [ɪ'nɪʃəl] *adj* anfänglich; **~**

stage Anfangsstadium nt ▷ vt mit Initialen unterschreiben; **initially** adv anfangs; **initials** npl Initialen pl

initiative [ɪˈnɪʃətɪv] n Initiative f

inject [ɪnˈdʒekt] vt (drug etc) einspritzen; **to ~ sb with sth** jdm etw (ein)spritzen; **injection** n ʃpritze f, Injektion f

in-joke [ˈɪndʒəʊk] n Insiderwitz m

injure [ˈɪndʒə*] vt verletzen; **to ~ one's leg** sich dat das Bein verletzen; **injury** n Verletzung f

injustice [ɪnˈdʒʌstɪs] n Ungerechtigkeit f

ink [ɪŋk] n Tinte f; **ink-jet printer** n Tintenstrahldrucker m

inland [ˈɪnlənd] adj Binnen- ▷ adv landeinwärts; **inland revenue** n (BRIT) Finanzamt nt

in-laws [ˈɪnlɔ:z] npl (fam) Schwiegereltern pl

inline skates [ˈɪnlaɪnskeɪts] npl Inlineskates pl, Inliner pl

inmate [ˈɪnmeɪt] n Insasse m

inn [ɪn] n Gasthaus nt

innate [ɪˈneɪt] adj angeboren

inner [ˈɪnə*] adj innere(r, s); **~ city** Innenstadt f

innocence [ˈɪnəsns] n Unschuld f; **innocent** adj unschuldig

innovation [ɪnəʊˈveɪʃən] n Neuerung f

innumerable [ɪˈnju:mərəbl] adj unzählig

inoculate [ɪˈnɒkjʊleɪt] vt impfen (against gegen); **inoculation** [ɪnɒkjʊˈleɪʃən] n Impfung f

in-patient [ˈɪnpeɪʃnt] n stationärer Patient, stationäre Patientin

input [ˈɪnpʊt] n (contribution) Beitrag m; (Inform) Eingabe f

inquest [ˈɪnkwest] n gerichtliche Untersuchung (einer Todesursache)

inquire [ɪnˈkwaɪə*] see **enquire**; **inquiry** [ɪnˈkwaɪərɪ] see **enquiry**

insane [ɪnˈseɪn] adj wahnsinnig; (Med) geisteskrank; **insanity** [ɪnˈsænɪtɪ] n Wahnsinn m

insatiable [ɪnˈseɪʃəbl] adj unersättlich

inscription [ɪnˈskrɪpʃən] n (on stone etc) Inschrift f

insect [ˈɪnsekt] n Insekt nt; **insecticide** n [ɪnˈsektɪsaɪd] n Insektenbekämpfungsmittel nt; **insect repellent** n Insektenschutzmittel nt

insecure [ɪnsɪˈkjʊə*] adj (person) unsicher; (shelves) instabil

insensitive [ɪnˈsensɪtɪv] adj unempfindlich (to gegen); (unfeeling) gefühllos; **insensitivity** [ɪnsensɪˈtɪvɪtɪ] n Unempfindlichkeit f (to gegen); (unfeeling nature) Gefühllosigkeit f

inseparable [ɪnˈsepərəbl] adj unzertrennlich

insert [ɪnˈsɜ:t] vt einfügen; (coin) einwerfen; (key etc) hineinstecken ▷ n (in magazine) Beilage f; **insertion** n (in text) Einfügen nt

inside [ɪnˈsaɪd] n **the ~** das Innere; (surface) die Innenseite; **from the ~** von innen ▷ adj innere(r, s), Innen-; **~ lane** (Aut) Innenspur f; (Sport) Innenbahn f ▷ adv (place) innen; (direction) hinein; **to go ~** hineingehen ▷ prep (place) in +dat; (into) in +akk ... hinein; (time, within) innerhalb +gen; **inside out** adv verkehrt herum; (know) in- und auswendig; **insider** n Eingeweihte(r) mf, Insider(in) m(f)

insight [ˈɪnsaɪt] n Einblick m (into in +akk)

insignificant [ɪnsɪgˈnɪfɪkənt] adj unbedeutend

insincere [ɪnsɪnˈsɪə*] adj unaufrichtig, falsch

insinuate [ɪnˈsɪnjʊeɪt] vt andeuten; **insinuation** [ɪnsɪnjʊˈeɪʃən] n

Andeutung f
insist [ɪnˈsɪst] vi darauf bestehen;
to ~ on sth auf etw dat bestehen;
insistent adj hartnäckig
insoluble [ɪnˈsɒljʊbl] adj unlösbar
insomnia [ɪnˈsɒmnɪə] n Schlaflosigkeit f
inspect [ɪnˈspekt] vt prüfen, kontrollieren; **inspection** n Prüfung f; (check) Kontrolle f; **inspector** n (police ~) Inspektor(in) m(f); (senior) Kommissar(in) m(f); (on bus etc) Kontrolleur(in) m(f)
inspiration [ɪnspɪˈreɪʃən] n Inspiration f; **inspire** [ɪnˈspaɪə*] vt (respect) einflößen (in dat); (person) inspirieren
install [ɪnˈstɔːl] vt (software) installieren; (furnishings) einbauen
installment, instalment [ɪnˈstɔːlmənt] n Rate f; (of story) Folge f; **to pay in ~s** auf Raten zahlen; **installment plan** n (US) Ratenkauf m
instance [ˈɪnstəns] n (of discrimination) Fall m; (example) Beispiel nt; **for ~** zum Beispiel
instant [ˈɪnstənt] n Augenblick m ▷ adj sofortig; **instant coffee** n Instantkaffee m; **instantly** adv sofort
instead [ɪnˈsted] adv stattdessen; **instead of** prep (an)statt +gen; ~ **of me** an meiner Stelle; ~ **of going** (an)statt zu gehen
instinct [ˈɪnstɪŋkt] n Instinkt m; **instinctive, instinctively** [ɪnˈstɪŋktɪv, -lɪ] adj, adv instinktiv
institute [ˈɪnstɪtjuːt] n Institut nt; **institution** [ɪnstɪˈtjuːʃən] n (organisation) Institution f, Einrichtung f; (home) Anstalt f
instruct [ɪnˈstrʌkt] vt anweisen; **instruction** [ɪnˈstrʌkʃən] n (teaching) Unterricht m; (command)

Anweisung f; **~s for use** Gebrauchsanweisung f; **instructor** n Lehrer(in) m(f); (US) Dozent(in) m(f)
instrument [ˈɪnstrʊmənt] n Instrument nt; **instrument panel** n Armaturenbrett nt
insufficient [ɪnsəˈfɪʃənt] adj ungenügend
insulate [ˈɪnsjʊleɪt] vt (Elec) isolieren; **insulating tape** n Isolierband nt; **insulation** [ɪnsjʊˈleɪʃən] n Isolierung f
insulin [ˈɪnsjʊlɪn] n Insulin nt
insult [ˈɪnsʌlt] n Beleidigung f ▷ [ɪnˈsʌlt] vt beleidigen; **insulting** [ɪnˈsʌltɪŋ] adj beleidigend
insurance [ɪnˈʃʊərəns] n Versicherung f; **~ company** Versicherungsgesellschaft f; **~ policy** Versicherungspolice f; **insure** [ɪnˈʃʊə*] vt versichern (against gegen)
intact [ɪnˈtækt] adj intakt
intake [ˈɪnteɪk] n Aufnahme f
integrate [ˈɪntɪgreɪt] vt integrieren (into in +akk); **integration** n Integration f
integrity [ɪnˈtegrɪtɪ] n Integrität f, Ehrlichkeit f
intellect [ˈɪntɪlekt] n Intellekt m; **intellectual** [ɪntɪˈlektjʊəl] adj intellektuell; (interests etc) geistig
intelligence [ɪnˈtelɪdʒəns] n (understanding) Intelligenz f; **intelligent** adj intelligent
intend [ɪnˈtend] vt beabsichtigen; **to ~ to do sth** vorhaben, etw zu tun
intense [ɪnˈtens] adj intensiv; (pressure) enorm; (competition) heftig; **intensity** n Intensität f; **intensive** adj intensiv; **intensive care unit** n Intensivstation f; **intensive course** n Intensivkurs m
intent [ɪnˈtent] n Absicht f; **to be ~ on doing sth** fest entschlossen sein, etw zu tun; **intention** [ɪnˈtenʃən] n Absicht f; **intentional, inten-**

tionally *adj, adv* absichtlich

interact [ɪntər'ækt] *vi* aufeinander einwirken; **interaction** *n* Interaktion *f*, Wechselwirkung *f*; **interactive** *adj* interaktiv

interchange ['ɪntətʃeɪndʒ] *n* (*of motorways*) Autobahnkreuz *nt*; **interchangeable** [ɪntə'tʃeɪndʒəbl] *adj* austauschbar

intercity [ɪntə'sɪtɪ] *n* Intercityzug *m*, IC *m*

intercom ['ɪntəkɒm] *n* (*Gegen*)sprechanlage *f*

intercourse ['ɪntəkɔːs] *n* (*sexual*) Geschlechtsverkehr *m*

interest ['ɪntrest] *n* Interesse *nt*; (*Fin: on money*) Zinsen *pl*; (*Comm: share*) Anteil *m*; **to be of ~** von Interesse sein (to für) *b vt* interessieren; **interested** *adj* interessiert (*in an +dat*); **to be ~ed in** sich interessieren für; **are you ~ in coming?** hast du Lust, mitzukommen?; **interest-free** *adj* zinsfrei; **interesting** *adj* interessant; **interest rate** *n* Zinssatz *m*

interface ['ɪntəfeɪs] *n* (*Inform*) Schnittstelle *f*

interfere [ɪntə'fɪə*] *vi* (*meddle*) sich einmischen (with, in in +akk); **interference** *n* Einmischung *f*; (*TV, Radio*) Störung *f*

interior [ɪn'tɪərɪə*] *adj* Innen- *b n* Innere(s) *nt*; (*of car*) Innenraum *m*; (*of house*) Innenausstattung *f*

intermediate [ɪntə'miːdɪət] *adj* Zwischen-; **~ stage** Zwischenstadium *nt*

intermission [ɪntə'mɪʃən] *n* Pause *f*

intern [ɪn'tɜːn] *n* Assistent(in) *m(f)*

internal [ɪn'tɜːnl] *adj* innere(r, s); (*flight*) Inlands-; **~ revenue** (*US*) Finanzamt *nt*, **internally** *adv* innen; (*in body*) innerlich

international [ɪntə'næʃnəl] *adj* international; **~ match** Länderspiel *nt*; **~ flight** Auslandsflug *m* *b n* (*Sport: player*) Nationalspieler(in) *m(f)*

Internet ['ɪntənet] *n* (*Inform*) Internet *nt*; **Internet banking** *n* Onlinebanking *nt*; **Internet café** *n* Internetcafé *nt*; **Internet provider** *n* Internetprovider *m*

interpret [ɪn'tɜːprɪt] *vi, vt* (*translate*) dolmetschen; (*explain*) interpretieren; **interpretation** [ɪntɜːprɪ'teɪʃən] *n* Interpretation *f*; **interpreter** [ɪn'tɜːprɪtə*] *n* Dolmetscher(in) *m(f)*

interrogate [ɪn'terəgeɪt] *vt* verhören; **interrogation** *n* Verhör *nt*

interrupt [ɪntə'rʌpt] *vt* unterbrechen; **interruption** [ɪntə'rʌpʃən] *n* Unterbrechung *f*

intersection [ɪntə'sekʃən] *n* (*of roads*) Kreuzung *f*

interstate [ɪntə'steɪt] *n* (*US*) zwischenstaatlich; **~ highway** ≈ Bundesautobahn *f*

interval ['ɪntəvəl] *n* (*space, time*) Abstand *m*; (*theatre etc*) Pause *f*

intervene [ɪntə'viːn] *vi* eingreifen (in in); **intervention** [ɪntə'venʃən] *n* Eingreifen *nt*; (*Pol*) Intervention *f*

interview ['ɪntəvjuː] *n* Interview *nt*; (*for job*) Vorstellungsgespräch *nt* *b vt* interviewen; (*job applicant*) ein Vorstellungsgespräch führen mit; **interviewer** *n* Interviewer(in) *m(f)*

intestine [ɪn'testɪn] *n* Darm *m*; **~s** *pl* Eingeweide *pl*

intimate ['ɪntɪmət] *adj* (*friends*) vertraut, eng; (*atmosphere*) gemütlich; (*sexually*) intim

intimidate [ɪn'tɪmɪdeɪt] *vt* einschüchtern; **intimidation** *n* Einschüchterung *f*

into ['ɪntə] *prep* in +akk; (*crash*) gegen; **to change ~ sth** (*turn ~*) zu etw werden; (put on) sich dat etw anziehen; **to translate ~ French** ins Französische übersetzen; **to be ~ sth** (fam) auf etw akk stehen

intolerable [ɪnˈtɒlərəbl] adj unerträglich

intolerant [ɪnˈtɒlərənt] adj intolerant

intoxicated [ɪnˈtɒksɪkeɪtɪd] adj betrunken; (fig) berauscht

intricate [ˈɪntrɪkət] adj kompliziert

intrigue [ɪnˈtriːg] vt faszinieren; **intriguing** adj faszinierend, fesselnd

introduce [ɪntrəˈdjuːs] vt (person) vorstellen (to sb jdm); (sth new) einführen (to in +akk); **introduction** [ɪntrəˈdʌkʃən] n Einführung f (to in +akk); (to book) Einleitung f (to zu); (to person) Vorstellung f

introvert [ˈɪntrəʊvɜːt] n Introvertierte(r) mf

intuition [ɪntjuːˈɪʃn] n Intuition f

invade [ɪnˈveɪd] vt einfallen in +akk

invalid [ˈɪnvəlɪd] n Kranke(r) mf; (disabled) Invalide m ▷ adj [ɪnˈvælɪd] (not valid) ungültig

invaluable [ɪnˈvæljʊəbl] adj äußerst wertvoll, unschätzbar

invariably [ɪnˈvɛərɪəblɪ] adv ständig; (every time) jedes Mal, ohne Ausnahme

invasion [ɪnˈveɪʒən] n Invasion f (of in +akk), Einfall m (of in +akk)

invent [ɪnˈvent] vt erfinden; **invention** [ɪnˈvenʃən] n Erfindung f; **inventor** n Erfinder(in) m(f)

inverted commas [ɪnˈvɜːtɪd ˈkɒmæz] npl Anführungszeichen pl

invest [ɪnˈvest] vt, vi investieren (in in +akk)

investigate [ɪnˈvestɪgeɪt] vt untersuchen; **investigation** [ɪnvestɪˈgeɪʃən] n Untersuchung f (into

+gen)

investment [ɪnˈvestmənt] n Investition f; (it'll be useful) es ist eine gute Anlage; (it'll be useful) es macht sich bezahlt

invigorating [ɪnˈvɪgəreɪtɪŋ] adj erfrischend, belebend; (tonic) stärkend

invisible [ɪnˈvɪzəbl] adj unsichtbar

invitation [ɪnvɪˈteɪʃən] n Einladung f; **invite** [ɪnˈvaɪt] vt einladen

invoice [ˈɪnvɔɪs] n (bill) Rechnung f

involuntary [ɪnˈvɒləntərɪ] adj unbeabsichtigt

involve [ɪnˈvɒlv] vt verwickeln (in sth in etw akk); (entail) zur Folge haben; **to be ~d in sth** (participate in) an etw dat beteiligt sein; **I'm not ~d** (affected) ich bin nicht betroffen

inward [ˈɪnwəd] adj innere(r, s); **inwardly** adv innerlich; **inwards** adv nach innen

iodine [ˈaɪədiːn] n Jod nt

IOU [aɪəʊˈjuː] abbr = **I owe you** Schuldschein m

IQ abbr = **intelligence quotient** IQ m

Iran [ɪˈrɑːn] n der Iran

Iraq [ɪˈrɑːk] n der Irak

Ireland [ˈaɪələnd] n Irland nt

iris [ˈaɪrɪs] n (flower) Schwertlilie f; (of eye) Iris f

Irish [ˈaɪrɪʃ] adj irisch; **~ coffee** Irishcoffee m; **~ Sea** die Irische See ▷ n (language) Irisch nt; **the ~** pl die Iren pl; **Irishman** (pl **-men**) n Ire m; **Irishwoman** (pl **-women**) n Irin f

iron [ˈaɪən] n Eisen nt; (for ironing) Bügeleisen nt ▷ adj eisern ▷ vt bügeln

ironic(al) [aɪˈrɒnɪk(əl)] adj ironisch

ironing board n Bügelbrett nt

irony [ˈaɪrənɪ] n Ironie f

irrational [ɪˈræʃənl] *adj* irrational

irregular [ɪˈregjʊlə*] *adj* unregelmäßig; *(shape)* ungleichmäßig

irrelevant [ɪˈreləvənt] *adj* belanglos, irrelevant

irreplaceable [ɪrɪˈpleɪsəbl] *adj* unersetzlich

irresistible [ɪrɪˈzɪstəbl] *adj* unwiderstehlich

irrespective of [ɪrɪˈspektɪv ɒv] *prep* ungeachtet +*gen*

irresponsible [ɪrɪˈspɒnsəbl] *adj* verantwortungslos

irretrievable [ɪrɪˈtriːvəbl] *adv* unwiederbringlich; *(loss)* unersetzlich

irritable [ˈɪrɪtəbl] *adj* reizbar; **irritate** [ˈɪrɪteɪt] *vt* *(annoy)* ärgern; *(deliberately)* reizen; **irritation** [ɪrɪˈteɪʃən] *n* *(anger)* Ärger *m*; *(Med)* Reizung *f*

IRS *abbr* = **Internal Revenue Service** *(US)* Finanzamt *nt*

is [ɪz] *present of* **be** ist

Islam [ˈɪzlɑːm] *n* Islam *m*; **Islamic** [ɪzˈlæmɪk] *adj* islamisch

island [ˈaɪlənd] *n* Insel *f*; **Isle** [aɪl] *n* *(in names)* the ~ **of Man** die Insel Man; **the ~ of Wight** die Insel Wight; **the British ~s** die Britischen Inseln

isn't [ˈɪznt] *contr of* **is not**

isolate [ˈaɪsəleɪt] *vt* isolieren; **isolated** *adj* *(remote)* abgelegen; *(cut off)* abgeschnitten *(from von)*; **an ~ case** ein Einzelfall; **isolation** [aɪsəˈleɪʃən] *n* Isolierung *f*

Israel [ˈɪzreɪl] *n* Israel *nt*; **Israeli** [ɪzˈreɪlɪ] *adj* israelisch ▷ *n* Israeli *m* o *f*

issue [ˈɪʃuː] *n* *(matter)* Frage *f*; *(problem)* Problem *nt*; *(subject)* Thema *nt*; *(of newspaper etc)* Ausgabe *f*; **that's not the ~** darum geht es nicht ▷ *vt* ausgeben; *(document)* ausstellen; *(orders)* erteilen; *(book)*

herausgeben

it [ɪt] *pron* *(as subject)* er / sie / es; *(as direct object)* ihn / sie / es; *(as indirect object)* ihm / ihr / ihm; **the worst thing about ~** das Schlimmste daran; **what is ~? - ~'s me / ~'s him** wer ist da? - ich bin's / er ist's; **~ 's your turn** du bist dran; **~ was she who went** sie war es, die gegangen ist; **that's ~** ja genau, **~'s raining** es regnet; **~'s Charlie here** hier spricht Charlie

IT *abbr* = **information technology** IT *f*

Italian [ɪˈtæljən] *adj* italienisch ▷ *n* Italiener(in) *m(f)*; *(language)* Italienisch *nt*

italic [ɪˈtælɪk] *adj* kursiv ▷ *npl* **in ~s** kursiv

Italy [ˈɪtəlɪ] *n* Italien *nt*

itch [ɪtʃ] *n* Juckreiz *m*; **I have an ~** mich juckt es ▷ *vi* jucken; **he is ~ing to ...** es juckt ihn, zu ...; **itchy** *adj* juckend

it'd [ˈɪtd] *contr of* **it would; it had**

item [ˈaɪtəm] *n* *(article)* Gegenstand *m*, *(in catalogue)* Artikel *m*; *(in accounts)* Posten *m*; *(on agenda)* Punkt *m*, *(in show programme)* Nummer *f*; *(in news)* Bericht *m*; *(Tv: radio)* Meldung *f*

itinerary [aɪˈtɪnərərɪ] *n* Reise route *f*

it'll [ˈɪtl] *contr of* **it will; it shall**

its [ɪts] *pron* sein; *(feminine form)* ihr

it's [ɪts] *contr of* **it is; it has**

itself [ɪtˈself] *pron* *(reflexive)* sich; *(emphatic)* **the house ~ is OK** das Haus selbst o an sich ist in Ordnung; **by ~** allein; **the door closes (by) ~** die Tür schließt sich von selbst

I've [aɪv] *contr of* **I have**

ivory [ˈaɪvərɪ] *n* Elfenbein *nt*

ivy [ˈaɪvɪ] *n* Efeu *m*

J

jab [dʒæb] vt (needle, knife) stechen
(into in +akk) ▷ n (fam) Spritze f

jack [dʒæk] n (Auto) Wagenheber
m; (Cards) Bube m; **jack in** vt (fam)
aufgeben, hinschmeißen; **jack up**
vt (car etc) aufbocken

jacket [dʒækɪt] n Jacke f; (of man's
suit) Jackett nt; (of book) Schutzumschlag m; **jacket potato** (pl **-es**) n
(in der Schale) gebackene Kartoffel

jack-knife [dʒæknaɪf] (pl **jack-
knives**) n Klappmesser nt ▷ vi
(truck) sich quer stellen

jackpot [dʒækpɒt] n Jackpot m

jacuzzi [dʒəˈkuːzɪ] n (bath)
Whirlpool® m

jail [dʒeɪl] n Gefängnis nt ▷ vt
einsperren

jam [dʒæm] n Konfitüre f, Marmelade f; (traffic ~) Stau m ▷ vt
(street) verstopfen; (machine) blockieren; **to be ~med** (stuck) klemmen; **to ~ on the brakes** eine
Vollbremsung machen

Jamaica [dʒəˈmeɪkə] n Jamaika nt

jam-packed adj proppenvoll

janitor [dʒænɪtəˈ] n (US) Haus-
meister(in) m(f)

Jan abbr = **January** Jan

January [dʒænjʊərɪ] n Januar m

Japan [dʒəˈpæn] n Japan nt; **Japanese** [dʒæpəˈniːz] adj japanisch
▷ n (person) Japaner(in) m(f); (language) Japanisch nt

jar [dʒɑːˈ] n Glas nt

jaundice [dʒɔːndɪs] n Gelbsucht f

javelin [dʒævlɪn] n Speer m;
(Sport) Speerwerfen nt

jaw [dʒɔː] n Kiefer m

jazz [dʒæz] n Jazz m

jealous [dʒeləs] adj eifersüchtig
(of auf +akk); **don't make me ~**
mach mich nicht neidisch; **jealousy** n Eifersucht f

jeans [dʒiːnz] npl Jeans pl

jeep® [dʒiːp] n Jeep® m

jelly [dʒelɪ] n Gelee nt; (on meat)
Gallert nt; (dessert) Götterspeise f;
(US: jam) Marmelade f; **jelly baby**
n (sweet) Gummibärchen nt; **jellyfish**
n Qualle f

jeopardize [dʒepədaɪz] vt gefährden

jerk [dʒɜːk] n Ruck m; (fam: idiot)
Trottel m ▷ vt ruckartig bewegen ▷
vi (rope) rucken; (muscles) zucken

Jerusalem [dʒəˈruːsələm] n Jerusalem nt

jet [dʒet] n (of water etc) Strahl m;
(nozzle) Düse f; (aircraft) Düsenflugzeug nt; **jet foil** n Tragflächenboot
nt; **jetlag** n Jetlag m (Müdigkeit nach
langem Flug)

jetty [dʒetɪ] n Landesteg m;
(larger) Landungsbrücke f

Jew [dʒuː] n Jude m, Jüdin f

jewel [dʒuːəl] n Edelstein m; (esp
fig) Juwel nt; **jeweller, jeweler** (US)
n Juwelier(in) m(f); **jewellery, jew-
elery** (US) n Schmuck m

Jewish [dʒuːɪʃ] adj jüdisch; **she's**

ala lat Jädln

jigsaw (puzzle) [ˈdʒɪgsɔː(ˈpʌzl)]
n Puzzle nt

jilt [dʒɪlt] vt den Laufpass geben
+dat

jingle [ˈdʒɪŋgl] n (advert) Jingle m;
(verse) Reim m

jitters [ˈdʒɪtərz] npl (fam) **to have
the ~** Bammel haben; **jittery** adj
(fam) ganz nervös

job [dʒɒb] n (piece of work) Arbeit f;
(task) Aufgabe f; (occupation) Stellung
f, Job m; **what's your ~?** was machen Sie beruflich?; **it's a good ~
you did that** gut, dass du das gemacht hast; **job-hunting** n **to go ~**
auf Arbeitssuche gehen; **jobless** adj arbeitslos; **job seeker** n Arbeitssu-
chende(r) mf; **jobseeker's allowance** n Arbeitslosengeld n; **job-
-sharing** n Arbeitsplatzteilung f

jockey [ˈdʒɒkɪ] n Jockey m

jog [dʒɒg] vt (person) anstoßen ▷ vi
(run) joggen; **jogging** n Jogging
nt; **to go ~** joggen gehen

john [dʒɒn] n (US fam) Klo nt

join [dʒɔɪn] vt (put together) verbinden; (club etc) beitreten
+dat; **to ~ sb** sich jdm anschließen;
(sit with) sich zu jdm setzen ▷ vi
(unite) sich vereinigen; (rivers) zu-
sammenfließen ▷ n Verbindungsstelle f; (seam) Naht f; **join in** vi, vt
mitmachen (sth bei etw)

joinery [ˈdʒɔɪnərɪ] n Schreinerei f

joint [dʒɔɪnt] n (of bones) Gelenk
nt; (in pipe etc) Verbindungsstelle f; (of
meat) Braten m; (of marijuana) Joint m
▷ adj gemeinsam; **joint account**
n Gemeinschaftskonto nt; **jointly**
adv gemeinsam

joke [dʒəʊk] n Witz m; (prank)
Streich m; **for a ~** zum Spaß; **it's no
~** das ist nicht zum Lachen ▷ vi

Witze machen; **you must be joking**
das ist ja wohl nicht dein Ernst!

jolly [ˈdʒɒlɪ] adj lustig, vergnügt

Jordan [ˈdʒɔːdən] n (country) Jordanien nt; (river) Jordan m

jot down [dʒɒt daʊn] vt sich
notieren; **jotter** n Notizbuch nt

journal [ˈdʒɜːnl] n (diary) Tagebuch nt; (magazine) Zeitschrift f;
journalism n Journalismus m;
journalist n Journalist(in) m(f)

journey [ˈdʒɜːnɪ] n Reise f; (esp on
stage, by car, train) Fahrt f

joy [dʒɔɪ] n Freude f (at über +akk);
joystick n (Inform) Joystick m; (Aviat)
Steuerknüppel m

judge [dʒʌdʒ] n Richter(in) m(f);
(Sport) Punktrichter(in) m(f) ▷ vt
beurteilen (by nach); **as far as I can
~** meinem Urteil nach ▷ vi urteilen
(by nach); **judg(e)ment** n (of law-
teil nt; (opinion) Ansicht f; **an error of
~** Fehleinschätzung f

judo [ˈdʒuːdəʊ] n Judo nt

jug [dʒʌg] n Krug m

juggle [ˈdʒʌgl] vi (lit, fig) jonglieren
(with mit)

juice [dʒuːs] n Saft m; **juicy** adj
saftig; (story, scandal) pikant

July [dʒuːˈlaɪ] n Juli m; see also
September

jumble [ˈdʒʌmbl] n Durcheinander nt ▷ vt **to ~ (up)** durcheinander
werfen; (facts) durcheinander bringen; **jumble sale** n (for charity)
Wohltätigkeitsbasar m

jumbo [ˈdʒʌmbəʊ] adj (sausage
etc) Riesen-; **jumbo jet** n Jumbojet
m

jump [dʒʌmp] vi springen; (nerv-
ously) zusammenzucken; **to ~ to
conclusions** voreilige Schlüsse ziehen; **to ~ from one thing to another** dauernd das Thema wechseln
▷ vt (a. fig: omit) überspringen; **to ~
the lights** bei Rot über die Kreuzung

fahren; **to ~ the queue** sich vor-
drängen ▷ n Sprung m; (for horses)
Hindernis nt; **jumper** n Pullover m;
(US: dress) Trägerkleid nt; (person,
horse) Springer(in) m(f); **jumper cables** npl (US), **jump leads** npl
(BRIT Auto) Starthilfekabel nt

junction ['dʒʌŋkʃən] n (of roads)
Kreuzung f; (Rail) Knotenpunkt m

June [dʒuːn] n Juni m; see also
September

jungle ['dʒʌŋgl] n Dschungel m

junior ['dʒuːnɪə*] adj (younger)
jünger; (lower position) untergeordnet (to sb jdm) ▷ n **she's two years
my ~** sie ist zwei Jahre jünger als ich;
junior high (school) n (US) ≈
Mittelschule f; **junior school** n
(BRIT) Grundschule f

junk [dʒʌŋk] n (trash) Plunder m;
junkfood n Nahrungsmittel pl mit
geringem Nährwert, Junkfood nt;
junkie n (fam) Junkie m, Fixer(in)
m(f); (fig: fan) Freak m; **junk mail** n
Reklame f; (Inform) Junkmail f; **junk
shop** n Trödelladen m

jury ['dʒʊərɪ] n Geschworene pl;
(in competition) Jury f

just [dʒʌst] adj gerecht ▷ adv
(recently) gerade; (exactly) genau; **~
as expected** genau wie erwartet; **~
as nice** genauso nett; (barely) **~ in
time** gerade noch rechtzeitig; (immediately) **~ before / after ...** gleich
vor / nach ...; (small distance) **~
round the corner** gleich um die
Ecke; (a little) **~ over an hour** etwas
mehr als eine Stunde; (only) **~ the
two of us** nur wir beide; **~ a moment** Moment mal; (absolutely,
simply) **it was ~ fantastic** es war
einfach klasse; **~ about** so etwa;
(more or less) mehr oder weniger; **~
about ready** fast fertig

justice ['dʒʌstɪs] n Gerechtigkeit
f; **justifiable** [dʒʌstɪ'faɪəbl] adj

berechtigt; **justifiably** adv zu
Recht; **justify** ['dʒʌstɪfaɪ] vt
rechtfertigen

jut [dʒʌt] vi **to ~ (out)** herausragen

juvenile ['dʒuːvənaɪl] n adj Ju-
gend-, jugendlich ▷ n Jugendli-
che(r) mf

K

k *abbr* = **thousand**; **15k** 15 000

K *abbr* = **kilobyte** KB

kangaroo [kæŋgə'ru:] *n* Känguru nt

karaoke [kærɪ'aʊkɪ] *n* Karaoke nt

karate [kə'rɑ:tɪ] *n* Karate nt

kart [kɑ:t] *n* Gokart m

kayak ['kaɪæk] *n* Kajak m o nt

Kazakhstan [kæzæk'stɑ:n] *n* Kasachstan nt

kebab [kə'bæb] *n* (shish ~) Schaschlik m o nt; (doner ~) Kebab m

keel [ki:l] *n* (Naut) Kiel m; **keel over** *vi* (boat) kentern; (person) umkippen

keen [ki:n] *adj* begeistert (on von); (hardworking) eifrig; (mind, wind) scharf; (interest, feeling) stark; **to be ~ on sb** von jdm angetan sein; **she's ~ on riding** sie reitet gern; **to be ~ to do sth** darauf erpicht sein, etw zu tun

keep [ki:p] (kept, kept) *vt* (retain) behalten; (secret) für sich behalten; (observe) einhalten; (promise) halten; (run: shop, diary, accounts) führen; (animals) halten; (support, family etc) unterhalten, versorgen; (store) aufbewahren; **to ~ sb waiting** jdn warten lassen; **to ~ sb from doing sth** jdn davon abhalten, etw zu tun; **to ~ sth clean/secret** etw sauber/geheim halten; **'~ clear'** (bitte) freihalten'; **~ this to yourself** behalten Sie das für sich ▷ *vi* (food) sich halten; (remain: with adj) bleiben; **~ quiet** sei ruhig!; **~ left** links fahren; **to ~ doing sth** (repeatedly) etw immer wieder tun; (continuously) etw am laufen halten; **to ~ at it** mach weiter so!; **it ~s happening** es passiert immer wieder ▷ *n* (livelihood) Unterhalt m; **keep back** *vi* zurückbleiben ▷ *vt* zurückhalten; (information) verschweigen (from sb jdm); **keep off** *vt* (person, animal) fernhalten; **'~ off the grass'** 'Betreten des Rasens verboten'; **keep on** *vi* weitermachen; (walking) weitergehen; (in car) weiterfahren; **to ~ doing sth** (persistently) etw immer wieder tun ▷ *vt* (coat etc) anbehalten; **keep out** *vt* nicht hereinlassen ▷ *vi* draußen bleiben; **~ (on sign)** Eintritt verboten; **keep to** *vt* (road, path) bleiben auf +dat; (plan etc) sich halten an +akk; **to ~ the point** bei der Sache bleiben; **keep up** *vi* Schritt halten (with mit) ▷ *vt* (maintain) aufrechterhalten; (speed) halten; **to ~ appearances** den Schein wahren; **keep it up!** (fam) weiter so!

keeper *n* (museum etc) Aufseher(in) m(f); (goal~) Torwart m; (zoo ~) Tierpfleger(in) m(f); **keep-fit** *n* Fitnesstraining nt; **~ exercises** Gymnastik f

kennel ['kɛnl] *n* Hundehütte f; **kennels** *n* Hundepension f

Kenya ['kɛnjə] *n* Kenia nt

kept [kɛpt] *pt, pp of* **keep**

kerb ['kɜ:b] *n* Randstein m

kerosene ['kɛrəsi:n] *n* (US) Petroleum nt

ketchup ['kɛtʃʌp] *n* Ket(s)chup nt

o m

kettle ['ketl] n Kessel m

key [ki:] n Schlüssel m; (of piano, computer) Taste f; (Mus) Tonart f; (for map etc) Zeichenerklärung f ▷ vt **to ~ (in)** (Inform) eingeben ▷ adj entscheidend; **keyboard** n (piano, computer) Tastatur f; **keyhole** n Schlüsselloch nt; **keypad** n (Inform) Nummernblock m; **keyring** n Schlüsselring m

kick [kɪk] n Tritt m; (Sport) Stoß m; **I get a ~ out of it** (fam) es turnt mich an ▷ vt, vi treten; **kick out** vt (fam) rausschmeißen (of aus); **kick-off** n (Sport) Anstoß m

kid [kɪd] n (child) Kind nt ▷ vt (tease) auf den Arm nehmen ▷ vi Witze machen; **you're ~ding** das ist doch nicht dein Ernst!; **no ~ding** aber echt!

kidnap ['kɪdnæp] vt entführen; **kidnapper** n Entführer(in) m(f); **kidnapping** n Entführung f

kidney ['kɪdnɪ] n Niere f; **kidney machine** n künstliche Niere

kill [kɪl] vt töten; (esp intentionally) umbringen; (weeds) vernichten; **killer** n Mörder(in) m(f)

kilo ['ki:ləʊ] (pl **-s**) n Kilo nt; **kilobyte** n Kilobyte nt; **kilogramme** n Kilogramm nt; **kilometer** (US), **kilometre** n Kilometer m; **~s per hour** Stundenkilometer pl; **kilowatt** n Kilowatt nt

kilt [kɪlt] n Schottenrock m

kind [kaɪnd] adj nett, freundlich (to zu) ▷ n Art f; (of coffee, cheese etc) Sorte f; **what ~ of ...?** was für ein(e) ...?; **this ~ of ...** so ein(e) ...; **~ of ...** (+ adj) irgendwie

kindergarten ['kɪndəga:tn] n Kindergarten m

kindly ['kaɪndlɪ] adj nett, freundlich ▷ adv liebenswürdigerweise; **kindness** ['kaɪndnəs] n Freundlichkeit f

king [kɪŋ] n König m; **kingdom** n Königreich nt; **kingfisher** n Eisvogel m; **king-size** adj im Großformat; (bed) extra groß

kipper ['kɪpə*] n Räucherhering m

kiss [kɪs] n Kuss m; **~ of life** Mund-zu-Mund-Beatmung f ▷ vt küssen

kit [kɪt] n (equipment) Ausrüstung f; (Brit) Sachen pl; (sports ~) Sportsachen pl; (belongings, clothes) Sachen pl; (for building sth) Bausatz m

kitchen ['kɪtʃɪn] n Küche f; **kitchen foil** n Alufolie f; **kitchen scales** n Küchenwaage f; **kitchen unit** n Küchenschrank m; **kitchenware** n Küchengeschirr nt

kite [kaɪt] n Drachen m

kitten [kɪtn] n Kätzchen nt

kiwi ['ki:wi:] n (fruit) Kiwi f

km abbr = **kilometres** km

knack [næk] n Dreh m, Trick m; **to get / have got the ~** den Dreh herausbekommen / heraushaben; **knackered** ['nækəd] adj (Brit fam) fix und fertig, kaputt

knee [ni:] n Knie nt; **kneecap** n Kniescheibe f; **knee-jerk** adj (reaction) reflexartig; **kneel** [ni:l] (knelt o kneeled, knelt o kneeled) vi knien; (action, ~ down) sich hinknien

knelt [nelt] pt, pp of **kneel**

knew [nju:] pt of **know**

knickers ['nɪkəz] npl (Brit) Schlüpfer m

knife [naɪf] (pl **knives**) n Messer nt

knight [naɪt] n Ritter m; (in chess) Pferd nt, Springer m

knit [nɪt] vt, vi stricken; **knitting** n (piece of work) Strickarbeit f; (activity) Stricken nt; **knitting needle** n Stricknadel f; **knitwear** n Strickwaren pl

knob [nɒb] n (on door) Knauf m; (on radio etc) Knopf m

knock [nɒk] vt (with hammer etc) schlagen; (accidentally) stoßen; **to ~**

one's head sich *dat* den Kopf anschlagen ▷ vi klopfen (on, at an +akk) ▷ n (blow) Schlag m; (on door) Klopfen nt; **there was a ~ (at the door)** es hat geklopft; **knock down** vt (object) umstoßen; (person) niederschlagen; (with car) anfahren; (building) abreißen; **knock out** vt (stun) bewusstlos schlagen; (boxer) k.o. schlagen; **knock over** vt umstoßen; (with car) anfahren; **knocker** n Türklopfer m; **knockout** n Knockout m, K.o. m

knot [nɒt] n Knoten m

know [nəʊ] (**knew, known**) vt, vi wissen; (be acquainted with: people, places) kennen; (recognize) erkennen; (language) können; **I'll let you ~** ich sage dir Bescheid; **I ~ some French** ich kann etwas Französisch; **to get to ~ sb** jdn kennen lernen; **to be ~ as** bekannt sein als; **know about** vt Bescheid wissen über +akk; (subject) sich auskennen in +dat; (cars, horses etc) sich auskennen mit; **know of** vt kennen; **not that I ~** nicht dass ich wüsste; **know-all** n (fam) Klugscheißer m; **know-how** n Kenntnis f, Know-how nt; **knowing** adj wissend; (look, smile) vielsagend; **knowledge** ['nɒlɪdʒ] n Wissen nt; (of a subject) Kenntnisse pl; **to (the best of) my ~** meines Wissens

known [nəʊn] pp of **know**

knuckle ['nʌkl] n (Finger)knöchel m; (Gastr) Hachse f; **knuckle down** vi sich an die Arbeit machen

Koran [kɔ'rɑːn] n Koran m

Korea [kə'rɪə] n Korea nt

Kosovo ['kɒsəvəʊ] n der Kosovo

kph abbr = kilometres per hour km/h

Kremlin ['kremlɪn] n **the ~** der Kreml

Kurd [kɜːd] n Kurde m, Kurdin f; **Kurdish** adj kurdisch

Kuwait [kʊ'weɪt] n Kuwait nt

L abbr (BRIT Auto) = **learner**

LA abbr = **Los Angeles**

lab [læb] n (fam) Labor nt

label ['leɪbl] n Etikett nt; (tied) Anhänger m; (adhesive) Aufkleber m; (record ~) Label nt ▷ vt etikettieren; (pej) abstempeln

laboratory [lə'bɒrətəri] n Labor nt

LABOR DAY

Der **Labor Day** ist in den USA und Kanada der Name für den Tag der Arbeit. Er wird dort als gesetzlicher Feiertag am ersten Montag im September begangen.

laborious [lə'bɔːriəs] adj mühsam; **labor** (US), **labour** ['leɪbə*] n Arbeit f; (Med) Wehen pl; **to be in ~** Wehen haben ▷ adj (Pol) Labour-; **Party** Labour Party f; **labor union** n (US) Gewerkschaft f; **labourer** n Arbeiter(in) m(f)

lace [leɪs] n (fabric) Spitze f; (of

shoe) Schnürsenkel *m* ▷ *vt* **to ~ (up)** zuschnüren; **lace-up** *n* Schnürschuh *m*

lack [læk] *vt*, *vi* **to be ~ing** fehlen; **sb ~s** is **~ing in sth** es fehlt jdm an etw *dat*; **we ~ the time** uns fehlt die Zeit ▷ *n* Mangel *m*; **for ~ of** aus Mangel an +*dat*

lacquer ['lækə*] *n* Lack *m*; (*BRIT*: *hair ~*) Haarspray *nt*

lad [læd] *n* Junge *m*

ladder ['lædə*] *n* Leiter *f*; (*in tight*) Laufmasche *f*

laddish ['lædɪʃ] *adj* (*BRIT*) machohaft

laden ['leɪdn] *adj* beladen (*with mit*)

ladies ['leɪdɪz] , **ladies' room** *n* Damentoilette *f*; **lady** ['leɪdɪ] *n* Dame *f*; (*as title*) Lady *f*; **ladybird**, **ladybug** (*US*) *n* Marienkäfer *m*

lag [læg] *vi* **to ~ (behind)** zurückliegen ▷ *vt* (*pipes*) isolieren

lager ['lɑ:gə*] *n* helles Bier; **~ lout** betrunkener Rowdy

lagging ['lægɪŋ] *n* Isolierung *f*

laid [leɪd] *pt*, *pp of* **lay**; **laid-back** *adj* (*fam*) cool, gelassen

lain [leɪn] *pp of* **lie**

lake [leɪk] *n* See *m*; **the Lake District** Seengebiet *nt* im Nordwesten Englands

lamb [læm] *n* Lamm *nt*; (*meat*) Lammfleisch *nt*; **lamb chop** *n* Lammkotelett *nt*

lame [leɪm] *adj* lahm; (*excuse*) faul; (*argument*) schwach

lament [lə'ment] *n* Klage *f* ▷ *vt* beklagen

laminated ['læmineɪtɪd] *adj* beschichtet

lamp [læmp] *n* Lampe *f*; (*in street*) Laterne *f*; (*in car*) Licht *nt*, Scheinwerfer *m*; **lamppost** *n* Laternenpfahl *m*; **lampshade** *n* Lampenschirm *m*

land [lænd] *n* Land *nt* ▷ *vi* (*from ship*) an Land gehen; (*Aviat*) landen ▷ *vt* (*passengers*) absetzen; (*goods*) abladen; (*plane*) landen; **landing** *n* Landung *f*; (*on stairs*) Treppenabsatz *m*; **landing stage** *n* Landesteg *m*; **landing strip** *n* Landebahn *f*

landlady *n* Hauswirtin *f*, Vermieterin *f*; **landlord** *n* (*of house*) Hauswirt *m*, Vermieter *m*; (*of pub*) Gastwirt *m*; **landmark** *n* Wahrzeichen *nt*; (*event*) Meilenstein *m*; **landowner** *n* Grundbesitzer(in) *m(f)*; **landscape** *n* Landschaft *f*; (*format*) Querformat *nt*; **landslide** *n* (*Geo*) Erdrutsch *m*

lane [leɪn] *n* (*in country*) Weg *m*; Landstraße, Weg *m*; (*in town*) Gasse *f*; (*of motorway*) Spur *f*; (*Sport*) Bahn *f*; **to get in ~** (*in car*) sich einordnen

language ['læŋgwɪdʒ] *n* Sprache *f*; (*style*) Ausdrucksweise *f*

lantern ['læntən] *n* Laterne *f*

lap [læp] *n* Schoß *m*; (*in race*) Runde *f* ▷ *vt* (*in race*) überholen

lapse [læps] *n* (*mistake*) Irrtum *m*; (*moral*) Fehltritt *m* ▷ *vi* ablaufen

laptop ['læptɒp] *n* Laptop *m*

large [lɑ:dʒ] *adj* groß; **by and ~** im Großen und Ganzen; **largely** *adv* zum größten Teil; **large-scale** *adv* groß angelegt, Groß-

lark [lɑ:k] *n* (*bird*) Lerche *f*

laryngitis [lærɪn'dʒaɪtɪs] *n* Kehlkopfentzündung *f*; **larynx** ['lærɪŋks] *n* Kehlkopf *m*

laser ['leɪzə*] *n* Laser *m*; **laser printer** *n* Laserdrucker *m*

lash [læʃ] *vt* peitschen; **lash out** *vi* (*with fists*) um sich schlagen; (*spend money*) sich in Unkosten stürzen (*on mit*)

lass [læs] *n* Mädchen *nt*

last [lɑ:st] *adj* letzte(r, s); **the ~ but one** der/die/das vorletzte; **~ night** gestern Abend; **~ but not**

least nicht zuletzt ▷ *adv* zuletzt; *(last time)* das letzte Mal; **at** – endlich ▷ *n (person)* Letzte(r) *mf*; *(thing)* Letzte(s) *nt*; **he was the ~ to leave** er ging als Letzter ▷ *vi (continue)* dauern; *(remain in good condition)* durchhalten; *(remain good)* sich halten; *(money)* ausreichen; **lasting** *adj* dauerhaft; *(impression)* nachhaltig; **lastly** *adv* schließlich; **last-minute** *adj* in letzter Minute; **last name** *n* Nachname *m*

late [leɪt] *adj* spät; *(after proper time)* zu spät; *(train etc)* verspätet; *(dead)* verstorben; **to be** ~ zu spät kommen; *(train etc)* Verspätung haben ▷ *adv* spät; *(after proper time)* zu spät; **late availibility flight** *n* Last-Minute-Flug *m*; **lately** *adv* in letzter Zeit; **late opening** *n* verlängerte Öffnungszeiten *pl*; **later** ['leɪtə*] *adj, adv* später; **see you** bis später; **latest** ['leɪtɪst] *adj* späteste(r, s); *(most recent)* neueste(r, s) ▷ *n* **the ~** *(news)* das Neueste; **at the ~** spätestens

Latin ['lætɪn] *n* Latein *nt* ▷ *adj* lateinisch; **Latin America** *n* Lateinamerika *nt*; **Latin-American** *adj* lateinamerikanisch ▷ *n* Lateinamerikaner(in) *m(f)*

latitude ['lætɪtjuːd] *n (Geo)* Breite *f*

latter ['lætə*] *adj (second of two)* letztere(r, s); *(last part, years)* letzte(r, s), später

Latvia ['lætvɪə] *n* Lettland *nt*

laugh [lɑːf] *n* Lachen *nt*; **for a ~** aus Spaß ▷ *vi* lachen *(at, about über +akk)*; **to ~ at sb** sich über jdn lustig machen; **it's no ~ing matter** es ist nicht zum Lachen; **laughter** ['lɑːftə*] *n* Gelächter *nt*

launch [lɔːntʃ] *n (launching, of ship)* Stapellauf *m*; *(of rocket)* Abschuss *m*; *(of product)* Markteinfüh-

rung *f*; *(with hype)* Lancierung *f*; *(event)* Eröffnungsfeier *f* ▷ *vt (ship)* vom Stapel lassen; *(rocket)* abschießen; *(product)* einführen; *(with hype)* lancieren; *(project)* in Gang setzen

launder ['lɔːndə*] *vt* waschen und bügeln; *(fig: money)* waschen; **laundrette** [lɔːn'dret] *n (BRIT)*, **laundromat** ['lɔːndrəmæt] *n (US)* Waschsalon *m*; **laundry** ['lɔːndrɪ] *n (place)* Wäscherei *f*; *(clothes)* Wäsche *f*

lavatory ['lævətrɪ] *n* Toilette *f*

lavender ['lævɪndə*] *n* Lavendel *m*

lavish ['lævɪʃ] *adj* verschwenderisch; *(furnishings etc)* üppig; *(gift)* großzügig

law [lɔː] *n* Gesetz *nt*; *(system)* Recht *nt*; *(for study)* Jura; *(of sport)* Regel *f*; **against the ~** gesetzwidrig; **law-abiding** *adj* gesetzestreu; **law court** *n* Gerichtshof *m*; **lawful** *adj* rechtmäßig

lawn [lɔːn] *n* Rasen *m*; **lawnmower** *n* Rasenmäher *m*

lawsuit ['lɔːsuːt] *n* Prozess *m*; **lawyer** ['lɔːjə*] *n* Rechtsanwalt *m*, Rechtsanwältin *f*

laxative ['læksətɪv] *n* Abführmittel *nt*

lay [leɪ] *pt of* **lie** ▷ *vt* **(laid, laid)** legen; *(table)* decken; *(vulg)* poppen, bumsen; *(egg)* legen ▷ *adj* Laien-; **lay down** *vt* hinlegen; **lay off** *vt (workers)* (vorübergehend) entlassen; *(stop attacking)* in Ruhe lassen; **lay on** *vt (provide)* anbieten; *(organize)* veranstalten, bereitstellen; **layabout** *n* Faulenzer(in) *m(f)*; **lay-by** *n* Parkbucht *f*; *(bigger)* Parkplatz *m*

layer ['leɪə*] *n* Schicht *f*

layman ['leɪmən] *n* Laie *m*

layout ['leɪaʊt] *n* Gestaltung *f*; *(of book etc)* Lay-out *nt*

laze [leɪz] *vi* faulenzen; **laziness**

lazy | 372

['leɪzɪnɪs] n Faulheit f; **lazy** ['leɪzɪ] adj faul; (day, time) gemütlich

lb abbr = **pound** Pfd.

lead [led] n Blei nt ▷ vt, vi [liːd] (**led, led**) führen; (group etc) leiten; **to ~ the way** vorangehen; **this is ~ing us nowhere** das bringt uns nicht weiter ▷ [liːd] n (race) Führung f; (distance, time ahead) Vorsprung m (over vor +dat); (of police) Spur f; (Theat) Hauptrolle f; (dog's) Leine f; (Elec: flex) Leitung f; **lead astray** vt irreführen; **lead away** vt wegführen; **lead back** vi zurückführen; **lead on** vt anführen; **lead to** vt (street) hinführen nach; (result in) führen zu; **lead up to** vt (drive) führen zu

leaded ['ledɪd] adj (petrol) verbleit

leader ['liːdə*] n Führer(in) m(f); (of party) Vorsitzende(r) mf; (of project, expedition) Leiter(in) m(f); (Sport: in race) der/die Erste; (in league) Tabellenführer m; **leadership** ['liːdəʃɪp] n Führung f

lead-free ['led'friː] adj (petrol) bleifrei

leading ['liːdɪŋ] adj führend, wichtig

leaf [liːf] (pl **leaves**) n Blatt nt; **leaflet** ['liːflɪt] n Prospekt m; (pamphlet) Flugblatt nt; (with instructions) Merkblatt nt

league [liːg] n Bund m; (Sport) Liga f

leak [liːk] n (gap) undichte Stelle; (escape) Leck nt; **to take a ~** (fam) pinkeln gehen ▷ vi (pipe etc) undicht sein; (liquid etc) auslaufen; **leaky** adj undicht

lean [liːn] adj (meat) mager; (face) schmal; (person) drahtig ▷ vi (**leant** o **leaned, leant** o **leaned**) (not vertical) sich neigen; (rest) **to ~ against sth** sich an etw akk lehnen; (support oneself) **to ~ on sth** sich auf etw akk

stützen ▷ vt lehnen (on, against an +akk); **lean back** vi sich zurücklehnen; **lean forward** vi sich vorbeugen; **lean over** vi sich hinüberbeugen; **lean towards** vt tendieren zu

leant [lent] pt, pp of **lean**

leap [liːp] n Sprung m ▷ vi (**lept** o **leaped, lept** o **leaped**) springen; **leap year** n Schaltjahr nt

learn [lɜːn] (**learnt** o **learned, learnt** o **learned**) vt, vi lernen; (find out) erfahren; **to ~ (how) to swim** schwimmen lernen; **learned** ['lɜːnɪd] adj gelehrt; **learner** n Anfänger(in) m(f); (BRIT: driver) Fahrschüler(in) m(f)

learnt [lɜːnt] pt, pp of **learn**

lease [liːs] n (of land, premises etc) Pacht f; (contract) Pachtvertrag m; (of house, car etc) Miete f; (contract) Mietvertrag m ▷ vt pachten; (house, car etc) mieten; **lease out** vt vermieten; **leasing** ['liːsɪŋ] n Leasing nt

least [liːst] adj wenigste(r, s); (slightest) geringste(r, s) ▷ adv am wenigsten; **~ expensive** billigste(r, s) ▷ n **the ~** das Mindeste; **not in the ~** nicht im geringsten; **at ~** wenigstens; (with number) mindestens

leather ['leðə*] n Leder nt ▷ adj ledern, Leder-

leave [liːv] n (time off) Urlaub m; **on ~** auf Urlaub; **to take one's ~** Abschied nehmen (of von) ▷ vt (left, left) (place, person) verlassen; (not remove, not change) lassen; (~ behind: message, scar etc) hinterlassen; (forget) hinter sich lassen; (after death) hinterlassen (to sb jdm); (entrust) überlassen (to sb jdm); **to be left** (remain) übrig bleiben; **~ me alone** lass mich in Ruhe!; **don't ~ it to the last minute** warte nicht bis zur letzten Minute ▷ vi (weg)gehen, (weg)fahren; (on journey) abreisen; (bus, train) abfahren (for nach); **leave behind** vt zurücklassen; (scar etc) hinterlassen; (forget) hinter sich lassen; **leave out** vt auslassen; (person) ausschließen (of von)

leaves [liːvz] pl of **leaf**

leaving do [ˈliːvɪŋduː] n Abschiedsfeier f

Lebanon [ˈlebənən] n **the ~** der Libanon

lecture [ˈlektʃəʳ] n Vortrag m; (at university) Vorlesung f; **to give a ~** einen Vortrag / eine Vorlesung halten; **lecturer** n Dozent(in) m(f);
lecture theatre n Hörsaal m

led [led] pt, pp of **lead**

LED abbr = **light-emitting diode** Leuchtdiode f

ledge [ledʒ] n Leiste f; (window ~) Sims m o nt

leek [liːk] n Lauch m

left [left] pt, pp of **leave** ▷ adj linke(r, s) ▷ adv (position) links; (movement) nach links ▷ n (side) linke Seite; **the Left** (Pol) die Linke; **on / to the ~** links (of von); **move / fall to the ~** nach links rücken / fallen; **left-hand** adj (drive) links-; **left-hand side** n linke Seite

left-luggage locker n Gepäckschließfach nt; **left-luggage office** n Gepäckaufbewahrung f

left-overs npl Reste pl

left wing n linker Flügel; **left-wing** adj (Pol) linksgerichtet

leg [leg] n Bein nt; (of meat) Keule f

legacy [ˈlegəsɪ] n Erbe nt, Erbschaft f

legal [ˈliːgəl] adj Rechts-, rechtlich; (allowed) legal; (limit, age) gesetzlich; **~ aid** Rechtshilfe f; **legalize** vt legalisieren; **legally** adv legal

legend [ˈledʒənd] n Legende f

legible [ˈledʒəbl, -blɪ] adj, adv leserlich

legislation [ledʒɪsˈleɪʃn] n Gesetze pl

legitimate [lɪˈdʒɪtɪmət] adj rechtmäßig, legitim

legroom [ˈlegrum] n Platz m für die Beine

leisure [ˈleʒəʳ] n (time) Freizeit f ▷ adj Freizeit-; **~ centre** Freizeitzentrum nt; **leisurely** [ˈleʒəlɪ] adj gemächlich

lemon [ˈlemən] n Zitrone f; **lemonade** [leməˈneɪd] n Limonade f; **lemon curd** n Brotaufstrich aus Zitronen, Butter, Eiern und Zucker; **lemon juice** n Zitronensaft m; **lemon sole** n Seezunge f

lend [lend] (**lent**, **lent**) vt leihen; **to ~ sb sth** jdm etw leihen; **to (sb) ~ a hand** (jdm) behilflich sein; **lending library** n Leihbücherei f

length [leŋθ] n Länge f; **4 metres in ~** 4 Meter lang; **what ~ is it?** wie lange ist es?; **for any ~ of time** für längere Zeit; **at ~** (lengthily) ausführlich; **lengthen** [ˈleŋθən] vt verlängern; **lengthy** adj sehr lange; (dragging) langwierig

lenient [ˈliːnɪənt] adj nachsichtig

lens [lenz] n Linse f; (Foto) Objektiv nt

lent [lent] pt, pp of **lend**

Lent [lent] n Fastenzeit f

lentil [ˈlentl] n (Bot) Linse f

Leo [ˈliːəʊ] (pl **-s**) n (Astr) Löwe m

leopard [ˈlepəd] n Leopard m

lept [lept] pt, pp of **leap**

lesbian [ˈlezbɪən] adj lesbisch ▷ n Lesbe f

less [les] adj, adv, n weniger; **~ and ~** immer weniger; (~ often) immer seltener; **lessen** [ˈlesn] vi abnehmen, nachlassen ▷ vt verringern; (pain) lindern; **lesser** ['lesə*] adj geringer; (amount) kleiner

lesson ['lesn] n (at school) Stunde f; (unit of study) Lektion f; (fig) Lehre f; (Rel) Lesung f; **~s start at 9** der Unterricht beginnt um 9

let [let] (**let, let**) vt lassen; (lease) vermieten; **to ~ sb have sth** jdm etw geben; **~'s go** gehen wir; **to ~ go (of sth)** (etw) loslassen; **let down** vt herunterlassen; (fail to help) im Stich lassen; (disappoint) enttäuschen; **let in** vt hereinlassen; **let off** vt (bomb) hochgehen lassen; (person) laufen lassen; **let out** vt hinauslassen; (secret) verraten; (scream etc) ausstoßen; **let up** vi nachlassen; (stop) aufhören

lethal ['li:θəl] adj tödlich

let's contr = let us

letter ['letə*] n (of alphabet) Buchstabe m; (message) Brief m; (official ~) Schreiben nt; **letter bomb** n Briefbombe f; **letterbox** n Briefkasten m

lettuce ['letɪs] n Kopfsalat m

leukaemia, **leukemia** (US) [lu:-'ki:mɪə] n Leukämie f

level ['levl] adj (horizontal) waagerecht; (ground) eben; (two things, two runners) auf selber Höhe; **to be ~ with sb / sth** mit jdm / etw auf gleicher Höhe sein; **~ on points** punktgleich ▷ adv (run etc) auf gleicher Höhe; **to draw ~** (in race) gleichziehen (with mit); (in game) ausgleichen ▷ n (altitude) Höhe f; (standard) Niveau nt; (amount, degree) Grad m; **to be on a ~ with** auf gleicher Höhe sein mit ▷ vt (ground) einebnen; **level crossing** n (BRIT) (schienengleicher) Bahnübergang m; **level-headed** adj vernünftig

lever ['li:və*], (US) ['levə*] n He-

bel m; (fig) Druckmittel nt; **lever up** vt hochstemmen

liability [laɪə'bɪlɪtɪ] n Haftung f; (burden) Belastung f; (obligation) Verpflichtung f; **liable** ['laɪəbl] adj **to be ~ for sth** (responsible) für etw haften; **~ for tax** steuerpflichtig

liar ['laɪə*] n Lügner(in) m(f)

Lib Dem [lɪb'dem] abbr = **Liberal Democrat**

liberal ['lɪbərəl] adj (generous) großzügig; (broad-minded) liberal; **Liberal Democrat** n (BRIT Pol) Liberaldemokrat(in) m(f) ▷ adj liberaldemokratisch; **the ~ Party** die Liberaldemokratische Partei

liberate ['lɪbəreɪt] vt befreien; **liberation** [lɪbə'reɪʃn] n Befreiung f

Liberia [laɪ'bɪərɪə] n Liberia nt

liberty ['lɪbətɪ] n Freiheit f

Libra ['li:brə] n (Astr) Waage f

library ['laɪbrərɪ] n Bibliothek f; (lending ~) Bücherei f

Libya ['lɪbɪə] n Libyen nt

lice [laɪs] pl of **louse**

licence ['laɪsəns] n (permit) Genehmigung f; (Comm) Lizenz f; (driving ~) Führerschein m; **license** ['laɪsəns] n (US) see **licence** ['laɪsəns] ▷ vt genehmigen; **licensed** adj (restaurant etc) mit Schankerlaubnis; **license plate** n (US Aut) Nummernschild nt; **licensing hours** npl Ausschankzeiten pl

lick [lɪk] vt lecken ▷ n Lecken nt

licorice ['lɪkərɪs] n Lakritze f

lid [lɪd] n Deckel m; (eye-) Lid nt

lie [laɪ] n Lüge f; **~ detector** Lügendetektor m ▷ vi lügen; **to ~ to sb** jdn belügen ▷ vi (**lay, lain**) (rest, be situated) liegen; (~ down) sich legen; (snow) liegen bleiben; **to be lying third** an dritter Stelle liegen; **lie about** vi herumliegen; **lie down** vi sich hinlegen

Liechtenstein ['lɪktənstaɪn] n
Liechtenstein nt

lie in [laɪ'ɪn] n **to have a** ~ ausschlafen

life [laɪf] (pl **lives**) n Leben nt; **to get** ~ lebenslänglich bekommen; **there isn't much** ~ here hier ist nicht viel los; **how many lives were lost?** wie viele sind ums Leben gekommen?; **life assurance** n Lebensversicherung f; **lifebelt** n Rettungsring m; **lifeboat** n Rettungsboot nt; **lifeguard** n Bademeister(in) m(f), Rettungsschwimmer(in) m(f); **life insurance** n Lebensversicherung f; **life jacket** n Schwimmweste f; **lifeless** adj (dead) leblos; **lifelong** adj lebenslang; **life preserver** n (US) Rettungsring m; **life-saving** adj lebensrettend; **life-size(d)** adj in Lebensgröße; **life span** n Lebensspanne f; **life style** n Lebensstil m; **lifetime** n Lebenszeit f

lift [lɪft] vt (hoch)heben; (ban) aufheben ▷ n (BRIT: elevator) Aufzug m, Lift m; **to give sb a** ~ jdn im Auto mitnehmen; **lift up** vt hochheben; **lift-off** n Start m

ligament ['lɪgəmənt] n Band nt

light [laɪt] (**lit** o **lighted**, **lit** o **lighted**) vt beleuchten; (fire, cigarette) anzünden ▷ n Licht nt; (lamp) Lampe f; ▷ **pl** (Aut) Beleuchtung f; (traffic ~s) Ampel f ▷ **in the** ~ **of** angesichts +gen ▷ adj (bright) hell; (not heavy, easy) leicht; (punishment) milde; (taxes) niedrig; ~ **blue/green** hellblau/hellgrün, **light up** vt (illuminate) beleuchten ▷ vi (a. eyes) aufleuchten

light bulb n Glühbirne f

lighten ['laɪtn] vt hell werden; ▷ vt (give light to) erhellen; (make less heavy) leichter machen; (fig) erleichtern

lighter ['laɪtə*] n (cigarette ~) Feuerzeug nt

light-hearted adj unbeschwert; **lighthouse** n Leuchtturm m; **lighting** n Beleuchtung f; **lightly** adv leicht; **light meter** n (Foto) Belichtungsmesser m

lightning ['laɪtnɪŋ] n Blitz m

lightweight adj leicht

like [laɪk] vt mögen, gern haben; **he** ~**s swimming** er schwimmt gern; **would you** ~ ...? hätten Sie gern ...?; **I'd** ~ **to go home** ich möchte nach Hause (gehen); **I don't** ~ **the film** der Film gefällt mir nicht ▷ prep wie; **what's it/he** ~? wie ist es/er?; **he looks** ~ **you** er sieht dir ähnlich; ~ **that/this** so; **likeable** ['laɪkəbl] adj sympathisch

likelihood ['laɪklɪhʊd] n Wahrscheinlichkeit f; **likely** ['laɪklɪ] adj wahrscheinlich; **the bus is** ~ **to be late** der Bus wird wahrscheinlich Verspätung haben; **he's not (at all)** ~ **to come** (höchst)wahrscheinlich kommt er nicht

like-minded [laɪk'maɪndɪd] adj gleich gesinnt

likewise ['laɪkwaɪz] adv ebenfalls; **to do** ~ das Gleiche tun

liking ['laɪkɪŋ] n (for person) Zuneigung f; (for type, things) Vorliebe f (for für)

lilac ['laɪlək] n Flieder m ▷ adj fliederfarben

lily ['lɪlɪ] n Lilie f; ~ **of the valley** Maiglöckchen nt

limb [lɪm] n Glied nt

limbo ['lɪmbəʊ] n **in** ~ (plans) auf Eis gelegt

lime [laɪm] n (tree) Linde f; (fruit) Limone f; (substance) Kalk m; **lime juice** n Limonensaft m; **limelight** n (fig) Rampenlicht nt

limerick ['lɪmərɪk] n Limerick m (fünfzeiliges komisches Gedicht)

limestone ['laɪmstəʊn] n Kalkstein m

limit ['lɪmɪt] n Grenze f; (for pollution etc) Grenzwert m; **there's a ~ to that** dem sind Grenzen gesetzt; **to drive over the ~** das Tempolimit überschreiten; **that's the ~** jetzt reicht's!, das ist die Höhe! ▷ vt beschränken (to auf +akk); (freedom, spending) einschränken; **limitation** [lɪmɪ'teɪʃən] n Beschränkung f; (of freedom, spending) Einschränkung f; **limited** adj begrenzt; **~ liability company** Gesellschaft f mit beschränkter Haftung, GmbH f; **public ~ company** Aktiengesellschaft f

limousine ['lɪməzi:n] n Limousine f

limp [lɪmp] vi hinken ▷ adj schlaff

line [laɪn] n Linie f; (written) Zeile f; (rope) Leine f; (on face) Falte f; (row) Reihe f; (US: queue) Schlange f; (Rail) Bahnlinie f; (between A and B) Strecke f; (Tel) Leitung f; (range of items) Kollektion f; **hold the ~** bleiben Sie am Apparat; **to stand in ~** Schlange stehen; **in ~ with** in Übereinstimmung mit; **something along those ~s** etwas in dieser Art; **~s** (Theat) Text m ▷ vt (clothes) füttern; (streets) säumen; **lined** adj (paper) liniert; (face) faltig; **line up** vi sich aufstellen; (US: form queue) sich anstellen

linen ['lɪnɪn] n Leinen nt; (sheets etc) Wäsche f

liner ['laɪnə*] n Überseedampfer m, Passagierschiff nt

linesman ['laɪnzmən] (pl **-men**) n (Sport) Linienrichter m

linger ['lɪŋɡə*] vi verweilen; (smell) nicht weggehen

lingerie ['lænʒəriː] n Damenunterwäsche f

lining ['laɪnɪŋ] n (of clothes) Futter nt; (brake ~) Bremsbelag m

link [lɪŋk] n (connection) Verbindung f; (of chain) Glied nt; (relationship) Beziehung f (with zu); (between events) Zusammenhang m; (Internet) Link m ▷ vt verbinden

lion ['laɪən] n Löwe m; **lioness** n Löwin f

lip [lɪp] n Lippe f; **lipstick** n Lippenstift m

liqueur [lɪ'kjʊə*] n Likör m

liquid ['lɪkwɪd] n Flüssigkeit f ▷ adj flüssig

liquidate ['lɪkwɪdeɪt] vt liquidieren

liquidizer ['lɪkwɪdaɪzə*] n Mixer m

liquor ['lɪkə*] n Spirituosen pl

liquorice ['lɪkərɪs] n Lakritze f

Lisbon ['lɪzbən] n Lissabon nt

lisp [lɪsp] vi, vt lispeln

list [lɪst] n Liste f ▷ vi (ship) Schlagseite haben ▷ vt auflisten, aufzählen; **~ed building** unter Denkmalschutz stehendes Gebäude

listen ['lɪsn] vi zuhören, horchen (for sth auf etw akk); **listen to** (person) zuhören +dat; (radio) hören; (advice) hören auf; **listener** n Zuhörer(in) m(f); (to radio) Hörer(in) m(f)

lit [lɪt] pt, pp of **light**

liter ['li:tə*] n (US) Liter m

literacy ['lɪtərəsɪ] n Fähigkeit f zu lesen und zu schreiben; **literal** ['lɪtərəl] adj (translation, meaning) wörtlich; (actual) buchstäblich; **literally** adv (translate, take sth) wörtlich; (really) buchstäblich, wirklich; **literary** ['lɪtərərɪ] adj literarisch; (critic, journal etc) Literatur-; (language) gehoben; **literature** ['lɪtrətʃə*] n Literatur f; (brochures etc) Informationsmaterial nt

Lithuania [lɪθjʊ'eɪnjə] n Litauen nt

litre ['li:tə*] n Liter m

litter ['lɪtə*] n Abfälle pl; (of animals) Wurf m ▷ vt **to be ~ed with**

übersät sein mit; **litter bin** n Ab falleimer m

little ['lɪtl] adj **(smaller, smallest)** klein, (in quantity) wenig; **a ~ while ago** vor kurzer Zeit ▷ adv, n **(fewer, fewest)** wenig; **a ~** ein bisschen, ein wenig; **as ~ as possible** so wenig wie möglich, **for as ~ as £5** ab nur 5 Pfund; **I see very ~ of them** ich sehe sie sehr selten; **~ by ~** nach und nach; **little finger** n kleiner Finger

live [laɪv] adj lebendig; (Elec) geladen, unter Strom; (Tv, Radio: event) live; **~ broadcast** Direktübertragung f ▷ [lɪv] vi leben; (to die) überleben; (dwell) wohnen, **you ~ and learn** man lernt nie aus ▷ vt (life) führen; **to ~ a life of luxury** im Luxus leben; **live on** vi weiterleben ▷ vt fus von etw leben; (feed) sich von etw ernähren; **to earn enough to ~** genug verdienen, um davon zu leben; **live together** vi zusammenleben; **live up to** vt (reputation) gerecht werden +dat; (expectations) entsprechen +dat; **live with** vt (parents etc) wohnen bei; (partner) zusammenleben mit; (difficulty) **you'll just have to ~ it** du musst dich eben damit abfinden

liveliness ['laɪvlɪnɪs] n Lebhaftigkeit f; **lively** ['laɪvlɪ] adj lebhaft
liver ['lɪvə*] n Leber f
lives [laɪvz] pl of **life**
livestock ['laɪvstɒk] n Vieh nt
living ['lɪvɪŋ] n Lebensunterhalt m; **what do you do for a ~?** was machen Sie beruflich? ▷ adj lebend; **living room** n Wohnzimmer nt
lizard ['lɪzəd] n Eidechse f
load [ləʊd] n Last f; (cargo) Ladung f; (Tech, fig) Belastung f; **~s of** massenhaft; **it was a ~ of rubbish** (fam) es war grottenschlecht ▷ vt (vehicle) beladen, (inform) laden, (film) einlegen

loaf [ləʊf] (pl **loaves**) n ~ (of bread) Brot nt; Laib m ▷ vi faulenzen
loan [ləʊn] n (item loan) Leihgabe f; (Fin) Darlehen nt; **on ~** geliehen ▷ vt leihen (to sb jdm)
loathe [ləʊð] vt verabscheuen
loaves [ləʊvz] pl of **loaf**
lobby ['lɒbɪ] n Vorhalle f, (Pol) Lobby f
lobster ['lɒbstə*] n Hummer m
local ['ləʊkəl] adj (traffic, time etc) Orts-; (radio, news, paper) Lokal-; (government, authority) Kommunal-; (anaesthetic) örtlich; **~ call** (Tel) Ortsgespräch nt; **~ elections** Kommunalwahlen pl; **~ time** Ortszeit f; **~ train** Nahverkehrszug m; **the ~ shops** die Geschäfte am Ort ▷ n (pub) Stammlokal nt; **the ~s** pl die Ortsansässigen pl; **locally** adv örtlich, am Ort
locate [ləʊ'keɪt] vt (find) ausfindig machen; (position) legen; (establish) errichten; **to be ~d** sich befinden (in, at in +dat); **location** [ləʊ'keɪʃən] n (position) Lage f; (Cine) Drehort m
loch [lɒx] n (SCOT) See m
lock [lɒk] n Schloss nt; (Naut) Schleuse f; (of hair) Locke f ▷ vt (door etc) abschließen ▷ vi (door etc) sich abschließen lassen; (wheels) blockieren; **lock in** vt einschließen, einsperren; **lock out** vt aussperren; **lock up** vt (house) abschließen; (person) einsperren
locker ['lɒkə*] n Schließfach nt; **locker room** n (US) Umkleideraum m
locksmith ['lɒksmɪθ] n Schlosser(in) m(f)
locust ['ləʊkəst] n Heuschrecke f
lodge [lɒdʒ] n (small house) Pförtnerhaus nt; (porter's ~) Pförtnerloge f ▷ vi in Untermiete wohnen (with bei); (get stuck) stecken bleiben;

lodger n Untermieter(in) m(f);
lodging n Unterkunft f
loft [lɔft] n Dachboden m
log [lɔg] n Klotz m; (Naut) Log nt; **to keep a ~ of sth** über etw Buch führen; **log in** vi (Inform) sich einloggen; **log off** vi (Inform) sich ausloggen; **log on** vi (Inform) sich einloggen; **log out** vi (Inform) sich ausloggen
logic [ˈlɔdʒɪk] n Logik f; **logical** adj logisch
logo [ˈləʊgəʊ] (pl -s) n Logo nt
loin [lɔɪn] n Lende f
loiter [ˈlɔɪtə*] vi sich herumtreiben
lollipop [ˈlɔlɪpɔp] n Lutscher m; **~ man / lady** (BRIT) Schülerlotse m, Schülerlotsin f
lolly [ˈlɔlɪ] n Lutscher m; (fam: money) Knete f
London [ˈlʌndən] n London nt; **Londoner** n Londoner(in) m(f)
loneliness [ˈləʊnlɪnɪs] n Einsamkeit f; **lonely** [ˈləʊnlɪ] n, (esp US) **lonesome** [ˈləʊnsəm] adj einsam
long [lɔŋ] adj lang; (distance) weit; **it's a ~ way** es ist weit (to nach); **for a ~ time** lange; **how ~ is the film?** wie lange dauert der Film?; **in the ~ run** auf die Dauer ▷ adv lange; **not for ~** nicht lange; **~ ago** vor langer Zeit; **before ~** bald; **all day ~** den ganzen Tag; **no ~er** nicht mehr; **as ~ as** solange ▷ vi sich sehnen (for nach); (be waiting) sehnsüchtig warten (for auf); **long-distance call** n Ferngespräch nt; **long drink** n Longdrink m; **long-haul flight** n Langstreckenflug m; **longing** n Sehnsucht f (for nach); **longingly** adv sehnsüchtig; **longitude** [ˈlɔŋgɪtjuːd] n Länge f; **long jump** n Weitsprung m; **long-life milk** n H-Milch f; **long-range** adj Langstrecken-, Fern-; **~ missile** Langstreckenrakete f; **long-sighted** adj weitsichtig; **long-standing** adj alt,

langjährig; **long-term** adj langfristig; (car park, effect etc) Langzeit-; **~ unemployment** Langzeitarbeitslosigkeit f; **long wave** n Langwelle f
loo [luː] n (BRIT fam) Klo nt
look [lʊk] n Blick m; (appearance) **~(s)** pl Aussehen nt; **I'll have a ~** ich schau mal nach; **to have a ~ at sth** sich dat etw ansehen; **can I have a ~?** darf ich mal sehen? ▷ vi schauen, gucken; (with prep) sehen; (search) nachsehen; (appear) aussehen; (I'm) **just ~ing** ich schaue nur; **it ~s like rain** es sieht nach Regen aus ▷ vt ~ **what you've done** sieh dir mal an, was du da angestellt hast; (appear) **he ~s his age** man sieht ihm sein Alter an; **to ~ one's best** sehr vorteilhaft aussehen; **look after** vt (care for) sorgen für; (keep an eye on) aufpassen auf +akk; **look at** vt ansehen, anschauen; **look back** vi sich umsehen; (fig) zurückblicken; **look down on** vt (fig) herabsehen auf +akk; **look for** vt suchen; **look forward to** vt sich freuen auf +akk; **look into** vt (investigate) untersuchen; **look out** vi hinaussehen (of the window zum Fenster); (watch out) Ausschau halten (for nach); (be careful) aufpassen, Acht geben (for auf +akk); **~!** Vorsicht!; **look up** vi aufsehen ▷ vt (word etc) nachschlagen; **look up to** vt aufsehen zu
loony [ˈluːnɪ] adj (fam) bekloppt
loop [luːp] n Schleife f
loose [luːs] adj locker; (knot, button) lose; **loosen** vt lockern; (knot) lösen
loot [luːt] n Beute f
lop-sided [ˈlɔpˈsaɪdɪd] adj schief
lord [lɔːd] n (ruler) Herr m; (BRIT: title) Lord m; **the Lord** (God) Gott der Herr; **the (House of) Lords** (BRIT) das Oberhaus

lorry ['lɒrɪ] n (BRIT) Lastwagen m

lose [luːz] (lost, lost) vt verlieren; (chance) verpassen; **to ~ weight** abnehmen; **to ~ one's life** umkommen ▷ vi verlieren; (clock, watch) nachgehen; **loser** n Verlierer(in) m(f);

loss [lɒs] n Verlust m; **lost** [lɒst] pt, pp of **lose**; **we've ~** = wir haben uns verlaufen ▷ adj verloren; **lost-and-found** (US), **lost property (office)** n Fundbüro nt

lot [lɒt] n (fam: batch) Menge f, Haufen m, Stoß m; **this is the first** = das ist die erste Ladung; **a ~** viel(e); **a ~ of money** viel Geld; **~s of people** viele Leute; **the (whole) ~** alles; (people) alle; **(parking) ~** (US) Parkplatz m

lotion ['ləʊʃən] n Lotion f

lottery ['lɒtərɪ] n Lotterie f

loud [laʊd] adj laut; (colour) schreiend; **loudspeaker** n Lautsprecher m; (of stereo) Box f

lounge [laʊndʒ] n Wohnzimmer nt, (in hotel) Aufenthaltsraum m; (at airport) Warteraum m ▷ vi sich herumlümmeln

louse [laʊs] (pl lice) n Laus f;
lousy ['laʊzɪ] adj (fam) lausig

lout [laʊt] n Rüpel m

lovable ['lʌvəbl] adj liebenswert

love [lʌv] n Liebe f (of zu); (person, address) Liebling m, Schatz m; (SPORT) null; **to be in ~** verliebt sein (with sb in jdn); **to fall in ~** sich verlieben (with sb in jdn); **to make ~** (= sexually) sich lieben; **to make ~ to** (= sexually) mit jdm schlafen; (in letter) **he sends his ~** er lässt grüßen; **give her my ~** grüße sie von mir; **~, Tom** liebe Grüße, Tom ▷ vt (person) lieben; (activity) sehr gerne mögen; **to ~ to do sth** etw für sein Leben gerne tun; **I'd ~ a cup of tea** ich hätte liebend gern eine Tasse Tee; **love affair** n (Liebes)verhältnis nt; **love letter** n

Liebesbrief m; **love life** n Liebesleben nt; **lovely** ['lʌvlɪ] adj schön, wunderschön; (charming) reizend; **we had a ~ time** es war sehr schön; **lover** ['lʌvə] n Liebhaber(in) m(f); **loving** adj liebevoll

low [ləʊ] adj niedrig; (rank) niedere(r, s); (level, note, neckline) tief; (intelligence, density, quality, standard) schlecht; (not loud) leise; (depressed) niedergeschlagen; **we're ~ on petrol** wir haben kaum noch Benzin ▷ n (Meteo) Tief nt; **low-calorie** adj kalorienarm; **lowcut** adj (dress) tief ausgeschnitten; **low-emission** adj schadstoffarm; **lower** ['ləʊə] adj niedriger; (storey, class etc) untere(r, s) ▷ vt herunterlassen; (eyes, price) senken; (pressure) verringern; **low-fat** adj fettarm; **low tide** n Ebbe f

loyal ['lɔɪəl] adj treu, **loyalty** n Treue f

lozenge ['lɒzɪndʒ] n Pastille f

Ltd abbr = **limited** ≈ GmbH f

lubricant ['luːbrɪkənt] n Schmiermittel nt, Gleitmittel nt

luck [lʌk] n Glück nt; **bad ~** Pech nt; **luckily** adv glücklicherweise, zum Glück; **lucky** adj (number, day etc) Glücks-; **to be ~** Glück haben; **~**

coincidence glücklicher Zufall

ludicrous ['luːdɪkrəs] *adj* grotesk

luggage ['lʌɡɪdʒ] *n* Gepäck *nt*; **luggage compartment** *n* Gepäckraum *m*; **luggage rack** *n* Gepäcknetz *nt*

lukewarm ['luːkwɔːm] *adj* lauwarm

lullaby ['lʌləbaɪ] *n* Schlaflied *nt*

lumbago [lʌm'beɪɡəʊ] *n* Hexenschuss *m*

luminous ['luːmɪnəs] *adj* leuchtend

lump [lʌmp] *n* Klumpen *m*; (*Med*) Schwellung *f*; (*in breast*) Knoten *m*; (*of sugar*) Stück *nt*; **lump sum** *n* Pauschalsumme *f*; **lumpy** *adj* klumpig

lunacy ['luːnəsɪ] *n* Wahnsinn *m*; **lunatic** ['luːnətɪk] *adj* wahnsinnig ▷ *n* Wahnsinnige(r) *mf*

lunch, luncheon [lʌntʃ, -ən] *n* Mittagessen *nt*; **to have ~** zu Mittag essen; **lunch break, lunch hour** *n* Mittagspause *f*; **lunch packet** *n* Lunchpaket *nt*; **lunchtime** *n* Mittagszeit *f*

lung [lʌŋ] *n* Lunge *f*

lurid ['ljʊərɪd] *adj* (*colour*) grell; (*details*) widerlich

lurk [lɜːk] *vi* lauern

lust [lʌst] *n* (sinnliche) Begierde (*for* nach)

luster (*US*), **lustre** ['lʌstə*] *n* Glanz *m*

Luxembourg ['lʌksəmbɜːɡ] *n* Luxemburg *nt*; **Luxembourger** [lʌksəm'bɜːɡə*] *n* Luxemburger(in) *m(f)*

luxurious [lʌɡ'zʊərɪəs] *adj* luxuriös, Luxus-; **luxury** ['lʌkʃərɪ] *n* (*a. luxuries pl*) Luxus *m*; **~ goods** Luxusgüter *pl*

lynx [lɪŋks] *n* Luchs *m*

lyrics *npl* (*words for song*) Liedtext *m*

m *abbr* = **metre** m

M *abbr* (*street*) = **Motorway** A; (*size*) = **medium** M

MA *abbr* = **Master of Arts** Magister Artium *m*

ma [maː] *n* (*fam*) Mutti *f*

mac [mæk] *n* (*BRIT fam*) Regenmantel *m*

Macedonia [mæsɪ'dəʊnɪə] *n* Mazedonien *nt*

machine [mə'ʃiːn] *n* Maschine *f*; **machine gun** *n* Maschinengewehr *nt*; **machinery** [mə'ʃiːnərɪ] *n* Maschinen *pl*; (*fig*) Apparat *m*; **machine washable** *adj* waschmaschinenfest

mackerel ['mækrəl] *n* Makrele *f*

macro ['mækrəʊ] (*pl* **-s**) *n* (*Inform*) Makro *nt*

mad [mæd] *adj* wahnsinnig, verrückt; (*dog*) tollwütig; (*angry*) wütend, sauer (*at* auf +*akk*); (*fam*) **~ about** (*fond of*) verrückt nach; **to work like ~** wie verrückt arbeiten; **are you ~?** spinnst du?

madam ['mædəm] n gnädige Frau

mad cow disease [mæd'kaʊdɪ'ziːz] n Rinderwahnsinn m; **maddening** adj zum Verrücktwerden

made [meɪd] pt, pp of **make**

made-to-measure ['meɪdtə'meʒə*] adj nach Maß; **~ suit** Maßanzug m

madly ['mædlɪ] adv wie verrückt (with adj) wahnsinnig; **madman** ['mædmən] (pl **-men**) n Verrückte(r) m; **madwoman** ['mædwomən] (pl **-women**) n Verrückte f; **madness** ['mædnɪs] n Wahnsinn m

magazine [mægə'ziːn] n Zeitschrift f

maggot ['mægət] n Made f

magic ['mædʒɪk] n Magie f; (activity) Zauberei f; (fig: effect) Zauber m; **as if by ~** wie durch Zauberei ▷ adj Zauber-; (powers) magisch; **magician** [mə'dʒɪʃən] n Zauberer m, Zaub(r)erin f

magnet ['mægnɪt] n Magnet m; **magnetic** [mæg'netɪk] adj magnetisch; **magnetism** ['mægnɪtɪzəm] n (fig) Anziehungskraft f

magnificent adv; **magnificently** [mæg'nɪfɪsənt, -lɪ] adj, adv herrlich, großartig

magnify ['mægnɪfaɪ] vt vergrößern; **magnifying glass** n Vergrößerungsglas nt, Lupe f

magpie ['mægpaɪ] n Elster f

maid [meɪd] n Dienstmädchen nt; **maiden name** n Mädchenname m; **maiden voyage** n Jungfernfahrt f

mail [meɪl] n Post f; (e-mail) Mail f ▷ vt (post) aufgeben; (send) mit der Post schicken (to an +akk); **mailbox** n (US) Briefkasten m; (Inform) Mailbox f; **mailing list** n Adressenliste f; **mailman** n (pl **-men**) (US) Briefträger m; **mail order** n Bestellung f

per Post; **mail order firm** n Versandhaus nt, **mailshot** n Mailing nt

main [meɪn] adj Haupt-; **~ course** Hauptgericht nt; **the ~ thing** die Hauptsache ▷ n (pipe) Hauptleitung f; **mainframe** n Großrechner m; **mainland** n Festland nt; **mainly** adv hauptsächlich; **main road** n Hauptverkehrsstraße f; **main street** n (US) Hauptstraße f

maintain [meɪn'teɪn] vt (keep up) aufrechterhalten; (machine, roads) instand halten; (service) warten; (claim) behaupten; **maintenance** ['meɪntənəns] n Instandhaltung f; (Tech) Wartung f

maize [meɪz] n Mais m

majestic [mə'dʒestɪk] adj majestätisch; **majesty** ['mædʒɪstɪ] n Majestät f; **his/her Majesty** seine/ihre Majestät

major ['meɪdʒə*] adj (bigger) größer; (important) bedeutend; **~ part** Großteil m; (role) wichtige Rolle; **~ road** Hauptverkehrsstraße f; (Mus) **A ~** A-Dur nt ▷ vi (US) **to ~ in sth** etw als Hauptfach studieren

Majorca [mə'jɔːkə] n Mallorca nt

majority [mə'dʒɒrɪtɪ] n Mehrheit f; **to be in the ~** in der Mehrzahl sein

make [meɪk] n Marke f ▷ vt (**made**, **made**) machen; (manufacture) herstellen; (clothes) anfertigen; (dress) nähen; (soup) zubereiten; (bread, cake) backen; (tea, coffee) kochen; (speech) halten; (earn) verdienen; (decision) treffen; **it's made of gold** es ist aus Gold; **to ~ sb do sth** jdn dazu bringen, etw zu tun; (force) jdn zwingen, etw zu tun; **she made us wait** sie ließ uns warten; **what ~s you think that?** wie kommen Sie darauf?; **it ~s the room look smaller** es lässt den Raum kleiner wirken; **to ~ (it to) the airport** (reach) den Flughafen erreichen; (in *time*) es zum Flughafen schaffen; **he never really made it** er hat es nie zu etwas gebracht; **she didn't ~ it through the night** sie hat die Nacht nicht überlebt; (*calculate*) **I ~ it £5/a quarter to six** nach meiner Rechnung kommt es auf 5 Pfund/ nach meiner Uhr ist es dreiviertel sechs; **he's just made for this job** er ist für diese Arbeit wie geschaffen; **make for** *vt* zusteuern auf +*akk*; **make of** *vt* (*think of*) halten von; **I couldn't ~ anything of it** ich wurde daraus nicht schlau; **make off** *vi* sich davonmachen (*with* mit); **make out** *vi* zurechtkommen ▷ *vt* (*cheque*) ausstellen; (*list*) aufstellen; (*understand*) verstehen; (*discern*) ausmachen; **to ~ (that) ...** es so hinstellen, als ob ...; **make up** *vt* (*team etc*) bilden; (*face*) schminken; (*invent: story etc*) erfinden; **to ~ one's mind** sich entscheiden; **to make it up with sb** sich mit jdm aussöhnen ▷ *vi* sich versöhnen; **make up for** *vi* ausgleichen; (*time*) aufholen

make-believe *adj* Fantasie-; **makeover** *n* gründliche Veränderung, Verschönerung *f*; **maker** *n* (*Comm*) Hersteller(in) *m(f)*; **makeshift** *adj* behelfsmäßig; **make-up** *n* Make-up *nt*, Schminke *f*; **making** ['meɪkɪŋ] *n* Machen *nt*

maladjusted [mælə'dʒʌstɪd] *adj* verhaltensgestört

malaria [mə'lɛərɪə] *n* Malaria *f*; **Malaysia** [mə'leɪʒɪə] *n* Malaysia *nt*

male [meɪl] *n* Mann *m*; (*animal*) Männchen *nt* ▷ *adj* männlich; **~ chauvinist** Chauvi *m*, Macho *m*; **~ nurse** Krankenpfleger *m*

malfunction [mæl'fʌŋkʃən] *vi* nicht richtig funktionieren ▷ *n* Defekt *m*

malice ['mælɪs] *n* Bosheit *f*; **malicious** [mə'lɪʃəs] *adj* boshaft; (*behaviour, action*) böswillig; (*damage*) mutwillig

malignant [mə'lɪgnənt] *adj* bösartig

mall [mɔːl] *n* (US) Einkaufszentrum *nt*

malnutrition [mælnju'trɪʃən] *n* Unterernährung *f*

malt [mɔːlt] *n* Malz *nt*

Malta ['mɔːltə] *n* Malta *nt*; **Maltese** [mɔːl'tiːz] *adj* maltesisch ▷ *n* (*person*) Malteser(in) *m(f)*; (*language*) Maltesisch *nt*

maltreat [mæl'triːt] *vt* schlecht behandeln; (*violently*) misshandeln

mammal ['mæməl] *n* Säugetier *nt*

mammoth ['mæməθ] *adj* Mammut-, Riesen-

man [mæn] (*pl* **men**) *n* (*male*) Mann *m*; (*human race*) der Mensch, die Menschen *pl*; (*in chess*) Figur *f* ▷ *vt* besetzen

manage ['mænɪdʒ] *vi* zurechtkommen; **can you ~?** schaffst du es?; **to ~ without sth** ohne etw auskommen, auf etw verzichten können ▷ *vt* (*control*) leiten; (*musician, sportsman*) managen; (*cope with*) fertig werden mit; (*task, portion, climb etc*) schaffen; **to ~ to do sth** es schaffen, etw zu tun; **manageable** *adj* (*object*) handlich; (*task*) zu bewältigen; **management** *n* Leitung *f*; (*directors*) Direktion *f*; (*subject*) Management *nt*, Betriebswirtschaft *f*; **management consultant** *n* Unternehmensberater(in) *m(f)*

manager *n* Geschäftsführer(in) *m(f)*; (*departmental ~*) Abteilungsleiter(in) *m(f)*; (*of branch, bank*) Filialleiter(in) *m(f)*; (*of musician, sportsman*) Manager(in) *m(f)*; **managing director** *n* Geschäftsführer(in) *m(f)*

mane [meɪn] n Mähne f

maneuver (US) see **manoeuvre**

mango ['mæŋgəʊ] (pl **-es**) n Mango f

man-hour n Arbeitsstunde f

manhunt n Fahndung f

mania ['meɪnɪə] n Manie f; **maniac** ['meɪnɪæk] n Wahnsinnige(r) mf; (fan) Fanatiker(in) m(f)

manicure ['mænɪkjʊə*] n Maniküre f

manipulate [mə'nɪpjʊleɪt] vt manipulieren

mankind [mæn'kaɪnd] n Menschheit f

manly ['mænlɪ] adj männlich

man-made ['mænmeɪd] adj (product) künstlich

manner ['mænə*] n Art f; **in this ~** auf diese Art und Weise; **~s** pl Manieren pl

manoeuvre [mə'nu:və*] n Manöver nt ▷ vt, vi manövrieren

manor ['mænə*] n **~ (house)** Herrenhaus nt

manpower ['mænpaʊə*] n Arbeitskräfte pl

mansion ['mænʃən] n Villa f; (of old family) Herrenhaus nt

manslaughter ['mænslɔ:tə*] n Totschlag m

mantelpiece ['mæntlpi:s] n Kaminsims m

manual ['mænjʊəl] adj manuell, Hand- ▷ n Handbuch nt

manufacture [mænjʊ'fæktʃə*] vt herstellen ▷ n Herstellung f; **manufacturer** n Hersteller m

manure [mə'njʊə*] n Dung m; (esp artificial) Dünger m

many ['menɪ] (more, most) adj, pron viele; **~ times** oft; **not ~ people** nicht viele Leute; **too ~ problems** zu viele Probleme

map [mæp] n Landkarte f; (of town) Stadtplan m

maple ['meɪpl] n Ahorn m

marathon ['mærəθən] n Marathon m

marble ['mɑ:bl] n Marmor m; (for playing) Murmel f

march [mɑ:tʃ] vi marschieren ▷ n Marsch m; (protest) Demonstration f

March [mɑ:tʃ] n März m; see also **September**

mare [meə] n Stute f

margarine [mɑ:dʒə'ri:n] n Margarine f

margin ['mɑ:dʒɪn] n Rand m; (extra amount) Spielraum m; (Comm) Gewinnspanne f; **marginal** adj (difference etc) geringfügig

marijuana [mærjʊ'ɑ:nə] n Marihuana nt

marinade ['mærɪneɪd] n (Gastr) Marinade f; **marinated** ['mærɪneɪtɪd] adj mariniert

marine [mə'ri:n] adj Meeres-

marital ['mærɪtl] adj ehelich; **~ status** Familienstand m

maritime ['mærɪtaɪm] adj See-

marjoram ['mɑ:dʒərəm] n Majoran m

mark [mɑ:k] n (spot) Fleck m; (at school) Note f; (sign) Zeichen nt ▷ vt (make ~) Flecken machen auf +akk; (indicate) markieren; (schoolwork) benoten, korrigieren, Flecken machen auf +akk; **markedly** ['mɑ:kɪdlɪ] adv merklich; (with comp adj) wesentlich; **marker** n (in book) Lesezeichen nt; (pen) Marker m

market ['mɑ:kɪt] n Markt m; (stock ~) Börse f ▷ vt (Comm: new product) auf den Markt bringen; (goods) vertreiben; **marketing** n Marketing nt; **market leader** n Marktführer m; **market place** n Marktplatz m; **market research** n Marktforschung f

marmalade ['mɑ:məleɪd] n Orangenmarmelade f

maroon [mə'ru:n] *adj* rötlich braun

marquee [mɑː'kiː] *n* großes Zelt

marriage ['mærɪdʒ] *n* Ehe *f*; (*wedding*) Heirat *f* (*to* mit); **married** ['mærɪd] *adj* (*person*) verheiratet

marrow ['mærəʊ] *n* (*bone ~*) Knochenmark *nt*; (*vegetable*) Kürbis *m*

marry ['mærɪ] *vt* heiraten; (*join*) trauen; (*take as husband, wife*) heiraten ▷ *vi* **to ~ / to get married** heiraten

marsh [mɑːʃ] *n* Marsch *f*, Sumpf *m*

marshal ['mɑːʃəl] *n* (*at rally etc*) Ordner *m*; (*US: police*) Bezirkspolizeichef *m*

martial arts ['mɑːʃəl'ɑːts] *npl* Kampfsportarten *pl*

martyr ['mɑːtə*] *n* Märtyrer(in) *m(f)*

marvel ['mɑːvəl] *n* Wunder *nt* ▷ *vi* staunen (*at* über *+akk*); **marvellous, marvelous** (*US*) *adj* wunderbar

marzipan [mɑːzɪ'pæn] *n* Marzipan *nt* o *m*

mascara [mæ'skɑːrə] *n* Wimperntusche *f*

mascot ['mæskɒt] *n* Maskottchen *nt*

masculine ['mæskjʊlɪn] *adj* männlich

mashed [mæʃt] *adj* **~ potatoes** *pl* Kartoffelbrei *m*, Kartoffelpüree *nt*

mask [mɑːsk] *n* (*a. Inform*) Maske *f* ▷ *vt* (*feelings*) verbergen

masochist ['mæsəʊkɪst] *n* Masochist(in) *m(f)*

mason ['meɪsn] *n* (*stone~*) Steinmetz(in) *m(f)*; **masonry** *n* Mauerwerk *nt*

mass [mæs] *n* Masse *f*; (*of people*) Menge *f*; (*Rel*) Messe *f*; **~es of** massenhaft

massacre ['mæsəkə*] *n* Blutbad *nt*

massage ['mæsɑːʒ] *n* Massage *f* ▷ *vt* massieren

massive ['mæsɪv] *adj* (*powerful*) gewaltig; (*very large*) riesig

mass media ['mæs'miːdɪə] *npl* Massenmedien *pl*; **mass-produce** *vt* in Massenproduktion herstellen; **mass production** *n* Massenproduktion *f*

master ['mɑːstə*] *n* Herr *m*; (*of dog*) Besitzer *m*, Herrchen *m*; (*teacher*) Lehrer *m*; (*artist*) Meister *m* ▷ *vt* meistern; (*language etc*) beherrschen; **masterly** *adj* meisterhaft; **masterpiece** *n* Meisterwerk *nt*

masturbate ['mæstəbeɪt] *vi* masturbieren

mat [mæt] *n* Matte *f*; (*for table*) Untersetzer *m*

match [mætʃ] *n* Streichholz *nt*; (*Sport*) Wettkampf *m*; (*ball games*) Spiel *nt*; (*tennis*) Match *nt* ▷ *vt* (*be like, suit*) passen zu; (*equal*) gleichkommen *+dat* ▷ *vi* zusammenpassen; **matchbox** *n* Streichholzschachtel *f*; **matching** *adj* (*one item*) passend; (*two items*) zusammenpassend

mate [meɪt] *n* (*companion*) Kumpel *m*; (*of animal*) Weibchen *nt* / Männchen *nt* ▷ *vi* sich paaren

material [mə'tɪərɪəl] *n* Material *nt*; (*for book etc, cloth*) Stoff *m*; **materialistic** [mətɪərɪə'lɪstɪk] *adj* materialistisch; **materialize** [mə'tɪərɪəlaɪz] *vi* zustande kommen; (*hope*) wahr werden

maternal [mə'tɜːnl] *adj* mütterlich; **maternity** [mə'tɜːnɪtɪ] *adj* **~ dress** Umstandskleid *nt*; **~ leave** Elternzeit *f* (*der Mutter*); **~ ward** Entbindungsstation *f*

math [mæθ] *n* (*US fam*) Mathe *f*; **mathematical** [mæθə'mætɪkəl]

adj mathematisch; **mathematics**
[mæθə'mætɪks] *nsing* Mathematik
f. **maths** [mæθs] *nsing* (BRIT fam)
Mathe f

matinée ['mætɪneɪ] *n* Nachmit-
tagsvorstellung f

matter ['mætə*] *n* (*substance*)
Materie f; (*affair*) Sache f; **a personal
~** eine persönliche Angelegenheit; **a
~ of taste** eine Frage des Ge-
schmacks; **no ~ how/what** egal
wie/was; **what is the ~?** was ist
los?; **as a ~ of fact** eigentlich; **a ~ of
time** eine Frage der Zeit ⊳ *vi* darauf
ankommen, wichtig sein; **it doesn't
~** es macht nichts; **matter-of-fact**
adj sachlich, nüchtern

mattress ['mætrəs] *n* Matratze f

mature [mə'tjʊə*] *adj* reif ⊳ *vi*
reif werden; **maturity** [mə'tjʊə-
rɪtɪ] *n* Reife f

maximum ['mæksɪməm] *adj*
Höchst-, höchste(r, s); **~ speed**
Höchstgeschwindigkeit f ⊳ *n* Ma-
ximum nt

may [meɪ] (**might**) *vb aux* (*be
possible*) können; (*have permission*)
dürfen; **it ~ rain** es könnte regnen; **~
I smoke?** darf ich rauchen?; **it ~ not
happen** es passiert vielleicht gar
nicht; **we ~ as well go** wir können
ruhig gehen

May [meɪ] *n* Mai m: *see also* **September**

maybe ['meɪbi:] *adv* vielleicht

May Day ['meɪdeɪ] *n* der erste
Mai

mayo ['meɪəʊ] (US *fam*), **mayonnaise** [meɪə'neɪz] *n* Mayo f, Mayonnaise f, Majonäse f

mayor [mɛə*] *n* Bürgermeister m

maze [meɪz] *n* Irrgarten m; (*fig*)
Wirrwarr *nt*

MB *abbr* = **megabyte** MB *nt*

me [mi:] *pron* (*direct object*) mich;
(*indirect object*) mir; **it's ~** ich bin's

meadow ['medəʊ] *n* Wiese f

meal [mi:l] *n* Essen nt, Mahlzeit f;
to go out for a ~ essen gehen; **meal
pack** n (US) tiefgekühltes Fertiggericht; **meal time** n Essenszeit f

mean [mi:n] (**meant, meant**) *vt*
(*signify*) bedeuten; (*have in mind*)
meinen; (*intend*) vorhaben; **I ~ it** ich
meine das ernst; **what do you ~ (by
that)?** was willst du damit sagen;
to ~ to do sth etw tun wollen; **it
was ~t for you** es war für dich bestimmt (⊳ *gedacht*); **it was ~t to be
a joke** es sollte ein Witz sein ⊳ *vi* **he
~s well** er meint es gut ⊳ *adj* (*stingy*)
geizig; (*spiteful*) gemein (to zu);
meaning ['mi:nɪŋ] *n* Bedeutung f;
(*of life, poem*) Sinn m; **meaningful**
adj sinnvoll; **meaningless** *adj*
(*text*) ohne Sinn

means [mi:nz] (*pl* **means**) *n* Mittel nt; (*pl: funds*) Mittel pl; **by ~ of**
durch, mittels; **by all ~** selbstverständlich; **by no ~** keineswegs; **~ of
transport** Beförderungsmittel

meant [ment] *pt, pp of* **mean**

meantime ['mi:ntaɪm] *adv* **in
the ~** inzwischen; **meanwhile**
['mi:nwaɪl] *adv* inzwischen

measles ['mi:zlz] *nsing* Masern pl;
German ~ Röteln pl

measure ['meʒə*] *vt, vi* messen ⊳
n (*unit, device for measuring*) Maß nt;
(*step*) Maßnahme f; **to take ~s**
Maßnahmen ergreifen; **measurement** *n* (*amount measured*) Maß nt

meat [mi:t] *n* Fleisch nt; **meat-
ball** n Fleischbällchen nt

mechanic [mɪ'kænɪk] *n* Mecha-
niker(in) m(f); **mechanical** *adj*
mechanisch; **mechanics** *nsing*
Mechanik f; **mechanism**
['mekənɪzəm] *n* Mechanismus m

medal ['medl] *n* Medaille f; (*decoration*) Orden m; **medalist** (US),
medallist ['medəlɪst] *n* Medail-

lengewinner(in) *m(f)*

media ['miːdɪə] *npl* Medien *pl*

median strip ['miːdɪən strɪp] *n* (US) Mittelstreifen *m*

mediate ['miːdɪeɪt] *vi* vermitteln

medical ['medɪkəl] *adj* medizinisch; (*treatment etc*) ärztlich; ~ **student** Medizinstudent(in) *m(f)* ▷ *n* Untersuchung *f*; **Medicare** ['medɪkeə*] *n* (US) Krankenkasse *f* für ältere Leute; **medication** [medɪ'keɪʃən] *n* Medikamente *pl*; **to be on** ~ Medikamente nehmen; **medicinal** [me'dɪsɪnl] *adj* Heil-; ~ **herbs** Heilkräuter *pl*; **medicine** ['medsɪn] *n* Arznei *f*; (*science*) Medizin *f*

medieval [medɪ'iːvəl] *adj* mittelalterlich

mediocre [miːdɪ'əʊkə*] *adj* mittelmäßig

meditate ['medɪteɪt] *vi* meditieren; (*fig*) nachdenken (*on* über *+akk*)

Mediterranean [medɪtə'reɪnɪən] *n* (*sea*) Mittelmeer *nt*; (*region*) Mittelmeerraum *m*

medium ['miːdɪəm] *adj* (*quality, size*) mittlere(r, s); (*steak*) halbdurch; ~ (**dry**) (*wine*) halbtrocken; ~ **sized** mittelgroß; ~ **wave** Mittelwelle *f* ▷ *n* (*pl* **media**) Medium *nt*; (*means*) Mittel *nt*

meet [miːt] (**met, met**) *vt* treffen; (*by arrangement*) sich treffen mit; (*difficulties*) stoßen auf *+akk*; (*get to know*) kennen lernen; (*requirement, demand*) gerecht werden *+dat*; (*deadline*) einhalten; **pleased to ~ you** sehr angenehm; **to ~ sb at the station** jdn vom Bahnhof abholen ▷ *vi* sich treffen; (*become acquainted*) sich kennen lernen; **we've met** (*before*) wir kennen uns schon; **meet up** *vt* sich treffen (*with* mit); **meet with** *vt* (*group*) zusammenkommen mit; (*difficulties, resistance*

etc) stoßen auf *+akk*; **meeting** *n* Treffen *nt*; (*business* ~) Besprechung *f*; (*of committee*) Sitzung *f*; (*assembly*) Versammlung *f*; **meeting place**, **meeting point** *n* Treffpunkt *m*

megabyte ['megəbaɪt] *n* Megabyte *nt*

melody ['melədɪ] *n* Melodie *f*

melon ['melən] *n* Melone *f*

melt [melt] *vt, vi* schmelzen

member ['membə*] *n* Mitglied *nt*; (*of tribe, species*) Angehörige(r) *m(f)*; **Member of Parliament** Parlamentsabgeordnete(r) *m(f)*; **membership** *n* Mitgliedschaft *f*; **membership card** *n* Mitgliedskarte *f*

memento [mə'mentəʊ] (*pl* **-es**) *n* Andenken *nt* (*of an +akk*)

memo ['meməʊ] (*pl* **-s**) *n* Mitteilung *f*, Memo *nt*; **memo pad** *n* Notizblock *m*

memorable ['memərəbl] *adj* unvergesslich; **memorial** [mɪ'mɔːrɪəl] *n* Denkmal *nt* (*to* für); **memorize** ['meməraɪz] *vt* sich einprägen, auswendig lernen; **memory** ['memərɪ] *n* Gedächtnis *nt*; (*Inform: of computer*) Speicher *m*; (*sth recalled*) Erinnerung *f*; **in ~ of** zur Erinnerung an *+akk*

men [men] *pl of* **man**

menace ['menɪs] *n* Bedrohung *f*; (*danger*) Gefahr *f*

mend [mend] *vt* reparieren; (*clothes*) flicken ▷ *n* **to be on the ~** auf dem Wege der Besserung sein

meningitis [menɪn'dʒaɪtɪs] *n* Hirnhautentzündung *f*

menopause ['menəʊpɔːz] *n* Wechseljahre *pl*

mental ['mentl] *adj* geistig; ~ **hospital** psychiatrische Klinik; **mentality** [men'tælɪtɪ] *n* Mentalität *f*; **mentally** ['mentəlɪ] *adv* geistig; ~ **handicapped** geistig behindert; ~ **ill** geisteskrank

mention ['menʃən] n Erwähnung f ▷ vt erwähnen (*to sb* jdm gegenüber); **don't ~ it** bitte sehr, gern geschehen

menu ['menju:] n Speisekarte f; (*Inform*) Menü nt

merchandise ['mɜːtʃəndaɪz] n Handelsware f; **merchant** ['mɜːtʃənt] adj Handels-

merciful ['mɜːsɪful] adj gnädig, **mercifully** adv glücklicherweise

mercury ['mɜːkjʊrɪ] n Quecksilber nt

mercy ['mɜːsɪ] n Gnade f

mere [mɪə*] adj bloß; **merely** ['mɪəlɪ] adv bloß, lediglich

merge [mɜːdʒ] vi verschmelzen; (*Auto*) sich einfädeln; (*Comm*) fusionieren; **merger** n (*Comm*) Fusion f

meringue [mə'ræŋ] n Baiser nt

merit ['merɪt] n Verdienst nt; (*advantage*) Vorzug m

merry ['merɪ] adj fröhlich; (*fam: tipsy*) angeheitert; **Merry Christmas** Fröhliche Weihnachten!; **merry-go-round** n Karussell nt

mess [mes] n Unordnung f; (*muddle*) Durcheinander nt; (*dirt*) Schweinerei f; (*trouble*) Schwierigkeiten pl; **in a ~** (*muddled*) durcheinander; (*untidy*) unordentlich; (*fig: person*) in der Klemme, **to make a ~ of sth** etw verpfuschen, **to look a ~** unmöglich aussehen; **mess about** vi (*tinker with*) herummurksen (*with* an +dat); (*play the fool*) herumalbern; (*do nothing in particular*) herumgammeln; **mess up** vt verpfuschen; (*make untidy*) in Unordnung bringen; (*dirty*) schmutzig machen

message ['mesɪdʒ] n Mitteilung f, Nachricht f; (*meaning*) Botschaft f; **can I give him a ~?** kann ich ihm etwas ausrichten?; **please leave a ~** (*on answerphone*) bitte hinterlassen Sie eine Nachricht; **I get the ~** ich

habe verstanden

messenger ['mesɪndʒə*] n Bote m

messy ['mesɪ] adj (*untidy*) unordentlich; (*situation etc*) verfahren

met [met] pt, pp of **meet**

metal ['metl] n Metall nt, **metallic** [mɪ'tælɪk] adj metallisch

meteorology [miːtɪə'rɒlədʒɪ] n Meteorologie f

meter ['miːtə*] n Zähler m; (*parking meter*) Parkuhr f; (*US*) see **metre**

method ['meθəd] n Methode f; **methodical** [mɪ'θɒdɪkəl] adj methodisch

meticulous [mɪ'tɪkjʊləs] adj (*peinlich*) genau

metre ['miːtə*] n Meter m o nt; **metric** ['metrɪk] adj metrisch; **~ system** Dezimalsystem nt

Mexico ['meksɪkəʊ] n Mexiko nt

mice [maɪs] pl of **mouse**

mickey ['mɪkɪ] n **to take the ~ (out of sb)** (*fam*) (jdn) auf den Arm nehmen

microchip ['maɪkrəʊtʃɪp] n (*Inform*) Mikrochip m; **microphone** n Mikrofon nt; **microscope** n Mikroskop nt, **microwave (oven)** n Mikrowelle(nherd) f(m)

mid [mɪd] adj: **in ~ January** Mitte Januar; **he's in his ~ forties** er ist Mitte vierzig

midday ['mɪddeɪ] n Mittag m; **at ~** mittags

middle ['mɪdl] n Mitte f; (*waist*) Taille f; **in the ~ of** mitten in +dat; **to be in the ~ of doing sth** gerade dabei sein etw zu tun ▷ adj mittlere(r, s), Mittel-; **the ~ one** der/die/das Mittlere; **middle-aged** adj mittleren Alters; **Middle Ages** npl **the ~** das Mittelalter; **middle-class** adj mittelständisch; (*bourgeois*) bürgerlich; **middle classes** npl **the ~** der Mittelstand; **Middle East** n the ~ der Nahe Osten; **middle name** n zweiter Vorname

Midlands ['mɪdləndz] npl the ~ Mittelengland nt

midnight ['mɪdnaɪt] n Mitternacht f

midst [mɪdst] n in the ~ of mitten in +dat

midsummer ['mɪdsʌmə*] n Hochsommer m; **Midsummer's Day** Sommersonnenwende f

midway [mɪd'weɪ] adv auf halbem Wege; ~ through the film nach der Hälfte des Films; **midweek** [mɪd'wiːk] adj, adv in der Mitte der Woche

midwife ['mɪdwaɪf] (pl -wives) n Hebamme f

midwinter [mɪd'wɪntə*] n tiefster Winter

might [maɪt] pt of **may**; (possibility) könnte; (permission) dürfte; (would) würde; **they ~ still come** sie könnten noch kommen; **he ~ have let me know** er hätte mir doch Bescheid sagen können; **I thought she ~ change her mind** ich dachte schon, sie würde sich anders entscheiden ▷ n Macht f, Kraft f

mighty ['maɪtɪ] adj gewaltig; (powerful) mächtig

migraine ['miːgreɪn] n Migräne f

migrant ['maɪgrənt] n (bird) Zugvogel m; ~ **worker** Gastarbeiter(in) m(f); **migrate** [maɪ'greɪt] vi abwandern; (birds) nach Süden ziehen

mike [maɪk] n (fam) Mikro nt

Milan [mɪ'læn] n Mailand nt

mild [maɪld] adj mild; (person) sanft; **mildly** adv to put it ~ gelinde gesagt; **mildness** n Milde f

mile [maɪl] n Meile f (= 1,609 km); **for ~s (and ~s)** kilometerweit; **~s per hour** Meilen pro Stunde; **~s better than** hundertmal besser als;

mileage n Meilen pl, Meilenzahl f; **mileometer** [maɪ'lɒmɪtə*] n ≈ Kilometerzähler m; **milestone** n (a. fig) Meilenstein m

militant ['mɪlɪtənt] adj militant; **military** ['mɪlɪtərɪ] adj Militär-, militärisch

milk [mɪlk] n Milch f ▷ vt melken; **milk chocolate** n Vollmilchschokolade f; **milkman** (pl -men) n Milchmann m; **milk shake** n Milkshake m, Milchmixgetränk nt

mill [mɪl] n Mühle f; (factory) Fabrik f

millennium [mɪ'leniəm] n Jahrtausend nt

millet ['mɪlɪt] n Hirse f

milligramme ['mɪlɪgræm] n Milligramm m; **milliliter** (US), **millilitre** n Milliliter m; **millimeter** (US), **millimetre** n Millimeter m

million ['mɪljən] n Million f; **five ~** fünf Millionen; **~s of people** Millionen von Menschen; **millionaire** [mɪljə'nɛə*] n Millionär(in) m(f)

mime [maɪm] n Pantomime f ▷ vt, vi mimen; **mimic** ['mɪmɪk] n Imitator(in) m(f) ▷ vt, vi nachahmen; **mimicry** ['mɪmɪkrɪ] n Nachahmung f

mince [mɪns] vt (zer)hacken ▷ n (meat) Hackfleisch nt; **mincemeat** n ≈ süße Gebäckfüllung aus Rosinen, Äpfeln, Zucker, Gewürzen und Talg; **mince pie** n mit 'mincemeat' gefülltes süßes Weihnachtsgebäck

mind [maɪnd] n (intellect) Verstand m; (also person) Geist m; **out of sight, out of** ~ aus den Augen, aus dem Sinn; **he is out of his ~** er ist nicht bei Verstand; **to keep sth in ~** etw im Auge behalten; **do you have sth in ~?** denken Sie an etwas Besonderes?; **I've a lot on my ~** mich beschäftigt so vieles im Moment; **to change one's ~** es sich dat anders überlegen ▷ vt (look after) aufpassen auf +akk; (object to) etwas haben gegen; ~ **you,** ... allerdings ...; **I wouldn't ~ ...** ich hätte nichts gegen ...; **'~ the step'** „Vorsicht Stufe!" ▷ vi etwas dagegen haben; **do you ~ if I ...** macht es Ihnen etwas aus, **nenn Ih ... I don't ~ es** ist mir egal, meinetwegen; **never** macht nichts

mine [maɪn] pron meine(r, s); **this is** ~ das gehört mir; **a friend of** ~ ein Freund von mir ▷ n (coalmine) Bergwerk nt, (Mil) Mine f; **miner** n Bergarbeiter m

mineral ['mɪnərəl] n Mineral nt; **mineral water** n Mineralwasser nt

mingle ['mɪŋgl] vi sich mischen (with unter +akk)

miniature ['mɪnɪtʃə*] adj Miniatur-

minibar ['mɪnɪbɑː] n Minibar f; **minibus** n Kleinbus m; **minicab** n Kleintaxi nt

minimal ['mɪnɪml] adj minimal; **minimize** ['mɪnɪmaɪz] vt auf ein Minimum reduzieren; **minimum** ['mɪnɪməm] n Minimum nt ▷ adj Mindest-

mining ['maɪnɪŋ] n Bergbau m

miniskirt ['mɪnɪskɜːt] n Minirock m

minister ['mɪnɪstə*] n (Pol) Minister(in) m(f); (Rel) Pastor(in) m(f), Pfarrer(in) m(f); **ministry** ['mɪnɪstrɪ] n (Pol) Ministerium nt

minor ['maɪnə*] adj kleiner; (insignificant) unbedeutend; (operation, offence) harmlos; ~ **road** Nebenstraße f; (Mus) **A** - a-Moll ▷ n (BRIT: under 18) Minderjährige(r) m(f); **minority** [maɪˈnɒrɪtɪ] n Minderheit f

mint [mɪnt] n Minze f; (sweet) Pfefferminz(bonbon) nt; **mint sauce** n Minzsoße f

minus ['maɪnəs] prep minus;

(without) ohne

minute [maɪˈnjuːt] adj winzig; **in ~ detail** genauestens ▷ ['mɪnɪt] n Minute f; **just a ~** Moment mal; **any ~** jeden Augenblick; **~s** pl (of meeting) Protokoll nt

miracle ['mɪrəkl] n Wunder nt; **miraculous** [mɪˈrækjʊləs] adj wunderbar

mirage ['mɪrɑːʒ] n Fata Morgana f, Luftspiegelung f

mirror ['mɪrə*] n Spiegel m

misbehave [mɪsbɪˈheɪv] vi sich schlecht benehmen

miscalculation ['mɪskælkjʊˈleɪʃən] n Fehlkalkulation f; (misjudgement) Fehleinschätzung f

miscarriage [mɪsˈkærɪdʒ] n (Med) Fehlgeburt f

miscellaneous [mɪsɪˈleɪnɪəs] adj verschieden

mischief ['mɪstʃɪf] n Unfug m; **mischievous** ['mɪstʃɪvəs] adj (person) durchtrieben; (glance) verschmitzt

misconception [mɪskənˈsepʃən] n falsche Vorstellung

misconduct [mɪsˈkɒndʌkt] n Vergehen nt

miser ['maɪzə*] n Geizhals m

miserable ['mɪzərəbl] adj (person) todunglücklich; (conditions, life) elend; (pay, weather) miserabel

miserly ['maɪzəlɪ] adj geizig

misery ['mɪzərɪ] n Elend nt; (suffering) Qualen pl

misfit ['mɪsfɪt] n Außenseiter(in) m(f)

misfortune [mɪsˈfɔːtʃən] n Pech nt

misguided [mɪsˈgaɪdɪd] adj irrig; (optimism) unangebracht

misinform [mɪsɪnˈfɔːm] vt falsch informieren

misinterpret [mɪsɪnˈtɜːprɪt] vt falsch auslegen

misjudge [mɪs'dʒʌdʒ] vt falsch beurteilen

mislay [mɪs'leɪ] irr vt verlegen

mislead [mɪs'liːd] irr vt -irreführen; **misleading** adj irreführend

misprint ['mɪsprɪnt] n Druckfehler m

mispronounce [mɪsprə'naʊns] vt falsch aussprechen

miss [mɪs] n (fail to hit, catch) verfehlen; (not notice, hear) nicht mitbekommen; (be too late for) verpassen; (chance) versäumen; (regret the absence of) vermissen; **I ~ you** du fehlst mir ▷ vi nicht treffen; (shooting) danebenschießen; (ball, shot etc) danebengehen; **miss out** vt auslassen ▷ vi **to ~ on** etw verpassen

Miss [mɪs] n (unmarried woman) Fräulein nt

missile ['mɪsaɪl] n Geschoss nt; (rocket) Rakete f

missing ['mɪsɪŋ] adj (person) vermisst; (thing) fehlend; **to be/go ~** vermisst werden, fehlen

mission ['mɪʃən] n (Pol, Mil, Rel) Auftrag m, Mission f; **missionary** ['mɪʃənrɪ] n Missionar(in) m(f)

mist [mɪst] n (feiner) Nebel m; (haze) Dunst m; **mist over**, **mist up** vi sich beschlagen

mistake [mɪs'teɪk] n Fehler m; **by ~** aus Versehen ▷ irr vt (mistook, mistaken) (misunderstand) falsch verstehen; (mix up) verwechseln (for mit); **there's no mistaking ...** ... ist unverkennbar; (meaning) ... ist unmissverständlich; **mistaken** adj (idea, identity) falsch; **to be ~** sich irren, falsch liegen

mistletoe ['mɪsltəʊ] n Mistel f

mistreat [mɪs'triːt] vt schlecht behandeln

mistress ['mɪstrɪs] n (lover) Geliebte f

mistrust [mɪs'trʌst] n Misstrauen nt (of gegen) ▷ vt misstrauen +dat

misty ['mɪstɪ] adj neblig; (hazy) dunstig

misunderstand [mɪsʌndə'stænd] irr vt, vi falsch verstehen; **misunderstanding** n Missverständnis nt; (disagreement) Differenz f

mitten ['mɪtn] n Fausthandschuh m

mix [mɪks] n (mixture) Mischung f ▷ vt mischen; (blend) vermischen (with mit); (drinks, music) mixen; **to ~ business with pleasure** das Angenehme mit dem Nützlichen verbinden ▷ vi (liquids) sich vermischen lassen; **mix up** vt (mix) zusammenmischen; (confuse) verwechseln (with mit); **mixed** adj gemischt; **a ~ bunch** eine bunt gemischte Truppe; **~ grill** Mixedgrill m; **~ vegetables** Mischgemüse nt; **mixer** n (for food) Mixer m; **mixture** ['mɪkstʃə*] n Mischung f; (Med) Saft m; **mix-up** n Durcheinander nt

ml abbr = **millilitre** ml

mm abbr = **millimetre** mm

moan [məʊn] n Stöhnen nt; (complaint) Gejammer nt ▷ vi stöhnen; (complain) jammern, meckern (about über +akk)

mobile ['məʊbaɪl] adj beweglich; (on wheels) fahrbar ▷ n (phone) Handy nt; **mobile phone** n Mobiltelefon nt, Handy nt; **mobility** [məʊ'bɪlɪtɪ] n Beweglichkeit f

mock [mɒk] vt verspotten ▷ adj Schein-; **mockery** n Spott m

mod cons ['mɒd'kɒnz] abbr = **modern conveniences** (moderner) Komfort

mode [məʊd] n Art f; (Inform) Modus m

model ['mɒdl] n Modell nt; (example) Vorbild nt; (fashion ~) Model nt ▷ adj (miniature) Modell-; (perfect) Muster- ▷ vt (make) formen ▷ vi she ~s for Versace sie arbeitet als Model bei Versace

modem ['məʊdem] n Modem nt

moderate [adj 'mɒdərət] adj mäßig; (views, politics) gemäßigt; (income, success) mittelmäßig ▷ n (Pol) Gemäßigte(r) mf ▷ [ˌmɒdəˈreɪt] vt mäßigen; moderation [ˌmɒdəˈreɪʃən] n Mäßigung f; in ~ mit Maßen

modern ['mɒdən] adj modern; ~ history neuere Geschichte; ~ Greek Neugriechisch nt; modernize ['mɒdənaɪz] vt modernisieren

modest ['mɒdɪst] adj bescheiden; modesty n Bescheidenheit f

modification [mɒdɪfɪˈkeɪʃən] n Abänderung f; modify ['mɒdɪfaɪ] vt abändern

moist [mɔɪst] adj feucht; moisten ['mɔɪsn] vt befeuchten; moisture ['mɔɪstʃə*] n Feuchtigkeit f; moisturizer n Feuchtigkeitscreme f

molar ['məʊlə*] n Backenzahn m

mould (US) see mould

mole [məʊl] n (spot) Leberfleck m; (animal) Maulwurf m

molecule ['mɒlɪkjuːl] n Molekül nt

molest [məʊˈlest] vt belästigen

molt (US) see moult

molten ['məʊltən] adj geschmolzen

mom [mɒm] n (US) Mutti f

moment ['məʊmənt] n Moment m, Augenblick m; just a ~ Moment mal!; at (of for) the ~ im Augenblick; in a ~ gleich

momentous [məˈmentəs] adj bedeutsam

Monaco ['mɒnəkəʊ] n Monaco nt

monarchy ['mɒnəkɪ] n Monar-

chie f

monastery ['mɒnəstrɪ] n (for monks) Kloster nt

Monday ['mʌndeɪ] n Montag m; see also Tuesday

monetary ['mʌnɪtərɪ] adj (reform, policy, union) Währungs-; ~ unit Geldeinheit f

money ['mʌnɪ] n Geld nt; to get one's ~'s worth auf seine Kosten kommen; money order n Postanweisung f

mongrel ['mʌŋɡrəl] n Promenadenmischung f

monitor ['mɒnɪtə*] n (screen) Monitor m ▷ vt (progress etc) überwachen; (broadcasts) abhören

monk [mʌŋk] n Mönch m

monkey ['mʌŋkɪ] n Affe m; ~ business Unfug m

monopolize [məˈnɒpəlaɪz] vt monopolisieren; (fig: person, thing) in Beschlag nehmen; monopoly [məˈnɒpəlɪ] n Monopol nt

monotonous [məˈnɒtənəs] adj eintönig, monoton

monsoon [mɒnˈsuːn] n Monsun m

monster ['mɒnstə*] n (animal, thing) Monstrum nt ▷ adj Riesen-; monstrosity [mɒnˈstrɒsɪtɪ] n Monstrosität f; (thing) Ungetüm nt

month [mʌnθ] n Monat m; monthly adj monatlich; (ticket, salary) Monats- ▷ adv monatlich ▷ n (magazine) Monats(zeit)schrift f

monty ['mɒntɪ] n to go the full ~ (fam: strip) alle Hüllen fallen lassen; (go the whole hog) aufs Ganze gehen

monument ['mɒnjʊmənt] n Denkmal nt (to für); monumental [mɒnjʊˈmentl] adj (huge) gewaltig

mood [muːd] n (of person) Laune f, (u. general) Stimmung f; to be in a good/bad ~ gute/schlechte Laune haben, gut/schlecht drauf sein; to

be in the ~ for sth zu etw aufgelegt sein; **I'm not in the ~** ich fühle mich nicht danach; **moody** *adj* launisch

moon [muːn] *n* Mond *m*; **to be over the ~** *(fam)* überglücklich sein; **moonlight** *n* Mondlicht *nt* ▷ *vi* schwarzarbeiten; **moonlit** *adj (night, landscape)* mondhell

moor [mɔː*] *n* Moor *nt* ▷ *vt, vi* festmachen; **moorings** *npl* Liegeplatz *m*; **moorland** *n* Moorland *nt*, Heideland *nt*

moose [muːs] *(pl -)* *n* Elch *m*

mop [mɒp] *n* Mopp *m*; **mop up** *vt* aufwischen

mope [məʊp] *vi* Trübsal blasen

moped ['məʊped] *n (BRIT)* Moped *nt*

moral ['mɒrəl] *adj* moralisch; *(values)* sittlich ▷ *n* Moral *f*; **~s** *pl* Moral *f*; **morale** [mɒ'rɑːl] *n* Stimmung *f*, Moral *f*; **morality** [mə'rælɪtɪ] *n* Ethik *f*

morbid ['mɔːbɪd] *adj* krankhaft

more [mɔː*] *adj, pron, adv* mehr; *(additional)* noch; **three ~** noch drei; **some ~ tea?** noch etwas Tee?; **are there any ~?** gibt es noch welche?; **I don't go there any ~** ich gehe nicht mehr hin; *(forming comparative)* **~ important** wichtiger; **~ slowly** langsamer; **~ and ~** immer mehr; **~ and ~ beautiful** immer schöner; **~ or less** mehr oder weniger; **moreish** *adj (food)* **these crisps are really ~** ich kann mit diesen Chips einfach nicht aufhören; **moreover** *adv* außerdem

morgue [mɔːg] *n* Leichenschauhaus *nt*

morning ['mɔːnɪŋ] *n* Morgen *m*; **in the ~** am Morgen, morgens; *(tomorrow)* morgen früh; **this ~** heute morgen ▷ *adj* Morgen-; *(early)* Früh-; *(walk etc)* morgendlich; **morning after pill** *n* die Pille danach; **morning sickness** *n* Schwangerschaftsübelkeit *f*

Morocco [mə'rɒkəʊ] *n* Marokko *nt*

moron ['mɔːrɒn] *n* Idiot(in) *m(f)*

morphine ['mɔːfiːn] *n* Morphium *nt*

morsel ['mɔːsl] *n* Bissen *m*

mortal ['mɔːtl] *adj* sterblich; *(wound)* tödlich ▷ *n* Sterbliche(r) *mf*; **mortality** [mɔː'tælɪtɪ] *n (death rate)* Sterblichkeitsziffer *f*; **mortally** *adv* tödlich

mortgage ['mɔːgɪdʒ] *n* Hypothek *f* ▷ *vt* mit einer Hypothek belasten

mortified ['mɔːtɪfaɪd] *adj* **I was ~** es war mir schrecklich peinlich

mortuary ['mɔːtjʊərɪ] *n* Leichenhalle *f*

mosaic [məʊ'zeɪɪk] *n* Mosaik *nt*

Moscow ['mɒskəʊ] *n* Moskau *nt*

Moslem ['mɒzləm] *adj, n see* **Muslim**

mosque [mɒsk] *n* Moschee *f*

mosquito [mɒs'kiːtəʊ] *(pl -es)* *n* (Stech)mücke *f*; *(tropical)* Moskito *m*; **~ net** Moskitonetz *nt*

moss [mɒs] *n* Moos *nt*

most [məʊst] *adj* meiste *pl*, die meisten; **in ~ cases** in den meisten Fällen ▷ *adv (with verbs)* am meisten; *(with adj)* ...ste; *(with adv)* am ...sten; *(very)* äußerst, höchst; **he ate (the) ~** er hat am meisten gegessen; **the ~ beautiful / interesting** der / die / das schönste / interessanteste; **~ interesting** hochinteressant! ▷ *n* beste, meiste, der größte Teil; *(people)* die meisten; **~ of the money / players** das meiste Geld / die meisten Spieler; **for the ~ part** zum größten Teil; **five at the ~** höchstens fünf; **to make the ~ of sth** etw voll ausnützen; **mostly** *adv (most of the time)* meistens; *(mainly)* hauptsächlich; *(for the most* *part*) größtenteils

MOT *abbr* = **Ministry of Transport**; ~ **(test)** ≈ TÜV *m*

motel [məʊˈtel] *n* Motel *nt*

moth [mɒθ] *n* Nachtfalter *m*; (*wool-eating*) Motte *f*; **mothball** *n* Mottenkugel *f*

mother ['mʌðə*] *n* Mutter *f* ▷ *vt* bemuttern; **mother-in-law** (*pl* **mothers-in-law**) *n* Schwiegermutter *f*; **mother-to-be** (*pl* **mothers-to-be**) *n* werdende Mutter

motif [məʊˈtiːf] *n* Motiv *nt*

motion ['məʊʃən] *n* Bewegung *f*; (*in meeting*) Antrag *m*; **motionless** *adj* bewegungslos

motivate ['məʊtɪveɪt] *vt* motivieren; **motive** ['məʊtɪv] *n* Motiv *nt*

motor ['məʊtə*] *n* Motor *m*; (*fam: car*) Auto *nt* ▷ *cpd* Motor-; **Motorail train** ® *n* (*BRIT*) Autoreisezug *m*; **motorbike** *n* Motorrad *nt*; **motorboat** *n* Motorboot *nt*; **motorcycle** *n* Motorrad *nt*; **motor industry** *n* Automobilindustrie *f*; **motoring** ['məʊtərɪŋ] *n* Autofahren *nt*; ~ **organization** Automobilklub *m*; **motorist** ['məʊtərɪst] *n* Autofahrer(in) *m(f)*; **motor oil** *n* Motorenöl *nt*; **motor racing** *n* Autorennsport *m*; **motor scooter** *n* Motorroller *m*; **motor show** *n* Automobilausstellung *f*; **motor vehicle** *n* Kraftfahrzeug *nt*; **motorway** *n* (*BRIT*) Autobahn *f*

motto ['mɒtəʊ] (*pl* -es) *n* Motto *nt*

mould [məʊld] *n* Form *f*; (*mildew*) Schimmel *m* ▷ *vt* (*a. fig*) formen; **mouldy** ['məʊldɪ] *adj* schimmelig

moult [məʊlt] *vi* sich mausern, haaren

mount [maʊnt] *n* (*horse*) steigen auf +*akk*, (*exhibition etc*) organisieren; (*painting*) mit einem Passepartout versehen ▷ *vi* **to ~ (up)** (an)steigen

▷ *n* Passepartout *nt*

mountain ['maʊntɪn] *n* Berg *m*; **mountain bike** *n* Mountainbike *nt*; **mountaineer** [maʊntɪ'nɪə*] *n* Bergsteiger(in) *m(f)*; **mountaineering** [maʊntɪ'nɪərɪŋ] *n* Bergsteigen *nt*; **mountainous** *adj* bergig; **mountainside** *n* Berghang *m*

mourn [mɔːn] *vt* betrauern ▷ *vi* trauern (*for* um); **mourner** *n* Trauernde(r) *mf*; **mournful** *adj* trauervoll; **mourning** *n* Trauer *f*; **to be in ~** trauern (*for* um)

mouse [maʊs] (*pl* **mice**) *n* (*a. Inform*) Maus *f*; **mouse mat**, **mouse pad** (*US*) *n* Mauspad *nt*; **mouse trap** *n* Mausefalle *f*

mousse [muːs] *n* (*Gastr*) Creme *f*; (*styling*) Schaumfestiger *m*

moustache [ma'staːʃ] *n* Schnurrbart *m*

mouth [maʊθ] *n* Mund *m*; (*of animal*) Maul *nt*; (*of cave*) Eingang *m*; (*of bottle etc*) Öffnung *f*; (*of river*) Mündung *f*; **to keep one's ~ shut** (*fam*) den Mund halten; **mouthful** *n* (*of drink*) Schluck *m*; (*of food*) Bissen *m*; **mouth organ** *n* Mundharmonika *f*; **mouthwash** *n* Mundwasser *nt*; **mouthwatering** *adj* appetitlich, lecker

move [muːv] *n* (*movement*) Bewegung *f*; (*in game*) Zug *m*; (*step*) Schritt *m*; (*moving house*) Umzug *m*; **to make a ~** (*in game*) ziehen; (*leave*) sich auf den Weg machen; **to get a ~ on (with sth)** sich (*mit etw*) beeilen ▷ *vt* bewegen; (*object*) rücken; (*car*) wegfahren; (*transport: goods*) befördern; (*people*) transportieren; (*in job*) versetzen; (*emotionally*) bewegen, rühren; **I can't ~ it** (*stuck, too heavy*) ich kriege es nicht von der Stelle; **to ~ house** umziehen ▷ *vi* sich bewegen; (*change place*) gehen; (*vehicle, ship*) fahren; (*move house,*

town etc) umziehen; (in game) ziehen;
move about vi sich bewegen;
(travel) unterwegs sein; **move
away** vi weggehen; (move town)
wegziehen; **move in** vi (to house)
einziehen; **move off** vi losfahren;
move on vi weitergehen; (vehicle)
weiterfahren; **move out** vi ausziehen; **move up** vi (in queue etc)
aufrücken; **movement** n Bewegung f

movie ['muːvɪ] n Film m; **the ~s**
(the cinema) das Kino

moving ['muːvɪŋ] adj (emotionally) ergreifend, berührend

mow [məʊ] (**mowed**, **mown** o
mowed) vt mähen; **mower** n
(lawn~) Rasenmäher m

mown [məʊn] pp of **mow**

Mozambique [məʊzæmˈbiːk] n
Mosambik nt

MP abbr = **Member of Parliament**
Parlamentsabgeordnete(r) mf

mph abbr = **miles per hour** Meilen
pro Stunde

MPV abbr = **multi-purpose vehicle**
Mehrzweckfahrzeug nt

MP3 n MP3 nt

Mr [ˈmɪstə*] n (form of address) Herr

Mrs [ˈmɪsɪz] n (form of address) Frau

Ms [məz] n (form of address for young
woman, married or unmarried) Frau

MS n abbr = **multiple sclerosis** MS
f

Mt abbr = **Mount** Berg m

much [mʌtʃ] (**more**, **most**) adj
viel; **we haven't got ~ time** wir
haben nicht viel Zeit; **how ~ money?** wie viel Geld? ▷ adv viel; (with
verb) sehr; **~ better** viel besser; **I like
it very ~** es gefällt mir sehr gut; **I
don't like it ~** ich mag es nicht
besonders; **thank you very ~** danke
sehr; **I thought as ~** das habe ich
mir gedacht; **~ as I like him** so sehr
ich ihn mag; **we don't see them ~**

wir sehen sie nicht sehr oft; **~ the
same** fast gleich ▷ n viel; **as ~ as
you want** so viel du willst; **he's not
~ of a cook** er ist kein großer Koch

muck [mʌk] n (fam) Dreck m;
muck about vi (fam) herumalbern;
muck up vt (fam) dreckig machen;
(spoil) vermasseln; **mucky** adj
dreckig

mucus [ˈmjuːkəs] n Schleim m

mud [mʌd] n Schlamm m

muddle [ˈmʌdl] n Durcheinander
nt; **to be in a ~** ganz durcheinander
sein ▷ vt **to ~ (up)** durcheinander
bringen; **muddled** adj konfus

muddy [ˈmʌdɪ] adj schlammig;
(shoes) schmutzig; **mudguard**
[ˈmʌdgɑːd] n Schutzblech nt

muesli [ˈmuːzlɪ] n Müsli nt

muffin [ˈmʌfɪn] n Muffin m;
(BRIT) weiches, flaches Milchbrötchen
aus Hefeteig, das meist getoastet und
mit Butter gegessen wird

muffle [ˈmʌfl] vt (sound) dämpfen; **muffler** n (US) Schalldämpfer
m

mug [mʌg] n (cup) Becher m; (fam:
fool) Trottel m ▷ vt (attack and rob)
überfallen; **mugging** n Raubüberfall m

muggy [ˈmʌgɪ] adj (weather)
schwül

mule [mjuːl] n Maulesel m

mull over [mʌl ˈəʊvə*] vt nachdenken über +akk

mulled [mʌld] adj **~ wine** Glühwein m

multicolored (US), **multicol-
oured** [ˈmʌltɪˈkʌləd] adj bunt;
multicultural adj multikulturell;
multi-grade adj **~ oil** Mehrbe-
reichsöl nt; **multilingual** adj
mehrsprachig; **multinational** n
(company) Multi m

multiple [ˈmʌltɪpl] n Vielfache(s)
nt ▷ adj mehrfach; (several) meh-

rere; **multiple-choice (method)** n Multiple-Choice-Verfahren nt; **multiple sclerosis** [ˈmʌltɪpləkleˈrəʊsɪs] n Multiple Sklerose f

multiplex [ˈmʌltɪpleks] adj. n ~ **(cinema)** Multiplexkino nt

multiplication [mʌltɪplɪˈkeɪʃən] n Multiplikation f; **multiply** [ˈmʌltɪplaɪ] vi multiplizieren (by mit) ▷ vt sich vermehren

multi-purpose [ˈmʌltɪˈpɜːpəs] adj Mehrzweck-; **multistorey (car park)** n Parkhaus nt, **multitasking** n (Inform) Multitasking nt

mum [mʌm] n (fam: mother) Mutti f, Mami f

mumble [ˈmʌmbl] vt, vi murmeln

mummy [ˈmʌmɪ] n (dead body) Mumie f; (fam: mother) Mutti f, Mami f

mumps [mʌmps] nsing Mumps m

munch [mʌntʃ] vt, vi mampfen

Munich [ˈmjuːnɪk] n München nt

municipal [mjuːˈnɪsɪpəl] adj städtisch

mural [ˈmjʊərəl] n Wandgemälde nt

murder [ˈmɜːdə*] n Mord m; **the traffic was ~** der Verkehr war die Hölle ▷ vt ermorden; **murderer** n Mörder(in) m(f)

murky [ˈmɜːkɪ] adj düster; (water) trüb

murmur [ˈmɜːmə*] vt, vi murmeln

muscle [ˈmʌsl] n Muskel m; **muscular** [ˈmʌskjʊlə*] adj (strong) muskulös; (cramp, pain etc) Muskel-

museum [mjuːˈzɪəm] n Museum nt

mushroom [ˈmʌʃruːm] n (essbarer) Pilz; (button ~) Champignon m ▷ vi (fig) emporschießen

mushy [ˈmʌʃɪ] adj breiig; **~ peas** Erbsenmus nt

music [ˈmjuːzɪk] n Musik f;

(printed) Noten pl, **musical** adj (sound) melodisch; (person) musikalisch; **~ instrument** Musikinstrument nt ▷ n (show) Musical nt; **musically** adv musikalisch; **musician** [mjuːˈzɪʃən] n Musiker(in) m(f)

Muslim [ˈmʊzlɪm] adj moslemisch ▷ n Moslem m, Muslime f

mussel [ˈmʌsl] n Miesmuschel f

must [mʌst] (had to, had to) vb aux (need to) müssen; (in negation) dürfen; **I ~n't forget that** ich darf das nicht vergessen; (certainty) **he ~ be there by now** er ist inzwischen bestimmt schon da; (assumption) **I ~ have lost it** ich habe es wohl verloren; **~ you?** muss das sein? ▷ n Muss nt

mustache [ˈmʌstæʃ] n (US) Schnurrbart m

mustard [ˈmʌstəd] n Senf m; **to cut the ~** es bringen

mustn't [ˈmʌsnt] contr of must not

mute [mjuːt] adj stumm

mutter [ˈmʌtə*] vt, vi murmeln

mutton [ˈmʌtn] n Hammelfleisch nt

mutual [ˈmjuːtjʊəl] adj gegenseitig, **by ~ consent** in gegenseitigem Einvernehmen

my [maɪ] adj mein; **I've hurt ~ leg** ich habe mir das Bein verletzt

Myanmar [ˈmaɪænmɑː] n Myanmar nt

myself [maɪˈself] pron (reflexive) mich akk, mir dat; **I've hurt ~** ich habe mich verletzt; **I've bought ~ a flat** ich habe mir eine Wohnung gekauft; **I need it for ~** ich brauche es für mich (selbst); (emphatic) **I did it ~** ich habe es selbst gemacht; **(all) by ~** allein

mysterious [mɪˈstɪərɪəs] adj geheimnisvoll, mysteriös; (inexplicable) rätselhaft; **mystery** ['mɪstərɪ] n Geheimnis nt; (puzzle) Rätsel nt; **it's a ~ to me** es ist mir schleierhaft; **mystify** ['mɪstɪfaɪ] vt verblüffen

myth [mɪθ] n Mythos m; (fig: untrue story) Märchen nt; **mythical** adj mythisch; (fig: untrue) erfunden; **mythology** [mɪ'θɒlədʒɪ] n Mythologie f

N abbr = **north** N
nag [næg] vt, vi herumnörgeln (sb an jdm); **nagging** n Nörgelei f
nail [neɪl] n Nagel m ▷ vt festnageln (to an); **nail down** vt festnageln; **nailbrush** n Nagelbürste f; **nail clippers** npl Nagelknipser m; **nailfile** n Nagelfeile f; **nail polish** n Nagellack m; **nail polish remover** n Nagellackentferner m; **nail scissors** npl Nagelschere f; **nail varnish** n Nagellack m
naive [naɪ'iːv] adj naiv
naked ['neɪkɪd] adj nackt
name [neɪm] n Name m; **his ~ is ...** er heißt ...; **what's your ~?** wie heißen Sie?; (reputation) **to have a good/bad ~** einen guten/schlechten Ruf haben ▷ vt nennen (after nach); (sth new) benennen; (nominate) ernennen (as als/zu); **a boy ~d ...** ein Junge namens ...; **namely** adv nämlich; **name plate** n Namensschild nt
nan bread ['nɑːnbred] n (warm

serviertes) indisches Fladenbrot
nanny ['nænɪ] n Kindermädchen nt
nap [næp] n **to have a ~** ein Nickerchen machen
napkin ['næpkɪn] n *(at table)* Serviette f
Naples ['neɪplz] n Neapel nt
nappy ['næpɪ] n *(BRIT)* Windel f
narcotic [nɑː'kɒtɪk] n Rauschgift nt

narrate [nə'reɪt] vt erzählen; **narration** [nə'reɪʃən], **narrative** ['nærətɪv] n Erzählung f; **narrator** [nə'reɪtə*] n Erzähler(in) m(f)
narrow ['nærəʊ] adj eng, schmal; *(victory, majority)* knapp; **to have a ~ escape** mit knapper Not davonkommen ▷ vi sich verengen; **narrow down** vt einschränken *(to sth auf etw akk)*, **narrow-minded** adj engstirnig

nasty ['nɑːstɪ] adj ekelhaft; *(person)* fies; *(remark)* gehässig; *(accident, wound etc)* schlimm
nation ['neɪʃən] n Nation f, **national** ['næʃənl] adj national; ~ **anthem** Nationalhymne f; **National Health Service** *(BRIT)* staatlicher Gesundheitsdienst; ~ **insurance** *(BRIT)* Sozialversicherung f; ~ **park** Nationalpark m, ~ **service** Wehrdienst m, ~ **socialism** *(Hist)* Nationalsozialismus m ▷ n Staatsbürger(in) m(f)

● **NATIONAL TRUST**
● Der **National Trust** ist ein 1895
● gegründeter Natur- und Denk-
● malschutzverband in Großbritan-
● nien, der Gebäude und Gelände
● von besonderem historischem
● oder ästhetischem Interesse erhält
● und der Öffentlichkeit zugänglich
● macht.

nationality [næʃ'nælɪtɪ] n Staatsangehörigkeit f, Nationalität f; **nationalize** ['næʃnəlaɪz] vt verstaatlichen; **nationwide** adj, adv landesweit
native ['neɪtɪv] adj einheimisch; *(inborn)* angeboren, natürlich; **Native American** Indianer(in) m(f); ~ **country** Heimatland nt; **a ~ German** ein gebürtiger Deutscher, eine gebürtige Deutsche; ~ **language** Muttersprache f; ~ **speaker** Muttersprachler(in) m(f) ▷ n Einheimische(r) mf; *(in colonial context)* Eingeborene(r) mf
nativity play [nə'tɪvətɪpleɪ] n Krippenspiel nt
NATO ['neɪtəʊ] acr = **North Atlantic Treaty Organization** Nato f
natural ['nætʃrəl] adj natürlich; *(law, science, forces etc)* Natur-; *(inborn)* angeboren; ~ **gas** Erdgas nt; ~ **resources** Bodenschätze pl; **naturally** adv natürlich; *(by nature)* von Natur aus; **it comes ~ to her** es fällt ihr leicht
nature ['neɪtʃə*] n Natur f; *(type)* Art f; **it is not in my ~** es entspricht nicht meiner Art; **by ~** von Natur aus; **nature reserve** n Naturschutzgebiet nt
naughty ['nɔːtɪ] adj *(child)* ungezogen; *(cheeky)* frech
nausea ['nɔːsɪə] n Übelkeit f
nautical ['nɔːtɪkəl] adj nautisch; ~ **mile** Seemeile f
nave [neɪv] n Hauptschiff nt
navel ['neɪvl] n Nabel m
navigate ['nævɪgeɪt] vi navigieren; *(in car)* lotsen, dirigieren; **navigation** [nævɪ'geɪʃən] n Navigation f; *(in car)* Lotsen nt
navy ['neɪvɪ] n Marine f; ~ **blue** Marineblau nt
Nazi ['nɑːtsɪ] n Nazi m
NB abbr = **nota bene** NB

NE abbr = **northeast** NO

near [nɪə*] adj nahe; **my ~est relations** meine nächsten Verwandten; **in the ~ future** in nächster Zukunft; **that was a ~ miss** (o thing) das war knapp; (with price) ... ▷ adv in der Nähe; **so ~** so nahe; **come ~er** näher kommen; (event) näher rücken ▷ prep ~ **(to)** (space) nahe an +dat; (vicinity) in der Nähe +gen; **~ the sea** nahe am Meer; **~ the station** in der Nähe des Bahnhofs, in Bahnhofsnähe; **nearby** adj nahe gelegen ▷ adv in der Nähe; **nearly** adv fast; **nearside** n (Auto) Beifahrerseite f; **nearsighted** adj kurzsichtig

neat [niːt] adj ordentlich; (work, writing) sauber; (undiluted) pur

necessarily [nesə'serəlɪ] adv notwendigerweise; **not ~** nicht unbedingt; **necessary** ['nesəsərɪ] adj notwendig, nötig; **it's ~ to ...** man muss ...; **it's not ~ for him to come** er braucht nicht mitzukommen; **necessity** [nɪ'sesɪtɪ] n Notwendigkeit f; **the bare necessities** das absolut Notwendigste; **there is no ~ to ...** man braucht nicht (zu) ..., man muss nicht ...

neck [nek] n Hals m; (size) Halsweite f; **back of the ~** Nacken m; **necklace** ['neklɪs] n Halskette f; **necktie** n (US) Krawatte f

nectarine ['nektərɪn] n Nektarine f

née [neɪ] adj geborene

need [niːd] n (requirement) Bedürfnis nt (for für); (necessity) Notwendigkeit f; (poverty) Not f; **to be in ~ of sth** etw brauchen; **if ~(s) be** wenn nötig; **there is no ~ to ...** man braucht nicht (zu) ..., man muss nicht ... ▷ vt brauchen; **I ~ to speak to you** ich muss mit dir reden; **you**

~n't go du brauchst nicht (zu) gehen, du musst nicht gehen

needle ['niːdl] n Nadel f

needless, **needlessly** ['niːdlɪs, -lɪ] adj, adv unnötig; **~ to say** selbstverständlich

needy ['niːdɪ] adj bedürftig

negative ['negətɪv] n (Ling) Verneinung f; (Foto) Negativ nt ▷ adj negativ; (answer) verneinend

neglect [nɪ'glekt] n Vernachlässigung f ▷ vt vernachlässigen; **to ~ to do sth** es versäumen, etw zu tun; **negligence** ['neglɪdʒəns] n Nachlässigkeit f; **negligent** adj nachlässig

negligible ['neglɪdʒəbl] adj unbedeutend; (amount) geringfügig

negotiate [nɪ'gəʊʃɪeɪt] vi verhandeln; **negotiation** [nɪgəʊʃɪ'eɪʃən] n Verhandlung f

neigh [neɪ] vi (horse) wiehern

neighbour (US), **neighbor** ['neɪbə*] n Nachbar(in) m(f); **neighbo(u)rhood** n Nachbarschaft f; **neighbo(u)ring** adj benachbart

neither ['naɪðə*] adj, pron keine(r, s) von beiden; **~ of you/us** keiner von euch/uns beiden ▷ adv **~ ... nor ...** weder ... noch ... ▷ conj **I'm not going – ~ am I** ich gehe nicht – ich auch nicht

neon ['niːɒn] n Neon nt; **~ sign** (advertisement) Leuchtreklame f

nephew ['nefjuː] n Neffe m

nerd [nɜːv] n (fam) Schwachkopf m; **he's a real computer ~** er ist ein totaler Computerfreak

nerve [nɜːv] n Nerv m; **he gets on my ~s** er geht mir auf die Nerven; (courage) **to keep/lose one's ~** die Nerven behalten/verlieren; (cheek) **to have the ~ to do sth** die Frechheit besitzen, etw zu tun; **nerve-racking** adj nervenaufreibend; **nervous** ['nɜːvəs] adj (ap-

prehensive) ängstlich; *(on edge)* nervös; **nervous breakdown** n Nervenzusammenbruch m

nest [nest] n Nest nt ▷ vi nisten

net [net] n Netz nt; **the Net** *(Internet)* das Internet; **on the ~** im Netz ▷ *adj (price, weight)* Netto-; **~ profit** Reingewinn m; **netball** n Netzball m

Netherlands ['neðələndz] *npl* **the ~** die Niederlande *pl*

nettle ['netl] n Nessel f

network ['netwɜːk] n Netz nt; *(TV, Radio)* Sendenetz nt; *(Inform)* Netzwerk nt

neurosis [njʊə'rəʊsɪs] n Neurose f; **neurotic** [njʊə'rɒtɪk] *adj* neurotisch

neuter ['njuːtə*] *adj (Bio)* geschlechtslos; *(Ling)* sächlich

neutral ['njuːtrəl] *adj* neutral ▷ n *(gear in car)* Leerlauf m

never ['nevə*] *adv* nie(mals); **~ before** noch nie; **~ mind** macht nichts!; **never-ending** *adj* endlos; **nevertheless** [nevəðə'les] *adv* trotzdem

new [njuː] *adj* neu; **this is all ~ to me** das ist für mich noch ungewohnt; **newcomer** n Neuankömmling m; *(in job, subject)* Neuling m

New England [njuː'ɪŋglənd] n Neuengland nt

Newfoundland ['njuːfəndlənd] n Neufundland nt

newly ['njuːlɪ] *adv* neu; **~ made** *(cake)* frisch gebacken; **newly-weds** *npl* Frischvermählte *pl*; **new moon** n Neumond m

news [njuːz] *nsing (item of ~)* Nachricht f; *(Radio, TV)* Nachrichten *pl*; **good ~** ein erfreuliche Nachricht; **what's the ~?** was gibt's Neues?; **have you heard the ~?** hast du das Neueste gehört?; **that's ~ to me** das

ist mir neu; **newsagent**, **news dealer** *(US)* n Zeitungshändler(in) m(f); **news bulletin** n Nachrichtensendung f; **news flash** n Kurzmeldung f; **newsgroup** n *(Inform)* Diskussionsforum nt, Newsgroup f; **newsletter** n Mitteilungsblatt nt; **newspaper** ['njuːspeɪpə*] n Zeitung f

New Year ['njuː'jɪə*] n das neue Jahr; **Happy ~** (ein) frohes Neues Jahr!; *(toast)* Prosit Neujahr!; **~'s Day** Neujahr nt, Neujahrstag m; **~'s Eve** Silvesterabend m; **~'s resolution** guter Vorsatz fürs neue Jahr

New York [njuː'jɔːk] n New York nt

New Zealand [njuː'ziːlənd] n Neuseeland nt ▷ *adj* neuseeländisch; **New Zealander** n Neuseeländer(in) m(f)

next [nekst] *adj* nächste(r, s); **the week after ~** übernächste Woche; **~ time I see him** wenn ich ihn das nächste Mal sehe; **you're ~** du bist jetzt dran ▷ *adv* als Nächstes; *(then)* dann, darauf; **~ to** neben +*dat*; **~ to last** vorletzte(r, s); **~ to impossible** nahezu unmöglich; **the ~ best thing** das Nächstbeste; **~ door** nebenan

NHS *abbr* = **National Health Service**

Niagara Falls [naɪ'ægrə'fɔːlz] *npl* Niagarafälle *pl*

nibble ['nɪbl] vt knabbern an +*dat*; **nibbles** *npl* Knabberzeug nt

Nicaragua [nɪkə'rægjʊə] n Nicaragua nt

nice [naɪs] *adj* nett, sympathisch; *(taste, food, drink)* gut; *(weather)* schön; **~ and ...** schön ...; **be ~ to him** sei nett zu ihm; **have a ~ day** *(US)* schönen Tag noch!; **nicely** *adv* nett; *(well)* gut; **that'll do ~** das genügt vollauf

nick [nɪk] vt (fam: steal) klauen; (capture) schnappen

nickel ['nɪkl] n (Chem) Nickel nt; (US: coin) Nickel nt

nickname ['nɪkneɪm] n Spitzname m

nicotine ['nɪkəti:n] n Nikotin nt; **nicotine patch** n Nikotinpflaster nt

niece [ni:s] n Nichte f

Nigeria [naɪ'dʒɪərɪə] n Nigeria nt

night [naɪt] n Nacht f; (before bed) Abend m; **good ~** gute Nacht!; **at (o by) ~** nachts; **to have an early ~** früh schlafen gehen; **nightcap** n Schlummertrunk m; **nightclub** n Nachtklub m; **nightdress** n Nachthemd nt; **nightie** ['naɪtɪ] n (fam) Nachthemd nt

nightingale ['naɪtɪŋgeɪl] n Nachtigall f

night life ['naɪtlaɪf] n Nachtleben nt; **nightly** adv (every evening) jeden Abend; (every night) jede Nacht; **nightmare** ['naɪtmeə*] n Albtraum m; **nighttime** n Nacht f; **at ~** nachts

nil [nɪl] n (Sport) null

Nile [naɪl] n Nil m

nine [naɪn] num neun; **~ times out of ten** so gut wie immer ▷ n (a. bus etc) Neun f; see also **eight**; **nineteen** [naɪn'ti:n] num neunzehn ▷ n (a. bus etc) Neunzehn f; see also **eight**; **nineteenth**(r, s); see also **eight**; **ninetieth** ['naɪntɪəθ] adj neunzigste(r, s); see also **eighth**; **ninety** ['naɪntɪ] num neunzig ▷ n Neunzig f; see also **eight**; **ninth** [naɪnθ] adj neunte(r, s) ▷ n (fraction) Neuntel nt; see also **eighth**

nipple ['nɪpl] n Brustwarze f

nitrogen ['naɪtrədʒən] n Stickstoff m

no [nəʊ] adv nein; (after compara-

tive) nicht; **I can wait ~ longer** ich kann nicht länger warten; **I have ~ more money** ich habe kein Geld mehr ▷ adj kein; **in ~ time** im Nu; **~ way** (fam) keinesfalls; **it's ~ use (o good)** es hat keinen Zweck; **~ smoking** Rauchen verboten ▷ n (pl **-es**) Nein nt

nobility [nəʊ'bɪlɪtɪ] n Adel m; **noble** ['nəʊbl] adj (rank) adlig; (quality) edel ▷ n Adlige(r) mf

nobody ['nəʊbədɪ] pron niemand; (emphatic) keiner; **~ knows** keiner weiß es; **~ else** sonst niemand, kein anderer ▷ n Niemand m

no-claims bonus [nəʊ'kleɪmz-bəʊnəs] n Schadenfreiheitsrabatt m

nod [nɒd] vi, vt nicken; **nod off** vi einnicken

noise [nɔɪz] n (loud) Lärm m; (sound) Geräusch nt; **noisy** adj laut; (crowd) lärmend

nominate ['nɒmɪneɪt] vt (in election) aufstellen; (appoint) ernennen

nominative ['nɒmɪnətɪv] n (Ling) Nominativ m

nominee [nɒmɪ'ni:] n Kandidat(in) m(f)

non- [nɒn] pref Nicht-; (with adj) nicht-, un-; **non-alcoholic** adj alkoholfrei

none [nʌn] pron keine(r, s); **~ of them** keiner von ihnen; **~ of it is any use** nichts davon ist brauchbar; **there are ~ left** es sind keine mehr da; (with comparative) **to be ~ the wiser** auch nicht schlauer sein; **I was ~ the worse for it** es hat mir nichts geschadet

nonentity [nɒ'nentɪtɪ] n Null f

nonetheless [nʌnðə'les] adv nichtsdestoweniger, dennoch

non-event n Reinfall m; **non-existent** adj nicht vorhanden; **non-**

fiction n Sachbücher pl; **non-iron** adj bügelfrei; **non-polluting** adj schadstofffrei; **non-resident** n 'open to ~s' "auch für Nichthotelgäste"; **non-returnable** adj ~ **bottle** Einwegflasche f

nonsense ['nɒnsəns] n Unsinn m; **don't talk ~** red keinen Unsinn

non-smoker [nɒn'sməʊkə*] n Nichtraucher(in) m(f); **non-smoking** adj Nichtraucher-; **~ area** Nichtraucherbereich m; **non-standard** adj nicht serienmäßig; **non-stop** adj (train) durchgehend; (flight) Nonstop-▷ adv (talk) ununterbrochen; (travel) ohne Unterbrechung; (fly) ohne Zwischenlandung; **non-violent** adj gewaltfrei

noodles ['nuːdlz] npl Nudeln pl

noon [nuːn] n Mittag m; **at ~** um 12 Uhr mittags

no one ['nəʊwʌn] pron niemand; (emphatic) keiner; **~ else** sonst niemand, kein anderer

nor [nɔː] conj **neither ... ~ ...** weder ... noch ...; **I don't smoke, ~ does he** Ich rauche nicht, er auch nicht

norm [nɔːm] n Norm f

normal ['nɔːml] adj normal; **to get back to ~** sich wieder normalisieren; **normally** adv (usually) normalerweise

north [nɔːθ] n Norden m **to the ~ of** nördlich von ▷ adv (go, face) nach Norden ▷ adj Nord-; **~ wind** Nordwind m; **North America** n Nordamerika nt; **northbound** adj (in) Richtung Norden; **northeast** n Nordosten m; **to the ~ of** nordöstlich von ▷ adv (go, face) nach Nordosten ▷ adj Nordost-; **northern** ['nɔːðən] adj nördlich; **~ France** Nordfrankreich nt; **Northern Ireland** n Nordirland nt; **North Pole** n Nordpol m; **North Sea** n

Nordsee f; **northwards** adv nach Norden; **northwest** n Nordwesten m; **to the ~ of** nordwestlich von ▷ adv (go, face) nach Nordwesten ▷ adj Nordwest-

Norway ['nɔːweɪ] n Norwegen nt; **Norwegian** [nɔːˈwiːdʒən] adj norwegisch ▷ n (person) Norweger(in) m(f); (language) Norwegisch nt

nos. abbr = **numbers** Nr.

nose [nəʊz] n Nase f; **nose around** vi herumschnüffeln; **nosebleed** n Nasenbluten nt; **nose-dive** n Sturzflug m; **to take a ~** abstürzen

nosey ['nəʊzɪ] see **nosy**

nostalgia [nɒˈstældʒɪə] n Nostalgie f (for nach); **nostalgic** adj

nostril ['nɒstrɪl] n Nasenloch nt

nosy ['nəʊzɪ] adj neugierig

not [nɒt] adv nicht; **~ a** kein; **~ one of them** kein einziger von ihnen; **he is ~ an expert** er ist kein Experte; **I told him ~ to (do it)** ich sagte ihm, er solle es nicht tun; **~ at all** überhaupt nicht, keineswegs; (don't mention it) gern geschehen; **~ yet** noch nicht

notable ['nəʊtəbl] adj bemerkenswert; **note** [nəʊt] n (written) Notiz f; (short letter) paar Zeilen pl; (on scrap of paper) Zettel m; (comment in book etc) Anmerkung f; (banknote) Schein m; (Mus: sign) Note f; (sound) Ton m; **to make a ~ of sth** sich etw notieren; **~s** (of lecture etc) Aufzeichnungen pl; **to take ~** sich dat Notizen machen (of über +akk) ▷ vt (notice) bemerken (that dass); (write down) notieren; **notebook** n Notizbuch nt; (Inform) Notebook nt; **notepad** n Notizblock m; **notepaper** n Briefpapier nt

nothing ['nʌθɪŋ] n nichts; **~ but ...** lauter ...; **for ~** umsonst; **he**

thinks ~ of it er macht sich nichts daraus

notice ['nəʊtɪs] n (announcement) Bekanntmachung f; (on ~ board) Anschlag m; (attention) Beachtung f; (advance warning) Ankündigung f; (to leave job, flat etc) Kündigung f; **at short ~** kurzfristig; **until further ~** bis auf weiteres; **to give sb ~** jdm kündigen; **to hand in one's ~** kündigen; **to take (no) ~ of (sth)** etw (nicht) beachten; **take no ~** kümmere dich nicht darum! ▷ vt bemerken; **noticeable** adj erkennbar; (visible) sichtbar; **to be ~** auffallen; **notice board** n Anschlagtafel f

notification [nəʊtɪfɪ'keɪʃən] n Benachrichtigung f (of von); **notify** ['nəʊtɪfaɪ] vt benachrichtigen (of von)

notion ['nəʊʃən] n Idee f

notorious [nəʊ'tɔːrɪəs] adj berüchtigt

nought [nɔːt] n Null f

noun [naʊn] n Substantiv nt

nourish ['nʌrɪʃ] vt nähren; **nourishing** adj nahrhaft; **nourishment** n Nahrung f

novel ['nɒvəl] n Roman m ▷ adj neuartig; **novelist** n Schriftsteller(in) m(f); **novelty** n Neuheit f

November [nəʊ'vembə*] n November m; see also **September**

novice ['nɒvɪs] n Neuling m

now [naʊ] adv (at the moment) jetzt; (introductory phrase) also; **right ~** jetzt gleich; **just ~** gerade; **by ~** inzwischen; **from ~ on** ab jetzt; **~ and again** (o then) ab und zu; **nowadays** adv heutzutage

nowhere ['nəʊwɛə*] adv nirgends; **we're getting ~** wir kommen nicht weiter; **~ near** noch lange nicht

nozzle ['nɒzl] n Düse f

nuclear ['njuːklɪə*] adj (energy etc) Kern-; **~ power station** Kernkraftwerk nt; **nuclear waste** n Atommüll m

nude [njuːd] adj nackt ▷ n (person) Nackte(r) mf; (painting etc) Akt m

nudge [nʌdʒ] vt stupsen; **nudist** ['njuːdɪst] n Nudist(in) m(f), FKK-Anhänger(in) m(f); **nudist beach** n FKK-Strand m

nuisance ['njuːsns] n Ärgernis nt; (person) Plage f; **what a ~** wie ärgerlich!

nuke [njuːk] n (bomb) Atombombe f ▷ vt eine Atombombe werfen auf +akk

numb [nʌm] adj taub, gefühllos ▷ vt betäuben

number ['nʌmbə*] n Nummer f; (Math) Zahl f; (quantity) (An)zahl f; **in small/large ~s** in kleinen / großen Mengen; **a ~ of times** mehrmals ▷ vt (give a number to) nummerieren; (count) zählen (among zu); **his days are ~ed** seine Tage sind gezählt; **number plate** n (BRIT Auto) Nummernschild nt

numeral ['njuːmərəl] n Ziffer f; **numerical** [njuː'merɪkəl] adj numerisch; (superiority) zahlenmäßig; **numerous** ['njuːmərəs] adj zahlreich

nun [nʌn] n Nonne f

Nuremberg ['njuərəmbɜːg] n Nürnberg n

nurse [nɜːs] n Krankenschwester f; (male ~) Krankenpfleger m ▷ vt (patient) pflegen; (baby) stillen; **nursery** n Kinderzimmer nt; (for plants) Gärtnerei f; (tree) Baumschule f; **nursery rhyme** n Kinderreim m; **nursery school** n Kindergarten m; **~ teacher** Kindergärtner(in) m(f), Erzieher(in) m(f); **nursing** n (profession) Krankenpflege f; **~ home**

Privatklinik f

nut [nʌt] n Nuss f; (Tech: for bolt) Mutter f; **nutcase** n (fam) Spinner(in) m(f); **nutcracker** n, **nutcrackers** npl Nussknacker m

nutmeg ['nʌtmɛg] n Muskat m, Muskatnuss f

nutrient ['njuːtrɪənt] n Nährstoff m

nutrition [njuːˈtrɪʃən] n Ernährung f; **nutritious** [njuːˈtrɪʃəs] adj nahrhaft

nuts [nʌts] (fam) adj verrückt; **to be ~ about sth** nach etw verrückt sein ▷ npl (testicles) Eier pl

nutshell ['nʌtʃel] n Nussschale f; **in a ~** kurz gesagt

nutter ['nʌtə*] n (fam) Spinner(in) m(f); **nutty** ['nʌtɪ] adj (fam) verrückt

NW abbr = **northwest** NW

nylon® ['naɪlɒn] n Nylon® nt ▷ adj Nylon-

O [əʊ] n (Tel) Null f

oak [əʊk] n Eiche f ▷ adj Eichen-

OAP abbr = **old-age pensioner** Rentner(in) m(f)

oar [ɔː*] n Ruder nt

oasis [əʊˈeɪsɪs] (pl **oases**) n Oase f

oatcake ['əʊtkeɪk] n Haferkeks m

oath [əʊθ] n (statement) Eid m

oats [əʊts] npl Hafer m; (Gastr) Haferflocken pl

obedience [əˈbiːdɪəns] n Gehorsam m; **obedient** adj gehorsam; **obey** [əˈbeɪ] vt, vi gehorchen +dat

object ['ɒbdʒekt] n Gegenstand m, (abstract) Objekt nt; (purpose) Ziel nt ▷ [əbˈdʒekt] vi dagegen sein; (raise objection) Einwände erheben (to gegen); (morally) Anstoß nehmen (to an +dat); **do you ~ to my smoking?** haben Sie etwas dagegen, wenn ich rauche?; **objection** [əbˈdʒekʃən] n Einwand m

objective [əbˈdʒektɪv] n Ziel nt ▷ adj objektiv, **objectivity** [ɒbdʒekˈtɪvɪtɪ] n Objektivität f

obligation [ɒblɪˈɡeɪʃən] n (duty) Pflicht f; (commitment) Verpflichtung f; **no ~** unverbindlich; **obligatory** [əˈblɪɡətərɪ] adj obligatorisch; **oblige** [əˈblaɪdʒ] vt **to ~ sb to do sth** jdn (dazu) zwingen, etw zu tun; **he felt ~d to accept the offer** er fühlte sich verpflichtet, das Angebot anzunehmen

oblique [əˈbliːk] adj schräg; (angle) schief

oblong [ˈɒblɒŋ] n Rechteck nt ▷ adj rechteckig

oboe [ˈəʊbəʊ] n Oboe f

obscene [əbˈsiːn] adj obszön

obscure [əbˈskjʊə*] adj unklar; (unknown) unbekannt

observant [əbˈzɜːvənt] adj aufmerksam; **observation** [ɒbzəˈveɪʃən] n (watching) Beobachtung f; (remark) Bemerkung f; **observe** [əbˈzɜːv] vt (notice) bemerken; (watch) beobachten; (customs) einhalten

obsessed [əbˈsest] adj besessen (with an idea etc von einem Gedanken etc); **obsession** [əbˈseʃən] n Manie f

obsolete [ˈɒbsəliːt] adj veraltet

obstacle [ˈɒbstəkl] n Hindernis nt (to für); **to be an ~ to sth** einer Sache im Weg stehen

obstinate [ˈɒbstɪnət] adj hartnäckig

obstruct [əbˈstrʌkt] vt versperren; (pipe) verstopfen; (hinder) behindern, aufhalten; **obstruction** [əbˈstrʌkʃən] n Blockierung f; (of pipe) Verstopfung f; (obstacle) Hindernis nt

obtain [əbˈteɪn] vt erhalten; **obtainable** adj erhältlich

obvious [ˈɒbvɪəs] adj offensichtlich; **it was ~ to me that ...** es war mir klar, dass ...; **obviously** adv offensichtlich

occasion [əˈkeɪʒən] n Gelegenheit f; (special event) (großes) Ereignis; **on the ~ of** anlässlich +gen; **special ~** besonderer Anlass; **occasional · occasionally** adj, adv gelegentlich

occupant [ˈɒkjʊpənt] n (of house) Bewohner(in) m(f); (of vehicle) Insasse m, Insassin f; **occupation** [ɒkjʊˈpeɪʃən] n Beruf m; (pastime) Beschäftigung f; (of country etc) Besetzung f; **occupied** adj (country, seat, toilet) besetzt; (person) beschäftigt; **to keep sb/oneself ~** jdn/sich beschäftigen; **occupy** [ˈɒkjʊpaɪ] vt (country) besetzen; (time) beanspruchen; (mind, person) beschäftigen

occur [əˈkɜː*] vi vorkommen; **~ to sb** jdm einfallen; **occurrence** [əˈkʌrəns] n (event) Ereignis nt; (presence) Vorkommen nt

ocean [ˈəʊʃən] n Ozean m; (US: sea) das Meer nt

o'clock [əˈklɒk] adv **5 ~** 5 Uhr; **at 10 ~** um 10 Uhr

octagon [ˈɒktəɡən] n Achteck nt

October [ɒkˈtəʊbə*] n Oktober m; see also **September**

octopus [ˈɒktəpəs] n Tintenfisch m

odd [ɒd] adj (strange) sonderbar; (not even) ungerade; (one missing) einzeln; **to be the ~ one out** nicht dazugehören; **~ jobs** Gelegenheitsarbeiten pl; **odds** npl Chancen pl; **against all ~** entgegen allen Erwartungen; **~ and ends** (fam) Kleinkram pl

odometer [əʊˈdɒmətə*] n (US Auto) Meilenzähler m

odor (US), **odour** [ˈəʊdə*] n Geruch m

of [ɒv, əv] prep gen von; (material, origin) aus; **the name ~ the hotel** der Name des Hotels; **the works ~**

Shakespeare Shakespeares Werke; **a friend ~ mine** ein Freund von mir; **the fourth ~ June** der vierte Juni; **a wall (made) ~ stone** eine Mauer aus Stein; *(quantity)* **a glass ~ water** ein Glas Wasser; **a litre ~ wine** ein Liter Wein; **a girl ~ ten** ein zehnjähriges Mädchen; *(US: in time)* **it's five ~ three** es ist fünf vor drei; *(cause)* **to die ~ cancer** an Krebs sterben

off [ɒf] *adv (away)* weg, fort; *(free)* frei; *(switch)* ausgeschaltet; *(milk)* sauer; **a mile ~** eine Meile entfernt. **I'll be ~ now** ich gehe jetzt; **to have the day/Monday ~** heute/Montag freihaben; **the lights are ~** die Lichter sind aus; **the concert is ~** das Konzert fällt aus; **I got 10% ~** ich habe 10% Nachlaß bekommen ▷ *prep (away from)* von; **to jump/fall ~ the roof** vom Dach springen/fallen; **to get ~ the bus** aus dem Bus aussteigen; **he's ~ work/school** er hat frei/schulfrei; **to take £20 ~ the price** den Preis um 20 Pfund herabsetzen

offence [ə'fɛns] *n (crime)* Straftat *f*; *(minor)* Vergehen *nt*; *(to feelings)* Kränkung *f*; **to cause/take ~** Anstoß erregen/nehmen; **offend** [ə'fɛnd] *vt* kränken; *(eye, ear)* beleidigen; **offender** *n* Straffällige(r) *m(f)*, **offense** (US) *see* **offence**; **offensive** [ə'fɛnsɪv] *adj* anstößig; *(insulting)* beleidigend; *(smell)* übel, abstoßend ▷ *n (Mil)* Offensive *f*

offer ['ɒfə*] *n* Angebot *nt*; **on ~** *(Comm)* im Angebot ▷ *vt* anbieten *(to sb jdm)*; *(money, a chance etc)* bieten

offhand [ɒf'hænd] *adj* lässig ▷ *adv (say)* auf Anhieb

office ['ɒfɪs] *n* Büro *nt*; *(position)* Amt *nt*, **doctor's ~** (US) Arztpraxis *f*; **office block** *n* Bürogebäude *nt*; **office hours** *npl* Dienstzeit *f*; *(notice)* Geschäftszeiten *pl*; **officer**

['ɒfɪsə*] *n (Mil)* Offizier(in) *m(f)*; *(official)* Polizeibeamte(r) *m*, Polizeibeamtin *f*; **office worker** ['ɒfɪs-wɜːkə*] *n* Büroangestellte(r) *mf*; **official** [ə'fɪʃl] *adj* offiziell; *(report etc)* amtlich; **~ language** Amtssprache *f* ▷ *n* Beamte(r) *m*, Beamtin *f*, Repräsentant(in) *m(f)*

off-licence ['ɒflaɪsəns] *n (BRIT)* Wein- und Spirituosenhandlung *f*; **off-line** *adj (Inform)* offline; **off-peak** *adj* außerhalb der Stoßzeiten; *(rate, ticket)* verbilligt; **off-putting** *adj* abstoßend, entmutigend, irritierend; **off-season** *adj* außerhalb der Saison

offshore ['ɒfʃɔː*] *adj* küstennah, Küsten-; *(oil rig)* im Meer; **offside** ['ɒf'saɪd] *n (Aut)* Fahrerseite *f*; *(Sport)* Abseits *nt*

often ['ɒfn] *adv oft;* **every so ~** von Zeit zu Zeit

oil [ɔɪl] *n* Öl *nt* ▷ *vt* ölen; **oil level** *n* Ölstand *m*; **oil painting** *n* Ölgemälde *nt*; **oil-rig** *n* (Öl)bohrinsel *f*; **oil slick** *n* Ölteppich *m*, **oil tanker** *n* Öltanker *m*; *(truck)* Tankwagen *m*; **oily** *adj* ölig; *(skin hair)* fettig

ointment ['ɔɪntmənt] *n* Salbe *f*

OK, okay [əʊ'keɪ] *adj (fam)* okay, in Ordnung; **that's ~ by** *(n with)* **me** das ist mir recht

old [əʊld] *adj* alt; **old age** *n* Alter *nt*, **~ pension** Rente *f*; **~ pensioner** Rentner(in) *m(f)*; **old-fashioned** *adj* altmodisch; **old people's home** *n* Altersheim *nt*

olive ['ɒlɪv] *n* Olive *f*; **olive oil** *n* Olivenöl *nt*

Olympic [əʊ'lɪmpɪk] *adj* olympisch; **the ~ Games, the ~s** *pl* die Olympischen Spiele *pl*, die Olympiade

omelette ['ɒmlət] *n* Omelett *nt*

omission [əʊ'mɪʃən] *n* Auslassung f; **omit** [əʊˈmɪt] vt auslassen

on [ɒn] prep (position) auf +dat; (with motion) auf +akk; (vertical surface, day) an +dat; (with motion) an +akk; **it's ~ the table** es ist auf dem Tisch; **hang it ~ the wall** häng es an die Wand; **I haven't got it ~ me** ich habe es nicht bei mir; **~ TV** im Fernsehen; **~ the main road** an der Hauptstraße; **~ the left** links; **~ the right** rechts; **~ the train/bus** im Zug/Bus; **~ the twelfth** am zwölften; **~ Sunday** am Sonntag; **~ Sundays** sonntags ▷ adj, adv (light etc) (Tv, Elec) an; **what's ~ at the cinema?** was läuft im Kino?; **I've nothing ~** (nothing arranged) ich habe nichts vor; (no clothes) ich habe nichts an; **to leave the light ~** das Licht brennen lassen

once [wʌns] adv (one time, in the past) einmal; **at ~** sofort; (at the same time) gleichzeitig; **~ more** noch einmal; **for ~** ausnahmsweise (einmal); **~ in a while** ab und zu mal ▷ conj wenn ... einmal; **~ you've got used to it** sobald Sie sich daran gewöhnt haben

oncoming [ˈɒnkʌmɪŋ] adj entgegenkommend; **~ traffic** Gegenverkehr m

one [wʌn] num eins ▷ adj ein, eine, ein; (only) einzige(r, s); **~ day** eines Tages; **the ~ and only ... ** der/die unvergleichliche ... ▷ pron eine(r, s); (people, you) man; **the ~ who/that ...** der(jenige), der/die(jenige), die/das(jenige), das ...; **this ~, that ~** dieser/diese/dieses; **the blue ~** der/die/das Blaue; **which ~?** welcher/welche/welches?; **~ another** einander; **one-off** adj einmalig ▷ n **a ~** etwas Einmaliges; **one-parent family** n Einelternfamilie f; **one-piece** adj einteilig; **oneself** pron (reflexive)

sich; **to cut ~** sich schneiden; **one-way** adj **~ street** Einbahnstraße f; **~ ticket** (US) einfache Fahrkarte

onion [ˈʌnjən] n Zwiebel f

on-line adj (Inform) on-line; **~ banking** Homebanking nt

only [ˈəʊnlɪ] adv nur; (with time) erst; **~ yesterday** erst gestern; **he's ~ four** er ist erst vier; **~ just arrived** gerade erst angekommen ▷ adj einzige(r, s); **~ child** Einzelkind nt

o.n.o. abbr = **or nearest offer** VB

onside [ˈɒnˈsaɪd] adv (Sport) nicht im Abseits

onto [ˈɒntʊ] prep auf +akk; (vertical surface) an +akk; **to be ~ sb** jdm auf die Schliche gekommen sein

onwards [ˈɒnwədz] adv voran, vorwärts; **from today ~** von heute an, ab heute

opaque [əʊˈpeɪk] adj undurchsichtig

open [ˈəʊpən] adj offen; **in the ~ air** im Freien; **~ to the public** für die Öffentlichkeit zugänglich; **the shop is ~ all day** das Geschäft hat den ganzen Tag offen ▷ vt öffnen, aufmachen; (meeting, account, new building) eröffnen; (road) dem Verkehr übergeben ▷ vi (door, window etc) aufgehen, sich öffnen; (shop, bank) öffnen, aufmachen; (begin) anfangen (with mit); **open-air** adj Freiluft-; **open day** n Tag m der offenen Tür; **opening** n Öffnung f; (beginning) Anfang m; (official, of exhibition etc) Eröffnung f; (opportunity) Möglichkeit f; **~ hours** (o times) Öffnungszeiten pl; **openly** adv offen; **open-minded** adj aufgeschlossen; **open-plan** adj **~ office** Großraumbüro nt

opera [ˈɒpərə] n Oper f; **opera glasses** npl Opernglas nt; **opera house** n Oper f, Opernhaus nt; **opera singer** n Opernsänger(in

operate ['ɔpəreɪt] vt (machine) bedienen; (brakes, lights) betätigen ▷ vi (machine) laufen; (bus etc) verkehren (between zwischen); **to ~ (on sb)** (Med) (jdn) operieren; **operating theatre** n Operationssaal m; **operation** [ɔpə'reɪʃən] n (of machine) Bedienung f; (functioning) Funktionieren nt; (Med) Operation f (on an +dat); (undertaking) Unternehmen nt; **in ~** (machine) in Betrieb; **to have an ~** operiert werden (for wegen); **operator** ['ɔpəreɪtə*] n **to phone the ~** die Vermittlung anrufen

opinion [ə'pɪnjən] n Meinung f (on zu); **in my ~** meiner Meinung nach

opponent [ə'pəunənt] n Gegner(in) m(f)

opportunity [ɔpə'tjuːnɪti] n Gelegenheit f

oppose [ə'pəuz] vt sich widersetzen +dat; (idea) ablehnen; **opposed adj to be ~ to sth** gegen etw sein; **as ~ to** im Gegensatz zu; **opposing adj** (team) gegnerisch; (points of view) entgegengesetzt

opposite ['ɔpəzɪt] adj (house) gegenüberliegend; (direction) entgegengesetzt, **the ~ sex** das andere Geschlecht ▷ adv gegenüber ▷ prep gegenüber; **~ me** mir gegenüber ▷ n Gegenteil nt

opposition [ɔpə'zɪʃən] n Widerstand m (to gegen); (Pol) Opposition f

oppress [ə'pres] vt unterdrücken; **oppressive adj** (heat) drückend

opt [ɔpt] vi **to ~ for sth** sich für etw entscheiden; **to ~ to do sth** sich entscheiden, etw zu tun

optician [ɔp'tɪʃən] n Optiker(in) m(f)

optimist ['ɔptɪmɪst] n Optimist(in) m(f); **optimistic** [ɔptɪ'mɪstɪk] adj optimistisch

optimum ['ɔptɪməm] adj optimal

option ['ɔpʃən] n Möglichkeit f; (Comm) Option f; **to have no ~** keine Wahl haben; **optional** adj freiwillig; **~ extras** (Auto) Extras pl

or [ɔː*] conj oder; (otherwise) sonst; (after neg) noch; **hurry up, ~ else** **we'll be late** beeil dich, sonst kommen wir zu spät

oral ['ɔːrəl] adj mündlich; **~ sex** Oralverkehr m ▷ n (exam) Mündliche(s) nt

orange ['ɔrɪndʒ] n Orange f ▷ adj orangefarben; **orange juice** n Orangensaft m

orbit ['ɔːbɪt] n Umlaufbahn f; **to be out of ~** (fam) nicht zu erreichen sein ▷ vt umkreisen

orchard ['ɔːtʃəd] n Obstgarten m

orchestra ['ɔːkɪstrə] n Orchester nt; (US Theat) Parkett nt

orchid ['ɔːkɪd] n Orchidee f

ordeal [ɔː'diːl] n Tortur f; (emotional) Qual f

order ['ɔːdə*] n (sequence) Reihenfolge f; (good arrangement) Ordnung f; (command) Befehl m; (Jur) Anordnung f; (condition) Zustand m; (Comm), Bestellung f; **out of ~** (not functioning) außer Betrieb; (unsuitable) nicht angebracht; **in ~** (tidy) richtig geordnet; (all right) in Ordnung; **in ~ to do sth** um etw zu tun ▷ vt (arrange) ordnen; (command) befehlen; **to ~ sb to do sth** jdm befehlen, etw zu tun; (food, product) bestellen; **order form** n Bestellschein m

ordinary ['ɔːdnrɪ] adj gewöhnlich, normal; (average) durchschnittlich

ore [ɔː*] n Erz nt

organ ['ɔːgən] n (Mus) Orgel f; (Anat) Organ nt

organic [ɔː'gænɪk] adj organisch;

(farming, vegetables) Bio-, Öko-; **~ farmer** Biobauer *m*, Biobäuerin *f*; **~ food** Biokost *f*

organization [ɔːgənaɪˈzeɪʃən] *n* Organisation *f*; *(arrangement)* Ordnung *f*; **organize** [ˈɔːgənaɪz] *vt* organisieren; **organizer** *n* (elektronisches) Notizbuch

orgasm [ˈɔːgæzəm] *n* Orgasmus *m*

orgy [ˈɔːdʒɪ] *n* Orgie *f*

oriental [ɔːrɪˈentəl] *adj* orientalisch

orientation [ɔːrɪenˈteɪʃən] *n* Orientierung *f*

origin [ˈɒrɪdʒɪn] *n* Ursprung *m*; *(of person)* Herkunft *f*; **original** [əˈrɪdʒɪnl] *adj (first)* ursprünglich; *(painting)* original; *(idea)* originell ▷ *n* Original *nt*. **originality** [ərɪdʒɪˈnælɪtɪ] *n* Originalität *f*; **originally** *adv* ursprünglich

Orkneys [ˈɔːknɪz] *npl*, **Orkney Islands** *npl* Orkneyinseln *pl*

ornament [ˈɔːnəmənt] *n* Schmuckgegenstand *m*; **ornamental** [ɔːnəˈmɛntl] *adj* dekorativ

orphan [ˈɔːfən] *n* Waise *f*, Waisenkind *nt*; **orphanage** [ˈɔːfənɪdʒ] *n* Waisenhaus *nt*

orthodox [ˈɔːθədɒks] *adj* orthodox

orthopaedic, **orthopedic** *(US)* [ɔːθəʊˈpiːdɪk] *adj* orthopädisch

ostentatious [ɒstɛnˈteɪʃəs] *adj* protzig

ostrich [ˈɒstrɪtʃ] *n (Zool)* Strauß *m*

other [ˈʌðə*] *adj*, *pron* andere(r, s); **any ~ questions?** sonst noch Fragen?; **the ~ day** neulich; **every ~ day** jeden zweiten Tag; **any person ~ than him** alle außer ihm; **someone/something or ~** irgend jemand/irgend etwas; **otherwise** *adv* sonst; *(differently)* anders

OTT *adj abbr* = **over the top**

übertrieben

otter [ˈɒtə*] *n* Otter *m*

ought [ɔːt] *vb aux (obligation)* sollte; *(probability)* dürfte; *(stronger)* müsste; **you ~ to do that** Sie sollten das tun; **he ~ to win** er müsste gewinnen; **that ~ to do** das müsste (o dürfte) reichen

ounce [aʊns] *n* Unze *f* (28,35 g)

our [aʊə*] *adj* unser; **ours** *pron* unsere(r, s); **this is ~** das gehört uns; **a friend of ~** ein Freund von uns; **ourselves** *pron (reflexive)* uns; **we enjoyed ~** wir haben uns amüsiert; **we've got the house to ~** wir haben das Haus für uns; *(emphatic)* **we did it ~** wir haben es selbst gemacht; *(all)* **by ~** allein

out [aʊt] *adv* hinaus /heraus; *(indoors)* draußen; *(not at home)* nicht zu Hause; *(not alight)* aus; *(unconscious)* bewusstlos; *(published)* herausgekommen; *(results)* bekannt gegeben; **have you been ~ yet?** waren Sie schon draußen?; **I was ~ when they called** ich war nicht da, als sie vorbeikamen; **to be ~ and about** unterwegs sein; **the sun is ~** die Sonne scheint; **the fire is ~** das Feuer ist ausgegangen; *(wrong)* **the calculation is (way) ~** die Kalkulation stimmt (ganz und gar) nicht; **they're ~ to get him** sie sind hinter ihm her

outback [ˈaʊtbæk] *n (in Australia)* **the ~** das Hinterland

outboard [ˈaʊtbɔːd] *adj* **~ motor** Außenbordmotor *m*

outbreak [ˈaʊtbreɪk] *n* Ausbruch *m*

outburst [ˈaʊtbɜːst] *n* Ausbruch *m*

outcome [ˈaʊtkʌm] *n* Ergebnis *nt*

outcry [ˈaʊtkraɪ] *n (public protest)* Protestwelle *f (against* gegen)

outdo [aʊtˈduː] *irr vt* übertreffen

outdoor ['autdɔ:*] adj Außen-; (Sport) im Freien; **~ swimming pool** Freibad nt; **outdoors** [aut'dɔ:z] adv draußen, im Freien

outer ['autə*] adj äußere(r, s); **outer space** n Weltraum m

outfit ['autfit] n Ausrüstung f, (clothes) Kleidung f

outgoing ['autɡəuŋ] adj kontaktfreudig

outgrow [aut'ɡrəu] irr vt (clothes) herauswachsen aus

outing ['autɪŋ] n Ausflug m

outlet ['autlet] n Auslass m, Abfluss m; (US) Steckdose f; (shop) Verkaufsstelle f

outline ['autlaɪn] n Umriss m; (summary) Abriss m

outlive [aut'lɪv] vt überleben

outlook ['autluk] n Aussicht(en) f(pl); (prospects) Aussichten pl; (attitude) Einstellung f (on zu)

outnumber [aut'nʌmbə*] vt zahlenmäßig überlegen sein +dat; **~ed** zahlenmäßig unterlegen

out of ['autɔv] prep (motion, motive, origin) aus; (position, away from) außerhalb +gen; **~ danger/sight/ breath** außer Gefahr/Sicht/Atem; **made ~ wood** aus Holz gemacht; **we are ~ bread** wir haben kein Brot mehr; **out-of-date** adj veraltet; **out-of-the-way** adj abgelegen

outpatient ['autpeɪʃnt] n ambulanter Patient, ambulante Patientin

output ['autput] n Produktion f; (of engine) Leistung f; (inform) Ausgabe f

outrage ['autreɪdʒ] n (great anger) Empörung f (at über); (wicked deed) Schandtat f; (crime) Verbrechen nt; (indecency) Skandal m; **outrageous** [aut'reɪdʒəs] adj unerhört; (clothes, behaviour etc) unmöglich, schrill

outright ['autraɪt] adv (killed) so-

lort ▷ adj total; (denial) völlig; (winner) unbestritten

outside [aut'saɪd] n Außenseite f; **on the ~** außen ▷ adj äußere(r, s), Außen-; (chance) sehr gering ▷ adv außen, to go **~** nach draußen gehen ▷ prep außerhalb +gen; **outsider** n Außenseiter(in) m(f)

outsize ['autsaɪz] adj übergroß; (clothes) in Übergröße

outskirts ['autskə:ts] npl (of town) Stadtrand m

outstanding [aut'stændɪŋ] adj hervorragend; (debts etc) ausstehend

outward ['autwəd] adj äußere(r, s); **~ journey** Hinfahrt f; **outwardly** adv nach außen hin; **outwards** adv nach außen

oval ['əuvəl] adj oval

ovary ['əuvərɪ] n Eierstock m

ovation [əu'veɪʃən] n Ovation f, Applaus m

oven ['ʌvn] n Backofen m; **oven glove** n Topfhandschuh m; **oven-proof** adj feuerfest; **oven-ready** adj bratfertig

over ['əuvə*] prep (position) über +dat, (motion) über +akk; **they spent a long time ~ it** sie haben lange dazu gebraucht; **from all ~ England** aus ganz England; **~ £20** mehr als 20 Pfund; **~ the phone/radio** am Telefon/im Radio; **to talk ~ a glass of wine** sich bei einem Glas Wein unterhalten; **~ and above** this darüber hinaus; **~ the summer** während des Sommers ▷ adv (across) hinüber/herüber; (finished) vorbei; (match, play etc) zu Ende; (left) übrig; (more) mehr; **~ there/in America** da drüben/drüben in Amerika; **~ to you** Sie sind dran; **it's (all) ~ between us** es ist aus zwischen uns; **~ and ~ again** immer wieder; **to start (all) ~ again** noch einmal von vorn anfangen; **children of 8 and ~** Kinder von 8 Jahren und darüber

over- ['əʊvə*] *pref* über-

overall ['əʊvɔ:l] *n* (BRIT) Kittel *m* ▷ *adj* (situation) allgemein; (length) Gesamt-; **~ majority** absolute Mehrheit ▷ *adv* insgesamt; **overalls** *npl* Overall *m*

overboard ['əʊvəbɔ:d] *adv* über Bord

overbooked [əʊvə'bʊkt] *adj* überbucht; **overbooking** *n* Überbuchung *f*

overcharge [əʊvə'tʃɑ:dʒ] *vt* zu viel verlangen von

overcoat ['əʊvəkəʊt] *n* Wintermantel *m*

overcome [əʊvə'kʌm] *irr vt* überwinden; **~ by sleep/emotion** von Schlaf/Rührung übermannt; **we shall ~** wir werden siegen

overcooked [əʊvə'kʊkt] *adj* zu lange gekocht; (meat) zu lange gebraten

overcrowded [əʊvə'kraʊdɪd] *adj* überfüllt

overdo [əʊvə'du:] *irr vt* übertreiben; **you're ~ing it** du übertreibst es; (doing too much) Sie übernehmen sich; **overdone** *adj* übertrieben; (food) zu lange gekocht; (meat) zu lange gebraten

overdose ['əʊvədəʊs] *n* Überdosis *f*

overdraft ['əʊvədrɑ:ft] *n* Kontoüberziehung *f*; **overdrawn** [əʊvə'drɔ:n] *adj* überzogen

overdue [əʊvə'dju:] *adj* überfällig

overestimate [əʊvər'estɪmeɪt] *vt* überschätzen

overexpose [əʊvərɪks'pəʊz] *vt* (Foto) überbelichten

overflow [əʊvə'fləʊ] *vi* überlaufen

overhead ['əʊvəhed] *adj* (Aviat) locker Gepäckfach *nt*; **~ projector** Overheadprojektor *m*; **~ railway** Hochbahn *f* ▷ [əʊvə'hed] *adv* oben

overhear [əʊvə'hɪə*] *irr vt* zufällig mit anhören

overheat [əʊvə'hi:t] *vi* (engine) heiß laufen

overjoyed [əʊvə'dʒɔɪd] *adj* überglücklich (at über)

overland ['əʊvəlænd] *adj* Überland- ▷ [əʊvə'lænd] *adv* (travel) über Land

overlap [əʊvə'læp] *vi* (dates etc) sich überschneiden; (objects) sich teilweise decken

overload [əʊvə'ləʊd] *vt* überladen

overlook [əʊvə'lʊk] *vt* (view from above) überblicken; (not notice) übersehen; (pardon) hinwegsehen über +akk

overnight [əʊvə'naɪt] *adj* (journey, train) Nacht-; **~ bag** Reisetasche *f*; **~ stay** Übernachtung *f* ▷ *adv* über Nacht

overpass ['əʊvəpɑ:s] *n* Überführung *f*

overpay [əʊvə'peɪ] *vt* überbezahlen

overrule [əʊvə'ru:l] *vt* verwerfen; (decision) aufheben

overseas [əʊvə'si:z] *adj* Übersee-; (fam) Auslands-; **~ students** Studenten aus Übersee ▷ *adv* (go) nach Übersee; (live, work) in Übersee

oversee [əʊvə'si:] *irr vt* beaufsichtigen

overshadow [əʊvə'ʃædəʊ] *vt* überschatten

overshoot [əʊvə'ʃu:t] *irr vt* (runway) hinausschießen über +akk; (turning) vorbeifahren +dat

oversight ['əʊvəsaɪt] *n* Versehen *nt*

oversimplify [əʊvə'sɪmplɪfaɪ] *vt* zu sehr vereinfachen

oversleep [əʊvə'sli:p] *irr vi* verschlafen

overtake [əʊvə'teɪk] irr vt, vi überholen

overtime ['əʊvətaɪm] n Überstunden pl

overturn [əʊvə'tɜːn] vt, vi umkippen

overweight [əʊvə'weɪt] adj **to be ~** Übergewicht haben

overwhelm [əʊvə'welm] vt überwältigen; **overwhelming** adj überwältigend

overwork [əʊvə'wɜːk] n Überarbeitung f ▷ vi sich überarbeiten; **overworked** adj überarbeitet

owe [əʊ] vt schulden; **to ~ sth to sb** (money) jdm etw schulden; (favour etc) jdm etw verdanken; **how much do I ~ you?** was bin ich Ihnen schuldig?; **owing to** prep wegen +gen

owl [aʊl] n Eule f

own [əʊn] vt besitzen ▷ adj eigen; **on one's ~** allein; **he has a flat of his ~** er hat eine eigene Wohung; **own up** vi **to ~ to sth** etw zugeben; **owner** n Besitzer(in) m(f); (of business) Inhaber(in) m(f); **ownership** n Besitz m; **under new ~** unter neuer Leitung

ox [ɒks] (pl **oxen**) n Ochse m; **oxtail** ['ɒksteɪl] n Ochsenschwanz m; **~ soup** Ochsenschwanzsuppe f; **oxygen** ['ɒksɪdʒən] n Sauerstoff m

oyster ['ɔɪstə*] n Auster f

oz abbr = **ounces** Unzen pl

Oz ['ɒz] n (fam) Australien nt

ozone ['əʊzəʊn] n Ozon nt; **~ layer** Ozonschicht f

p abbr = **page** S., abbr = **penny**, **pence**

p.a. abbr = **per annum**

pace [peɪs] n (speed) Tempo nt; (step) Schritt m; **pacemaker** n (Med) Schrittmacher m

Pacific [pə'sɪfɪk] n **the ~** (Ocean) der Pazifik; **Pacific Standard Time** n pazifische Zeit

pacifier ['pæsɪfaɪə] n (US: for baby) Schnuller m

pack [pæk] n (of cards) Spiel nt; (esp US: of cigarettes) Schachtel f; (gang) Bande f; (US: backpack) Rucksack m ▷ vt (case) packen; (clothes) einpacken ▷ vi (for holiday) packen; **pack in** vt (BRIT fam: job) hinschmeißen; **package** ['pækɪdʒ] n (a. Inform, fig) Paket nt; **package deal** n Pauschalangebot nt; **package holiday** n Pauschalreise f; **package tour** n Pauschalreise f; **packaging** n (material) Verpackung f; **packed lunch** n (BRIT) Lunchpaket nt; **packet** n Päckchen nt; (of cigarettes) Schachtel f

pad [pæd] n (of paper) Schreibblock m; (padding) Polster nt; **padded envelope** n wattierter Umschlag; **padding** n (material) Polsterung f

paddle ['pædl] n (for boat) Paddel nt ▷ vi (in boat) paddeln; **paddling pool** n (BRIT) Planschbecken nt

padlock ['pædlɒk] n Vorhängeschloss nt

page [peɪdʒ] n (of book etc) Seite f

pager ['peɪdʒə*] n Piepser m

paid [peɪd] pt, pp of **pay** ▷ adj bezahlt

pain [peɪn] n Schmerz m; **to be in ~** Schmerzen haben; **she's a (real) ~** sie nervt; **painful** adj (physically) schmerzhaft; (embarrassing) peinlich; **painkiller** n schmerzstillendes Mittel

painstaking adj sorgfältig

paint [peɪnt] n Farbe f ▷ vt anstreichen; (picture) malen; **paintbrush** n Pinsel m; **painter** n Maler(in) m(f); **painting** n (picture) Bild nt, Gemälde nt

pair [pɛə*] n **a ~ of shoes** ein Paar Schuhe; **a ~ of scissors** eine Schere; **a ~ of trousers** eine Hose

pajamas [pəˈdʒɑːməz] npl (US) Schlafanzug m

Pakistan [pɑːkɪˈstɑːn] n Pakistan nt

pal [pæl] n (fam) Kumpel m

palace ['pæləs] n Palast m

pale [peɪl] adj (face) blass, bleich; (colour) hell

palm [pɑːm] n (of hand) Handfläche f; **~ (tree)** Palme f; **palmtop (computer)** n Palmtop(computer) m

pamper ['pæmpə*] vt verhätscheln

pan [pæn] n (saucepan) Topf m; (frying pan) Pfanne f; **pancake** ['pænkeɪk] n Pfannkuchen m; **Pancake Day** n (BRIT) Fastnachtsdienstag m

panda ['pændə] n Panda m

pane [peɪn] n Scheibe f

panel ['pænl] n (of wood) Tafel f; (in discussion) Diskussionsteilnehmer pl

panic ['pænɪk] n Panik f ▷ vi in Panik geraten; **panicky** ['pænɪkɪ] adj panisch

pansy ['pænzɪ] n (flower) Stiefmütterchen nt

panties ['pæntɪz] npl (Damen)slip m

pantomime ['pæntəmaɪm] n (BRIT) um die Weihnachtszeit aufgeführte Märchenkomödie

pants [pænts] npl Unterhose f; (esp US: trousers) Hose f

pantyhose ['pæntɪhəʊz] npl (US) Strumpfhose f; **panty-liner** n Slipeinlage f

paper ['peɪpə*] n Papier nt; (newspaper) Zeitung f; (exam) Klausur f; (for reading at conference) Referat nt; **~s** pl (identity papers) Papiere pl; **~ bag** n Papiertüte f; **~ cup** Pappbecher m ▷ vt (wall) tapezieren; **paperback** n Taschenbuch nt; **paper clip** n Büroklammer f; **paper feed** n (of printer) Papiereinzug m; **paper round** n **to do a ~** Zeitungen austragen; **paperwork** n Schreibarbeit f

parachute ['pærəʃuːt] n Fallschirm m ▷ vi abspringen

paracetamol [pærəˈsiːtəmɒl] n (tablet) Paracetamoltablette f

parade [pəˈreɪd] n (procession) Umzug m; (Mil) Parade f ▷ vi vorbeimarschieren

paradise ['pærədaɪs] n Paradies nt

paragliding ['pærəɡlaɪdɪŋ] n Gleitschirmfliegen nt

paragraph ['pærəɡrɑːf] n Absatz m

parallel ['pærəlel] adj parallel ▷ n (Math, fig) Parallele f

paralyze ['pærəlaɪz] vt lähmen; (fig) lahm legen

paranoid ['pærənɔɪd] adj paranoid

paraphrase ['pærəfreɪz] vt umschreiben, (sth spoken) anders ausdrücken

parasailing ['pærəseɪlɪŋ] n Parasailing nt

parasol ['pærəsɒl] n Sonnenschirm m

parcel ['pɑːsl] n Paket nt

pardon ['pɑːdn] n (Jur) Begnadigung f: ~ **me/I beg your ~** verzeihen Sie bitte; (objection) aber ich hitte Sie; **I beg your ~?/ ~ me?** wie bitte?

parent ['pɛərənt] n Elternteil m; **~s** pl Eltern pl; **~s-in-law** pl Schwiegereltern pl; **parental** [pə'rentl] adj elterlich, Eltern-

parish ['pærɪʃ] n Gemeinde f

park [pɑːk] n Park m ▷ vt, vi parken; **parking** n Parken nt; **'no Parken verboten'**; **parking brake** n (US) Handbremse f; **parking disc** n Parkscheibe f; **parking fine** n Geldbuße f für falsches Parken; **parking lights** npl (US) Standlicht nt, **parking lot** n (US) Parkplatz m; **parking meter** n Parkuhr f; **parking place, parking space** n Parkplatz m; **parking ticket** n Strafzettel m

parliament ['pɑːləmənt] n Parlament nt

parrot ['pærət] n Papagei m

parsley ['pɑːslɪ] n Petersilie f

parsnip ['pɑːsnɪp] n Pastinake f (längliches, weißes Wurzelgemüse)

part [pɑːt] n Teil m; (of machine) Teil nt; (Theat) Rolle f; (US: in hair) Scheitel m; **to take ~** teilnehmen (in an +dat); **for the most ~** zum größten Teil ▷ adj Teil- ▷ vt (separate) trennen; (hair) scheiteln ▷ vi (people) sich trennen

partial ['pɑːʃəl] adj (incomplete) teilweise, Teil-; (biased) parteiisch

participant [pɑː'tɪsɪpənt] n Teilnehmer(in) m(f); **participate** [pɑː'tɪsɪpeɪt] vi teilnehmen (in an +dat)

particular [pə'tɪkjʊlə*] adj (specific) bestimmt; (exact) genau; (fussy) eigen; **in ~** insbesondere ▷ n **~s** pl (details) Einzelheiten pl; (about person) Personalien pl; **particularly** adv besonders

parting ['pɑːtɪŋ] n (farewell) Abschied m; (BRIT: in hair) Scheitel m

partly ['pɑːtlɪ] adv teilweise

partner ['pɑːtnə*] n Partner(in) m(f); **partnership** n Partnerschaft f

partridge ['pɑːtrɪdʒ] n Rebhuhn nt

part-time ['pɑːt'taɪm] adj Teilzeit- ▷ adv **to work ~** Teilzeit arbeiten

party ['pɑːtɪ] n (celebration) Party f; (Pol, Jur) Partei f; (group) Gruppe f ▷ vi feiern

pass [pɑːs] vt (on foot) vorbeigehen an +dat; (in car etc) vorbeifahren an +dat; (time) verbringen; (exam) bestehen; (law) verabschieden; **to ~ sth to sb, to ~ sb sth** jdm etw reichen; **to ~ the ball to sb** jdm den Ball zuspielen ▷ vi (on foot) vorbeigehen; (in car etc) vorbeifahren; (years) vergehen; (in exam) bestehen ▷ n (document) Ausweis m; (Sport) Pass m; **pass away** vi (die) verscheiden; **pass by** vi (on foot) vorbeigehen; (in car etc) vorbeifahren ▷ vt (on foot) vorbeigehen an +dat; (in car etc) vorbeifahren an +dat; **pass on** vt weitergeben (to an +akk); (disease) übertragen (to auf +akk); **pass out** vi (faint) ohnmächtig werden; **pass round** vt herumreichen

passage ['pæsɪdʒ] n (corridor)

Gang m; (in book, music) Passage f;
passageway n Durchgang m

passenger ['pæsɪndʒə*] n Passagier(in) m(f); (on bus) Fahrgast m,
(on train) Reisende(r) mf; (in car)
Mitfahrer(in) m(f)

passer-by ['pɑːsə'baɪ] (pl passers-by) n Passant(in) m(f)

passion ['pæʃən] n Leidenschaft f;
passionate ['pæʃənɪt] adj leidenschaftlich; **passion fruit** n Passionsfrucht

passive ['pæsɪv] adj passiv ▷ n ~
(voice) (Ling) Passiv nt

passport ['pɑːspɔːt] n (Reise)pass
m; **passport control** n Passkontrolle f

password ['pɑːswɜːd] n (Inform)
Passwort nt

past [pɑːst] n Vergangenheit f ▷
adv (by) vorbei; it's ~ es ist fünf
nach ▷ adj (years) vergangen;
(president etc) ehemalig; in the ~
two months in den letzten zwei
Monaten ▷ prep (telling time) nach;
it's half ~ 10 es ist halb 11; to go ~
sth an etw dat vorbeigehen / -fahren

pasta ['pæstə] n Nudeln pl

paste [peɪst] vt (stick) kleben; (Inform) einfügen ▷ n (glue) Kleister m

pastime ['pɑːstaɪm] n Zeitvertreib m

pastry ['peɪstrɪ] n Teig m; (cake)
Stückchen

pasty ['pæstɪ] n (BRIT) Pastete f

patch [pætʃ] n (area) Fleck m; (for
mending) Flicken ▷ vt flicken;
patchy adj (uneven) ungleichmäßig

pâté ['pæteɪ] n Pastete f

paternal [pə'tɜːnl] adj väterlich;
~ **grandmother** Großmutter f väterlicherseits; **paternity leave**
[pə'tɜːnɪtɪliːv] n Elternzeit f (des
Vaters)

path [pɑːθ] n (a. Inform) Pfad m; (a.
fig) Weg m

pathetic [pə'θetɪk] adj (bad)
kläglich, erbärmlich; it's ~ es ist zum
Heulen

patience ['peɪʃəns] n Geduld f;
(BRIT Cards) Patience f; **patient** adj
geduldig ▷ n Patient(in) m(f)

patio ['pætɪəʊ] n Terrasse f

patriotic [pætrɪ'ɒtɪk] adj patriotisch

patrol car [pə'trəʊlkɑː*] n Streifenwagen m; **patrolman** (pl -men)
n (US) Streifenpolizist m

patron ['peɪtrən] n (sponsor) Förderer m, Förderin f; (in shop) Kunde
m, Kundin f

patronize ['pætrənaɪz] vt (treat
condescendingly) von oben herab
behandeln; **patronizing** adj (attitude) herablassend

pattern ['pætən] n Muster nt

pause [pɔːz] n Pause f ▷ vi
(speaker) innehalten

pavement n (BRIT) Bürgersteig m;
(US) Pflaster nt

pay [peɪ] (paid, paid) vt bezahlen;
he paid (me) £20 for it er hat (mir)
20 Pfund dafür gezahlt; to ~ attention Acht geben (to auf +akk); to
~ sb a visit jdn besuchen ▷ vi
zahlen; (be profitable) sich bezahlt
machen; to ~ for sth etw bezahlen
▷ n Bezahlung f, Lohn m; **pay back**
vt (money) zurückzahlen; **pay in** vt
(into account) einzahlen; **payable**
adj zahlbar; (due) fällig; **payday** n
Zahltag m; **payee** [peɪ'iː] n Zahlungsempfänger(in) m(f); **payment**
n Bezahlung f; (money) Zahlung f;
pay-per-view adj Pay-per-View-;
pay phone n Münzfernsprecher m;
pay TV n Pay-TV nt

PC abbr = **personal computer** PC m;
abbr = **politically correct** politisch
korrekt

PDA abbr = **personal digital assistant** PDA n

PE abbr = **physical education** (school) Sport m

pea [pi:] n Erbse f

peace [pi:s] n Frieden m; **peaceful** adj friedlich

peach [pi:tʃ] n Pfirsich m

peacock ['pi:kɔk] n Pfau m

peak [pi:k] n (of mountain) Gipfel m; (fig) Höhepunkt m; **peak period** n Stoßzeit f; (season) Hochsaison f

peanut ['pi:nʌt] n Erdnuss f; **peanut butter** n Erdnussbutter f

pear [peə*] n Birne f

pearl [pɜ:l] n Perle f

pebble ['pebl] n Kiesel m

pecan [pɪ'kæn] n Pekannuss f

peck [pek] vt, vi picken; **peckish** adj (BRIT fam) ein bisschen hungrig

peculiar [pɪ'kju:lɪə*] adj (odd) seltsam; **~ to** charakteristisch für; **peculiarity** [pɪkju:lɪ'ærɪtɪ] n (singular quality) Besonderheit f; (strangeness) Eigenartigkeit f

pedal ['pedl] n Pedal nt

pedestrian [pɪ'destrɪən] n Fußgänger(in) m(f); **pedestrian crossing** n Fußgängerüberweg m

pee [pi:] vi (fam) pinkeln

peel [pi:l] n Schale f ▷ vt schälen ▷ vi (paint etc) abblättern; (skin etc) sich schälen

peer [pɪə*] n Gleichaltrige(r) mf ▷ vi starren

peg [peg] n (for coat etc) Haken m; (for tent) Hering m; (clothes) **~** (Wäsche)klammer f

pelvis ['pelvɪs] n Becken nt

pen [pen] n (ball-point) Kuli m, Kugelschreiber m; (fountain **~**) Füller m

penalize ['pi:nəlaɪz] vt (punish) bestrafen; **penalty** ['penltɪ] n (punishment) Strafe f; (in football) Elfmeter m

pence [pens] pl of **penny**

pencil ['pensl] n Bleistift m; **pencil sharpener** n (Bleistift)spitzer m

penetrate ['penɪtreɪt] vt durchdringen; (enter into) eindringen in +akk

penfriend ['penfrend] n Brieffreund(in) m(f)

penguin ['peŋgwɪn] n Pinguin m

penicillin [penɪ'sɪlɪn] n Penizillin nt

peninsula [pɪ'nɪnsjələ] n Halbinsel f

penis ['pi:nɪs] n Penis m

penknife ['pennaɪf] (pl **penknives**) n Taschenmesser nt

penny ['penɪ] n (pl **pence** o **pennies**) n (BRIT) Penny m; (US) Centstück nt

pension ['penʃən] n Rente f; (for civil servants, executives etc) Pension f; **pensioner** n Rentner(in) m(f); **pension plan**, **pension scheme** n Rentenversicherung f

penultimate [pɪ'nʌltɪmət] adj vorletzte(r, s)

people ['pi:pl] npl (persons) Leute pl; (von Staat) Volk nt; (inhabitants) Bevölkerung f; **people carrier** n Minivan m

pepper ['pepə*] n Pfeffer m; (vegetable) Paprika m; **peppermint** n (sweet) Pfefferminz m

per [pɜ:*] prep pro; **~ annum** pro Jahr; **~ cent** Prozent nt

percentage [pə'sentɪdʒ] n Prozentsatz m

perceptible [pə'septəbl] adj wahrnehmbar

percolator ['pɜ:kəleɪtə*] n Kaffeemaschine f

percussion [pə'kʌʃən] n (Mus) Schlagzeug nt

perfect ['pɜ:fɪkt] adj perfekt; (utter) völlig ▷ [pə'fekt] vt vervollkommnen; **perfectly** adv perfekt; (utterly) völlig

perform [pə'fɔ:m] vt (task) ausführen; (play) aufführen; (Med: operation) durchführen ▷ vi (Theat) auftreten; **performance** n (show) Vorstellung f; (efficiency) Leistung f

perfume ['pɜːfjuːm] n Duft m; (substance) Parfüm nt

perhaps [pə'hæps] adv vielleicht

peril ['perɪl] n Gefahr f

period ['pɪərɪəd] n (length of time) Zeit f; (in history) Zeitalter nt; (school) Stunde f; (Med) Periode f; (US: full stop) Punkt m; **for a ~ of three years** für einen Zeitraum von drei Jahren; **periodical** [pɪərɪ'ɒdɪkəl] n Zeitschrift f

peripheral [pə'rɪfərəl] n (Inform) Peripheriegerät nt

perish ['perɪʃ] vi (die) umkommen; (material) verderben

perjury ['pɜːdʒərɪ] n Meineid m

perm [pɜːm] n Dauerwelle f

permanent, permanently ['pɜːmənənt, -lɪ] adj, adv ständig

permission [pə'mɪʃən] n Erlaubnis f; **permit** ['pɜːmɪt] n Genehmigung f ▷ [pə'mɪt] vt erlauben, zulassen; **to ~ sb to do sth** jdm erlauben, etw zu tun

persecute ['pɜːsɪkjuːt] vt verfolgen

perseverance [pɜːsɪ'vɪərəns] n Ausdauer f

Persian ['pɜːʃən] adj persisch

persist [pə'sɪst] vi (in belief etc) bleiben (in bei); (rain, smell) andauern; **persistent** adj beharrlich

person ['pɜːsn] n Mensch m; (in official context) Person f; **in ~** persönlich; **personal** adj persönlich; (private) privat; **personality** [pɜːsə'nælɪtɪ] n Persönlichkeit f; **personal organizer** n Organizer m; **personal stereo** (pl **-s**) n Walkman® m; **personnel** [pɜːsə'nel] n Personal nt

perspective [pə'spektɪv] n Perspektive f

perspire [pə'spaɪə*] vi schwitzen

persuade [pə'sweɪd] vt überreden; (convince) überzeugen; **persuasive** [pə'sweɪsɪv] adj überzeugend

perverse [pə'vɜːs] adj pervers; (obstinate) eigensinnig; **pervert** ['pɜːvɜːt] n Perverse(r) mf ▷ [pə'vɜːt] vt (morally) verderben

pessimist ['pesɪmɪst] n Pessimist(in) m(f); **pessimistic** [pesɪ'mɪstɪk] adj pessimistisch

pest [pest] n (insect) Schädling m; (fig: person) Nervensäge f; (thing) Plage f; **pester** ['pestə*] vt plagen; **pesticide** ['pestɪsaɪd] n Schädlingsbekämpfungsmittel nt

pet [pet] n (animal) Haustier nt; (person) Liebling m

petal ['petl] n Blütenblatt nt

petition [pə'tɪʃən] n Petition f

petrol ['petrəl] n (BRIT) Benzin nt; **petrol pump** n (at garage) Zapfsäule f; **petrol station** n Tankstelle f; **petrol tank** n Benzintank m

pharmacy ['faːməsɪ] n (shop) Apotheke f

phase [feɪz] n Phase f

PhD abbr = **Doctor of Philosophy** Dr. phil; (dissertation) Doktorarbeit f; **to do one's ~** promovieren

pheasant ['feznt] n Fasan m

phenomenon [fɪ'nɒmɪnən] (pl **phenomena**) n Phänomen nt

Philippines ['fɪlɪpiːnz] npl Philippinen pl

philosophical [fɪlə'sɒfɪkəl] adj philosophisch; (fig) gelassen; **philosophy** [fɪ'lɒsəfɪ] n Philosophie f

phone [fəʊn] n Telefon nt ▷ vt, vi anrufen; **phone book** n Telefonbuch nt; **phone bill** n Telefonrechnung f; **phone booth, phone box** (BRIT) n Telefonzelle f; **phonecall** n Telefonanruf m; **phonecard** n Telefonkarte f; **phone-in** n Rundfunkprogramm, bei dem der Hörer anrufen können; **phone**

number n Telefonnummer f
photo ['fəʊtəʊ] (pl -s) n Foto nt;
photo booth n Fotoautomat m;
photocopier ['fəʊtəʊ'kɒpɪə*] n
Kopiergerät nt; **photocopy** ['fəʊ-
təʊkɒpɪ] n Fotokopie f ▷ vt fotokopieren; **photograph** ['fəʊtə-
grɑːf] n Fotografie f, Aufnahme f ▷
vt fotografieren; **photographer**
[fə'tɒgrəfə*] n Fotograf(in) m(f);
photography [fə'tɒgrəfi] n Fotografie f

phrase [freɪz] n (expression) Redewendung f, Ausdruck m; **phrase
book** n Sprachführer m

physical ['fɪzɪkəl] adj (bodily)
körperlich, physisch ▷ n ärztliche
Untersuchung; **physically** adv
(bodily) körperlich, physisch; ~
handicapped körperbehindert

physician [fɪ'zɪʃən] n Arzt m,
Ärztin f

physics ['fɪzɪks] nsing Physik f
physiotherapy [fɪzɪə'θerəpɪ] n
Physiotherapie f

physique [fɪ'ziːk] n Körperbau m
piano ['pjɑːnəʊ] (pl -s) n Klavier nt
pick [pɪk] vt (flowers, fruit) pflücken; (choose) auswählen; (team)
aufstellen; **pick out** vt auswählen;
pick up vt (lift up) aufheben; (collect) abholen; (learn) lernen

pickle ['pɪkl] n (food) (Mixed) Pickles pl ▷ vt einlegen

pickpocket ['pɪkpɒkɪt] n Ta-
schendieb(in) m(f)

picnic ['pɪknɪk] n Picknick nt

picture ['pɪktʃə*] n Bild nt, **to go
to the ~s** (BRIT) ins Kino gehen ▷ vt
(visualize) sich vorstellen; **picture
book** n Bilderbuch nt; **picturesque** [pɪktʃə'resk] adj malerisch

pie [paɪ] n (meat) Pastete f; (fruit)
Kuchen m

piece [piːs] n Stück nt; (part) Teil
nt; (in chess) Figur f; (in draughts)

Stein m; **a ~ of cake** ein Stück Kuchen; **to fall to ~s** auseinanderfallen

pier [pɪə*] n Pier m

pierce [pɪəs] vt durchstechen,
durchbohren; (cold, sound) durchdringen; **pierced** adj (part of body)
geplerct, **piercing** adj durchdrin-
gend

pig [pɪg] n Schwein nt

pigeon ['pɪdʒən] n Taube f; **pi-
geonhole** n (compartment) Ablege-
fach nt

piggy ['pɪgɪ] adj (fam) verfressen;
pigheaded ['pɪg'hedɪd] adj dick-
köpfig; **piglet** ['pɪglət] n Ferkel nt;
pigsty ['pɪgstaɪ] n Schweinestall
m; **pigtail** ['pɪgteɪl] n Zopf m

pile [paɪl] n (heap) Haufen m; (one
on top of another) Stapel m; **pile up**
vi (accumulate) sich anhäufen

piles [paɪlz] npl Hämorr(ho)iden pl

pile-up ['paɪlʌp] n (Auto) Massenkarambolage f

pilgrim ['pɪlgrɪm] n Pilger(in) m(f)

pill [pɪl] n Tablette f; **the ~** die
(Antibaby)pille; **to be on the ~** die
Pille nehmen

pillar ['pɪlə*] n Pfeiler m

pillow ['pɪləʊ] n (Kopf)kissen nt;
pillowcase n (Kopf)kissenbezug m

pilot ['paɪlət] n (Aviat) Pilot(in) m(f)

pimple ['pɪmpl] n Pickel m

pin [pɪn] n (for fixing) Nadel f; (in
sewing) Stecknadel f; (Tech) Stift m,
I've got ~s and needles in my leg
mein Bein ist mir eingeschlafen ▷ vt
(fix with ~) heften (to an +akk)

PIN [pɪn] acr = **personal identification number ~ (number)** PIN f,
Geheimzahl f

pincers ['pɪnsəz] npl (tool) Kneifzange f

pinch [pɪntʃ] n (of salt) Prise f ▷ vt
zwicken; (fam: steal) klauen ▷ vi
(shoe) drücken

pine [paɪn] n Kiefer f

pineapple ['paɪnæpl] n Ananas f
pink [pɪŋk] adj rosa
pinstripe(d) ['pɪnstraɪp(t)] adj Nadelstreifen-
pint [paɪnt] n Pint nt (BRIT: 0,57 l, US: 0,473l); (BRIT: glass of beer) Bier nt
pious ['paɪəs] adj fromm
pip [pɪp] n (of fruit) Kern m
pipe [paɪp] n (for smoking) Pfeife f; (for water, gas) Rohrleitung f
pirate ['paɪərɪt] n Pirat(in) m(f); **pirated copy** n Raubkopie f
Pisces ['paɪsiːz] nsing (Astr) Fische pl; **she's a ~** sie ist Fisch
piss [pɪs] vi (vulg) pissen ▷ n (vulg) Pisse f; **to take the ~ out of sb** jdn verarschen; **the ~ out of sb** (vulg) sich verpissen; **~I** verpiss dich!; **pissed** adj (BRIT fam: drunk) sturzbesoffen; (US fam: annoyed) stocksauer
pistachio [pɪ'stɑːʃɪəʊ] (pl **-s**) n Pistazie f
piste [piːst] n (Ski) Piste f
pistol ['pɪstl] n Pistole f
pit [pɪt] n (hole) Grube f; (coalmine) Zeche f; **the ~s** (in motor racing) die Box; **to be the ~s** (fam) grottenschlecht sein
pitch [pɪtʃ] n (Sport) Spielfeld nt; (Mus: of instrument) Tonlage f; (of voice) Stimmlage f ▷ vt (tent) aufschlagen; (throw) werfen; **pitch-black** adj pechschwarz
pitcher ['pɪtʃə*] n (US: jug) Krug m
pitiful ['pɪtɪfʊl] adj (contemptible) jämmerlich
pitta bread ['pɪtəbred] n Pitta-brot nt
pity ['pɪtɪ] n Mitleid nt; **what a ~** wie schade; **it's a ~** es ist schade ▷ vt Mitleid haben mit
pizza ['piːtsə] n Pizza f
place [pleɪs] n m (spot, in text) Stelle f; (town etc) Ort; (house) Haus nt; (position, seat, on course) Platz m; **~ of birth** Geburtsort m; **at my ~** bei

mir; **in third ~** auf dem dritten Platz; **to three decimal ~s** bis auf drei Stellen nach dem Komma; **out of ~** nicht an der richtigen Stelle; (fig: remark) unangebracht; **in ~ of** anstelle von; **in the first ~** (firstly) erstens; (immediately) gleich; (in any case) überhaupt ▷ vt (put) stellen, setzen; (lay flat) legen; (advertisement) setzen (in in +akk); (Comm: order) aufgeben; **place mat** n Set nt
plague [pleɪg] n Pest f
plaice [pleɪs] n Scholle f
plain [pleɪn] adj (clear) klar, deutlich; (simple) einfach; (not beautiful) unattraktiv; (yoghurt) Natur-; (BRIT: chocolate) (Zart)bitter- ▷ n Ebene f; **plainly** adv (frankly) offen; (simply) einfach; (obviously) eindeutig
plait [plæt] n Zopf m ▷ vt flechten
plan [plæn] n Plan m; (for essay etc) Konzept nt ▷ vt planen; **to ~ to do sth, to ~ on doing sth** vorhaben, etw zu tun ▷ vi planen
plane [pleɪn] n (aircraft) Flugzeug nt; (tool) Hobel m; (Math) Ebene f
planet ['plænɪt] n Planet m
plank [plæŋk] n Brett nt
plant [plɑːnt] n Pflanze f; (equipment) Maschinen pl; (factory) Werk nt ▷ vt (tree etc) pflanzen; **plantation** [plæn'teɪʃən] n Plantage f
plaque [plæk] n Gedenktafel f; (on teeth) Zahnbelag m
plaster ['plɑːstə*] n (BRIT Med: sticking ~) Pflaster nt; (on wall) Verputz m; **to have one's arm in ~** den Arm in Gips haben
plastered ['plɑːstəd] adj (fam) besoffen; **to get (absolutely) ~** sich besaufen
plastic ['plæstɪk] n Kunststoff m; **to pay with ~** mit Kreditkarte bezahlen ▷ adj Plastik-; **plastic bag** n Plastiktüte f; **plastic surgery** n plastische Chirurgie f

plate [pleɪt] n (for food) Teller m; (flat sheet) Platte f; (plaque) Schild nt

platform ['plætfɔːm] n (Rail) Bahnsteig m; (at meeting) Podium nt

platinum ['plætɪnəm] n Platin nt

play [pleɪ] n Spiel nt; (Theat) (Theater)stück nt ▷ vt spielen; (another player or team) spielen gegen; **to ~ the piano** Klavier spielen; **to ~ a part in** (fig) eine Rolle spielen bei ▷ vi spielen; **play at** vt what are you ~ing at? was soll das?; **play back** vt abspielen; **play down** vt herunterspielen

playacting n Schauspielerei f; **playback** n Wiedergabe f; **player** n Spieler(in) m(f); (Mus) (person) verspielt; (remark) scherzhaft; **playground** n Spielplatz m; (in school) Schulhof m; **playgroup** n Spielgruppe f; **playing card** n Spielkarte f; **playing field** n Sportplatz m; **playmate** n Spielkamerad(in) m(f); **playwright** n Dramatiker(in) m(f)

plc abbr = **public limited company** AG f

plea [pliː] n Bitte f (for um)

plead [pliːd] vi dringend bitten (with sb jdn); (Jur) **to ~ guilty** sich schuldig bekennen

pleasant, pleasantly ['pleznt, -lɪ] adj, adv angenehm

please [pliːz] adv bitte; **more tea? - yes, ~** noch Tee? - ja, bitte (if be agreeable to) gefallen +dat; **~ yourself** wie du willst; **pleased** adj zufrieden, (glad) erfreut; **~ to meet you** freut mich, angenehm; **pleasing** adj erfreulich; **pleasure** ['pleʒə*] n Vergnügen nt, Freude f; **it's a ~** gern geschehen

pledge [pledʒ] n (promise) Versprechen nt ▷ vt (promise) versprechen

plenty ['plentɪ] n **~ of** eine Menge, viel(e); **to be ~** genug sein, reichen; **I've got ~** ich habe mehr als genug ▷ adv (US fam) ganz schön

pliable ['plaɪəbl] adj biegsam

pliers ['plaɪəz] npl (Kombi)zange f

plimsolls ['plɪmsəlz] npl (BRIT) Turnschuhe pl

plot [plɒt] n (of story) Handlung f; (conspiracy) Komplott nt; (of land) Stück nt Land, Grundstück nt ▷ vi ein Komplott schmieden

plough, plow (US) [plaʊ] n Pflug m ▷ vt, vi (Agr) pflügen; **ploughman's lunch** n (BRIT) in einer Kneipe serviertes Gericht aus Käse, Brot, Mixed Pickles etc

pluck [plʌk] vt (eyebrows, guitar) zupfen; (chicken) rupfen; **pluck up** vt **to ~ (one's) courage** Mut aufbringen

plug [plʌg] n (for sink, bath) Stöpsel m; (Elec) Stecker m; (Auto) (Zünd)kerze f; (fam: publicity) Schleichwerbung f ▷ vt (fam: advertise) Reklame machen für; **plug in** vt anschließen

plum [plʌm] n Pflaume f ▷ adj (fam: job etc) Super-

plumber ['plʌmə*] n Klempner(in) m(f); **plumbing** ['plʌmɪŋ] n (fittings) Leitungen pl; (craft) Installieren nt

plump [plʌmp] adj rundlich

plunge [plʌndʒ] n (of knife) stoßen; (into water) tauchen ▷ vi stürzen; (into water) tauchen

plural ['plʊərəl] n Plural m

plus [plʌs] prep (as well as) und ▷ adj Plus-; **20 ~ mehr** als 20 ▷ n (fig) Plus nt

plywood ['plaɪwʊd] n Sperrholz nt

pm abbr = **post meridiem** at **3 ~** um 3 Uhr nachmittags; **at 8 ~** um 8 Uhr abends

pneumonia [njuːˈməʊnɪə] n Lungenentzündung f

poached [pəʊtʃt] adj (egg) pochiert, verloren

PO Box abbr = **post office box** Postfach nt

pocket [ˈpɒkɪt] n Tasche f ▷ vt (put in ~) einstecken; **pocketbook** n (US: wallet) Brieftasche f; **pocket calculator** n Taschenrechner m; **pocket money** n Taschengeld nt

poem [ˈpəʊɪm] n Gedicht nt; **poet** [ˈpəʊɪt] n Dichter(in) m(f); **poetic** [pəʊˈetɪk] adj poetisch; **poetry** [ˈpəʊɪtrɪ] n (art) Dichtung f; (poems) Gedichte pl

point [pɔɪnt] n Punkt m; (spot) Stelle f; (sharp tip) Spitze f; (moment) Zeitpunkt m; (purpose) Zweck m; (idea) Argument nt; (decimal) Dezimalstelle f; **-s** pl (Rail) Weiche f; **~ of view** Standpunkt m; **three ~ two** drei Komma zwei; **at some ~** irgendwann (mal); **to get to the ~** zur Sache kommen; **there's no ~ es** hat keinen Sinn; **I was on the ~ of leaving** ich wollte gerade gehen ▷ vt (gun etc) richten (at auf +akk); **to ~ one's finger at** mit dem Finger zeigen auf +akk ▷ vi (with finger etc) zeigen (at, to auf +akk); **point out** vt (indicate) aufzeigen; (mention) hinweisen auf +akk; **pointed** adj spitz; (question) gezielt; **pointer** n (on dial) Zeiger m; (tip) Hinweis m; **pointless** adj sinnlos

poison [ˈpɔɪzn] n Gift nt ▷ vt vergiften; **poisonous** adj giftig

poke [pəʊk] vt (with stick, finger) stoßen, stupsen; (put) stecken

Poland [ˈpəʊlənd] n Polen nt

polar [ˈpəʊlə*] adj Polar-, polar; **~ bear** Eisbär m

pole [pəʊl] n Stange f; (Geo, Elec) Pol m

Pole [pəʊl] n Pole m, Polin f

pole vault n Stabhochsprung m

police [pəˈliːs] n Polizei f; **police car** n Polizeiwagen m; **policeman** (pl **-men**) n Polizist m; **police station** n (Polizei)wache f; **policewoman** (pl **-women**) n Polizistin f

policy [ˈpɒlɪsɪ] n (plan) Politik f; (principle) Grundsatz m; (insurance ~) (Versicherungs)police f

polio [ˈpəʊlɪəʊ] n Kinderlähmung f

polish [ˈpɒlɪʃ] n (for furniture) Politur f; (for floor) Wachs nt; (for shoes) Creme f; (shine) Glanz m; (fig) Schliff m ▷ vt polieren; (shoes) putzen; (fig) den letzten Schliff geben +dat

Polish [ˈpəʊlɪʃ] adj polnisch ▷ n Polnisch nt

polite [pəˈlaɪt] adj höflich; **politeness** n Höflichkeit f

political, politically [pəˈlɪtɪkəl, -lɪ] adj, adv politisch; **~ly correct** politisch korrekt; **politician** [pɒlɪˈtɪʃən] n Politiker(in) m(f); **politics** [ˈpɒlɪtɪks] nsing o pl Politik f

poll [pəʊl] n (election) Wahl f; (opinion ~) Umfrage f

pollen [ˈpɒlən] n Pollen m, Blütenstaub m; **pollen count** n Pollenflug m

polling station [ˈpəʊlɪŋsteɪʃən] n Wahllokal nt

pollute [pəˈluːt] vt verschmutzen; **pollution** [pəˈluːʃən] n Verschmutzung f

pompous [ˈpɒmpəs] adj aufgeblasen; (language) geschwollen

pond [pɒnd] n Teich m

ponder [ˈpɒndə*] vt nachdenken über +akk

pony [ˈpəʊnɪ] n Pony nt; **ponytail** n Pferdeschwanz m

poodle [ˈpuːdl] n Pudel m

pool [puːl] n (swimming ~) Schwimmbad nt; (private) Swim-

mingpool m; (of spilt liquid, blood)
Lache f; (game) Poolbillard nt ▷ vt
(money etc) zusammenlegen

poor [pɔ:*] adj arm; (not good)
schlecht ▷ npl **the ~** die Armen pl;
poorly adv (badly) schlecht ▷ adj
(BRIT) krank

pop [pɒp] n (music) Pop m; (noise)
Knall m ▷ vt (put) stecken; (balloon)
platzen lassen ▷ vi (balloon) platzen; (cork) knallen; **to ~ in** (person)
vorbeischauen; **pop concert** n
Popkonzert nt; **popcorn** n Popcorn
nt

Pope [pəʊp] n Papst m

pop group [ˈpɒpgruːp] n Pop
gruppe f; **pop music** n Popmusik f

poppy [ˈpɒpɪ] n Mohn m

Popsicle® [ˈpɒpsɪkl] n (US) Eis nt
am Stiel

pop star [ˈpɒpstaː*] n Popstar m

popular [ˈpɒpjʊlə*] adj (well-liked)
beliebt (with bei); (widespread) weit
verbreitet

population [pɒpjʊˈleɪʃən] n Bevölkerung f; (of town) Einwohner pl

porcelain [ˈpɔːslɪn] n Porzellan nt

porch [pɔːtʃ] n Vorbau m; (US:
verandah) Veranda f

porcupine [ˈpɔːkjʊpaɪn] n Stachelschwein nt

pork [pɔːk] n Schweinefleisch nt;
pork chop n Schweinekotelett;
pork pie n Schweinefleischpastete
f

porn [pɔːn] n Porno m; **pornographic** [pɔːnəˈɡræfɪk] adj pornografisch; **pornography** [pɔːˈnɒ-
grafɪ] n Pornografie f

porridge [ˈpɒrɪdʒ] n Haferbrei m

port [pɔːt] n (harbour) Hafen m;
(town) Hafenstadt f (Naut: left side)
Backbord nt; (wine) Portwein m; (Inf:
form) Anschluss m

portable [ˈpɔːtəbl] adj tragbar;
(radio) Koffer-

portal [ˈpɔːtl] n (Inform) Portal nt

porter [ˈpɔːtə*] n Pförtner(in) m(f);
(for luggage) Gepäckträger m

porthole [ˈpɔːthəʊl] n Bullauge nt

portion [ˈpɔːʃən] n Teil m; (of food)
Portion f

portrait [ˈpɔːtrɪt] n Porträt nt

portray [pɔːˈtreɪ] vt darstellen

Portugal [ˈpɔːtʃʊɡl] n Portugal nt;
Portuguese [pɔːtʃʊˈɡiːz] adj portugiesisch ▷ n Portugiese m, Portugiesin f; (language) Portugiesisch nt

pose [pəʊz] n Haltung f ▷ vi posieren ▷ vt (threat, problem) darstellen

posh [pɒʃ] adj (Inf) piekfein

position [pəˈzɪʃən] n (place) Position f, Lage f; (job) Stelle f; (opinion) Standpunkt m; **to be in a ~ to do sth** in der Lage sein, etw zu tun; **in third ~** auf dem dritten Platz

positive [ˈpɒzɪtɪv] adj positiv; (convinced) sicher; (definite) eindeutig

possess [pəˈzes] vt besitzen; **possession** [pəˈzeʃən] n **~(s** pl)
Besitz m; **possessive** adj (person)
Besitz ergreifend

possibility [pɒsəˈbɪlɪtɪ] n Möglichkeit f; **possible** [ˈpɒsəbl] adj
möglich; **if ~** wenn möglich; **as big / soon as ~** so groß / bald wie möglich; **possibly** adv (perhaps) vielleicht; **I've done all I ~ can** ich habe mein Möglichstes getan

post [pəʊst] n (mail) Post f; (pole)
Pfosten m; (job) Stelle f ▷ vt (letters)
aufgeben; **to keep sb ~ed** jdn auf
dem Laufenden halten; **postage**
[ˈpəʊstɪdʒ] n Porto nt; **~ and packing** Porto und Verpackung;
postal adj Post-; (BRIT) **~ order** –
Postanweisung f; **postbox** n
Briefkasten m; **postcard** n Postkarte f; **postcode** n (BRIT) Post-

leitzahl f
poster ['pəʊstə*] n Plakat nt,
Poster nt
postgraduate [pəʊst'grædjuɪt]
n jmd, der seine Studien nach dem
ersten akademischen Grad weiterführt
postman ['pəʊstmən] (pl **-men**) n
Briefträger m; **postmark** n Poststempel m
postmortem [pəʊst'mɔːtəm] n
Autopsie f
post office ['pəʊstɒfɪs] n Post® f;
post office box n Postfach nt
postpone [pə'spəʊn] vt verschieben (till auf +akk)
posture ['pɒstʃə*] n Haltung f
pot [pɒt] n Topf m; (tea~, coffee ~)
Kanne f; (fam: marijuana) Pot nt ▷ vt
(plant) eintopfen
potato [pə'teɪtəʊ] (pl **-es**) n Kartoffel f; **potato chips** (US) npl Kartoffelchips pl; **potato peeler** n
Kartoffelschäler m
potent ['pəʊtənt] adj stark
potential [pə'tenʃəl] adj potenziell ▷ n Potenzial nt; **potentially**
adv potenziell
pothole ['pɒthəʊl] n Höhle f; (in
road) Schlagloch nt
potter about ['pɒtərəbaʊt] vi
herumhantieren
pottery ['pɒtərɪ] n (objects) Töp-
ferwaren pl
potty ['pɒtɪ] adj (BRIT fam) verrückt ▷ n Töpfchen nt
poultry ['pəʊltrɪ] n Geflügel nt
pounce [paʊns] vi to ~ on sich
stürzen auf +akk
pound [paʊnd] n (money) Pfund
nt; (weight) Pfund nt (0,454 kg); **a ~ of**
cherries ein Pfund Kirschen; **ten-**
note Zehnpfundschein m
pour [pɔː*] vt (liquid) gießen; (rice,
sugar etc) schütten; **to ~ sb sth**
(drink) jdm etw eingießen; **pouring**
adj (rain) strömend

poverty ['pɒvətɪ] n Armut f
powder ['paʊdə*] n Pulver nt;
(cosmetic) Puder m; **powdered milk**
n Milchpulver nt; **powder room** n
Damentoilette f
power ['paʊə*] n Macht f; (ability)
Fähigkeit f; (strength) Stärke f; (Elec)
Strom m; **to be in ~** an der Macht
sein ▷ vt betreiben, antreiben;
power-assisted steering n Servolenkung f; **power cut** n Stromausfall m; **powerful** adj (politician
etc) mächtig; (engine, government)
stark; (argument) durchschlagend;
powerless adj machtlos; **power**
station n Kraftwerk nt
p&p abbr = **postage and packing**
PR abbr = **public relations** ▷ abbr =
proportional representation
practical, **practically** ['præktɪkəl,
-I] adj, adv praktisch; **practice**
['præktɪs] n (training) Übung f;
(custom) Gewohnheit f; (doctor's,
lawyer's) Praxis f; **in ~** (in reality) in
der Praxis; **out of ~** außer Übung; **to**
put sth into ~ etw in die Praxis
umsetzen ▷ vt, vi (US) see **practise**;
practise ['præktɪs] vt (instrument,
movement) üben; (profession) ausüben ▷ vi üben; (doctor, lawyer)
praktizieren
Prague [prɑːg] n Prag nt
praise [preɪz] n Lob nt ▷ vt loben
pram [præm] n (BRIT) Kinderwagen m
prawn [prɔːn] n Garnele f, Krabbe
f; **prawn crackers** npl Krabben-
chips pl
pray [preɪ] vi beten; **to ~ for sth**
(fig) stark auf etw akk hoffen;
prayer ['preə*] n Gebet nt
pre- [priː] pref vor-, prä-
preach [priːtʃ] vi predigen
prearrange [priːə'reɪndʒ] vt im
Voraus vereinbaren
precaution [prɪ'kɔːʃən] n Vor-

sichtsmaßnahme f

precede [prɪ'siːd] vt vorausgehen +dat; **preceding** adj vorhergehend

precinct ['priːsɪŋkt] n (BRIT: pedestrian ~) Fußgängerzone f; (BRIT: shopping ~) Einkaufsviertel nt; (US: district) Bezirk m

precious ['prɛʃəs] adj kostbar; **~ stone** Edelstein m

précis ['preɪsiː] n Zusammenfassung f

precise [prɪ'saɪs], **precisely** [prɪ'saɪs, -lɪ] adj, adv genau

precondition [priːkən'dɪʃən] n Vorbedingung f

predecessor ['priːdɪsɛsə*] n Vorgänger(in) m(f)

predicament [prɪ'dɪkəmənt] n missliche Lage

predict [prɪ'dɪkt] vt voraussagen; **predictable** adj vorhersehbar; (person) berechenbar

predominant [prɪ'dɒmɪnənt] adj vorherrschend; **predominantly** adv überwiegend

preface ['prɛfɪs] n Vorwort nt

prefer [prɪ'fɜː*] vt vorziehen (to dat), lieber mögen (to als); **to ~ to do sth** etw lieber tun; **preferably** ['prɛfrəblɪ] adv vorzugsweise, am liebsten; **preference** ['prɛfərəns] n (liking) Vorliebe f; **preferential** [prɛfə'rɛnʃəl] adj **to get ~ treatment** bevorzugt behandelt werden

prefix ['priːfɪks] n (Sprach) Vorsilbe f

pregnancy ['prɛgnənsɪ] n Schwangerschaft f; **pregnant** ['prɛgnənt] adj schwanger; **two months ~** im zweiten Monat schwanger

prejudice ['prɛdʒʊdɪs] n Vorurteil nt; **prejudiced** adj (person) voreingenommen

preliminary [prɪ'lɪmɪnərɪ] adj (measures) vorbereitend; (results)

vorläufig; (remarks) einleitend

premature ['prɛmətʃʊə*] adj vorzeitig; (hasty) voreilig

premiere ['prɛmɪeə*] n Premiere f

premises ['prɛmɪsɪz] npl (offices) Räumlichkeiten pl; (of factory, school) Gelände nt

premium-rate ['priːmɪəmreɪt] adj (Tel) zum Höchsttarif

preoccupied [priː'ɒkjʊpaɪd] adj **to be ~ with sth** mit etw sehr beschäftigt sein

prepaid [priː'peɪd] adj vorausbezahlt; (envelope) frankiert

preparation [prɛpə'reɪʃən] n Vorbereitung f; **prepare** [prɪ'pɛə*] vt vorbereiten (for auf +akk); (food) zubereiten; **to be ~d to do sth** bereit sein, etw zu tun ♦ vi sich vorbereiten (for auf +akk)

prerequisite [priː'rɛkwɪzɪt] n Voraussetzung f

prescribe [prɪ'skraɪb] vt vorschreiben; (Med) verschreiben; **prescription** [prɪ'skrɪpʃən] n Rezept nt

presence ['prɛzəns] n Gegenwart f; **present** [prɛznt] adj (in attendance) anwesend (at bei); (current) gegenwärtig; **~ tense** Gegenwart f, Präsens nt ♦ n Gegenwart f; (gift) Geschenk nt; **at ~** zurzeit ♦ [prɪ'zɛnt] vt (Tv, Radio) präsentieren; (problem) darstellen; (report etc) vorlegen; **to ~ sb with sth** jdm etw überreichen; **present-day** adj heutig; **presently** adv bald; (at present) zurzeit

preservative [prɪ'zɜːvətɪv] n Konservierungsmittel nt; **preserve** [prɪ'zɜːv] vt erhalten; (food) einmachen, konservieren

president ['prɛzɪdənt] n Präsident(in) m(f); **presidential** [prɛzɪ'dɛnʃəl] adj Präsidenten-; (election)

Präsidentschafts-

press [pres] *n* (*newspapers, machine*) Presse *f* ▷ *vt* (*push*) drücken; **to ~ a button** auf einen Knopf drücken ▷ *vi* (*push*) drücken; **pressing** *adj* dringend; **press-stud** *n* Druckknopf *m*; **press-up** *n* (BRIT) Liegestütz *m*; **pressure** ['preʃə*] *n* Druck *m*; **to be under ~** unter Druck stehen; **to put ~ on sb** jdn unter Druck setzen; **pressure cooker** *n* Schnellkochtopf *m*; **pressurize** ['preʃəraɪz] *vt* (*person*) unter Druck setzen

presumably [prɪ'zjuːməblɪ] *adv* vermutlich; **presume** [prɪ'zjuːm] *vt, vi* annehmen

presumptuous [prɪ'zʌmptʃʊəs] *adj* anmaßend

presuppose [priːsə'pəʊz] *vt* voraussetzen

pretend [prɪ'tend] *vt* **to ~ that** so tun als ob; **to ~ to do sth** vorgeben, etw zu tun ▷ *vi* **she's ~ing** sie tut nur so

pretentious [prɪ'tenʃəs] *adj* anmaßend; (*person*) wichtigtuerisch

pretty ['prɪtɪ] *adj* hübsch ▷ *adv* ziemlich

prevent [prɪ'vent] *vt* verhindern; **to ~ sb from doing sth** jdn daran hindern, etw zu tun

preview ['priːvjuː] *n* (Cine) Voraufführung *f*; (*trailer*) Vorschau *f*

previous ['priːvɪəs], **previously** [-lɪ] *adj, adv* früher

prey [preɪ] *n* Beute *f*

price [praɪs] *n* Preis *m* ▷ *vt* **it's ~d at £10** es ist mit 10 Pfund ausgezeichnet; **priceless** *adj* unbezahlbar; **price list** *n* Preisliste *f*; **price tag** *n* Preisschild *m*

prick [prɪk] *n* Stich *m*; (vulg: *penis*) Schwanz *m*; (vulg: *person*) Arsch *m* ▷ *vt* stechen in +akk; **to ~ one's finger** sich *dat* in den Finger stechen

prickly ['prɪklɪ] *adj* stachelig

pride [praɪd] *n* Stolz *m*; (*arrogance*) Hochmut *m* ▷ *vt* **to ~ oneself on sth** auf etw akk stolz sein

priest [priːst] *n* Priester *m*

primarily ['praɪmərɪlɪ] *adv* vorwiegend; **primary** ['praɪmərɪ] *adj* Haupt-; **~ education** Grundschulausbildung *f*; **~ school** Grundschule *f*

prime [praɪm] *adj* Haupt-; (*excellent*) erstklassig ▷ *n* **in one's ~** in den besten Jahren; **prime minister** *n* Premierminister(in) *m(f)*; **prime time** *n* (TV) Hauptsendezeit *f*

primitive ['prɪmɪtɪv] *adj* primitiv

primrose ['prɪmrəʊz] *n* Schlüsselblume *f*

prince [prɪns] *n* Prinz *m*; (*ruler*) Fürst *m*; **princess** [prɪn'ses] *n* Prinzessin *f*; (*wife of ruler*) Fürstin *f*

principal ['prɪnsɪpəl] *adj* Haupt-, wichtigste(r, s) ▷ *n* (*school*) Rektor(in) *m(f)*

principle ['prɪnsəpl] *n* Prinzip *nt*; **in ~** im Prinzip; **on ~** aus Prinzip

print [prɪnt] *n* (*picture*) Druck *m*; (Foto) Abzug *m*; (*made by feet, fingers*) Abdruck *m*; **out of ~** vergriffen ▷ *vt* drucken; (*photo*) abziehen; (*write in block letters*) in Druckschrift schreiben; **print out** *vt* (Inform) ausdrucken; **printed matter** *n* Drucksache *f*; **printer** *n* Drucker *m*; **print-out** *n* (Inform) Ausdruck *m*

prior ['praɪə*] *adj* früher; **a ~ engagement** eine vorher getroffene Verabredung; **~ to sth** vor etw *dat*; **~ to going abroad, she had ...** bevor sie ins Ausland ging, hatte sie ...

priority [praɪ'ɒrɪtɪ] *n* (*thing having precedence*) Priorität *f*

prison ['prɪzn] *n* Gefängnis *nt*; **prisoner** *n* Gefangene(r) *mf*; **~ of war** Kriegsgefangene(r) *mf*

privacy ['prɪvəsɪ] *n* Privatleben

nt; **private** ['praɪvɪt] adj privat, (confidential) vertraulich ▷ n einfacher Soldat; **in ~** privat; **privately** adv privat; (confidentially) vertraulich; **privatize** ['praɪvətaɪz] vt privatisieren

privilege ['prɪvɪlɪdʒ] n Privileg nt; **privileged** adj privilegiert

prize [praɪz] n Preis m, Prize; **money** n Preisgeld nt, **prizewinner** n Gewinner(in) m(f); **prizewinning** adj preisgekrönt

pro [prəʊ] (pl **-s**) n (professional) Profi m; **the ~s and cons** pl das Für und Wider

pro- [prəʊ] pref pro-

probability [probəˈbɪlɪtɪ] n Wahrscheinlichkeit f; **probable**, **probably** ['probəbl, -blɪ] adj, adv wahrscheinlich

probation [prəˈbeɪʃən] n Probezeit f; (Jur) Bewährung f

probe [prəʊb] n (investigation) Untersuchung f ▷ vt untersuchen

problem ['probləm] n Problem nt; **no ~** kein Problem!

procedure [prəˈsiːdʒə*] n Verfahren nt

proceed [prəˈsiːd] vi (continue) fortfahren; (set about sth) vorgehen ▷ vt **to ~ to do sth** anfangen, etw zu tun; **proceedings** npl (Jur) Verfahren nt; **proceeds** ['prəʊsiːdz] npl Erlös m

process ['prəʊses] n Prozess m, Vorgang m; (method) Verfahren n ▷ vt (application etc) bearbeiten; (food, data) verarbeiten; (film) entwickeln

procession [prəˈseʃən] n Umzug m

processor ['prəʊsesə*] n (Inform) Prozessor m; (Gastr) Küchenmaschine f

produce ['prodjuːs] n (Agr) Produkte pl, Erzeugnisse pl ▷ [prəˈdjuːs] vt (manufacture) herstellen,

produzieren; (on farm) erzeugen; (film, play, record) produzieren; (cause) hervorrufen; (evidence, results) liefern; **producer** n (manufacturer) Hersteller(in) m(f); (of film, play, record) Produzent(in) m(f); **product** ['prodʌkt] n Produkt nt, Erzeugnis nt; **production** [prəˈdʌkʃən] n Produktion f; (Theat) Inszenierung f; **productive** [prəˈdʌktɪv] adj produktiv; (land) ertragreich

prof [prof] n (fam) Professor(in) m(f)

profession [prəˈfeʃən] n Beruf m; **professional** [prəˈfeʃənl] n Profi m ▷ adj beruflich; (expert) fachlich; (sportsman, actor etc) Berufs-

professor [prəˈfesə*] n Professor(in) m(f); (US: lecturer) Dozent(in) m(f)

proficient [prəˈfɪʃənt] adj kompetent (in in +dat)

profile ['prəʊfaɪl] n Profil nt; **to keep a low ~** sich rar machen

profit ['profɪt] n Gewinn m ▷ vi profitieren (by, from von); **profitable** adj rentabel

profound [prəˈfaʊnd] adj tief; (idea, thinker) tiefgründig; (knowledge) profund

program ['prəʊgræm] n (Inform) Programm nt; (US) see **programme** ▷ vt (Inform) programmieren; (US) see **programme**

programme ['prəʊgræm] n Programm nt; (Tv, Radio) Sendung f ▷ vt programmieren; **programmer** n Programmierer(in) m(f); **programming** n (Inform) Programmiersprache f; **~ language** Programmiersprache f

progress ['prəʊgres] n Fortschritt m; **to make ~** Fortschritte machen ▷ [prəˈgres] vi (work, illness etc) fortschreiten; (improve) Fortschritte machen; **progressive** [prəˈgresɪv] *adj* (*person, policy*) fortschrittlich; **progressively** [prə'gresɪvlɪ] *adv* zunehmend

prohibit [prə'hɪbɪt] *vt* verbieten

project ['prɒdʒekt] *n* Projekt *nt*

projector [prə'dʒektə*] *n* Projektor *m*

prolong [prə'lɒŋ] *vt* verlängern

prom [prɒm] *n* (*at seaside*) Promenade *f*; (*BRIT: concert*) Konzert *nt* (*bei dem ein Großteil des Publikums im Parkett Stehplätze hat*); (*US: dance*) Ball *m* für die Schüler und Studenten von Highschools oder Colleges

prominent ['prɒmɪnənt] *adj* (*politician, actor etc*) prominent; (*easily seen*) auffallend

promiscuous [prə'mɪskjʊəs] *adj* promisk

promise ['prɒmɪs] *n* Versprechen *nt* ▷ *vt* versprechen; **to ~ sb sth** etw versprechen; **to ~ to do sth** versprechen, etw zu tun ▷ *vi* versprechen; **promising** *adj* viel versprechend

promote [prə'məʊt] *vt* (*in rank*) befördern; (*help on*) fördern; (*Comm*) werben für; **promotion** [prə'məʊʃən] *n* (*in rank*) Beförderung *f*; (*Comm*) Werbung *f* (*for* für)

prompt [prɒmpt] *adj* prompt; (*punctual*) pünktlich ▷ *adv* **at two o'clock ~** Punkt zwei Uhr ▷ *vt* (*Theat: actor*) soufflieren +*dat*

prone [prəʊn] *adj* **to be ~ to sth** zu etw neigen

pronounce [prə'naʊns] *vt* (*word*) aussprechen; **pronounced** *adj* ausgeprägt; **pronunciation** [prənʌnsɪ'eɪʃən] *n* Aussprache *f*

proof [pruːf] *n* Beweis *m*; (*of alcohol*) Alkoholgehalt *m*

prop [prɒp] *n* Stütze *f*; (*Theat*) Requisit *nt* ▷ *vt* **to ~ sth against sth** etw gegen etw lehnen; **prop up** *vt* stützen; (*fig*) unterstützen

proper ['prɒpə*] *adj* richtig; (*morally correct*) anständig

property ['prɒpətɪ] *n* (*possession*) Eigentum *nt*; (*house*) Haus *nt*; (*land*) Grundbesitz *m*; (*characteristic*) Eigenschaft *f*

proportion [prə'pɔːʃən] *n* Verhältnis *nt*; (*share*) Teil *m*; **~s** *pl* (*size*) Proportionen *pl*; **in ~ to** im Verhältnis zu; **proportional** *adj* proportional; **~ representation** Verhältniswahlrecht *nt*

proposal [prə'pəʊzl] *n* Vorschlag *m*; **~ (of marriage)** (Heirats)antrag *m*; **propose** [prə'pəʊz] *vt* vorschlagen ▷ *vi* (*offer marriage*) einen Heiratsantrag machen (*to* jdm)

proprietor [prə'praɪətə*] *n* Besitzer(in) *m(f)*; (*of pub, hotel*) Inhaber(in) *m(f)*

prose [prəʊz] *n* Prosa *f*

prosecute ['prɒsɪkjuːt] *vt* verfolgen (*for* wegen)

prospect ['prɒspekt] *n* Aussicht *f*

prosperity [prɒ'sperɪtɪ] *n* Wohlstand *m*; **prosperous** *adj* wohlhabend; (*business*) gut gehend

prostitute ['prɒstɪtjuːt] *n* Prostituierte(r) *mf*

protect [prə'tekt] *vt* schützen (*from, against* vor +*dat*, gegen); **protection** [prə'tekʃən] *n* Schutz *m* (*from, against* vor +*dat*, gegen); **protective** *adj* beschützend; (*clothing etc*) Schutz-

protein ['prəʊtiːn] *n* Protein *nt*, Eiweiß *nt*

protest [prə'test] *n* Protest *m*; (*demonstration*) Protestkundgebung *f* ▷ [prə'test] *vi* protestieren (*against* gegen); (*demonstrate*) demonstrieren

Protestant ['prɒtəstənt] *adj* protestantisch ▷ *n* Protestant(in) *m(f)*

proud, proudly [praʊd, -lɪ] *adj, adv* stolz (*of* auf +*akk*)

prove [pruːv] vt beweisen; (turn out to be) sich erweisen als

proverb ['prɒvɜːb] n Sprichwort nt

provide [prə'vaɪd] vt zur Verfügung stellen; (drinks, music etc) sorgen für; (person) versorgen (with mit), **provide for** vt (family etc) sorgen für; **provided** conj ~ (that) vorausgesetzt, dass; **provider** n (Inform) Provider m

provision [prə'vɪʒən] n (condition) Bestimmung f; **~s** pl (food) Proviant m

provisional, provisionally [prə'vɪʒənl, -ɪ] adj, adv provisorisch

provoke [prə'vəʊk] vt provozieren; (cause) hervorrufen

proximity [prɒk'sɪmɪtɪ] n Nähe f

prudent ['pruːdənt] adj klug; (person) umsichtig

prudish ['pruːdɪʃ] adj prüde

prune [pruːn] n Backpflaume f ▷ vt (tree etc) zurechtstutzen

PS abbr = **postscript** PS nt

psalm [sɑːm] n Psalm m

pseudo ['sjuːdəʊ] adj pseudo-, Pseudo-; **pseudonym** ['sjuːdənɪm] n Pseudonym nt

PST abbr = **Pacific Standard Time**

psychiatric [saɪkɪ'ætrɪk] adj psychiatrisch; (illness) psychisch; **psychiatrist** [saɪ'kaɪətrɪst] n Psychiater(in) m(f); **psychiatry** [saɪ'kaɪətrɪ] n Psychiatrie f; **psychic** ['saɪkɪk] adj übersinnlich; **I'm not** ~ Ich kann keine Gedanken lesen; **psychoanalysis** [saɪkəʊə-'næləsɪs] n Psychoanalyse f; **psychoanalyst** [saɪkəʊ'ænəlɪst] n Psychoanalytiker(in) m(f); **psychological** [saɪkə'lɒdʒɪkəl] adj psychologisch; **psychology** [saɪ'kɒlədʒɪ] n Psychologie f; **psychopath** ['saɪkəʊpæθ] n Psychopath(in) m(f)

pt abbr = **pint**

pto abbr = **please turn over** b.w.

pub [pʌb] n (BRIT) Kneipe f

● **PUB**

Ein **pub** ist ein Gasthaus mit einer Lizenz zum Ausschank von alkoholischen Getränken. Ein „Pub" besteht meist aus verschiedenen gemütlichen (**lounge, snug**) oder einfacheren (**public bar**) Räumen, in denen oft auch Spiele wie Darts, Domino und Poolbillard zur Verfügung stehen. In „Pubs" werden vor allem mittags auch Mahlzeiten angeboten (**pub lunch**). „Pubs" sind normalerweise von 11 bis 23 Uhr geöffnet, aber manchmal nachmittags geschlossen.

puberty ['pjuːbətɪ] n Pubertät f

public ['pʌblɪk] n the (general) ~ die (breite) Öffentlichkeit; **in** ~ in der Öffentlichkeit ▷ adj öffentlich; (relating to the State) Staats-; ~ **convenience** (BRIT) öffentliche Toilette; ~ **holiday** gesetzlicher Feiertag; ~ **opinion** die öffentliche Meinung; ~ **relations** pl Öffentlichkeitsarbeit f, Public Relations pl; ~ **school** (BRIT) Privatschule f; **publication** [pʌblɪ-'keɪʃən] n Veröffentlichung f; **publicity** [pʌb'lɪsɪtɪ] n Publicity f; (advertisements) Werbung f; **publish** ['pʌblɪʃ] vt veröffentlichen; **publisher** n Verleger(in) m(f); (company) Verlag m; **publishing** n Verlagswesen nt

pub lunch ['pʌb'lʌntʃ] n (oft einfacheres) Mittagessen in einer Kneipe

pudding ['pʊdɪŋ] n (course) Nachtisch m

puddle ['pʌdl] n Pfütze f

puff [pʌf] vi (pant) schnaufen

puffin ['pʌfɪn] n Papageientaucher m

puff paste (US), **puff pastry**
['pʌf,peɪstrɪ] n Blätterteig m
pull [pʊl] n Ziehen nt; **to give sth
a ~** an etw dat ziehen ▷ vt (cart,
tooth) ziehen; (rope, handle) ziehen
an +dat; (fam: date) abschleppen; **to
~ a muscle** sich dat einen Muskel
zerren; **to ~ sb's leg** jdn auf den Arm
nehmen ▷ vi ziehen; **pull apart** vt
(separate) auseinander ziehen; **pull
down** vt (blind) herunterziehen;
(house) abreißen; **pull in** vi hineinfahren; (stop) anhalten; **pull off** vt
(clothes) ausziehen; (deal etc) zuwege
bringen; **pull on** vt (clothes) anziehen; **pull out** vi (car from lane)
ausscheren; (train) abfahren; (withdraw) aussteigen (of aus) ▷ vt herausziehen; (tooth) ziehen; (troops)
abziehen; **pull round, pull
through** vi durchkommen; **pull
up** vt (raise) hochziehen; (chair)
heranziehen ▷ vi anhalten
pullover ['pʊləʊvə*] n Pullover m
pulp [pʌlp] n Brei m; (of fruit)
Fruchtfleisch nt
pulpit ['pʊlpɪt] n Kanzel f
pulse [pʌls] n Puls m
pump [pʌmp] n Pumpe f; (in petrol
station) Zapfsäule f; **pump up** vt
(tyre etc) aufpumpen
pumpkin ['pʌmpkɪn] n Kürbis m
pun [pʌn] n Wortspiel nt
punch [pʌntʃ] n (blow) (Faust-)
schlag m; (tool) Locher m; (hot drink)
Punsch m; (cold drink) Bowle f ▷ vt
(strike) schlagen; (ticket, paper) lochen
punctual, punctually ['pʌŋktjʊəl,
-ɪ] adj, adv pünktlich
punctuation [pʌŋktjʊ'eɪʃən] n
Interpunktion f; **punctuation
mark** n Satzzeichen nt
puncture ['pʌŋktʃə*] n (flat tyre)
Reifenpanne f
punish ['pʌnɪʃ] vt bestrafen;

punishment n Strafe f; (action)
Bestrafung f
pupil ['pju:pl] n (school) Schü-
ler(in) m(f)
puppet ['pʌpɪt] n Puppe f; (string
~) Marionette f
puppy ['pʌpɪ] n junger Hund
purchase ['pɜ:tʃɪs] n Kauf m ▷ vt
kaufen
pure [pjʊə*] adj rein; (clean) sauber; (utter) pur; **purely** ['pjʊəlɪ]
adv rein; **purify** ['pjʊərɪfaɪ] vt
reinigen; **purity** ['pjʊərɪtɪ] n
Reinheit f
purple ['pɜ:pl] adj violett
purpose ['pɜ:pəs] n Zweck m; (of
person) Absicht f; **on ~** absichtlich
purr [pɜ:*] vi (cat) schnurren
purse [pɜ:s] n Geldbeutel m; (US:
handbag) Handtasche f
pursue [pə'sju:] vt (person, car)
verfolgen; (hobby, studies) nachgehen +dat; **pursuit** [pə'sju:t] n
(chase) Verfolgung f; (occupation) Beschäftigung f; (hobby) Hobby nt
pus [pʌs] n Eiter m
push [pʊʃ] n Stoß m ▷ vt (person)
stoßen; (car, chair etc) schieben;
(button) drücken; (drugs) dealen ▷ vi
(in crowd) drängeln; **push in** vi (in
queue) sich vordrängeln; **push off**
vi (fam: leave) abhauen; **push on** vi
(with job) weitermachen; **push up**
vt (prices) hochtreiben; **pushchair**
n (BRIT) Sportwagen m; **pusher**
n (of drugs) Dealer(in) m(f); **push-up**
n (US) Liegestütz m; **pushy** adj
(fam) aufdringlich, penetrant
put [pʊt] (put, put) vt tun; (upright) stellen; (flat) legen; (express)
ausdrücken; (write) schreiben; **he ~
his hand in his pocket** er steckte
die Hand in die Tasche; **he ~ his
hand on her shoulder** er legte ihr
die Hand auf die Schulter; **to ~
money into one's account** Geld

auf sein Konto einzahlen; **put aside** vt (money) zurücklegen; **put away** vt (tidy away) wegräumen; **put back** vt zurücklegen; (clock) zurückstellen; **put down** vt (in writing) aufschreiben; (BRIT: animal) einschläfern; (rebellion) niederschlagen; **to put the phone down** (den Hörer) auflegen; **to put one's name down for sth** sich für etw eintragen; **put forward** vt (idea) vorbringen; (name) vorschlagen; (clock) vorstellen; **put in** vt (install) einbauen; (submit) einreichen; **put off** vt (switch off) ausschalten; (postpone) verschieben; **to put sb off doing sth** jdn davon abbringen, etw zu tun; **put on** vt (switch on) anmachen; (clothes) anziehen; (hat, glasses) aufsetzen; (make-up, CD) auflegen; (play) aufführen; **to put the kettle on** Wasser aufsetzen; **to put weight on** zunehmen; **put out** vt (hand, foot) ausstrecken; (light, cigarette) ausmachen; **put up** vt (hand) hochheben; (picture) aufhängen; (tent) aufstellen; (building) errichten; (price) erhöhen; (person) unterbringen; **to ~ with** sich abfinden mit; **I won't ~ with it** das lasse ich mir nicht gefallen

putt [pʌt] vt, vi (Sport) putten

puzzle ['pʌzl] n Rätsel nt; (toy) Geduldsspiel nt; (jigsaw) ~ Puzzle nt ▷ vt vor ein Rätsel stellen; **It ~s me** es ist mir ein Rätsel; **puzzling** adj rätselhaft

pyjamas [pɪ'dʒɑːmaz] npl Schlafanzug m

pylon ['paɪlən] n Mast m

pyramid ['pɪrəmɪd] n Pyramide f

quack [kwæk] vi quaken

quaint [kweɪnt] adj (idea, tradition) kurios; (picturesque) malerisch

qualification [kwɒlɪfɪ'keɪʃən] n (for job) Qualifikation f; (from school, university) Abschluss m; **qualified** ['kwɒlɪfaɪd] adj (for job) qualifiziert; **qualify** vt (limit) einschränken; **to be qualified to do sth** berechtigt sein, etw zu tun ▷ vi (finish training) seine Ausbildung abschließen; (Sport) sich qualifizieren

quality ['kwɒlɪtɪ] n Qualität f; (characteristic) Eigenschaft f

quantity ['kwɒntɪtɪ] n Menge f, Quantität f

quarantine ['kwɒrəntiːn] n Quarantäne f

quarrel ['kwɒrəl] n Streit m ▷ vi sich streiten; **quarrelsome** adj streitsüchtig

quarter ['kwɔːtə*] n Viertel nt; (of year) Vierteljahr nt; (US: coin) Vierteldollar m; **a ~ of an hour** eine Viertelstunde; **~ to/past** (BRIT) (~ o -

of / after (US) **three** Viertel vor / nach drei ▷ vt vierteln; **quarter final** n Viertelfinale nt; **quarters** npl (Mil) Quartier nt

quartet [kwɔː'tet] n Quartett nt

quay [kiː] n Kai m

queasy ['kwiːzɪ] adj **I feel ~** mir ist übel

queen [kwiːn] n Königin f; (in cards, chess) Dame f

queer [kwɪə*] adj (strange) seltsam, sonderbar; (pej: homosexual) schwul ▷ n (pej) Schwule(r) m

quench [kwentʃ] vt (thirst) löschen

query ['kwɪərɪ] n Frage f ▷ vt in Frage stellen; (bill) reklamieren

question ['kwestʃən] n Frage f; **that's out of the ~** das kommt nicht in Frage ▷ vt (person) befragen; (suspect) vernehmen; (express doubt about) bezweifeln; **questionable** adj zweifelhaft; (improper) fragwürdig; **question mark** n Fragezeichen nt; **questionnaire** [kwestʃə'neə*] n Fragebogen m

queue [kjuː] n (BRIT) Schlange f; **to jump the ~** sich vordrängeln ▷ vi **to ~ (up)** Schlange stehen

quibble ['kwɪbl] vi kleinlich sein; (argue) streiten

quiche [kiːʃ] n Quiche

quick [kwɪk] adj schnell; (short) kurz; **be ~** mach schnell!; **quickly** adv schnell

quid [kwɪd] (pl **quid**) n (BRIT fam) Pfund nt; **20 ~** 20 Pfund

quiet ['kwaɪət] adj (not noisy) leise; (peaceful, calm) still, ruhig; **be ~** sei still!; **to keep ~ about sth** über etw akk nichts sagen ▷ n Stille f, Ruhe f; **quiet down** (US), **quieten down** ['kwaɪətən'daʊn] vi sich beruhigen ▷ vt beruhigen; **quietly** adv leise; (calmly) ruhig

quilt [kwɪlt] n (Stepp)decke f

quit [kwɪt] (**quit** o **quitted**, **quit** o **quitted**) vt (leave) verlassen; (job) aufgeben; **to ~ doing sth** aufhören, etw zu tun ▷ vi aufhören; (resign) kündigen

quite [kwaɪt] adv (fairly) ziemlich; (completely) ganz, völlig; **I don't ~ understand** ich verstehe das nicht ganz; **~ a few** ziemlich viele; **~ so** richtig!

quits [kwɪts] adj **to be ~ with sb** mit jdm quitt sein

quiver ['kwɪvə*] vi zittern

quiz [kwɪz] n (competition) Quiz nt

quota ['kwəʊtə] n Anteil m; (Comm, Pol) Quote f

quotation [kwəʊ'teɪʃən] n Zitat nt; (price) Kostenvoranschlag m; **quotation marks** npl Anführungszeichen pl; **quote** [kwəʊt] vt (text, author) zitieren; (price) nennen ▷ n Zitat nt; (price) Kostenvoranschlag m; **in ~s** in Anführungszeichen

rabbi ['ræbaɪ] n Rabbiner m
rabbit ['ræbɪt] n Kaninchen nt
rabies ['reɪbiːz] nsing Tollwut f
raccoon [rə'kuːn] n Waschbär m
race [reɪs] n (competition) Rennen
nt; (people) Rasse f ▷ vt um die
Wette laufen/fahren ▷ vi (rush)
rennen; **racecourse** n Rennbahn f;
racehorse n Rennpferd nt; **racetrack** n Rennbahn f
racial ['reɪʃəl] adj Rassen-; **~ discrimination** Rassendiskriminierung
f
racing ['reɪsɪŋ] n (horse) **~** Pferderennen nt; (motor) **~** Autorennen
nt; **racing car** n Rennwagen m
racism ['reɪsɪzəm] n Rassismus
m; **racist** n Rassist(in) m(f) ▷ adj
rassistisch
rack [ræk] n Ständer m, Gestell nt
▷ vt **to ~ one's brains** sich darüber
den Kopf zerbrechen
racket ['rækɪt] n (Sport) Schläger
m; (noise) Krach m
radar ['reɪdɑː*] n Radar nt o m;

radar trap n Radarfalle f
radiation [ˌreɪdɪ'eɪʃən] n (radioactive) Strahlung f
radiator ['reɪdɪeɪtə*] n Heizkörper m; (Auto) Kühler m
radical ['rædɪkəl] adj radikal
radio ['reɪdɪəʊ] (pl **-s**) n Rundfunk
m, Radio nt
radioactivity [ˌreɪdɪəʊæk'tɪvɪtɪ] n
Radioaktivität f
radio alarm [ˌreɪdɪəʊə'lɑːm] n
Radiowecker m; **radio station** n
Rundfunkstation f
radiotherapy [ˌreɪdɪəʊ'θerəpɪ] n
Strahlenbehandlung f
radish ['rædɪʃ] n Radieschen nt
radius ['reɪdɪəs] n Radius m;
within a five-mile ~ im Umkreis
von fünf Meilen (of um)
raffle ['ræfl] n Tombola f; **raffle
ticket** n Los nt
raft [rɑːft] n Floß nt
rag [ræɡ] n Lumpen m; (for cleaning) Lappen m
rage [reɪdʒ] n Wut f; **to be all the
~** der letzte Schrei sein ▷ vi toben;
(disease) wüten
raid [reɪd] n Überfall m (on auf
+akk); (by police) Razzia f (on gegen)
▷ vt (bank etc) überfallen; (by police)
eine Razzia machen in +dat
rail [reɪl] n (on stairs, balcony etc)
Geländer nt; (of ship) Reling f; (Rail)
Schiene f; **railcard** n (BRIT) ≈
Bahncard® f; **railing** n Geländer nt;
~s pl (fence) Zaun m; **railroad** n (US)
Eisenbahn f; **railroad station** n
(US) Bahnhof m; **railway** n (BRIT)
Eisenbahn f; **railway line** n Bahnlinie f; (track) Gleis nt; **railway station** n Bahnhof m
rain [reɪn] n Regen m ▷ vi regnen;
it's ~ing es regnet; **rainbow** n
Regenbogen m; **raincoat** n Regenmantel m; **rainfall** n Niederschlag m; **rainforest** n Regenwald

m; **rainy** adj regnerisch

raise [reɪz] n (US: of wages / salary)
Gehalts-/Lohnerhöhung f ▷ vt (lift)
hochheben; (increase) erhöhen;
(family) großziehen; (livestock) züchten; (money) aufbringen; (objection)
erheben; **to ~ one's voice** (in anger)
laut werden

raisin ['reɪzən] n Rosine f

rally ['rælɪ] n (Pol) Kundgebung f;
(Auto) Rallye f; (Tennis) Ballwechsel m

RAM [ræm] acr = **random access
memory** RAM m

ramble ['ræmbl] n Wanderung f
▷ vi (walk) wandern; (talk) schwafeln

ramp [ræmp] n Rampe f

ran [ræn] pt of **run**

ranch [rɑːntʃ] n Ranch f

rancid ['rænsɪd] adj ranzig

random ['rændəm] adj willkürlich ▷ n **at ~** (choose) willkürlich;
(fire) ziellos

randy ['rændɪ] adj (BRIT fam) geil,
scharf

rang [ræŋ] pt of **ring**

range [reɪndʒ] n (selection) Auswahl f (of an +dat); (Comm) Sortiment
nt (of an +dat); (of missile, telescope)
Reichweite f; (of mountains) Kette f;
in this price ~ in dieser Preisklasse
▷ vi **to ~ from ... to ...** gehen von
... bis ...; (temperature, sizes, prices)
liegen zwischen ... und ...

rank [ræŋk] n (Mil) Rang m; (social
position) Stand m ▷ vt einstufen ▷
vi **to ~ among** zählen zu

ransom ['rænsəm] n Lösegeld nt

rap [ræp] n (Mus) Rap m

rape [reɪp] n Vergewaltigung f ▷
vt vergewaltigen

rapid, rapidly ['ræpɪd, -lɪ] adj, adv
schnell

rapist ['reɪpɪst] n Vergewaltiger m

rare [rɛə*] adj selten, rar; (especially good) vortrefflich; (steak) blutig;

rarely adv selten; **rarity** ['rɛərɪtɪ]
n Seltenheit f

rash [ræʃ] adj unbesonnen ▷ n
(Med) (Haut)ausschlag m

rasher ['ræʃə*] n ~ **(of bacon)**
(Speck)scheibe f

raspberry ['rɑːzbərɪ] n Himbeere
f

rat [ræt] n Ratte f; (pej: person)
Schwein nt

rate [reɪt] n (proportion, frequency)
Rate f; (speed) Tempo nt; ~ **(of exchange)** (Wechsel)kurs m; ~ **of inflation** Inflationsrate f; ~ **of interest** Zinssatz m; **at any ~** auf jeden
Fall ▷ vt (evaluate) einschätzen (as
als)

rather ['rɑːðə*] adv (in preference)
lieber; (fairly) ziemlich; **I'd ~ stay
here** ich würde lieber hier bleiben;
I'd ~ not lieber nicht; **or ~** (more
accurately) vielmehr

ratio ['reɪʃɪəʊ] (pl -s) n Verhältnis
nt

rational ['ræʃənl] adj rational;
rationalize ['ræʃnəlaɪz] vt ratio-
nalisieren

rattle ['rætl] n (toy) Rassel f ▷ vt
(keys, coins) klimpern mit; (person)
durcheinander bringen ▷ vi (window) klappern; (bottles) klirren; **rattle off** vt herunterrasseln; **rattlesnake** n Klapperschlange f

rave [reɪv] vi (talk wildly) fanta-
sieren; (rage) toben; (enthuse)
schwärmen (about von) ▷ n (BRIT:
event) Raveparty f

raven ['reɪvn] n Rabe m

raving ['reɪvɪŋ] adv ~ **mad** total
verrückt

ravishing ['rævɪʃɪŋ] adj hin-
reißend

raw [rɔː] adj (food) roh; (skin)
wund; (climate) rau

ray [reɪ] n (of light) Strahl m; ~ **of
hope** Hoffnungsschimmer m

razor ['reɪzə*] n Rasierapparat m; **razor blade** n Rasierklinge f

Rd n abbr = **road** Str.

re [riː] prep (Comm) betreffs +gen

RE abbr = **religious education**

reach [riːtʃ] n within/out of (sb's) ~ in/außer (jds) Reichweite; **within easy ~ of the shops** nicht weit von den Geschäften ▷ vt (arrive at contact) erreichen; (come down / un as far as) reichen bis zu; (contact) **can you ~ it?** kommen Sie dran?; **reach for** vt greifen nach; **reach out** vi die Hand ausstrecken; **to ~ for** greifen nach

react [riːˈækt] vi reagieren (to auf +akk); **reaction** [riːˈækʃən] n Reaktion f (to auf +akk); **reactor** [riːˈæktə*] n Reaktor m

read [riːd] (read, read) vt lesen; (meter) ablesen; **to ~ sth to sb** jdm etw vorlesen ▷ vi lesen; **to ~ to sb** jdm vorlesen; **it ~s well** es liest sich gut, **it ~s as follows** es lautet folgendermaßen; **read out** vt vorlesen; **read through** vt durchlesen; **read up on** vt nachlesen über +akk; **readable** adj (book) lesenswert; (handwriting) lesbar; **reader** n Leser(in) m(f)

readily ['redɪlɪ] adv (willingly) bereitwillig; **~ available** leicht erhältlich

reading ['riːdɪŋ] n (action) Lesen nt; (from meter) Zählerstand m; **reading glasses** npl Lesebrille f; **reading lamp** n Leselampe f; **reading list** n Leseliste f; **reading matter** n Lektüre f

readjust [riːəˈdʒʌst] vt (mechanism etc) neu einstellen ▷ vi sich wieder anpassen (to an +akk)

ready ['redɪ] adj fertig, bereit; **to be ~ to do sth** (willing) bereit sein, etw zu tun; **are you ~ to go?** bist du so weit?; **to get sth ~** etw fertig machen; **to get (oneself) ~** sich fertig machen; **ready cash** n Bargeld nt; **ready-made** adj (product) Fertig-; (clothes) Konfektions-; **meal** Fertiggericht nt

real [rɪəl] adj wirklich; (actual) eigentlich; (genuine) echt; (idiot etc) richtig; **for ~** echt. **this time it's for ~** diesmal ist es ernst; **get ~** sei realistisch! (sagt fam, esp US) echt ▷ n **for ~** echt; **this time it's for ~** diesmal ist es ernst; **get ~** sei realistisch!; **real ale** n Ale nt; **real estate** n Immobilien pl

realistic, realistically [rɪəˈlɪstɪk, -əlɪ] adj, adv realistisch; **reality** [rɪˈælɪtɪ] n Wirklichkeit f; **in ~** in Wirklichkeit; **reality TV** n Reality-TV nt; **realization** [rɪəlaɪˈzeɪʃən] n (awareness) Erkenntnis f; **realize** ['rɪəlaɪz] vt (understand) begreifen; (plan, idea) realisieren; **I ~d (that) ...** mir wurde klar, dass ...

really ['rɪəlɪ] adv wirklich

real time [rɪəl'taɪm] n (Inform) **in ~** in Echtzeit

realtor ['rɪəltɔ*] n (US) Grundstücksmakler(in) m(f)

reappear [riːəˈpɪə*] vi wieder erscheinen

rear [rɪə*] adj hintere(r, s), Hinter- ▷ n (of building, vehicle) hinterer Teil; **at the ~ of** hinter +dat; (inside) hinten in +dat; **rear light** n (Auto) Rücklicht nt

rearm [riːˈɑːm] vi wieder aufrüsten

rearrange [riːəˈreɪndʒ] vt (furniture, system) umstellen; (meeting) verlegen (for auf +akk)

rear-view mirror ['rɪəvjuː-'mɪrə*] n Rückspiegel m; **rear window** n (Auto) Heckscheibe f

reason ['riːzn] n (cause) Grund m (for für); (ability to think) Verstand m; (common sense) Vernunft f; **for some**

~ aus irgendeinem Grund ▷ vi **to ~
with sb** mit jdm vernünftig reden;
reasonable adj (person, price) vernünftig; (offer) akzeptabel; (chance)
reell; (food, weather) ganz gut; **reasonably** adv vernünftig; (fairly)
ziemlich

reassure [riːəˈʃʊə*] vt beruhigen;
she ~d me that ... sie versicherte
mir, dass ...

rebel [ˈrebl] n Rebell(in) m(f) ▷
[rɪˈbel] vi rebellieren; **rebellion**
[rɪˈbeljən] n Aufstand m

reboot [riːˈbuːt] vt, vi (Inform) rebooten

rebound [rɪˈbaʊnd] vi (ball etc)
zurückprallen

rebuild [riːˈbɪld] irr vt wieder
aufbauen

recall [rɪˈkɔːl] vt (remember) sich
erinnern an +akk; (call back) zurückrufen

recap [ˈriːkæp] vt, vi rekapitulieren

receipt [rɪˈsiːt] n (document)
Quittung f; (receiving) Empfang m; **~s**
pl (money) Einnahmen pl

receive [rɪˈsiːv] vt (news etc) erhalten, bekommen; (visitor) empfangen; **receiver** n (Tel) Hörer m;
(Radio) Empfänger m

recent [ˈriːsnt] adj (event) vor
kurzem stattgefunden; (photo) neueste(r,s); (invention) neu; **in ~ years**
in den letzten Jahren; **recently** adv
vor kurzem; (in the last few days or
weeks) in letzter Zeit

reception [rɪˈsepʃən] n Empfang
m; **receptionist** n (in hotel) Empfangschef m, Empfangsdame f;
(woman in firm) Empfangsdame f;
(Med) Sprechstundenhilfe f

recess [rɪˈses] n (in wall) Nische f;
(US: in school) Pause f

recession [rɪˈseʃən] n Rezession f

recharge [riːˈtʃɑːdʒ] vt (battery)

aufladen; **rechargeable** [riːˈtʃɑː-
dʒəbl] adj wieder aufladbar

recipe [ˈresɪpɪ] n Rezept nt (for
für)

recipient [rɪˈsɪpɪənt] n Empfänger(in) m(f)

reciprocal [rɪˈsɪprəkəl] adj gegenseitig

recite [rɪˈsaɪt] vt vortragen; (details) aufzählen

reckless [ˈrekləs] adj leichtsinnig;
(driving) gefährlich

reckon [ˈrekən] vt (calculate)
schätzen; (think) glauben ▷ vi **to ~
with** rechnen mit

reclaim [rɪˈkleɪm] vt (baggage)
abholen; (expenses, tax) zurückverlangen

recline [rɪˈklaɪn] vi (person) sich
zurücklehnen; **reclining seat** n
Liegesitz m

recognition [rekəgˈnɪʃən] n (acknowledgement) Anerkennung f; **in ~
of** in Anerkennung +gen; **recognize**
[ˈrekəgnaɪz] vt erkennen; (approve
officially) anerkennen

recommend [rekəˈmend] vt
empfehlen; **recommendation** [rekəmənˈdeɪʃən] n Empfehlung f

reconcile [ˈrekənsaɪl] vt (people)
versöhnen; (facts) (miteinander)
vereinbaren

reconsider [riːkənˈsɪdə*] vt noch
einmal überdenken ▷ vi es sich dat
noch einmal überlegen

reconstruct [riːkənˈstrʌkt] vt
wieder aufbauen; (crime) rekonstruieren

record [ˈrekɔːd] n (Mus) (Schall)-
platte f; (best performance) Rekord m;
~s pl (files) Akten pl; **to keep a ~ of**
Buch führen über +akk ▷ adj (time
etc) Rekord- ▷ [rɪˈkɔːd] vt (write
down) aufzeichnen; (on tape etc)
aufnehmen; **~ed message** Ansage f;
recorded delivery n (BRIT) by ~

per Einschreiben

recorder [rɪˈkɔːdə*] n (Mus) Blockflöte f; **(cassette) ~** (Kassetten)rekorder m; **recording** [rɪˈkɔːdɪŋ] n (on tape etc) Aufnahme f; **record player** [ˈrekɔːdpleɪə*] n Plattenspieler m

recover [rɪˈkʌvə*] vt (money, item) zurückbekommen; (appetite, strength) wiedergewinnen ⊳ vi sich erholen

recreation [rekrɪˈeɪʃən] n Erholung f; **recreational** adj Freizeit-; **vehicle** (US) Wohnmobil nt

recruit [rɪˈkruːt] n (Mil) Rekrut(in) m(f); (in firm, organization) neues Mitglied ⊳ vt (Mil) rekrutieren; (members) anwerben; (staff) einstellen; **recruitment agency** n Personalagentur f

rectangle [ˈrektæŋgl] n Rechteck nt; **rectangular** [rekˈtæŋgʊlə*] adj rechteckig

rectify [ˈrektɪfaɪ] vt berichtigen

recuperate [rɪˈkuːpəreɪt] vi sich erholen

recyclable [riːˈsaɪkləbl] adj recycelbar, wieder verwertbar; **recycle** [iːˈsaɪkl] vt recyceln, wieder verwerten; **~d paper** Recyclingpapier nt; **recycling** n Recycling nt, Wiederverwertung f

red [red] adj rot ⊳ n **in the ~** in den roten Zahlen; **Red Cross** n Rotes Kreuz; **red cabbage** n Rotkohl m; **redcurrant** n (rote) Johannisbeere

redeem [rɪˈdiːm] vt (Comm) einlösen

red-handed [redˈhændɪd] adj **to catch sb ~** jdn auf frischer Tat ertappen; **redhead** n Rothaarige(r) mf

redial [riːˈdaɪəl] vt, vi nochmals wählen

redirect [riːdaɪˈrekt] vt (traffic) umleiten; (forward) nachsenden

red light [redˈlaɪt] n (traffic signal) rotes Licht; **to go through the ~** bei Rot über die Ampel fahren; **red meat** n Rind-, Lamm-, Rehfleisch

redo [riːˈduː] irr vt nochmals machen

reduce [rɪˈdjuːs] vt reduzieren (to auf +akk, by um); **reduction** [rɪˈdʌkʃən] n Reduzierung f; (in price) Ermäßigung f

redundant [rɪˈdʌndənt] adj überflüssig; **to be made ~** entlassen werden

red wine [redˈwaɪn] n Rotwein m

reef [riːf] n Riff nt

reel [riːl] n Spule f; (on fishing rod) Rolle f; **reel off** vt herunterrasseln

ref [ref] n (fam: referee) Schiri m

refectory [rɪˈfektərɪ] n (at college) Mensa f

refer [rɪˈfɜː*] vt **to ~ sb to sb/sth** jdn an jdn/etw verweisen; **to ~ sth to sb** (query, problem) etw an jdn weiterleiten ⊳ vi **to ~ to** (mention, allude to) sich beziehen auf +akk, (book) nachschlagen in +dat

referee [refəˈriː] n Schiedsrichter(in) m(f); (in boxing) Ringrichter m, (BRIT: for job) Referenz f

reference [ˈrefrəns] n (allusion) Anspielung f (to auf +akk); (for job) Referenz f; (in book) Verweis m; **~ (number)** (in document) Aktenzeichen nt; **with ~ to** mit Bezug auf +akk; **reference book** n Nachschlagewerk nt

referendum [refəˈrendəm] (pl **referenda**) n Referendum nt

refill [riːˈfɪl] vt [riːˈfɪl] nachfüllen ⊳ n (for ballpoint pen) Ersatzmine f

refine [rɪˈfaɪn] vt (purify) raffinieren; (improve) verfeinern; **refined** adj (genteel) fein

reflect [rɪˈflekt] vt reflektieren; (fig) widerspiegeln ⊳ vi nachdenken

(on über +akk); **reflection** [rɪˈflek-
ʃən] n (image) Spiegelbild nt;
(thought) Überlegung f

reflex [ˈriːfleks] n Reflex m

reform [rɪˈfɔːm] n Reform f ▷ vt
reformieren; (person) bessern

refrain [rɪˈfreɪn] vi **from
doing sth** es unterlassen, etw zu
tun

refresh [rɪˈfreʃ] vt erfrischen; **re-
fresher course** n Auffrischungs-
kurs m; **refreshing** adj erfrischend;
refreshments npl Erfrischungen pl

refrigerator [rɪˈfrɪdʒəreɪtə*] n
Kühlschrank m

refuel [riːˈfjʊəl] vt, vi auftanken

refuge [ˈrefjuːdʒ] n Zuflucht f
(from vor +dat); **to take** ~ sich
flüchten (from vor +dat, in in +akk);
refugee [refjuˈdʒiː] n Flüchtling m

refund [ˈriːfʌnd] n (of money)
Rückerstattung f; **to get a** ~ (on
sth) sein Geld (für etw) zurückbekommen ▷ [rɪˈfʌnd] vt zurücker-
statten

refusal [rɪˈfjuːzəl] n (to do sth)
Weigerung f; **refuse** [ˈrefjuːs] n
Müll m, Abfall m ▷ [rɪˈfjuːz] vt
ablehnen; **to** ~ **sb sth** jdm etw
verweigern; **to** ~ **to do sth** sich
weigern, etw zu tun ▷ vi sich weigern

regain [rɪˈgeɪn] vt wiedergewinnen, wiedererlangen; **to** ~ **consciousness** wieder zu Bewusstsein
kommen

regard [rɪˈgɑːd] n **with** ~ **to** in
Bezug auf +akk; **in this** ~ in dieser
Hinsicht; **-s** (at end of letter) mit
freundlichen Grüßen; **give my ~s to**
... viele Grüße an ... +akk; betriff;
sb/sth as sth jdn/etw als etw
betrachten; **as ~s** ... was ... betrifft;
regarding prep bezüglich +gen;
regardless adj ~ **of** ohne Rücksicht
auf +akk ▷ adv trotzdem; **to carry**

on ~ einfach weitermachen

regime [reɪˈʒiːm] n (Pol) Regime
nt

region [ˈriːdʒən] n (of country)
Region f, Gebiet nt; **in the** ~ **of**
(about) ungefähr; **regional** adj regional

register [ˈredʒɪstə*] n Register nt;
(school) Namensliste f ▷ vt (with an
authority) registrieren lassen; (birth,
death, vehicle) anmelden ▷ vi (at
hotel, for course) sich anmelden; (at
university) sich einschreiben; **registered** adj eingetragen; (letter) ein-
geschrieben; **by** ~ **post** per Einschreiben; **registration** [redʒɪ-
ˈstreɪʃən] n (for course) Anmeldung
f; (at university) Einschreibung f;
(Auto: number) (polizeiliches) Kennzeichen; **registration form** n Anmeldeformular nt; **registration
number** n (Auto) (polizeiliches)
Kennzeichen; **registry office**
[ˈredʒɪstrɪɒfɪs] n Standesamt nt

regret [rɪˈgret] n Bedauern nt ▷
vt bedauern; **regrettable** adj bedauerlich

regular [ˈregjʊlə*] adj regelmäßig; (size) normal ▷ n (client)
Stammkunde m, Stammkundin f; (in
bar) Stammgast m; (petrol) Normalbenzin nt; **regularly** adv regelmäßig

regulate [ˈregjʊleɪt] vt regulieren; (using rules) regeln; **regulation**
[regjʊˈleɪʃən] n (rule) Vorschrift f

rehabilitation [riːəbɪlɪˈteɪʃən] n
Rehabilitation f

rehearsal [rɪˈhɜːsəl] n Probe f;
rehearse vt, vi proben

reign [reɪn] n Herrschaft f ▷ vi
herrschen (over über +akk)

reimburse [riːɪmˈbɜːs] vt (person)
entschädigen; (expenses) zurücker-
statten

reindeer [ˈreɪndɪə*] n Rentier nt

reinforce [riːɪnˈfɔːs] vt verstärken

reinstate [riːɪnˈsteɪt] vt (employee) wieder einstellen; (passage in text) wieder aufnehmen

reject [ˈriːdʒekt] n (Comm) Ausschussartikel m ▷ [rɪˈdʒekt] vt ablehnen; **rejection** [rɪˈdʒekʃən] n Ablehnung f

relapse [rɪˈlæps] n Rückfall m

relate [rɪˈleɪt] vt (story) erzählen; (connect) in Verbindung bringen (to mit) ▷ vi **to ~ to** (refer) sich beziehen auf +akk; **related** adj verwandt (to mit); **relation** [rɪˈleɪʃən] n (relative) Verwandte(r) mf; (connection) Beziehung f; **~s** pl (dealings) Beziehungen pl; **relationship** n (connection) Beziehung f; (between people) Verhältnis nt

relative [ˈrelətɪv] n Verwandte(r) mf ▷ adj relativ; **relatively** adv relativ, verhältnismäßig

relax [rɪˈlæks] vi sich entspannen; **~! reg** dich nicht auf! ▷ vt (grip, conditions) lockern; **relaxation** [riːlækˈseɪʃən] n (rest) Entspannung f; **relaxed** adj entspannt; **relaxing** adj entspannend

release [rɪˈliːs] n (from prison) Entlassung f, **new/recent ~** (film, CD) Neuerscheinung f ▷ vt (animal, hostage) freilassen; (prisoner) entlassen; (handbrake) lösen; (news) veröffentlichen; (film, CD) herausbringen

relent [rɪˈlent] vi nachgeben; **relentless, relentlessly** adj, adv (merciless) erbarmungslos; (neverending) unaufhörlich

relevance [ˈreləvəns] n Relevanz f (to für); **relevant** adj relevant (to für)

reliable, reliably [rɪˈlaɪəbl, -blɪ] adj, adv zuverlässig; **reliant** [rɪˈlaɪənt] adj **~ on** abhängig von

relic [ˈrelɪk] n (from past) Relikt nt

relief [rɪˈliːf] n (from anxiety, pain)

Erleichterung f; (assistance) Hilfe f;
relieve [rɪˈliːv] vt (pain) lindern; (boredom) überwinden; (take over from) ablösen; **I'm ~d** ich bin erleichtert

religion [rɪˈlɪdʒən] n Religion f, **religious** [rɪˈlɪdʒəs] adj religiös

relish [ˈrelɪʃ] n (for food) würzige Soße f ▷ vt (enjoy) genießen; **I don't ~ the thought of getting up early** der Gedanke, früh aufzustehen, behagt mir gar nicht

reluctant [rɪˈlʌktənt] adj widerwillig; **to be ~ to do sth** etw nur ungern tun; **reluctantly** adv widerwillig

rely [rɪˈlaɪ] vi **~ on** sich verlassen auf +akk; (depend on) abhängig sein von

remain [rɪˈmeɪn] vi bleiben; (be left over) übrig bleiben; **remainder** n (a. Math) Rest m; **remaining** adj übrig; **remains** npl Überreste pl

remark [rɪˈmɑːk] n Bemerkung f ▷ vt **to ~ that** bemerken, dass ▷ vi **to ~ on sth** über etw akk eine Bemerkung machen; **remarkable, remarkably** adj, adv bemerkenswert

remarry [riːˈmærɪ] vi wieder heiraten

remedy [ˈremədɪ] n Mittel nt (for gegen) ▷ vt abhelfen +dat

remember [rɪˈmembə*] vt sich erinnern an +akk, **to ~ to do sth** daran denken, etw zu tun; **I ~ seeing her** ich erinnere mich daran, sie gesehen zu haben; **I must ~ that** das muss ich mir merken ▷ vi sich erinnern

Remembrance Day [rɪˈmembrənsˈdeɪ] n (BRIT) ≈ Volkstrauertag m

● REMEMBRANCE DAY

● Remembrance Sunday/Day ist
● der britische Gedenktag für die

remind | 438

Gefallenen der beiden Weltkriege und anderer Kriege. Er fällt auf einen Sonntag vor oder nach dem 11. November (am 11.11.1918 endete der Erste Weltkrieg) und wird mit einer Schweigeminute, Kranzniederlegungen an Kriegerdenkmälern und dem Tragen von Anstecknadeln in Form einer Mohnblume begangen.

remind [rɪˈmaɪnd] *vt* to ~ **sb of/about sb/sth** jdn an jdn/etw erinnern; **to ~ sb to do sth** jdn daran erinnern, etw zu tun; **that ~s me** dabei fällt mir ein ...; **reminder** *n* (to pay) Mahnung *f*

reminisce [remɪˈnɪs] *vi* in Erinnerungen schwelgen (about an +akk); **reminiscent** [remɪˈnɪsənt] *adj* **to be ~ of** erinnern an +akk

remittance *n* Überweisung *f* (to an +akk)

remnant [ˈremnənt] *n* Rest *m*

remote [rɪˈməʊt] *adj* (place) abgelegen; (slight) gering *b* *n* (TV) Fernbedienung *f*; **remote control** *n* Fernsteuerung *f*; (device) Fernbedienung *f*

removal [rɪˈmuːvəl] *n* Entfernung *f*; (BRIT: move from house) Umzug *m*; **removal firm** *n* (BRIT) Spedition *f*; **remove** [rɪˈmuːv] *vt* entfernen; (lid) abnehmen; (clothes) ausziehen; (doubt, suspicion) zerstreuen

rename [riːˈneɪm] *vt* umbenennen

renew [rɪˈnjuː] *vt* erneuern; (licence, passport, library book) verlängern lassen

renounce [rɪˈnaʊns] *vt* verzichten auf +akk; (faith, opinion) abschwören +dat

renovate [ˈrenəveɪt] *vt* renovieren

renowned [rɪˈnaʊnd] *adj* berühmt (for für)

rent [rent] *n* Miete *f*; **for ~** (US) zu vermieten *b* *vt* (as hirer, tenant) mieten; (as owner) vermieten; **~ed car** Mietwagen *m*; **rent out** *vt* vermieten; **rental** *n* Miete *f*; (for car, TV etc) Leihgebühr *f* *b* *adj* Miet-

reorganize [riːˈɔːgənaɪz] *vt* umorganisieren

rep [rep] *n* (Comm) Vertreter(in) *m(f)*

repair [rɪˈpeə*] *n* Reparatur *f* *b* *vt* reparieren; (damage) wieder gutmachen; **repair kit** *n* Flickzeug *nt*

repay [riːˈpeɪ] *irr vt* (money) zurückzahlen; **to ~ sb for sth** (fig) sich bei jdm für etw revanchieren

repeat [rɪˈpiːt] *n* (Radio, TV) Wiederholung *f* *b* *vt* wiederholen; **repetition** [repəˈtɪʃən] *n* Wiederholung *f*; **repetitive** [rɪˈpetɪtɪv] *adj* sich wiederholend

rephrase [riːˈfreɪz] *vt* anders formulieren

replace [rɪˈpleɪs] *vt* ersetzen (with durch); (put back) zurückstellen, zurücklegen; **replacement** *n* (thing, person) Ersatz *m*; (temporarily in job) Vertretung *f*; **replacement part** *n* Ersatzteil *nt*

replay [ˈriːpleɪ] *n* (action) Wiederholung *f* *b* [riːˈpleɪ] *vt* (game) wiederholen

replica [ˈreplɪkə] *n* Kopie *f*

reply [rɪˈplaɪ] *n* Antwort *f* *b* *vi* antworten; **to ~ to sb/sth** jdm/auf etw akk antworten *b* *vt* **to ~ that** antworten, dass

report [rɪˈpɔːt] *n* Bericht *m*; (school) Zeugnis *nt* *b* *vt* (tell) berichten; (give information against) melden; (to police) anzeigen *b* *vi* (present oneself) sich melden; **to ~ sick** sich krankmelden; **report card** *n* (US: school) Zeugnis *nt*; **reporter**

n Reporter(in) m(f)

represent [repri'zent] vt darstellen; (speak for) vertreten; **representation** [reprizen'teɪʃən] n (picture etc) Darstellung f; **representative** [repri'zentətiv] n Vertreter(in) m(f); (US Pol) Abgeordnete(r) mf ▷ adj repräsentativ (of für)

reprimand ['reprimɑːnd] n Tadel m ▷ vt tadeln

reprint ['riːprɪnt] n Nachdruck m

reproduce [riːprə'djuːs] vt (copy) reproduzieren ▷ vi (Bio) sich fortpflanzen; **reproduction** [riːprə'dʌkʃən] n (copy) Reproduktion f; (Bio) Fortpflanzung f

reptile ['reptaɪl] n Reptil nt

republic [rɪ'pʌblɪk] n Republik f; **republican** adj republikanisch ▷ n Republikaner(in) m(f)

repulsive [rɪ'pʌlsɪv] adj abstoßend

reputable ['repjʊtəbl] adj seriös

reputation [repjʊ'teɪʃən] n Ruf m; **he has a ~ for being difficult** er hat den Ruf, schwierig zu sein

request [rɪ'kwest] n Bitte f (for um); **on ~** auf Wunsch ▷ vt bitten um; **to ~ sb to do sth** jdn bitten, etw zu tun

require [rɪ'kwaɪə*] vt (need) brauchen; (desire) verlangen; **what qualifications are ~d?** welche Qualifikationen sind erforderlich?; **required** adj erforderlich; **requirement** n (condition) Anforderung f; (need) Bedingung f

rerun ['riːrʌn] n Wiederholung f

rescue ['reskjuː] n Rettung f; **to come to sb's ~** jdm zu Hilfe kommen ▷ vt retten; **rescue party** n Rettungsmannschaft f

research [rɪ'sɜːtʃ] n Forschung f ▷ vi forschen (into über +akk) ▷ vt erforschen; **researcher** n Forscher(in) m(f)

resemblance [rɪ'zembləns] n Ähnlichkeit f (to mit); **resemble** [rɪ'zembl] vt ähneln +dat

resent [rɪ'zent] vt übel nehmen

reservation [rezə'veɪʃən] n (booking) Reservierung f; (doubt) Vorbehalt m; **I have a ~** (in hotel, restaurant) ich habe reserviert; **reserve** [rɪ'zɜːv] n (store) Vorrat m (of an +dat); (manner) Zurückhaltung f; (Sport) Reservespieler(in) m(f); (game ~) Naturschutzgebiet nt ▷ vt (book in advance) reservieren; **reserved** adj reserviert

reservoir ['rezəvwɑː*] n (for water) Reservoir nt

reside [rɪ'zaɪd] vi wohnen; **residence** ['rezɪdəns] n Wohnsitz m; (living) Aufenthalt m; **~ permit** Aufenthaltsgenehmigung f; **~ hall** Studentenwohnheim nt; **resident** ['rezɪdənt] n (in house) Bewohner(in) m(f); (in town, area) Einwohner(in) m(f)

resign [rɪ'zaɪn] vt (post) zurücktreten von; (job) kündigen ▷ vi (from post) zurücktreten; (from job) kündigen; **resignation** [rezɪg'neɪʃən] n (from post) Rücktritt m; (from job) Kündigung f; **resigned** adj resigniert; **he is ~ to it** er hat sich damit abgefunden

resist [rɪ'zɪst] vt widerstehen +dat; **resistance** n Widerstand m (to gegen)

resit [riː'sɪt] (BRIT) irr vt wiederholen ▷ ['riːsɪt] n Wiederholungsprüfung f

resolution [rezə'luːʃən] n (intention) Vorsatz m; (decision) Beschluss m

resolve [rɪ'zɒlv] vt (problem) lösen

resort [rɪ'zɔːt] n (holiday ~) Urlaubsort m; (health ~) Kurort m; **as a last ~** als letzter Ausweg ▷ vi **to ~ to** greifen zu; (violence) anwenden

resources [rɪ'sɔːsɪz] npl (money) (Geld)mittel pl; (mineral ~) Bodenschätze pl

respect [rɪ'spekt] n Respekt m (for vor +dat); (consideration) Rücksicht f (for auf +akk); **with ~ to** in Bezug auf +akk; **in this ~** in dieser Hinsicht; **in all due ~** bei allem Respekt ▷ vt respektieren; **respectable** [rɪ'spektəbl] adj (person, family) angesehen; (district) anständig; (achievement, result) beachtlich; **respected** [rɪ'spektɪd] adj angesehen

respective [rɪ'spektɪv] adj jeweilig; **respectively** adv **5% and 10% ~** 5% beziehungsweise 10%

respiratory [rɪ'spɪrətərɪ] adj **~ problems** (ø **trouble**) Atembeschwerden pl

respond [rɪ'spɒnd] vi antworten (to auf +akk); (react) reagieren (to auf +akk); (to treatment) ansprechen (to auf +akk); **response** [rɪ'spɒns] n Antwort f; (reaction) Reaktion f; **in ~ to** als Antwort auf +akk

responsibility [rɪspɒnsə'bɪlɪtɪ] n Verantwortung f; **that's her ~** dafür ist sie verantwortlich; **responsible** [rɪ'spɒnsəbl] adj verantwortlich (for für); (trustworthy) verantwortungsbewusst; (job) verantwortungsvoll

rest [rest] n (relaxation) Ruhe f; (break) Pause f; (remainder) Rest m; **to have** (ø **take**) **a ~** sich ausruhen; (break) Pause machen; **the ~ of the wine / the people** der Rest des Weins / der Leute ▷ vi (relax) sich ausruhen; (lean) lehnen (on, against an +dat, gegen)

restaurant ['restərɒnt] n Restaurant nt; **restaurant car** n (BRIT) Speisewagen m

restful ['restfʊl] adj (holiday etc) erholsam, ruhig; **restless** ['restləs]
adj unruhig

restore [rɪ'stɔː] vt (painting, building) restaurieren; (order) wiederherstellen; (give back) zurückgeben

restrain [rɪ'streɪn] vt (person, feelings) zurückhalten; **to ~ oneself** sich beherrschen

restrict [rɪ'strɪkt] vt beschränken (to auf +akk); **restricted** adj beschränkt; **restriction** [rɪ'strɪkʃən] n Einschränkung f (on +gen)

rest room ['restruːm] n (US) Toilette f

result [rɪ'zʌlt] n Ergebnis nt; (consequence) Folge f; **as a ~ of** infolge +gen ▷ vi **to ~ in** führen zu; **to ~ from** sich ergeben aus

resume [rɪ'zjuːm] vt (work, negotiations) wieder aufnehmen; (journey) fortsetzen

résumé ['rezjʊmeɪ] n Zusammenfassung f; (US: curriculum vitae) Lebenslauf m

resuscitate [rɪ'sʌsɪteɪt] vt wieder beleben

retail ['riːteɪl] adv im Einzelhandel; **retailer** n Einzelhändler(in) m(f)

retain [rɪ'teɪn] vt behalten; (heat) halten

rethink [riː'θɪŋk] irr vt noch einmal überdenken

retire [rɪ'taɪə*] vi (from work) in den Ruhestand treten; (withdraw) sich zurückziehen; **retired** adj (person) pensioniert; **retirement** n (time of life) Ruhestand m; **retirement age** n Rentenalter nt

retrace [rɪ'treɪs] vt zurückverfolgen

retrain [riː'treɪn] vi sich umschulen lassen

retreat [rɪ'triːt] n (Mil) Rückzug m (from aus); (refuge) Zufluchtsort m ▷ vi (Mil) sich zurückziehen; (step back) zurückweichen

retrieve [rɪ'triːv] vt (recover) wiederbekommen; (rescue) retten; (data) abrufen

retrospect ['retrəspekt] n **in ~** rückblickend; **retrospective** [retrəʊ'spektɪv] adj rückblickend; (pay rise) rückwirkend

return [rɪ'tɜːn] n (going back) Rückkehr f; (going back) Rückkehr f; (profit) Gewinn m; (BRIT: = ticket) Rückfahrkarte f; (plane ticket) Rückflugticket nt; (Tennis), Return m; **in ~** als Gegenleistung (for für); **many happy ~s (of the day)** herzlichen Glückwunsch zum Geburtstag! ▷ vi (person) zurückkehren; (doubts, symptoms) wieder auftreten; **to ~ to school/work** wieder in die Schule/die Arbeit gehen ▷ vt (give back) zurückgeben; **I ~ed his call** ich habe ihn zurückgerufen; **returnable** adj (bottle) Pfand-; **return flight** n (BRIT) Rückflug m; (both ways) Hin- und Rückflug m; **return key** n (in form) Eingabetaste f; **return ticket** n (BRIT) Rückfahrkarte f; (for plane) Rückflugticket nt

reunification [riːjuːnɪfɪ'keɪʃən] n Wiedervereinigung f

reunion [riː'juːnjən] n (party) Treffen nt; **reunite** [riːjuː'naɪt] vt wieder vereinigen

reusable [riː'juːzəbl] adj wieder verwendbar

reveal [rɪ'viːl] vt (make known) enthüllen; (secret) verraten; (show) zeigen; **revealing** adj aufschlussreich; (dress) freizügig

revenge [rɪ'vendʒ] n Rache f; (in game) Revanche f; **to take ~ (for sth)** sich an jdm (für etw) rächen

revenue ['revənjuː] n Einnahmen pl

reverse [rɪ'vɜːs] n (back) Rückseite

f; (opposite) Gegenteil nt; (Auto) ~ **(gear)** Rückwärtsgang m ▷ adj **in ~ order** in umgekehrter Reihenfolge ▷ vt (order) umkehren; (decision) umstoßen; (car) zurücksetzen; **to ~ the charges** (BRIT) ein R-Gespräch führen ▷ vi (Auto) rückwärts fahren

review [rɪ'vjuː] n (of book, film etc) Rezension f; **to be under ~** überprüft werden ▷ vt (book, film etc) rezensieren; (re-examine) überprüfen

revise [rɪ'vaɪz] vt revidieren; (text) überarbeiten; (BRIT: in school) wiederholen ▷ vi (BRIT: in school) den Stoff wiederholen; **revision** [rɪ'vɪʒən] n (of text) Überarbeitung f; (BRIT: in school) Wiederholung f

revitalize [riː'vaɪtəlaɪz] vt neu beleben

revive [rɪ'vaɪv] vt (person) wieder beleben; (tradition, interest) wieder aufleben lassen ▷ vi (regain consciousness) wieder zu sich kommen

revolt [rɪ'vəʊlt] n Aufstand m; **revolting** adj widerlich

revolution [revə'luːʃən] n (Pol, fig) Revolution f; (turn) Umdrehung f; **revolutionary** adj revolutionär ▷ n Revolutionär(in) m(f)

revolve [rɪ'vɒlv] vi sich drehen (around um); **revolver** n Revolver m; **revolving door** n Drehtür f

reward [rɪ'wɔːd] n Belohnung f ▷ vt belohnen; **rewarding** adj lohnend

rewind [riː'waɪnd] irr vt (tape) zurückspulen

rewrite [riː'raɪt] irr vt (write again; recast) umschreiben

rheumatism ['ruːmətɪzəm] n Rheuma nt

Rhine [raɪn] n Rhein m

rhinoceros [raɪ'nɒsərəs] n Nashorn nt

Rhodes [rəʊdz] n Rhodos nt

rhubarb ['ruːbɑːb] n Rhabarber m

rhyme [raɪm] n Reim m ▷ vi sich reimen (*with* auf +*akk*)

rhythm [ˈrɪðəm] n Rhythmus m

rib [rɪb] n Rippe f

ribbon [ˈrɪbən] n Band nt

rice [raɪs] n Reis m; **rice pudding** n Milchreis m

rich [rɪtʃ] *adj* reich; (*food*) schwer ▷ *npl* **the ~** die Reichen pl

rickety [ˈrɪkɪtɪ] *adj* wackelig

rid [rɪd] (**rid, rid**) vt **to get ~ of sb/sth** jdn/etw loswerden

ridden [ˈrɪdn] pp of **ride**

riddle [ˈrɪdl] n Rätsel nt

ride [raɪd] (**rode, ridden**) vt (*horse*) reiten; (*bicycle*) fahren ▷ vi (*on horse*) reiten; (*on bike*) fahren ▷ n (*in vehicle, on bike*) Fahrt f; (*on horse*) (Aus)ritt m; **to go for a ~** (*in car, on bike*) spazieren fahren; (*on horse*) reiten gehen; **to take sb for a ~** (*fam*) jdn verarschen; **rider** n (*on horse*) Reiter(in) m(f); (*on bike*) Fahrer(in) m(f)

ridiculous [rɪˈdɪkjʊləs] *adj* lächerlich; **don't be ~** red keinen Unsinn!

riding [ˈraɪdɪŋ] n Reiten nt; **to go ~** reiten gehen ▷ *adj* Reit-

rifle [ˈraɪfl] n Gewehr nt

rig [rɪɡ] n **oil ~** Bohrinsel f ▷ vt (*election etc*) manipulieren

right [raɪt] *adj* (*correct, just*) richtig; (*opposite of left*) rechte(r, s); (*clothes, job etc*) passend; **to be ~** (*person*) Recht haben; (*clock*) richtig gehen; **that's ~** das stimmt! ▷ n Recht nt (*to* auf +*akk*); (*side*) rechte Seite; **the Right** (*Pol*) die Rechte; **to take a ~** (*Auto*) rechts abbiegen; **on the ~** rechts (*of* von); **to the ~** nach rechts; (*of*) rechts (*of* von) ▷ *adv* (*towards the ~*) nach rechts; (*directly, exactly*) genau; **to turn ~** (*Auto*) rechts abbiegen; **~ away** sofort; **~ now** im Moment;

(*immediately*) sofort; **right angle** n rechter Winkel; **right-hand drive** n Rechtssteuerung f ▷ *adj* rechtsgesteuert; **right-handed** *adj* **he is ~** er ist Rechtshänder; **right-hand side** n rechte Seite; **on the ~** auf der rechten Seite; **rightly** *adv* zu Recht; **right of way** n **to have ~** (*Auto*) Vorfahrt haben; **right wing** n (*Pol, Sport*) rechter Flügel; **right-wing** *adj* Rechts-; **~ extremist** Rechtsradikale(r) mf

rigid [ˈrɪdʒɪd] *adj* (*stiff*) starr; (*strict*) streng

rigorous, rigorously [ˈrɪɡərəs, -lɪ] *adj, adv* streng

rim [rɪm] n (*of cup etc*) Rand m; (*of wheel*) Felge f

rind [raɪnd] n (*of cheese*) Rinde f; (*of bacon*) Schwarte f; (*of fruit*) Schale f

ring [rɪŋ] (**rang, rung**) vt, vi (*bell*) läuten; (*Tel*) anrufen ▷ n (*on finger, in boxing*) Ring m; (*circle*) Kreis m; (*at circus*) Manege f; **to give sb a ~** (*Tel*) jdn anrufen; **ring back** vt, vi zurückrufen; **ring up** vt, vi anrufen

ring binder n Ringbuch nt

ringing tone n (*Tel*) Rufzeichen nt

ringleader n Anführer(in) m(f)

ring road n (*BRIT*) Umgehungsstraße f

ringtone n Klingelton m

rink [rɪŋk] n (*ice ~*) Eisbahn f; (*for roller-skating*) Rollschuhbahn f

rinse [rɪns] vt spülen

riot [ˈraɪət] n Aufruhr m

rip [rɪp] n Riss m ▷ vt zerreißen; **to ~ sth open** etw aufreißen ▷ vi reißen; **rip off** vt (*fam: person*) übers Ohr hauen; **rip up** vt zerreißen

ripe [raɪp] *adj* (*fruit*) reif; **ripen** vi reifen

rip-off [ˈrɪpɒf] n **that's a ~** (*fam: too expensive*) das ist Wucher

rise [raɪz] (**rose, risen**) vi (*from sitting, lying*) aufstehen; (*sun*) aufgehen; (prices, temperature) steigen; (ground) ansteigen; (in revolt) sich erheben ▷ n (increase) Anstieg m (in +gen); (pay ~) Gehaltserhöhung f; (to power, fame) Aufstieg m (to zu); (slope) Steigung f, risen ['rɪzn] pp of **rise**

risk [rɪsk] n Risiko nt ▷ vt riskieren; **to ~ doing sth** es riskieren, etw zu tun; **risky** adj riskant

risotto [rɪ'zɔtəu] (pl **-s**) n Risotto nt

ritual ['rɪtjuəl] n Ritual nt ▷ adj rituell

rival ['raɪvəl] n Rivale m, Rivalin f (for um); (Comm) Konkurrent(in) m(f), **rivalry** n Rivalität f; (Comm, Sport) Konkurrenz f

river ['rɪvə*] n Fluss m; **the River Thames** (BRIT), **the Thames River** (US) die Themse; **riverside** n Flussufer nt ▷ adj am Flussufer

road [rəud] n Straße f; (fig) Weg m; **on the ~** (travelling) unterwegs; mit dem Auto / Bus etc fahren; **roadblock** n Straßensperre f; **roadmap** n Straßenkarte f; **road rage** n aggressives Verhalten im Straßenverkehr; **roadside** n at ▷ (o by) **the ~** am Straßenrand; **roadsign** n Verkehrsschild nt; **road tax** n Kraftfahrzeugsteuer f; **roadworks** npl Straßenarbeiten pl; **roadworthy** adj fahrtüchtig

roar [rɔ:*] n (of person, lion) Brüllen nt, (von Verkehr) Donnern nt ▷ vi (person, lion) brüllen (with vor +dat)

roast [rəust] n Braten m ▷ adj ~ **beef** n Rinderbraten m; ~ **chicken** n Brathähnchen nt; ~ **pork** Schweinebraten m; ~ **potatoes** pl im Backofen gebratene Kartoffeln ▷ vt (meat) braten

rob [rɔb] vt bestehlen; (bank, shop) ausrauben; **robber** n Räuber(in) m(f); **robbery** n Raub m

robe [rəub] n (US: dressing gown) Morgenrock m; (of judge, priest etc) Robe f, Talar m

robin ['rɔbɪn] n Rotkehlchen nt

robot ['rəubɔt] n Roboter m

robust [rəu'bʌst] adj robust; (defence) stark

rock [rɔk] n (substance) Stein m, (boulder) Felsbrocken m; (Mus) Rock m; **stick of ~** (BRIT) Zuckerstange f; **on the ~s** (drink) mit Eis; (marriage) gescheitert ▷ vt, vi (swing) schaukeln; (dance) rocken; **rock climbing** n Klettern nt; **to go ~** klettern gehen

rocket ['rɔkɪt] n Rakete f; (in salad) Rucola f

rocking chair ['rɔkɪŋtʃeə*] n Schaukelstuhl m

rocky ['rɔkɪ] adj (landscape) felsig; (path) steinig

rod [rɔd] n (bar) Stange f; (fishing ~) Rute f

rode [rəud] pt of ride

rogue [rəug] n Schurke m, Gauner m

role [rəul] n Rolle f; **role model** n Vorbild nt

roll [rəul] n (of film, paper etc) Rolle f; (bread) Brötchen nt ▷ vt (move by ~ing) rollen; (cigarette) drehen ▷ vi (move by ~ing) rollen; (ship) schlingern; (camera) laufen; **roll out** vt (pastry) ausrollen; **roll over** vi (person) sich umdrehen; **roll up** vi (fam: arrive) antanzen ▷ vt (carpet) aufrollen; **to roll one's sleeves** up die Ärmel hochkrempeln

roller n (hair ~) (Locken)wickler m; **Rollerblades®** npl Inlineskates pl; **rollerblading** n Inlineskaten nt; **roller coaster** n Achterbahn f; **roller skates** npl Rollschuhe pl; **roller-skating** n Rollschuhlaufen nt; **rolling pin** n Nudelholz nt; **roll-on** (deodorant) n Deoroller m

ROM [rɔm] acr = read only

memory ROM *m*

Roman ['rəʊmən] *adj* römisch ▷
n Römer(in) *m(f)*; **Roman Catholic**
adj römisch-katholisch ▷ *n* Ka-
tholik(in) *m(f)*

romance [rəʊ'mæns] *n* Romantik *f*; (*love affair*) Romanze *f*

Romania [rəʊ'meɪnɪə] *n* Rumänien *nt*; **Romanian** *adj* rumänisch
▷ *n* Rumäne *m*, Rumänin *f*; (*language*) Rumänisch *nt*

romantic [rəʊ'mæntɪk] *adj* romantisch

roof [ruːf] *n* Dach *nt*; **roof rack** *n*
Dachgepäckträger *m*

rook [rʊk] *n* (*in chess*) Turm *m*

room [ruːm] *n* Zimmer *nt*, Raum
m; (*large, for gatherings etc*) Saal *m*;
(*space*) Platz *m*; (*fig*) Spielraum *m*; **to
make ~ for** Platz machen für;
roommate *n* Zimmergenosse *m*,
Zimmergenossin *f*; (*US: sharing
apartment*) Mitbewohner(in) *m(f)*;
room service *n* Zimmerservice *m*;
roomy *adj* geräumig; (*garment*)
weit

root [ruːt] *n* Wurzel *f*; **root out**
vt (*eradicate*) ausrotten; **root vegetable** *n* Wurzelgemüse *nt*

rope [rəʊp] *n* Seil *nt*; **to know the
~s** (*fam*) sich auskennen

rose [rəʊz] *pt of* **rise** ▷ *n* Rose *f*

rosé ['rəʊzeɪ] *n* Rosé(wein) *m*

rot [rɒt] *vi* verfaulen

rota ['rəʊtə] *n* (*BRIT*) Dienstplan *m*

rotate [rəʊ'teɪt] *vt* (*turn*) rotieren
lassen ▷ *vi* rotieren; **rotation**
[rəʊ'teɪʃən] *n* (*turning*) Rotation *f*;
in ~ abwechselnd

rotten ['rɒtn] *adj* (*decayed*) faul;
(*mean*) gemein; (*unpleasant*) scheußlich; (*ill*) elend

rough [rʌf] *adj* (*not smooth*) rau;
(*path*) uneben; (*coarse, violent*) grob;
(*crossing*) stürmisch; (*without com-
forts*) hart; (*unfinished, makeshift*)

grob; (*approximate*) ungefähr; **~**
draft Rohentwurf *m*; **I have a ~**
idea ich habe eine ungefähre Vorstellung ▷ *adv* **to sleep ~** im Freien
schlafen ▷ *vt* **to ~ it** primitiv leben
▷ *n* **to write sth in ~** etw ins Un-
reine schreiben; **roughly** *adv* grob;
(*approximately*) ungefähr

round [raʊnd] *adj* rund ▷ *adv* **all**
~ (*on all sides*) rundherum; **the long**
way ~ der längere Weg; **I'll be ~ at 8**
ich werde um acht Uhr da sein; **the**
other way ~ umgekehrt ▷ *prep*
(*surrounding*) um (... herum); **~**
(*about*) (*approximately*) ungefähr; **~**
the corner um die Ecke; **to go ~ the**
world um die Welt reisen; **she lives**
~ here sie wohnt hier in der Gegend
▷ *n* Runde *f*; (*of bread, toast*) Scheibe
f; **it's my ~** (*of drinks*) die Runde geht
auf mich ▷ *vt* (*corner*) biegen um;
round off *vt* abrunden; **round up**
vt (*number, price*) aufrunden

roundabout *n* (*BRIT Auto*) Kreisverkehr *m*; (*BRIT: merry-go-round*)
Karussell *nt* ▷ *adj* umständlich;
round-the-clock *adj* rund um die
Uhr; **round trip** *n* Rundreise *f*;
round-trip ticket *n* (*US*) Rückfahrkarte *f*; (*for plane*) Rückflugticket
nt

rouse [raʊz] *vt* (*from sleep*) wecken

route [ruːt] *n* Route *f*; (*bus, plane
etc service*) Linie *f*; (*fig*) Weg *m*

routine [ruː'tiːn] *n* Routine *f* ▷
adj Routine-

row [rəʊ] *n* (*line*) Reihe *f*; **three**
times in a ~ dreimal hintereinander
▷ *vt, vi* (*boat*) rudern ▷ [raʊ] *n*
(*noise*) Krach *m*; (*dispute*) Streit *m*

rowboat ['rəʊbəʊt] *n* (*US*) Ruderboot *nt*

row house ['rəʊhaʊs] *n* (*US*)
Reihenhaus *nt*

rowing ['rəʊɪŋ] *n* Rudern *nt*;
rowing boat *n* (*BRIT*) Ruderboot

nt: **rowing machine** n Rudergerät nt

royal ['rɔɪəl] adj königlich; **royalty** n (family) Mitglieder pl der königlichen Familie; **royalties** pl (from book, music) Tantiemen pl

RSPCA abbr = **Royal Society for the Prevention of Cruelty to Animals** britischer Tierschutzverein

RSPCC abbr = **Royal Society for the Prevention of Cruelty to Children** britischer Kinderschutzverein

RSVP abbr = **répondez s'il vous plaît** u. A. w. g.

rub [rʌb] vt reiben; **rub in** vt einmassieren; **rub out** vt (with eraser) ausradieren

rubber ['rʌbə*] n Gummi m; (BRIT: eraser) Radiergummi m; (US fam: contraceptive) Gummi m; **rubber band** n Gummiband nt; **rubber stamp** n Stempel m

rubbish ['rʌbɪʃ] n Abfall m, (nonsense) Quatsch m; (poor-quality thing) Mist m; **don't talk ~** red keinen Unsinn!; **rubbish bin** n Mülleimer m; **rubbish dump** n Mülladeplatz m

rubble ['rʌbl] n Schutt m

ruby ['ru:bi] n (stone) Rubin m

rucksack ['rʌksæk] n Rucksack m

rude [ru:d] adj (impolite) unhöflich; (indecent) unanständig

rug [rʌg] n Teppich m; (next to bed) Bettvorleger m; (for knees) Wolldecke f

rugby ['rʌgbɪ] n Rugby nt

rugged ['rʌgɪd] adj (coastline) zerklüftet; (features) markant

ruin ['ru:ɪn] n Ruine f; (financial, social) Ruin m ▷ vt ruinieren

rule [ru:l] n Regel f; (governing) Herrschaft f; **as a ~** in der Regel ▷ vt, vi (govern) regieren; (decide) entscheiden; **ruler** n Lineal nt; (person) Herrscher(in) m(f)

rum [rʌm] n Rum m

rumble ['rʌmbl] vi (stomach) knurren; (train, truck) rumpeln

rummage ['rʌmɪdʒ] vi ~ **(around)** herumstöbern

rumor (US), **rumour** ['ru:mə*] n Gerücht nt

run [rʌn] (ran, run) vt (race, distance) laufen; (machine, engine, computer program, water) laufen lassen; (manage) leiten, führen; (car) unterhalten; **I ran her home** ich habe sie nach Hause gefahren ▷ vi (move quickly) rennen; (bus, train) fahren; (path etc) verlaufen; (machine, engine, computer program) laufen; (flow) fließen; (colours, make-up) verlaufen; **to ~ for President** für die Präsidentschaft kandidieren; **to be ~ning low** knapp werden; **my nose is ~ning** mir läuft die Nase; **it ~s in the family** es liegt in der Familie ▷ n (on foot) Lauf m; (in car) Spazierfahrt f; (series) Reihe f; (sudden demand) Ansturm m (on auf +akk); (in tights) Laufmasche f; (in cricket, baseball) Lauf m; **to go for a ~** laufen gehen; (in car) eine Spazierfahrt machen; **in the long ~** auf die Dauer; **on the ~** auf der Flucht (from vor +dat); **run about** vi herumlaufen; **run away** vi weglaufen; **run down** vt (with car) umfahren; (criticize) heruntermachen; **to be ~** (tired) abgespannt sein; **run into** vt (meet) zufällig treffen; (problem) stoßen auf (+akk); **run off** vi weglaufen; **run out** vi (person) hinausrennen; (liquid) auslaufen; (lease, time) ablaufen; (money, supplies) ausgehen; **he ran ~ of money** ihm ging das Geld aus; **run over** vt (with car) überfahren; **run up** vt (debt, bill) machen

rung [rʌŋ] pp of **ring**

runner ['rʌnə*] n (athlete) Läu-

fer(in) *m(f)*; **to do a ~** *(fam)* weg-
rennen; **runner beans** *npl* *(BRIT)*
Stangenbohnen *pl*

running ['rʌnɪŋ] *n* *(Sport)* Laufen
nt; *(management)* Leitung *f*, Führung
f ▷ *adj* *(water)* fließend; **~ costs**
Betriebskosten *pl*; *(for car)* Unter-
haltskosten *pl*; **3 days ~** 3 Tage
hintereinander

runny ['rʌnɪ] *adj* *(food)* flüssig;
(nose) laufend

runway ['rʌnweɪ] *n* Start- und
Landebahn *f*

rural ['ruərəl] *adj* ländlich

rush [rʌʃ] *n* Eile *f*; *(for tickets etc)*
Ansturm *m* *(for auf +akk)*; **to be in a
~** es eilig haben; **there's no ~** es eilt
nicht ▷ *vt* *(do too quickly)* hastig
machen; *(meal)* hastig essen; **to ~ sb
to hospital** jdn auf dem schnellsten
Weg ins Krankenhaus bringen;
don't ~ me dräng mich nicht ▷ *vi*
(hurry) eilen; **don't ~** lass dir Zeit;
rush hour *n* Hauptverkehrszeit *f*

rusk [rʌsk] *n* Zwieback *m*

Russia ['rʌʃə] *n* Russland *nt*;
Russian *adj* russisch ▷ *n* Russe *m*,
Russin *f*; *(language)* Russisch *nt*

rust [rʌst] *n* Rost *m* ▷ *vi* rosten;
rustproof ['rʌstpru:f] *adj* rostfrei;
rusty ['rʌstɪ] *adj* rostig

ruthless ['ru:θləs] *adj* rücksichtslos; *(treatment, criticism)* scho-
nungslos

rye [raɪ] *n* Roggen *m*; **rye bread**
n Roggenbrot *nt*

S *abbr* = **south** S

sabotage ['sæbətɑ:ʒ] *vt* sabotieren

sachet ['sæʃeɪ] *n* Päckchen *nt*

sack [sæk] *n* *(bag)* Sack *m*; **to get
the ~** *(fam)* rausgeschmissen werden ▷ *vt* *(fam)* rausschmeißen

sacred ['seɪkrɪd] *adj* heilig

sacrifice ['sækrɪfaɪs] *n* Opfer *nt* ▷
vt opfern

sad [sæd] *adj* traurig

saddle ['sædl] *n* Sattel *m*

sadistic [sə'dɪstɪk] *adj* sadistisch

sadly ['sædlɪ] *adv* *(unfortunately)*
leider

safari [sə'fɑ:rɪ] *n* Safari

safe [seɪf] *adj* *(free from danger)*
sicher; *(out of danger)* in Sicherheit;
(careful) vorsichtig; **have a ~ journey** gute Fahrt! ▷ *n* Safe *m*; **safe-
guard** *n* Schutz *m* ▷ *vt* schützen
(against vor +dat); **safely** *adv* sicher; *(arrive)* wohlbehalten; *(drive)*
vorsichtig; **safety** *n* Sicherheit *f*;
safety belt *n* Sicherheitsgurt *m*;

safety pin n Sicherheitsnadel f

Sagittarius [sædʒɪˈtɛərɪəs] n (Astr) Schütze m

Sahara [səˈhɑːrə] n **the ~** (Desert) die (Wüste) Sahara

said [sɛd] pt, pp of **say**

sail [seɪl] n Segel nt; **to set ~** losfahren (for nach) ▷ vi (in yacht) segeln; (on ship) mit dem Schiff fahren; (ship) auslaufen (for nach) ▷ vt (yacht) segeln mit; (ship) steuern; **sailboat** n (US) Segelboot nt; **sailing** n **to go ~** segeln gehen; **sailing boat** n (BRIT) Segelboot nt; **sailor** n Seemann m; (in navy) Matrose m

saint [seɪnt] n Heilige(r) mf

sake [seɪk] n **for the ~** of um +gen ... willen; **for your ~** deinetwegen, dir zuliebe

salad [ˈsæləd] n Salat m; **salad cream** n (BRIT) majonäseartige Salatsoße; **salad dressing** n Salatsoße f

salary [ˈsælərɪ] n Gehalt nt

sale [seɪl] n Verkauf m; (at reduced prices) Ausverkauf m; **the ~s** pl (in summer, winter) der Schlussverkauf; **for ~** zu verkaufen; **sales clerk** n (US) Verkäufer(in) mf; **salesman** (pl **-men**) n Verkäufer m; (rep) Vertreter m; **sales rep** n Vertreter(in) mf; **sales tax** n (US) Verkaufssteuer f; **saleswoman** (pl **-women**) n Verkäuferin f; (rep) Vertreterin f

saliva [səˈlaɪvə] n Speichel m

salmon [ˈsæmən] n Lachs m

saloon [səˈluːn] n (ship's lounge) Salon m; (US: bar) Kneipe f

salt [sɔːlt] n Salz nt ▷ vt salzen; (roads) mit Salz streuen; **salt cellar**, **salt shaker** (US) n Salzstreuer m; **salty** adj salzig

salvage [ˈsælvɪdʒ] vt bergen (from aus); (fig) retten

same [seɪm] adj **the ~** (similar) der/die/das gleiche, die gleichen

pl; (identical) der/die/dasselbe, dieselben pl; **they live in the ~ house** sie wohnen im selben Haus ▷ pron **the ~** (similar) der/die/das Gleiche, die Gleichen pl; (identical) der/die/dasselbe, dieselben pl; **I'll have the ~ again** ich möchte noch mal das Gleiche; **all the ~** trotzdem; **the ~ to you** gleichfalls; **it's all the ~ to me** es ist mir egal ▷ adv **the ~** gleich; **they look the ~** sie sehen gleich aus

sample [ˈsɑːmpl] n Probe f; (of fabric) Muster nt ▷ vt probieren

sanctions [ˈsæŋkʃənz] npl (Pol) Sanktionen pl

sanctuary [ˈsæŋktjʊərɪ] n (refuge) Zuflucht f; (for animals) Schutzgebiet nt

sand [sænd] n Sand m

sandal [ˈsændl] n Sandale f

sandpaper n Sandpapier nt ▷ vt schmirgeln

sandwich [ˈsænwɪdʒ] n Sandwich nt

sandy [ˈsændɪ] adj (full of sand) sandig; **~ beach** Sandstrand m

sane [seɪn] adj geistig gesund, normal; (sensible) vernünftig

sang [sæŋ] pt of **sing**

sanitary [ˈsænɪtərɪ] adj hygienisch; **sanitary napkin** (US), **sanitary towel** n Damenbinde f

sank [sæŋk] pt of **sink**

Santa (Claus) [ˌsæntəˈklɔːz] n der Weihnachtsmann

sarcastic [sɑːˈkæstɪk] adj sarkastisch

sardine [sɑːˈdiːn] n Sardine f

Sardinia [sɑːˈdɪnɪə] n Sardinien nt

sari [ˈsɑːrɪ] n Sari m (von indischen Frauen getragenes Gewand)

sat [sæt] pt, pp of **sit**

Sat abbr = **Saturday** Sa.

satellite [ˈsætəlaɪt] n Satellit m; **satellite dish** n Satellitenschüssel f; **satellite TV** n Satellitenfernsehen nt

satin ['sætɪn] n Satin m

satisfaction [sætɪs'fækʃən] n (contentment) Zufriedenheit f; **is that to your ~?** sind Sie damit zufrieden?; **satisfactory** [sætɪs'fæktərɪ] adj zufrieden stellend; **satisfied** ['sætɪsfaɪd] adj zufrieden (with mit); **satisfy** ['sætɪsfaɪ] vt zufrieden stellen; (convince) überzeugen; (conditions) erfüllen; (need, demand) befriedigen; **satisfying** adj befriedigend

Saturday ['sætədeɪ] n Samstag m, Sonnabend m; see also **Tuesday**

sauce [sɔːs] n Soße f; **saucepan** n Kochtopf m; **saucer** n Untertasse f

saucy ['sɔːsɪ] adj frech

Saudi Arabia ['saʊdɪə'reɪbɪə] n Saudi-Arabien nt

sauna ['sɔːnə] n Sauna f

sausage ['sɒsɪdʒ] n Wurst f; **sausage roll** n mit Wurst gefülltes Blätterteigröllchen

savage ['sævɪdʒ] adj (person, attack) brutal; (animal) wild

save [seɪv] vt (rescue) retten (from vor +dat); (money, time, electricity etc) sparen; (strength) schonen; (Inform) speichern; **to ~ sb's life** jdm das Leben retten ▷ vi sparen ▷ n (in football) Parade f; **save up** vi sparen (for auf +akk); **saving** n (of money) Sparen nt; **~s** pl Ersparnisse pl; **~s account** Sparkonto nt

savory (US), **savoury** ['seɪvərɪ] adj (not sweet) pikant

saw [sɔː] (**sawed, sawn**) vt, vi sägen ▷ n (tool) Säge f ▷ pt of **see**; **sawdust** n Sägemehl nt

saxophone ['sæksəfəʊn] n Saxophon nt

say [seɪ] (**said, said**) vt sagen (to sb jdm); (prayer) sprechen; **what** does the letter ~? was steht im Brief?; **the rules ~ that ...** in den Regeln heißt es, dass ...; **he's said to be rich** er soll reich sein ▷ n **to have a ~ in sth** bei etw ein Mitspracherecht haben ▷ adv zum Beispiel; **saying** n Sprichwort nt

scab [skæb] n (on cut) Schorf m

scaffolding ['skæfəʊldɪŋ] n (Bau)gerüst nt

scale [skeɪl] n (of map etc) Maßstab m; (on thermometer etc) Skala f; (of pay) Tarifsystem nt; (Mus) Tonleiter f; (of fish, snake) Schuppe f; **to ~** maßstabsgerecht; **on a large/small ~** in großem / kleinem Umfang; **scales** npl (for weighing) Waage f

scalp [skælp] n Kopfhaut f

scan [skæn] vt (examine) genau prüfen; (read quickly) überfliegen; (Inform) scannen ▷ n (Med) Ultraschall m; **scan in** vt (Inform) einscannen

scandal ['skændl] n Skandal m; **scandalous** adj skandalös

Scandinavia [skændɪ'neɪvɪə] n Skandinavien nt; **Scandinavian** adj skandinavisch ▷ n Skandinavier(in) m(f)

scanner ['skænə*] n Scanner m

scapegoat ['skeɪpgəʊt] n Sündenbock m

scar [skɑː*] n Narbe f

scarce ['skɛəs] adj selten; (in short supply) knapp; **scarcely** adv kaum

scare ['skɛə*] n (general alarm) Panik f ▷ vt erschrecken; **to be ~d** Angst haben (of vor +dat)

scarf [skɑːf] (pl **-scarves**) n Schal m; (on head) Kopftuch nt

scarlet ['skɑːlət] adj scharlachrot; **scarlet fever** n Scharlach m

scary ['skɛərɪ] adj (film, story) gruselig

scatter ['skætə*] vt verstreuen;

(seed, gravel) streuen; *(disperse)* auseinander treiben

scene [si:n] *n (location)* Ort *m*; *(division of play)* (Theat) Szene *f*; *(view)* Anblick *m*; **to make a ~** eine Szene machen; **scenery** ['si:nərɪ] *n (landscape)* Landschaft *f*; *(Theat)* Kulissen *pl*; **scenic** ['si:nɪk] *adj (landscape)* malerisch; **~ route** landschaftlich schöne Strecke

scent [sent] *n (perfume)* Parfüm *nt*; *(smell)* Duft *m*

sceptical ['skeptɪkəl] *adj (BRIT)* skeptisch

schedule ['ʃedju:l, 'skedʒʊəl] *n (plan)* Programm *nt*; *(of work)* Zeitplan *m*; *(list)* Liste *f*; *(US: of trains, buses, air traffic)* Fahr-, Flugplan *m*; **on ~** planmäßig; **to be behind ~ with sth** mit etw in Verzug sein ▷ *vt* the meeting is **~d for next Monday** die Besprechung ist für nächsten Montag angesetzt; **scheduled** *adj (departure, arrival)* planmäßig; **~ flight** Linienflug *m*

scheme [ski:m] *n (plan)* Plan *m*; *(project)* Projekt *nt*; *(dishonest)* Intrige *f* ▷ *vi* intrigieren

schizophrenic [skɪtsə'frenɪk] *adj* schizophren

scholar ['skɒlə*] *n* Gelehrte(r) *mf*; **scholarship** *n (grant)* Stipendium *nt*

school [sku:l] *n* Schule *f*; *(university department)* Fachbereich *m*; *(US: university)* Universität *f*; **school bag** *n* Schultasche *f*; **schoolbook** *n* Schulbuch *nt*; **schoolboy** *n* Schüler *m*; **school bus** *n* Schulbus *m*; **schoolgirl** *n* Schülerin *f*; **schoolteacher** *n* Lehrer(in) *mf*; **schoolwork** *n* Schularbeiten *pl*

sciatica [saɪ'ætɪkə] *n* Ischias *m*

science ['saɪəns] *n* Wissenschaft *f*; *(natural ~)* Naturwissenschaft *f*; **science fiction** *n* Sciencefiction *f*;

scientific [saɪən'tɪfɪk] *adj* wissenschaftlich; **scientist** ['saɪəntɪst] *n* Wissenschaftler(in) *mf*; *(in natural sciences)* Naturwissenschaftler(in) *mf*)

scissors ['sɪzəz] *npl* Schere *f*

scone [skɒn] *n* kleines süßes Hefebrötchen mit oder ohne Rosinen, das mit Butter oder Biskuit und Marmelade gegessen wird

scoop [sku:p] *n (exclusive story)* Exklusivbericht *m*; **a ~ of ice-cream** eine Kugel Eis ▷ *vt* **to ~ (up)** schaufeln

scooter ['sku:tə*] *n* (Motor)roller *m*; *(toy)* (Tret)roller *m*

scope [skəʊp] *n* Umfang *m*; *(opportunity)* Möglichkeit *f*

score [skɔ:*] *n (Sport)* Spielstand *m*; *(final result)* Spielergebnis *nt*; *(in quiz etc)* Punktestand *m*; *(Mus)* Partitur *f*; **to keep (the) ~** mitzählen ▷ *vt (goal)* schießen; *(points)* machen ▷ *vi (keep ~)* mitzählen: **scoreboard** *n* Anzeigetafel *f*

scorn ['skɔ:n] *n* Verachtung *f*; **scornful** *adj* verächtlich

Scorpio ['skɔ:pɪəʊ] *(pl -s)* *n (Astr)* Skorpion *m*

scorpion ['skɔ:pɪən] *n* Skorpion *m*

Scot [skɒt] *n* Schotte *m*, Schottin *f*; **Scotch** [skɒtʃ] *adj* schottisch ▷ *(whisky)* schottischer Whisky, Scotch *m*

Scotch tape® *n (US)* Tesafilm® *m*

Scotland ['skɒtlənd] *n* Schottland *nt*; **Scotsman** *(pl -men)* *n* Schotte *m*; **Scotswoman** *(pl -women)* *n* Schottin *f*; **Scottish** *adj* schottisch

scout [skaʊt] *n (boy ~)* Pfadfinder *m*

scowl [skaʊl] *vi* finster blicken

scrambled eggs *npl* Rührei *nt*

scrap [skræp] *n (bit)* Stückchen *nt*, Fetzen *m*; *(metal)* Schrott *m* ▷ *vt* (car) verschrotten; (plan) verwerfen; **scrapbook** n Sammelalbum nt

scrape [skreip] n (scratch) Kratzer m ▷ vt (car) schrammen; (wall) streifen; **to ~ one's knee** sich das Knie schürfen; **scrape through** vi (exam) mit knapper Not bestehen

scrap heap ['skræphi:p] n Schrotthaufen m; **scrap metal** n Schrott m; **scrap paper** n Schmierpapier nt

scratch [skrætʃ] n (mark) Kratzer m; **to start from ~** von vorne anfangen ▷ vt kratzen; (car) zerkratzen; **to ~ one's arm** sich am Arm kratzen ▷ vi kratzen; (~ oneself) sich kratzen

scream [skri:m] n Schrei m ▷ vi schreien (with vor +dat); **to ~ at sb** jdn anschreien

screen [skri:n] n (TV, Inform) Bildschirm m; (Cine) Leinwand f ▷ vt (protect) abschirmen; (hide) verdecken; (film) zeigen; (applicants, luggage) überprüfen; **screenplay** n Drehbuch nt; **screen saver** n (Inform) Bildschirmschoner m

screw [skru:] n Schraube f ▷ vt (vulg: have sex with) poppen; **to ~ sth to sth** etw an etw akk schrauben; **to ~ off/on** (lid) ab-/aufschrauben; **screw up** vt (paper) zusammenknüllen; (make a mess of) vermasseln; **screwdriver** n Schraubenzieher m; **screw top** n Schraubverschluss m

scribble ['skribl] vt, vi kritzeln

script [skript] n (of play) Text m; (of film) Drehbuch nt; (style of writing) Schrift f

scroll down ['skrəʊl'daʊn] vi (Inform) runterscrollen; **scroll up** vi (Inform) raufscrollen; **scroll bar** n (Inform) Scrollbar f

scrub [skrʌb] vt schrubben; **scrubbing brush, scrub brush** (US) n Scheuerbürste f

scruffy ['skrʌfi] adj vergammelt

scrupulous, scrupulously ['skru:pjʊləs, -li] adj, adv gewissenhaft; (painstaking) peinlich genau

scuba-diving ['sku:bədaɪvɪŋ] n Sporttauchen nt

sculptor ['skʌlptə*] n Bildhauer(in) m(f); **sculpture** ['skʌlptʃə*] n (Art) Bildhauerei f; (statue) Skulptur f

sea [si:] n Meer nt, See f; **seafood** n Meeresfrüchte pl; **sea front** n Strandpromenade f; **seagull** n Möwe f

seal [si:l] n (animal) Robbe f; (stamp, impression) Siegel nt; (Tech) Dichtung f; (ring etc) Dichtung f ▷ vt versiegeln; (envelope) zukleben

seam [si:m] n Naht f

seaport [si:pɔ:t] n Seehafen m

search [sɜ:tʃ] n Suche f (for nach); **to do a ~ for** (Inform) suchen nach; **in ~ of** auf der Suche nach ▷ vi suchen (for nach) ▷ vt durchsuchen; **search engine** n (Inform) Suchmaschine f

seashell ['si:fel] n Muschel f; **seashore** n Strand m; **seasick** adj seekrank; **seaside** n **at the ~** am Meer; **to go to the ~** ans Meer fahren; **seaside resort** n Seebad nt

season ['si:zn] n Jahreszeit f; (Comm) Saison f; **high/low ~** Hoch-/Nebensaison f ▷ vt (flavour) würzen; **seasoning** n Gewürz nt; **season ticket** n (Rail) Zeitkarte f; (Theat) Abonnement nt; (Sport) Dauerkarte f

seat [si:t] n (place) Platz m; (chair) Sitz m; **take a ~** setzen Sie sich ▷ vt **the hall ~s 300** der Saal hat 300 Sitzplätze; **please be ~ed** bitte setzen Sie sich; **to remain ~ed** sitzen bleiben; **seat belt** n Sicherheitsgurt m

sea view ['si:vju:] n Seeblick m; **seaweed** n Seetang m

secluded [sɪ'klu:dɪd] adj abgelegen

second ['sekənd] *adj* zweite(r, s); **the ~ of June** der zweite Juni ▷ *adv* (*in ~ position*) an zweiter Stelle; (*secondly*) zweitens; **he came ~** er ist Zweiter geworden ▷ *n* (*of time*) Sekunde *f*; (*moment*) Augenblick *m*; ~ (**gear**) *der* zweite Gang; (~ *helping*) zweite Portion; **just a ~** (einen) Augenblick! **secondary** *adj* (*less important*) zweitrangig; ~ **education** höhere Schulbildung *f*; ~ **school** weiterführende Schule; **second-class** *adj* (*ticket*) zweiter Klasse; ~ **stamp** Briefmarke *f* für nicht bevorzugt beförderte Sendungen ▷ *adv* (*travel*) zweiter Klasse; **secondhand** *adj*, *adv* gebraucht; (*information*) aus zweiter Hand; **secondly** *adv* zweitens; **second-rate** *adj* (*pej*) zweitklassig

secret ['si:krət] *n* Geheimnis *nt* ▷ *adj* geheim; (*admirer*) heimlich
secretary ['sekrətrɪ] *n* Sekretär(in) *m(f)*; (*minister*) Minister(in) *m(f)*; **Secretary of State** *n* (*US*) Außenminister(in) *m(f)*
secretive ['si:krətɪv] *adj* (*person*) geheimnistuerisch; **secretly** ['si:krətlɪ] *adv* heimlich
sect [sekt] *n* Sekte *f*
section ['sekʃən] *n* (*part*) Teil *m*; (*of document*) Abschnitt *m*; (*department*) Abteilung *f*
secure [sɪ'kjuə*] *adj* (*safe*) sicher (*from vor +dat*), (*firmly fixed*) fest ▷ *vt* (*make firm*) befestigen; (*window, door*) fest verschließen; (*obtain*) sich sichern; **securely** *adv* fest; (*safely*) sicher, **security** [sɪ'kjuərɪtɪ] *n* Sicherheit *f*
sedative ['sedətɪv] *n* Beruhigungsmittel *nt*
seduce [sɪ'dju:s] *vt* verführen; **seductive** [sɪ'dʌktɪv] *adj* verführerisch; (*offer*) verlockend

see [si:] (**saw, seen**) *vt* sehen; (*understand*) verstehen; (*check*) nachsehen; (*accompany*) bringen; (*visit*) besuchen; (*talk to*) sprechen; **to ~ the doctor** zum Arzt gehen; **to ~ sb home** jdn nach Hause begleiten; **I saw him swimming** ich habe ihn schwimmen sehen; ~ **you** tschüs!; ~ **you on Friday** bis Freitag! ▷ *vi* sehen; (*understand*) verstehen; (*check*) nachsehen; (*you*) ~ siehst du; **we'll ~** mal sehen; **see about** *vt* (*attend to*) sich kümmern um; **see off** *vt* (*say goodbye to*) verabschieden; **see out** *vt* (*show out*) zur Tür bringen; **see through** *vt* **to see sb/sth** jdn/etw durchschauen; **see to** *vt* sich kümmern um; ~ **it that ...** sieh zu, dass ...

seed [si:d] *n* (*of plant*) Samen *m*; (*in fruit*) Kern *m*; **seedless** *adj* kernlos
seek [si:k] (**sought, sought**) *vt* suchen; (*fame*) streben nach; **to ~ sb's advice** jdn um Rat fragen
seem [si:m] *vi* scheinen; **he ~s (to be)** honest er scheint ehrlich zu sein; **it ~s to me that ...** es scheint mir, dass ...
seen [si:n] *pp* of **see**
seesaw ['si:sɔ:] *n* Wippe *f*
segment ['segmənt] *n* Teil *m*
seize [si:z] *vt* packen; (*confiscate*) beschlagnahmen; (*opportunity, power*) ergreifen
seldom ['seldəm] *adv* selten
select [sɪ'lekt] *adj* (*exclusive*) exklusiv ▷ *vt* auswählen; **selection** [sɪ'lekʃən] *n* Auswahl *f* (*of +dat*); **selective** *adj* (*choosy*) wählerisch
self [self] (*pl* **selves**) *n* Selbst *nt*, Ich *nt*; **he's his old ~ again** er ist wieder ganz der Alte; **self-adhesive** *adj* selbstklebend; **self-assured** *n* selbstsicher; **self-catering** *adj* für Selbstversorger; **self-centred** *adj*

egozentrisch; **self-confidence** n Selbstbewusstsein nt; **self-confident** adj selbstbewusst; **self-conscious** adj befangen, verklemmt; **self-contained** adj (flat) separat; **self-control** n Selbstbeherrschung f; **self-defence** n Selbstverteidigung f; **self-employed** adj selbstständig; **self-evident** adj offensichtlich

selfish, selfishly ['selfɪʃ, -lɪ] adj, adv egoistisch, selbstsüchtig; **selfless, selflessly** adj, adv selbstlos

self-pity [self'pɪtɪ] n Selbstmitleid nt; **self-portrait** n Selbstporträt nt; **self-respect** n Selbstachtung f; **self-service** n Selbstbedienung f ▷ adj Selbstbedienungs-

sell [sel] (**sold, sold**) vt verkaufen; **to ~ sb sth, to ~ sth to sb** jdm etw verkaufen; **do you ~ postcards?** haben Sie Postkarten? ▷ vi (product) sich verkaufen; **sell out** vt to be sold ~ ausverkauft sein; **sell-by date** n Haltbarkeitsdatum nt

Sellotape® ['seləteɪp] n (BRIT) Tesafilm® m

semester [sɪ'mestə*] n Semester nt

semi ['semɪ] n (BRIT: house) Doppelhaushälfte f; **semicircle** n Halbkreis m; **semicolon** n Semikolon nt; **semidetached (house)** n (BRIT) Doppelhaushälfte f; **semifinal** n Halbfinale nt

seminar ['semɪnɑː*] n Seminar nt

semiskimmed milk ['semɪskɪmd'mɪlk] n Halbfettmilch f

senate ['senət] n Senat m; **senator** n Senator(in) m(f)

send [send] (**sent, sent**) vt schicken; **to ~ sb sth, to ~ sth to sb** jdm etw schicken; **~ her my best wishes** grüße sie von mir; **send away** vt wegschicken ▷ vi **to ~ for** etw anfordern; **send back** vt zurückschicken; **send for** vt (person) holen lassen; (by post) anfordern; **send off** vt (by post) abschicken; **send out** vt (invitations etc) verschicken ▷ vi **to ~ for sth** etw holen lassen

sender ['sendə*] n Absender(in) m(f)

senior ['siːnɪə*] adj (older) älter; (high-ranking) höher; (pupils) älter; **he is ~ to me** er ist mir übergeordnet ▷ n **he's eight years my ~** er ist acht Jahre älter als ich; **senior citizen** n Senior(in) m(f)

sensation [sen'seɪʃən] n Gefühl nt; (excitement, person, thing) Sensation f; **sensational** adj sensationell

sense [sens] n (faculty, meaning) Sinn m; (feeling) Gefühl nt; (understanding) Verstand m; **~ of smell / taste** Geruchs-/Geschmackssinn m; **to have a ~ of humour** Humor haben; **to make ~** (sentence etc) einen Sinn ergeben; (be sensible) Sinn machen; **in a ~** gewissermaßen ▷ vt spüren; **senseless** adj (stupid) sinnlos

sensible, sensibly ['sensəbl, -blɪ] adj, adv vernünftig

sensitive ['sensɪtɪv] adj empfindlich (to gegen); (easily hurt) sensibel; (subject) heikel

sensual ['sensjʊəl] adj sinnlich

sensuous ['sensjʊəs] adj sinnlich

sent [sent] pt, pp of **send**

sentence ['sentəns] n (Ling) Satz m; (Jur) Strafe f ▷ vt **to ~** verurteilen (to zu)

sentiment ['sentɪmənt] n (sentimentality) Sentimentalität f; (opinion) Ansicht f; **sentimental** [sentɪ'mentl] adj sentimental

separate ['sepərət] adj getrennt, separat; (individual) einzeln ▷ ['sepəreɪt] vt trennen (from von); **they are ~d** (couple) sie leben getrennt vi sich trennen: **separately** adv getrennt, (singly) einzeln

September [sep'tembə*] n September m; **in** ~ im September; **on the 2nd of** ~ am 2. September; **at the beginning/in the middle/at the end of** ~ Anfang/Mitte/Ende September; **last/next** ~ letzten/nächsten September

septic ['septik] adj vereitert

sequel ['si:kwəl] n (to film, book) Fortsetzung f (to von)

sequence ['si:kwəns] n (order) Reihenfolge f

Serb ['sɜ:b] n Serbe m, Serbin f; **Serbia** ['sɜ:bjə] n Serbien nt

sergeant ['sɑ:dʒənt] n (Police) Polizeimeister(in) m(f); (Mil) Feldwebel(in) m(f)

serial ['sɪərɪəl] n (TV) Serie f; (in newspaper etc) Fortsetzungsroman m ▷ adj (Inform) seriell; ~ **number** Seriennummer f

series ['sɪəri:z] nsing Reihe f; (TV, Radio) Serie f

serious ['sɪərɪəs] adj ernst; (injury, illness, mistake) schwer; (discussion) ernsthaft; **are you ~?** ist das dein Ernst?; **seriously** adv ernsthaft; (hurt) schwer; **~?** im Ernst?; **to take sb ~** jdn ernst nehmen

sermon ['sɜːmən] n (Rel) Predigt f

servant ['sɜːvənt] n Diener(in) m(f); **serve** [sɜːv] vt (customer) bedienen; (food) servieren; (one's country etc) dienen +dat; (sentence) verbüßen; **I'm being ~d** ich werde schon bedient; **it ~s him right** es geschieht ihm recht ▷ vi dienen (as als), aufschlagen ▷ n Aufschlag m

server n (Inform) Server m

service ['sɜːvɪs] n (in shop, hotel) Bedienung f; (activity, amenity) Dienstleistung f; (set of dishes) Service nt; (Auto) Inspektion f; (Tech)

Wartung f; (Rel) Gottesdienst m, Aufschlag m; **train/bus** ~ Zug-/Busverbindung f; **'~ not included'** „Bedienung nicht inbegriffen" ▷ vt (Auto, Tech) warten; **service area** n (on motorway) Raststätte f (mit Tankstelle); **service charge** n Bedienung f; **service provider** n (inform) Provider m; **service station** n Tankstelle f

serving ['sɜːvɪŋ] n (portion) Portion f

session ['seʃən] n (of court, assembly) Sitzung f

set [set] (**set, set**) vt (place) stellen; (lay flat) legen; (arrange) anordnen; (table) decken; (trap, record) aufstellen; (time, price) festsetzen; (watch, alarm) stellen (for auf +akk); **to** ~ **sb a task** jdm eine Aufgabe stellen; **to** ~ **free** freilassen; **to** ~ **a good example** ein gutes Beispiel geben, **the novel is** ~ **in London** der Roman spielt in London ▷ vi (sun) untergehen; (become hard) fest werden; (bone) zusammenwachsen ▷ n (collection of things) Satz m; (of cutlery, furniture) Garnitur f; (group of people) Kreis m; (Radio, TV) Apparat m, Satz m; (Theat) Bühnenbild nt; (Cine, Film)kulisse f ▷ adj (agreed, prescribed) festgelegt; (ready) bereit; ~ **meal** Menü nt; **set aside** vt (money) beiseite legen; (time) einplanen; **set off** vi aufbrechen (for nach) ▷ vt (alarm) auslösen; (enhance) hervorheben; **set out** vi aufbrechen (for nach) ▷ vt (chairs, chesspieces etc) aufstellen; (state) darlegen; **to** ~ **to do sth** (intend) beabsichtigen, etw zu tun; **set up** vt (firm, organization) gründen; (stall, tent, camera) aufbauen; (meeting) vereinbaren ▷ vi **to** ~ **as a doctor** sich als Arzt niederlassen

setback n Rückschlag m

settee [se'ti:] n Sofa nt, Couch f

setting ['setɪŋ] n (of novel, film) Schauplatz m; (surroundings) Umgebung f

settle ['setl] vt (bill, debt) begleichen; (dispute) beilegen; (question) klären; (stomach) beruhigen ▷ vi to ~ (**down**) (feel at home) sich einleben; (calm down) sich beruhigen; **settle in** vi (in place) sich einleben; (in job) sich eingewöhnen; **settle up** vi (be)zahlen; to ~ **with sb** mit jdm abrechnen; **settlement** n (of bill, debt) Begleichung f; (colony) Siedlung f; **to reach a** ~ sich einigen

setup ['setʌp] n (organization) Organisation f; (situation) Situation f

seven ['sevn] num sieben ▷ n Sieben f; see also **eight**; **seventeen** ['sevn'ti:n] num siebzehn ▷ n Siebzehn f; see also **eight**; **seventeenth** adj siebzehnte(r, s); see also **eighth**; **seventh** ['sevnθ] adj siebte(r, s) ▷ n (fraction) Siebtel nt; see also **eighth**; **seventieth** ['sevntɪθ] adj siebzigste(r, s); see also **eighth**; **seventy** ['sevntɪ] num siebzig; **~one** einundsiebzig ▷ n Siebzig f; **to be in one's seventies** in den Siebzigern sein; see also **eight**

several ['sevrəl] adj, pron mehrere

severe [sɪ'vɪə*] adj (strict) streng; (serious) schwer; (pain) stark; (winter) hart; **severely** adv (harshly) hart; (seriously) schwer

sew [səʊ] (sewed, sewn) vt, vi nähen

sewage ['su:ɪdʒ] n Abwasser nt; **sewer** ['sʊə*] n Abwasserkanal m

sewing ['səʊɪŋ] n Nähen nt; **sewing machine** n Nähmaschine f

sewn [səʊn] pp of **sew**

sex [seks] n Sex m; (gender) Geschlecht nt; **to have** ~ Sex haben (with mit); **sexism** ['seksɪzəm] n

---

Sexismus m; **sexist** ['seksɪst] adj sexistisch ▷ n Sexist(in) m(f); **sex life** n Sex(ual)leben nt

sexual ['seksjʊəl] adj sexuell; ~ **discrimination / harassment** sexuelle Diskriminierung / Belästigung; ~ **intercourse** Geschlechtsverkehr m; **sexuality** [seksjʊ'ælɪtɪ] n Sexualität f; **sexually** adv sexuell

sexy ['seksɪ] adj sexy

Seychelles ['seɪʃelz] npl Seychellen pl

shabby ['ʃæbɪ] adj schäbig

shack [ʃæk] n Hütte f

shade [ʃeɪd] n (shadow) Schatten m; (for lamp) (Lampen)schirm m; (colour) Farbton m; ~**s** (US: sunglasses) Sonnenbrille f ▷ vt (from sun) abschirmen; (in drawing) schattieren

shadow ['ʃædəʊ] n Schatten m

shady ['ʃeɪdɪ] adj schattig; (fig) zwielichtig

shake [ʃeɪk] (shook, shaken) vt schütteln; (shock) erschüttern; **to ~ hands with sb** jdm die Hand geben; **to ~ one's head** den Kopf schütteln ▷ vi (tremble) zittern; (building, ground) schwanken; **shake off** vt abschütteln; **shaken** ['ʃeɪkn] pp of **shake**; **shaky** ['ʃeɪkɪ] adj (trembling) zittrig; (table, chair, position) wackelig; (weak) unsicher

shall [ʃæl] (**should**) vb aux werden; (in questions) sollen; **I ~ do my best** ich werde mein Bestes tun; ~ **I come too?** soll ich mitkommen?; **where ~ we go?** wo gehen wir hin?

shallow ['ʃæləʊ] adj (a. fig) seicht; (person) oberflächlich

shame [ʃeɪm] n (feeling of ~) Scham f; (disgrace) Schande f; **what a** ~ wie schade!; ~ **on you** schäm dich!; **it's a** ~ **that ...** schade, dass ...

shampoo [ʃæm'pu:] n Shampoo nt; **to have a** ~ **and set** sich die Haare waschen und legen lassen ▷

vt (hair) waschen; (carpet) schamponieren

shandy ['ʃændı] n Radler m, Alsterwasser nt

shan't [ʃɑːnt] contr of **shall not**

shape [ʃeɪp] n Form f; (undentified figure) Gestalt f; **in the ~ of** in Form ~gen, **to be in good ~** (healthwise) in guter Verfassung sein; **to take ~** (plan, idea) Gestalt annehmen ▷ vt (clay, person) formen; **-shaped** [ʃeɪpt] suf **-förmig; heart~** herzförmig; **shapeless** adj formlos

share [ʃeə*] n Anteil +dat (in, of an m); (Fin) Aktie f ▷ vt, vi teilen; **shareholder** n Aktionär(in) m(f)

shark [ʃɑːk] n (Zool) Haifisch m

sharp [ʃɑːp] adj scharf; (pin) spitz; (person) scharfsinnig; (pain) heftig; (increase, fall) abrupt; **C/F ~** (Mus) Cis / Dis nt ▷ adv **at 2 o'clock ~** Punkt 2 Uhr; **sharpen** vt (knife) schärfen; (pencil) spitzen; **sharpener** n (pencil ~) Spitzer m

shatter [ʃætə*] vt zerschmettern; (fig) zerstören ▷ vi zerspringen; **shattered** adj (exhausted) kaputt

shave [ʃeɪv] (shaved, shaved or shaven) vt rasieren ▷ vi sich rasieren ▷ n Rasur f; **that was a close ~** (fig) das war knapp; **shave off** vt **to shave one's beard off** sich den Bart abrasieren; **shaven** [ʃeɪvn] pp of **shave** ▷ adj (head) kahl geschoren; **shaver** n (Elec) Rasierapparat m; **shaving brush** n Rasierpinsel m; **shaving foam** n Rasierschaum m

shawl [ʃɔːl] n Tuch nt

she [ʃiː] pron sie

shed [ʃed] (shed, shed) n Schuppen m ▷ vt (tears, blood) vergießen; (hair, leaves) verlieren

she'd [ʃiːd] contr of **she had; she would**

sheep [ʃiːp] n (pl -) n Schaf nt;

sheepdog n Schäferhund m; **sheepskin** n Schaffell nt

sheer [ʃɪə*] adj (madness) rein; (steep) steil; (transparent) hauchdünn; **by ~ chance** rein zufällig

sheet [ʃiːt] n (on bed) Betttuch nt; (of paper) Blatt nt, (of metal) Platte f; (of glass) Scheibe f; **a ~ of paper** ein Blatt Papier

shelf [ʃelf] (pl **shelves**) n Bücherbord nt, Regal nt; **shelves** pl (item of furniture) Regal nt

she'll [ʃiːl] contr of **she will; she shall**

shell [ʃel] n (of egg, nut) Schale f; (sea~) Muschel f ▷ vt (peas, nuts) schälen; **shellfish** n (as food) Meeresfrüchte pl

shelter [ʃeltə*] n (protection) Schutz m; (accommodation) Unterkunft f; (bus ~) Wartehäuschen nt ▷ vt schützen (from vor +dat) ▷ vi sich unterstellen; **sheltered** adj (spot) geschützt; (life) behütet

shelve [ʃelv] vt (fig) aufschieben; **shelves** pl of **shelf**

shepherd [ʃepəd] n Schäfer m; **shepherd's pie** n Hackfleischauflauf mit Decke aus Kartoffelpüree

sherry [ʃerɪ] n Sherry m

she's [ʃiːz] contr of **she is; she has**

shield [ʃiːld] n Schild m; (fig) Schutz m ▷ vt schützen (from vor +dat)

shift [ʃɪft] n (change) Veränderung f; (period at work, workers) Schicht f; (on keyboard) Umschalttaste f ▷ vt (furniture etc) verrücken; (stain) entfernen; **to ~ gear(s)** (US Auto) schalten ▷ vi (move) sich bewegen; (move up) rutschen; **shift key** n Umschalttaste f

shin [ʃɪn] n Schienbein nt

shine [ʃaɪn] (shone, shone) n (be shiny) glänzen; (sun) scheinen; (lamp) leuchten ▷ vt (polish) polieren ▷ n

Glanz m

shingles ['ʃɪŋglz] nsing (Med) Gürtelrose f

shiny ['ʃaɪnɪ] adj glänzend

ship [ʃɪp] n Schiff nt ▷ vt (send) versenden; (by ship) verschiffen; **shipment** n (goods) Sendung f; (sent by ship) Ladung f; **shipwreck** n Schiffbruch m; **shipyard** n Werft f

shirt [ʃɜːt] n Hemd nt

shit [ʃɪt] n (vulg) Scheiße f; (person) Arschloch nt; **~!** Scheiße!; **shitty** ['ʃɪtɪ] adj (fam) beschissen

shiver ['ʃɪvə*] vi zittern (with vor +dat)

shock [ʃɒk] n (mental, emotional) Schock m; **to be in ~** unter Schock stehen; **to get a ~** (Elec) einen Schlag bekommen ▷ vt schockieren; **shock absorber** n Stoßdämpfer m; **shocked** adj schockiert (by über +akk); **shocking** adj schockierend; (awful) furchtbar

shoe [ʃuː] n Schuh m; **shoehorn** n Schuhlöffel m; **shoelace** n Schnürsenkel m; **shoe polish** n Schuhcreme f

shone [ʃɒn] pt, pp of **shine**

shook [ʃʊk] pt of **shake**

shoot [ʃuːt] n (shot, shot) vt (wound) anschießen; (kill) erschießen; (Cine) drehen; (fam: heroin) drücken ▷ vi (with gun, move quickly) schießen; **to ~ at sb** auf jdn schießen ▷ n (of plant) Trieb m; **shooting** n (exchange of gunfire) Schießerei f; (killing) Erschießung f

shop [ʃɒp] n Geschäft nt, Laden m ▷ vi einkaufen; **shop assistant** n Verkäufer(in) m(f); **shopkeeper** n Geschäftsinhaber(in) m(f); **shoplifting** n Ladendiebstahl m; **shopper** n Käufer(in) m(f); **shopping** n (activity) Einkaufen nt; (goods) Einkäufe pl; **to do the ~** einkaufen; **to**

go ~ einkaufen gehen; **shopping bag** n Einkaufstasche f; **shopping cart** n (US) Einkaufswagen m; **shopping center** (US), **shopping centre** n Einkaufszentrum nt; **shopping list** n Einkaufszettel m; **shopping trolley** n (BRIT) Einkaufswagen m; **shop window** n Schaufenster nt

shore [ʃɔː*] n Ufer nt; **on ~** an Land

short [ʃɔːt] adj kurz; (person) klein; **to be ~ of money** knapp bei Kasse sein; **to be ~ of time** wenig Zeit haben; **~ of breath** kurzatmig; **to cut ~** (holiday) abbrechen; **we are two ~** wir haben zwei zu wenig; **it's ~ for ...** das ist die Kurzform von ... ▷ n (drink, Elec) Kurze(r) m; **shortage** n Knappheit f (of an +dat); **shortbread** n Buttergebäck nt; **short circuit** n Kurzschluss m; **shortcoming** n Unzulänglichkeit f; (of person) Fehler m; **shortcut** n (quicker route) Abkürzung f; (Inform) Shortcut m; **shorten** vt kürzen; (in time) verkürzen; **shorthand** n Stenografie f; **shortlist** n **to be on the ~** in der engeren Wahl sein; **short-lived** adj kurzlebig; **shortly** adv bald; **shorts** npl Shorts pl; **short-sighted** adj (a. fig) kurzsichtig; **short-sleeved** adj kurzärmelig; **short-stay car park** n Kurzzeitparkplatz m; **short story** n Kurzgeschichte f; **short-term** adj kurzfristig; **short wave** n Kurzwelle f

shot [ʃɒt] pt, pp of **shoot** ▷ n (from gun, in football) Schuss m; (Foto, Cine) Aufnahme f; (injection) Spritze f; (of alcohol) Schuss m

should [ʃʊd] pt of **shall** ▷ vb aux **I ~ go now** ich sollte jetzt gehen; **what ~ I do?** was soll ich tun?; **you ~n't have said that** das hättest du nicht sagen sollen; **that ~ be**

enough das müsste reichen
shoulder [ˈʃəʊldəʳ] n Schulter f
shouldn't [ˈʃʊdnt] contr of **should not**
should've [ˈʃʊdəv] contr of **should have**
shout [ʃaʊt] n Schrei m; (call) Ruf m ▷ vt rufen; (order) brüllen ▷ vi schreien; **to ~ at** anschreien; **to ~ for help** um Hilfe rufen
shove [ʃʌv] vt (person) schubsen, (car, table etc) schieben ▷ vi (in crowd) drängeln
shovel [ˈʃʌvl] n Schaufel f ▷ vt schaufeln
show [ʃəʊ] (showed, shown) vt zeigen; **to ~ sb sth, to ~ sth to sb** jdm etw zeigen; **to ~ sb in** jdn hereinführen; **to ~ sb out** jdn zur Tür bringen ▷ n (Cine, Theat) Vorstellung f; (TV) Show f; (exhibition) Ausstellung f; **show off** vi (pej) angeben; **show round** vt herumführen; **to show sb round the house/the town** jdm das Haus/die Stadt zeigen; **show up** vi (arrive) auftauchen
shower [ˈʃaʊəʳ] n Dusche f; (rain) Schauer m; **to have** (◊ **take**) **a ~** duschen ▷ vi (wash) duschen
showing [ˈʃəʊɪŋ] n (Cine) Vorstellung f
shown [ʃəʊn] pp of **show**
showroom [ˈʃəʊruːm] n Ausstellungsraum m
shrank [ʃræŋk] pt of **shrink**
shred [ʃred] n (of paper, fabric) Fetzen m ▷ vt (in shredder) (im Reißwolf) zerkleinern; **shredder** n (for paper) Reißwolf m
shrimp [ʃrɪmp] n Garnele f
shrink [ʃrɪŋk] (shrank, shrunk) vi schrumpfen; (clothes) eingehen
shrivel [ˈʃrɪvl] vt ▷ vi **~ (up)** schrumpfen; (skin) runzlig werden; (plant) welken
Shrove Tuesday [ˈʃrəʊvˈtjuːzdeɪ]

n Fastnachtsdienstag m
shrub [ʃrʌb] n Busch m, Strauch m
shrug [ʃrʌg] vt, vi **to ~ (one's shoulders)** mit den Achseln zucken
shrunk [ʃrʌŋk] pp of **shrink**
shudder [ˈʃʌdəʳ] vi schaudern; (ground, building) beben
shuffle [ˈʃʌfl] vt vi mischen
shut [ʃʌt] (shut, shut) vt zumachen, schließen ▷ vi schließen; **~ your mouth** (fam) halt den Mund! ▷ schließen; **shut down** (computer) ausschalten ▷ vi schließen; (computer) sich ausschalten; **shut in** vt einschließen; **shut out** vt (lock out) aussperren; **to shut oneself out** sich aussperren; **shut up** vi (lock up) abschließen; (silence) zum Schweigen bringen ▷ vi (keep quiet) den Mund halten; **~! halt** den Mund!; **shutter** n (on window) (Fenster)laden m; **shutter release** n Auslöser m; **shutter speed** n Belichtungszeit f
shuttle bus [ˈʃʌtlbʌs] n Shuttlebus m
shuttlecock [ˈʃʌtlkɒk] n Federball m
shuttle service [ˈʃʌtlsɜːvɪs] n Pendelverkehr m
shy [ʃaɪ] adj schüchtern; (animal) scheu
Siberia [saɪˈbɪərɪə] n Sibirien nt
Sicily [ˈsɪsɪlɪ] n Sizilien nt
sick [sɪk] adj krank; (joke) makaber; **to be ~** (BRIT: vomit) sich übergeben; **to be ~ off** wegen Krankheit fehlen; **I feel ~** mir ist schlecht; **to be ~ of sb/sth** jdn/etw satt haben; **it makes me ~** (fig) es ekelt mich an; **sickbag** n Spucktüte f; **sick leave** n **to be on ~** krankgeschrieben sein; **sickness** n Krankheit f; (BRIT: nausea) Übelkeit f; **sickness benefit** n (BRIT)

Krankengeld nt

side [saɪd] n Seite f; (of road) Rand m; (of mountain) Hang m; (Sport) Mannschaft f; **by my ~** neben mir; **~ by ~** nebeneinander ▷ adj (door, entrance) Seiten-; **sideboard** n Anrichte f; **sideboards**, **sideburns** (US) npl Koteletten pl; **side dish** n Beilage f; **side effect** n Nebenwirkung f; **sidelight** n (BRIT Auto) Parklicht nt; **side order** n Beilage f; **side road** n Nebenstraße f; **side street** n Seitenstraße f; **sidewalk** n (US) Bürgersteig m; **sideways** adv seitwärts

sieve [sɪv] n Sieb nt

sift [sɪft] vt (flour etc) sieben

sigh [saɪ] vi seufzen

sight [saɪt] n (power of seeing) Sehvermögen nt; (view, thing seen) Anblick m; **~s** pl (of city etc) Sehenswürdigkeiten pl; **to have bad ~** schlecht sehen; **to lose ~ of** aus den Augen verlieren; **out of ~** außer Sicht; **sightseeing** n **to go ~** Sehenswürdigkeiten besichtigen; **~ tour** Rundfahrt f

sign [saɪn] n Zeichen nt; (notice, road ~) Schild nt ▷ vt unterschreiben ▷ vi unterschreiben; **to ~ for sth** den Empfang einer Sache gen bestätigen; **to ~ in/out** sich ein-/austragen; **sign on** vi (BRIT: register as unemployed) sich arbeitslos melden; **sign up** vi (for course) sich einschreiben; (Mil) sich verpflichten

signal ['sɪɡnl] n Signal nt ▷ vi (car driver) blinken

signature ['sɪɡnətʃə*] n Unterschrift f

significant [sɪɡ'nɪfɪkənt] adj (important) bedeutend, wichtig; (meaning sth) bedeutsam; **significantly** adv (considerably) bedeutend

sign language ['saɪnlæŋwɪdʒ]

n Zeichensprache f; **signpost** n Wegweiser m

silence ['saɪləns] n Stille f; (of person) Schweigen nt; **~!** Ruhe! ▷ vt zum Schweigen bringen; **silent** adj still; (taciturn) schweigsam; **she remained ~** sie schwieg

silk [sɪlk] n Seide f ▷ adj Seiden-

silly ['sɪlɪ] adj dumm, albern; **don't do anything ~** mach keine Dummheiten

silver ['sɪlvə*] n Silber nt; (coins) Silbermünzen pl ▷ adj Silber-, silbern; **silver-plated** adj versilbert; **silver wedding** n silberne Hochzeit

similar ['sɪmɪlə*] adj ähnlich (to dat); **similarity** [sɪmɪ'lærɪtɪ] n Ähnlichkeit f (to mit); **similarly** adv (equally) ebenso

simple ['sɪmpl] adj einfach; (unsophisticated) schlicht; **simplify** ['sɪmplɪfaɪ] vt vereinfachen; **simply** adv einfach; (merely) bloß; (dress) schlicht

simulate ['sɪmjʊleɪt] vt simulieren

simultaneous, **simultaneously** [sɪməl'teɪnɪəs, -lɪ] adj, adv gleichzeitig

sin [sɪn] n Sünde f ▷ vi sündigen

since [sɪns] adv seitdem; (in the meantime) inzwischen ▷ prep seit +dat; **ever ~ 1995** schon seit 1995 ▷ conj (time) seit, seitdem; (because) da, weil; **ever ~ I've known her** seit ich sie kenne; **it's ages ~ I've seen him** ich habe ihn seit langem nicht mehr gesehen

sincere [sɪn'sɪə*] adj aufrichtig; **sincerely** adv aufrichtig; **Yours ~** mit freundlichen Grüßen

sing [sɪŋ] (**sang, sung**) vt, vi singen

Singapore [sɪŋɡə'pɔ:*] n Singapur m

singer ['sɪŋə*] n Sänger(in) m(f)

single ['sɪŋgl] adj (one only) einzig; (not double) einfach; (bed, room) Einzel-; (unmarried) ledig; (BRIT: ticket) einfach ▷ n (BRIT: ticket) einfache Fahrkarte; (Mus) Single f; **a ~ to London, please** (BRIT Rail) einfach nach London, bitte; **single out** vt (choose) auswählen; **single-handed, single-handedly** adv im Alleingang; **single parent** n Alleinerziehende(r) mf; **single supplement** n (for hotel room) Einzelzimmerzuschlag m

singular ['sɪŋgjulə*] n Singular m

sinister ['sɪnɪstə*] adj unheimlich

sink [sɪŋk] (**sank, sunk**) vt (ship) versenken ▷ vi sinken ▷ n Spülbecken nt; (in bathroom) Waschbecken nt

sip [sɪp] vt nippen an +dat

sir [sɜ:*] n **yes, ~** ja(, mein Herr); **can I help you, ~?** kann ich Ihnen helfen?; **Sir James** (title) Sir James

sister ['sɪstə*] n Schwester f; (BRIT: nurse) Oberschwester f; **sister-in-law** (pl **sisters-in-law**) n Schwägerin f

sit [sɪt] (**sat, sat**) vi (be sitting) sitzen; (~ down) sich setzen; (committee, court) tagen ▷ vt (BRIT: exam) machen; **sit down** vi sich hinsetzen; **sit up** vi (from lying position) sich aufsetzen

sitcom ['sɪtkɒm] n Situationskomödie f

site [saɪt] n Platz m; (building ~) Baustelle f; (web~) Site f

sitting ['sɪtɪŋ] n (meeting, for portrait) Sitzung f; **sitting room** n Wohnzimmer nt

situated ['sɪtjʊeɪtɪd] adj **to be ~** liegen

situation [sɪtjʊ'eɪʃən] n (circumstances) Situation f, Lage f; (job) Stelle f; **'~s vacant/wanted'** (BRIT)

"Stellenangebote/Stellengesuche"

six [sɪks] num sechs ▷ n Sechs f; see also **eight**; **sixpack** n (of beer etc) Sechserpack m; **sixteen** ['sɪks'ti:n] num sechzehn ▷ n Sechzehn f, see also **eight**; **sixteenth** adj sechzehnte(r, s); see also **eighth**; **sixth** [sɪksθ] adj sechste(r, s), **~-form** (BRIT) ≈ Oberstufe f ▷ n (fraction) Sechstel nt; see also **eighth**; **sixtieth** ['sɪkstɪɪθ] adj sechzigste(r, s); see also **eighth**; **sixty** ['sɪkstɪ] num sechzig; **~-one** ein-undsechzig ▷ n Sechzig f; **to be in one's sixties** in den Sechzigern sein; see also **eight**

size [saɪz] n Größe f; **what ~ are you?** welche Größe haben Sie?; **a ~ too big** eine Nummer zu groß

sizzle ['sɪzl] vi (Gastr) brutzeln

skate [skeɪt] n Schlittschuh m; (roller ~) Rollschuh m ▷ vi Schlittschuh laufen; (roller ~) Rollschuh laufen; **skateboard** n Skateboard nt; **skating** n Eislauf m; (roller~~) Rollschuhlauf m; **skating rink** n Eisbahn f; (for roller-skating) Rollschuhbahn f

skeleton ['skelɪtn] n (a. fig) Skelett nt

skeptical n (US) see **sceptical**

sketch [sketʃ] n Skizze f; (Theat) Sketch m ▷ vt skizzieren; **sketchbook** n Skizzenbuch f

ski [ski:] n Ski m ▷ vi Ski laufen; **ski boot** n Skistiefel m

skid [skɪd] vi (Auto) schleudern

skier ['ski:ə*] n Skiläufer(in) m(f)

skiing n Skilaufen nt; **to go ~** Ski laufen gehen; **~ holiday** Skiurlaub m; **skiing instructor** n Skilehrer(in) m(f)

skilful, skilfully ['skɪlful, -fəlɪ] adj, adv geschickt

ski-lift ['ski:lɪft] n Skilift m

skill [skɪl] n Geschick nt; (acquired

technique) Fertigkeit f; **skilled** adj
geschickt (*at, in* in +dat); (*worker*)
Fach-; (*work*) fachmännisch

skim [skɪm] vt **to ~ (off)** (*fat etc*)
abschöpfen; **to ~ (through)** (*read*)
überfliegen; **skimmed milk** n Magermilch f

skin [skɪn] n Haut f; (*fur*) Fell nt;
(*peel*) Schale f; **skin diving** n
Sporttauchen nt; **skinny** adj dünn

skip [skɪp] vi hüpfen; (*with rope*)
Seil springen ▷ vt (*miss out*) überspringen; (*meal*) ausfallen lassen;
(*school, lesson*) schwänzen

ski pants ['skiːpænts] npl Skihose f; **ski pass** n Skipass m; **ski pole**
n Skistock m; **ski resort** n Skiort m

skirt [skɜːt] n Rock m

ski run ['skiːrʌn] n (Ski)abfahrt f;
ski stick n Skistock m; **ski tow** n
Schlepplift m

skittle ['skɪtl] n Kegel m; **~s** (*game*)
Kegeln nt

skive [skaɪv] vi **to ~ (off)** (*BRIT
fam*) sich drücken; (*from school*)
schwänzen; (*from work*) blaumachen

skull [skʌl] n Schädel m

sky [skaɪ] n Himmel m; **skydiving**
n Fallschirmspringen nt; **skylight**
n ʾDachfenster nt; **skyscraper** n
Wolkenkratzer m

slam [slæm] vt (*door*) zuschlagen;
slam on vt **to slam the brakes on**
voll auf die Bremse treten

slander ['slɑːndə*] n Verleumdung f ▷ vt verleumden

slang [slæŋ] n Slang m

slap [slæp] n Klaps m; (*across face*)
Ohrfeige f ▷ vt schlagen; **to ~ sb's
face** jdn ohrfeigen

slash [slæʃ] n (*punctuation mark*)
Schrägstrich m ▷ vt (*face, tyre*) aufschlitzen; (*prices*) stark herabsetzen

slate [sleɪt] n (*rock*) Schiefer m;
(*roof ~*) Schieferplatte f

slaughter ['slɔːtə*] vt (*animals*)

schlachten; (*people*) abschlachten

Slav [slɑːv] adj slawisch ▷ n Sla-
we m, Slawin f

slave [sleɪv] n Sklave m, Sklavin f;
slave away vi schuften; **slave-
-driver** n (*fam*) Sklaventreiber(in)
m(f); **slavery** ['sleɪvərɪ] n Sklave-
rei f

sleaze [sliːz] n (*corruption*) Kor-
ruption f; **sleazy** adj (*bar, district*)
zwielichtig

sledge [sledʒ] n Schlitten m

sleep [sliːp] (**slept, slept**) vi
schlafen; **to ~ with sb** mit jdm
schlafen ▷ n Schlaf m; **to put to ~**
(*animal*) einschläfern; **sleep in** vi
(*lie in*) ausschlafen; **sleeper** n (Rail:
train) Schlafwagenzug m; (*carriage*)
Schlafwagen m; **sleeping bag** n
Schlafsack m; **sleeping car** n
Schlafwagen m; **sleeping pill** n
Schlaftablette f; **sleepless** adj
schlaflos; **sleepy** adj schläfrig;
(*place*) verschlafen

sleet [sliːt] n Schneeregen m

sleeve [sliːv] n Ärmel m; **sleeveless** adj ärmellos

sleigh [sleɪ] n (Pferde)schlitten m

slender ['slendə*] adj schlank;
(*fig*) gering

slept [slept] pt, pp of **sleep**

slice [slaɪs] n Scheibe f; (*of cake,
tart, pizza*) Stück nt ▷ vt **to ~ (up)** in
Scheiben schneiden; **sliced bread**
n geschnittenes Brot

slid [slɪd] pt, pp of **slide**

slide [slaɪd] (**slid, slid**) vt gleiten
lassen; (*push*) schieben ▷ vi gleiten;
(*slip*) rutschen ▷ n (*foto*) Dia nt; (*in
playground*) Rutschbahn f; (*BRIT: for
hair*) Spange f

slight [slaɪt] adj leicht; (*problem,
difference*) klein; **not in the ~est**
nicht im Geringsten; **slightly** adv
etwas; (*injured*) leicht

slim [slɪm] adj (*person*) schlank;

(book) dünn; *(chance, hope)* gering ▷ vi abnehmen

slime [slaɪm] n Schleim m; **slimy** adj schleimig

sling [slɪŋ] **(slung, slung)** vt werfen ▷ n *(for arm)* Schlinge f

slip [slɪp] n *(mistake)* Flüchtigkeitsfehler m, **~ of paper** Zettel m ▷ vt *(put)* stecken: **to ~ on/off** *(garment)* an-/ausziehen; **it ~ped my mind** ich habe es vergessen ▷ vi *(lose balance)* (aus)rutschen; **slip away** vi *(leave)* sich wegstehlen; **slipper** n Hausschuh m; **slippery** adj *(path, road)* glatt; *(soap, fish)* glitschig; **slip-road** n *(BRIT: onto motorway)* Auffahrt f; *(: off motorway)* Ausfahrt f

slit [slɪt] vt aufschlitzen ▷ n Schlitz m

slope [sləʊp] n Neigung f; *(side of hill)* Hang m ▷ vi *(be sloping)* schräg sein, **slope down** vi *(land, road)* abfallen; **sloping** adj *(floor, roof)* schräg

sloppy ['slɒpɪ] adj *(careless)* schlampig; *(sentimental)* rührselig

slot [slɒt] n *(opening)* Schlitz m; *(inform)* Steckplatz m; **we have a ~ free at 2** *(free time)* um 2 ist noch ein Termin frei: **slot machine** n Automat m; *(for gambling)* Spielautomat m

Slovak ['sləʊvæk] adj slowakisch ▷ n *(person)* Slowake m, Slowakin f; *(language)* Slowakisch nt; **Slovakia** [sləʊ'vækɪə] n Slowakei f

Slovene ['sləʊviːn], **Slovenian** [sləʊ'viːnɪən] adj slowenisch ▷ n *(person)* Slowene m, Slowenin f; *(language)* Slowenisch nt; **Slovenia** [sləʊ'viːnɪə] n Slowenien nt

slow [sləʊ] adj langsam; *(business)* flau; **to be ~** *(clock)* nachgehen; *(stupid)* begriffsstutzig sein; **slow down** vi langsamer werden; *(when*

driving/walking) langsamer fahren/gehen, **slowly** adv langsam; **slow motion** n **in ~** in Zeitlupe

slug [slʌg] n *(Zool)* Nacktschnecke f

slum [slʌm] n Slum m

slump [slʌmp] n Rückgang m *(in an +dat)* ▷ vi *(onto chair etc)* sich fallen lassen; *(prices)* stürzen

slung [slʌŋ] pt, pp of **sling**

slur [slɜː*] n *(insult)* Verleumdung f; **slurred** [slɜːd] adj undeutlich

slush [slʌʃ] n *(snow)* Schneematsch m; **slushy** adj matschig; *(fig)* schmalzig

slut [slʌt] n *(pej)* Schlampe f

smack [smæk] n Klaps m ▷ vt **to ~ sb** jdm einen Klaps geben ▷ vi **to ~ of** riechen nach

small [smɔːl] adj klein; **small ads** npl *(BRIT)* Kleinanzeigen pl; **small change** n Kleingeld nt; **small letters** npl **in ~** in Kleinbuchstaben; **smallpox** n Pocken pl; **small print** n **the ~** das Kleingedruckte; **small-scale** adj *(map)* in kleinem Maßstab; **small talk** n Konversation f, Smalltalk m

smart [smɑːt] adj *(elegant)* schick; *(clever)* clever; **smart card** n Chipkarte f; **smartly** adv *(dressed)* schick

smash [smæʃ] n *(car crash)* Zusammenstoß m, Schmetterball m ▷ vt *(break)* zerschlagen; *(fig: record)* brechen, deutlich übertreffen ▷ vi *(break)* zerbrechen; **to ~ into** *(car)* krachen gegen; **smashing** adj *(fam)* toll

smear [smɪə*] n *(mark)* Fleck m; *(Med)* Abstrich m; *(fig)* Verleumdung f ▷ vt *(spread)* schmieren; *(make dirty)* beschmieren; *(fig)* verleumden

smell [smel] **(smelt** o **smelled, smelt** o **smelled)** vt riechen ▷ vi riechen *(of* nach); *(unpleasantly)* stinken ▷ n Geruch m; *(unpleasant)* Gestank m; **smelly** adj übel riechend; **smelt** [smelt] *pt, pp of* **smell**

smile [smaɪl] *n* Lächeln *nt* ▷ *vi* lächeln; **to ~ at sb** jdn anlächeln

smock [smɒk] *n* Kittel *m*

smog [smɒg] *n* Smog *m*

smoke [sməʊk] *n* Rauch *m* ▷ *vt* rauchen; (*food*) räuchern ▷ *vi* rauchen; **smoke alarm** *n* Rauchmelder *m*; **smoked** *adj* (*food*) geräuchert; **smoke-free** *adj* (*zone, building*) rauchfrei; **smoker** *n* Raucher(in) *m(f)*; **smoking** *n* Rauchen *nt*; **'no ~'** „Rauchen verboten"

smooth [smuːð] *adj* glatt; (*flight, crossing*) ruhig; (*movement*) geschmeidig; (*without problems*) reibungslos; (*pej: person*) aalglatt ▷ *vt* (*hair, dress*) glatt streichen; (*surface*) glätten; **smoothly** *adv* reibungslos; **to run ~** (*engine*) ruhig laufen

smudge [smʌdʒ] *n* (*writing, lipstick*) Fleck *m* ▷ *vt* verschmieren

smug [smʌg] *adj* selbstgefällig

smuggle ['smʌgl] *vt* schmuggeln; **to ~ in/out** herein-/herausschmuggeln

smutty ['smʌtɪ] *adj* (*obscene*) schmutzig

snack [snæk] *n* Imbiss *m*; **to have a ~** eine Kleinigkeit essen; **snack bar** *n* Imbissstube *f*

snail [sneɪl] *n* Schnecke *f*; **snail mail** *n* (*fam*) Schneckenpost *f*

snake [sneɪk] *n* Schlange *f*

snap [snæp] *n* (*photo*) Schnappschuss *m* ▷ *adj* (*decision*) spontan ▷ *vt* (*break*) zerbrechen; (*rope*) zerreißen ▷ *vi* (*break*) brechen; (*rope*) reißen; (*bite*) schnappen (*at* nach); **snap off** *vt* (*break*) abbrechen; **snap fastener** *n* (*US*) Druckknopf *m*; **snapshot** *n* Schnappschuss *m*

snatch [snætʃ] *vt* (*grab*) schnappen

sneak [sniːk] *vi* (*move*) schleichen;

sneakers *npl* (*US*) Turnschuhe *pl*

sneeze [sniːz] *vi* niesen

sniff [snɪf] *vi* schniefen; (*smell*) schnüffeln (*at* an +*dat*) ▷ *vt* schnuppern an +*dat*; (*glue*) schnüffeln

snob [snɒb] *n* Snob *m*; **snobbish** *adj* versnobt

snog [snɒg] *vi, vt* knutschen

snooker ['snuːkə*] *n* Snooker *nt*

snoop [snuːp] *vi* **to ~ (around)** (herum)schnüffeln

snooze [snuːz] *n, vi* **to (have a) ~** ein Nickerchen machen

snore [snɔː*] *vi* schnarchen

snorkel ['snɔːkl] *n* Schnorchel *m*; **snorkelling** *n* Schnorcheln *nt*; **to go ~** schnorcheln gehen

snout [snaʊt] *n* Schnauze *f*

snow [snəʊ] *n* Schnee *m* ▷ *vi* schneien; **snowball** *n* Schneeball *m*; **snowboard** *n* Snowboard *nt*; **snowboarding** *n* Snowboarding *nt*; **snowdrift** *n* Schneewehe *f*; **snowdrop** *n* Schneeglöckchen *nt*; **snowflake** *n* Schneeflocke *f*; **snowman** (*pl* **-men**) *n* Schneemann *m*; **snowplough**, **snowplow** (*US*) *n* Schneepflug *m*; **snowstorm** *n* Schneesturm *m*; **snowy** *adj* (*region*) schneereich; (*landscape*) verschneit

snug [snʌg] *adj* (*person, place*) gemütlich

snuggle up ['snʌglʌp] *vi* **to ~ to sb** sich an jdn ankuscheln

so [səʊ] *adv* so; **~ many/much** so viele/viel; **~ big that** so groß dass; **~ do I** ich auch; **I hope ~** hoffentlich; **30 or ~** etwa 30; **~ what?** na und?; **and ~ on** und so weiter ▷ *conj* (*therefore*) also, deshalb

soak [səʊk] *vt* durchnässen; (*leave in liquid*) einweichen; **I'm ~ed** ich bin durchnässt; **soaking** *adj* **~ (wet)** durchnässt

soap [səʊp] n Seife f; **soap (opera)** n Seifenoper f; **soap powder** n Waschpulver nt

sob [sɒb] vi schluchzen

sober ['səʊbə*] adj nüchtern; **sober up** vi nüchtern werden

so-called ['səʊ'kɔːld] adj so genannt

soccer ['sɒkə*] n Fußball m

sociable ['səʊʃəbl] adj gesellig

social ['səʊʃəl] adj sozial, (sociable) gesellig; **socialist** adj sozialistisch ▷ n Sozialist(in) m(f); **socialize** vi unter die Leute gehen; **social security** n (BRIT) Sozialhilfe f; (US) Sozialversicherung f

society [sə'saɪətɪ] n Gesellschaft f; (club) Verein m

sock [sɒk] n Socke f

socket ['sɒkɪt] n (Elec) Steckdose f

soda ['səʊdə] n (~ water) Soda f; (US: pop) Limo f; **soda water** n Sodawasser nt

sofa ['səʊfə] n Sofa nt; **sofa bed** n Schlafcouch f

soft [sɒft] adj weich, (quiet) leise; (lighting) gedämpft; (kind) gutmütig; (weak) nachgiebig; **~ drink** alkoholfreies Getränk; **softly** adv sanft, (quietly) leise; **software** n (Inform) Software f

soil [sɔɪl] n Erde f; (ground) Boden m

solar ['səʊlə*] adj Sonnen-, Solar-

solarium [sə'lɛərɪəm] n Solarium nt

sold [səʊld] pt, pp of **sell**

soldier ['səʊldʒə*] n Soldat(in) m(f)

sole [səʊl] n Sohle f; (fish) Seezunge f ▷ vt besohlen ▷ adj einzig; (owner, responsibility) alleinig; **solely** adv nur

solemn ['sɒləm] adj feierlich; (person) ernst

solicitor [sə'lɪsɪtə*] n (BRIT)

Rechtsanwalt m, Rechtsanwältin f

solid ['sɒlɪd] adj (hard) fest; (gold, oak etc) massiv; (~ly built) solide; (meal) kräftig; **three hours ~** drei volle Stunden

solitary ['sɒlɪtərɪ] adj einsam; (single) einzeln; **solitude** ['sɒlɪtjuːd] n Einsamkeit f

solo ['səʊləʊ] n (Mus) Solo nt

soluble ['sɒljʊbl] adj löslich; (problem) lösbar; **solution** [sə'luːʃən] n Lösung f (to +gen); **solve** [sɒlv] vt lösen

somber (US), **sombre** ['sɒmbə*] adj düster

some [sʌm] adj etwas; (with plural nouns) einige; **~ woman** or **other** irgendeine Frau; **would you like ~ more (wine)?** möchten Sie noch etwas (Wein)? ▷ pron etwas; (plural) einige; **~ of the team** einige (aus) der Mannschaft; **would you like ~ more?** möchten Sie noch etwas? ▷ adv **~ 50 people** (or so) etwa 50 Leute

somebody pron jemand; **~ (or other)** irgendjemand; **~ else** jemand anders; **someday** adv irgendwann; **somehow** adv irgendwie; **someone** pron see **somebody**; **someplace** adv (US) see **somewhere**; **something** ['sʌmθɪŋ] pron etwas; **~ (or other)** irgendetwas; **~ else** etwas anderes; **~ nice** etwas Nettes; **would you like ~ to drink?** möchten Sie etwas trinken? ▷ adv **~ like 20** ungefähr 20; **sometime** adv irgendwann; **sometimes** adv manchmal; **somewhat** adv ein wenig; **somewhere** adv irgendwo; (to a place) irgendwohin; **~ else** irgendwo anders; (to another place) irgendwo anders hin; **~ around 6** ungefähr 6

son [sʌn] n Sohn m

song [sɒŋ] n Lied nt

son-in-law ['sʌnɪnlɔ:] (pl **sons-in-law**) n Schwiegersohn m

soon [su:n] adv bald; (early) früh; **too ~** zu früh; **as ~ as I ...** sobald ich ...; **as ~ as possible** so bald wie möglich; **sooner** adv (time) früher; (for preference) lieber

soot [sut] n Ruß m

soothe [su:ð] vt beruhigen; (pain) lindern

sophisticated [sə'fɪstɪkeɪtɪd] adj (person) kultiviert; (machine) hoch entwickelt; (plan) ausgeklügelt

sophomore ['sɔfəmɔ:] n (US) College-Student(in) m(f) im zweiten Jahr

soppy ['sɔpɪ] adj (fam) rührselig

soprano [sə'prɑ:nəʊ] n Sopran m

sore [sɔ:*] adj **to be ~** weh tun; **to have a ~ throat** Halsschmerzen haben ▷ n wunde Stelle

sorrow ['sɔrəʊ] n Kummer m

sorry ['sɔrɪ] adj (sight, figure) traurig; (I'm ~) (excusing) Entschuldigung!; **I'm ~** (regretful) es tut mir leid; **~?** wie bitte?; **I feel ~ for him** er tut mir leid

sort [sɔ:t] n Art f; **what ~ of film is it?** was für ein Film ist das?; **a ~ of** eine Art +gen; **all ~s of things** alles Mögliche ▷ adv **~ of** (fam) irgendwie ▷ vt sortieren; **everything's ~ed** (dealt with) alles ist geregelt; **sort out** vt (classify etc) sortieren; (problems) lösen

sought [sɔ:t] pt, pp of **seek**

soul [səʊl] n Seele f; (music) Soul m

sound [saʊnd] adj (healthy) gesund; (safe) sicher; (sensible) vernünftig; (theory) stichhaltig; (thrashing) tüchtig ▷ adv **to be ~ asleep** fest schlafen ▷ n (noise) Geräusch nt; (Mus) Klang m; (Tel) Ton m ▷ vt **to ~ the alarm** Alarm schlagen; **to ~ one's horn** hupen ▷ vi (seem) klingen (like wie); **soundcard** n (Inform)

Soundkarte f; **sound effects** npl Klangeffekte pl; **soundproof** adj schalldicht; **soundtrack** n (of film) Filmmusik f, Soundtrack m

soup [su:p] n Suppe f

sour ['saʊə*] adj sauer; (fig) mürrisch

source [sɔ:s] n Quelle f; (fig) Ursprung m

sour cream [saʊə'kri:m] n saure Sahne

south [saʊθ] n Süden m; **to the ~ of** südlich von ▷ adv (go, face) nach Süden ▷ adj Süd-; **South Africa** n Südafrika nt; **South African** adj südafrikanisch ▷ n Südafrikaner(in) m(f); **South America** n Südamerika nt; **South American** adj südamerikanisch ▷ n Südamerikaner(in) m(f); **southbound** adj (in) Richtung Süden; **southern** ['sʌðən] adj Süd-, südlich; **~ Europe** Südeuropa nt; **southwards** ['saʊθwədz] adv nach Süden

souvenir [su:və'nɪə*] n Andenken nt (of an +akk)

sow [saʊ] (sowed, sown o sowed) vt (a. fig) säen; (field) besäen ▷ [saʊ] n (pig) Sau f

soya bean ['sɔɪə'bi:n] n Sojabohne f

soy sauce ['sɔɪ'sɔ:s] n Sojasoße f

spa [spɑ:] n (place) Kurort m

space [speɪs] n (room) Platz m, Raum m; (outer ~) Weltraum m; (gap) Zwischenraum m; (for parking) Lücke f; **space bar** n Leertaste f; **spacecraft** (pl -) n Raumschiff m; **space ship** n Raumschiff nt; **space shuttle** n Raumfähre f

spacing ['speɪsɪŋ] n (in text) Zeilenabstand m; **double ~** zweizeiliger Abstand

spacious ['speɪʃəs] adj geräumig

spade [speɪd] n Spaten m; **~s** Pik nt

spaghetti [spə'getɪ] nsing Spaghetti pl

Spain [speɪn] n Spanien nt

spam [spæm] n (Inform) Spam m

Spaniard ['spænɪəd] n Spanier(in) m(f); **Spanish** ['spænɪʃ] adj spanisch ▷ n (language) Spanisch nt

spanner ['spænə*] n (BRIT) Schraubenschlüssel m

spare [spɛə*] adj (as replacement) Ersatz-, ~ **part** Ersatzteil nt; ~ **room** Gästezimmer nt; ~ **time** Freizeit f; ~ **tyre** Ersatzreifen m ▷ n (~ part) Ersatzteil nt ▷ vt (lives, feelings) verschonen; **can you ~ (me) a moment?** hätten Sie einen Moment Zeit?

spark [spɑːk] n Funke m; **sparkle** ['spɑːkl] vi funkeln; **sparkling wine** n Schaumwein m, Sekt m; **spark plug** n ['spɑːkplʌg] n Zündkerze f

sparrow ['spærəʊ] n Spatz m

sparse [spɑːs] adj spärlich; **sparsely** adv ~ **populated** dünn besiedelt

spasm ['spæzəm] n (Med) Krampf m

spat [spæt] pt, pp of **spit**

speak [spiːk] (**spoke, spoken**) vt sprechen; **can you ~ French?** sprechen Sie Französisch?; **to ~ one's mind** seine Meinung sagen ▷ vi sprechen (to mit, zu); (make speech) reden; **~ing** (Tel) am Apparat; **so as to** sozusagen; **~ for yourself** das meinst auch nur du!; **speak up** vi (louder) lauter sprechen; **speaker** n Sprecher(in) m(f); (public ~) Redner(in) m(f); (loud~) Lautsprecher m

spear [spɪə*] n Speer m

special ['spɛʃəl] adj besondere(r, s); special n (on menu) Tagesgericht nt; (Tv, Radio) Sondersendung f; **special delivery** n Eilzustellung f; **special effects** npl Spezialeffekte

pl; **specialist** n Spezialist(in) m(f); (Tech) Fachmann m, Fachfrau f; (Med) Facharzt m, Fachärztin f; **speciality** [spɛʃɪ'ælɪtɪ] n Spezialität f; **specialize** vi sich spezialisieren (in auf +akk); **specially** adv besonders; (specifically) extra; **special offer** n Sonderangebot nt; **specialty** n (US) see **speciality**

species ['spiːʃiːz] nsing Art f

specific [spə'sɪfɪk] adj spezifisch; (precise) genau; **specify** ['spɛsɪfaɪ] vt genau angeben

specimen ['spɛsɪmən] n (sample) Probe f; (example) Exemplar nt

specs [spɛks] npl (fam) Brille f

spectacle ['spɛktəkl] n Schauspiel nt

spectacles npl Brille f

spectacular [spɛk'tækjʊlə*] adj spektakulär

spectator [spɛk'teɪtə*] n Zuschauer(in) m(f)

sped [spɛd] pt, pp of **speed**

speech [spiːtʃ] n (address) Rede f; (faculty) Sprache f; **to make a ~** eine Rede halten; **speechless** adj sprachlos (with vor +dat)

speed [spiːd] (**sped** o **speeded, sped** o **speeded**) vi rasen; (exceed ~ limit) zu schnell fahren ▷ n Geschwindigkeit f; (of film) Lichtempfindlichkeit f; **speed up** vt beschleunigen ▷ vi schneller werden / fahren; (drive faster) schneller fahren; **speedboat** n Rennboot nt; **speed bump** n Bodenschwelle f; **speed camera** n Blitzgerät nt; **speed limit** n Geschwindigkeitsbegrenzung f; **speedometer** [spɪ'dɒmɪtə*] n Tacho(meter) m; **speed trap** n Radarfalle f; **speedy** adj schnell

spell [spɛl] (**spelt** o **spelled, spelt** o **spelled**) vt buchstabieren; **how do you ~ ...?** wie schreibt man ...? ▷

n (period) Weile *f*; (enchantment)
Zauber *m*; **a cold/hot ~** (weather)
ein Kälteeinbruch/eine Hitzewelle;
spellchecker *n* (Inform) Recht-
schreibprüfung *f*; **spelling** *n*
Rechtschreibung *f*; (of a word)
Schreibweise *f*; **~ mistake** Schreibfehler *m*

spelt [spelt] *pt, pp of* **spell**

spend [spend] (**spent, spent**) *vt*
(money) ausgeben (on für); (time)
verbringen; **spending money** *n*
Taschengeld *nt*

spent [spent] *pt, pp of* **spend**

sperm [spɜːm] *n* Sperma *nt*

sphere [sfɪə*] *n* (globe) Kugel *f*;
(fig) Sphäre *f*

spice [spaɪs] *n* Gewürz *nt*; (fig)
Würze *f* ▷ *vt* würzen; **spicy**
['spaɪsɪ] *adj* würzig; (fig) pikant

spider ['spaɪdə*] *n* Spinne *f*

spike [spaɪk] *n* (on railing etc)
Spitze *f*; (on shoe, tyre) Spike *m*

spill [spɪl] (**spilt** *o* **spilled, spilt** *o*
spilled) *vt* verschütten

spin [spɪn] (**spun, spun**) *vi* (turn)
sich drehen; (washing) schleudern;
my head is ~ning mir dreht sich
alles ▷ *vt* (turn) drehen; (coin)
hochwerfen ▷ *n* (turn) Drehung *f*

spinach ['spɪnɪtʃ] *n* Spinat *m*

spin-drier ['spɪndraɪə*] *n* Wäscheschleuder *f*; **spin-dry** *vt*
schleudern

spine [spaɪn] *n* Rückgrat *nt*; (of
animal, plant) Stachel *m*; (of book)
Rücken *m*

spiral ['spaɪərəl] *n* Spirale *f* ▷ *adj*
spiralförmig; **spiral staircase** *n*
Wendeltreppe *f*

spire [spaɪə*] *n* Turmspitze *f*

spirit ['spɪrɪt] *n* (essence, soul) Geist
m; (humour, mood) Stimmung *f*;
(courage) Mut *m*; (verve) Elan *m*; **~s** *pl*
(drinks) Spirituosen *pl*

spiritual ['spɪrɪtjʊəl] *adj* geistig;

(Rel) geistlich

spit [spɪt] (**spat, spat**) *vi* spucken
▷ *n* (for roasting) (Brat)spieß *m*;
(saliva) Spucke *f*; **spit out** *vt* aus-
spucken

spite [spaɪt] *n* Bosheit *f*; **in ~
of** trotz +*gen*; **spiteful** *adj* boshaft

spitting image ['spɪtɪŋ'ɪmɪdʒ] *n*
he's the ~ of you er ist dir wie aus
dem Gesicht geschnitten

splash [splæʃ] *vt* (person, object)
bespritzen ▷ *vi* (liquid) spritzen;
(play in water) planschen

splendid ['splendɪd] *adj* herrlich

splinter ['splɪntə*] *n* Splitter *m*

split [splɪt] (**split, split**) *vt* (stone,
wood) spalten; (share) teilen ▷ *vi*
(stone, wood) sich spalten; (seam)
platzen ▷ *n* (in stone, wood) Spalt *m*;
(in clothing) Riss *m*; (fig) Spaltung *f*;
split up *vi* (couple) sich trennen ▷
vt (divide up) aufteilen; **split ends**
npl (Haar)spliss *m*; **splitting** *adj*
(headache) rasend

spoil [spɔɪl] (**spoiled** *o* **spoilt,
spoiled** *o* **spoilt**) *vt* verderben;
(child) verwöhnen ▷ *vi* (food) verderben

spoilt [spɔɪlt] *pt, pp of* **spoil**

spoke [spəʊk] *pt of* **speak** ▷ *n*
Speiche *f*

spoken ['spəʊkən] *pp of* **speak**

spokesperson ['spəʊkspɜːsən] (*pl*
-people) *n* Sprecher(in) *m(f)*

sponge [spʌndʒ] *n* (for washing)
Schwamm *m*; **sponge bag** *n* Kulturbeutel *m*; **sponge cake** *n* Bis-
kuitkuchen *m*

sponsor ['spɒnsə*] *n* (of event,
programme) Sponsor(in) *m(f)* ▷ *vt*
unterstützen; (event, programme)
sponsern

spontaneous, spontaneously
[spɒn'teɪnɪəs, -lɪ] *adj, adv* spontan

spool [spuːl] *n* Spule *f*

spoon [spuːn] *n* Löffel *m*

sport [spɔ:t] n Sport m, **sports**
car n Sportwagen m; **sports cen-**
tre n Sportzentrum nt; **sports**
club n Sportverein m; **sportsman**
(pl **-men**) n Sportler m; **sports-**
wear n Sportkleidung f; **sports-**
woman (pl **-women**) n Sportlerin f;
sporty adj sportlich

spot [spɒt] n (dot) Punkt m; (in
paint, blood etc) Fleck m; (place) Stelle
f; (pimple) Pickel m; **on the ~** n vor Ort;
(at once) auf der Stelle ▷ vt (notice)
entdecken; (difference) erkennen;
spotless adj (clean) blitzsauber;
spotlight n (lamp) Scheinwerfer m;
spotty adj (pimply) pickelig

spouse [spaʊs] n Gatte m, Gattin f

spout [spaʊt] n Schnabel m

sprain [spreɪn] n Verstauchung f
▷ vt **to ~ one's ankle** sich den
Knöchel verstauchen

sprang [spræŋ] pt of **spring**

spray [spreɪ] n (liquid in can) Spray
nt o m; (~ can) Spraydose f ▷ vt
(plant, insects) besprühen; (car)
spritzen

spread [spred] (**spread, spread**)
vt (open out) ausbreiten; (news, disease) verbreiten; (butter, jam) streichen; (bread, surface) bestreichen ▷
vi (news, disease, fire) sich verbreiten
▷ n (of disease, religion etc) Verbrei-
tung f; (for bread) Aufstrich m;
spreadsheet n (Inform) Tabellen-
kalkulation f

spring [sprɪŋ] (**sprang, sprung**)
vi (leap) springen ▷ n (season)
Frühling m; (coil) Feder f; (water)
Quelle f, Sprung m ▷ n Sprung-
brett nt; **spring onion** n (BRIT)
Frühlingszwiebel f; **spring roll** n
(BRIT) Frühlingsrolle f; **springy** adj
(mattress) federnd

sprinkle ['sprɪŋkl] vt streuen;
(liquid) beträufeln; **to ~ sth with**
sth etw mit etw bestreuen; (with

liquid) etw mit etw besprengen;
sprinkler n (for lawn) Rasenspren-
ger m; (for fire) Sprinkler m

sprint [sprɪnt] vi rennen; (Sport)
sprinten

sprout [spraʊt] vi (of plant) Trieb
m; (from seed) Keim m; (**Brussels**) **~s**
pl Rosenkohl m ▷ vi sprießen

sprung [sprʌŋ] pp of **spring**

spun [spʌn] pt, pp of **spin**

spy [spaɪ] n Spion(in) m(f) ▷ vi
spionieren; **to ~ on sb** jdm nach-
spionieren ▷ vt erspähen

squad [skwɒd] n (Sport) Mannschaft f; (police ~) Kommando nt

square [skweə*] n (shape) Quadrat nt; (open space) Platz m; (on
chessboard etc) Feld nt ▷ adj (in
shape) quadratisch; **2 ~ metres** 2
Quadratmeter; **2 metres ~** 2 Meter
im Quadrat ▷ vt **3 ~d** 3 hoch 2;
square root n Quadratwurzel f

squash [skwɒʃ] n (drink) Frucht-
saftgetränk nt; (Sport) Squash nt; (US:
vegetable) Kürbis m ▷ vt zerquetschen

squat [skwɒt] vi (be crouching)
hocken; **to ~ (down)** sich (hin)ho-
cken

squeak [skwi:k] vi (door, shoes etc)
quietschen; (animal) quieken

squeal [skwi:l] vi (person) kreischen (with vor +dat)

squeeze [skwi:z] vt drücken; (orange) auspressen ▷ vi **to ~ into the**
car sich in den Wagen hineinzwän-
gen, **squeeze up** vi (on bench etc)
zusammenrücken

squid [skwɪd] n Tintenfisch m

squint [skwɪnt] vi schielen; (in
bright light) blinzeln

squirrel ['skwɪrəl] n Eichhörnchen nt

squirt [skwɜ:t] vt, vi (liquid)
spritzen

Sri Lanka [sri:'læŋkə] n Sri Lanka

nt

st abbr = **stone** Gewichtseinheit (6,35 kg)

St abbr = **saint** St.; abbr = **street** Str.

stab [stæb] vt (person) einstechen auf +akk; (to death) erstechen; **stabbing** adj (pain) stechend

stabilize ['steɪbəlaɪz] vt stabilisieren ▷ vi sich stabilisieren

stable ['steɪbl] n Stall m ▷ adj stabil

stack [stæk] n (pile) Stapel m ▷ vt **to ~ (up)** (auf)stapeln

stadium ['steɪdɪəm] n Stadion nt

staff [stɑːf] n (personnel) Personal nt, Lehrkräfte pl

stag [stæg] n Hirsch m

stag night n (BRIT) Junggesellenabschied m

stage [steɪdʒ] n (Theat) Bühne f; (of project, life etc) Stadium nt; (of journey) Etappe f; **at this ~** zu diesem Zeitpunkt ▷ vt (Theat) aufführen, inszenieren; (demonstration) veranstalten

stagger ['stægə*] vi wanken ▷ vt (amaze) verblüffen; **staggering** adj (amazing) umwerfend; (amount, price) Schwindel erregend

stagnant ['stægnənt] adj (water) stehend; **stagnate** [stæg'neɪt] vi (fig) stagnieren

stain [steɪn] n Fleck m; **stained-glass window** n Buntglasfenster nt; **stainless steel** n rostfreier Stahl; **stain remover** n Fleck(en)entferner m

stair [steə*] n (Treppen)stufe f; **~s** pl Treppe f; **staircase** n Treppe f

stake [steɪk] n (post) Pfahl m; (in betting) Einsatz m; (Fin) Anteil m (in an +dat); **to be at ~** auf dem Spiel stehen

stale [steɪl] adj (bread) alt; (beer) schal

stalk [stɔːk] n Stiel m ▷ vt (wild animal) sich anpirschen an +akk; (person) nachstellen +dat

stall [stɔːl] n (in market) (Verkaufs)stand m; (in stable) Box f; **~s** pl (Theat) Parkett nt ▷ vt (engine) abwürgen ▷ vi (driver) den Motor abwürgen; (car) stehen bleiben; (delay) Zeit schinden

stamina ['stæmɪnə] n Durchhaltevermögen nt

stammer ['stæmə*] n, vt stottern

stamp [stæmp] n (postage ~) Briefmarke f; (for document) Stempel m ▷ vt (passport etc) stempeln; (mail) frankieren; **stamped addressed envelope** n frankierter Rückumschlag

stand [stænd] (stood, stood) vi stehen; (as candidate) kandidieren ▷ vt (place) stellen; (endure) aushalten; **I can't ~ her** ich kann sie nicht ausstehen ▷ n (stall) Stand m; (seats in stadium) Tribüne f; (for coats, bicycles) Ständer m; (for small objects) Gestell nt; **stand around** vi herumstehen; **stand by** vi (be ready) sich bereithalten; (be inactive) danebenstehen ▷ vt (fig: person) halten zu; (decision, promise) stehen zu; **stand for** vt (represent) stehen für; (tolerate) hinnehmen; **stand in for** vt einspringen für; **stand out** vi (be noticeable) auffallen; **stand up** vi (get up) aufstehen ▷ vt (girlfriend, boyfriend) versetzen; **stand up for** vt sich einsetzen für; **stand up to** vt **to ~ to ~ sb** jdm die Stirn bieten

standard ['stændəd] n (norm) Norm f; **~ of living** Lebensstandard m ▷ adj Standard-

standardize ['stændədaɪz] vt vereinheitlichen

stand-by ['stændbaɪ] n (thing in reserve) Reserve f; **on ~** in Bereitschaft ▷ adj (flight, ticket) Standby-;

standing order n (at bank) Dauerauftrag m; **standpoint** ['stændpɔɪnt] n Standpunkt m; **standstill** ['stændstɪl] n Stillstand m; **to come to a ~** stehen bleiben; (fig) zum Erliegen kommen

stank [stæŋk] pt of **stink**

staple ['steɪpl] n (for paper) Heftklammer f ▷ vt heften (to an +akk); **stapler** n Hefter m

star [staː*] n Stern m; (person) Star m ▷ vt **the film ~s Hugh Grant** der Film zeigt Hugh Grant in der Hauptrolle ▷ vi die Hauptrolle spielen

starch [staːtʃ] n Stärke f

stare [steə*] vi starren; **to ~ at** anstarren

starfish ['staːfɪʃ] n Seestern m

star sign ['staːsaɪn] n Sternzeichen nt

start [staːt] n (beginning) Anfang m, Beginn m; (Sport) Start m; (lead) Vorsprung m; **from the ~** von Anfang an ▷ vi anfangen; (car, engine) starten; (business, family) gründen; **to ~ to do sth, to ~ doing sth** anfangen, etw zu tun ▷ vt anfangen; (car) anspringen; (on journey) aufbrechen; (Sport) starten; (jump) zusammenfahren; **~ing from Monday** ab Montag: **start off** vt (discussion, process etc) anfangen, beginnen ▷ vi (begin) anfangen, beginnen; (on journey) aufbrechen; **start over** vi (US) wieder anfangen; **start up** vi (in business) anfangen ▷ vt (car, engine) starten; (business) gründen; **starter** n (BRIT: first course) Vorspeise f; (Auto) Anlasser m; **starting point** n (a. fig) Ausgangspunkt m

startle ['staːtl] vt erschrecken; **startling** adj überraschend

starve [staːv] vi hungern; (to death) verhungern; **I'm ~ing** ich habe einen Riesenhunger

state [steɪt] n (condition) Zustand m; (Pol) Staat m; **~ of health/mind** Gesundheits-/Geisteszustand m; **the (United) States** die (Vereinigten) Staaten ▷ adj Staats-; (control, education) staatlich ▷ vt erklären; (facts, name etc) angeben; **stated** adj (fixed) festgesetzt

statement ['steɪtmənt] n (official declaration) Erklärung f; (to police) Aussage f; (from bank) Kontoauszug m

state-of-the-art [steɪtəvðiˈaːt] adj hochmodern, auf dem neuesten Stand der Technik

static ['stætɪk] adj (unchanging) konstant

station ['steɪʃən] n (for trains, buses) Bahnhof m; (underground ~) Station f; (police ~; fire ~) Wache f; (TV, Radio) Sender m ▷ vt (Mil) stationieren

stationer's ['steɪʃənəz] n ~ (shop) Schreibwarengeschäft nt; **stationery** n Schreibwaren pl

station wagon ['steɪʃənwægən] n (US) Kombiwagen m

statistics [stəˈtɪstɪks] nsing (science) Statistik f; (figures) Statistiken pl

statue ['stætjuː] n Statue f

status ['steɪtəs] n Status m; (prestige) Ansehen nt; **status bar** n (Inform) Statuszeile f

stay [steɪ] n Aufenthalt m ▷ vi bleiben; (with friends, in hotel) wohnen (with bei); **to ~ the night** übernachten; **stay away** vi wegbleiben; **to ~ from sb** sich von jdm fern halten; **stay behind** vi zurückbleiben; (at work) länger bleiben; **stay in** vi (at home) zu Hause bleiben; **stay out** vi (not come home) wegbleiben; **stay up** vi (at night) aufbleiben

steady ['stedɪ] adj (speed) gleichmäßig; (progress, increase) stetig;
(job, income, girlfriend) fest; (worker)
zuverlässig; (hand) ruhig; **they've
been going ~ for two years** sie sind
seit zwei Jahren fest zusammen ▷
vt (nerves) beruhigen; **to ~ oneself**
Halt finden

steak [steɪk] n Steak nt; (of fish)
Filet nt

steal [stiːl] (**stole, stolen**) vt
stehlen; **to ~ sth from sb** jdm etw
stehlen

steam [stiːm] n Dampf m ▷ vt
(Gastr) dämpfen; **steam up** vi
(window) beschlagen; **steamer** n
(Gastr) Dampfkochtopf m; (ship)
Dampfer m; **steam iron** n
Dampfbügeleisen nt

steel [stiːl] n Stahl m ▷ adj Stahl-

steep [stiːp] adj steil

steeple ['stiːpl] n Kirchturm m

steer [stɪə*] vt, vi steuern; (car,
bike etc) lenken; **steering** n (Auto)
Lenkung f; **steering wheel** n
Steuer nt, Lenkrad nt

stem [stem] n (of plant, glass) Stiel
m

step [step] n Schritt m; (stair) Stufe
f; (measure) Maßnahme f; **~ by ~**
Schritt für Schritt ▷ vi treten; **~ this
way, please** hier entlang, bitte;
step down vi (resign) zurücktreten

stepbrother n Stiefbruder m;
stepchild (pl **-children**) n Stiefkind
nt; **stepfather** n Stiefvater m

stepladder n Trittleiter f

stepmother n Stiefmutter f;
stepsister n Stiefschwester f

stereo ['steriəʊ] (pl **-s**) n **~ (system)** Stereoanlage f

sterile ['steraɪl] adj steril; **sterilize** ['sterɪlaɪz] vt sterilisieren

sterling ['stɜːlɪŋ] n (Fin) das Pfund
Sterling

stern [stɜːn] adj streng ▷ n Heck
nt

stew [stjuː] n Eintopf m

steward ['stjuːəd] n (on plane,
ship) Steward m; **stewardess** n
Stewardess f

stick [stɪk] (**stuck, stuck**) vt (with
glue etc) kleben; (pin etc) stecken;
(fam: put) tun ▷ vi (get jammed)
klemmen; (hold fast) haften ▷ n
Stock m; (hockey ~) Schläger m; (of
chalk) Stück nt; (of celery, rhubarb)
Stange f; **stick out** vt **to stick
one's tongue out (at sb)** (jdm) die
Zunge herausstrecken ▷ vi (pro-
trude) vorstehen; (ears) abstehen; (be
noticeable) auffallen; **stick to** vt
(rules, plan etc) sich halten an +akk;
sticker ['stɪkə*] n Aufkleber m;
sticky ['stɪkɪ] adj klebrig; (weather) schwül; **~ label** Aufkleber m; **~
tape** Klebeband nt

stiff [stɪf] adj steif

stifle ['staɪfl] vt (yawn etc, opposition) unterdrücken; **stifling** adj
drückend

still [stɪl] adj still; (drink) ohne
Kohlensäure ▷ adv (yet, even now)
(immer) noch; (all the same) immer-
hin; (sit, stand) still; **he ~ doesn't
believe me** er glaubt mir immer
noch nicht; **keep ~** halt still!; **big-
ger/better ~** noch größer/besser

still life (pl **still lives**) n Stillleben nt

stimulate ['stɪmjʊleɪt] vt anre-
gen, stimulieren; **stimulating** adj
anregend; **stimulus** ['stɪmjʊləs] n
(incentive) Anreiz m

sting [stɪŋ] (**stung, stung**) vt
(wound with ~) stechen ▷ vi (eyes,
ointment etc) brennen ▷ n (insect
wound) Stich m

stingy ['stɪndʒɪ] adj (fam) geizig

stink [stɪŋk] (**stank, stunk**) vi
stinken (of nach) ▷ n Gestank m

stir [stɜː*] vt (mix) (um)rühren; **stir
up** vt (mob) aufhetzen; (memories)

wachrufen: **to ~ trouble** Unruhe stiften; **stir-fry** vt (unter Rühren) kurz anbraten

stitch ['stɪtʃ] n (in sewing) Stich m; (in knitting) Masche f; **to have a ~** (pain) Seitenstechen haben; **he had to have ~es** er musste genäht werden; **she had her ~es out** ihr wurden die Fäden gezogen; **to be in ~es** (fam) sich kanuttlachen ▷ vt nähen; **stitch up** vt (hole, wound) nähen

stock [stɔk] n (supply) Vorrat m (of an +dat); (of shop) Bestand m; (for soup etc) Brühe f; **~s and shares** pl Aktien und Wertpapiere pl; **to be in/out of ~** vorrätig/nicht vorrätig sein; **to take ~** Inventur machen; (fig) Bilanz ziehen ▷ vt (keep in shop) führen; **stock up** vi sich eindecken (on, with mit)

stockbroker n Börsenmakler(in) m(f)

stock cube n Brühwurfel m

stock exchange n Börse f

stocking ['stɔkɪŋ] n Strumpf m

stock market n ['stɔkmɑːkɪt] n Börse f

stole [stəʊl] pt of **steal**; **stolen** ['stəʊlən] pp of **steal**

stomach ['stʌmək] n Magen m; (belly) Bauch m; **on an empty ~** auf leeren Magen; **stomach-ache** n Magenschmerzen pl; **stomach upset** n Magenverstimmung f

stone [stəʊn] n Stein m; (seed) Kern m, Stein m; (weight) britische Gewichtseinheit (6,35 kg) ▷ adj Stein-, aus Stein; **stony** adj (ground) steinig

stood [stʊd] pt, pp of **stand**

stool [stuːl] n Hocker m

stop [stɔp] n Halt m; (for bus, train) Haltestelle f; **to come to a ~** anhalten ▷ vt (vehicle, passer-by) anhalten; (put an end to) ein Ende

machen +dat; (cease) aufhören mit; (prevent from happening) verhindern; (bleeding) stillen; (engine, machine) abstellen; (payments) einstellen; (cheque) sperren; **to ~ doing sth** aufhören, etw zu tun; **to ~ sb (from) doing sth** jdn daran hindern, etw zu tun, ~ **it** hör auf (damit)! ▷ vi (vehicle) anhalten; (during journey) Halt machen; (vegetarian, clock, heart) stehen bleiben; (rain, noise) aufhören; **stop by** vi vorbeischauen; **stop over** vi Halt machen; (overnight) übernachten; **stopover** n (on journey) Zwischenstation f; **stopper** n Stöpsel m; **stop sign** n Stoppschild nt; **stopwatch** n Stoppuhr f

storage ['stɔːrɪdʒ] n Lagerung f; **store** [stɔː*] n (supply) Vorrat m (of an +dat); (place for storage) Lager nt; (large shop) Kaufhaus nt; (US: shop) Geschäft nt ▷ vt lagern; (inform) speichern; **storecard** n Kundenkreditkarte f; **storeroom** n Lagerraum m

storey ['stɔːrɪ] n (BRIT) Stock m, Stockwerk nt

storm [stɔːm] n Sturm m; (thunder~) Gewitter nt ▷ vt, vi (with movement) stürmen; **stormy** adj stürmisch

story ['stɔːrɪ] n Geschichte f; (plot) Handlung f; (US: of building) Stock m, Stockwerk nt

stout [staʊt] adj (fat) korpulent; (shoes) fest

stove [stəʊv] n Herd m; (for heating) Ofen m

stow [stəʊ] vt verstauen; **stowaway** n blinder Passagier

straight [streɪt] adj (not curved) gerade; (hair) glatt, (honest) ehrlich (with zu); (fam: heterosexual) hetero ▷ adv (directly) direkt; (immediately) sofort; (drink) pur; (think) klar; **~**

ahead geradeaus; **to go ~ on** geradeaus weitergehen/weiterfahren; **straightaway** adv sofort; **straightforward** adj einfach; (person) aufrichtig

strain [streɪn] n Belastung f ▷ vt (eyes) überanstrengen; (rope, relationship) belasten; (vegetables) abgießen; **to ~ a muscle** sich einen Muskel zerren; **strained** adj (laugh, smile) gezwungen; (relations) gespannt; **~ muscle** Muskelzerrung f; **strainer** n Sieb nt

strand [strænd] n (of wool) Faden m; (of hair) Strähne f ▷ vt **to be (left) ~ed** (person) festsitzen

strange [streɪndʒ] adj seltsam; (unfamiliar) fremd; **strangely** adv seltsam; **~ enough** seltsamerweise; **stranger** n Fremde(r) mf; **I'm a ~ here** ich bin hier fremd

strangle ['stræŋgl] vt (kill) erdrosseln

strap [stræp] n Riemen m; (on dress etc) Träger m; (on watch) Band nt ▷ vt (fasten) festschnallen (to an +dat); **strapless** adj trägerlos

strategy ['strætɪdʒɪ] n Strategie f

straw [strɔ:] n Stroh nt; (drinking ~) Strohhalm m

strawberry n Erdbeere f

stray [streɪ] n streunendes Tier ▷ adj (cat, dog) streunend ▷ vi streunen

streak [stri:k] n (of colour, dirt) Streifen m; (in hair) Strähne f; (in character) Zug m

stream [stri:m] n (flow of liquid) Strom m; (brook) Bach m ▷ vi strömen; **streamer** n (of paper) Luftschlange f

street [stri:t] n Straße f; **streetcar** n (US) Straßenbahn f; **street lamp**, **street light** n Straßenlaterne f; **street map** n Stadtplan m

strength [streŋθ] n Kraft f,

Stärke f; **strengthen** vt verstärken; (fig) stärken

strenuous ['strenjʊəs] adj anstrengend

stress [stres] n Stress m; (on word) Betonung f; **to be under ~** im Stress sein ▷ vt betonen; (put under ~) stressen; **stressed** adj **~ (out)** gestresst

stretch [stretʃ] n (of land) Stück nt; (of road) Strecke f ▷ vt (material, shoes) dehnen; (rope, canvas) spannen; (person in job etc) fordern; **to ~ one's legs** (walk) sich die Beine vertreten ▷ vi (person) sich erstrecken; (area) sich erstrecken (to bis zu); **stretch out** vi **to stretch one's hand/legs out** die Hand/die Beine ausstrecken, ausstrecken ▷ vt (reach) sich strecken; (lie down) sich ausstrecken; **stretcher** n Tragbahre f

strict, strictly [strɪkt, -lɪ] adj, adv (severe(ly)) streng; (exact(ly)) genau

strike [straɪk] n (of workers) Streik m ▷ (struck, struck) vt (match) anzünden; (hit) schlagen; (find) finden; **it struck me as strange** es kam mir seltsam vor ▷ vi (stop work) streiken; (attack) zuschlagen; (clock) schlagen ▷ n (by workers) Streik m; **to be on ~** streiken; **strike up** vt (conversation) anfangen; (friendship) schließen; **striking** adj auffallend; (resemblance) verblüffend

string [strɪŋ] n (for tying) Schnur f; (Mus, Tennis) Saite f; **the ~s** pl (section of orchestra) die Streicher pl

strip [strɪp] n Streifen m; (Brit: of footballer etc) Trikot nt ▷ vt (undress) ausziehen ▷ vi (undress) sich ausziehen, strippen

stripe [straɪp] n Streifen m; **striped** adj gestreift

stripper ['strɪpə*] n Stripper(in) m(f); (paint ~) Farbentferner m

strip search ['strɪpsɜːtʃ] n Leibesvisitation f (bei der man sich ausziehen muss)

striptease ['strɪptiːz] n Striptease m

strive [straɪv] (**strove, striven**) vi **to ~ to do sth** bemüht sein, etw zu tun; **to ~ for sth** nach etw streben

stroke [strəʊk] n (Med, Tennis etc) Schlag m; (of pen, brush) Strich m ▷ vt streicheln

stroll [strəʊl] n Spaziergang m ▷ vi spazieren; **stroller** n (US: for baby) Buggy m

strong [strɒŋ] adj stark; (healthy) robust; (wall, table) stabil; (shoes) fest; (influence, force) groß; **strongly** adv stark; (believe) fest; (constructed) stabil

strove [strəʊv] pt of **strive**

struck [strʌk] pt, pp of **strike**

structural . structurally ['strʌktʃərəl, -lɪ] adj strukturell; **structure** ['strʌktʃəʳ] n Struktur f; (building, bridge) Konstruktion f, Bau m

struggle ['strʌgl] n Kampf m (for um) ▷ vi (fight) kämpfen (for um); (do sth with difficulty) sich abmühen; **to ~ to do sth** sich abmühen, etw zu tun

stub [stʌb] n (of cigarette) Kippe f; (of ticket, cheque) Abschnitt m ▷ vt **to ~ one's toe** sich dat den Zeh stoßen (on an +dat)

stubble ['stʌbl] n Stoppeln pl

stubborn ['stʌbən] adj (person) stur

stuck [stʌk] pt, pp of **stick** ▷ adj **to be ~** (jammed) klemmen; (at a loss) nicht mehr weiterwissen; **to get ~** (car in snow etc) stecken bleiben

student ['stjuːdənt] n Student(in) m(f), Schüler(in) m(f)

studio ['stjuːdɪəʊ] (pl **-s**) n Studio nt

studious ['stjuːdɪəs] adj fleißig

study ['stʌdɪ] n (investigation) Untersuchung f; (studying) Studium nt; (room) Arbeitszimmer nt ▷ vt, vi studieren; **to ~ for an exam** sich auf eine Prüfung vorbereiten

stuff [stʌf] n Zeug nt, Sachen pl ▷ vt (push) stopfen; (Gastr) füllen; **to ~ oneself** (fam) sich voll stopfen; **stuffing** n (Gastr) Füllung f

stuffy ['stʌfɪ] adj (room) stickig; (person) spießig

stumble ['stʌmbl] vi stolpern; (when speaking) stocken

stun [stʌn] vt (shock) fassungslos machen; **I was ~ned** ich war fassungslos (o völlig überrascht)

stung [stʌŋ] pt, pp of **sting**

stunk [stʌŋk] pp of **stink**

stunning ['stʌnɪŋ] adj (marvellous) fantastisch; (beautiful) atemberaubend; (very surprising, shocking) überwältigend, unfassbar

stunt [stʌnt] n (Cine) Stunt m

stupid ['stjuːpɪd] adj dumm, **stupidity** [stjuːˈpɪdɪtɪ] n Dummheit f

sturdy ['stɜːdɪ] adj robust; (building, car) stabil

stutter ['stʌtəʳ] vi, vt stottern

stye [staɪ] n (Med) Gerstenkorn nt

style [staɪl] n Stil m ▷ vt (hair) stylen; **styling mousse** n Schaumfestiger m; **stylish** ['staɪlɪʃ] adj elegant

subconscious [ˌsʌbˈkɒnʃəs] adj unterbewusst ▷ n **the ~** das Unterbewusstsein

subdivide [ˌsʌbdɪˈvaɪd] vt unterteilen

subject ['sʌbdʒɪkt] n (topic) Thema nt; (in school) Fach nt; (citizen) Staatsangehörige(r), (of kingdom) Untertan(in) m(f); (Ling) Subjekt nt; **to change the ~** das Thema wechseln ▷ adj [səbˈdʒekt] **to be ~ to** (dependent on) abhängen von; (under

control of) unterworfen sein +dat
subjective [səb'dʒεktɪv] adj
subjektiv
sublet [sʌb'lεt] irr vt untervermieten (to an +akk)
submarine [sʌbmə'riːn] n
U-Boot nt
submerge [səb'mɜːdʒ] vt (put in water) eintauchen ▷ vi tauchen
submit [səb'mɪt] vt (application, claim) einreichen ▷ vi (surrender) sich ergeben
subordinate [sə'bɔːdɪnət] adj untergeordnet (to +dat) ▷ n Untergebene(r) mf
subscribe [səb'skraɪb] vi **to ~ to** (magazine etc) abonnieren; **subscription** [səb'skrɪpʃən] n (to magazine etc) Abonnement nt; (to club etc) (Mitglieds)beitrag m
subsequent ['sʌbsɪkwənt] adj nach(folgend); **subsequently** adv später, anschließend
subside [səb'saɪd] vi (floods) zurückgehen; (storm) sich legen; (building) sich senken
substance ['sʌbstəns] n Substanz f
substantial [səb'stænʃəl] adj beträchtlich; (improvement) wesentlich; (meal) reichhaltig; (furniture) solide
substitute ['sʌbstɪtjuːt] n Ersatz m; (Sport) Ersatzspieler(in) m(f) ▷ vt **to ~ A for B** B durch A ersetzen
subtitle ['sʌbtaɪtl] n Untertitel m
subtle ['sʌtl] adj (difference, taste) fein; (plan) raffiniert
subtotal ['sʌbtəʊtl] n Zwischensumme f
subtract [səb'trækt] vt abziehen (from von)
suburb ['sʌbɜːb] n Vorort m; **in the ~s** im Stadtrand; **suburban** [sə'bɜːbən] adj vorstädtisch, Vorstadt-

subway ['sʌbweɪ] n (BRIT) Unterführung f; (US Rail) U-Bahn f
succeed [sək'siːd] vi erfolgreich sein; **he ~ed (in doing it)** es gelang ihm(, es zu tun) ▷ vt nachfolgen +dat; **succeeding** adj nachfolgend; **success** [sək'sεs] n Erfolg m; **successful, successfully** adj, adv erfolgreich
successive [sək'sεsɪv] adj aufeinander folgend; **successor** n Nachfolger(in) m(f)
succulent ['sʌkjʊlənt] adj saftig
succumb [sə'kʌm] vi erliegen (to +dat)
such [sʌtʃ] adj solche(r, s); **~ a book** so ein Buch, ein solches Buch; **it was ~ a success that ...** es war solch ein Erfolg, dass ...; **~ as** wie ▷ adv so; **~ a hot day** so ein heißer Tag ▷ pron **as ~** als solche(r, s); **suchlike** adj derartig ▷ pron dergleichen
suck [sʌk] vt (toffee etc) lutschen; (liquid) saugen; **it ~s** (fam) das ist beschissen
Sudan [suˈdɑːn] n (**the**) **~** der Sudan
sudden ['sʌdn] adj plötzlich; **all of a ~** ganz plötzlich; **suddenly** adv plötzlich
sue [suː] vt verklagen
suede [sweɪd] n Wildleder nt
suffer ['sʌfə*] vt erleiden ▷ vi leiden; **to ~ from** (Med) leiden an +dat
sufficient, sufficiently [sə'fɪʃənt, -lɪ] adj, adv ausreichend
suffocate ['sʌfəkeɪt] vt, vi ersticken
sugar ['ʃʊgə*] n Zucker m ▷ vt zuckern; **sugar bowl** n Zuckerdose f; **sugary** adj (sweet) süß
suggest [sə'dʒεst] vt vorschlagen; (imply) andeuten; **I ~ saying nothing** ich schlage vor, nichts zu

sayen, **suggestion** [sə'dʒestʃən] n (proposal) Vorschlag m: **suggestive** adj vielsagend; (sexually) anzüglich

suicide ['suɪsaɪd] n (act) Selbstmord m

suit [suːt] n (man's clothes) Anzug m: (lady's clothes) Kostüm nt; (Cards) Farbe f ▷ vt (be convenient for) passen +dat, (clothes, colour) stehen +dat, (climate, food) bekommen +dat; **suitable** adj geeignet (for für); **suitcase** n Koffer m

suite [swiːt] n (of rooms) Suite f; (sofa and chairs) Sitzgarnitur f

sulk [sʌlk] vi schmollen; **sulky** adj eingeschnappt

sultana [sʌl'tɑːnə] n (raisin) Sultanine f

sum [sʌm] n Summe f; (money a.) Betrag m; (calculation) Rechenaufgabe f; **sum up** vt, vi (summarize) zusammenfassen

summarize ['sʌməraɪz] vt, vi zusammenfassen; **summary** n Zusammenfassung f

summer ['sʌmə*] n Sommer m; **summer camp** n (US) Ferienlager nt; **summer holidays** n Sommerferien pl; **summertime** n in (the) ~ im Sommer

summit ['sʌmɪt] n (a. Pol) Gipfel m

summon ['sʌmən] vt (doctor, fire brigade etc) rufen, (to one's office) zitieren; **summon up** vt (courage, strength) zusammennehmen

summons ['sʌmənz] nsing (Jur) Vorladung f

sumptuous ['sʌmptjʊəs] adj luxuriös; (meal) üppig

sun [sʌn] n Sonne f ▷ vt to ~ oneself sich sonnen

Sun abbr = **Sunday** So.

sunbathe vi sich sonnen; **sunbathing** n Sonnenbaden nt; **sunbed** n Sonnenbank f, **sunblock** n Sunblocker m; **sunburn** n

Sonnenbrand m; **sunburnt** adj to be / get ~ einen Sonnenbrand haben / bekommen

sundae ['sʌndeɪ] n Eisbecher m

Sunday ['sʌndɪ] n Sonntag m; see also **Tuesday**

sung [sʌŋ] pp of **sing**

sunglasses ['sʌnɡlɑːsɪz] npl Sonnenbrille f; **sunhat** n Sonnenhut m

sunk [sʌŋk] pp of **sink**

sunlamp n ['sʌnlæmp] n Höhensonne f; **sunlight** n Sonnenlicht nt; **sunny** ['sʌnɪ] adj sonnig; **sun protection factor** n Lichtschutzfaktor m; **sunrise** n Sonnenaufgang m; **sunroof** n (Auto) Schiebedach nt; **sunscreen** n Sonnenschutzmittel nt; **sunset** n Sonnenuntergang m; **sunshade** n Sonnenschirm m; **sunshine** n Sonnenschein m; **sunstroke** n Sonnenstich m; **suntan** n (Sonnen)bräune f; **to get / have a ~** braun werden / sein; **~ lotion** (o oil) Sonnenöl nt

super ['suːpə*] adj (fam) toll

superb [suː'pɜːb, sjuː-] adj, adv ausgezeichnet

superficial, superficially [suːpə'fɪʃəl, -ɪ] adj, adv oberflächlich

superfluous [suː'pɜːflʊəs] adj überflüssig

superglue ['suːpəɡluː] n Sekundenkleber m

superior [suː'pɪərɪə*] adj (better) besser (to als); (higher in rank) höher gestellt (to als), höher ▷ n (in rank) Vorgesetzte(r) mf

supermarket ['suːpəmɑːkɪt] n Supermarkt m

supersede [suːpə'siːd] vt ablösen; **supersonic** [suːpə'sɒnɪk] adj Überschall-

superstitious [suːpə'stɪʃəs] adj abergläubisch

superstore ['su:pəstɔ:*] n Verbrauchermarkt m

supervise ['su:pəvaɪz] vt beaufsichtigen; **supervisor** ['su:pəvaɪzə] n Aufsicht f; (at university) Doktorvater m

supper ['sʌpə*] n Abendessen nt; (late-night snack) Imbiss

supplement ['sʌplɪmənt] n (extra payment) Zuschlag m; (of newspaper) Beilage f ▷ vt ergänzen; **supplementary** [sʌplɪ'mentərɪ] adj zusätzlich

supplier [sə'plaɪə*] n Lieferant(in) m(f); **supply** [sə'plaɪ] vt (deliver) liefern; (drinks, music etc) sorgen für; **to ~ sb with sth** (provide) jdn mit etw versorgen ▷ n (stock) Vorrat m (of an +dat)

support [sə'pɔ:t] n Unterstützung f; (Tech) Stütze f ▷ vt (hold up) tragen, stützen; (provide for) ernähren, unterhalten; (speak in favour of) unterstützen; **he ~ s Manchester United** er ist Manchester-United-Fan

suppose [sə'pəʊz] vt (assume) annehmen; **I ~ so** ich denke schon; **I ~ not** wahrscheinlich nicht; **you're not ~d to smoke here** du darfst hier nicht rauchen; **supposedly** [sə'pəʊzɪdlɪ] adv angeblich; **supposing** conj angenommen

suppress [sə'pres] vt unterdrücken

surcharge ['sɜ:tʃɑ:dʒ] n Zuschlag m

sure [ʃʊə*] adj sicher; **I'm (not) ~** ich bin mir (nicht) sicher; **make ~ you lock up** vergiss nicht abzuschließen ▷ adv **~ I!** klar!; **~ enough** tatsächlich; **surely** adv **~ you don't mean it?** das ist nicht dein Ernst, oder?

surf [sɜ:f] n Brandung f ▷ vi (Sport) surfen ▷ vt **to ~ the net** im Internet

surfen

surface ['sɜ:fɪs] n Oberfläche f ▷ vi auftauchen; **surface mail** n **by ~** auf dem Land-/Seeweg

surfboard ['sɜ:fbɔ:d] n Surfbrett nt; **surfer** n Surfer(in) m(f); **surfing** n Surfen nt; **to go ~** surfen gehen

surgeon ['sɜ:dʒən] n Chirurg(in) m(f); **surgery** ['sɜ:dʒərɪ] n (operation) Operation f; (room) Praxis f, Sprechzimmer nt; (consulting time) Sprechstunde f; **to have ~** operiert werden

surname ['sɜ:neɪm] n Nachname m

surpass [sɜ:'pɑ:s] vt übertreffen

surplus ['sɜ:pləs] n Überschuss m (of an +dat)

surprise [sə'praɪz] n Überraschung f ▷ vt überraschen; **surprising** adj überraschend; **surprisingly** adv überraschenderweise, erstaunlicherweise

surrender [sə'rendə*] vi sich ergeben (to +dat) ▷ vt (weapon, passport) abgeben

surround [sə'raʊnd] vt umgeben; (stand all round) umringen; **surrounding** adj (countryside) umliegend ▷ n **~s** pl Umgebung f

survey ['sɜ:veɪ] n (opinion poll) Umfrage f; (of literature etc) Überblick m (of über +akk); (of land) Vermessung f ▷ [sɜ:'veɪ] vt (look out over) überblicken; (land) vermessen

survive [sə'raɪv] vt, vi überleben

susceptible [sə'septəbl] adj empfänglich (to für); (Med) anfällig (to für)

suspect ['sʌspekt] n Verdächtige(r) mf ▷ adj verdächtig ▷ [sə'spekt] vt verdächtigen (of +gen); (think likely) vermuten

suspend [sə'spend] vt (from work) suspendieren; (payment) vorübergehend einstellen; (*player*) sperren; (*hang up*) aufhängen; **suspender** n (BRIT) Strumpfhalter m; **~s** pl (US: *for trousers*) Hosenträger pl

suspense [sə'spɛns] n Spannung f

suspicious [sə'spɪʃəs] adj misstrauisch (*of sb / sth* jdm / etw gegenüber); (*causing suspicion*) verdächtig

swallow ['swɒləʊ] n (*bird*) Schwalbe f ⊳ vt, vi schlucken

swam [swæm] pt of **swim**

swamp [swɒmp] n Sumpf m

swan [swɒn] n Schwan m

swap [swɒp] vt, vi tauschen; **to ~ sth for sth** etw gegen etw eintauschen

sway [sweɪ] vi schwanken

swear [swɛə*] (**swore, sworn**) vi (*promise*) schwören; (*curse*) fluchen; **to ~ at sb** jdn beschimpfen; **swear by** vt (*have faith in*) schwören auf +akk; **swearword** n Fluch m

sweat [swɛt] n Schweiß m ⊳ vi schwitzen; **sweatband** n Schweißband nt; **sweater** n Pullover m; **sweatshirt** n Sweatshirt nt; **sweaty** adj verschwitzt

swede [swiːd] n Steckrübe f

Swede [swiːd] n Schwede m, Schwedin f; **Sweden** n Schweden nt, **Swedish** adj schwedisch ⊳ n (*language*) Schwedisch nt

sweep [swiːp] (**swept, swept**) vt, vi (*with brush*) kehren, fegen; **sweep up** vt (*dirt etc*) zusammenkehren, zusammenfegen

sweet [swiːt] n (BRIT: *candy*) Bonbon nt; (*dessert*) Nachtisch m ⊳ adj süß; (*kind*) lieb; **sweet-and-sour** adj süßsauer; **sweetcorn** n Mais m; **sweeten** vt (*tea etc*) süßen; **sweetener** n (*substance*) Süßstoff m

swell [swɛl] (**swelled, swollen** o

swelled) vi **to ~ (up)** (an)schwellen ⊳ adj (US fam) toll; **swelling** n (Med) Schwellung f

sweltering ['swɛltərɪŋ] adj (*heat*) drückend

swept [swɛpt] pt, pp of **sweep**

swift, swiftly [swɪft] adj, adv schnell

swig [swɪg] n (*fam*) Schluck m

swim [swɪm] (**swam, swum**) vi schwimmen ⊳ n **to go for a ~** schwimmen gehen; **swimmer** n Schwimmer(in) m(f); **swimming** n Schwimmen nt; **to go ~** schwimmen gehen; **swimming cap** n (BRIT) Badekappe f; **swimming costume** n (BRIT) Badeanzug m; **swimming pool** n Schwimmbad nt; (*private, in hotel*) Swimmingpool m; **swimming trunks** npl (BRIT) Badehose f; **swimsuit** n Badeanzug m

swindle ['swɪndl] vt betrügen (*out of* um)

swine [swaɪn] n (*person*) Schwein nt

swing [swɪŋ] (**swung, swung**) vt, vi (*object*) schwingen ⊳ n (*for child*) Schaukel f

swipe [swaɪp] vt (*credit card etc*) durchziehen; (*fam: steal*) klauen; **swipe card** n Magnetkarte f

Swiss [swɪs] adj schweizerisch ⊳ n Schweizer(in) m(f)

switch [swɪtʃ] n (Elec) Schalter m ⊳ vt change) wechseln; **to ~ sth for sth** etw gegen etw eintauschen ⊳ vi (change) wechseln (to zu); **switch off** vt ausschalten, ausmachen; **switch on** vt anschalten, einschalten; **switchboard** n (Tel) Vermittlung f

Switzerland ['swɪtsələnd] n die Schweiz

swivel ['swɪvl] vi sich drehen ⊳ vt drehen; **swivel chair** n Drehstuhl m

swollen ['swəʊlən] pp of **swell** ▷ adj (Med) geschwollen; (stomach) aufgebläht

swop [swɒp] see **swap**

sword [sɔːd] n Schwert nt

swore [swɔː*] pt of **swear**

sworn [swɔːn] pp of **swear**

swot [swɒt] vi (BRIT fam) büffeln (for für)

swum [swʌm] pp of **swim**

swung [swʌŋ] pt, pp of **swing**

syllable ['sɪləbl] n Silbe f

syllabus ['sɪləbəs] n Lehrplan m

symbol ['sɪmbəl] n Symbol nt; **symbolic** [sɪm'bɒlɪk] adj symbolisch; **symbolize** vt symbolisieren

symmetrical [sɪ'metrɪkəl] adj symmetrisch

sympathetic [sɪmpə'θetɪk] adj mitfühlend; (understanding) verständnisvoll; **sympathize** ['sɪmpəθaɪz] vi mitfühlen (with sb mit jdm); **sympathy** ['sɪmpəθɪ] n Mitleid nt; (after death) Beileid nt; (understanding) Verständnis nt

symphony ['sɪmfənɪ] n Sinfonie f

symptom ['sɪmptəm] n (a. fig) Symptom nt

synagogue ['sɪnəgɒg] n Synagoge f

synonym ['sɪnənɪm] n Synonym nt; **synonymous** [sɪ'nɒnɪməs] adj synonym (with mit)

synthetic [sɪn'θetɪk] adj (material) synthetisch

syphilis ['sɪfɪlɪs] n Syphilis f

Syria ['sɪrɪə] n Syrien nt

syringe [sɪ'rɪndʒ] n Spritze f

system ['sɪstəm] n System nt; **systematic** [sɪstə'mætɪk] adj systematisch; **system disk** n (Inform) Systemdiskette f; **system(s) software** n (Inform) Systemsoftware f

tab [tæb] n (for hanging up coat etc) Aufhänger m; (Inform) Tabulator m; **to pick up the –** (fam) die Rechnung übernehmen

table ['teɪbl] n Tisch m; (list) Tabelle f; **– of contents** Inhaltsverzeichnis nt; **tablecloth** n Tischdecke f; **tablelamp** n Tischlampe f; **tablemat** n Set nt; **tablespoon** n Serviertöffel m; (in recipes) Esslöffel m

tablet ['tæblət] n (Med) Tablette f

table tennis ['teɪbltenɪs] n Tischtennis nt; **table wine** n Tafelwein m

tabloid ['tæblɔɪd] n Boulevardzeitung f

taboo [tə'buː] n Tabu nt ▷ adj tabu

tacit, tacitly ['tæsɪt, -lɪ] adj, adv stillschweigend

tack [tæk] n (small nail) Stift m; (US: thumb~) Reißzwecke f

tackle ['tækl] n (Sport) Angriff m; (equipment) Ausrüstung f ▷ vt (deal with) in Angriff nehmen; (Sport) an-

greifen; (verbally) zur Rede stellen
(about wegen)

tact [tækt] n Takt m; **tactful,
tactfully** adj,adv taktvoll; **tactic(s)**
['tæktɪk(s)] n(pl) Taktik f; **tactless,
tactlessly** ['tæktlɪs, -lɪ] adj, adv
taktlos

tag [tæg] n (label) Schild nt; (with
maker's name) Etikett nt

Tahiti [tə'hiːtɪ] n Tahiti nt

tail [teɪl] n Schwanz m; **heads or
~s?** Kopf oder Zahl?; **tailback** n
(BRIT) Rückstau m; **taillight** n
(Auto) Rücklicht nt

tailor ['teɪlə] n Schneider(in) m(f)

tailpipe ['teɪlpaɪp] n (US Auto)
Auspuffrohr nt

tainted ['teɪntɪd] adj (US: food)
verdorben

Taiwan [taɪ'wæn] n Taiwan nt

take [teɪk] (took, taken) vt nehmen; (~ along with one) mitnehmen;
(~ to a place) bringen; (subtract) abziehen (from von); (capture: person)
fassen; (gain, obtain) bekommen;
(Fin, Comm) einnehmen; (train, taxi)
nehmen, fahren mit; (trip, walk, holiday, exam course photo) machen;
(bath) nehmen; (phone call) entge-
gennehmen; (decision, precautions)
treffen; (risk) eingehen; (advice, job)
annehmen; (consume) zu sich nehmen; (tablets) nehmen; (heat, pain)
ertragen; (react to) aufnehmen; (have
room for) Platz haben für; **I'll ~ it**
(item in shop) ich nehme es; **how
long does it ~?** wie lange dauert es?;
it ~s 4 hours man braucht 4 Stunden; **do you ~ sugar?** nehmen Sie
Zucker?; **I ~ it that ...** ich nehme an,
dass ...; **to ~ place** stattfinden; **take
after** vt nachschlagen +dat; **take
along** vt mitnehmen; **take apart**
vt auseinander nehmen; **take
away** vt (remove) wegnehmen
(from sb jdm); (subtract) abziehen

(from von), **take back** vt (return)
zurückbringen; (retract) zurücknehmen; (remind) zurückversetzen (to in
+akk); **take down** vt (picture, cur-
tains) abnehmen; (write down) aufschreiben; **take in** vt (understand)
begreifen; (give accommodation to)
aufnehmen; (deceive) hereinlegen;
(include) einschließen; (show, film etc)
mitnehmen; **take off** vi (plane)
starten ▷ vt (clothing) ausziehen;
(hat, lid) abnehmen; (deduct) abziehen; (BRIT: imitate) nachmachen; **to
take a day off** sich einen Tag frei-
nehmen; **take on** vt (undertake)
übernehmen; (employ) einstellen;
(Sport) antreten gegen; **take out** vt
(wallet etc) herausnehmen; (person,
dog) ausführen; (insurance) abschließen; (money from bank) abheben;
(book from library) ausleihen; **take
over** vt übernehmen ▷ vi **he took
over (from me)** er hat mich abge-
löst; **take to** vt **I've taken to her/
it** ich mag sie/es; **to ~ doing sth**
(begin) anfangen, etw zu tun; **take
up** vt (carpet) hochnehmen; (space)
einnehmen; (time) in Anspruch nehmen; (hobby) anfangen mit; (new job)
antreten; (offer) annehmen

takeaway n (BRIT: meal) Essen nt
zum Mitnehmen

taken ['teɪkn] pp of **take** ▷ adj
(seat) besetzt; **to be ~ with** angetan
sein von

takeoff ['teɪkɒf] n (Aviat) Start m;
(imitation) Nachahmung f; **takeout**
(US) see **takeaway**; **takeover** n
(Comm) Übernahme f

takings ['teɪkɪŋz] npl Einnahmen
pl

tale [teɪl] n Geschichte f

talent ['tælənt] n Talent nt; **talented** adj begabt

talk [tɔːk] n (conversation) Gespräch nt; (rumour) Gerede nt; (to

audience) Vortrag m ▷ vi sprechen, reden; (have conversation) sich unterhalten; **to ~ to** (ø **with**) **sb** (about sth) mit jdm (über etw akk) sprechen ▷ vt (language) sprechen; (nonsense) reden; (politics, business) reden über +akk; **to ~ sb into doing/out of doing sth** jdn überreden/jdm ausreden, etw zu tun; **talk over** vt besprechen

talkative adj gesprächig; **talk show** n Talkshow f

tall [tɔːl] adj groß; (building, tree) hoch; **he is 6ft ~** er ist 1,80m groß

tame [teɪm] adj zahm; (joke, story) fade ▷ vt (animal) zähmen

tampon ['tæmpɒn] n Tampon m

tan [tæn] n (on skin) (Sonnen)bräune f; **to get/have a ~** braun werden/sein ▷ vi braun werden

tangerine [tændʒə'riːn] n Mandarine f

tango ['tæŋgəʊ] n Tango m

tank [tæŋk] n Tank m; (for fish) Aquarium nt; (Mil) Panzer m

tanker ['tæŋkə*] n (ship) Tanker m; (vehicle) Tankwagen m

tanned [tænd] adj (by sun) braun

tantalizing ['tæntəlaɪzɪŋ] adj verlockend

Tanzania [tænzə'nɪə] n Tansania nt

tap [tæp] n (for water) Hahn m ▷ vt, vi (strike) klopfen; **to ~ sb on the shoulder** jdm auf die Schulter klopfen; **tap-dance** vi steppen

tape [teɪp] n (adhesive ~) Klebeband nt; (for tape recorder) Tonband nt; (cassette) Kassette f; (video) Video nt ▷ vt (record) aufnehmen; **tape up** vt (parcel) zukleben; **tape measure** n Maßband nt; **tape recorder** n Tonbandgerät nt

tapestry ['tæpɪstrɪ] n Wandteppich m

tap water ['tæpwɔːtə*] n Lei-

tungswasser nt

tar [tɑː*] n Teer m

target ['tɑːgɪt] n Ziel nt; (board) Zielscheibe f

tariff ['tærɪf] n (price list) Preisliste f; (tax) Zoll m

tarmac [tɑːmæk] n (Aviat) Rollfeld nt

tart [tɑːt] n (fruit ~) (Obst)kuchen m; (small) (Obst)törtchen nt; (fam, pej: prostitute) Nutte f; **tfam:** promiscuous person) Schlampe f

tartan ['tɑːtən] n Schottenkaro nt; (material) Schottenstoff m

tartar(e) sauce ['tɑːtə'sɔːs] n Remouladensoße f

task [tɑːsk] n Aufgabe f; (duty) Pflicht f; **taskbar** n (Inform) Taskbar f

Tasmania [tæz'meɪnɪə] n Tasmanien nt

taste [teɪst] n Geschmack m; (sense of ~) Geschmacksinn m; (small quantity) Kostprobe f; **it has a strange ~** es schmeckt komisch ▷ vt schmecken; (try) probieren ▷ vi (food) schmecken (of nach); **to ~ good/strange** gut/komisch schmecken; **tasteful, tastefully** adj, adv geschmackvoll; **tasteless** adj, adv geschmacklos; **tasty** adj schmackhaft

tattered ['tætəd] adj (clothes) zerlumpt; (fam: person) angespannt; **I'm absolutely ~** ich bin mit den Nerven am Ende

tattoo [tə'tuː] n (on skin) Tätowierung f

taught [tɔːt] pt, pp of **teach**

Taurus ['tɔːrəs] n (Astr) Stier m

tax [tæks] n Steuer f (on auf +akk) ▷ vt besteuern; **taxable** adj steuerpflichtig; **taxation** [tæk'seɪʃən] n Besteuerung f; **tax bracket** n Steuerklasse f; **tax disc** n (BRIT Auto) Steuermarke f; **tax-free**

steuerfrei

taxi ['tæksɪ] n Taxi nt ▷ vi (plane) rollen; **taxi driver** n Taxifahrer(in) m(f); **taxi rank** (BRIT), **taxi stand** n Taxistand m

tax return ['tæksrɪ'tɜːn] n Steuererklärung f

tea [tiː] n Tee m; (afternoon ~) ≈ Kaffee und Kuchen; (meal) frühes Abendessen; **teabag** n Teebeutel m; **tea break** n (Tee)pause f

teach [tiːtʃ] (taught, taught) vt (person, subject) unterrichten; **to ~ sb (how) to do sth** jdm das Tanzen beibringen ▷ vi unterrichten; **teacher** n Lehrer(in) m(f); **teaching** n (activity) Unterrichten nt; (profession) Lehrberuf m

teacup ['tiːkʌp] n Teetasse f

team [tiːm] n (Sport) Mannschaft f, Team nt; **teamwork** n Teamarbeit f

teapot ['tiːpɒt] n Teekanne f

tear [tɪə*] n (in eye) Träne f

tear [tɛə*] (tore, torn) vt zerreißen; **to ~ a muscle** sich einen Muskel zerren ▷ n (in material etc) Riss m; **tear down** vt (building) abreißen; **tear up** vt (paper) zerreißen

tearoom ['tiːrʊm] n Teestube f, Café, in dem in erster Linie Tee serviert wird

tease [tiːz] vt (person) necken (about wegen)

tea set ['tiːset] n Teeservice nt; **teashop** n Teestube f, **teaspoon** n Teelöffel m; **tea towel** n Geschirrtuch nt

technical ['teknɪkəl] adj technisch; (knowledge, term, dictionary) Fach-; **technically** adv technisch; **technique** [tek'niːk] n Technik f

techno ['teknəʊ] n Techno f

technological [teknə'lɒdʒɪkəl] adj technologisch; **technology** [tek'nɒlədʒɪ] n Technologie f

tedious ['tiːdɪəs] adj langweilig

teen(age) ['tiːn(eɪdʒ)] adj (fashions etc) Teenager-; **teenager** n Teenager m, Teenager m; **teens** [tiːnz] npl **in one's ~** im Teenageralter

teeth [tiːθ] pl of tooth

teetotal [tiː'təʊtl] adj abstinent

telegraph pole ['telɪɡrɑːfpəʊl] n (BRIT) Telegrafenmast m

telephone ['telɪfəʊn] n Telefon nt ▷ vi telefonieren ▷ vt anrufen; **telephone banking** n Telefonbanking nt; **telephone book** n Telefonbuch nt; **telephone booth**, **telephone box** (BRIT) n Telefonzelle f; **telephone call** n Telefonanruf m; **telephone directory** n Telefonbuch nt; **telephone number** n Telefonnummer f

telephoto lens ['telɪfəʊtəʊ'lenz] n Teleobjektiv nt

telescope ['telɪskəʊp] n Teleskop nt

televise ['telɪvaɪz] vt im Fernsehen übertragen; **television** ['telɪvɪʒən] n Fernsehen nt; **television programme** n Fernsehsendung f; **television set** n Fernsehapparat m

teleworking ['telɪwɜːkɪŋ] n Telearbeit f

tell [tel] (told, told) vt (say, inform) sagen (sb sth jdm etw); (story) erzählen; (truth) sagen; (difference) erkennen; (reveal secret) verraten; **to ~ sb about sth** jdm von etw erzählen; **to ~ sth from sth** etw von etw unterscheiden ▷ vi (be sure) wissen; **tell apart** vt unterscheiden; **tell off** vt schimpfen

telling [tel] adj aufschlussreich

telly ['telɪ] n (BRIT fam) Glotze f; **on (the) ~** in der Glotze

temp [temp] n Aushilfskraft f ▷ vi als Aushilfskraft arbeiten

temper ['tempə*] n (anger) Wut f,

(mood) Laune f; **to lose one's ~** die Beherrschung verlieren; **to have a bad ~** jähzornig sein; **temperamental** [tempərə'mentl] *adj (moody)* launisch

temperature ['temprɪtʃə*] n Temperatur f; *(Med: high ~)* Fieber nt; **to have a ~** Fieber haben

temple ['templ] n Tempel m; *(Anat)* Schläfe f

tempo ['tempəʊ] *(pl* **-s)** n Tempo nt

temporarily ['tempərɪlɪ] *adv* vorübergehend; **temporary** ['tempərərɪ] *adj* vorübergehend; *(road, building)* provisorisch

tempt [tempt] vt in Versuchung führen; **I'm ~ed to accept** ich bin versucht anzunehmen; **temptation** [temp'teɪʃən] n Versuchung f; **tempting** *adj* verlockend

ten [ten] *num* zehn ▷ n Zehn f; *see also* **eight**

tenant ['tenənt] n Mieter(in) m(f); *(of land)* Pächter(in) m(f)

tend [tend] vi **to ~ to do sth** *(person)* dazu neigen, etw zu tun; **to ~ towards** neigen zu; **tendency** ['tendənsɪ] n Tendenz f; **to have a ~ to do sth** *(person)* dazu neigen, etw zu tun

tender ['tendə*] *adj (loving)* zärtlich; *(sore)* empfindlich; *(meat)* zart

tendon ['tendən] n Sehne f

Tenerife [tenə'ri:f] n Teneriffa nt

tenner ['tenə*] n *(BRIT fam: note)* Zehnpfundschein m; *(amount)* zehn Pfund

tennis ['tenɪs] n Tennis nt; **tennis ball** n Tennisball m; **tennis court** n Tennisplatz m; **tennis racket** n Tennisschläger m

tenor ['tenə*] n Tenor m

tenpin bowling, **tenpins** (US) ['tenpɪn'bəʊlɪŋ, 'tenpɪnz] n Bowling nt

tense [tens] *adj* angespannt; *(stretched tight)* gespannt; **tension** ['tenʃən] n Spannung f; *(strain)* Anspannung f

tent [tent] n Zelt nt

tenth [tenθ] *adj* zehnte(r, s) ▷ n *(fraction)* Zehntel nt; *see also* **eighth**

tent peg ['tentpeg] n Hering m; **tent pole** n Zeltstange f

term [tɜ:m] n *(in school, at university)* Trimester nt; *(expression)* Ausdruck m; **~s** pl *(conditions)* Bedingungen pl; **to be on good ~s with sb** mit jdm gut auskommen; **to come to ~s with sth** sich mit etw abfinden; **in the long/short ~** langfristig/kurzfristig; **in ~s of ...** was ... betrifft

terminal ['tɜ:mɪnl] n *(bus – etc)* Endstation f; *(Aviat)* Terminal m; *(Inform)* Terminal nt; *(Elec)* Pol m ▷ *adj (Med)* unheilbar; **terminally** *adv (ill)* unheilbar

terminate ['tɜ:mɪneɪt] vt *(contract)* lösen; *(pregnancy)* abbrechen ▷ vi *(train, bus)* enden

terminology [tɜ:mɪ'nɒlədʒɪ] n Terminologie f

terrace ['terəs] n *(of houses)* Häuserreihe f; *(in garden etc)* Terrasse f; **terraced** *adj (garden)* terrassenförmig angelegt; **terraced house** n *(BRIT)* Reihenhaus nt

terrible ['terɪbl] *adj* schrecklich

terrific [tə'rɪfɪk] *adj (very good)* fantastisch

terrify ['terɪfaɪ] vt erschrecken; **to be terrified** schreckliche Angst haben *(of* vor *+dat)*

territory ['terɪtərɪ] n Gebiet nt

terror ['terə*] n Schrecken m; *(Pol)* Terror m; **terrorism** n Terrorismus m; **terrorist** n Terrorist(in) m(f)

test [test] n Test m, Klassenarbeit f; *(driving ~)* Prüfung f; **to put to the ~** auf die Probe stellen ▷ vt testen, prüfen; (patience, courage etc) auf die Probe stellen

Testament ['testəmənt] n **the Old/New** ~ das Alte/Neue Testament

test-drive ['testdraɪv] vt Probe fahren

testicle ['testɪkl] n Hoden m

testify ['testɪfaɪ] vi (jur) aussagen

test tube ['testtjuːb] n Reagenzglas nt

tetanus ['tetənəs] n Tetanus m

text [tekst] n Text m; (of document) Wortlaut m; (sent by mobile phone) SMS f ▷ vt (message) simsen, SMSen; **to ~ sb** jdm simsen, jdm eine SMS schicken; **I'll ~ it to you** ich schicke es dir per SMS

textbook n Lehrbuch nt

texting ['tekstɪŋ] n SMS-Messaging nt; **text message** n SMS f; **text messaging** n SMS-Messaging nt

texture ['tekstʃə*] n Beschaffenheit f

Thailand ['taɪlænd] n Thailand nt

Thames [temz] n Themse f

than [ðæn] prep, conj als; **bigger/faster ~ me** größer/schneller als ich; **I'd rather walk ~ drive** ich gehe lieber zu Fuß als mit dem Auto

thank [θæŋk] vt danken +dat; **~ you** danke, **~ you very much** vielen Dank; **thankful** adj dankbar, **thankfully** adv (luckily) zum Glück; **thankless** adj undankbar; **thanks** npl Dank m; **~ dankel**; **~ to** dank +gen

● **THANKSGIVING DAY**

● **Thanksgiving (Day)** ist ein Feiertag in den USA, der auf den vierten ● Donnerstag im November fällt. Er ● soll daran erinnern, wie die Pilgerväter die gute Ernte im Jahre ● 1621 feierten. In Kanada gibt es ei-

● nen ähnlichen Erntedanktag (, der ● aber nichts mit den Pilgervätern zu ● tun hat) am zweiten Montag im ● Oktober.

that [ðæt, ðət] adj der/die/das; (opposed to this) jene(r, s); **who's ~ woman?** wer ist die Frau?; **like ~** one ich mag das da ▷ pron das; (in relative clauses) der/die/das, die pl; **~ is very good** das ist sehr gut; **the wine – I drank** der Wein, den ich getrunken habe, **~ is (to say)** das heißt ▷ conj dass; **I think ~ ...** ich denke, dass ... ▷ adv so; **~ good** so gut

that's [ðæts] contr of that is; that has

thaw [θɔː] vi tauen; (frozen food) auftauen ▷ vt auftauen lassen

the [ðə, ðiː] art der/die/das, die pl; **in ~ room** im Zimmer, in dem Zimmer; **Henry ~ Eighth** Heinrich der Achte; **by ~ hour** pro Stunde; **~ ... better** je ..., desto besser

theater (US), **theatre** ['θɪətə*] n Theater nt; (for lectures etc) Saal m

theft [θeft] n Diebstahl m

their [ðeə*] adj ihr; (unidentified person) sein; **they cleaned ~ teeth** sie putzten sich die Zähne; **someone has left ~ umbrella here** je mand hat seinen Schirm hier vergessen; **theirs** pron ihre(r, s); (unidentified person) seine(r, s); **it's ~ es** gehört ihnen, **a friend of ~** ein Freund von ihnen; **someone has left ~ here** jemand hat seins hier liegen lassen

them [ðem, ðəm] pron (direct object) sie; (indirect object) ihnen; (unidentified person) ihn/ihm, sie/ihr; **do you know ~?** kennst du sie?; **can you help ~?** kannst du ihnen helfen?; **it's ~** sie sind's; **if anyone has a problem you should help ~** wenn jemand ein Problem hat, solltest du ihm helfen

theme [θiːm] n Thema nt; (Mus) Motiv nt; ~ **park** Themenpark m; ~ **song** Titelmusik f

themselves [ðəmˈselvz] pron sich; **they hurt** ~ sie haben sich verletzt; **they** ~ **were not there** sie selbst waren nicht da; **they did it** ~ sie haben es selbst gemacht; **they are not dangerous in** ~ an sich sind sie nicht gefährlich; (**all**) **by** ~ allein

then [ðen] adv (at that time) damals; (next) dann; (therefore) also; (furthermore) ferner; **from** ~ **on** von da an; **by** ~ bis dahin ▷ adj damalig; **our** ~ **boss** unser damaliger Chef

theoretical adj, **theoretically** [θɪəˈretɪkəl, -lɪ] adj theoretisch

theory [ˈθɪərɪ] n Theorie f; **in** ~ theoretisch

therapy [ˈθerəpɪ] n Therapie f

there [ðeə*] adv dort; (to a place) dorthin; ~ **is/are** (exists/exist) es gibt; **it's over** ~ es ist da drüben; ~ **you are** (when giving) bitte schön; **thereabouts** adv (approximately) so ungefähr; **therefore** adv daher, deshalb

thermometer [θəˈmɒmɪtə*] n Thermometer nt

Thermos® [ˈθɜːməs] n ~ (**flask**) Thermosflasche® f

these [ðiːz] pron, adj diese; **I don't like** ~ **apples** ich mag diese Äpfel nicht; ~ **are not my books** das sind nicht meine Bücher

thesis [ˈθiːsɪs] (pl **theses**) n (for PhD) Doktorarbeit f

they [ðeɪ] pron pl sie; (people in general) man; (unidentified person) er/sie; ~ **are rich** sie sind reich; ~ **say that** ... man sagt, dass ...; **if anyone looks at this,** ~ **will see that** ... wenn sich jemand dies ansieht, wird er erkennen, dass ...

they'd [ðeɪd] contr of **they had**; **they would**

they'll [ðeɪl] contr of **they will**; **they shall**

they're [ðeɪv] contr of **they have**

thick [θɪk] adj dick; (fog) dicht; (liquid) dickflüssig; (fam: stupid) dumm; **thicken** vi (fog) dichter werden; (sauce) dick werden ▷ vt (sauce) eindicken

thief [θiːf] (pl **thieves**) n Dieb(in) m(f)

thigh [θaɪ] n Oberschenkel m

thimble [ˈθɪmbl] n Fingerhut m

thin [θɪn] adj dünn

thing [θɪŋ] n Ding nt; (affair) Sache f; **my** ~**s** meine Sachen pl; **how are** ~**s**? wie geht's?; **I can't see a** ~ ich kann nichts sehen; **he knows a** ~ **or two about cars** er kennt sich mit Autos aus

think [θɪŋk] (**thought, thought**) vt, vi denken; (believe) meinen; **I** ~ **so** ich denke schon; **I don't** ~ **so** ich glaube nicht; **think about** vt denken an +akk; (reflect on) nachdenken über +akk; (have opinion of) halten von; **think of** vt denken an +akk; (devise) sich ausdenken; (have opinion of) halten von; (remember) sich erinnern an +akk; **think over** vt überdenken; **think up** vt sich ausdenken

third [θɜːd] adj dritte(r, s); **the Third World** die Dritte Welt ▷ n (fraction) Drittel nt; **in** ~ (gear) im dritten Gang; see also **eight**; **thirdly** adv drittens; **third-party insurance** n Haftpflichtversicherung f

thirst [θɜːst] n Durst m (for nach); **thirsty** adj **to be** ~ Durst haben

thirteen [θɜːˈtiːn] num dreizehn ▷ n Dreizehn f; see also **eight**; **thirteenth** adj dreizehnte(r, s); see also **eighth**; **thirtieth** [ˈθɜːtɪɪθ] adj

dreißigste(r, s); *see also* eighth;
thirty ['θɜ:tɪ] *num* dreißig; ■na
einunddreißig ▷ *n* Dreißig f; to be
in one's thirties in den Dreißigern
sein; *see also* eight

this [ðɪs] *adj* diese(r, s); I don't like
~ wine ich mag diesen Wein nicht; ~
morning heute Morgen ▷ *pron* das
dies; ~ is not my book das ist nicht
mein Buch; is Mark (*on the phone*)
hier spricht Mark

thistle ['θɪsl] *n* Distel f

thorn [θɔ:n] *n* Dorn m, Stachel m

thorough ['θʌrə] *adj* gründlich;
thoroughly *adv* gründlich; (*agree
etc*) völlig

those [ðəʊz] *pron* die da, jene; ~
who diejenigen, die ▷ *adj* die, jene

though [ðəʊ] *conj* obwohl; as ~
als ob ▷ *adv* aber

thought [θɔ:t] *pt, pp of* think ▷ *n*
Gedanke m; (*thinking*) Überlegung f;
thoughtful *adj* (*kind*) rücksichtsvoll; (*attentive*) aufmerksam; (*in Gedanken versunken*) nachdenklich;
thoughtless *adj* (*unkind*) rücksichtslos, gedankenlos

thousand ['θaʊzənd] *num* (one)
~, a ~ tausend; five ~ fünftausend;
~s of Tausende von

thrash [θræʃ] *vt* (*hit*) verprügeln;
(*defeat*) vernichtend schlagen

thread [θred] *n* Faden m ▷ *vt*
(*needle*) einfädeln; (*beads*) auffädeln

threat [θret] *n* Drohung f; (*danger*)
Bedrohung f (*to für*); threaten *vt*
bedrohen; threatening *adj* be-
drohlich

three [θri:] *num* drei ▷ *n* Drei f;
see also eight; three-dimensional
adj dreidimensional; three-piece
suit *n* Anzug m mit Weste; three-
quarters *npl* drei Viertel *pl*

threshold ['θreʃhəʊld] *n*
Schwelle f

threw [θru:] *pt of* throw

thrifty ['θrɪftɪ] *adj* sparsam

thrilled [θrɪld] *adj* to be ~ (with
sth) sich (über etw *akk*) riesig freu-
en; thriller *n* Thriller m; thrilling
adj aufregend

thrive [θraɪv] *vi* gedeihen (*on* bei);
(*fig, business*) florieren

throat [θrəʊt] *n* Hals m, Kehle f

throbbing ['θrɒbɪŋ] *adj* (*pain,
headache*) pochend

thrombosis [θrɒm'bəʊsɪs] *n*
Thrombose f; deep vein ~ tiefe Ve-
nenthrombose f

throne [θrəʊn] *n* Thron m

through [θru:] *prep* durch; (*time*)
während +gen; (*because of*) aus,
durch; (US: up to and including) bis;
arranged ~ him durch ihn arrangiert ▷ *adv* durch; to put sb ~ (*Tel*)
jdn verbinden (to mit) ▷ *adj* (*ticket,
train*) durchgehend; ~ flight Direktflug m; to be ~ with sb/sth mit
jdm/etw fertig sein; throughout
[θru:'aʊt] *prep* (*place*) überall in
+dat; (*time*) während +gen; ~ the
night die ganze Nacht hindurch ▷
adv überall; (*time*) die ganze Zeit

throw [θrəʊ] (threw, thrown) *vt*
werfen; (*rider*) abwerfen; (*party*) geben; to ~ sth to sb, to ~ sb sth jdm
etw zuwerfen; I was ~n by his
question seine Frage hat mich aus
dem Konzept gebracht ▷ *n* Wurf m;
throw away *vt* wegwerfen; throw
in *vt* (*include*) dazugeben; throw
out *vt* (*unwanted object*) wegwerfen; (*person*) hinauswerfen (of aus);
throw up *vt, vi* (*fam: vomit*) sich
übergeben; throw-in *n* Einwurf m

thrown [θrəʊn] *pp of* throw

thru (US) *see* through

thrush [θrʌʃ] *n* Drossel f

thrust [θrʌst] (thrust, thrust) *vt,
vi* (*push*) stoßen

thruway ['θru:weɪ] *n* (US)
Schnellstraße f

thumb [θʌm] n Daumen m ▷ vt **to ~ a lift** per Anhalter fahren; **thumbtack** n (US) Reißzwecke f

thunder ['θʌndə*] n Donner m ▷ vi donnern; **thunderstorm** n Gewitter nt

Thur(s) abbr = **Thursday** Do.

Thursday ['θɜːzdɪ] n Donnerstag m; see also **Tuesday**

thus [ðʌs] adv (in this way) so; (therefore) somit, also

thyme [taɪm] n Thymian m

Tibet [tɪ'bet] n Tibet nt

tick [tɪk] n (BRIT: mark) Häkchen nt ▷ vt (name) abhaken; (box, answer) ankreuzen ▷ vi (clock) ticken

ticket ['tɪkɪt] n (for train, bus) (Fahr)karte f; (plane ~) Flugschein m, Ticket nt; (for theatre, match, museum etc) (Eintritts)karte f; (price ~) (Preis)schild nt; (raffle ~) Los nt; (for car park) Parkschein m; (for traffic offence) Strafzettel m; **ticket collector, ticket inspector** (BRIT) n Fahrkartenkontrolleur(in) m(f); **ticket machine** n (for public transport) Fahrscheinautomat m; (in car park) Parkscheinautomat m; **ticket office** n (Rail) Fahrkartenschalter m; (Theat) Kasse f

tickle ['tɪkl] vt kitzeln; **ticklish** ['tɪklɪʃ] adj kitzlig

tide [taɪd] n Gezeiten pl; **the ~ is in/out** es ist Flut/Ebbe

tidy ['taɪdɪ] adj ordentlich ▷ vt aufräumen; **tidy up** vt, vi aufräumen

tie [taɪ] n (neck~) Krawatte f; (Sport) Unentschieden nt; (bond) Bindung f ▷ vt (attach, do up) binden (to an +akk); (~ together) zusammenbinden; (knot) machen ▷ vi (Sport) unentschieden spielen; **tie down** vt festbinden (to an +dat); (fig) binden; **tie up** vt (dog) anbinden; (parcel) verschnüren; (shoelace) binden;

(boat) festmachen; **I'm tied up** (fig) ich bin beschäftigt

tiger ['taɪgə*] n Tiger m

tight [taɪt] adj (clothes) eng; (knot) fest; (screw, lid) fest sitzend; (control, security measures) streng; (timewise) knapp; (schedule) eng ▷ adv (shut) fest; (pull) stramm; **hold ~** festhalten; **sleep ~** schlaf gut!; **tighten** vt (knot, rope, screw) anziehen; (belt) enger machen; (restrictions, control) verschärfen; **tights** npl (BRIT) Strumpfhose f

tile [taɪl] n (on roof) Dachziegel m; (on wall, floor) Fliese f; **tiled** adj (roof) Ziegel-; (floor, wall) gefliest

till [tɪl] n Kasse f ▷ prep, conj see **until**

tilt [tɪlt] vt kippen; (head) neigen ▷ vi sich neigen

time [taɪm] n Zeit f; (occasion) Mal nt; (Mus) Takt m; **local ~** Ortszeit; **what ~ is it?, what's the ~?** wie spät ist es?, wie viel Uhr ist es?; **to take one's ~** (over sth) sich (bei etw) Zeit lassen; **to have a good ~** Spaß haben; **in two weeks' ~** in zwei Wochen; **at ~s** manchmal; **at the same ~** gleichzeitig; **all the ~** die ganze Zeit; **by the ~ ...** bis er ...; (in past) als er ...; **for the ~ being** vorläufig; **in ~** (not late) rechtzeitig; **on ~** pünktlich; **the first ~** das erste Mal; **this ~** diesmal; **five ~s** fünfmal; **five × six** fünf mal sechs; **four ~s a year** viermal im Jahr; **three at a ~** drei auf einmal ▷ vt (with stopwatch) stoppen; **you ~d that well** das hast du gut getimt; **time difference** n Zeitunterschied m; **time limit** n Frist f; **timer** n Timer m; (switch) Schaltuhr f; **time-saving** adj Zeit sparend; **time switch** n Schaltuhr f; **timetable** n (for public transport) Fahrplan m; (school) Stundenplan m; **time zone** n Zeitzone f

timid ['tɪmɪd] *adj* ängstlich

timing ['taɪmɪŋ] *n* (*coordination*) Timing *nt*, zeitliche Abstimmung

tin [tɪn] *n* (*metal*) Blech *nt*; (BRIT: *can*) Dose *f*; **tinfoil** *n* Alufolie *f*; **tinned** *adj* (BRIT) aus der Dose; **tin opener** *n* (BRIT) Dosenöffner *m*

tinsel ['tɪnsəl] *n* ≈ Lametta *nt*

tint [tɪnt] *n* (Farb)ton *m*; (*in hair*) Tönung *f*; **tinted** *adj* getönt

tiny ['taɪnɪ] *adj* winzig

tip [tɪp] *n* (*money*) Trinkgeld *nt*; (*hint*) Tipp *m*; (*end*) Spitze *f*; (*of cigarette*) Filter *m*; (BRIT: *rubbish*) Müllkippe *f* ▷ *vt* (*waiter*) Trinkgeld geben +*dat*; **tip over** *vt, vi* (*overturn*) umkippen

tipsy ['tɪpsɪ] *adj* beschwipst

tiptoe ['tɪptəʊ] *n* **on ~** auf Zehenspitzen

tire [taɪə*] *n* (US) see **tyre** ▷ *vt* müde machen ▷ *vi* müde werden; **tired** *adj* müde, **to be ~ of sb/sth** jdn/etw satt haben; **to be ~ of doing sth** es satt haben, etw zu tun; **tireless, tirelessly** *adv* unermüdlich; **tiresome** *adj* lästig; **tiring** *adj* ermüdend

Tirol [tɪˈrəʊl] see **Tyrol**

tissue ['tɪʃuː] *n* (Anat) Gewebe *nt*; (*paper handkerchief*) Tempotaschentuch® *nt*, Papier(taschen)tuch *nt*; **tissue paper** *n* Seidenpapier *nt*

tit [tɪt] *n* (*bird*) Meise *f*; (*fam*: *breast*) Titte *f*

title ['taɪtl] *n* Titel *m*

to [tuː, tə] *prep* (*towards*) zu; (*with countries, regions*) nach; (*as far as*) bis; (*with infinitive of verb*) zu; **~ Rome / Switzerland** nach Rom / in die Schweiz; **I've been ~ London** ich war schon mal in London; **to go ~ town / ~ the theatre** in die Stadt / Ins Theater gehen; **from Monday ~ Thursday** von Montag bis Donnerstag; **he came ~ say sorry** er kam, um sich zu entschuldigen; **the key ~ my room** der Schlüssel zu meinem Zimmer; **20 minutes ~ 4** 20 Minuten vor 4; **12 kilometres ~ the litre** 12 Kilometer pro Liter; **they won by 4 goals ~ 3** sie haben mit 4 zu 3 Toren gewonnen

toad [təʊd] *n* Kröte *f*; **toadstool** *n* Giftpilz *m*

toast [təʊst] *n* (*bread, drink*) Toast *m*; **a piece (o slice) of ~** eine Scheibe Toast; **to propose a ~ to sb** einen Toast auf jdn ausbringen ▷ *vt* (*bread*) toasten; (*person*) trinken auf +*akk*, **toaster** *n* Toaster *m*

tobacco [təˈbækəʊ] (*pl* **-es**) *n* Tabak *m*; **tobacconist's** [təˈbækənɪsts] *n* ~ (**shop**) Tabakladen *m*

toboggan [təˈbɒgən] *n* Schlitten *m*

today [təˈdeɪ] *adv* heute; **a week ~** heute in einer Woche; **~'s newspaper** die Zeitung von heute

toddler ['tɒdlə*] *n* Kleinkind *nt*

toe [təʊ] *n* Zehe *f*, Zeh *m*; **toenail** *n* Zehennagel *m*

toffee ['tɒfɪ] *n* (*sweet*) Karamellbonbon *nt*; **toffee apple** *n* kandierter Apfel

tofu ['təʊfuː] *n* Tofu *m*

together [təˈgeðə*] *adv* zusammen; **I tied them ~** ich habe sie zusammengebunden

toilet ['tɔɪlət] *n* Toilette *f*; **to go to the ~** auf die Toilette gehen; **toilet bag** *n* Kulturbeutel *m*; **toilet paper** *n* Toilettenpapier *nt*; **toiletries** ['tɔɪlətrɪz] *npl* Toilettenartikel *pl*; **toilet roll** *n* Rolle *f* Toilettenpapier

token ['təʊkən] *n* Marke *f*; (*in casino*) Spielmarke *f*; (*voucher, gift ~*) Gutschein *m*; (*sign*) Zeichen *nt*

Tokyo ['təʊkɪəʊ] *n* Tokio *nt*

told [təʊld] *pt, pp of* **tell**

tolerant ['tɒlərənt] *adj* tolerant (of gegenüber); **tolerate** ['tɒləreɪt] *vt* tolerieren; (noise, pain, heat) ertragen

toll [təʊl] *n* (charge) Gebühr *f*; **the death** ~ die Zahl der Toten; **toll-free** *adj, adv* (US Tel) gebührenfrei; **toll road** *n* gebührenpflichtige Straße

tomato [tə'mɑːtəʊ] (*pl* **-es**) *n* Tomate *f*; **tomato juice** *n* Tomatensaft *m*; **tomato ketchup** *n* Tomatenket(s)chup *m o nt*; **tomato sauce** *n* Tomatensoße *f*; (BRIT: ketchup) Tomatenket(s)chup *m o nt*

tomb [tuːm] *n* Grabmal *nt*; **tombstone** *n* Grabstein *m*

tomorrow [tə'mɒrəʊ] *adv* morgen; ~ **morning** morgen früh; ~ **evening** morgen Abend; **the day after** ~ übermorgen; **a week (from)** ~/~ **week** morgen in einer Woche

ton [tʌn] *n* (BRIT) Tonne *f* (1016 kg); (US) Tonne *f* (907 kg); **~s of books** (fam) eine Menge Bücher

tone [təʊn] *n* Ton *m*; **tone down** *vt* mäßigen; **toner** ['təʊnə*] *n* (for printer) Toner *m*; **toner cartridge** *n* Tonerpatrone *f*

tongs [tɒŋz] *npl* Zange *f*; (curling ~) Lockenstab *m*

tongue [tʌŋ] *n* Zunge *f*

tonic ['tɒnɪk] *n* (Med) Stärkungsmittel *nt*; ~ **(water)** Tonic *nt*; **gin and** ~ Gin *m* Tonic

tonight [tə'naɪt] *adv* heute Abend; (during night) heute Nacht

tonsils ['tɒnslz] *n* Mandeln *pl*; **tonsillitis** [tɒnsɪ'laɪtɪs] *n* Mandelentzündung *f*

too [tuː] *adv* zu; (also) auch; ~ **fast** zu schnell; ~ **much/many** zu viel/viele; **me** ~ ich auch; **she liked it** ~ ihr gefiel es auch

took [tʊk] *pt of* **take**

tool [tuːl] *n* Werkzeug *nt*; **tool-**

bar *n* (Inform) Symbolleiste *f*; **toolbox** *n* Werkzeugkasten *m*

tooth [tuːθ] (*pl* **teeth**) *n* Zahn *m*; **toothache** *n* Zahnschmerzen *pl*; **toothbrush** *n* Zahnbürste *f*; **toothpaste** *n* Zahnpasta *f*; **toothpick** *n* Zahnstocher *m*

top [tɒp] *n* (of tower, class, company etc) Spitze *f*; (of mountain) Gipfel *m*; (of tree) Krone *f*; (of street) oberes Ende; (of tube, pen) Kappe *f*; (of box) Deckel *m*; (of bikini) Oberteil *nt*; (sleeveless) Top *nt*; **at the ~ of the page** oben auf der Seite; **at the ~ of the league** an der Spitze der Liga; **on** ~ oben ▷ **on** ~ **of** auf +dat; (in addition to) zusätzlich zu; **in** ~ **(gear)** im höchsten Gang; **over the** ~ übertrieben ▷ *adj* (floor, shelf) oberste(r, s); (price, note) höchste(r, s); (best) Spitzen-; (pupil, school) beste(r, s) ▷ *vt* (exceed) übersteigen; (be better than) übertreffen; **an erster Stelle liegen in** +dat; **~ped with cream** mit Sahne obendrauf; **top up** *vt* auffüllen; **can I top you up?** darf ich dir nachschenken?

topic ['tɒpɪk] *n* Thema *nt*; **topical** *adj* aktuell

topless ['tɒpləs] *adj, adv* oben ohne

topping ['tɒpɪŋ] *n* (on top of pizza, ice-cream etc) Belag *m*, Garnierung *f*

top-secret ['tɒp'siːkrət] *adj* streng geheim

torch [tɔːtʃ] *n* (BRIT) Taschenlampe *f*

tore [tɔː*] *pt of* **tear**

torment [tɔː'ment] *vt* quälen

torn [tɔːn] *pp of* **tear**

tornado [tɔː'neɪdəʊ] (*pl* **-es**) *n* Tornado *m*

torrential [tə'renʃəl] *adj* (rain) sintflutartig

tortoise ['tɔːtəs] *n* Schildkröte *f*

torture ['tɔːtʃə*] *n* Folter *f*; (fig)

Qual f ▷ vt foltern

Tory ['tɔːrɪ] n Tory m, Konservative(r) mf ▷ adj Tory-

toss [tɒs] vt (throw) werfen; (salad) anmachen; **to ~ a coin** eine Münze werfen ▷ n **I don't give a ~** (fam) es ist mir scheißegal

total ['təutl] n (of figures, money) Gesamtsumme f; **a ~ of 30** insgesamt 30; **in ~** insgesamt ▷ adj total; (sum etc) Gesamt- ▷ vt (amount to) sich belaufen auf +akk; **totally** adv total

touch [tʌtʃ] n (act of ~ing) Berührung f; (sense of ~) Tastsinn m; (trace) Spur f; **to be/keep in ~ with sb** mit jdm in Verbindung stehen/bleiben; **to get in ~ with sb** sich mit jdm in Verbindung setzen; **to lose ~ with sb** den Kontakt zu jdm verlieren ▷ vt (feel) berühren; (emotionally) bewegen; **touch on** vt (topic) berühren; **touchdown** n (Aviat) Landung f; (Sport) Touchdown m; **touching** adj (moving) rührend; **touch screen** n Touchscreen m, Berührungsbildschirm m; **touchy** adj empfindlich, zickig

tough [tʌf] adj hart; (meat) zäh; (material) robust; (meat) zäh

tour ['tuə*] n Tour f (of durch); (of town, building) Rundgang m (of durch); (of pop group etc) Tournee f ▷ vt eine Tour / einen Rundgang / eine Tournee machen durch ▷ vi (on holiday) umherreisen; **tour guide** n Reiseleiter(in) m(f)

tourism ['tuərɪzəm] n Tourismus m, Fremdenverkehr m; **tourist** n Tourist(in) m(f); **tourist class** n Touristenklasse f; **tourist guide** n (book) Reiseführer m; (person) Fremdenführer(in) m(f); **tourist office** n Fremdenverkehrsamt nt

tournament ['tuənəmənt] n Turnier nt

tour operator ['tuərɒpəreɪtə*] n Reiseveranstalter m

tow [təu] vt abschleppen; (caravan, trailer) ziehen; **tow away** vt abschleppen

towards [tə'wɔːdz] prep **~ me** mir entgegen, auf mich zu; **we walked ~ the station** wir gingen in Richtung Bahnhof; **my feelings ~ him** meine Gefühle ihm gegenüber; **she was kind ~ me** sie war nett zu mir

towel ['tauəl] n Handtuch nt

tower ['tauə*] n Turm m; **tower block** n (BRIT) Hochhaus nt

town [taun] n Stadt f; **town center** (US), **town centre** n Stadtmitte f, Stadtzentrum nt; **town hall** n Rathaus nt

towrope ['təurəup] n Abschleppseil nt; **tow truck** n (US) Abschleppwagen m

toxic ['tɒksɪk] adj giftig, Gift-

toy [tɔɪ] n Spielzeug nt; **toy with** vt spielen mit; **toyshop** n Spielwarengeschäft nt

trace [treɪs] n Spur f; **without ~** spurlos ▷ vt (find) ausfindig machen; **tracing paper** n Pauspapier nt

track [træk] n (mark) Spur f; (path) Weg m; (Rail) Gleis nt; (on CD, record) Stück nt; **to keep/lose ~ of sb/sth** jdn / etw im Auge behalten / aus den Augen verlieren; **track down** vt ausfindig machen; **trackball** n (inform) Trackball m; **tracksuit** n Trainingsanzug m

tractor ['træktə*] n Traktor m

trade [treɪd] n (commerce) Handel m; (business) Geschäft nt; (skilled job) Handwerk nt ▷ vi handeln (in mit) ▷ vt (exchange) tauschen (for gegen); **trademark** n Warenzeichen nt; **tradesman** (pl -**men**) n (shopkeeper) Geschäftsmann m; (workman) Handwerker m; **trade(s) union** n

(BRIT) Gewerkschaft f

tradition [trə'dɪʃən] n Tradition f;
traditional, **traditionally** adj, adv
traditionell

traffic ['træfɪk] n Verkehr m; (pej:
trading) Handel m (in mit); **traffic
circle** n (US) Kreisverkehr m; **traffic island** n Verkehrsinsel f; **traffic
jam** n Stau m; **traffic lights** npl
Verkehrsampel f; **traffic warden** n
(BRIT) ≈ Politesse f

tragedy ['trædʒədɪ] n Tragödie f;
tragic ['trædʒɪk] adj tragisch

trail [treɪl] n Spur f; (path) Weg m
▷ vt (follow) verfolgen; (drag)
schleppen; (drag behind) hinter sich
herziehen; (Sport) zurückliegen hinter +dat ▷ vi (hang loosely) schleifen;
(Sport) weit zurückliegen; **trailer** n
Anhänger m; (US: caravan) Wohnwagen m; (Cine) Trailer m

train [treɪn] n (Rail) Zug m ▷ vt
(teach) ausbilden; (Sport) trainieren ▷
vi (Sport) trainieren; **to ~ as** (o **to be**)
a teacher eine Ausbildung als Lehrer machen; **trained** adj (person,
voice) ausgebildet; **trainee** n Aus-
zubildende(r) mf; (academic, practical) Praktikant(in) mf; **trainer** n
(Sport) Trainer(in) mf; **~s** (BRIT:
shoes) Turnschuhe pl; **training** n
Ausbildung f; (Sport) Training m;
train station n Bahnhof m

tram [træm] n (BRIT) Straßenbahn f

tramp [træmp] n Landstrei-
cher(in) mf) ▷ vi trotten

tranquillizer ['træŋkwɪlaɪzə*] n
Beruhigungsmittel nt

transaction n (piece of business)
Geschäft nt

transatlantic ['trænzæt'læntɪk]
adj transatlantisch; **~ flight** Trans-
atlantikflug m

transfer ['trænsfə*] n (of money)
Überweisung f; (US: ticket) Umstei-

gekarte f ▷ [træns'fɜː*] vt (money)
überweisen (to sb an jdn); (patient)
verlegen; (employee) versetzen;
(Sport) transferieren ▷ vi (on journey)
umsteigen; **transferable** [træns-
'fɜːrəbl] adj übertragbar

transform [træns'fɔːm] vt umwandeln; **transformation** [træns-
fə'meɪʃən] n Umwandlung f

transfusion [træns'fjuːʒən] n
Transfusion f

transistor [træn'zɪstə*] n Transistor m; **~ (radio)** Transistorradio nt

transition [træn'zɪʃən] n Übergang m (from ... to von ... zu)

transit lounge ['trænzɪtlaʊndʒ]
n Transitraum m; **transit passenger** n Transitreisende(r) mf

translate [trænz'leɪt] vt, vi
übersetzen; **translation** [trænz-
'leɪʃən] n Übersetzung f; **translator** [trænz'leɪtə*] n Übersetzer(in)
mf)

transmission [trænz'mɪʃən] n
(Tv, Radio) Übertragung f; (Auto) Getriebe nt

transparent [træns'pærənt] adj
durchsichtig; (fig) offenkundig

transplant [træns'plɑːnt] (Med)
vt transplantieren ▷
['trænsplɑːnt] n (operation) Transplantation f

transport [n] [n] ['trænspɔːt] n (of
goods, people) Beförderung f; **public
~** öffentliche Verkehrsmittel pl ▷
[træns'pɔːt] vt befördern, transportieren; **transportation** [træns-
pɔː'teɪʃən] n see **transport**

trap [træp] n Falle f ▷ vt **to be
~ped** (in snow, job etc) festsitzen

trash [træʃ] n (book, film etc)
Schund m; (US: refuse) Abfall m;
trash can n (US) Abfalleimer m;
trashy adj niveaulos; (novel)
Schund-

traumatic [trɔː'mætɪk] adj traumatisch

travel ['trævl] n Reisen nt ▷ vi
(journey) reisen ▷ vt (distance) zurücklegen; (country) bereisen; **travel
agency, travel agent** n (company)
Reisebüro nt; **traveler** (US) see
traveller traveler's check (US) see
**traveller's cheque; travel insur-
ance** n Reiseversicherung f; **traveller** n Reisende(r) mf; **traveller's
cheque** n (BRIT) Reisescheck m;
travelsick n reisekrank

tray [treɪ] n Tablett nt; (for mail etc)
Ablage f; (of printer, photocopier) Fach
nt

tread [tred] n (on tyre) Profil nt;
tread on [tred] (**trod, trodden**) vt
treten auf +akk

treasure ['treʒə*] n Schatz m ▷
vt schätzen

treat [triːt] n besondere Freude;
it's my ~ das geht auf meine Kosten
▷ vt behandeln; **to ~ sb (to sth)** jdn
(zu etw) einladen; **to ~ oneself to
sth** sich etw leisten; **treatment**
['triːtmənt] n Behandlung f

treaty ['triːtɪ] n Vertrag m

tree [triː] n Baum m

tremble ['trembl] vi zittern

tremendous [trə'mendəs] adj
gewaltig; (fam: very good) toll

trench [trentʃ] n Graben m

trend [trend] n Tendenz f; (fashion) Mode f, Trend m; **trendy** adj
trendy

trespass ['trespəs] vi **'no ~ing'**
„Betreten verboten"

trial ['traɪəl] n (Jur) Prozess m;
(test) Versuch m; **by ~ and error**
durch Ausprobieren; **trial period** n
(for employee) Probezeit f

triangle ['traɪæŋgl] n Dreieck nt;
(Mus) Triangel m; **triangular** [traɪ-
'æŋgjʊlə*] adj dreieckig

tribe [traɪb] n Stamm m

trick [trɪk] n Trick m; (mischief)

Streich m ▷ vt hereinlegen

tricky ['trɪkɪ] adj (difficult)
schwierig; (situation) verzwickt

trifle ['traɪfl] n Kleinigkeit f; (BRIT
Gastr) Trifle nt (Nachspeise aus Biskuit,
Wackelpudding, Obst, Vanillesoße und
Sahne)

trigger ['trɪgə*] n (of gun) Abzug m
▷ vt **to ~ (off)** auslösen

trim [trɪm] vt (hair, beard) nachschneiden; (nails) schneiden; (hedge)
stutzen ▷ n **just a ~**, bitte etwas
nachschneiden; **trim-
mings** npl (decorations) Verzierun-
gen pl; (extras) Zubehör nt; (Gastr)
Beilagen pl

trip [trɪp] n Reise f; (outing) Ausflug
m ▷ vi stolpern (over über +akk)

triple ['trɪpl] adj dreifach ▷ adv ~
the price dreimal so teuer ▷ vi sich
verdreifachen; **triplets** ['trɪplɪts]
npl Drillinge pl

tripod ['traɪpɒd] n (Foto) Stativ nt

trite [traɪt] adj banal

triumph ['traɪʌmf] n Triumph m

trivial ['trɪvɪəl] adj trivial

trod [trɒd] pt of **tread**

trodden pp of **tread**

trolley ['trɒlɪ] n (BRIT: in shop)
Einkaufswagen m; (for luggage) Kof-
ferkuli m; (serving ~) Teewagen m

trombone [trɒm'bəʊn] n Posaune f

troops [truːps] npl (Mil) Truppen pl

trophy ['trəʊfɪ] n Trophäe f

tropical ['trɒpɪkl] adj tropisch

trouble ['trʌbl] n (problems)
Schwierigkeiten pl; (worry) Sorgen pl;
(effort) Mühe f; (unrest) Unruhen pl;
(Med) Beschwerden pl; **to be in ~** in
Schwierigkeiten sein; **to get into ~**
(with authority) Ärger bekommen; **to
make ~** Schwierigkeiten machen ▷
vt (worry) beunruhigen; (disturb)
stören; **my back's troubling me**
mein Rücken macht mir zu schaffen;

sorry to ~ you ich muss dich leider kurz stören; **troubled** adj (worried) beunruhigt; **trouble-free** adj problemlos; **troublemaker** n Unruhestifter(in) m(f); **troublesome** adj lästig

trousers [ˈtraʊzəz] npl Hose f; **trouser suit** n (BRIT) Hosenanzug m

trout [traʊt] n Forelle f

truck [trʌk] n Lastwagen m; (BRIT Rail) Güterwagen m; **trucker** n (US: driver) Lastwagenfahrer(in) m(f)

true [truː] adj (factually correct) wahr; (genuine) echt; **to come ~** wahr werden

truly [ˈtruːlɪ] adv wirklich; **Yours ~** (in letter) mit freundlichen Grüßen

trump [trʌmp] n (Cards) Trumpf m

trumpet [ˈtrʌmpɪt] n Trompete f

trunk [trʌŋk] n (of tree) Stamm m; (Anat) Rumpf m; (of elephant) Rüssel m; (piece of luggage) Überseekoffer m; (US Auto) Kofferraum m; **trunks** npl (swimming) ~ Badehose f

trust [trʌst] n (confidence) Vertrauen nt (in zu) ▷ vt vertrauen +dat; **trusting** adj vertrauensvoll; **trustworthy** adj vertrauenswürdig

truth [truːθ] n Wahrheit f; **truthful** adj ehrlich; (statement) wahrheitsgemäß

try [traɪ] n Versuch m ▷ vt (attempt) versuchen; (~ out) ausprobieren; (sample) probieren; (Jur: person) vor Gericht stellen ▷ vi versuchen; (make effort) sich bemühen; **~ and come** versuch zu kommen; **try on** vt (clothes) anprobieren; **try out** vt ausprobieren

T-shirt [ˈtiːʃɜːt] n T-Shirt nt

tub [tʌb] n (for ice-cream, margarine) Becher m

tube [tjuːb] n (pipe) Rohr nt; (of rubber, plastic) Schlauch m; (for toothpaste, glue etc) Tube f; **the Tube** (in London) die U-Bahn

tube station [ˈtjuːbsteɪʃən] n U-Bahn-Station f

tuck [tʌk] vt (put) stecken; **tuck in** vt (shirt) in die Hose stecken; (blanket) feststecken; (person) zudecken ▷ vi (eat) zulangen

Tue(s) abbr = **Tuesday** Di.

Tuesday [ˈtjuːzdɪ] n Dienstag m; **on ~** (am) Dienstag; **on ~s** dienstags; **this / last / next ~** diesen / letzten / nächsten Dienstag; **(on) ~ morning / afternoon / evening** (am) Dienstag Morgen / Nachmittag / Abend; **every ~** jeden Dienstag; **a week on ~ / ~ week** Dienstag in einer Woche

tug [tʌg] vt ziehen; **she ~ged his sleeve** sie zog an seinem Ärmel ▷ vi ziehen (at an +dat)

tuition [tjuːˈɪʃən] n Unterricht m; (US: fees) Studiengebühren pl; **~ fees** pl Studiengebühren pl

tulip [ˈtjuːlɪp] n Tulpe f

tumble [ˈtʌmbl] vi (person, prices) fallen; **tumble dryer** n Wäschetrockner m; **tumbler** n (glass) (Becher)glas nt

tummy [ˈtʌmɪ] n (fam) Bauch m; **tummyache** n (fam) Bauchweh nt

tumor (US), **tumour** [ˈtjuːmə*] n Tumor m

tuna [ˈtjuːnə] n Thunfisch m

tune [tjuːn] n Melodie f; **to be in / out of ~** (instrument) gestimmt / verstimmt sein; (singer) richtig / falsch singen ▷ vt (instrument) stimmen; (radio) einstellen (to auf +akk); **tuner** n (in stereo system) Tuner m

Tunisia [tjuːˈnɪzɪə] n Tunesien nt

tunnel [ˈtʌnl] n Tunnel m; (under road, railway) Unterführung f

turban [ˈtɜːbən] n Turban m

turbulence ['tɜːbjʊləns] n (Aviat) Turbulenzen pl; **turbulent** adj stürmisch

Turk [tɜːk] n Türke m, Türkin f

turkey ['tɜːkɪ] n Truthahn m

Turkey ['tɜːkɪ] n die Türkei, **Turkish** adj türkisch ▷ n (language) Türkisch nt

turmoil ['tɜːmɔɪl] n Aufruhr m

turn [tɜːn] n (rotation) Drehung f; (performance) Nummer f; **to make a left** ~ nach links abbiegen; **at the** ~ **of the century** um die Jahrhundertwende; **it's your** ~ du bist dran; **in** ~, **by** ~**s** abwechselnd; **to take** ~**s** sich abwechseln ▷ vt (wheel, key, screw) drehen; (to face other way) umdrehen; (corner) biegen um; (page) umblättern; (transform) verwandeln (into in +akk) ▷ vi (rotate) sich drehen; (to face other way) sich umdrehen; (change direction: driver, car) abbiegen; (become) werden; (weather) umschlagen; **to** ~ **into sth** (become) sich in etw akk verwandeln; **to** ~ **cold/green** kalt/grün werden; **to** ~ **left/right** links/rechts abbiegen; **turn away** vt (person) abweisen ▷ vi (go back) umkehren; **turn back** vt (person) zurückweisen ▷ vi (go back) umkehren; **turn down** vt (refuse) ablehnen; (radio, TV) leiser stellen; (heating) kleiner stellen; **turn off** vi abbiegen ▷ vt (switch off) ausschalten; (tap) zudrehen; (engine, electricity) abstellen; **turn on** vt (switch on) einschalten; (tap) aufdrehen; (engine, electricity) anstellen; (fam: person) anmachen, antörnen; **turn out** vt (light) ausmachen; (pockets) leeren ▷ vi (develop) sich entwickeln; **as it turned out** wie sich herausstellte; **turn over** vt (onto other side, umdrehen; (page) umblättern ▷ vi (person) sich umdrehen; (car) sich überschlagen; (TV) umschalten (to auf +akk); **turn**

round vt (to face other way) umdrehen ▷ vi (person) sich umdrehen; (go back) umkehren; **turn to** vt sich zuwenden +dat; **turn up** vi (person, lost object) auftauchen ▷ vt (radio, TV) lauter stellen; (heating) höher stellen; **turning** n (in road) Abzweigung f; **turning point** n Wendepunkt m

turnip ['tɜːnɪp] n Rübe f

turnover ['tɜːnəʊvə*] n (Fin) Umsatz m

turnpike ['tɜːnpaɪk] n (US) gebührenpflichtige Autobahn

turntable ['tɜːnteɪbl] n (on record player) Plattenteller m

turn-up ['tɜːnʌp] n (BRIT: on trousers) Aufschlag m

turquoise ['tɜːkwɔɪz] adj türkis

turtle ['tɜːtl] n (BRIT) Wasserschildkröte f; (US) Schildkröte f

tutor ['tjuːtə*] n (private) Privatlehrer(in) m(f); (BRIT: at university) Tutor(in) m(f)

tuxedo [tʌk'siːdəʊ] (pl -s) n (US) Smoking m

TV ['tiː'viː] n Fernsehen nt; (~ set) Fernseher m; **to watch** ~ fernsehen; **on** ~ im Fernsehen ▷ adj Fernseh-; ~ **programme** Fernsehsendung f

tweed [twiːd] n Tweed m

tweezers ['twiːzəz] npl Pinzette f

twelfth [twelfθ] adj zwölfte(r, s); see also **eighth**; **twelve** [twelv] num zwölf ▷ n Zwölf f; see also **eight**

twentieth ['twentɪθ] adj zwanzigste(r, s); see also **eighth**; **twenty** ['twentɪ] num zwanzig; ~**-one** einundzwanzig ▷ n Zwanzig f; **to be in one's twenties** in den Zwanzigern sein; see also **eight**

twice [twaɪs] adv zweimal; ~ **as much/many** doppelt so viel/viele

twig [twɪg] n Zweig m

twilight ['twaɪlaɪt] n (in evening)

Dämmerung f

twin [twɪn] n Zwilling m ▷ adj (brother etc) Zwillings-; **~ beds** zwei Einzelbetten

twinge [twɪndʒ] n (pain) stechender Schmerz

twinkle ['twɪŋkl] vi funkeln

twin room [twɪn'ruːm] n Zweibettzimmer nt; **twin town** n Partnerstadt f

twist [twɪst] vt (turn) drehen, winden; (distort) verdrehen; **I've ~ed my ankle** ich bin mit dem Fuß umgeknickt

two [tuː] num zwei; **to break sth in ~** etw in zwei Teile brechen ▷ n Zwei f; **the ~ of them** die beiden; see also **eight**; **two-dimensional** adj zweidimensional; (fig) oberflächlich; **two-faced** adj falsch, heuchlerisch; **two-piece** adj zweiteilig; **two-way** adj **~ traffic** Gegenverkehr

type [taɪp] n (sort) Art f; (typeface) Schrift(art) f; **what ~ of car is it?** was für ein Auto ist das?; **he's not my ~** er ist nicht mein Typ; **typeface** n Schrift(art) f; **typewriter** n Schreibmaschine f

typhoid ['taɪfɔɪd] n Typhus m

typhoon [taɪ'fuːn] n Taifun m

typical ['tɪpɪkəl] adj typisch (of für)

typing error ['taɪpɪŋerə*] n Tippfehler m

tyre [taɪə*] n (BRIT) Reifen m; **tyre pressure** n Reifendruck m

Tyrol [tɪ'rəʊl] n **the ~** Tirol nt

UFO ['juːfəʊ] acr = **unidentified flying object** Ufo nt

Uganda [juː'gændə] n Uganda nt

ugly ['ʌglɪ] adj hässlich; (bad) schlimm

UHT adj abbr = **ultra-heat treated ~ milk** H-Milch f

UK abbr = **United Kingdom**

Ukraine [juː'kreɪn] n **the ~** die Ukraine

ulcer ['ʌlsə*] n Geschwür nt

ulterior [ʌl'tɪərɪə*] adj **~ motive** Hintergedanke m

ultimate ['ʌltɪmət] adj (final) letzte(r, s); (authority) höchste(r, s); **ultimately** adv letzten Endes; (eventually) schließlich; **ultimatum** [ʌltɪ'meɪtəm] n Ultimatum nt

ultra- ['ʌltrə] pref ultra-

ultrasound ['ʌltrəsaʊnd] n (Med) Ultraschall m

umbrella [ʌm'brelə] n Schirm m

umpire ['ʌmpaɪə*] n Schiedsrichter(in) m(f)

umpteen ['ʌmptiːn] num (fam)

zig; ~ **times** zigmal
un- [ʌn] *pref* un-
UN *nsing abbr* = **United Nations**
UNO f
unable [ʌn'eɪbl] *adj* **to be ~ to do sth** etw nicht tun können
unacceptable [ʌnə'kseptəbl] *adj* unannehmbar
unaccountably [ʌnə'kauntəblɪ] *adv* unerklärlicherweise
unaccustomed [ʌnə'kʌstəmd] *adj* **to be ~ to sth** etw nicht gewohnt sein
unanimous, unanimously [ju:-'nænɪməs, -lɪ] *adj, adv* einmütig
unattached [ʌnə'tætʃt] *adj* (*without partner*) ungebunden
unattended [ʌnə'tendɪd] *adj* (*luggage, car*) unbeaufsichtigt
unauthorized [ʌn'ɔ:θəraɪzd] *adj* unbefugt
unavailable [ʌnə'veɪləbl] *adj* nicht erhältlich; (*person*) nicht erreichbar
unavoidable [ʌnə'vɔɪdəbl] *adj* unvermeidlich
unaware [ʌnə'weə*] *adj* **to be ~ of sth** sich einer Sache *dat* nicht bewusst sein; **I was ~ that ...** ich wusste nicht, dass ...
unbalanced [ʌn'bælənst] *adj* unausgewogen; (*mentally*) gestört
unbearable [ʌn'beərəbl] *adj* unerträglich
unbeatable [ʌn'bi:təbl] *adj* unschlagbar
unbelievable [ʌnbɪ'li:vəbl] *adj* unglaublich
unblock [ʌn'blɒk] *vt* (*pipe*) frei machen
unbutton [ʌn'bʌtn] *vt* aufknöpfen
uncertain [ʌn'sɜ:tən] *adj* unsicher
uncle [ʌŋkl] *n* Onkel m
uncomfortable [ʌn'kʌmfətəbl] *adj* unbequem
unconditional [ʌnkən'dɪʃənl] *adj* bedingungslos
unconscious [ʌn'kɒnʃəs] *adj* (*Med*) bewusstlos; **to be ~ of sth** sich einer Sache *dat* nicht bewusst sein; **unconsciously** *adv* unbewusst
uncork [ʌn'kɔ:k] *vt* entkorken
uncover [ʌn'kʌvə*] *vt* aufdecken
undecided [ʌndɪ'saɪdɪd] *adj* unschlüssig
undeniable [ʌndɪ'naɪəbl] *adj* unbestreitbar
under [ʌndə*] *prep* (*beneath*) unter +*dat*; (*with motion*) unter +*akk*; **children ~ sth** Kinder unter acht; **~ an hour** weniger als eine Stunde ▷ *adv* (*beneath*) unten; (*with motion*) darunter; **children aged eight and ~** Kinder bis zu acht Jahren; **under-age** *adj* minderjährig
undercarriage ['ʌndəkærɪdʒ] *n* Fahrgestell *nt*
underdog ['ʌndədɒg] *n* Unterlegene(r) *mf*; (*outsider*) Außenseiter(in) *m(f)*
underdone [ʌndə'dʌn] *adj* (*Gastr*) nicht gar, durch; (*deliberately*) nicht durchgebraten
underestimate [ʌndər'estɪmeɪt] *vt* unterschätzen
underexposed [ʌndərɪk'spəuzd] *adj* (*Foto*) unterbelichtet
undergo [ʌndə'gəu] *irr vt* (*experience*) durchmachen; (*operation, test*) sich unterziehen +*dat*
undergraduate [ʌndə'grædjuət] *n* Student(in) *m(f)*
underground ['ʌndəgraund] *adj* unterirdisch ▷ *n* (*BRIT Rail*) U-Bahn *f*; **underground station** *n* U-Bahn-Station *f*
underlie [ʌndə'laɪ] *irr vt* zugrunde liegen +*dat*
underline [ʌndə'laɪn] *vt* unterstreichen

underlying [ˌʌndəˈlaɪɪŋ] adj zugrunde liegend
underneath [ˌʌndəˈniːθ] prep
unter; (with motion) unter +akk ▷
adv darunter
underpants [ˈʌndəpænts] npl
Unterhose f; **undershirt** [ˈʌndəʃɜːt] n (US) Unterhemd nt; **under-
shorts** [ˈʌndəʃɔːts] npl (US) Un-
terhose f
understand [ˌʌndəˈstænd] irr vt,
vi verstehen; **I ~ that ...** (been told)
ich habe gehört, dass ...; (sympathize) ich habe Verständnis dafür,
dass ...; **to make oneself under-
stood** sich verständlich machen;
understandable adj verständlich;
understanding adj verständnisvoll
undertake [ˌʌndəˈteɪk] irr vt (task)
übernehmen; **to ~ to do sth** sich
verpflichten, etw zu tun; **under-
taker** n Leichenbestatter(in) m(f);
~'s (firm) Bestattungsinstitut nt
underwater [ˌʌndəˈwɔːtəˀ] adv
unter Wasser ▷ adj Unterwasser-
underwear [ˈʌndəwɛəˀ] n Unterwäsche f
undesirable [ˌʌndɪˈzaɪərəbl] adj
unerwünscht
undo [ʌnˈduː] irr vt
aufmachen; (work) zunichte machen; (Inform) rückgängig machen
undoubtedly [ʌnˈdaʊtɪdlɪ] adv
zweifellos
undress [ʌnˈdres] vt ausziehen;
to get ~ed sich ausziehen ▷ vi sich
ausziehen
undue [ʌnˈdjuː] adj übermäßig
unduly [ʌnˈdjuːlɪ] adv übermäßig
unearth [ʌnˈɜːθ] vt (dig up) ausgraben; (find) aufstöbern
unease [ʌnˈiːz] n Unbehagen nt;
uneasy [ʌnˈiːzɪ] adj (person) unbehaglich;
I'm ~ about it mir ist nicht wohl
dabei

unemployed [ˌʌnɪmˈplɔɪd] adj
arbeitslos ▷ ▷ npl **the ~** die Ar-
beitslosen pl; **unemployment**
[ˌʌnɪmˈplɔɪmənt] n Arbeitslosigkeit f; **unemployment benefit** n
Arbeitslosengeld nt
unequal [ʌnˈiːkwəl] adj ungleich
uneven [ʌnˈiːvən] adj (surface,
road) uneben; (contest) ungleich
unexpected [ˌʌnɪkˈspektɪd] adj
unerwartet
unfair [ʌnˈfɛəˀ] adj unfair
unfamiliar [ˌʌnfəˈmɪljəˀ] adj **to
be ~ with sb/sth** jdn/etw nicht
kennen
unfasten [ʌnˈfɑːsn] vt aufmachen
unfit [ʌnˈfɪt] adj ungeeignet (for
für); (in bad health) nicht fit
unforeseen [ˌʌnfɔːˈsiːn] adj un-
vorhergesehen
unforgettable [ˌʌnfəˈgɪvəbl] adj
unvergesslich
unforgivable [ˌʌnfəˈgɪvəbl] adj
unverzeihlich
unfortunate [ʌnˈfɔːtʃnət] adj
(unlucky) unglücklich; **it is ~ that ...**
es ist bedauerlich, dass ...; **unfortunately** adv leider
unfounded [ʌnˈfaʊndɪd] adj un-
begründet
unhappy [ʌnˈhæpɪ] adj (sad) unglücklich, unzufrieden; **to be ~ with**
sth mit etw unzufrieden sein
unhealthy [ʌnˈhelθɪ] adj ungesund
unheard-of [ʌnˈhɜːdɒv] adj (unknown) gänzlich unbekannt; (outrageous) unerhört
unhelpful [ʌnˈhelpfʊl] adj nicht
hilfreich
unhitch [ʌnˈhɪtʃ] vt (caravan,
trailer) abkoppeln
unhurt [ʌnˈhɜːt] adj unverletzt
uniform [ˈjuːnɪfɔːm] n Uniform f
▷ adj einheitlich

unify ['ju:nɪfaɪ] vt vereinigen

unimportant [ʌnɪm'pɔːtənt] adj unwichtig

uninhabited [ʌnɪn'hæbɪtɪd] adj unbewohnt

uninstall [ʌnɪn'stɔːl] vt (Inform) deinstallieren

unintentional [ʌnɪn'tenʃənl] adj unabsichtlich

union ['juːnjən] n (uniting) Vereinigung f; (alliance) Union f; Union Jack n Union Jack m (britische Nationalflagge)

unique [juːˈniːk] adj einzigartig

unit ['juːnɪt] n Einheit f; (of system, machine) Teil nt; (in school) Lektion f

unite [juːˈnaɪt] vt vereinigen; the United Kingdom das Vereinigte Königreich; the United Nations pl die Vereinten Nationen pl; the United States (of America) pl die Vereinigten Staaten (von Amerika) pl ▷ vi sich vereinigen

universe ['juːnɪvɜːs] n Universum nt

university [juːnɪ'vɜːsɪtɪ] n Universität f

unkind [ʌn'kaɪnd] adj unfreundlich (to zu)

unknown [ʌn'nəʊn] adj unbekannt (to i dat)

unloaded [ʌn'ləʊdɪd] adj bleifrei

unless [ɒn'les] conj es sei denn, wenn ... nicht; don't do it - I tell you to mach das nicht, es sei denn, ich sage es dir; ~ I'm mistaken ... wenn ich mich nicht irre ...

unlicensed [ʌn'laɪsənst] adj (to sell alcohol) ohne Lizenz

unlike [ʌn'laɪk] prep (in contrast to) im Gegensatz zu; it's ~ her to be late es sieht ihr gar nicht ähnlich, zu spät zu kommen; unlikely [ʌn'laɪklɪ] adj unwahrscheinlich

unload [ʌn'ləʊd] vt ausladen

unlock [ʌn'lɒk] vt aufschließen

unlucky [ʌn'lʌkɪ] adj unglücklich; to be ~ Pech haben

unmistakable [ʌnmɪ'steɪkəbl] adj unverkennbar

unnecessary [ʌn'nesəsərɪ] adj unnötig

unobtainable [ʌnəb'teɪnəbl] adj nicht erhältlich

unoccupied [ʌn'ɒkjʊpaɪd] adj (seat) frei; (building, room) leer stehend

unpack [ʌn'pæk] vt, vi auspacken

unpleasant [ʌn'pleznt] adj unangenehm

unplug [ʌn'plʌg] vt to ~ sth den Stecker von etw herausziehen

unprecedented [ʌn'presɪdəntɪd] adj beispiellos

unpredictable [ʌnprɪ'dɪktəbl] adj (person, weather) unberechenbar

unreasonable [ʌn'riːznəbl] adj unvernünftig; (demand) übertrieben

unreliable [ʌnrɪ'laɪəbl] adj unzuverlässig

unsafe [ʌn'seɪf] adj nicht sicher; (dangerous) gefährlich

unscrew [ʌn'skruː] vt abschrauben

unsightly [ʌn'saɪtlɪ] adj unansehnlich

unskilled [ʌn'skɪld] adj (worker) ungelernt

unsuccessful [ʌnsək'sesfʊl] adj erfolglos

unsuitable [ʌn'suːtəbl] adj ungeeignet (for für)

until [ɒn'tɪl] prep bis; not ~ erst, from Monday ~ Friday von Montag bis Freitag; he didn't come home ~ midnight er kam erst um Mitternacht nach Hause; ~ then bis dahin ▷ conj bis; she won't come ~ you invite her sie kommt erst, wenn du sie einlädst

unusual, unusually [ʌn'juːʒʊəl, -ɪ] adj, adv ungewöhnlich

unwanted [ʌn'wɒntɪd] *adj* unerwünscht, ungewollt

unwell [ʌn'wel] *adj* krank; **to feel ~** sich nicht wohl fühlen

unwilling [ʌn'wɪlɪŋ] *adj* **to be ~ to do sth** nicht bereit sein, etw zu tun

unwind [ʌn'waɪnd] *irr vt* abwickeln ▷ *vi (relax)* sich entspannen

unwrap [ʌn'ræp] *vt* auspacken

unzip [ʌn'zɪp] *vt* den Reißverschluss aufmachen an +*dat*; *(Inform)* entzippen

up [ʌp] *prep* **to climb ~ a tree** einen Baum hinaufklettern; **to go ~ the street / the stairs** die Straße entlanggehen / die Treppe hinaufgehen; **further ~ the hill** weiter oben auf dem Berg ▷ *adv (in higher position)* oben; *(to higher position)* nach oben; *(out of bed)* auf; **~ there** dort oben; **~ and down** *(walk, jump)* auf und ab; **what's ~?** *(fam)* was ist los?; **~ to £100** bis zu 100 Pfund; **what's she ~ to?** was macht sie da?; *(planning)* was hat sie vor?; **it's ~ to you** das liegt bei dir; **I don't feel ~ to it** ich fühle mich dem nicht gewachsen; *(not well enough)* ich fühle mich nicht wohl genug dazu

upbringing ['ʌpbrɪŋɪŋ] *n* Erziehung *f*

update [ʌp'deɪt] *n (list etc)* Aktualisierung *f; (software)* Update *nt* ▷ *vt (list etc, person)* auf den neuesten Stand bringen, aktualisieren

upgrade [ʌp'greɪd] *vt (computer)* aufrüsten; **we were ~d** das Hotel hat uns ein besseres Zimmer gegeben

upheaval [ʌp'hi:vəl] *n* Aufruhr *m; (Pol)* Umbruch *m*

uphill [ʌp'hɪl] *adv* bergauf

upon [ə'pɒn] *prep see* **on**

upper ['ʌpə*] *adj* obere(r, s); *(arm, deck)* Ober-

upright ['ʌpraɪt] *adj, adv* aufrecht

uprising ['ʌpraɪzɪŋ] *n* Aufstand *m*

uproar ['ʌprɔ:*] *n* Aufruhr *m*

upset [ʌp'set] *irr vt (overturn)* umkippen; *(disturb)* aufregen; *(sadden)* bestürzen; *(offend)* kränken; *(plans)* durcheinander bringen ▷ *adj (disturbed)* aufgeregt; *(sad)* bestürzt; *(offended)* gekränkt; **~ stomach** ['ʌpset] Magenverstimmung *f*

upside down [ʌpsaɪd'daʊn] *adv* verkehrt herum; *(fig)* drunter und drüber; **to turn sth ~** *(box etc)* etw umdrehen / durchwühlen

upstairs [ʌp'steəz] *adv* oben; *(go, take)* nach oben

up-to-date [ʌptə'deɪt] *adj* modern; *(fashion, information)* aktuell; **to keep sb ~** jdn auf dem Laufenden halten

upwards ['ʌpwədz] *adv* nach oben

urban ['ɜːbən] *adj* städtisch, Stadt-

urge [ɜːdʒ] *n* Drang *m* ▷ *vt* **to ~ sb to do sth** jdn drängen, etw zu tun; **urgent, urgently** ['ɜːdʒənt, -lɪ] *adj, adv* dringend

urine ['jʊərɪn] *n* Urin *m*

us [ʌs] *pron* uns; **do they know ~?** kennen sie uns?; **can he help ~?** kann er uns helfen?; **it's ~** wir sind's; **both of ~** wir beide

US, USA *nsing abbr* = **United States (of America)** USA *pl*

use [ju:s] *n (using)* Gebrauch *m; (for specific purpose)* Verwendung *f;* **to make ~ of** Gebrauch machen von; **in / out of ~** in / außer Gebrauch; **it's no ~ (doing that)** es hat keinen Zweck, das zu tun; **it's (of) no ~ to me** das kann ich nicht brauchen ▷ [ju:z] *vt* benutzen, gebrauchen; *(for specific purpose)* verwenden; *(method)* anwenden; **use up** *vt* aufbrauchen

used [ju:zd] *adj* (secondhand) gebraucht ▷ *vb aux* **to be ~d to sb/
sth** an jdn/etw gewöhnt sein; **to
get ~d to sb/sth** sich an jdn/etw
gewöhnen; **she ~d to live here** sie
hat früher mal hier gewohnt; **useful** *adj* nützlich; **useless** *adj*
nutzlos; (unusable) unbrauchbar;
(pointless) zwecklos; **user** [ˈjuːzə*]
n Benutzer(in) *m(f)*; **user-friendly**
adj benutzerfreundlich

usual [ˈjuːʒəl] *adj* üblich, gewöhnlich; **as ~** wie üblich; **usually**
adv normalerweise

utensil [juːˈtensl] *n* Gerät *nt*

uterus [ˈjuːtərəs] *n* Gebärmutter *f*

utilize [ˈjuːtɪlaɪz] *vt* verwenden

utmost [ˈʌtməʊst] *adj* äußerst; **to
do one's ~** sein Möglichstes tun

utter [ˈʌtə*] *adj* völlig ▷ *vt* von
sich geben; **utterly** *adv* völlig

U-turn [ˈjuːtɜːn] *n* (Auto) Wende *f*;
to do a ~ wenden; (fig) eine Kehrt-
wendung machen

vacancy [ˈveɪkənsɪ] *n* (job) offene
Stelle; (room) freies Zimmer; **vacant**
[ˈveɪkənt] *adj* (room, seat) frei;
(post) offen; (building) leer stehend;
vacate [vəˈkeɪt] *vt* (room, building)
räumen; (seat) frei machen

vacation [vəˈkeɪʃən] *n* (US) Ferien
pl, Urlaub *m*; (at university) (Semester)ferien *pl*; **to go on ~** in Urlaub
fahren; **~ course** Ferienkurs *m*

vaccinate [ˈvæksɪneɪt] *vt* impfen; **vaccination** [væksɪˈneɪʃən] *n*
Impfung *f*; **~ card** Impfpass *m*

vacuum [ˈvækjʊm] *n* Vakuum *nt*
▷ *vt, vi* (staub)saugen; **vacuum
cleaner** *n* Staubsauger *m*

vagina [vəˈdʒaɪnə] *n* Scheide *f*

vague [veɪg] *adj* (imprecise) vage;
(resemblance) entfernt; **vaguely** *adv*
in etwa, irgendwie

vain [veɪn] *adj* (attempt) vergeblich; (conceited) eitel; **vainly** *adv* (in
vain) vergeblich

valentine (card) [ˈvæləntaɪn(-
kɑːd)] *n* Valentinskarte *f*, valen-

valid | 500

tine's Day n Valentinstag m

valid ['vælɪd] adj (ticket, passport etc) gültig; (argument) stichhaltig; (claim) berechtigt

valley ['vælɪ] n Tal nt

valuable ['væljʊəbl] adj wertvoll; (time) kostbar; **valuables** npl Wertsachen pl

value ['væljuː] n Wert m ▷ vt (appreciate) schätzen; **value added tax** n Mehrwertsteuer f

valve [vælv] n Ventil nt

van [væn] n (Auto) Lieferwagen m

vanilla [və'nɪlə] n Vanille f

vanish ['vænɪʃ] vi verschwinden

vanity ['vænɪtɪ] n Eitelkeit f; **vanity case** n Schminkkoffer m

vapor ['veɪpə], **vapour** ['veɪpə*] n (mist) Dunst m; (steam) Dampf m

variable ['vɛərɪəbl] adj (weather, mood) unbeständig; (quality) unterschiedlich; (speed, height) regulierbar; **varied** ['vɛərɪd] adj (interests, selection) vielseitig; (career) bewegt; (work, diet) abwechslungsreich; **variety** [və'raɪətɪ] n (diversity) Abwechslung f; (assortment) Vielfalt f (of an +dat); (type) Art f; **various** ['vɛərɪəs] adj verschieden

varnish ['vɑːnɪʃ] n Lack m ▷ vt lackieren

vary ['vɛərɪ] vt (alter) verändern ▷ vi (be different) unterschiedlich sein; (fluctuate) sich verändern; (prices) schwanken

vase [vɑːz, ɑ veɪz] (US) n Vase f

vast [vɑːst] adj riesig; (area) weit

VAT abbr = **value added tax** Mehrwertsteuer f, MwSt.

Vatican ['vætɪkən] n the ~ der Vatikan

VCR abbr = **video cassette recorder** Videorekorder m

VD abbr = **venereal disease**

VDU abbr = **visual display unit**

veal [viːl] n Kalbfleisch nt

vegan ['viːgən] n Veganer(in) m(f)

vegetable ['vedʒtəbl] n Gemüse nt

vegetarian [vedʒɪ'tɛərɪən] n Vegetarier(in) m(f) ▷ adj vegetarisch

vehicle ['viːɪkl] n Fahrzeug nt

veil [veɪl] n Schleier m

vein [veɪn] n Ader f

Velcro® ['velkrəʊ] n Klettband nt

velvet ['velvɪt] n Samt m

vending machine ['vendɪŋmə-ʃiːn] n Automat m

venereal disease [vɪ'nɪərəldɪz-iːz] n Geschlechtskrankheit f

venetian blind [vɪ'niːʃən'blaɪnd] n Jalousie f

Venezuela [vene'zweɪlə] n Venezuela nt

vengeance ['vendʒəns] n Rache f

Venice ['venɪs] n Venedig nt

venison ['venɪsn] n Rehfleisch nt

vent [vent] n Öffnung f

ventilate ['ventɪleɪt] vt lüften; **ventilation** [ventɪ'leɪʃən] n Belüftung f; **ventilator** ['ventɪleɪtə*] n (in room) Ventilator m; **to be on a ~** (Med) künstlich beatmet werden

venture ['ventʃə*] n (project) Unternehmung f; (Comm) Unternehmen nt ▷ vi (go) (sich) wagen

venue ['venjuː] n (for concert etc) Veranstaltungsort m; (Sport) Austragungsort m

verb [vɜːb] n Verb nt; **verbal** adj (agreement) mündlich; (skills) sprachlich; **verbally** adv mündlich

verdict ['vɜːdɪkt] n Urteil nt

verge [vɜːdʒ] n (of road) (Straßen)rand m; **to be on the ~ of doing sth** im Begriff sein, etw zu tun ▷ vi **to ~ on** grenzen an +akk

verification [verɪfɪ'keɪʃən] n (confirmation) Bestätigung f; (check) Überprüfung f; **verify** ['verɪfaɪ] vt (confirm) bestätigen; (check) überprüfen vermin ['vɜːmɪn] npl Schädlinge pl; (Insects) Ungeziefer nt

verruca [ve'ruːkə] n Warze f

versatile ['vɜːsətaɪl] adj vielseitig

verse [vɜːs] n (poetry) Poesie f; (stanza) Strophe f

version ['vɜːʃən] n Version f

versus ['vɜːsəs] prep gegen; (in contrast to) im Gegensatz zu

vertical ['vɜːtɪkəl] adj senkrecht, vertikal

very ['verɪ] adv sehr; ~ much sehr ▷ adj the ~ book I need genau das Buch, das ich brauche; at that ~ moment gerade in dem Augenblick; at the ~ top ganz oben; the ~ best der/die/das Allerbeste

vest [vest] n (BRIT) Unterhemd nt; (US: waistcoat) Weste f

vet [vet] n Tierarzt m, Tierärztin f

veto ['viːtəʊ] (pl ~es) n Veto nt ▷ vt sein Veto einlegen gegen

VHF abbr = very high frequency UKW

via ['vaɪə] prep über +akk

viable ['vaɪəbl] adj (plan) realisierbar; (company) rentabel

vibrate [vaɪ'breɪt] vi vibrieren; vibration [vaɪ'breɪʃən] n Vibration f

vicar ['vɪkə*] n Pfarrer(in) m(f)

vice [vaɪs] n (evil) Laster nt; (Tech) Schraubstock m ▷ pref Vize-; ~-chairman stellvertretender Vorsitzender; ~-president Vizepräsident(in) m(f)

vice versa [vaɪs'vɜːsə] adv umgekehrt

vicinity [vɪ'sɪnɪtɪ] n in the ~ in der Nähe (of +gen)

vicious ['vɪʃəs] adj (violent) brutal; (malicious) gemein; vicious circle n Teufelskreis m

victim ['vɪktɪm] n Opfer nt

Victorian [vɪk'tɔːrɪən] adj viktorianisch

victory ['vɪktərɪ] n Sieg m

video ['vɪdɪəʊ] (pl ~s) adj Video- ▷ n Video nt; (recorder) Videorekorder m ▷ vt (auf Video) aufnehmen; video camera n Videokamera f; video cassette n Videokassette f; video clip n Videoclip m; video game n Videospiel nt; video recorder n Videorecorder m; video shop n Videothek f; videotape n Videoband nt ▷ vt (auf Video) aufnehmen

Vienna [vɪ'enə] n Wien nt

Vietnam [vjet'næm] n Vietnam nt

view [vjuː] n (sight) Blick m (of auf +akk); (vista) Aussicht f; (opinion) Ansicht f, Meinung f; in ~ of angesichts +gen ▷ vt (situation, event) betrachten; (house) besichtigen; viewer n (for slides) Diabetrachter m; (TV) Zuschauer(in) m(f); viewpoint n (fig) Standpunkt m

vigilant ['vɪdʒɪlənt] adj wachsam

vile [vaɪl] adj (weather, food) scheußlich; (smell) abscheulich

village ['vɪlɪdʒ] n Dorf nt; villager n Dorfbewohner(in) m(f)

villain ['vɪlən] n Schurke m; (in film, story) Bösewicht m

vine [vaɪn] n (Weinrebe f

vinegar ['vɪnɪgə*] n Essig m

vineyard ['vɪnjəd] n Weinberg m

vintage ['vɪntɪdʒ] n (of wine) Jahrgang m; vintage wine n edler Wein

vinyl ['vaɪnɪl] n Vinyl nt

viola [vɪ'əʊlə] n Bratsche f

violate ['vaɪəleɪt] vt (treaty) brechen; (rights, rule) verletzen

violence ['vaɪələns] n (brutality) Gewalt f; (of person) Gewalttätigkeit f; violent adj (brutal) brutal; (death) gewaltsam

violet ['vaɪələt] n Veilchen f

violin [vaɪə'lɪn] n Geige f, Violine f

VIP abbr = very important person VIP m(f)

virgin ['vɜːdʒɪn] n Jungfrau f

Virgo ['vɜːgəʊ] n (Astr) Jungfrau f

virile ['vɪraɪl] adj (man) männlich

virtual ['vɜːtjʊəl] adj (Inform) virtuell; **virtually** adv praktisch; **virtual reality** n virtuelle Realität

virtue ['vɜːtjuː] n Tugend f; **by ~ of** aufgrund +gen; **virtuous** ['vɜːtjʊəs] adj tugendhaft

virus ['vaɪrəs] n (Med, Inform) Virus nt

visa ['viːzə] n Visum nt

visibility [vɪzɪ'bɪlɪtɪ] n (Meteo) Sichtweite f; **good/poor ~** gute/ schlechte Sicht; **visible** ['vɪzəbl] adj sichtbar; (evident) sichtlich; **visibly** adv sichtlich

vision ['vɪʒən] n (power of sight) Sehvermögen nt; (foresight) Weitblick m; (dream, image) Vision f

visit ['vɪzɪt] n Besuch m; (stay) Aufenthalt m ▷ vt besuchen; **visiting hours** npl Besuchszeiten pl; **visitor** n (to house etc) Besucher(in) m(f); **~'s book** Gästebuch nt; **visitor centre** n Informationszentrum nt

visor ['vaɪzə*] n (on helmet) Visier nt; (Auto) Blende f

visual ['vɪzjʊəl] adj Seh-; (image, joke) visuell; **~ aid** Anschauungsmaterial nt; **~ display unit** Monitor m; **visualize** vt sich vorstelle; **visually** adv visuell; **~impaired** sehbehindert

vital ['vaɪtl] adj (essential) unerlässlich, wesentlich; (argument, moment) entscheidend; **vitality** [vaɪ'tælɪtɪ] n Vitalität f; **vitally** adv äußerst

vitamin ['vɪtəmɪn] n Vitamin nt

vivacious [vɪ'veɪʃəs] adj lebhaft

vivid ['vɪvɪd] adj (description) anschaulich; (memory) lebhaft; (colour) leuchtend

V-neck ['viːnek] n V-Ausschnitt m

vocabulary [vəʊ'kæbjʊlərɪ] n Wortschatz m, Vokabular nt

vocal ['vəʊkəl] adj (of the voice)

Stimm-; (group) Gesangs-; (protest, person) lautstark

vocation [vəʊ'keɪʃən] n Berufung f; **vocational** adj Berufs-

vodka ['vɒdkə] n Wodka m

voice [vɔɪs] n Stimme f ▷ vt äußern; **voice mail** n Voicemail f

void [vɔɪd] n Leere f ▷ adj (Jur) ungültig; **~ of** (ganz) ohne

volcano [vɒl'keɪnəʊ] (pl **-es**) n Vulkan m

volley ['vɒlɪ] n (Tennis) Volley m; **volleyball** n Volleyball m

volt [vəʊlt] n Volt nt; **voltage** n Spannung f

volume ['vɒljuːm] n (of sound) Lautstärke f; (space occupied by sth) Volumen nt; (size, amount) Umfang m; (book) Band m; **volume control** n Lautstärkeregler m

voluntary, **voluntarily** ['vɒləntərɪ, -lɪ] adj, adv freiwillig; (unpaid) ehrenamtlich; **volunteer** [vɒlən-'tɪə*] n Freiwillige(r) mf ▷ vi sich freiwillig melden ▷ vt **to ~ to do sth** sich anbieten, etw zu tun

voluptuous [və'lʌptjʊəs] adj sinnlich

vomit ['vɒmɪt] vi sich übergeben

vote [vəʊt] n Stimme f; (ballot) Wahl f; (result) Abstimmungsergebnis nt; (right to vote) Wahlrecht nt ▷ vt (elect) wählen; **they ~d him chairman** sie wählten ihn zum Vorsitzenden ▷ vi wählen; **to ~ for/against sth** für/gegen etw stimmen; **voter** n Wähler(in) m(f)

voucher ['vaʊtʃə*] n Gutschein m

vow [vaʊ] n Gelöbnis nt ▷ vt **to ~ to do sth** geloben, etw zu tun

vowel ['vaʊəl] n Vokal m

voyage ['vɔɪdʒ] n Reise f

vulgar ['vʌlgə*] adj vulgär, ordinär

vulnerable ['vʌlnərəbl] adj verwundbar; (sensitive) verletzlich

vulture ['vʌltʃə*] n Geier m

W

W abbr = **west** W

wade [weɪd] vi (in water) waten

wafer ['weɪfə*] n Waffel f; (Rel) Hostie f; **wafer-thin** adj hauchdünn

waffle ['wɒfl] n Waffel f; (BRIT fam: empty talk) Geschwafel nt ▷ vi (BRIT fam) schwafeln

wag [wæg] vt (tail) wedeln mit

wage [weɪdʒ] n Lohn m

waggon (BRIT), **wagon** ['wægən] n (horse-drawn) Fuhrwerk nt; (BRIT Rail) Waggon m; (US Auto) Wagen m

waist [weɪst] n Taille f; **waistcoat** (BRIT) n Weste f; **waistline** n Taille f

wait [weɪt] n Wartezeit f ▷ vi warten (for auf +Akk); **to ~ and see** abwarten; **~ a minute** Moment mal; **wait up** vi aufbleiben

waiter n Kellner m; **~!** Herr Ober!

waiting n 'no ~' „Halteverbot"; **waiting list** n Warteliste f; **waiting room** n (Med) Wartezimmer nt; (Rail) Wartesaal m

waitress n Kellnerin f

wake [weɪk] (woke o **waked**, **woken** o **waked**) vt wecken ▷ vi aufwachen; **wake up** vt aufwecken ▷ vi aufwachen; **wake-up call** n (Tel) Weckruf m

Wales ['weɪlz] n Wales nt

walk [wɔːk] n Spaziergang m; (ramble) Wanderung f; (route) Weg m, **to go for a ~** spazieren gehen, **it's only a five minute ~** es sind nur fünf Minuten zu Fuß ▷ vi gehen; (stroll) spazieren gehen; (ramble) wandern ▷ vt (dog) ausführen; **walking** n **to go ~** wandern; **walking shoes** npl Wanderschuhe pl; **walking stick** n Spazierstock m

Walkman® (pl **-s**) n Walkman® m

wall [wɔːl] n (inside) Wand f; (outside) Mauer f

wallet ['wɒlɪt] n Brieftasche f

wallpaper ['wɔːlpeɪpə*] n Tapete f; (Inform) Bildschirmhintergrund m ▷ vt tapezieren

walnut ['wɔːlnʌt] n (nut) Walnuss f

waltz [wɔːlts] n Walzer m

wander ['wɒndə*] vi (person) herumwandern

want [wɒnt] n (lack) Mangel m (of an +dat); (need) Bedürfnis nt; **for ~ of** aus Mangel an +dat ▷ vt (desire) wollen; (need) brauchen; **I ~ to stay here** ich will hier bleiben; **he doesn't ~ to** er will nicht

WAP phone n ['wæpfəʊn] n WAP-Handy nt

war [wɔː*] n Krieg m

ward [wɔːd] n (in hospital) Station f; (child) Mündel nt

warden ['wɔːdən] n Aufseher(in) m(f); (in youth hostel) Herbergsvater m, Herbergsmutter f

wardrobe ['wɔːdrəʊb] n Kleiderschrank m

warehouse ['weəhaʊs] n Lagerhaus *nt*

warfare ['wɔːfɛə*] *n* Krieg *m*; *(techniques)* Kriegsführung *f*

warm [wɔːm] *adj* warm; *(welcome)* herzlich; **I'm ~** mir ist warm ▷ *vt* wärmen; *(food)* aufwärmen; **warm over** *vt* (US: *food)* aufwärmen; **warm up** *(food)* aufwärmen; *(room)* erwärmen ▷ *vi* *(food, room)* warm werden; *(Sport)* sich aufwärmen; **warmly** *adv* warm; *(welcome)* herzlich; **warmth** *n* Wärme *f*; *(of welcome)* Herzlichkeit *f*

warn [wɔːn] *vt* warnen *(of, against* vor +*dat)*; **to ~ sb not to do sth** jdn davor warnen, etw zu tun; **warning** *n* Warnung *f*; **warning light** *n* Warnlicht *nt*; **warning triangle** *n* (Auto) Warndreieck *n*

warranty ['wɒrəntɪ] *n* Garantie *f*

wart [wɔːt] *n* Warze *f*

wary ['wɛərɪ] *adj* vorsichtig; *(suspicious)* misstrauisch

was [wɒz, wəz] *pt of* **be**

wash [wɒʃ] *n* to have a ~ sich waschen; **it's in the ~** es ist in der Wäsche ▷ *vt* waschen; *(plates, glasses etc)* abwaschen; **to ~ one's hands** sich *dat* die Hände waschen; **to ~ the dishes** (das Geschirr) abwaschen ▷ *vi* *(clean oneself)* sich waschen; **wash off** *vt* abwaschen; **wash up** *vi* (BRIT: *wash dishes)* abwaschen; *(US: clean oneself)* sich waschen; **washable** *adj* waschbar; **washbag** *n* (US) Kulturbeutel *m*; **washbasin** *n* Waschbecken *n*; **washcloth** *n* (US) Waschlappen *m*; **washer** *n* (Tech) Dichtungsring *m*; *(washing machine)* Waschmaschine *f*; **washing** *n* *(laundry)* Wäsche *f*; **washing machine** *n* Waschmaschine *f*; **washing powder** *n* Waschpulver *nt*; **washing-up** *n* (BRIT) Abwasch *m*; **to do the ~** abwaschen; **washing-up liquid** *n*

(BRIT) Spülmittel *nt*; **washroom** *n* (US) Toilette *f*

wasn't ['wɒznt] *contr of* **was not**

wasp [wɒsp] *n* Wespe *f*

waste [weɪst] *n* *(materials)* Abfall *m*; *(wasting)* Verschwendung *f*; **it's a ~ of time** das ist Zeitverschwendung ▷ *adj* *(superfluous)* überschüssig ▷ *vt* verschwenden *(on an* +*akk)*; *(opportunity)* vertun; **waste bin** *n* Abfalleimer *m*; **wastepaper basket** *n* Papierkorb *m*

watch [wɒtʃ] *n* *(timepiece)* (Armband)uhr *f* ▷ *vt* *(observe)* beobachten; *(guard)* aufpassen auf +*akk*; *(film, play, programme)* sich ansehen; **to ~ TV** fernsehen ▷ *vi* zusehen; *(guard)* Wache halten; **to ~ for sb/sth** nach jdm/etw Ausschau halten; **~ out** pass auf!; **watchdog** *n* Wachhund *m*; *(fig)* Aufsichtsbehörde *f*; **watchful** *adj* wachsam

water ['wɔːtə*] *n* Wasser *nt*; **~s** *pl* *(territory)* Gewässer *pl* ▷ *vt* *(plant)* gießen ▷ *vi* *(eye)* tränen; **my mouth is ~ing** mir läuft das Wasser im Mund zusammen; **water down** *vt* verdünnen; **watercolor** (US), **watercolour** *n* *(painting)* Aquarell *f*; *(paint)* Wasserfarbe *f*; **watercress** *n* (Brunnen)kresse *f*; **waterfall** *n* Wasserfall *m*; **watering can** *n* Gießkanne *f*; **water level** *n* Wasserstand *m*; **watermelon** *n* Wassermelone *f*; **waterproof** *adj* wasserdicht; **water-skiing** *n* Wasserskilaufen *nt*; **water sports** *npl* Wassersport *m*; **watertight** *adj* wasserdicht; **water wings** *npl* Schwimmflügel *pl*; **watery** *adj* wässerig

wave [weɪv] *n* Welle *f* ▷ *vt* *(move to and fro)* schwenken; *(hand, flag)* winken mit ▷ *vi* *(person)* winken; *(flag)* wehen; **wavelength** *n* Wellenlänge f; **to be on the same ~ (fig)** die gleiche Wellenlänge haben; **wavy** ['weivi] adj wellig

wax [wæks] n Wachs nt; (in ear) Ohrenschmalz m

way [wei] n Weg m; (direction) Richtung f; (manner) Art f; **can you tell me the ~ to ...?** wie komme ich (am besten) zu ...?; **we went the wrong ~** wir sind in die falsche Richtung gefahren/gegangen; **to lose one's ~** sich verirren; **to make ~ for sb/sth** jdm/etw Platz machen; **to get one's own ~** seinen Willen durchsetzen; **'give ~'** (Auto) „Vorfahrt achten"; **the other ~ round** andersherum; **one ~ or another** irgendwie; **in a ~** in gewisser Weise; **in the ~** im Weg; **by the ~** übrigens; **'~ in'** „Eingang"; **'~ out'** „Ausgang"; **no ~** (fam) kommt nicht infrage!

we [wi:] pron wir

weak [wi:k] adj schwach; **weaken** vt schwächen ▷ vi schwächer werden

wealth [welθ] n Reichtum m; **wealthy** adj reich

weapon ['wepən] n Waffe f

wear [weə*] (wore, worn) vt (have on) tragen; **what shall I ~?** was soll ich anziehen? ▷ vi (become worn) sich abnutzen ▷ ~ **(and tear)** Abnutzung f; **wear off** vi (diminish) nachlassen; **wear out** vt abnutzen; (person) erschöpfen ▷ vi sich abnutzen

weary ['wiəri] adj müde

weather ['weðə*] n Wetter nt; **I'm feeling under the ~** ich fühle mich nicht ganz wohl; **weather forecast** n Wettervorhersage f

weave [wi:v] (wove o weaved, woven o weaved) vt (cloth) weben; (basket etc) flechten

web [web] n (a. fig) Netz nt; **the**

Web das Web, das Internet; **webcam** ['webkæm] n Webcam f; **web page** n Webseite f; **website** n Website f

we'd [wi:d] contr of **we had; we would**

Wed abbr = **Wednesday** Mi

wedding ['wedɪŋ] n Hochzeit f; **wedding anniversary** n Hochzeitstag m; **wedding dress** n Hochzeitskleid nt; **wedding ring** n Ehering m

wedding shower n (US) Party für die zukünftige Braut

wedge [wedʒ] n (under door etc) Keil m; (of cheese etc) Stück nt, Ecke f

Wednesday ['wenzdei] n Mittwoch m; see also **Tuesday**

wee [wi:] adj klein ▷ vi (fam) Pipi machen

weed [wi:d] n Unkraut nt ▷ vt jäten

week [wi:k] n Woche f, **twice a ~** zweimal in der Woche; **a ~ on Friday/Friday ~** Freitag in einer Woche; **a ~ last Friday** letzten Freitag vor einer Woche; **in two ~s' time, in two ~s** in zwei Wochen; **for ~s** wochenlang; **weekday** n Wochentag m; **weekend** n Wochenende nt; **weekly** adj, adv wöchentlich; (magazine) Wochen-

weep [wi:p] (wept, wept) vi weinen

weigh [wei] vt, vi wiegen; **it ~s 20 kilos** es wiegt 20 Kilo; **weigh up** vt abwägen; (person) einschätzen; **weight** [weit] n Gewicht nt; **to lose/put on ~** abnehmen/zunehmen; **weightlifting** n Gewichtheben nt; **weight training** n Krafttraining nt; **weighty** adj (important) schwer wiegend

weird [wiəd] adj seltsam; **weirdo** ['wiədəu] n Spinner(in) m(f)

welcome ['welkəm] n Empfang

m ▷ *adj* willkommen; (*news*) angenehm; **~ to London** willkommen in London! ▷ *vt* begrüßen; **welcoming** *adj* freundlich

welfare ['welfeə*] *n* Wohl *nt*; (US: *social security*) Sozialhilfe *f*; **welfare state** *n* Wohlfahrtsstaat *m*

well [wel] *n* Brunnen *m* ▷ *adj* (*in good health*) gesund; **are you ~?** geht es dir gut?; **to feel ~** sich wohl fühlen; **get ~ soon** gute Besserung! ▷ *interj* nun; **~, I don't know** nun, ich weiß nicht ▷ *adv* gut; **~ done** gut gemacht!; **it may ~ be** das kann wohl sein; **~** (*in addition*) auch; **~ over 60** weit über 60

we'll [wi:l] *contr of* **we will**; **we shall**

well-behaved [welbɪ'heɪvd] *adj* brav; **well-being** *n* Wohl *nt*; **well-built** *adj* (*person*) gut gebaut; **well-done** *adj* (*steak*) durchgebraten; **well-earned** *adj* wohlverdient

wellingtons ['welɪŋtənz] *npl* Gummistiefel *pl*

well-known [wel'nəʊn] *adj* bekannt; **well-off** *adj* (*wealthy*) wohlhabend; **well-paid** *adj* gut bezahlt

Welsh [welʃ] *adj* walisisch ▷ *n* (*language*) Walisisch *nt*; **the ~** *pl* die Waliser *pl*; **Welshman** (*pl* **-men**) *n* Waliser *m*; **Welshwoman** (*pl* **-women**) *n* Waliserin *f*

went [went] *pt of* **go**

wept [wept] *pt, pp of* **weep**

were [wɜ:*] *pt of* **be**

we're [wɪə*] *contr of* **we are**

weren't [wɜ:nt] *contr of* **were not**

west [west] *n* Westen *m*; **the West** (Pol) der Westen ▷ *adv* (*go, face*) nach Westen ▷ *adj* West-; **westbound** *adj* (*in*) Richtung Westen; **western** *adj* West-, westlich; **Western Europe** Westeuropa *nt* ▷ *n* (Cine) Western *m*;

West Germany *n* (**the former**) ~ (das ehemalige) Westdeutschland, Westdeutschland *nt*; **westwards** ['westwədz] *adv* nach Westen

wet [wet] (**wet, wet**) *vt* **to ~ oneself** in die Hose machen ▷ *adj* nass, feucht; **'~ paint'** ,frisch gestrichen"; **wet suit** *n* Taucheranzug *m*

we've [wi:v] *contr of* **we have**

whale [weɪl] *n* Wal *m*

wharf [wɔ:f] (*pl* **-s** *or* **wharves**) *n* Kai *m*

what [wɒt] *pron, interj* was; **~'s that?** was ist das?; **~'s your name?** wie heißt du?; **~ is the letter about?** worum geht es in dem Brief?; **~ are they talking about?** worüber reden sie?; **~ for?** wozu? ▷ *adj* welche(r, s); **~ colour is it?** welche Farbe hat es?; **whatever** *pron* **I'll do ~ you want** ich tue alles, was du willst; **~ he says** egal, was er sagt

what's [wɒts] *contr of* **what is**; **what has**

wheat [wi:t] *n* Weizen *m*

wheel [wi:l] *n* Rad *nt*; (*steering wheel*) Lenkrad *nt* ▷ *vt* (*bicycle, trolley*) schieben; **wheelbarrow** *n* Schubkarren *m*; **wheelchair** *n* Rollstuhl *m*; **wheel clamp** *n* Parkkralle *f*

when [wen] *adv* (*in questions*) wann; **on the day ~** an dem Tag, als; **she asked me ~ I would be finished** sie fragte mich, wann ich fertig wäre ▷ *conj* wenn; (*in past*) als; **~ I was younger** als ich jünger war; **whenever** *adv* (*every time*) immer wenn; **come ~ you like** komm wann immer du willst

where [wɛə*] *adv* wo; **~ are you going?** wohin gehst du?; **~ are you from?** woher kommst du? ▷ *conj* wo; **that's ~ I used to live** da habe ich früher gewohnt; **whereabouts**

[weərə'bauts] *adv* wo ▷ *npl*
['weərəbauts] Aufenthaltsort *m*;
whereas [weər'æz] *conj* während,
wohingegen; **whereby** *adv* wodurch; **wherever** [weər'evə*] *conj*
wo immer; **~ that may be** wo immer das sein mag; **~ I go** überall,
wohin ich gehe

whether ['weðə*] *conj* ob

which [wɪtʃ] *adj* welche(r, s) **~ car
is yours?** welches Auto gehört dir?;
~ one? welche(r, s)? ▷ *pron* (*in
questions*) welche(r, s); (*in relative
clauses*) der / die / das, die *pl*; **it
rained, ~ upset his plans** es regnete, was seine Pläne durcheinander
brachte; **whichever** *adj, pron* welche(r, s) auch immer

while [waɪl] *n* a ~ eine Weile; **for
a ~** eine Zeit lang; **a short ~ ago** vor
kurzem ▷ *conj* während; (*although*)
obwohl

whine [waɪn] *vi* (*person*) jammern

whip [wɪp] *n* Peitsche *f* ▷ *vt* (*beat*)
peitschen; **~ped cream** Schlagsahne *f*

whirl [wɜːl] *vt, vi* herumwirbeln;
whirlpool *n* (*in river, sea*) Strudel *m*;
(*pool*) Whirlpool *m*

whisk [wɪsk] *n* Schneebesen *m* ▷
vt (*cream etc*) schlagen

whisker ['wɪskə*] *n* (*of animal*)
Schnurrhaar *nt*; **~s** *pl* (*of man*) Backenbart *m*

whisk(e)y ['wɪskɪ] *n* Whisky *m*

whisper ['wɪspə*] *vi, vt* flüstern;
to ~ sth to sb jdm etw zuflüstern

whistle ['wɪsl] *n* Pfiff *m*; (*instrument*) Pfeife *f* ▷ *vt, vi* pfeifen

white [waɪt] *n* (*of egg*) Eiweiß *nt*;
(*of eye*) Weiße *nt* ▷ *adj* weiß; (*with
fear*) blass; (*coffee*) mit Milch; **White
House** *n* the ~ das Weiße Haus;
white lie *n* Notlüge *f*; **white
meat** *n* helles Fleisch; **white
sauce** *n* weiße Soße; **white water**

rafting *n* Rafting *nt*; **white wine**
n Weißwein *m*

Whitsun ['wɪtsn] *n* Pfingsten *nt*

who [huː] *pron* (*in questions*) wer;
(*in relative clauses*) der / die / das, die
pl; **~ do you see?** wen hast du gesehen?; **~ does that belong to?**
wem gehört das?; **the people ~ live
next door** die Leute, die nebenan
wohnen; **whoever** [huː'evə*] *pron*
wer auch immer; **~ you choose** wen
auch immer du wählst

whole [həʊl] *adj* ganz ▷ *n* Ganze(s) *nt*; **the ~ of my family** meine
ganze Familie; **on the ~** im Großen
und Ganzen; **wholefood** *n* (*BRIT*)
Vollwertkost *f*; **wholeheartedly**
adv voll und ganz; **wholemeal** *adj*
(*BRIT*) Vollkorn-; **wholesale** *adj*
(*buy, sell*) im Großhandel; **wholesome** *adj* gesund; **wholewheat**
adj Vollkorn-; **wholly** ['həʊlɪ] *adv*
völlig

whom [huːm] *pron* (*in questions*)
wen; (*in relative clauses*) den / die /
das, die *pl*; **with ~ did you speak?**
mit wem haben Sie gesprochen?

whooping cough ['huːpɪŋkɒf]
n Keuchhusten *m*

whose [huːz] *adj* (*in questions*)
wessen; (*in relative clauses*) dessen /
deren / dessen, deren *pl*; **~ bike is
that?** wessen Fahrrad ist das? ▷
pron (*in questions*) wessen; **~ is this?**
wem gehört das?

why [waɪ] *adv, conj* warum; **that's
~** deshalb

wicked ['wɪkɪd] *adj* böse; (*fam:
great*) geil

wide [waɪd] *adj* breit; (*skirt, trousers*) weit; (*selection*) groß ▷ *adv*
weit; **wide-angle lens** *n* Weitwinkelobjektiv *nt*; **wide-awake** *adj*
hellwach; **widely** *adv* weit; **~
known** allgemein bekannt; **widen**
vt verbreitern; (*fig*) erweitern; **wide-**

open adj weit offen; **widescreen TV** n Breitbildfernseher m; **widespread** adj weit verbreitet

widow ['wɪdəʊ] n Witwe f; **widowed** adj verwitwet; **widower** n Witwer m

width [wɪdθ] n Breite f

wife [waɪf] (pl **wives**) n (Ehe)frau f

wig [wɪg] n Perücke f

wiggle ['wɪgl] vt wackeln mit

wild [waɪld] adj wild; (violent) heftig; (plan, idea) verrückt ▷ n **in the ~** in freier Wildbahn; **wildlife** n Tier- und Pflanzenwelt f; **wildly** adv wild; (enthusiastic, exaggerated) maßlos

will [wɪl] vb aux **he / they ~ come** er wird / sie werden kommen; **I won't be back until late** ich komme erst spät zurück; **the car won't start** das Auto will nicht anspringen; **~ you have some coffee?** möchten Sie eine Tasse Kaffee? ▷ n Wille m; (wish) Wunsch m; (document) Testament nt; **against her ~** gegen ihren Willen; **willing** adj bereitwillig; **to be ~ to do sth** bereit sein, etw zu tun; **willingly** adv gern(e)

willow ['wɪləʊ] n Weide f

willpower ['wɪlpaʊə*] n Willenskraft f

wimp [wɪmp] n Weichei nt

win [wɪn] (won, won) vt, vi gewinnen ▷ n Sieg m; **win over, win round** vt für sich gewinnen

wind [waɪnd] (wound, wound) vt (rope, bandage) wickeln; **wind down** vt (car window) herunterkurbeln; **wind up** vt (clock) aufziehen; (car window) hochkurbeln; (meeting, speech) abschließen; (person) aufziehen, ärgern

wind [wɪnd] n Wind m; (Med) Blähungen pl

wind instrument ['wɪndɪnstru-](wiederholt)

mənt} n Blasinstrument nt;

windmill n Windmühle f

window ['wɪndəʊ] n Fenster nt; (counter) Schalter m; **window box** n Blumenkasten m; **windowpane** n Fensterscheibe f; **window-shopping** n **to go ~** einen Schaufensterbummel machen; **windowsill** n Fensterbrett nt

windpipe ['wɪndpaɪp] n Luftröhre f; **windscreen** n (BRIT) Windschutzscheibe f; **windscreen wiper** n (BRIT) Scheibenwischer m; **windshield** n (US) Windschutzscheibe f; **windshield wiper** n (US) Scheibenwischer m; **windsurfer** n Windsurfer(in) m(f); (board) Surfbrett nt; **windsurfing** n Windsurfen nt

windy ['wɪndɪ] adj windig

wine [waɪn] n Wein m; **wine bar** n Weinlokal nt; **wineglass** n Weinglas nt; **wine list** n Weinkarte f; **wine tasting** n (event) Weinprobe f

wing [wɪŋ] n Flügel m; (BRIT Auto) Kotflügel m; **~s** pl (Theat) Kulissen pl

wink [wɪŋk] vi zwinkern; **to ~ at sb** jdm zuzwinkern

winner ['wɪnə*] n Gewinner(in) m(f); (Sport) Sieger(in) m(f); **winning** adj (team, horse etc) siegreich; **~ number** Gewinnzahl f ▷ n **~s** pl Gewinn m

winter ['wɪntə*] n Winter m; **winter sports** npl Wintersport m; **wint(e)ry** ['wɪntrɪ] adj winterlich

wipe [waɪp] vt abwischen; **to ~ one's nose** sich dat die Nase putzen; **to ~ one's feet** sich (on mat) die Schuhe abtreten; **wipe off** vt abwischen; **wipe out** vt (destroy) vernichten; (data, debt) löschen; (epidemic etc) ausrotten

wire ['waɪə*] n Draht m; (Elec) Leitung f; (US: telegram) Telegramm nt ▷ vt (plug in) anschließen; (US Tel)

telegrafieren (sb sth jdm etw);
wireless ['waɪələs] adj drahtlos
wisdom ['wɪzdəm] n Weisheit f;
wisdom tooth n Weisheitszahn m
wise [waɪz, -lɪ] adj, adv
weise

wish [wɪʃ] n Wunsch m (for nach);
with best ~es (in letter) herzliche
Grüße ▷ vt wünschen wollen; **to ~
sb good luck/Merry Christmas**
jdm viel Glück/frohe Weihnachten
wünschen; **I ~ I'd never seen him**
ich wünschte, ich hätte ihn nie gesehen

witch [wɪtʃ] n Hexe f
with [wɪð] prep mit; (cause) vor
+dat; **I'm pleased ~ it** ich bin damit
zufrieden; **to shiver ~ cold** vor Kälte
zittern; **he lives ~ his aunt** er wohnt
bei seiner Tante

withdraw [wɪð'drɔː] irr vt zurückziehen; (money) abheben; (comment) zurücknehmen ▷ vi sich zurückziehen

wither ['wɪðə*] vi (plant) verwelken

withhold [wɪð'həʊld] irr vt vorenthalten (from sb jdm)

within [wɪð'ɪn] prep innerhalb
+gen; **~ walking distance** zu Fuß
erreichbar

without [wɪð'aʊt] prep ohne; **~
asking** ohne zu fragen

withstand [wɪð'stænd] irr vt
standhalten +dat

witness ['wɪtnəs] n Zeuge m,
Zeugin f ▷ vt Zeuge sein; **witness
box, witness stand** (US) n Zeugenstand m

witty ['wɪtɪ] adj geistreich
wives [waɪvz] pl of **wife**
wobble ['wɒbl] vi wackeln; **wobbly** adj wackelig
wok [wɒk] n Wok m
woke [wəʊk] pt of **wake**
woken ['wəʊkn] pp of **wake**

wolf [wʊlf] (pl **wolves**) n Wolf m
woman ['wʊmən] (pl **women**) n
Frau f
womb [wuːm] n Gebärmutter f
women ['wɪmɪn] pl of **woman**
won [wʌn] pt, pp of **win**
wonder ['wʌndə*] n (marvel)
Wunder nt; (surprise) Staunen nt ▷ vt,
vi (speculate) sich fragen; **I ~ what /
if ...** ich frage mich, was / ob ...;
wonderful, wonderfully adj, adv
wunderbar

won't [wəʊnt] contr of **will not**
wood [wʊd] n Holz nt; (forest) Wald m;
wooden adj Holz-; (fig) hölzern;
woodpecker n Specht m; **woodwork** n (wooden parts) Holzteile pl;
(in school) Werken nt

wool [wʊl] n Wolle f; **woollen,
woolen** (US) adj Woll-
word [wɜːd] n Wort nt; (promise)
Ehrenwort nt; **~s** pl (of song) Text m;
to have a ~ with sb mit jdm sprechen; **in other ~s** mit anderen
Worten ▷ vt formulieren; **wording**
n Wortlaut m, Formulierung f; **word
processing** n Textverarbeitung f;
word processor n (program) Textverarbeitungsprogramm nt

wore [wɔː*] pt of **wear**
work [wɜːk] n Arbeit f; (of art, literature) Werk nt; **~ of art** Kunstwerk
nt; **he's at ~** er ist in / auf der Arbeit;
out of ~ arbeitslos ▷ vi arbeiten (at,
on an +dat); (machine, plan) funktionieren; (medicine) wirken; (succeed)
klappen ▷ vt (machine) bedienen;
work out vi (plan) klappen; (sum)
aufgehen; (person) trainieren ▷ vt
(price, speed etc) ausrechnen; (plan)
ausarbeiten; **work up** vt **to get
worked up** sich aufregen; **workaholic** [wɜːkə'hɒlɪk] n Arbeitstier
nt; **worker** n Arbeiter(in) m(f);
working class n Arbeiterklasse f;
workman (pl **-men**) n Handwerker

m; **workout** n (Sport) Fitnesstraining nt, Konditionstraining nt; **work permit** n Arbeitserlaubnis f; **workplace** n Arbeitsplatz m; **workshop** n Werkstatt f; (meeting) Workshop m; **work station** n (inform) Workstation f

world [wɜːld] n Welt f; **world championship** n Weltmeisterschaft f; **World War** ~ I/II, **the First/Second** ~ der Erste/Zweite Weltkrieg; **world-wide** adj, adv weltweit; **World Wide Web** n World Wide Web nt

worm [wɜːm] n Wurm m

worn [wɔːn] pp of **wear** ▷ adj (clothes) abgetragen; (tyre) abgefahren; **worn-out** adj abgenutzt; (person) erschöpft

worried ['wʌrɪd] adj besorgt; **be ~ about** sich dat Sorgen machen um; **worry** ['wʌrɪ] n Sorge f ▷ vt Sorgen machen +dat ▷ vi sich Sorgen machen (about um); **don't ~** keine Sorge!; **worrying** adj beunruhigend

worse [wɜːs] adj comparative of **bad**; schlechter; (pain, mistake etc) schlimmer ▷ adv comparative of **badly**; schlechter; **worsen** vt verschlechtern ▷ vi sich verschlechtern

worship ['wɜːʃɪp] vt anbeten, anhimmeln

worst [wɜːst] adj superlative of **bad**; schlechteste(r, s); (pain, mistake etc) schlimmste(r, s) ▷ adv superlative of **badly**; am schlechtesten ▷ n **the ~ is over** das Schlimmste ist vorbei; **at (the) ~** schlimmstenfalls

worth [wɜːθ] n Wert m; **£10 ~ of food** Essen für 10 Pfund ▷ adj **it is ~ £50** es ist 50 Pfund wert; **~ seeing** sehenswert; **it's ~ it** (rewarding) es lohnt sich; **worthless** adj wertlos; **worthwhile** adj lohnend, lohnenswert; **worthy** ['wɜːðɪ] adj

(deserving respect) würdig; **to be ~ of sth** etw verdienen

would [wʊd] vb aux **if you asked he ~ come** wenn Sie ihn fragten, würde er kommen; **I ~ have told you, but ...** ich hätte es dir gesagt, aber ...; **~ you like a drink?** möchten Sie etwas trinken?; **he ~n't help me** er wollte mir nicht helfen

wouldn't ['wʊdnt] contr of **would not**

would've ['wʊdəv] contr of **would have**

wound [wuːnd] n Wunde f ▷ vt verwunden; (fig) verletzen ▷ [waʊnd] pt, pp of **wind**

wove [wəʊv] pt of **weave**

woven ['wəʊvn] pp of **weave**

wrap [ræp] n (parcel, present) einwickeln; **to ~ sth round sth** etw um etw wickeln; **wrap up** (parcel, present) einwickeln ▷ vi (dress warmly) sich warm anziehen; **wrapper** n (of sweet) Papier nt; **wrapping paper** n Packpapier nt; (giftwrap) Geschenkpapier nt

wreath [riːθ] n Kranz m

wreck [rek] n (ship, plane, car) Wrack nt; **a nervous ~** ein Nervenbündel m ▷ vt (car) zu Schrott fahren; (fig) zerstören; **wreckage** ['rekɪdʒ] n Trümmer pl

wrench [rentʃ] n (tool) Schraubenschlüssel m

wrestling ['reslɪŋ] n Ringen nt

wring out ['rɪŋ'aʊt] (**wrung**, **wrung**) vt auswringen

wrinkle ['rɪŋkl] n Falte f

wrist [rɪst] n Handgelenk nt; **wristwatch** n Armbanduhr f

write [raɪt] (**wrote**, **written**) vt schreiben; (cheque) ausstellen ▷ vi schreiben; **to ~ to sb** jdm schreiben; **write down** vt aufschreiben; **write off** vt (debt, person) abschreiben; (car) zu Schrott fahren ▷

vi **to ~ off** for sth etw anfordern; **write out** vt (name etc) ausschreiben; (cheque) ausstellen; **write-protected** adj (Inform) schreibgeschützt; **writer** n Verfasser(in) m(f); (author) Schriftsteller(in) m(f); **writing** n Schrift f, (profession) Schreiben nt; **writing paper** n Schreibpapier nt

written ['rɪtən] pp of **write**
wrong [rɒŋ] adj (incorrect) falsch, (morally) unrecht; **you're ~** du hast Unrecht; **what's ~ with your leg?** was ist mit deinem Bein los?; **you've got the ~ number** Sie sind falsch verbunden; **I dialled the ~ number** ich habe mich verwählt; **don't get me ~** versteh mich nicht falsch; **to go ~** (plan) schief gehen; **wrongly** adv falsch; (unjustly) zu Unrecht

wrote [rəʊt] pt of **write**
WWW abbr = **World Wide Web** WWW

X, y

xenophobia [zenəˈfəʊbɪə] n Ausländerfeindlichkeit f
XL abbr = **extra large** XL; übergroß
Xmas ['eksməs] n Weihnachten nt
X-ray ['eksreɪ] n (picture) Röntgenaufnahme f ▷ vt röntgen
xylophone ['zaɪləfəʊn] n Xylophon nt

yacht [jɒt] n Jacht f; **yachting** n Segeln nt; **to go ~** segeln gehen
yard [jɑːd] n Hof m; (US: garden) Garten m; (measure) Yard nt (0,91 m)
yawn [jɔːn] vi gähnen
yd abbr = **yard(s)**
year ['jɪə] n Jahr nt; **this / last / next ~** dieses/letztes/nächstes Jahr; **he is 28 ~s old** er ist 28 Jahre alt; **~s ago** vor Jahren; **a five-year-old** ein(e) Fünfjährige(r); **yearly** adj, adv jährlich
yearn [jɜːn] vi sich sehnen (for nach +dat); **to ~ to do sth** sich danach sehnen, etw zu tun
yeast [jiːst] n Hefe f
yell [jel] vi, vt schreien; **to ~ at sb**

jdn anschreien

yellow ['jeləʊ] *adj* gelb; ~ **card** (*Sport*) gelbe Karte; ~ **fever** Gelbfieber *nt*; ~ **line** (BRIT) ≈ Halteverbot *nt*; **double ~ line** (BRIT) ≈ absolutes Halteverbot; **the Yellow Pages®** *pl* die Gelben Seiten *pl*

yes [jes] *adv* ja; (*answering negative question*) doch; **to say ~ to sth** ja zu etw sagen ▷ *n* Ja *nt*

yesterday ['jestədeɪ] *adv* gestern; ~ **morning/evening** gestern Morgen/Abend; **the day before ~** vorgestern; ~**'s newspaper** die Zeitung von gestern

yet [jet] *adv* (*still*) noch; (*up to now*) bis jetzt; (*in a question: already*) schon; **he hasn't arrived ~** er ist noch nicht gekommen; **have you finished ~?** bist du schon fertig?; ~ **again** schon wieder; **as ~** bis jetzt ▷ *conj* doch

yield [jiːld] *n* Ertrag *m* ▷ *vt* (*result, crop*) hervorbringen; (*profit, interest*) bringen ▷ *vi* nachgeben (*to* +*dat*); (*Mil*) sich ergeben (*to* +*dat*); '~' (US *Auto*) "Vorfahrt beachten"

yoga ['jəʊgə] *n* Joga *nt*

yog(h)urt ['jɒgət] *n* Jog(h)urt *m*

yolk [jəʊk] *n* Eigelb *nt*

Yorkshire pudding ['jɔːkʃə-'pʊdɪŋ] *n* gebackener Eierteig, der meist zum Roastbeef gegessen wird

you [juː] *pron* (*as subject*) du/Sie/ihr; (*as direct object*) dich/Sie/euch; (*as indirect object*) dir/Ihnen/ihnen; ~ **never can tell** man weiß nie; **it's good for ~** das tut dir gut; (*people in general*) das tut einem gut

you'd [juːd] *contr of* **you had; you would**; ~ **better leave** du solltest gehen

you'll [juːl] *contr of* **you will; you shall**

young [jʌŋ] *adj* jung ▷ *n* **the ~** *pl*

(~ *people*) die jungen Leute *pl*; (*animals*) die Jungen *pl*; **youngster** ['jʌŋstə*] *n* Jugendliche(r) *mf*

your ['jɔː*] *adj sing* dein; *polite form* Ihr; *pl* euer; *polite form* Ihr; **have you hurt ~ leg?** hast du dir das Bein verletzt?

you're ['jʊə*] *contr of* **you are**

yours ['jɔːz] *pron sing* deine(r, s); *polite form* Ihre(r, s); *pl* eure(r, s); *polite form* Ihre(r, s); **is this ~?** gehört das dir/Ihnen?; **a friend of ~** ein Freund von dir/Ihnen; ~ **...,** dein/deine ..., Ihr/Ihre ...

yourself [jɔː'self] *pron sing* dich; *polite form* sich; **have you hurt ~?** hast du dich/haben Sie sich verletzt?; **did you do it ~?** hast du es selbst gemacht?; **(all) by ~** allein; **yourselves** *pron pl* euch; *polite form* sich; **have you hurt ~?** habt ihr euch/haben Sie sich verletzt?; **did you do it ~?** habt ihr es selbst gemacht?; **(all) by ~** allein

youth [juːθ] *n* (*period*) Jugend *f*; (*young man*) junger Mann; (*young people*) Jugend *f*; **youth hostel** *n* Jugendherberge *f*

you've [juːv] *contr of* **you have**

yucky ['jʌkɪ] *adj* (*fam*) eklig

Yugoslav [juːgə'slɑːv] *adj* jugoslawisch ▷ *n* Jugoslawe *m*, Jugoslawin *f*; **Yugoslavia** *n* (*hist*) Jugoslawien *nt*; **the former ~** das ehemalige Jugoslawien; **Yugoslavian** *see* **Yugoslav**

yummy ['jʌmɪ] *adj* (*fam*) lecker

yuppie, yuppy ['jʌpɪ] *n* Yuppie *m*

zit [zɪt] n (fam) Pickel m
zodiac ['zəʊdɪæk] n Tierkreis m; **sign of the ~** Tierkreiszeichen nt
zone [zəʊn] n Zone f; (area) Gebiet nt; (in town) Bezirk m
zoo [zu:] n Zoo m
zoom [zu:m] vi (move fast) brausen; **zoom ▷ vi** (lens) Zoomobjektiv nt; **zoom in** vi (film) heranzoomen (an an +akk)
zucchini [zʊ'ki:nɪ] (pl (a)) n (US) Zucchini f

Z

zap [zæp] vt (Inform) löschen; (in computer game) abknallen ▷ vi (TV) zappen; **zapper** n (TV) Fernbedienung f; **zapping** n (TV) ständiges Umschalten, Zapping nt
zebra ['zebrə, d 'zi:brə] (US) n Zebra nt; **zebra crossing** n (BRIT) Zebrastreifen m
zero ['zɪərəʊ] (pl -es) n Null f; **10 degrees below ~** 10 Grad unter null
zest [zest] n (enthusiasm) Begeisterung f
zigzag ['zɪgzæg] n Zickzack m ▷ vi (person, vehicle) im Zickzack gehen/fahren; (path) im Zickzack verlaufen
zinc [zɪŋk] n Zink nt
zip [zɪp] n (BRIT) Reißverschluss m ▷ vt **to ~ (up)** den Reißverschluss zumachen; (Inform) zippen; **zip code** n (US) Postleitzahl f; **Zip disk®** n (Inform) ZIP-Diskette® n (Inform) **Zip drive®** n (Inform) ZIP-Laufwerk® nt; **Zip file®** n (Inform) ZIP-Datei® f; **zipper** n (US) Reißverschluss m

Kleines Reise-ABC

Mini Phrasefinder

THEMEN | TOPICS

THEMEN | TOPICS

AUTO | CARS

Autovermietung	Car hire
Ich möchte ... mieten.	I want to hire ...
ein Auto	*a car.*
ein Moped	*a moped.*
ein Motorrad	*a motorbike.*
Einen Kleinwagen, bitte.	A small car, please.
Einen Mittelklassewagen, bitte.	A mid-range car, please.
Ein Auto mit Automatikgetriebe, bitte.	An automatic, please.
Was kostet das für ...?	How much is it for ...?
einen Tag	*one day*
eine Woche	*a week*
Ich möchte das Auto in ... abgeben.	I'd like to leave the car in ...
Verlangen Sie eine Kilometergebühr?	Is there a kilometre charge?
Was ist alles im Preis inbegriffen?	What is included in the price?
Ich möchte ... vereinbaren.	I'd like to arrange ...
Haftungsausschluss	*a super collision damage waiver.*
Haftungsbeschränkung	*a collision damage waiver.*
eine Diebstahlversicherung	*theft protection.*
eine Insassen-Unfallversicherung	*personal accident insurance.*
Ich möchte einen Kindersitz für ein ... Jahre altes Kind.	I'd like a child seat for a ...-year-old child.
Bitte erklären Sie mir die Schalter.	Please show me the controls.
Was tue ich bei einem Unfall/einer Panne?	What do I do if I have an accident/if I break down?

Pannen	Breakdowns
Ich habe eine Panne.	My car has broken down.
Bitte rufen Sie die Pannenhilfe.	Call the breakdown service, please.

AUTO | CARS

Ich bin Mitglied in einem Automobilklub.	I'm a member of a rescue service.
Ich bin allein.	I'm on my own.
Ich habe Kinder dabei.	I have children in the car.
Bitte schleppen Sie mich zur nächsten Werkstatt.	Can you tow me to the next garage, please?
Wo ist die nächste Werkstatt?	Where is the next garage?
... ist kaputt.	... is broken.
Der Auspuff	*The exhaust*
Das Getriebe	*The gearbox*
Die Windschutzscheibe	*The windscreen*
... funktionieren nicht.	... are not working.
Die Bremsen	*The brakes*
Die Scheinwerfer	*The headlights*
Die Scheibenwischer	*The windscreen wipers*
Die Batterie ist leer.	The battery is flat.
Der Motor springt nicht an.	The car won't start.
Der Motor wird zu heiß.	The engine is overheating.
Die Ölwarnlampe geht nicht aus.	The oil warning light won't go off.
Die Ölwanne/der Tank ist leck.	The oil/petrol tank is leaking.
Ich habe einen Platten.	I have a flat tyre.
Können Sie das reparieren?	Can you repair it?
Wann ist das Auto fertig?	When will the car be ready?
Haben Sie Ersatzteile für ...?	Do you have the parts for ...?
Das Auto ist noch unter Garantie.	The car is still under warranty.

Parken	Parking
Kann ich hier parken?	Can I park here?
Wie lange kann ich hier parken?	How long can I park here?
Brauche ich eine Parkscheibe?	Do I need a parking disc?

AUTO | CARS

Wo kann ich eine Parkscheibe bekommen?	Where can I get a parking disc?
Muss ich einen Parkschein lösen?	Do I need to buy a (car-parking) ticket?
Wo ist der Parkscheinautomat?	Where is the ticket machine?
Der Parkscheinautomat funktioniert nicht.	The ticket machine isn't working.
Wo kann ich das Bußgeld bezahlen?	Where do I pay the fine?

Tankstelle | Petrol Station

Wo ist die nächste Tankstelle?	Where is the nearest petrol station?
Voll tanken bitte.	Fill it up, please.
Für 40 Euro ... bitte.	40 euros worth of ..., please.
Diesel	*diesel*
Normalbenzin	*(unleaded economy petrol)*
Super	*premium unleaded*
Säule Nummer ... bitte.	Pump number ... please.
Bitte überprüfen Sie ...	Please check ...
das Wasser.	*the water.*
den Reifendruck.	*the tyre pressure.*
das Öl.	*the oil.*
Eine Marke für die Waschanlage bitte.	A token for the car wash, please.
Waschprogramm Nummer ...	Programme number ...

Unfall | Accident

Bitte rufen Sie ...	Please call ...
die Polizei.	*the police.*
den Notarzt.	*the emergency doctor.*
Hier sind meine Versicherungsangaben.	Here are my insurance details.

AUTO | CARS

Bitte geben Sie mir Ihre Versicherungsangaben.	Give me your insurance details, please.
Würden Sie das bezeugen?	Can you be a witness for me?
Sie sind zu schnell gefahren.	You were driving too fast.
Sie haben die Vorfahrt nicht beachtet.	It wasn't your right of way.

Unterwegs mit dem Auto — Car Travel

Wie kommt man am besten nach/zu ...?	What's the best route to ...?
Wo kann ich die Maut bezahlen?	Where can I pay the toll?
Ich möchte einen Aufkleber für die Autobahngebühr/ eine Vignette ...	I'd like a motorway tax sticker ...
für eine Woche.	for a week.
für einen Monat.	for a month.
für ein Jahr.	for a year.
Haben Sie eine Straßenkarte von dieser Gegend?	Do you have a road map of this area?

BANK | CHANGING MONEY

Wo kann ich hier Geld wechseln?	Where can I change money?
Gibt es hier eine Bank/eine Wechselstube?	Is there a bank/bureau de change here?
Wann ist die Bank/Wechselstube geöffnet?	When is the bank/bureau de change open?
Ich möchte ... Euro/Franken in Pfund/Dollar umtauschen.	I'd like to change ... euros/francs into pounds/dollars.
Ich möchte diese Reiseschecks/Euroschecks einlösen.	I'd like to cash these traveller's cheques/eurocheques.
Wie hoch ist die Gebühr?	What's the commission?
Kann ich hier mit meiner Kreditkarte Bargeld bekommen?	Can I use my credit card to get cash?
Wo gibt es hier einen Geldautomaten?	Where is the nearest cash machine?
Der Geldautomat hat meine Karte geschluckt.	The cash machine swallowed my card.
Bitte geben Sie mir etwas Kleingeld.	Can you give me some change, please?

BEHINDERTE | DISABLED TRAVELLERS

Kann man ... auch im Rollstuhl besuchen?	Is it possible to visit ... with a wheelchair?
Wo ist der Eingang für Rollstuhlfahrer?	Where is the wheelchair-accessible entrance?
Ist Ihr Hotel rollstuhlgerecht?	Is your hotel accessible to wheelchairs?
Ich brauche ein Zimmer ...	I need a room ...
im Erdgeschoss.	*on the ground floor.*
für Rollstuhlfahrer.	*with wheelchair access.*
Haben Sie einen Aufzug für Rollstühle?	Do you have a lift for wheelchairs?
Haben Sie Rollstühle?	Do you have wheelchairs?
Wo ist die Behindertentoilette?	Where is the disabled toilet?
Kann ich als Rollstuhlfahrer in diesem Zug mitfahren?	Is the train wheelchair accessible?
Bitte helfen Sie mir beim Einsteigen/Aussteigen.	Can you help me get on/off, please?
Wo gibt es hier eine Werkstatt für Rollstühle?	Where is the nearest repair shop for wheelchairs?
Ein Reifen ist geplatzt.	A tyre has burst.
Die Batterie ist leer.	The battery has run down.
Die Räder blockieren.	The wheels lock.

BESCHWERDEN | COMPLAINTS

Ich möchte mich beschweren.	I'd like to make a complaint.
Bei wem kann ich mich beschweren?	To whom can I complain?
Ich möchte mit dem Geschäftsführer sprechen.	I'd like to speak to the manager, please.
... funktioniert nicht.	... doesn't work.
Das Licht	*The light*
Die Heizung	*The heating*
Die Toilette	*The toilet*
Das Zimmer ist ...	The room is ...
schmutzig.	*dirty.*
zu klein.	*too small.*
zu kalt.	*too cold.*
Bitte machen Sie das Zimmer sauber.	Can you clean the room, please?
Bitte stellen Sie den Fernseher/das Radio leiser.	Can you turn down the TV/the radio, please?
Das Essen ist ...	The food is ...
kalt.	*cold.*
versalzen.	*too salty.*
Das habe ich nicht bestellt.	This isn't what I ordered.
Wir warten schon sehr lange.	We've been waiting for a very long time.
Die Rechnung stimmt nicht.	The bill is not correct.
Ich möchte mein Geld zurück.	I want my money back.
Ich möchte das umtauschen.	I'd like to exchange this.
Ich bin damit nicht zufrieden.	I'm not satisfied with this.

BESICHTIGUNGEN | SIGHTSEEING

Wo ist die Touristeninformation?	Where is the tourist office?
Haben Sie Broschüren über ...?	Do you have any leaflets about ...?
Welche Sehenswürdigkeiten gibt es hier?	What sights can you visit here?
Gibt es eine Stadtrundfahrt/ einen Stadtrundgang auf Englisch?	Is there a guided tour in English?
Wann ist ... geöffnet?	When is ... open?
das Museum	the museum
die Kirche	the church
das Schloss	the castle
Was kostet der Eintritt?	How much does it cost to get in?
Gibt es eine Ermäßigung ...?	Are there any reductions ...?
für Studenten	for students
für Kinder	for children
für Rentner	for pensioners
für Arbeitslose	for the unemployed
Gibt es eine Führung auf Deutsch?	Is there a guided tour in German?
Ich möchte einen Katalog.	I'd like a catalogue.
Kann ich hier fotografieren?	Can I take photos here?
Kann ich hier filmen?	Can I film here?

DIENSTREISE | BUSINESS TRAVEL

Ich möchte eine Besprechung mit ... ausmachen.	I'd like to arrange a meeting with ...
Ich habe einen Termin mit Herrn/Frau ...	I have an appointment with Mr/Ms ...
Hier ist meine Karte.	Here is my card.
Ich arbeite für ...	I work for ...
Wie komme ich ...?	How do I get to ...?
zu Ihrem Büro	*your office*
zum Büro von Herrn/Frau ...	*Mr/Ms ...'s office*
zur Kantine	*the canteen*
Ich brauche einen Dolmetscher.	I need an interpreter.
Bitte kopieren Sie das für mich.	Can you copy that for me, please?
Darf ich ... benutzen?	May I use ...?
Ihr Telefon	*your phone*
Ihren Computer	*your computer*
Ihren Schreibtisch	*your desk*

EINKAUFEN | SHOPPING

Ich suche ...	I'm looking for ...
Ich möchte ...	I'd like ...
Haben Sie ...?	Do you have ...?
Bitte zeigen Sie mir ...	Can you show me ..., please?
Wo gibt es hier ein Geschäft mit ...?	Where is the nearest shop which sells ...?
Fotoartikeln	*photographic equipment*
Schuhen	*shoes*
Souvenirs	*souvenirs*
Haben Sie das ...?	Do you have this ...?
in einer anderen Größe	*in another size*
in einer anderen Farbe	*in another colour*
mit einem anderen Muster	*in another design*
Ich trage Größe ...	I take size ...
Ich nehme das.	I'll take it.
Haben Sie noch etwas anderes?	Do you have anything else?
Das ist zu teuer.	That's too expensive.
Ich sehe mich nur um.	I'm just looking.
Nehmen Sie ...?	Do you take ...?
Kreditkarten	*credit cards*
Euroschecks	*eurocheques*

Lebensmittel | Food shopping

Wo ist hier ...?	Where is the nearest ...?
ein Supermarkt	*supermarket*
eine Bäckerei	*baker's*
eine Metzgerei	*butcher's*
ein Obst- und Gemüseladen	*greengrocer's*
Wo kann man hier Lebensmittel kaufen?	Where can you buy groceries?
Wo ist der Markt?	Where is the market?
Wann ist Markt?	When is the market on?
ein Kilo ...	*a kilo of ...*
ein Pfund ...	*a pound of ...*

EINKAUFEN | SHOPPING

200 Gramm ...	200 grams of ...
... Scheiben ...	... slices ...
ein Liter ...	a litre of ...
eine Flasche ...	a bottle of ...
ein Päckchen ...	a packet of ...

ERKUNDIGUNGEN | ASKING THE WAY

Wo ist der/die/das nächste ...?	Where is the nearest ...?
Wie komme ich dahin?	How do I get there?
Wie komme ich zum/zur/ nach ...?	How do I get to ...?
Ist es weit?	Is it far?
Wie weit ist es?	How far is it?
Bin ich hier richtig zum/ zur/nach ...?	Is this the right way to ...?
Ich habe mich verlaufen/ verfahren.	I'm lost.
Können Sie mir das auf der Karte zeigen?	Can you show me on the map?
Welchen Hinweisschildern muss ich folgen?	Which signs should I follow?
Kehren Sie um.	You have to turn round.
Fahren Sie geradeaus.	Go straight on.
Biegen Sie nach links/rechts ab.	Turn left/right.
Nehmen Sie die zweite Straße links/rechts.	Take the second street on the left/right.

FOTO UND VIDEO | PHOTOS AND VIDEOS

Einen Farbfilm/Diafilm bitte.	A colour film/slide film, please.
Mit 24/36 Bildern.	With 24/36 exposures.
Eine Kassette für diese Videokamera bitte.	Can I have a tape for this video camera, please?
Batterien für diesen Apparat bitte.	Can I have batteries for this camera, please?
Der Apparat klemmt.	The camera is sticking.
Bitte nehmen Sie den Film heraus.	Take the film out, please.
Bitte entwickeln Sie diesen Film.	Can you develop this film, please?
Ich hätte die Bilder gern ...	I'd like the photos ...
matt.	*matt.*
Hochglanz.	*glossy.*
im Format 10 mal 15.	*10 by 15 centimetres.*
Die Dias ... bitte.	I'd like the slides ..., please.
mit Rahmung	*mounted*
ohne Rahmung	*developed only*
Bitte helfen Sie mir, den Umschlag auszufüllen.	Can you help me to fill out the envelope, please?
Wann sind die Fotos fertig?	When will the photos be ready?
Wie viel kosten die Bilder?	How much do the photos cost?
Darf man hier fotografieren?	Are you allowed to take photos here?
Könnten Sie bitte ein Foto von uns machen?	Could you take a photo of us, please?

GESUNDHEIT | HEALTH

Apotheke	Pharmacy
Wo gibt es hier eine Apotheke?	Where is the nearest pharmacy?
Welche Apotheke hat Bereitschaft?	Which pharmacy provides emergency service?
Ich möchte etwas gegen ...	I'd like something for ...
Durchfall.	*diarrhoea.*
Fieber.	*a temperature.*
Reisekrankheit.	*travel sickness.*
Kopfschmerzen.	*a headache.*
Erkältung.	*a cold.*
Ich möchte ...	I'd like ...
Pflaster.	*plasters.*
einen Verband.	*a bandage.*
ein Dreieckstuch.	*a triangular bandage.*
Ich vertrage kein ...	I can't take ...
Aspirin.	*aspirin.*
Penizillin.	*penicillin.*
Kann man das Kindern geben?	Is it safe to give children?
Wie soll ich das einnehmen?	How should I take it?

Beim Arzt	At the doctor
Ich brauche einen Arzt.	I need a doctor.
Wo ist die Notaufnahme?	Where is casualty?
Ich habe hier Schmerzen.	I have a pain here.
Mir ist ...	I feel ...
heiß.	*hot.*
kalt.	*cold.*
übel.	*sick.*
schwindlig.	*dizzy.*
Ich bin allergisch gegen ...	I'm allergic to ...
Ich bin ...	I am ...
schwanger.	*pregnant.*

GESUNDHEIT | HEALTH

Diabetiker.	*diabetic.*
HIV-positiv.	*HIV-positive.*
Ich nehme dieses Medikament.	I'm on this medication.
Meine Blutgruppe ist ...	My blood group is ...

Krankenhaus | At the hospital

Auf welcher Station liegt ...?	Which ward is ... in?
Wann ist die Besuchszeit?	When are visiting hours?
Ich möchte mit ... sprechen.	I'd like to speak to ...
einem Arzt	*a doctor.*
einer Krankenschwester	*a nurse.*
Ich möchte ein Telefon mieten.	I'd like to hire a phone.
Ich möchte Kopfhörer für das Fernsehen, bitte.	I'd like headphones for the TV, please.
Wann werde ich entlassen?	When will I be discharged?

Beim Zahnarzt | At the dentist

Ich brauche einen Zahnarzt.	I need a dentist.
Dieser Zahn tut weh.	This tooth hurts.
Mir ist eine Füllung herausgefallen.	One of my fillings has fallen out.
Ich habe einen Abszess.	I have an abscess.
Ich möchte eine/keine Spritze gegen die Schmerzen.	I want/don't want an injection for the pain.
Können Sie mein Gebiss reparieren?	Can you repair my dentures?
Ich brauche eine Quittung für die Versicherung.	I need a receipt for the insurance.

KENNENLERNEN | MEETING PEOPLE

Guten Tag!	Hello
Guten Abend!	Good evening
Gute Nacht!	Good night
Auf Wiedersehen!	Goodbye
Wie heißen Sie?	What's your name?
Mein Name ist ...	My name is ...
Das ist ...	This is
meine Frau.	*my wife.*
mein Mann.	*my husband.*
mein Partner/meine Partnerin.	*my partner.*
Wo kommen Sie her?	Where are you from?
Ich komme aus ...	I come from ...
Wie geht es Ihnen?	How are you?
Danke, gut.	Fine, thanks.
Und Ihnen?	And you?
Sprechen Sie Englisch?	Do you speak English?
Ich verstehe kein Deutsch.	I don't understand German.
Vielen Dank!	Thanks very much.

NOTFALLDIENSTE | EMERGENCY SERVICES

Hilfe!	Help!
Feuer!	Fire!
Bitte rufen Sie ...	Please call ...
den Notarzt.	*the emergency doctor.*
die Feuerwehr.	*the fire brigade.*
die Polizei.	*the police.*
Ich muss dringend telefonieren.	I need to make an urgent phone call.
Ich brauche einen Dolmetscher.	I need an interpreter.
Wo ist die Polizeiwache?	Where is the police station?
Wo ist das nächste Krankenhaus?	Where is the nearest hospital?
Ich möchte einen Diebstahl melden.	I want to report a theft.
... ist gestohlen worden.	... has been stolen.
Es ist ein Unfall passiert.	There's been an accident.
Es gibt ... Verletzte.	There are ... people injured.
Mein Standort ist ...	My location is ...
Ich bin ... worden.	I've been ...
beraubt	*robbed*
überfallen	*attacked*
vergewaltigt	*raped*
Ich möchte mit meiner Botschaft sprechen.	I'd like to phone my embassy.

PASS/ZOLL | PASSPORT/CUSTOMS

Hier ist ...	Here is ...
mein Pass.	*my passport.*
mein Personalausweis.	*my identity card.*
mein Führerschein.	*my driving licence.*
meine grüne Versicherungskarte.	*my green card.*
Hier sind meine Fahrzeug-papiere.	Here are my vehicle documents.
Die Kinder stehen in diesem Pass.	The children are on this passport.
Muss ich das verzollen?	Do I have to pay duty on this?
Das ist ...	This is ...
ein Geschenk.	*a present.*
ein Warenmuster.	*a sample.*
Das ist für meinen persönlichen Gebrauch.	This is for my own personal use.
Ich bin auf der Durchreise nach ...	I'm on my way to ...

POST | POST OFFICE

Wo ist die nächste Post?	Where is the nearest post office?
Wann hat die Post geöffnet?	When does the post office open?
Wo kann ich Briefmarken kaufen?	Where can I buy stamps?
Ich möchte ... Briefmarken für Postkarten/Briefe nach Deutschland/in die Schweiz.	I'd like ... stamps for postcards/ letters to Germany/ Switzerland.
Ich möchte ... aufgeben.	I'd like to post/send ...
diesen Brief	*this letter.*
dieses Päckchen	*this small packet.*
dieses Paket	*this parcel.*
Per Luftpost/Express/ Einschreiben	By airmail/express mail/ registered mail
Ich möchte ein Telegramm aufgeben.	I'd like to send a telegram.
Hier ist der Text.	Here is the text.
Sind für mich postlagernde Sendungen da?	Is there any poste restante mail for me?
Wo ist hier ein Briefkasten?	Where is the nearest postbox?

FAHRRAD | CYCLING

Gibt es eine Fahrradkarte von dieser Gegend?	Is there a cycle map of this area?
Wo ist der Radwanderweg nach ...?	Where is the cycle path to ...?
Wie weit ist es noch bis ...?	How far is it now to ...?
Kann ich hier mein Fahrrad unterstellen?	Can I keep my bike here?
Bitte verschließen Sie mein Fahrrad an einem sicheren Ort.	Please lock my bike in a secure place.
Mein Fahrrad ist gestohlen worden.	My bike has been stolen.
Wo gibt es hier eine Fahrradwerkstatt?	Where is the nearest bike repair shop?
Der Rahmen ist verbogen.	The frame is twisted.
Die Bremse funktioniert nicht.	The brake isn't working.
Die Gangschaltung funktioniert nicht.	The gears aren't working.
Die Kette ist gerissen.	The chain is broken.
Ich habe einen Platten.	I've got a flat tyre.
Ich brauche Reifenflickzeug.	I need a puncture repair kit.

REISEN MIT KINDERN | TRAVELLING WITH CHILDREN

Können wir die Kinder mitbringen?	Is it ok to bring children here?
Ist der Eintritt auch Kindern gestattet?	Are children allowed in, too?
Gibt es eine Ermäßigung für Kinder?	Is there a reduction for children?
Haben Sie Kinderportionen?	Do you have children's portions?
Haben Sie ...?	Do you have ...?
einen Kinderstuhl	*a high chair*
ein Kinderbett	*a cot*
einen Kindersitz	*a child's seat*
einen Wickeltisch	*a baby's changing table*
Wo kann ich das Baby wickeln?	Where can I change the baby?
Wo kann ich das Baby stillen?	Where can I breast-feed the baby?
Können Sie das bitte aufwärmen?	Can you warm this up, please?
Was können Kinder hier unternehmen?	What is there for children to do?
Wo gibt es hier einen Spielplatz?	Where is the nearest playground?
Gibt es hier eine Kinderbetreuung?	Is there a childminding service?
Mein Sohn/meine Tochter ist krank.	My son/daughter is ill.

REPARATUREN | REPAIRS

Wo kann ich das reparieren lassen?	Where can I get this repaired?
Können Sie ... reparieren?	Can you repair ...?
diese Schuhe	*these shoes*
diese Uhr	*this watch*
dieses Jackett	*this jacket*
Lohnt sich die Reparatur?	Is it worth repairing?
Was kostet die Reparatur?	How much will the repairs cost?
Wo kann ich neue Absätze an meine Schuhe machen lassen?	Where can I have my shoes reheeled?
Wann ist es fertig?	When will it be ready?
Können Sie das gleich machen?	Can you do it straight away?

RESTAURANT | FOOD AND DRINK

Einen Tisch für ... Personen bitte.	A table for ... people, please.
Die Speisekarte bitte.	The menu, please.
Die Weinkarte bitte.	The wine list, please.
Was empfehlen Sie?	What do you recommend?
Haben Sie ...?	Do you have ...?
vegetarische Gerichte	*any vegetarian dishes*
Kinderportionen	*children's portions*
Enthält das ...?	Does that contain ...?
Erdnüsse	*peanuts*
Alkohol	*alcohol*
Bitte bringen Sie (noch) ...	Can you bring (more) ..., please
Ich nehme ...	I'll have ...
Zahlen bitte.	The bill, please.
Bitte alles zusammen.	All together, please.
Getrennte Rechnungen bitte.	Separate bills, please.
Stimmt so.	Keep the change.
Das habe ich nicht bestellt.	I didn't order this.
Die Rechnung stimmt nicht.	The bill is wrong.
Das Essen ist kalt/versalzen.	The food is cold/too salty.

SKI | SKIING

Wo kann ich eine Skiaus-rüstung ausleihen?	Where can I hire skiing equipment?
Ich möchte ... ausleihen.	I'd like to hire ...
Abfahrtski	*downhill skis.*
Langlaufski	*cross-country skis*
Skischuhe	*ski boots*
Skistöcke	*ski poles.*
Bitte stellen Sie meine Bindung ein.	Can you tighten my bindings, please?
Wo kann ich einen Skipass kaufen?	Where can I buy a ski pass?
Ich möchte einen Skipass ...	I'd like a ski pass ...
für einen Tag.	*for a day.*
für fünf Tage.	*for five days.*
für sieben Tage.	*for a week.*
Wie viel kostet der Skipass?	How much is a ski pass?
Wann fährt der erste/letzte Lift?	When does the first/last chair lift leave?
Haben Sie eine Pistenkarte?	Do you have a map of the ski runs?
Wo sind die Abfahrten für Anfänger?	Where are the beginners' slopes?
Welchen Schwierigkeitsgrad hat diese Abfahrt?	How difficult is this slope?
Gibt es eine Skischule?	Is there a ski school?
Wo ist die nächste Station der Bergwacht?	Where is the nearest mountain rescue service post?
Wo ist die nächste Berg-hütte?	Where is the nearest mountain hut?
Wie ist der Wetterbericht?	What's the weather forecast?
Wie ist der Schnee?	What's the snow like?
Besteht Lawinengefahr?	Is there a danger of avalanches?

SPORT | SPORT

Wo kann man hier ...?	Where can we ...?
Tennis/Golf spielen	*play tennis/golf*
schwimmen	*go swimming*
reiten	*go riding*
angeln	*go fishing*
rudern	*go rowing*
Wie viel kostet es pro Stunde?	How much is it per hour?
Wo kann ich einen Platz buchen?	Where can I book a court?
Wo kann ich Schläger ausleihen?	Where can I hire rackets?
Wo kann ich ein Ruderboot/ ein Tretboot mieten?	Where can I hire a rowing boat/ a pedal boat?
Braucht man einen Angelschein?	Do you need a fishing permit?
Wo bekomme ich einen Angelschein?	Where will I get a fishing permit?
Welche Sportveranstaltungen kann man hier besuchen?	Which sporting events can we go to?
Ich möchte ... ansehen.	I'd like to see ...
ein Fußballspiel	*a football match.*
ein Pferderennen	*a horse race.*

AM STRAND | AT THE BEACH

Kann man hier/in diesem See baden?	Can you swim here/in this lake?
Wo gibt es hier einen ruhigen Strand?	Where is the nearest quiet beach?
Gibt es einen bewachten Strand?	Is there a beach with lifeguards?
Wie tief ist das Wasser?	How deep is the water?
Wie viel Grad hat das Wasser?	What is the water temperature?
Gibt es hier Strömungen?	Are there currents?
Gibt es hier einen Rettungs- schwimmer?	Is there a lifeguard?
Wo kann man hier ...?	Where can you ...?
surfen	*go surfing*
Wasserski fahren	*go waterskiing*
tauchen	*go diving*
Gleitschirm fliegen	*go paragliding*
Ich möchte ... mieten.	I'd like to hire ...
einen Strandkorb	*a beach chair.*
einen Liegestuhl	*a deckchair.*
einen Sonnenschirm	*a sunshade.*
Ich möchte ... ausleihen.	I'd like to hire ...
ein Surfbrett	*a surfboard.*
einen Jetski	*a jet-ski.*
ein Ruderboot	*a rowing boat.*
ein Tretboot	*a pedal boat.*

TELEFON | TELEPHONE

Wo kann ich hier telefonieren?	Where can I make a phone call?
Wo ist das nächste Kartentelefon?	Where is the nearest card phone?
Wo ist der nächste Münzfernsprecher?	Where is the nearest coin box?
Ich möchte eine Telefonkarte für 10 Euro.	I'd like a ten euro phone card.
Ich möchte Münzen für das Telefon bitte.	I'd like some coins for the phone, please.
Ich möchte ein R-Gespräch anmelden.	I'd like to make a reverse charge call.
Hallo.	Hello.
Hier ist ...	This is ...
Wer spricht dort bitte?	Who's speaking, please?
Kann ich bitte mit Herrn/ Frau ... sprechen?	Can I speak to Mr/Ms ..., please?
Apparat ... bitte.	Extension ..., please.
Ich rufe später wieder an.	I'll phone back later.
Wo kann ich mein Handy aufladen?	Where can I charge my mobile phone?
Ich brauche einen neuen Akku.	I need a new battery.
Hier ist kein Netz.	I can't get a network.

UNTERHALTUNG | ENTERTAINMENT

Was kann man hier unternehmen?	What is there to do here?
Haben Sie einen Veranstaltungskalender?	Do you have a list of events?
Wo kann man hier ...?	Where can we ...?
tanzen gehen	*go dancing*
Livemusik hören	*hear live music*
Wo gibt es hier ...?	Where is there ...?
eine nette Kneipe	*a nice pub*
eine gute Disko	*a good disco*
Was gibt es heute Abend ...?	What's on tonight ...?
im Kino	*at the cinema*
im Theater	*at the theatre*
in der Oper	*at the opera*
in der Konzerthalle	*at the concert hall*
Wo kann ich Karten für ... kaufen?	Where can I buy tickets for ...?
das Theater	*the theatre*
das Konzert	*the concert*
die Oper	*the opera*
das Ballett	*the ballet*
Was kostet der Eintritt?	How much is it to get in?
Ich möchte eine Karte/ ... Karten für ...	I'd like a ticket/... tickets for ...
Gibt es eine Ermäßigung für ...?	Are there any reductions for ?
Kinder	*children*
Rentner	*pensioners*
Studenten	*students*
Arbeitslose	*the unemployed*

UNTERKUNFT | ACCOMMODATION

Camping	Camping
Gibt es hier einen Camping-platz?	Is there a campsite here?
Wir möchten einen Platz für ...	We'd like a site for ...
ein Zelt.	a tent.
ein Wohnmobil.	a camper van.
einen Wohnwagen.	a caravan.
Wir möchten eine Nacht/ ... Nächte bleiben.	We'd like to stay one night/ ... nights.
Was kostet die Nacht?	How much is it per night?
Wo sind ...?	Where are ...?
die Toiletten	the toilets
die Duschen	the showers
die Mülltonnen	the dustbins
Wo ist ...?	Where is ...?
der Laden	the shop
die Verwaltung	the site office
das Restaurant	the restaurant
Können wir über Nacht hier zelten?	Can we camp here overnight?
Können wir unser Wohn-mobil/unseren Wohnwagen hier über Nacht parken?	Can we park our camper van/ caravan here overnight?

Ferienwohnung/-haus	Self-Catering
Wo bekommen wir den Schlüssel für die Wohnung/ das Haus?	Where do we get the key for the apartment/house?
Welcher Schlüssel ist für diese Tür?	Which is the key for this door?
Müssen wir Strom/Gas extra bezahlen?	Do we have to pay extra for electricity/gas?
Wo sind die Sicherungen?	Where are the fuses?
Wo ist der Stromzähler?	Where is the electricity meter?

UNTERKUNFT | ACCOMMODATION

Wo ist die Gasuhr?	Where is the gas meter?
Wie funktioniert ...?	How does ... work?
die Waschmaschine	*the washing machine*
der Herd	*the cooker*
die Heizung	*the heating*
der Heißwasserboiler	*the water heater*
Bitte zeigen Sie uns, wie das funktioniert.	Please show us how this works.
An wen kann ich mich bei Problemen wenden?	Whom do I contact if there are any problems?
Wir brauchen ...	We need ...
einen zweiten Schlüssel.	*a second key.*
mehr Bettwäsche.	*more sheets.*
mehr Geschirr.	*more crockery.*
Das Gas ist alle.	The gas has run out.
Es gibt keinen Strom.	There is no electricity.
Wo geben wir die Schlüssel bei der Abreise ab?	Where do we hand in the keys when we're leaving?
Müssen wir die Wohnung/ das Haus vor der Abreise sauber machen?	Do we have to clean the apartment/the house before we leave?

Hotel | Hotel

Haben Sie ein ... für heute Nacht?	Do you have a ... for tonight?
Einzelzimmer	*single room*
Doppelzimmer	*double room*
Zimmer für ... Personen	*room for ... people*
mit Bad	*with bath*
mit Dusche	*with shower*
Ich möchte eine Nacht/ ... Nächte bleiben.	I want to stay for one night/ ... nights.
Ich habe ein Zimmer auf den Namen ... reserviert.	I booked a room in the name of ...

UNTERKUNFT | ACCOMMODATION

Ich möchte ein anderes Zimmer.	I'd like another room.
Wann gibt es Frühstück?	What time is breakfast?
Wo gibt es Frühstück?	Where is breakfast served?
Können Sie mir das Frühstück aufs Zimmer bringen?	Can I have breakfast in my room?
Wo ist …?	Where is …?
das Restaurant	*the restaurant*
die Bar	*the bar*
der Fitnessraum	*the gym*
der Swimmingpool	*the swimming pool*
Bitte legen Sie das in den Safe.	Put that in the safe, please.
Bitte wecken Sie mich morgen früh um …	I'd like an alarm call for tomorrow morning at …
Ich möchte diese Sachen waschen/reinigen lassen.	I'd like to get these things washed/cleaned.
Bitte bringen Sie mir …	Please bring me …
… funktioniert nicht.	… doesn't work.
Den Schlüssel bitte.	The key, please.
Zimmer Nummer …	Room number …
Sind Nachrichten für mich da?	Are there any messages for me
Bitte machen Sie die Rechnung fertig.	Please prepare the bill.

VERKEHRSMITTEL | TRANSPORT

Eisenbahn	Train
Eine einfache Fahrt nach ... bitte.	A single to ..., please.
1./2. Klasse	first/second class
Zweimal hin und zurück nach ... bitte.	Two returns to ..., please.
Gibt es eine Ermäßigung ...?	Is there a reduction ...?
für Studenten	for students
für Rentner	for pensioners
für Kinder	for children
mit diesem Pass	with this pass
Eine Platzkarte für den Zug nach ... bitte.	I'd like to reserve a seat on the train to ..., please.
Nichtraucher/Raucher bitte.	Non smoking/Smoking, please.
In Fahrtrichtung bitte.	Facing the front, please.
Ich möchte einen Liegewagenplatz/Schlafwagenplatz nach ... buchen.	I want to book a couchette/a berth to ...
Wann geht der nächste Zug nach ...?	When is the next train to ...?
Muss ich einen Zuschlag kaufen?	Is there a supplement to pay?
Muss ich umsteigen?	Do I need to change?
Wo muss ich umsteigen?	Where do I change?
Wartet der Anschlusszug?	Will my connecting train wait?
Ist das der Zug nach ...?	Is this the train for ...?
Entschuldigung, das ist mein Platz.	Excuse me, that's my seat.
Ich habe eine Platzkarte/Reservierung.	I have a reservation.
Ist dieser Platz noch frei?	Is this seat free?
Bitte sagen Sie mir, wann wir in ... ankommen.	Please let me know when we get to ...
Wo ist der Speisewagen?	Where is the buffet car?
Wo ist Wagen Nummer ...?	Where is coach number ...?

VERKEHRSMITTEL | TRANSPORT

Fähre	Ferry
Gibt es eine Fähre nach ...?	Is there a ferry to ...?
Wann geht die nächste Fähre nach ...?	When is the next ferry to ...?
Wann geht die erste/letzte Fähre nach ...?	When is the first/last ferry to ...?
Was kostet ...?	How much is ...?
die einfache Fahrt	*a single*
die Hin- und Rückfahrt	*a return*
Was kostet es für ein Auto/ Wohnmobil mit ... Personen?	How much is it for a car/ camper with ... people?
Wo fährt das Schiff ab?	Where does the boat leave from?
Wie lange dauert die Überfahrt?	How long does the crossing take?
Wann sind wir in ...?	When do we get to ...?
Kann man auf dem Schiff etwas zu essen bekommen?	Is there somewhere to eat on the boat?
Wo ist ...?	Where is ...?
das Restaurant	*the restaurant*
die Bar	*the bar*
der Dutyfreeshop	*the duty-free shop*
Wie komme ich zum Autodeck?	How do I get to the car deck?
Wo ist Kabine Nummer ...?	Where is cabin number ...?
Haben Sie etwas gegen Seekrankheit?	Do you have anything for seasickness?

Flugzeug	Plane
Wo ist das Gepäck vom Flug aus ...?	Where is the luggage for the flight from ...?
Wo kann ich hier Geld wechseln?	Where can I change some money?
Wie komme ich von hier zu/ nach ...?	How do I get to ... from here?

VERKEHRSMITTEL | TRANSPORT

Wo ist ...?	Where is ...?
der Taxistand	the taxi rank
die Bushaltestelle	the bus stop
die Information	the information office
Ich möchte mit einem Vertreter von Lufthansa sprechen.	I'd like to speak to a representative of Lufthansa.
Mein Gepäck ist nicht angekommen.	My luggage hasn't arrived.
Können Sie ... ausrufen lassen?	Can you page ...?
Wo ist der Check in für den Flug nach ...?	Where do I check in for the flight to ...?
Von welchem Ausgang geht der Flug nach ...?	Which gate for the flight to ...?
Bis wann muss ich spätestens eingecheckt haben?	When is the latest I can check in?
Wann beginnt das Einsteigen?	When does boarding begin?
Fenster/Gang bitte.	Window/aisle, please.
Wo ist der Dutyfreeshop?	Where is the duty free?
Ich habe meine Einsteigekarte/meinen Flugschein verloren.	I've lost my boarding pass/my ticket.
Ich möchte meinen Flug umbuchen/stornieren.	I'd like to change/cancel my flight.

Öffentlicher Nahverkehr | Local public transport

Wie komme ich zum/zur/nach ...?	How do I get to ...?
Welche Linie fährt zum/zur/nach ...?	Which number goes to ...?
Wo ist die nächste ...?	Where is the nearest ...?
Bushaltestelle	bus stop
Straßenbahnhaltestelle	tram stop

VERKEHRSMITTEL | TRANSPORT

U-Bahn-Station	*underground station*
S-Bahn-Station	*suburban railway station*
Wo ist der Busbahnhof?	Where is the bus station?
Einen Fahrschein bitte.	A ticket, please.
... Fahrscheine bitte.	... tickets, please.
Bis ...	To ...
Für eine Zone.	For one zone.
Für ... Zonen.	For ... zones.
Gibt es eine Ermäßigung ...?	Is there a reduction ...?
für Studenten	*for students*
für Rentner	*for pensioners*
für Kinder	*for children*
für Arbeitslose	*for the unemployed*
mit diesem Ausweis	*with this card*
Gibt es Mehrfahrtenkarten/ Tageskarten?	Do you have multi-journey tickets/day tickets?
Wie funktioniert der Automat?	How does the (ticket) machine work?
Haben Sie eine Karte mit dem Streckennetz?	Do you have a map of the rail network?
Bitte sagen Sie mir, wann ich aussteigen muss.	Please tell me when to get off.
Was ist die nächste Haltestelle?	What is the next stop?
Darf ich bitte mal vorbei?	Can I get past, please?

Taxi | Taxi

Wo bekomme ich hier ein Taxi?	Where can I get a taxi?
Bitte rufen Sie mir ein Taxi.	Call me a taxi, please.
Bitte bestellen Sie mir ein Taxi für ... Uhr.	Please order me a taxi for ... o'clock.
Zum/zur/nach ... bitte.	To ..., please.
Zum Flughafen/Bahnhof bitte.	To the airport/station, please.

VERKEHRSMITTEL | TRANSPORT

Zum Hotel ... bitte.	To the ... hotel, please.
Zu dieser Adresse bitte.	To this address, please.
Ich habe es sehr eilig.	I'm in a hurry.
Was kostet die Fahrt?	How much is it?
Ich brauche eine Quittung.	I need a receipt.
Ich habe es nicht kleiner.	I don't have anything smaller.
Stimmt so.	Keep the change.
Bitte halten Sie hier.	Stop here, please.